UNIVERSITY CASEBOOK SERIES®

CASES ON REPRODUCTIVE RIGHTS AND JUSTICE

SECOND EDITION

MELISSA MURRAY
Frederick I. and Grace Stokes Professor of Law
New York University, School of Law

KRISTIN LUKER
Elizabeth Josselyn Boalt Professor of Law Emerita
Professor of Sociology Emerita
Founding Director, Berkeley Center on Reproductive Rights and Justice
University of California, Berkeley

FOUNDATION
PRESS

University Casebook Series is a trademark registered in the U.S. Patent and Trademark Office.

© 2015 LEG, Inc. d/b/a West Academic
© 2023 LEG, Inc. d/b/a West Academic
     860 Blue Gentian Road, Suite 350
     Eagan, MN 55121
     1-877-888-1330

Printed in the United States of America

ISBN: 978-1-64708-806-4

This second edition is dedicated to our children.

ACKNOWLEDGMENTS

The authors are grateful to NYU Law students Kelsey Brown, Alon Handler, Nina Haug, Asha McLachlan, Hilarie Meyers, and Ry Walker for all of their editorial assistance. We are forever grateful to Jill E. Adams and Yvonne Lindgren for their support of the first edition and the ongoing effort to keep the casebook up to date.

The authors thank Berkeley Law librarians Joseph Cera, Michael Levy, Edna Lewis, Ramona Martinez, and Dean Rowan for their determination and efforts, as well as NYU Law librarian Dana Rubin for her amazing assistance, persistence, and support.

We commend the longstanding efforts of if/when/how (formerly Law Students for Reproductive Justice) to cultivate and facilitate law school courses dedicated to reproductive rights and justice issues, including a reader and memo from which we drew inspiration and ideas for structure and content of the first and second editions. Leading contributors to these efforts include: Jill Adams, Sabrina Andrus, Elizabeth R. Kukura, Mariko Miki, and Jessica Rubenstein.

Finally, we express our most sincere appreciation for our late colleague, Herma Hill Kay. Her sage advice and motivating example were pivotal in launching this project. Her influence on this casebook— and our lives—cannot be overstated.

Finally, we are extraordinarily grateful for the support and patience that we have received from family and friends as we worked to bring the second edition to fruition.

INTRODUCTION

Confronted with the title of this casebook, a student might reasonably ask, "what is reproductive *justice*[1] and how is it different from reproductive *rights*?"[2] Reproductive justice, as both a concept and a social movement, grew out of the experiences and vision of women of color involved in struggles for gender equity, reproductive health care, social justice, and civil and human rights.[3] These pioneering activists situated reproductive rights within a social justice framework to capture the complex, interlocking forms of oppression that often keep their communities from fully enjoying reproductive autonomy, and to compel the elimination of these oppressions in a quest for comprehensive and inclusive justice.

The advocacy and movement-building organization Forward Together (formerly Asian Communities for Reproductive Justice) defines reproductive justice as a state of being. As they conceive it, "Reproductive Justice exists when all people have the social, political and economic power and resources to make healthy decisions about our gender, bodies, sexuality and families for ourselves and our communities."[4]

Central to the reproductive justice framework is an understanding that people's reproductive choices and experiences are shaped by more than internal motivations that can be protected entirely by rights and privileges forbidding governmental involvement in decision-making. It acknowledges the external forces, such as social structures, economic systems, and government institutions that may influence or impede the realization of reproductive rights. On this account, reproductive justice

---

[1] A comprehensive description of reproductive justice theory and praxis lies beyond the scope of this book. *See generally* Jael Silliman et al., *The Political Context for Women of Color Organizing, in* UNDIVIDED RIGHTS: WOMEN OF COLOR ORGANIZING FOR REPRODUCTIVE JUSTICE (2004); ASIAN COMMUNITIES FOR REPROD. JUSTICE, A NEW VISION FOR ADVANCING OUR MOVEMENT FOR REPRODUCTIVE HEALTH, REPRODUCTIVE RIGHTS, AND REPRODUCTIVE JUSTICE (2005); SISTERSONG WOMEN OF COLOR REPROD. HEALTH COLLECTIVE, REPRODUCTIVE JUSTICE BRIEFING BOOK (2007).

[2] Generally speaking, reproductive rights, captured by laws, policies, regulations, and other legal instruments, encompass a broad array of needs a person may have in his or her lifetime, including but not limited to sexuality education; prevention, testing, and treatment for sexually transmitted infections; maternity care; birthing options; parental rights; public assistance; assisted reproductive technologies; and access to volitional use of abortion, contraception, and sterilization.

[3] *What Is RJ?*, SISTERSONG (2014), https://books.google.com/books?id=JZqtCQAAQBAJ& pg=PA27&lpg=PA27&dq=%22all+individuals+are+part+of+families+and+communities+and+ that+our+strategies+must+lift+up+entire+communities+in+order+to+support+individuals %22&source=bl&ots=CnbxFjWhB-&sig=ACfU3U39kBPmkaIkUntKy8x1-ka0FOCLww&hl= en&sa=X&ved=2ahUKEwjk3sjVu5r4AhVpt4QIHVsnCeAQ6AF6BAgYEAM#v=onepage&q=%2 2all%20individuals%20are%20part%20of%20families%20and%20communities%20and%20that %20our%20strategies%20must%20lift%20up%20entire%20communities%20in%20order%20to %20support%20individuals%22&f=false.

[4] ASIAN COMMUNITIES FOR REPROD. JUSTICE, WINNING REPRODUCTIVE JUSTICE: CONTRIBUTIONS TO POLICY CHANGE FROM THE REPRODUCTIVE JUSTICE MOVEMENT 1 (2008).

is about fundamentally "transform[ing] power inequities and creat[ing] long-term systemic change."[5]

Rather than focusing exclusively on individual rational actors operating in a free market, as the law is prone to do, "[t]he reproductive justice framework recognizes that all individuals are part of families and communities and that our strategies must lift up entire communities in order to support individuals."[6]

At the same time, reproductive justice activists and scholars insist that it is impossible to speak of entire groups (e.g., women, parents, or people, for that matter) as if they were all fungible. As they make clear, race, class, gender, and other social forces shape lives in ways large and small, making the experience of reproduction deeply personal and individualized. In short, no single story could represent the reproductive experiences of all people.

Relatedly, an important dimension of reproductive justice is its emphasis on what legal scholars Kimberlé Crenshaw[7] and Angela Harris[8] (among others) have termed "intersectionality." Intersectionality posits that the traditional conceptualizations of oppression within society, such as racism, sexism, classism, homophobia, transphobia, and other forms of bigotry, do not act independently of one another. Instead, intersectionality maintains that these forms of oppression and discrimination are inextricably intertwined, creating a complex system of subordination that is informed by multiple types of discrimination. In the context of reproductive justice, an intersectional approach assumes that impositions on the individual's or community's reproductive autonomy reflect the interaction of gender with class, race, ability, sexual orientation, immigration status, age, gender identity, and other aspects of social stratification and control.

This intersectional approach to reproductive rights and justice issues informs this casebook. For example, mainstream rhetoric has emphasized women's reproductive "choices" and framed them as empowering. Yet, as we demonstrate, it is difficult to think of reproductive choices without considering the ways in which social determinants may limit or coerce the deeply contingent options available to each individual, reflecting a "least worst" alternative, rather than a truly empowering decision.

This book is the product of collaboration between a legal scholar and a social scientist interested in sociolegal issues. This is not accidental. We feel very strongly that in the rapidly evolving world of reproductive

[5] *What Is Reproductive Justice?*, FORWARD TOGETHER (2022), http://strongfamilies movement.org/what-is-reproductive-justice.
[6] *Id.*
[7] Kimberlé Crenshaw, *Demarginalizing the Intersection of Race and Sex*, 1989 U. CHI. LEGAL F. 139 (1989).
[8] Angela P. Harris, *Race and Essentialism in Feminist Legal Theory*, 42 STAN. L. REV. 581 (1990).

rights and justice, interested law students will be disadvantaged if they do not understand the historical and political context in which legal doctrine and discourse have evolved. Because the majority of the issues examined in the casebook are newly (or continually) controversial, a strong background of knowledge will enable the student to think rigorously about the present and future legal landscape.

We have taken the insights of reproductive rights and justice seriously and have sought to illuminate the way the law instantiates and reproduces gendered, raced, and classed stratification. Although abortion and privacy have served as the centerpiece for most education about reproductive rights, we have chosen to disrupt this orthodoxy by instead focusing on the way in which law controls bodies and relationships at all points of the human life cycle. In this vein, the casebook reflects our best effort to provide structure to an intellectual and legal inquiry about how the law regulates all realms of reproduction, and in so doing, shapes our daily lives.

As this second edition goes to press, the legal landscape for reproductive rights and justice has never been more bleak. The developments that this edition chronicles make clear the ongoing efforts to roll back reproductive freedom—as well as the effort to occlude or ignore entirely other persistent reproductive injustices.

Given the state of the law, it would be easy to throw up our hands and lament all that has transpired since the first edition of this casebook went to press in 2014. This second edition, however, is a repudiation of that impulse. It is a clarion call to all who are invested in these issues to continue the work—and to cultivate the next generation of reproductive justice advocates.

MELISSA MURRAY

KRISTIN LUKER

SUMMARY OF CONTENTS

TABLE OF CONTENTS

TABLE OF CASES

The principal cases are in bold type.

UNIVERSITY CASEBOOK SERIES®

CASES ON REPRODUCTIVE RIGHTS AND JUSTICE

SECOND EDITION

CHAPTER 1

REGULATING SEX

The contest over reproductive rights and justice might also be understood as a contest over the legal and social regulation of sex and sexuality. This chapter provides background material on the legal regulation of sex that may usefully inform more particularized discussions of reproductive rights and justice (and their gendered dimensions) that appear in subsequent chapters.

A. INTRODUCTION

In accordance with a state statute that permitted any adult of good character and sufficient training to be admitted to the bar, Myra Bradwell applied for a law license. Because she was a woman, however, the Illinois Supreme Court denied her admission. Bradwell appealed the decision to the United States Supreme Court, arguing that her right to practice law was protected by the Privileges and Immunities Clause of the Fourteenth Amendment. A majority of the Court concluded that the right to practice law was not among the privileges and immunities protected by the Fourteenth Amendment. Although it was one of the first cases to parse the meaning of the various provisions of the Fourteenth Amendment, Bradwell *is best known for Justice Joseph Bradley's concurring opinion.*

Bradwell v. Illinois

83 U.S. 130 (1872).

■ BRADLEY, J., [concurring].

. . .

The claim that, under the [F]ourteenth [A]mendment of the Constitution, which declares that no State shall make or enforce any law which shall abridge the privileges and immunities of citizens of the United States, the statut[ory] law of Illinois, or the common law prevailing in that State, can no longer be set up as a barrier against the right of females to pursue any lawful employment for a livelihood (the practice of law included), assumes that it is one of the privileges and immunities of women as citizens to engage in any and every profession, occupation, or employment in civil life.

It certainly cannot be affirmed, as an historical fact, that this has ever been established as one of the fundamental privileges and immunities of the sex. On the contrary, the civil law, as well as nature herself, has always recognized a wide difference in the respective spheres and destinies of man and woman. Man is, or should be, woman's protector and defender. The natural and proper timidity and delicacy which belongs to the female sex evidently unfits it for many of the occupations of civil life. The constitution of the family organization, which is founded in the divine ordinance, as well as in the nature of things, indicates the domestic sphere as that which properly belongs to the domain and functions of womanhood. The harmony, not to say identity, of interest and views which belong, or should belong, to the family institution is repugnant to the idea of a woman adopting a distinct and independent career from that of her husband. So firmly fixed was this sentiment in the founders of the common law that it became a maxim of that system of jurisprudence that a woman had no legal existence separate from her husband, who was regarded as her head and representative in the social state; and, notwithstanding some recent modifications of this civil status, many of the special rules of law flowing from and dependent upon this cardinal principle still exist in full force in most States. One of these is, that a married woman is incapable, without her husband's consent, of making contracts which shall be binding on her or him. This very incapacity was one circumstance which the Supreme Court of Illinois deemed important in rendering a married woman incompetent fully to perform the duties and trusts that belong to the office of an attorney and counsellor.

It is true that many women are unmarried and not affected by any of the duties, complications, and incapacities arising out of the married state, but these are exceptions to the general rule. The paramount destiny and mission of woman are to fulfil the noble and benign offices of wife and mother. This is the law of the Creator. And the rules of civil society must be adapted to the general constitution of things, and cannot be based upon exceptional cases.

The humane movements of modern society, which have for their object the multiplication of avenues for woman's advancement, and of occupations adapted to her condition and sex, have my heartiest concurrence. But I am not prepared to say that it is one of her fundamental rights and privileges to be admitted into every office and position, including those which require highly special qualifications and demanding special responsibilities. In the nature of things it is not every citizen of every age, sex, and condition that is qualified for every calling and position. It is the prerogative of the legislator to prescribe regulations founded on nature, reason, and experience for the due admission of qualified persons to professions and callings demanding special skill and confidence. This fairly belongs to the police power of the State; and, in my opinion, in view of the peculiar characteristics, destiny, and mission of woman, it is within the province of the legislature to ordain what offices, positions, and callings shall be filled and discharged by men, and shall receive the benefit of those energies and responsibilities, and that decision and firmness which are presumed to predominate in the sterner sex.

. . .

NOTES

1. *Natural law.* When Justice Bradley affirms that the legislature can make rules "founded on nature, reason, and experience," he is drawing on a deep tradition in Western legal thought that relies on a belief in "natural law." Springing most directly from Thomas Aquinas's thinking, natural law posits that there are rules of morality that exist across time and context, inherent in the "natural order." Rules that may be "socially constructed"—by humans who are located in distinct social locations with distinct interests—would be roundly rejected in this tradition. Understandably, this outlook tends to lead to traditional views on reproduction, sexuality, and gender roles, as indicated by Justice Bradley's comment that denying Myra Bradwell the right to practice law was "the law of the Creator." For an overview, see ROBERT P. GEORGE, IN DEFENSE OF NATURAL LAW (rev. ed. 2001). Although natural law theories tend toward the traditional in the areas relevant to this casebook, natural law is not solely the province of conservative theorists. Martin Luther King, Jr., who trained as a seminarian, based his opposition to segregation on Thomas Aquinas's famous natural law proposition that "an unjust law is no law at all." MARTIN LUTHER KING, JR., LETTER FROM A BIRMINGHAM JAIL 3 (1963).

2. *Separate spheres.* In *Bradwell*, Justice Bradley notes that men and women are intended "to occupy different spheres of action." However, the ideology of the separate spheres pre-dates *Bradwell*. The concept dates back to the ancient Greeks who divided society into two sectors, the *oikos* (home) and the *polis* (city). One of the first modern social critics to examine the separate spheres was Alexis de Tocqueville. In his 1840 book, *Democracy in America*, Tocqueville observed that "[i]n no country has such constant care been taken as in America to trace two clearly distinct lines of action for the two sexes and to make them keep pace one with the other, but in two pathways that are always different." ALEXIS DE TOCQUEVILLE, DEMOCRACY IN AMERICA 698 (1840). Tocqueville went on to note that "in the United States the inexorable opinion of the public carefully circumscribes woman within the narrow circle of domestic interests and duties and forbids her to step beyond it." *Id.* at 688. Although Tocqueville considered separate spheres a positive development, modern feminists were more critical. Some have argued that the separate spheres ideology resulted in the devaluation of the domestic sphere and the exclusion of women from essential aspects of public life.

B. THE GENESIS OF SEXUAL REGULATION

1. THE BIBLE

"Patriarchy" literally once meant the rule of the father over his wife (or wives) and his children, because children—and hence fertile women—were scarce and highly valued resources. Written more than two thousand years ago, much of the Bible testifies to the centrality of reproduction in human history. Promises and injunctions to "[b]e fruitful and multiply" occur no fewer than ten times in the book of Genesis alone. And when

Yahweh executes a contract ("covenant") with Abraham, the Lord's part of the bargain is human fertility.

Genesis 15:5–6.

. . . And [the Lord] took [Abraham] outside and He said, "look up to the heavens and count the stars, if you can count them." And He said, "so shall be your seed." And [Abraham] trusted in the LORD and He reckoned it to his merit.

ROBERT ALTER, THE FIVE BOOKS OF MOSES 74 (W.W. Norton 2008).

When the Lord renews his covenant, this time with Moses, again fertility is center stage in the contract between humans and the Lord.

Deuteronomy 7:12–15.

[Speaking directly to Moses, the Lord says:] "And it shall come about in consequence of your heeding these laws when you keep and do them, that the Lord your God will keep the covenant and the faith for you that he swore to your fathers. And he will love you and bless you and multiply you and bless the fruit of your womb and the fruit of your soil, your grain and your wine and your oil, the spawn of your herds and calvings of your flock, upon the soil that he swore to your fathers to give to you. Blessed shall you be more than all the people. There shall be no sterile male or female among you nor among your beasts . . . ."

ROBERT ALTER, THE FIVE BOOKS OF MOSES 918 (W.W. Norton 2008).

NOTE

What is patriarchy? Social scientists often speak of "hegemony," by which they mean those ideas so deeply ingrained in a culture that they seem to be "natural," or as Justice Bradley declares, "the law of the Creator." Patriarchy has been a "hegemonic" idea in Western law for millennia, and originally referred to men's control over their women and children. Critically, patriarchy is rooted in the scarcity (and value) of children, and men's interests in making sure that they have access to their own genetic offspring.

2. ENGLISH COMMON LAW ON MARRIAGE AND BASTARDY

The regulation of sex and reproduction achieved two other tasks besides delineating who had claim to the valuable resource a child represented. Control of marriage (and the chastity of women) was designed to reassure men that property was bequeathed only to legitimate heirs, and to assign each child a designated father, as the following section illuminates.

William Blackstone, Commentaries on the Laws of England, Book the First: Chapter the Sixteenth: Of Parent and Child

(1765–1769).

[The] duty of parents to provide for the maintenance of their children is a principle of natural law; an obligation . . . laid on them not only by nature herself, but by their own proper act, in bringing them into the world: for they would be in the highest manner injurious to their issue, if they only gave the children life, that they might afterwards see them perish. By begetting them therefore they have entered into a voluntary obligation, to endeavor, as far as in them lies, that the life which they have bestowed shall be supported and preserved. And thus the children will have a perfect right of receiving maintenance from their parents. And the prescient Montesquieu has a very just observation upon this head [sic]: that the establishment of marriage in all civilized states is built on this natural obligation of the father to provide for his children; for [marriage] ascertains and makes known the person who is bound to fulfil [sic] this obligation: whereas, in promiscuous and illicit conjunctions, the father is unknown; and the mother finds a thousand obstacles in her way;—shame, remorse, the constraint of her sex, and the rigor of laws;—that stifle her inclinations to perform this duty.

. . .

[Who] are bastards? A bastard, by our English laws, is one that is not only begotten, but born out of lawful matrimony. . . . [Legal systems based on Roman law] do not allow a child to remain a bastard, if the parents afterwards intermarry: and herein they differ most materially from our [English common] law, which, though not so strict as to require that the child shall be begotten, yet it makes it an indispensable condition that it shall be born after lawful wedlock. And the reason of our English law is surely much superior to that of the Roman, if we consider the principal end and design of establishing the contract of marriage, taken in a civil light, abstractedly from any religious view, which has nothing to do with the legitimacy or illegitimacy of the children. The main end and design of marriage therefore being to ascertain and fix upon some certain person, to whom the care, the protection, the maintenance, and the education of the children should belong; this end is undoubtedly better answered by legitimating all issue born after wedlock, than by legitimating all issue of the same parties, even born before wedlock, so as wedlock afterwards ensues . . . . [B]ecause of the very great uncertainty there will generally be, in the proof that the issue was really begotten by the same man; whereas, by confining the proof to the birth, and not to the begetting, our law has rendered it perfectly certain, what child is legitimate, and who is to take care of the child. . . . [T]his rule of the Roman laws admits of no limitations as to the time, or number, of bastards so to be legitimated; but a dozen of them may, twenty years after their birth, by the subsequent marriage of their parents, be admitted to all the privileges of legitimate children. This is plainly a great discouragement to the matrimonial state; to which one main inducement is usually not only the desire of having children, but also the desire of procreating lawful heirs.

NOTES

1.   *Slavery and matrilineal descent.* Although English common law traced descent through the father, the sexual exploitation of slave women and the economic realities of chattel slavery prompted a change in the laws of descent. Lest children born of free white men and enslaved African women take on the status of their fathers, colonial legislatures fashioned new rules of matrilineal descent to govern the status of children born to enslaved women. Drawing on the Blackstonian axiom *partus sequitur ventrem*, or "the offspring follows the belly," which was used to determine the ownership of livestock, the colonial assembly of Virginia enacted the following rules of matrilineal descent in 1662:

> Whereas some doubts have arrisen [sic] whether children got by any Englishman upon a Negro woman should be slave or free, [b]e it therefore enacted and declared by this present grand assembly, that all children borne in this country shall be held bond or free only according to the condition of the mother . . . .

Negro Women's Children to Serve According to the Condition of the Mother, Act XII (1662), *reprinted in* 2 THE STATUTES AT LARGE; BEING A COLLECTION OF ALL THE LAWS OF VIRGINIA, FROM THE FIRST SESSION OF THE LEGISLATURE IN THE YEAR 1619, at 170 (William Waller Hening ed., 1823).

Other colonies soon followed suit, using matrilineal descent to dictate the status of children born to enslaved women.

2.   *Matrilineal descent and tribal law.* Descent has always been a product of larger social and historical needs. In 1939, the Pueblo Tribe changed its matrilineal rules for membership out of concern that tribeswomen were out-marrying at alarming rates. Prior to 1939, the Tribe followed a rule of matrilineal descent and children born to Pueblo mothers were deemed tribal members. The 1939 change stated that any child born to a Pueblo mother who had married a Navajo man *would not* be considered a member of the Pueblo Tribe. Critically, male tribal members who out-married were able to pass their tribal membership on to their children.

> In 1978's *Santa Clara Pueblo v. Martinez*, 436 U.S. 49 (1978), Pueblo women challenged the new rules, arguing that they violated the Indian Civil Rights Act. The U.S. Supreme Court held that the Tribe's traditional sovereign immunity from suit on issues of membership barred federal courts from ruling on the merits of these claims. *Id.* at 72. In upholding the tribal laws, the Court emphasized tribal sovereignty, a development hailed as progressive by multiculturalists. Yet as political scientist Sarah Song observes, multiculturalists (and the Court) "tend to assume that indigenous cultures are distinct, self-contained wholes. . . . The federal

government has played a strong role in shaping Native American identity and membership practices, sometimes in patriarchal ways. In some cases, . . . deference to tribal sovereignty has been driven not so much by respect for indigenous difference but by congruence of patriarchal norms across cultures. . . . [I]ndigenous ways of life are a hybrid product of intercultural interactions. The struggles over the Santa Clara Pueblo membership rule flesh out this difficulty." SARAH SONG, JUSTICE, GENDER, AND THE POLITICS OF MULTICULTURALISM 115 (2007).

* * *

As American society shifted in the nineteenth and early twentieth centuries from an agricultural, kin-based society to an urban, industrial one, the regulation of sexuality and reproduction also shifted from the assumptions we find in the Bible and in Blackstone. Far from being valuable assets, children became "economically useless and emotionally priceless," as sociologist Viviana Zelizer notes. Accordingly, sex was transformed from a primarily procreative endeavor at the core of economic production to being the foundation of an intimate, affective relationship whose value resided in its capacity to encourage emotional bonding rather than the production of children. In the following selection—an amicus brief filed before the U.S. Supreme Court in 2003's Lawrence v. Texas—*a group of historians note the degree to which anti-sodomy laws were originally animated by an interest in promoting procreative sex.*

Brief for Professors of History et al. as Amici Curiae, *Lawrence v. Texas*

539 U.S. 558 (2003) (No. 02–102).

. . .

In colonial America, regulation of non-procreative sexual practices—regulation that carried harsh penalties but was rarely enforced—stemmed from Christian religious teachings and reflected the need for procreative sex to increase the population. Colonial sexual regulation included such non-procreative acts as masturbation, and sodomy laws applied equally to male-male, male-female, and human-animal sexual activity. "Sodomy" was not the equivalent of "homosexual conduct." It was understood as a particular, discrete act, not as an indication of a person's sexuality or sexual orientation.

Not until the end of the nineteenth century did lawmakers and medical writing recognize sexual "inversion" or what we would today call homosexuality. The phrase "homosexual sodomy" would have been literally incomprehensible to the Framers of the Constitution, for the very concept of homosexuality as a discrete psychological condition and source of personal identity was not available until the late 1800s. . . .

Proscriptive laws designed to suppress all forms of non-procreative and non-marital sexual conduct existed through much of the last millennium. Widespread discrimination against a class of people on the basis of their homosexual status developed only in the twentieth century, however, and peaked from the 1930s to the 1960s. Gay men and women were labeled "deviants," "degenerates," and "sex criminals" by the medical profession, government officials, and the mass media. . . .

. . .

Prohibitions against sodomy are rooted in the teachings of Western Christianity, but those teachings have always been strikingly inconsistent in their definition of the acts encompassed by the term. When the term "sodomy" was first emphasized by medieval Christian theologians in the eleventh century, they applied it inconsistently to a diverse group of nonprocreative sexual practices. . . .

. . .

The English Reformation Parliament of 1533 turned the religious injunction against sodomy into the secular crime of buggery when it made "the detestable and abominable vice of buggery committed with mankind or beast" punishable by death. The English courts interpreted this to apply to sexual intercourse between a human and animal and anal intercourse between a man and woman as well as anal intercourse between two men.

Colonial American statutes variously drew on the religious and secular traditions and shared their imprecision in the definition of the offense. Variously defining the crime as (the religious) sodomy or (the secular) buggery, they generally proscribed anal sex between men and men, men and women, and humans and animals, but their details and their rationale varied, and the New England colonies penalized a wider range of "carnall knowledge," including (but by no means limited to) "men lying with men." Puritan leaders in the New England colonies were especially vigorous in their denunciation of sodomitical sins as contrary to God's will, but their condemnation was also motivated by the pressing need to increase the population and to secure the stability of the family. Thus John Winthrop mused that the main offense of one man hanged in New Haven in 1646 for having engaged in masturbation with numerous youths—not, in other words, for "sodomy" as it is usually understood today—was his "frustratinge of the Ordinance of marriage & the hindringe the generation of mankinde."

Another indication that the sodomy statutes were not the equivalent of a statute against "homosexual conduct" is that with one brief exception they applied exclusively to acts performed by men, whether with women, girls, men, boys, or animals, and not to acts committed by two women. . . .

. . .

It was only beginning in the 1970s that a handful of States, including Texas, passed legislation specifying homosexual sodomy while decriminalizing heterosexual sodomy. This legislation had no historical precedent, but resulted from a uniquely twentieth-century form of animus directed at homosexuals . . . .

. . .

   . . . In our judgment as historians, the lessons of this history are clear. The history of antigay discrimination is short, not millennial. In early American history, "sodomy" was indeed condemned, but the concept of "the homosexual" and the notion of singling out "homosexual sodomy" for condemnation were foreign. Through most of our Nation's history, sodomy laws prohibited some forms of same-sex conduct only as one aspect of a more general (and historically variable) prohibition.

   It was only in the twentieth century that the government began to classify and discriminate against certain of its citizens on the basis of their homosexual status. . . .

C. THEORETICAL PERSPECTIVES ON THE REGULATION OF SEX

Gayle S. Rubin, *Thinking Sex: Notes for a Radical Theory of the Politics of Sexuality, in* Deviations: A Gayle Rubin Reader
(2011).

. . .

   . . . Contemporary conflicts over sexual values and erotic conduct have much in common with the religious disputes of earlier centuries. They acquire immense symbolic weight. Disputes over sexual behaviour often become the vehicles for displacing social anxieties, and discharging their attendant emotional intensity. . . .

. . .

   A radical theory of sex must identify, describe, explain, and denounce erotic injustice and sexual oppression. Such a theory needs refined conceptual tools which can grasp the subject and hold it in view. It must build rich descriptions of sexuality as it exists in society and history. It requires a convincing critical language that can convey the barbarity of sexual persecution.

. . .

   Modern Western societies appraise sex acts according to a hierarchical system of sexual value. Marital, reproductive heterosexuals are alone at the top erotic pyramid. Clamouring below are unmarried monogamous heterosexuals in couples, followed by most other heterosexuals. Solitary sex floats ambiguously. The powerful nineteenth-century stigma on masturbation lingers in less potent, modified forms, such as the idea that masturbation is an inferior substitute for partnered encounters. Stable, long-term lesbian and gay male couples are verging on respectability, but bar dykes and promiscuous gay men are hovering just above the groups at the very bottom of the pyramid. The most despised sexual castes currently include transsexuals, transvestites, fetishists, sadomasochists, sex workers such as prostitutes and porn models, and the lowliest of all, those whose eroticism transgresses generational boundaries.

Individuals whose behaviour stands high in this hierarchy are rewarded with certified mental health, respectability, legality, social and physical mobility, institutional support, and material benefits. As sexual behaviours or occupations fall lower on the scale, the individuals who practice them are subjected to a presumption of mental illness, disreputability, criminality, restricted social and physical mobility, loss of institutional support, and economic sanctions.

Extreme and punitive stigma maintains some sexual behaviours as low status and is an effective sanction against those who engage in them. The intensity of this stigma is rooted in Western religious traditions. But most of its contemporary content derives from medical and psychiatric opprobrium.

The old religious taboos were primarily based on kinship forms of social organization. They were meant to deter inappropriate unions and to provide proper kin. Sex laws derived from Biblical pronouncements were aimed at preventing the acquisition of the wrong kinds of affinal partners: consanguineous kin (incest), the same gender (homosexuality), or the wrong species (bestiality). When medicine and psychiatry acquired extensive powers over sexuality, they were less concerned with unsuitable mates than with unfit forms of desire. If taboos against incest best characterized kinship systems of sexual organization, then the shift to an emphasis on taboos against masturbation was more apposite to the newer systems organized around qualities of erotic experience. . . .

NOTE

The charmed circle. Professor Rubin suggests that sexual acts similar to those performed by the procreative married couple fall within the charmed circle of normative sexuality.

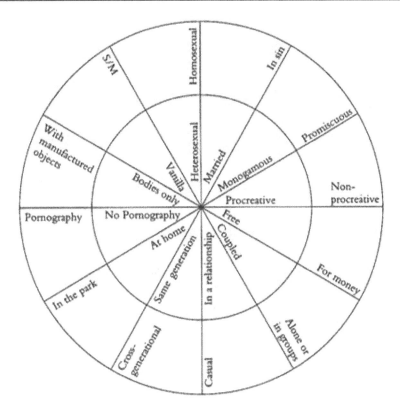

Id. at 152. In the thirty years since Rubin wrote *Thinking Sex*, are there other acts that have come to be accepted within the charmed circle? Is there only one charmed circle, or is there a series of concentric circles? Or, as Rubin suggests, is there a series of circles that overlap in the manner of a Venn diagram? If the latter, how do we gauge the normative value of the various sexual acts contained within the overlapping circles?

* * *

In his seminal work, Discipline and Punish, *Michel Foucault noted the degree to which the sovereign exercised ultimate authority over the populace through his use of the power of death, namely the spectacle of public executions and other forms of public and painful punishment. In* The History of Sexuality, *Foucault expanded upon these ideas, and more particularly, related them to the development of the nation-state. As the nation-state emerges as the authoritative figure in the lives of the populace, power is exercised through the control of life, rather than death. On this account, the state seeks to cultivate a disciplined polity by controlling the discourse—indeed, the way we talk and think—about such quotidian processes as sex and reproduction. In the following selection from* The History of Sexuality, *Foucault makes clear that discourses about sex and reproduction are neither natural nor inevitable. Instead, they are socially constructed by—and disseminated under the authority of—the state, which uses these discourses to control and discipline the populace.*

Michel Foucault, *Right of Death and Power Over Life, in* The History of Sexuality, Vol. 1: An Introduction

(1978).

. . .

The old power of death that symbolized sovereign power was now carefully supplanted by the administration of bodies and the calculated management of life. During the classical period, there was a rapid development of various disciplines—universities, secondary schools, barracks, workshops; there was also the emergence in the field of political practices and economic observation, of the problems of birthrate, longevity, public health, housing, and migration. Hence there was an explosion of numerous and diverse techniques for achieving this subjugation of bodies and the control of populations, marking the beginning of an era of "bio-power." . . .

. . .

NOTES

1. *The two poles.* Foucault imagined two extremes—discipline and state administration of the population—through which the state achieved dominion over individual bodies within the polity. How does the state achieve dominion over bodies today? Does it rely on discipline and various state administrative vehicles, as Foucault imagined, or are other technologies deployed? Is the state principally interested in regulating *bodies* or in regulating those bodies engaged in *sex*?

2. *Regulating sex and sexuality through marriage and crime.* Foucault suggests that there are various state vehicles that are used to cultivate a disciplined citizenry. One obvious state apparatus for imposing discipline is criminal law. Professor Melissa Murray suggests, however, that "the criminal law is not the only institution" that is used in this manner. According to Murray, "[t]he idea of an institution that communicates and internalizes modes of discipline has long been a part of the understanding of marriage . . . ." Melissa Murray, *Marriage as Punishment*, 112 COLUM. L. REV. 1, 52 (2012). What would Foucault make of Murray's assessment of marriage as a form of discipline and a means of regulating sex and sexuality? How does this vision of marriage square with popular discussions of marriage as a (beneficial) social institution?

D. CREATING THE CATEGORY OF NORMATIVE SEX AND SEXUALITY

1. MARRIAGE

Maynard v. Hill

125 U.S. 190 (1888).

Maynard v. Hill involves marriage, divorce, and the challenges of westward expansion. In 1828, David and Lydia Maynard were married in Vermont. Financially strapped after a series of unsuccessful business ventures, the Maynards, along with their two grown sons, relocated to Ohio in 1850. Thereafter, Maynard "left his family in Ohio and started overland for California, under a promise to his wife that he would either return or send for her and the children within two years, and that [in] the mean time [sic] he would send her the means of support." He did neither. Somewhere along the Oregon Trail, Maynard met and fell in love with Catherine Brashears, a fellow settler. Upon arriving in what is now Washington State, Maynard "settled upon and claimed, as a married man, a tract of land of 640 acres." He also petitioned the legislature for a bill of divorce, which was granted in 1852. In 1853, he married Brashears. The lawsuit arose over a property dispute concerning the title to Maynard's claimed 670 acres—and ultimately turned on the question of the validity of Maynard's legislative divorce. In deciding that question, the U.S. Supreme Court took the opportunity to opine on the importance of marriage in society and the constitutional order.

■ FIELD, J.

. . .

As seen by the statement of the case, two questions are presented for our consideration: *First*, was the act of the legislative assembly of the territory of Oregon of the 22d of December, 1852, declaring the bonds of matrimony between David S. Maynard and his wife dissolved, valid and effectual to divorce the parties? [A]nd, *second*, if valid and effectual for that purpose, did such divorce defeat any rights of the wife to a portion of the donation claim?

The [A]ct of [C]ongress creating the territory of Oregon and establishing a government for it, passed on the 14th of August, 1848, . . . declared that the legislative power of the territory should "extend to all rightful subjects of legislation not inconsistent with the [C]onstitution and laws of the United States" . . . . What were "rightful subjects of legislation," when these acts organizing the territories were passed, is not to be settled by reference to the distinctions usually made between legislative acts and such as are judicial or administrative in their character, but by an examination of the subjects upon which legislatures had been in the practice of acting with the consent and approval of the people they represented. A long acquiescence in repeated acts of legislation on particular matters is evidence that those matters have been generally considered by the people as properly within legislative control. Such acts are not to be set aside or treated as invalid, because, upon a careful consideration of their character, doubts may arise as to the competency of the legislature to pass them. . . . With special force does this observation apply, when the validity of acts dissolving the bonds of matrimony is assailed; the legitimacy of many children, the peace of many families, and the settlement of many estates depending upon its being sustained. . . .

Marriage, as creating the most important relation in life, as having more to do with the morals and civilization of a people than any other institution, has always been subject to the control of the legislature. That body prescribes the age at which parties may contract to marry, the procedure or form essential to constitute marriage, the duties and obligations it creates, its effects upon the property rights of both, present and prospective, and the acts which may constitute grounds for its dissolution.

. . .

If within the competency of the legislative assembly of the territory, we cannot inquire into its motives in passing the act granting the divorce; its will was a sufficient reason for its action. One of the parties, the husband, was a resident within the territory, and, as he acted soon afterwards upon the dissolution and married again, we may conclude that the act was passed upon his petition. . . .

The facts alleged in the bill of complaint, that no cause existed for the divorce, and that it was obtained without the knowledge of the wife, cannot affect the validity of the act. Knowledge or ignorance of parties of intended legislation does not affect its validity, if within the competency of the legislature. The facts mentioned as to the neglect of the husband to send to his wife, whom he left in Ohio, any means for her support or that of her children, in disregard of his promise, shows conduct meriting the strongest reprobation, and, if the facts stated had been brought to the attention of congress, that body might and probably would have annulled the act. Be that as it may, the loose morals and shameless conduct of the husband can have no bearing upon the question of the existence or absence of power in the assembly to pass the act. . . . It is also to be observed that, while marriage is often termed by text writers and in decisions of courts as a civil contract, generally to indicate that it must be founded upon the agreement of the parties, and does not require any religious ceremony for its solemnization, it is something more than a mere contract. The consent of the parties is of course essential to its existence, but when the contract to marry is executed by the marriage, a relation between the parties is created which they cannot change. Other contracts may be modified, restricted, or enlarged, or entirely released upon the consent of the parties. Not so with marriage. The relation once formed, the law steps in and holds the parties to various obligations and liabilities. It is an institution, in the maintenance of which in its purity the public is deeply interested, for it is the foundation of the family and of society, without which there would be neither civilization nor progress.

NOTES

1. *State regulation of "irregular" marriages.* Because the laws of slavery did not recognize formal marriage among enslaved persons, sexual and intimate relationships among this population were much more diverse, irregular, and subject to disruption. Following emancipation, there was a strong federal effort to regularize intimate relationships among newly-freed persons. Professor Katherine Franke argues that "[f]or many newly freed slaves in the latter half of the nineteenth century, the ability to marry was a powerfully important aspect of freedom . . . ." Yet at the same time, the right to marry made newly-freed slaves responsible for the support of wives and children, giving rise to both penury (for women and children) and imprisonment for the men who had scarce economic resources to comply with these legal mandates. Franke further notes that the pressure to participate in monogamous marriage, and the nuclear family form, was also difficult for newly-freed persons who may have had multiple intimate relationships due to the many familial disruptions that slavery imposed. Katherine M. Franke, *Becoming a Citizen: Reconstruction Era Regulation of African American Marriages*, 11 YALE J.L. & HUMAN. 251, 252–53 (1999).

2. *Political dimensions of marriage and state regulation of marriage.* In 1878, the U.S. Supreme Court presaged *Maynard*'s meditation on marriage and its importance to civil society in another case involving a newly-settled territory: *Reynolds v. United States*, 98 U.S. 145 (1878). There, George Reynolds, a member of the Mormon faith, challenged his criminal conviction under the Utah Territory's anti-bigamy law on the ground that the law, *inter alia*, violated his right to free exercise of religion. The Court upheld Reynolds's conviction, noting that although the Free Exercise Clause of the First Amendment prevented the government from "interfer[ing] with mere religious beliefs and opinions," it did not go so far as to prohibit the state from interfering with religious practices, including polygamy. *Id.* at 166. However, the Court went further, justifying state regulation of polygamy and marriage by noting that "[p]olygamy has always been odious among the northern and western nations of Europe, and, until the establishment of the Mormon Church, was almost exclusively a feature of the life of Asiatic and of African people." *Id.* at 165. It then went on to explain that monogamous marriage was the foundation upon which civilized societies were built:

> In fact, according as monogamous or polygamous marriages are allowed, do we find the principles on which the government of the people, to a greater or less extent, rests. Professor Lieber says, polygamy leads to the patriarchal principle, and which, when applied to large communities, fetters the people in stationary despotism, while that principle cannot long exist in connection with monogamy.

Id. at 165–66.

3.   *The rise of marriage licensing restrictions.* In broad terms, before the end of the nineteenth century and by the beginning of the twentieth, both ordinary people and legal actors thought of marriage licensing as a way of registering, rather than restricting, marriage. But eugenic concerns and concerns about venereal diseases led to a Progressive Era expansion of control over entry into marriage. By the 1930s, twenty-nine states barred the "feeble-minded" from marriage, and nineteen states made venereal disease a reason for denying marriage licenses. Matthew J. Lindsay, *Reproducing a Fit Citizenry: Dependency, Eugenics, and the Law of Marriage in the United States, 1860–1920,* 23 LAW & SOC. INQUIRY 541, 542–43 (1998).

4.   *David Maynard and the history of Seattle.* David "Doc" Maynard is credited as one of the founders of Seattle, Washington. For more on Maynard and the landmark lawsuit that bears his name, see Steven H. Hobbs, *Love on the Oregon Trail: What the Story of* Maynard v. Hill *Teaches Us About Marriage and Democratic Self-Governance,* 32 HOFSTRA L. REV. 111 (2003).

Skinner v. Oklahoma
316 U.S. 535 (1942).

■ DOUGLAS, J.

This case touches a sensitive and important area of human rights. Oklahoma deprives certain individuals of a right which is basic to the perpetuation of a race—the right to have offspring. . . .

The statute involved is Oklahoma's Habitual Criminal Sterilization Act. That Act defines an "habitual criminal" as a person who, having been convicted two or more times for crimes "amounting to felonies involving moral turpitude" either in an Oklahoma court or in a court of any other State, is thereafter convicted of such a felony in Oklahoma and is sentenced to a term of imprisonment in an Oklahoma penal institution. Machinery is provided for the institution by the Attorney General of a proceeding against such a person in the Oklahoma courts for a judgment that such person shall be rendered sexually sterile. Notice, an opportunity to be heard, and the right to a jury trial are provided. The issues triable in such a proceeding are narrow and confined. If the court or jury finds that the defendant is an "habitual criminal" and that he "may be rendered sexually sterile without detriment to his or her general health," then the court "shall render judgment to the effect that said defendant be rendered sexually sterile," by the operation of vasectomy in case of a male and of salpingectomy in case of a female. Only one other provision of the Act is material here and [it] provides that "offenses arising out of the violation of the prohibitory laws, revenue acts, embezzlement, or political offenses, shall not come or be considered within the terms of this Act."

Petitioner was convicted in 1926 of the crime of stealing chickens and was sentenced to the Oklahoma State Reformatory. In 1929 he was convicted of the crime of robbery with fire arms [sic] and was sentenced to the reformatory. In 1934 he was convicted again of robbery with firearms and was sentenced to the penitentiary. He was confined there in 1935 when the Act was passed. In 1936 the Attorney General instituted proceedings against him. . . . A jury trial was had. The court instructed the jury that the crimes of which petitioner had been convicted were felonies involving moral turpitude and that the only question for the jury was whether the operation of vasectomy could be performed on petitioner without detriment to his general health. The jury found that it could be. A judgment directing that the operation of vasectomy be performed on petitioner was affirmed by the Supreme Court of Oklahoma . . . .

Several objections to the constitutionality of the Act have been pressed upon us. It is urged that the Act cannot be sustained as an exercise of the police power in view of the state of scientific authorities respecting inheritability of criminal traits. It is argued that due process is lacking because under this Act, unlike the act upheld in *Buck v. Bell*, the defendant is given no opportunity to be heard on the issue as to whether he is the probable potential parent of socially undesirable offspring. It is also suggested that the Act is penal in character and that the sterilization provided for is cruel and unusual punishment and violative of the Fourteenth Amendment. We pass those points without intimating an opinion on them, for there is a feature of the Act which clearly condemns it. That is its failure to meet the requirements of the [E]qual [P]rotection [C]lause of the Fourteenth Amendment.

. . . In Oklahoma grand larceny is a felony. Larceny is grand larceny when the property taken exceeds $20 in value. Embezzlement is punishable "in the manner prescribed for feloniously stealing property of the value of that embezzled." Hence he who embezzles property worth more than $20 is guilty of a felony. A clerk who appropriates over $20 from his employer's till and a stranger who steals the same amount are thus both guilty of felonies. If the latter repeats his act and is convicted three times, he may be sterilized. But the clerk is not subject to the pains and penalties of the Act no matter how large his embezzlements nor how frequent his convictions. A person who enters a chicken coop and steals chickens commits a felony; and he may be sterilized if he is thrice convicted. If, however, he is a bailee of the property and fraudulently appropriates it, he is an embezzler. Hence no matter how habitual his proclivities for embezzlement are and no matter how often his conviction, he may not be sterilized. Thus the nature of the two crimes is intrinsically the same and they are punishable in the same manner.

. . . Under our constitutional system the States in determining the reach and scope of particular legislation need not provide "abstract symmetry." They may mark and set apart the classes and types of problems according to the needs and as dictated or suggested by experience. . . . For a State is not constrained in the exercise of its police power to ignore experience which marks a class of offenders or a family of offenses for special treatment. Nor is it prevented by the [E]qual [P]rotection [C]lause from confining "its restrictions to those classes of cases where the need is deemed to be clearest". . . .

But the instant legislation runs afoul of the [E]qual [P]rotection [C]lause. . . . We are dealing here with legislation which involves one of the basic civil rights of man. Marriage and procreation are fundamental to the very existence and survival of the race. The power to sterilize, if exercised, may have subtle, farreaching [sic] and devastating effects. In evil or reckless hands it can cause races or types which are inimical to the dominant group to wither and disappear. There is no redemption for the individual whom the law touches. Any experiment which the State conducts is to his irreparable injury. He is forever deprived of a basic liberty. We mention these matters not to reexamine the scope of the police power of the States. We advert to them merely in emphasis of our view that strict scrutiny of the classification which a State makes in a sterilization law is essential, lest unwittingly or otherwise invidious discriminations are made against groups or types of individuals in violation of the constitutional guaranty of just and equal laws. The guaranty of "equal protection of the laws is a pledge of the protection of equal laws." When the law lays an unequal hand on those who have committed intrinsically the same quality of offense and sterilizes one and not the other, it has made as an invidious a discrimination [sic] as if it had selected a particular race or nationality for oppressive treatment. Sterilization of those who have thrice committed grand larceny with immunity for those who are embezzlers is a clear, pointed, unmistakable discrimination. Oklahoma makes no attempt to say that he who commits larceny by trespass or trick or fraud has biologically inheritable traits which he who commits embezzlement lacks. . . . We have not the slightest basis for inferring that that line has any significance in eugenics nor that the inheritability of criminal traits follows the neat legal distinctions which the law has marked between those two offenses. In terms of fines and imprisonment the crimes of larceny and embezzlement rate the same under the Oklahoma code. Only when it comes to sterilization are the pains and penalties of the law different. The [E]qual [P]rotection [C]lause would indeed be a formula of empty words if such conspicuously artificial lines could be drawn. In *Buck v. Bell*, the Virginia statute was upheld though it applied only to feebleminded persons in institutions of the State. But it was pointed out that "so far as the operations enable those who otherwise must be kept confined to be returned to the world, and thus open the asylum to others, the equality aimed at will be more nearly reached." Here there is no such saving feature. Embezzlers are forever free. Those who steal or take in other ways are not. . . .

Reversed.

■ STONE, C.J., concurring.

I concur in the result, but I am not persuaded that we are aided in reaching it by recourse to the [E]qual [P]rotection [C]lause.

If Oklahoma may resort generally to the sterilization of criminals on the assumption that their propensities are transmissible to future generations by inheritance, I seriously doubt that the [E]qual [P]rotection [C]lause requires it to apply the measure to all criminals in the first instance, or to none.

. . . I think the real question we have to consider is not one of equal protection, but whether the wholesale condemnation of a class to such an invasion of personal liberty, without opportunity to any individual to show that his is not the type of case which would justify resort to it, satisfies the demands of due process.

There are limits to the extent to which the presumption of constitutionality can be pressed, especially where the liberty of the person is concerned and where the presumption is resorted to only to dispense with a procedure which the ordinary dictates of prudence would seem to demand for the protection of the individual from arbitrary action. Although petitioner here was given a hearing to ascertain whether sterilization would be detrimental to his health, he was given none to discover whether his criminal tendencies are of an inheritable type. Undoubtedly a state may, after appropriate inquiry, constitutionally interfere with the personal liberty of the individual to prevent the transmission by inheritance of his socially injurious tendencies. But until now we have not been called upon to say that it may do so without giving him a hearing and opportunity to challenge the existence as to him of the only facts which could justify so drastic a measure.

Science has found and the law has recognized that there are certain types of mental deficiency associated with delinquency which are inheritable. But the State does not contend—nor can there be any pretense—that either common knowledge or experience, or scientific investigation, has given assurance that the criminal tendencies of any class of habitual offenders are universally or even generally inheritable. In such circumstances, inquiry whether such is the fact in the case of any particular individual cannot rightly be dispensed with. Whether the procedure by which a statute carries its mandate into execution satisfies due process is a matter of judicial cognizance. A law which condemns, without hearing, all the individuals of a class to so harsh a measure as the present because some or even many merit condemnation, is lacking in the first principles of due process. And so, while the state may protect itself from the demonstrably inheritable tendencies of the individual which are injurious to society, the most elementary notions of due process would seem to require it to take appropriate steps to safeguard the liberty of the individual by affording him, before he is condemned to an irreparable injury in his person, some opportunity to show that he is without such inheritable tendencies. The state is called on to sacrifice no permissible end when it is required to reach its objective by a reasonable and just procedure adequate to safeguard rights of the individual which concededly the Constitution protects.

. . .

NOTES

1.   *Eugenics, totalitarianism, and* Skinner. In striking down the Oklahoma statute at issue in *Skinner*, the Court did an abrupt about-face from an earlier case, *Buck v. Bell*, 274 U.S. 200 (1927), *infra* at pp. 1058–1060, in which it upheld a similar sterilization law. Writing for the Court in *Buck v. Bell*, Justice Oliver Wendell Holmes infamously justified that law on the ground that "[t]hree generations of imbeciles are enough." *Id.* at 207. What explains the Court's retreat from sterilization laws in *Skinner*? Some scholars have argued that the "widespread revulsion" to the eugenics and sterilization policies practiced in Nazi Germany contributed to the Court's reconsideration of sterilization laws in *Skinner*. *See* CARL N. DEGLER, IN SEARCH OF HUMAN NATURE: THE DECLINE AND REVIVAL OF DARWINISM IN AMERICAN SOCIAL THOUGHT 203–05 (1991) (discussing the shift in English and American attitudes toward eugenics as a result of the brutal example of genocidal eugenics in Nazi Germany); VICTORIA F. NOURSE, IN RECKLESS HANDS: *SKINNER V. OKLAHOMA* AND THE NEAR TRIUMPH OF AMERICAN EUGENICS 126–32 (2008) (describing the conflation of eugenics with totalitarianism and specifically Nazism); Mary Ziegler, *Reinventing Eugenics: Reproductive Choice and Law Reform After World War II*, 14 CARDOZO J.L. & GENDER 319, 319–21 (2008) (noting that scholars attribute the shift in post-war eugenics rhetoric to "widespread revulsion" of Nazi sterilization policies).

2.   *Sex and* Skinner. Legal historian Ariela Dubler has argued that the concern with eugenics and totalitarianism provides only one frame for reading *Skinner* and its discussion of marriage and procreation. Also of likely concern to the *Skinner* Court, Dubler maintains, was the deep-seated fear that compulsory sterilization would offer the possibility of sex solely for pleasure and without the deterrent of pregnancy. As Dubler makes clear, the prospect of unrestrained sexuality was not only a threat to society generally, but to marriage's place in the social order. The ability to have sex without the deterrent of pregnancy would, it was feared, encourage promiscuity and adultery, undermining marriage, the marital family, and their roles in maintaining sexual order. "[F]ar from imposing social order . . . [sterilization] actually could bring about sexual chaos." *See* Ariela R. Dubler, *Sexing* Skinner: *History and the Politics of the Right to Marry*, 110 COLUM. L. REV. 1348, 1361 (2010).

3.   *Sterilization and disability.* Victoria Nourse notes that Skinner had lost a foot in a childhood accident, thus making him a "cripple," in the language of the times. While eugenicists believed "unfitness" was a global category, the restriction of reproductive rights for both mentally and physically disabled people would later be justified in paternalistic language. VICTORIA F. NOURSE, IN RECKLESS HANDS: *SKINNER V. OKLAHOMA* AND THE NEAR TRIUMPH OF AMERICAN EUGENICS 91 (2008).

Turner v. Safley

482 U.S. 78 (1987).

■ O'CONNOR, J.

This case requires us to determine the constitutionality of regulations promulgated by the Missouri Division of Corrections relating to inmate marriages .... [W]e conclude that the marriage restriction cannot be sustained.

. . .

The challenged marriage regulation, which was promulgated while this litigation was pending, permits an inmate to marry only with the permission of the superintendent of the prison, and provides that such approval should be given only "when there are compelling reasons to do so." The term "compelling" is not defined, but prison officials testified at trial that generally only a pregnancy or the birth of an illegitimate child would be considered a compelling reason. Prior to the promulgation of this rule, the applicable regulation did not obligate Missouri Division of Corrections officials to assist an inmate who wanted to get married, but it also did not specifically authorize the superintendent of an institution to prohibit inmates from getting married.

. . .

In support of the marriage regulation, petitioners first suggest that the rule does not deprive prisoners of a constitutionally protected right. They concede that the decision to marry is a fundamental right under *Zablocki v. Redhail* and *Loving v. Virginia*, but they imply that a different rule should obtain "in ... a prison forum." Petitioners then argue that even if the regulation burdens inmates' constitutional rights, the restriction should be tested under a reasonableness standard. They urge that the restriction is reasonably related to legitimate security and rehabilitation concerns.

We disagree with petitioners that *Zablocki* does not apply to prison inmates. It is settled that a prison inmate "retains those [constitutional] rights that are not inconsistent with his status as a prisoner or with the legitimate penological objectives of the corrections system." The right to marry, like many other rights, is subject to substantial restrictions as a result of incarceration. Many important attributes of marriage remain, however, after taking into account the limitations imposed by prison life. First, inmate marriages, like others, are expressions of emotional support and public commitment. These elements are an important and significant aspect of the marital relationship. In addition, many religions recognize marriage as having spiritual significance; for some inmates and their spouses, therefore, the commitment of marriage may be an exercise of religious faith as well as an expression of personal dedication. Third, most inmates eventually will be released by parole or commutation, and therefore most inmate marriages are formed in the expectation that they ultimately will be fully consummated. Finally, marital status often is a precondition to the receipt of government benefits (e.g., Social Security benefits), property rights (e.g., tenancy by the entirety, inheritance rights), and other, less tangible benefits (e.g., legitimation of children born out of wedlock). These incidents of marriage, like the religious and personal aspects of the marriage commitment, are unaffected by the fact of confinement or the pursuit of legitimate corrections goals.

Taken together, we conclude that these remaining elements are sufficient to form a constitutionally protected marital relationship in the prison context. . . .

. . .

Petitioners have identified both security and rehabilitation concerns in support of the marriage prohibition. The security concern emphasized by petitioners is that "love triangles" might lead to violent confrontations between inmates. With respect to rehabilitation, prison officials testified that female prisoners often were subject to abuse at home or were overly dependent on male figures, and that this dependence or abuse was connected to the crimes they had committed. The superintendent at Renz, petitioner William Turner, testified that in his view, these women prisoners needed to concentrate on developing skills of self-reliance and that the prohibition on marriage furthered this rehabilitative goal. Petitioners emphasize that the prohibition on marriage should be understood in light of Superintendent Turner's experience with several ill-advised marriage requests from female inmates.

We conclude that on this record, the Missouri prison regulation, as written, is not reasonably related to these penological interests. No doubt legitimate security concerns may require placing reasonable restrictions upon an inmate's right to marry, and may justify requiring approval of the superintendent. The Missouri regulation, however, represents an exaggerated response to such security objectives. There are obvious, easy alternatives to the Missouri regulation that accommodate the right to marry while imposing a *de minimis* burden on the pursuit of security objectives. *See, e.g.,* 28 CFR § 551.10 (1986) (marriage by inmates in federal prison generally permitted, but not if warden finds that it presents a threat to security or order of institution, or to public safety). We are aware of no place in the record where prison officials testified that such ready alternatives would not fully satisfy their security concerns. Moreover, with respect to the security concern emphasized in petitioners' brief—the creation of "love triangles"—petitioners have pointed to nothing in the record suggesting that the marriage regulation was viewed as preventing such entanglements. Common sense likewise suggests that there is no logical connection between the marriage restriction and the formation of love triangles: surely in prisons housing both male and female prisoners, inmate rivalries are as likely to develop without a formal marriage ceremony as with one. Finally, this is not an instance where the "ripple effect" on the security of fellow inmates and prison staff justifies a broad restriction on inmates' rights—indeed, where the inmate wishes to marry a civilian, the decision to marry (apart from the logistics of the wedding ceremony) is a completely private one.

Nor, on this record, is the marriage restriction reasonably related to the articulated rehabilitation goal. First, in requiring refusal of permission absent a finding of a compelling reason to allow the marriage, the rule sweeps much more broadly than can be explained by petitioners' penological objectives. Missouri prison officials testified that generally they had experienced no problem with the marriage of male inmates, and the District Court found that such marriages had routinely been allowed as a matter of practice at Missouri correctional institutions prior to adoption of the rule. The proffered justification thus does not explain the adoption of a rule banning marriages by these inmates. Nor does it account for the prohibition on inmate marriages to civilians. Missouri prison officials testified that generally they had no objection to inmate-civilian marriages, and Superintendent Turner testified that he usually did not object to the marriage of either male or female prisoners to civilians. The rehabilitation concern appears from the record to have been centered almost exclusively on female inmates marrying other inmates or ex-felons; it does not account for the ban on inmate-civilian marriages.

Moreover, although not necessary to the disposition of this case, we note that on this record the rehabilitative objective asserted to support the regulation itself is suspect. Of the several female inmates whose marriage requests were discussed by prison officials at trial, only one was refused on the basis of fostering excessive dependency. The District Court found that the Missouri prison system operated on the basis of excessive paternalism in that the proposed marriages of all female inmates were scrutinized carefully even before adoption of the current regulation—only one was approved at Renz in the period from 1979–1983—whereas the marriages of male inmates during the same period were routinely approved. That kind of lopsided rehabilitation concern cannot provide a justification for the broad Missouri marriage rule.

It is undisputed that Missouri prison officials may regulate the time and circumstances under which the marriage ceremony itself takes place. On this record, however, the almost complete ban on the decision to marry is not reasonably related to legitimate penological objectives. We conclude, therefore, that the Missouri marriage regulation is facially invalid.

. . .

NOTES

1.   Turner *and same-sex marriage*. Today, marriage equality advocates frequently invoke *Turner v. Safley*, citing it for the proposition that marriage

is a fundamental right. *Turner* also has been used by marriage equality advocates to highlight the injustice of allowing certain constituencies (prisoners) to enter into civil marriage, while prohibiting other constituencies (same-sex couples) from doing so. Consider the following excerpt from the petitioners' brief filed in *Perry v. Schwarzenegger*, the federal challenge to California's Proposition 8:

> None of Proponents' purported state interests can withstand the slightest scrutiny. Indeed, California law prohibits gay and lesbian individuals from marrying the person of their choice, even while it allows murderers, child molesters, rapists, abusers, serial divorcers, and philanderers to marry. It even guarantees incarcerated inmates the right to marry.

Plaintiffs' and Plaintiff-Intervenor's Trial Memorandum at 10, *Perry v. Schwarzenegger*, 704 F. Supp. 2d 291 (N.D. Cal. 2010) (No. 09–CV–2292 VRW), 2009 WL 4718815.

It is not just advocates who use *Turner* to highlight the injustice of restricting gay men and lesbians from civil marriage. Courts have made similar arguments in same-sex marriage cases. *See Varnum v. Brien*, 763 N.W.2d 862, 900 (Iowa 2009) (noting that the state's purported interest in denying marriage to same-sex couples to protect children cannot be justified where "child abusers, sexual predators, . . . [and] violent felons" are allowed to marry).

2. *Marriage and discipline.* Critically, the *Turner* petitioners also challenged the state's restrictions on prisoner correspondence on First Amendment grounds. The Court upheld the correspondence restrictions, even in the face of other fundamental rights concerns. What explains the difference in the Court's treatment of these two claims? According to one scholar,

> The difference . . . can be explained by reference to marriage's disciplinary force. In the 1980s, when *Turner* was litigated, an extant penological literature maintained that marriage and family ties could play a salutary role in the rehabilitation and socialization of prisoners (and male prisoners especially) during and after their period of incarceration . . . .
>
> . . .
>
> While the *Turner* Court did not advert directly to the corrections scholarship identifying the salutary benefits of marriage and family ties in reducing disciplinary problems and fostering an atmosphere conducive to prisoner rehabilitation during incarceration, it nonetheless recognized that marriage's benefits went beyond the physical acts of sex and procreation.

Melissa Murray, *Marriage as Punishment*, 112 COLUM. L. REV. 1, 48–49 (2012).

Obergefell v. Hodges

576 U.S. 644 (2015).

■ KENNEDY, J.

The Constitution promises liberty to all within its reach, a liberty that includes certain specific rights that allow persons, within a lawful realm, to define and express their identity. The petitioners in these cases seek to find that liberty by marrying someone of the same sex and having their marriages deemed lawful on the same terms and conditions as marriages between persons of the opposite sex.

. . . . The petitioners claim the respondents violate the Fourteenth Amendment by denying them the right to marry or to have their marriages, lawfully performed in another State, given full recognition.

. . . .

From their beginning to their most recent page, the annals of human history reveal the transcendent importance of marriage. The lifelong union of a man and a woman always has promised nobility and dignity to all persons, without regard to their station in life. Marriage is sacred to those who live by their religions and offers unique fulfillment to those who find meaning in the secular realm. Its dynamic allows two people to find a life that could not be found alone, for a marriage becomes greater than just the two persons. Rising from the most basic human needs, marriage is essential to our most profound hopes and aspirations.

The centrality of marriage to the human condition makes it unsurprising that the institution has existed for millennia and across civilizations. . . . It is fair and necessary to say these references were based on the understanding that marriage is a union between two persons of the opposite sex.

That history is the beginning of these cases. The respondents say it should be the end as well. To them, it would demean a timeless institution if the concept and lawful status of marriage were extended to two persons of the same sex. Marriage, in their view, is by its nature a gender-differentiated union of man and woman. This view long has been held—and continues to be held—in good faith by reasonable and sincere people here and throughout the world.

The petitioners acknowledge this history but contend that these cases cannot end there. Were their intent to demean the revered idea and reality of marriage, the petitioners' claims would be of a different order. But that is neither their purpose nor their submission. To the contrary, it is the enduring importance of marriage that underlies the petitioners' contentions. . . . Far from seeking to devalue marriage, the petitioners seek it for themselves because of their respect—and need—for its privileges and responsibilities. And their immutable nature dictates that same-sex marriage is their only real path to this profound commitment.

. . . .

The ancient origins of marriage confirm its centrality, but it has not stood in isolation from developments in law and society. The history of marriage is one of both continuity and change. That institution—even as confined to opposite-sex relations—has evolved over time.

. . . .

These new insights have strengthened, not weakened, the institution of marriage. Indeed, changed understandings of marriage are characteristic of a Nation where new dimensions of freedom become apparent to new generations, often through perspectives that begin in pleas or protests and then are considered in the political sphere and the judicial process.

This dynamic can be seen in the Nation's experiences with the rights of gays and lesbians. Until the mid-20th century, same-sex intimacy long had been condemned as immoral by the state itself in most Western nations, a belief often embodied in the criminal law. For this reason, among others, many persons did not deem homosexuals to have dignity in their own distinct identity. A truthful declaration by same-sex couples of what was in their hearts had to remain unspoken. Even when a greater awareness of the humanity and integrity of homosexual persons came in the period after World War II, the argument that gays and lesbians had a just claim to dignity was in conflict with both law and widespread social conventions. Same-sex intimacy remained a crime in many States. Gays and lesbians were prohibited from most government employment, barred from military service, excluded under immigration laws, targeted by police, and burdened in their rights to associate.

For much of the 20th century, moreover, homosexuality was treated as an illness. When the American Psychiatric Association published the first Diagnostic and Statistical Manual of Mental Disorders in 1952, homosexuality was classified as a mental disorder, a position adhered to until 1973. Only in more recent years have psychiatrists and others recognized that sexual orientation is both a normal expression of human sexuality and immutable.

Under the Due Process Clause of the Fourteenth Amendment, no State shall "deprive any person of life, liberty, or property, without due process of law." The fundamental liberties protected by this Clause include most of the rights enumerated in the Bill of Rights. In addition these liberties extend to certain personal choices central to individual dignity and autonomy, including intimate choices that define personal identity and beliefs.

The identification and protection of fundamental rights is an enduring part of the judicial duty to interpret the Constitution. That responsibility, however, "has not been reduced to any formula." Rather, it requires courts to exercise reasoned judgment in identifying interests of the person so fundamental that the State must accord them its respect. That process is guided by many of the same considerations relevant to analysis of other constitutional provisions that set forth broad principles rather than specific requirements. History and tradition guide and discipline this inquiry but do not set its outer boundaries. That method respects our history and learns from it without allowing the past alone to rule the present.

The nature of injustice is that we may not always see it in our own times. The generations that wrote and ratified the Bill of Rights and the Fourteenth Amendment did not presume to know the extent of freedom in all of its dimensions, and so they entrusted to future generations a charter protecting the right of all persons to enjoy liberty as we learn its meaning. When new insight reveals discord between the Constitution's central protections and a received legal stricture, a claim to liberty must be addressed.

Applying these established tenets, the Court has long held the right to marry is protected by the Constitution. In *Loving v. Virginia* (1967), which invalidated bans on interracial unions, a unanimous Court held marriage is "one of the vital personal rights essential to the orderly pursuit of happiness by free men." The Court reaffirmed that holding in *Zablocki v. Redhail* (1978), which held the right to marry was burdened by a law prohibiting fathers who were behind on child support from marrying. The Court again applied this principle in *Turner v. Safley* (1987), which held the right to marry was abridged by regulations limiting the privilege of prison inmates to marry. Over time and in other contexts, the Court has reiterated that the right to marry is fundamental under the Due Process Clause.

It cannot be denied that this Court's cases describing the right to marry presumed a relationship involving opposite-sex partners. The Court, like many institutions, has made assumptions defined by the world and time of which it is a part. . . .

Still, there are other, more instructive precedents. This Court's cases have expressed constitutional principles of broader reach. In defining the right to marry these cases have identified essential attributes of that right based in history, tradition, and other constitutional liberties inherent in this intimate bond. And in assessing whether the force and rationale of its cases apply to same-sex couples, the Court must respect the basic reasons why the right to marry has been long protected.

This analysis compels the conclusion that same-sex couples may exercise the right to marry. The four principles and traditions to be discussed demonstrate that the reasons marriage is fundamental under the Constitution apply with equal force to same-sex couples.

A first premise of the Court's relevant precedents is that the right to personal choice regarding marriage is inherent in the concept of individual autonomy. This abiding connection between marriage and liberty is why . . . [l]ike choices concerning contraception, family relationships, procreation, and childrearing, all of which are protected by the Constitution, decisions concerning marriage are among the most intimate that an individual can make. Indeed, the Court has noted it would be contradictory "to recognize a right of privacy with respect to other matters of family life and not with respect to the decision to enter the relationship that is the foundation of the family in our society."

Choices about marriage shape an individual's destiny.... The nature of marriage is that, through its enduring bond, two persons together can find other freedoms, such as expression, intimacy, and spirituality. This is true for all persons, whatever their sexual orientation. There is dignity in the bond between two men or two women who seek to marry and in their autonomy to make such profound choices.

A second principle in this Court's jurisprudence is that the right to marry is fundamental because it supports a two-person union unlike any other in its importance to the committed individuals. This point was central to *Griswold v. Connecticut* (1965), which held the Constitution protects the right of married couples to use contraception....

Marriage responds to the universal fear that a lonely person might call out only to find no one there. It offers the hope of companionship and understanding and assurance that while both still live there will be someone to care for the other.

As this Court held in *Lawrence*, same-sex couples have the same right as opposite-sex couples to enjoy intimate association. *Lawrence* invalidated laws that made same-sex intimacy a criminal act.... But while *Lawrence* confirmed a dimension of freedom that allows individuals to engage in intimate association without criminal liability, it does not follow that freedom stops there. Outlaw to outcast may be a step forward, but it does not achieve the full promise of liberty.

A third basis for protecting the right to marry is that it safeguards children and families and thus draws meaning from related rights of childrearing, procreation, and education. The Court has recognized these connections by describing the varied rights as a unified whole: "[T]he right to 'marry, establish a home and bring up children' is a central part of the liberty protected by the Due Process Clause." Under the laws of the several States, some of marriage's protections for children and families are material. But marriage also confers more profound benefits. By giving recognition and legal structure to their parents' relationship, marriage allows children "to understand the integrity and closeness of their own family and its concord with other families in their community and in their daily lives." Marriage also affords the permanency and stability important to children's best interests.

As all parties agree, many same-sex couples provide loving and nurturing homes to their children, whether biological or adopted. And hundreds of thousands of children are presently being raised by such couples. Most States have allowed gays and lesbians to adopt, either as individuals or as couples, and many adopted and foster children have same-sex parents. This provides powerful confirmation from the law itself that gays and lesbians can create loving, supportive families.

Excluding same-sex couples from marriage thus conflicts with a central premise of the right to marry. Without the recognition, stability, and predictability marriage offers, their children suffer the stigma of knowing their families are somehow lesser. They also suffer the significant material costs of being raised by unmarried parents, relegated through no fault of their own to a more difficult and uncertain family life. The marriage laws at issue here thus harm and humiliate the children of same-sex couples.

That is not to say the right to marry is less meaningful for those who do not or cannot have children. An ability, desire, or promise to procreate is not and has not been a prerequisite for a valid marriage in any State. In light of precedent protecting the right of a married couple not to procreate, it cannot be said the Court or the States have conditioned the right to marry on the capacity or commitment to procreate. The constitutional marriage right has many aspects, of which childbearing is only one.

Fourth and finally, this Court's cases and the Nation's traditions make clear that marriage is a keystone of our social order. . . . For that reason, just as a couple vows to support each other, so does society pledge to support the couple, offering symbolic recognition and material benefits to protect and nourish the union. Indeed, while the States are in general free to vary the benefits they confer on all married couples, they have throughout our history made marriage the basis for an expanding list of governmental rights, benefits, and responsibilities. These aspects of marital status include: taxation; inheritance and property rights; rules of intestate succession; spousal privilege in the law of evidence; hospital access; medical decisionmaking authority; adoption rights; the rights and benefits of survivors; birth and death certificates; professional ethics rules; campaign finance restrictions; workers' compensation benefits; health insurance; and child custody, support, and visitation rules. . . .

There is no difference between same- and opposite-sex couples with respect to this principle. Yet by virtue of their exclusion from that institution, same-sex couples are denied the constellation of benefits that the States have linked to marriage. This harm results in more than just material burdens. Same-sex couples are consigned to an instability many opposite-sex couples would deem intolerable in their own lives. As the State itself makes marriage all the more precious by the significance it attaches to it, exclusion from that status has the effect of teaching that gays and lesbians are unequal in important respects. It demeans gays and lesbians for the State to lock them out of a central institution of the Nation's society. Same-sex couples, too, may aspire to the transcendent purposes of marriage and seek fulfillment in its highest meaning.

The limitation of marriage to opposite-sex couples may long have seemed natural and just, but its inconsistency with the central meaning of the fundamental right to marry is now manifest. With that knowledge must come the recognition that laws excluding same-sex couples from the marriage right impose stigma and injury of the kind prohibited by our basic charter. . . .

. . . . If rights were defined by who exercised them in the past, then received practices could serve as their own continued justification and new groups could not invoke rights once denied. This Court has rejected that approach, both with respect to the right to marry and the rights of gays and lesbians.

. . . .

The right of same-sex couples to marry that is part of the liberty promised by the Fourteenth Amendment is derived, too, from that Amendment's guarantee of the equal protection of the laws. The Due Process Clause and the Equal Protection Clause are connected in a profound way, though they set forth independent principles. Rights implicit in liberty and rights secured by equal protection may rest on different precepts and are not always co-extensive, yet in some instances each may be instructive as to the meaning and reach of the other. In any particular case one Clause may be thought to capture the essence of the right in a more accurate and comprehensive way, even as the two Clauses may converge in the identification and definition of the right. This interrelation of the two principles furthers our understanding of what freedom is and must become.

. . . .

. . . . It is now clear that the challenged laws burden the liberty of same-sex couples, and it must be further acknowledged that they abridge central precepts of equality. Here the marriage laws enforced by the respondents are in essence unequal: same-sex couples are denied all the benefits afforded to opposite-sex couples and are barred from exercising a fundamental right. Especially against a long history of disapproval of their relationships, this denial to same-sex couples of the right to marry works a grave and continuing harm. The imposition of this disability on gays and lesbians serves to disrespect and subordinate them. And the Equal Protection Clause, like the Due Process Clause, prohibits this unjustified infringement of the fundamental right to marry.

These considerations lead to the conclusion that the right to marry is a fundamental right inherent in the liberty of the person, and under the Due Process and Equal Protection Clauses of the Fourteenth Amendment couples of the same-sex may not be deprived of that right and that liberty. The Court now holds that same-sex couples may exercise the fundamental right to marry. No longer may this liberty be denied to them. . . .

There may be an initial inclination in these cases to proceed with caution—to await further legislation, litigation, and debate. . . . Yet there has been far more deliberation than this argument acknowledges. There have been referenda, legislative debates, and grassroots campaigns, as well as countless studies, papers, books, and other popular and scholarly writings. There has been extensive litigation in state and federal courts. . . .

Of course, the Constitution contemplates that democracy is the appropriate process for change, so long as that process does not abridge fundamental rights. . . .

The dynamic of our constitutional system is that individuals need not await legislative action before asserting a fundamental right. The Nation's courts are open to injured individuals who come to them to vindicate their own direct, personal stake in our basic charter. An individual can invoke a right to constitutional protection when he or she is harmed, even if the broader public disagrees and even if the legislature refuses to act. . . .

Finally, it must be emphasized that religions, and those who adhere to religious doctrines, may continue to advocate with utmost, sincere conviction that, by divine precepts, same-sex marriage should not be condoned. The First Amendment ensures that religious organizations and persons are given proper protection as they seek to teach the principles that are so fulfilling and so central to their lives and faiths, and to their own deep aspirations to continue the family structure they have long revered. The same is true of those who oppose same-sex marriage for other reasons. In turn, those who believe allowing same-sex marriage is proper or indeed essential, whether as a matter of religious conviction or secular belief, may engage those who disagree with their view in an open and searching debate. The Constitution, however, does not permit the State to bar same-sex couples from marriage on the same terms as accorded to couples of the opposite sex.

. . . .

No union is more profound than marriage, for it embodies the highest ideals of love, fidelity, devotion, sacrifice, and family. In forming a marital union, two people become something greater than once they were. As some of the petitioners in these cases demonstrate, marriage embodies a love that may endure even past death. It would misunderstand these men and women to say they disrespect the idea of marriage. Their plea is that they do respect it, respect it so deeply that they seek to find its fulfillment for themselves. Their hope is not to be condemned to live in loneliness, excluded from one of civilization's oldest institutions. They ask for equal dignity in the eyes of the law. The Constitution grants them that right.

. . . .

■ ROBERTS, C.J., with whom SCALIA, J., and THOMAS, J. join, dissenting.

. . . .

Today . . . the Court takes the extraordinary step of ordering every State to license and recognize same-sex marriage. Many people will rejoice at this decision, and I begrudge none their celebration. But for those who believe in a government of laws, not of men, the majority's approach is deeply disheartening. Supporters of same-sex marriage have achieved considerable success persuading their fellow citizens—through the democratic process—to adopt their view. That ends today. Five lawyers have closed the debate and enacted their own vision of marriage as a matter of constitutional law. Stealing this issue from the people will for many cast a cloud over same-sex marriage, making a dramatic social change that much more difficult to accept.

The majority's decision is an act of will, not legal judgment. The right it announces has no basis in the Constitution or this Court's precedent. The majority expressly disclaims judicial "caution" and omits even a pretense of humility, openly relying on its desire to remake society according to its own "new insight" into the "nature of injustice." As a result, the Court invalidates the marriage laws of more than half the States and orders the transformation of a social institution that has formed the basis of human society for millennia, for the Kalahari Bushmen and the Han Chinese, the Carthaginians and the Aztecs. Just who do we think we are?

It can be tempting for judges to confuse our own preferences with the requirements of the law. But as this Court has been reminded throughout our history, the Constitution "is made for people of fundamentally differing views." *Lochner v. New York* (1905) (Holmes, J., dissenting). Accordingly, "courts are not concerned with the wisdom or policy of legislation." The majority today neglects that restrained conception of the judicial role. It seizes for itself a question the Constitution leaves to the people, at a time when the people are engaged in a vibrant debate on that question. And it answers that question based not on neutral principles of constitutional law, but on its own "understanding of what freedom is and must become." I have no choice but to dissent.

Understand well what this dissent is about: It is not about whether, in my judgment, the institution of marriage should be changed to include same-sex couples. It is instead about whether, in our democratic republic, that decision should rest with the people acting through their elected representatives, or with five lawyers who happen to hold commissions authorizing them to resolve legal disputes according to law. The Constitution leaves no doubt about the answer.

. . . .

It is striking how much of the majority's reasoning would apply with equal force to the claim of a fundamental right to plural marriage. If "[t]here is dignity in the bond between two men or two women who seek to marry and in their autonomy to make such profound choices," why would there be any less dignity in the bond between three people who, in exercising their autonomy, seek to make the profound choice to marry? If a same-sex couple has the constitutional right to marry because their children would otherwise "suffer the stigma of knowing their families are somehow lesser," why wouldn't the same reasoning apply to a family of three or more persons raising children? If not having the opportunity to marry "serves to disrespect and subordinate" gay and lesbian couples, why wouldn't the same "imposition of this disability," serve to disrespect and subordinate people who find fulfillment in polyamorous relationships?

I do not mean to equate marriage between same-sex couples with plural marriages in all respects. There may well be relevant differences that compel different legal analysis. But if there are, petitioners have not pointed to any. When asked about a plural marital union at oral argument, petitioners asserted that a State "doesn't have such an institution." But that is exactly the point: the States at issue here do not have an institution of same-sex marriage, either.

. . . .

The majority's understanding of due process lays out a tantalizing vision of the future for Members of this Court: If an unvarying social institution enduring over all of recorded history cannot inhibit judicial policymaking, what can? But this approach is dangerous for the rule of law. The purpose of insisting that implied fundamental rights have roots in the history and tradition of our people is to ensure that when unelected judges strike down democratically enacted laws, they do so based on something more than their own beliefs. The Court today not only overlooks our country's entire history and tradition but actively repudiates it, preferring to live only in the heady days of the here and now. I agree with the majority that the "nature of injustice is that we may not always see it in our own times." As petitioners put it, "times can blind." But to blind yourself to history is both prideful and unwise. "The past is never dead. It's not even past." W. Faulkner, Requiem for a Nun 92 (1951).

In addition to their due process argument, petitioners contend that the Equal Protection Clause requires their States to license and recognize same-sex marriages. The majority does not seriously engage with this claim. Its discussion is, quite frankly, difficult to follow. The central point seems to be that there is a "synergy between" the Equal Protection Clause and the Due Process Clause, and that some precedents relying on one Clause have also relied on the other. Absent from this portion of the opinion, however, is anything resembling our usual framework for deciding equal protection cases. . . .

The majority goes on to assert in conclusory fashion that the Equal Protection Clause provides an alternative basis for its holding. Yet the majority fails to provide even a single sentence explaining how the Equal Protection Clause supplies independent weight for its position, nor does it attempt to justify its gratuitous violation of the canon against unnecessarily resolving constitutional questions. . . .

. . . .

Those who founded our country would not recognize the majority's conception of the judicial role. They after all risked their lives and fortunes for the precious right to govern themselves. They would never have imagined yielding that right on a question of social policy to unaccountable and unelected judges. And they certainly would not have been satisfied by a system empowering judges to override policy judgments so long as they do so after "a quite extensive discussion." In our democracy, debate about the content of the law is not an exhaustion requirement to be checked off before courts can impose their will. . . .

The Court's accumulation of power does not occur in a vacuum. It comes at the expense of the people. And they know it. Here and abroad, people are in the midst of a serious and thoughtful public debate on the issue of same-sex marriage. They see voters carefully considering same-sex marriage, casting ballots in favor or opposed, and sometimes changing their minds. They see political leaders similarly reexamining their positions, and either reversing course or explaining adherence to old convictions confirmed anew. They see governments and businesses modifying policies and practices with respect to same-sex couples, and participating actively in the civic discourse. They see countries overseas democratically accepting profound social change, or declining to do so. This deliberative process is making people take seriously questions that they may not have even regarded as questions before.

When decisions are reached through democratic means, some people will inevitably be disappointed with the results. But those whose views do not prevail at least know that they have had their say, and accordingly are—in the tradition of our political culture—reconciled to the result of a fair and honest debate. In addition, they can gear up to raise the issue later, hoping to persuade enough on the winning side to think again. "That is exactly how our system of government is supposed to work."

But today the Court puts a stop to all that. By deciding this question under the Constitution, the Court removes it from the realm of democratic decision. There will be consequences to shutting down the political process on an issue of such profound public significance. Closing debate tends to close minds. People denied a voice are less likely to accept the ruling of a court on an issue that does not seem to be the sort of thing courts usually decide. As a thoughtful commentator observed about another issue, "The political process was moving . . . , not swiftly enough for advocates of quick, complete change, but majoritarian institutions were listening and acting. Heavy-handed judicial intervention was difficult to justify and appears to have provoked, not resolved, conflict." [Ruth Bader] Ginsburg, Some Thoughts on Autonomy and Equality in Relation to *Roe v. Wade*, 63 N.C. L. Rev. 375, 385–386 (1985). Indeed, however heartened the proponents of same-sex marriage might be on this day, it is worth acknowledging what they have lost, and lost forever: the opportunity to win the true acceptance that comes from persuading their fellow citizens of the justice of their cause. And they lose this just when the winds of change were freshening at their backs.

Federal courts are blunt instruments when it comes to creating rights. They have constitutional power only to resolve concrete cases or controversies; they do not have the flexibility of legislatures to address concerns of parties not before the court or to anticipate problems that may arise from the exercise of a new right. Today's decision, for example, creates serious questions about religious liberty. Many good and decent people oppose same-sex marriage as a tenet of faith, and their freedom to exercise religion is—unlike the right imagined by the majority—actually spelled out in the Constitution.

Respect for sincere religious conviction has led voters and legislators in every State that has adopted same-sex marriage democratically to include accommodations for religious practice. The majority's decision imposing same-sex marriage cannot, of course, create any such accommodations. The majority graciously suggests that religious believers may continue to "advocate" and "teach" their views of marriage. The First Amendment guarantees, however, the freedom to *"exercise"* religion. Ominously, that is not a word the majority uses.

Hard questions arise when people of faith exercise religion in ways that may be seen to conflict with the new right to same-sex marriage— when, for example, a religious college provides married student housing only to opposite-sex married couples, or a religious adoption agency declines to place children with same-sex married couples. Indeed, the Solicitor General candidly acknowledged that the tax exemptions of some religious institutions would be in question if they opposed same-sex marriage. There is little doubt that these and similar questions will soon be before this Court. Unfortunately, people of faith can take no comfort in the treatment they receive from the majority today.

. . . .

If you are among the many Americans—of whatever sexual orientation—who favor expanding same-sex marriage, by all means celebrate today's decision. Celebrate the achievement of a desired goal. Celebrate the opportunity for a new expression of commitment to a partner. Celebrate the availability of new benefits. But do not celebrate the Constitution. It had nothing to do with it.

■ SCALIA, J., with whom THOMAS, J. joins, dissenting.

I join the Chief Justice's opinion in full. I write separately to call attention to this Court's threat to American democracy.

. . . .

The Constitution places some constraints on self-rule—constraints adopted *by the People themselves* when they ratified the Constitution and its Amendments. Forbidden are laws "impairing the Obligation of Contracts," denying "Full Faith and Credit" to the "public Acts" of other

States, prohibiting the free exercise of religion, abridging the freedom of speech, infringing the right to keep and bear arms, authorizing unreasonable searches and seizures, and so forth. Aside from these limitations, those powers "reserved to the States respectively, or to the people" can be exercised as the States or the People desire. These cases ask us to decide whether the Fourteenth Amendment contains a limitation that requires the States to license and recognize marriages between two people of the same sex. Does it remove *that* issue from the political process?

Of course not. It would be surprising to find a prescription regarding marriage in the Federal Constitution since, as the author of today's opinion reminded us only two years ago (in an opinion joined by the same Justices who join him today):

> "[R]egulation of domestic relations is an area that has long been regarded as a virtually exclusive province of the States." "[T]he Federal Government, through our history, has deferred to state-law policy decisions with respect to domestic relations."

But we need not speculate. When the Fourteenth Amendment was ratified in 1868, every State limited marriage to one man and one woman, and no one doubted the constitutionality of doing so. That resolves these cases. When it comes to determining the meaning of a vague constitutional provision—such as "due process of law" or "equal protection of the laws"—it is unquestionable that the People who ratified that provision did not understand it to prohibit a practice that remained both universal and uncontroversial in the years after ratification. We have no basis for striking down a practice that is not expressly prohibited by the Fourteenth Amendment's text, and that bears the endorsement of a long tradition of open, widespread, and unchallenged use dating back to the Amendment's ratification. Since there is no doubt whatever that the People never decided to prohibit the limitation of marriage to opposite-sex couples, the public debate over same-sex marriage must be allowed to continue.

But the Court ends this debate, in an opinion lacking even a thin veneer of law. Buried beneath the mummeries and straining-to-be-memorable passages of the opinion is a candid and startling assertion: No matter *what* it was the People ratified, the Fourteenth Amendment protects those rights that the Judiciary, in its "reasoned judgment," thinks the Fourteenth Amendment ought to protect. . . . This is a naked judicial claim to legislative—indeed, *super*-legislative—power; a claim fundamentally at odds with our system of government. Except as limited by a constitutional prohibition agreed to by the People, the States are free to adopt whatever laws they like, even those that offend the esteemed Justices' "reasoned judgment." A system of government that makes the People subordinate to a committee of nine unelected lawyers does not deserve to be called a democracy.

. . . .

■ THOMAS, J., with whom SCALIA, J., joins, dissenting.

. . . .

The majority's decision today will require States to issue marriage licenses to same-sex couples and to recognize same-sex marriages entered in other States largely based on a constitutional provision guaranteeing "due process" before a person is deprived of his "life, liberty, or property." I have elsewhere explained the dangerous fiction of treating the Due Process Clause as a font of substantive rights. It distorts the constitutional text, which guarantees only whatever "process" is "due" before a person is deprived of life, liberty, and property. Worse, it invites judges to do exactly what the majority has done here—" 'roa[m] at large in the constitutional field' guided only by their personal views" as to the " 'fundamental rights' " protected by that document.

By straying from the text of the Constitution, substantive due process exalts judges at the expense of the People from whom they derive their authority. Petitioners argue that by enshrining the traditional definition of marriage in their State Constitutions through voter-approved amendments, the States have put the issue "beyond the reach of the normal democratic process." But the result petitioners seek is far less democratic. They ask nine judges on this Court to enshrine their definition of marriage in the Federal Constitution and thus put it beyond the reach of the normal democratic process for the entire Nation. That a "bare majority" of this Court, is able to grant this wish, wiping out with a stroke of the keyboard the results of the political process in over 30 States, based on a provision that guarantees only "due process" is but further evidence of the danger of substantive due process.

Even if the doctrine of substantive due process were somehow defensible—it is not—petitioners still would not have a claim. To invoke the protection of the Due Process Clause at all—whether under a theory of "substantive" or "procedural" due process—a party must first identify a deprivation of "life, liberty, or property." The majority claims these state laws deprive petitioners of "liberty," but the concept of "liberty" it conjures up bears no resemblance to any plausible meaning of that word as it is used in the Due Process Clauses.

. . . .

Even assuming that the "liberty" in those Clauses encompasses something more than freedom from physical restraint, it would not include the types of rights claimed by the majority. In the American legal tradition, liberty has long been understood as individual freedom *from* governmental action, not as a right *to* a particular governmental entitlement.

. . . .

Whether we define "liberty" as locomotion or freedom from governmental action more broadly, petitioners have in no way been deprived of it.

Petitioners cannot claim, under the most plausible definition of "liberty," that they have been imprisoned or physically restrained by the States for participating in same-sex relationships. To the contrary, they have been able to cohabitate and raise their children in peace. They have been able to hold civil marriage ceremonies in States that recognize same-sex marriages and private religious ceremonies in all States. They have been able to travel freely around the country, making their homes where they please. Far from being incarcerated or physically restrained, petitioners have been left alone to order their lives as they see fit.

Nor, under the broader definition, can they claim that the States have restricted their ability to go about their daily lives as they would be able to absent governmental restrictions. Petitioners do not ask this Court to order the States to stop restricting their ability to enter same-sex relationships, to engage in intimate behavior, to make vows to their partners in public ceremonies, to engage in religious wedding ceremonies, to hold themselves out as married, or to raise children. The States have imposed no such restrictions. Nor have the States prevented petitioners from approximating a number of incidents of marriage through private legal means, such as wills, trusts, and powers of attorney.

Instead, the States have refused to grant them governmental entitlements. Petitioners claim that as a matter of "liberty," they are entitled to access privileges and benefits that exist solely *because of* the government. They want, for example, to receive the State's *imprimatur* on their marriages—on state issued marriage licenses, death certificates, or other official forms. And they want to receive various monetary benefits, including reduced inheritance taxes upon the death of a spouse, compensation if a spouse dies as a result of a work-related injury, or loss of consortium damages in tort suits. But receiving governmental recognition and benefits has nothing to do with any understanding of "liberty" that the Framers would have recognized.

. . . .

Our Constitution—like the Declaration of Independence before it— was predicated on a simple truth: One's liberty, not to mention one's dignity, was something to be shielded from—not provided by—the State. Today's decision casts that truth aside. In its haste to reach a desired result, the majority misapplies a clause focused on "due process" to afford substantive rights, disregards the most plausible understanding of the "liberty" protected by that clause, and distorts the principles on which this Nation was founded. Its decision will have inestimable consequences for our Constitution and our society. I respectfully dissent.

■ ALITO, J., with whom SCALIA, J., and THOMAS, J., join, dissenting.

. . . .

The Constitution says nothing about a right to same-sex marriage, but the Court holds that the term "liberty" in the Due Process Clause of the Fourteenth Amendment encompasses this right. . . . To prevent five unelected Justices from imposing their personal vision of liberty upon the American people, the Court has held that "liberty" under the Due Process Clause should be understood to protect only those rights that are " 'deeply rooted in this Nation's history and tradition.' " *Washington v. Glucksberg* (1997). And it is beyond dispute that the right to same-sex marriage is not among those rights. *See United States v. Windsor* (2003) (Alito, J., dissenting).

For today's majority, it does not matter that the right to same-sex marriage lacks deep roots or even that it is contrary to long-established tradition. The Justices in the majority claim the authority to confer constitutional protection upon that right simply because they believe that it is fundamental.

Attempting to circumvent the problem presented by the newness of the right found in these cases, the majority claims that the issue is the right to equal treatment. Noting that marriage is a fundamental right, the majority argues that a State has no valid reason for denying that right to same-sex couples. This reasoning is dependent upon a particular understanding of the purpose of civil marriage. . . .

This understanding of marriage, which focuses almost entirely on the happiness of persons who choose to marry, is shared by many people today, but it is not the traditional one. For millennia, marriage was inextricably linked to the one thing that only an opposite-sex couple can do: procreate.

. . . .

Today's decision usurps the constitutional right of the people to decide whether to keep or alter the traditional understanding of marriage. The decision will also have other important consequences.

It will be used to vilify Americans who are unwilling to assent to the new orthodoxy. In the course of its opinion, the majority compares traditional marriage laws to laws that denied equal treatment for African-Americans and women. The implications of this analogy will be exploited by those who are determined to stamp out every vestige of dissent.

Perhaps recognizing how its reasoning may be used, the majority attempts, toward the end of its opinion, to reassure those who oppose same-sex marriage that their rights of conscience will be protected. We will soon see whether this proves to be true. I assume that those who cling to old beliefs will be able to whisper their thoughts in the recesses of their homes, but if they repeat those views in public, they will risk being labeled as bigots and treated as such by governments, employers, and schools.

The system of federalism established by our Constitution provides a way for people with different beliefs to live together in a single nation. If the issue of same-sex marriage had been left to the people of the States, it is likely that some States would recognize same-sex marriage and others would not. It is also possible that some States would tie recognition to protection for conscience rights. The majority today makes that impossible. By imposing its own views on the entire country, the majority facilitates the marginalization of the many Americans who have traditional ideas. Recalling the harsh treatment of gays and lesbians in the past, some may think that turnabout is fair play. But if that sentiment prevails, the Nation will experience bitter and lasting wounds.

Today's decision will also have a fundamental effect on this Court and its ability to uphold the rule of law. If a bare majority of Justices can invent a new right and impose that right on the rest of the country, the only real limit on what future majorities will be able to do is their own sense of what those with political power and cultural influence are willing to tolerate. Even enthusiastic supporters of same-sex marriage should worry about the scope of the power that today's majority claims. . . .

NOTES

1.   *Marriage's "constellation of benefits"*. A principal question arising out of *Obergefell* is the issue of breadth. The decision requires states to make marriage available to same-sex and opposite-sex couples alike. But does it require the state to make other benefits with which marriage is associated equally available as well? In *Pavan v. Smith*, 137 S. Ct. 2075 (2017), the Court considered whether married same-sex couples were eligible to be recognized as legal parents for purposes of Arkansas's birth certificate registration scheme, which allowed married opposite-sex parents to be listed as legal parents. In a per curiam opinion issued without briefing on the merits or oral argument, the Court rejected Arkansas' argument that the registration of parents on a birth certificate had nothing to do with marriage. As the Court explained, because "Arkansas law makes birth certificates about more than just genetics," the different treatment of married same-sex and opposite-sex couples impermissibly denied same-sex couples "the constellation of benefits that the State has linked to marriage." *Id.* at 2078–79.

The decision drew a spirited dissent from Justice Neil Gorsuch, who had recently joined the Court. In an opinion joined by Justices Thomas and Alito, Gorsuch acknowledged that *Obergefell* "addressed the question whether a State must recognize same-sex marriages." But, he continued, "nothing in *Obergefell* indicates that a birth registration regime based on biology, one no doubt with many analogues across the country and throughout history, offends the Constitution." *Id.* at 2079 (Gorsuch, J., dissenting).

2.   *Employment benefits and same-sex marriage.* In 2013, the mayor of Houston, Texas extended spousal benefits to city employees in same-sex marriages legally obtained in other states. Although same-sex marriages weren't legal in Texas at the time, the city maintained that marriages outside the state were still legal and state employees who fit that criteria should be extended the same benefits as legal opposite-sex couples. Houston

taxpayers Jack Pidgeon and Larry Hicks filed a lawsuit against the mayor and the City of Houston, alleging that the extension of benefits to same-sex couples violated the Texas Constitution and the Texas Family Code. A trial court granted a temporary injunction that prevented the city from providing the spousal benefits to city employees in same-sex marriages. But in July 2015, the state intermediate appellate court reversed the injunction in light of *Obergefell*. Although the Texas Supreme Court originally declined to hear to case, pressure from conservative constituents and politicians around the state prompted the court to hear the case on appeal. On June 30, 2017, the Texas Supreme Court remanded the case back to the trial court for new arguments and reconsideration in light of *Obergefell*. On September 15, 2017, the city of Houston asked the United States Supreme Court to review the case, arguing that the Texas Supreme Court ignored United States Supreme Court rulings. On December 4, 2017, the Court denied the petition, sending the case back to the state trial court. On February 18, 2019, a state-level trial court ruled in favor of the city of Houston and dismissed the lawsuit.

3.   *Marriage equality and illegitimacy.* Although *Obergefell* expanded civil marriage to include same-sex couples, some worry that the decision "is likely to have negative repercussions for those—gay or straight—who, by choice or by circumstance, live their lives outside of marriage." Melissa Murray, Obergefell v. Hodges *and Nonmarriage Inequality*, 104 CALIF. L. REV. 1207, 1210 (2016). That is, "*Obergefell* builds the case for equal access to marriage on the premise that marriage is the most profound, dignified, and fundamental institution into which individuals may enter. Alternatives to marriage . . . are by comparison undignified, less profound, and less valuable." *Id.* at 1209–10. Do you agree? Does the rationale for marriage equality render other relationships and kinship forms fundamentally unequal?

4.   *Paths forsaken? Obergefell v. Hodges* was a set of four consolidated cases. One of those cases, *DeBoer v. Snyder*, involved two women who were coparenting foster children. When they filed their lawsuit against the state of Michigan, Jayne Rowse and April DeBoer were not challenging their exclusion from civil marriage. Instead, they were challenging Michigan's adoption laws, which prevented unmarried persons from jointly adopting. In presenting their challenge to the adoption laws, Rowse and DeBoer initially drew upon cases like *Levy v. Louisiana* and *Weber* to argue that the Michigan adoption policy discriminated against children based upon their adult caregivers' unmarried status. *Id.* However, as Rowse and DeBoer's lawsuit progressed through the courts, they were advised to reframe the underlying legal claim. Instead of challenging the adoption policy and seeking its modification to permit joint adoptions by unmarried couples, Rowse and DeBoer were encouraged to challenge Michigan's marriage laws. As a legally married couple, there would be no impediment to a joint adoption. With this in mind, the couple filed an amended complaint, focusing their claims on the consequences of their exclusion from civil marriage. *See* Melissa Murray, Obergefell v. Hodges *and Nonmarriage Inequality*, 104 CALIF. L. REV. 1207, 1252–53 (2016). Obviously, with the *Obergefell* decision, Rowse and DeBoer

were able to legally marry in Michigan, and thus, were eligible to adopt
under the state's laws. But in amending their legal claim to challenge the
state's marriage laws, did they sacrifice an opportunity to champion a more
inclusive understanding of family and kinship?

5.   Masterpiece Cakeshop v. Colorado Civil Rights Commission. The
Obergefell decision leaves open, but did not resolve, the prospect of
permissible religious objections to same-sex marriage. Since *Obergefell*, the
question of how to reconcile religious liberty with antidiscrimination
protections for LGBTQ persons and their relationships has continued to
percolate. In *Masterpiece Cakeshop Ltd. v. Colorado Civil Rights
Commission*, 138 S. Ct. 1719 (2018), the Supreme Court considered whether
a business owner's religious beliefs insulated him from a state law
prohibiting discrimination on the basis of sexual orientation. The facts of the
case were compelling: Charlie Craig and David Mullins went to the
Masterpiece Bakeshop in Lakewood, Colorado to order a cake for a party
celebrating their recent Massachusetts wedding. The bakery's owner, Jack
Phillips, refused to design and bake the cake, explaining that gay marriage
violated his religious beliefs. To provide the cake, he argued, would make
him "complicit" in the sin of same-sex marriage. To be clear, Phillips insisted
he had no objection to homosexuality—his objection was to same-sex
marriage itself. He would be happy to provide baked goods to gay customers
for other purposes.

The Colorado Anti-Discrimination Act prohibits businesses from
discriminating, including on the basis of sexual orientation. Pursuant to the
law, Craig and Mullins filed a discrimination claim against Phillips and the
bakery. Craig and Mullins prevailed in the administrative process and in the
state courts. The United States Supreme Court, however, reversed in a 7–2
decision written by Justice Anthony Kennedy. Critically, the Court did not
resolve the central issue in the case: whether an antidiscrimination law that
required business owners to serve all comers violated the First Amendment.
Instead, the majority found that the Colorado Civil Rights Commission had
expressed impermissible hostility to religion in its administrative
adjudication of the claim. In particular, Justice Kennedy took issue with a
commissioner's statement that " '[f]reedom of religion and religion has been
used to justify all kinds of discrimination throughout history . . . . And to me,
it is one of the most despicable pieces of rhetoric that people can use to—to
use their religion to hurt others.' " As he explained, "[t]o describe a man's
faith as 'one of the most despicable pieces of rhetoric that people can use' is
to disparage his religion in at least two distinct ways: by describing it as
despicable, and also by characterizing it as merely rhetorical—something
insubstantial and even insincere." The majority also concluded that the
Commission's rejection of claims brought by religious believers against
bakers who refused to bake cakes with messages the bakers found offensive
also evinced hostility to religion. Because the Court found that members of
the Colorado Civil Rights Commission had expressed hostility to religion, the
Court concluded that the Establishment Clause had been violated without
reaching the question of whether it would violate other aspects of the First

Amendment to hole Phillips liable for his refusal to provide a cake for a same-sex wedding.

6.   *Revisiting* Obergefell? Just days after the opening of October Term 2020, Justices Alito and Thomas issued a broadside against the Court's 2015 decision in *Obergefell v. Hodges*. The Justices's statement arose in the context of the Court's refusal to hear a case brought by Kim Davis, a former Kentucky county clerk who refused to issue a marriage license for such couples. *Davis v. Ermold*, 141 S. Ct. 3 (2020). Although both Justices Alito and Thomas agreed with the decision not to grant certiorari, they nonetheless used the occasion to underscore their objections to *Obergefell*. Writing for himself and Alito, Justice Thomas argued that *Obergefell* "enables courts and governments to brand religious adherents who believe that marriage is between one man and one woman as bigots, making their religious liberty concerns that much easier to dismiss." *Id*. Although Thomas and Alito agreed that Davis's case did not "cleanly" present issues to be resolved by the Court, the case nonetheless "provides a stark reminder" of *Obergefell*'s "ruinous consequences for religious liberty." *Id*. Critically, this unorthodox writing came just a month before the Court heard oral arguments in *Fulton v. City of Philadelphia*, a challenge to Philadelphia's decision to terminate a contract with Catholic Social Services for screening and certifying parents for foster care because the agency, citing its religious objections, refused to certify qualified same-sex couples as foster parents. 140 S. Ct. 1104 (2020).

2.   CRIMINAL LAW

United States v. Bitty

208 U.S. 393 (1908).

■ HARLAN, J.

This is a criminal prosecution under an act of Congress regulating the immigration of aliens into the United States.

. . .

By the act of March 3d, 1903, chap. 1012, it was provided: "That the importation into the United States of any woman or girl for the purposes of prostitution is hereby forbidden; and whoever shall import or attempt to import any woman or girl into the United States for the purposes of prostitution, or shall hold or attempt to hold any woman or girl for such purposes in pursuance of such illegal importation, shall be deemed guilty of a felony, and, on conviction thereof, shall be imprisoned not less than one nor more than five years, and pay a fine not exceeding five thousand dollars."

A more comprehensive statute regulating the immigration of aliens into the United States was passed on February 20th, 1907. By that act the prior [immigration] act of 1903 (except one section) was repealed. The [thir]d section of this last statute was in these words: "That the importation into the United States of any alien woman or girl for the purpose of prostitution, *or for any other immoral purpose*, is hereby forbidden; and whoever shall, directly or indirectly, import, or attempt to import, into the United States, any alien woman or girl for the purpose of prostitution, or for any other immoral purpose, or whoever shall hold or attempt to hold any alien woman or girl for any such purpose in pursuance of such illegal importation, or whoever shall keep, maintain, control, support, or harbor in any house or other place, for the purpose of prostitution, or for any other immoral purpose, any alien woman or girl, within three years after she shall have entered the United States, shall, in every such case, be deemed guilty of a felony, and, on conviction thereof, be imprisoned not more than five years and pay a fine of not more than five thousand dollars. . . ."

The defendant in error, Bitty, was charged by indictment . . . with the offense of having unlawfully, wilfully [sic], and feloniously imported into the United States from England a certain named alien woman for "an immoral purpose," namely, "that she should live with him as his concubine."

. . .

. . . [The 1903 Act and other immigration statutes] were directed against the importation into this country of alien women for the purposes of prostitution. But the last statute, on which the indictment rests, is, we have seen, directed against the importation of an alien woman "for the purpose of prostitution *or* for any other immoral purpose;" and the indictment distinctly charges that the defendant imported the alien woman in question "that she should live with him as his concubine;" that is, in illicit intercourse, not under the sanction of a valid or legal marriage. Was that an immoral purpose within the meaning of the statute? The circuit court held, in effect, that it was not, the bringing of an alien woman into the United States that she may live with the person importing her as his concubine not being, in its opinion, an act *ejusdem generis* with the bringing of such a woman to this country for the purposes of "prostitution." Was that a sound construction of the statute?

All will admit that full effect must be given to the intention of Congress as gathered from the words of the statute. There can be no doubt as to what class was aimed at by the clause forbidding the importation of alien women for purposes of "prostitution." It refers to women who, for hire or without hire, offer their bodies to indiscriminate intercourse with men. The lives and example of such persons are in hostility to "the idea of the family as consisting in and springing from the union for life of one man and one woman in the holy estate of matrimony; the sure foundation of all that is stable and noble in our civilization; the best guaranty of that reverent morality which is the source of all beneficent progress in social and political improvement." Congress, no doubt, proceeded on the ground that contact with society on the part of alien women leading such lives would be hurtful to the cause of sound private and public morality and to the general well-being of the people. Therefore the importation of alien women for purposes of prostitution was forbidden and made a crime against the United States. Now, the addition in the last statute of the words, "or for any other immoral purpose," after the word "prostitution," must have been made for some practical object. Those added words show beyond question that Congress had in view the protection of society against another class of alien women other than those who might be brought here merely for purposes of "prostitution." In forbidding the importation of alien women "for any other immoral purpose," Congress evidently thought that there were purposes in connection with the importations of alien women which, as in the case of importations for prostitution, were to be deemed immoral. It may be admitted that, in accordance with the familiar rule of *ejusdem generis*, the immoral purpose referred to by the words "any other immoral purpose," must be one of the same general class or kind as the particular purpose of "prostitution" specified in the same clause of the statute. But that rule cannot avail the accused in this case; for the immoral purpose charged in the indictment is of the same general class or kind as the one that controls in the importation of an alien woman for the purpose strictly of prostitution. The prostitute may, in the popular sense, be more degraded in character than the concubine, but the latter none the less must be held to lead an immoral life, if any regard whatever be had to the views that are almost universally held in this country as to the relations which may rightfully, from the standpoint of morality, exist between man and woman in the matter of sexual intercourse. We must assume that, in using the words "or for any other immoral purposes," Congress had reference to the views commonly entertained among the people of the United States as to what is moral or immoral in the relations between man and woman in the matter of such intercourse. Those views may not be overlooked in determining questions involving the morality or immorality of sexual intercourse between particular persons. Chief Justice Marshall, speaking for the court, said that "though penal laws are to be construed strictly, they are not to be construed so strictly as to defeat the obvious intention of the legislature. The maxim is not to be so applied as to narrow the words of the statute to the exclusion of cases which those words, in their ordinary acceptation, or in that sense in which the legislature has obviously used them, would comprehend. The intention of the legislature is to be collected from the words they employ. . . . The case must be a strong one indeed which would justify a court in departing from the plain meaning of words, especially in a penal act, in search of an intention which the words themselves did not suggest." . . . Guided by these considerations and rules, we must hold that Congress intended by the words "or for any other immoral purpose," to include the case of anyone who imported into the United States an alien woman that she might live with him as his concubine. The statute in question, it must be remembered, was intended to keep out of this country immigrants whose permanent residence here would not be desirable or for the common good, and we cannot suppose either that Congress intended to exempt from the operation of the statute the importation of an alien woman brought here only that she might live in a state of concubinage with the man importing her, or that it did not regard such an importation as being for an immoral purpose.

The judgment must be reversed . . . .

It is so ordered.

NOTES

1. *Immoral purposes.* As legal historian Ariela Dubler notes, the 1907 Immigration Act was not the only federal statute to deploy the terms "immoral purposes." In 1910, Congress enacted the Mann Act, which made it a federal crime to transport or aid in the transportation in interstate or foreign commerce of "any woman or girl for the purpose of prostitution or debauchery, or for any other immoral purpose." The Mann Act was aimed at combating the so-called "white slave trade"—the trafficking of white women into prostitution. *See* Ariela R. Dubler, *Immoral Purposes: Marriage and the Genus of Illicit Sex*, 115 YALE L.J. 756, 787–94 (2006). However, as Dubler makes clear, both the Mann Act and the 1907 Immigration Act reflected a broader fear that nonmarital sex and sexuality threatened marriage and the social order that that institution supported.

2. *Discrimination and immoral purposes.* Perhaps the most (in)famous Mann Act prosecution took place in 1912 when world-champion boxer Jack Johnson was charged with transporting Lucille Cameron, his girlfriend, across state lines in violation of the Mann Act. Most recognized that the prosecution was animated by the fact that Johnson was African American and Cameron was white. Cameron, soon to become Johnson's second wife, refused to cooperate, causing the government's case to flounder. Less than a month later, Johnson was arrested again on similar charges. This time, the woman, an alleged prostitute with whom Johnson had been involved in 1909 and 1910, testified against him. An all-white jury convicted Johnson in June 1913, despite the fact that the incidents that formed the basis for the prosecution took place before the Mann Act was enacted. Johnson was sentenced to a year and a day in prison. *See* DAVID J. LANGUM, CROSSING OVER THE LINE: LEGISLATING MORALITY AND THE MANN ACT 180–82 (2007).

3. *Marriage as punishment?* Criminal laws, like the Mann Act, have long served as a crucial means for state regulation of sex and sexuality. However, Professor Melissa Murray observes that marriage and criminal law have often worked in tandem to regulate sex and sexuality. In the nineteenth and early twentieth centuries, marriage served as a defense to the crime of seduction. In more than thirty American jurisdictions it was a criminal offense to "[seduce] and ha[ve] sexual intercourse with an unmarried female of previously chaste character . . . under a promise of marriage." Melissa Murray, *Marriage as Punishment*, 112 COLUM. L. REV. 1, 1 (2012). The penalty for seduction could be harsh—in Georgia, the punishment for seduction was twenty years' imprisonment in the state penitentiary. *Id.* at 5 n.16. However, most seduction statutes prescribed a specific defense to the

crime: marriage. The defendant "could simply marry the victim, thereby avoiding liability for the crime." According to Murray, marriage's role in the administration and enforcement of criminal seduction statutes went beyond simply serving as a defense to the crime. She argues that it also served as a means of punishment and rehabilitation. "Though marriage did not require the physical deprivations of incarceration, it nonetheless deprived the defendant (and the victim) of other liberties by imposing upon him a particular set of burdens and responsibilities—fidelity, sobriety, responsibility, wage-earning—that could not be cast off lightly." *Id.* at 31. What would Foucault make of Murray's assessment of marriage as punishment? Could marriage redeem the illicit acts contemplated by the 1907 Immigration Act and the Mann Act?

Lovisi v. Slayton
539 F.2d 349 (4th Cir. 1976).

■ HAYNSWORTH, C.J.,

The petitioners in this habeas corpus proceeding, Aldo and Margaret Lovisi, husband and wife, were convicted in the state court of sodomy with each other in violation of Va. Code Ann. § 18.1–212.[1] They challenged the constitutionality of the statute, as applied to them, through the state court system and then sought federal habeas corpus relief. After a hearing, the district judge concluded that the Lovisis had waived their constitutional right to privacy in their marital conduct and, consequently, their right to contest their state convictions of sodomy with one another by carelessly exposing erotic photographs to Mrs. Lovisi's young daughters. We affirm.

From time to time the Lovisis had placed advertisements in a magazine, "Swinger's Life," in which they sought contact with others interested in erotic sexual experiences. Earl Romeo Dunn answered one such advertisement, and the three met together on three occasions. The last occasion was in the Lovisis' home in Virginia Beach, Virginia. The three engaged in sexual activity in the Lovisis' bedroom, during which Margaret Lovisi performed fellatio upon her husband and upon Dunn. Polaroid pictures were made of this activity, and Mrs. Lovisi's daughters by a former marriage, then 13 and 11 years old, testified that they were present in the bedroom at the time, described what they saw and testified that they took the Polaroid pictures. Dunn[2] and Lovisi denied the presence of the young girls and testified that they took the pictures, sometimes with the aid of a time-delay device.

---

[1] Section 18.1–212. Crimes against nature. If any person shall carnally know in any manner any brute animal, or carnally know any male or female person by the anus or by or with the mouth, or voluntarily submit to such carnal knowledge, he or she shall be guilty of a felony and shall be confined in the penitentiary not less than one year nor more than three years.

[2] Dunn testified for the prosecution. His participation in the incident, however, resulted in his deportation to his native Jamaica.

The general verdict of guilty in the state court did not resolve the dispute in the testimony about the presence of the young girls and their taking the pictures. The district judge was disinclined to accept the disputed testimony of the girls, but he did find that the Lovisis had relinquished their right of privacy by carelessly exposing pictures of their sexual activity to the girls. The entire matter had come to light when one of the girls appeared in school with a picture, subsequently destroyed, said to have been of her and of an adult male, both completely unclothed. This resulted in the execution of a search warrant, and the policeman testified that hundreds of erotic pictures were found in the house. Lovisi, however, testified that the pictures taken of himself and his wife and their companions were kept in a box in a gun cabinet which, as described by him, was quite insecure, and these were among the pictures seized by the police.

The Constitution recognizes a right of privacy with respect to those rights regarded as "fundamental" or "implicit in the concept of ordered liberty." *Roe v. Wade*, 410 U.S. 113, 152 (1973). The personal intimacies of marriage, the home, procreation, motherhood, childbearing and the family have been held "fundamental" by the Supreme Court and, hence, have been encompassed within the protected rights of privacy. We may thus assume that the marital intimacies shared by the Lovisis when alone and in their own bedroom are within their protected right of privacy. What they do in the privacy of the marital boudoir is beyond the power of the state to scrutinize. The question we face, however, is whether they preserve any right of privacy when they admit others to observe their intimacies.

Married couples engage in acts of sexual intimacy. That they do is no secret. Though they converse with friends or write books about their sexual relations, recounting in explicit detail their own intimacies and techniques, they remain protected in their expectation of privacy within their own bedroom. State law protects them from unwelcome intruders, and the federal constitution protects them from the state in the guise of an unwelcome intruder.

What the federal constitution protects is the right of privacy in circumstances in which it may reasonably be expected. Once a married couple admits strangers as onlookers, federal protection of privacy dissolves. It matters not whether the audience is composed of one, fifty, or one hundred, or whether the onlookers pay for their titillation. If the couple performs sexual acts for the excitation or gratification of welcome onlookers, they cannot selectively claim that the state is an intruder. They possess the freedom to follow their own inclinations in privacy, but once they accept onlookers, whether they are close friends, chance acquaintances, observed "peeping Toms" or paying customers, they may not exclude the state as a constitutionally forbidden intruder.

. . .

The presence of the onlooker, Dunn, in the Lovisis' bedroom dissolved the reasonable expectation of privacy shared by the Lovisis when alone. Hence, we affirm the district court's refusal to issue the writ.

. . .

ADDENDUM

After this opinion was prepared and circulated, but before it was filed, the Supreme Court summarily affirmed a decision of a statutory three-judge court dealing with this same statute as applied to adult homosexuals alleging that they were engaged in homosexual activity in private. *Doe v. Commonwealth's Attorney for City of Richmond*, 403 F. Supp. 1199 (E.D. Va. 1975), *aff'd* 425 U.S. 901 (1976).

In upholding the statute as applied to homosexual acts between two consenting adults in private places, the Supreme Court necessarily confined the constitutionally protected right of privacy to heterosexual conduct, probably even that only within the marital relationship. At least it reinforces our conclusion that the oral sexual activity of the Lovisis in the presence of Dunn and a camera was not within the area of the constitution's protection.

■ WINTER, J., dissenting.

We accept as settled law the majority's assumption that marital intimacies shared by the Lovisis when alone and in their own bedroom are within their protected right of privacy. We reject, however, the majority's implied premise that this marital right of privacy is restricted to those situations in which it is enjoyed in secret. . . . From the majority's contrary conclusion, we respectfully dissent.

. . .

That there exists a marital right of privacy need not be merely assumed; it is positive law. Beginning with the early decisions of *Meyer v. Nebraska*, 262 U.S. 390 (1923), which invalidated a statute regulating the teaching of modern foreign languages in schools, and *Pierce v. Society of Sisters*, 268 U.S. 510 (1925), which invalidated a statute requiring that children be sent to public schools, the Supreme Court has gradually evolved a concept of liberty applying to family life which has elevated the marital relationship to a place of near inviolable sanctity. . . .

. . .

In *Griswold v. Connecticut*, 381 U.S. 479 (1965), the Court invalidated Connecticut's statute rendering the use or the giving of advice about the use of contraceptives a criminal offense. A majority of the Court concurred in an opinion which stated:

> We deal with a right of privacy older than the Bill of Rights older than our political parties, older than our school system. Marriage is a coming together for better or for worse, hopefully enduring, and intimate to the degree of being sacred. It is an association that promotes a way of life, not causes; a harmony

in living, not political faiths; a bilateral loyalty, not commercial or social projects. Yet it is an association for as noble a purpose as any involved in our prior decisions.

. . .

Following *Griswold*, the Court invalidated Virginia's statute prohibiting interracial marriage as unconstitutional under the [E]qual [P]rotection and [D]ue [P]rocess [C]lauses of the Fourteenth Amendment, *Loving v. Virginia*, 388 U.S. 1 (1967); and in *Eisenstadt v. Baird*, 405 U.S. 438 (1972), invalidated a statute which made the exhibition of contraceptives and the giving of contraceptives to an unmarried person criminal acts. The Court found an insufficient state interest, i.e., health or morals, to justify the prohibition and concluded that it denied equal protection of the laws to unmarried persons. . . .

Finally, in *Roe v. Wade*, 410 U.S. 113 (1973), and *Doe v. Bolton*, 410 U.S. 179 (1973), the Court recognized a related right of privacy the right of a woman to terminate a pregnancy by an abortion, unqualified to the end of the first trimester of pregnancy and qualified thereafter by proper state regulation to preserve the state's interest in the preservation and protection of maternal health and preservation of the life of a viable fetus.

From these cases we would conclude that certainly within the marital relationship, and perhaps in some instances even without, the nature and kind of consensual sexual intimacy is beyond the power of the state to regulate or even to inquire. If the state may not restrict marital sexual relations to those whose object or risk is that of procreation, we think that the state is powerless to brand as sodomitic other consensual sexual practice within the marital relationship.

. . .

Given the premise that a sufficient state interest to regulate or to inquire into consensual marital intimacies does not exist, we turn to the question of whether this marital right of privacy exists only if the consensual conduct is carried on in secrecy. We think that existence of the right is not conditioned upon secrecy.

. . .

Certainly *Meyer v. Nebraska*, *Pierce v. Society of Sisters*, and *Skinner v. Oklahoma*, the foundations from which the right of marital privacy was developed, had nothing to do with secrecy. Their outcome depended upon the nature of the activity sought to be regulated and the relationship of that activity to a protected right. In *Griswold*, the Court invalidated Connecticut's ban on the use of contraceptives at the behest of a doctor who was permitted to assert the rights of his patients who came to him for advice about contraceptives. These patients were admitting an outsider into their marital intimacies by seeking counseling and advice about contraception, yet they were not held to have lost their right to constitutional protection. Most recently, in *Roe v. Wade*, the Court, in upholding a woman's exercise of her right to "privacy" by having an abortion, explicitly noted that "[t]he pregnant woman cannot be isolated in her privacy." Not only was the developing fetus involved, but the abortion would have to be performed by a doctor, probably with the assistance of others.

Based on these authorities, we conclude that secrecy is not a necessary element of the right and that therefore the right exists, whether or not exercised in secret.[2]

We are at a loss to understand how or why the majority concludes otherwise. Its conclusion is unsupported by any authority; nor do we think it supported by reason. The majority assumes that the Lovisis have a constitutional right to practice marital sodomy in secret, and further suggests that this right would not be lost or "waived" if they talked or wrote about their sexual activities. Presumably this protection would extend to non-obscene but explicit photographs and movies even if sold on a commercial basis; yet, if a husband and wife were to seek certain types of medical help in an attempt to save a marriage endangered by sexual maladjustment, or if due to economic necessity, or for any other reason, they share a bedroom with other family members, under the majority's holding the state may prosecute them for certain types of consensual marital acts. Surely these absurd results suggest that the presence of Dunn is irrelevant to the question before us. What would not be punishable sodomy in Dunn's absence is not rendered punishable sodomy by his presence, although his presence may, of course, give rise to other prosecution for other crimes.

. . .

Finally, we comment on the majority's claim of support for its holding from the recent summary affirmance in *Doe v. Commonwealth's Attorney for City of Richmond*, 403 F. Supp. 1199 (E.D. Va. 1975), *aff'd*, 425 U.S. 901 (1976). That case upheld the validity of an application of the statute with which we are concerned to consensual homosexual acts between adults in private.

The Supreme Court's affirmance was summary. . . . Until the Supreme Court speaks more definitively, no one can tell [whether the right to privacy does not encompass consensual homosexual acts]. Of course, we would apply the holding in a case in which Virginia sought to punish consensual homosexual acts between adults, but we decline to go further and speculate whether it constitutes an adjudication, confirming or detracting from the principles on which we and the majority rely, or indicating what we should decide here.

---

[2] Just as secrecy is not essential to the assertion of a "privacy" right claim, the fact that conduct is carried on in secret does not itself entitle it to protection. "[I]t would be an absurdity to suggest either that offenses may not be committed in the bosom of the family or that the home can be made a sanctuary for crime. . . . Thus, I would not suggest that adultery, homosexuality, fornication and incest are immune from criminal enquiry, however, privately practiced." Poe v. Ullman, 367 U.S. 497, 552–53 (1961). See *Doe v. Commonwealth's Attorney for City of Richmond*, 403 F.Supp. 1199 (E.D. Va. 1975), *aff'd*, 425 U.S. 901 (1976).

■ CRAVEN, J., dissenting.

I dissent because I think it is dangerous to withdraw from any citizen the protection of the Constitution because he or she is amoral, immoral or just plain nasty. The point I make is a factual one. It will not be understood without knowing what the case is about, and to make that clear I begin by stating what it is not about. It is not about group sex. It is not about sexual activity, deviant or otherwise, in public. The Lovisis attack their charges and convictions under a statute making their conduct with each other while married criminal whether or not in public and without regard to the presence or participation of a third person.

Most of the court's opinion consists of a narrative of the sort found in "adult" bookstores. Had the case been properly tried in the Virginia state court, we would not even know this sordid story because Dunn's participation is irrelevant and highly prejudicial to the question of the Lovisis' guilt of a violation of Virginia's crime against nature by their conduct with each other. Just as a jury cannot forget such evidence erroneously received, neither, apparently, can we.

. . .

The "right of privacy," apt in some cases, is a misleading misnomer in others including this one. This freedom may be termed more accurately "the right to be let alone," or personal autonomy, or simply "personhood." One thing for sure it is not limited to the conduct of persons in private. Marriage, normally a public ceremony, is protected. Mrs. Roe does not lose her right to be let alone to abort because her doctor permits the intrusion of a nurse to assist him [in performing an abortion]. Baird[, the defendant in *Eisenstadt*,] may not be prosecuted for failure to be discreet and secret in lecturing students on contraception.

It is therefore unclear to me why the Lovisis forfeit their right to be let alone in their conjugal relationship because they allowed a third person to be present. The only valid reason I can think of is a moral value judgment that deviant sex is so odious[6] that not even the Constitution may be successfully interposed to protect a husband and wife so despicably disposed. However right the court may be as to morals, I do not believe it to be a proper principle of constitutional law.

. . .

NOTES

1.   *Sex in public and private.* One of the crucial distinctions that has made sex subject to state regulation is its location. Sex that occurs in public settings is far more likely to offend the sensibilities of others, thereby justifying state efforts to regulate and/or prohibit it. By contrast, sex that takes place within the confines of the private sphere (and occurs between consenting adults) is likely to be viewed as beyond the state's regulatory

---

[6]   Dunn's participation makes it even more odious but that is another case. I reiterate these cases relate only to the Lovisis' conduct with each other.

purview. What then explains the outcome in *Lovisi*? Does the presence of a third person negate the fact that the sex acts occurred within the privacy of the Lovisis' bedroom?

2.   *Sex in quasi-public places.* If it is axiomatic that the state may regulate "public sex," how do we draw the line between the public and private spheres? If a bedroom is private and the street is public, how should we categorize places of public accommodation where individuals have an expectation of privacy, such as a public restroom stall, or a private club that is open to members of the public? In *832 Corporation v. Gloucester Township*, 404 F. Supp. 2d 614 (D.N.J. 2005), a federal district court concluded that the right of privacy did not go so far as to insulate from state regulation sex acts that took place in a members-only sex club. Emphasizing the associations between privacy, the home, and intimate relationships, the court concluded that it "did not recognize a broad right to engage in sexual conduct outside of private settings." *Id.* at 623. How can the decision in *832 Corporation* be reconciled with *Lovisi*?

Bowers v. Hardwick
478 U.S. 186 (1986).

■ WHITE, J.

In August 1982, respondent Hardwick . . . was charged with violating the Georgia statute criminalizing sodomy[1] by committing that act with another adult male in the bedroom of respondent's home. . . .

. . .

This case does not require a judgment on whether laws against sodomy between consenting adults in general, or between homosexuals in particular, are wise or desirable. It raises no question about the right or propriety of state legislative decisions to repeal their laws that criminalize homosexual sodomy, or of state-court decisions invalidating those laws on state constitutional grounds. The issue presented is whether the Federal Constitution confers a fundamental right upon homosexuals to engage in sodomy and hence invalidates the laws of the many States that still make such conduct illegal and have done so for a very long time. The case also calls for some judgment about the limits of the Court's role in carrying out its constitutional mandate.

We first register our disagreement with . . . respondent that the Court's prior cases have construed the Constitution to confer a right of privacy that extends to homosexual sodomy and for all intents and purposes have decided this case. The reach of this line of cases was sketched in *Carey v. Population Services International*, 431 U.S. 678, 685

---

[1]   Georgia Code Ann. § 16–6–2 (1984) provides, in pertinent part, as follows:

(a) A person commits the offense of sodomy when he performs or submits to any sexual act involving the sex organs of one person and the mouth or anus of another. . . .

(b) A person convicted of the offense of sodomy shall be punished by imprisonment for not less than one nor more than 20 years. . . ."

(1977). *Pierce v. Society of Sisters* and *Meyer v. Nebraska* were described as dealing with child rearing and education; *Prince v. Massachusetts*, with family relationships; *Skinner v. Oklahoma ex rel. Williamson*, with procreation; *Loving v. Virginia*, with marriage; *Griswold v. Connecticut* and *Eisenstadt v. Baird*, with contraception; and *Roe v. Wade*, with abortion. The latter three cases were interpreted as construing the Due Process Clause of the Fourteenth Amendment to confer a fundamental individual right to decide whether or not to beget or bear a child.

Accepting the decisions in these cases and the above description of them, we think it evident that none of the rights announced in those cases bears any resemblance to the claimed constitutional right of homosexuals to engage in acts of sodomy that is asserted in this case. No connection between family, marriage, or procreation on the one hand and homosexual activity on the other has been demonstrated, either by the Court of Appeals or by respondent. Moreover, any claim that these cases nevertheless stand for the proposition that any kind of private sexual conduct between consenting adults is constitutionally insulated from state proscription is unsupportable. . . .

. . .

Striving to assure itself and the public that announcing rights not readily identifiable in the Constitution's text involves much more than the imposition of the Justices' own choice of values on the States and the Federal Government, the Court has sought to identify the nature of the rights qualifying for heightened judicial protection. In *Palko v. Connecticut*, 302 U.S. 319, 325 (1937), it was said that this category includes those fundamental liberties that are "implicit in the concept of ordered liberty," such that "neither liberty nor justice would exist if [they] were sacrificed." A different description of fundamental liberties appeared in *Moore v. East Cleveland*, 431 U.S. 494, 503 (1977) (opinion of Powell, J.), where they are characterized as those liberties that are "deeply rooted in this Nation's history and tradition."

It is obvious to us that neither of these formulations would extend a fundamental right to homosexuals to engage in acts of consensual sodomy. Proscriptions against that conduct have ancient roots. Sodomy was a criminal offense at common law and was forbidden by the laws of the original thirteen States when they ratified the Bill of Rights. In 1868, when the Fourteenth Amendment was ratified, all but 5 of the 37 States in the Union had criminal sodomy laws. In fact, until 1961, all 50 States outlawed sodomy, and today, 24 States and the District of Columbia continue to provide criminal penalties for sodomy performed in private and between consenting adults. Against this background, to claim that a right to engage in such conduct is "deeply rooted in this Nation's history and tradition" or "implicit in the concept of ordered liberty" is, at best, facetious.

Nor are we inclined to take a more expansive view of our authority to discover new fundamental rights imbedded in the Due Process Clause.

The Court is most vulnerable and comes nearest to illegitimacy when it deals with judge-made constitutional law having little or no cognizable roots in the language or design of the Constitution. That this is so was painfully demonstrated by the face-off between the Executive and the Court in the 1930's, which resulted in the repudiation of much of the substantive gloss that the Court had placed on the Due Process Clauses of the Fifth and Fourteenth Amendments. There should be, therefore, great resistance to expand the substantive reach of those Clauses, particularly if it requires redefining the category of rights deemed to be fundamental. Otherwise, the Judiciary necessarily takes to itself further authority to govern the country without express constitutional authority. The claimed right pressed on us today falls far short of overcoming this resistance.

Respondent, however, asserts that the result should be different where the homosexual conduct occurs in the privacy of the home. He relies on *Stanley v. Georgia*, 394 U.S. 557 (1969), where the Court held that the First Amendment prevents conviction for possessing and reading obscene material in the privacy of one's home: "If the First Amendment means anything, it means that a State has no business telling a man, sitting alone in his house, what books he may read or what films he may watch."

Stanley did protect conduct that would not have been protected outside the home, and it partially prevented the enforcement of state obscenity laws; but the decision was firmly grounded in the First Amendment. The right pressed upon us here has no similar support in the text of the Constitution, and it does not qualify for recognition under the prevailing principles for construing the Fourteenth Amendment. Its limits are also difficult to discern. Plainly enough, otherwise illegal conduct is not always immunized whenever it occurs in the home. Victimless crimes, such as the possession and use of illegal drugs, do not escape the law where they are committed at home. *Stanley* itself recognized that its holding offered no protection for the possession in the home of drugs, firearms, or stolen goods. And if respondent's submission is limited to the voluntary sexual conduct between consenting adults, it would be difficult, except by fiat, to limit the claimed right to homosexual conduct while leaving exposed to prosecution adultery, incest, and other sexual crimes even though they are committed in the home. We are unwilling to start down that road.

Even if the conduct at issue here is not a fundamental right, respondent asserts that there must be a rational basis for the law and that there is none in this case other than the presumed belief of a majority of the electorate in Georgia that homosexual sodomy is immoral and unacceptable. This is said to be an inadequate rationale to support the law. The law, however, is constantly based on notions of morality, and if all laws representing essentially moral choices are to be invalidated under the Due Process Clause, the courts will be very busy indeed. Even respondent makes no such claim, but insists that majority sentiments about the morality of homosexuality should be declared inadequate. We do not agree, and are unpersuaded that the sodomy laws of some 25 States should be invalidated on this basis.[8]

Accordingly, the judgment of the Court of Appeals is

Reversed.

. . .

■ BLACKMUN, J., with whom BRENNAN, J., MARSHALL, J., and STEVENS, J., join, dissenting.

This case is no more about "a fundamental right to engage in homosexual sodomy," as the Court purports to declare, than *Stanley v. Georgia*, 394 U.S. 557 (1969), was about a fundamental right to watch obscene movies, or *Katz v. United States*, 389 U.S. 347 (1967), was about a fundamental right to place interstate bets from a telephone booth. Rather, this case is about "the most comprehensive of rights and the right most valued by civilized men," namely, "the right to be let alone." *Olmstead v. United States*, 277 U.S. 438 (1928) (Brandeis, J., dissenting).

The statute at issue . . . denies individuals the right to decide for themselves whether to engage in particular forms of private, consensual sexual activity. The Court concludes that § 16–6–2 is valid essentially because "the laws of . . . many States . . . still make such conduct illegal and have done so for a very long time." But the fact that the moral judgments expressed by statutes like § 16–6–2 may be " 'natural and familiar . . . ought not to conclude our judgment upon the question whether statutes embodying them conflict with the Constitution of the United States.' " *Roe v. Wade*, 410 U.S. 113, 117 (1973), quoting *Lochner v. New York*, 198 U.S. 45, 76 (1905) (Holmes, J., dissenting). . . . I believe we must analyze Hardwick's claim in the light of the values that underlie the constitutional right to privacy. If that right means anything, it means that, before Georgia can prosecute its citizens for making choices about the most intimate aspects of their lives, it must do more than assert that the choice they have made is an " 'abominable crime not fit to be named among Christians.' " *Herring v. State*, 46 S.E. 876 (Ga. 1904).

. . .

First, the Court's almost obsessive focus on homosexual activity is particularly hard to justify in light of the broad language Georgia has used. Unlike the Court, the Georgia Legislature has not proceeded on the assumption that homosexuals are so different from other citizens that their lives may be controlled in a way that would not be tolerated if it limited the choices of those other citizens. Rather, Georgia has provided that "[a] person commits the offense of sodomy when he performs or submits to any sexual act involving the sex organs of one person and the

---

[8]   Respondent does not defend the judgment below based on the Ninth Amendment, the Equal Protection Clause, or the Eighth Amendment.

mouth or anus of another." Ga. Code Ann. § 16–6–2(a) (1984). The sex or status of the persons who engage in the act is irrelevant as a matter of state law. In fact, to the extent I can discern a legislative purpose for Georgia's 1968 enactment of § 16–6–2, that purpose seems to have been to broaden the coverage of the law to reach heterosexual as well as homosexual activity. I therefore see no basis for the Court's decision to treat this case as an "as applied" challenge to § 16–6–2, *see ante*, at n.2, or for Georgia's attempt, both in its brief and at oral argument, to defend § 16–6–2 solely on the grounds that it prohibits homosexual activity. Michael Hardwick's standing may rest in significant part on Georgia's apparent willingness to enforce against homosexuals a law it seems not to have any desire to enforce against heterosexuals. But his claim that § 16–6–2 involves an unconstitutional intrusion into his privacy and his right of intimate association does not depend in any way on his sexual orientation.

. . .

The Court concludes today that none of our prior cases dealing with various decisions that individuals are entitled to make free of governmental interference "bears any resemblance to the claimed constitutional right of homosexuals to engage in acts of sodomy that is asserted in this case." While it is true that these cases may be characterized by their connection to protection of the family, see *Roberts v. United States Jaycees*, 468 U.S. 609 (1984), the Court's conclusion that they extend no further than this boundary ignores the warning in *Moore v. City of East Cleveland*, 431 U.S. 494 (1977) (plurality opinion), against "clos[ing] our eyes to the basic reasons why certain rights associated with the family have been accorded shelter under the Fourteenth Amendment's Due Process Clause." We protect those rights not because they contribute, in some direct and material way, to the general public welfare, but because they form so central a part of an individual's life. "[T]he concept of privacy embodies the 'moral fact that a person belongs to himself and not others nor to society as a whole.'" *Thornburgh v. American College of Obstetricians & Gynecologists*, 476 U.S., at 777, n.5 (Stevens, J., concurring), quoting Fried, Correspondence, 6 Phil. & Pub. Affairs 288–289 (1977). And so we protect the decision whether to marry precisely because marriage "is an association that promotes a way of life, not causes; a harmony in living, not political faiths; a bilateral loyalty, not commercial or social projects." *Griswold v. Connecticut*, 381 U.S. at 486. We protect the decision whether to have a child because parenthood alters so dramatically an individual's self-definition, not because of demographic considerations or the Bible's command to be fruitful and multiply. And we protect the family because it contributes so powerfully to the happiness of individuals, not because of a preference for stereotypical households. The Court recognized in *Roberts*, 468 U.S. at 619, that the "ability independently to define one's identity that is central to any concept of liberty" cannot truly be exercised in a vacuum; we all depend on the "emotional enrichment from close ties with others."

Only the most willful blindness could obscure the fact that sexual intimacy is "a sensitive, key relationship of human existence, central to family life, community welfare, and the development of human personality[.]" *Paris Adult Theatre I. v. Slaton*, 413 U.S. 49, 63 (1973). The fact that individuals define themselves in a significant way through their intimate sexual relationships with others suggests, in a Nation as diverse as ours, that there may be many "right" ways of conducting those relationships, and that much of the richness of a relationship will come from the freedom an individual has to *choose* the form and nature of these intensely personal bonds.

In a variety of circumstances we have recognized that a necessary corollary of giving individuals freedom to choose how to conduct their lives is acceptance of the fact that different individuals will make different choices. For example, in holding that the clearly important state interest in public education should give way to a competing claim by the Amish to the effect that extended formal schooling threatened their way of life, the Court declared: "There can be no assumption that today's majority is 'right' and the Amish and others like them are 'wrong.' A way of life that is odd or even erratic but interferes with no rights or interests of others is not to be condemned because it is different." *Wisconsin v. Yoder*, 406 U.S. 205, 223–24 (1972). The Court claims that its decision today merely refuses to recognize a fundamental right to engage in homosexual sodomy; what the Court really has refused to recognize is the fundamental interest all individuals have in controlling the nature of their intimate associations with others.

. . .

NOTES

1.   *Sodomy within marriage.* A married couple, John and Mary Doe, sought to join Hardwick's suit, claiming that they were "[c]hilled and deterred [from engaging in private sexual activity] by the existence of the [Georgia sodomy] statute and the recent arrest of Hardwick." *Hardwick v. Bowers*, 760 F.2d 1202, 1204 (11th Cir. 1985) (discussing the decision below). "[B]ecause they had neither sustained, nor were in immediate danger of sustaining, any direct injury from the enforcement of the statute," the district court concluded that the Does lacked standing to sue. *Bowers v. Hardwick*, 478 U.S. 186, 188 n.2 (1986). The Eleventh Circuit agreed, and the Does did not challenge this holding at the Supreme Court. *Id.*

2.   *The* Bowers *back-story.* Because there was no trial record, the story of how Michael Hardwick came to be arrested for sodomy in the privacy of his own bedroom has been left to investigative journalists and historians to describe. As Randy Shilts documents:

> The debate centered on a twenty-nine-year-old bartender named Michael Hardwick, arrested by Atlanta police on the night of

August 2, 1982. The police officer had knocked on Hardwick's front door to serve a warrant for public intoxication; a house guest pointed the officer toward Hardwick's bedroom door. The policeman opened the door and saw Hardwick engaged in oral sex with another man. When the policeman said he was serving his warrant, Hardwick explained he had already cleared the matter with the court and offered to show the officer his receipt. That no longer mattered, the policeman said, because he had found Hardwick engaging in a violation of the Georgia law that banned oral and anal sex. Hardwick and his companion spent the next twelve hours in jail.

RANDY SHILTS, CONDUCT UNBECOMING: GAYS AND LESBIANS IN THE U.S. MILITARY 522 (1994).

Given the several departures from usual police procedure in this account, might other factors explain Hardwick's arrest?

* * *

Even as Bowers v. Hardwick *underscored the continued criminality of sodomy in the United States, attitudes toward so-called "deviant" sexual behavior were changing in other parts of the world. Indeed, in the United Kingdom, efforts to liberalize sodomy laws were undertaken in the 1960s. Of course, these efforts were not uncontroversial, as the following selections from the Hart-Devlin Debate make clear. The United Kingdom's 1957 Wolfenden Report animated the debates between Professor H. L. A. Hart and Lord Patrick Devlin. Convened after a succession of high-profile men were convicted of homosexual offenses, the Departmental Committee on Homosexual Offences and Prostitution, led by Lord Wolfenden, considered the criminalization of sodomy and other morals crimes, like prostitution. Ultimately, the Wolfenden Committee recommended decriminalizing "homosexual behaviour between consenting adults in private" on the ground that it was not the duty of the law to enforce norms concerning morality and immorality. In the debates, Hart defended the Committee's position, noting that criminal law should be concerned principally with preventing harm to others, not enforcing morality. By contrast, Devlin argued that criminal law must respect and reinforce the moral norms of society in order to keep social order from unraveling.*

3. THE HART-DEVLIN DEBATES

H. L. A. Hart, *Immorality and Treason*, The Listener
July 30, 1959, at 162.

. . . .

No doubt we would all agree that a consensus of moral opinion on certain matters is essential if society is to be worth living in. Laws against murder, theft, and much else would be of little use if they were not supported by a widely diffused conviction that what these laws forbid is also immoral. So much is obvious. But it does not follow that everything to which the moral vetoes of accepted morality attach is of equal importance to society; nor is there the slightest reason for thinking of morality as a seamless web: one which will fall to pieces carrying society with it, unless all its emphatic vetoes are enforced by law. Surely even in the face of the moral feeling that is up to concert pitch—the trio of intolerance, indignation, and disgust—we must pause to think. We must ask a question at two different levels . . . . First, we must ask whether a practice which offends moral feeling is harmful, independently of its repercussion on the general moral code. Secondly, what about repercussion on the moral code? Is it really true that failure to translate this item of general morality into criminal law will jeopardize the whole fabric of morality and so of society?

. . . .

Nothing perhaps shows more clearly the inadequacy of [the criminalization of immorality] to this problem than [the] comparison between the suppression of sexual immorality and the suppression of treason or subversive activity. Private subversive activity is, of course, a contradiction in terms because 'subversion' means overthrowing government, which is a public thing. But it is grotesque, even where moral feeling against homosexuality is up to concert pitch, to think of the homosexual behaviour of two adults in private as in any way like treason or sedition either in intention or effect. We can make it seem like treason only if we assume that deviation from a general moral code is bound to affect that code, and to lead not merely to its modification but to its destruction. The analogy could begin to be plausible only if it was clear that offending against this item of morality was likely to jeopardize the whole structure. But we have ample evidence for believing that people will not abandon morality, will not think any better of murder, cruelty, and dishonesty, merely because some private sexual practice which they abominate is not punished by the law.

. . . .

As Mill saw, and de Tocqueville showed in detail long ago in his critical but sympathetic study of democracy, it is fatally easy to confuse the democratic principle that power should be in the hands of the majority with the utterly different claim that the majority, with power in their hands, need respect no limits. Certainly there is a special risk in a democracy that the majority may dictate how all should live. This is the risk we run, and should gladly run; for it is the price of all that is so good in democratic rule. But loyalty to democratic principles does not require us to maximize this risk: yet this is what we shall do if we mount the man in the street on the top of the Clapham omnibus and tell him that if only he feels sick enough about what other people do in private to demand its suppression by law no theoretical criticism can be made of his demand.

Patrick Devlin, The Enforcement of Morals

(1965).

What is the connection between crime and sin and to what extent, if at all, should the criminal law of England concern itself with the enforcement of morals and punish sin or immorality as such?

. . . .

. . . . The criminal law of England has from the very first concerned itself with moral principles. A simple way of testing this point is to consider the attitude which the criminal law adopts towards consent.

Subject to certain exceptions inherent in the nature of particular crimes, the criminal law has never permitted consent of the victim to be used as a defense. In rape, for example, consent negatives an essential element. But consent of the victim is no defense to a charge of murder. It is not a defense to any form of assault that the victim thought his punishment well deserved and submitted to it; to make a good defense the accused must prove that the law gave him the right to chastise and that he exercised it reasonably. Likewise, the victim may not forgive the aggressor and require the prosecution to desist; the right to enter a *nolle prosequi* belongs to the Attorney-General alone.

Now, if the law existed for the protection of the individual, there would be no reason why he should avail himself of it if he did not want it. The reason why a man may not consent to the commission of an offense against himself beforehand or forgive it afterwards is because it is an offense against society. It is not that society is physically injured; that would be impossible. Nor need any individual be shocked, corrupted, or exploited; everything may be done in private. Nor can it be explained on the practical ground that a violent man is a potential danger to others in the community who have therefore a direct interest in his apprehension and punishment as being necessary to their own protection. That would be true of a man whom the victim is prepared to forgive but not of one who gets his consent first; a murderer who acts only upon the consent, and maybe the request of his victim is no menace to others, but he does threaten one of the great moral principles upon which society is based, that is, the sanctity of human life. There is only one explanation of what has hitherto been accepted as the basis of criminal law and that is that there are certain standards of behavior or moral principles which society requires to be observed; and the breach of them is an offense not merely against the person who is injured but against society as a whole.

Thus, if the criminal law were to be reformed so as to eliminate from it everything that was not designed to preserve order and decency or to protect citizens (including the protection of youth from corruption), it would overturn a fundamental principle. It would also end a number of specific crimes. Euthanasia, or the killing of another at his own request, suicide, attempted suicide and suicide pacts, dueling, abortion, incest between brother and sister, are all acts which can be done in private and without offense to others and need not involve the corruption or exploration of others . . . .

I think it is clear that the criminal law as we know it is based upon moral principle. In a number of crimes its function is simply to enforce a moral principle and nothing else. . . .

. . . . What makes a society of any sort is community of ideas, not only political ideas but also ideas about the way its members should behave and govern their lives; these latter ideas are its morals. Every society has a moral structure as well as a political one; or rather, since that might suggest two independent systems, I should say that the structure of every society is made up both of politics and morals. . . .

. . . [W]ithout shared ideas on politics, morals, and ethics no society can exist. Each one of us has ideas about what is good and what is evil; they cannot be kept private from the society in which we live. If men and women try to create a society in which there is no fundamental agreement about good and evil they will fail; if having based it on common agreement, the agreement goes, the society will disintegrate. For society is not something that is kept together physically; it is held by the invisible bonds of common thought. If the bonds were too far relaxed the members would drift apart. A common morality is part of the bondage. The bondage is part of the price of society; and mankind, which needs society, must pay its price. . . .

I think, therefore, that it is not possible to set theoretical limits to the power of the State to legislate against immorality. It is not possible to settle in advance exceptions to the general rule or to define inflexibly areas of morality into which the law is in no circumstances to be allowed to enter. Society is entitled by means of its laws to protect itself from dangers, whether from within or without. Here again I think that the political parallel is legitimate. The law of treason is directed against aiding the king's enemies and against sedition from within. The justification for this is that established government is necessary for the existence of society and therefore its safety against violent overthrow must be secured. But an established morality is as necessary as good government to the welfare of society. Societies disintegrate from within more frequently than they are broken up by external pressures. There is disintegration when no common morality is observed and history shows that the loosening of moral bonds is often the first state of disintegration, so that society is justified in taking the same steps to preserve its moral code as it does to preserve its government and other essential institutions. The suppression of vice is as much the law's business as the suppression of subversive activities; it is no more possible to define a sphere of private morality than it is to define one of private subversive activity. . . .

. . . But . . . the individual has a locus standi too; he cannot be expected to surrender to the judgment of society the whole conduct of his life. It is the old and familiar question of striking a balance between the rights and interests of society and those of the individual. . . .

. . . There must be toleration of the maximum individual freedom that is consistent with the integrity of society. . . . The principle appears to me to be peculiarly appropriate to all questions of morals. Nothing should be punished by the law that does not lie beyond the limits of tolerance. It is not nearly enough to say that a majority dislike a practice; there must be a real feeling of reprobation. Those who are dissatisfied with the present law on homosexuality often say that the opponents of reform are swayed simply by disgust. If that were so it would be wrong, but I do not think one can ignore disgust if it is deeply felt and not manufactured. Its presence is a good indication that the bounds of toleration are being reached. Not everything is to be tolerated. No society can do without intolerance, indignation, and disgust; they are the forces behind the moral law, and indeed it can be argued that if they or something like them are not present the feelings of society cannot be weighty enough to deprive the individual of freedom of choice. . . .

NOTES

1.   *The Wolfenden Committee.* As noted above, the Hart-Devlin Debate arose in the wake of the 1957 Wolfenden Committee Report. In its report, the Departmental Committee on Homosexual Offences and Prostitution, led by Lord Wolfenden, recommended decriminalizing homosexual sodomy on the ground that "part of the function of the law is to preserve public order and decency, to protect the citizen from what is offensive or injurious, and to provide sufficient safeguards against exploitation and corruption of others. . . . We do not think that is it proper for the law to concern itself with what a man does in private. . . ." REPORT OF THE COMMITTEE ON HOMOSEXUAL OFFENCES AND PROSTITUTION (1957). Critically, the Committee considered whether to decriminalize a wide array of "morals" offenses. Although the Committee's report recommended decriminalizing homosexual sodomy (when conducted in private), it did not recommend decriminalizing prostitution, which it associated with "community instability" and the "weakening of the family." *Id.*

2.   *The Model Penal Code.* In 1962, the American Law Institute (ALI) published its Model Penal Code (MPC), a massive reform project aimed at rationalizing and modernizing the hodgepodge of statutory and common law criminal law principles at work in U.S. jurisdictions. Perhaps the MPC's most radical reform was its treatment of sexual offenses. The MPC recommended eliminating criminal laws prohibiting consensual, private sexual activity between adults. As a result, the MPC made no provisions for the criminalization of fornication, adultery, and private consensual sodomy—all of which were standard crimes in the penal codes of most American jurisdictions at the time. The MPC's sexual offense reforms were prompted by a number of concerns. Some argued that these laws were only rarely enforced, and more troublingly, when they were enforced, the prosecutions were animated by discrimination or extortion. Others argued

that the criminalization of such acts diverted scarce resources away from more pressing criminal justice issues. Finally—and perhaps most importantly—many believed that the criminalization of private, consensual sexuality allowed the state to intrude too far into the private realm. For an overview of the motivations behind the MPC, see Herbert Wechsler, *The Challenge of a Model Penal Code*, 65 HARV. L. REV. 1097 (1952). For a discussion of the debate within the ALI over the decriminalization of sodomy, see Ellen Ann Andersen, *The Stages of Sodomy Reform*, 23 T. MARSHALL L. REV. 283, 289–91 (1997).

3.   *Competing visions of law and morality.* At the core of the Hart-Devlin Debate are different notions of the relationship between law and morality. Hart is a legal pragmatist, arguing that law cannot and should not uphold popular morality in the absence of concrete harms. This position was arguably dominant in the United States during the 1960s and 1970s. Devlin, by contrast, took the view that law should articulate an ideal of moral behavior. Of late, Devlin's "idealist" position has gained more traction, as legal idealists argue that even when there is no concrete harm, there is always a victim when morality is ignored, namely "society." *See, e.g.*, Andrew Koppelman, *Does Obscenity Cause Moral Harm?*, 105 COLUM. L. REV. 1635, 1636 (2005) (discussing contemporary conservatives' argument that obscenity is a moral harm to all). What is left unclear in an increasingly diverse society is who is included in the term "society," and who is allowed to determine what is moral and what is not.

4.   *The* Spanner *case.* In the U.K. case *R v. Brown*, [1994] 1 AC 212 (known as the *Spanner* case, after Operation Spanner, the investigation that led to the arrests that formed the basis for the legal challenge), a group of men challenged their convictions under sections 20 and 47 of the Offences Against the Person Act of 1861. Specifically, the men were charged with unlawful and malicious wounding and assault occasioning actual bodily harm, stemming from their involvement in sadomasochistic activities. The men challenged their convictions on the ground that, in all instances, they consented to the acts for which they were convicted. In taking up the appeal to the convictions, the House of Lords confronted the question of whether, in the context of bodily harm incurred in the course of a sadomasochistic encounter, the prosecution must prove the victim's lack of consent in order to convict the defendant. A bare majority of the panel concluded that the victim's consent was no defense to the charges. What would Hart and Devlin have made of Operation Spanner and the convictions and appeal that followed?

E. REDEFINING AND REFINING THE CATEGORIES OF NORMATIVE AND DEVIANT SEX

Loving v. Virginia

388 U.S. 1 (1967).

■ WARREN, C.J.

This case presents a constitutional question never addressed by this Court: whether a statutory scheme adopted by the State of Virginia to prevent marriages between persons solely on the basis of racial classifications violates the Equal Protection and Due Process Clauses of the Fourteenth Amendment. . . .

In June 1958, two residents of Virginia, Mildred Jeter, a Negro woman, and Richard Loving, a white man, were married in the District of Columbia pursuant to its laws. Shortly after their marriage, the Lovings returned to Virginia and established their marital abode in Caroline County. At the October Term, 1958, of the Circuit Court of Caroline County, a grand jury issued an indictment charging the Lovings with violating Virginia's ban on interracial marriages. On January 6, 1959, the Lovings pleaded guilty to the charge and were sentenced to one year in jail; however, the trial judge suspended the sentence for a period of 25 years on the condition that the Lovings leave the State and not return to Virginia together for 25 years. He stated in an opinion that:

> Almighty God created the races white, black, yellow, malay and red, and he placed them on separate continents. And but for the interference with his arrangement there would be no cause for such marriages. The fact that he separated the races shows that he did not intend for the races to mix.

. . .

Virginia is . . . one of 16 States which prohibit and punish marriages on the basis of racial classifications.[5] Penalties for miscegenation arose as an incident to slavery and have been common in Virginia since the

---

[5] After the initiation of this litigation, Maryland repealed its prohibitions against interracial marriage, Md. Laws 1967, c. 6, leaving Virginia and 15 other States with statutes outlawing interracial marriage: Alabama, Ala. Const., Art. 4, § 102, Ala. Code, Tit. 14, § 360 (1958); Arkansas, Ark. Stat. Ann. § 55–104 (1947); Delaware, Del. Code Ann., Tit. 13, § 101 (1953); Florida, Fla. Const., Art. 16, § 24, F.S.A., Fla. Stat. § 741.11 (1965); Georgia, Ga. Code Ann. § 53–106 (1961); Kentucky, Ky. Rev. Stat. Ann. § 402.020 (Supp.1966); Louisiana, La. Rev. Stat. § 14:79 (1950); Mississippi, Miss. Const., Art. 14, § 263, Miss. Code Ann. § 459 (1956); Missouri, Mo. Rev. Stat. § 451.020 (Supp. 1966); North Carolina, N.C. Const., Art. XIV, § 8, N.C. Gen. Stat. § 14–181 (1953); Oklahoma, Okla. Stat., Tit. 43, § 12 (Supp. 1965); South Carolina, S.C. Const., Art. 3, § 33, S.C.Code Ann. § 20–7 (1962); Tennessee, Tenn. Const., Art. 11, § 14; Tenn. Code. Ann. § 36–402 (1955); Vernon's Ann. Texas, Tex. Pen. Code, Art. 492 (1952); West Virginia, W.Va. Code Ann. § 4697 (1961).

Over the past 15 years, 14 States have repealed laws outlawing interracial marriages: Arizona, California, Colorado, Idaho, Indiana, Maryland, Montana, Nebraska, Nevada, North Dakota, Oregon, South Dakota, Utah, and Wyoming.

The first state court to recognize that miscegenation statutes violate the Equal Protection Clause was the Supreme Court of California. *Perez v. Sharp*, 32 Cal.2d 711 (1948).

colonial period. . . . The present statutory scheme dates from the adoption
of the Racial Integrity Act of 1924, passed during the period of extreme
nativism which followed the end of the First World War. The central
features of this Act, and current Virginia law, are the absolute
prohibition of a "white person" marrying other than another "white
person," a prohibition against issuing marriage licenses until the issuing
official is satisfied that the applicants' statements as to their race are
correct, certificates of "racial composition" to be kept by both local and
state registrars, and the carrying forward of earlier prohibitions against
racial intermarriage.

In upholding the constitutionality of these provisions in the decision
below, the Supreme Court of Appeals of Virginia referred to its 1955
decision in *Naim v. Naim* as stating the reasons supporting the validity
of these laws. In *Naim*, the state court concluded that the State's
legitimate purposes were "to preserve the racial integrity of its citizens,"
and to prevent "the corruption of blood," "a mongrel breed of citizens,"
and "the obliteration of racial pride," obviously an endorsement of the
doctrine of White Supremacy. The court also reasoned that marriage has
traditionally been subject to state regulation without federal
intervention, and, consequently, the regulation of marriage should be left
to exclusive state control by the Tenth Amendment.

While the state court is no doubt correct in asserting that marriage
is a social relation subject to the State's police power, the State does not
contend in its argument before this Court that its powers to regulate
marriage are unlimited notwithstanding the commands of the
Fourteenth Amendment. . . . Instead, the State argues that the meaning
of the Equal Protection Clause, as illuminated by the statements of the
Framers, is only that state penal laws containing an interracial element
as part of the definition of the offense must apply equally to whites and
Negroes in the sense that members of each race are punished to the same
degree. Thus, the State contends that, because its miscegenation statutes
punish equally both the white and the Negro participants in an
interracial marriage, these statutes, despite their reliance on racial
classifications do not constitute an invidious discrimination based upon
race. . . .

Because we reject the notion that the mere "equal application" of a
statute containing racial classifications is enough to remove the
classifications from the Fourteenth Amendment's proscription of all
invidious racial discriminations, we do not accept the State's contention
that these statutes should be upheld if there is any possible basis for
concluding that they serve a rational purpose. The mere fact of equal
application does not mean that our analysis of these statutes should
follow the approach we have taken in cases involving no racial
discrimination. . . . In the case at bar . . . we deal with statutes containing
racial classifications, and the fact of equal application does not immunize
the statute from the very heavy burden of justification which the

Fourteenth Amendment has traditionally required of state statutes drawn according to race.

. . .

The State finds support for its "equal application" theory in the decision of the Court in *Pace v. Alabama*, 106 U.S. 583 (1883). In that case, the Court upheld a conviction under an Alabama statute forbidding adultery or fornication between a white person and a Negro which imposed a greater penalty than that of a statute proscribing similar conduct by members of the same race. The Court reasoned that the statute could not be said to discriminate against Negroes because the punishment for each participant in the offense was the same. However, as recently as the 1964 Term, in rejecting the reasoning of that case, we stated "*Pace* represents a limited view of the Equal Protection Clause which has not withstood analysis in the subsequent decisions of this Court." *McLaughlin v. Florida*, 379 U.S. 184 (1964). As we there demonstrated, the Equal Protection Clause requires the consideration of whether the classifications drawn by any statute constitute an arbitrary and invidious discrimination. . . .

There can be no question but that Virginia's miscegenation statutes rest solely upon distinctions drawn according to race. The statutes proscribe generally accepted conduct if engaged in by members of different races. Over the years, this Court has consistently repudiated "[d]istinctions between citizens solely because of their ancestry" as being "odious to a free people whose institutions are founded upon the doctrine of equality." *Hirabayashi v. United States*, 320 U.S. 81 (1943). At the very least, the Equal Protection Clause demands that racial classifications, especially suspect in criminal statutes, be subjected to the "most rigid scrutiny," *Korematsu v. United States*, 323 U.S. 214 (1944), and, if they are ever to be upheld, they must be shown to be necessary to the accomplishment of some permissible state objective, independent of the racial discrimination which it was the object of the Fourteenth Amendment to eliminate. . . .

There is patently no legitimate overriding purpose independent of invidious racial discrimination which justifies this classification. The fact that Virginia prohibits only interracial marriages involving white persons demonstrates that the racial classifications must stand on their own justification, as measures designed to maintain White Supremacy. We have consistently denied the constitutionality of measures which restrict the rights of citizens on account of race. There can be no doubt that restricting the freedom to marry solely because of racial classifications violates the central meaning of the Equal Protection Clause.

These statutes also deprive the Lovings of liberty without due process of law in violation of the Due Process Clause of the Fourteenth Amendment. The freedom to marry has long been recognized as one of the vital personal rights essential to the orderly pursuit of happiness by free men.

Marriage is one of the "basic civil rights of man," fundamental to our very existence and survival. *Skinner v. Oklahoma*, 316 U.S. 535 (1942). To deny this fundamental freedom on so unsupportable a basis as the racial classifications embodied in these statutes, classifications so directly subversive of the principle of equality at the heart of the Fourteenth Amendment, is surely to deprive all the State's citizens of liberty without due process of law. The Fourteenth Amendment requires that the freedom of choice to marry not be restricted by invidious racial discriminations. Under our Constitution, the freedom to marry or not marry, a person of another race resides with the individual and cannot be infringed by the State.

These convictions must be reversed. It is so ordered.

NOTES

1.   *Race and eugenics.* Virginia's Racial Integrity Act of 1924, which was challenged in *Loving*, was enacted amidst a period of broader social interest in eugenics. *See* An Act to Preserve Racial Integrity, 1924 Va. Acts 534. Indeed, in 1924, Virginia also enacted the eugenics-inflected sterilization statute upheld in *Buck v. Bell*, 274 U.S. 200 (1927). *See infra* at pp. 1058–1060. As Professor Paul Lombardo observes, the Racial Integrity Act "was drafted by men who argued for its value in the name of the 'science' of eugenics." Paul A. Lombardo, *Miscegenation, Eugenics, and Racism: Historical Footnotes to* Loving v. Virginia, 21 U.C. DAVIS L. REV. 421, 422 (1988). According to one of the Act's supporters, the law was "the most perfect expression of the white ideal, and the most important eugenical effort that has been made in 4000 years." *Id.* at 439.

2.   *From outlaws to in-laws.* Professor Katherine Franke observes that the *Loving* decision presents decriminalization and legalization as two sides of the same regulatory coin. According to Franke:

> . . . On June 11, 1967, the Lovings were criminals in the Commonwealth of Virginia, but on June 12, 1967 (the day the Supreme Court issued the decision in their favor), they were not. On June 11, 1967, the Lovings were not legally married in the Commonwealth of Virginia, but on June 12, 1967, they were. In this frame, when a court invalidates the criminalization of a particular behavior, the logical consequence of the court's action is to render the group subject to positive legal regulation. In this circumstance, there is no social or legal daylight between being subject to the regulation of criminal laws and being subject to the regulation of civil laws. The effect of winning the constitutional challenge to a status-based disadvantage of this kind is that the district attorney walks the file containing your criminal case over to the clerk in the marriage license office. You and your relationship never leave the building. . . .

Katherine M. Franke, *Longing for* Loving, 76 FORDHAM L. REV. 2685, 2687 (2008). What is Franke's point? How should we think about the Lovings' transformation from outlaws to in-laws? To connect the point to Gayle Rubin's discussion of the charmed circle of sexuality, see *supra* p. 11, what does it mean for the Lovings to be relocated from the periphery to the center of Rubin's charmed circle?

3. *In the shadow of* Griswold v. Connecticut. Arguably, the foundational case in the creation of a jurisprudence of reproductive and sexual privacy is *Griswold v. Connecticut*, the 1965 Supreme Court decision finding Connecticut's law forbidding the use of contraceptives unconstitutional. In that case, Justice Douglas painted a grim portrait of jackbooted police officers entering "the sacred precincts of the marital bedroom" in search of "telltale signs of the use of contraceptives." *Griswold v. Connecticut*, 381 U.S. 479, 485 (1965). Justice Douglas suggested that such an idea would be "repulsive to the notions of privacy surrounding the marriage relationship." *Id.* at 486. Yet, this is exactly what happened in *Loving*. "[I]n the early morning of July 11, 1958, five weeks after their wedding ... the county sheriff and two deputies, acting on an anonymous tip, burst into [the Lovings'] bedroom and shined flashlights in their eyes." Douglas Martin, *Mildred Loving, Who Battled Ban on Mixed-Race Marriage, Dies at 68*, N.Y. TIMES, May 6, 2008, at B7. One of the officers asked Richard Loving, who "this women you're sleeping with" was, and Mildred Loving answered that she was Richard's wife. When Richard gestured to the couple's marriage certificate, the sheriff dismissed it. *Id.*

Lawrence v. Texas
539 U.S. 558 (2003).

■ KENNEDY, J.

Liberty protects the person from unwarranted government intrusions into a dwelling or other private places. In our tradition the State is not omnipresent in the home. And there are other spheres of our lives and existence, outside the home, where the State should not be a dominant presence. Freedom extends beyond spatial bounds. Liberty presumes an autonomy of self that includes freedom of thought, belief, expression, and certain intimate conduct. The instant case involves liberty of the person both in its spatial and in its more transcendent dimensions.

The question before the Court is the validity of a Texas statute making it a crime for two persons of the same sex to engage in certain intimate sexual conduct.

In Houston, Texas, officers of the Harris County Police Department were dispatched to a private residence in response to a reported weapons disturbance. They entered an apartment where one of the petitioners, John Geddes Lawrence, resided. The right of the police to enter does not seem to have been questioned. The officers observed Lawrence and another man, Tyron Garner, engaging in a sexual act. The two petitioners were arrested, held in custody overnight, and charged and convicted before a Justice of the Peace.

The complaints described their crime as "deviate sexual intercourse, namely anal sex, with a member of the same sex (man)." The applicable state law is Tex. Penal Code Ann. § 21.06(a) (2003). It provides: "A person commits an offense if he engages in deviate sexual intercourse with another individual of the same sex." The statute defines "[d]eviate sexual intercourse" as follows:

(A) any contact between any part of the genitals of one person and the mouth or anus of another person; or

(B) the penetration of the genitals or the anus of another person with an object.

§ 21.01(1).

. . . The petitioners, having entered a plea of *nolo contendere,* were each fined $200 and assessed court costs of $141.25.

The Court of Appeals for the Texas Fourteenth District considered the petitioners' federal constitutional arguments under both the Equal Protection and Due Process Clauses of the Fourteenth Amendment. After hearing the case en banc the court, in a divided opinion, rejected the constitutional arguments and affirmed the convictions. The majority opinion indicates that the Court of Appeals considered our decision in *Bowers v. Hardwick*, 478 U.S. 186 (1986), to be controlling on the federal due process aspect of the case. *Bowers* then being authoritative, this was proper.

We granted certiorari to consider three questions:

1.   Whether petitioners' criminal convictions under the Texas "Homosexual Conduct" law—which criminalizes sexual intimacy by same-sex couples, but not identical behavior by different-sex couples—violate the Fourteenth Amendment guarantee of equal protection of the laws.

2.   Whether petitioners' criminal convictions for adult consensual sexual intimacy in the home violate their vital interests in liberty and privacy protected by the Due Process Clause of the Fourteenth Amendment.

3.   Whether *Bowers v. Hardwick* should be overruled.

The petitioners were adults at the time of the alleged offense. Their conduct was in private and consensual.

We conclude the case should be resolved by determining whether the petitioners were free as adults to engage in the private conduct in the exercise of their liberty under the Due Process Clause of the Fourteenth Amendment to the Constitution. For this inquiry we deem it necessary to reconsider the Court's holding in *Bowers*.

. . .

The Court began its substantive discussion in *Bowers* as follows: "The issue presented is whether the Federal Constitution confers a fundamental right upon homosexuals to engage in sodomy and hence invalidates the laws of the many States that still make such conduct illegal and have done so for a very long time." That statement, we now conclude, discloses the Court's own failure to appreciate the extent of the liberty at stake. To say that the issue in *Bowers* was simply the right to engage in certain sexual conduct demeans the claim the individual put forward, just as it would demean a married couple were it to be said marriage is simply about the right to have sexual intercourse. The laws involved in *Bowers* and here are, to be sure, statutes that purport to do no more than prohibit a particular sexual act. Their penalties and purposes, though, have more far-reaching consequences, touching upon the most private human conduct, sexual behavior, and in the most private of places, the home. The statutes do seek to control a personal relationship that, whether or not entitled to formal recognition in the law, is within the liberty of persons to choose without being punished as criminals.

This, as a general rule, should counsel against attempts by the State, or a court, to define the meaning of the relationship or to set its boundaries absent injury to a person or abuse of an institution the law protects. It suffices for us to acknowledge that adults may choose to enter upon this relationship in the confines of their homes and their own private lives and still retain their dignity as free persons. When sexuality finds overt expression in intimate conduct with another person, the conduct can be but one element in a personal bond that is more enduring. The liberty protected by the Constitution allows homosexual persons the right to make this choice.

Having misapprehended the claim of liberty there presented to it, and thus stating the claim to be whether there is a fundamental right to engage in consensual sodomy, the *Bowers* Court said: "Proscriptions against that conduct have ancient roots." . . . [T]he following considerations counsel against adopting the definitive conclusions upon which *Bowers* placed such reliance.

At the outset it should be noted that there is no longstanding history in this country of laws directed at homosexual conduct as a distinct matter. Beginning in colonial times there were prohibitions of sodomy derived from the English criminal laws passed in the first instance by the Reformation Parliament of 1533. The English prohibition was understood to include relations between men and women as well as relations between men and men. Nineteenth-century commentators similarly read American sodomy, buggery, and crime-against-nature statutes as criminalizing certain relations between men and women and between men and men. . . . Thus early American sodomy laws were not directed at homosexuals as such but instead sought to prohibit nonprocreative sexual activity more generally. This does not suggest approval of homosexual conduct. It does tend to show that this particular form of conduct was not thought of as a separate category from like conduct between heterosexual persons.

. . .

It was not until the 1970's that any State singled out same-sex relations for criminal prosecution, and only nine States have done so. Post-*Bowers* even some of these States did not adhere to the policy of suppressing homosexual conduct. Over the course of the last decades, States with same-sex prohibitions have moved toward abolishing them.

In summary, the historical grounds relied upon in *Bowers* are more complex than the majority opinion and the concurring opinion by Chief Justice Burger indicate. Their historical premises are not without doubt and, at the very least, are overstated.

It must be acknowledged, of course, that the Court in *Bowers* was making the broader point that for centuries there have been powerful voices to condemn homosexual conduct as immoral. The condemnation has been shaped by religious beliefs, conceptions of right and acceptable behavior, and respect for the traditional family. For many persons these are not trivial concerns but profound and deep convictions accepted as ethical and moral principles to which they aspire and which thus determine the course of their lives. These considerations do not answer the question before us, however. The issue is whether the majority may use the power of the State to enforce these views on the whole society through operation of the criminal law

Chief Justice Burger joined the opinion for the Court in *Bowers* and further explained his views as follows: "Decisions of individuals relating to homosexual conduct have been subject to state intervention throughout the history of Western civilization. Condemnation of those practices is firmly rooted in Judeao-Christian [sic] moral and ethical standards." As with Justice White's assumptions about history, scholarship casts some doubt on the sweeping nature of the statement by Chief Justice Burger as it pertains to private homosexual conduct between consenting adults. In all events we think that our laws and traditions in the past half century are of most relevance here. These references show an emerging awareness that liberty gives substantial protection to adult persons in deciding how to conduct their private lives in matters pertaining to sex. . . .

This emerging recognition should have been apparent when *Bowers* was decided. In 1955 the American Law Institute promulgated the Model Penal Code and made clear that it did not recommend or provide for "criminal penalties for consensual sexual relations conducted in private." ALI, Model Penal Code § 213.2, Comment 2, p. 372 (1980). It justified its decision on three grounds: (1) The prohibitions undermined respect for the law by penalizing conduct many people engaged in; (2) the statutes regulated private conduct not harmful to others; and (3) the laws were arbitrarily enforced and thus invited the danger of blackmail. ALI, Model Penal Code, Commentary 277–280 (Tent. Draft No. 4, 1955). In 1961 Illinois changed its laws to conform to the Model Penal Code. Other States soon followed.

. . .

The sweeping references by Chief Justice Burger to the history of Western civilization and to Judeo-Christian moral and ethical standards did not take account of other authorities pointing in an opposite direction. A committee advising the British Parliament recommended in 1957 repeal of laws punishing homosexual conduct. *The Wolfenden Report: Report of the Committee on Homosexual Offenses and Prostitution* (1963). Parliament enacted the substance of those recommendations 10 years later.

Of even more importance, almost five years before *Bowers* was decided the European Court of Human Rights considered a case with parallels to *Bowers* and to today's case. An adult male resident in Northern Ireland alleged he was a practicing homosexual who desired to engage in consensual homosexual conduct. The laws of Northern Ireland forbade him that right. He alleged that he had been questioned, his home had been searched, and he feared criminal prosecution. The court held that the laws proscribing the conduct were invalid under the European Convention on Human Rights. *Dudgeon v. United Kingdom*, 45 Eur. Ct. H.R. (1981) & ¶ 52. Authoritative in all countries that are members of the Council of Europe (21 nations then, 45 nations now), the decision is at odds with the premise in *Bowers* that the claim put forward was insubstantial in our Western civilization.

In our own constitutional system the deficiencies in *Bowers* became even more apparent in the years following its announcement. The 25 States with laws prohibiting the relevant conduct referenced in the *Bowers* decision are reduced now to 13, of which 4 enforce their laws only against homosexual conduct. In those States where sodomy is still proscribed, whether for same-sex or heterosexual conduct, there is a pattern of nonenforcement with respect to consenting adults acting in private. . . .

. . .

Two principal cases decided after *Bowers* cast its holding into even more doubt. In *Planned Parenthood of Southeastern Pennsylvania v. Casey*, 505 U.S. 833 (1992), the Court reaffirmed the substantive force of the liberty protected by the Due Process Clause. The *Casey* decision again confirmed that our laws and tradition afford constitutional protection to personal decisions relating to marriage, procreation, contraception, family relationships, child rearing, and education. . . .

Persons in a homosexual relationship may seek autonomy for these purposes, just as heterosexual persons do. The decision in *Bowers* would deny them this right.

. . .

As an alternative argument in this case, counsel for the petitioners and some *amici* contend that *Romer* [*v. Evans*, 517 U.S. 620 (1996)] provides the basis for declaring the Texas statute invalid under the Equal Protection Clause. That is a tenable argument, but we conclude the instant case requires us to address whether *Bowers* itself has continuing validity. Were we to hold the statute invalid under the Equal Protection Clause some might question whether a prohibition would be valid if drawn differently, say, to prohibit the conduct both between same-sex and different-sex participants.

Equality of treatment and the due process right to demand respect for conduct protected by the substantive guarantee of liberty are linked in important respects, and a decision on the latter point advances both interests. If protected conduct is made criminal and the law which does so remains unexamined for its substantive validity, its stigma might remain even if it were not enforceable as drawn for equal protection reasons. When homosexual conduct is made criminal by the law of the State, that declaration in and of itself is an invitation to subject homosexual persons to discrimination both in the public and in the private spheres. The central holding of *Bowers* has been brought in question by this case, and it should be addressed. Its continuance as precedent demeans the lives of homosexual persons.

The stigma this criminal statute imposes, moreover, is not trivial. The offense, to be sure, is but a class C misdemeanor, a minor offense in the Texas legal system. Still, it remains a criminal offense with all that imports for the dignity of the persons charged. The petitioners will bear on their record the history of their criminal convictions. . . . Furthermore, the Texas criminal conviction carries with it the other collateral consequences always following a conviction, such as notations on job application forms, to mention but one example.

. . .

Bowers was not correct when it was decided, and it is not correct today. It ought not to remain binding precedent. *Bowers v. Hardwick* should be and now is overruled.

The present case does not involve minors. It does not involve persons who might be injured or coerced or who are situated in relationships where consent might not easily be refused. It does not involve public conduct or prostitution. It does not involve whether the government must give formal recognition to any relationship that homosexual persons seek to enter. The case does involve two adults who, with full and mutual consent from each other, engaged in sexual practices common to a homosexual lifestyle. The petitioners are entitled to respect for their private lives. The State cannot demean their existence or control their destiny by making their private sexual conduct a crime. Their right to liberty under the Due Process Clause gives them the full right to engage in their conduct without intervention of the government. . . . The Texas statute furthers no legitimate state interest which can justify its intrusion into the personal and private life of the individual.

Had those who drew and ratified the Due Process Clauses of the Fifth Amendment or the Fourteenth Amendment known the components of liberty in its manifold possibilities, they might have been more specific. They did not presume to have this insight. They knew times can blind us to certain truths and later generations can see that laws once thought necessary and proper in fact serve only to oppress. As the Constitution endures, persons in every generation can invoke its principles in their own search for greater freedom.

The judgment of the Court of Appeals for the Texas Fourteenth District is reversed, and the case is remanded for further proceedings not inconsistent with this opinion.

It is so ordered.

. . .

■ SCALIA, J., with whom THE CHIEF JUSTICE and THOMAS, J., join, dissenting.

"Liberty finds no refuge in a jurisprudence of doubt." *Planned Parenthood of Southeastern Pa. v. Casey*, 505 U.S. 833, 844 (1992). That was the Court's sententious response, barely more than a decade ago, to those seeking to overrule *Roe v. Wade*, 410 U.S. 113 (1973). The Court's response today, to those who have engaged in a 17-year crusade to overrule *Bowers v. Hardwick*, 478 U.S. 186 (1986), is very different. . . .

. . .

. . . I do not myself believe in rigid adherence to *stare decisis* in constitutional cases; but I do believe that we should be consistent rather than manipulative in invoking the doctrine. Today's opinions in support of reversal do not bother to distinguish—or indeed, even bother to mention—the paean to *stare decisis* coauthored by three Members of today's majority in *Planned Parenthood v. Casey*. There, when *stare decisis* meant preservation of judicially invented abortion rights, the widespread criticism of *Roe* was strong reason to *reaffirm* it . . . .

. . .

Today, however, the widespread opposition to *Bowers*, a decision resolving an issue as "intensely divisive" as the issue in *Roe*, is offered as a reason in favor of *overruling* it. . . .

Bowers, the Court says, has been subject to "substantial and continuing [criticism], disapproving of its reasoning in all respects, not just as to its historical assumptions." . . . Of course, *Roe* too (and by extension *Casey*) had been (and still is) subject to unrelenting criticism. . . .

... "[T]here has been," the Court says, "no individual or societal reliance on *Bowers* of the sort that could counsel against overturning its holding. . . ." It seems to me that the "societal reliance" on the principles confirmed in *Bowers* and discarded today has been overwhelming. Countless judicial decisions and legislative enactments have relied on the ancient proposition that a governing majority's belief that certain sexual behavior is "immoral and unacceptable" constitutes a rational basis for regulation. . . . State laws against bigamy, same-sex marriage, adult incest, prostitution, masturbation, adultery, fornication, bestiality, and obscenity are likewise sustainable only in light of *Bowers*' validation of laws based on moral choices. Every single one of these laws is called into question by today's decision . . . .

What a massive disruption of the current social order, therefore, the overruling of *Bowers* entails. Not so the overruling of *Roe*, which would simply have restored the regime that existed for centuries before 1973, in which the permissibility of, and restrictions upon, abortion were determined legislatively State by State. *Casey*, however, chose to base its *stare decisis* determination on a different "sort" of reliance. "[P]eople," it said, "have organized intimate relationships and made choices that define their views of themselves and their places in society, in reliance on the availability of abortion in the event that contraception should fail." This falsely assumes that the consequence of overruling *Roe* would have been to make abortion unlawful. It would not; it would merely have *permitted* the States to do so. Many States would unquestionably have declined to prohibit abortion, and others would not have prohibited it within six months (after which the most significant reliance interests would have expired). Even for persons in States other than these, the choice would not have been between abortion and childbirth, but between abortion nearby and abortion in a neighboring State.

To tell the truth, it does not surprise me, and should surprise no one, that the Court has chosen today to revise the standards of *stare decisis* set forth in *Casey*. It has thereby exposed *Casey*'s extraordinary deference to precedent for the result-oriented expedient that it is.

. . .

I turn now to the ground on which the Court squarely rests its holding: the contention that there is no rational basis for the law here under attack. This proposition is so out of accord with our jurisprudence—indeed, with the jurisprudence of *any* society we know—that it requires little discussion.

The Texas statute undeniably seeks to further the belief of its citizens that certain forms of sexual behavior are "immoral and unacceptable,"—the same interest furthered by criminal laws against fornication, bigamy, adultery, adult incest, bestiality, and obscenity. *Bowers* held that this *was* a legitimate state interest. The Court today reaches the opposite conclusion. The Texas statute, it says, "furthers *no legitimate state interest* which can justify its intrusion into the personal and private life of the individual. The Court embraces instead Justice Stevens' declaration in his *Bowers* dissent, that "the fact that the governing majority in a State has traditionally viewed a particular practice as immoral is not a sufficient reason for upholding a law prohibiting the practice." This effectively decrees the end of all morals legislation. If, as the Court asserts, the promotion of majoritarian sexual morality is not even a *legitimate* state interest, none of the above-mentioned laws can survive rational-basis review.

. . .

Finally, I turn to petitioners' equal-protection challenge . . . . On its face § 21.06(a) applies equally to all persons. Men and women, heterosexuals and homosexuals, are all subject to its prohibition of deviate sexual intercourse with someone of the same sex. To be sure, § 21.06 does distinguish between the sexes insofar as concerns the partner with whom the sexual acts are performed: men can violate the law only with other men, and women only with other women. But this cannot itself be a denial of equal protection, since it is precisely the same distinction regarding partner that is drawn in state laws prohibiting marriage with someone of the same sex while permitting marriage with someone of the opposite sex.

The objection is made, however, that the antimiscegenation laws invalidated in *Loving v. Virginia*, 388 U.S. 1 (1967), similarly were applicable to whites and blacks alike, and only distinguished between the races insofar as the *partner* was concerned. In *Loving*, however, we correctly applied heightened scrutiny, rather than the usual rational-basis review, because the Virginia statute was "designed to maintain White Supremacy." A racially discriminatory purpose is always sufficient to subject a law to strict scrutiny, even a facially neutral law that makes no mention of race. No purpose to discriminate against men or women as a class can be gleaned from the Texas law, so rational-basis review applies. That review is readily satisfied here by the same rational basis that satisfied it in *Bowers*—society's belief that certain forms of sexual behavior are "immoral and unacceptable." This is the same justification that supports many other laws regulating sexual behavior that make a distinction based upon the identity of the partner—for example, laws against adultery, fornication, and adult incest, and laws refusing to recognize homosexual marriage.

Justice O'Connor argues that the discrimination in this law which must be justified is not its discrimination with regard to the sex of the partner but its discrimination with regard to the sexual proclivity of the principal actor.

. . .

Of course the same could be said of any law. A law against public nudity targets "the conduct that is closely correlated with being a nudist," and hence "is targeted at more than conduct"; it is "directed toward nudists as a class." . . . Even if the Texas law *does* deny equal protection to "homosexuals as a class," that denial *still* does not need to be justified by anything more than a rational basis, which our cases show is satisfied by the enforcement of traditional notions of sexual morality.

Justice O'Connor simply decrees application of "a more searching form of rational basis review" to the Texas statute. . . . [This] must at least mean . . . that laws exhibiting "a desire to harm a politically unpopular group," are invalid *even though* there may be a conceivable rational basis to support them.

This reasoning leaves on pretty shaky grounds state laws limiting marriage to opposite-sex couples. Justice O'Connor seeks to preserve them by the conclusory statement that "preserving the traditional institution of marriage" is a legitimate state interest. But "preserving the traditional institution of marriage" is just a kinder way of describing the State's *moral disapproval* of same-sex couples. Texas's interest in § 21.06 could be recast in similarly euphemistic terms: "preserving the traditional sexual mores of our society." In the jurisprudence Justice O'Connor has seemingly created, judges can validate laws by characterizing them as "preserving the traditions of society" (good); or invalidate them by characterizing them as "expressing moral disapproval" (bad).

. . .

Today's opinion is the product of a Court, which is the product of a law-profession culture, that has largely signed on to the so-called homosexual agenda, by which I mean the agenda promoted by some homosexual activists directed at eliminating the moral opprobrium that has traditionally attached to homosexual conduct. . . .

. . . It is clear from this that the Court has taken sides in the culture war, departing from its role of assuring, as neutral observer, that the democratic rules of engagement are observed. Many Americans do not want persons who openly engage in homosexual conduct as partners in their business, as scoutmasters for their children, as teachers in their children's schools, or as boarders in their home. They view this as protecting themselves and their families from a lifestyle that they believe to be immoral and destructive. The Court views it as "discrimination" which it is the function of our judgments to deter. So imbued is the Court with the law profession's anti-anti-homosexual culture, that it is seemingly unaware that the attitudes of that culture are not obviously "mainstream." . . .

Let me be clear that I have nothing against homosexuals, or any other group, promoting their agenda through normal democratic means. Social perceptions of sexual and other morality change over time, and every group has the right to persuade its fellow citizens that its view of such matters is the best. That homosexuals have achieved some success in that enterprise is attested to by the fact that Texas is one of the few remaining States that criminalize private, consensual homosexual acts. But persuading one's fellow citizens is one thing, and imposing one's views in absence of democratic majority will is something else. I would no more *require* a State to criminalize homosexual acts—or, for that matter, display *any* moral disapprobation of them—than I would *forbid* it to do so. What Texas has chosen to do is well within the range of traditional democratic action, and its hand should not be stayed through the invention of a brand-new "constitutional right" by a Court that is impatient of democratic change. It is indeed true that "later generations can see that laws once thought necessary and proper in fact serve only to oppress," and when that happens, later generations can repeal those laws. But it is the premise of our system that those judgments are to be made by the people, and not imposed by a governing caste that knows best.

. . .

NOTES

1. *The facts of* Lawrence. Although Justice Kennedy depicts John Geddes Lawrence and Tyron Garner as a couple living a life in common, there was scant evidence for this conclusion. Indeed, Professor Dale Carpenter maintains that the true circumstances of the *Lawrence* petitioners depart considerably from Justice Kennedy's vision of cozy domesticity. According to Carpenter, at the time of the arrest, Lawrence and Garner may have been occasional sexual partners, but were not in a long-term, committed relationship. Indeed, Carpenter argues that Garner was romantically involved with Robert Eubanks, the man believed to have made the call alerting the police to a gun disturbance at Lawrence's apartment. DALE CARPENTER, FLAGRANT CONDUCT: THE STORY OF *LAWRENCE V. TEXAS* 62 (2012).

2. *Interracial sex on trial . . . again.* It should be noted that *Lawrence*, like *Loving*, involved an interracial pairing. John Geddes Lawrence was white, while Tyron Garner was black. Though it is unmentioned in the Court's opinion, race played a critical role in the facts of the case. According to Professor Dale Carpenter, the police were called to Lawrence's apartment, after Robert Eubanks reported a black male "going crazy with a gun." Upon arriving at the apartment, the police claimed to have witnessed Lawrence and Garner engaged in sexual activity, though there is evidence that this was not the case. DALE CARPENTER, FLAGRANT CONDUCT: THE STORY OF *LAWRENCE V. TEXAS* 62–63, 71 (2012). Why are the racial dimensions of the story absent in the *Lawrence* opinions?

3. *Domesticating gay sex.* Some scholars have argued that *Lawrence*'s protection for gay sex is deeply contingent. Professor Teemu Ruskola suggests that the Court's depiction of Lawrence and Garner as a couple in a relationship was intended to establish this type of monogamous, coupled intimacy as the norm for same-sex sexuality. *See* Teemu Ruskola, *Gay Rights versus Queer Theory: What is Left of Sodomy After* Lawrence v. Texas?, 23 SOC. TEXT 235, 241 (2005). According to Ruskola, the *Lawrence* decision

"leaves little or no justification for protecting less-than-transcendental sex that is not part of an ongoing relationship." *Id.* at 239. Likewise, Professor Katherine Franke maintains that *Lawrence*'s conception of privacy hearkens back to earlier privacy cases, like *Griswold v. Connecticut*, where the right of privacy was "both relational, in the sense of applying to the marital relationship, and spatially domesticated, in the sense of pertaining to activities in the most private confines of the home." Katherine M. Franke, *The Domesticated Liberty of* Lawrence v. Texas, 104 COLUM. L. REV. 1399, 1404 (2004).

4.   *Same-sex marriage and* Lawrence. Critically, *Lawrence v. Texas* was not even remotely about marriage—same-sex or otherwise. Yet, many have embraced the decision as an "opening salvo" in the fight to secure same-sex marriage. *See* Melissa Murray, *Strange Bedfellows: Criminal Law, Family Law, and the Legal Construction of Intimate Life*, 94 IOWA L. REV. 1253, 1305 (2009). Moreover, in his dissent in *Lawrence*, Justice Scalia made clear that he viewed the decriminalization of sodomy as leading inexorably to same-sex marriage. How did a case challenging criminal sodomy laws become a conduit to same-sex marriage? Professor Melissa Murray argues that this view is rooted in criminal law and marriage law's cooperative efforts to regulate and organize sex and sexuality. As she explains:

> [D]ecriminalizing same-sex sodomy necessarily gestures towards expanding marriage to include same-sex couples because that is the way we have always organized sex. If it is not marital, it must be criminal. And if it is not criminal, it must be marital. . . . [T]he idea of sex that is not criminal, but not eligible for marriage is completely unintelligible. Sex always has been subject to law— whether criminal law or family law. The idea of a zone where law is not present—where neither of these two doctrines governs—is preposterous and untenable.

Id. at 1304–05.

Obergefell v. Hodges

576 U.S. 644 (2015).

The Obergefell *decision is reproduced at pp. 25–40.*

NOTES

1.   Hollingsworth v. Perry, U.S. v. Windsor, *and the road to* Obergefell. In October Term 2012, the Supreme Court took up two separate but related challenges involving same-sex marriage. *Hollingsworth v. Perry*, 570 U.S. 693 (2013), was a constitutional challenge to Proposition 8, the California ballot initiative that amended the California state constitution to prohibit legal recognition of same-sex marriage. *United States v. Windsor*, 570 U.S. 744 (2013), was a challenge to section 3 of the Defense of Marriage Act (DOMA), which specified, for purposes of all federal laws and regulations, that marriage was a union between a man and a woman. The Court dismissed *Hollingsworth v. Perry* on jurisdictional grounds. It reached the

merits in *Windsor*, striking down section 3 on equal protection grounds. Although *Windsor* was limited to the constitutionality of section 3 of DOMA and did not take up the ancillary question of whether the Constitution's right to marry included the right to marry a person of the same sex, lower federal courts relied on *Windsor* in considering the constitutionality of state laws limiting marriage to opposite sex couples. *See, e.g., Baskin v. Bogan*, 766 F.3d 648 (7th Cir. 2014); *Bostic v. Schaefer*, 760 F.3d 375 (4th Cir. 2014); *Bishop v. Smith*, 760 F.3d 1070 (10th Cir. 2014); *Kitchen v. Herbert*, 755 F.3d 1193 (10th Cir. 2014); *Bishop v. United States ex rel. Holder*, 962 F. Supp. 2d 1252 (N.D. Okla. 2014); *Bourke v. Beshear*, 996 F. Supp. 2d 542 (W.D. Ky. 2014); *Bostic v. Rainey*, 970 F. Supp. 2d 456 (E.D. Va. 2014); *Lee v. Orr*, No. 13–cv–8719, 2014 WL 683680 (N.D. Ill. Feb. 21, 2014); *De Leon v. Perry*, 975 F. Supp. 2d 632 (W.D. Tex. 2014); *Tanco v. Haslam*, 7 F. Supp. 3d 759 (M.D. Tenn. 2014); *DeBoer v. Snyder*, 973 F. Supp. 2d 757 (E.D. Mich. 2014); *Henry v. Himes*, 14 F. Supp. 3d 1036 (S.D. Ohio 2014); *Obergefell v. Wymyslo*, 962 F. Supp. 2d 968 (S.D. Ohio 2013); *Kitchen v. Herbert*, 961 F. Supp. 2d 1181 (D. Utah 2013). Two years later, the Court took up the question of the constitutionality of same-sex marriage in *Obergefell.*

2.   *LGBT persons and the charmed circle of marriage.* With *Goodridge v. Department of Public Health*, 798 N.E.2d 941 (Mass. 2003), decided just a few months after *Lawrence v. Texas*, Massachusetts became the first American jurisdiction to legalize same-sex marriage. Almost twelve years later, *Obergefell* legalized same-sex marriage in the remaining U.S. jurisdictions. What does the legalization of same-sex marriage mean for the legal regulation of LGBT sex and sexuality? How does the inclusion of LGBT persons in the charmed circle of sexuality, see *supra* p. 11, impact LGBT persons—and other populations—who are unmarried?

3.   Obergefell *and* Lawrence. In his in dissent in *Lawrence v. Texas*, Justice Scalia predicted that, despite the majority's efforts to avoid the question of same-sex marriage, the decriminalization of same-sex sodomy would lead inexorably to the legalization of gay marriage.

4.   *Changing social norms.* As the National Opinion Research Center has pointed out:

> From 1973 through 1991 there was little change in public attitudes towards homosexual behavior. From two-thirds to three-quarters [of the public] consistently said it was "always wrong" while 10–15% considered it "not wrong at all." . . . In 1991, 72% considered [homosexuality] "always wrong" and this declined to 44% in 2010 . . . . [F]rom 1991 to 2010, the percentage saying homosexual behavior was "not wrong at all" rose from 14% to 41% . . . .

TOM W. SMITH, NAT'L OP. RESEARCH CTR. AT THE UNIV. OF CHI., PUBLIC ATTITUDES TOWARD HOMOSEXUALITY 1 (2011). Reflecting back on the Hart-Devlin Debate, how should these figures, which portray a deeply divided—but rapidly changing—society, be reflected in law?

5.   *Perfect and imperfect plaintiffs.* It is worth noting the role of plaintiff selection in *Goodridge* and in other marriage equality lawsuits. As some scholars have acknowledged, those selected to front marriage equality

lawsuits are carefully chosen in an effort to emphasize certain traits and downplay others. *See* Katherine M. Franke, *The Politics of Same-Sex Marriage Politics*, 15 COLUM. J. GENDER & L. 236, 239 (2006) (discussing the selection of plaintiffs in marriage equality litigation); Douglas NeJaime, Note, *Marriage, Cruising, and Life in Between: Clarifying Organizational Positionalities in Pursuit of Polyvocal Gay-Based Advocacy*, 38 HARV. C.R.-C.L. L. REV. 511, 545 (2003) (noting that the plaintiffs in *Goodridge* were selected, in part, based on their comportment with heteronormative family ideals). By and large, the plaintiffs in these marriage equality lawsuits are in "long term, committed, marriage-like relationships" in which they are raising children. Nancy Levit, *Theorizing and Litigating the Rights of Sexual Minorities*, 19 COLUM. J. GENDER & L. 21, 32–33 (2010); *see also* Franke, *supra*, at 239 (discussing the selection of "perfect plaintiffs").

> Critically, this strategic impulse is not exclusive to marriage equality litigation. Gay rights litigation, more generally, has operated in this fashion. According to Professor Kenji Yoshino, when we look at "the gay plaintiffs presented to the courts and the world as the public face of gay rights, we see 'straight-acting' men . . . . We see less of Perry Watkins—an African-American army service member with an . . . exemplary [service] record who performed as the drag queen Simone." KENJI YOSHINO, COVERING: THE HIDDEN ASSAULT ON OUR CIVIL RIGHTS 80 (2006). A similar strategy of emphasizing respectability was deployed by those advocating for the civil rights of racial minorities during the Civil Rights Movement. *See* TOMIKO BROWN-NAGIN, COURAGE TO DISSENT: ATLANTA AND THE LONG HISTORY OF THE CIVIL RIGHTS MOVEMENT 32 (2011) (noting that black leaders cultivated norms of "respectability" to combat stereotypes justifying discrimination).

American Law Institute: Principles of the Law of Family Dissolution: Analysis and Recommendations
(2002).

The primary challenge in shaping the law that governs allocation of responsibility for children is to determine how to facilitate thoughtful planning by cooperative parents while minimizing the harm to children who are caught in a cycle of conflict. Several unavoidable tensions in the law's objectives and its design complicate this task.

    a. Predictability vs. individualized decision-making. There is a significant tension in custody law between the goals of *predictability* and *individualization.* The predictability of outcomes helps to reduce litigation, as well as strategic and manipulative behavior by parents. Predictable outcomes are insufficient, however, unless they are also sound. And it is difficult to imagine sound outcomes in custody cases unless the diverse range of circumstances in which family breakdown occurs are taken into account. In short, predictability is important, but so is the customization of a result to the individual, sometimes unique, facts of a case.

. . .

Throughout the first two-thirds of the 20th century in the United States, the best-interests-of-the-child test was implemented through maternal preference rules that produced results that were both uniform, and generally regarded as sound. The relatively recent elimination of explicit sex-based preferences and the erosion of the ideology on which it was based left the best-interests test without concrete mooring. Today, the test is uniformly disparaged.

. . .

Another criticism of the best-interests test is that it sets an unrealistic goal for the law. The standard tells courts to do what is best for a child, as if what is best can be determined and is within their power to achieve. In fact, what is best for children depends upon values and norms upon which reasonable people sometimes differ. Even when consensus exists, there are substantial limits on the ability of courts to predict outcomes for children and to compel individuals to act in ways most beneficial to children.

. . .

An alternative for achieving greater determinacy is an approach that builds in a preference in favor of, or against, a particular form of custody. For example, some states express a presumption that joint custody is in a child's best interests; other states have a presumption in favor of the primary custodian. Such presumptions add determinacy to the decisionmaking process, but they are based necessarily on factual and normative assumptions about families and children that (1) are not accurate across the board, and (2) run counter to the commitment this society avows toward family diversity.

. . .

b. Finality v. flexibility. Another tension in custodial rule-making is created by the desire for both finality of results and flexibility in the face of changing circumstances. Finality forces parents to accept and live with the results of judicial decisionmaking, leading potentially to greater stability for the child. Yet flexibility is necessary to be responsive to children's needs and parental circumstances as they change over time. In the two-parent, intact family, finality and flexibility typically are achieved through an ongoing process of consensus, negotiation, and compromise. When parents no longer live together in a single family unit, more structured mechanisms are often necessary.

. . .

The best legal approaches to conflict over children at divorce would assume the likelihood of future changes and disagreements, and provide for them. Rules should require planning for the child's future needs, anticipate disruptions, and provide a process for defusing and resolving conflict.

    c.   Judicial supervision v. private ordering. Generally speaking, responsibility for children is allocated on a decentralized basis, to a child's parents. That responsibility is broad and near-absolute.[8] The degree of confidence placed in parents is not based on the certainty that all parents will do best for their children; some children would undoubtedly be better off if they had been assigned to someone other than their parents, or if their parents were more heavily supervised. It is assumed, however, that children on the whole will be better off, because (1) parents are the adults most likely to love their children; (2) love inspires parents to act responsibly toward their children[;] and (3) parental autonomy not only makes parents able to care for their children but more committed to doing so. Society, in turn, benefits from the diverse social fabric that is created by the de-centralized manner in which their care is provided.

    At divorce, ... under most states' laws a court must review an agreement to determine whether it is in the child's best interests. ... Despite the appearance of review, however, independent judicial inquiry is difficult because of the inaccessibility of facts that might dictate a different result. The result is the worst of both worlds: parents enter the divorce process with their autonomy to make arrangements for their children officially abridged, and yet arrangements that might truly be detrimental to children are unlikely to be identified.

    d.   Biological v. de facto parenthood. As noted above, a child's legal parents are given comprehensive authority to make decisions for their children, in part to reinforce their maximum commitment to the parenting enterprise. In practice, however, children are often cared for by adults other than parents. These adults include stepparents, grandparents, and parental partners who function as co-parents. Giving rights to de facto parents may serve to weaken the commitment society has to legal parents, on which the ideology of responsible parenting is based; yet disregarding their connection to a child at the time of family dissolution ignores child-parent relationships that may be fundamental to the child's sense of stability.

    Traditionally, parenthood is an exclusive, all-or-nothing status. A child can have only one mother and only one father; others have no rights, regardless of their functional roles. ... Yet states have carved out an exception for one group of non-parents—grandparents—who may be given rights sometimes without regard to their prior contact with the child. These two sets of principles are difficult to reconcile from a child-centered perspective.

---

    [8] *See* Katharine T. Bartlett, *Rethinking Parenthood as an Exclusive Status: The Need for Legal Alternatives When the Premise of the Nuclear Family Has Failed*, 70 VA. L. REV. 879, 883–85 (1984).

The law's challenge is to identify an approach applicable to all cases that allows continued contacts by de facto parents whose participation in the child's life is critically important to the child's welfare and recognizes the importance that some families place on extended family, and yet is consistent with the autonomy of parents that is essential to their meaningful exercise of responsibility.

e. *Protection v. privacy.* The final tension concerns the conflict between the state's interest in protecting individuals from harm and the freedom of families to have their privacy undisturbed. There is increasing awareness of the prevalence and danger of domestic abuse both to the physical security of individuals and to domestic tranquility. At the same time, there is a traditional resistance to interference in the family, rooted in ideologies of family privacy that are supported in constitutional jurisprudence. The law's difficult task is to provide protection for individuals who need it, within an institution valued primarily for the privacy from law that it provides.

NOTES

1. *Privileging marriage and marriage-like relationships?* The ALI's *Principles of Family Dissolution* are an attempt to deal with, among other things, the proliferation of nonmarital relationships between parents of children, which are increasingly common in the United States. The National Center for Health Statistics in 2013 noted that almost half of all women interviewed from 2006 to 2010 had their first sexual "union" as a cohabiting relationship rather than marriage, and 41% of births in 2010 were to unmarried women. For historical reasons, longitudinal data exist for women but not for men. Yet the *Principles* suggest that legal treatment of a relationship or parentage may depend on the extent to which the relationship resembles a marriage. *See* Casey E. Copen et al., *First Premarital Cohabitation in the United States: 2006–2010, National Survey of Family Growth,* NAT'L HEALTH STATS. REPS. (Ctrs. for Disease Control & Prevention, Hyattsville, Md.), Apr. 4, 2013, at 3.

2. *Recognizing nonmarital relationships. Maglica v. Maglica,* 78 Cal. Rptr. 2d 101 (Ct. App. 1998), reflects the tension between recognizing nonmarital relationships and using marital norms as indicia for such recognition. In 1971, Anthony Maglica and Claire Halasz moved in together, and Claire began using Anthony's last name. *Id.* at 103. The couple built a very successful business together, developing a brand of popular flashlights ("Maglights"). *Id.* In 1992, Halasz-Maglica discovered that Maglica was transferring his assets to his children from a prior marriage. *Id.* She filed a "palimony" suit, claiming a share of the company's assets on the ground that her ideas had been instrumental in developing the successful flashlight line. Halasz-Maglica was awarded an $84 million judgment, then thought to be the nation's largest palimony award. *Id.* On appeal, however, the judgment was reversed, as the California Court of Appeal tried to parse out the couple's sexual and intimate relationship and their business relationship. *Id.* at 108–10. In the end, the court concluded that because Halasz-Maglica could not

clearly claim status as a wife (because the couple were not married and because they worked together in a manner inconsistent with marriage) or as a business partner (because their sexual relationship belied a working relationship), she could not prevail on her claims. *Id.* Halasz-Maglica eventually settled with Mag Instrument for $29 million.

3.   *Nonmarital recognition, comparatively.* Starting in the late 1980s and early 1990s, many European countries (and some American municipalities) established civil unions or registered domestic partnerships, typically to provide same-sex couples access to some of the benefits of marriage. In both Europe and the United States, however, many opposite-sex couples have come to prefer these more flexible relationships. For example, in 1999, France established the Pacte Civil De Solidarité (PACS) as a civil partnership that provided an array of legal protections and benefits to couples who could not or wished not to enter into legal marriage. While same-sex couples can and do enter into PACS relationships, increasingly it is opposite-sex couples who value the relative flexibility of the PACS, although the text of the law makes clear that it is indifferent to sexual orientation. Amended in 2006, PACS provide some, but not all, of the benefits of marriage and makes clear that it is to cover both same-sex and opposite-sex relationships. *See* Joëlle Goddard, *PACS Seven Years On: Is It Moving Towards Marriage?*, 21 INT'L J.L. POL'Y & FAM. 310, 310 (2007). As of 2012, 94% of PACS are between opposite-sex couples. Gilles Wullus, *Il n'y a Pas de Mariage Homosexual, Il y a un Mariage pour Tous*, LIBÉRATION (July 18, 2012), http://www.liberation.fr/societe/2012/07/18/il-n-y-a-pas-de-mariage-homosexuel-il-y-a-un-mariage-pour-tous_834152. In 2013, France extended marriage and adoption rights to same-sex couples. Since 2013, PACS remain available to both same- and opposite-sex couples. Would similar forms of recognition be useful in the United States?

* * *

The prior excerpts suggest a progression in which once-deviant relationships are recast as valid and valuable. For example, same-sex sexual relationships are no longer considered per se deviant, and instead may be included within the charmed circle of marriage. But does this progression signal the end of sexual deviance entirely? As the following excerpts make clear, even as some relationships come to be regarded as valuable and socially productive, others continue to be regarded as deviant and continue to be subject to state regulation.

Doe v. Jindal
851 F. Supp. 2d 995 (E.D. La. 2012).

■ FELDMAN, J.

. . .

In Louisiana, the solicitation of oral or anal sex for compensation can be prosecuted under two different statutes: the solicitation for compensation provision of the Prostitution statute, and the Crime

Against Nature by Solicitation statute.[2] Nine anonymous plaintiffs, all of whom were convicted of violating Louisiana's Crime Against Nature by Solicitation statute based on their agreement to engage in oral sex for compensation prior to August 15, 2011, bring this civil rights suit. They challenge that statute's requirement that, as a result of their conviction, they must register as sex offenders under Louisiana's sex offender registry law. They complain that if, instead, they had been convicted of solicitation of sex for money under the state Prostitution law, they would not have been required to register as sex offenders.[3] It is the State's more lenient treatment of those convicted under the solicitation provision of the Prostitution statute, they urge, compared to those convicted under the Crime Against Nature by Solicitation statute, that anchors their civil rights claim in which they advance their constitutional challenge under the Fourteenth Amendment to the U.S. Constitution. . . .

Louisiana's approach to punishing solicitation of sex, until recently, depended in part on the particular sex act solicited: solicitation for money of oral or anal sex. Because the law dictated that a second-offense was a felony, if the conviction was for a Crime Against Nature by Solicitation, it was punished by longer prison sentences and larger fines, and the accused also had to register as a sex offender. But the solicitation of "indiscriminate sexual intercourse" (which encompasses oral and anal, as well as vaginal sexual intercourse) has always been by law a misdemeanor offense when statutorily identified as Prostitution, and those convicted of solicitation of Prostitution have never been required to register as sex offenders.

On February 15, 2011, these nine anonymous plaintiffs sued the defendants in their official capacities under 42 U.S.C. § 1983 to challenge the constitutionality of Louisiana's mandatory inclusion on the State's sex offender registry under the Crime Against Nature by Solicitation statute but not the Prostitution statute. . . . Each of the nine plaintiffs alleges that they have been convicted of Crime Against Nature by Solicitation for agreeing to perform oral sex for money, and must register as sex offenders for 15 years, or in some cases for their lifetime, solely as a result of their Crime Against Nature by Solicitation convictions. . . . Plaintiffs urge that no rational basis exists for criminally distinguishing between what is otherwise identical criminal conduct and that their constitutional right to [e]qual [p]rotection of the laws continues to be

---

[2]   The solicitation provision of the Prostitution statute outlaws "[t]he solicitation by one person of another with the intent to engage in indiscriminate sexual intercourse with the latter for compensation." La. Rev. Stat. Ann. § 14:82(A)(2). The Prostitution statute defines "sexual intercourse" as "anal, oral, or vaginal sexual intercourse." La. Rev. Stat. Ann. § 14:82(B). The Crime Against Nature by Solicitation statute forbids "solicitation by a human being of another with the intent to engage in any unnatural carnal copulation for compensation." La. Rev. Stat. Ann. § 14:89.2(A). "Unnatural carnal copulation" is also defined as oral or anal sexual intercourse. *See, e.g., Louisiana v. Smith*, 766 So.2d 501, 504–05 (La. 2000).

[3]   They also point out that they would not have been subjected to longer prison sentences and stricter fines had they been convicted of Prostitution. But they seek no relief regarding these harsher sentences.

violated because they remain by law subject to the sex offender registration requirements when others similarly situated are not.

. . .

To prove an [e]qual [p]rotection violation, and thereby satisfy their burden of proving a [c]onstitutional violation sufficient to warrant § 1983 relief, the plaintiffs must show that they have been treated differently by the state from others similarly situated, and that there is no rational basis for the difference in treatment. They have done so as a matter of law. The plaintiffs contend that they have demonstrated a violation of the Equal Protection Clause: they observe that an examination of the two statutes reflects that they treat differently identically-situated individuals, because plaintiffs are required to register as sex offenders simply because they were convicted of Crime Against Nature by Solicitation, rather than solicitation of Prostitution (conduct chargeable by and covered under either statute). Plaintiffs draw the conclusion that the statutory classification drawn between individuals convicted of Crime Against Nature by Solicitation and those convicted of Prostitution is not rationally related to achieving any legitimate state interest.[23] The Court agrees.

The plaintiffs contend that their Equal Protection claim turns on the obvious situation that, because the Crime Against Nature by Solicitation and the solicitation provision of the Prostitution statute have identical elements and punish, as to them, identical conduct, the State cannot point to any constitutionally acceptable rationale for requiring those convicted of Crime Against Nature by Solicitation, but not Prostitution, to register as sex offenders. The plaintiffs correctly lean heavily on *Eisenstadt v. Baird*, 405 U.S. 438, 454 (1972), which they argue supports their assertion that the State cannot have a legitimate interest in imposing a sanction on one group of people and not another when the "evil, as perceived by the State, [is] identical." The Court finds that *Eisenstadt* supports their contentions and is binding here.

In *Eisenstadt*, the Supreme Court invalidated a Massachusetts law that criminalized the distribution of contraception to unmarried persons because of the different statutory treatment of married persons, who were allowed access to contraception. In so doing, the high court rejected various arguments that the government offered for treating these groups differently. The Court announced that "whatever the rights of the individual to access to contraceptives may be, the rights must be the same for the unmarried and the married alike." Those words resonate here. For example, the Supreme Court rejected the asserted public health purpose of the law, on the ground that such a purpose would apply equally to married people not subject to the restriction and, also, that any

---

[23] The parties concede that no fundamental right has been infringed, nor any suspect classification is involved; accordingly, the parties agree that the classification need only bear a rational relationship to some legitimate objective. Again, "[r]ational basis scrutiny requires only that the classification rationally promote a legitimate governmental objective."

concern over the dangerousness of the contraceptives themselves was already addressed by federal and state public health regulations in place. In holding that criminally outlawing the distribution of contraceptives to unmarried persons but not the distribution to married persons violated the Equal Protection Clause, the Supreme Court explained: "the evil, as perceived by the State, would be identical, and the underinclusion would be invidious." *Eisenstadt* reaches far into this dispute and the State unconvincingly seeks to run from it.

. . . [T]he State has created two classifications of similarly (in fact, identical) situated individuals who were treated differently (only one class is subject to mandatory sex offender registration).[25] Second, the classification has no rational relation to any legitimate government objective: there is no legitimating rationale in the record to justify targeting only those convicted of Crime Against Nature by Solicitation for mandatory sex offender registration. The defendants' arguments fail, as the similar ones did under *Eisenstadt*. The very same public health and moral purposes apply to both statutes.

. . .

The defendants . . . contend that persons convicted of Crime Against Nature by Solicitation are not similarly situated to persons convicted of Prostitution and, thus, state law has created no impermissible classification. In support of their argument that the Crime Against Nature by Solicitation and Prostitution statutes punish different conduct differently, the defendants invoke the Louisiana Supreme Court case of *State v. Baxley*, 656 So.2d 973 (La. 1995), and mistakenly argue that this Court is bound by the state high court's interpretation of the statutes at issue.

The plaintiffs respond that *Baxley* was limited to a finding that it does not "facially punish homosexuals more severely than heterosexuals", whereas the plaintiffs' Equal Protection claim here is premised upon the classification that exists between individuals convicted of Crime Against Nature by Solicitation and those convicted under the solicitation provision of the Prostitution statute. That question, whether a classification exists between these two groups, this Court concludes, was not reached by the Louisiana Supreme Court in *Baxley*.

In *State v. Baxley*, the Louisiana Supreme Court rejected a state constitutional challenge that the Crime Against Nature by Solicitation statute punished homosexuals more harshly than heterosexuals; the state high court narrowly found that both the Crime Against Nature by Solicitation and the Prostitution statutes facially apply to homosexuals

---

[25] Simply comparing the statutes demonstrates the inequality: a defendant convicted of Crime Against Nature by Solicitation is a "sex offender" as defined by the registry law and such a conviction is a "sex offense," which mandates registration for 15 years (to life) under the registry law, although no individual convicted of solicitation of Prostitution is ever defined as a "sex offender" and, therefore, has never been required to register as such.

and heterosexuals equally. That narrow setting provides no guide here. Also it seems useful to repeat that the state high court's analysis was limited to the state constitution and this Court is no less empowered to hear this federal constitutional challenge. "It is well established," it is instructive to note, "that a state court's interpretation of its statutes is binding on the federal courts unless a state law is inconsistent with the federal Constitution."

. . .

Finally, focusing again in their search for a rational basis, the defendants assert that requiring sex offender registration protects the public's safety, health, and welfare. They insist that conviction is an imperfect indicator of the underlying charge and, because Crime Against Nature by Solicitation is a lesser offense to which other registrable offenses can be pleaded down to, it is possible that prosecutors pleaded down "more heinous" solicitation charges (such as solicitation of persons under 17, human trafficking, and intentional exposure to the AIDS virus if the exposure occurred during the course of a commercial sex act). The Court has no duty to indulge such patent hypothetical speculation; no suggestion exists in the record that the state legislature's purpose for requiring those convicted of Crime Against Nature by Solicitation to register as sex offenders was anchored to a legislative desire that prosecutors plead down other registrable offenses. The defendants add that requiring individuals convicted of Crime Against Nature by Solicitation protects public morality. But the Court has already observed that public health and moral concerns apply equally to prostitution. The defendants fail to credibly serve up even one unique legitimating governmental interest that can rationally explain the registration requirement imposed on those convicted of Crime Against Nature by Solicitation. The Court is left with no other conclusion but that the relationship between the classification is so shallow as to render the distinction wholly arbitrary.

. . . [T]he plaintiffs have shown that they are entitled to judgment as a matter of law that they have been deprived of equal protection of the laws in violation of the Fourteenth Amendment to the U.S. Constitution. Accordingly, the plaintiffs' motion for summary judgment is GRANTED. . . .

NOTES

1. *Criminalizing same-sex sex after* Lawrence. Though *Lawrence v. Texas* decriminalized private consensual adult sodomy, the Court made clear that the state still had the authority to use the criminal law to regulate sex that did not comport with *Lawrence*'s template of domesticated, marriage-like sex. *Doe v. Jindal* makes clear that *Lawrence*'s privacy protections do not extend so far as to insulate commercial sex from state regulation. Still, given *Lawrence*'s interest in affirming the dignity of LGBT persons, is there an argument to be made that criminalizing same-sex commercial sex more

rigorously than different-sex commercial sex contradicts the spirit of *Lawrence*?

2. *Discriminatory enforcement.* Though the Crime Against Nature by Solicitation (CANS) statute challenged in *Doe* reflects an impulse toward criminalizing deviant sex, attorney and activist Andrea Ritchie argues that suspicion of deviant sexual acts and actors is only part of the story. As she observes, in deciding what charge to bring against an individual arrested for prostitution, street-level law enforcement officers in Louisiana routinely charged white female prostitutes under the prostitution statute, while charging LGBT persons and persons of color under the CANS statute, which carried a harsher penalty and required sex offender registration. Accordingly, "a significant percentage of individuals on Louisiana's sex offender registry are women and LGBTQ people of color, overwhelmingly as a result of CANS convictions." Andrea J. Ritchie, *Crimes Against Nature: Challenging Criminalization of Queerness and Black Women's Sexuality*, 14 LOY. J. PUB. INT. L. 355, 356 (2013).

* * *

Doe v. Jindal *suggests that, even after* Lawrence v. Texas, *criminal law continues to be a force in the legal regulation of same-sex sex and sexuality. However, criminal law is not the only means of legally regulating sex and sexuality. As the following selection makes clear, in the midst of* Griswold *and* Eisenstadt's *"privacy revolution," administrative regulations became a potent means of signaling—and punishing— deviant sexuality.*

King v. Smith

392 U.S. 309 (1968).

■ WARREN, C.J.

. . . At issue is the validity of Alabama's so-called "substitute father" regulation which denies [Aid to Families With Dependent Children or "AFDC"] payments to the children of a mother who "cohabits" in or outside her home with any single or married able-bodied man. . . . A properly convened three-judge District Court . . . found the regulation to be inconsistent with the Social Security Act and the Equal Protection Clause. We . . . affirm without reaching the constitutional issue.

The AFDC program is one of three major categorical public assistance programs established by the Social Security Act of 1935. The category singled out for welfare assistance by AFDC is the "dependent child," who is defined in § 406 of the Act as an age-qualified "needy child . . . who has been deprived of parental support or care by reason of the death, continued absence from the home or physical or mental incapacity of a parent, and who is living with" any one of several listed relatives. Under this provision, and, insofar as relevant here, aid can be granted only if "a parent" of the needy child is continually absent from the home. Alabama considers a man who qualifies as a "substitute father" under its regulation to be a nonabsent parent within the federal statute. The State therefore denies aid to an otherwise eligible needy child on the basis that his substitute parent is not absent from the home.

Under the Alabama regulation, an "able-bodied man, married or single, is considered a substitute father of all the children of the applicant . . . mother" in three different situations: (1) if "he lives in the home with the child's natural or adoptive mother for the purpose of cohabitation"; or (2) if "he visits (the home) frequently for the purpose of cohabiting with the child's natural or adoptive mother"; or (3) if "he does not frequent the home but cohabits with the child's natural or adoptive mother elsewhere." Whether the substitute father is actually the father of the children is irrelevant. It is also irrelevant whether he is legally obligated to support the children, and whether he does in fact contribute to their support. What is determinative is simply whether he "cohabits" with the mother.

The testimony below by officials responsible for the administration of Alabama's AFDC program establishes that "cohabitation," as used in the regulation, means essentially that the man and woman have "frequent" or "continuing" sexual relations. . . . The regulation itself provides that pregnancy or a baby under six months of age is prima facie evidence of a substitute father.

. . .

. . . As applied in this case, the regulation has caused the termination of all AFDC payments to the appellees, Mrs. Sylvester Smith and her four minor children.

. . . This action was taken by the Dallas County welfare authorities pursuant to the substitute father regulation, on the ground that a Mr. Williams came to [Mrs. Smith's] home on weekends and had sexual relations with her.

Three of Mrs. Smith's children have not received parental support or care from a father since their natural father's death in 1955. The fourth child's father left home in 1963, and the child has not received the support or care of his father since then. All the children live in the home of their mother, and except for the substitute father regulation are eligible for aid. The family is not receiving any other type of public assistance, and has been living, since the termination of AFDC payments, on Mrs. Smith's salary of between $16 and $20 per week which she earns working from 3:30 a.m. to 12 noon as a cook and waitress.

Mr. Williams, the alleged "substitute father" of Mrs. Smith's children, has nine children of his own and lives with his wife and family, all of whom are dependent upon him for support. Mr. Williams is not the father of any of Mrs. Smith's children. He is not legally obligated, under Alabama law, to support any of Mrs. Smith's children. Further, he is not willing or able to support the Smith children, and does not in fact support them. His wife is required to work to help support the Williams household.

The AFDC program is based on a scheme of cooperative federalism. It is financed largely by the Federal Government, on a matching fund basis, and is administered by the States. . . .

One of the statutory requirements [of the AFDC program] is that "aid to families with dependent children . . . shall be furnished with reasonable promptness to all eligible individuals. . . ." As noted above, § 406(a) of the Act defines a "dependent child" as one who has been deprived of "parental" support or care by reason of the death, continued absence, or incapacity of a "parent." In combination, these two provisions of the Act clearly require participating States to furnish aid to families with children who have a parent absent from the home, if such families are in other respects eligible.

The State argues that its substitute father regulation simply defines who is a nonabsent "parent" under § 406(a) of the Social Security Act. The State submits that the regulation is a legitimate way of allocating its limited resources available for AFDC assistance, in that it reduces the caseload of its social workers and provides increased benefits to those still eligible for assistance. Two state interests are asserted in support of the allocation of AFDC assistance achieved by the regulation: first, it discourages illicit sexual relationships and illegitimate births; second, it puts families in which there is an informal "marital" relationship on [par] with those in which there is an ordinary marital relationship, because families of the latter sort are not eligible for AFDC assistance.

. . .

. . . There is no question that States have considerable latitude in allocating their AFDC resources, since each State is free to set its own standard of need and to determine the level of benefits by the amount of funds it devotes to the program. Further, there is no question that regular and actual contributions to a needy child, including contributions from the kind of person Alabama calls a substitute father, can be taken into account in determining whether the child is needy. . . . The appellees here, however, meet Alabama's need requirements; their alleged substitute father makes no contribution to their support; and they have been denied assistance solely on the basis of the substitute father regulation. Further, the regulation itself is unrelated to need, because the actual financial situation of the family is irrelevant in determining the existence of a substitute father.

Also not involved in this case is the question of Alabama's general power to deal with conduct it regards as immoral and with the problem of illegitimacy. This appeal raises only the question whether the State may deal with these problems in the manner that it has here—by flatly denying AFDC assistance to otherwise eligible dependent children. Alabama's argument based on its interests in discouraging immorality and illegitimacy would have been quite relevant at one time in the history of the AFDC program. However, subsequent developments clearly establish that these state interests are not presently legitimate justifications for AFDC disqualification. Insofar as this or any similar regulation is based on the State's asserted interest in discouraging illicit sexual behavior and illegitimacy, it plainly conflicts with federal law and policy.

. . .

. . . [I]n 1960, Louisiana enacted legislation requiring, as a condition precedent for AFDC eligibility, that the home of a dependent child be "suitable," and specifying that any home in which an illegitimate child had been born subsequent to the receipt of public assistance would be considered unsuitable. In the summer of 1960, approximately 23,000 children were dropped from Louisiana's AFDC rolls. In disapproving this legislation, then Secretary of Health, Education, and Welfare [("HEW")] Flemming issued what is now known as the Flemming Ruling, stating that as of July 1, 1961,

> A State plan . . . may not impose an eligibility condition that would deny assistance with respect to a needy child on the basis that the home conditions in which the child lives are unsuitable, while the child continues to reside in the home. Assistance will therefore be continued during the time efforts are being made either to improve the home conditions or to make arrangements for the child elsewhere.

Congress quickly approved the Flemming Ruling, while extending until September 1, 1962, the time for state compliance. . . .

In 1962, Congress made permanent the provision for AFDC assistance to children placed in foster homes and extended such coverage to include children placed in child-care institutions. At the same time, Congress modified the Flemming Ruling by amending § 404(b) of the Act. As amended, the statute permits States to disqualify from AFDC aid children who live in unsuitable homes, provided they are granted other "adequate care and assistance."

Thus, under the 1961 and 1962 amendments to the Social Security Act, the States are permitted to remove a child from a home that is judicially determined to be so unsuitable as to "be contrary to the welfare of such child." The States are also permitted to terminate AFDC assistance to a child living in an unsuitable home, if they provide other adequate care and assistance for the child under a general welfare program. The statutory approval of the Flemming Ruling, however, precludes the States from otherwise denying AFDC assistance to dependent children on the basis of their mothers' alleged immorality or to discourage illegitimate births.

. . .

In sum, Congress has determined that immorality and illegitimacy should be dealt with through rehabilitative measures rather than measures that punish dependent children, and that protection of such children is the paramount goal of AFDC. In light of the Flemming Ruling and the [subsequent] amendments to the Social Security Act, it is simply inconceivable, as HEW has recognized, that Alabama is free to discourage immorality and illegitimacy by the device of absolute disqualification of needy children. Alabama may deal with these problems by several different methods under the Social Security Act. But the method it has chosen plainly conflicts with the Act.

Alabama's second justification for its substitute father regulation is that "there is a public interest in a State not undertaking the payment of these funds to families who because of their living arrangements would be in the same situation as if the parents were married, except for the marriage." In other words, the State argues that since in Alabama the needy children of married couples are not eligible for AFDC aid so long as their father is in the home, it is only fair that children of a mother who cohabits with a man not her husband and not their father be treated similarly. The difficulty with this argument is that it fails to take account of the circumstance that children of fathers living in the home are in a very different position from children of mothers who cohabit with men not their fathers: the child's father has a legal duty to support him, while the unrelated substitute father, at least in Alabama, does not. We believe Congress intended the term "parent" in § 406(a) of the Act to include only those persons with a legal duty of support.

. . .

The question for decision here is whether Congress could have intended that a man was to be regarded as a child's parent so as to deprive the child of AFDC eligibility despite the circumstances: (1) that the man did not in fact support the child; and (2) that he was not legally obligated to support the child. The State correctly observes that the fact that the man in question does not actually support the child cannot be determinative, because a natural father at home may fail actually to support his child but his presence will still render the child ineligible for assistance. On the question whether the man must be legally obligated to provide support before he can be regarded as the child's parent, the State has no such cogent answer. We think the answer is quite clear: Congress must have meant by the term "parent" an individual who owed to the child a state-imposed legal duty of support.

. . .

. . . [W]e think that Congress must have intended that the children in such a situation remain eligible for AFDC assistance notwithstanding their mother's impropriety. AFDC was intended to provide economic security for children whom Congress could not reasonably expect would be provided for by simply securing employment for family breadwinners. We think it apparent that neither Congress nor any reasonable person would believe that providing employment for some man who is under no legal duty to support a child would in any way provide meaningful economic security for that child.

. . .

Alabama's substitute father regulation, as written and as applied in this case, requires the disqualification of otherwise eligible dependent children if their mother "cohabits" with a man who is not obligated by Alabama law to support the children. The regulation is therefore invalid because it defines "parent" in a manner that is inconsistent with § 406(a) of the Social Security Act. In denying AFDC assistance to appellees on the basis of this invalid regulation, Alabama has breached its federally imposed obligation to furnish "aid to families with dependent children . . . with reasonable promptness to all eligible individuals. . . ." Our conclusion makes unnecessary consideration of appellees' equal-protection claim, upon which we intimate no views.

We think it well, in concluding, to emphasize that no legitimate interest of the State of Alabama is defected by the decision we announce today. The State's interest in discouraging illicit sexual behavior and illegitimacy may be protected by other means, subject to constitutional limitations, including state participation in AFDC rehabilitative programs. Its interest in economically allocating its limited AFDC resources may be protected by its undisputed power to set the level of benefits and the standard of need, and by its taking into account in determining whether a child is needy all actual and regular contributions to his support.

All responsible governmental agencies in the Nation today recognize the enormity and pervasiveness of social ills caused by poverty. The causes of and cures for poverty are currently the subject of much debate. We hold today only that Congress has made at least this one determination: that destitute children who are legally fatherless cannot be flatly denied federally funded assistance on the transparent fiction that they have a substitute father.

Affirmed.

■ DOUGLAS, J., concurring.

The Court follows the statutory route in reaching the result that I reach on constitutional grounds. . . .

. . .

The Alabama regulation describes three situations in which needy children, otherwise eligible for relief, are to be denied financial assistance. In none of these is the child to blame. The disqualification of the family, and hence the needy child, turns upon the "sin" of the mother.

. . .

. . . [In this way,] the Alabama regulation is aimed at punishing mothers who have nonmarital sexual relations. The economic need of the children, their age, their other means of support, are all irrelevant. The standard is the so-called immorality of the mother.

The other day in [*Levy v. Louisiana*, 391 U.S. 68 (1968)], we held that the Equal Protection Clause of the Fourteenth Amendment barred discrimination against illegitimate children. We held that they cannot be denied a cause of action because they were conceived in "sin," that the making of such a disqualification was an invidious discrimination. I would think precisely the same result should be reached here. I would say that the immorality of the mother has no rational connection with the need of her children under any welfare program.

. . .

NOTES

1. *Statutory v. constitutional grounds.* In *King*, the Court made clear that its decision invalidating the Alabama regulation rested on statutory interpretation grounds, rather than on constitutional grounds. What are the consequences of the Court's decision to avoid determining whether the regulation violated the Constitution? What constitutional arguments might have been made to strike down—or uphold—the challenged regulation?

2. *Signaling disapproval of nonmarital sex and promiscuity.* In offering a rationale for the challenged regulation, Alabama was forthright about its aims. The regulation was at once a means of discouraging promiscuity and nonmarital sex, while also preserving scarce public resources. Intriguingly, the state also noted that the regulation prevented the state from treating marital and nonmarital families differently (ostensibly, marital families would be ineligible for public assistance).

3. *"Man in the house" regulations amidst other constitutional changes.* Aimed at curbing promiscuity and nonmarital sexuality, "man in the house" regulations were proliferating as many jurisdictions were dismantling criminal regulations prohibiting various forms of nonmarital sex and sexuality. Likewise, these regulations were contemporaneous with the emergence of constitutional protections for illegitimate children, a point that Justice Douglas notes in his dissent in *King v. Smith*.

* * *

As King v. Smith *suggests, public assistance remains a vital site of state sexual regulation. Indeed, concerns about public assistance and limited state resources can prompt efforts to regulate access to marriage. In this sense, the following excerpt,* Zablocki v. Redhail, *reflects the collision of multiple forms of state sexual regulation. In this landmark Supreme Court decision, the Court grapples with the interest in preserving scarce public assistance resources while also permitting access to marriage as a vehicle of state sexual regulation.*

Zablocki v. Redhail

434 U.S. 374 (1978).

■ MARSHALL, J.

At issue in this case is the constitutionality of a Wisconsin statute, Wis. Stat. §§ 245.10(1), (4), (5) (1973), which provides that members of a certain class of Wisconsin residents may not marry, within the State or elsewhere, without first obtaining a court order granting permission to marry. The class is defined by the statute to include any "Wisconsin resident having minor issue not in his custody and which he is under obligation to support by any court order or judgment." The statute specifies that court permission cannot be granted unless the marriage applicant submits proof of compliance with the support obligation and, in addition, demonstrates that the children covered by the support order "are not then and are not likely thereafter to become public charges." No marriage license may lawfully be issued in Wisconsin to a person covered by the statute, except upon court order; any marriage entered into without compliance with § 245.10 is declared void; and persons acquiring marriage licenses in violation of the section are subject to criminal penalties.

After being denied a marriage license because of his failure to comply with § 245.10, appellee brought this class action . . . challenging the statute as violative of the Equal Protection and Due Process Clauses of the Fourteenth Amendment and seeking declaratory and injunctive relief. The United States District Court for the Eastern District of Wisconsin held the statute unconstitutional under the Equal Protection Clause and enjoined its enforcement. We . . . now affirm.

Appellee Redhail is a Wisconsin resident who, under the terms of § 245.10, is unable to enter into a lawful marriage in Wisconsin or elsewhere so long as he maintains his Wisconsin residency. . . . In January 1972, when appellee was a minor and a high school student, a paternity action was instituted against him in Milwaukee County Court, alleging that he was the father of a baby girl born out of wedlock on July 5, 1971. After he appeared and admitted that he was the child's father, the court entered an order on May 12, 1972, adjudging appellee the father and ordering him to pay $109 per month as support for the child until she reached 18 years of age. From May 1972 until August 1974, appellee was unemployed and indigent, and consequently was unable to make any support payments. On September 27, 1974, appellee filed an application for a marriage license with appellant Zablocki, the County Clerk of Milwaukee County, and a few days later the application was denied on the sole ground that appellee had not obtained a court order granting him permission to marry, as required by § 245.10. Although appellee did not petition a state court thereafter, it is stipulated that he would not have been able to satisfy either of the statutory prerequisites for an order granting permission to marry. First, he had not satisfied his support obligations to his illegitimate child, and as of December 1974 there was an arrearage in excess of $3,700. Second, the child had been a public charge since her birth, receiving benefits under the Aid to Families with Dependent Children program. It is stipulated that the child's benefit payments were such that she would have been a public charge even if appellee had been current in his support payments.

On December 24, 1974, appellee filed his complaint in the District Court, on behalf of himself and the class of all Wisconsin residents who had been refused a marriage license pursuant to § 245.10(1) by one of the county clerks in Wisconsin. . . . The complaint alleged, among other things, that appellee and the woman he desired to marry were expecting a child in March 1975 and wished to be lawfully married before that time. . . .

. . .

The leading decision of this Court on the right to marry is *Loving v. Virginia*, 388 U.S. 1 (1967). . . .

Although *Loving* arose in the context of racial discrimination, prior and subsequent decisions of this Court confirm that the right to marry is of fundamental importance for all individuals. Long ago, in *Maynard v. Hill*, 125 U.S. 190 (1888), the Court characterized marriage as "the most important relation in life," and as "the foundation of the family and of society, without which there would be neither civilization nor progress."

. . .

More recent decisions have established that the right to marry is part of the fundamental "right of privacy" implicit in the Fourteenth Amendment's Due Process Clause. . . .

. . .

It is not surprising that the decision to marry has been placed on the same level of importance as decisions relating to procreation, childbirth, child rearing, and family relationships. As the facts of this case illustrate, it would make little sense to recognize a right of privacy with respect to other matters of family life and not with respect to the decision to enter the relationship that is the foundation of the family in our society. The woman whom appellee desired to marry had a fundamental right to seek an abortion of their expected child, see *Roe v. Wade*, [410 U.S. 113 (1973),] or to bring the child into life to suffer the myriad social, if not economic, disabilities that the status of illegitimacy brings. Surely, a decision to marry and raise the child in a traditional family setting must receive equivalent protection. And, if appellee's right to procreate means anything at all, it must imply some right to enter the only relationship in which the State of Wisconsin allows sexual relations legally to take place.

By reaffirming the fundamental character of the right to marry, we do not mean to suggest that every state regulation which relates in any way to the incidents of or prerequisites for marriage must be subjected to rigorous scrutiny. To the contrary, reasonable regulations that do not significantly interfere with decisions to enter into the marital relationship may legitimately be imposed. The statutory classification at issue here, however, clearly does interfere directly and substantially with the right to marry.

Under the challenged statute, no Wisconsin resident in the affected class may marry in Wisconsin or elsewhere without a court order, and marriages contracted in violation of the statute are both void and punishable as criminal offenses. Some of those in the affected class, like appellee, will never be able to obtain the necessary court order, because they either lack the financial means to meet their support obligations or cannot prove that their children will not become public charges. These persons are absolutely prevented from getting married. Many others, able in theory to satisfy the statute's requirements, will be sufficiently burdened by having to do so that they will in effect be coerced into forgoing their right to marry. And even those who can be persuaded to meet the statute's requirements suffer a serious intrusion into their freedom of choice in an area in which we have held such freedom to be fundamental.[12]

When a statutory classification significantly interferes with the exercise of a fundamental right, it cannot be upheld unless it is supported by sufficiently important state interests and is closely tailored to effectuate only those interests. Appellant asserts that two interests are served by the challenged statute: the permission-to-marry proceeding furnishes an opportunity to counsel the applicant as to the necessity of fulfilling his prior support obligations; and the welfare of the out-of-custody children is protected. We may accept for present purposes that these are legitimate and substantial interests, but, since the means selected by the State for achieving these interests unnecessarily impinge on the right to marry, the statute cannot be sustained.

There is evidence that the challenged statute, as originally introduced in the Wisconsin Legislature, was intended merely to establish a mechanism whereby persons with support obligations to children from prior marriages could be counseled before they entered into new marital relationships and incurred further support obligations. Court permission to marry was to be required, but apparently permission was automatically to be granted after counseling was completed. The

---

[12] The directness and substantiality of the interference with the freedom to marry distinguish the instant case from *Califano v. Jobst,* 434 U.S. 47 (1977). In *Jobst,* we upheld sections of the Social Security Act providing, *inter alia,* for termination of a dependent child's benefits upon marriage to an individual not entitled to benefits under the Act. As the opinion for the Court expressly noted, the rule terminating benefits upon marriage was not "an attempt to interfere with the individual's freedom to make a decision as important as marriage." 434 U.S. at 54. The Social Security provisions placed no direct legal obstacle in the path of persons desiring to get married, and—notwithstanding our Brother Rehnquist's imaginative recasting of the case, there was no evidence that the laws significantly discouraged, let alone made "practically impossible," any marriages. Indeed, the provisions had not deterred the individual who challenged the statute from getting married, even though he and his wife were both disabled.

statute actually enacted, however, does not expressly require or provide for any counseling whatsoever, nor for any automatic granting of permission to marry by the court, and thus it can hardly be justified as a means for ensuring counseling of the persons within its coverage. Even assuming that counseling does take place—a fact as to which there is no evidence in the record—this interest obviously cannot support the withholding of court permission to marry once counseling is completed.

With regard to safeguarding the welfare of the out-of-custody children, appellant's brief does not make clear the connection between the State's interest and the statute's requirements. At argument, appellant's counsel suggested that, since permission to marry cannot be granted unless the applicant shows that he has satisfied his court-determined support obligations to the prior children and that those children will not become public charges, the statute provides incentive for the applicant to make support payments to his children. This "collection device" rationale cannot justify the statute's broad infringement on the right to marry.

First, with respect to individuals who are unable to meet the statutory requirements, the statute merely prevents the applicant from getting married, without delivering any money at all into the hands of the applicant's prior children. More importantly, regardless of the applicant's ability or willingness to meet the statutory requirements, the State already has numerous other means for exacting compliance with support obligations, means that are at least as effective as the instant statute's and yet do not impinge upon the right to marry. Under Wisconsin law, whether the children are from a prior marriage or were born out of wedlock, court-determined support obligations may be enforced directly via wage assignments, civil contempt proceedings, and criminal penalties. And, if the State believes that parents of children out of their custody should be responsible for ensuring that those children do not become public charges, this interest can be achieved by adjusting the criteria used for determining the amounts to be paid under their support orders.

There is also some suggestion that § 245.10 protects the ability of marriage applicants to meet support obligations to prior children by preventing the applicants from incurring new support obligations. But the challenged provisions of § 245.10 are grossly underinclusive with respect to this purpose, since they do not limit in any way new financial commitments by the applicant other than those arising out of the contemplated marriage. The statutory classification is substantially overinclusive as well: Given the possibility that the new spouse will actually better the applicant's financial situation, by contributing income from a job or otherwise, the statute in many cases may prevent affected individuals from improving their ability to satisfy their prior support obligations. And, although it is true that the applicant will incur support obligations to any children born during the contemplated marriage, preventing the marriage may only result in the children being born out of wedlock, as in fact occurred in appellee's case. Since the support obligation is the same whether the child is born in or out of wedlock, the net result of preventing the marriage is simply more illegitimate children.

The statutory classification created by §§ 245.10(1), (4), (5) thus cannot be justified by the interests advanced in support of it. The judgment of the District Court is, accordingly,

Affirmed.

. . .

■ STEWART, J., concurring in the judgment.

I cannot join the opinion of the Court. . . .

. . .

I do not agree with the Court that there is a "right to marry" in the constitutional sense. That right, or more accurately that privilege, is under our federal system peculiarly one to be defined and limited by state law. A State may not only "significantly interfere with decisions to enter into marital relationship," but may in many circumstances absolutely prohibit it. Surely, for example, a State may legitimately say that no one can marry his or her sibling, that no one can marry who is not at least 14 years old, that no one can marry without first passing an examination for venereal disease, or that no one can marry who has a living husband or wife. But, just as surely, in regulating the intimate human relationship of marriage, there is a limit beyond which a State may not constitutionally go.

The Constitution does not specifically mention freedom to marry, but it is settled that the "liberty" protected by the Due Process Clause of the Fourteenth Amendment embraces more than those freedoms expressly enumerated in the Bill of Rights. And the decisions of this Court have made clear that freedom of personal choice in matters of marriage and family life is one of the liberties so protected. It is evident that the Wisconsin law now before us directly abridges that freedom. The question is whether the state interests that support the abridgment can overcome the substantive protections of the Constitution.

The Wisconsin law makes permission to marry turn on the payment of money in support of one's children by a previous marriage or liaison. Those who cannot show both that they have kept up with their support obligations and that their children are not and will not become wards of the State are altogether prohibited from marrying.

If Wisconsin had said that no one could marry who had not paid all of the fines assessed against him for traffic violations, I suppose the constitutional invalidity of the law would be apparent. For while the state interest would certainly be legitimate, that interest would be both disproportionate and unrelated to the restriction of liberty imposed by the State. But the invalidity of the law before us is hardly so clear, because its restriction of liberty seems largely to be imposed only on those who have abused the same liberty in the past.

Looked at in one way, the law may be seen as simply a collection device additional to those used by Wisconsin and other States for enforcing parental support obligations. But since it operates by denying permission to marry, it also clearly reflects a legislative judgment that a person should not be permitted to incur new family financial obligations until he has fulfilled those he already has. Insofar as this judgment is paternalistic rather than punitive, it manifests a concern for the economic well-being of a prospective marital household. These interests are legitimate concerns of the State. But it does not follow that they justify the absolute deprivation of the benefits of a legal marriage.

. . .

■ POWELL, J., concurring in the judgment.

I concur in the judgment of the Court that Wisconsin's restrictions on the exclusive means of creating the marital bond, erected by Wis. Stat. §§ 245.10(1), (4), and (5) (1973), cannot meet applicable constitutional standards. I write separately because the majority's rationale sweeps too broadly in an area which traditionally has been subject to pervasive state regulation. The Court apparently would subject all state regulation which "directly and substantially" interferes with the decision to marry in a traditional family setting to "critical examination" or "compelling state interest" analysis. Presumably, "reasonable regulations that do not significantly interfere with decisions to enter into the marital relationship may legitimately be imposed." The Court does not present, however, any principled means for distinguishing between the two types of regulations. Since state regulation in this area typically takes the form of a prerequisite or barrier to marriage or divorce, the degree of "direct" interference with the decision to marry or to divorce is unlikely to provide either guidance for state legislatures or a basis for judicial oversight. . . . On several occasions, the Court has acknowledged the importance of the marriage relationship to the maintenance of values essential to organized society. . . . Thus, it is fair to say that there is a right of marital and familial privacy which places some substantive limits on the regulatory power of government. But the Court has yet to hold that all regulation touching upon marriage implicates a "fundamental right" triggering the most exacting judicial scrutiny.

The principal authority cited by the majority is *Loving v. Virginia*, 388 U.S. 1 (1967). . . .

. . .

[But] *Loving* involved a denial of a "fundamental freedom" on a wholly unsupportable basis—the use of classifications "directly subversive of the principle of equality at the heart of the Fourteenth Amendment. . . ." It does not speak to the level of judicial scrutiny of, or governmental justification for, "supportable" restrictions on the "fundamental freedom" of individuals to marry or divorce.

In my view, analysis must start from the recognition of domestic relations as "an area that has long been regarded as a virtually exclusive province of the States." *Sosna v. Iowa*, 419 U.S. 393 (1975). The marriage relation traditionally has been subject to regulation, initially by the ecclesiastical authorities, and later by the secular state. As early as *Pennoyer v. Neff*, 95 U.S. 714, 734–735 (1878), this Court noted that a State "has absolute right to prescribe the conditions upon which the marriage relation between its own citizens shall be created, and the causes for which it may be dissolved." The State, representing the collective expression of moral aspirations, has an undeniable interest in ensuring that its rules of domestic relations reflect the widely held values of its people. . . .

State regulation has included bans on incest, bigamy, and homosexuality, as well as various preconditions to marriage, such as blood tests. Likewise, a showing of fault on the part of one of the partners traditionally has been a prerequisite to the dissolution of an unsuccessful union. A "compelling state purpose" inquiry would cast doubt on the network of restrictions that the States have fashioned to govern marriage and divorce. . . . State power over domestic relations is not without constitutional limits. The Due Process Clause requires a showing of justification "when the government intrudes on choices concerning family living arrangements" in a manner which is contrary to deeply rooted traditions. Due process constraints also limit the extent to which the State may monopolize the process of ordering certain human relationships while excluding the truly indigent from that process. Furthermore, under the Equal Protection Clause the means chosen by the State in this case must bear "a fair and substantial relation" to the object of the legislation.

The Wisconsin measure in this case does not pass muster under either due process or equal protection standards. Appellant identifies three objectives which are supposedly furthered by the statute in question: (i) a counseling function; (ii) an incentive to satisfy outstanding support obligations; and (iii) a deterrent against incurring further obligations. The opinion of the Court amply demonstrates that the asserted counseling objective bears no relation to this statute. . . .

The so-called "collection device" rationale presents a somewhat more difficult question. I do not agree with the suggestion in the Court's opinion that a State may never condition the right to marry on satisfaction of existing support obligations simply because the State has alternative methods of compelling such payments. To the extent this restriction applies to persons who are able to make the required support payments but simply wish to shirk their moral and legal obligation, the Constitution interposes no bar to this additional collection mechanism. The vice inheres, not in the collection concept, but in the failure to make provision for those without the means to comply with child-support obligations. . . . The monopolization present in this case is total, for Wisconsin will not recognize foreign marriages that fail to conform to the requirements of § 245.10.

The third justification, only obliquely advanced by appellant, is that the statute preserves the ability of marriage applicants to support their prior issue by preventing them from incurring new obligations. The challenged provisions of § 245.10 are so grossly underinclusive with respect to this objective, given the many ways that additional financial obligations may be incurred by the applicant quite apart from a contemplated marriage, that the classification "does not bear a fair and substantial relation to the object of the legislation."

The marriage applicant is required by the Wisconsin statute not only to submit proof of compliance with his support obligation, but also to demonstrate—in some unspecified way—that his children "are not then and are not likely thereafter to become public charges." This statute does more than simply "fail to alleviate the consequences of differences in economic circumstances that exist wholly apart from any state action." *Griffin v. Illinois*, 351 U.S. 12, 34 (1956) (Harlan, J., dissenting). It tells the truly indigent, whether they have met their support obligations or not, that they may not marry so long as their children are public charges or there is a danger that their children might go on public assistance in the future. Apparently, no other jurisdiction has embraced this approach as a method of reducing the number of children on public assistance. Because the State has not established a justification for this unprecedented foreclosure of marriage to many of its citizens solely because of their indigency, I concur in the judgment of the Court.

■ STEVENS, J., concurring in the judgment.

. . .

When a State allocates benefits or burdens, it may have valid reasons for treating married and unmarried persons differently. Classification based on marital status has been an accepted characteristic of tax legislation, Selective Service rules, and Social Security regulations. As cases like *Jobst* demonstrate, such laws may "significantly interfere with decisions to enter into the marital relationship." That kind of interference, however, is not a sufficient reason for invalidating every law reflecting a legislative judgment that there are relevant differences between married persons as a class and unmarried persons as a class.

A classification based on marital status is fundamentally different from a classification which determines who may lawfully enter into the marriage relationship. The individual's interest in making the marriage decision independently is sufficiently important to merit special constitutional protection. It is not, however, an interest which is constitutionally immune from evenhanded regulation. Thus, laws prohibiting marriage to a child, a close relative, or a person afflicted with venereal disease, are unchallenged even though they "interfere directly and substantially with the right to marry." This Wisconsin statute has a different character.

Under this statute, a person's economic status may determine his eligibility to enter into a lawful marriage. A noncustodial parent whose children are "public charges" may not marry even if he has met his court-ordered obligations. Thus, within the class of parents who have fulfilled their court-ordered obligations, the rich may marry and the poor may not. This type of statutory discrimination is, I believe, totally unprecedented, as well as inconsistent with our tradition of administering justice equally to the rich and to the poor.

The statute appears to reflect a legislative judgment that persons who have demonstrated an inability to support their offspring should not be permitted to marry and thereafter to bring additional children into the world.[6] Even putting to one side the growing number of childless marriages and the burgeoning number of children born out of wedlock, that sort of reasoning cannot justify this deliberate discrimination against the poor.

The statute prevents impoverished parents from marrying even though their intended spouses are economically independent. Presumably, the Wisconsin Legislature assumed (a) that only fathers would be affected by the legislation, and (b) that they would never marry employed women. The first assumption ignores the fact that fathers are sometimes awarded custody,[7] and the second ignores the composition of today's work force. To the extent that the statute denies a hard-pressed parent any opportunity to prove that an intended marriage will ease rather than aggravate his financial straits, it not only rests on unreliable premises, but also defeats its own objectives.

These questionable assumptions also explain why this statutory blunderbuss is wide of the target in another respect. The prohibition on marriage applies to the noncustodial parent but allows the parent who has custody to marry without the State's leave. Yet the danger that new children will further strain an inadequate budget is equally great for custodial and non-custodial parents, unless one assumes (a) that only mothers will ever have custody and (b) that they will never marry unemployed men.

---

[6] The "public charge" provision, which falls on parents who have faithfully met their obligations, but who are unable to pay enough to remove their children from the welfare rolls, obviously cannot be justified by a state interest in assuring the payment of child support. And, of course, it would be absurd for the State to contend that an interest in providing paternalistic counseling supports a total ban on marriage.

[7] The Wisconsin Legislature has itself provided:

"In determining the parent with whom a child shall remain, the court shall consider all facts in the best interest of the child and shall not prefer one parent over the other solely on the basis of the sex of the parent." Wis. Stat. § 247.24(3) (1977).

Characteristically, this law fails to regulate the marriages of those parents who are least likely to be able to afford another family, for it applies only to parents under a court order to support their children. The very poorest parents are unlikely to be the objects of support orders.[9] If the State meant to prevent the marriage of those who have demonstrated their inability to provide for children, it overlooked the most obvious targets of legislative concern.

In sum, the public-charge provision is either futile or perverse insofar as it applies to childless couples, couples who will have illegitimate children if they are forbidden to marry, couples whose economic status will be improved by marriage, and couples who are so poor that the marriage will have no impact on the welfare status of their children in any event. Even assuming that the right to marry may sometimes be denied on economic grounds, this clumsy and deliberate legislative discrimination between the rich and the poor is irrational in so many ways that it cannot withstand scrutiny under the Equal Protection Clause of the Fourteenth Amendment.[10]

■ REHNQUIST, J., dissenting.

I substantially agree with my Brother Powell's reasons for rejecting the Court's conclusion that marriage is the sort of "fundamental right" which must invariably trigger the strictest judicial scrutiny. I disagree with his imposition of an "intermediate" standard of review, which leads him to conclude that the statute, though generally valid as an "additional collection mechanism" offends the Constitution by its "failure to make provision for those without the means to comply with child-support obligations." For similar reasons, I disagree with my Brother Stewart's conclusion that the statute is invalid for its failure to exempt those persons who "simply cannot afford to meet the statute's financial requirements." I would view this legislative judgment in the light of the traditional presumption of validity. I think that under the Equal Protection Clause the statute need pass only the "rational basis test," and that under the Due Process Clause it need only be shown that it bears a rational relation to a constitutionally permissible objective. The statute so viewed is a permissible exercise of the State's power to regulate family

---

[9] Although Wisconsin precedents are scarce, the State's courts seem to follow the general rule that child-support orders are heavily influenced by the parent's ability to pay. *See* H. CLARK, LAW OF DOMESTIC RELATIONS 496 (1968); *see also Miller v. Miller*, 227 N.W.2d 626 (Wis. 1975). A parent who is so disabled that he will never earn enough to pay child support is unlikely to be sued, and a court order is unlikely to be granted. *Cf. Ponath v. Hedrick*, 126 N.W.2d 28 (1964) (social security benefits not to be included in determining relative's ability to make support payments).

[10] Neither the fact that the appellee's interest is constitutionally protected, nor the fact that the classification is based on economic status is sufficient to justify a "level of scrutiny" so strict that a holding of unconstitutionality is virtually foreordained. On the other hand, the presence of these factors precludes a holding that a rational expectation of occasional and random benefit is sufficient to demonstrate compliance with the constitutional command to govern impartially. *See Craig v. Boren*, 429 U.S. 190, 211 (1976) (Stevens, J., concurring).

life and to assure the support of minor children, despite its possible imprecision in the extreme cases envisioned in the concurring opinions.

. . .

. . . Because of the limited amount of funds available for the support of needy children, the State has an exceptionally strong interest in securing as much support as their parents are able to pay. Nor does the extent of the burden imposed by this statute so differentiate it from that considered in *Jobst* as to warrant a different result. In the case of some applicants, this statute makes the proposed marriage legally impossible for financial reasons; in a similar number of extreme cases, the Social Security Act makes the proposed marriage practically impossible for the same reasons. I cannot conclude that such a difference justifies the application of a heightened standard of review to the statute in question here. In short, I conclude that the statute, despite its imperfections, is sufficiently rational to satisfy the demands of the Fourteenth Amendment.

* * *

Since Zablocki, *there has been increased interest in limiting access to public assistance resources and increasing private sources of support for families. Indeed, much of the effort to curb public assistance dependence focuses on welfare as a vehicle for encouraging promiscuity and unchecked fertility. The following excerpts reflect efforts to reform public assistance, while strengthening the marital family as a site for the privatization of dependency.*

The Personal Responsibility and Work Opportunity Reconciliation Act of 1996

Pub. L. No. 104–193, 110 Stat. 2105 (1996) (codified in scattered sections of 42 U.S.C.).

One Hundred Fourth Congress of the United States of America, Second Session January 3, 1996. This Act may be cited as the "Personal Responsibility and Work Opportunity Reconciliation Act of 1996."

Sec. 101. FINDINGS.

The Congress makes the following findings:

(1)   Marriage is the foundation of a successful society.

(2)   Marriage is an essential institution of a successful society which promotes the interests of children.

(3)   Promotion of responsible fatherhood and motherhood is integral to successful child rearing and the well-being of children.

. . .

(5)   The number of individuals receiving aid to families with dependent children (in this section referred to as "AFDC") has more than tripled since 1965. More than two-thirds of these recipients are children.

Eighty-nine percent of children receiving AFDC benefits now live in homes in which no father is present.

. . .

(C) The increase in the number of children receiving public assistance is closely related to the increase in births to unmarried women.

. . .

(B) Children born out-of-wedlock have a substantially higher risk of being born at a very low or moderately low birth weight.

(C) Children born out-of-wedlock are more likely to experience low verbal cognitive attainment, as well as more child abuse, and neglect.

(D) Children born out-of-wedlock were more likely to have lower cognitive scores, lower educational aspirations, and a greater likelihood of becoming teenage parents themselves.

. . .

(F) Children born out-of-wedlock are 3 times more likely to be on welfare when they grow up.

. . .

(C) Children born into families receiving welfare assistance are 3 times more likely to be on welfare when they reach adulthood than children not born into families receiving welfare.

. . .

(G) Between 1985 and 1990, the public cost of births to teenage mothers under the aid to families with dependent children program, the food stamp program, and the Medicaid program has been estimated at $120,000,000,000.

(H) The absence of a father in the life of a child has a negative effect on school performance and peer adjustment.

. . .

(M) Of those youth held for criminal offenses within the State juvenile justice system, only 29.8 percent lived primarily in a home with both parents. In contrast to these incarcerated youth, 73.9 percent of the 62,800,000 children in the Nation's resident population were living with both parents.

(10) Therefore, in light of this demonstration of the crisis in our Nation, it is the sense of the Congress that prevention of out-of-wedlock pregnancy and reduction in out-of-wedlock birth are very important Government interests and the policy contained in part A of title IV of the Social Security Act (as amended by section 103(a) of this Act) is intended to address the crisis.

NOTES

1.   *Rhetorical slippage?* The 1996 welfare reforms ("PRWORA") did more than "end welfare as we know it." The original welfare program, Aid to Dependent Children (ADC), grew out of Progressive Era mothers' pensions, and was consciously aimed at providing assistance to needy families, typically widowed or abandoned single mothers with children. Not only did PRWORA restructure the grant-in-aid program, it fundamentally transformed its aims. This transformation in purpose is reflected in the statute's text, which shifts from a discussion of poor children to problematizing the (apparent) increase in unmarried teen motherhood. This shift, arguably, is rooted in conservative criticisms of ADC and its successor, Aid to Families with Dependent Children (AFDC). According to critics, these original public assistance programs "incentivized" nonmarital births and cultivated an unhealthy dependency on government aid. Does this discursive shift capture all of the factors that may have exerted pressure on the welfare system during the 1970s and 1980s? How do rising levels of income inequality affect rates of welfare dependency? Why don't these critiques engage these empirical facts, as well as statistics regarding teen pregnancy and nonmarital births? What are we to make of this rhetorical shift from attributing poverty to systemic and institutional challenges toward blaming individuals (and their choices) for the indignity of poverty? *See* Joyce A. Martin et al., *Births: Final Data for 2011*, NAT'L VITAL STATS. REP. (Ctrs. for Disease Control & Prevention, Hyattsville, Md.), June 28, 2013, at 1, 7.

2.   *Causing poverty?* It is worth noting that the welfare-reform effort links teen pregnancy and poverty in ways that identify teen pregnancy as a root cause of poverty. However, empirical evidence suggests that this linkage is misguided. Although children born to younger mothers are more likely to live in poverty, the data suggest that it is actually *poverty* that causes teen births, rather than teen births causing poverty. *See* KRISTIN LUKER, DUBIOUS CONCEPTIONS: THE POLITICS OF TEENAGE PREGNANCY, 107–08 (1997). Further, institutional and systemic factors might play a role in the (many) challenges that children living in poverty routinely face. What other systemic and institutional factors might give rise to the high levels of teen births among those living in poverty?

3.   *Blaming poor mothers?* The rhetoric of welfare reform holds poor mothers responsible for two social problems: the proliferation of teen pregnancies and nonmarital births, and the escalation of crime in poor, urban communities. As the logic goes, teenage motherhood lends itself to a cycle of "babies having babies" without the structure and support of the marital family. More troublingly, it is argued that the children of poor teenage mothers are, because of the circumstances of their births and rearing, more likely to become involved in crime. Can such broad systemic issues be reduced to individual failures, as this rhetoric suggests?

Wade F. Horn, Assistant Secretary for Children and Families, Department of Health and Human Services, *Testimony to Discuss Policies That Help Strengthen the Institution of Marriage: Hearing Before the Senate Subcommittee on Children and Families of the Committee on Health, Education, Labor and Pensions*

108th Cong. 2 (2004).

. . .

Why should government be in the business of supporting the formation and stability of healthy marriages? Because the research literature is now replete with studies showing that children raised in stable, healthy marriages are less at risk for a host of negative developmental outcomes compared to children raised in unstable, unhealthy and dysfunctional married households. We know, for example, that children raised in healthy married households are less likely to be poor, less likely to fail at school, and less likely to have an emotional or behavioral problem[s] requiring psychiatric treatment, compared to those who are not. Moreover, as adolescents, they are less likely to commit crime, develop substance abuse problems or to commit suicide. Healthy marriages, it appears, are the best environment for rearing healthy children.

And it is not just children who benefit from healthy marriages. Research shows that adults in healthy marriages are happier, healthier and accumulate more wealth compared to those who are not. And communities with high rates of healthy marriages evidence fewer social pathologies, such as crime and welfare dependency, compared to those with low rates of healthy marriages.

. . .

. . . A critical mass of healthy marriages help[s] all societies to function well, and without that critical mass, they will forever be seeking new programs and services to cope with the ever increasing social problems that result from its absence.

NOTES

1. *Marriage promotion and patriarchy?* Professor Kaaryn Gustafson argues that marriage-promotion efforts are steeped in a patriarchal account of marriage and the marital family. As she explains:

> [S]ome social scientists and members of the religious Right have joined forces in arguing that families should be hierarchical groups, with fathers exercising ultimate authority in the home and women and children serving subordinate roles. The religious-based marriage promotion activists specifically advocate patriarchal family structures: families where there is a clear gendered division

of wage work and household labor, and where men serve as authority figures in the family.

Kaaryn Gustafson, *Breaking Vows: Marriage Promotion, the New Patriarchy, and the Retreat from Egalitarianism*, 5 STAN. J. CIV. RTS. & CIV. LIBERTIES 269, 282–83 (2009) (footnotes omitted).

2.   *The marriageable male index.* Sociologist William Julius Wilson constructed a "male marriageable pool index (MMPI)," which calculates the pool of employed "marriageable" men by age and race, and compares this figure to the pool of similarly-situated women. The MMPI for white men remained roughly steady between the 1950s and 1980s. For African American men, however, there was a "long-term decline in the proportion of black men [who are marriageable], and particularly young black men. . . ." WILLIAM JULIUS WILSON, THE TRULY DISADVANTAGED: THE INNER CITY, THE UNDERCLASS, AND PUBLIC POLICY 82 (2d ed. 2012). Given these data, do efforts to improve marriage rates at the individual level make sense, or are interventions aimed at systemic and structural impediments to marriage— like unemployment, education, and the like—also required?

* * *

In advance of the 2012 Republican presidential primary, the FAMiLY [sic] Leader, a Christian conservative group, exhorted Republican presidential candidates to sign on to its "Marriage Vow: A Declaration of Dependence Upon Marriage and FAMiLY." Locating itself within the tradition of founding documents like the Declaration of Independence, the "Marriage Vow" aims to restore America's greatness by recommitting its leaders to the defense of marriage and the marital family and the denunciation of non-conforming family forms and kinship models.

The FAMiLY Leader, The Marriage Vow: A Declaration of Dependence Upon Marriage and FAMiLY
(2012).

Faithful monogamy is at the very heart of a designed and purposeful order—as conveyed by Jewish and Christian Scripture, by Classical Philosophers, by Natural Law, and by the American Founders—upon which our concepts of Creator-endowed human rights, racial justice and gender equality all depend.

Enduring marital fidelity between one man and one woman protects innocent children, vulnerable women, the rights of fathers, the stability of families, and the liberties of all American citizens under our republican form of government. Our exceptional and free society simply cannot endure without the transmission of personal virtue, from one generation to the next, by means of nurturing, nuclear families comprised of sexually-faithful husbands and wives, fathers and mothers. We acknowledge and regret the widespread hypocrisy of many who defend marriage yet turn a blind eye toward the epidemic of infidelity and the anemic condition of marriages in their own communities. Unmistakably, the Institution of Marriage in America [sic] is in great crisis:

- Slavery had a disastrous impact on African-American families, yet sadly a child born into slavery in 1860 was more likely to be raised by his mother and father in a two-parent household than was an African-American baby born after the election of the USA's first African-American President.

- LBJ's 1965 War on Poverty was triggered in part by the famous "Moynihan Report" finding that the black out-of-wedlock birthrate had hit 26%; today, the white rate exceeds that, the overall rate is 41%, and over 70% of African-American babies are born to single parents—a prime sociological indicator for poverty, pathology and prison regardless of race or ethnicity.

- About one million U.S. children suffer through divorce each year—the outcome of about half of all first marriages and about 60 percent of remarriages, disproportionately affecting economically-vulnerable families.

- The taxpayer-borne social costs of family fragmentation exceeds $112 billion per year, especially when all costs to the justice system are recognized.

- Social protections, especially for women and children, have been evaporating as we have collectively "debased the currency" of marriage. This debasement continues as a function of adultery; "quickie divorce;" physical and verbal spousal abuse; non-committal co-habitation; exemplary infidelity and "unwed cheating" among celebrities, sports figures and politicians; anti-scientific bias which holds, in complete absence of empirical proof, that non-heterosexual inclinations are genetically determined, irresistible and akin to innate traits like race, gender and eye color; as well as anti-scientific bias which holds, against all empirical evidence, that homosexual behavior in particular, and sexual promiscuity in general, optimizes individual or public health.

The Candidate Vow:

Therefore, in any elected or appointed capacity by which I may have the honor of serving our fellow citizens in these United States, I the undersigned do hereby solemnly vow* to honor and to cherish, to defend

---

* NOTE: Or, "solemnly attest". Each signatory signs only in his or her individual capacity as an American citizen and current or potential leader; affiliations herein are for identification purposes only and do not necessarily imply formal embrace of this vow or the sentiments herein by any institution or organization.

and to uphold, the Institution of Marriage as only between one man and one woman. I vow to do so through my:

- Personal fidelity to my spouse.

- Respect for the marital bonds of others.

- Official fidelity to the U.S. Constitution, supporting the elevation of none but faithful constitutionalists as judges or justices.

- Vigorous opposition to any redefinition of the Institution of Marriage—faithful monogamy between one man and one woman—through statutory-, bureaucratic-, or court-imposed recognition of intimate unions which are bigamous, polygamous, polyandrous, same-sex, etc.

- Recognition of the overwhelming statistical evidence that married people enjoy better health, better sex, longer lives, greater financial stability, and that children raised by a mother and a father together experience better learning, less addiction, less legal trouble, and less extramarital pregnancy.

- Support for prompt reform of uneconomic, anti-marriage aspects of welfare policy, tax policy, and marital/divorce law, and extended "second chance" or "cooling-off" periods for those seeking a "quickie divorce."

- Earnest, bona fide legal advocacy for the Defense of Marriage Act (DOMA) at the federal and state levels.

- Steadfast embrace of a federal Marriage Amendment to the U.S. Constitution which protects the definition of marriage as between one man and one woman in all of the United States.

- Humane protection of women and the innocent fruit of conjugal intimacy—our next generation of American children—from human trafficking, sexual slavery, seduction into promiscuity, and all forms of pornography and prostitution, infanticide, abortion and other types of coercion or stolen innocence.

- Support for the enactment of safeguards for all married and unmarried U.S. Military and National Guard personnel, especially our combat troops, from inappropriate same-gender or opposite-gender sexual harassment, adultery or intrusively intimate commingling among attracteds [sic] (restrooms, showers, barracks, tents, etc.); plus prompt termination of military policymakers who would expose American wives and daughters to rape or sexual harassment, torture, enslavement or sexual leveraging by the enemy in forward combat roles.

- Rejection of Sharia Islam and all other anti-woman, anti-human rights forms of totalitarian control.

- Recognition that robust childbearing and reproduction is beneficial to U.S. demographic, economic, strategic and actuarial health and security.

- Commitment to downsizing government and the enormous burden upon American families of the USA's $14.3 trillion public debt, its $77 trillion in unfunded liabilities, its $1.5 trillion federal deficit, and its $3.5 trillion federal budget.

- Fierce defense of the First Amendment's rights of Religious Liberty and Freedom of Speech [sic], especially against the intolerance of any who would undermine law-abiding American citizens and institutions of faith and conscience for their adherence to, and defense of, faithful heterosexual monogamy.

The Vow of Civic, Religious, Lay, Business, and Social Leaders:

We the undersigned do hereby solemnly vow that no U.S. Presidential primary candidate—nor any primary candidate for the U.S. House, Senate, Governor, state or municipal office—will, in his or her public capacity, benefit from any substantial form of aid, support, endorsement, contribution, independent expenditure, or affirmation from any of us without first affirming this Marriage Vow. Furthermore, to uphold and advance the natural Institution of Marriage, we ourselves also hereby vow our own fidelity to this Declaration and especially, to our spouses.

So help us God.

NOTES

1. *Blaming poor women.* Much has been made of the propensity of women in recent years to give birth out of wedlock. While critics decry the moral decline represented by these births, social science research has made clear that the main culprit is the decline in labor-market prospects for both men and women who are not well-educated. Given our earlier discussion of the marriageable male index, do you find confirmation of that thesis in the following graphic? Keep in mind that education is a rough measure of class and socio-economic status.

Trends in Single Motherhood, 1960–2000

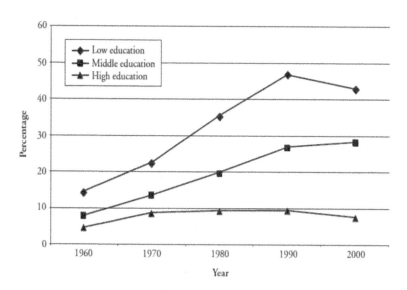

Sara McLanahan, *Diverging Destinies: How Children Are Faring Under the Second Demographic Transition*, 41 DEMOGRAPHY 607, 612 (2004).

2.   *Marriage and socio-economic status.* Sociologist Sara McLanahan argues that "feminism, new birth control technologies, changes in labor market opportunities and welfare state policies" drive differences in family formation (and marriage in particular). She contends that these forces cause those who are affluent to have greater opportunities to enter into dual-income marriages. This fact, she maintains, leads to "diverging destinies" between the children of the poor and the affluent, with the affluent being able to invest more resources (time and money) into their children. In her view, marriage is a driver as well as an outcome of economic inequality. *Id.* at 607–08. Given this argument, what should public policy be with respect to marriage?

CHAPTER 2

REGULATING BODIES: PREGNANCY AND BIRTH

A. INTRODUCTION

Feminist scholars have long argued that important social issues and anxieties are fought on the terrain of women's bodies. Concerns about proper mothering, gender behavior, drug use, population control, poverty, and race are manifested in the regulation of women's bodies. While it is obvious that women's bodies are at issue when it comes to contraception and abortion, less readily apparent are legal and medical controls that are imposed on women's bodies during pregnancy and in the very act of giving birth.

Because reproductive justice seeks to ensure reproductive autonomy for all women across a range of arenas, the following section examines ways in which the state (primarily through the legal system, though often with the assistance of the medical system) tries to make women conform to views of what is "best" for them during pregnancy and childbirth. Upon closer examination, there is very little concrete evidence that many of these efforts to regulate women's bodies are needed to improve the pregnancies or lives of women, and the health and wellbeing of their offspring.

B. REGULATING PREGNANCY

Muller v. Oregon

208 U.S. 412 (1908).

■ BREWER, J.

On February 19, 1903, the legislature of the state of Oregon passed an act (Session Laws 1903, p. 148) the first section of which is in these words:

> Sec. 1. That no female (shall) be employed in any mechanical establishment, or factory, or laundry in this state more than ten hours during any one day. The hours of work may be so arranged as to permit the employment of females at any time so that they shall not work more than ten hours during the twenty-four hours of any one day.

> Sec. 3 made a violation of the provisions of the prior sections a misdemeanor subject to a fine of not less than $10 nor more than $25. . . .

The single question is the constitutionality of the statute under which the defendant was convicted, so far as it affects the work of a female in a laundry . . . .

. . .

It is the law of Oregon that women, whether married or single, have equal contractual and personal rights with men. . . .

. . .

It thus appears that, putting to one side the elective franchise, in the matter of personal and contractual rights [women] stand on the same plane as the other sex. Their rights in these respects can no more be infringed than the equal rights of their brothers. We held in *Lochner v. New York* that a law providing that no laborer shall be required or permitted to work in bakeries more than sixty hours in a week or ten hours in a day was not as to men a legitimate exercise of the police power of the state, but an unreasonable, unnecessary, and arbitrary interference with the right and liberty of the individual to contract in relation to his labor, and as such was in conflict with, and void under, the Federal Constitution. That decision is invoked by plaintiff in error as decisive of the question before us. But this assumes that the difference between the sexes does not justify a different rule respecting a restriction of the hours of labor.

. . . It may not be amiss, in the present case, before examining the constitutional question, to notice the course of legislation, as well as expressions of opinion from other than judicial sources. In the brief filed by Mr. Louis D. Brandeis for the defendant in error is a very copious collection of all these matters, an epitome of which is found in the margin.

. . .

The legislation . . . referred to in the margin may not be, technically speaking, authorities, and in them is little or no discussion of the constitutional question presented to us for determination, yet they are significant of a widespread belief that woman's physical structure, and the functions she performs in consequence thereof, justify special legislation restricting or qualifying the conditions under which she should be permitted to toil. Constitutional questions, it is true, are not settled by even a consensus of present public opinion, for it is the peculiar value of a written constitution that it places in unchanging form limitations upon legislative action, and thus gives a permanence and stability to popular government which otherwise would be lacking. At the same time, when a question of fact is debated and debatable, and the extent to which a special constitutional limitation goes is affected by the truth in respect to that fact, a widespread and long-continued belief concerning it is worthy of consideration. We take judicial cognizance of all matters of general knowledge.

It is undoubtedly true, as more than once declared by this court, that the general right to contract in relation to one's business is part of the liberty of the individual, protected by the 14th Amendment to the Federal Constitution; yet it is equally well settled that this liberty is not absolute and extending to all contracts, and that a state may, without conflicting with the provisions of the 14th Amendment, restrict in many respects the individual's power of contract.

. . .

That woman's physical structure and the performance of maternal functions place her at a disadvantage in the struggle for subsistence is obvious. This is especially true when the burdens of motherhood are upon her. Even when they are not, by abundant testimony of the medical fraternity continuance for a long time on her feet at work, repeating this from day to day, tends to injurious effects upon the body, and, as healthy mothers are essential to vigorous offspring, the physical well-being of woman becomes an object of public interest and care in order to preserve the strength and vigor of the race.

Still again, history discloses the fact that woman has always been dependent upon man. He established his control at the outset by superior physical strength, and this control in various forms, with diminishing intensity, has continued to the present. As minors, though not to the same extent, she has been looked upon in the courts as needing especial care that her rights may be preserved. Education was long denied her, and while now the doors of the schoolroom are opened and her opportunities for acquiring knowledge are great, yet even with that and the consequent increase of capacity for business affairs it is still true that in the struggle for subsistence she is not an equal competitor with her brother. Though limitations upon personal and contractual rights may be removed by legislation, there is that in her disposition and habits of life which will operate against a full assertion of those rights. She will still be where some legislation to protect her seems necessary to secure a real equality of right. Doubtless there are individual exceptions, and there are many respects in which she has an advantage over him; but looking at it from the viewpoint of the effort to maintain an independent position in life, she is not upon an equality. Differentiated by these matters from the other sex, she is properly placed in a class by herself, and legislation designed for her protection may be sustained, even when like legislation is not necessary for men, and could not be sustained. It is impossible to close one's eyes to the fact that she still looks to her brother and depends upon him. Even though all restrictions on political, personal, and contractual rights were taken away, and she stood, so far as statutes are concerned, upon an absolutely equal plane with him, it would still be true that she is so constituted that she will rest upon and look to him for protection; that her physical structure and a proper discharge of her maternal functions—having in view not merely her own health, but the well-being of the race—justify legislation to protect her from the greed as well as the passion of man. The limitations which this statute places upon her contractual powers, upon her right to agree with her employer as to the time she shall labor, are not imposed solely for her benefit, but also largely for the benefit of all. Many words cannot make this plainer. The two sexes differ in structure of body, in the functions to be performed by each, in the amount of physical strength, in the capacity for long-continued labor, particularly when done standing, the influence of vigorous health upon the future well-being of the race, the self-reliance which enables one to assert full rights, and in the capacity to maintain the struggle for subsistence. This difference justifies a difference in legislation, and upholds that which is designed to compensate for some of the burdens which rest upon her.

We have not referred in this discussion to the denial of the elective franchise in the state of Oregon, for while that may disclose a lack of political equality in all things with her brother, that is not of itself decisive. The reason runs deeper, and rests in the inherent difference between the two sexes, and in the different functions in life which they perform.

For these reasons, and without questioning in any respect the decision in *Lochner v. New York*, we are of the opinion that it cannot be adjudged that the act in question is in conflict with the Federal Constitution, so far as it respects the work of a female in a laundry, and the judgment of the Supreme Court of Oregon is affirmed.

NOTES

1.   Muller *in context*. Three years before the Supreme Court decided *Muller*, it struck down similar maximum hours legislation in *Lochner v. New York*, 198 U.S. 45 (1905). Though the Bakeshop Act challenged in *Lochner* was animated by health concerns, and was unanimously passed by the New York legislature, the Supreme Court struck down the Act as an infringement of the individual's freedom to contract for the terms of his employment. *Id.* However, three years after it decided *Lochner*, the Court had little trouble upholding maximum hours legislation in *Muller*. The critical difference? The workers at issue in *Muller* were women, who were "essential to [the production of] vigorous offspring" and thus, necessary "to preserve the strength and vigor of the race." *Muller*, 208 U.S. at 421. With women's maternal functions firmly in mind, the Court had little trouble distinguishing between the Bakeshop Act invalidated in *Lochner* and Oregon's protective labor law.

2.   *The Brandeis Brief.* Written by future Supreme Court Justice Louis Brandeis, the famed Brandeis Brief, submitted in support of the challenged Oregon statute, compiled testimony by physicians, social scientists, and male workers arguing that long working hours had a negative effect on the "health, safety, morals, and general welfare of women." At over 100 pages—only two of which were devoted to legal arguments—the Brandeis Brief reshaped the nature of Supreme Court advocacy by combining legal argument with scientific evidence. *See generally* Noga Morag-Levine, *Facts, Formalism and the Brandeis Brief: the Origins of a Myth*, 2013 U. ILL. L. REV. 59 (discussing the origins and impact of the Brandeis Brief).

3. *Racing* Muller. The Oregon act challenged in *Muller* was upheld, in part because it served the state's interest in ensuring the "future well-being of the race." In referencing "the race," the *Muller* Court ostensibly meant the human race. However, the discourse of the time might suggest a more particularized reading of the term "race." That is, when the *Muller* Court referred to "the race," they understood the term to mean the white race. *See* Patricia A. Cooper, *"A Masculinist Vision of Useful Labor": Popular Ideologies About Women and Work in the United States, 1820 to 1939*, 84 KY. L.J. 827, 845–46 (1995). Does this reading complicate *Muller*?

American College of Obstetricians and Gynecologists (ACOG) & American Academy of Pediatrics, Guidelines for Perinatal Care

95–136 (7th ed. 2012).

Preconception and Antepartum Care

A comprehensive antepartum care program involves a coordinated approach to medical care, continuous risk assessment, and psychosocial support that optimally begins before conception and extends throughout the postpartum period and interconceptional period. Health care professionals should integrate the concept of family-centered care into antepartum care. . . . Care should include an assessment of the expectant mother's attitude toward her pregnancy (as well as the family's attitudes, if this is so desired by the expectant mother)[,] the support systems available, and the need for parenting education. To the extent it is desired by the expectant mother, she and her family should be encouraged to work with her caregivers in order to make well-informed decisions about pregnancy, labor, delivery, the postpartum period, and the interconceptional period.

. . .

Preconception Care

Optimizing a woman's health, health behaviors, and knowledge before she plans and conceives a pregnancy is known as preconception care. Preconception care is a component of a larger health care goal—optimizing the health of every woman. Because reproductive capacity spans almost four decades for most women, optimizing women's health before and between pregnancies is an ongoing process that requires access to and the full participation of all segments of the health care system. Increasingly it is apparent that few women seek a specific visit before conception for preconception counseling, which would be the ideal situation. Therefore, all health encounters during a woman's reproductive years should include counseling on appropriate medical care and behavior to optimize pregnancy outcomes.

. . .

Preconception Counseling and Interventions

During episodic or focused health care visits in women who could become pregnant, in addition to performing a physical exam and obtaining her obstetric and gynecologic histories, there are core topics in preconception care that should be addressed. The following topics may serve as the basis for such counseling:

- Family planning and pregnancy spacing
- Immunity and immunization status
- Risk factors for sexually transmitted infections (STIs)
- Substance use, including alcohol, tobacco, and recreational and illicit drugs
- Exposure to violence and intimate partner violence
- Medical, surgical, and psychiatric histories
- Current medications (prescription and nonprescription)
- Family history
- Genetic history (both maternal and paternal)
- Nutrition
- Teratogens; environmental and occupational exposures
- Assessment of socioeconomic, educational, and cultural context

. . .

In addition, women should be counseled regarding the benefits of maximizing their personal health status; maintaining a menstrual calendar to assist with estimating the conception date; and practicing safe sex to avoid STIs, including human immunodeficiency virus (HIV).

Reproductive Health Plan

Physicians should encourage women to formulate a reproductive health plan and discuss it in a nonjudgmental way at each visit. Such a plan would address the individual's or couple's desire for a child or children (or desire not to have children); the optimal number, spacing, and timing of children in the family; and age-related changes in fertility. Because many women's plans change over time, creating a reproductive health plan requires an ongoing conscientious assessment of the desirability of a future pregnancy, determination of steps that need to be taken either to prevent or to plan for and optimize a pregnancy, and evaluation of current health status and other issues relevant to the health of a pregnancy. If pregnancy is not desired, a woman's current contraceptive use and options should be discussed to assist in the identification of the most appropriate and effective method for her. If a woman's request for care is in conflict with her primary caregiver's recommendations or preferences, consultation or referral may be indicated.

Preconception Immunization

Preconception care offers the opportunity to review immunization status. Although there is no evidence of adverse fetal effects from vaccinating pregnant women with an inactivated virus or bacterial vaccines or toxoids, ideally vaccinations should be administered before conception in order to avoid unnecessary exposure to the fetus. Live vaccines do pose a theoretical risk for the fetus. . . .

. . .

Preconception Nutritional Counseling

Consumption of a balanced diet with the appropriate distribution of the basic food pyramid groups is especially important during pregnancy. Diet can be affected by food preferences, cultural beliefs, and eating patterns. A woman who is a vegan or who has special dietary restrictions secondary to medical illnesses, such as diabetes mellitus, inflammatory bowel disease, renal disease or PKU, will require special dietary measures as well as vitamin and mineral supplements. Women who frequently diet to lose weight, fast, skip meals, or have eating disorders or unusual eating habits should be identified and counseled. Additional risk factors for nutritional problems include adolescence, tobacco and substance abuse, history of pica during a previous pregnancy, high parity, and mental illness . . . . The patient's access to food and the ability to purchase food can be pertinent.

Ideally, women should be advised to achieve a near-normal body mass index (BMI) before attempting conception because infertility as well as both maternal and fetal complications are associated with abnormal BMI . . . . All women should be encouraged to exercise at least 30 minutes on most days of the week. Obese women should be advised regarding their increased risk of adverse perinatal outcomes, including difficulty becoming pregnant, conception of a fetus with a variety of birth defects, preterm delivery, diabetes, cesarean delivery, hypertensive disease, and thromboembolic disease. Weight loss before pregnancy reduces these risks.

. . .

Folic acid supplementation is recommended before pregnancy and during pregnancy, despite the fortification of fortified grain products in the United States, because the amount of folic acid consumed in fortified grain products may be less than the amount recommended to prevent NTDs. The CDC and the U.S. Public Health Service recommend the daily intake of 400 micrograms of folic acid for all women who could become pregnant.

. . .

Antepartum Care

Women who receive early and regular prenatal care are more likely to have healthier infants. Prenatal care includes a process of ongoing risk identification and assessment in order to develop appropriate care plans. This plan of care should take into consideration the medical, nutritional, psychosocial, cultural and educational needs of the patient and her family, and it should be periodically reevaluated and revised in accordance with the progress of the pregnancy. Health care providers of antepartum care must be able to either primarily provide or easily refer to others to provide a wide array of services to pregnant women. These services include the following:

- Readily available and regularly scheduled obstetric care, beginning in early pregnancy and continuing through the postpartum period

- Access to unscheduled visits or emergency visits on a 24-hour basis. Timing of access varies depending on the nature of the problem

- Timely transmittal of prenatal records to the site of the patient's planned delivery so that her records are readily accessible at the time of delivery

- Medical interpretation services exclusive of family members for women with limited English language ability

- Referral network of reliable, competent, culturally sensitive, accessible social service, mental health, and specialist medical care providers.

. . .

NOTES

1. *Reproductive awareness.* In its 2002 Guidelines for Perinatal Care, ACOG asserts that "[r]eproductive awareness must be integrated more effectively into the health care system and society at large." AMERICAN COLLEGE OF OBSTETRICIANS AND GYNECOLOGISTS (ACOG) & AMERICAN ACADEMY OF PEDIATRICS, GUIDELINES FOR PERINATAL CARE 2 (5th ed. 2002). To this end, it suggests that "[e]very encounter with the health care system, including those with adolescents and men, as well as those with women of childbearing age should be viewed as an opportunity to reinforce reproductive awareness." *Id.* at 3. Does "reproductive awareness" go too far in its assumption that everyone who can bear a child, will—at some point—do so? Recall the Court's opinion in *Muller.* Does it evince a preoccupation with "reproductive awareness"?

2. *Assuming a middle-class pregnancy?* The ACOG guidelines for perinatal care set forth "best practices" for perinatal care. These standards assume certain things: regular access to health care, a relationship of trust and comfort between the patient and her physician, as well as the financial wherewithal to achieve all of these things. With that in mind, do these guidelines assume a certain income level? Can women accessing perinatal care through government-provided services like Medicaid achieve these "best

practices" in perinatal care? Put simply, are *all* pregnant women able to comport with these guidelines?

3.   *Expanding access to prenatal care.* Enacted in 1965 as part of the Social Security Act, Medicaid is a cooperative venture jointly funded by the federal and state governments (including the District of Columbia and the territories) to assist states in furnishing medical assistance to eligible needy persons. Medicaid is one of the largest sources of funding for medical and health-related services for indigent Americans. States generally have broad discretion to determine eligibility criteria for Medicaid. To be eligible for federal funds, however, states must provide Medicaid coverage to the "categorically needy"—a group that has been defined to include pregnant women whose family income is below 133 percent of the federal poverty level (services to these women are limited to those related to pregnancy, complications of pregnancy, delivery, and postpartum care), and infants born to Medicaid-eligible women for the first year of life (subject to certain restrictions). *See* CTRS. FOR MEDICARE & MEDICAID SERVS., DEP'T OF HEALTH & HUMAN SERVS., BRIEF SUMMARIES OF MEDICARE & MEDICAID: TITLE XVIII & TITLE XIX OF THE SOCIAL SECURITY ACT 23–25 (Nov. 15, 2019). In what ways does the federal law requiring prenatal care for low-income pregnant women respond to the ACOG guidelines? Is the federal interest in expanding access to prenatal care a good thing, or might such access come at a cost for low-income women?

4.   *Prenatal care as a condition of access to other benefits.* It should be noted that, despite the ACOG guidelines for prenatal care, submitting to prenatal care is not a legal requirement—at least for those women who have access to private health care and health insurance. For those women who lack these resources, prenatal care is often a condition of access to other important public benefits. In these contexts, why does prenatal care rise to the level of a mandate?

* * *

Not all impositions on prenatal decision-making come in the form of direct mandates from the state. As we saw in the context of the ACOG guidelines, the medical community, in conjunction with the state, may issue "best practices" for prenatal decision-making that are strongly recommended in the course of prenatal care. Though these measures are nominally optional—or may not relate to pregnancy per se—they have become normalized as an expected practice. As we will see, these "best practices" may not be entirely discretionary and may affect pregnant and non-pregnant persons alike.

Centers for Disease Control, Morbidity and Mortality Weekly Report, Trends in Wheat-Flour Fortification with Folic Acid and Iron—Worldwide, 2004 and 2007

(2008), http://www.cdc.gov/mmwr/preview/mmwrhtml/mm5701a4.htm.

Consumption of adequate amounts of folic acid by women before pregnancy and during early pregnancy decreases their risk for having a pregnancy affected by neural tube defects (NTDs), the most common preventable type of birth defects worldwide.... Although certain populations consume substantial amounts of rice and corn, worldwide, the consumption of wheat flour is greater than that of any other cereal grain. Fortification of wheat flour is an effective, simple, and inexpensive strategy for supplying folic acid, iron, and other vitamins and minerals to large segments of the world population. To assess the global change from 2004 to 2007 in 1) the percentage of wheat flour being fortified with folic acid and iron; 2) the total number of persons overall and women in particular with access to fortified wheat flour; and 3) the total number of newborns whose mothers had access to fortified wheat flour during pregnancy, CDC analyzed data from the Flour Fortification Initiative (FFI). This report summarizes the results of that assessment, which indicated that the worldwide percentage of wheat-flour fortification increased from 18% in 2004 to 27% in 2007. The estimated number of persons with access to fortified wheat flour increased by approximately 540 million, and the annual number of newborns whose mothers had access to fortified wheat flour during pregnancy increased by approximately 14 million. Nonetheless, approximately two thirds of the world population lacks access to fortified wheat flour....

. . .

From 2004 to 2007, the number of countries with documented national regulations for mandatory wheat-flour fortification increased from 33 to 54. Fifty of the 54 countries with mandatory fortification in 2007 required fortification with both iron and folic acid, two with folic acid but not iron, and two with iron but not folic acid. Twenty-four of those countries also mandated wheat-flour fortification with thiamin, riboflavin, and niacin; two with thiamin and riboflavin; and two with thiamin. The percentage of wheat flour processed in roller mills that was fortified increased from 18% in 2004 to 27% in 2007. Nearly 540 million additional persons, including 167 million additional women aged 15–60 years, had access to fortified wheat flour in 2007 compared with 2004, and the annual number of newborns whose mothers had access to fortified wheat flour during pregnancy increased by approximately 14 million (Table). By region, the greatest increase in the percentage of wheat flour being fortified was in the Eastern Mediterranean Region: from 5% in 2004 to 44% in 2007 (Figure). The portion of wheat flour being fortified increased from 90% to 97% in the Americas Region (the region with the highest percentage of wheat flour being fortified), from 26% to 31% in the African Region, from 16% to 21% in the South-East Asia Region, from 3% to 6% in the European Region, and from 2% to 4% in the Western Pacific Region.

TABLE. Estimated number and percentage of persons and women who had access to fortified wheat flour and of newborns whose mothers had access to fortified wheat flour during pregnancy — worldwide, 2004 and 2007

Category	Total population	2004 No.*	2004 (%)	2007 No.*	2007 (%)	Change from 2004 to 2007 No.	Change from 2004 to 2007 (%)
Total persons	6,512,822[†]	1,271,363	(19.5)	1,810,659	(27.8)	539,297	(8.3)
Women aged 15–60 yrs	2,142,225[†]	410,091	(19.1)	577,461	(27.0)	167,370	(7.8)
Newborns whose mothers had access	133,804[§]	27,052	(20.2)	41,060	(30.7)	14,007	(10.5)

* In thousands. Calculated from data from the Flour Fortification Initiative, available at http://www.sph.emory.edu/wheatflour.
[†] In thousands, mid-2006 estimate. From U.S. Central Intelligence Agency, available at http://www.cia.gov.
[§] In thousands. From United Nations International Children's Emergency Fund (UNICEF) birth rate estimates, available at http://www.unicef.org.

FIGURE. Percentage of wheat flour processed in roller mills that was fortified — worldwide and by World Health Organization (WHO) region, 2004 and 2007

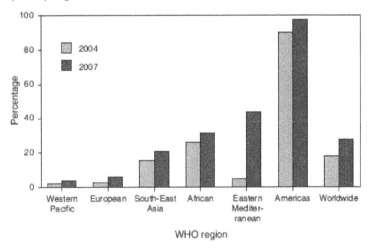

NOTES

1. *Folic acid mandates in the United States.* In 1992, the Public Health Service recommended that all women of childbearing age consume 0.4 mg of folic acid per day in order to reduce their risk of having a child affected with spina bifida or other neural tube disorders (NTDs). J. DAVID ERICKSON, FOLIC ACID AND PREVENTION OF SPINA BIFIDA AND ANENCEPHALY: 10 YEARS

AFTER THE U.S. PUBLIC HEALTH SERVICE RECOMMENDATION 1 (2002). Because folic acid supplements were unlikely to have sufficient penetration, especially in populations less likely to use supplements, which included subpopulations with a higher incidence of NTDs, alternative interventions were deemed necessary. *Id.* In 1996, the U.S. Food and Drug Administration mandated that by January 1998, all flour and grain products labeled as "enriched" would contain folic acid. *Id.* Today, the vast majority of flour and cereal products in the United States are labeled "enriched" and contain added folic acid.

2.   *Mandates as governmental coercion?* Some have argued that mandatory folic acid fortification presents ethical issues. *See, e.g., Objections to the Mandatory Fortification of Bread with Folic Acid*, HEALTH FREEDOM N.Z. (Apr. 4, 2009), https://healthfreedom.org.nz/campaigns/safefood/objections-to-the-mandatory-fortification-of-bread-with-folic-acid (outlining various ethical and practical objections to mandatory fortification). Specifically, it has been argued that mandatory fortification amounts to governmental coercion, as those who do not wish to consume additional quantities of folic acid have few options for opting out. Others have argued that mandatory fortification presumes that all women of childbearing age *will* become mothers, and that those who are unable to bear children (i.e., men, children, the elderly, and infertile women) are conscripted into consuming additional folic acid in order to reduce the incidence of NTDs among a smaller subset of the overall population.

Geduldig v. Aiello — Pregnancy disability
417 U.S. 484 (1974).   coverage under
EPC

■ STEWART, J.

For almost 30 years California has administered a disability insurance system that pays benefits to persons in private employment who are temporarily unable to work because of disability not covered by workmen's compensation. The appellees brought this action to challenge the constitutionality of a provision of the California program that, in defining 'disability,' excludes from coverage certain disabilities resulting from pregnancy. . . .

An individual is eligible for disability benefits if, during a one-year base period prior to his disability, he has contributed one percent of a minimum income of $300 to the Disability Fund. . . .

In return for his one-percent contribution to the Disability Fund, the individual employee is insured against the risk of disability stemming from a substantial number of "mental or physical illness(es) and mental or physical injur(ies)." It is not every disabling condition, however, that triggers the obligation to pay benefits under the program. . . . [Section] 2626 of the Unemployment Insurance Code excludes from coverage certain disabilities that are attributable to pregnancy. It is this provision that is at issue in the present case.

It is clear that California intended to establish this benefit system as an insurance program that was to function essentially in accordance with insurance concepts. Since the program was instituted in 1946, it has been totally self-supporting, never drawing on general state revenues to finance disability or hospital benefits. . . .

Over the years California has demonstrated a strong commitment not to increase the contribution rate above the one-percent level. The State has sought to provide the broadest possible disability protection that would be affordable by all employees, including those with very low incomes. Because any larger percentage or any flat dollar-amount rate of contribution would impose an increasingly regressive levy bearing most heavily upon those with the lowest incomes, the State has resisted any attempt to change the required contribution from the one-percent level. The program is thus structured, in terms of the level of benefits and the risks insured, to maintain the solvency of the Disability Fund at a one-percent annual level of contribution.

In ordering the State to pay benefits for disability accompanying normal pregnancy and delivery, the District Court acknowledged the State's contention "that coverage of these disabilities is so extraordinarily expensive that it would be impossible to maintain a program supported by employee contributions if these disabilities are included." There is considerable disagreement between the parties with respect to how great the increased costs would actually be, but they would clearly be substantial. For purposes of analysis the District Court accepted the State's estimate, which was in excess of $100 million annually, and stated: "[I]t is clear that including these disabilities would not destroy the program The increased costs could be accommodated quite easily by making reasonable changes in the contribution rate, the maximum benefits allowable, and the other variables affecting the solvency of the program." . . .

We cannot agree that the exclusion of this disability from coverage amounts to invidious discrimination under the Equal Protection Clause. . . . Although California has created a program to insure most risks of employment disability, it has not chosen to insure all such risks, and this decision is reflected in the level of annual contributions exacted from participating employees. This Court has held that, consistently with the Equal Protection Clause, a State "may take one step at a time, addressing itself to the phase of the problem which seems most acute to the legislative mind. . . . The legislature may select one phase of one field and apply a remedy there, neglecting the others. . . ." Particularly with respect to social welfare programs, so long as the line drawn by the State is rationally supportable, the courts will not interpose their judgment as to the appropriate stopping point. "[T]he Equal Protection Clause does not require that a State must choose between attacking every aspect of a problem or not attacking the problem at all."

. . .

It is evident that a totally comprehensive program would be substantially more costly than the present program and would inevitably require state subsidy, a higher rate of employee contribution, a lower scale of benefits for those suffering insured disabilities, or some combination of these measures. There is nothing in the Constitution, however, that requires the State to subordinate or compromise its legitimate interests solely to create a more comprehensive social insurance program than it already has.

The State has a legitimate interest in maintaining the self-supporting nature of its insurance program. Similarly, it has an interest in distributing the available resources in such a way as to keep benefit payments at an adequate level for disabilities that are covered, rather than to cover all disabilities inadequately. Finally, California has a legitimate concern in maintaining the contribution rate at a level that will not unduly burden participating employees, particularly low-income employees who may be most in need of the disability insurance.

These policies provide an objective and wholly noninvidious basis for the State's decision not to create a more comprehensive insurance program than it has. There is no evidence in the record that the selection of the risks insured by the program worked to discriminate against any definable group or class in terms of the aggregate risk protection derived by that group or class from the program.[20] There is no risk from which men are protected and women are not. Likewise, there is no risk from which women are protected and men are not.[21]

The appellee simply contends that, although she has received insurance protection equivalent to that provided all other participating employees, she has suffered discrimination because she encountered a risk that was outside the program's protection. For the reasons we have

---

[20] The dissenting opinion to the contrary, this case is thus a far cry from cases like *Reed v. Reed*, 404 U.S. 71 (1971), and *Frontiero v. Richardson*, 411 U.S. 677 (1973), involving discrimination based upon gender as such. The California insurance program does not exclude anyone from benefit eligibility because of gender but merely removes one physical condition—pregnancy—from the list of compensable disabilities. While it is true that only women can become pregnant it does not follow that every legislative classification concerning pregnancy is a sex-based classification like those considered in *Reed* and *Frontiero*. Normal pregnancy is an objectively identifiable physical condition with unique characteristics. Absent a showing that distinctions involving pregnancy are mere pretexts designed to effect an invidious discrimination against the members of one sex or the other, lawmakers are constitutionally free to include or exclude pregnancy from the coverage of legislation such as this on any reasonable basis, just as with respect to any other physical condition.

The lack of identity between the excluded disability and gender as such under this insurance program becomes clear upon the most cursory analysis. The program divides potential recipients into two groups—pregnant women and nonpregnant persons. While the first group is exclusively female, the second includes members of both sexes. The fiscal and actuarial benefits of the program thus accrue to members of both sexes.

[21] Indeed, the appellant submitted to the District Court data that indicated that both the annual claim rate and the annual claim cost are greater for women than for men. As the District Court acknowledged, "women contribute about 28 percent of the total disability insurance fund and receive back about 38 percent of the fund in benefits." Several amici curiae have represented to the Court that they have had a similar experience under private disability insurance programs.

stated, we hold that this contention is not a valid one under the Equal Protection Clause of the Fourteenth Amendment.

Reversed.

■ BRENNAN, J., with whom DOUGLAS, J., and MARSHALL, J., join, dissenting.

. . .

California's disability insurance program was enacted to supplement the State's unemployment insurance and workmen's compensation programs by providing benefits to wage earners to cushion the economic effects of income loss and medical expenses resulting from sickness or injury. . . .

To achieve the Act's broad humanitarian goals, the legislature fashioned a pooled-risk disability fund covering all employees at the same rate of contribution, regardless of individual risk.[2] The only requirement that must be satisfied before an employee becomes eligible to receive disability benefits is that the employee must have contributed one percent of a minimum income of $300 during a one-year base period. . . . Benefits are payable for a maximum of 26 weeks, but may not exceed one-half of the employee's total base-period earnings. Finally, compensation is paid for virtually all disabling conditions without regard to cost, voluntariness, uniqueness, predictability, or "normalcy" of the disability. Thus, for example, workers are compensated for costly disabilities such as heart attacks, voluntary disabilities such as cosmetic surgery or sterilization, disabilities unique to sex or race such as prostatectomies or sickle-cell anemia, pre-existing conditions inevitably resulting in disability such as degenerative arthritis or cataracts, and "normal" disabilities such as removal of irritating wisdom teeth or other orthodontia.

Despite the Code's broad goals and scope of coverage, compensation is denied for disabilities suffered in connection with a 'normal' pregnancy—disabilities suffered only by women. Disabilities caused by pregnancy, however, like other physically disabling conditions covered by the Code, require medical care, often include hospitalization, anesthesia and surgical procedures, and may involve genuine risk to life. Moreover, the economic effects caused by pregnancy-related disabilities are functionally indistinguishable from the effects caused by any other disability: wages are lost due to a physical inability to work, and medical expenses are incurred for the delivery of the child and for postpartum care.[5] In my view, by singling out for less favorable treatment a gender-

---

[2]   California deliberately decided not to classify employees on the basis of actuarial data. Thus, the contribution rate for a particular group of employees is not tied to that group's predicted rate of disability claims.

[5]   Nearly two-thirds of all women who work do so of necessity: either they are unmarried or their husbands earn less than $7,000 per year. *See* United States Department of Labor, Women's Bureau, *Why Women Work* (rev. ed. 1972); United States Department of Labor, Employment Standards Administration, The Myth and The Reality (May 1974 rev.). Moreover,

linked disability peculiar to women, the State has created a double standard for disability compensation: a limitation is imposed upon the disabilities for which women workers may recover, while men receive full compensation for all disabilities suffered, including those that affect only or primarily their sex, such as prostatectomies, circumcision, hemophilia, and gout. In effect, one set of rules is applied to females and another to males. Such dissimilar treatment of men and women, on the basis of physical characteristics inextricably linked to one sex, inevitably constitutes sex discrimination.

. . .

. . . California's legitimate interest in fiscal integrity could easily have been achieved through a variety of less drastic, sexually neutral means. As the District Court observed:

> "Even using (the State's) estimate of the cost of expanding the program to include pregnancy-related disabilities, however, it is clear that including these disabilities would not destroy the program. The increased costs could be accommodated quite easily by making reasonable changes in the contribution rate, the maximum benefits allowable, and the other variables affecting the solvency of the program."

. . .

I would therefore affirm the judgment of the District Court.

NOTES

1. *Equality and difference.* To modern readers the reasoning in these cases may have an "Alice in Wonderland" quality to them. How could the Court conclude that pregnancy was not sex discrimination but merely discrimination against pregnant people? Especially in view of the fact, as Professor Katharine Bartlett notes, that at the time of *Geduldig*, eighty-four percent of married women were or would be pregnant, on average two and a half times each. Bartlett notes that excluding pregnancy from disability coverage de facto affected pregnant people (all of whom were women), potentially pregnant people (all of whom were women), and fundamentally shaped how women (but in most cases not men) thought about work and family. It reinscribed, she argues, the conclusion in *Bradwell v. Illinois*, 83 U.S. 130 (1872), the notorious Supreme Court case that barred women from the practice of law on the grounds that women's primary role was in the family. *See* Katharine T. Bartlett, *Pregnancy and the Constitution: The Uniqueness Trap*, 62 CALIF. L. REV. 1532, 1533–35 (1974). In all fairness however, at the time *Geduldig* was decided, feminist theorists themselves (like the Court) were debating whether society should treat motherhood as a private decision ("equality feminists") or recognize the unique status of

---

this Court recognized in *Kahn v. Shevin*, 416 U.S. 351, 353 (1974), that "data compiled by the Women's Bureau of the United States Department of Labor show that in 1972 a woman working full time had a median income which was only 57.9% of the median for males—a figure actually six points lower than had been achieved in 1955."

[Handwritten margin notes:]
double standard: female: only services not covered, but men only are
this is sex discrim
proposes alternative

motherhood ("difference feminists"). *See* Mary Hawkesworth, *Feminist Rhetoric: Discourses on the Male Monopoly of Thought*, 16 POL. THEORY 444, 448–49 (1988).

2. *The Pregnancy Discrimination Act.* In response to the decisions in *Geduldig*, *supra* p. 128, and *General Electric Co. v. Gilbert*, *infra* p. 133, Congress rebuked the Court, enacting the Pregnancy Discrimination Act of 1978, see *infra* pp. 140–141. Thirty-six years later, however, pregnant women still lose their jobs due to their pregnancies. Or, as a *New York Times* op-ed put it in 2012, "[f]ew people realize that getting pregnant can mean losing your job. Imagine a woman who, seven months into her pregnancy, is fired from her position as a cashier because she needed a few extra bathroom breaks." Dina Bakst, *Pregnant, and Pushed Out of a Job*, N.Y. TIMES, Jan. 30, 2012, at A25.

General Electric Co. v. Gilbert — Pregnancy disability coverage under Title VII

429 U.S. 125 (1976).

■ REHNQUIST, J.

Petitioner, General Electric Co., provides for all of its employees a disability plan which pays weekly nonoccupational sickness and accident benefits. Excluded from the plan's coverage, however, are disabilities arising from pregnancy. Respondents, on behalf of a class of women employees, brought this action seeking . . . a declaration that this exclusion constitutes sex discrimination in violation of Title VII of the Civil Rights Act of 1964 . . . .

I

As part of its total compensation package, General Electric provides nonoccupational sickness and accident benefits to all employees under its . . . Plan . . . in an amount equal to 60% of an employee's normal straight-time weekly earnings. These payments are paid to employees who become totally disabled as a result of a nonoccupational sickness or accident. Benefit payments normally start with the eighth day of an employee's total disability (although if an employee is earlier confined to a hospital as a bed patient, benefit payments will start immediately), and continue up to a maximum of 26 weeks for any one continuous period of disability or successive periods of disability due to the same or related causes.

The individual named respondents are present or former hourly paid production employees . . . . Each . . . was pregnant . . . and each presented a claim to the company for disability benefits under the Plan to cover the period while absent from work as a result of the pregnancy. These claims were routinely denied on the ground that the Plan did not provide disability-benefit payments for any absence due to pregnancy. . . . The [plaintiffs] asserted a violation of Title VII. Damages were sought as well as an injunction directing General Electric to include pregnancy disabilities within the Plan on the same terms and conditions as other nonoccupational disabilities.

. . . [T]he District Court made findings of fact and conclusions of law, and entered an order in which it determined that General Electric, by excluding pregnancy disabilities from the coverage of the Plan, had engaged in sex discrimination in violation of . . . Title VII. The District Court found that normal pregnancy, while not necessarily either a "disease" or an "accident," was disabling for a period of six to eight weeks; that approximately "(t)en per cent of pregnancies are terminated by miscarriage, which is disabling"; and that approximately 10% of pregnancies are complicated by diseases which may lead to additional disability. The District Court noted the evidence introduced during the trial . . . concerning the relative cost to General Electric of providing benefits under the Plan to male and female employees, all of which indicated that, with pregnancy-related disabilities excluded, the cost of the Plan to General Electric per female employee was at least as high as, if not substantially higher than, the cost per male employee.

The District Court found that the inclusion of pregnancy-related disabilities within the scope of the Plan would "increase G.E.'s [disability benefits plan] costs by an amount which, though large, is at this time undeterminable." . . .

. . .

Between the date on which the District Court's judgment was rendered and the time this case was decided by the Court of Appeals, we decided *Geduldig v. Aiello*, 417 U.S. 484 (1974), where we rejected a claim that a very similar disability program established under California law violated the Equal Protection Clause of the Fourteenth Amendment because that plan's exclusion of pregnancy disabilities represented sex discrimination. . . .

. . .

. . . We think, therefore, that our decision in *Geduldig v. Aiello* . . . is quite relevant in determining whether or not the pregnancy exclusion did discriminate on the basis of sex. In *Geduldig* . . . [w]e rejected appellee's equal protection challenge to this statutory scheme . . . [, noting:]

. . . The California insurance program does not exclude anyone from benefit eligibility because of gender but merely removes one physical condition pregnancy from the list of compensable disabilities. While it is true that only women can become pregnant, it does not follow that every legislative classification concerning pregnancy is a sex-based classification . . . . Normal pregnancy is an objectively identifiable physical condition with unique characteristics. . . .

The lack of identity between the excluded disability and gender as such under this insurance program becomes clear upon the most cursory analysis. The program divides potential recipients into two groups pregnant women and nonpregnant persons. While the first group is exclusively female, the second includes members of both sexes.

[*Geduldig*, 417 U.S. at 496–497 n.20.]

The quoted language . . . leaves no doubt that our reason for rejecting appellee's equal protection claim in that case was that the exclusion of pregnancy from coverage under California's disability-benefits plan was not in itself discrimination based on sex.

We recognized in *Geduldig*, of course, that the fact that there was no sex-based discrimination as such was not the end of the analysis, should it be shown "that distinctions involving pregnancy are mere pretexts designed to effect an invidious discrimination against the members of one sex or the other." But . . . no semblance of such a showing had been made:

. . . There is no risk from which men are protected and women are not. Likewise, there is no risk from which women are protected and men are not." *Id.* at 496–497.

. . .

. . . *Geduldig* is precisely [o]n point in its holding that an exclusion of pregnancy from a disability-benefits plan providing general coverage is not a gender-based discrimination at all.

. . . [W]e have here no question of excluding a disease or disability comparable in all other respects to covered diseases or disabilities and yet confined to the members of one race or sex. Pregnancy is, of course, confined to women, but it is in other ways significantly different from the typical covered disease or disability. The District Court found that it is not a "disease" at all, and is often a voluntarily undertaken and desired condition. We do not therefore infer that the exclusion of pregnancy disability benefits from petitioner's plan is a simple pretext for discriminating against women. . . .

The instant suit was grounded on Title VII rather than the Equal Protection Clause, and our cases recognize that a prima facie violation of Title VII can be established in some circumstances upon proof that the effect of an otherwise facially neutral plan or classification is to discriminate against members of one class or another. *See Washington v. Davis*, 426 U.S. 229, 246–248 (1976). For example, in the context of a challenge, under the provisions of [Title VII] to a facially neutral employment test, this Court held that a prima facie case of discrimination would be established if, even absent proof of intent, the consequences of the test were "invidiously to discriminate on the basis of racial or other impermissible classification," *Griggs v. Duke Power Co.*, 401 U.S. 424, 431 (1971). Even assuming that it is not necessary in this case to prove intent to establish a prima facie violation of [Title VII] the respondents have not made the requisite showing of gender-based effect.

... The Plan, in effect ... is nothing more than an insurance package, which covers some risks, but excludes others .... As there is no proof that the package is in fact worth more to men than to women, it is impossible to find any gender-based discriminatory effect in this scheme simply because women disabled as a result of pregnancy do not receive benefits; that is to say, gender-based discrimination does not result simply because an employer's disability-benefits plan is less than all-inclusive. For all that appears, pregnancy-related disabilities constitute an additional risk, unique to women, and the failure to compensate them for this risk does not destroy the presumed parity of the benefits, accruing to men and women alike, which results from the facially evenhanded inclusion of risks. ...

. . .

■ BRENNAN, J., with whom MARSHALL, J., concurs, dissenting.

. . .

This case is unusual in that it presents a question the resolution of which at first glance turns largely upon the conceptual framework chosen to identify and describe the operational features of the challenged disability program. By directing their focus upon the risks excluded from the otherwise comprehensive program, and upon the purported justifications for such exclusions, the Equal Employment Opportunity Commission, the women plaintiffs, and the lower courts reason that the pregnancy exclusion constitutes a prima facie violation of Title VII. This violation is triggered, they argue, because the omission of pregnancy from the program has the intent and effect of providing that "only women [are subjected] to a substantial risk of total loss of income because of temporary medical disability." Brief for EEOC as [A]micus [C]uriae [at] 12.

The Court's framework is diametrically different. It views General Electric's plan as representing a gender-free assignment of risks in accordance with normal actuarial techniques. From this perspective the lone exclusion of pregnancy is not a violation of Title VII insofar as all other disabilities are mutually covered for both sexes. ...

... I believe that the [consideration of General Electric's practices and policies] compels the conclusion that the Court's assumption that General Electric engaged in a gender-neutral risk-assignment process is purely fanciful. [Further,] the EEOC's interpretation that the exclusion of pregnancy from a disability insurance plan is incompatible with the overall objectives of Title VII has been unjustifiably rejected.

. . .

Considered most favorably to the Court's view, *Geduldig* established the proposition that a pregnancy classification standing alone cannot be said to fall into the category of classifications that rest explicitly on "gender as such," 417 U.S. at 496 n. 20. ... Surely it offends common sense to suggest that a classification revolving around pregnancy is not, at the minimum, strongly "sex related." *See, e.g., Cleveland Board of Education v. LaFleur*, 414 U.S. 632, 652 (1974) (Powell, J., concurring). Indeed, even in the insurance context where neutral actuarial principles were found to have provided a legitimate and independent input into the decisionmaking process, *Geduldig*'s outcome was qualified by the explicit reservation of a case where it could be demonstrated that a pregnancy-centered differentiation is used as a "mere pretext . . . designed to effect an invidious discrimination against the members of one sex . . . ." 417 U.S. at 496–497, n. 20.

Thus, *Geduldig* itself obliges the Court to determine whether the exclusion of a sex-linked disability from the universe of compensable disabilities was actually the product of neutral, persuasive actuarial considerations, or rather stemmed from a policy that purposefully downgraded women's role in the labor force. . . . [Here,] the Court simply disregards a history of General Electric practices that have served to undercut the employment opportunities of women who become pregnant while employed. Moreover, the Court studiously ignores the undisturbed conclusion of the District Court that General Electric's "discriminatory attitude" toward women was "a motivating factor in its policy," and that the pregnancy exclusion was "neutral (neither) on its face" nor "in its intent."

Plainly then, the Court's appraisal of General Electric's policy as a neutral process of sorting risks and "not a gender-based discrimination at all," cannot easily be squared with the historical record in this case. The Court, therefore, proceeds to a discussion of purported neutral criteria that suffice to explain the lone exclusion of pregnancy from the program. The Court argues that pregnancy is not "comparable" to other disabilities since it is a "voluntary" condition rather than a "disease." The fallacy of this argument is that even if "non-voluntariness" and "disease" are to be construed as the operational criteria for inclusion of a disability in General Electric's program, application of these criteria is inconsistent with the Court's gender-neutral interpretation of the company's policy.

For example, the characterization of pregnancy as "voluntary" is not . . . persuasive . . . for as the Court of Appeals correctly noted, "other than for childbirth disability, [General Electric] had never construed its plan as eliminating all so-called 'voluntary' disabilities," including sport injuries, attempted suicides, venereal disease, disabilities incurred in the commission of a crime or during a fight, and elective cosmetic surgery. 519 F.2d at 665. Similarly, the label "disease" rather than "disability" cannot be deemed determinative since General Electric's pregnancy disqualification also excludes the 10% of pregnancies that end in debilitating miscarriages, the 10% of cases where pregnancies are complicated by "diseases" in the intuitive sense of the word, and cases where women recovering from childbirth are stricken by severe diseases unrelated to pregnancy.[4]

... [A]lthough all mutually contractible risks are covered irrespective of gender ... the plan also insures risks such as prostatectomies, vasectomies, and circumcisions that are specific to the reproductive system of men and for which there exist no female counterparts covered by the plan. ... Again, pregnancy affords the only disability, sex-specific or otherwise, that is excluded from coverage. Accordingly, the District Court appropriately remarked "[T[he concern of defendants in reference to pregnancy risks, coupled with the apparent lack of concern regarding the balancing of other statistically sex-linked disabilities, buttresses the Court's conclusion that the discriminatory attitude characterized elsewhere in the Court's findings was in fact a motivating factor in its policy."

If decision of this case, therefore, turns upon acceptance of the Court's view of General Electric's disability plan as a sex-neutral assignment of risks, or plaintiffs' perception of the plan as a sex-conscious process expressive of the secondary status of women in the company's labor force, the history of General Electric's employment practices and the absence of definable gender-neutral sorting criteria under the plan warrant rejection of the Court's view in deference to the plaintiffs'. Indeed, the fact that the Court's frame of reference lends itself to such intentional, sex-laden decisionmaking makes clear the wisdom and propriety of the EEOC's contrary approach to employment disability programs.

III

Of course, the demonstration of purposeful discrimination is not the only ground for recovery under Title VII. ... [T]his Court, and every Court of Appeals now have firmly settled that a prima facie violation of Title VII ... also is established by demonstrating that a facially neutral classification has the effect of discriminating against members of a defined class.

General Electric's disability program has three divisible sets of effects. First, the plan covers all disabilities that mutually afflict both sexes. ... Second, the plan insures against all disabilities that are male-specific or have a predominant impact on males. Finally, all female-specific and female-impacted disabilities are covered, except for the most prevalent, pregnancy. The Court focuses on the first factor ... and therefore understandably can identify no discriminatory effect arising from the plan. In contrast, the EEOC and plaintiffs rely upon the unequal

---

[4] The experience of one of the class plaintiffs is instructive of the reach of the pregnancy exclusion. On April 5, 1972, she took a pregnancy leave, delivering a stillborn baby some nine days later. Upon her return home, she suffered a blood clot in the lung, a condition unrelated to her pregnancy, and was rehospitalized. The company declined her claim for disability payments on the ground that pregnancy severed her eligibility under the plan. Had she been separated from work for any other reason for example, during a work stoppage the plan would have fully covered the embolism.

exclusion manifested in effects two and three to pinpoint an adverse impact on women. However one defines the profile of risks protected by General Electric, the determinative question must be whether the social policies and aims to be furthered by Title VII . . . fairly forbid an ultimate pattern of coverage that insures all risks except a commonplace one that is applicable to women but not to men.

. . .

. . . Unlike the hypothetical situations conjectured by the Court, contemporary disability programs are not creatures of a social or cultural vacuum devoid of stereotypes and signals concerning the pregnant woman employee. Indeed, no one seriously contends that General Electric or other companies actually conceptualized or developed their comprehensive insurance programs disability-by-disability in a strictly sex-neutral fashion. Instead, the company has devised a policy that, but for pregnancy, offers protection for all risks, even those that are "unique to" men or heavily male dominated. . . .

I would affirm the judgment of the Court of Appeals.

■ STEVENS, J., dissenting.

The word "discriminate" does not appear in the Equal Protection Clause. Since the plaintiffs' burden of proving a prima facie violation of that constitutional provision is significantly heavier than the burden of proving a prima facie violation of [Title VII], the constitutional holding in *Geduldig* does not control . . . this case. . . . We are . . . presented with a fresh, and rather simple, question of statutory construction: Does a contract between a company and its employees which treats the risk of absenteeism caused by pregnancy differently from any other kind of absence discriminate against certain individuals because of their sex?

Geduldig doesn't control here → that was an equal pro case

. . .

. . . [T]he rule at issue places the risk of absence caused by pregnancy in a class by itself.[5] By definition, such a rule discriminates on account of sex; for it is the capacity to become pregnant which primarily differentiates the female from the male. . . . I conclude that the language of the statute plainly requires the result which the Courts of Appeals have reached unanimously.

this is sex discrimination → tied to capacity to become pregnant that makes difference here

* * *

---

[5] It is not accurate to describe the program as dividing "potential recipients into two groups pregnant women and nonpregnant persons." Insurance programs, company policies, and employment contracts all deal with future risks rather than historic facts. The classification is between persons who face a risk of pregnancy and those who do not.

Nor is it accurate to state that under the plan "[t]here is no risk from which men are protected and women are not." If the word "risk" is used narrowly, men are protected against the risks associated with a prostate operation whereas women are not. If the word is used more broadly to describe the risk of uncompensated unemployment caused by physical disability, men receive total protection (subject to the 60% and 26-week limitations) against that risk whereas women receive only partial protection.

The Pregnancy Discrimination Act of 1978 amended Title VII as Congress's direct attempt to overrule the Supreme Court's decisions in Geduldig *and* Gilbert.

Pregnancy Discrimination Act

Pub. L. No. 95–555, 92 Stat. 2076 (1978) (codified as amended at 42 U.S.C. § 2000e).

An Act to amend title VII of the Civil Rights Act of 1964 to prohibit sex discrimination on the basis of pregnancy.

Be it enacted by the Senate and House of Representatives of the United States of America in Congress assembled, That section 701 of the Civil Rights Act of 1964, 42 U.S.C. 2000e, is amended by adding at the end thereof the following new subsection:

(k) The terms "because of sex" or "on the basis of sex" include, but are not limited to, because of or on the basis of pregnancy, childbirth, or related medical conditions; and women affected by pregnancy, childbirth, or related medical conditions shall be treated the same for all employment-related purposes, including receipt of benefits under fringe benefit programs, as other persons not so affected but similar in their ability or inability to work, and nothing in section 703(h) of this title, 42 U.S.C. 2000e–2, shall be interpreted to permit otherwise. This subsection shall not require an employer to pay for health insurance benefits for abortion, except where the life of the mother would be endangered if the fetus were carried to term, or except where medical complications have arisen from an abortion: Provided, That nothing herein shall preclude an employer from providing abortion benefits or otherwise affect bargaining agreements in regard to abortion.

Sec. 2. (a) Except as provided in subsection (b), the amendment made by this Act, 42 U.S.C. 2000e, shall be effective on the date of enactment.

(b) The provisions of the amendment made by the first section of this Act shall not apply to any fringe benefit program or fund, or insurance program which is in effect on the date of enactment of this Act until 180 days after enactment of this Act.

Sec. 3. Until the expiration of a period of one year from the date of enactment of this Act, 42 U.S.C. 2000e, or, if there is an applicable collective-bargaining agreement in effect on the date of enactment of this Act, until the termination of that agreement, no person who, on the date of enactment of this Act is providing either by direct payment or by making contributions to a fringe benefit fund or insurance program, benefits in violation with this Act shall, in order to come into compliance with this Act, reduce the benefits or the compensation provided any employee on the date of enactment of this Act, either directly or by failing to provide sufficient contributions to a fringe benefit fund or insurance program: Provided, That where the costs of such benefits on the date of enactment of this Act are apportioned between employers and employees, the payments or contributions required to comply with this Act may be made by employers and employees in the same proportion: And provided further, That nothing in this section shall prevent the readjustment of benefits or compensation for reasons unrelated to compliance with this Act.

Cleveland Board of Education v. LaFleur

414 U.S. 632 (1974).

■ STEWART, J.

. . .

I

Jo Carol LaFleur and Ann Elizabeth Nelson . . . are junior high school teachers employed by the Board of Education of Cleveland, Ohio. Pursuant to a rule first adopted in 1952, the school board requires every pregnant school teacher to take maternity leave without pay, beginning five months before the expected birth of her child. . . . A teacher on maternity leave is not allowed to return to work until the beginning of the next regular school semester which follows the date when her child attains the age of three months. . . . The teacher on maternity leave is not promised re-employment after the birth of the child; she is merely given priority in reassignment to a position for which she is qualified. Failure to comply with the mandatory maternity leave provisions is ground for dismissal.

Neither Mrs. LaFleur nor Mrs. Nelson wished to take an unpaid maternity leave; each wanted to continue teaching until the end of the school year. Because of the mandatory maternity leave rule, however, each was required to leave her job in March 1971. The two women then filed separate suits . . . , challenging the constitutionality of the maternity leave rule. . . .

. . .

This Court has long recognized that freedom of personal choice in matters of marriage and family life is one of the liberties protected by the Due Process Clause of the Fourteenth Amendment. As we noted in *Eisenstadt v. Baird*, 405 U.S. 438, 453 (1972), there is a right "to be free from unwarranted governmental intrusion into matters so fundamentally affecting a person as the decision whether to bear or beget a child."

By acting to penalize the pregnant teacher for deciding to bear a child, overly restrictive maternity leave regulations can constitute a heavy burden on the exercise of these protected freedoms. Because public school maternity leave rules directly affect "one of the basic civil rights of man," *Skinner v. Oklahoma*, 316 U.S. [535, 541 (1942)], the Due Process Clause of the Fourteenth Amendment requires that such rules must not needlessly, arbitrarily, or capriciously impinge upon this vital area of a teacher's constitutional liberty. The question before us in these cases is whether the interests advanced in support of the rules of the Cleveland . . . School Board[ ] can justify the particular procedures . . . adopted.

. . . [The school board] contend[s] that the firm cutoff dates are necessary to maintain continuity of classroom instruction, since advance knowledge of when a pregnant teacher must leave facilitates the finding and hiring of a qualified substitute. Secondly, the school board[ ] seek[s] to justify [its] maternity rules by arguing that at least some teachers become physically incapable of adequately performing certain of their duties during the latter part of pregnancy. By keeping the pregnant teacher out of the classroom during these final months, the maternity leave rules are said to protect the health of the teacher and her unborn child, while at the same time assuring that students have a physically capable instructor in the classroom at all times.[9]

It cannot be denied that continuity of instruction is a significant and legitimate educational goal. Regulations requiring pregnant teachers to provide early notice of their condition to school authorities undoubtedly facilitate administrative planning toward the important objective of continuity. But, as the Court of Appeals for the Second Circuit noted in *Green v. Waterford Board of Education*, 473 F.2d 629, 635 [(2d Cir. 1973)]:

> Where a pregnant teacher provides the Board with a date certain for commencement of leave . . . that value (continuity) is preserved; an arbitrary leave date set at the end of the fifth month is no more calculated to facilitate a planned and orderly transition between the teacher and a substitute than is a date fixed closer to confinement. Indeed, the latter . . . would afford the Board more, not less, time to procure a satisfactory long-term substitute. . . .

Thus, while the advance-notice provisions in the . . . rules are wholly rational and may well be necessary to serve the objective of continuity of instruction, the absolute requirements of termination at the end of the fourth or fifth month of pregnancy are not. Were continuity the only goal,

---

[9]   The records in these cases suggest that the maternity leave regulations may have originally been inspired by other, less weighty, considerations. For example, Dr. Mark C. Schinnerer, who served as Superintendent of Schools in Cleveland at the time the leave rule was adopted, testified . . . that the rule had been adopted in part to save pregnant teachers from embarrassment at the hands of giggling schoolchildren; the cutoff date at the end of the fourth month was chosen because this was when the teacher "began to show." Similarly, at least several members of the Chesterfield County School Board thought a mandatory leave rule was justified in order to insulate schoolchildren from the sight of conspicuously pregnant women. One member of the school board thought that it was "not good for the school system" for students to view pregnant teachers, "because some of the kids say, my teacher swallowed a water melon, things like that." The school board[ ] ha[s] not contended in this Court that these considerations can serve as a legitimate basis for a rule requiring pregnant women to leave work; we thus note the comments only to illustrate the possible role of outmoded taboos in the adoption of the rules.

cutoff dates much later during pregnancy would serve as well as or better than the challenged rules, providing that ample advance notice requirements were retained. Indeed, continuity would seem just as well attained if the teacher herself were allowed to choose the date upon which to commence her leave, at least so long as the decision were required to be made and notice given of it well in advance of the date selected.

. . .

We thus conclude that the arbitrary cutoff dates embodied in the mandatory leave rules before us have no rational relationship to the valid state interest of preserving continuity of instruction. As long as the teachers are required to give substantial advance notice of their condition, the choice of firm dates later in pregnancy would serve the boards' objectives just as well, while imposing a far lesser burden on the women's exercise of constitutionally protected freedom.

The question remains as to whether the cutoff dates at the beginning of the fifth and sixth months can be justified on the other ground advanced by the school boards—the necessity of keeping physically unfit teachers out of the classroom. There can be no doubt that such an objective is perfectly legitimate, both on educational and safety grounds. And, despite the plethora of conflicting medical testimony in these cases, we can assume, *arguendo*, that at least some teachers become physically disabled from effectively performing their duties during the latter stages of pregnancy.

The mandatory termination provisions . . . surely operate to insulate the classroom from the presence of potentially incapacitated pregnant teachers. But the question is whether the rules sweep too broadly. That question must be answered in the affirmative, for the provisions amount to a conclusive presumption that every pregnant teacher who reaches the fifth or sixth month of pregnancy is physically incapable of continuing. There is no individualized determination by the teacher's doctor—or the school board's—as to any particular teacher's ability to continue at her job. The rules contain an irrebuttable presumption of physical incompetency, and that presumption applies even when the medical evidence as to an individual woman's physical status might be wholly to the contrary.

. . .

. . . While the medical experts in these cases differed on many points, they unanimously agreed on one—the ability of any particular pregnant woman to continue at work past any fixed time in her pregnancy is very much an individual matter. Even assuming, arguendo, that there are some women who would be physically unable to work past the particular cutoff dates embodied in the challenged rules, it is evident that there are large numbers of teachers who are fully capable of continuing work for longer than the . . . regulations will allow. Thus, the conclusive

*substantive?
or
procedural?* ←

presumption embodied in these rules ... is neither "necessarily (nor) universally true," and is violative of the Due Process Clause.

The school boards have argued that the mandatory termination dates serve the interest of administrative convenience, since there are many instances of teacher pregnancy, and the rules obviate the necessity for case-by-case determinations. ...

While it might be easier for the school boards to conclusively presume that all pregnant women are unfit to teach past the fourth or fifth month or even the first month, of pregnancy, administrative convenience alone is insufficient to make valid what otherwise is a violation of due process of law. The Fourteenth Amendment requires the school boards to employ alternative administrative means, which do not so broadly infringe upon basic constitutional liberty, in support of their legitimate goals.

We conclude, therefore, that neither the necessity for continuity of instruction nor the state interest in keeping physically unfit teachers out of the classroom can justify the sweeping mandatory leave regulations that the Cleveland and Chesterfield County School Boards have adopted. While the regulations no doubt represent a good-faith attempt to achieve a laudable goal, they cannot pass muster under the Due Process Clause of the Fourteenth Amendment, because they employ irrebuttable presumptions that unduly penalize a female teacher for deciding to bear a child.

Post-birth restrictions

In addition to the mandatory termination provisions, ... the ... rules contain limitations upon a teacher's eligibility to return to work after giving birth. Again, the school boards offer two justifications for the return rules—continuity of instruction and the desire to be certain that the teacher is physically competent when she returns to work. As is the case with the leave provisions, the question is not whether the school board's goals are legitimate, but rather whether the particular means chosen to achieve those objectives unduly infringe upon the teacher's constitutional liberty.

. . .

The respondents ... do not seriously challenge either the medical requirements of the Cleveland rule or the policy of limiting eligibility to return to the next semester following birth. The provisions concerning a medical certificate or supplemental physical examination are narrowly drawn methods of protecting the school board's interest in teacher fitness; these requirements allow an individualized decision as to the teacher's condition, and thus avoid the pitfalls of the presumptions inherent in the leave rules. Similarly, the provision limiting eligibility to return to the semester following delivery is a precisely drawn means of serving the school board's interest in avoiding unnecessary changes in classroom personnel during any one school term.

The Cleveland rule, however, does not simply contain these reasonable medical and next-semester eligibility provisions. In addition, the school board requires the mother to wait until her child reaches the age of three months before the return rules begin to operate. The school board has offered no reasonable justification for this supplemental limitation, and we can perceive none. To the extent that the three-month provision reflects the school board's thinking that no mother is fit to return until that point in time, it suffers from the same constitutional deficiencies that plague the irrebuttable presumption in the termination rules. The presumption, moreover, is patently unnecessary, since the requirement of a physician's certificate or a medical examination fully protects the school's interests in this regard. And finally, the three-month provision simply has nothing to do with continuity of instruction, since the precise point at which the child will reach the relevant age will obviously occur at a different point throughout the school year for each teacher.

[handwritten margin note: no reasonable reason for 3 month limit]

Thus, we conclude that the . . . return rule, insofar as it embodies the three-month age provision, is wholly arbitrary and irrational, and hence violates the Due Process Clause of the Fourteenth Amendment. The age limitation serves no legitimate state interest, and unnecessarily penalizes the female teacher for asserting her right to bear children. . . .

We perceive no such constitutional infirmities in the Chesterfield County rule. In that school system, the teacher becomes eligible for re-employment upon submission of a medical certificate from her physician; return to work is guaranteed no later than the beginning of the next school year following the eligibility determination. The medical certificate is both a reasonable and narrow method of protecting the school board's interest in teacher fitness, while the possible deferring of return until the next school year serves the goal of preserving continuity of instruction. . . .

It is so ordered.

United Auto Workers v. Johnson Controls, Inc.
499 U.S. 187 (1991).

■ BLACKMUN, J.

In this case we are concerned with an employer's gender-based fetal-protection policy. May an employer exclude a fertile female employee from certain jobs because of its concern for the health of the fetus the woman might conceive?

[handwritten margin note: issue]

I

Respondent Johnson Controls, Inc., manufactures batteries. In the manufacturing process, the element lead is a primary ingredient. Occupational exposure to lead entails health risks, including the risk of harm to any fetus carried by a female employee.

Before the Civil Rights Act of 1964 became law, Johnson Controls did not employ any woman in a battery-manufacturing job. In June 1977, however, it announced its first official policy concerning its employment of women in lead-exposure work:

> [P]rotection of the health of the unborn child is the immediate and direct responsibility of the prospective parents. While the medical profession and the company can support them in the exercise of this responsibility, it cannot assume it for them without simultaneously infringing their rights as persons.

> . . . Since not all women who can become mothers wish to become mothers (or will become mothers), it would appear to be illegal discrimination to treat all who are capable of pregnancy as though they will become pregnant.

Consistent with that view, Johnson Controls "stopped short of excluding women capable of bearing children from lead exposure," but emphasized that a woman who expected to have a child should not choose a job in which she would have such exposure. The company also required a woman who wished to be considered for employment to sign a statement that she had been advised of the risk of having a child while she was exposed to lead. . . .

Five years later, in 1982, Johnson Controls shifted from a policy of warning to a policy of exclusion. . . . The company [announced] a broad exclusion of women from jobs that exposed them to lead:

> . . . [I]t is [Johnson Controls'] policy that women who are pregnant or who are capable of bearing children will not be placed into jobs involving lead exposure or which could expose them to lead through the exercise of job bidding, bumping, transfer or promotion rights.

The policy defined "women . . . capable of bearing children" as "[a]ll women except those whose inability to bear children is medically documented." It further stated that an unacceptable work station was one where, "over the past year," an employee had recorded a blood lead level of more than 30 micrograms per deciliter or the work site had yielded an air sample containing a lead level in excess of 30 micrograms per cubic meter.

II

In April 1984, petitioners filed in the United States District Court for the Eastern District of Wisconsin a class action challenging Johnson Controls' fetal-protection policy as sex discrimination that violated Title VII of the Civil Rights Act of 1964, as amended. Among the individual plaintiffs were petitioners Mary Craig, who had chosen to be sterilized in order to avoid losing her job, Elsie Nason, a 50-year-old divorcee, who had suffered a loss in compensation when she was transferred out of a job where she was exposed to lead, and Donald Penney, who had been denied a request for a leave of absence for the purpose of lowering his lead level because he intended to become a father. Upon stipulation of the parties, the District Court certified a class consisting of "all past, present and future production and maintenance employees" in United Auto Workers bargaining units at nine of Johnson Controls' plants "who have been and continue to be affected by [the employer's] Fetal Protection Policy . . . ."

The District Court granted summary judgment for defendant-respondent Johnson Controls. Applying a three-part business necessity defense derived from fetal-protection cases in the Courts of Appeals for the Fourth and Eleventh Circuits, the District Court concluded that while "there is a disagreement among the experts regarding the effect of lead on the fetus," . . . "[e]xpert opinion has been provided which holds that lead [. . .] affects the reproductive abilities of men and women" . . .; and that petitioners had "failed to establish that there is an acceptable alternative policy which would protect the fetus." The court stated that, in view of this disposition of the business necessity defense, it did not "have to undertake a bona fide occupational qualification's [sic] (BFOQ) analysis."

The Court of Appeals for the Seventh Circuit, sitting en banc, affirmed the summary judgment . . . . The majority held that the proper standard for evaluating the fetal-protection policy was the defense of business necessity; that Johnson Controls was entitled to summary judgment under that defense; and that even if the proper standard was a BFOQ, Johnson Controls still was entitled to summary judgment.

. . .

With its ruling, the Seventh Circuit became the first Court of Appeals to hold that a fetal-protection policy directed exclusively at women could qualify as a BFOQ. We granted certiorari to resolve [a circuit split] on this issue, and to address the important and difficult question whether an employer, seeking to protect potential fetuses, may discriminate against women just because of their ability to become pregnant.

III

The bias in Johnson Controls' policy is obvious. Fertile men, but not fertile women, are given a choice as to whether they wish to risk their reproductive health for a particular job. Section 703(a) of the Civil Rights Act of 1964 prohibits sex-based classifications in terms and conditions of employment, in hiring and discharging decisions, and in other employment decisions that adversely affect an employee's status. Respondent's fetal-protection policy explicitly discriminates against women on the basis of their sex. The policy excludes women with childbearing capacity from lead-exposed jobs and so creates a facial classification based on gender.

Nevertheless, the Court of Appeals assumed, as did the two appellate courts that already had confronted the issue, that sex-specific fetal-protection policies do not involve facial discrimination. . . . That assumption, however, was incorrect.

... And facial discrimination

First, Johnson Controls' policy classifies on the basis of gender and childbearing capacity, rather than fertility alone. Respondent does not seek to protect the unconceived children of all its employees. Despite evidence in the record about the debilitating effect of lead exposure on the male reproductive system, Johnson Controls is concerned only with the harms that may befall the unborn offspring of its female employees. . . . Johnson Controls' policy is facially discriminatory because it requires only a female employee to produce proof that she is not capable of reproducing.

looks @ gender rather than fertility

Our conclusion is bolstered by the Pregnancy Discrimination Act (PDA), in which Congress explicitly provided that, for purposes of Title VII, discrimination "on the basis of sex" includes discrimination "because of or on the basis of pregnancy, childbirth, or related medical conditions."[3] "The Pregnancy Discrimination Act has now made clear that, for all Title VII purposes, discrimination based on a woman's pregnancy is, on its face, discrimination because of her sex." In its use of the words "capable of bearing children" in the 1982 policy statement as the criterion for exclusion, Johnson Controls explicitly classifies on the basis of potential for pregnancy. Under the PDA, such a classification must be regarded, for Title VII purposes, in the same light as explicit sex discrimination. Respondent has chosen to treat all its female employees as potentially pregnant; that choice evinces discrimination on the basis of sex.

pregnancy discrim in employment = sex discrim

Moreover, the absence of a malevolent motive does not convert a facially discriminatory policy into a neutral policy with a discriminatory effect. Whether an employment practice involves disparate treatment through explicit facial discrimination does not depend on why the employer discriminates but rather on the explicit terms of the discrimination. . . . The beneficence of an employer's purpose does not undermine the conclusion that an explicit gender-based policy is sex discrimination under § 703(a) and thus may be defended only as a BFOQ.

. . .

In sum, Johnson Controls' policy "does not pass the simple test of whether the evidence shows 'treatment of a person in a manner which but for that person's sex would be different.'" We hold that Johnson Controls' fetal-protection policy is sex discrimination forbidden under

---

[3] The Act added subsection (k) to § 701 of the Civil Rights Act of 1964 and reads in pertinent part:

The terms "because of sex" or "on the basis of sex" [in Title VII] include, but are not limited to, because of or on the basis of pregnancy, childbirth, or related medical conditions; and women affected by pregnancy, childbirth, or related medical conditions shall be treated the same for all employment-related purposes . . . as other persons not so affected but similar in their ability or inability to work. . . .

Title VII unless respondent can establish that sex is a "bona fide occupational qualification."

IV   *Occupational qualification?*

Under § 703(e)(1) of Title VII, an employer may discriminate on the basis of "religion, sex, or national origin in those certain instances where religion, sex, or national origin is a bona fide occupational qualification reasonably necessary to the normal operation of that particular business or enterprise." We therefore turn to the question whether Johnson Controls' fetal-protection policy is one of those "certain instances" that come within the BFOQ exception.

discrim reasonably necessary?

. . .

The wording of the BFOQ defense contains several terms of restriction that indicate that the exception reaches only special situations. The statute thus limits the situations in which discrimination is permissible to "certain instances" where sex discrimination is "reasonably necessary" to the "normal operation" of the "particular" business. Each one of these terms—certain, normal, particular—prevents the use of general subjective standards and favors an objective, verifiable requirement. But the most telling term is "occupational"; this indicates that these objective, verifiable requirements must concern job-related skills and aptitudes.

. . .

Johnson Controls argues that its fetal-protection policy falls within the so-called safety exception to the BFOQ. Our cases have stressed that discrimination on the basis of sex because of safety concerns is allowed only in narrow circumstances. In *Dothard v. Rawlinson,* this Court indicated that danger to a woman herself does not justify discrimination. We there allowed the employer to hire only male guards in contact areas of maximum-security male penitentiaries only because more was at stake than the "individual woman's decision to weigh and accept the risks of employment." We found sex to be a BFOQ inasmuch as the employment of a female guard would create real risks of safety to others if violence broke out because the guard was a woman. Sex discrimination was tolerated because sex was related to the guard's ability to do the job—maintaining prison security. We also required in *Dothard* a high correlation between sex and ability to perform job functions and refused to allow employers to use sex as a proxy for strength although it might be a fairly accurate one.

Similarly, some courts have approved airlines' layoffs of pregnant flight attendants at different points during the first five months of pregnancy on the ground that the employer's policy was necessary to ensure the safety of passengers. In two of these cases, the courts pointedly indicated that fetal, as opposed to passenger, safety was best left to the mother.

We considered safety to third parties in *Western Air Lines, Inc. v. Criswell*, in the context of the [Age Discrimination in Employment Act ("ADEA")]. We focused upon "the nature of the flight engineer's tasks," and the "actual capabilities of persons over age 60" in relation to those tasks. Our safety concerns were not independent of the individual's ability to perform the assigned tasks, but rather involved the possibility that, because of age-connected debility, a flight engineer might not properly assist the pilot, and might thereby cause a safety emergency. Furthermore, although we considered the safety of third parties in *Dothard* and *Criswell*, those third parties were indispensable to the particular business at issue. In *Dothard*, the third parties were the inmates; in *Criswell*, the third parties were the passengers on the plane. We stressed that in order to qualify as a BFOQ, a job qualification must relate to the "essence," or to the "central mission of the employer's business."

Justice White ignores the "essence of the business" test and so concludes that "protecting fetal safety while carrying out the duties of battery manufacturing is as much a legitimate concern as is safety to third parties in guarding prisons (*Dothard*) or flying airplanes (*Criswell*)." By limiting his discussion to cost and safety concerns and rejecting the "essence of the business" test that our case law has established, he seeks to expand what is now the narrow BFOQ defense. Third-party safety considerations properly entered into the BFOQ analysis in *Dothard* and *Criswell* because they went to the core of the employee's job performance. Moreover, that performance involved the central purpose of the enterprise. Justice White attempts to transform this case into one of customer safety. The unconceived fetuses of Johnson Controls' female employees, however, are neither customers nor third parties whose safety is essential to the business of battery manufacturing. No one can disregard the possibility of injury to future children; the BFOQ, however, is not so broad that it transforms this deep social concern into an essential aspect of battery making.

Our case law, therefore, makes clear that the safety exception is limited to instances in which sex or pregnancy actually interferes with the employee's ability to perform the job. This approach is consistent with the language of the BFOQ provision itself, for it suggests that permissible distinctions based on sex must relate to ability to perform the duties of the job. Johnson Controls suggests, however, that we expand the exception to allow fetal-protection policies that mandate particular standards for pregnant or fertile women. We decline to do so. Such an expansion contradicts not only the language of the BFOQ and the narrowness of its exception, but also the plain language and history of the PDA.

The PDA's amendment to Title VII contains a BFOQ standard of its own: Unless pregnant employees differ from others "in their ability or inability to work," they must be "treated the same" as other employees "for all employment-related purposes." This language clearly sets forth Congress' remedy for discrimination on the basis of pregnancy and potential pregnancy. Women who are either pregnant or potentially pregnant must be treated like others "similar in their ability . . . to work." In other words, women as capable of doing their jobs as their male counterparts may not be forced to choose between having a child and having a job.

. . .

The legislative history confirms what the language of the PDA compels. Both the House and Senate Reports accompanying the legislation indicate that this statutory standard was chosen to protect female workers from being treated differently from other employees simply because of their capacity to bear children.

This history counsels against expanding the BFOQ to allow fetal-protection policies. The Senate Report . . . states that employers may not require a pregnant woman to stop working at any time during her pregnancy unless she is unable to do her work. Employment late in pregnancy often imposes risks on the unborn child, but Congress indicated that the employer may take into account only the woman's ability to get her job done. With the PDA, Congress made clear that the decision to become pregnant or to work while being either pregnant or capable of becoming pregnant was reserved for each individual woman to make for herself.

We conclude that the language of both the BFOQ provision and the PDA which amended it, as well as the legislative history and the case law, prohibit an employer from discriminating against a woman because of her capacity to become pregnant unless her reproductive potential prevents her from performing the duties of her job. We reiterate our holdings in *Criswell* and *Dothard* that an employer must direct its concerns about a woman's ability to perform her job safely and efficiently to those aspects of the woman's job-related activities that fall within the "essence" of the particular business.

V

We have no difficulty concluding that Johnson Controls cannot establish a BFOQ. Fertile women, as far as appears in the record, participate in the manufacture of batteries as efficiently as anyone else. Johnson Controls' professed moral and ethical concerns about the welfare of the next generation do not suffice to establish a BFOQ of female sterility. Decisions about the welfare of future children must be left to the parents who conceive, bear, support, and raise them rather than to the employers who hire those parents. . . .

Nor can concerns about the welfare of the next generation be considered a part of the "essence" of Johnson Controls' business. . . .

. . .

The judgment of the Court of Appeals is reversed. . . .

■ WHITE, J., concurring in part and concurring in the judgment.

The Court properly holds that Johnson Controls' fetal-protection policy overtly discriminates against women, and thus is prohibited by Title VII of the Civil Rights Act of 1964 unless it falls within the bona fide occupational qualification (BFOQ) exception, set forth at 42 U.S.C. § 2000e–2(e). The Court erroneously holds, however, that the BFOQ defense is so narrow that it could never justify a sex-specific fetal-protection policy. I nevertheless concur in the judgment of reversal because on the record before us summary judgment in favor of Johnson Controls was improperly entered by the District Court and affirmed by the Court of Appeals.

In evaluating the scope of the BFOQ defense, the proper starting point is the language of the statute. Title VII forbids discrimination on the basis of sex, except "in those certain instances where . . . sex . . . is a bona fide occupational qualification reasonably necessary to the normal operation of that particular business or enterprise." For the fetal-protection policy involved in this case to be a BFOQ, therefore, the policy must be "reasonably necessary" to the "normal operation" of making batteries, which is Johnson Controls' "particular business." Although that is a difficult standard to satisfy, nothing in the statute's language indicates that it could *never* support a sex-specific fetal-protection policy.[1]

Prior decisions construing the BFOQ defense confirm that the defense is broad enough to include considerations of cost and safety of the sort that could form the basis for an employer's adoption of a fetal-protection policy. In *Dothard v. Rawlinson*, 433 U.S. 321 (1977), the Court held that being male was a BFOQ for "contact" guard positions in Alabama's maximum-security male penitentiaries. The Court first took note of the actual conditions of the prison environment: "In a prison system where violence is the order of the day, where inmate access to guards is facilitated by dormitory living arrangements, where every institution is understaffed, and where a substantial portion of the inmate population is composed of sex offenders mixed at random with other prisoners, there are few visible deterrents to inmate assaults on women custodians." The Court also stressed that "[m]ore [was] at stake" than a risk to individual female employees: "The likelihood that inmates would assault a woman because she was a woman would pose a real threat not only to the victim of the assault but also to the basic control of the penitentiary and protection of its inmates and the other security

---

[1]   The Court's heavy reliance on the word "occupational" in the BFOQ statute . . . is unpersuasive. *Any* requirement for employment can be said to be an occupational qualification, since "occupational" merely means related to a job. *See* Webster's Third New International Dictionary 1560 (1976). Thus, Johnson Controls' requirement that employees engaged in battery manufacturing be either male or non-fertile clearly is an "occupational qualification." The issue, of course, is whether that qualification is "reasonably necessary to the normal operation" of Johnson Controls' business. It is telling that the Court offers no case support, either from this Court or the lower federal courts, for its interpretation of the word "occupational."

personnel." Under those circumstances, the Court observed that "it would be an oversimplification to characterize [the exclusion of women] as an exercise in 'romantic paternalism.' "

We revisited the BFOQ defense in *Western Air Lines, Inc. v. Criswell*, 472 U.S. 400 (1985), this time in the context of the Age Discrimination in Employment Act of 1967 (ADEA). There, we endorsed [a] two-part inquiry for evaluating a BFOQ defense .... First, the job qualification must not be "so peripheral to the central mission of the employer's business" that no discrimination could be "reasonably *necessary* to the normal operation of the particular business." Although safety is *not* such a peripheral concern, the inquiry "adjusts to the safety factor"—"[t]he greater the safety factor, measured by the likelihood of harm and the probable severity of that harm in case of an accident, the more stringent may be the job qualifications." Second, the employer must show either that all or substantially all persons excluded "would be unable to perform safely and efficiently the duties of the job involved," or that it is "impossible or highly impractical" to deal with them on an individual basis. We further observed that this inquiry properly takes into account an employer's interest in safety—"[w]hen an employer establishes that a job qualification has been carefully formulated to respond to documented concerns for public safety, it will not be overly burdensome to persuade a trier of fact that the qualification is 'reasonably necessary' to safe operation of the business."

Dothard and *Criswell* make clear that avoidance of substantial safety risks to third parties is *inherently* part of both an employee's ability to perform a job and an employer's "normal operation" of its business. Indeed, . . . an employer could establish a BFOQ defense by showing that "all or substantially all women would be unable to perform *safely and efficiently* the duties of the job involved." [There is] no support [for the Court's] conclusion that a fetal-protection policy could never be justified as a BFOQ. On the facts of this case, for example, protecting fetal safety while carrying out the duties of battery manufacturing is as much a legitimate concern as is safety to third parties in guarding prisons (*Dothard*) or flying airplanes (*Criswell*).

. . .

→ can't is wrong to foreclose this possibility altogether

NOTES

1.   *Deference to professional authority*. In *Muller, Johnson Controls*, and *LaFleur*, professional authority played an important role in determining whether women would be admitted to the workforce. In *Muller*, the Court deferred to the opinions of physicians (among others) claiming that excessive participation in paid work would have negative consequences for women (and indirectly, their children and the human race). In *Johnson Controls*, medical proof of infertility was required to hold a job in the company's battery-making operations. In *LaFleur*, the Court found that the provisions requiring pregnant women to obtain a physician's approval before returning

from maternity leave did not violate the Constitution. Should the opinions of medical personnel carry such weight? Do physicians serve a similar gatekeeping function for men in the workplace? Why or why not?

2.   *Gender roles.* In a footnote, the *LaFleur* Court conceded that the school board's rule requiring new mothers to wait until their infants were three months old before returning to work might have been "based upon another theory—that new mothers are too busy with their children within the first three months to allow a return to work." To what extent does such a view reflect particular gender roles for men and women? Are gendered assumptions about family roles at play in the policies challenged in *Johnson Controls* and *Muller*?

3.   *Motherhood and work.* To what extent did the policies challenged in these three cases evince a tension between motherhood and paid employment outside of the home? Do these tensions present themselves in other contexts in which women seek to exercise reproductive freedom?

4.   *Fatherhood and care.* In *Johnson Controls*, plaintiff Donald Penney was "denied a request for a leave of absence for the purpose of lowering his lead level because he intended to become a father." Would Penney's request have been denied if he were a woman preparing for motherhood? What gendered family roles did the challenged policy in *Johnson Controls* underwrite?

5.   *Pregnancy and minors.* In *LaFleur*, the Court noted that, at least originally, the school board's rules were animated by concerns regarding the visibility of the pregnant female body in a school setting. Though the school board ultimately justified its policies on concerns regarding the physical capabilities of pregnant women, were these newly proffered concerns pretextual?

6.   Johnson *and "reproductive awareness."* Recall the ACOG Guidelines for Perinatal Care, *supra* p. 121. In what ways is Johnson Controls' policy defining " 'women . . . capable of bearing children' as '[a]ll women except those whose inability to bear children is medically documented' " consistent with an ethos of "reproductive awareness"?

* * *

In recent years, advance health directives have become increasingly common. Advance health directives are written instructions regarding an individual's medical care preferences. In the event that an individual is incapacitated and is unable to make her own medical decisions, her family and doctors will consult the advance directive in determining future medical treatment. Advance directives were created in response to the increasing sophistication, prevalence, and rising costs of medical technology, which allowed medical professionals to prolong life, even in circumstances where the long-term prognosis was grim. Today, there is a range of advance health directives forms, including the living will, the durable power of attorney, and the health care proxy. In the United States, most states recognize advance health directives. However, as we will see, many provide exceptions where the advance directive pertains to a patient who is pregnant.

University Health Services, Inc. v. Piazzi

No. CV86–RCCV–464, 1986 WL 1167470 (Ga. Super. Ct. Aug. 4, 1986).

Order

On July 25, 1986, this case came before the Court for a hearing on University Health Service[s], Inc.'s petition for a declaratory judgment that life support systems should be maintained for Donna Piazzi in order to preserve the life of her unborn child. . . . On the basis of the evidence and arguments of counsel, the Court renders the following findings of fact and conclusions of law:

Findings of Fact

1.   University Health Services, Inc., which operates University Hospital, filed a petition for declaratory relief requesting an order and judgment of this court declaring the rights and relations of the parties and, in particular, an order that life support systems be maintained to give the unborn child of Donna Piazzi the opportunity to develop and be delivered.

2.   On June 27, 1986, Donna Piazzi was brought to University Hospital in an unconscious condition. Since her arrival at the hospital, Donna Piazzi's condition has deteriorated until the point that she is now brain dead.

3.   As of July 25, 1986, Mrs. Piazzi was approximately 20–1/2 weeks pregnant. The fetus is "quickened," meaning it is moving in the womb. The fetus is not now capable of surviving outside the mother's womb and, therefore, is not viable.

4.   There exists a reasonable possibility that with continued life support Donna Piazzi's body can remain functioning until the point that the fetus would be viable and could be delivered with a reasonable possibility of survival.

5.   If the fetus is delivered and survives there is a possibility it will suffer from abnormalities such as mental retardation, but it was and is impossible to determine the existence of such abnormalities prior to birth. There also exists a reasonable possibility that the child, if it survives, will be normal.

6.   Robert Piazzi is the lawful husband of Donna Piazzi. David Hadden, although not the husband of Donna Piazzi, claims to be the father of the fetus, and this claim was not disputed by Robert Piazzi.

7.   Robert Piazzi has requested that the hospital terminate life support for Donna Piazzi, a decision that would render death to the fetus a medical certainty at this time.

8.   David Hadden has requested that the hospital maintain life support systems for Donna Piazzi in order that the fetus be given the opportunity to develop and survive.

9.   The Division of Family and Children Services has taken the position that the decision in this case is a medical, not legal, decision; therefore, the Division argues that the court has no jurisdiction in the case and requests the hospital's petition be dismissed.

10. A guardian ad litem was appointed by the Court to represent the interest of the unborn child. The guardian ad litem requests that life support systems be maintained.

Conclusions of Law

This case poses two related questions of law: whether the Court has jurisdiction to decide a dispute involving the maintenance of life support systems for a non-viable fetus, and, if the Court does have jurisdiction, whether the Court should order that life support systems be maintained in order to give the fetus the opportunity to develop and be delivered.

Contrary to the contention of the Division of Family and Children Services in its motion to dismiss, this Court does have jurisdiction to decide whether the life of the unborn fetus should be protected. The Division of Family and Children Services contends that *Roe v. Wade*, 410 U.S. 113 (1973), deprives the Court of jurisdiction. Such is not the case. In *Roe v. Wade*, the United States Supreme Court held that the privacy interests of the mother are sufficiently strong to preclude the State from regulating the mother's right to an abortion of a non-viable fetus. The Supreme Court did not preclude a state court's jurisdiction to hear a dispute with regard to the life of an unborn fetus; moreover, the privacy rights of the mother are not a factor in this case because the mother is dead .... *Roe v. Wade* expressly recognizes that a state may assert interest in protecting potential life, and this court is a proper forum for determination of the fate of this fetus. Therefore, the motion to dismiss based on lack of jurisdiction is denied.

Turning to the merits of this case, the Court notes that it is confronted with a question of first impression. The law is settled that prior to viability the mother may decide to abort a fetus, and that after viability the state can both prohibit abortions and require that the mother undergo necessary treatment to protect the life of the fetus. These well-settled principles of law do not apply here because the mother is brain dead and the fetus is not yet viable. Because of the lack of authority directly on point, this Court must discern the policy of the State from the law as developed in analogous situations.

In *Jefferson v. Griffin Spalding County Hospital Authority*, the Georgia Supreme Court refused to stay the order of a lower court requiring a mother to undergo a caesarean section delivery even though such a procedure violated the mother's religious beliefs. Although *Jefferson v. Griffin Spalding County Hospital Authority* is factually distinguishable because the fetus in that case was viable, the court's ruling clearly showed the state's interest in, and preference for, the preservation of life or potential life.

In *In re L.H.R.*[,] 321 S.E.2d 716, 23 (1984), the Georgia Supreme Court found that "the State has an interest in the prolongation of life." The court held that the state has a duty to preserve the possibility of meaningful life and that a family member or guardian has no right to terminate life unless the patient is diagnosed terminally ill with no hope of recovery and in a chronic vegetative state with no reasonable possibility of attaining cognitive functions. The clear implication of *In re L.H.R.* is a public policy favoring the maintenance of every reasonably possible chance for life.

In addition to the case authority discussed above, the Georgia legislature has enacted several statutes which further support the policy of protecting life. The Georgia legislature has enacted a law permitting a competent adult to sign a living will providing for the termination of the person's life support systems under certain circumstances O.C.G.A. § 31–32–1, et seq. The legislature specifically restricted the statute so that the living will would have no effect if the adult were pregnant. O.C.G.A. §§ 31–32–3(b),–8(a)(1). Accordingly, even though the law permits a patient to choose whether or not life support systems will be maintained for that patient, the legislature has specifically provided that the patient cannot make the decision if it will affect an unborn child.

The legislature has also enacted a feticide statute, O.C.G.A. § 16–5–80, which makes the killing of a quickened fetus a crime. This statute evidences a state interest in a quickened fetus and a policy of protecting the potential life of that fetus.

Based on the foregoing cases and statutes, the Court concludes that public policy in Georgia requires the maintenance of life support systems for a brain dead mother so long as there exists a reasonable possibility that the fetus may develop and survive. The Court furthermore finds no case law or authority in Georgia which supports the right of anyone other than a mother to terminate a quickened fetus that is not yet viable. Finally, the United States Supreme Court decisions upholding the rights of women to abort non-viable fetuses, are inapplicable because those decisions are based on the mother's right of privacy, which right was extinguished upon the brain death of Donna Piazzi. Accordingly, the Court concludes that so long as there exists a reasonable possibility that a non-viable fetus can develop and survive with the maintenance life support systems for its brain dead mother, then those life support systems must be maintained.

. . .

IT IS HEREBY ORDERED, ADJUDGED, AND DECREED that the petition of University Health Services, Inc., for a declaratory judgment be granted and that life support systems for Donna Piazzi be maintained.

Molly C. Dyke, Note, *A Matter of Life and Death: Pregnancy Clauses in Living Will Statutes*
70 B.U. L. REV. 867 (1990).

Recently, some courts and legislatures have recognized that meaningful life may cease for persons who are utterly dependent upon medical technology. In such circumstances, it may make little sense to keep a patient "alive" when she is terminally ill. A majority of state legislatures have enacted living will statutes that permit a person to choose whether to forego or discontinue life-sustaining medical treatment. . . .

Conflicting interests arise, however, when a woman on a life-support system is pregnant. The patient's right to refuse treatment is juxtaposed with the fetus's alleged right to life. A number of states with living will statutes have determined that the right to refuse medical treatment, or the right to bodily integrity, carries less weight when the individual asserting the right is pregnant. These states have included pregnancy clauses in their living will statutes. The clauses automatically invalidate the living will during the course of the patient's pregnancy in order to protect the life of the fetus. . . .

Living wills authorize the withholding or withdrawal of life-support systems. Statutory authorization of living wills is a relatively recent way of allowing individuals to formalize their desire to refuse future medical care. Currently, thirty-eight states and the District of Columbia have enacted living will statutes which grant competent adults the right to terminate medical treatment if they should become terminally ill. The living will takes effect when the attending physician (some states require two physicians) determines that the individual's condition is terminal. Generally, the individual can revoke the declaration at any time.

The pregnancy clauses contained in many living will statutes reflect the state's concern for fetal life. States that have enacted pregnancy clauses have, in effect, determined that the state interest in protecting the fetus outweighs the patient's right to determine whether to forego medical treatment.

The typical pregnancy clause removes all force from the living will during the course of pregnancy. Only six states restrict the application of the pregnancy clause to cases in which the fetus is viable. A majority of the states, however, make no distinction based on viability. The Supreme Court's holding in *Roe v. Wade* that states may proscribe a woman's right to have an abortion only after viability, has led some to argue that pregnancy clauses which interfere with a woman's right to have an abortion in order to protect a nonviable fetus are unconstitutional.

NOTE

Pregnancy exceptions to end-of-life directives. Currently, all fifty states and the District of Columbia have enacted living will or advance directive acts in some form. Of these fifty-one jurisdictions, only fourteen (California, D.C., Hawaii, Maine, Massachusetts, Mississippi, New Mexico, New York, North Carolina, Oregon, Tennessee, Virginia, West Virginia, and Wyoming) are silent as to the effectiveness of such provisions if a patient is found to be pregnant. Six (Arizona, Connecticut, Florida, Maryland, New Jersey, and Vermont) leave the determination as to the effectiveness of a directive in a pregnancy scenario completely to the discretion of the patient. In contrast, eleven states (Alabama, Idaho, Indiana, Kansas, Michigan, Missouri, South Carolina, Texas, Utah, Washington, and Wisconsin) completely stay the effectiveness of a living will or directive in the instance of a pregnant woman. Thirteen (Alaska, Arkansas, Colorado, Delaware, Georgia, Illinois, Iowa, Louisiana, Montana, Nebraska, Nevada, Ohio, and Rhode Island) stay the living will or directive if a fetus is viable or live birth would be possible with continued life-sustaining treatment. Five (Kentucky, New Hampshire, North Dakota, Pennsylvania, and South Dakota) do so unless life-sustaining treatment would not have the effect of allowing the fetus to continue to live birth, such treatment would be physically harmful to the woman, or such action would prolong severe pain which cannot be alleviated with medication. The last two jurisdictions (Minnesota and Oklahoma) impose a rebuttable presumption that a female patient would not want life-sustaining treatment withdrawn were she found to be pregnant. *See* Kristeena L. Johnson, Note, *Forcing Life on the Dead: Why the Pregnancy Exemption Clause of the Kentucky Living Will Directive Act Is Unconstitutional*, 100 KY. L.J. 209, 210–11 & nn.7–12 (2012); Nikolas Youngsmith, Note, *The Muddled Milieu of Pregnancy Exceptions and Abortion Restrictions*, 49 COLUM. HUM. RTS. L. REV. 415, 423–26 & nn.27–30 (2018).

C. REGULATING PREGNANCY AT THE MARGINS

The recommendations of the American College of Obstetricians and Gynecologists seem to suggest that all women should be treated as "pre-pregnant," creating the possibility that every woman of childbearing age, rich or poor, is potentially subject to reproductive regulation. Yet the regulation of pregnancy and birth can be seen most clearly among women at the margins—women on public assistance, incarcerated women, and women who use drugs. The excerpts that follow make clear the state's force in regulating the reproductive lives of such women.

**Khiara M. Bridges, Reproducing Race:
An Ethnography of Pregnancy
as a Site of Racialization**

41 (2011).

The following excerpt discusses the author's research during the mid-2000s at "Alpha" Hospital, a large public hospital in Manhattan.

. . .

... [O]ver time, patterns began to emerge. I learned that bodies could be dichotomized into categories of "patient" and "employee." Of the "patient" bodies, some were "obstetric patients" and some were "gynecology patients"; some sought abortions and other infertility services; some were "medically high risk" and would be seen by doctors specializing in maternal-fetal medicine, and others were "low risk" and would be seen by midwives. ... It would be a long time before I learned all of the myriad ways in which patient bodies could be classified.

Similarly, it would take months before I understood the different employee bodies. I came to realize that in addition to the nurses and doctors, a host of professionals work in the obstetrics clinic: abortion counselors, patient advocates, geneticists, HIV counselors, nurse/health educators, nutritionists, social workers, and financial officers. I eventually learned that many people were located in the clinic because all pregnant patients at Alpha are required to meet with them upon beginning prenatal care.

. . .

At Alpha Hospital, a woman must first take an Alpha Hospital-administered urine test to confirm her pregnancy (without regard to whether she has already confirmed her pregnancy with an at-home test) before she is given her initial [Prenatal Care Assistance Program ("PCAP")] appointment. . . .

. . .

On the day of her PCAP appointment, a woman meets with a registered nurse/health educator, HIV counselor, nutritionist, social worker, and financial officer. . . .

. . .

Registered Nurse/Health Educator

During the PCAP patient's meeting with the nurse, the latter takes the woman's medical history, asking if she has ever had any of a number of medical problems (e.g., diabetes, hypertension, heart disease, gynecologic surgery, anesthetic complications, and uterine anomalies). The nurse also records information about any past pregnancies a woman has had—whether any were ectopic or multiple, whether she carried the pregnancy to term or had a spontaneous or induced abortion, and whether she suffered any complications during the pregnancy, labor, or delivery. The nurse documents whether the woman has had any history of mental illness, whether she has experienced trauma or violence in the past, and whether she consumes tobacco, alcohol, or any other "illicit/recreational drugs" (and, if so, in what amounts). . . . Additionally, the nurse draws blood and takes a urine sample from the patient in order to conduct a battery of tests, including blood type, Rh type, and hemoglobin electrophoresis.

The nurse also refers the patient to the Women, Infants, and Children Program for Pregnant, Breastfeeding, and Postpartum Women (WIC) by completing a medical referral form. . . .

The nurse's final task it to provide the patient with what is called "education" involving a number of matters that could conceivably affect the patient's pregnancy (e.g., sexual activity, exercise, travel, domestic violence, seatbelt usage, and the use of any medications, "including supplements, vitamins, herbs, or O[ver] T[he] C[ounter] drugs"). . . .

HIV Counselor

As per [New York State Department of Health] guidelines, all PCAP patients must receive counseling as to the "benefits of HIV testing as early in pregnancy as possible to reduce perinatal transmission" and the "meaning of the test results for both mother and newborn." Further, all patients receive an "explanation that all cases of HIV infection and names of all partners known to the provider will be reported to the NYSDOH for epidemiological and partner/spousal notification purposes only." Hence, all PCAP patients meet with a counselor who discharges this duty. . . .

. . .

Nutritionist

Each patient meets with a nutritionist who records any known food or non-food allergies, notes whether the patient has had any difficulty eating due to nausea or vomiting, and provides information to the patient about the nutritional needs of pregnant women. Furthermore, during the meeting with the nutritionist, patients are asked to record (in exacting detail) what they ate for breakfast, lunch, and dinner the day before. Afterwards, they are given a chart with an itemization of foods (e.g., milk, cheese, meat, eggs, fruit, cereal); then they are asked to circle the number of times per day (or alternatively, per week) foods are consumed. After the assessment, they are given information about the prenatal diet's relationship to a "healthy baby," dietary recommendations for pregnancy, and "tips" on how to increase or control weight gain, as needed. Should the nutritionist find the patient's diet unsatisfactory, she checks a box labeled "inadequate/unusual dietary habits" and asks the patient to make a verbal commitment to meet the nutritional needs of herself and her fetus.

The nutritionist's assessment of the patient's diet has a direct relationship to a woman's eligibility for WIC. Because, by statutory caveat, WIC food vouchers are only available to those pregnant women who are at "nutritional risk," it is in the interest of a patient that wants to receive WIC vouchers that the nutritionist find fault with her diet and, concurrently, enable her eligibility for WIC. . . .

WIC eligibility

. . .

Social Worker

Although oddly paired, the screening that the nutritionist performs is identified as a "Nursing Nutrition/Psychosocial Assessment." . . . If the nutritionist deems a social work referral appropriate for a patient, she escorts the patient to the social worker's office. The social worker then acquires more information from the patient . . . and if necessary, puts her in contact with additional professionals who can assist her.

In practice, . . . the expectation is that the social worker will see *all* of the PCAP patients who come through the obstetrics clinic. As explained to me by one of the social workers . . . Medicaid eligibility is sufficient to establish the woman as "at social risk," thereby making a social work referral appropriate. . . .

Accordingly, all PCAP patients meet with a social worker and are encouraged to divulge personal information. . . .

To a pregnant woman expecting solely routine prenatal care during her visit to the hospital, it may seem relatively counterintuitive that, prior to having a standard and routine medical examination by someone qualified to do so, she must meet with a social worker and detail intensely personal and intimate facts about her life.

. . .

One may find the social workers' interventions . . . unproblematic, even laudable as an indication of Alpha Hospital's commitment to all aspects of the health of their pregnant and unborn patients. . . . However, one must bear in mind that this "holistic" approach to prenatal care . . . is made compulsory for patients who do not have private insurance and made optional for their private insurance-holding counterparts. That is, while private insurance-holding expectant mothers can forego the requirement of a social work assessment by electing to receive prenatal care from a private hospital or physician that eschews such a requirement, the poor-qua-public-insurance-holders have no choice in the matter.

Medicaid Financial Officer

Patients are required to meet with the financial officer only if they do not have Medicaid when they present themselves to the hospital for prenatal care. . . .

. . .

. . . [T]he financial officer explains to the patient that she needs to submit documents establishing proof of pregnancy, identity, address, and income in order to qualify for Medicaid and, thus, have her medical expenses covered by the state. . . .

. . .

. . . [M]uch is extracted from the poor woman when she finds herself pregnant and in need of government assistance with her medicals bills.

The state essentially says to her "We will pay your bills in exchange for state surveillance of your pregnant body and the private arena in which it exists together with the possibility of a sustained, regulatory relationship." . . .

. . . [S]ome may find state intervention into women's private lives completely unproblematic and potentially desirable understanding it as a laudable effort to provide pregnant women with a wealth of information that they could use to make their pregnancies healthy events on multiple levels. . . .

However, subsequent to all meetings with patients, Alpha Hospital employees must make a written notation inside the patient's medical records of the topics discussed. Upon review of these notations, it is difficult to squelch skepticism toward hopeful articulations that Medicaid-mandated services are provided for the benefit of the woman alone. . . .

. . .

. . . That the state pays the medical bills accrued by pregnant women for their prenatal care is benign, in and of itself; however, the endeavor appears more disciplinary, surveillance-intensive, regulatory, and punitive when one considers what the state requires the woman to give in exchange: access to her private life.

All of this is to say: the pregnant women who decide to attempt prenatal care with state assistance find themselves, along with their male partners, most decidedly within the reach of the disciplinary, regulatory, and biopolitical state. . . .

. . .

In sum, the fact of pregnancy alone does not bring a woman within the jurisdiction of the state. Yet, pregnancy combined with the woman's attempted receipt of state aid not only does so, but becomes an opportunity for the state to create a legal subject whose private life is exposed to state supervision and surveillance. . . .

. . .

NOTES

1.   *Prenatal care as a gateway to other contacts with the state.* As Professor Bridges recounts, prenatal care can serve as a gateway for other contacts with the state's regulatory apparatus. The women at Alpha Hospital submitted to the interventions of various state agencies in order to become eligible for prenatal care under the Medicaid program. Critically, these interactions with the state do not end upon completion of a pregnancy. They may continue for some time, making the state a persistent presence in the lives of the woman and her child. *See* Khiara M. Bridges, *Privacy Rights and Public Families*, 34 HARV. J.L. & GENDER 113, 116–17 (2011).

2.   *Prenatal care and drug testing.* The failure to obtain prenatal care can trigger other forms of state surveillance. For example, in *State v. McKnight, infra* p. 184, a physician noted that a pregnant patient had failed to secure adequate prenatal care during her pregnancy. This observation prompted further prenatal screenings, including drug testing.

3.   *Public families and private families.* As Professor Martha Fineman has argued, the "private" family becomes "public" whenever the husband/father figure is absent, obliging the state to intervene into the family to fill the void created by his absence. MARTHA ALBERTSON FINEMAN, THE NEUTERED MOTHER, THE SEXUAL FAMILY, AND OTHER TWENTIETH CENTURY TRAGEDIES 177–78 (1995). Bridges's account of Alpha Hospital complicates this argument by showing that it is not necessarily the *physical* absence of a father/husband figure that transforms the "private" family into a "public" family with a thick relationship to the state. According to Bridges, a family can be rendered "public"—even when a father/husband is present—so long as the family relies on public services and other forms of state assistance. In this sense, privacy is associated with (relative) wealth—and the ability to be financially independent of the state.

1.   PROTECTING THE FETUS FROM DRUG USE

Johnson v. State

602 So. 2d 1288 (Fla. 1992).

■ HARDING, J.

. . .

The issue before the court is whether section 893.13(1)(c)1., Florida Statutes (1989), permits the criminal prosecution of a mother, who ingested a controlled substance prior to giving birth, for delivery of a controlled substance to the infant during the thirty to ninety seconds following the infant's birth, but before the umbilical cord is severed.

. . .

Johnson appeals from two convictions for delivering a controlled substance to her two minor children in violation of section 893.13(1)(c)1., Florida Statutes (1989).[1]

. . .

---

[1]   Section 893.13(1)(c)1., Florida Statutes (1989) provides as follows:
893.13 Prohibited acts; penalties.—

* * *

(c)   Except as authorized by this chapter, it is unlawful for any person 18 years of age or older to deliver any controlled substance to a person under the age of 18 years, or to use or hire a person under the age of 18 years as an agent or employee in the sale or delivery of such a substance, or to use such person to assist in avoiding detection or apprehension for a violation of this chapter. Any person who violates this provision with respect to:

1.   A controlled substance . . . is guilty of a felony of the first degree. . . .

The record in this case establishes the following facts. On October 3, 1987, Johnson delivered a son. The birth was normal with no complications. There was no evidence of fetal distress either within the womb or during the delivery. About one and one-half minutes elapsed from the time the son's head emerged from his mother's birth canal to the time he was placed on her stomach and the cord was clamped.

The obstetrician who delivered Johnson's son testified he presumed that the umbilical cord was functioning normally and that it was delivering blood to the baby after he emerged from the birth canal and before the cord was clamped. Johnson admitted to the baby's pediatrician that she used cocaine the night before she delivered. A basic toxicology test performed on Johnson and her son was positive for benzoylecgonine, a metabolite or "breakdown" product of cocaine.

In December 1988, Johnson, while pregnant with a daughter, suffered a crack overdose. Johnson told paramedics that she had taken $200 of crack cocaine earlier that evening and that she was concerned about the effects of the drug on her unborn child. Johnson was then taken to the hospital for observation.

Johnson was hospitalized again on January 23, 1989, when she was in labor. Johnson told Dr. Tompkins, an obstetrician, that she had used rock cocaine that morning while she was in labor. With the exception of finding meconium stain fluid in the amniotic sack, there were no other complications with the birth of Johnson's baby daughter. Approximately sixty-to-ninety seconds elapsed from the time the child's head emerged from her mother's birth canal until her umbilical cord was clamped.

. . .

[T]he primary question in this case is whether section 893.13(1)(c)1. was intended by the Legislature to apply to the birthing process. Before Johnson can be prosecuted under this statute, it must be clear that the Legislature intended for it to apply to the delivery of cocaine derivatives to a newborn during a sixty-to-ninety second interval, before severance of the umbilical cord. I can find no case where "delivery" of a drug was based on an involuntary act such as diffusion and blood flow. . . .

. . . My review of other pertinent legislative enactments . . . leads me to conclude in this case that the Legislature expressly chose to treat the problem of drug dependent mothers and newborns as a public health problem and that it considered but rejected imposing criminal sanctions, via section 893.13(1)(c)1.

In 1982, sections 415.501–514 were enacted to deal with the problem of child abuse and neglect. The Legislature determined that because of the impact that abuse or neglect has on a victimized child, siblings, family structure, and inevitably on all citizens of the state, the prevention of child abuse and neglect is a priority of this state. To further this end, the Legislature required that a comprehensive approach for the prevention of abuse and neglect of children be developed for the state.

The statute defined an "abused or neglected child" as a child whose physical or mental health or welfare was harmed, or threatened with harm, by the acts of omissions of the parent or other person responsible for the child's welfare. As originally defined, "harm" included physical or mental injury, sexual abuse, exploitation, abandonment, and neglect.

In 1987, a bill was proposed to broaden the definition of "harm" to include physical dependency of a newborn infant upon certain controlled drugs. However, there was a concern among legislators that this language might authorize criminal prosecutions of mothers who give birth to drug-dependent children. The bill was then amended to provide that no parent of a drug-dependent newborn shall be subject to criminal investigation solely on the basis of the infant's drug dependency. In the words of the sponsor of the House bill:

> This clearly states that the individual would not be subject to any investigation solely upon the basis of the infant's drug dependency.

> The prime purpose of this bill is to keep the families intact. It's not for the purpose of investigation.

. . .

From this legislative history, it is clear that the Legislature *considered* and *rejected* a specific statutory provision authorizing criminal penalties against mothers for delivering drug-affected children who received transfer of an illegal drug derivative metabolized by the mother's body, *in utero*. In light of this express legislative statement, I conclude that the Legislature never intended for the general drug delivery statute to authorize prosecutions of those mothers who take illegal drugs close enough in time to childbirth that a doctor could testify that a tiny amount passed from mother to child in the few seconds before the umbilical cord was cut. Criminal prosecution of mothers like Johnson will undermine Florida's express policy of "keeping families intact" and could destroy the family by incarcerating the child's mother when alternative measures could protect the child and stabilize the family.

. . .

There can be no doubt that drug abuse is one of the most serious problems confronting our society today. Of particular concern is the alarming rise in the number of babies born with cocaine in their systems as a result of cocaine use by pregnant women. . . .

It is well-established that the effects of cocaine use by a pregnant woman on her fetus and later on her newborn can be severe. On average, cocaine-exposed babies have lower birth weights, shorter body lengths at birth, and smaller head circumferences than normal infants. Cocaine use may also result in sudden infant death syndrome, neural-behavioral deficiencies as well as other medical problems and long-term developmental abnormalities. The basic problem of damaging the fetus by drug use during pregnancy should not be addressed piecemeal, however, by prosecuting users who deliver their babies close in time to use of drugs and ignoring those who simply use drugs during their pregnancy.

Florida could possibly have elected to make *in utero* transfers criminal. But it chose to deal with this problem in other ways. One way is to allow evidence of drug use by women as a ground for removal of the child to the custody of protective services, as was done in this case. Some states have responded to this crisis by charging women with child abuse and neglect.

However, prosecuting women for using drugs and "delivering" them to their newborns appears to be the least effective response to this crisis.[5] Rather than face the possibility of prosecution, pregnant women who are substance abusers may simply avoid prenatal or medical care for fear of being detected. Yet the newborns of these women are, as a group, the most fragile and sick, and most in need of hospital neonatal care. A decision to deliver these babies "at home" will have tragic and serious consequences. As the [American Medical Association] Board of Trustees Reports notes:

> [C]riminal penalties may exacerbate the harm done to fetal health by deterring pregnant substance abusers from obtaining help or care from either the health or public welfare professions, the very people who are best able to prevent future abuse. . . .

might deter care

Florida's Secretary of Health and Rehabilitative Services has also observed that potential prosecution under existing child abuse or drug use statutes already "makes many potential reporters reluctant to identify women as substance abusers."

. . . Prosecution of pregnant women for engaging in activities harmful to their fetuses or newborns may also unwittingly increase the incidence of abortion.

Such considerations have led the American Medical Association Board of Trustees to oppose criminal sanctions for harmful behavior by a pregnant woman toward her fetus and to advocate that pregnant substance abusers be provided with rehabilitative treatment appropriate to their specific psychological and physiological needs. Likewise, the American Public Health Association has adopted the view that the use of illegal drugs by pregnant women is a public health problem. It also recommends that no punitive measures be taken against pregnant

Punishment ≠ deterrent

---

[5] As the AMA Board of Trustees Report notes, possession of illicit drugs already results in criminal penalties and pregnant women who use illegal substances obviously are not deterred by existing sanctions. Thus the goal of deterrence is not served. To punish a person for substance abuse ignores the impaired capacity of these individuals to make rational decisions concerning their drug use. "In all but a few cases, taking a harmful substance such as cocaine is not meant to harm the fetus but to satisfy an acute psychological and physical need for that particular substance. If a pregnant woman suffers from a substance dependency, it is the physical impossibility of avoiding an impact on fetal health that causes severe damage to the fetus, not an intentional or malicious wish to cause harm." Punishment is simply not an effective way of curing a dependency or preventing future substance abuse. . . .

women who are users of illicit drugs when no other illegal acts, including drug-related offenses, have been committed.

In summary, I would hold that section 893.13(1)(c)1. does not encompass "delivery" of an illegal drug derivative from womb to placenta to umbilical cord to newborn after a child's birth. If that is the intent of the Legislature, then this statute should be redrafted to clearly address the basic problem of passing illegal substances from mother to child *in utero*, not just in the birthing process.

. . .

NOTES

1. *Statutory construction.* If the "primary question in this case is whether section 893.13(1)(c)1. was intended by the legislature to apply to the birthing process," why does the court consider the physiological aspects of placentas, umbilical cords, and blood flow during the birthing process? What aspects of this analysis are necessary for the interpretation of the statute on which the court ultimately based its decision?

2. *The use of judicial discretion.* It is important to recognize that the use of judicial power to influence pregnancy-related decisions may also extend into control over a woman's right to access abortion. Although expression and exercise of such power is usually off the record and therefore uncaptured by any opinions issued in the case, such incidents occasionally are exposed in a more public fashion. Consider the following sentencing colloquy between a judge and a pregnant defendant. In a letter sent to the court two weeks before the sentencing hearing, the defendant "revealed that she was pregnant . . . and expressed a desire to obtain an abortion." The defendant "begged" to either sentence her to probation, so that she might return to her home state to have an abortion, or allow her to "bond out," so that she might obtain an abortion in that jurisdiction.

> THE COURT: With regard to your child, though, would you be placing your child or keeping your child?
>
> . . .
>
> THE DEFENDANT: . . . This was an unwanted pregnancy.
>
> THE COURT: I understand that, but it happened.
>
> THE DEFENDANT: . . . I have talked to the doctors, and I have talked to the social workers, and if I am released, I will be trying to have a procedure done.
>
> THE COURT: But if that doesn't happen, if you are sentenced to an institution, or if you [are] placed on a term of probation, and it's too late for you to have an abortion, what I am asking you is this: What are your plans in that regard?
>
> . . .
>
> THE DEFENDANT: I would be giving it up for adoption.

THE COURT: All right. What I am going to do at this time, I'm sentencing you to the Ohio State Reformatory for Women at Marysville for six months, credit for time served, and costs are imposed in this case.

[DEFENSE COUNSEL]: Your Honor, I want to understand what you are suggesting.

THE COURT: *I'm saying that she is not having a second term abortion.*

In reviewing the judge's appeal from an administrative board's disciplinary recommendation, the Ohio Supreme Court noted that the judge appeared to be "offering a sentencing 'quid pro quo.' That is, if [defendant] agreed to have her baby, [the judge] would sentence her to probation; if, however, [defendant] insisted on pursuing an abortion, [the judge] would sentence her to a six-month prison term." *Cleveland Bar Association v. Cleary*, 754 N.E.2d 235, 239 (Ohio 2001).

3.   *The rhetoric of choice.* Although her conviction was ultimately reversed, Jennifer Johnson was originally sentenced to fifteen years' probation. The judge justified the sentence on the ground that "the defendant . . . made a choice to become pregnant and to allow those pregnancies to come to term" and because the "choice to use or not to use cocaine is just that—a choice." *State v. Johnson*, No. E89–890–CFA (Fla. Cir. Ct. July 13, 1989). Consider Lynn Paltrow's discussion of the role that "choice" rhetoric plays in cases like *Johnson*:

> The term "choice" is often applied to both reproductive decisionmaking and to drug use. Women have a right to "choose" to have an abortion and drug addicts make a "choice" to use drugs. In both areas, however, it is a term that obscures the lack of choice that many people have and the larger economic and institutional barriers that deny people, and disproportionately deny people of color, particularly low-income women of color, the ability to make consumer-like choices.
>
> . . . Since the late 1970's, approximately 200 women have been arrested based on their status as pregnant, drug-using women, thousands of others—and their families—are being affected by state laws that equate a pregnant woman's drug use with evidence of civil child neglect, and new calls for sterilization of drug using women are receiving significant media attention and private financial support. These laws, policies and practices combine the seemingly unrelated arguments that fetal rights should be recognized under the law and the argument that the war on drugs should be expanded to women's wombs.
>
> . . . [In *Johnson*,] the word "choice" as used by the judge contained numerous assumptions and judgments about Ms. Johnson. . . . He assumed that she had "chosen" not to use contraceptives, . . . and assumed that contraceptive services were easily accessible to her. The judge also assumed that she made a choice not to have an abortion and clearly believed that was the wrong decision. He

undoubtedly ignored that fact that Florida ... does not fund abortion services—thus making an abortion inaccessible even if her moral and ethical beliefs had allowed her to seek termination of the pregnancy. Hiding behind the language of "choice" the judge felt justified in punishing a low income African-American woman for having a child.

Lynn Paltrow, *The War on Drugs and the War on Abortion: Some Initial Thoughts on the Connections, Intersections and the Effects*, 28 S.U. L. REV. 201, 227–30 (2001) (footnotes omitted).

4.   *The fiction of choice.* Professor Rickie Solinger argues that the rhetoric of choice is framed from the perspective of economically privileged, middle-class Americans. This understanding of "choice," which pervades debates over reproductive rights and autonomy, often has little relevance in the lives of marginalized populations. As Solinger explains:

> When Americans began to refer to reproductive liberty by the simple name "choice," they obscured the fact that millions of women in the United States—and abroad—lived in conditions of poverty and oppression that precluded many of the kinds of choices that middle-class American women thought of as a matter of personal decision making. Then and now, many Americans have glossed over this: poor and/or culturally oppressed women in the United States and abroad may lack the money to "choose" abortion. They may live where abortion is inaccessible, illegal, or life-threatening. They may lack the resources to feed the children they have, much less a new baby. They may want to be mothers but lack the resources to escape stigma, punishment, or death for having a baby under the wrong conditions. They may lack the resources to avoid pregnancy from sexual violence. Can women in any of these circumstances be described as being in a position to exercise their "choice" in the way that middle-class Americans generally use that term?

RICKIE SOLINGER, BEGGARS AND CHOOSERS: HOW THE POLITICS OF CHOICE SHAPES ADOPTION, ABORTION, AND WELFARE IN THE UNITED STATES 21–22 (2002).

New Jersey v. Ikerd

850 A.2d 516 (N.J. Super. Ct. App. Div. 2004).

■ PAYNE, J.

We hold in this appeal that a pregnant, drug-addicted woman who has violated the conditions of her probation cannot be sentenced to prison for the avowed purpose of safeguarding the health of her fetus. To have done so is contrary to law and constituted an abuse of discretion.

The facts follow: On January 29, 1998, defendant Simmone Ikerd pled guilty to one count of third-degree theft by deception (welfare fraud). It was her first indictable conviction. Ikerd was sentenced on March 16 of that year to a five-year period of probation, conditioned upon entry into and completion of drug treatment and restitution . . . .

On February 14, 2003, Ikerd appeared before a different judge as the result of a reported violation of probation (VOP). At the time, she had paid only nineteen or twenty dollars in restitution and allegedly had been noncompliant with other probationary conditions. She remained drug-addicted, but she stated that she was undergoing drug treatment through a methadone clinic.

. . .

At the time of the February hearing, Ikerd was eleven weeks pregnant, a fact that she confirmed upon questioning by the judge. Although there had been some concern regarding the condition of her fetus, hospital tests had found that it remained viable. Ikerd sought continuation of her probation so that she could attempt to finish her drug treatment; the State requested incarceration in State prison because of the risk to both mother and fetus from drug abuse. The prosecutor argued: "There is nothing—no conditions of probation—that will help Miss [Ikerd] away from her addiction, help the life of her baby, and they will both be at risk."

The judge characterized Ikerd's situation as creating a "dilemma." She had acknowledged that she desired her present pregnancy. Yet . . . methadone maintenance was necessary to the preservation of that pregnancy, and, as the judge recognized, it was not available in county jail. Medical treatment in a hospital setting, the judge observed, would cause "[t]he taxpayers to pay out a fortune." However, if Ikerd's probation were continued, there was no assurance that she would seek the high-risk pre-natal care that had been recommended as medically necessary. The judge believed that [the] only place where Ikerd's addiction and the health of her fetus could be adequately addressed was the Edna Mahan Correctional Facility. He observed:

> I dare say, that there isn't a person in this group, who has a personal opinion, you know, put her in jail. Not because we want to punish her; but because we want to save the baby. Because we know, once we release her on the street, she's going to kill herself, she's going to kill the baby, if she doesn't kill herself. It's only because she's developed a tolerance that is beyond words. Because this bright lady, this educated lady, who is a public employee for years, is going to use drugs no matter what we do.
>
> So, we all agree. But how can I ignore the fact that she is pregnant?

. . .

[The judge] then directed defense counsel to discuss punishment with Ikerd, stating:

If you want to make my weekend, tell me that Miss Ikerd said, "Judge, sentence me to the minimum amount of time at Edna Mahan [State Prison], so I know that this child can be born." Please do that. Tell me that she wants to go to jail, so she can save the baby.

Ikerd responded through her counsel that she sought "mercy from the Court" and that she was "asking for the minimum time at Edna Mahan State Prison."

A factual basis for the VOP was established, consisting of Ikerd's acknowledgment of a urine test that was positive for opiates on March 30, 2001, failure to pay "fines" in the approximate amount of $3,000, and failure to cooperate with prenatal testing . . . . The court thereupon found a sufficient factual basis to permit acceptance of Ikerd's "plea of guilty."

An extended discussion then occurred regarding sentencing. . . . [To avoid the possibility that Ikerd would be paroled before the birth of her child], [t]he prosecutor suggested the imposition of a period of parole ineligibility, to which the court agreed, with thanks. The judge stated:

. . .

. . . I am going to sentence her to a three-year term, with an 18-month period of parole ineligibility. . . .

Now, [defense counsel] Fleming, if she loses the baby, if there is a problem, and she has the baby, I'll consider, since this is a Violation of Probation, any application that you wish to make at that time. . . . But the point is, I want to keep her off the street. I don't want her using drugs. The only way I can do it is by putting her in jail.

Ikerd appealed her sentence. . . .

. . .

II.

We recognize that punishment, including the imposition of a term of incarceration in the custody of the Department of Corrections, can legally be imposed on a defendant as the result of an inexcusable failure to comply with a condition of probation. However, the February hearing in Ikerd's case clearly demonstrated that the extent of the punishment imposed upon Ikerd resulted solely from her status as a pregnant addict. It bore no relationship to the offense that she initially committed, was excessively punitive, and accomplished no legitimate penal aim. It thus violated New Jersey law, and likely violated Ikerd's constitutional rights.

We commence our analysis with a discussion of New Jersey sentencing law and the bedrock principle that sentences should be oriented toward the offense, not the offender. Accordingly, when imposing a sentence on a VOP, the focus of the sentencing judge must be upon the underlying crime and the sentence appropriate to that crime when considered in conjunction with the aggravating factors found by the court at the time the initial sentence was imposed and any mitigating factors surviving the probationary violation.

. . .

In the present case, the VOP judge considered . . . not only the need to deter [Ikerd and others from future drug use], found initially, but also the previously uncited risk that Ikerd would commit another offense, as well as Ikerd's "disinclination to cooperate with probation in any respect." The precedent that we have discussed demonstrates that neither of the latter two factors should have been considered.[3] The judge was likewise wrong in seeking to address Ikerd's addiction in the fashion that he did. "By emphasizing the potential rehabilitative effect of incarceration, the court departed from the Code's mandate to forego defendant's capacity for rehabilitation and to concentrate on fitting the penalty to the crime."

. . .

Finally, we are satisfied that the judge's reasons for sentencing Ikerd to prison had no relationship whatsoever to the Criminal Code, as is required. No where [sic] was there any real consideration given to the impact of the probation violation that was demonstrated and to which Ikerd admitted guilt (essentially, the use of drugs in 2001) .... The transcript of the February hearing clearly discloses that the only reason that the judge sent Ikerd to prison was to protect the health of her fetus, a consideration wholly unrelated to Ikerd's underlying crime of welfare fraud. That the court was willing to reconsider its sentence if Ikerd's pregnancy terminated constitutes disturbing but compelling proof of this proposition. Ikerd was punished by being subjected to the extended prison term because she was pregnant and addicted, and for no other reason.

. . .

III.

Our decision to vacate the sentence imposed in this matter finds ample support in state law, and thus we do not discuss at length the constitutional implications of the court's action. However, we recognize that the VOP judge's sentencing rationale touches upon, at least, intertwined principles underlying federal and state safeguards against cruel and unusual punishment.

. . .

NOTES

1. *Proportionality, punishment, and constitutional law.* The *Ikerd* court based its decision on New Jersey's sentencing law, which states that punishment should reflect the nature of the offense, rather than the offender. Such a view is rooted in deeply-held criminal law principles regarding the

---

[3] Although not addressed by the VOP judge, Ikerd's drug use during pregnancy did not, at time of sentencing, by virtue of the pregnancy constitute a crime.

proportionality of punishment. These principles, in turn, are reflected in the Eighth Amendment's requirement that punishment be proportional to the crime committed. U.S. CONST. amend. VIII. Other than the Eighth Amendment and the proportionality principle, what other constitutional provisions and principles might the *Ikerd* court have invoked in reviewing this case?

Maybe cobal pro? ←

2. *The judicial role.* Some have argued that judges should only decide the issues before them and nothing more. *See, e.g.,* Cass R. Sunstein, *The Supreme Court, 1995 Term: Foreword: Leaving Things Undecided,* 110 HARV. L. REV. 4, 20 (1996) ("Judges should allow . . . room [for minimalism] because their judgments might be wrong, and even if right, their judgments may be counterproductive."). In *Ikerd*, the sentencing judge was charged with fashioning an appropriate punishment for Ikerd's violation of her probation requirements. Yet, in determining Ikerd's punishment, the sentencing judge seemed to go beyond this narrow charge. On what grounds did the sentencing judge feel justified in doing so? Was this justified? Could it ever be justified?

Whitner v. State
492 S.E.2d 777 (S.C. 1997).

■ TOAL, J.

. . .

FACTS

On April 20, 1992, Cornelia Whitner . . . pled guilty to criminal child neglect for causing her baby to be born with cocaine metabolites in its system by reason of Whitner's ingestion of crack cocaine during the third trimester of her pregnancy. The circuit court judge sentenced Whitner to eight years in prison. Whitner did not appeal her conviction.

Thereafter, Whitner filed a petition for Post Conviction Relief (PCR), pleading the circuit court's lack of subject matter jurisdiction to accept her guilty plea as well as ineffective assistance of counsel. Her claim of ineffective assistance of counsel was based upon her lawyer's failure to advise her the statute under which she was being prosecuted might not apply to prenatal drug use. The petition was granted on both grounds. The State appeals.

LAW/ANALYSIS

A. Subject Matter Jurisdiction

. . .

Under South Carolina law, a circuit court lacks subject matter jurisdiction to accept a guilty plea to a nonexistent offense. For the sentencing court to have had subject matter jurisdiction to accept Whitner's plea, criminal child neglect under section 20–7–50 would have to include an expectant mother's use of crack cocaine after the fetus is viable. All other issues are ancillary to this jurisdictional issue.

TIDE: this wasn't a law?

S.C. Code Ann. § 20–7–50 (1985) provides:

Any person having the legal custody of any *child* or helpless person, who shall, without lawful excuse, refuse or neglect to provide, as defined in § 20–7–490, the proper care and attention for such *child* or helpless person, so that the life, health or comfort of such *child* or helpless person is endangered or is likely to be endangered, shall be guilty of a misdemeanor and shall be punished within the discretion of the circuit court. (emphasis added).

. . .

Under the Children's Code, "child" means a "person under the age of eighteen." The question for this Court, therefore, is whether a viable fetus is a "person" for purposes of the Children's Code.   } issue

In interpreting a statute, this Court's primary function is to ascertain the intent of the legislature. Of course, where a statute is complete, plain, and unambiguous, legislative intent must be determined from the language of the statute itself. We should consider, however, not merely the language of the particular clause being construed, but the word and its meaning in conjunction with the purpose of the whole statute and the policy of the law. Finally, there is a basic presumption that the legislature has knowledge of previous legislation as well as of judicial decisions construing that legislation when later statutes are enacted concerning related subjects.

South Carolina law has long recognized that viable fetuses are persons holding certain legal rights and privileges. In 1960, this Court decided *Hall v. Murphy*. That case concerned the application of South Carolina's wrongful death statute to an infant who died four hours after her birth as a result of injuries sustained prenatally during viability. The Appellants argued that a viable fetus was not a person within the purview of the wrongful death statute, because, *inter alia,* a fetus is thought to have no separate being apart from the mother.

We found such a reason for exclusion from recovery "unsound, illogical and unjust," and concluded there was "no medical or other basis" for the "assumed identity" of mother and viable unborn child. In light of that conclusion, this Court unanimously held: "We have no difficulty in concluding that a fetus having reached that period of prenatal maturity where it is capable of independent life apart from its mother *is a person*."

Four years later, in *Fowler v. Woodward,* we interpreted *Hall* as supporting a finding that a viable fetus injured while still in the womb need not be born alive for another to maintain an action for the wrongful death of the fetus.

. . .

More recently, we held the word "person" as used in a *criminal* statute includes viable fetuses. *State v. Horne* concerned South Carolina's murder statute. The defendant in that case stabbed his wife, who was nine months' pregnant, in the neck, arms, and abdomen. Although doctors performed an emergency caesarean section to deliver the child, the child died while still in the womb. The defendant was convicted of voluntary manslaughter and appealed his conviction on the ground South Carolina did not recognize the crime of feticide.

This Court disagreed. In a unanimous decision, we held it would be "grossly inconsistent . . . to construe a viable fetus as a 'person' for the purposes of imposing civil liability while refusing to give it a similar classification in the criminal context." Accordingly, the Court recognized the crime of feticide with respect to viable fetuses.

Similarly, we do not see any rational basis for finding a viable fetus is not a "person" in the present context. Indeed, it would be absurd to recognize the viable fetus as a person for purposes of homicide laws and wrongful death statutes but not for purposes of statutes proscribing child abuse. Our holding in *Hall* that a viable fetus is a person rested primarily on the plain meaning of the word "person" in light of existing medical knowledge concerning fetal development. We do not believe that the plain and ordinary meaning of the word "person" has changed in any way that would now deny viable fetuses status as persons.

The policies enunciated in the Children's Code also support our plain meaning reading of "person." . . . The abuse or neglect of a child at *any* time during childhood can exact a profound toll on the child herself as well as on society as a whole. However, the consequences of abuse or neglect which takes place after birth often pale in comparison to those resulting from abuse suffered by the viable fetus before birth. This policy of prevention supports a reading of the word "person" to include viable fetuses. Furthermore, the scope of the Children's Code is quite broad. It applies "to *all* children who have need of services." When coupled with the comprehensive remedial purposes of the [Children's] Code, this language supports the inference that the legislature intended to include viable fetuses within the scope of the Code's protection.

Whitner advances several arguments against an interpretation of "person" as used in the Children's Code to include viable fetuses. We shall address each of Whitner's major arguments in turn.

Whitner's first argument concerns the number of bills introduced in the South Carolina General Assembly in the past five years addressing substance abuse by pregnant women. Some of these bills would have criminalized substance abuse by pregnant women; others would have addressed the issue through mandatory reporting, treatment, or intervention by social service agencies. Whitner suggests that the introduction of several bills touching the specific issue at hand evinces a belief by legislators that prior legislation had not addressed the issue. Whitner argues the introduction of the bills proves that section 20–7–50 was not intended to encompass abuse or neglect of a viable fetus.

We disagree with Whitner's conclusion about the significance of the proposed legislation. Generally, the legislature's subsequent acts "cast no light on the intent of the legislature which enacted the statute being construed." Rather, this Court will look first to the *language* of the statute to discern legislative intent, because the language itself is the best guide to legislative intent. Here, we see no reason to look beyond the statutory language. Additionally, our existing case law strongly supports our conclusion about the meaning of the statute's language.

Whitner also argues [that] . . . if we interpret "child" to include viable fetuses, *every* action by a pregnant woman that endangers or is likely to endanger a fetus, whether otherwise legal or illegal, would constitute unlawful neglect under the statute. For example, a woman might be prosecuted under section 20–7–50 for smoking or drinking during pregnancy. Whitner asserts these "absurd" results could not have been intended by the legislature and, therefore, the statute should not be construed to include viable fetuses.

We disagree for a number of reasons. First, the same arguments against the statute can be made whether or not the child has been born. After the birth of a child, a parent can be prosecuted under section 20–7–50 for an action that is likely to endanger the child without regard to whether the action is illegal in itself. For example, a parent who drinks excessively could, under certain circumstances, be guilty of child neglect or endangerment even though the underlying act—consuming alcoholic beverages—is itself legal. Obviously, the legislature did not think it "absurd" to allow prosecution of parents for such otherwise legal acts when the acts actually or potentially endanger the "life, health or comfort" of the parents' born children. We see no reason such a result should be rendered absurd by the mere fact the child at issue is a viable fetus.

Moreover, we need not address this potential parade of horribles advanced by Whitner. In *this* case, which is the only case we are called upon to decide here, certain facts are clear. Whitner admits to having ingested crack cocaine during the third trimester of her pregnancy, which caused her child to be born with cocaine in its system. Although the precise effects of maternal crack use during pregnancy are somewhat unclear, it is well documented and within the realm of public knowledge that such use can cause serious harm to the viable unborn child. There can be no question here Whitner endangered the life, health, and comfort of her child. We need not decide any cases other than the one before us.

We are well aware of the many decisions from other states' courts throughout the country holding maternal conduct before the birth of the child does not give rise to criminal prosecution under state child abuse/endangerment or drug distribution statutes. Many of these cases were prosecuted under statutes forbidding delivery or distribution of illicit substances and depended on statutory construction of the terms "delivery" and "distribution." Obviously, such cases are inapplicable to the present situation. The cases concerning child endangerment statutes or construing the terms "child" and "person" are also distinguishable, because the states in which these cases were decided have entirely different bodies of case law from South Carolina. . . .

Massachusetts, however, has a body of case law substantially similar to South Carolina's, yet [in *Commonwealth v. Pellegrini*] a Massachusetts trial court has held that a mother pregnant with a viable fetus is not criminally liable for transmission of cocaine to the fetus.[5] Specifically, Massachusetts law allows wrongful death actions on behalf of viable fetuses injured *in utero* who are not subsequently born alive. Similarly, Massachusetts law permits homicide prosecutions of third parties who kill viable fetuses. Because of the similarity of the case law in Massachusetts to ours, the *Pellegrini* decision merits examination.

In *Pellegrini,* the Massachusetts Superior Court found that state's distribution statute does not apply to the distribution of an illegal substance to a viable fetus. The statute at issue forbade distribution of cocaine to persons under the age of eighteen. Rather than construing the word "distribution," however, the superior court found that a viable fetus is not a "person under the age of eighteen" within the meaning of the statute. In so finding, the court had to distinguish [two prior cases, *Commonwealth v. Lawrence* and *Commonwealth v. Cass,*] both of which held viable fetuses are "persons" for purposes of criminal laws in Massachusetts.

The Massachusetts trial court found *Lawrence* and *Cass* "accord legal rights to the unborn only where the mother's or parents' interest in the potentiality of life, not the state's interest, are sought to be vindicated." In other words, a viable fetus should only be accorded the rights of a person for the sake of its mother or both its parents. Under this rationale, the viable fetus lacks rights of its own that deserve vindication. Whitner suggests we should interpret our decisions in *Hall, Fowler,* and *Horne* to accord rights to the viable fetus only when doing so protects the special parent-child relationship rather than any individual rights of the fetus or any State interest in potential life. We do not think *Hall, Fowler,* and *Horne* can be interpreted so narrowly.

. . . First, *Hall, Fowler,* and *Horne* were decided primarily on the basis of the meaning of "person" as understood in the light of existing medical knowledge, rather than based on any policy of protecting the relationship between mother and child. . . . Because the rationale underlying our body of law—protection of the viable fetus—is radically different from that underlying the law of Massachusetts, we decline to follow the decision of the Massachusetts Superior Court in *Pellegrini.*

The dissent contends that our holding in this case is inconsistent with *Doe v. Clark.* Specifically, it suggests that *Doe v. Clark,* in which we

---

[5] We note that *Pellegrini* was decided by a Massachusetts superior court. To date, no appellate court in Massachusetts has addressed this issue directly.

construed another provision of the Children's Code, stands for the proposition that the definition of "child" in S.C. Code Ann. § 20–7–50 (1985) means a "child in being and not a fetus." Contrary to the dissent's characterization of that case, *Doe* turned on the specific language in the consent provisions of the Adoption Act.

In *Doe*, Wylanda Clark, who was pregnant, signed a consent form allowing the Does to adopt the child upon its birth. After the child was born, Clark decided she wanted to keep the baby and attempted to argue that the consent she executed was void because it did not contain certain information required by statute. The trial judge held Clark's consent was valid. Clark appealed.

On appeal, we reversed the trial court. However, the basis for our reversal was not that "child" as defined in the Children's Code only includes born children, but that the adoption statutes contemplate that the natural mother's consent to the adoption must be given after the birth of the child to be adopted. Specifically, section 20–7–1700(A)(3) requires the consent form to contain the race, sex, and *date of birth* of the adoptee, as well as any names by which the adoptee has been known. Clearly, the date of birth requirement could not be fulfilled until after the birth of the child. Furthermore, section 20–7–1690, which specifies who must consent to an adoption, provides that consent is required of "the mother of a child *born* when the mother was not married." (emphasis added). Citing these sections as well as the Children's Code's definition of child, we concluded that a natural mother cannot consent to adoption until after the birth of her child. We did *not* hold that the term "child" excludes viable fetuses, nor do we think our holding in *Doe* can be read so broadly.

Finally, the dissent implies that we have ignored the rule of lenity requiring us to resolve any ambiguities in a criminal statute in favor of the defendant. The dissent argues that "[a]t most, the majority only suggests that the term 'child' as used in § 20–7–50 is ambiguous," and that the ambiguity "is created not by reference to our decisions under the Children's Code or by reference to the statutory language and applicable rules of statutory construction, but by reliance on decisions in two different fields of the law, civil wrongful death and common law feticide."

Plainly, the dissent misunderstands our opinion. First, we do not believe the statute is ambiguous and, therefore, the rule of lenity does not apply. Furthermore, our interpretation of the statute is based primarily on the plain meaning of the word "person" as contained *in the statute.* We need not go beyond that language. However, because our prior decisions . . . support our reading of the statute, we have discussed the rationale underlying those holdings. We conclude that both statutory language and case law compel the conclusion we reach. We see no ambiguity.

. . .

2. Right to Privacy

. . .

Whitner argues that section 20–7–50 burdens her right of privacy, a right long recognized by the United States Supreme Court. She cites *Cleveland Board of Education v. LaFleur* as standing for the proposition that the Constitution protects women from measures penalizing them for choosing to carry their pregnancies to term.

In *LaFleur*, two junior high school teachers challenged their school systems' maternity leave policies. The policies required "every pregnant school teacher to take maternity leave without pay, beginning [four or] five months before the expected birth of her child." A teacher on maternity leave could not return to work "until the beginning of the next regular school semester which follows the date when her child attains the age of three months." The two teachers, both of whom had become pregnant and were required against their wills to comply with the school systems' policies, argued that the policies were unconstitutional.

The United States Supreme Court agreed. It found that "[b]y acting to penalize the pregnant teacher for deciding to bear a child, overly restrictive maternity leave regulations can constitute a heavy burden on the exercise of these protected freedoms." . . .

Whitner argues that the alleged violation here is far more egregious than that in *LaFleur*. She first suggests that imprisonment is a far greater burden on her exercise of her freedom to carry the fetus to term than was the unpaid maternity leave in *LaFleur*. Although she is, of course, correct that imprisonment is more severe than unpaid maternity leave, Whitner misapprehends the fundamentally different nature of her own interests and those of the government in this case as compared to those at issue in *LaFleur*.

First, the State's interest in protecting the life and health of the viable fetus is not merely legitimate. It is compelling. The United States Supreme Court [has] recognized that the State possesses a profound interest in the potential life of the fetus, not only after the fetus is viable, but *throughout* the expectant mother's pregnancy.

. . . [Further, i]t strains belief for Whitner to argue that using crack cocaine during pregnancy is encompassed within the constitutionally recognized right of privacy. Use of crack cocaine is illegal, period. No one here argues that laws criminalizing the use of crack cocaine are themselves unconstitutional. If the State wishes to impose additional criminal penalties on pregnant women who engage in this already illegal conduct because of the effect the conduct has on the viable fetus, it may do so. We do not see how the fact of pregnancy elevates the use of crack cocaine to the lofty status of a fundamental right.

Moreover, as a practical matter, we do not see how our interpretation of section 20–7–50 imposes a burden on Whitner's right to carry her child to term. In *LaFleur*, the Supreme Court found that the mandatory maternity leave policies burdened women's rights to carry their pregnancies to term because the policies prevented pregnant teachers from exercising a freedom they would have enjoyed but for their pregnancies. In contrast, during her pregnancy after the fetus attained viability, Whitner enjoyed the same freedom to use cocaine that she enjoyed earlier in and predating her pregnancy—none whatsoever. Simply put, South Carolina's child abuse and endangerment statute as applied to this case does not restrict Whitner's freedom in any way that it was not already restricted. The State's imposition of an additional penalty when a pregnant woman with a viable fetus engages in the already proscribed behavior does not burden a woman's right to carry her pregnancy to term; rather, the additional penalty simply recognizes that a third party (the viable fetus or newborn child) is harmed by the behavior.

[handwritten margin note: never had to freedom to use cocaine]

. . .

CONCLUSION

For the foregoing reasons, the decision of the PCR Court is REVERSED.

■ FINNEY, C.J.[, dissenting]:

I respectfully dissent, and would affirm the grant of post-conviction relief to respondent Whitner.

The issue before the Court is whether a fetus is a "child" within the meaning of S.C. Code Ann. § 20–7–50 (1985), a statute which makes it a misdemeanor for a "person having legal custody of any child or helpless person" to unlawfully neglect that child or helpless person. Since this is a penal statute, it is strictly construed against the State and in favor of respondent.

The term child for purposes of § 20–7–50 is defined as a "person under the age of eighteen" unless a different meaning is required by the circumstances. We have already held [in *Doe v. Clark*] that this same definition found in another part of the Children's Code means a child in being and not a fetus. It would be incongruous at best to hold the definition of "child" in the civil context of *Doe* is more restrictive than it is in the criminal context we consider today.

[handwritten margin note: the code means child, not fetus]

More importantly, it is apparent from a reading of the entire statute that the word child in § 20–7–50 means a child in being and not a fetus. A plain reading of the entire child neglect statute demonstrates the intent to criminalize only acts directed at children, and not those which may harm fetuses. First, § 20–7–50 does not impose criminal liability on every person who neglects a child, but only on a person having legal custody of that child. The statutory requirement of legal custody is evidence of intent to extend the statute's reach only to children, because the concept of legal custody is simply inapplicable to a fetus. Second, § 20–7–50 refers to S.C. Code Ann. § 20–7–490 for the definition of neglect. Section 20–7–490 defines a neglected child as one harmed or

[handwritten margin note: legal custody]

[handwritten margin note: neglected child]

threatened with harm, and further defines harm. The vast majority of acts which constitute statutory harm under § 20–7–490 are acts which can only be directed against a child, and not towards a fetus.[2] The reliance upon § 20–7–490 in § 20–7–50 is further evidence that the term child as used in the child neglect statute does not encompass a fetus. Read in context, and in light of the statutory purpose of protecting persons of tender years, it is clear that "child" as used in § 20–7–50 means a child in being.

At most, the majority only suggests that the term "child" as used in § 20–7–50 is ambiguous. This suggestion of ambiguity is created not by reference to our decisions under the Children's Code or by reference to the statutory language and applicable rules of statutory construction, but by reliance on decisions in two different fields of the law, civil wrongful death and common law feticide. . . . Even if these wrongful death, common law, and Children's Code decisions are sufficient to render the term child in § 20–7–50 ambiguous, it is axiomatic that the ambiguity must be resolved in respondent's favor.

If ambiguous, should be resolved in D's favor

I would affirm.

■ MOORE, J.[, dissenting]:

I concur with the dissent in this case but write separately to express my concerns with today's decision.

In my view, the repeated failure of the legislature to pass proposed bills addressing the problem of drug use during pregnancy is evidence the child abuse and neglect statute is not intended to apply in this instance. This Court should not invade what is clearly the sole province of the legislative branch. At the very least, the legislature's failed attempts to enact a statute regulating a pregnant woman's conduct indicate the complexity of this issue. While the majority opinion is perhaps an argument for what the law *should* be, it is for the General Assembly, and not this Court, to make that determination by means of a clearly drawn statute. With today's decision, the majority not only ignores legislative intent but embarks on a course of judicial activism rejected by every other court to address the issue.

this is province of legislative branch

. . .

NOTES

1.   *Expanding fetal personhood.* The *Whitner* decision has furnished ample grounds for expanding the concept of fetal personhood in order to punish pregnant women who are viewed as engaging in risky behavior while pregnant. For example, a pregnant South Carolina woman was arrested for using alcohol while pregnant. *See* Melissa Manware, *Infant Born Drunk*, THE STATE (Columbia, S.C.), Sept. 24, 1998, at A1. Similarly, the parents of a

---

[2] Examples include condoning delinquency, using excessive corporal punishment, committing sexual offenses against the child, and depriving her of adequate food, clothing, shelter or education.

thirteen-year-old who gave birth to a stillborn child were arrested and charged with, *inter alia*, "unlawful conduct to a child" based on their alleged failure to properly care for the fetus. *See Parents, Girls Face Charges in Stillborn Birth*, SUN NEWS (S.C.), July 22, 1999, at C2. *Whitner* has also been used to support at least two other stillbirth prosecutions, including one in which the stillbirth resulted in a homicide charge, despite lack of conclusive causal evidence that drug use contributed to the stillbirth. *See State v. McKnight*, 576 S.E.2d 168 (S.C. 2003) (concluding that a fetus is a child for purposes of South Carolina's child endangerment statute) *infra* p. 184; *Ankrom v. State*, CR–09–1148, 2011 WL 3781258, at *5–8 (Ala. Crim. App. Aug. 26, 2011). Finally, *Whitner* was used as an authority in a case seeking a court order compelling a woman to have a cesarean section against her will. *See* NAT'L ADVOCATES FOR PREGNANT WOMEN, *WHITNER V. SOUTH CAROLINA* FACT SHEET (2006), http://www.advocatesforpregnantwomen.org/issues/ whitner.htm.

2.   *Institutional competency.* The dissenters in *Whitner* suggest that the majority has gone beyond the judiciary's institutional role of interpreting the language and meaning of statutes. Indeed, they argue that in interpreting the term "child" to include a fetus, the judiciary has expanded the scope of the statute, and in so doing, has assumed a legislative role. These questions of institutional competency frequently arise in the context of reproductive rights and justice. To what extent are the *Whitner* dissenters justified in making this charge? Did the *Whitner* majority exceed its judicial role and improperly engage in lawmaking?

3.   *The rule of lenity.* An established principle of statutory interpretation, the rule of lenity requires that ambiguities in a criminal statute relating to prohibitions and penalties be resolved in favor of the defendant, so long as doing so would not be contrary to legislative intent. The *Whitner* majority concluded that there were no statutory ambiguities, and thus, no reason to invoke the rule of lenity. Do you agree with this conclusion?

4.   *Fetal rights in the balance.* Some scholars have noted the connection between the prosecution of pregnant women who use drugs and arguments that the unborn have a right to be born with a sound mind and body. Does such a right exist? Should it? Consider the following excerpt from Professor Michelle Oberman:

> Recently, some courts have recognized a child's "legal right to begin life with a sound mind and body." This right does not reflect a state interest in protecting the fetus, but instead sidesteps the issue of the fetus' legal status by addressing the live born child. However, if this right is to have any beneficial impact on newborn health other than providing potential financial compensation for an injured newborn, a mechanism for protecting the well being of a developing fetus must be discerned. This is the heart of the legal dilemma. The only way to prevent harm to the fetus entails regulating maternal behavior, and such regulation infringes upon the mother's fundamental constitutional rights to liberty and privacy.

Michelle Oberman, *Sex, Drugs, Pregnancy, and the Law: Rethinking the Problems of Pregnant Women Who Use Drugs*, 43 HASTINGS L.J. 505, 529 (1992). Do you agree with Oberman? If so, to what extent does recognizing fetal rights impinge upon the autonomy of pregnant women?

State v. McKnight
576 S.E.2d 168 (S.C. 2003).

■ WALLER, J.

Appellant, Regina McKnight was convicted of homicide by child abuse; she was sentenced to twenty years, suspended upon service of twelve years. We affirm.

FACTS

On May 15, 1999, [Regina] McKnight gave birth to a stillborn five-pound baby girl. The baby's gestational age was estimated to be between 34–37 weeks old. An autopsy revealed the presence of benzoylecgonine, a substance which is metabolized by cocaine. The pathologist, Dr. Proctor, testified that the only way for the infant to have the substance present was through cocaine, and that the cocaine had to have come from the mother. Dr. Proctor testified that the baby died one to three days prior to delivery. Dr. Proctor determined the cause of death to be intra-uterine fetal demise with mild chorioamnionitis, funisitis and cocaine consumption. He ruled the death a homicide. McKnight was indicted for homicide by child abuse. A first trial held Jan. 8–12, 2002 resulted in a mistrial. At the second trial held May 14–16, 2001, the jury returned a guilty verdict. McKnight was sentenced to twenty years, suspended to service of twelve years.

. . .

1.   DIRECTED VERDICT

McKnight asserts the trial court erred in refusing to direct a verdict for her on the grounds that a) there was insufficient evidence of the cause of death, b) there was no evidence of criminal intent, and c) there was no evidence the baby was viable when McKnight ingested the cocaine. We disagree.

A defendant is entitled to a directed verdict when the State fails to produce evidence of the offense charged. In reviewing a motion for directed verdict, the trial judge is concerned with the existence of the evidence, not with its weight. On appeal from the denial of a directed verdict, an appellate court must view the evidence in the light most favorable to the State. If there is any direct evidence or substantial circumstantial evidence reasonably tending to prove the guilt of the accused, we must find the case was properly submitted to the jury.

a. Cause of Death

McKnight asserts the state failed to introduce sufficient evidence demonstrating that cocaine caused the stillbirth. We disagree.

Dr. Proctor, who performed the autopsy and who was qualified as an expert in criminal pathology, testified that the only way for the infant to have benzoylecgonine present was through cocaine, and that the cocaine had to have come from the mother. Dr. Proctor determined the cause of death to be intrauterine fetal demise with mild chorioamnionitis, funisitis and cocaine consumption. Dr. Proctor ruled the death a homicide.

Another pathologist, Dr. Woodward, . . . testified that the gestational age of the infant was between 35–37 weeks, and that it was viable. He then described how one determines the cause of death of a viable fetus, by looking for abnormalities, placental defects, infections, and the chemical constituency of the child. He explained the effect that cocaine would have on both an adult and a child. . . . He stated that he found areas of pinkish red degeneration of the blood vessels which were consistent with cocaine exposure. He testified that he did not see any other indications of the cause of death, and found a lack of evidence of other infections, lack of other abnormalities, otherwise normal development of the child . . . . He also opined that neither syphilis, nor placental abruption killed the infant. He concluded that, to a reasonable degree of medical certainty, the cause of death was intrauterine cocaine exposure. . . .

Although McKnight's expert, Dr. Conradi, would not testify that cocaine had caused the stillbirth, she did testify that cocaine had been in the baby at one point. She also ruled out the possibility of chorioamnionitis, funisitis or syphilis as the cause of death.

Viewing the expert testimony in the light most favorable to the state, we find sufficient evidence to withstand a directed verdict. . . .

b. Criminal Intent

McKnight next asserts she was entitled to a directed verdict as the state failed to prove she had the requisite criminal intent to commit homicide by child abuse. We disagree.

Under S.C. Code Ann. § 16–3–85(A), a person is guilty of homicide by child abuse if the person causes the death of a child under the age of eleven while committing child abuse or neglect, and the death occurs under circumstances manifesting an extreme indifference to human life. McKnight claims there is no evidence she acted with extreme indifference to human life as there was no evidence of how likely cocaine is to cause stillbirth, or that she knew the risk that her use of cocaine could result in the stillbirth of her child.

. . .

... [W]e have held that reckless disregard for the safety of others signifies an indifference to the consequences of one's acts. It denotes a conscious failure to exercise due care or ordinary care or a conscious indifference to the rights and safety of others or a reckless disregard thereof.

In *Whitner v. State*, this Court noted that although the precise effects of maternal crack use during pregnancy are somewhat unclear, it is well documented and within the realm of public knowledge that such use can cause serious harm to the viable unborn child.... Indeed, more than twelve years ago, Justice Toal wrote:

... It is common knowledge that the drug is highly addictive and potentially fatal....

Here, it is undisputed that McKnight took cocaine on numerous occasions while she was pregnant, that the urine sample taken immediately after she gave birth had very high concentrations of cocaine, and that the baby had benzoylecgonine in its system. The DSS investigator who interviewed McKnight shortly after the birth testified that McKnight admitted she knew she was pregnant and that she had been using cocaine when she could get it, primarily on weekends. Given the fact that it is public knowledge that usage of cocaine is potentially fatal, we find the fact that McKnight took cocaine knowing she was pregnant was sufficient evidence to submit to the jury on whether she acted with extreme indifference to her child's life....

c.   Viability

Finally, McKnight asserts she was entitled to a directed verdict as there was no evidence the baby was viable at the time she ingested cocaine....

2.   DIMISSAL [sic] OF HOMICIDE INDICTMENT

McKnight next asserts the trial court erred in refusing to dismiss the homicide by child abuse indictment on the grounds that a) the more specific criminal abortion statute governs, b) the homicide by child abuse statute does not apply to the facts of this case, and c) the legislature did not intend the statute to apply to fetuses. We disagree.

a.   Criminal Abortion Statute

Initially, McKnight asserts the criminal abortion statute, S.C. Code Ann. § 44–41–80 ... controls under the circumstances of this case. McKnight did not raise this contention to the trial court. Contrary to the assertions in her reply brief, although McKnight did argue that the statute was inapplicable to the circumstances of this case, at no time did she assert that the criminal abortion statute was the more specific, controlling statute. Accordingly, this issue is unpreserved....

b.   Application of Homicide by Abuse Statute in This Case

McKnight next asserts the Legislature did not intend the homicide by child abuse statute [to] apply to the stillbirth of a fetus. We disagree.

McKnight asserts the term child, as used in the statute, is most naturally read as including only children already born. In several cases this Court has specifically held that the Legislature's use of the term child includes a viable fetus. McKnight cites to portions of the statute defining harm as relating to corporal punishment and/or abandonment; she asserts this demonstrates that the statute was clearly intended to apply only to children already born. However, section 16–3–85(B) also defines harm as inflicting or allowing to be inflicted on the child physical injury [ ] and failing to supply the child with adequate health care[.] Either of these provisions may clearly be applied to an unborn child. . . . [W]e find the plain language of the statute does not preclude its application to the present case.

c.   Legislative History

McKnight lastly asserts that the legislative history of section 16–3–85 conclusively demonstrates that it does not apply to unborn children. We find this contention unpersuasive.

. . .

There is a presumption that the legislature has knowledge of previous legislation as well as of judicial decisions construing that legislation when later statutes are enacted concerning related subjects. The homicide by child abuse statute was amended in May 2000, some three years after this Court, in *Whitner*, had specifically held that the term child includes a viable fetus. The fact that the legislature was well aware of this Court's opinion in *Whitner*, yet failed to omit viable fetus from the statute's applicability, is persuasive evidence that the legislature did not intend to exempt fetuses from the statute's operation. . . .

3.   DUE PROCESS/NOTICE

McKnight next asserts [that] application of the homicide by child abuse statute to her violates due process; she contends she had no notice the statute could be applied to a woman whose fetus is stillborn. We disagree.

In numerous cases dating since 1960, we have held that a viable fetus is a person. In *Whitner*, we reiterated the fact that a viable fetus is a child within the meaning of the child abuse and endangerment statute. Most recently, we held that a viable fetus is both "person" and "child" as used in statutory aggravating circumstances which provide for death penalty eligibility.

A penal statute offends due process only when it fails to give fair notice of the conduct it proscribes. . . .

. . . Given the ample authority in this state finding a viable fetus to be a person, we find McKnight was on notice that her conduct in ingesting cocaine would be proscribed.

4.   RIGHT TO PRIVACY

McKnight next asserts application of the homicide by child abuse statute to women for conduct during pregnancy violates the constitutional rights of privacy and autonomy.

. . .

   . . . [In *Whitner*], this Court specifically rejected the claim that prosecution for abuse and neglect of a viable fetus due to the mother's ingestion of cocaine violates any fundamental right. . . . Accordingly, we find McKnight's right of privacy was not violated.

5.   EIGHTH AMENDMENT

McKnight next asserts the trial court erred in refusing to dismiss the indictment on Eighth Amendment grounds. We disagree.

   The cruel and unusual punishment clause requires the duration of a sentence not be grossly out of proportion with the severity of the crime. . . . [T]his Court reviews three factors in assessing proportionality: (1) the gravity of the offense compared to the harshness of the penalty; (2) sentences imposed on other criminals in the same jurisdiction; and (3) sentences for the same crime in other jurisdictions.

   Here, the gravity of the offense is severe; McKnight is charged with homicide. The sentence for homicide by child abuse . . . is twenty years to life, and McKnight received a twenty year sentence, suspended upon service of twelve years. The penalty is no harsher than that imposed upon any other individual charged with murder. . . .

   Finally, although other states have not defined a viable fetus as a child for purposes of criminal prosecution of a pregnant mother, other states impose severe sentences on those who are guilty of the murder or neglect of a child. . . . We find no Eighth Amendment violation.

6.   EQUAL PROTECTION

McKnight next asserts that application of the homicide by child abuse statute to her violates equal protection inasmuch as a person charged under the criminal abortion statute is subjected to a maximum of two years imprisonment, while one prosecuted under the homicide by child abuse statute is subjected to the possibility of life imprisonment.

   This issue is procedurally barred from review. While McKnight did file a pre-trial motion to dismiss based upon equal protection, and renewed that motion at trial, her arguments at trial were premised upon the statute's applicability only to women and its disparate impact upon women. At no time did she raise the contention she now raises concerning the disproportionality of the criminal abortion statute. Accordingly, this argument is unpreserved and we therefore decline to address it.

7.   SUPRESSION [sic] OF URINE SAMPLE

Finally, McKnight asserts the trial court erred in refusing to suppress the results of a urine sample taken at the hospital after the stillbirth, contending the sample was taken in violation of her [F]ourth [A]mendment rights. We disagree.

. . .

Here, an initial drug screen was ordered by the obstetrician, Dr. Niles, due to McKnight's lack of prenatal care. When the initial screen tested positive for cocaine, Mary McBride, a labor and delivery nurse, was instructed to obtain a forensic urine sample from McKnight. Before doing so, McBride read an Informed Consent to Drug Testing form to McKnight. McBride testified she read the form to McKnight, and advised her that it could be used for legal purposes; she did not, however, specifically advise McKnight that police would possibly arrest her. The form states that McKnight acknowledges she has testified [sic] positive for cocaine, and is being requested to give consent for a medical-legal (forensic) test . . . . McKnight signed the form indicating her consent. The second sample also tested positive for cocaine.

McKnight asserts the forensic/legal sample was taken in violation of her [F]ourth [A]mendment rights, contrary to the United States Supreme Court's opinion in *Ferguson v. City of Charleston*. We disagree. . . .

. . .

[In *Ferguson*, t]he Supreme Court held [the] performance of diagnostic tests to obtain evidence of the women's criminal conduct for law enforcement purposes was an unreasonable search if the patient had not consented to the procedure. . . .

. . .

. . . Conway Hospital's testing was not done surreptitiously, but was done with McKnight's knowledge and consent. . . .

We find the state sufficiently demonstrated . . . that McKnight consented to the search. . . .

Finally, even assuming *arguendo* that McKnight did not consent to the urine specimen, and that it was illegally obtained, we find any error in its admission was harmless. The DSS caseworker testified, without objection, that McKnight told her she knew she was pregnant and that she had been using crack cocaine when she could get it. Further, the defenses' own expert, Dr. Conradi, testified that cocaine was in the baby at some point. . . . Given this evidence, even assuming the urine sample was erroneously admitted, it could not have impacted the jury's verdict.

McKnight's conviction and sentence are affirmed.

AFFIRMED.

■ TOAL, C.J., and BURNETT, J., concur[red in the court's decision].

■ MOORE, J.[, dissenting]

I respectfully dissent. Once again, I must part company with the majority for condoning the prosecution of a pregnant woman under a statute that could not have been intended for such a purpose. Our abortion statute, S.C. Code Ann. § 44–41–80(b) (2002), carries a maximum punishment of two years or a $1,000 fine for the intentional killing of a viable fetus by its mother. In penalizing this conduct, the legislature recognized the unique situation of a feticide by the mother. I do not believe the legislature intended to allow the prosecution of a pregnant woman for homicide by child abuse under S.C. Code Ann. § 16–3–85(A)(1) (Supp. 2001) which provides a disproportionately greater punishment of twenty years to life.

. . . [I]t is for the legislature to determine whether to penalize a pregnant woman's abuse of her own body because of the potential harm to her fetus. It is not the business of this Court to expand the application of a criminal statute to conduct not clearly within its ambit. To the contrary, we are constrained to strictly construe penal statutes in the defendant's favor. . . .

NOTES

1.   *From* Whitner *to* McKnight. Interestingly, *State v. McKnight*, like *Whitner*, was decided by the South Carolina Supreme Court—with much of the same court personnel as *Whitner*. Are the rationales undergirding these decisions the same? If not, what has changed? What accounts for these changes?

2.   *The role of experts.* In McKnight's appeal of her conviction, the South Carolina Supreme Court noted that "it is well documented and within the realm of public knowledge that [crack] use can cause serious harm to the viable unborn child." This echoed the Florida Supreme Court's decision in *Johnson v. State, supra* p. 164, which observed that "[i]t is well-established that the effects of cocaine use by a pregnant woman on her fetus and later on her newborn can be severe," and, relying on several medical authorities, proceeded to detail the harm caused to cocaine-exposed babies. Critically, the research that was widely relied upon to stoke fears about the crack-baby epidemic has since been discredited. *See* Susan Okie, *The Epidemic That Wasn't*, N.Y. TIMES, Jan. 27, 2009, at D1. Despite the fact that this empirical evidence was later debunked, it undeniably shaped the legislative and judicial response to fetal exposure to maternal drug use. Interestingly, this is not the only venue in which we have seen such expertise used to shape policy responses. In *Muller*, for example, medical evidence concerning the alleged effects of labor-force participation on women's reproductive functions guided the Court's decision-making. Likewise, in *Johnson Controls*, physicians' opinions regarding women's exposure to chemicals informed workplace policies and the Court's review of those policies. *See supra* p. 145. Given this reliance, should we be concerned when these "expert opinions" are later debunked as "junk science"?

3.   *Viability of the fetus.* In appealing her conviction, McKnight presented an argument to the court regarding the viability of the fetus—that is, that the state had not established that the fetus was viable at the time she ingested cocaine. The court rejected this argument on the ground that it was

not presented at trial and could not be considered on appeal. Why do you think McKnight raised this claim on appeal, but neglected to do so at trial?

* * *

Regina McKnight subsequently brought a claim for post-conviction relief, arguing that her trial counsel had been ineffective. In an initial post-conviction relief proceeding, her claims were denied. She appealed the post-conviction relief court's decision to the South Carolina Supreme Court—the same court that previously had upheld her criminal conviction.

McKnight v. State

661 S.E.2d 354 (S.C. 2008).

■ TOAL, C.J.

. . .

FACTUAL/PROCEDURAL BACKGROUND

Petitioner Regina McKnight gave birth to a nearly full-term stillborn baby girl in May 1999. An autopsy revealed . . . the presence of benzoylecgonine (BZE), a by-product of cocaine. The autopsy report concluded that death occurred one to two days earlier "secondary to chorioamnionitis, funisitis and cocaine consumption" and labeled the baby's death a homicide. McKnight was subsequently charged with homicide by child abuse pursuant to S.C. Code Ann. § 16–3–85 (2003).

The public defender for Horry County represented McKnight in each of two trials for homicide by child abuse. The first trial . . . ended in a mistrial. At the second, . . . a jury convicted McKnight of homicide by child abuse. This Court affirmed the jury's verdict on direct appeal.

McKnight filed a petition for P[ost-]C[onviction] R[elief] [("PCR")] alleging ineffective assistance of counsel on numerous grounds. The PCR court held that counsel was not ineffective and denied McKnight relief as to each of her claims. This Court granted certiorari to review the PCR court's decision . . . .

STANDARD OF REVIEW

In order to establish a claim of ineffective assistance of counsel, a PCR applicant must prove: (1) counsel failed to render reasonably effective assistance under prevailing professional norms; and (2) counsel's deficient performance prejudiced the applicant's case. . . .

LAW/ANALYSIS

I. Failure to prepare an adequate defense

McKnight argues that counsel was ineffective in her preparation of McKnight's defense through expert testimony and cross-examination. We agree.

. . . At [the first] trial, the State tendered Dr. Edward Proctor, the pathologist who performed the autopsy, to opine as to the cause of death. Consistent with his autopsy report, Dr. Proctor testified that the chorioamnionitis and the funisitis in conjunction with cocaine caused the fetus to die. The doctor said that he based his finding of cocaine on the presence of the cocaine metabolite BZE in the fetus . . . . Although Dr. Proctor made general statements on the lethal effects of maternal cocaine consumption on fetuses, he also admitted it was possible for chorioamnionitis or funisitis alone to have caused the death of McKnight's fetus. Dr. Brett Woodard, . . . the State's second witness on the issue, testified that by ruling out other possible causes of death, including syphilis, thyroid problems, or other substance use, it was his opinion that McKnight's cocaine use alone caused the chorioamnionitis and funisitis in the fetus which resulted in fetal death. . . .

Counsel for McKnight called two expert witnesses to testify as to possible alternative causes of death. Dr. Steven Karch, a cardiac pathologist and expert in drug-related deaths, opined that although he could not determine the underlying cause of the chorioamnionitis and funisitis found in the fetus, these conditions alone were responsible for its death. Dr. Karch . . . additionally testified that it was impossible to rule out syphilis as a cause of death.

Dr. Karch also rebutted the State's experts' testimony on the harmful effects of cocaine and the notion of "crack babies" by explaining . . . that although cocaine is a potentially dangerous drug, it is not as dangerous as the medical community once believed. Dr. Karch went on to describe recent studies which had been unable to conclusively link cocaine to stillbirth, and discussed the flaws in earlier studies that had shown otherwise. . . .

Counsel for McKnight also called Dr. Sandra Conradi . . . to testify on the cause of death. Similar to Dr. Karch, Dr. Conradi rebutted the State's testimony on the harmful effects of cocaine by pointing to a published medical study showing fetal exposure to levels of cocaine even higher than McKnight's fetus was no more likely to give rise to an adverse pregnancy than exposure to other harmful conditions. Dr. Conradi also stated that she would have ruled the cause of death "undetermined," rather than a homicide. However, upon further questioning, the doctor eliminated all potential natural causes of death, testifying that it was "unlikely, but possible" that the chorioamnionitis and funisitis led to stillbirth and that her tests for syphilis were negative. On the other hand, Dr. Conradi testified that she could not rule out cocaine as a cause of death.

In its closing argument at the first trial, the State . . . repeatedly emphasiz[ed] that McKnight's own expert [Dr. Conradi] had eliminated all potential causes of death except exposure to cocaine. The jury deliberated for over seven hours without reaching a verdict and was sent home for the night. The next morning, upon learning that several jurors had researched medical issues related to the case on the internet overnight, the trial court declared a mistrial.

At the second trial, . . . the State again called Dr. Proctor and Dr. Woodard to testify to their belief that cocaine caused baby McKnight's stillbirth. Counsel for McKnight did not call Dr. Karch back to testify and only called Dr. Conradi, who again testified that although she could not precisely determine the cause of death, neither chorioamnionitis, funisitis, nor syphilis caused the fetus to die. Counsel did not examine Dr. Conradi on the published study favorable to McKnight's defense that the doctor had mentioned at the first trial. Furthermore, counsel did not call any other expert to rebut or discredit the medical studies cited by the State's experts as Dr. Karch had done previously, nor did counsel cross-examine the State's experts on the matter.

As in the closing arguments of the first trial, the State began by pointing out Dr. Conradi's failure to eliminate cocaine as a cause of fetal demise and declared that in conjunction with the testimony of Dr. Woodard, Dr. Conradi "really helped us out in figuring out the cause of death in this particular case" by eliminating all other relevant causes of death. The jury returned a guilty verdict in thirty minutes.

a.   Expert witnesses

McKnight argues that counsel was ineffective in calling an expert witness whose testimony undermined the defense and in failing to call an expert witness whose testimony supported the defense. We agree.

. . .

In the instant case, upon learning that an extended trip abroad would prevent Dr. Karch from testifying at the second trial, counsel stated at the PCR hearing that she believed at the time of trial that Dr. Conradi's testimony alone would be sufficient. . . . For this reason, counsel testified that she never thought to request a continuance or elicit Dr. Karch's testimony via videotape as the State had with Dr. Woodard. Counsel also admitted that due to her case load, she did not have time to find another expert who could, as Dr. Karch did, effectively rule out cocaine as the cause of death.

We find that it was unreasonable for counsel to produce a single expert witness at the second trial whose testimony had clearly benefitted the State's case in the first trial, and that her reasons for doing so do not qualify as a valid trial strategy. . . . Although Dr. Conradi ultimately concluded that the cause of death was indeterminable while Dr. Woodard concluded that cocaine caused fetal demise, counsel was certainly cognizant of the fact that the State's closing argument at the first trial used these experts' similar methods of analysis to its advantage. From this, counsel should have reasonably concluded that regardless of Dr. Conradi's ultimate conclusion, her testimony went to the heart of the State's case, and that substitute and/or additional testimony was needed.

Furthermore, Petitioner showed that even if Dr. Karch was unavailable, another expert was available to testify that cocaine did not cause the stillbirth. Dr. Kimberly Collins, ... an expert witness in numerous cases, testified at the PCR hearing that she agreed with Dr. Karch's view of the evidence and would have testified on behalf of McKnight at the second trial had she been contacted by counsel. ... Although we accept counsel's assertion that she was pressed for time in preparing for the second trial, in light of counsel's familiarity with the first trial and the relative ease with which counsel could have procured favorable expert testimony at the second trial, we conclude that counsel's decision to call Dr. Conradi alone to testify at the second trial was unreasonable.

We further find that there is a reasonable probability that this deficiency prejudiced McKnight. The methodology used by the *only* expert witness for the defense in determining the cause of fetal death mimicked that of the State's star expert and, in this way, Dr. Conradi's testimony primarily served to bolster the State's theory of the case. ...

In our opinion, counsel's two-fold error in calling an expert witness whose testimony was known to have previously been used to bolster the State's case, while neglecting to elicit favorable testimony from other experts when such testimony was known to exist and readily available, represents counsel's inadequate preparation for trial rather than a valid trial strategy. ... [W]e hold that the PCR court erred in determining that counsel was not ineffective on these grounds.

b.   Failure to investigate

McKnight also argues that counsel was ineffective in failing to investigate medical evidence contradicting the State's experts' testimony on the link between cocaine and stillbirth, and in further failing to investigate methods to challenge Dr. Woodard's conclusions ruling out natural causes of death. We agree.

A criminal defense attorney has the duty to conduct a reasonable investigation to discover all reasonably available mitigation evidence and all reasonably available evidence tending to rebut any aggravating evidence introduced by the State. In this case, counsel testified that her failure to rebut the medical research ... was due to her belief that Dr. Conradi's testimony alone was adequate and that she did not otherwise have time to interview additional experts. Counsel, however, did not attempt to rebut the medical studies she knew the State's experts would cite, nor did she examine Dr. Conradi on the study the doctor cited at the first trial that concluded cocaine is no more harmful to fetuses than other adverse factors during pregnancy. In light of counsel's thorough investigation and examination of witnesses at the first trial, counsel, in our view, was deficient in failing to conduct a reasonable investigation which resulted in a substantially weaker defense at the second trial.

Furthermore, in the absence of testimony from the defense on medical research to the contrary, there is a reasonable probability that the jury used the adverse and apparently outdated scientific studies propounded by the State's witnesses to find additional support for the State's experts' conclusions that cocaine caused the death of the fetus. Accordingly, we hold that the PCR court erred in determining that counsel was not ineffective on these grounds.

II.   Jury instructions

a.   Criminal intent under the Homicide
by Child Abuse statute

McKnight argues that counsel was ineffective in failing to object to the trial court's charge on the measure of criminal intent required for conviction under the Homicide by Child Abuse (HCA) statute. We agree.

... At trial, the trial court began by instructing the jury, in accordance with the HCA statute, that the State must prove beyond a reasonable doubt that "death occurred in circumstances showing extreme indifference to human life." The court continued with the general charge on criminal intent from the Circuit Court Bench Book. Specifically, the court explained:

> In any case in order to establish criminal liability criminal intent is required.... Criminal intent is a mental state, a conscious wrongdoing. It is up to you to determine what the defendant intended to do based on the circumstances shown to have existed. Criminal intent can arise from actions or failure to act. It may arise from negligence, recklessness or indifference to duty or consequences therefore. It is considered by law to be the equivalent of criminal intent.

Ten minutes after dismissing the jury for deliberations, the jury asked, "Can we have a definition of criminal intent? If we do have to confirm criminal intent?" The court then recharged the jury, again using the general charge on criminal intent. Counsel for McKnight did not object to either the primary charge or the supplemental charge.

McKnight argues that trial court improperly charged the jury that it could convict if it found negligence, recklessness, or mere indifference when a conviction for homicide by child abuse requires a finding of extreme indifference to human life. For purposes of the HCA statute, "extreme indifference" has been defined as "a mental state akin to intent characterized by a deliberate act culminating in death." In a similar vein, this Court has held that "reckless disregard for the safety of others" in reckless homicide cases is "a conscious failure to exercise due care or ordinary care or a conscious indifference to the rights and safety of others or a reckless disregard thereof." Accordingly, the specification of the *mens rea* in the HCA statute in conjunction with the general charge on criminal intent was proper and counsel was not deficient in failing to object to the primary charge.

However, the propriety of using the general criminal intent charge alone in the supplemental charge is not so clear. The foreman's note appears to question what specific level of criminal intent was required to find McKnight guilty, indicating that the jury was confused on this point. Although the references in the criminal intent charge to recklessness and indifference are consistent with this Court's HCA jurisprudence regarding the meaning of "extreme indifference to human life," we believe that the trial court's recitation of the general criminal intent charge alone in response to the jury's inquiry only served to further confuse the jury by referencing mere negligence and otherwise failing to clarify the particular mental state required for a conviction of homicide by child abuse. . . .

. . . [B]ecause the erroneous charge occurred in a supplemental instruction and likely attained a special significance in the minds of the jurors, there is a reasonable probability that counsel's deficient performance prejudiced McKnight. That the jury returned a guilty verdict five minutes after the trial court issued the supplemental charge indicates that counsel's failure to object to the erroneous charge was prejudicial in fact. . . .

. . .

III. Equal protection

McKnight argues that counsel was ineffective for failing to move to dismiss the charges on the grounds that the disparity between the sentences for criminal abortion and homicide by child abuse violates the Equal Protection Clause. We disagree.

The criminal abortion statute provisions relevant to this case provide that any woman who intentionally procures an illegal abortion will be guilty of a misdemeanor and upon conviction, may be imprisoned for no more than two years. The relevant HCA statute provisions state that a person who causes the death of a child under age eleven while committing child abuse or neglect under circumstances manifesting extreme indifference to human life may be imprisoned for life, and for no less than a term of twenty years.

The Equal Protection Clause provides that no State shall deny to any person within its jurisdiction the equal protection of the laws. A classification does not violate the Equal Protection Clause if (1) "similarly situated" members in a class are treated alike; (2) the classification rests on some reasonable basis; and (3) the classification bears a reasonable relation to a legitimate legislative purpose.

. . . [A] legislative history of the statutes is instructive in analyzing whether there is a legitimate legislative purpose for the different sentences. In 1974, the General Assembly amended the criminal abortion statute to its current form in accordance with the United States Supreme Court's decision in *Roe v. Wade*. Our jurisprudence on the applicability of South Carolina criminal law to viable fetuses, on the other hand, did not substantively develop until the 1980's and 1990's, and in 1992, nearly twenty years after *Roe v. Wade*, the General Assembly enacted the HCA statute. This time differential between the enactment of the two statutes, as well as the placement of the HCA statute in the Crimes and Offenses section of the Code in contrast to the placement of the criminal abortion statute in the Health section of the Code, reflects the General Assembly's legitimate interest in the protection of unborn children, separate and distinct from its interest in the health of expectant mothers and their own unborn children.

For these same reasons, we believe that any sentencing differences in the two statutes reflect a valid legislative determination for the need to target a specific societal problem. Accordingly, we hold that the PCR court correctly determined that counsel was not ineffective in failing to argue that the HCA statute violated the Equal Protection Clause.

IV. Autopsy report

McKnight argues that counsel was ineffective for failing to introduce the autopsy report into evidence. We agree.

After introducing the report at the first trial, counsel's only reason for neglecting to introduce the report at the second trial is that she "just forgot." The PCR court found that this error did not prejudice McKnight because the author of the autopsy report testified to its contents, and therefore, the report itself would have merely been cumulative evidence.

We find that the autopsy was a powerful piece of documentary evidence that was crucial to McKnight's defense because it contradicted the State's theory of the case. The State's own expert authored the autopsy report which listed three causes of death: chorioamnionitis, funisitis, and cocaine. After McKnight's own expert could not rule out cocaine as a cause of death, the autopsy report itself would have served as hard evidence to (1) undermine the conclusion of Dr. Woodard, the only expert who opined that cocaine alone caused the fetal demise, and (2) remind jurors of the inconsistencies in the State's experts' testimony.

For these reasons, we hold that counsel's failure to introduce the autopsy report into evidence was deficient, and that this deficiency, in the absence of otherwise helpful testimony from her own expert, was prejudicial to McKnight. Accordingly, the PCR court erred in determining counsel was not ineffective on these grounds.

V.   Intent

McKnight argues that counsel was ineffective in failing to argue that there was no evidence on the record suggesting that McKnight knew that using cocaine risked harming her fetus's life. We disagree.

. . .

. . . This Court correctly acknowledged in *Whitner* that men of common understanding are familiar with the harmful effects of cocaine. Therefore, a reasonable jury would certainly not be persuaded by the argument that McKnight did not know that her cocaine use posed risks to her unborn child. Accordingly, even if counsel erred in failing to argue that McKnight did not know using cocaine posed risks to her unborn child, this deficient performance was not prejudicial. Therefore, we hold that the PCR court did not err in determining that counsel was not ineffective on these grounds.

. . .

CONCLUSION

For the foregoing reasons, we reverse the PCR court's denial of relief.

NOTES

1.   *The role of amici*. Regina McKnight was convicted of homicide by child abuse as the result of her stillbirth, and was sentenced to twenty years' imprisonment, suspended to twelve years' imprisonment with no chance for parole. The medical community opposed her prosecution and conviction, with organizations such as the South Carolina Medical Association, the South Carolina Nurses Association, the South Carolina Association of Alcoholism and Drug Abuse Counselors, and the South Carolina Coalition for Healthy Families submitting an amicus brief challenging the state's evidence regarding the cause of the stillbirth and arguing that women do not lose their constitutional rights upon becoming pregnant. *See* Brief for S.C. Med. Ass'n et al. as Amici Curiae Supporting Appellant, *State v. McKnight*, 576 S.E.2d 168 (2003) (No. 2003–cp–26–5752), 2007 WL 4966966. When McKnight petitioned the U.S. Supreme Court for certiorari, a broad array of national medical and public health organizations joined the South Carolina organizations as amici to argue that inconclusive medical and scientific research did not support a causal link between McKnight's cocaine use and the stillbirth. *See* Brief of Am. Pub. Health Ass'n et al. as Amici Curiae Supporting Petitioner at 15, *McKnight v. South Carolina*, 540 U.S. 819 (2003) (No. 02–1741), 2003 WL 22428153. Amici also challenged the *McKnight* decision on the basis that it would deter pregnant women from seeking prenatal care and undermine standards of care for treating women who experience stillbirth. *See id*. At 16.

2.   *Using extant criminal laws and procedures to address prenatal drug use*. A *Journal of the American Medical Association* (JAMA) study found that criminal prosecution of pregnant women is often pursued via existing criminal statutes—specifically, statutes prohibiting: 1) child endangerment/ abuse; 2) illegal drug delivery to a minor; and 3) fetal murder/manslaughter. Lisa H. Harris & Lynn Paltrow, *The Status of Pregnant Women and Fetuses in U.S. Criminal Law*, 289 J. AM. MED. ASS'N 1697, 1697–99 (2003). From 2014 to 2016, Tennessee became the first state to enact a law that uniquely criminalized drug abuse among pregnant women. *See* Act of Apr. 29, 2014, 2014 Tenn. Pub. Acts ch. 820 ("[N]othing in this section shall preclude prosecution of a woman for assault . . . for the illegal use of a narcotic drug, . . . while pregnant, if her child is born addicted to or harmed by the narcotic drug. . . .") (expired 2016). Nevertheless, each individual prosecution under extant criminal statutes presents an opportunity for courts to determine if

these statutes can—and should—be interpreted to cover this conduct. For example, in *Ferguson v. City of Charleston*, 532 U.S. 67, 68 (2001), the U.S. Supreme Court determined that a state hospital regulation requiring the drug testing of pregnant women and the reporting of positive test results to law enforcement violated the Fourth Amendment as an unreasonable search. The *Ferguson* Court narrowed its holding to the issue of evidence collection for the purpose of prosecuting pregnant women. The Court neglected to answer the greater question of whether the prosecution of pregnant women for behavior during their pregnancies is permissible. *See* IF/WHEN/HOW: LAWYERING FOR REPRODUCTIVE JUSTICE, REGULATION OF PREGNANCY: ISSUE BRIEF 7–8 (2017).

3.   *Southern (dis)comfort?* Prosecution of pregnant women and forced interventions in pregnancy are not randomly distributed by state. Jeanne Flavin and Lynn Paltrow combed legal records, interviewed knowledgeable insiders, and searched newspaper databases to identify cases where women were punished for engaging in certain conduct while pregnant, or where women were confronted with forced medical procedures in order to protect the fetus. Of the 413 cases that they found, 93 cases or twenty-two percent of the total, occurred in South Carolina, where *McKnight* and *Whitner* took place. More strikingly, fifty-six percent of the cases took place in states that were once part of the Confederacy. Perhaps unsurprisingly, these regional trends also had a decidedly racialized cast. Of the cases that Flavin and Paltrow identified, fifty-two percent involved African American women. As troublingly, of the total number of women, seventy percent were represented by lawyers for the indigent. *See* Lynn M. Paltrow & Jeanne Flavin, *Arrests of and Forced Interventions on Pregnant Women in the United States, 1973– 2005: Implications for Women's Legal Status and Public Health*, 38 J. HEALTH POL. POL'Y & L. 299, 309–10 (2013).

4.   *The collateral consequences of drug screening.* Some hospitals, particularly those serving low-income patients and public assistance recipients, regularly test pregnant women for marijuana use and turn over positive test results to child welfare authorities. Oren Yaniv, *Weed Out: More than a Dozen City Maternity Wards Regularly Test New Moms for Marijuana and Other Drugs*, N.Y. DAILY NEWS, Dec. 25, 2012, at 22. Although the *Ferguson* Court invalidated involuntary drug testing of pregnant women that could lead to *criminal* charges, the decision did not reach the issue of whether involuntary drug testing of pregnant women could be used to inform *civil* proceedings, like child welfare proceedings. As of 2017, twenty-five U.S. jurisdictions considered substance use during pregnancy to be child abuse, and three states considered it grounds for civil commitment. IF/WHEN/HOW: LAWYERING FOR REPRODUCTIVE JUSTICE, *supra* note 2, at 8.

5.   *Who gets screened?* Critically, a well-known study based in Pinellas County, Florida found that white women were more likely to use marijuana than African American women, although African American women were *ten times* more likely to be screened for marijuana use than their white counterparts. *See* Ira Chasnoff et. Al., *The Prevalence of Illicit-Drug or Alcohol Use During Pregnancy and Discrepancies in Mandatory Reporting in Pinellas County, Florida*, 322 NEW ENG. J. MED. 1202, 1204 (1990).

6.   *Pregnancy and the opioid epidemic.* In recent years, concerns about the effects of drug use on pregnant persons has centered on the growing opioid crisis. Unlike the crack cocaine "epidemic," the impact of the opioid crisis has fallen largely on white communities. *See* Helena Hansen & Julie Netherland, Editorial, *Is the Prescription Opioid Epidemic a White Problem?*, 106 AM. J. PUB. HEALTH 2127 (2016). As many have noted, this demographic feature has influenced the public policy response to the crisis. Rather than casting opioid abuse as an opportunity for *criminal* intervention, it has largely been cast as a public health crisis, requiring treatment and rehabilitative intervention. *See* Louise Radnofsky & Jon Kamp, *Trump Announces Opioid Crisis a Public Health Emergency*, WALL ST. J., (https://www.wsj. com/articles/president-trump-to-announce-opioid-crisis-a-public-health- emergency-1509024286) [https://perma.cc/T8GX-48T7]. Except in those circumstances where opioid use coincides with pregnancy. As Professor Khiara Bridges observes, drug use during pregnancy continues to be criminalized, even when it results in the punishment of a largely white population. *See* Khiara M. Bridges, *Race, Pregnancy, and the Opioid Epidemic: White Privilege and the Criminalization of Opioid Use During Pregnancy*, 133 HARV. L. REV. 770 (2020). In this regard, the prosecution of white women for using opioids speaks to two distinct impulses. First, it underscores the victimhood of the white fetuses who are "endangered" by opioid use. *Id.* at 836. And relatedly, such prosecutions not only punish opioid use during pregnancy, they are also a means by which the state identifies and punishes "a population of people who," through their poverty, drug uses, and criminal activity, "have been disloyal to their whiteness." *Id.* at 843. In this way, the criminalization of drug use during pregnancy continues "to reinforce racial meanings as well as the social order that is built around those meanings." *Id.*

2.   PROTECTING THE FETUS FROM HIV/AIDS

New Jersey Division of Youth & Family Services v. L.V. & C.M.

889 A.2d 1153 (N.J. Super. Ct., Ch. Div. 2005).

■ ROTHSTADT, J.S.C.

The Division of Youth and Family Services ("DYFS") filed an action against the defendant, L.V. (hereinafter "the mother"), alleging her abuse and neglect of her baby, who was born on January 10, 2005. . . . That allegation related solely to the mother's refusal to take certain medications, during her pregnancy, to reduce the risk that the baby would be born HIV positive. . . .

. . . The mother admitted that while she was pregnant with her child she learned, for the first time, that she was HIV positive. Further, the mother admitted that despite advice she received from the nurse who treated her, she refused to regularly take medication that was intended to reduce the chance that her baby would be HIV positive. She refused to take the medication on a regular basis because she simply could not accept the fact that she contracted the disease.

DYFS supplemented the mother's admission with the testimony of the nurse practitioner who provided prenatal treatment for the mother. That nurse, Ann M. Scanlon-Smith . . . testified credibly both as to her treatment and conversations with the mother and as to her expert opinion regarding current treatment methods available to HIV-positive pregnant women. Those treatments include antiretroviral (drug) therapy, which is designed to reduce the risk of the virus being passed to a newborn baby.

However, Scanlon also reported that all babies born to mothers who are HIV positive carry their mother's antibody to HIV in their blood, even if the medication is taken during the pregnancy. Therefore, initial tests on all children of HIV-positive mothers can [test] positive for HIV. However, as the mother's antibodies die off and the baby's immune system matures and produces antibodies to environmental antigens, the child can ultimately test negative for the virus. This is known as seroreversion. At the hearing, the parties therefore agreed that, even where the virus initially appears in a child, the virus can disappear from the child within its first eighteen months of development. They also agreed that an initial negative result can change to a positive result during that time.

According to Ms. Scanlon, the recommended therapy reduced the risk of passing the virus to the baby from twenty-eight percent to seven percent. In other words, pregnant women who test positive for HIV and who do not take the medication expose their babies to a twenty-eight percent chance that the virus will be transmitted at birth. The same women who take the medication reduce the risk to approximately a seven percent chance of passing the virus to their babies. Moreover, in Scanlon-Smith's experience, none of her patients who strictly followed their therapeutic regimes ever passed the virus to their child.

Thus, even when a pregnant mother does not take the medication at all, there is a seventy-two percent chance that the child will not be HIV positive. Further, even if a baby is HIV positive at birth, the virus may disappear. Whenever a baby is exposed to the virus, it, however, is standard procedure to treat the baby for the virus using various medications until the virus disappears. The medication, however, does not cause that disappearance. Instead, its disappearance is evidently attributable to the child's development during its first eighteen months.

. . .

As noted, the mother gave birth to the baby on January 10, 2005. Although the parties agreed that the child was exposed to the virus, there was no evidence that the baby actually tested positive for HIV.[4] Also,

---

4   In fact, counsel all agreed during summations that the only test administered to the baby to date came back negative for HIV.

DYFS did not present any evidence that the baby suffered any physical harm, injury, or disability as a result of being exposed to the virus. The baby evidently suffered from other serious health problems, unrelated to her exposure to HIV.

After the hospital medically cleared the baby, DYFS transferred her to foster care and then to a hospital for medically fragile infants. She is now receiving all of the medical treatment she requires. The mother confirmed that she would insure that the baby continue to receive her necessary medical treatment if the court were to place the baby back in her custody and care. (The mother made this promise even though it is not clear if she has the financial ability to insure that such treatment will be provided).

... Pursuant to New Jersey's child abuse, neglect and cruelty statutes ("the Act"), DYFS must establish at a fact-finding hearing, by a preponderance of the evidence, that the baby was an abused or neglected child. The fact-finding process under the Act is a significant and necessary check on DYFS's actions. Its focus centers upon the question of whether the parent under consideration caused injury to the child and, if not, whether the parent is likely to do so in the future.

The Act defines an "abused or neglected child" as a child, less than eighteen years of age, whose parent;

(1) inflicts or allows to be inflicted upon such child physical injury by other than accidental means which causes or creates a substantial risk of death, or serious or protracted disfigurement, or protracted impairment of physical or emotional health or protracted loss or impairment of the function of any bodily organ;

(2) creates or allows to be created a substantial or ongoing risk of physical injury to such child by other than accidental means which would be likely to cause death or serious or protracted disfigurement, or protracted loss or impairment of the function of any bodily organ; ...

(4) or a child whose physical, mental, or emotional condition has been impaired or is in imminent danger of becoming impaired as the result of the failure of his parent or guardian, as herein defined, to exercise a minimum degree of care

(a) in supplying the child with adequate food, clothing, shelter, education, medical or surgical care though financially able to do so or though offered financial or other reasonable means to do so . . . .

The question here then was whether the mother's failure to take the prescribed medication during her pregnancy, after being told of its benefits, constituted . . . an act of abuse or neglect.

Apparently, there is no case law in this state that previously addressed these narrow circumstances. . . .

Since there is no applicable case law, DYFS argued to the court that the situation *sub judice* was analogous to a pregnant mother's use of illegal drugs during her pregnancy. Clearly, it is well settled that where a mother abuses narcotics or alcohol during her pregnancy, and her abuse results in her child being born addicted to drugs and forced to suffer the consequences of that addiction, the mother can be shown to have abused or neglected her child. However, it is the attendant suffering to the child, after birth, that a court must rely on in making a finding of abuse or neglect under those circumstances. The mother's decision to use narcotics or alcohol during her pregnancy alone is an insufficient basis for a finding of abuse or neglect. To otherwise hold a mother culpable for her incorrect decision would be an unauthorized punishment for her "past transgressions against the child in utero or in esse."

This proscription against finding that a mother committed an act of abuse or neglect against her child by her actions before the child's birth, without attendant suffering or injury after birth, recognizes that the protections afforded by the Act are limited to the child's situation after his or her birth and not while a fetus. Also, since the Act clearly does not expressly include a fetus in its definition of a child, its protection does not extend to the child before birth. This conclusion is equally supported by the express provisions of the Act, which contemplate the removal and placement of an abused and neglected child into DYFS's custody. Those provisions simply could not apply to a fetus.

The Act, therefore, does not and cannot be construed to permit government interference with a woman's protected right to control her body and her future during her pregnancy. . . . The decisions she makes as to what medications she will take during her pregnancy, (as compared to controlled dangerous substances), are left solely to her discretion after consultation with her treating physicians. The right to make that decision is part of her constitutional right to privacy, which includes her right to control her own body and destiny. Those rights include the ability to refuse medical treatment, even at the risk of her death or the termination of her pregnancy.

While the mother's decision here may not have been one that another would have made (especially one who did not walk in her shoes), it cannot, therefore, be the basis for a finding of abuse or neglect. . . .

In addition, even if the court considered the mother's refusal to take the recommended medication during her pregnancy to be questionable, there simply was no evidence that the baby even tested positive for HIV or suffered from any condition relating to her exposure to that virus. Even if there was evidence that the baby initially tested positive for the virus, the evidence also established that the virus could disappear as the baby developed. Moreover, the evidence established that even if the mother took the medication, there was no guarantee that the baby would not be born HIV positive. The medication only reduced that risk; it did not eliminate the risk.

. . .

After considering the safety of the baby in the light of the evidence presented at the fact-finding hearing, this court was satisfied that DYFS failed to meet its burden. Although the baby suffered from several maladies, none of them were shown to be the result of the mother's actions. Specifically, there was no evidence that the mother harmed the child or refused to insure that the child received that which she required, including necessary medical care. There simply was no proof of abuse or neglect.

Today, the mother is not interfering with the baby's treatment and agrees to continue the treatment when her child is returned to her. Thus, there is no evidence that the mother is likely to abuse or neglect the baby in the future. Under these circumstances, it cannot be said that the mother caused or will cause the baby to suffer any pain or injury or that she seeks to deprive her of any necessary medical treatment. The baby is therefore neither an abused or neglected child as defined by the Act.

As there is no finding of abuse or neglect, the complaint alleging abuse or neglect will be dismissed. However, the baby's legal custody will not be transferred back to the mother. The court is concerned about the mother's present ability to provide the continued medical treatment the baby requires. Thus, the action for custody, care and supervision is sustained and will continue for a period of six months, unless extended after a summary hearing to be scheduled on notice to all parties. DYFS is to insure that the baby and the mother are able to receive all necessary treatment to address the baby's medical needs. The mother is not to make any attempt to remove the baby from her placement at the O'Neill Center at St. Joseph's Hospital Medical Center without further order from the court.

NOTES

1.   *Administrative law as a site of reproductive regulation.* The conventional wisdom suggests that reproductive rights and justice issues arise in the context of constitutional law, but have little to do with other areas of the law. *L.V.*, however, makes clear that this is not the case. *L.V.* arises in the course of an administrative proceeding concerning a statute governing the abuse and neglect of children—a statute that is regulated by an administrative agency. How does this shift to the terrain of administrative agencies transform the struggle for reproductive rights and justice?

2.   *Going beyond legislative intent.* As seen in *Whitner, supra* p. 174, extant criminal laws have been used to further policy ends for which they were not originally intended. In *L.V.*, a similar concern arises in the context of the administrative state. There, New Jersey's child welfare agency, the Department of Youth and Family Services ("DYFS"), invites the court to interpret the child abuse statute (which it is charged with administering) in

a way that is consistent with existing case law on drug use during pregnancy. It is unlikely that these issues were contemplated by the New Jersey legislature at the time it enacted the child abuse and neglect statute. Is it problematic to conflate these two very different issues?

3. *Medical standards for prenatal care for HIV-positive women.* The Center for HIV Law and Policy, drawing on guidelines developed by the U.S. Public Health Service Task Force for Pregnant Women and Newborns, articulates the following core principles for perinatal HIV care:

- Women have the right to the highest quality reproductive and HIV health care available;

- Women have the right to initiate, prevent, maintain, or terminate pregnancies, irrespective of their HIV status;

- Women need and are entitled to comprehensive, accurate, accessible, and linguistically and culturally appropriate information about HIV treatment, prevention of mother-to-child transmission, and their own health, so that they can make the best possible decisions in their particular circumstances;

- Misinformation about HIV and AIDS is a threat to the health of women and children;

- A healthy mother is one of a child's greatest health assets, which means that she must consider her own health and treatment carefully when making decisions about PMTCT health care;

- Imposing mandates for unconsented testing and coercive prophylaxis and care is counterproductive. The best outcomes will follow when women are supported in making informed, autonomous decisions in respectful partnership with knowledgeable doctors and other health care providers; and

- There is no one right course of action or treatment regimen for all HIV-positive pregnant women. Each woman must balance a complicated set of risks and advantages to her child and herself in making her decisions.

CATHERINE HANSSENS, ET AL., CTR. FOR HIV LAW & POLICY, HIV AND PREGNANCY: MEDICAL AND LEGAL CONSIDERATIONS FOR WOMEN AND THEIR ADVOCATES 5 (2009).

Do these criteria make sense for all pregnant HIV-positive women? What assumptions are being made about access to prenatal health care and HIV care? What kind of health care access do these criteria presuppose? Are aspects of these criteria problematic for some women, but not others?

4. *Losing by winning?* The pregnant HIV-positive defendant in *L.V.* was vindicated when the court confirmed her right to decline treatment for HIV during her pregnancy. But was she a winner? It is worth noting that while her ability to make decisions about health care was affirmed, the court nonetheless imposed conditions on the exercise of her parental rights. In this context, what was the price of exercising her reproductive autonomy?

D. REGULATING BIRTH

In 2002, Childbirth Connection, a national non-profit organization founded in 1918 that aims "to improve the quality and value of maternity care," fielded a national survey polling women about their maternity experiences. A follow-up study to poll women who gave birth in U.S. hospitals in 2005 about their experiences giving birth. Below are some of the findings gleaned from the 2005 study.

Childbirth Connection, Listening to Mothers II: Report of the Second National U.S. Survey of Women's Childbearing Experiences
(2006).

Despite the primarily healthy population and the fact that birth is not intrinsically pathologic, technology-intensive care *was* the norm during childbirth. Each of the following interventions was experienced by most mothers: continuous electronic fetal monitoring, one or more vaginal exams, intravenous drip, epidural or spinal analgesia, and urinary catheter. Half of the mothers experienced one or more methods of inducing labor (attempted medical and/or self-inductions), and a notable minority experienced each of the following: labor that was induced, synthetic oxytocin (Pitocin) during labor, artificially ruptured membranes during labor, narcotics, cesarean section, episiotomy, perineal stitches, staff-directed pushing and a staff member pressing on the mother's belly to help push the baby out. The combination of interventions depended to a large degree on whether the birth was vaginal or cesarean. Nearly one-third (32%) had cesareans, evenly divided between first-time and repeat cesareans.

NOTES

1.   *Increased medicalization of labor and delivery.* The *Listening to Mothers II* study suggests that labor and delivery in the U.S. has become increasingly medicalized. What explains this development? Some have argued that the rise of induction, caesarean sections, and fetal monitoring is part of an effort to improve infant and maternal mortality rates. *See* Sora Song, *Too Posh to Push?*, TIME, Apr. 19, 2004, at 58. Others suggest that these developments respond to the prospect of increased tort liability for medical personnel. *Id.*

2.   *Maternal and infant mortality.* The United States has one of the worst records for infant and maternal mortality in the developed world, despite spending more money on childbirth than peer countries. *See* Ina May Gaskin, *Maternal Death in the United States: A Problem Solved or a Problem Ignored?*, 17 J. PERINATAL EDUC. 9, 9 (2008).

3.   *Racial disparities in infant and maternal mortality.* According to the United Nations Commission on the Elimination of Racial Discrimination (CERD) Working Group on Health and Environmental Health:

[W]omen of color in the United States fare significantly worse than white women in nearly every aspect of reproductive health. The U.S. has one of the highest rates of maternal mortality among western developed nations and ranks 30th in the world with respect to maternal mortality rate. Racial disparities in maternal mortality help explain why this rate is so high. African American women are nearly four times more likely to die in childbirth than white women (30.5 vs. 8.7 deaths per 100,000 live births). These disparities have remained unchanged over the past five decades. This disparity is largely attributable to the fact that women of color, especially those who are low-income, disproportionately lack access to prenatal care that is essential for healthy birth outcomes.

not entirely true

CERD WORKING GRP. ON HEALTH & ENVTL. HEALTH, UNEQUAL HEALTH OUTCOMES IN THE UNITED STATES 6 (2008).

4. *Factors in rising maternal and infant mortality rates.* The World Health Organization (WHO) has identified complications from caesarean sections and anesthesia as the primary cause of maternal death in industrialized nations. *See* Khalid S. Khan et al., *WHO Analysis of Causes of Maternal Death: A Systematic Review*, 367 LANCET 1066, 1066–74 (2006).

1. FORCED MEDICAL TREATMENT FOR PREGNANT WOMEN

As we have seen, women may experience difficulty exercising their civil rights when they are pregnant. Upon becoming pregnant, a woman's civil rights must be balanced against the state's interests in the potential life of the fetus and the mother's health. In the following cases, as in the cases concerning advance health directives, courts must grapple with these competing concerns. In some cases, courts have determined that a woman's autonomy must be subordinated in order to bring a pregnancy safely to term. In making these decisions, courts may rely on—or in some cases, defer completely to—medical accounts of how pregnancies should and must proceed.

Burton v. Florida

49 So. 3d 263 (Dist. Ct. Fla. 2010).

■ CLARK, J.

This is an appeal of a circuit court order compelling a pregnant woman to submit to any medical treatment deemed necessary by the attending obstetrician, including detention in the hospital for enforcement of bed rest, administration of intra-venous medications, and anticipated surgical delivery of the fetus. The action was initiated in the circuit court by the State Attorney under the procedure described in *In re Dubreuil*, 629 So. 2d 819 (Fla. 1994). As provided in *Dubreuil,* after the State Attorney received notification from a health care provider that a patient refused medical treatment, the State Attorney exercised his

issue

discretion to determine that a sufficient state interest was at stake to justify legal action.

. . .

. . . [C]ase precedent governing the use of a *Dubreuil* proceeding to compel a pregnant woman to undergo medical confinement, treatment and procedures against her wishes for the benefit of her unborn fetus is not found in Florida's jurisprudence. In an effort to assist trial courts and counsel involved in these expedited, if not emergency proceedings, we exercise our discretionary authority to address this appeal.

The trial court found that the appellant had failed to follow the doctor's instructions and recommendations, rendering her pregnancy "high-risk," and found a "substantial and unacceptable" risk of severe injury or death to the unborn child if the appellant continued to fail to follow the recommended course of treatment. The trial court stated the rule that "as between parent and child, the ultimate welfare of the child is the controlling factor," and concluded that the State's interests in the matter "override Ms. Burton's privacy interests at this time." The court ordered Samantha Burton to comply with the physician's orders "including, but not limited to" bed rest, medication to postpone labor and prevent or treat infection, and eventual performance of a cesarean section delivery.

The law in Florida is clear: Every person has the right "to be let alone and free from government intrusion into the person's private life." Art. I, sec. 23, Fla. Const. This fundamental right to privacy encompasses a person's "right to the sole control of his or her person" and the "right to determine what shall be done with his own body." The Florida Supreme Court has specifically recognized that "a competent person has the constitutional right to choose or refuse medical treatment, and that right extends to all relevant decisions concerning one's health."

A patient's fundamental constitutional right to refuse medical intervention "can only be overcome if the state has a compelling state interest great enough to override this constitutional right." Thus, the threshold issue in this situation is whether the state established a compelling state interest sufficient to trigger the court's consideration and balance of that interest against the appellant's right to refuse to submit to the medical intervention the obstetrician prescribed. The state's interest in the potentiality of life of an unborn fetus becomes compelling "at the point in time when the fetus becomes viable," defined as "the time at which the fetus becomes capable of meaningful life outside the womb, albeit with artificial aid." The Legislature has defined "viability" as "that stage of fetal development when the life of the unborn child may with a reasonable degree of medical probability be continued indefinitely outside the womb." § 390.0111(4), Fla. Stat. No presumption of viability is provided in the statute.

Because there is no statutory or precedential presumption of viability, in terms of the stage of pregnancy or otherwise, there must be some evidence of viability via testimony or otherwise. Only after the threshold determination of viability has been made may the court weigh the state's compelling interest to preserve the life of the fetus against the patient's fundamental constitutional right to refuse medical treatment.

Even if the State had made the threshold showing of viability and the court had made the requisite determination, the legal test recited in the order on appeal was a misapplication of the law. The holding in *M.N. v. Southern Baptist Hosp. of Florida*, 648 So. 2d 769 (Fla. 1st DCA 1994), "that as between parent and child, the ultimate welfare of the child is the controlling factor," does not apply to this case. Unlike this case, in *M.N.*, the parents refused consent for a blood transfusion and chemotherapy for their 8-month-old infant. No privacy rights of a pregnant woman were involved.

The test to overcome a woman's right to refuse medical intervention in her pregnancy is whether the state's compelling state interest is sufficient to override the pregnant woman's constitutional right to the control of her person, including her right to refuse medical treatment. In addition, where the state does establish a compelling state interest and the court has found the state's interest sufficient to override a pregnant patient's right to determine her course of medical treatment, the state must then show that the method for pursuing that compelling state interest is "narrowly tailored in the least intrusive manner possible to safeguard the rights of the individual."

REVERSED.

. . .

■ BERGER, A. J., dissenting.

I agree with the majority that the trial judge applied the wrong legal standard. If this case were not moot, I would reverse and remand for consideration using the correct, compelling state interest standard. However, because I disagree with the majority view that this is a case capable of repetition yet evading review, I would dismiss the appeal as moot. Accordingly, I dissent.

This court was not presented with a case of first impression warranting an opinion to assist trial courts and counsel in similar future expedited cases. It matters not that the case before us involves a hospital's desire to compel medical treatment over the objection of a pregnant woman. The law to be followed is clear and unambiguous. The proper test to be applied when a trial court is presented with a request to override a competent adult's constitutional right to refuse medical treatment was decided in *In re Guardianship of Browning*, 568 So. 2d 4 (Fla. 1990) (State has a duty to assure that a person's wishes regarding medical treatment are respected unless the State has a compelling interest great enough to override this constitutional right.). The proper procedure to be followed when a healthcare provider wishes to override a patient's decision to refuse medical treatment was outlined in *In re Matter of Dubreuil,* 629 So. 2d 819 (Fla. 1994) (Healthcare provider must immediately provide notice to both the state attorney, who is responsible for deciding whether to engage in legal action, and to interested third parties known to the provider.). Additionally, it is well settled that the State's interest in preserving the life of an unborn child becomes compelling upon viability. *Roe v. Wade,* 410 U.S. 113 (1973); *In re T.W.,* 551 So. 2d 1186, 1194 (Fla. 1989) (Viability under Florida law occurs at that point in time when the fetus becomes capable of meaningful life outside the womb through standard medical measures. Under current standards, this point generally occurs upon completion of the second trimester.). Here the trial judge followed the correct procedure but applied the wrong legal standard. Instead of determining whether the State had a compelling interest in overriding the appellant's right to refuse medical treatment, the judge determined forced treatment was in the best interest of the child.

The trial court specifically found that the risk of severe injury or death to the unborn child was substantial and unacceptable and that the interests of the State in this matter overrode appellant's privacy interests. While I believe the balancing of interests employed by the trial judge would have been appropriate under *Browning,* it was the trial court's application of the State's *parens patriae* authority to override the appellant's right to refuse medical treatment for an existing child that was in error. However, since the principles of law to be applied in this case are not new . . . I would dismiss the appeal.

NOTES

1. *Bed rest or bust?* In *Burton,* Ms. Burton's physicians prescribed extended bed rest for her for the remainder of her pregnancy. Does bed rest assume a particular patient with specific circumstances and resources? That is, though bed rest may be deemed medically necessary, are all women in a position to comply with such an order? Would all workplaces willingly accommodate a physician's order regarding extended bed rest for their employees?

2. *Refusal as resistance?* For some, refusing medical treatment may simply be an effort to assert control and autonomy in the birthing process. Indeed, Professor Nancy Ehrenreich argues that these decisions should be understood as "power struggles—struggles over the control of reproduction and the meaning of motherhood." On this account, a woman's refusal to submit to medical advice may take on a political dimension:

> In refusing [medical directives], a woman is resisting a patriarchal view of herself and her role in reproduction. A high-income white woman who rejects the medical model of childbirth is resisting a vision of herself as an object to be "managed," as passive, incompetent, selfless, and emotional. Moreover, she is resisting an

image of the reproductive process as a pathological, flawed undertaking fraught with danger, and of her own body as incompetent, threatening, and out of control. A low-income woman of color who refuses [medical directives] is rejecting not only the notion that her body is dangerous but also an image of herself as stupid, irresponsible, and selfish and as impervious to pain, discomfort, or inconvenience. Moreover, she is also engaging in an act of self-preservation, challenging the very profession that has so often hurt women like her before. In a profound way, she is claiming her humanity and fighting for her survival.

Nancy Ehrenreich, *The Colonization of the Womb*, 43 DUKE L.J. 492, 553 (1993).

In re Madyun

114 Daily Wash. L. Rptr. 2233 (D.C. Super. Ct. July 26, 1986).

■ LEVIE, A.J.

Upon the oral petition of D.C. General Hospital ("Hospital") for an order that the Hospital be authorized to perform a Caesarean section upon Ayesha Madyun to deliver her fetus, a hearing was convened at the Hospital at 10:30 p.m. on July 25, 1986. . . . After hearing testimony and arguments of counsel, the Court orally granted the Hospital's petition at 1:05 a.m., on July 26 and then denied the parents' motion for a stay. A telephonic appeal was heard and the decision of this Court was affirmed. . . .

FINDINGS OF FACT

The mother of the infant, Ayesha Madyun, is a 19-year-old woman experiencing her first pregnancy. She arrived at the Hospital on July 25, 1986, at approximately 1:45 a.m., after previously having been to Greater Southeast Community Hospital for an unknown period of time. Upon admission to the Hospital, it was determined that she was at term; she related that her membrane had ruptured (water broken) some 48 hours earlier. Mrs. Madyun indicated throughout the entire time prior to the performance of the Caesarean section that she wanted a natural delivery. By 11:00 a.m. on July 25 she was seven centimeters dilated. When the hearing convened at the Hospital almost 12 hours later, Mrs. Madyun was still dilated at seven centimeters. By the time of the hearing her contractions were coming at intervals approximately five minutes apart.

Mr. and Mrs. Madyun met with the medical staff at approximately 4:00 p.m. and again at 8:00 p.m. on July 25 to discuss the available options. When no progress toward completing a natural (vaginal) delivery was evidenced by 8:00 p.m., it was recommended that Mrs. Madyun consent to undergo Caesarean section to deliver the fetus. Consent to perform a Caesarean section was denied. When questioned during the hearing, some four hours after the 8:00 p.m. conference, Mrs. Madyun reiterated her preference for a natural delivery and expressed her belief that a Caesarean section was not necessary. She understood the risks of infection to the fetus resulting from continuation of labor without delivery, but sought to explain her decision to decline a Caesarean section by reference to her religious beliefs. Mrs. Madyun testified that a Muslim woman has the right to decide whether or not to risk her own health to eliminate a possible risk to the life of her undelivered fetus.

During a separate, longer interview, Mr. Madyun explained that his refusal to consent to the performance of a Caesarean was based upon his belief that there was no demonstrable danger at that point to either Mrs. Madyun or the fetus. . . . Further, it was his belief that there had been insufficient opportunity for his wife to deliver vaginally. He also expressed his view that the Hospital had failed to permit Mrs. Madyun to engage in certain potentially natural acts of assisting delivery, such as standing up or walking around. Mr. Madyun similarly explained that a Muslim woman, confronted with a life or death situation, had the right to decide whether to risk her health or life to save an unborn fetus. The risks of infection and possible death to the fetus in the absence of a Caesarean section were likewise explained to and understood by Mr. Madyun.

The medical basis for the Hospital's emergency oral petition was presented through the testimony of Dr. Cummings. . . .

According to Dr. Cummings, normal labor for an uncomplicated first pregnancy is 10–15 hours. For a woman in her first pregnancy to remain dilated at seven centimeters for 12 hours was, in his opinion, abnormal. Normal obstetrical procedures with a term pregnancy call for delivery of a baby within 24 hours of the membrane's rupture.

Failure to adhere to this procedure increases the risk of chorioamnionitis (inflammation of the fetal placental membranes) which can lead to fetal sepsis (infection). This, in turn, can result in the death of the baby or brain damage. Sepsis can start at any time 24 hours after rupture of the membrane. The likelihood of infection to the baby (fetus) increases greatly in proportion to the length of time between rupture of the membrane and delivery of the baby. It was the opinion of Dr. Cummings that each passing hour increased the risk of fetal sepsis.

As Dr. Cummings explained, one of the most insidious dangers in the situation presented by Mrs. Madyun was that sepsis could begin without detection and advance to the point of causing the death of the baby with little, or possibly no, warning. Prior to birth, it is difficult to determine the commencement of fetal sepsis. While there are certain symptoms of fetal sepsis (maternal temperature, foul smelling discharge, and fetal heartbeat), evidence of them may not become apparent until the baby is already septic. Given the fact that, by the time of hearing, Mrs. Madyun's membrane had ruptured between 60 and 70 hours earlier, Dr. Cummings believed that the risk of fetal sepsis here was 50–75%. In contrast, the risk to Mrs. Madyun undergoing a Caesarean section was said to be 0.25%.

Against this background, the Hospital was seeking authorization to deliver the baby by the most expedient means—a Caesarean section. On behalf of the unborn child, Mr. Baach joined in the Hospital's request that authorization for the Caesarean section be granted.

CONCLUSIONS OF LAW

When a competent adult declines medical treatment on religious grounds, the Court is obligated to respect this decision, even in a life or death situation, unless the state can "demonstrate a compelling interest that would justify overriding the individual's choice."

standard of law

In the case of children, the state acting as *parens patriae* has the ability, in appropriate situations, to "restrict" a parent's control of a child, even where the parent's claim to control is founded upon religious rights or a more generalized "right[] of parenthood. . . ." Thus, where the requisite factual predicate has been established, courts have ordered medical treatment of children over parental objections.

parens patriae

Counsel for the parents, while not challenging these general propositions of law, questioned whether consideration of the state's interest affecting a child already born applies with the same force to an unborn child. Under the facts here, the answer is yes.

Makes difference that child unborn? not here

The state has an "important and legitimate interest in protecting the potentiality of human life." *Roe v. Wade,* 410 U.S. 113 (1973). At the point of "viability" the state's interest becomes "compelling." To be sure, by the third trimester the state's interest "become[s] sufficiently compelling to justify unduly burdensome state interference with the woman's constitutionally protected privacy interest." A "compelling interest" of the state may likewise justify overriding religious convictions in cases of unborn infants.

compelling state interest here overrides religious convictions

Because Mrs. Madyun was at term, there was no issue as to viability. All that stood between the Madyun fetus and its independent existence, separate from its mother, was, put simply, a doctor's scalpel. In these circumstances, the life of the infant inside its mother's womb was entitled to be protected.

. . .

In the instant case, the Court was confronted with a 50–75% risk of infection for the infant, in view of the extended period of time (60 hours) since rupture of the mother's membrane. The testimony adduced at the hearing was that the onset of infection to the infant could begin and progress to a potentially fatal point before symptoms of the infection became evident. To have required the doctors to continue a "wait and see" attitude could have had potentially fatal consequences to the infant. It is one thing for an adult to gamble with nature regarding his or her own life; it is quite another when the gamble involves the life or death of an unborn infant.

The Court had before it parents who, in part, refused a Caesarean section on the basis of religious beliefs. Although both parents impressed the Court as sincere, it was evident that the stronger basis for their individual decisions was the belief that the surgical procedure was not necessary and that additional steps could be taken to enhance the possibility of a vaginal delivery. Neither parent, however, is a trained physician. To ignore the undisputed opinion of a skilled and trained physician to indulge the desires of the parents where, as here, there is a substantial risk to the unborn infant, is something the Court cannot do. Indeed, even if the religious beliefs of the parents were the primary or sole reason for refusing a Caesarean, the state had a compelling interest in ensuring this infant could be born. . . . On these facts, the parents may not make a martyr of their unborn infant.

Accordingly, the Hospital is ordered to take such steps as medically indicated, including but not limited to a C-section, to preserve and protect the birth and safety of the fetus.

Interim Findings and Conclusions

. . .

Given the significant risks to the fetus versus the minimal risks to the mother, the Court concludes that there is a compelling interest to intervene and protect the life and safety of the fetus.

Accordingly, the Hospital is ordered to take such steps as are medically indicated, including but not limited to a C-section, to preserve and protect the birth and safety of the fetus.

NOTES

1. *Religious concerns and forced medical treatment.* The Madyuns argued that their opposition to a forced caesarean section was motivated in part by their Muslim beliefs. The court, however, concluded that their objections were insufficiently tethered to their religious beliefs. Do you agree with this conclusion? By what standard does the court determine the veracity of religious belief?

2. *Skepticism of minority religions?* Though the opinion notes that Ayesha Madyun was a Muslim, in fact, she was a *Black* Muslim. Does the fact that Madyun belonged to a minority religious sect play a role in the court's reluctance to credit her interest in a natural birth to genuine religious beliefs? In other contexts, courts have been reluctant to credit the views of those belonging to minority religious sects when those religious beliefs have conflicted with other normative commitments. *See, e.g., Prince v. Massachusetts*, 321 U.S. 158 (1944), *infra* p. 283 (upholding a state child labor law over objection of child's guardian, who was a Jehovah's Witness); *Church of the Lukumi Babalu Aye, Inc. v. Hialeah*, 508 U.S. 520 (1993)

this isn't correct!

(upholding a local ordinance prohibiting animal sacrifices over the objections of a Santeria sect).

3.   *Freedom to birth?* Mrs. Madyun wanted the opportunity to allow her labor to progress naturally. To speed her labor, she wanted to walk around—a common practice among laboring women. The hospital, however, refused this request. Did this refusal violate Madyun's rights? John Robertson has argued that "[a] woman's interest in an aesthetically pleasing or emotionally satisfying birth should not be satisfied at the expense of the child's safety." *See* John A. Robertson, *Procreative Liberty and the Control of Conception, Pregnancy, and Childbirth*, 69 VA. L. REV. 405, 453 (1983). Do laboring women have a right to give birth in the manner of their choosing? Or should these concerns be subordinated to the child's safety?

4.   *Pregnancy and pathology.* Professor Lisa Ikemoto observes a seachange in the way that pregnancy is viewed in modern medical practice:

> The understanding of childbirth as a pathology, a set of risks to be controlled, developed during the twentieth century as doctors became participants in caring for pregnant women. . . . As a corollary to the medicalization of pregnancy and childbirth, women have been displaced as actors in the reproductive process; they have become sources of risk and conflict.

Lisa C. Ikemoto, *Furthering the Inquiry: Race, Class, and Culture in the Forced Medical Treatment of Pregnant Women*, 59 TENN. L. REV. 487, 505 (1991).

5.   *Professional "facts" vs. lay "preferences."* Professor Nancy Ehrenreich suggests that *In re Madyun* reflects the legal system's deference to medical professionals—and skepticism of lay views:

> In his opinion . . . Judge Levie made it clear that he viewed the Madyuns' position that the surgery was unnecessary as unfounded. In describing the couple's reasons for saying that a C-section was unnecessary, he emphasized at every turn that those were merely *beliefs*, not the reality of the situation. In contrast, the judge unquestioningly accepted the doctor's conclusions, relating the "risks" posed by foregoing the surgery as statements of fact, rather than as statements of medical opinion. Accepting the medical vision of reproduction as a pathological process, Judge Levie treated nature (i.e., childbirth) as a dangerous and unpredictable force that needed to be controlled by the physicians. To him, the Madyuns, in trying to face it on their own, unprotected by experts, were playing with fire.

Nancy Ehrenreich, *The Colonization of the Womb*, 43 DUKE L.J. 492, 557–58 (1993).

Mom w/
terminal
cancer   — **In re A.C.**

533 A.2d 611 (D.C. App. 1987).

■ NEBEKER, A. J., RET.

. . .

A.C. was diagnosed with leukemia when she was thirteen years old. As part of her treatment, she underwent a number of major surgical procedures, therapy, and chemotherapy. When she was twenty-seven years old, after her cancer had been in remission for three years, A.C. married. At the time she became pregnant, she had not undergone chemotherapy for more than a year. In her fifteenth week of pregnancy, she was referred to the hospital's high-risk pregnancy clinic.

When A.C. was approximately twenty-five weeks pregnant, she went to her regularly scheduled prenatal visit complaining of shortness of breath and some pain in her back. Her physicians subsequently discovered that she had a tumor mass in her lung which was most likely a metastatic oxygenic carcinoma. She was admitted to the hospital on June 11 and her prognosis was terminal.

On June 15, during A.C.'s twenty-sixth week of pregnancy, A.C., her physicians, her mother, and her husband discussed the possibility of providing A.C. with radiation therapy or chemotherapy to relieve her pain and to continue her pregnancy. Her physicians believed that her unborn child's chances of viability would be greatly increased if it were delivered when it had reached twenty-eight weeks gestational age. By June 16, the date on which the hospital sought the declaratory order in the Superior Court, A.C. had been heavily sedated so that she could continue to breathe. Her condition was declining, and the attending medical staff concluded that passive treatment was appropriate because the mother would not survive and the child's chances of survival were grim. The hospital administration then decided to test this decision in the Superior Court.

The trial court appointed counsel for A.C. and the fetus, respectively. The District of Columbia was permitted to intervene for the fetus as parens patriae. A hearing was held at the hospital and was transcribed.

There was some dispute about whether A.C. would have chosen to have a Caesarean section on June 16. Before she was sedated, A.C. indicated that she would choose to relinquish her life so that the fetus could survive should such a choice present itself at the fetus' gestational age of twenty-eight weeks. Her physicians never discussed with her what her choice would be if such a choice had to be made before the fetus reached the twenty-eight-week point. The fetus was suffering oxygen starvation and resultant rapid heart rate. There was at that point less than 20 percent chance that it would be afflicted with cerebral palsy, neurological defects, deafness and blindness. There was not a clear medical consensus on the course of A.C.'s treatment. Those physicians who objected to the proposed surgery did so because A.C. refused her consent to the procedure, not because the surgery was medically objectionable. One physician testified that he believed that A.C. would not have wanted to deliver a baby that might have to undergo the pain of having handicaps that are associated with premature delivery. Another physician believed that A.C. would not have refused permission for the Caesarean section to be performed. During the course of her pregnancy, however, A.C. was aware that a number of medications she was taking might harm the fetus. Nevertheless, she expressed a desire to her physicians to be kept as comfortable as possible throughout her pregnancy and to maintain the quality of her life.

[handwritten margin note: Physicians disagreed about what mom wanted]

[handwritten note: → but she wanted comfort + quality of life]

The trial court determined that the fetus was viable and that the District of Columbia had an interest in protecting the potential life of the fetus. See Roe v. Wade, 410 U.S. 113 (1973). . . .

Shortly after the trial judge made his decision, A.C. was informed of it. She stated, during a period of lucidity, that she would agree to the surgery although she might not survive it. When another physician went to A.C. to verify her decision, she apparently changed her mind, mouthing the words, "I don't want it done." There was no explanation for either decision.

After our Clerk was advised of the desire to appeal, a telephonic hearing was had before a hastily assembled division of the court. The trial judge's findings were read to us, and we heard from counsel and an attending physician. The latter answered questions respecting the relative chances of survival of both A.C. and the fetus with and without the surgery. He also informed us of the rapid decline of A.C. and the need to proceed promptly with the surgery, if it was decided to do so. There was no time to have the transcript read or to do effective research. The atypical nature of the appellate hearing included our hearing directly from one of the physicians.

The court based its decision to deny a stay on the medical judgment that A.C. would not survive for a significant time after the surgery and that the fetus had a better, though slim, chance if taken before A.C.'s imminent death. If A.C. died before delivery, the fetus would die as well. Though A.C. might have lived twenty-four to forty-eight hours, the surgery might have hastened her death. The ordinary question of likelihood of ultimate success on the merits was deemed subsumed in the immediate necessity to balance the delicate interests of fetus survival with the mother's condition and options on her behalf.

[The Caesarean section was performed; both mother and child died soon thereafter.]

. . .

This is a case of first impression for this court. In fact, only one other appellate court in the nation has reported that it squarely addressed the issue of whether and when a court should order or permit that a Caesarean section be performed on a woman.

It is appropriate here to state that this case is not about abortion. . . . [A]s a matter of law, the right of a woman to an abortion is different and distinct from her obligations to the fetus once she has decided not to timely terminate her pregnancy. With a viable fetus, a balancing of interests must replace the single interest of the mother, and as in this case, time can be a critical factor.

We next view this case within the context of its closest legal analogues: the right of an adult to refuse medical treatment and the right of a parent to refuse medical treatment on behalf of offspring.

. . .

The fundamental right to bodily integrity encompasses an adult's right to refuse medical treatment, even if the refusal will result in death. The right of an adult to refuse medical treatment is not absolute, however. The state has four countervailing interests in sustaining a person's life: preserving life, preventing suicide, maintaining the integrity of the medical profession, and protecting innocent third parties. . . .

The state's interest in preserving life usually will not override an adult's right to refuse medical treatment. In most cases where a court orders an adult to receive medical treatment against his consent, it will be to protect innocent third parties who would be harmed by the adult's decision.

. . .

Courts have used this reasoning to hold that parents may not withhold life-saving treatment from their children because of the parents' religious beliefs. The state may intervene even when a parent's refusal of medical treatment for his or her child does not place the child in danger of imminent death.

. . .

There is a significant difference, however, between a court authorizing medical treatment for a child already born and a child who is yet unborn, although the state has compelling interests in protecting the life and health of both children and viable unborn children. Where birth has occurred, the medical treatment does not infringe on the mother's right to bodily integrity. With an unborn child, the state's interest in preserving the health of the child may run squarely against the mother's interest in her bodily integrity.

It can be argued that the state may not infringe upon the mother's right to bodily integrity to protect the life or health of her unborn child unless to do so will not significantly affect the health of the mother and unless the child has a significant chance of being born alive. Performing Caesarean sections will, in most instances, have an effect on the condition of the mother. That effect may be temporary in otherwise normal patients. The surgery presents a number of common complications, including infection, hemorrhage, gastric aspiration of the stomach contents, and postoperative embolism. It also produces considerable discomfort. In some cases, the surgery will result in the mother's death.

Even though we recognize these considerations, we think they should not have been dispositive here. The Caesarean section would not significantly affect A.C.'s condition because she had, at best, two days left of sedated life; the complications arising from the surgery would not significantly alter that prognosis. The child, on the other hand, had a chance of surviving delivery, despite the possibility that it would be born handicapped. Accordingly, we concluded that the trial judge did not err in subordinating A.C.'s right against bodily intrusion to the interests of the unborn child and the state, and hence we denied the motion for stay.

. . .

In re A.C.
573 A.2d 1235 (D.C. Ct. App. 1990).

■ TERRY, A. J.

. . .

We are confronted here with two profoundly difficult and complex issues. First, we must determine who has the right to decide the course of medical treatment for a patient who, although near death, is pregnant with a viable fetus. Second, we must establish how that decision should be made if the patient cannot make it for herself—more specifically, how a court should proceed when faced with a pregnant patient, in extremis, who is apparently incapable of making an informed decision regarding medical care for herself and her fetus. . . .

. . .

There was no evidence before the court showing that A.C. consented to, or even contemplated, a caesarean section before her twenty-eighth week of pregnancy. There was, in fact, considerable dispute as to whether she would have consented to an immediate caesarean delivery at the time the hearing was held. . . .

[The court found that, despite the fact that A.C. and her baby were dead, the case was not moot because the hospital treated high-risk pregnancy and was likely to face a similar situation again.]

[O]ur analysis of this case begins with the tenet common to all medical treatment cases: that any person has the right to make an informed choice, if competent to do so, to accept or forego medical treatment. . . .

. . .

In the same vein, courts do not compel one person to permit a significant intrusion upon his or her bodily integrity for the benefit of another person's health. McFall v. Shimp, 10 Pa.D. & C.3d 90 (Allegheny County Ct. 1978). In McFall the court refused to order Shimp to donate bone marrow which was necessary to save the life of his cousin, McFall. . . .

Even though Shimp's refusal would mean death for McFall, the court would not order Shimp to allow his body to be invaded. It has been suggested that fetal cases are different because a woman who "has chosen to lend her body to bring [a] child into the world" has an enhanced duty to assure the welfare of the fetus, sufficient even to require her to undergo caesarean surgery. Surely, however, a fetus cannot have rights in this respect superior to those of a person who has already been born.

. . .

What we distill from the cases . . . is that every person has the right, under the common law and the Constitution, to accept or refuse medical treatment. This right of bodily integrity belongs equally to persons who are competent and persons who are not. Further, it matters not what the quality of a patient's life may be; the right of bodily integrity is not extinguished simply because someone is ill, or even at death's door. To protect that right against intrusion by others—family members, doctors, hospitals, or anyone else, however well-intentioned—we hold that a court must determine the patient's wishes by any means available, and must abide by those wishes unless there are truly extraordinary or compelling reasons to override them. When the patient is incompetent, or when the court is unable to determine competency, the substituted judgment procedure must be followed.

. . .

Under the substituted judgment procedure, the court as decision-maker must "substitute itself as nearly as may be for the incompetent, and . . . act upon the same motives and considerations as would have moved her. . . ." In recent times the procedure has been used to authorize organ "donations" by incompetents . . . and to prohibit the forced administration of medical treatment to incompetents, over religious objections, where life itself was not at stake. Most cases involving substituted judgment, however, have arisen in the "right to die" context, and the courts have generally concluded that giving effect to the perceived decision of the incompetent is the proper course, even though doing so will result in the incompetent's death.

. . .

Because it is the patient's decisional rights which the substituted judgment inquiry seeks to protect, courts are in accord that the greatest weight should be given to the previously expressed wishes of the patient. This includes prior statements, either written or oral, even though the treatment alternatives at hand may not have been addressed. . . . [I]n a case such as this it would be highly relevant that A.C. had consented to intrusive and dangerous surgeries in the past, and that she chose to become pregnant and to protect her pregnancy by seeking treatment at the hospital's high-risk pregnancy clinic. It would also be relevant that she accepted a plan of treatment which contemplated caesarean intervention at the twenty-eighth week of pregnancy, even though the possibility of a caesarean during the twenty-sixth week was apparently unforeseen. On the other hand, A.C. agreed to a plan of palliative treatment which posed a greater danger to the fetus than would have been necessary if she were unconcerned about her own continuing care. Further, when A.C. was informed of the fatal nature of her illness, she was equivocal about her desire to have the baby.

In short, to determine the subjective desires of the patient, the court must consider the totality of the evidence, focusing particularly on written or oral directions concerning treatment to family, friends, and health-care professionals. The court should also take into account the patient's past decisions regarding medical treatment, and attempt to ascertain from what is known about the patient's value system, goals, and desires what the patient would decide if competent.

... When the patient is pregnant, however, she may not be concerned exclusively with her own welfare. Thus it is proper for the court, in a case such as this, to weigh (along with all the other factors) the mother's prognosis, the viability of the fetus, the probable result of treatment or non-treatment for both mother and fetus, and the mother's likely interest in avoiding impairment for her child together with her own instincts for survival.

... Finally, in making a substituted judgment, the court should become as informed about the patient's condition, prognosis, and treatment options as one would expect any patient to become before making a treatment decision. Obviously, the weight accorded to all of these factors will vary from case to case.

. . .

... In this case there is an understandable paucity of factual findings, which necessarily limits our review. The trial court, faced with an issue affecting life and death, was forced to make a decision with almost no time for deliberation. Nevertheless, after reviewing the transcript of the hearing and the court's oral findings, it is clear to us that the trial court did not follow the substituted judgment procedure....

... Instead, the court said that it was "still not clear what her intent is" and again ordered the caesarean.

It is that order which we must now set aside. What a trial court must do in a case such as this is to determine, if possible, whether the patient is capable of making an informed decision about the course of her medical treatment. If she is, and if she makes such a decision, her wishes will control in virtually all cases. If the court finds that the patient is incapable of making an informed consent (and thus incompetent), then the court must make a substituted judgment. This means that the court must ascertain as best it can what the patient would do if faced with the particular treatment question. Again, in virtually all cases the decision of the patient, albeit discerned through the mechanism of substituted judgment, will control. We do not quite foreclose the possibility that a conflicting state interest may be so compelling that the patient's wishes must yield, but we anticipate that such cases will be extremely rare and truly exceptional. This is not such a case.

Having said that, we go no further. We need not decide whether, or in what circumstances, the state's interests can ever prevail over the interests of a pregnant patient. We emphasize, nevertheless, that it would be an extraordinary case indeed in which a court might ever be justified in overriding the patient's wishes and authorizing a major surgical procedure such as a caesarean section. Throughout this opinion we have stressed that the patient's wishes, once they are ascertained, must be followed in "virtually all cases," unless there are "truly extraordinary or compelling reasons to override them," ante at 1247. Indeed, some may doubt that there could ever be a situation extraordinary or compelling enough to justify a massive intrusion into a person's body, such as a caesarean section, against that person's will. Whether such a situation may someday present itself is a question that we need not strive to answer here. We see no need to reach out and decide an issue that is not presented on the record before us; this case is difficult enough as it is. . . .

Ordinarily, when the factual record in a case is insufficient to support the trial court's decision, we remand for additional findings. In this case, however, a remand for supplemental findings would be inappropriate and futile because the caesarean has been performed and cannot be undone. . . .

Accordingly, we vacate the order of the trial court and remand the case for such further proceedings as may be appropriate. We note, in doing so, that the trial court's order allowing the hospital to perform the caesarean section was presumptively valid from the date it was entered until today. What the legal effect of that order may have been during its lifetime is a matter on which we express no opinion here.

Vacated and remanded.

NOTES

1. *The patient-physician relationship.* The dynamics of the patient-physician relationship can play a crucial role in the provision of medical care—and in efforts to compel particular medical interventions. Forced decision-making—and the overriding of the pregnant patient's desires—is more likely to occur in circumstances where the patient-physician relationship is not well-established, or is acrimonious. With that in mind, in what circumstances is a productive, trusting, respectful patient-physician

relationship likely to be cultivated? What circumstances might impede the formation of such a relationship between the patient and her doctor?

2. *Incidence of caesarean births.* According to the Department of Health and Human Services' Division of Vital Statistics, the rate of cesarean deliveries peaked in 2009 at 32.9% after increasing every year since 1996 (20.7%). The cesarean delivery rate has since decreased to 31.9% in 2018. BRADY E. HAMILTON ET AL., NAT'L VITAL STATISTICS REPORT, BIRTHS: FINAL DATA FOR 2018 (2019). The current cesarean-delivery rate in the U.S. far exceeds the World Health Organization's recommendation that caesarean sections comprise ten to fifteen percent of all births. World Health Org. [WHO], *WHO Statement on Caesarean Section Rates*, at 1, WHO/RHR/15.02 (April 2015).

3. *In the shadow of abortion.* In *In re A.C.*, the court goes to great lengths to clarify that "this case is not about abortion." Why did the court believe it was necessary to make this statement? In what ways does the specter of abortion haunt *In re A.C.* and other cases that are decidedly *not* about abortion?

2. VAGINAL BIRTH AFTER CAESAREAN SECTION

Pemberton v. Tallahassee Memorial Regional Medical Center, Inc.
66 F. Supp. 2d 1247 (N.D. Fla. 1999).

■ HINKLE, D.J.

This action arises from a state court's order compelling plaintiff Laura L. Pemberton, who was in labor attempting vaginal delivery at home at the conclusion of a full-term pregnancy, to submit to a caesarean section that was medically necessary in order to avoid a substantial risk that her baby would die during delivery. Based on the state court's order, physicians on the medical staff of the defendant hospital performed the caesarean section, resulting in the birth of a healthy baby. Ms. Pemberton suffered no complications.

Ms. Pemberton asserts the procedure was not medically necessary. She claims the physicians who rendered opinions that the procedure *was* medically necessary (and for whose actions the hospital has accepted responsibility), as well as the hospital itself, acted under color of state law. Ms. Pemberton claims the hospital and physicians violated her substantive constitutional rights . . . . Concluding that Ms. Pemberton's constitutional rights were not violated . . . I grant summary judgment in favor of the hospital.

Background

Ms. Pemberton delivered a prior baby in 1995 by caesarean section. Most caesarian sections are performed using a horizontal incision. Ms. Pemberton's 1995 [caesarean], however, was performed using a vertical incision. Moreover, the vertical incision extended well beyond a traditional low vertical incision up into the thickened myometrium. The nature of this caesarean presented a greater risk of uterine rupture during any subsequent vaginal delivery than would be the case with a more typical caesarean section.

When she became pregnant again in 1996, Ms. Pemberton attempted to find a physician who would allow her to deliver vaginally. She was unable to find any physician who would do so. . . .

Undeterred, Ms. Pemberton made arrangements to deliver her baby at home, attended by a midwife, without any physician attending or standing by and without any backup arrangement with a hospital. On January 13, 1996, after more than a full day of labor, Ms. Pemberton determined she needed an intravenous infusion of fluids . . . . She went with her husband, plaintiff Kent Pemberton, to the emergency room of defendant Tallahassee Memorial Regional Medical Center ("the hospital"), where she requested an IV.

Ms. Pemberton first saw a family practice resident on call for obstetrics, who brought the case to the attention of Dr. Wendy Thompson, a board-certified family practice physician whose practice included obstetrics. Dr. Thompson advised Ms. Pemberton that she needed a caesarean section. Ms. Pemberton refused, saying she wanted only an IV so she could return home to deliver vaginally. Dr. Thompson declined to assist in that plan by ordering only an IV and instead notified hospital officials of the situation. Hospital officials set about securing additional opinions from board certified obstetricians Dr. A.J. Brickler and Dr. David R. O'Bryan, the chairman of the hospital's obstetrics staff. Dr. Brickler and Dr. O'Bryan each separately concurred in the determination that a caesarean was medically necessary. Meanwhile, the Pembertons left the hospital against medical advice, apparently surreptitiously.

. . . The hospital called its long-time attorney, John D. Buchanan, Jr., who in turn called William N. Meggs, the State Attorney for Florida's Second Judicial Circuit, where Tallahassee is located. Mr. Meggs, who had the responsibility under Florida law to institute any court proceeding seeking to compel a medical procedure without a patient's consent, deputized Mr. Buchanan as a special assistant state attorney for purposes of dealing with this matter. Mr. Buchanan contacted Second Circuit Chief Judge Phillip J. Padovano, advised him of the situation and of Mr. Buchanan's intent to file a petition on behalf of the State of Florida seeking a court order requiring Ms. Pemberton to submit to a caesarean section, and requested a hearing.

Judge Padovano went to the hospital and convened a hearing in the office of hospital Senior Vice President and Chief Medical Officer Dr. Jack MacDonald. In response to the judge's questions, Drs. Thompson, Brickler and O'Bryan testified unequivocally that vaginal birth would pose a substantial risk of uterine rupture and resulting death of the baby.

Judge Padovano ordered Ms. Pemberton returned to the hospital. Mr. Meggs and a law enforcement officer went to Ms. Pemberton's home and advised her she had been ordered to return to the hospital. She returned to the hospital by ambulance against her will.

Judge Padovano then continued the hearing in Ms. Pemberton's room at the hospital. Both she and Mr. Pemberton were allowed to express their views. The judge ordered that a caesarean section be performed.

Dr. Brickler and Dr. Kenneth McAlpine performed a caesarean section, resulting in delivery of a healthy baby boy. Ms. Pemberton suffered no complications.

. . .

Ms. Pemberton now seeks in this federal court an award of damages against the hospital. She has not named the physicians as defendants because the hospital has agreed, for purposes only of the claims at issue in this lawsuit, that the physicians acted as agents of the hospital, thus allowing entry of a judgment against the hospital for any claim established against any or all of the physicians.

Ms. Pemberton claims that the forced caesarean violated her substantive constitutional rights . . . .

The hospital has moved for summary judgment. For the reasons that follow, I grant the motion.

Discussion

. . .

Ms. Pemberton invokes a variety of theories in support of her claim that requiring her to undergo a caesarean section was unconstitutional. She asserts a right to bodily integrity, a right to refuse unwanted medical treatment, and a right to make important personal and family decisions regarding the bearing of children without undue governmental interference. . . .

All of these are important interests of constitutional dimension. . . . [T]he Constitution does not explicitly address these various interests, but their constitutional stature has been recognized repeatedly. . . . While the precise reach of these various constitutional principles in this context remains unclear, it cannot be doubted that Ms. Pemberton had important constitutional interests that were implicated by the events the hospital set in motion.

Recognizing these constitutional interests, however, is only the beginning, not the end, of the analysis. Ms. Pemberton was at full term and actively in labor. It was clear that one way or the other, a baby would be born (or stillborn) very soon, certainly within hours. Whatever the scope of Ms. Pemberton's personal constitutional rights in this situation, they clearly did not outweigh the interests of the State of Florida in preserving the life of the unborn child.

This is confirmed by *Roe v. Wade*. There the Court recognized the state's increasing interest in preserving a fetus as it progresses toward viability. The Court concluded that by the point of viability—roughly the third trimester of pregnancy—the state's interest in preserving the life of the fetus outweighs the mother's own constitutional interest in determining whether she will bear a child.

The balance tips far more strongly in favor of the state in the case at bar, because here the full-term baby's birth was imminent, and more importantly, here the mother sought only to avoid a particular procedure for giving birth, not to avoid giving birth altogether. Bearing an unwanted child is surely a greater intrusion on the mother's constitutional interests than undergoing a caesarean section to deliver a child that the mother affirmatively desires to deliver. Thus the state's interest here was greater, and the mother's interest less, than during the third trimester situation addressed in *Roe*. Here, as there, the state's interest outweighed the mother's.[10]

Ms. Pemberton of course does not explicitly argue that her interest in avoiding a caesarean was greater than the baby's interest in living. . . .

Ms. Pemberton does assert, however, that what was at stake was not the baby's interest in living, because, she says, vaginal delivery did not pose an appreciable risk of the baby's death as the doctors claimed. She says she could and would have delivered her baby vaginally without harming him in any way.

The medical evidence belies Ms. Pemberton's bravado. The evidence is this. After a caesarean section of the type Ms. Pemberton previously had undergone . . . it is possible for a woman to deliver vaginally without uterine rupture or other complications. Nonetheless, there is a very substantial risk of uterine rupture and resulting death of the baby (as well as serious injury to the mother).

The record includes testimony of six physicians on this subject. Five—those whose testimony has been offered by the hospital—uniformly assert the risk of uterine rupture from any vaginal delivery in these circumstances is unacceptably high and the standard of care therefore requires a [caesarean]. . . .

In response, Ms. Pemberton offered the affidavit of a sixth physician, Dr. Marsden G. Wagner.[15] . . .

---

[10] In *Roe*, the Court held a fetus not a "person" imbued with its own constitutional rights. Whether that conclusion is equally applicable when labor is in progress and birth imminent need not be addressed here, because the state's interest in a viable, full-term fetus whose delivery is imminent is sufficient to defeat a claim of the type advanced by Ms. Pemberton, even if such a fetus is not deemed a "person" with his or her own constitutional rights.

[15] Dr. Wagner has impressive credentials but was based in Denmark, not the United States, from the 1980s until 1997, after the events at issue. For all this record indicates, in recent years he has lectured, consulted or attended rounds but apparently has not practiced. The tenor of his testimony is that of an advocate, not a witness. I nonetheless accept his testimony (though not all his rhetoric and legal conclusions) as true.

... Dr. Wagner's analysis assumes a delivery in a hospital attended by a physician. In fact, however, Ms. Pemberton was in the process of attempting vaginal delivery at home without a physician either participating or standing by. Prior to attempting to deliver vaginally at home, Ms. Pemberton was unable to locate a single physician willing to attend the birth; this shows just how widely held was the view that this could not be done safely. Ms. Pemberton's request to the hospital was not that she be allowed to deliver vaginally at the hospital but instead that the hospital provide an IV so that she could return home to deliver there. Even Dr. Wagner does not suggest that Ms. Pemberton could have delivered safely at home without an attending or even a standby physician.

[handwritten margin note: reject testimony supporting P's claim]

... In anything other than an extraordinary and overwhelming case, the right to decide would surely rest with the mother, not with the state. But based on the evidence disclosed by this record, this was an extraordinary and overwhelming case; no reasonable or even unreasonable argument could be made in favor of vaginal delivery at home with the attendant risk of death to the baby (and concomitant grave risk to the mother). On the clear and uncontradicted evidence, the interests of the baby required a caesarean section.[18]

Because of the very substantial risk that the course Ms. Pemberton was attempting to pursue would result in the death of her baby, requiring her to undergo an unconsented caesarean section did not violate her constitutional rights. . . .

Conclusion

Because Ms. Pemberton's constitutional rights were not violated . . . [t]he motions of defendant Tallahassee Memorial Regional Medical Center, Inc. for summary judgment . . . are GRANTED. . . .

[handwritten margin note: holding → rights not violated]

NOTES

1. *Additional claims.* In their complaint, the Pembertons alleged a series of common law tort claims, including negligence (medical malpractice), false imprisonment, and loss of consortium (on behalf of Mr. Pemberton). They also alleged that the hospital's procedures for imposing a caesarean birth over a patient's objections violated Laura Pemberton's procedural due process rights. The district court granted summary judgment to the defendants on all of these claims.

2. *In re A.C.* In *In re A.C.*, the court suggested that the circumstances in which a caesarean birth would be imposed over a competent patient's objections would be "extremely rare and truly exceptional." In your view, do the circumstances of *Pemberton* comport with this standard? *[handwritten: no]*

---

[18] Ms. Pemberton notes that performing a caesarean section was not without risk. Medical procedures rarely are. . . . The risk from a caesarean was far less, by orders of magnitude, than the risk from vaginal delivery . . . .

Elizabeth Kukura, *Choice in Birth: Preserving Access to VBAC*

114 PENN ST. L. REV. 955 (2010).

Reproductive rights as commonly understood in American society today emphasize the right to be free from unwanted reproduction—through the availability of contraception and abortion—at the expense of the freedom to reproduce and freedom within reproduction. . . .

One consequence of the cordoning off of pregnancy and childbirth from other forms of sexual and reproductive empowerment—and from human rights in general—is that many women are unaware of their rights in childbirth. . . . One area of particular controversy in today's hospitals and doctors' offices is the availability of vaginal birth after cesarean surgery ("VBAC") for women who have previously given birth by cesarean and wish to deliver subsequent babies vaginally. After a period in the 1990s when VBAC was promoted as a relatively low-risk alternative to repeat cesarean surgery and the number of successful VBACs increased significantly, the last several years have seen a reversal in the trend. The decline in VBAC rates is not simply a function of women opting for cesareans over vaginal delivery but is rather, at least in part, the result of a growing number of hospitals that refuse to accept women who intend to have VBACs and physicians who refuse to attend such births. A recent survey found that more than 800 hospitals—in every state of the United States—have banned VBAC, with women served by smaller and more rural medical facilities suffering disproportionately from such outright refusals to perform the services they seek. Another nearly 400 hospitals have de facto VBAC bans in place, due to the unavailability of providers willing to attend VBACs or rules about conditions for VBAC that are strict enough to make VBACs highly unlikely to occur.

VBAC restrictions constrain women's choices in childbirth and often lead them to undergo a medical procedure they do not want. Such a broad violation of the right to liberty and reproductive choice calls for a legal challenge. . . . A successful legal challenge must articulate the ways in which VBAC restrictions breathe new life into the medical profession's patriarchal roots and promote a downgrading of women's knowledge about their own bodies. . . .

I.   Trends in Birthing Practices: VBAC in Context

The twentieth century saw a major shift in our society's approach to the birthing process—from a practice that took place largely in the home and was overseen by midwives to one that occurs in a hospital setting with doctors and nurses (and the occasional midwife) shepherding a woman through labor and delivery. As such, the medicalization of birth is a relatively recent phenomenon. . . .

A.   Growth in Cesarean Births

At the turn of the twentieth century, developments in surgical methods, the use of anesthesia, and understanding about sterility made cesareans a safer, more reasonable option when complications arose during childbirth; its safety continued to improve over the course of the century. In the 1970s, the introduction of electronic fetal monitoring ("EFM") to monitor fetal heart rate and uterine contractions was widely believed to improve doctors' ability to predict fetal distress in labor. Widespread introduction of this technology led to a dramatic increase in the cesarean rate out of concern for fetal distress . . . . [I]n 1980, the National Institutes of Health convened an expert panel to discuss concern over the rapid growth in cesareans in American birthing practices. The panel concluded that promoting VBAC was an appropriate way to attempt to reverse the increasing cesarean rates. The advantages of VBAC include a shorter hospital stay, faster recovery time, and lower medical costs. Accordingly, it called for those hospitals with appropriate facilities, services, and staff for prompt cesarean birth to "permit a safe trial of labor and vaginal delivery for women who have had a previous low segment transverse cesarean birth."

By the mid-1980s, obstetricians had adopted a more widespread practice of using low transverse cuts instead of vertical incisions, and VBACs had become more common. Support for VBAC was bolstered by new studies at the time suggesting that about 75% of women with previous cesareans who tried to give birth vaginally would succeed, as well as continued concern about the growing rates of cesarean surgery by public health officials and insurance companies. . . .

In 1990, the VBAC rate for women who had previous cesareans had risen to 19.9%, a dramatic increase from ten years earlier. But in the same year, the cesarean rate rose to 22.7% of all births; it declined slightly during the mid-1990s, reaching its lowest point for the decade in 1996 at a rate of 20.7%—the year when VBACs reached an all-time high of 28.3%—but returned to 22.9% by 2000. VBAC rates saw a dramatic 33% increase from 1991 to 1996 and a subsequent 17% decline from 1996 to 1999; both trends were true across age groups and major races and ethnicities, as well as for almost all states and for most risk factors and complications. During the height of VBAC popularity, the overall VBAC rate was highest for non-Hispanic white women and lowest for Hispanic women, with non-Hispanic African American women falling in the middle. The push to reduce the cesarean rate continued throughout the 1990s, driven in part by awareness that the United States was out of step with other countries, including those with lower infant mortality rates, and that the U.S. cesarean rate was higher than the WHO recommendation. . . .

B.   Impact of [the American College of Obstetricians and Gynecologists (ACOG)] Guidelines

. . . In 1999, ACOG issued new, stricter guidelines for VBAC, which precipitated a marked decline in VBAC rates in the following years. Having previously called for medical personnel to be "readily" available, the guidelines now announced a "need for those institutions offering VBAC to have the facilities and personnel, including obstetric, anesthesia, and nursing personnel immediately available to perform emergency cesarean delivery when conducting a trial of labor for women with a prior uterine scar." Previously, the guidelines for those attempting VBAC were no different from the general standard for obstetric services, which ACOG defined as requiring the availability of a physician to evaluate labor and perform a cesarean surgery within thirty minutes of a decision to do so. But the new standard requiring the presence of a physician capable of performing a cesarean during the entire VBAC trial of labor exceeded the capabilities of many doctors. Practitioners who regularly attended VBACs had to close their VBAC practices because they could not treat patients in the clinic setting while attending the entire labor of a VBAC patient at a community hospital. The 1999 ACOG guidelines had a "chilling effect" on the ability of women to give birth vaginally if they had previously had a cesarean surgery, with the vast majority of VBACs available only in university and tertiary-level hospitals, where surgeons and anesthesiologists are continually available. A woman wishing to have a VBAC in an area without one of these facilities must bear the burden and expense of traveling to give birth at a medical center far from where she has been receiving pre-natal care (if there is such a center close enough for her to reach when labor begins), choose the riskier option of a VBAC homebirth, or abandon the hope for a VBAC and consent to a repeat cesarean. Declining VBAC rates reported by the National Center for Health Statistics reflect this tightening of VBAC availability: VBAC rates decreased from 23.4% in 1999 to 16.4% just two years later and sank to 10.6% in 2003, only four years after the ACOG guidelines were published.

. . .

By 2002, the International Cesarean Awareness Network (ICAN) was reporting an increase in calls from women who were unable to find a hospital where they could have a VBAC. Periodic reporting in the aftermath of the ACOG guidelines has highlighted the impact of ACOG's new standard. In 2004, the *New York Times* reported that half of all hospitals in New Hampshire and Vermont have banned VBAC. The *Washington Post* ran a story in 2005 about the VBAC ban adopted by Frederick Memorial Hospital in Frederick, MD, which inspired a media-friendly protest of mothers and children. The *Listening to Mothers* survey found that when asked a hypothetical question about choosing a cesarean in the future—even if no medical reason existed for the surgery—women preferred vaginal birth by a margin of five to one (83% to 16%). A follow-up study four years later found that 85% of women supported the right to choose VBAC.

3. REGULATION AND MARGINALIZATION OF MIDWIFERY

Charles Edward Ziegler, *The Elimination of the Midwife*
60 J. AM. MED. ASS'N 32 (1913).*

It is most gratifying to note the interest which has been awakened in the midwife problem during the past few years. . . . My own feeling is that the great danger lies in the possibility of attempting to educate the midwife and in licensing her to practice midwifery, giving her thereby a legal status which later cannot perhaps be altered. If she once becomes a fixed element in our social and economic system, as she now is in the British Isles and on the Continent, we may never be able to get rid of her. . . . Midwifery is the most poorly done of all medical work, not alone because about 50 percent of all labors are in the hands of midwives, but largely because of the low standards of midwifery existent among physicians and laity alike. . . . The argument that large numbers of physicians do as poor obstetrics as the midwives is entirely beside the question. We are quite ready to admit this, but to claim that for this reason we must retain the midwife, if we retain the physician, is absurd. . . . The fact is . . . we can get along very nicely without the midwife, whereas all are agreed that the physician is indispensable. It thus seems that the sensible thing to do is to train the physician until he is capable of doing good obstetrics, and then making it financially possible for him to do it, by eliminating the midwife and giving him such other support as may be necessary. . . .

. . .

The practice of obstetrics carries with it much more than standing by while the natural forces of labor complete the act as best they may. Obstetrics is an important branch of medicine, and to practice it safely and successfully implies a knowledge of general medicine, as well as a knowledge and appreciation of the physiology and pathology, the normal and the abnormal, of the childbearing process. The function of the physician in midwifery cases is to secure for the woman the best possible preparation for her labor, to accomplish her delivery safely and to leave her, so far as possible, in good physical condition; to prepare the mother for and to teach her the importance of nursing her baby, and to do everything that is possible to bring this about. . . . This means that pregnancy in each case must be carefully supervised, labor scientifically conducted and the mother and baby left so far as possible in good physical

---

* Read before the American Association for Study and Prevention of Infant Mortality at the Annual Meeting in Cleveland, October 1912.—Eds.

condition, which cannot be accomplished by untrained, non-medical individuals as are the midwives. . . .

. . .

It is, at present, impossible to secure cases sufficient for the proper training of physicians in obstetrics, since 75 percent of the material otherwise available for clinical purposes is utilized in providing a livelihood for midwives. If schools for midwives were established in all the larger cities of the country, a large number of additional cases would become necessary for training the midwives and we should soon find ourselves in the anomalous position of favoring the elimination of physicians from the practice of obstetrics, by still further depriving them of clinical material for their training in order to provide trained midwives to supplant them. If, moreover, the money which would be necessary for establishing and maintaining 200 schools for midwives, together with what would be necessary to supervise the midwives properly in their practice afterward, were used to pay physicians and nurses to care for the midwife cases, sufficient money would be available, to say nothing of the five million dollars which it is estimated is collected annually by midwives in this country and which should be paid to physicians and nurses for doing the work properly.

. . .

I believe that the midwife should be eliminated as rapidly as possible, but I do not believe that this can be accomplished at once nor perhaps even very rapidly. Legislation will not eliminate the midwife, unless hand in hand with such legislation provision is made to take her place. While a substitute is being provided she must be supervised in her work. She should, however, not be given a license but should be given a certificate, to be renewed from time to time or canceled as deemed advisable under the circumstances. Licensing her will not add to her knowledge, and will not make her more efficient, but will place on the state permanent responsibility for her work. No attempt should be made to establish schools for midwives, since, in my opinion, they are to be endured in ever-decreasing numbers, while substitutes are being created to displace them. . . .

. . .

. . . [T]he midwife can, in time, be entirely eliminated through the establishment and extension of obstetric charities—hospitals and dispensaries. The vast majority of cases, unable to pay physicians, can be cared for by medical students, provided the requirements for graduation are increased so as to give students the necessary training in obstetrics.

My own feeling is that before going into private practice each student should be required to deliver personally not less than fifty cases under careful supervision, and should also be taught to do on the living subject all the obstetric operations which the granting of his diploma gives him license to perform . . . . The average practitioner who gains his experience in obstetrics by operating solely on his own responsibility rarely ever learns to do it safely, and, therefore, always remains a menace to his patients, and should he eventually become an accomplished operator, his knowledge has been gained at the cost of much invalidism and a number of deaths. My argument, therefore, is that if he must acquire the knowledge, it is much better that he should do so under careful supervision and instruction. The public should learn that it is the duty of every citizen, if for no other reason than that of the safety of his own family, to insist that students of medicine be not only supplied with clinical material, but that they be required to utilize it in acquiring the knowledge which is indispensable to efficiency in the practice of obstetrics.

. . .

. . . The creations of obstetric education of the people will, in time, make the midwife unnecessary and her elimination inevitable.

NOTES

1.   *The rise of doctors and the decline of midwives.* In their 1973 book *Witches, Midwives, and Nurses: A History of Women Healers,* Professors Barbara Ehrenreich and Deirdre English note that although the modern medical community is largely populated by male doctors, with women assuming ancillary roles, this was not always the case. Ehrenreich and English thus link the decline of midwifery—and other female-populated medical roles—to a concerted effort by physicians, allied with an "emerging American business establishment," to monopolize medicine and shut women healers out:

> . . . For the first time in American history, there were sufficient concentrations of corporate wealth to allow for massive, organized philanthropy, i.e., organized ruling class intervention in the social, cultural, and political life of the nation. Foundations were created as the lasting instruments of this intervention—the Rockefeller and Carnegie foundations appeared in the first decade of the 20th century. One of the earliest and highest items on their agenda was medical "reform," the creation of a respectable, scientific American medical profession.

> The group of American medical practitioners that the foundations chose to put their money behind was, naturally enough, the scientific elite of the "regular" doctors. (Many of these men were themselves ruling class, and all were urbane, university-trained gentlemen.) Starting in 1903, foundation money began to pour into medical schools by the millions. . . .

> . . .

> . . . The Flexner Report, published in 1910, was the foundations' ultimatum to American medicine. In its wake, medical schools closed by the score, including six of America's eight black medical schools and the majority of the "irregular" schools which had been

a haven for female students. Medicine was established once and for all as a branch of "higher" learning, accessible only through lengthy and expensive university training. . . . Medicine had become a white, male, middle class occupation.

BARBARA EHRENREICH & DEIRDRE ENGLISH, WITCHES, MIDWIVES, AND NURSES: A HISTORY OF WOMEN HEALERS 31, 32 (1973).

2. *Race, gender, and class concerns.* Professors Ehrenreich and English further note that the professionalization of the medical profession had profound consequences for women, racial minorities, and those with fewer economic resources. Prior to the Flexner Report, "medical practice was traditionally open to anyone who could demonstrate healing skills—regardless of formal training, race, or sex." According to Ehrenreich and English, those responsible for the Flexner Report and its professionalizing impulse "had no intention of making [medical] training available to the great mass of lay healers and 'irregular' doctors. Instead, doors were slammed shut to blacks, to the majority of women and to poor white men." BARBARA EHRENREICH & DEIRDRE ENGLISH, WITCHES, MIDWIVES, AND NURSES: A HISTORY OF WOMEN HEALERS 33 (1973).

Danielle Pergament, *The Midwife as Status Symbol*
N.Y. TIMES, June 15, 2012, at 12.

Besides being impossibly gorgeous mothers, what else do Christy Turlington, Karolina Kurkova and Gisele Bündchen have in common?

Each could probably afford to buy her own private wing at a hospital, but instead of going to a top-notch obstetrician, all chose a midwife to deliver their babies.

"When I met my midwife, her whole approach felt closer to home," said Ms. Turlington, who delivered both her children—Grace, 9, and Finn, 6—with a midwife at St. Luke's-Roosevelt Hospital in New York, one with the help of an obstetrician because of complications. A former model, she founded . . . a nonprofit organization devoted to maternal health. "I knew I wanted a natural childbirth."

Are midwives becoming trendy . . . ? It seems that way, at least among certain well-dressed pockets of New York society, where midwifery is no longer seen as a weird, fringe practice favored by crunchy types, but as an enlightened, more natural choice for the famous and fashionable. "The perception of midwives has completely shifted," said Dr. Jacques Moritz, director of the gynecology division at St. Luke's-Roosevelt and a consulting obstetrician for three midwife practices. "It used to be just the hippies who wanted to go to midwives. Now it's the women in the red-bottom shoes."

. . .

Like obstetricians, midwives are medically trained and licensed to deliver babies. The main practical difference is that only obstetricians can perform surgeries, including Caesarean sections, and oversee high-risk pregnancies. On the other hand, midwives tend to approach childbirth holistically, and more of them provide emotional as well as physical care. This can involve staying by a laboring mother's side for 12 or more hours and making house calls.

Nevertheless, misconceptions remain. "There will always be people who have no idea what we do—they think we're witches who perform séances and burn candles," said Barbara Sellars, who runs CBS Midwifery, a small practice in Manhattan's financial district. "Sure, some women want a hippie-dippy spiritual birth and I can't guarantee that. I can guarantee the quality of care."

Ms. Sellars is considered one of the more respected midwives in New York, and her patients have included opera singers, actresses, bankers and models like Ms. Turlington. . . .

It was that high degree of care that led Kate Young, a stylist in New York, to seek out CBS Midwifery when she became pregnant with her son, Stellan, in 2008.

"My friends who had the best birth experiences all went to midwives," said Ms. Young . . . . "When you go to a doctor, you're left alone a lot. You don't have someone sitting there, looking you in the eye, getting you through it. When I thought about what I wanted for my child and how I wanted to have my child, every sign pointed to going to a midwife."

The rising popularity of midwifery among cosmopolitan women also coincides with larger cultural shifts toward all things natural, whether it's organic foods, raw diets or homeopathic remedies.

"Pregnancy is not a disease, it's a condition," said Dr. Moritz, whose own children were delivered by midwives. "We need fewer OB's and more midwives."

For other women, midwives offer a sense of control. "This is a time when women are asking more questions, getting healthy, wanting to be more empowered," said Ms. Kurkova, the 28-year-old model, who gave birth to her son, Tobin, in 2009. "I didn't want a hospital to take away my power. I didn't want to risk someone cutting me open and taking the baby out that way."

While midwife deliveries typically take place in the hospital, Ms. Kurkova is among those who have given birth at home.

"A home birth is more relaxed," said Miriam Schwarzschild, a home midwife for 25 years who lives in Brooklyn. "I wash my hands, listen to the baby's heartbeat, take the mother's vital signs and that's it. There are no routines. You step outside the bureaucracy at home."

A big selling point for midwives—both at home and in the hospital— is that, barring medical complications, the baby is not separated from the mother after the birth.

Another at-home advocate is Ms. Bündchen, who gave birth in 2010 to her son, Benjamin, in her Boston penthouse.

"We say Gisele delivered her own baby but I was in attendance," said Deborah Allen, a midwife in Cambridge, Mass., who, along with Mayra Calvette, a Brazilian midwife, was present at the birth. "Obviously, privacy is of the utmost importance. You are completely exposed. You need to be in a place where you feel comfortable to do that. Gisele was extremely prepared."

But not everyone is ready to go that route.

When Esther Haynes, deputy editor at Lucky Magazine, decided to go to a midwife, she quickly rejected an at-home birth. "This is New York, and if there was an emergency, I didn't want my story being, 'I called 911 and the ambulance took 45 minutes because of traffic!' " Ms. Haynes said.

"Also my apartment is kind of cluttered," she added. "I hated the thought of going into labor thinking, I wish I'd thrown out more magazines."

NOTES

1. *Class concerns in midwifery use.* The women quoted in this article are well-heeled (often wealthy) Manhattanites. Do their experiences suggest that midwifery is now a conceit of the economically privileged? Compare this account with that of Marsden Wagner, who credits contemporary midwifery with offering a significantly less expensive method of childbirth—a fact that may make it appealing to women with fewer economic resources. MARSDEN WAGNER, BORN IN THE USA: HOW A BROKEN MATERNITY SYSTEM MUST BE FIXED TO PUT WOMEN AND CHILDREN FIRST 102 (2006).

2. *Racial and cultural concerns.* While the CDC has noted a twenty-nine percent rise in the number of home births from 2004 to 2009, it is white women who are driving the increase. MARIAN F. MACDORMAN ET AL., NAT'L CTR. FOR HEALTH STATISTICS NO. 84, HOME BIRTHS IN THE UNITED STATES, 1990–2009, at 1 (2012); *see* Figure 1.

Figure 1. Percentage of Births That Were Home Births, by
Maternal Race/Ethnicity—United States, 1990–2009

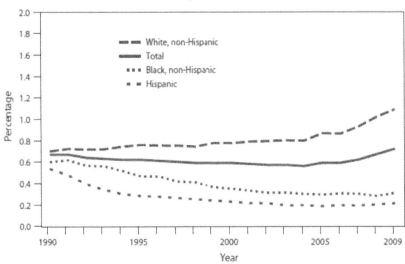

Because African Americans, and to a lesser extent, Latinas, may face higher
risks in giving birth, they may be reluctant to pursue home births. Further,
the fact that racial minorities historically have had uneven access to quality
medical care may contribute to the preference for hospital births over home
births.

3.   *Midwifery at home and in the hospital.* According to the National Center
for Health Statistics, in 2009, ninety-two percent of hospital births and five
percent of home births were attended by physicians, whereas seven percent
of hospital births and sixty-two percent of home births were attended by
midwives. MARIAN F. MACDORMAN ET AL., NAT'L CTR. FOR HEALTH
STATISTICS NO. 84, HOME BIRTHS IN THE UNITED STATES, 1990–2009, at 3
(2012).

4.   *Additional rationales for midwife use.* In addition to economic and
cultural concerns, other factors may account for the increasing use of
midwifery in the United States. Greater access to information about
pregnancy and the birthing process may have prompted a greater level of
comfort with midwifery. Similarly, a desire for greater autonomy in
pregnancy and birth may accord with the choice to use a midwife. Critically,
though midwifery remains a small (but growing) aspect of birthing practices
in the United States, it remains an accepted mainstream birthing practice
in other countries. *See* U.N. Population Fund, The State of the World's
Midwifery 2011: Delivering Health, Saving Lives, at 18 (2011).

Pemberton v. Tallahassee Memorial
Regional Medical Center, Inc.

66 F. Supp. 2d 1247 (N.D. Fla. 1999).

For an excerpt of Pemberton v. Tallahassee Memorial Regional Medical Center, Inc., *please see* supra *p. 223.*

NOTES

1.   Pemberton *and home birth.* Though *Pemberton* is often understood as a case about a forced caesarean section, it is worth noting that Laura Pemberton presented herself at the hospital in order to get an IV so that she could return to her home to give birth there with the assistance of a midwife.

2.   *Comparative developments.* Home births are the norm throughout much of the developing world. Though hospital births are more common in developed countries, there has been growing interest in home births. However, this burgeoning interest may be fragile. The January 2012 death of Caroline Lovell, an advocate in the Australian home-birth movement, a day after delivering her second daughter in a home birth, raised new questions about the safety of home births. *See* Richard Shears, *Woman, 36, Who Campaigned for Home Births Dies Having Baby Daughter at Home*, DAILY MAIL ONLINE (U.K.) (Jan. 31, 2012), http://www.dailymail.co.uk/health/article-2094348/Caroline-Lovell-Home-birth-advocate-dies-delivering-baby-daughter-home.html.

* * *

In recent years, a number of American jurisdictions have taken steps to legally regulate midwifery practice. The following is an excerpt from California's statute, which provides one of the nation's most comprehensive midwifery licensing schemes.

California Business & Professions Code § 2507

(2015).

2507.

(a)   The license to practice midwifery authorizes the holder to attend cases of normal childbirth, as defined in paragraph (1) of subdivision (b), and to provide prenatal, intrapartum, and postpartum care, including family-planning care, for the mother, and immediate care for the newborn.

(b)   As used in this article, the practice of midwifery constitutes the furthering or undertaking by any licensed midwife to assist a woman in childbirth as long as progress meets criteria accepted as normal.

(1)   Except as provided in paragraph (2), a licensed midwife shall only assist a woman in normal pregnancy and childbirth, which is defined as meeting all of the following conditions:

(A) There is an absence of both of the following:

(i) Any preexisting maternal disease or condition likely to affect the pregnancy.

(ii) Significant disease arising from the pregnancy.

(B) There is a singleton fetus.

(C) There is a cephalic presentation.

(D) The gestational age of the fetus is greater than 37 0/7 weeks and less than 42 0/7 completed weeks of pregnancy.

(E) Labor is spontaneous or induced in an outpatient setting.

(2) If a potential midwife client meets the conditions specified in subparagraphs (B) to (E), inclusive, of paragraph (1), but fails to meet the conditions specified in subparagraph (A) of paragraph (1), and the woman still desires to be a client of the licensed midwife, the licensed midwife shall provide the woman with a referral for an examination by a physician and surgeon trained in obstetrics and gynecology. A licensed midwife may assist the woman in pregnancy and childbirth only if an examination by a physician and surgeon trained in obstetrics and gynecology is obtained and the physician and surgeon who examined the woman determines that the risk factors presented by her disease or condition are not likely to significantly affect the course of pregnancy and childbirth.

(3) The board shall adopt regulations pursuant to the Administrative Procedure Act (Chapter 3.5 (commencing with Section 11340) of Part of 1 of Division 3 of Title 2 of the Government Code) specifying the conditions described in subparagraph (A) of paragraph (1).

(c)(1) If at any point during pregnancy, childbirth, or postpartum care a client's condition deviates from normal, the licensed midwife shall immediately refer or transfer the client to a physician and surgeon. The licensed midwife may consult and remain in consultation with the physician and surgeon after the referral or transfer.

(2) If a physician and surgeon determines that the client's condition or concern has been resolved such that the risk factors presented by a woman's disease or condition are not likely to significantly affect the course of pregnancy or childbirth, the licensed midwife may resume primary care of the client and resume assisting the client during her pregnancy, childbirth, or postpartum care.

(3) If a physician and surgeon determines the client's condition or concern has not been resolved as specified in paragraph (2), the licensed midwife may provide concurrent care with a physician and surgeon and, if authorized by the client, be present during the labor and childbirth, and resume postpartum care, if appropriate. A licensed midwife shall not resume primary care of the client.

(d) A licensed midwife shall not provide or continue to provide midwifery care to a woman with a risk factor that will significantly affect the course of pregnancy and childbirth, regardless of whether the woman has consented to this care or refused care by a physician or surgeon, except as provided in paragraph (3) of subdivision (c).

(e) The practice of midwifery does not include the assisting of childbirth by any artificial, forcible, or mechanical means, nor the performance of any version of these means.

(f) A midwife is authorized to directly obtain supplies and devices, obtain and administer drugs and diagnostic tests, order testing, and receive reports that are necessary to his or her practice of midwifery and consistent with his or her scope of practice.

(g) This article does not authorize a midwife to practice medicine or to perform surgery.

NOTES

1. *Licensing midwives—the national landscape.* Currently, thirty-five U.S. jurisdictions legally regulate midwifery practice by licensing Certified Professional Midwives (CPMs), sometimes called direct-entry midwives, who are trained to attend out-of-hospital births. Eleven U.S. jurisdictions are actively considering licensure for CPMs. *See CPMs Legal Status by State*, BIG PUSH FOR MIDWIVES CAMPAIGN, http://pushformidwives.org (last updated July 29, 2020).

2. *Dueling models of care.* According to Citizens for Midwifery, midwifery subscribes to a particular model of care that is distinguishable from the standard medical model. The Midwives Model of Care is based on the fact that pregnancy and birth are normal life events. The Midwives Model of Care includes:

- monitoring the physical, psychological, and social well-being of the mother throughout the childbearing cycle
- providing the mother with individualized education, counseling, and prenatal care, continuous hands-on assistance during labor and delivery, and postpartum support
- minimizing technological interventions[;] and . . .
- identifying and referring women who require obstetrical attention

According to midwifery advocates, the application of this model has been proven to reduce the incidence of birth injury, trauma, and caesarean section. *See Midwives Model of Care*, CITIZENS FOR MIDWIFERY, https://www.citizensformidwifery.org/mmoc#:~:text=The%20Midwives%20Model%20of%20Care%20includes%3A,and%20delivery%2C%20and%20postpartum%20support (last visited June 13, 2022). In what ways does the Midwives Model of Care depart from the standard medical model? Are there similarities between these two approaches?

3.   *Regulation as concession?* Proponents of midwifery licensing regimes argue that licensing is a practical—and responsible—response to the growing popularity of home births. Licensing midwives, they maintain, will improve access to home births, and will promote safer home births. With this in mind, does the shift towards regulating midwifery signal the medical community's grudging acceptance of home birth and natural birthing methods? Or does it signal the midwifery community's desire to be embraced as legitimate and accepted?

4.   REGULATING BIRTH AT THE MARGINS

Clifton v. Eubank

418 F. Supp. 2d 1243 (D. Colo. 2006).*

■ KANE, J.

. . . Pamela Clifton, an inmate of the Colorado Department of Corrections Women's Correctional Facility in Canon City, Colorado . . . seeks declaratory relief and damages against defendants, Nurse Ilona Eubanks, Officer Dawn Anaya, and Officer Ira Wilks. The action arises out of the stillbirth of Plaintiff Clifton's fetus. Clifton claims that the deprivation of her constitutional rights, in the form of improper medical care received in prison, resulted in the loss of her fetus. Defendants filed a Motion for Summary Judgment, arguing the suit is barred by the Prison Litigation Reform Act (PLRA). . . . Plaintiff has responded with a Motion to Recognize the Constitutional Rights of Prison Inmates, asserting that if the PLRA bars her suit it should be found unconstitutional.

I.   Background.

. . . On the morning of December 25, 1998, Pamela Clifton, an inmate housed by the Colorado Department of Corrections at the Women's Correctional Facility in Canon City, Colorado, went into labor. At the time, Clifton was approximately eight months pregnant. Four days earlier, on December 21, 1998, at an appointment with Dr. Mark Sindler, Sindler had reported that Clifton's pregnancy was proceeding normally.

Upon experiencing contractions, Clifton told Defendant Anaya, a guard at the correctional facility, that she was in labor and needed medical assistance. Defendant Anaya did not provide Clifton with medical assistance at that time, but instead sent Clifton back to her unit. At lunchtime, Clifton then told Defendant Wilks that she was in labor and needed help. Defendant Wilks also declined to provide Clifton with medical assistance and told Clifton to return to her unit. Upon Clifton's third request for medical assistance, another prison guard sent Clifton to the facility's medical unit.

---

*   The name of this case is "Clifton v. Eubank," despite the fact that the title defendant's name is "Eubanks," as evidenced in the text of the opinion.—Eds.

At the facility's medical unit, Defendant Nurse Eubanks examined Clifton. Nurse Eubanks reported finding no evidence that Clifton's water had broken. Clifton asked Defendant Eubanks to send her to the hospital despite the absence of amniotic fluid because with prior pregnancies she had required assistance with smooth induction of labor and breaking her water. However, Nurse Eubanks called Clifton's labor a "false alarm" and sent her back to her unit rather than to the hospital. During the examination, Nurse Eubanks did not use a fetal heart monitor to evaluate the status of Clifton's fetus, apparently because she did not know how to use the monitor.

water heant broken so deemed false alarm. Diant check status of baby

The next day, another prison guard noticed Clifton's distress and sent her to the medical unit. At this point, Clifton reported sensing no fetal movement. She was sent from the prison to a hospital, where it was determined that her fetus was dead. Clifton was required to undergo a stillbirth. Clifton claims that proper treatment, which was denied by the defendants, would have resulted in the healthy, live birth of her child.

II. Standard of Review

Summary judgment is appropriate "if the pleadings, depositions, answers to interrogatories, and admissions on file, together with the affidavits, if any, show that there is no genuine issue as to any material fact and that the moving party is entitled to a judgment as a matter of law."

. . .

III. Merits

Plaintiff's claims survive summary judgment because the PLRA's physical injury requirement does not bar a prisoner's claim for damages for violations of her constitutional rights when she alleges a deprivation of medical care that resulted in the loss of her fetus. The relevant section of the PLRA, entitled "Limitations on Recovery," states, "No Federal civil action may be brought by a prisoner confined in a jail, prison, or other correctional facility, for mental or emotional injury suffered while in custody without a prior showing of physical injury." Defendants argue the loss of a fetus requiring the mother to undergo a stillbirth does not constitute a physical injury that satisfies the physical injury requirement of the PLRA. The Plaintiff argues regardless of the presence or absence of physical injury attendant to undergoing a stillbirth, the PLRA should be deemed unconstitutional if it bars a claim in these circumstances. I address both arguments in turn . . . .

PS arguments

D argues that not bound by PLRA

Should to physical injury wrong

A.

. . .

The PLRA provides no statutory definition for the term "physical injury." Appeals courts confronting the issue have held that although a de minimis showing of physical injury does not satisfy the PLRA's physical injury requirement, an injury need not be significant to satisfy the statutory requirement. Physical pain, standing alone, is a de minimis injury that may be characterized as a mental or emotional injury and, accordingly, fails to overcome the PLRA's bar; but, when paired with allegations of physical effects, physical pain may support a claim under the PLRA. To define the contours of those more significant injuries that, standing alone, satisfy the PLRA, courts have looked to principles of tort law. . . . [M]any holdings support the notion that experiencing prolonged labor and stillbirth constitutes a physical injury to the mother, and, thus, provide a sufficient basis for surmounting the prior physical injury showing requirement of the PLRA.

1. pain + tangible effects (death of fetus) sufficient to overcome PLRA

. . .

. . . [T]he Tenth Circuit has suggested that although allegations of physical pain alone may be insufficient to overcome the PLRA bar, when paired with allegations of more tangible physical effects, they state a valid claim. Furthermore, allegations that a plaintiff suffered a miscarriage are sufficient to establish a question for the fact-finder as to whether the plaintiff suffered a more significant physical injury sufficient to overcome the PLRA's bar.

physical pain + physical injury

. . .

The physical injuries, including prolonged labor and the death of her otherwise viable fetus, that Plaintiff in the instant case alleges she experienced as a result of the deprivation of her constitutional rights, far surpass the de minimis physical injuries of headaches, insomnia, and stomach anxiety alleged [in other cases]. . . . Indeed, in all of the cited cases where courts found the physical injury to be de minimis, the plaintiffs failed to allege they endured any lasting, detrimental physical effects, whereas in the case at hand, Plaintiff alleges the prolonged labor she endured resulted in the death of her fetus. The tangible, physical effects in the matter at hand are undeniable, and, accordingly, should provide a sufficient basis for a cognizable claim, the PLRA notwithstanding.

this is not a de minimis physical injury

In addition, the claimants in cases where courts found de minimis injuries did not allege they experienced any heightened or prolonged physical pain as a result of their de minimis injuries. These facts readily distinguish the denied claimants from the Plaintiff in the case at hand, who alleges she experienced the pain of prolonged labor and the death of her fetus. . . .

. . .

[Here], Plaintiff demonstrates pain accompanied by tangible physical effects . . . significantly, the death of her otherwise viable fetus— sufficient to overcome the PLRA's bar.

. . . [Accordingly,] the degree to which Plaintiff's miscarriage resulted in physical harm is a question of fact, not law, that must be

reserved for the fact-finder, not dismissed on summary judgment for
want of a showing of physical injury. . . .

2.

. . .

The PLRA contains no definition of the term "physical injury."
However, tort law can inform notions of what constitutes a physical
injury under the PLRA. Tort law suggests that miscarriage constitutes a
physical injury to the mother. Accordingly, principles of tort law suggest
this Plaintiff has satisfied the PLRA physical injury requirement by
alleging that prolonged labor resulted in the death of her otherwise viable
fetus.

. . .

Colorado and the Tenth Circuit are joined by a number of states and
districts that have recognized the prolonged labor and miscarriage
attendant to the loss of a fetus as a compensable injury. In *Burgess v.
Superior Court*, the California Supreme Court explicitly rejected the
notion that an obstetrician providing medical services to a mother and
her fetus could "physically injure one and not the other." In *Burgess*, the
plaintiff alleged that negligent medical treatment resulted in the
deprivation of oxygen to her fetus for forty-four minutes before delivery,
resulting in injuries to his brain and nervous system and ultimately
causing his death one month later. The *Burgess* court held that to state
a cognizable claim, a physical injury is not required when a serious
emotional injury has been alleged. However, the *Burgess* court found a
physical injury had been alleged. Because an injury to one is, necessarily,
an injury to the other, the court reasoned, the failure of a mother to plead
a physical injury more specific and egregious than one inflicted upon "her
'nervous system and person,'" when her fetus was alleged to have been
fatally injured during delivery, was not a failure to state a cognizable
claim for a physical injury to herself.

Similarly, [in *Brown v. Green*,] the D.C. [C]ircuit has held that,
particularly when a fetus is not independently viable, an "injury to the
fetus is an injury to the mother." The plaintiff in *Brown* experienced a
prolonged pre-term labor that resulted in the premature birth and
subsequent death of her pre-viable twins. The *Brown* court reasoned
that, "[T]he physical event of a miscarriage at the stage of Ms. Brown's
pregnancy may in itself be considered a physical harm that could place
Ms. Brown in the zone of danger," and found that the nature and extent
of the physical injuries accruing to a mother when her fetus allegedly dies
as a result of negligent medical treatment are questions for the trier of
fact.

Indeed, [in *Daniel v. Jones*,] the pain of prolonged labor has been
held to constitute a physical injury in and of itself. As in *Brown*, the
plaintiff in *Daniel* experienced the premature birth and subsequent
death of her pre-viable twins after a prolonged pre-term labor and

delivery. In her complaint, the *Brown* plaintiff alleged she had suffered "great pain of body and mind," but had not specifically alleged other physical injuries. In denying the defendants' motion for judgment as a matter of law, the *Daniel* court reasoned a jury could reasonably return a verdict for plaintiff on a physical injury claim arising out of the miscarriage when "plaintiff was in excruciating pain for days before her ultimate delivery."

Even those courts that declin[e] to hold a miscarriage or still birth is a de facto injury to the mother have suggested miscarriages and stillbirths are in a class of their own and should be recognized as compensable injuries to the mother regardless of the presence or absence of any physical injury allegation. . . .

3.

. . .

An additional basis, along with recognizing a unique class of claim deserving of special accommodation, supports the recognition that allegations that prolonged labor resulted in the death of an otherwise viable fetus state a compensable claim, the PLRA's physical injury requirement notwithstanding. The Second Circuit, addressing the question of whether an emotional injury claim arising out of an alleged sexual assault was properly dismissed for lack of showing a prior "physical injury" under the PLRA, endorsed a "common sense" approach that seems wholly appropriate here. . . . Under the Second Circuit's common-sense approach, allegations that a deprivation of medical care resulted in prolonged labor and the death of a mother's otherwise viable fetus undoubtedly satisfy the PLRA's prior physical injury requirement. . . . The negative effects on Plaintiff's physical well-being that resulted from prolonged labor and subsequent death and stillbirth of her fetus are surely comparable to, if not potentially more physically injurious than, a sexual assault. . . . [C]ommon sense dictates Plaintiff's claim should survive the PLRA's bar.

. . .

In the matter at hand, because the damage inflicted by the alleged violation is terminal and irreversible, and because no relief, if not damages, is available to Plaintiff, who is no longer incarcerated, the PLRA should not operate to bar her claim. It was of central importance to the [Tenth Circuit in a prior case] that, although damages were barred, other forms of relief were available to the plaintiff, should his claim succeed. Because that is not the case here, the PLRA should not operate to bar damages. . . .

. . .

Accordingly, because this matter is so readily distinguishable, with facts indicating such clear physical effects, and because no other remedy would be available to Plaintiff if the PLRA were allowed to bar damages, it is well within the bounds of Tenth Circuit precedent to find that constitutionally the PLRA may not operate to bar the claim of a woman who alleges the deprivation of proper medical treatment resulted in prolonged labor and the death and stillbirth of her fetus.

Based on the foregoing, Defendants' Motion for Summary Judgment is DENIED. . . .

Doe v. Gustavus

294 F. Supp. 2d 1003 (E.D. Wis. 2003).

■ GRIESBACH, DISTRICT JUDGE.

Plaintiff Jane Doe brought this action under 42 U.S.C. § 1983 against ten defendants, all of whom are security or nursing staff at the Taycheedah Correctional Institute for women in Fond du Lac, Wisconsin. The plaintiff alleges that each of the defendants was deliberately indifferent to her serious medical needs while she was in custody. Specifically, many of the defendants allegedly ignored her cries for help and her medical needs while she went into labor in April 2001. . . . The defendants have moved for summary judgment on the grounds that there is no basis to find deliberate indifference, that two defendants had legitimate institutional objectives in their motives, and that they are all entitled to qualified immunity.

I. Background

1. The Delivery of the Baby

The plaintiff was incarcerated at Taycheedah Correctional Institution (TCI) as of February 21, 2001. At that time, she was well along in her pregnancy, with due date estimates ranging between April 10 and May 2 of that year. On April 18, Doe was told that she was being taken to have labor induced. She refused, but agreed to be induced sometime the next week.

According to the plaintiff, her refusal to be induced on April 18 caused a "stir" at TCI. Lt. Patricia Reese made Doe aware, apparently against prison policy, that her next induction appointment would be April 25. Since knowledge of an off-site appointment could pose a security risk, defendant Gustavus ordered Doe put into segregated confinement on April 20. In "seg," there is less interaction with guards and other inmates, and the cells are more spartan, with doors instead of bars.

Around 1:00 AM on April 21, Doe's water broke in a "big gush," and she was able to get a set of dry clothes from a guard. Four hours later, Nurse Engelmann tested Doe's pants, but no amniotic fluid was found because, according to the plaintiff, the pants had dried out by this point. Nurse Engelmann did not apparently ever speak to Doe.

At 7:30 AM Doe pressed an emergency buzzer in her room and asked defendant Camp, a guard, whether she would be taken to the hospital soon because her water had broken. Camp replied in the negative, apparently relying on the Nurse Engelmann's test indicating that Doe's water had not broken. Camp also said that no pain medication would be forthcoming and a nurse would not arrive until there was a crowning. . . .

[T]he plaintiff did not see a nurse until approximately 1:00 PM, when Nurse Vande Kolk-Stamm was handing out medications. The nurse checked Doe's contractions through the small tray door in Doe's cell, noting that they were five to six minutes apart and lasted some thirty seconds. The nurse concluded that the plaintiff was in false labor. At 9:15 that night the plaintiff was seen by Nurse Rockow. She also observed the plaintiff through the tray door, felt for contractions, and concluded that the plaintiff was in false labor. During the second shift of the 21st, Doe was called a "dumb bitch" by Sgt. Garrett Noyons, who also said that Doe would have to clean up her own vomit if she got sick again.

Around midnight, the plaintiff pressed the emergency button because she "just could not stand the pain anymore." Sgt. Rawson responded and called Nurse James Hebel. Doe complained of constant pain, and Hebel gave her some ibuprofen. He timed her contractions, which were between fifteen and thirty seconds, and stated that if she were really in labor, the contractions would last about one minute. Hebel observed that Doe's skin appeared sweaty and that she was in pain, but he told her that the pain she was experiencing was in the wrong place for it to signify labor. Around 1:10 AM on April 22, the plaintiff felt a "wet gush" down her legs, pressed the emergency button, and Sgt. Rawson again called Nurse Hebel. Hebel tested the discharge and then called the hospital to determine the meaning of the color blue on the nitrazine paper he used for the test. He also phoned the doctor on call, but was unable to reach him. He returned to Doe's cell at 2:01 AM and felt the plaintiff's abdomen, which felt soft to him. He asserts that the staff at St. Agnes Hospital (who were apparently advising him over the phone) told him the abdomen should be hard during a contraction, and since the plaintiff's was soft, he did not believe she was about to deliver. The plaintiff asserts that the information from St. Agnes was flawed because Hebel did not explain the entire situation to them, i.e., the plaintiff's symptoms and other signs of labor.

In any event, the situation at about 2:00 AM was that Hebel did not think the plaintiff was in immediate need of medical attention. The plaintiff was still in pain and, while changing into some dry clothes, felt some movement between her legs. She reached down and felt the baby's head and exclaimed, "the head, the head!" Eventually she felt the baby's mouth and scooped some "gook" out of it. She then found it "pretty easy" to complete the delivery, and wrapped the baby in a dirty towel. Nurse Hebel was contacted by radio at 2:16 AM, and he went to provide assistance.

Doe and the baby were taken to the hospital by ambulance, and Doe returned to TCI around 2:00 PM, some twelve hours later. Upon her return, she met with Capt. Gustavus, who allegedly stated that "she knew Doe had pushed that baby out on purpose, just to get out of segregation." Doe was then placed in maximum security on temporary lock-up (TLU), apparently due to Gustavus' belief that Doe had conspired with an inmate who had called Doe's parents regarding the delivery. While in TLU, Doe states that she was provided with no post-birth provisions such as ice or pads until 7:00 AM the next morning when pads were brought.

. . .

II. Analysis

Summary judgment is proper if the pleadings, depositions, answers to interrogatories, and admissions on file, together with any affidavits, show that there is no genuine issue of material fact and the moving party is entitled to judgment as a matter of law.

. . .

The legal claim brought here is for deliberate indifference, which is a particular subset of those forms of cruel and unusual punishment prohibited by the Eighth Amendment. The plaintiff in such a case must demonstrate two things. First, "that her condition was serious," which is an objective standard. A condition is "serious" if "the failure to treat a prisoner's condition could result in further significant injury or the unnecessary and wanton infliction of pain." Second, the plaintiff must show that each defendant acted with the "deliberately indifferent" culpable state of mind, which is a subjective standard. That is, state officials are deliberately indifferent if they know of and disregard "an excessive risk to inmate health or safety;" they must both be "aware of facts from which the inference could be drawn that a substantial risk of serious harm exists, and [they] must also draw the inference."

Thus, the first question which must be answered is: was plaintiff's condition "serious" for Eighth Amendment purposes? That is, could the failure to treat the plaintiff's condition (i.e., pre-birth, birth, and post-birth) have resulted in significant injury or the unnecessary and wanton infliction of pain? I conclude that Doe's condition was, in fact, serious. . . . Having medical assistance immediately preceding and during a birth is, in today's society, taken for granted. This is why the prison had a policy of taking women to St. Agnes Hospital for births. . . . [T]he defendants do not seriously contest the issue of medical seriousness . . . .

1. The Nursing Defendants

. . .

The recurring theme of the allegations against the defendant nurses is that they dropped the ball so egregiously that the only reasonable explanation is that they knowingly disregarded the risks to the plaintiff. That is, their treatment errors were so beyond the pale that a jury could conclude that they were not errors at all, but intentional or reckless actions. [According to plaintiff's expert witness], a professor of nursing at Marquette University in Milwaukee. . . .

All the symptoms presented by the plaintiff indicated the need for her immediate transport. These include patient feeling rectal pressure, vaginal discharge with some blood, pulse increasing, pain increasing, vomiting. . . . *Any nurse eligible for licensure in the State of Wisconsin would have known to send this patient to the hospital based on these signs and symptoms that labor was progressing and the patient needed monitoring and professional care only available in a hospital setting.*

While the nurse defendants argue that there is no evidence to suggest that they were deliberately indifferent, what they really mean is that there is no *direct* evidence of their subjective mental state. That is, no one heard any of the nurses say, "let's all delay treating Jane Doe so that she suffers." The lack of direct evidence is not surprising, however, as most claims involving a mental state must be proved without a clear view into the mind of the accused. Instead, such claims commonly rely on a jury's ability to make inferences based on the circumstances involved. Here . . . the expert will testify that any nurse would have known that the plaintiff was in labor. The jury could then connect the dots and find that, because the defendants are nurses, they must have known that the plaintiff was in labor. A jury could proceed to find that some, or all, of their actions constituted deliberate indifference. Thus, while the defendants are correct that the expert nursing witness cannot testify to the ultimate legal issue of deliberate indifference, she can certainly present testimony from which a jury could reasonably conclude that the performance of the nursing staff was so far below acceptable standards that the behavior of any given nurse was deliberate. Accordingly, construing the evidence in the light most favorable to the plaintiff, I conclude that a reasonable jury could find in the plaintiff's favor. I therefore will deny the motion for summary judgment as to the nursing defendants.

2.   The Security Defendants

. . .

[Likewise, d]ismissal on summary judgment is unwarranted as to any of [the security] defendants [Lt. Reese, Sgt. Noyons, Sgt. Rawson, and Sgt. Camp]. As to each, there is evidence in the record from which a jury could reasonably find that he or she deliberately ignored Doe's medical condition and suffering. A jury could find that these defendants were aware that the plaintiff was in pain and might be going into labor, and that in failing to assist her they knowingly subjected her to a substantial risk of harm.

3.   Supervisor Defendants

Finally, the plaintiff has sued Capt. Jeanette Gustavus . . . . Gustavus is alleged to be involved in the decision to put Doe in seg on the trumped-up grounds that Doe was a security risk. Gustavus also accused Doe of pushing the baby out on purpose (in order to get out of seg). Placing a prisoner in seg is not, in itself, cruel and unusual punishment. But putting a late term pregnant woman in seg is something different, and a jury could find that it was part the plan of Gustavus and Lt. Reese to ignore Doe's medical condition and to make life as difficult as possible for Doe, so difficult in fact that their actions resulted in cruel and unusual punishment. A jury could find that these actions constituted deliberate indifference, particularly when it is alleged, as here, that the defendants based their decisions on an animus against the plaintiff.

. . .

4. Qualified Immunity

Finally, the defendants make an attempt to assert that all of the above allegations, even if true, are barred by the qualified immunity that the defendants enjoy as state actors. But qualified immunity does not insulate state actors from violations of clearly established law. As the Seventh Circuit has noted, the Eighth Amendment prohibition against deliberate indifference to a prisoner's medical needs has been clearly established . . . . Thus, I do not find that qualified immunity applies here.

. . .

5. Conclusion

. . . I find that genuine issues of material fact remain in this case and the resolution of those facts is, of course, the province of the factfinder. . . . [D]efendants' motion for summary judgment is . . . DENIED.

[handwritten margin note: holding: Ps denied MSJ granted]

NOTES

1. *PLRA and pregnancy.* The Prison Litigation Reform Act (PLRA) was enacted for the purpose of curbing lawsuits brought by incarcerated persons. Prison Litigation Reform Act of 1995, 110 Stat. 1321 (1996) (codified as amended at 18 U.S.C. § 3626 (2014)). With this in mind, it is not surprising that the PLRA presented a significant procedural hurdle for the plaintiff in *Clifton.* Should there be an exception to the PLRA for those bringing suits for inadequate medical services and similar claims? Is the commitment to judicial economy and reducing frivolous lawsuits in tension with the interest in providing quality prenatal medical care?

[handwritten margin note: judicial econ]

2. *Professional competency in the carceral context.* In *Doe v. Gustavus,* the plaintiff argued that the nursing staff failed to meet general standards of professional competency in their interactions with her during her labor and delivery. Can we expect prison health care providers to perform their jobs with the same level of competence as we would expect outside of prison? Or is the professional bar lowered in the carceral context?

[handwritten margin note: people who deserve mgt qual care — still NO]

3. *The ever-expanding carceral state.* The American prison system has seen such a vast expansion over the last three decades that it has become common to speak of the "carceral" (prison) state. As of 2020, approximately .7% of the American population is incarcerated in a federal or state prison or local jail— that's 698 people incarcerated per 100,000 people. Peter Wagner & Wanda

Bertram, *"What Percent of the US Is Incarcerated?" (And Other Ways to Measure Mass Incarceration)*, PRISON POL'Y INITIATIVE (Jan. 16, 2020), https://www.prisonpolicy.org/blog/2020/01/16/percent-incarcerated/. That's more than any other country in the world. Peter Sawyer & Wendy Sawyer, *States of Incarceration: The Global Context 2018*, PRISON POL'Y INITIATIVE (June 2018), https://www.prisonpolicy.org/global/2018.html. Nationally, 6.7 million adults—or one in every thirty-seven—are under correctional control, which includes incarceration, probation, and parole. Alexi Jones, *Correctional Control 2018*, PRISON POL'Y INITIATIVE (Dec. 2018), https://www.prisonpolicy.org/reports/correctionalcontrol2018.html. Women are only an estimated seven percent of those incarcerated in state or federal prisons on drug offenses. *See* BUREAU OF JUSTICE STATISTICS, DEP'T OF JUSTICE, DRUG OFFENDERS IN FEDERAL PRISON: ESTIMATES OF CHARACTERISTICS: BASED ON LINKED DATA 3, tbl.3 (Oct. 2015) (authors' calculations). Racial disparities among incarcerated women are striking, yet there have been some interesting developments. The rate of imprisonment for African American women has been declining since 2000, In fact, between 2000 and 2017, the rate of imprisonment in state and federal prisons declined by 55% for black women, while the rate of imprisonment for white women rose by 44%. Nevertheless, by 2017, the imprisonment rate for African American women (92 per 100,000) was nearly twice the rate of imprisonment for white women (49 per 100,000). These statistical trends likely reflect both decreasing rates of incarceration among African American women and the increasing incarceration of white women. *See* THE SENTENCING PROJECT, INCARCERATED WOMEN AND GIRLS 2 (June 6, 2019).

4.   *Pregnancy at the margins.* Both *Clifton* and *Doe* make clear the difficulties that incarcerated women face during pregnancy. To what extent are the problems presented in these cases—uneven access to prenatal care, indifferent health care providers—limited to pregnant women in prisons? To what extent do these issues plague women who are marginalized in other ways?

→ Pain ignored, inadequate access to resources, etc

5.   *Shackling during labor and delivery.* According to the *New York Times*, correctional facilities across the United States routinely shackle pregnant prisoners during labor and delivery in order to prevent escape. *See* Adam Liptak, *Prisons Often Shackle Pregnant Inmates in Labor*, N.Y. TIMES, Mar. 2, 2006, at A16. Professor Priscilla Ocen has argued that the shackling of pregnant prisoners is rooted in antebellum slavery and postbellum convict leasing systems, and thus, "attach[ ] to Black women in particular through the historical devaluation, regulation, and punishment of their exercise of reproductive capacity . . . ." Priscilla A. Ocen, *Punishing Pregnancy: Race, Incarceration, and the Shackling of Pregnant Prisoners*, 100 CALIF. L. REV. 1239, 1239 (2012). As the following case illustrates, the shackling of pregnant women is not unique to the prison system.

Villegas v. Metropolitan Government of Nashville

709 F.3d 563 (6th Cir. 2013).

■ CLAY, CIRCUIT JUDGE.

in custody of
ble of the infraction,
to the infraction,
police fund
She wasn't
here
legally

Plaintiff Juana Villegas brought suit under 42 U.S.C. § 1983, claiming violations of her Eighth Amendment rights (made applicable to pretrial detainees through the Fourteenth Amendment) as a result of her being restrained and shackled prior to and following giving birth while in the custody of law enforcement authorities employed by Defendant Metropolitan Government of Nashville and Davidson County. On cross-motions for summary judgment, the district court granted summary judgment to Plaintiff .... For the reasons that follow, we reverse the district court's grant of summary judgment to Plaintiff and remand for further proceedings.

BACKGROUND

Plaintiff Juana Villegas's saga began on July 3, 2008 when her car was stopped by Berry Hill, Tennessee police officer Tim Coleman. At the time of the stop, Plaintiff was nine months pregnant. When Plaintiff failed to produce a valid driver's license, Coleman arrested Plaintiff and transported her to the jail operated by the Davi[d]son County Sheriff's Office ("the jail").[1] Once there, a jail employee, working as an agent of the United States through Immigration and Customs Enforcement's 287(g) program, *see* 8 U.S.C. § 1357(g), inquired into Plaintiff's immigration status and determined that Plaintiff was not lawfully in the United States. Due to her illegal status, a detainer was placed on Plaintiff, which meant that federal immigration officials would delay taking any action until after resolution of Plaintiff's then-pending state charges. After being unable to post bond, Plaintiff was, as a result of the immigration detainer, classified as a medium-security inmate.

Plaintiff was held in the jail from Thursday, July 3, 2008 until late on Saturday, July 5, 2008. At 10:00 p.m. on July 5, 2008, Plaintiff informed a jail guard that her amniotic fluid (or "water") had "broke" and that she was about to have her baby. Plaintiff was transported to the jail infirmary where a nurse confirmed that Plaintiff's water had broken and summoned an ambulance to take Plaintiff to Nashville General Hospital (the "Hospital"). For transportation in the ambulance, Plaintiff was placed on a stretcher with her wrists handcuffed together in front of her body and her legs restrained together. ...

... Shortly after Plaintiff arrived at the Hospital, officer Brandi Moore arrived to relieve [officers] Barshaw and Farragher[, who had transported Plaintiff to the hospital]. Farragher informed Moore that Plaintiff was a "medium-security inmate" with a "hold" or "detainer" in her file and gave Moore a "charge sheet," indicating Plaintiff's name,

---

[1] The jail accepts and houses individuals arrested by local law enforcement agencies without inquiry into whether the arrest was proper.

charge, and custody level. After Farragher and Barshaw left, Moore removed Plaintiff's handcuffs but kept one of Plaintiff's legs restrained to the hospital bed.

As if she isn't sprinting off during labor!

At some point during Moore's shift, Moore overheard Hospital staff talking to a doctor about a "No Restraint Order" but claims that she never received such an order from the Hospital. Additionally, Moore admitted to having been told by a nurse that she "shouldn't put leg irons on [Plaintiff]," but the conversation ended there. At 11:20 p.m., a Hospital doctor signed a physician's order stating: "Please remove shackles," and this order was placed in Plaintiff's hospital file, though never specifically given to any officer. Moore was relieved by officer David Peralta at 11:00 p.m. on June 5th and told Peralta to "be prepared for a no restraint order."

Shortly after the shift change, Peralta removed Plaintiff's restraints. According to hospital records, when the shackles were removed, Plaintiff had only dilated to 3 centimeters ("cm"). Plaintiff did not become dilated to 4 cm, a point that Defendant contends is medically relevant, until 11:45 p.m. It was around this time that Plaintiff also first requested pain medication, which she received in the form of an epidural. Plaintiff gave birth without any complications at approximately 1:00 a.m. on July 6, 2008—roughly two hours after Peralta removed her shackles. Plaintiff remained unshackled until shortly before Peralta's shift ended at 7:00 a.m., when he re-restrained Plaintiff to the bed at one of her ankles. Plaintiff was never handcuffed postpartum.

. . . .

DISCUSSION

I.   Deliberate Indifference

PS claim

Plaintiff . . . claims that by shackling her while she was in labor and postpartum, in the manner it did, Defendant was deliberately indifferent to her need to be unrestrained during this time. . . .

A.   Standard of Review

We review a district court's grant of summary judgment *de novo*, applying the same standards as the district court. Summary judgment is appropriate "if the pleadings, depositions, answers to interrogatories, and admissions on file, together with any affidavits, 'show that there is no genuine issue as to any material fact' " such that " 'the movant is entitled to a judgment as a matter of law.' " "A genuine issue of material fact exists when there are 'disputes over facts that might affect the outcome of the suit.' " . . .

B.   General Principles

"The Eighth Amendment prohibition on cruel and unusual punishment protects prisoners from the 'unnecessary and wanton infliction of pain.' " *Barker v. Goodrich,* 649 F.3d 428, 434 (6th Cir. 2011). Pretrial detainee claims, though they sound in the Due Process Clause of the Fourteenth Amendment rather than the Eighth Amendment, are analyzed under the same rubric as Eighth Amendment claims brought by prisoners. . . .

Proving an Eighth Amendment claim requires that the plaintiff make a showing of deliberate indifference. *Harrison v. Ash,* 539 F.3d 510, 518 (6th Cir. 2008). Deliberate indifference has two components to it: objective and subjective. The objective component first demands a showing that the detainee faced a substantial risk of serious harm. But the objective component is not met by proof of such a substantial risk of serious harm alone. The objective component further "requires a court to assess whether society considers the risk that the prisoner complains of to be so grave that it violates contemporary standards of decency"—that is, it "is not one that today's society chooses to tolerate." Therefore, the objective component of deliberate indifference is met upon a showing that a detainee faced a substantial risk of serious harm and that such a risk is one that society chooses not to tolerate.

As to the subjective component, a plaintiff must show that the defendant had "a sufficiently culpable state of mind." This state of mind is shown "where 'the official knows of and disregards'" the substantial risk of serious harm facing the detainee. That is, "the official must both be aware of facts from which the inference could be drawn that a substantial risk of serious harm exists, and he must also draw the inference." Direct evidence about a defendant's knowledge is not necessary, but rather, the knowledge aspect of the subjective component can be inferred from the obviousness of the harm stemming from the risk.

C.   Shackling Claim

Plaintiff predicates her first deliberate indifference claim on her being shackled during labor and postpartum recovery. . . . [S]adly, [shackling during labor and delivery] is a practice that has been around for at least a century. In spite of this history, the law on the shackling of pregnant women is underdeveloped, and this Court has not previously decided a deliberate indifference claim based on the practice. Therefore, we must at the outset determine a framework under which to analyze such a claim.

1.   Framework

In dealing with deliberate indifference claims in the past, this Court has enumerated some specific types of claims for factual scenarios that frequently arise. These types include, but are not limited to, conditions-of-confinement, excessive-force, and medical-needs. . . .

A typical medical-needs claim deals with a deprivation of medical care. . . .

Another typical medical-needs claim involves the interference with a prescribed treatment plan . . . .

... [T]his Court has stated that the objective component of deliberate indifference in a medical-needs case is met where a plaintiff produces evidence of a "serious medical need." *Blackmore v. Kalamazoo Cnty.*, 390 F.3d 890, 896 (6th Cir. 2004). We have further defined a serious medical need as either "one that has been diagnosed by a physician as mandating treatment or one that is so obvious that even a lay person would easily recognize the necessity for a doctor's attention." *Harrison*, 539 F.3d at 518. The problem with viewing a shackling claim, like Plaintiff's, solely as a medical-needs claim is that it ... does not necessarily involve the denial of or interference with medical treatment; rather, it may be premised on the notion that the shackles increase Plaintiff's risk of medical complications. We should hasten to add that there may be circumstances where shackling could interfere with medical treatment—where, for example, the shackles are not removed so that the medical treatment may proceed unimpeded; however, such were not the circumstances in this case.

This problem led one court to analyze the shackling claim it faced as a conditions-of-confinement claim. *See Women Prisoners of D.C. Dep't of Corr. v. District of Columbia*, 877 F. Supp. 634, 668–69 (D.D.C.1994), *modified in part on other grounds*, 899 F. Supp. 659 (1995), *vacated in part and remanded on other grounds* (93 F.3d 910 (D.C. Cir. 1996)). Under our case law, the objective component of a conditions-of-confinement claim is proven where the detainee or prisoner is denied "the minimal civilized measure of life's necessities." *Barker*, 649 F.3d at 434 (internal quotation marks omitted). This includes deprivations of "adequate food, clothing, shelter, [medical care, and safety]." *Farmer [v. Brennan]*, 511 U.S. [511], 832 [(1994)]. A typical conditions-of-confinement case is *Spencer v. Bouchard*, 449 F.3d 721 (6th Cir. 2006), *abrogated on other grounds by Jones v. Bock*, 549 U.S. 199 (2007), where the prisoner complained of being held in an unbearably cold and leaky cell. While a shackling claim does in some respects resemble some of our conditions-of-confinement cases, the nature of the medical proof offered by Plaintiff is different than we have previously addressed in the conditions-of-confinement context.

Similarly, we believe that the excessive-force type of claim is also not well adapted for analysis of Plaintiff's claim. The inquiry in excessive-force cases is about "whether force was applied in a good-faith effort to maintain or restore discipline, or maliciously and sadistically to cause harm," a formulation that does not harmonize with the way Plaintiff has presented her claim. In sum, it seems to us that none of the refinements we have made to the general deliberate indifference principles in order to more easily analyze common factual scenarios are particularly well-suited to the theory and proof offered by Plaintiff.

The Eighth Circuit in *Nelson v. Correctional Medical Services*, 583 F.3d 522 (8th Cir. 2009) (*en banc*), seems to have similarly recognized the crossover nature of a pregnant shackling claim. In dealing with such a claim the Eighth Circuit identified the "relevant questions" as: "(1) whether [the plaintiff] had a serious medical need or whether a substantial risk to her health or safety existed, and (2) whether [the official] had knowledge of such serious medical need or substantial risk to [the plaintiff's] health or safety but nevertheless disregarded it." *Id.* at 529. This formulation used by the *Nelson* court combines both medical-needs language ("serious medical need") as well as language that points to conditions-of-confinement ("substantial risk to health or safety"). In light of this language, rather than attempt to pigeonhole Plaintiff's shackling claim into a more specific subcategory of deliberate indifference claims, we think it best to analyze her claim under the general deliberate indifference principles.[3]

Consistent with the general principles discussed above, we analyze Plaintiff's claim in two steps, addressing first the objective component and then the subjective one. . . .

2.   Analysis

a.   Objective Component

In attempting to prove the objective component of her shackling claim, Plaintiff points us to prior pregnancy shackling cases, like *Nelson,* as well as statements from notable public health organizations. Turning first to the case law, each of the three courts to deal with a deliberate indifference shackling claim found the practice of shackling women in labor to be violative of contemporary standards of decency.

. . . .

All of these courts found that shackling the pregnant women under the circumstances of their respective cases violated the Eighth Amendment. In addition to these analogous cases, as the Eighth Amendment " 'must draw its meaning from the evolving standards of decency that mark the progress of a maturing society,' . . . an assessment of contemporary values concerning the infliction of a challenged sanction is relevant." *Gregg v. Georgia,* 428 U.S. 153, 173 (1976). In this vein, Plaintiff has adduced evidence from the American Medical Association, the American College of Obstetricians and Gynecologists, the United Nations, and Amnesty International decrying the practice of shackling pregnant women, especially while in labor.

In its *Standard Minimum Rules for the Treatment of Prisoners,* the United Nations stated that restraints including handcuffs and leg irons should only be used "[a]s a precaution against escape," "[o]n medical grounds by direction of the medical officer," or "if other methods of control

---

[3]   We note that while *Nelson* is informative with respect to the appropriate framework to apply, the majority would not go as far as the dissent in making *Nelson* dispositive of this case. There [is a] key distinction[ ] between this case and *Nelson* that [is] relevant. . . . *Nelson* did not involve a potential flight risk. The facts of *Nelson* are therefore quite different than the facts of this case where Plaintiff had an immigration detainer placed on her due to her previous removal from the country. . . .

fail, in order to prevent a prisoner from injuring himself or others or from damaging property."

With respect to pregnant detainees, the American Medical Association has passed a resolution that provides:

> No restraints of any kind shall be used on an inmate who is in labor, delivering her baby or recuperating from the delivery unless there are compelling grounds to believe that the inmate presents:

> An immediate and serious threat of harm to herself, staff or others; or a substantial flight risk and cannot be reasonably contained by other means.

Am. Med. Ass'n, "Shackling of Pregnant Women in Labor," Policy H-420.957 (June 2010).

Also with respect to pregnant detainees, the American College of Obstetricians and Gynecologists found:

> Physical restraints have interfered with the ability of physicians to safely practice medicine by reducing their ability to assess and evaluate the physical condition of the mother and the fetus, and have similarly made the labor and delivery process more difficult than it needs to be; thus, overall putting the health and lives of the women and unborn children at risk. . . .

> The practice of shackling an incarcerated woman in labor may not only compromise her health care but is demeaning and unnecessary. . . . Testimonials from incarcerated women who went through labor with shackles confirm the emotional distress and the physical pain caused by the restraints. Women describe the inability to move to allay the pains of labor, the bruising caused by chain belts across the abdomen, and the deeply felt loss of dignity.

Letter from Ralph Hale, Exec. Dir., Am. Coll. of Obstetricians & Gynecologists, to Malika Saada Saar, Exec. Dir., The Rebecca Project for Human Rights (Jun. 12, 2007).

Finally, Amnesty International has formulated a policy directive that states, in relevant part:

> Routine use of restraints on pregnant women is cruel, inhumane and degrading treatment, and given medical and other factors impeding pregnant or birthing women from attempting escape or becoming violent, the presumption must be that no restraints should be applied. . . .

> All Departments of Corrections should have an explicit policy dealing with the use of restraints on pregnant women. The following principles should be incorporated into such a policy:

> Leg irons, shackles, belly chains or handcuffs behind the body may not be used at any time during pregnancy.
>
> For pregnant women in the third trimester no restraints may be applied, including during transportation.
>
> Under no circumstances may restraints of any kind may [sic] be used on a woman in labor or while she is giving birth.
>
> . . .
>
> No restraints should be applied while a woman remains in the hospital during recovery. . . .

AMNESTY INT'L USA, USE OF RESTRAINTS ON PREGNANT WOMEN IN THE USA: POLICY GUIDELINES (2009).

However, as the United Nations and American Medical Association recognize, Amnesty International's policy also recognizes that there may be "rare instances" that deviations may be warranted—specifically, "where there are serious and imminent grounds to believe that a woman may attempt to harm herself or others or presents a credible risk of escape that cannot be contained through other methods."

Two things are clear from Plaintiff's evidence on the objective component. First, the shackling of pregnant detainees while in labor offends contemporary standards of human decency such that the practice violates the Eighth Amendment's prohibition against the "unnecessary and wanton infliction of pain"—i.e., it poses a substantial risk of serious harm. . . .

Second, it is equally clear, however, from both courts and commentators that the right to be free from shackling during labor is not unqualified. The sources establishing the potential violation also recognize that in certain circumstances, despite the fact that the woman is in labor, shackles may nonetheless be tolerated by society. . . .

These same caveats are found in the cases applying the Eighth Amendment to shackled pregnant detainees. The court in the *Women Prisoners* case left the door open for a situation where a prison "may need to shackle a woman prisoner who has a history of assaultive behavior or escapes." 877 F. Supp. at 668. Additionally, *Nelson* stated that Eighth Amendment would not afford a detainee a claim where a jail put forth "clear evidence that she is a security or flight risk." 583 F.3d at 534. Therefore, we must consider whether there is evidence in the record of the instant case that supports Defendant's claim that Plaintiff was a flight risk.

Defendant concedes that Plaintiff was restrained because of her status as a medium-security inmate, a status she obtained by virtue of the federal immigration check, which established that she was illegally present in this country, after having been previously removed. As Defendant's expert Richard Stalder, former president of both the

American Correctional Association and the Association of State Correctional Administrators, declared, Plaintiff's "security restrictions" (including the restraints) were "consistent with the custody level assignment": medium-security. Additionally, with respect to Plaintiff, "the stress of pending deportation could easily promote what otherwise may be uncharacteristic unlawful behaviors, including flight from custody and subsequent illegal activity." ... Finally, he opined that the jail's policy was consistent with the American Correctional Association Policy that mirrors the American Medical Association resolution in light of Plaintiff's "custody classification resulting from multiple immigration and customs enforcement violations." To be sure, this evidence shows that the jail's classification procedures were followed in this case. However, because of Plaintiff's obvious, physical condition as a pregnant woman in labor, a reasonable factfinder could nonetheless conclude that Plaintiff was not a flight risk despite the jail's conformity with its classification procedures. This potential dispute renders summary judgment inappropriate.

b.   Subjective Component

Turning to the subjective component, as stated above, the question is whether the officers had knowledge of the substantial risk, recognized the serious harm that such a risk could cause, and, nonetheless, disregarded it. On this point, Plaintiff has produced testimony from both fact and expert witnesses in an attempt to prove that Defendant had the knowledge to have "had a sufficiently culpable state of mind."

. . . .

. . . Plaintiff attempts to establish that Defendant was subjectively aware of the risks that the shackles posed by virtue of the fact that Hospital staff ordered the shackles removed. Knowledge of such a "no restraint order" would, at minimum, evince knowledge of a substantial risk of serious harm. Plaintiff's evidence on this front, however, falls short. Although it is clear from the record that a no restraint order was placed in Plaintiff's file at 11:20 p.m., no testimony reveals that Defendant or its officers ever knew about the existence of this order. Moore's testimony only discloses her knowledge that Hospital staff were contemplating a no restraint order, not that one was ever disclosed to her. Moore states that she told Peralta that she had been told that Hospital staff "were trying to get a no restraint order but no one had specifically talked to me about it." For his part, Peralta stated that Moore had "said that there was going to be a no restraint order" but does not mention whether he ever saw it. At worst, this evidence confirms Defendant's contention that it never knew about a no restraint order; at best, it shows the existence of a factual dispute concerning Defendant's officers' knowledge.

Both sides also presented expert testimony as to the specific harm faced by Plaintiff and the potential obviousness of this harm to Defendant's officers. Plaintiff offered two different witnesses: a gynecologist, Dr. Sandra Torrente, to opine on the physical risks associated with shackling, and a psychiatrist, Dr. Jill DeBona, to opine on the psychological risks. Defendant also presented a gynecologist, Dr. Bennett Spetalnick.

Spetalnick, who is the head of Obstetrics and Gynecology at Vanderbilt University Medical Center, opined that "[a]lthough the risk of a DVT (deep venous thrombosis) and PE (pulmonary embolism) is increased with pregnancy and postpartum, my medical opinion, based on the literature and personal experience, is that these risks are not enhanced by a leg restraint and/or handcuffs." Further, "[a]mbulation is encouraged in the peripartum period, but the amount of ambulation recommended to prevent a DVT is not prevented by leg restraints as they were used in [Plaintiff's] situation." Spetalnick explained that "[a]lthough labor is very painful, it is medically anticipated that the pain experienced in latent labor is less severe than that experienced in active labor [(defined as dilation to 4 cm)]. The facts of the case indicate that . . . she was in latent labor until at least 23:30 . . . [and] that all of her restraints were removed prior to active labor." In sum, as to shackling, Spetalnick concluded: "There is no significant risk to the patient with a leg restrained up to the time of delivery and immediately post partum and none in this case with no leg restrained for 7 hrs.—2 hrs. prior and for 5 hours after delivery."

Torrente, an assistant professor of Obstetrics and Gynecology at Meharry Medical College, on the other hand, stated: "Placing a pregnant woman in leg irons or shackles increases her risk of developing a potentially life-threatening blood clot. This risk is increased and present throughout a woman's entire pregnancy; however, it is at the greatest risk post-partum," and therefore women should be "ambulatory . . . as often as possible" during this period. Additionally, Torrente detailed the importance of being unrestrained due to "potential occurrence of umbilical cord prolapse" and "the increased risk in falling due to a pregnant woman's impaired balance." Finally, restraints would create "discomfort" and would not allow the woman to "safely handle a newborn child." Torrente further opined that Plaintiff was shackled during "active labor" and because she had previously given birth, "the risk created by shackling her during labor are even greater because of her potential to begin giving birth much sooner following the onset of labor than the average woman in labor." Specifically in response to Spetalnick, she disagreed "that there was no significant risk to [Plaintiff] because she happened to be unshackled two hours before she delivered[, and] . . . Spetalnick is incorrect that [Defendant's] conduct did not substantially elevate [Plaintiff's] risk of DVT and PE."

Lastly, psychiatrist DeBona, in detailing the various "episode[s] of shackling" that Plaintiff experienced, described the psychological effects of the shackling on Plaintiff:

While in the ambulance, [Plaintiff] had to face the terror that her baby might die. She did not realize that an officer was in the ambulance. She believed that there was no one to remove the shackles. . . . [S]he feared that her son would not be able to be delivered. . . . Her trust in people had been eroded by her treatment, especially the shackling. . . .

In her opinion, DeBona diagnosed Plaintiff with post traumatic stress disorder (PTSD) and major depressive disorder, among other things. Comparing the testimony of Spetalnick, Torrente, and DeBona indicates a further factual dispute about the specific risk of harm to Plaintiff and the obviousness to the officers of harm to Plaintiff.

In light of the material factual disputes surrounding whether Plaintiff was shown to be a flight risk, whether Defendant's officers had any knowledge about a no restraint order, and the conflicting expert testimony about the ill effects of Plaintiff's shackling, we conclude that the district court improperly granted summary judgment to Plaintiff on her shackling claim. On remand, a jury will need to determine whether Plaintiff was a flight risk in her condition and whether Defendant had knowledge of the substantial risk, recognized the serious harm that such a risk could cause, and, nonetheless, disregarded it, recognizing that such knowledge may be established through the obviousness of the risk.

. . . .

For the reasons stated above, we reverse the district court's grant of summary judgment to Plaintiff and remand for further proceedings consistent with this opinion.

■ WHITE, CIRCUIT JUDGE, dissenting.

. . . .

Villegas established that shackling created an objectively substantial risk of serious harm in two ways; by showing that her condition as a laboring and then lactating woman 1) resulted in medically prescribed treatment and 2) was obvious to lay persons as a serious medical need. *See Harrison v. Ash*, 539 F.3d 510, 518 (6th Cir. 2008); *see also Havard v. Wayne Cnty.*, 436 Fed. Appx. 451, 454 (6th Cir. 2011) ("The birth of a child always presents a risk of serious injury to both mother and child."); *Nelson v. Corr. Med. Servs.*, 583 F.3d 522, 530 n. 5 (8th Cir. 2009) (en banc) ("That labor is inherently risky is well known . . . and the hazards associated with labor and childbirth have entered the collective consciousness.") . . .

The majority observes that Villegas's right to be free from shackling during labor must be balanced against Defendant's penological interest, and concludes that a question of material fact remained whether Villegas was a flight risk. I disagree.

First, deliberate indifference to a prisoner's serious medical need "can typically be established or disproved without the necessity of

(Handwritten margin notes:) delib indifference can be established w/out balancing States penological interest; nothing in record shows assessment that she was actually a flight risk; facility wasn't "unsecured" building itself locked and armed guards all around; TODR no reason to shackle P

balancing competing institutional concerns for the safety of prison staff." *Nelson*, 583 F.3d at 530.

Here, Defendant maintained that Villegas's restraints were "consistent with" her medium-security designation and that illegal immigrants *in general* pose a danger of flight. But Villegas's medium-security designation did not take into account her late-term pregnancy or that she had gone into labor, nor was it based on any assessment of flight risk or risk of harm—it was automatic because of the Immigration and Customs Enforcement (ICE) detainer. Villegas was not being held for a crime of violence and had not been convicted of any crime. She was not individually assessed for flight risk or risk of harm to herself or others, and she had not engaged in any conduct evidencing such. Neither the ICE detainer's automatic designation of Villegas as "medium-security" nor generalized evidence that illegal immigrants may pose a flight danger constitute "clear evidence" that Villegas was a security or flight risk.

Defendant's asserted penological interest in shackling Villegas while she was being transported to and then hospitalized, to maintain control over her in an *unsecured* facility, suffers from another flaw. It is undisputed that at least one armed officer was present in the ambulance, at least one armed officer was present in the hospital room or outside the room at all times, and the maternity ward at Metro General Hospital is locked down at all times, that is, a nurse must unlock the doors and authorize persons to enter and exit. In order to flee or pose a threat, Villegas would have had to harm or elude armed officer(s) and the nurse authorizing entry and exit from the maternity ward charged with unlocking the doors.

Finally, I note that even though Villegas went through labor and gave birth without threat of escape or harm to anyone, Defendant's officers shackled her legs *together* postpartum while she walked, showered and used the toilet. This despite the fact that before the birth, a physician had ordered in writing that the shackles be removed.

In sum, Defendant made no showing, and the facts belied, that shackling Villegas at any time was necessary, whether to effect their purported penological interest or otherwise.

Villegas satisfied the subjective component by demonstrating that Defendant's officers acted with deliberate indifference to her serious medical needs, i.e., knew of and disregarded the substantial risk of harm posed by shackling her during labor and postpartum. An Eighth Amendment claimant "need not show that a prison official acted or failed to act believing that harm actually would befall an inmate; it is enough to [sic] that the official acted or failed to act despite his knowledge of a substantial risk of serious harm." *Harrison*, 539 F.3d at 518.

The district court's opinion sets forth the evidence establishing that Defendant's officers were aware of the substantial medical risks posed by shackling women while in labor and during postpartum recovery and disregarded it. The majority concludes that "no testimony reveals that Defendant or its officers ever knew about the existence of [the no-restraint order]" and thus that a factual dispute existed regarding Defendant's officers' knowledge of a substantial risk of serious harm. This determination erroneously presumes that Defendant's officers could know or become aware of the substantial medical risks shackling posed to Villegas only by entry of a written no-restraint order in her hospital file *and* the officers being "shown" the order. Even if this were the case, the record is clear that before the no-restraint order was placed in Villegas's file, hospital nursing staff had asked the officers to remove Villegas's shackles several times, had advised the officers that a no-restraint order was coming, and had advised officers of the high risk of blood clots after giving birth if the shackles were not removed.

Officer had good reason to know that shackling could cause harm

The majority also concludes that conflicting expert testimony about the ill effects of Villegas's shackling raised a material factual dispute. I disagree. Given the long-established law on shackling during labor and postpartum and the undisputed facts, I agree with the district court that the declaration of defense expert Dr. Spetalnick did not raise an issue of *material* fact.

Dr. Spetalnick opined that restraining Villegas did not enhance the medical risks of deep venous thrombosis and pulmonary embolism or cause her excessive pain under the circumstance that she was restrained while in *latent* labor, the restraints were removed while she was in active labor, and remained off until hours after the delivery. He opined that the amount of ambulation recommended to prevent deep venous thrombosis "is not prevented by leg restraints as they were used" in Villegas's case; that although a leg restraint is a theoretical impediment in the case of an emergency, a restraint would not prevent, significantly impede, or make less accurate the vaginal exam; and that although leg restraints can carry bacteria, there was no evidence that the use of restraints in this case created a significant infectious risk to Villegas.

Villegas's expert witness Dr. Torrente opined that shackling increased the risk of injury to both Villegas and her unborn child, that Defendant's officers subjected Villegas to unnecessary pain and suffering by shackling her after her water broke, and that Dr. Spetalnick's claim that Villegas was only in latent labor while shackled did not mean from a medical standpoint that Villegas was not in pain or that birth could not have progressed very quickly. Among Dr. Torrente's points unaddressed by Dr. Spetalnick were that shackling a woman after her water has broken is extremely dangerous because of a potential for umbilical cord prolapse, that once a woman's membranes have ruptured a cervical exam should be performed as soon as possible for potential umbilical cord prolapse, that a proper cervical exam and monitoring cannot be conducted while shackled, and that shackling may restrict or delay the ability to provide emergency medical care; that medical personnel need

D's expert didn't address these medical concerns w/shackling ↓

constant unrestricted access to a woman in labor for complications that can occur including a non-reassuring fetal heart tracing, for which the patient needs to be able to move to her left lateral decubitus position to increase blood flow to the baby; that a woman must be able to *freely* move and walk as often as possible to reduce risk of blood clots; that restraining a woman in labor and postpartum enhances the risk of injury to both woman and child because a woman should have *full range of movement of limbs and remain ambulatory* because of pain; that use of shackles during labor and postpartum is extremely unsanitary; and that the stress Villegas was placed under by shackling her increased the risk of injury to her and her unborn child. Dr. Torrente opined based on her review of Villegas's medical charts and personal history (i.e., having had three children), that she could have easily progressed to the final phase of labor while shackled in the ambulance or in the hospital room, and pointed to the fact that she progressed from being dilated at 3 cm to 10 cm in only two hours as support, noting that Dr. Spetalnick apparently overlooked this point.

Nor did Dr. Spetalnick rebut Villegas's expert and treating psychiatrist, Dr. DeBona, who stated that because Villegas's legs were shackled together while in the ambulance, she could not move or open her legs and faced the terror that her baby might die, believing there was no one to remove the shackles and that her labor would be short, as it had been with two of her children.

. . . .

NOTES

1. *Shackling before the Eighth Circuit.* In her lawsuit, Juana Villegas relies extensively on *Nelson v. Correctional Medical Services*, 583 F.3d 522 (8th Cir. 2009) (en banc), where the Eighth Circuit, sitting *en banc*, concluded that the shackling of a pregnant prisoner during labor constituted a violation of the Eighth Amendment. Why does the Sixth Circuit find *Nelson* inapposite in *Villegas*?

2. *Flight risk?* In *Villegas*, the majority goes to great lengths to distinguish the factual circumstances from those in *Nelson*. Of particular importance to the court was the fact that Villegas, whose immigration status was in question, was being held in immigration detention. This fact, according to the court suggested that she was a likely flight risk—and thus, the state's interest in shackling was justified. Critically, the dissent objected to treating immigration detention status as *per se* evidence of a flight risk. According to Judge White, Villegas, who was nine months pregnant at the time of her detention, and in labor at the time she was shackled, was unlikely to attempt an escape. Do you agree?

3. *Lactation and breastfeeding.* Villegas also filed a second claim, arguing that the defendant's refusal to allow her to take the breast pump provided to her by the hospital violated her Eighth Amendment rights. *Villegas*, 709 F.3d at 567. The defendant justified the decision on the ground that the breast

pump was not considered "a critical medical device." *Id.* at 579. Noting that
hospital staff had not "prescribed" expressing milk as part of Villegas's
postpartum treatment, *id.* at 579, the majority maintained that it was not
obvious that defendant has failed to meet Villegas's medical needs. In her
dissent, Judge White observed that "if a woman is unable to express milk for
several days because she does not have access to her child or to a breast
pump, she can develop engorged breasts and mastitis, and infection of the
breast tissue that results in severe breast pain, swelling, significant fever,
rigors and chills." *Id.* at 584 (White, J., dissenting). Indeed, Villegas's expert
witness, Dr. Torrente, opined that Villegas's development of mastitis was
"almost certainly caused by her inability to use a breast pump . . . following
her release from the hospital." *Id.* at 584.

4.   *Reproductive justice, birthright citizenship, and the immigration debate.*
As Allison Hartry observes, cases like *Villegas* may reflect the terms of
broader debate over immigration policies, and, in particular birthright
citizenship. Under U.S. law, any person born within the United States
(including the territories of Puerto Rico, Guam, the U.S. Virgin Islands, and
the Northern Mariana Islands) and subject to its jurisdiction is
automatically granted U.S. citizenship upon birth (as are many, though not
all, children born to American citizens overseas). In recent years, opponents
of undocumented immigration have argued that birthright citizenship
incentivizes foreign women to enter the United States unlawfully so that
their children will be born U.S. citizens. According to critics, as citizens,
these so-called "anchor babies" may then facilitate the immigration of foreign
family members. As Hartry argues, Immigration and Customs Enforcement
officials' targeting of pregnant immigrant women for deportation and
removal is likely an effort to prevent these women from giving birth in the
United States. *See* Allison S. Hartry, *Birthright Justice: The Attack on
Birthright Citizenship and Immigrant Women of Color*, 36 N.Y.U. REV. L. &
SOC. CHANGE 57 (2012).

                                    * * *

   *Some states have responded to critiques of the practice of shackling
pregnant inmates during labor and delivery. Below is California's effort
to confront the issue of shackling through legislation.*

California Assembly Bill No. 2530
(2012).

   An act to amend Section 6030 of, to add Section 3407 to, and to repeal
Section 5007.7 of, the Penal Code, and to amend Sections 222 and 1774
of the Welfare and Institutions Code, relating to inmates.

   [Approved by Governor September 28, 2012. Filed with Secretary of
State September 28, 2012.]

The people of the State of California do enact as follows:

SECTION 1. Section 3407 is added to the Penal Code, to read:

3407.

(a) An inmate known to be pregnant or in recovery after delivery shall not be restrained by the use of leg irons, waist chains, or handcuffs behind the body.

(b) A pregnant inmate in labor, during delivery, or in recovery after delivery, shall not be restrained by the wrists, ankles, or both, unless deemed necessary for the safety and security of the inmate, the staff, or the public.

(c) Restraints shall be removed when a professional who is currently responsible for the medical care of a pregnant inmate during a medical emergency, labor, delivery, or recovery after delivery determines that the removal of restraints is medically necessary.

(d) This section shall not be interpreted to require restraints in a case where restraints are not required pursuant to a statute, regulation, or correctional facility policy.

(e) Upon confirmation of an inmate's pregnancy, she shall be advised, orally or in writing, of the standards and policies governing pregnant inmates, including, but not limited to, the provisions of this chapter, the relevant regulations, and the correctional facility policies.

(f) For purposes of this section, "inmate" means an adult or juvenile who is incarcerated in a state or local correctional facility.

. . .

SEC. 3. Section 6030 of the Penal Code is amended to read:

6030.

(a) The Board of State and Community Corrections shall establish minimum standards for local correctional facilities. The board shall review those standards biennially and make any appropriate revisions.

. . .

(e) The standards shall require that inmates who are received by the facility while they are pregnant be notified, orally or in writing, of and provided all of the following:

(1) A balanced, nutritious diet approved by a doctor.

(2) Prenatal and post partum information and health care, including, but not limited to, access to necessary vitamins as recommended by a doctor.

(3) Information pertaining to childbirth education and infant care.

(4) A dental cleaning while in a state facility.

(f) The standards shall provide that a woman known to be pregnant or in recovery after delivery shall not be restrained, except as provided in Section 3407. The board shall develop standards regarding the restraint of pregnant women at the next biennial review of the standards after the enactment of the act amending this subdivision and shall review the individual facilities' compliance with the standards.

. . .

CHAPTER 3

REGULATING FAMILY AUTONOMY

A. INTRODUCTION

Sex and reproduction are often regulated in unobtrusive and even invisible ways. For example, the state may confine "legitimate" sex and reproduction to marriage, a kind of legal regulation that may seem unproblematic on its face. As a consequence of their location in marriage, these relationships—and any sexual acts that occur within them—are afforded a great deal of privacy and respect. However, when sexual and reproductive arrangements (or behaviors) deviate in some way from the traditional marital family ideal, respect and recognition are more contingent. In the selections that follow, we see the way in which law grapples with "troublesome" relationships or "threatening" behaviors. Almost all of these cases occur against the backdrop of the normative ideal of a heterosexual, married, procreative family, whose autonomy is largely protected by law. As the law examines non-traditional relationships and conduct against this backdrop of sexual normativity, assumptions about "normal" sex and relationships are revealed and reinstantiated.

Alice Ristroph & Melissa Murray, *Disestablishing the Family*
119 YALE L.J. 1236 (2010).

In this excerpt, Alice Ristroph and Melissa Murray reflect on the constitutional prohibition on establishing a state religion. As they recount, this prohibition plays an important role in creating alternative sources of moral authority that can potentially curb the excesses of government control. This "anti-totalitarian" argument in favor of disestablishment of religion, they argue, can also inform our understanding of the family and the state's regulation of the family. In their view, the state should remain neutral as to what kinds of family forms will be acceptable—resisting the urge to "establish" any particular familial model. Yet far from remaining neutral, the state consistently "establishes" a single form of family—the mutually-monogamous procreative couple.

INTRODUCTION

Congress shall make no law respecting an establishment of a family, or prohibiting the free exercise thereof. . . .

. . .

II.   FAMILIAL ESTABLISHMENT: ENCOUNTERS
WITH THE CONSTITUTION

Families are often sites of value creation and moral development, as philosophers and political leaders alike have long recognized. It is often simply taken for granted that a state will encourage, or even require, the kind of familial institutions most likely to produce the right kind of citizens. The right kind of citizen, and thus the best form of family, may vary from one regime to another, but the power of the regime to regulate the family for these purposes is rarely questioned.

Of course, churches too are sites of value creation and moral development, and at one time it was taken for granted that a state would encourage or require the kind of religious institutions most likely to produce the right kind of citizens. The puzzle, then, is why the liberal commitment to religious disestablishment has never led to any similar call for familial disestablishment. One possible explanation is that the family is not seen as posing the same threats as an established religion. That is, the state's promotion of a particular form of family—the marital, nuclear family—does not entail the same thick ideological content as an ecclesiastical establishment because the values associated with the marital family are perceived as broad and inclusive values whose active promotion by the state poses no threat to ideological diversity or healthy political debate.

But is this right? ... [W]e suggest that the particular normative framework promoted by the model legal family is more ideologically specific than a set of general principles easily acceptable to all members of a democratic society. We begin with the constitutional construction of the marital, nuclear family as an ideal family, and explore the underlying ideological implications of that model. We then examine constitutional challenges to criminal laws that regulate the family. We identify a thick, aggressive version of familial establishment in a criminal ban on polygamy, and a somewhat thinner form of familial establishment in the Supreme Court's decisions concerning parental control over their children's education.

A.   The Marriage Model

. . .

Constitutional doctrine's clear preference for the marital nuclear family above other alternatives is evident in a number of contexts. Take, for example, the Supreme Court's decisions concerning unmarried fathers. On its face, *Stanley v. Illinois* appeared to diminish the importance of the marital model. There the Court struck down a state law requiring the children of unwed fathers to become wards of the state upon the death of the mother. Yet, even as the Court emphasized constitutional protections for biological fathers, whether married or not, it noted with favor the ways in which Peter Stanley had discharged his paternal role in the years preceding his partner's death. Stanley was not a fly-by-night father. He shared in the parenting of his children, living with the children and their mother for eighteen years and sharing responsibility for their upkeep. Stanley acted like a father, but perhaps more importantly, he acted like a husband, performing his paternal role in a manner consistent with marital family norms.

The close association of legally cognizable fatherhood with the marital family is even clearer in two subsequent cases involving unmarried fathers. In *Quilloin v. Walcott* and *Lehr v. Robertson* the Court rejected petitions for paternal rights by two unmarried biological fathers. According to the Court, what distinguished *Quilloin* and *Lehr* from *Stanley* was the fact that neither father had been a consistent presence in his child's life. . . . They had not cohabited with their children and had provided little in the way of financial or emotional support. In short, they had failed to act in the manner of married fathers, as Stanley had done. . . .

The force of the marital family in the disposition of *Quilloin* and *Lehr* also is visible from another perspective. In each case, the biological father raised his claim for paternal rights to challenge an adoption petition filed by the child's stepfather (the mother's husband). In each case, there was another father figure, one who functioned in the family in the manner of a father and a husband. . . .

. . .

The Court's preference for the marital family is still more explicit in *Michael H. v. Gerald D*. Carole D. was married to Gerald D. when she became pregnant by Michael H. following an extramarital affair. Their child, Victoria, grew up in what the plurality opinion dismissed as a "quasi-family." Victoria regarded both Gerald and Michael as her fathers, and each man held himself out as Victoria's father. In denying Michael's claim for recognition of his rights as Victoria's biological father, a plurality of the Court made clear its affinity for the marital family: "The family unit accorded traditional respect in our society" is the " 'unitary family,' " a model "typified, of course, by the marital family." . . .

. . .

The claim that law favors the marital family as the normative ideal for family life may prompt resistance. In constitutional and state law alike, several efforts have been made to update the legal understanding of the family to reflect the increasing diversity of family life. . . . However, these seeming departures from the marital family ideal may be less radical than they first appear. Just as unmarried fathers were recognized as fathers when they acted like husbands, unmarried couples have sometimes enjoyed legal protection because they acted as though they were married.

 . . . Before we turn to a discussion of familial establishment, it is worth specifying the constellation of values that shape the legal understanding of what it is to act like a family. The marital, nuclear family is one that encourages monogamy, procreation, industriousness, insularity, and—seemingly paradoxically—a certain kind of visibility. . . .

. . .

By visibility, we mean that the state has encouraged the view that public recognition as a family is something to be prized. Given the association of the family with privacy, it may seem odd to associate it also with visibility. But familial privacy, insofar as it is protected, is a privacy of decisions and spaces. It is not a privacy of status. Instead, familial status is observed, recorded, and regulated by the state. . . .

The established family is a site of domestication, of discipline through interdependency and visibility. From the antitotalitarian perspective, this point bears special emphasis: the marital family is as important for what it discourages as for what it encourages. Specifically, it discourages nonconformity and rebelliousness by encouraging discipline through dependency among family members. In the traditional family recognized in early American law, men were disciplined by their obligations to support wives and children, women were disciplined by their caregiving obligations and their financial dependence on their husbands, and children were disciplined by their disciplined parents. . . .

Against this model, families that resist, rebel, or simply fail to conform may be perceived as threats to the political order. Historically the state has responded to such threats in many ways. Of particular interest . . . are responses that involve criminal sanctions. To be clear, the criminal law was a central tool of ecclesiastical establishment, but it was not the only way in which the state enforced religious conformity. Nor are criminal sanctions the only way in which the state has established a particular model of the family. But criminal punishment is among the most coercive forms of state action, and it is often an especially moralized state practice. So if establishment entails the state's enforcement of a particular ideology in nonstate institutions, it makes sense to consider criminal laws that punish nonconforming ideologies— and families' efforts to resist such laws.

B.   Thick Establishment

It is no coincidence (but too rarely noted) that many of the Supreme Court's encounters with the family involve efforts by states to use criminal sanctions against unruly families. . . . As is true of religion, the difference between establishment and disestablishment is a continuum rather than a stark binary dichotomy. In this section, we examine the thick form of establishment evident in *Reynolds v. United States*, an 1878 case involving a criminal ban on bigamy. Here, the link between political ideology and family structure is closely regulated. . . .

Convicted of bigamy under a federal statute in force in the Utah Territory, George Reynolds appealed his conviction on the ground that although he had taken a second wife in violation of the law, his religious beliefs shielded him from criminal liability. Among the "accepted doctrine[s]" of the Mormon Church was the belief "that it was the duty of male members of [the] church . . . to practise polygamy." The United States Supreme Court upheld the statute, finding it "impossible" to conclude that the Free Exercise Clause precluded the criminalization of plural marriage and other "actions . . . in violation of social duties or subversive of good order."

. . .

. . . At the time the *Reynolds* decision was announced, the traditional model of monogamous marriage was one that consigned husbands and wives to specific roles within their "separate spheres." A critical component of this separate spheres ideology was the construction of the wife as the moral center of the household. The wife was responsible for making the home a haven from the vulgarities and immoralities of the public sphere, all while inculcating their children with the values and virtues necessary for citizenship.

According to the antipolygamists, the role of women in polygamous households was wholly at odds with the notion of womanhood represented by the separate spheres and monogamous marriage. The notion of the woman as the moral center of the household presumed not only her moral superiority, but her possession of the virtues of good citizenship. Tethered to tyrannical husbands in a "virtual harem," polygamous wives were hardly models of wifely morality. Indeed, they appeared to be willing, or at least unobjecting, participants in the licentiousness and vice that characterized plural marriage for most of the country. Utterly immoral and unfit for citizenship themselves, polygamous wives, it was feared, would fail to inculcate their children with the moral virtue and freedom-loving values necessary to sustain a vital democracy.

. . .

Viewed through this lens, the *Reynolds* decision is as much (or more) a pronouncement on family-state relationships as it is a judgment of the proper church-state relationship. . . .

As such, *Reynolds* is a case about deploying the criminal law to denounce the polygamous family as immoral and antidemocratic while vindicating—indeed, establishing—the marital family and its mission to cultivate future citizens for the state. And importantly, the thick version of establishment seen in *Reynolds* is uncompromising in its stance. There is conformity with law, and there is nonconformity, which must be reordered by the force of the criminal law. There is no middle ground where families might resist conformity, but nevertheless be understood as serving the state.

C.   Thin Establishment

Although the *Reynolds* Court made clear that the marital family was an important site for the cultivation of civic virtue and "American values," the family is certainly not the only locus for such activities. In particular, public education has emerged as an important conduit for imparting democratic values and respect for national civic traditions. This means that family and school sometimes stand in an uneasy relationship. . . . In adjudicating these conflicts, the Court has continued to underscore the importance of the family in inculcating civic values. But it has also explicitly endorsed the family as a source of ideological diversity. Accordingly, in the education cases, the state tolerates nonconforming families—up to a point. Familial establishment is thinner in this context, but it is not abandoned altogether.

In *Meyer v. Nebraska*, the Court struck down a statute criminalizing the teaching of any subject in any language other than English in any school, or the teaching of languages other than English below the eighth grade. . . . [T]he adoption of the statute was animated by fears that children raised in foreign households speaking another language as their mother tongue would develop into unreliable citizens. The familial dimensions are less immediately obvious, because the law was challenged not by a parent, but by a schoolteacher convicted for teaching German to his students. But in reversing the teacher's conviction, the Court endorsed "the power of parents to control the education of their own" as one of many liberties protected by the Constitution.

Those who supported the ban on foreign language teaching saw immigrant families as a political threat, much as antipolygamists saw Mormon families as a political threat. But the Supreme Court's evaluations of the perceived danger to the state differ sharply. Meaningfully, the German-American families discussed in *Meyer* were not raising their children in the polygamous arrangements seen in *Reynolds*. . . . [A]s the Court noted, the immigrant families were not sufficiently threatening to democracy to require the state to usurp the parents' role in raising their children. Indeed, the Court suggested that the linguistic and cultural diversity of immigrant families could actually be "helpful and desirable" in a democratic society.

Meyer may be read to adopt the kind of antitotalitarian argument for institutional and ideological diversity explored [above]. . . . [T]he Court maintained that laws intended to "foster a homogenous people," though well-intended, may go too far in their desire to cultivate good citizens. . . .

The Court later elaborated this point in *Pierce v. Society of Sisters*. Under Oregon's Compulsory Education Act, parents who failed to enroll their children in public schools were subject to criminal sanctions. Here, the perceived threat was Catholicism (and again, immigration). Citing *Meyer* approvingly, the *Pierce* Court struck down the statute, deeming fundamental "the liberty of parents and guardians to direct the upbringing and education of children under their control." As in *Meyer*, the Court referenced . . . the democratic potential of the family as a check on such governmental excesses. "The child," the Court declared, "is not the mere creature of the State; those who nurture him and direct his destiny have the right, coupled with the high duty, to recognize and prepare him for additional obligations."

. . .

The specter of nonconforming polygamous family denounced in *Reynolds* is present but unmentioned in *Pierce* and *Meyer*. Some degree of linguistic, cultural, or educational pluralism can enhance democracy by challenging state impulses toward homogeneity. But familial pluralism—deviations from the form and substantive values of the marital family—is less amenable to democratic life. As the *Reynolds* Court suggests, such departures breed chaos, tyranny, and despotism— everything that is inimical to (and threatening to) democracy.

In this way, *Pierce* and *Meyer* offer a more nuanced conception of familial establishment than that seen in *Reynolds*. *Reynolds*'s thick notion of establishment draws a line in the sand. There is an acceptable family and a clearly unacceptable family, and nothing in between. . . . As *Pierce* and *Meyer* make clear, parents have broad authority to raise their children, particularly when they do so within the structure and normative parameters of the marital family.

To see that rights of familial free exercise are conditioned on conformity with the established family norm, consider a case that explicitly combines the free exercise issues of *Reynolds* with the education concerns of *Pierce* and *Meyer*: *Wisconsin v. Yoder*, 406 U.S. 205 (1972). In *Yoder*, three Amish fathers challenged a law mandating high school attendance on the ground that it impermissibly conflicted with the sect's religious values and practices.

Given the parents' explicit free exercise claim, *Yoder* looks a lot like *Reynolds*. . . . But importantly, the facts of *Yoder* and *Reynolds* are not solely about limitations on religious exercise; they also are about state-imposed limitations on the exercise of particular *family* commitments. At bottom, both cases involved laws that challenged the rights of families to live their family lives in the manner of their choosing.

. . .

Although their religious traditions marked them as distinctive in modern America, the form and substance of Amish family life was nonetheless consistent with the essential attributes of the marital family and the project of cultivating good citizens for the state. As individual families, and as a community, they were "productive and very law-abiding" and, importantly, self-sustaining and financially independent. Tellingly, the Court explicitly noted that none of members of the Amish community "had . . . been known to commit crimes, that none had been known to receive public assistance, and that none were unemployed." Unlike the polygamous families denounced in *Reynolds* as despotic and un-American, Amish families reflected the essential attributes of the marital family established in the American legal tradition, while also offering the safe, tolerable pluralism recognized in *Meyer* and *Pierce*.

Without attention to familial form, it is not easy to reconcile *Reynolds* and *Yoder*. . . .

Of course, the cases arose in distinct historical and jurisprudential contexts and were separated by almost a century. But there is also something more basic at work—at least in part. The pluralism embodied in Mormon family life was not the sort of democracy-enhancing diversity celebrated in *Meyer*, *Prince*, and later, *Yoder*. . . . The Mormons' deviation from the marital family betrayed their deviation from the substance of democratic principles.

The Amish families in *Yoder*, by contrast, presented a vision of family life rooted in democratic principles even as they lived apart from modern society. . . . Theirs was a family life consistent with "the simple life of the early Christian era" and the families that shaped and cultivated American democracy "during much of our early national life." Accordingly, their deviations from the norms and standards of modern America—their dress, their insularity, and their antipathy toward high school—could be accepted as pluralistic traditions that fostered and nurtured democracy.

III. THE FAMILY-STATE RELATIONSHIP, REIMAGINED

Disestablishing the family: our use of the present participle is deliberate. Many forms of familial establishment have already been dismantled: legitimacy classifications, adultery prohibitions, and sodomy bans are just a few examples. The law of marriage is in flux, but there is little doubt that the trend in recent years is toward a thinner form of establishment, if not disestablishment. Whether legal developments continue on this path remains to be seen. Also uncertain are the political benefits of disestablishment. As we have emphasized, disestablishment offers no guarantees. Indeed, it poses risks—it may shield illiberal families and produce illiberal citizens. The antitotalitarian approach thus raises an enduring question about the extent to which a liberal government should tolerate illiberal practices and institutions. We have not sought to resolve that debate here, but we have suggested reasons to think that a liberal government might need to endure certain risks in order to survive as liberal.

. . .

NOTES

1.   *The family's anti-totalitarian role.* Ristroph and Murray argue that, like religion, the family may inculcate values, equipping citizens to resist the state's efforts to impose its own values. In this way, the family serves as a bulwark against the totalitarian impulses of the state. Critically, Ristroph and Murray argue that this anti-totalitarian function is entirely consistent with democracy, as it fosters a skeptical, independent citizenry that is attentive to—and intolerant of—government encroachments on liberty.

2. *A tolerable pluralism?* Ristroph and Murray argue that family autonomy is tolerated only "up to a point." When families depart from the traditional marital procreative family form or espouse values that depart substantially from those the state holds, they are deemed ill-equipped to inculcate the values necessary for democratic government to flourish. Looking back at Gayle Rubin's "charmed circle" of sexuality, *supra* p. 11, what kinds of families might you predict would not be tolerated?

3. *Nuclear family norms.* As Ristroph and Murray recount, families whose kinship arrangements do not mimic the nuclear family form are often seen as deviant. Yet, non-nuclear kinship family forms are common, especially among racial minorities and immigrant groups. *See* CAROL STACK, ALL OUR KIN: STRATEGIES FOR SURVIVAL IN A BLACK COMMUNITY 93–107 (1974). Indeed, as discussed *infra* p. 359, the Indian Child Welfare Act of 1978 specifically notes the prevalence of communal child-rearing norms among Native Americans. To what extent does the emphasis on the nuclear family norm privilege white, middle-class families as the ideal?

B. STATE REGULATION OF PARENTING

Meyer v. State of Nebraska
262 U.S. 390 (1923).

■ McREYNOLDS, J.

Plaintiff in error was tried and convicted . . . under an information which charged that on May 25, 1920, while an instructor in Zion Parochial School he unlawfully taught the subject of reading in the German language to Raymond Parpart, a child of 10 years, who had not attained and successfully passed the eighth grade. The information is based upon "An act relating to the teaching of foreign languages in the state of Nebraska," approved April 9, 1919, which follows:

> Section 1. No person, individually or as a teacher, shall, in any private, denominational, parochial or public school, teach any subject to any person in any language than the English language.

> Sec. 2. Languages, other than the English language, may be taught as languages only after a pupil shall have attained and successfully passed the eighth grade as evidenced by a certificate of graduation issued by the county superintendent of the county in which the child resides.

> Sec. 3. Any person who violates any of the provisions of this act shall be deemed guilty of a misdemeanor and upon conviction, shall be subject to a fine of not less than twenty-five dollars ($25), nor more than one hundred dollars ($100), or be confined in the county jail for any period not exceeding thirty days for each offense.

Sec. 4. Whereas, an emergency exists, this act shall be in force from and after its passage and approval.

The Supreme Court of the state affirmed the judgment of conviction. It declared the offense charged and established was "the direct and intentional teaching of the German language as a distinct subject to a child who had not passed the eighth grade," in the parochial school maintained by Zion Evangelical Lutheran Congregation, a collection of Biblical stories being used therefore. And it held that the statute forbidding this . . . was a valid exercise of the police power. . . .

. . .

The problem for our determination is whether the statute as construed and applied unreasonably infringes the liberty guaranteed to the plaintiff in error by the Fourteenth Amendment:

No state . . . shall deprive any person of life, liberty or property without due process of law.

While this court has not attempted to define with exactness the liberty thus guaranteed, the term has received much consideration. . . . Without doubt, it denotes not merely freedom from bodily restraint but also the right of the individual to contract, to engage in any of the common occupations of life, to acquire useful knowledge, to marry, establish a home and bring up children, to worship God according to the dictates of his own conscience, and generally to enjoy those privileges long recognized at common law as essential to the orderly pursuit of happiness by free men. The established doctrine is that this liberty may not be interfered with, under the guise of protecting the public interest, by legislative action which is arbitrary or without reasonable relation to some purpose within the competency of the state to effect. Determination by the Legislature of what constitutes proper exercise of police power is not final or conclusive but is subject to supervision by the courts.

The American people have always regarded education and acquisition of knowledge as matters of supreme importance which should be diligently promoted. . . .

Corresponding to the right of control, it is the natural duty of the parent to give his children education suitable to their station in life; and nearly all the states, including Nebraska, enforce this obligation by compulsory laws.

Practically, education of the young is only possible in schools conducted by especially qualified persons who devote themselves thereto. The calling always has been regarded as useful and honorable, essential, indeed, to the public welfare. Mere knowledge of the German language cannot reasonably be regarded as harmful. Heretofore it has been commonly looked upon as helpful and desirable. Plaintiff in error taught this language in school as part of his occupation. His right thus to teach and the right of parents to engage him so to instruct their children, we think, are within the liberty of the amendment.

. . .

It is said the purpose of the legislation was to promote civic development by inhibiting training and education of the immature in foreign tongues and ideals before they could learn English and acquire American ideals, and "that the English language should be and become the mother tongue of all children reared in this state." It is also affirmed that the foreign born population is very large, that certain communities commonly use foreign words, follow foreign leaders, move in a foreign atmosphere, and that the children are thereby hindered from becoming citizens of the most useful type and the public safety is imperiled.

That the state may do much, go very far, indeed, in order to improve the quality of its citizens, physically, mentally and morally, is clear; but the individual has certain fundamental rights which must be respected. The protection of the Constitution extends to all, to those who speak other languages as well as to those born with English on the tongue. Perhaps it would be highly advantageous if all had ready understanding of our ordinary speech, but this cannot be coerced by methods which conflict with the Constitution—a desirable end cannot be promoted by prohibited means.

. . .

The desire of the Legislature to foster a homogeneous people with American ideals prepared readily to understand current discussions of civic matters is easy to appreciate. Unfortunate experiences during the late war and aversion toward every character of truculent adversaries were certainly enough to quicken that aspiration. But the means adopted, we think, exceed the limitations upon the power of the state and conflict with rights assured to plaintiff. . . .

. . . No emergency has arisen which renders knowledge by a child of some language other than English so clearly harmful as to justify its inhibition with the consequent infringement of rights long freely enjoyed. We are constrained to conclude that the statute as applied is arbitrary and without reasonable relation to any end within the competency of the state.

As the statute undertakes to interfere only with teaching which involves a modern language, leaving complete freedom as to other matters, there seems no adequate foundation for the suggestion that the purpose was to protect the child's health by limiting his mental activities. It is well known that proficiency in a foreign language seldom comes to one not instructed at an early age, and experience shows that this is not injurious to the health, morals or understanding of the ordinary child.

The judgment of the court below must be reversed. . . .

NOTES

1. *The realpolitik of* Meyer v. Nebraska. The statute at issue in *Meyer*— popularly known as the "Foreign Language Statute"—was enacted after

World War I amid a wave of anti-German hysteria. Indeed, the Court's opinion took note of the statute's xenophobic roots. In a section of the opinion (not included in the casebook's excerpt), the Court observed that the statute was intended to prevent "foreigners, who had taken residence in this country, to rear and educate their children in the language of their native land." According to the Nebraska legislature, this kind of linguistic pluralism was "inimical to our own safety," as children reared in the language of another country would "always think in that language," and, as a consequence, would naturally adopt "ideas and sentiments foreign to the best interests of this country." *See Meyer*, 262 U.S. at 397–98.

2.   *The Wilson Administration and the Foreign Language Act*. It is easy to dismiss the Foreign Language Act as the product of state-level parochialism. However, the anti-foreigner fervor that produced the Act was not limited to Nebraska. Indeed, during and after World War I, the federal government—under the leadership of the Wilson Administration—participated in the effort to rid the country of the influence of "hyphenated Americans." Under the auspices of the Committee on Public Information (CPI), the Wilson Administration wrote and distributed literature throughout the country justifying its war policies and restrictions on civil liberties. Echoing nativist themes, the CPI literature had a wide circulation, including extensive use in schools and universities. In particular, one popular series argued that the country was being "Germanized" by immigration, that pacifists opposed to the war were German sympathizers, and that German agents sought to subvert the American economy by provoking labor strikes. For a more comprehensive discussion of the political milieu that animated *Meyer*, see William G. Ross, *A Judicial Janus:* Meyer v. Nebraska *in Historical Perspective*, 57 U. CIN. L. REV. 125, 129, 165–66 (1988).

Pierce v. Society of the Sisters of the Holy Names of Jesus and Mary
268 U.S. 510 (1925).

■ MCREYNOLDS, J.

. . .

The challenged act, effective September 1, 1926, requires every parent, guardian, or other person having control or charge or custody of a child between 8 and 16 years to send him "to a public school for the period of time a public school shall be held during the current year" in the district where the child resides; and failure so to do is declared a misdemeanor. There are exemptions—not specially important here—for children who are not normal, or who have completed the eighth grade, or whose parents or private teachers reside at considerable distances from any public school, or who hold special permits from the county superintendent. The manifest purpose is to compel general attendance at public schools by normal children, between 8 and 16, who have not completed the eight[h] grade. And without doubt enforcement of the statute would seriously impair, perhaps destroy, the profitable features of appellees' business and greatly diminish the value of their property.

Appellee the Society of Sisters is an Oregon corporation, organized in 1880, with power to care for orphans, educate and instruct the youth, establish and maintain academies or schools, and acquire necessary real and personal property. . . .

. . .

No question is raised concerning the power of the state reasonably to regulate all schools, to inspect, supervise and examine them, their teachers and pupils; to require that all children of proper age attend some school, that teachers shall be of good moral character and patriotic disposition, that certain studies plainly essential to good citizenship must be taught, and that nothing be taught which is manifestly inimical to the public welfare.

The inevitable practical result of enforcing the act under consideration would be destruction of appellees' primary schools, and perhaps all other private primary schools for normal children within the state of Oregon. Appellees are engaged in a kind of undertaking not inherently harmful, but long regarded as useful and meritorious. Certainly there is nothing in the present records to indicate that they have failed to discharge their obligations to patrons, students, or the state. And there are no peculiar circumstances or present emergencies which demand extraordinary measures relative to primary education.

Under the doctrine of *Meyer v. Nebraska*, 262 U. S. 390 (1923), we think it entirely plain that the Act of 1922 unreasonably interferes with the liberty of parents and guardians to direct the upbringing and education of children under their control. As often heretofore pointed out, rights guaranteed by the Constitution may not be abridged by legislation which has no reasonable relation to some purpose within the competency of the state. The fundamental theory of liberty upon which all governments in this Union repose excludes any general power of the state to standardize its children by forcing them to accept instruction from public teachers only. The child is not the mere creature of the state; those who nurture him and direct his destiny have the right, coupled with the high duty, to recognize and prepare him for additional obligations.

Appellees are corporations, and therefore, it is said, they cannot claim for themselves the liberty which the Fourteenth Amendment guarantees. Accepted in the proper sense, this is true. But they have business and property for which they claim protection. These are threatened with destruction through the unwarranted compulsion which appellants are exercising over present and prospective patrons of their schools. And this court has gone very far to protect against loss threatened by such action.

The courts of the state have not construed the act, and we must determine its meaning for ourselves. Evidently it was expected to have general application and cannot be construed as though merely intended to amend the charters of certain private corporations, as in *Berea College v. Kentucky*, 211 U.S. 45 (1908). No argument in favor of such view has been advanced.

Generally, it is entirely true, as urged by counsel, that no person in any business has such an interest in possible customers as to enable him to restrain exercise of proper power of the state upon the ground that he will be deprived of patronage. But the injunctions here sought are not against the exercise of any proper power. Appellees asked protection against arbitrary, unreasonable, and unlawful interference with their patrons and the consequent destruction of their business and property. . . .

The suits were not premature. The injury to appellees was present and very real, not a mere possibility in the remote future. If no relief had been possible prior to the effective date of the act, the injury would have become irreparable. Prevention of impending injury by unlawful action is a well-recognized function of courts of equity.

The decrees below are affirmed.

NOTES

1.   *Parochial schools and anti-Americanism.* In *Meyer v. Nebraska, supra* p. 277, the Court invalidated a Nebraska law that criminally prohibited foreign language instruction on the ground that children should be raised with English as their first language. As with the Foreign Language Act invalidated in *Meyer*, the Compulsory Education Act, which "compel[led] general attendance at public schools by normal children, between eight and sixteen, who have not completed the eighth grade," was animated by xenophobic sentiment. As Professor Stephen Carter observes, immigrants were believed to bring with them "foreign religions"—namely, Roman Catholicism and Judaism. In the interest of "Protestantizing" the children of immigrants, "[m]any states established their [public] schools with the clear and often openly stated intention of wiping out the 'foreign religions.' " When Catholic parents responded by exiting the public school system and enrolling their children in parochial schools, the voters of Oregon adopted the Compulsory Education Act "with a clear intention of making it impossible for the Catholic schools to exist." *See* Stephen L. Carter, *Religious Freedom as if Family Matters*, 48 U. DET. MERCY L. REV. 1, 5 (2000).

2.   *Xenophobia, moral panics, and sexual regulation.* The kinds of state intervention seen in *Pierce* and *Meyer* relate to a broader literature concerning moral panics in times of intense social crisis. As scholars of moral panics have argued, in periods of deep anxiety and uncertainty, some behaviors may not only prompt concern, but may also give rise to moral-panic-fueled state regulation. *See* Stanley Coben, *A Study in Nativism: The American Red Scare of 1919–20*, 79 POL. SCI. Q. 52, 72–73 (1964). In this vein, not only was teaching German to schoolchildren viewed as a national security threat, the sexual practices of American women were likewise

suspect. For example, the Chamberlain-Kahn Act of 1918 sought to detain American women on the ground that nonmarital sex—and the "venereal diseases" that resulted from such sexual contact—were more threatening to the U.S. military effort than enemy bullets. *See* Kristin Luker, *Sex, Social Hygiene, and the State: The Double-Edged Sword of Social Reform*, 27 THEORY & SOC'Y 601, 617–18 (1998).

3. *Overbreadth and the Establishment Clause.* Although the Oregon Compulsory Education Act at issue in *Pierce* was intended to eliminate parochial schools—and by extension, Catholicism, Judaism, and other "foreign" religions—its reach was perhaps over-inclusive. By its terms, the Act made it a misdemeanor for parents to send their children to *any* school but an Oregon public school. As a result, private schools, whether parochial or not, ran afoul of the Act. With this in mind, it is perhaps unsurprising that one of the appellees in *Pierce* was the Hill Military Academy, a military school with no religious affiliation.

4. *The family and the state.* Both *Meyer* and *Pierce* recognize the principle of parental autonomy in the face of state encroachment. What is the relationship between the family and the state that *Pierce* and *Meyer* contemplate? Are the family and the state partners in the effort to cultivate good citizens? Or are they adversaries?

Prince v. Commonwealth of Massachusetts
321 U.S. 158 (1944).

■ RUTLEDGE, J.

The case brings for review another episode in the conflict between Jehovah's Witnesses and state authority. This time Sarah Prince appeals from convictions for violating Massachusetts' child labor laws, by acts said to be a rightful exercise of her religious convictions.

When the offenses were committed she was the aunt and custodian of Betty M. Simmons, a girl nine years of age. . . .

. . .

. . . Mrs. Prince, living in Brockton, is the mother of two young sons. She also has legal custody of Betty Simmons who lives with them. The children too are Jehovah's Witnesses and both Mrs. Prince and Betty testified they were ordained ministers. The former was accustomed to go each week on the streets of Brockton to distribute "Watchtower" and "Consolation," according to the usual plan. She had permitted the children to engage in this activity previously, and had been warned against doing so by the school attendance officer, Mr. Perkins. But, until December 18, 1941, she generally did not take them with her at night.

That evening . . . she yielded. Arriving downtown, . . . Betty . . . and Mrs. Prince took positions about twenty feet apart near a street intersection. Betty held up in her hand, for passersby to see, copies of "Watch Tower" and "Consolation." From her shoulder hung the usual canvas magazine bag, on which was printed "Watchtower and

Consolation 5¢ per copy." No one accepted a copy from Betty that evening and she received no money. Nor did her aunt. But on other occasions, Betty had received funds and given out copies.

. . .

. . . [T]wo claimed liberties are at stake. One is the parent's, to bring up the child in the way he should go, which for appellant means to teach him the tenets and the practices of their faith. The other freedom is the child's, to observe these; and among them is "to preach the gospel . . . by public distribution" of "Watchtower" and "Consolation," in conformity with the scripture: "A little child shall lead them."

. . .

The rights of children to exercise their religion, and of parents to give them religious training and to encourage them in the practice of religious belief, as against preponderant sentiment and assertion of state power voicing it, have had recognition here, most recently in *West Virginia State Board of Education v. Barnette*, 319 U.S. 624 (1943). Previously in *Pierce v. Society of Sisters*, 268 U.S. 510 (1925), this Court had sustained the parent's authority to provide religious with secular schooling, and the child's right to receive it, as against the state's requirement of attendance at public schools. And in *Meyer v. Nebraska*, 262 U.S. 390 (1923), children's rights to receive teaching in languages other than the nation's common tongue were guarded against the state's encroachment. It is cardinal with us that the custody, care and nurture of the child reside first in the parents, whose primary function and freedom include preparation for obligations the state can neither supply nor hinder. And it is in recognition of this that these decisions have respected the private realm of family life which the state cannot enter.

But the family itself is not beyond regulation in the public interest, as against a claim of religious liberty. *Reynolds v. United States*, 98 U.S. 145 (1878); *Davis v. Beason*, 133 U.S. 333 (1890). And neither rights of religion nor rights of parenthood are beyond limitation. Acting to guard the general interest in youth's well being, the state as *parens patriae* may restrict the parent's control by requiring school attendance, regulating or prohibiting the child's labor, and in many other ways. Its authority is not nullified merely because the parent grounds his claim to control the child's course of conduct on religion or conscience. Thus, he cannot claim freedom from compulsory vaccination for the child more than for himself on religious grounds. The right to practice religion freely does not include liberty to expose the community or the child to communicable disease or the latter to ill health or death. The catalogue need not be lengthened. It is sufficient to show what indeed appellant hardly disputes, that the state has a wide range of power for limiting parental freedom and authority in things affecting the child's welfare; and that this includes, to some extent, matters of conscience and religious conviction.

. . .

. . . The case reduces itself therefore to the question whether the presence of the child's guardian puts a limit to the state's power. That fact may lessen the likelihood that some evils the legislation seeks to avert will occur. But it cannot forestall all of them. The zealous though lawful exercise of the right to engage in propagandizing the community, whether in religious, political or other matters, may and at times does create situations difficult enough for adults to cope with and wholly inappropriate for children, especially of tender years, to face. Other harmful possibilities could be stated, of emotional excitement and psychological or physical injury. Parents may be free to become martyrs themselves. But it does not follow they are free, in identical circumstances, to make martyrs of their children before they have reached the age of full and legal discretion when they can make that choice for themselves. Massachusetts has determined that an absolute prohibition, though one limited to streets and public places and to the incidental uses proscribed, is necessary to accomplish its legitimate objectives. Its power to attain them is broad enough to reach these peripheral instances in which the parent's supervision may reduce but cannot eliminate entirely the ill effects of the prohibited conduct. We think that with reference to the public proclaiming of religion, upon the streets and in other similar public places, the power of the state to control the conduct of children reaches beyond the scope of its authority over adults, as is true in the case of other freedoms, and the rightful boundary of its power has not been crossed in this case.

. . .

The judgment is affirmed.

. . .

■ MURPHY, J., dissenting.

This attempt by the state of Massachusetts to prohibit a child from exercising her constitutional right to practice her religion on the public streets cannot, in my opinion, be sustained.

. . .

Religious training and activity, whether performed by adult or child, are protected by the Fourteenth Amendment against interference by state action, except insofar as they violate reasonable regulations adopted for the protection of the public health, morals and welfare. Our problem here is whether a state, under the guise of enforcing its child labor laws, can lawfully prohibit girls under the age of eighteen and boys under the age of twelve from practicing their religious faith insofar as it involves the distribution or sale of religious tracts on the public streets. . . .

In dealing with the validity of statutes which directly or indirectly infringe religious freedom and the right of parents to encourage their children in the practice of a religious belief, we are not aided by any strong presumption of the constitutionality of such legislation. On the contrary, the human freedoms enumerated in the First Amendment and carried over into the Fourteenth Amendment are to be presumed to be invulnerable and any attempt to sweep away those freedoms is *prima facie* invalid. It follows that any restriction or prohibition must be justified by those who deny that the freedoms have been unlawfully invaded. The burden was therefore on the state of Massachusetts to prove the reasonableness and necessity of prohibiting children from engaging in religious activity of the type involved in this case.

The burden in this instance, however, is not met by vague references to the reasonableness underlying child labor legislation in general. The great interest of the state in shielding minors from the evil vicissitudes of early life does not warrant every limitation on their religious training and activities. The reasonableness that justifies the prohibition of the ordinary distribution of literature in the public streets by children is not necessarily the reasonableness that justifies such a drastic restriction when the distribution is part of their religious faith. If the right of a child to practice its religion in that manner is to be forbidden by constitutional means, there must be convincing proof that such a practice constitutes a grave and immediate danger to the state or to the health, morals or welfare of the child. . . .

The state, in my opinion, has completely failed to sustain its burden of proving the existence of any grave or immediate danger to any interest which it may lawfully protect. There is no proof that Betty Simmons' mode of worship constituted a serious menace to the public. It was carried on in an orderly, lawful manner at a public street corner. And "one who is rightfully on a street which the state has left open to the public carries with him there as elsewhere the constitutional right to express his views in an orderly fashion. This right extends to the communication of ideas by handbills and literature as well as by the spoken word." The sidewalk, no less than the cathedral or the evangelist's tent, is a proper place, under the Constitution, for the orderly worship of God. Such use of the streets is as necessary to the Jehovah's Witnesses, the Salvation Army and others who practice religion without benefit of conventional shelters as is the use of the streets for purposes of passage.

It is claimed, however, that such activity was likely to affect adversely the health, morals and welfare of the child. Reference is made in the majority opinion to "the crippling effects of child employment, more especially in public places, and the possible harms arising from other activities subject to all the diverse influences of the street." To the extent that they flow from participation in ordinary commercial activities, these harms are irrelevant to this case. And the bare possibility that such harms might emanate from distribution of religious literature is not, standing alone, sufficient justification for restricting freedom of conscience and religion. Nor can parents or guardians be subjected to criminal liability because of vague possibilities that their religious teachings might cause injury to the child. The evils must be grave, immediate, substantial. Yet there is not the slightest indication in this record, or in sources subject to judicial notice, that children engaged in distributing literature pursuant to their religious beliefs have been or are likely to be subject to any of the harmful "diverse influences of the street." Indeed, if probabilities are to be indulged in, the likelihood is that children engaged in serious religious endeavor are immune from such influences. Gambling, truancy, irregular eating and sleeping habits, and the more serious vices are not consistent with the high moral character ordinarily displayed by children fulfilling religious obligations. Moreover, Jehovah's Witness children invariably make their distributions in groups subject at all times to adult or parental control, as was done in this case. The dangers are thus exceedingly remote, to say the least. And the fact that the zealous exercise of the right to propagandize the community may result in violent or disorderly situations difficult for children to face is no excuse for prohibiting the exercise of that right.

. . . From ancient times to the present day, the ingenuity of man has known no limits in its ability to forge weapons of oppression for use against those who dare to express or practice unorthodox religious beliefs. And the Jehovah's Witnesses are living proof of the fact that even in this nation, conceived as it was in the ideals of freedom, the right to practice religion in unconventional ways is still far from secure. Theirs is a militant and unpopular faith, pursued with a fanatical zeal. They have suffered brutal beatings; their property has been destroyed; they have been harassed at every turn by the resurrection and enforcement of little used ordinances and statutes. To them, along with other present-day religious minorities, befalls the burden of testing our devotion to the ideals and constitutional guarantees of religious freedom. We should therefore hesitate before approving the application of a statute that might be used as another instrument of oppression. . . .

NOTE

Minority religions and family autonomy. As in *Pierce* and *Meyer, Prince* involved the state's efforts to curb parental autonomy. Yet, the *Prince* Court reached the opposite conclusion than the Court reached in *Pierce* and *Meyer*. What explains the difference? As the majority noted, the state retains *parens patriae* authority to intervene in the family to protect the health and welfare of children. Certainly, one could view the child labor law at issue in *Prince* as this kind of permissible health and welfare intervention. Yet, as Justice Murphy observes in his dissent, laws of general application—like the child-labor law—may be selectively enforced against minority groups like the Jehovah's Witnesses. Justice Murphy notes that the Witnesses were "a militant and unpopular faith" subjected to "brutal beatings." The Witnesses refused to serve in World War II, salute the flag, or support the war effort; and throughout the war, they refused to seek conscientious objector status, as they believed in using force when Jehovah commanded them to do so. Their unpopular views made them targets of persecution during the fight against Nazi Germany and the Axis Powers. *See* RICHARD J. REGAN, THE AMERICAN CONSTITUTION AND RELIGION 207–09 (2013).

C. REGULATION THROUGH DEFINITION—WHO COUNTS AS A PARENT?

The following cases, Stanley v. Illinois, Quilloin v. Walcott, *and* Lehr v. Robertson *offer a view of the State's understanding of parenthood—and fatherhood. As you review these cases, consider what unites the Court's approach. What are points of departure?*

Stanley v. Illinois — Violates EPC
to deny
parental rights
to unmarried dad w/
no hearing

405 U.S. 645 (1972).

■ WHITE, J.

Joan Stanley lived with Peter Stanley intermittently for 18 years, during which time they had three children. When Joan Stanley died, Peter Stanley lost not only her but also his children. Under Illinois law, the children of unwed fathers become wards of the State upon the death of the mother. Accordingly, upon Joan Stanley's death, in a dependency proceeding instituted by the State of Illinois, Stanley's children were declared wards of the State and placed with court-appointed guardians. Stanley appealed, claiming that he had never been shown to be an unfit parent and that since married fathers and unwed mothers could not be deprived of their children without such a showing, he had been deprived of the equal protection of the laws guaranteed him by the Fourteenth Amendment. . . .

[EPC claim]

. . .

. . . [W]e are faced with a dependency statute that empowers state officials to circumvent neglect proceedings on the theory that an unwed father is not a "parent" whose existing relationship with his children must be considered. "Parents," says the State, "means the father and mother of a legitimate child, or the survivor of them, or the natural mother of an illegitimate child, and includes any adoptive parent," Ill. Rev. Stat., ch. 37, § 701–14, but the term does not include unwed fathers.

Under Illinois law, therefore, while the children of all parents can be taken from them in neglect proceedings, that is only after notice, hearing, and proof of such unfitness as a parent as amounts to neglect, an unwed father is uniquely subject to the more simplistic dependency proceeding. By use of this proceeding, the State, on showing that the father was not married to the mother, need not prove unfitness in fact, because it is presumed at law. Thus, the unwed father's claim of parental qualification is avoided as "irrelevant."

. . .

The private interest here, that of a man in the children he has sired and raised, undeniably warrants deference and, absent a powerful countervailing interest, protection. It is plain that the interest of a parent in the companionship, care, custody, and management of his or her children "come(s) to this Court with a momentum for respect lacking when appeal is made to liberties which derive merely from shifting economic arrangements." *Kovacs v. Cooper*, 336 U.S. 77, 95 (1949) (Frankfurter, J., concurring).

The Court has frequently emphasized the importance of the family. The rights to conceive and to raise one's children have been deemed "essential," *Meyer v. Nebraska*, 262 U.S. 390, 399 (1923), "basic civil rights of man," *Skinner v. Oklahoma*, 316 U.S. 535, 541 (1942), and "[r]ights far more precious . . . than property rights," *May v. Anderson*, 345 U.S. 528, 533 (1953). "It is cardinal with us that the custody, care and nurture of the child reside first in the parents, whose primary function and freedom include preparation for obligations the state can neither supply nor hinder." *Prince v. Massachusetts*, 321 U.S. 158, 166 (1944). The integrity of the family unit has found protection in the Due Process Clause of the Fourteenth Amendment, *Meyer*, 262 U.S. at 399, the Equal Protection Clause of the Fourteenth Amendment, *Skinner*, 316 U.S. at 541, and the Ninth Amendment, *Griswold v. Connecticut*, 381 U.S. 479, 496 (1965) (Goldberg, J., concurring).

right to conceive / raise child = essential

Nor has the law refused to recognize those family relationships unlegitimized by a marriage ceremony. The Court has declared unconstitutional a state statute denying natural, but illegitimate, children a wrongful-death action for the death of their mother, emphasizing that such children cannot be denied the right of other children because familial bonds in such cases were often as warm, enduring, and important as those arising within a more formally organized family unit. *Levy v. Louisiana*, 391 U.S. 68, 71–72 (1968). "To say that the test of equal protection should be the 'legal' rather than the biological relationship is to avoid the issue. For the Equal Protection Clause necessarily limits the authority of a State to draw such 'legal' lines as it chooses." *Glona v. American Guarantee & Liability Ins. Co.*, 391 U.S. 73, 75–76 (1968).

These authorities make it clear that, at the least, Stanley's interest in retaining custody of his children is cognizable and substantial.

For its part, the State has made its interest quite plain: Illinois has declared that the aim of the Juvenile Court Act is to protect "the moral, emotional, mental, and physical welfare of the minor and the best interests of the community" and to "strengthen the minor's family ties whenever possible, removing him from the custody of his parents only when his welfare or safety or the protection of the public cannot be adequately safeguarded without removal. . . ." Ill. Rev. Stat., ch. 37, § 701–2. These are legitimate interests, well within the power of the

State to implement. We do not question the assertion that neglectful parents may be separated from their children.

But we are here not asked to evaluate the legitimacy of the state ends, rather, to determine whether the means used to achieve these ends are constitutionally defensible. What is the state interest in separating children from fathers without a hearing designed to determine whether the father is unfit in a particular disputed case? We observe that the State registers no gain towards its declared goals when it separates children from the custody of fit parents. Indeed, if Stanley is a fit father, the State spites its own articulated goals when it needlessly separates him from his family.

It may be, as the State insists, that most unmarried fathers are unsuitable and neglectful parents. It may also be that Stanley is such a parent and that his children should be placed in other hands. But all unmarried fathers are not in this category; some are wholly suited to have custody of their children. This much the State readily concedes, and nothing in this record indicates that Stanley is or has been a neglectful father who has not cared for his children. Given the opportunity to make his case, Stanley may have been seen to be deserving of custody of his offspring. Had this been so, the State's statutory policy would have been furthered by leaving custody in him.

. . .

. . . [I]t may be argued that unmarried fathers are so seldom fit that Illinois need not undergo the administrative inconvenience of inquiry in any case, including Stanley's. The establishment of prompt efficacious procedures to achieve legitimate state ends is a proper state interest worthy of cognizance in constitutional adjudication. But the Constitution recognizes higher values than speed and efficiency. Indeed, one might fairly say of the Bill of Rights in general, and the Due Process Clause in particular, that they were designed to protect the fragile values of a vulnerable citizenry from the overbearing concern for efficiency and efficacy that may characterize praiseworthy government officials no less, and perhaps more, than mediocre ones.

Procedure by presumption is always cheaper and easier than individualized determination. But when, as here, the procedure forecloses the determinative issues of competence and care, when it explicitly disdains present realities in deference to past formalities, it needlessly risks running roughshod over the important interests of both parent and child. It therefore cannot stand.

. . .

The State of Illinois assumes custody of the children of married parents, divorced parents, and unmarried mothers only after a hearing and proof of neglect. The children of unmarried fathers, however, are declared dependent children without a hearing on parental fitness and without proof of neglect. Stanley's claim in the state courts and here is that failure to afford him a hearing on his parental qualifications while extending it to other parents denied him equal protection of the laws. We have concluded that all Illinois parents are constitutionally entitled to a hearing on their fitness before their children are removed from their custody. It follows that denying such a hearing to Stanley and those like him while granting it to other Illinois parents is inescapably contrary to the Equal Protection Clause.

. . .

   Reversed and remanded.

■ BURGER, J., with whom BLACKMUN, J. concurs, dissenting.

. . .

   . . . I agree with the State's argument that the Equal Protection Clause is not violated when Illinois gives full recognition only to those father-child relationships that arise in the context of family units bound together by legal obligations arising from marriage or from adoption proceedings. Quite apart from the religious or quasi-religious connotations that marriage has—and has historically enjoyed—for a large proportion of this Nation's citizens, it is in law an essentially contractual relationship, the parties to which have legally enforceable rights and duties, with respect both to each other and to any children born to them. Stanley and the mother of these children never entered such a relationship. . . . Stanley did not seek the burdens when he could have freely assumed them.

   Where there is a valid contract of marriage, the law of Illinois presumes that the husband is the father of any child born to the wife during the marriage; as the father, he has legally enforceable rights and duties with respect to that child. When a child is born to an unmarried woman, Illinois recognizes the readily identifiable mother, but makes no presumption as to the identity of the biological father. It does, however, provide two ways, one voluntary and one involuntary, in which that father may be identified. First, he may marry the mother and acknowledge the child as his own; this has the legal effect of legitimating the child and gaining for the father full recognition as a parent. Second, a man may be found to be the biological father of the child pursuant to a paternity suit initiated by the mother; in this case, the child remains illegitimate, but the adjudicated father is made liable for the support of the child until the latter attains age 18 or is legally adopted by another.

. . .

   The Illinois Supreme Court correctly held that the State may constitutionally distinguish between unwed fathers and unwed mothers. Here, Illinois' different treatment of the two is part of that State's statutory scheme for protecting the welfare of illegitimate children. In almost all cases, the unwed mother is readily identifiable, generally from hospital records, and alternatively by physicians or others attending the *but the not case here!*

child's birth. Unwed fathers, as a class, are not traditionally quite so easy to identify and locate. Many of them either deny all responsibility or exhibit no interest in the child or its welfare; and, of course, many unwed fathers are simply not aware of their parenthood.

stronger bonds w/ mom?

Furthermore, I believe that a State is fully justified in concluding, on the basis of common human experience, that the biological role of the mother in carrying and nursing an infant creates stronger bonds between her and the child than the bonds resulting from the male's often casual encounter. This view is reinforced by the observable fact that most unwed mothers exhibit a concern for their offspring either permanently or at least until they are safely placed for adoption, while unwed fathers rarely burden either the mother or the child with their attentions or loyalties. Centuries of human experience buttress this view of the realities of human conditions and suggest that unwed mothers of illegitimate children are generally more dependable protectors of their children than are unwed fathers. While these, like most generalizations, are not without exceptions, they nevertheless provide a sufficient basis to sustain a statutory classification whose objective is not to penalize unwed parents but to further the welfare of illegitimate children in fulfillment of the State's obligations as *parens patriae*.

. . .

. . . The Court today pursues that serious business by expanding its legitimate jurisdiction beyond . . . the permissible limits contemplated by Congress. In doing so, it invalidates a provision of critical importance to Illinois' carefully drawn statutory system governing family relationships and the welfare of the minor children of the State. And in so invalidating that provision, it ascribes to that statutory system a presumption that is simply not there and embarks on a novel concept of the natural law for unwed fathers that could well have strange boundaries as yet undiscernible.

biological dad of "illegitimate" daughter lost her to mother's new husband

mom's husband (wants to adopt)

biological dad

Quilloin v. Walcott
434 U.S. 246 (1978).

■ MARSHALL, J.

issue: as applied challenge to GA adoption law

The issue in this case is the constitutionality of Georgia's adoption laws as applied to deny an unwed father authority to prevent adoption of his illegitimate child. The child was born in December 1964 and has been in the custody and control of his mother, appellee Ardell Williams Walcott, for his entire life. The mother and the child's natural father, appellant Leon Webster Quilloin, never married each other or established a home together, and in September 1967 the mother married appellee Randall Walcott. In March 1976, she consented to adoption of the child by her husband, who immediately filed a petition for adoption. Appellant attempted to block the adoption and to secure visitation rights, but he did not seek custody or object to the child's continuing to live with appellees. Although appellant was not found to be an unfit parent, the adoption was granted over his objection.

. . .

I

Generally speaking, under Georgia law a child born in wedlock cannot be adopted without the consent of each living parent who has not voluntarily surrendered rights in the child or been adjudicated an un[fit] parent. Even where the child's parents are divorced or separated at the time of the adoption proceedings, either parent may veto the adoption. In contrast, only the consent of the mother is required for adoption of an illegitimate child. Ga. Code § 74–403(3) (1975). To acquire the same veto authority possessed by other parents, the father of a child born out of wedlock must legitimate his offspring, either by marrying the mother and acknowledging the child as his own, § 74–101, or by obtaining a court order declaring the child legitimate and capable of inheriting from the father, § 74–103. But unless and until the child is legitimated, the mother is the only recognized parent and is given exclusive authority to exercise all parental prerogatives, § 74–203, including the power to veto adoption of the child.

Appellant did not petition for legitimation of his child at any time during the 11 years between the child's birth and the filing of Randall Walcott's adoption petition. However, in response to Walcott's petition, appellant filed an application for a writ of habeas corpus seeking visitation rights, a petition for legitimation, and an objection to the adoption. . . .

The petitions for adoption, legitimation and writ of habeas corpus were consolidated for trial. . . . After receiving extensive testimony from the parties and other witnesses, the trial court found that, although the child had never been abandoned or deprived, appellant had provided support only on an irregular basis. Moreover, while the child previously had visited with appellant on "many occasions," and had been given toys and gifts by appellant "from time to time," the mother had recently concluded that these contacts were having a disruptive effect on the child and on appellees' entire family.[10] The child himself expressed a desire to be adopted by Randall Walcott and to take on Walcott's name, and the court found Walcott to be a fit and proper person to adopt the child. On the basis of these findings, as well as findings relating to appellees' marriage and the mother's custody of the child for all of the child's life, the trial court determined that the proposed adoption was in the "best interests of [the] child." The court concluded, further, that granting either the legitimation or the visitation rights requested by appellant would not be in the "best interests of the child," and that both should

---

[10] In addition to Darrell, appellees' family included a son born several years after appellees were married. The mother testified that Darrell's visits with appellant were having unhealthy effects on both children.

consequently be denied. . . . [S]ince appellant had failed to obtain a court order granting legitimation, he was found to lack standing to object to the adoption. Ruling that appellant's constitutional claims were without merit, the court granted the adoption petition and denied the legitimation and visitation petitions.

. . .

We have recognized on numerous occasions that the relationship between parent and child is constitutionally protected. *See, e. g., Wisconsin v. Yoder*, 406 U.S. 205, 231–233 (1972); *Stanley v. Illinois*, 5 U.S. 645 (1972); *Meyer v. Nebraska*, 262 U.S. 390, 399–401(1923). . . . And it is now firmly established that "freedom of personal choice in matters of . . . family life is one of the liberties protected by the Due Process Clause of the Fourteenth Amendment." *Cleveland Board of Education v. LaFleur*, 414 U.S. 632, 639–640 (1974).

We have little doubt that the Due Process Clause would be offended "[i]f a State were to attempt to force the breakup of a natural family, over the objections of the parents and their children, without some showing of unfitness and for the sole reason that to do so was thought to be in the children's best interest." *Smith v. Organization of Foster Families*, 431 U.S. 816, 862–863 (1977) (Stewart, J., concurring). But this is not a case in which the unwed father at any time had, or sought, actual or legal custody of his child. Nor is this a case in which the proposed adoption would place the child with a new set of parents with whom the child had never before lived. Rather, the result of the adoption in this case is to give full recognition to a family unit already in existence, a result desired by all concerned, except appellant. Whatever might be required in other situations, we cannot say that the State was required in this situation to find anything more than that the adoption, and denial of legitimation, were in the "best interests of the child."

B

Appellant contends that even if he is not entitled to prevail as a matter of due process, principles of equal protection require that his authority to veto an adoption be measured by the same standard that would have been applied to a married father. In particular, appellant asserts that his interests are indistinguishable from those of a married father who is separated or divorced from the mother and is no longer living with his child, and therefore the State acted impermissibly in treating his case differently. We think appellant's interests are readily distinguishable from those of a separated or divorced father, and accordingly believe that the State could permissibly give appellant less veto authority than it provides to a married father.

Although appellant was subject, for the years prior to these proceedings, to essentially the same child-support obligation as a married father would have had . . . he has never exercised actual or legal custody over his child, and thus has never shouldered any significant responsibility with respect to the daily supervision, education, protection, or care of the child. Appellant does not complain of his exemption from these responsibilities and, indeed, he does not even now seek custody of his child. In contrast, legal custody of children is, of course, a central aspect of the marital relationship, and even a father whose marriage has broken apart will have borne full responsibility for the rearing of his children during the period of the marriage. Under any standard of review, the State was not foreclosed from recognizing this difference in the extent of commitment to the welfare of the child.

For these reasons, we conclude that §§ 74–203 and 74–403(3), as applied in this case, did not deprive appellant of his asserted rights under the Due Process and Equal Protection Clauses. The judgment of the Supreme Court of Georgia is accordingly,

Affirmed.

Lehr v. Robertson

463 U.S. 248 (1983).

■ STEVENS, J.

The question presented is whether New York has sufficiently protected an unmarried father's inchoate relationship with a child whom he has never supported and rarely seen in the two years since her birth. The appellant, Jonathan Lehr, claims that the Due Process and Equal Protection Clauses of the Fourteenth Amendment, as interpreted in *Stanley v. Illinois*, 405 U.S. 645 (1972), and *Caban v. Mohammed*, 441 U.S. 380 (1979), give him an absolute right to notice and an opportunity to be heard before the child may be adopted. We disagree.

Jessica M. was born out of wedlock on November 9, 1976. Her mother, Lorraine Robertson, married Richard Robertson eight months after Jessica's birth. On December 21, 1978, when Jessica was over two years old, the Robertsons filed an adoption petition in the Family Court of Ulster County, New York. The court heard their testimony and received a favorable report from the Ulster County Department of Social Services. On March 7, 1979, the court entered an order of adoption. In this proceeding, appellant contends that the adoption order is invalid because he, Jessica's putative father, was not given advance notice of the adoption proceeding.

The State of New York maintains a "putative father registry." A man who files with that registry demonstrates his intent to claim paternity of a child born out of wedlock and is therefore entitled to receive notice of any proceeding to adopt that child. Before entering Jessica's adoption order, the Ulster County Family Court had the putative father registry examined. Although appellant claims to be Jessica's natural father, he had not entered his name in the registry.

In addition to the persons whose names are listed on the putative father registry, New York law requires that notice of an adoption proceeding be given to several other classes of possible fathers of children born out of wedlock—those who have been adjudicated to be the father, those who have been identified as the father on the child's birth certificate, those who live openly with the child and the child's mother and who hold themselves out to be the father, those who have been identified as the father by the mother in a sworn written statement, and those who were married to the child's mother before the child was six months old.[5] Appellant admittedly was not a member of any of those classes. He had lived with appellee prior to Jessica's birth and visited her in the hospital when Jessica was born, but his name does not appear on Jessica's birth certificate. He did not live with appellee or Jessica after Jessica's birth, he has never provided them with any financial support, and he has never offered to marry appellee. Nevertheless, he contends that the following special circumstances gave him a constitutional right to notice and a hearing before Jessica was adopted.

On January 30, 1979, one month after the adoption proceeding was commenced in Ulster County, appellant filed a "visitation and paternity petition" in the Westchester County Family Court. In that petition, he asked for a determination of paternity, an order of support, and reasonable visitation privileges with Jessica. Notice of that proceeding was served on appellee on February 22, 1979. Four days later appellee's attorney informed the Ulster County Court that appellant had commenced a paternity proceeding in Westchester County; the Ulster County judge then entered an order staying appellant's paternity proceeding until he could rule on a motion to change the venue of that proceeding to Ulster County. On March 3, 1979, appellant received notice

---

[5]   At the time Jessica's adoption order was entered, subdivisions 2–4 of § 111–a of the New York Domestic Relations Law provided:

2.   Persons entitled to notice, pursuant to subdivision one of this section, shall include:

(a) any person adjudicated by a court in this state to be the father of the child;

(b) any person adjudicated by a court of another state or territory of the United States to be the father of the child, when a certified copy of the court order has been filed with the putative father registry, pursuant to section three hundred seventy-two of the social services law;

(c) any person who has timely filed an unrevoked notice of intent to claim paternity of the child, pursuant to section three hundred seventy-two of the social services law;

(d) any person who is recorded on the child's birth certificate as the child's father;

(e) any person who is openly living with the child and the child's mother at the time the proceeding is initiated and who is holding himself out to be the child's father;

(f) any person who has been identified as the child's father by the mother in written, sworn statement; and

(g) any person who was married to the child's mother within six months subsequent to the birth of the child and prior to the execution of a surrender instrument or the initiation of a proceeding pursuant to section three hundred eighty-four-b of the social services law.

3.   The sole purpose of notice under this section shall be to enable the person served pursuant to subdivision two to present evidence to the court relevant to the best interests of the child.

of the change of venue motion and, for the first time, learned that an adoption proceeding was pending in Ulster County.

On March 7, 1979, appellant's attorney telephoned the Ulster County judge to inform him that he planned to seek a stay of the adoption proceeding pending the determination of the paternity petition. In that telephone conversation, the judge advised the lawyer that he had already signed the adoption order earlier that day. According to appellant's attorney, the judge stated that he was aware of the pending paternity petition but did not believe he was required to give notice to appellant prior to the entry of the order of adoption.

Thereafter, the Family Court in Westchester County granted appellee's motion to dismiss the paternity petition, holding that the putative father's right to seek paternity ". . . must be deemed severed so long as an order of adoption exists." Appellant did not appeal from that dismissal. On June 22, 1979, appellant filed a petition to vacate the order of adoption on the ground that it was obtained by fraud and in violation of his constitutional rights. The Ulster County Family Court received written and oral argument on the question whether it had "dropped the ball" by approving the adoption without giving appellant advance notice. After deliberating for several months, it denied the petition, explaining its decision in a thorough written opinion.

The Appellate Division of the Supreme Court affirmed. . . . One justice dissented on the ground that the filing of the paternity proceeding should have been viewed as the statutory equivalent of filing a notice of intent to claim paternity with the putative father registry.

The New York Court of Appeals also affirmed by a divided vote . . . it addressed what it described as the only contention of substance advanced by appellant: that it was an abuse of discretion to enter the adoption order without requiring that notice be given to appellant. The court observed that the primary purpose of the notice provision of § 111–a was to enable the person served to provide the court with evidence concerning the best interest of the child, and that appellant had made no tender indicating any ability to provide any particular or special information relevant to Jessica's best interest. Considering the record as a whole, and acknowledging that it might have been prudent to give notice, the court concluded that the family court had not abused its discretion either when it entered the order without notice or when it denied appellant's petition to reopen the proceedings. The dissenting judges concluded that the family court had abused its discretion, both when it entered the order without notice and when it refused to reopen the proceedings.

Appellant has now invoked our appellate jurisdiction. He offers two alternative grounds for holding the New York statutory scheme unconstitutional. First, he contends that a putative father's actual or potential relationship with a child born out of wedlock is an interest in liberty which may not be destroyed without due process of law; he argues therefore that he had a constitutional right to prior notice and an opportunity to be heard before he was deprived of that interest. Second, he contends that the gender-based classification in the statute, which both denied him the right to consent to Jessica's adoption and accorded him fewer procedural rights than her mother, violated the Equal Protection Clause.

The Due Process Claim.

. . .

. . . This Court has examined the extent to which a natural father's biological relationship with his illegitimate child receives protection under the Due Process Clause in precisely three cases: *Stanley v. Illinois*, 405 U.S. 645 (1972), *Quilloin v. Walcott*, 434 U.S. 246 (1978), and *Caban v. Mohammed*, 441 U.S. 380 (1979).

Stanley involved the constitutionality of an Illinois statute that conclusively presumed every father of a child born out of wedlock to be an unfit person to have custody of his children. The father in that case had lived with his children all their lives and had lived with their mother for eighteen years. There was nothing in the record to indicate that Stanley had been a neglectful father who had not cared for his children. . . . [T]he Court held that the Due Process Clause was violated by the automatic destruction of the custodial relationship without giving the father any opportunity to present evidence regarding his fitness as a parent.

Quilloin involved the constitutionality of a Georgia statute that authorized the adoption of a child born out of wedlock over the objection of the natural father. The father in that case had never legitimated the child. It was only after the mother had remarried and her new husband had filed an adoption petition that the natural father sought visitation rights and filed a petition for legitimation. The trial court found adoption by the new husband to be in the child's best interests, and we unanimously held that action to be consistent with the Due Process Clause.

Caban involved the conflicting claims of two natural parents who had maintained joint custody of their children from the time of their birth until they were respectively two and four years old. The father challenged the validity of an order authorizing the mother's new husband to adopt the children; he relied on both the Equal Protection Clause and the Due Process Clause. Because this Court upheld his equal protection claim, the majority did not address his due process challenge. The comments on the latter claim by the four dissenting Justices are nevertheless instructive, because they identify the clear distinction between a mere biological relationship and an actual relationship of parental responsibility.

Justice Stewart correctly observed:

Even if it be assumed that each married parent after divorce has some substantive due process right to maintain his or her parental relationship . . . it by no means follows that each unwed parent has any such right. *Parental rights do not spring full-blown from the biological connection between parent and child. They require relationships more enduring. Caban*, 441 U.S. at 397 (emphasis added).

. . .

The difference between the developed parent-child relationship that was implicated in *Stanley* and *Caban*, and the potential relationship involved in *Quilloin* and this case, is both clear and significant. When an unwed father demonstrates a full commitment to the responsibilities of parenthood by "com[ing] forward to participate in the rearing of his child," *Caban*, 441 U.S. at 392, his interest in personal contact with his child acquires substantial protection under the due process clause. At that point it may be said that he "act[s] as a father toward his children." *Id.* at 389, n. 7. . . . But the mere existence of a biological link does not merit equivalent constitutional protection. The actions of judges neither create nor sever genetic bonds. "[T]he importance of the familial relationship, to the individuals involved and to the society, stems from the emotional attachments that derive from the intimacy of daily association, and from the role it plays in 'promot[ing] a way of life' through the instruction of children as well as from the fact of blood relationship." *Smith v. Organization of Foster Families for Equality and Reform*, 431 U.S. 816, 844 (1977).

The significance of the biological connection is that it offers the natural father an opportunity that no other male possesses to develop a relationship with his offspring. If he grasps that opportunity and accepts some measure of responsibility for the child's future, he may enjoy the blessings of the parent-child relationship and make uniquely valuable contributions to the child's development. If he fails to do so, the Federal Constitution will not automatically compel a state to listen to his opinion of where the child's best interests lie.

In this case, we are not assessing the constitutional adequacy of New York's procedures for terminating a developed relationship. Appellant has never had any significant custodial, personal, or financial relationship with Jessica, and he did not seek to establish a legal tie until after she was two years old.[19] We are concerned only with whether New

---

[19] This case happens to involve an adoption by the husband of the natural mother, but we do not believe the natural father has any greater right to object to such an adoption than to an adoption by two total strangers. If anything, the balance of equities tips the opposite way in a case such as this. In denying the putative father relief in *Quilloin*, we made an observation equally applicable here:

"Nor is this a case in which the proposed adoption would place the child with a new set of parents with whom the child had never before lived. Rather, the result of the adoption in this case is to give full recognition to a family unit already in existence, a result desired by all concerned, except appellant. Whatever might be required in other situations, we cannot say that the State was required in this situation to find anything more than that the adoption, and denial of legitimation, were in the 'best interests of the child.' " *Quilloin*, 434 U.S. at 255.

York has adequately protected his opportunity to form such a relationship.

II

The most effective protection of the putative father's opportunity to develop a relationship with his child is provided by the laws that authorize formal marriage and govern its consequences. But the availability of that protection is, of course, dependent on the will of both parents of the child. Thus, New York has adopted a special statutory scheme to protect the unmarried father's interest in assuming a responsible role in the future of his child.

marriage

After this Court's decision in *Stanley,* the New York Legislature appointed a special commission to recommend legislation that would accommodate both the interests of biological fathers in their children and the children's interest in prompt and certain adoption procedures. The commission recommended, and the legislature enacted, a statutory adoption scheme that automatically provides notice to seven categories of putative fathers who are likely to have assumed some responsibility for the care of their natural children. If this scheme were likely to omit many responsible fathers, and if qualification for notice were beyond the control of an interested putative father, it might be thought procedurally inadequate. Yet, as all of the New York courts that reviewed this matter observed, the right to receive notice was completely within appellant's control. By mailing a postcard to the putative father registry, he could have guaranteed that he would receive notice of any proceedings to adopt Jessica. The possibility that he may have failed to do so because of his ignorance of the law cannot be a sufficient reason for criticizing the law itself. The New York legislature concluded that a more open-ended notice requirement would merely complicate the adoption process, threaten the privacy interests of unwed mothers, create the risk of unnecessary controversy, and impair the desired finality of adoption decrees. Regardless of whether we would have done likewise if we were legislators instead of judges, we surely cannot characterize the state's conclusion as arbitrary.

but burden of notice not usually on person whose rights are being denied

Appellant argues, however, that even if the putative father's opportunity to establish a relationship with an illegitimate child is adequately protected by the New York statutory scheme in the normal case, he was nevertheless entitled to special notice because the court and the mother knew that he had filed an affiliation proceeding in another court. This argument amounts to nothing more than an indirect attack on the notice provisions of the New York statute. The legitimate state interests in facilitating the adoption of young children and having the adoption proceeding completed expeditiously that underlie the entire statutory scheme also justify a trial judge's determination to require all interested parties to adhere precisely to the procedural requirements of the statute. The Constitution does not require either a trial judge or a litigant to give special notice to nonparties who are presumptively capable of asserting and protecting their own rights. Since the New York statutes adequately protected appellant's inchoate interest in establishing a relationship with Jessica, we find no merit in the claim that his constitutional rights were offended because the family court strictly complied with the notice provisions of the statute.

The Equal Protection Claim.

. . .

The legislation at issue in this case . . . is intended to establish procedures for adoptions. Those procedures are designed to promote the best interests of the child, protect the rights of interested third parties, and ensure promptness and finality. To serve those ends, the legislation guarantees to certain people the right to veto an adoption and the right to prior notice of any adoption proceeding. The mother of an illegitimate child is always within that favored class, but only certain putative fathers are included. Appellant contends that the gender-based distinction is invidious.

As we noted above, the existence or nonexistence of a substantial relationship between parent and child is a relevant criterion in evaluating both the rights of the parent and the best interests of the child. . . . Because appellant . . . has never established a substantial relationship with his daughter, the New York statutes at issue in this case did not operate to deny appellant equal protection.

We have held that these statutes may not constitutionally be applied in that class of cases where the mother and father are in fact similarly situated with regard to their relationship with the child. In *Caban v. Mohammed*, 441 U.S. 380 (1979), the Court held that it violated the Equal Protection Clause to grant the mother a veto over the adoption of a four-year-old girl and a six-year-old boy, but not to grant a veto to their father, who had admitted paternity and had participated in the rearing of the children. The Court made it clear, however, that if the father had not "come forward to participate in the rearing of his child, nothing in the Equal Protection Clause [would] preclude[ ] the State from withholding from him the privilege of vetoing the adoption of that child." *Caban*, 441 U.S. at 392.

Jessica's parents are not like the parents involved in *Caban*. Whereas appellee had a continuous custodial responsibility for Jessica, appellant never established any custodial, personal, or financial relationship with her. If one parent has an established custodial relationship with the child and the other parent has either abandoned or never established a relationship, the Equal Protection Clause does not prevent a state from according the two parents different legal rights.

The judgment of the New York Court of Appeals is

Affirmed.

■ WHITE, J., with whom MARSHALL, J., and BLACKMUN, J., join, dissenting.

The question in this case is whether the State may, consistent with the Due Process Clause, deny notice and an opportunity to be heard in an adoption proceeding to a putative father when the State has actual notice of his existence, whereabouts, and interest in the child.

I

. . .

According to Lehr, he and Jessica's mother met in 1971 and began living together in 1974. The couple cohabited for approximately 2 years, until Jessica's birth in 1976. Throughout the pregnancy and after the birth, Lorraine acknowledged to friends and relatives that Lehr was Jessica's father; Lorraine told Lehr that she had reported to the New York State Department of Social Services that he was the father. Lehr visited Lorraine and Jessica in the hospital every day during Lorraine's confinement. According to Lehr, from the time Lorraine was discharged from the hospital until August, 1978, she concealed her whereabouts from him. During this time Lehr never ceased his efforts to locate Lorraine and Jessica and achieved sporadic success until August, 1977, after which time he was unable to locate them at all. On those occasions when he did determine Lorraine's location, he visited with her and her children to the extent she was willing to permit it. When Lehr, with the aid of a detective agency, located Lorraine and Jessica in August, 1978, Lorraine was already married to Mr. Robertson. Lehr asserts that at this time he offered to provide financial assistance and to set up a trust fund for Jessica, but that Lorraine refused. Lorraine threatened Lehr with arrest unless he stayed away and refused to permit him to see Jessica. Thereafter Lehr retained counsel who wrote to Lorraine in early December, 1978, requesting that she permit Lehr to visit Jessica and threatening legal action on Lehr's behalf. On December 21, 1978, perhaps as a response to Lehr's threatened legal action, appellees commenced the adoption action at issue here.

. . .

Lehr's version of the "facts" paints a far different picture than that portrayed by the majority. The majority's recitation, that "[a]ppellant has never had any significant custodial, personal, or financial relationship with Jessica, and he did not seek to establish a legal tie until after she was two years old," obviously does not tell the whole story. Appellant has never been afforded an opportunity to present his case. The legitimation proceeding he instituted was first stayed, and then dismissed, on appellees' motions. Nor could appellant establish his interest during the adoption proceedings, for it is the failure to provide Lehr notice and an opportunity to be heard there that is at issue here. We cannot fairly make a judgment based on the quality or substance of a relationship without a complete and developed factual record. This case requires us to assume that Lehr's allegations are true—that but for the actions of the child's mother there would have been the kind of significant relationship that the majority concedes is entitled to the full panoply of procedural due process protections.

I reject the peculiar notion that the only significance of the biological connection between father and child is that "it offers the natural father an opportunity that no other male possesses to develop a relationship with his offspring." A "mere biological relationship" is not as unimportant in determining the nature of liberty interests as the majority suggests.

"[T]he usual understanding of 'family' implies biological relationships, and most decisions treating the relation between parent and child have stressed this element." The "biological connection" is itself a relationship that creates a protected interest. Thus the "nature" of the interest is the parent-child relationship; how well-developed that relationship has become goes to its "weight," not its "nature." Whether Lehr's interest is entitled to constitutional protection does not entail a searching inquiry into the quality of the relationship but a simple determination of the *fact* that the relationship exists—a fact that even the majority agrees must be assumed to be established.

Beyond that, however, because there is no established factual basis on which to proceed, it is quite untenable to conclude that a putative father's interest in his child is lacking in substance, that the father in effect has abandoned the child, or ultimately that the father's interest is not entitled to the same minimum procedural protections as the interests of other putative fathers. Any analysis of the adequacy of the notice in this case must be conducted on the assumption that the interest involved here is as strong as that of *any* putative father. That is not to say that due process requires actual notice to every putative father or that adoptive parents or the State must conduct an exhaustive search of records or an intensive investigation before a final adoption order may be entered. The procedures adopted by the State, however, must at least represent a reasonable effort to determine the identity of the putative father and to give him adequate notice.

II

In this case, of course, there was no question about either the identity or the location of the putative father. The mother knew exactly who he was and both she and the court entering the order of adoption knew precisely where he was and how to give him actual notice that his parental rights were about to be terminated by an adoption order. Lehr was entitled to due process, and the right to be heard is one of the fundamentals of that right, which "has little reality or worth unless one is informed that the matter is pending and can choose for himself whether to appear or default, acquiesce or contest."

. . .

The State asserts that any problem in this respect is overcome by the seventh category of putative fathers to whom notice must be given, namely those fathers who have identified themselves in the putative father register maintained by the State. Since Lehr did not take advantage of this device to make his interest known, the State contends, he was not entitled to notice and a hearing even though his identity, location and interest were known to the adoption court prior to entry of the adoption order. I have difficulty with this position. First, it represents a grudging and crabbed approach to due process. The State is quite willing to give notice and a hearing to putative fathers who have made themselves known by resorting to the putative fathers' register. It makes little sense to me to deny notice and hearing to a father who has not placed his name in the register but who has unmistakably identified himself by filing suit to establish his paternity and has notified the adoption court of his action and his interest. I thus need not question the statutory scheme on its face. Even assuming that Lehr would have been foreclosed if his failure to utilize the register had somehow disadvantaged the State, he effectively made himself known by other means, and it is the sheerest formalism to deny him a hearing because he informed the State in the wrong manner.

. . .

Because in my view the failure to provide Lehr with notice and an opportunity to be heard violated rights guaranteed him by the Due Process Clause, I need not address the question whether § 111–a violates the Equal Protection Clause by discriminating between categories of unwed fathers or by discriminating on the basis of gender.

Respectfully, I dissent.

NOTES

1.   *The marital model.* In *Stanley*, the Court credited Peter Stanley's status as the legal parent of his biological children. Yet, in *Quilloin* and *Lehr*, the biological fathers' claims were discredited. What explains the difference in the disposition of these cases? According to the Court, the difference lies in the fact that beyond their biological connection, the fathers in *Quilloin* and *Lehr* had—at best—an uneven and itinerant relationship with their children. In the absence of more robust paternal ties, it did not make sense to credit an unmarried father's rights. However, Professor Melissa Murray argues that it is not just a particular understanding of fatherhood that informs the Court's disposition of these cases. As she explains, the Court implicitly links fatherhood with marriage in a manner that shapes these decisions. In *Stanley*, she argues, it is meaningful that Peter Stanley "was a strong presence in his children's lives, living with them and supporting them financially for many years." As importantly, Peter was a consistent presence in the life of Joan, his children's mother. As Murray explains, the Court's embrace of Peter Stanley—and its antipathy for the fathers in *Lehr* and *Quilloin*—can be explained by the fact that Peter Stanley "had not only

behaved like a father; he had behaved like a husband," living with his partner and raising a family in a long-term, marriage-like relationship. *See* Melissa Murray, *What's So New About the New Illegitimacy?*, 20 AM. U. J. GENDER SOC. POL'Y & L. 387, 402 (2011).

2. *Adoption and illegitimacy.* Anxieties about illegitimacy—and adoption's role in "curing" illegitimate birth—also shadow the Court's decisions in *Lehr* and *Quilloin*. Professor Melissa Murray argues it is meaningful that in each case, the child's mother had remarried and the stepfather sought to adopt the child, creating a new marital family. *See* Melissa Murray, *What's So New About the New Illegitimacy?*, 20 AM. U. J. GENDER SOC. POL'Y & L. 387, 404–05 (2011). Indeed, as the Court noted in an earlier case, *Caban v. Mohammed*, 441 U.S. 380 (1979), allowing unmarried fathers to block the adoption of their biological children would "have the overall effect of . . . depriving innocent children of the . . . blessings of adoption," including ridding them of the "cruel and undeserved" stigma of illegitimacy. *Id.* at 390.

3. *Defending the unitary family.* As Professors Ristroph and Murray discuss in the excerpt of *Disestablishing the Family*, *supra* p. 269, *Michael H. v. Gerald D.*, 491 U.S. 110 (1989), is the capstone of the line of unmarried fathers cases. There, despite blood tests that indicated a 98.07% probability that he was the biological father of the child in question, and the fact that he had developed a close relationship with the child, a plurality of the Court rejected Michael H.'s paternity claim. Of particular importance to the plurality was the fact that the child was born of an adulterous affair between Michael and Carole, who, at the time of the child's birth, remained married to her husband, Gerald. Affirming a statutory presumption (long-derived from the common law) that "the issue of a wife cohabiting with her husband, who is not impotent or sterile, is conclusively presumed to be a child of the marriage," *id.* at 117, the plurality emphasized its commitment to preserving the "unitary family"—a structure, in the plurality's view, that was "typified, of course, by the marital family." *Id.* at 123 n.3. Although the plurality conceded that the unitary family could "include[ ] the household of unmarried parents and their children," as in *Stanley*, it could not be "stretched so far as to include the relationship established between a married woman, her lover, and their child." *Id.*

4. *A new illegitimacy?* Some courts have recognized the legitimate parentage of both lesbian mothers who have conceived and/or raised a child together. But as Professor Nancy Polikoff makes clear, this development echoes a persistent preoccupation with marriage and the marriage-like family credited in *Stanley*. As Polikoff explains, the parentage link is recognized only if the two women are married or comport with norms associated with married couples. Polikoff describes these cases as "winning backward," because same-sex parents' court victories come at the cost of entrenching marriage as the normative ideal for family structure. *See* Nancy D. Polikoff, *The New Illegitimacy: Winning Backward in the Protection of the Children of Lesbian Couples*, 20 AM. U. J. GENDER SOC. POL'Y & L. 721, 722 (2012).

5. *Constitutional protection for the extended family.* As Professors Ristroph and Murray argue, cases like *Stanley*, *Quilloin*, and *Lehr* all evince a

preference for the nuclear family. But, as we know, many families do not comport with the nuclear family model. Indeed, some families include intergenerational networks of extended family members. Are these family ties eligible for constitutional protection? In 1977's *Moore v. City of East Cleveland*, 431 U.S. 494 (1977), the U.S. Supreme Court considered whether the extended family was subject to the constitutional protections traditionally afforded the marital family. *Moore* involved an East Cleveland zoning ordinance that, in an effort to stem the influx of children from Cleveland to East Cleveland's schools, limited the occupancy of a dwelling unit to members of a single family—i.e. the nuclear family. Inez Moore, who resided with her adult son, his son, and another grandson, was criminally charged and convicted for violating the ordinance. In a 5–4 decision, the Court invalidated the ordinance on the ground that it "slic[ed] deeply into the family itself." *Id.* at 498. As the *Moore* Court acknowledged, "[o]urs is by no means a tradition limited to respect for the bonds uniting the members of the nuclear family. The tradition of uncles, aunts, cousins, and especially grandparents sharing a household along with parents and children has roots equally venerable and equally deserving of constitutional recognition." *Id.* at 504. Is *Moore* a radical departure from the traditional privileging of the nuclear family?

D. REGULATING FAMILIES AND CITIZENS

Nguyen v. INS
533 U.S. 53 (2001).

■ KENNEDY, J.

... Title 8 U.S.C. § 1409 governs the acquisition of United States citizenship by persons born to one United States citizen parent and one noncitizen parent when the parents are unmarried and the child is born outside of the United States or its possessions. The statute imposes different requirements for the child's acquisition of citizenship depending upon whether the citizen parent is the mother or the father. The question before us is whether the statutory distinction is consistent with the equal protection guarantee embedded in the Due Process Clause of the Fifth Amendment.

Petitioner Tuan Anh Nguyen was born in Saigon, Vietnam, on September 11, 1969, to copetitioner Joseph Boulais and a Vietnamese citizen. Boulais and Nguyen's mother were not married. Boulais always has been a citizen of the United States, and he was in Vietnam under the employ of a corporation. After he and Nguyen's mother ended their relationship, Nguyen lived for a time with the family of Boulais' new Vietnamese girlfriend. In June 1975, Nguyen, then almost six years of age, came to the United States. He became a lawful permanent resident and was raised in Texas by Boulais.

In 1992, when Nguyen was 22, he pleaded guilty in a Texas state court to two counts of sexual assault on a child. He was sentenced to eight years in prison on each count. Three years later, the United States Immigration and Naturalization Service (INS) initiated deportation proceedings against Nguyen as an alien who had been convicted of two crimes involving moral turpitude, as well as an aggravated felony. . . .

Nguyen appealed to the Board of Immigration Appeals and, in 1998, while the matter was pending, his father obtained an order of parentage from a state court, based on DNA testing. By this time, Nguyen was 28 years old. The Board dismissed Nguyen's appeal, rejecting his claim to United States citizenship because he had failed to establish compliance with 8 U.S.C. § 1409(a), which sets forth the requirements for one who was born out of wedlock and abroad to a citizen father and a noncitizen mother.

Nguyen and Boulais appealed to the Court of Appeals for the Fifth Circuit, arguing that § 1409 violates equal protection by providing different rules for attainment of citizenship by children born abroad and out of wedlock depending upon whether the one parent with American citizenship is the mother or the father. The court rejected the constitutional challenge to § 1409(a).

. . .

The general requirement for acquisition of citizenship by a child born outside the United States and its outlying possessions and to parents who are married, one of whom is a citizen and the other of whom is an alien, is set forth in 8 U.S.C. § 1401(g). The statute provides that the child is also a citizen if, before the birth, the citizen parent had been physically present in the United States for a total of five years, at least two of which were after the parent turned 14 years of age.

As to an individual born under the same circumstances, save that the parents are unwed, § 1409(a) sets forth the following requirements where the father is the citizen parent and the mother is an alien:

(1) a blood relationship between the person and the father is established by clear and convincing evidence,

(2) the father had the nationality of the United States at the time of the person's birth,

(3) the father (unless deceased) has agreed in writing to provide financial support for the person until the person reaches the age of 18 years, and

(4) while the person is under the age of 18 years—

(A) the person is legitimated under the law of the person's residence or domicile,

(B) the father acknowledges paternity of the person in writing under oath, or

(C) the paternity of the person is established by adjudication of a competent court.

In addition, § 1409(a) incorporates by reference, as to the citizen parent, the residency requirement of § 1401(g).

When the citizen parent of the child born abroad and out of wedlock is the child's mother, the requirements for the transmittal of citizenship are described in § 1409(c):

> (c) Notwithstanding the provision of subsection (a) of this section, a person born, after December 23, 1952, outside the United States and out of wedlock shall be held to have acquired at birth the nationality status of his mother, if the mother had the nationality of the United States at the time of such person's birth, and if the mother had previously been physically present in the United States or one of its outlying possessions for a continuous period of one year.

Section 1409(a) thus imposes a set of requirements on the children of citizen fathers born abroad and out of wedlock to a noncitizen mother that are not imposed under like circumstances when the citizen parent is the mother. All concede the requirements of §§ 1409(a)(3) and (a)(4), relating to a citizen father's acknowledgment of a child while he is under 18, were not satisfied in this case. . . .

For a gender-based classification to withstand equal protection scrutiny, it must be established "at least that the [challenged] classification serves 'important governmental objectives and that the discriminatory means employed' are 'substantially related to the achievement of those objectives.'" For reasons to follow, we conclude § 1409 satisfies this standard. . . .

. . .

The statutory distinction relevant in this case, then, is that § 1409(a)(4) requires one of three affirmative steps to be taken if the citizen parent is the father, but not if the citizen parent is the mother: legitimation; a declaration of paternity under oath by the father; or a court order of paternity. Congress' decision to impose requirements on unmarried fathers that differ from those on unmarried mothers is based on the significant difference between their respective relationships to the potential citizen at the time of birth. Specifically, the imposition of the requirement for a paternal relationship, but not a maternal one, is justified by two important governmental objectives. We discuss each in turn.

The first governmental interest to be served is the importance of assuring that a biological parent-child relationship exists. In the case of the mother, the relation is verifiable from the birth itself. The mother's status is documented in most instances by the birth certificate or hospital records and the witnesses who attest to her having given birth.

In the case of the father, the uncontestable fact is that he need not be present at the birth. If he is present, furthermore, that circumstance is not incontrovertible proof of fatherhood. . . . Fathers and mothers are not similarly situated with regard to the proof of biological parenthood. The imposition of a different set of rules for making that legal determination with respect to fathers and mothers is neither surprising nor troublesome from a constitutional perspective. Section 1409(a)(4)'s provision of three options for a father seeking to establish paternity— legitimation, paternity oath, and court order of paternity—is designed to ensure an acceptable documentation of paternity.

Petitioners argue that the requirement of § 1409(a)(1), that a father provide clear and convincing evidence of parentage, is sufficient to achieve the end of establishing paternity, given the sophistication of modern DNA tests. . . . With respect to DNA testing, the expense, reliability, and availability of such testing in various parts of the world may have been of particular concern to Congress. The requirement of § 1409(a)(4) represents a reasonable conclusion by the legislature that the satisfaction of one of several alternatives will suffice to establish the blood link between father and child required as a predicate to the child's acquisition of citizenship. Given the proof of motherhood that is inherent in birth itself, it is unremarkable that Congress did not require the same affirmative steps of mothers.

Finally, to require Congress to speak without reference to the gender of the parent with regard to its objective of ensuring a blood tie between parent and child would be to insist on a hollow neutrality. . . . Congress could have required both mothers and fathers to prove parenthood within 30 days or, for that matter, 18 years, of the child's birth. Given that the mother is always present at birth, but that the father need not be, the facially neutral rule would sometimes require fathers to take additional affirmative steps which would not be required of mothers, whose names will appear on the birth certificate as a result of their presence at the birth, and who will have the benefit of witnesses to the birth to call upon. The issue is not the use of gender specific terms instead of neutral ones. Just as neutral terms can mask discrimination that is unlawful, gender specific terms can mark a permissible distinction. The equal protection question is whether the distinction is lawful. Here, the use of gender specific terms takes into account a biological difference between the parents. The differential treatment is inherent in a sensible statutory scheme, given the unique relationship of the mother to the event of birth.

The second important governmental interest furthered in a substantial manner by § 1409(a)(4) is the determination to ensure that the child and the citizen parent have some demonstrated opportunity or potential to develop not just a relationship that is recognized, as a formal matter, by the law, but one that consists of the real, everyday ties that provide a connection between child and citizen parent and, in turn, the United States. In the case of a citizen mother and a child born overseas, the opportunity for a meaningful relationship between citizen parent and child inheres in the very event of birth, an event so often critical to our constitutional and statutory understandings of citizenship. The mother knows that the child is in being and is hers and has an initial point of contact with him. There is at least an opportunity for mother and child to develop a real, meaningful relationship.

The same opportunity does not result from the event of birth, as a matter of biological inevitability, in the case of the unwed father. Given the 9-month interval between conception and birth, it is not always certain that a father will know that a child was conceived, nor is it always clear that even the mother will be sure of the father's identity. This fact takes on particular significance in the case of a child born overseas and out of wedlock. One concern in this context has always been with young people, men for the most part, who are on duty with the Armed Forces in foreign countries.

When we turn to the conditions which prevail today, we find that the passage of time has produced additional and even more substantial grounds to justify the statutory distinction. The ease of travel and the willingness of Americans to visit foreign countries have resulted in numbers of trips abroad that must be of real concern when we contemplate the prospect of accepting petitioners' argument, which would mandate, contrary to Congress' wishes, citizenship by male parentage subject to no condition save the father's previous length of residence in this country. . . .

Principles of equal protection do not require Congress to ignore this reality. To the contrary, these facts demonstrate the critical importance of the Government's interest in ensuring some opportunity for a tie between citizen father and foreign born child which is a reasonable substitute for the opportunity manifest between mother and child at the time of birth. Indeed, especially in light of the number of Americans who take short sojourns abroad, the prospect that a father might not even know of the conception is a realistic possibility. Even if a father knows of the fact of conception, moreover, it does not follow that he will be present at the birth of the child. Thus, unlike the case of the mother, there is no assurance that the father and his biological child will ever meet. Without an initial point of contact with the child by a father who knows the child is his own, there is no opportunity for father and child to begin a relationship. Section 1409 takes the unremarkable step of ensuring that such an opportunity, inherent in the event of birth as to the mother-child relationship, exists between father and child before citizenship is conferred upon the latter.

The importance of the governmental interest at issue here is too profound to be satisfied merely by conducting a DNA test. The fact of paternity can be established even without the father's knowledge, not to say his presence. . . . Yet scientific proof of biological paternity does nothing, by itself, to ensure contact between father and child during the child's minority.

Congress is well within its authority in refusing, absent proof of at least the opportunity for the development of a relationship between citizen parent and child, to commit this country to embracing a child as a citizen entitled as of birth to the full protection of the United States, to the absolute right to enter its borders, and to full participation in the political process. If citizenship is to be conferred by the unwitting means petitioners urge, so that its acquisition abroad bears little relation to the realities of the child's own ties and allegiances, it is for Congress, not this Court, to make that determination. Congress has not taken that path but has instead chosen, by means of § 1409, to ensure in the case of father and child the opportunity for a relationship to develop, an opportunity which the event of birth itself provides for the mother and child. It should be unobjectionable for Congress to require some evidence of a minimal opportunity for the development of a relationship with the child in terms the male can fulfill.

. . .

Petitioners and their *amici* argue in addition that, rather than fulfilling an important governmental interest, § 1409 merely embodies a gender-based stereotype. . . . There is nothing irrational or improper in the recognition that at the moment of birth—a critical event in the statutory scheme and in the whole tradition of citizenship law—the mother's knowledge of the child and the fact of parenthood have been established in a way not guaranteed in the case of the unwed father. This is not a stereotype. . . .

Having concluded that facilitation of a relationship between parent and child is an important governmental interest, the question remains whether the means Congress chose to further its objective—the imposition of certain additional requirements upon an unwed father— substantially relate to that end. Under this test, the means Congress adopted must be sustained.

First, it should be unsurprising that Congress decided to require that an opportunity for a parent-child relationship occur during the formative years of the child's minority. In furtherance of the desire to ensure some tie between this country and one who seeks citizenship, various other statutory provisions concerning citizenship and naturalization require some act linking the child to the United States to occur before the child reaches 18 years of age.

Second, petitioners argue that § 1409(a)(4) is not effective. In particular, petitioners assert that, although a mother will know of her child's birth, "knowledge that one is a parent, no matter how it is acquired, does not guarantee a relationship with one's child." They thus maintain that the imposition of the additional requirements of § 1409(a)(4) only on the children of citizen fathers must reflect a stereotype that women are more likely than men to actually establish a relationship with their children.

This line of argument misconceives the nature of both the governmental interest at issue and the manner in which we examine statutes alleged to violate equal protection. . . . Congress enacted an easily administered scheme to promote the different but still substantial interest of ensuring at least an opportunity for a parent-child relationship to develop. Petitioners' argument confuses the means and ends of the equal protection inquiry; § 1409(a)(4) should not be invalidated because Congress elected to advance an interest that is less demanding to satisfy than some other alternative.

Even if one conceives of the interest Congress pursues as the establishment of a real, practical relationship of considerable substance between parent and child in every case, as opposed simply to ensuring the potential for the relationship to begin, petitioners' misconception of the nature of the equal protection inquiry is fatal to their argument. A statute meets the equal protection standard we here apply so long as it is "substantially related to the achievement of" the governmental objective in question. It is almost axiomatic that a policy which seeks to foster the opportunity for meaningful parent-child bonds to develop has a close and substantial bearing on the governmental interest in the actual formation of that bond. None of our gender-based classification equal protection cases have required that the statute under consideration must be capable of achieving its ultimate objective in every instance.

In this difficult context of conferring citizenship on vast numbers of persons, the means adopted by Congress are in substantial furtherance of important governmental objectives. The fit between the means and the important end is "exceedingly persuasive." We have explained that an "exceedingly persuasive justification" is established "by showing at least that the classification serves 'important governmental objectives and that the discriminatory means employed' are 'substantially related to the achievement of those objectives.'" Section 1409 meets this standard.

C

In analyzing § 1409(a)(4), we are mindful that the obligation it imposes with respect to the acquisition of citizenship by the child of a citizen father is minimal. This circumstance shows that Congress has not erected inordinate and unnecessary hurdles to the conferral of citizenship on the children of citizen fathers in furthering its important objectives. Only the least onerous of the three options provided for in § 1409(a)(4) must be satisfied. If the child has been legitimated under the law of the relevant jurisdiction, that will be the end of the matter. In the alternative, a father who has not legitimated his child by formal means need only make a written acknowledgment of paternity under oath in order to transmit citizenship to his child, hardly a substantial burden. Or, the father could choose to obtain a court order of paternity. The statute can be satisfied on the day of birth, or the next day, or for the next 18 years. In this case, the unfortunate, even tragic, circumstance is that Boulais did not pursue, or perhaps did not know of, these simple steps and alternatives. Any omission, however, does not nullify the statutory scheme.

Section 1409(a), moreover, is not the sole means by which the child of a citizen father can attain citizenship. An individual who fails to comply with § 1409(a), but who has substantial ties to the United States, can seek citizenship in his or her own right, rather than via reliance on ties to a citizen parent. This option now may be foreclosed to Nguyen, but any bar is due to the serious nature of his criminal offenses, not to an equal protection denial or to any supposed rigidity or harshness in the citizenship laws.

. . .

To fail to acknowledge even our most basic biological differences— such as the fact that a mother must be present at birth but the father need not be—risks making the guarantee of equal protection superficial, and so disserving it. Mechanistic classification of all our differences as stereotypes would operate to obscure those misconceptions and prejudices that are real. The distinction embodied in the statutory scheme here at issue is not marked by misconception and prejudice, nor does it show disrespect for either class. The difference between men and women in relation to the birth process is a real one, and the principle of equal protection does not forbid Congress to address the problem at hand in a manner specific to each gender.

The judgment of the Court of Appeals is *Affirmed.* *Holding*

NOTES

1.   Nguyen v. I.N.S. *and the plight of the "Amerasian."* Nobel Prize-winning author Pearl Buck popularized the term "Amerasian" in 1966 to describe children born to American servicemen and Asian women, although she suggests that it was perhaps the State Department that coined the term. PEARL S. BUCK, FOR SPACIOUS SKIES: JOURNEY IN DIALOGUE 54 (1966). Subsequent American military presence in Korea, Vietnam, Laos, Cambodia and Thailand have continued to raise questions and concerns about the status and citizenship rights of "Amerasian" children, giving rise to cases such as *Nguyen v. I.N.S. See* Sue-Je Lee Gage, *The Amerasian Problem: Blood, Duty, and Race,* 21 INT'L REL. 86, 86–87 (2007). To answer these concerns, the term "Amerasian" was given legal meaning by the Amerasian Immigration Act of 1982, Pub. L. No. 97–359, 96 Stat. 1716 (codified as amended at 8 U.S.C. § 1154 (2014)), which provided for the immigration of children born in Cambodia, Korea, Laos, Thailand, or Vietnam to a U.S. citizen father and a non-citizen Asian mother, if the children were born after December 31, 1950 and before October 22, 1982. Critically, children born in the Philippines and Japan were excluded from the Act's ambit. *See id.* What do these special immigration allowances tell us about how the U.S.

government views the role of fathers, as well as its own role in cultivating the conditions in which fatherhood occurs?

2.   *Fathers' rights and mothers' duties.* Professor Kristin Collins argues that cases like *Nguyen* reflect deeply entrenched principles that date back to the common law of coverture. As Collins explains:

> Under coverture, men had full legal rights and responsibilities regarding children born in marriage, while women had full legal rights and responsibilities regarding children born out of marriage. In order to protect men from claims on property and status by illegitimate children, the law imposed no obligation to support or care for their nonmarital children. Recognizing this legal arrangement, legislators, judges, and administrators limited citizenship transmission from citizen fathers to foreign-born nonmarital children.

Kristin Collins, Note, *When Fathers' Rights Are Mothers' Duties: The Failure of Equal Protection in* Miller v. Albright, 109 YALE L.J. 1669, 1672 (2000). As she observes, it is only when we recognize the gendered underpinnings of the statute at issue in *Nguyen,* do broader failures of equal protection analysis come into view. Indeed, "the principal gender injustice caused by § 1409 is not its truncation of fathers' rights, but its creation and perpetuation of a legal regime in which mothers assume full responsibility for foreign-born nonmarital children." *Id.* at 1673.

United States v. Flores-Villar

536 F.3d 990 (9th Cir. 2008).

■ RYMER, CIRCUIT JUDGE:

Ruben Flores-Villar raises a challenge under the equal protection component of the Fifth Amendment's due process clause on the basis of . . . gender to two former sections of the Immigration and Nationality Act, 8 U.S.C. §§ 1401(a)(7) and 1409 (1974), which impose a five-year residence requirement, after the age of fourteen, on United States citizen fathers—but not on United States citizen mothers—before they may transmit citizenship to a child born out of wedlock abroad to a non-citizen. This precise question has not been addressed before, but the answer follows from the Supreme Court's opinion in *Nguyen v. INS,* 533 U.S. 53 (2001). There the Court held that § 1409's legitimation requirements for citizen fathers, but not for citizen mothers, did not offend principles of equal protection. Assuming, as the Court did in *Nguyen,* that intermediate scrutiny applies to Flores-Villar's gender-based claim and rational basis review applies to his age-based claim, we conclude that the residence requirements of §§ 1401(a)(7) and 1409 survive. . . .

Flores-Villar was born in Tijuana, Mexico on October 7, 1974 to Ruben Trinidad Floresvillar-Sandez, his United States citizen biological father who was sixteen at the time, and Maria Mercedes Negrete, his non-United States citizen biological mother. Floresvillar-Sandez had been issued a Certificate of Citizenship on May 24, 1999 based on the fact that his mother—Flores Villar's paternal grandmother—is a United States citizen by birth.

His father and grandmother brought Flores-Villar to the United States for medical treatment when he was two months old. He grew up in San Diego with his grandmother and father. Floresvillar-Sandez is not listed on Flores-Villar's birth certificate, but he acknowledged Flores-Villar as his son by filing an acknowledgment of paternity with the Civil Registry in Mexico on June 2, 1985. On March 17, 1997 Flores-Villar was convicted of importation of marijuana in violation of 21 U.S.C. §§ 952 and 960; and on June 16, 2003 he was convicted of two counts of illegal entry into the United States in violation of 8 U.S.C. § 1325. He was removed from the United States pursuant to removal orders on numerous occasions. . . .

He was arrested again on February 24, 2006, and this time was charged with being a deported alien found in the United States after deportation in violation of 8 U.S.C. § 1326(a) and (b). He sought to defend on the footing that he believed he was a United States citizen through his father. Meanwhile, Flores-Villar filed an N–600 application seeking a Certificate of Citizenship, which was denied on the ground that it was physically impossible for his father, who was sixteen when Flores-Villar was born, to have been present in the United States for five years after his fourteenth birthday as required by § 1401(a)(7). The government filed a motion *in limine* to exclude evidence of derivative citizenship for the same reason, which the district court granted. The court denied Flores-Villar's corresponding motion *in limine*, to be allowed to present evidence that he believed he was a United States citizen.

The district court found Flores-Villar guilty following a bench trial on stipulated facts. It denied his motion for judgment of acquittal. Flores-Villar timely appeals his conviction.

When Flores-Villar was born, § 1401(a)(7) provided, in relevant part:

(a) The following shall be nationals and citizens of the United States at birth:

. . .

(7) a person born outside the geographic limits of the United States and its outlying possessions of parents one of whom is an alien, and the other a citizen of the United States who, prior to the birth of such person, was physically present in the United States or its outlying possessions for a period or periods totaling not less than ten years, at least five of which were after attaining the age of fourteen years.

8 U.S.C. § 1401(a)(7) (1974). Section 1409 provided:

> The provisions of paragraphs (3) to (5) and (7) of section 1401(a) of this title, and of paragraph (2) of section 1408, of this title shall apply as of the date of birth to a child born out of wedlock . . . if the paternity of such child is established while such child is under the age of twenty-one years by legitimation.
>
> . . .
>
> (c) Notwithstanding the provision of subsection (a) of this section, a person born . . . outside the United States and out of wedlock shall be held to have acquired at birth the nationality status of his mother, if the mother had the nationality of the United States at the time of such person's birth, and if the mother had previously been physically present in the United States or one of its outlying possessions for a continuous period of one year.

Thus, if a United States citizen father had a child out of wedlock abroad, with a non-United States citizen mother, the father must have resided in the United States for at least five years after his fourteenth birthday to confer citizenship on his child. But a United States citizen mother had to reside in the United States for a continuous period of only one year prior to the child's birth to pass on citizenship. It is this difference that Flores-Villar claims makes an impermissible classification on the basis of gender. . . .

In *Nguyen*, the United States citizen father of a child born in Vietnam to a Vietnamese mother challenged § 1409s imposition of different rules for obtaining citizenship depending upon whether the one parent with American citizenship is the mother or the father. There, the father complained about the affirmative steps a citizen father, but not a citizen mother, was required by § 1409(a)(4) to take: legitimation; a declaration of paternity under oath by the father; or a court order of paternity. Assuming, without deciding, that the intermediate level of scrutiny normally applied to a gender-based classification applies even when the statute is within Congress' immigration and naturalization power, and drawing on Justice Stevens's prior opinion in *Miller v. Albright*, 523 U.S. 420 (1998), the Court identified two important governmental interests substantially furthered by § 1409's distinction between citizen fathers and citizen mothers. The first is "assuring that a biological parent-child relationship exists." Mothers and fathers are not similarly situated in this respect; the relation is verifiable from the birth itself in the case of the mother, while a father's biological relationship to the child is not so easily established. The second interest is ensuring "that the child and the citizen parent have some demonstrated opportunity or potential to develop not just a relationship that is recognized, as a formal matter, by the law, but one that consists of the real, everyday ties that provide a connection between child and citizen parent and, in turn, the United States." The mother knows that the child is in being and has immediate contact at birth such that an opportunity for a meaningful relationship exists, whereas, as the Court put it, "[t]he same opportunity does not result from the event of birth, as a matter of biological inevitability, in the case of the unwed father." Unlike an unwed mother, there is no assurance that the father and his biological child will ever meet, or have the kind of contact from which there is a chance for a meaningful relationship to develop. The Court emphasized that Congress need not ignore these realities for purposes of equal protection, and found that the means chosen—additional requirements for an unwed citizen father to confer citizenship upon his child—are substantially related to the objective of a relationship between parent and child, and in turn, the United States.

Although the means at issue are different in this case—an additional residence requirement for the unwed citizen father—the government's interests are no less important, and the particular means no less substantially related to those objectives, than in *Nguyen*.[2] The government argues that avoiding stateless children is an important objective that is substantially furthered by relaxing the residence requirement for women because many countries confer citizenship based on bloodline (*jus sanguinis*) rather than, as the United States does, on place of birth (*jus soli*). We explained the conundrum in *Runnett v. Shultz*:

> One obvious rational basis for a more lenient policy towards illegitimate children of U.S. citizen mothers is that illegitimate children are more likely to be "stateless" at birth. . . . As the government notes, if the U.S. citizen mother is not a dual national, and the illegitimate child is born in a country that does not recognize citizenship by *jus soli* (citizenship determined by place of birth) alone, the child can acquire no citizenship other than his mother's at birth. This policy clearly demonstrates a "rational basis" for Congress' more lenient policy towards illegitimate children born abroad to U.S. citizen mothers.

. . .

Avoiding statelessness, and assuring a link between an unwed citizen father, and this country, to a child born out of wedlock abroad who is to be a citizen, are important interests. The means chosen substantially further the objectives. Though the fit is not perfect, it is sufficiently persuasive in light of the virtually plenary power that Congress has to legislate in the area of immigration and citizenship.

---

[2]   Like the Supreme Court in *Nguyen*, we will assume that intermediate scrutiny applies. The government makes a forceful argument that rational basis review should apply given Congress' broad authority under Article I, Section 8 of the Constitution in matters related to citizenship and immigration. But we do not need to decide which level of review is the most appropriate, and we do not, for the equal protection challenge fails regardless of whether §§ 1401(a)(7) and 1409 are analyzed under intermediate scrutiny, a rational basis standard, or some other level of review in between.

Flores-Villar acknowledges that the prevention of stateless children is a legitimate goal, but contends that it cannot be furthered by penalizing fathers. In his view, the real purpose of the statute is to perpetuate the stereotypical notion that women should have custody of illegitimate children. Further, he suggests, the length of residence in the United States says nothing about the father-child relationship or the biological basis of that relationship. And understandably, Flores-Villar emphasizes that his father in fact had a custodial relationship with him. However, the Court rejected similar submissions by the father in *Nguyen*. As it explained:

> This line of argument misconceives the nature of both the governmental interest at issue and the manner in which we examine statutes alleged to violate equal protection. As to the former, Congress would of course be entitled to advance the interest of ensuring an actual, meaningful relationship in every case before citizenship is conferred. Or Congress could excuse compliance with the formal requirements when an actual father-child relationship is proved. It did neither here, perhaps because of the subjectivity, intrusiveness, and difficulties of proof that might attend an inquiry into any particular bond or tie. Instead, Congress enacted an easily administered scheme to promote the different but still substantial interest of ensuring at least an opportunity for a parent-child relationship to develop. Petitioners' argument confuses the means and ends of the equal protection inquiry; § 1409(a)(4) should not be invalidated because Congress elected to advance an interest that is less demanding to satisfy than some other alternative.

533 U.S. at 69. The residence differential is directly related to statelessness; the one-year period applicable to unwed citizen mothers seeks to insure that the child will have a nationality at birth. Likewise, it furthers the objective of developing a tie between the child, his or her father, and this country. Accordingly, we conclude that even if intermediate scrutiny applies, §§ 1401(a)(7) and 1409 survive.

. . . Having passed intermediate scrutiny, the statutory scheme necessarily is rationally related to a legitimate government purpose. This follows from *Runnett*. There we held that it was rational to adopt a more lenient policy for illegitimate children of United States citizen mothers who satisfied a residence requirement than for legitimate children whose mothers failed to meet a higher residency requirement.

Flores-Villar contends that there is no rational reason to entrust an eighteen year old male to vote and serve in the military, yet restrict his ability to confer citizenship on his child when a woman, who has greater ability to choose where a child is born, can transmit citizenship to her children without a lengthy residence requirement. However, it is not irrational to believe that residence in the United States advances the objective of a link between the citizen, this country, and a foreign-born child born out of wedlock, and that the children of citizen mothers born out of wedlock abroad run a greater risk of being stateless than the children of citizen fathers. *Wauchope v. United States Department of State*, 985 F.2d 1407 (9th Cir. 1993), upon which Flores-Villar relies, does not suggest otherwise. There, we found no rational reason for § 1993 of the Revised Statutes of 1874, which accorded to American citizen males, but not American citizen females, the right to pass on citizenship to their foreign-born offspring. The statutory scheme at issue here is different, and is supported by a different rationale that is in accord with *Miller*, *Nguyen*, and *Runnett*.

. . .

Flores-Villar also argues that §§ 1401 and 1409 violate substantive due process because these provisions interfere with personal decisions relating to marriage, procreation, family relationships, child rearing, and education, as well as with the child's fundamental right to parental involvement. He lacks standing to pursue rights that belong to his father, however, as most of them do. Floresvillar-Sandez is not a party, and the record discloses no obstacle that would prevent him from asserting his own constitutional rights. The claimed right to parental involvement is personal to Flores-Villar, but he fails precisely to describe a right deeply rooted in the nation's history, as he must do in order to sustain a substantive due process violation. In any event, we have already upheld similar requirements against similar challenges.

. . .

[The decision is] affirmed.

E. REGULATING POOR FAMILIES

Jill Quadagno, The Color of Welfare: How Racism Undermined the War on Poverty
19–20 (1994).

. . .

Franklin Delano Roosevelt took office in 1932 with a mandate to inaugurate a new era in government intervention. The cornerstone of his New Deal was the Social Security Act of 1935, which provided old-age insurance and unemployment compensation for the industrial labor force. Under the old-age insurance program, workers paid payroll taxes of 1 percent on the first $3,000 earned, matched by their employers, in exchange for a $15 pension upon retirement. Under the unemployment insurance program, states levied a payroll tax on employers to protect workers against downturns in the business cycle. Although the unemployment program was technically voluntary, generous tax credits that offset most of the payroll tax provided incentives to employers to participate.

The Social Security Act also included two means-tested social assistance programs, Aid to Dependent Children and Old Age Assistance, in which state expenditures were matched by federal funds. These programs provided minimal support to those outside the wage labor pool. Old-age assistance paid eligible elderly men and women a maximum grant of $30 a month, though most states, especially those in the South, paid less. Aid to Dependent Children was restricted to single-parent families and paid benefits only to children.

. . .

The Personal Responsibility and Work Opportunity Reconciliation Act of 1996

Pub. L. No. 104–193, 110 Stat. 2105 (1996) (codified in scattered sections of 42 U.S.C.).

For an excerpt of The Personal Responsibility and Work Opportunity Reconciliation Act of 1996, please see supra p. 108.

NOTES

1. *Race and welfare.* The Social Security Act of 1935 excluded about half of all American workers, and these workers were disproportionately women and African Americans. Domestic and agricultural workers (a group comprised largely of African Americans and women) were not covered, and thus were ineligible for Old Age Insurance, unemployment, and other support programs. *See* LINDA GORDON, PITIED BUT NOT ENTITLED: THE HISTORY OF WELFARE, 1890–1935, at 4–6 (1994). In the period immediately after the passage of the Social Security Act, Congress granted broad discretion to states to impose "other eligibility requirements—as to means, moral character, etc.—as [the states] see[ ] fit." S. REP. No. 74–628, at 36 (1935). States used this discretion to create, among others, "suitable home" and "man in the house" requirements that limited African Americans' access to the Aid to Dependent Children (ADC) program. *See* WINIFRED BELL, AID TO DEPENDENT CHILDREN 44–45, 63–68, 75 (1966).

2. *Welfare reform in the 1960s.* In the wake of the civil rights movement, mobilization by the National Welfare Rights Organization (NWRO) drew attention to the state-level denial or delay of benefits to children—most egregiously to African-American children in the South—because of their parents' behavior. In 1960, after Louisiana excluded 23,000 children from the welfare rolls because they were residing in "unsuitable home[s]," Arthur Flemming, the Secretary of Health, Education, and Welfare, directed states to offer due process protections to recipients excluded from public assistance because of noncompliance with state "suitable home" requirements. He further directed the states to provide services to assist welfare recipients in their efforts to comply with the suitable home requirement. *See* Memorandum from Secretary Flemming to the Comm'r 4–5 (Jan. 16, 1961) (on file with National Association for the Advancement of Colored People Records Collection, Record Group III, U.S. National Archives, Washington, DC); WINIFRED BELL, AID TO DEPENDENT CHILDREN 142–45 (1966). For the

history of the National Welfare Rights Organization, see FELICIA KORNBLUH, THE BATTLE FOR WELFARE RIGHTS: POLITICS AND POVERTY IN MODERN AMERICA (2007). The Flemming Rule permitted many more African Americans and unmarried women to use Aid to Dependent Children (ADC), and its successor Aid to Families with Dependent Children (AFDC), and perhaps not coincidentally, initiated a conservative critique of a "culture of dependency." *See* Claudia Lawrence-Webb, *African American Children in the Modern Child Welfare System: A Legacy of the Flemming Rule*, in SERVING AFRICAN AMERICAN CHILDREN: CHILD WELFARE PERSPECTIVES 23–25 (Sondra Jackson & Sheryl Brissett-Chapman eds., 1999).

3. *"Reforming" the reforms*. Since the creation of ADC in 1935, there have been considerable efforts to reform welfare. As Professors Susan Bennett and Kathleen Sullivan document, as the federal government shifted toward funding public assistance through generous grants to the states, the "fragile concept of federal supremacy in welfare administration" was dismantled. Further, as African Americans and single mothers became eligible for aid, there was increasing conservative mobilization against "welfare." *See* Susan Bennett & Kathleen A. Sullivan, *Disentitling the Poor: Waivers and Welfare "Reform"*, 26 U. MICH. J.L. REFORM 742, 753 (1993). Indeed, by 1988, Professor David Ellwood could proclaim, "[e]veryone hates welfare." DAVID T. ELLWOOD, POOR SUPPORT: POVERTY IN THE AMERICAN FAMILY 4 (1988). This sentiment was reflected in the welfare reform efforts of the 1990s, which purported to "end welfare as we know it," imposing time limits on welfare receipt, and recreating behavioral requirements for welfare recipients. *See* Jason DeParle, *From Pledge to Plan: The Campaign to End Welfare—A Special Report*, N.Y. TIMES, July 15, 1994, at A1.

Sojourner A. v. N.J. Department of Human Services
828 A.2d 306 (N.J. 2003).

■ PORITZ, C.J.

In this appeal, plaintiffs challenge the constitutionality of a provision in the Work First New Jersey Act (WFNJ) that "caps" the amount of cash assistance for families at the level set when the family enters into the State welfare system. *N.J.S.A.* 44:10–61a. Although families in the assistance program are eligible to receive additional Medicaid and food stamp benefits on the birth of another child, the statute prohibits an increase in cash assistance benefits for any child born more than ten months after the family initially applies for and obtains such benefits. *N.J.S.A.* 44:10–61a, b, and e. Plaintiffs claim that the "family cap" violates the right to privacy and equal protection guarantees of the New Jersey Constitution. More specifically, plaintiffs allege that Section 61a impinges on a welfare recipient's right to bear a child and, if she chooses to have that child, denies her and her unsupported child equal treatment under the law.

. . .

In 1987, shortly after giving birth to her first child, plaintiff Angela B. began receiving family Medicaid benefits in addition to a monthly allowance in the form of food stamps and cash assistance. Subsequently, in 1988, 1989, and 1995 Angela B. gave birth to three more children. She received an increase in combined welfare benefits for the two children born in 1988 and 1989, but due to the enactment of New Jersey's first family cap provision in the interim, was unable to obtain additional cash assistance when her fourth child was born.

In 1994, also after bearing her first child, plaintiff Sojourner A. began receiving Medicaid family coverage as well as monthly assistance in food stamps and cash payments. When Sojourner A. became pregnant with her second child in 1996, however, the State notified her that she was not eligible for an increase in cash assistance as her child would be born more than ten months after she had started receiving welfare benefits. According to Sojourner A., she again became pregnant in 1997 and 1998, but terminated those pregnancies because of financial difficulties and because "she was not ready . . . for more children." By 1998, Sojourner A. was working five days a week and was therefore ineligible for cash assistance under WFNJ, although her family remained entitled to Medicaid and an increase in food stamps.

Both Angela B. and Sojourner A. have stated in depositions that the lack of additional cash assistance has imposed an extreme financial hardship on their families and left them without adequate food, shelter and other necessities. At the time of filing, Sojourner A. was receiving $322 in cash assistance, $163 in food stamps, and Medicaid benefits for her two children. Angela B. was receiving $424 in cash assistance, $396 in food stamps, and Medicaid benefits for the three children then residing with her.

. . . The gravamen of plaintiffs' complaint is that the family cap provision has been designed impermissibly to coerce the procreative and child-bearing decisions of plaintiffs and other women similarly situated by penalizing them for "exercis[ing] their fundamental right to bear children." Plaintiffs further contend that the "family cap" violates the equal protection rights of certain classes of poor children "based on their parents' reproductive choices and the timing of [their] birth."

. . .

Subsequently, plaintiffs and the DHS filed a motion and cross-motion for summary judgment.

On December 18, 2000, the court entered an order granting the Department's cross-motion and dismissing plaintiffs' complaint with prejudice. . . . In respect of plaintiffs' right to privacy claim, the . . . court concluded:

> [T]he State has demonstrated a legitimate and a substantial relationship between the statutory classification and the ends asserted. The interest here of the Legislature, [which]

represents all of us, in promoting self-sufficient citizens, diminishing the dependency upon welfare and creating [parity] between welfare recipients and working people ... greatly outweighs an[y] slight imposition or mere burden on ... the plaintiffs' right to privacy.

The Appellate Division affirmed the trial court in a published opinion issued on April 2, 2002. . . .

As had the trial court, the Appellate Division ... acknowledged the fundamental nature of a woman's right to make procreative decisions under Article I, paragraph 1 of the New Jersey Constitution, and found that the family cap "at best, indirect[ly] and insignificant[ly]" intrudes on that right. The panel concluded that the cap "does not present a direct obstacle to bearing children. It merely introduces one of many factors that a woman considers when deciding whether to become pregnant and carry the child to term[,] a choice that remains hers and hers alone." Similarly, the panel found that the cap does not

> completely deprive either the family unit of the benefits it is already receiving, or eliminate all benefits to the newborn child. Although the welfare recipient will not receive an additional cash stipend for the child, she continues to receive benefits designed to assist her to obtain and retain employment, and significantly, Medicaid coverage and food stamps are provided for the additional child.

Agreeing with the trial court that the purposes of the statute—reducing the welfare rolls and putting welfare families on the same footing as working families—are " 'laudable state objectives,' " the Appellate Division held that the family cap provision bears a substantial relationship to those legitimate and reasonable goals. . . .

New Jersey has, since 1959, engaged in a cooperative effort with the federal government to provide aid to families in need of assistance. In a shift in approach related to that effort, the State Legislature enacted the FDA in 1992 to "offer[ ] intensified and coordinated services that ... address the educational, vocational and other needs of the public assistance recipient's family. . . ." That legislation included a provision that denied an incremental increase in benefits for children who were born when the family was eligible for AFDC benefits. . . .

In 1996, Congress replaced AFDC with the Temporary Assistance to Needy Families (TANF) block grant program. Under TANF, Congress provided the states with the flexibility to implement welfare reform in their jurisdictions, subject to a mandatory national welfare-to-work feature similarly designed to motivate welfare recipients to become self-sufficient. In March of 1997, the New Jersey Legislature responded to the federal initiative by replacing the FDA with WFNJ.

Under WFNJ, the level of cash benefits is determined pursuant to a schedule administered by the DHS. That schedule, with certain important limitations, provides incremental increases based on the size and need of the family. One such limitation is the family cap found at *N.J.S.A.* 44:10–61a, which states:

> The level of cash assistance benefits payable to an assistance unit with dependent children shall not increase as a result of the birth of a child during the period in which the assistance unit is eligible for benefits. . . .

The Act defines an "[a]ssistance unit" as

> a single person without dependent children; . . . dependent children only; or a person or couple with one or more dependent children who are legally or blood-related, or who is their legal guardian, and who live together as a household unit.

As noted earlier, the family cap does not apply "to an individual . . . who gives birth to a child fewer than 10 months after applying for and receiving cash assistance benefits." *N.J.S.A.* 44:10–61e. The family cap also does not apply when the new child is the product of rape or incest. *N.J.S.A.* 44:10–61f.

Like its predecessor New Jersey statute, and consonant with the TANF approach, the primary purpose of WFNJ is to encourage employment, self-sufficiency and family stability. Toward that end, WFNJ contains mechanisms designed to promote independence and decrease long-term reliance on welfare payments. One such mechanism reallocates the savings achieved by application of the family cap to a variety of programs aimed at developing adult welfare recipients' educational and vocational skills to enable them to get and keep stable employment.

Prior to receiving benefits, eligible welfare recipients are assessed as to their educational level, prior work experience and other indicators of their "potential . . . readiness for work." *N.J.S.A.* 44:10–62f. After the assessment is completed, "individual responsibility plan[s]" are developed to set specific goals in respect of employment, education obligations, medical care and schooling for the recipient's dependent children. Once recipients agree to follow the plan, they must "continuously and actively seek employment" or accept placement in an approved "work activity" to continue in the program. *N.J.S.A.* 44:10–62a. Recipients are not on their own in this endeavor; WFNJ provides or subsidizes a panoply of such activities, including actual "employment; on-the-job training; job search and job readiness assistance; vocational educational training; job skills training related directly to employment; community work experience; alternative work experience; supportive work; community service programs . . . [and] education that is necessary for employment. . . ." The statute encourages education by reducing the hourly work requirements for adult recipients who are "full time post-secondary student[s]," and permitting young parents under the age of nineteen to fulfill the "work activity" requirement by completing high school or a high school equivalency program.

WFNJ also aims to remove barriers so that persons receiving welfare can maintain employment or stay in school. Under *N.J.S.A.* 44:10–38, recipients receive "supportive services" such as child care, transportation to and from work, and stipends for necessary "work-related expenses, . . . as determined by the commissioner." Moreover, to enable those who have gained steady employment to remain in the workforce, the State continues to subsidize medical and child care expenses for two years after recipients have become ineligible for cash benefits.

. . .

The Fourteenth Amendment of the United States Constitution provides that the state governments shall not "deny to any person within [their] jurisdiction the equal protection of the law," and shall not "deprive any person of life, liberty, or property[ ] without due process of law." Under the latter provision, citizens enjoy the right to be free from governmental intrusion in making procreative decisions. The extent to which statutory provisions are scrutinized under federal equal protection and right to privacy claims depends on the class of persons affected, the nature of the right implicated, and the level of interference. When a state statute directly impinges on a fundamental right or a suspect class, then the provision is strictly scrutinized, when a statute impairs a lesser interest, the federal courts ask only whether it is "rationally related to legitimate government interests." It follows, then, that the rational basis test is applied when economic legislation, including statutes that establish benefit programs, is challenged.

. . . [T]he Third Circuit Court of Appeals and the federal District Court for New Jersey have considered the same claims that are now before this Court. In *C.K. v. Shalala*, 883 F. Supp. 991 (D.N.J. 1995), plaintiffs brought a class action challenging a decision of the Secretary of the United States Department of Health and Human Services to waive certain federal welfare requirements and thereby to permit implementation of the family cap provision under FDA. In addition to contesting the Secretary's authority to grant the waiver, plaintiffs claimed that the family cap violated their equal protection and fundamental privacy rights. The court held that the family cap provision was "rationally related to the legitimate state interests of altering the cycle of welfare dependency . . . [and] promoting individual responsibility and family stability." It reasoned that "by maintaining the level of . . . benefits despite the arrival of an additional child, [the family cap] puts the welfare household in the same situation as that of a working family, which does not automatically receive a wage increase" when a new child is born.

C.K. also rejected plaintiffs' privacy claims. The court observed that the birth of an additional child in a family on welfare does not result in a decrease in benefits under the cap. Rather, it "remove[s] the automatic benefit increase associated with an additional child under the federal program." The court held that although women have a fundamental right to make procreative decisions, there is no constitutional right to government subsidies in furtherance of that right.

The Third Circuit "ha[d] nothing to add to the district court's opinion [that plaintiffs' procreative rights are not burdened by the family cap] except to observe that it would be remarkable to hold that a state's failure to subsidize a reproductive choice burdens that choice."

In the New Jersey Constitution, both equal protection and the right to privacy derive from the same broad constitutional language, which states: "All persons are by nature free and independent, and have certain natural and unalienable rights, among which are those of enjoying and defending life and liberty, of acquiring, possessing and protecting property, and of pursuing and obtaining safety and happiness." Although Article I does not contain the terms "equal protection" or "right to privacy," it is well settled law that the expansive language of that provision is the source for both of those fundamental constitutional guarantees.

Thirty years ago, Chief Justice Weintraub ... described the balancing process by which a court "[u]ltimately" decides equal protection and due process challenges:

> [A] court must weigh the nature of the restraint or the denial against the apparent public justification, and decide whether the State action is arbitrary. In that process, if the circumstances sensibly so require, the court may call upon the State to demonstrate the existence of a sufficient public need for the restraint or the denial.

Later ... the Court reaffirmed that approach, finding that it provided a more flexible analytical framework for the evaluation of equal protection and due process claims. In keeping with Chief Justice Weintraub's direction, we " 'consider [ ] the nature of the affected right, the extent to which the governmental restriction intrudes upon it, and the public need for the restriction.' " By deviating from the federal tiered model, we are able to examine each claim on a continuum that reflects the nature of the burdened right and the importance of the governmental restriction. We point out, however, that although our mode of analysis differs in form from the federal tiered approach, the tests weigh the same factors and often produce the same result.

We turn not to plaintiffs' claims that the family cap provision of WFNJ unconstitutionally infringes on a woman's right to make procreative decisions by penalizing her for choosing to bear a child and, further, that the cap improperly singles out classes of poor children "based on their parents' reproductive choices and the timing of [their] birth."

Our discussion begins with an inquiry into the nature of the affected right. In [past cases] . . . we emphasized "the importance of a woman's right to control her body and her future, a right we as a society consider fundamental to individual liberty." . . . That most basic right, plaintiffs allege, has been burdened impermissibly by the family cap provision of WFNJ.

It is, then, the nature of that burden or the extent of the governmental intrusion that we must consider. Plaintiffs claim that the family cap functions as a coercive tool designed to encourage poor women to avoid having children or to abort their pregnancies when the family unit is receiving welfare. By withholding an incremental increase in cash assistance, plaintiffs argue, the State unduly influences their procreative choices. But even if we assume that procreative choices are influenced by a cap on cash assistance to the family unit, we do not find that influence to be "undue," or that a new burden is thereby created. We expect that the income of a family unit, whatever the source, is likely to influence a woman's decision to conceive or bear a child. That is true for most families in New Jersey. As noted by the federal courts, working families do not receive automatic wage increases when additional children are born. Indeed, the family cap appears to do no more than place welfare families "on a par with working families."

We also find that the DHS has presented ample justification for the family cap. The record informs us that resources available as a result of the cap have been diverted to job training, child care, and other programs established and expanded under WFNJ. The goals of promoting self-sufficiency and decreased dependency on welfare are laudable; the focus on education, job training and child care should advance those goals and, ultimately, result in improving the lives of children born into welfare families.

In [a prior case] the Court was presented with a challenge to legislation that denied Medicaid funding for abortions except when an abortion was medically necessary to save the life of the mother. On considering plaintiffs' equal protection challenge, we stated:

> [T]here [is no] fundamental right to funding for an abortion. The right to choose whether to have an abortion, however, is a fundamental right of all pregnant women, including those entitled to Medicaid reimbursement for necessary medical treatment. *As to that group of women,* the challenged statute discriminates between those for whom medical care is necessary for childbirth and those for whom an abortion is medically necessary. Under [the statute] those needing abortions receive funds only when their lives are at stake. By granting funds when life is at risk, but withholding them when health is endangered, the statute denies equal protection to those women entitled to necessary medical services under Medicaid.

. . . [This] dichotomy is directly relevant to this case. There we held that the State could not distinguish between "those for whom medical care is necessary for childbirth and those for whom an abortion is medically necessary." Most important, we also held that "[e]lective, nontherapeutic abortions . . . do not involve the life or health of the mother, and the State may pursue its interest in potential life by excluding those abortions from the Medicaid program." Here, the life or health of the mother is not at issue. Whatever the impact of the family cap on the family unit, that impact is no different from the impact of another child on any family with a fixed income. Like most women in New Jersey, a woman receiving welfare assistance will likely weigh the extent of the economic strain caused by the addition of a child to the family unit. Ultimately, however, the decision to bring a child to term or to have an abortion remains wholly with the woman.

Plaintiffs also rely on the distinction created in WFNJ between children born before the family begins receiving welfare benefits, and similarly situated children born ten months after the receipt of such benefits. The family cap treats these classes disparately, plaintiffs argue, based on when mothers choose to exercise their fundamental right to conceive and bear children. In fact, the *family* does not receive additional cash assistance when a new child is born, although the family does receive additional food stamps and Medicaid benefits. All of the children in the family unit share presumably in the total amount of cash assistance available, as is the case in other similarly situated family units.

This case is not about a woman's right to choose whether and when to bear children, but rather, about whether the State must subsidize that choice. . . . [W]e [have] held that the State may decline to fund a woman's choice to obtain an abortion when the abortion is not medically necessary. We hold today that the State is not required to provide additional cash assistance when a woman chooses to bear a child more than ten months after her family has received welfare benefits. In so holding, we reject plaintiffs' claim that the family cap provision of WFNJ violates the equal protection and due process guarantees of our State Constitution.

The judgment of the Appellate Division is affirmed.

NOTES

1. *Maximum family grants and fertility.* Maximum family grants were established in the belief that public assistance "incentivized" both teenage motherhood and out-of-wedlock births. Under the Personal Responsibility and Work Opportunity Reconciliation Act (PRWORA), states were granted wide latitude to implement maximum family grants ("caps"). By 2006, twenty-four states had implemented some version of these caps. *See* Rebekah J. Smith, *Family Caps in Welfare Reform: Their Coercive Effects and Damaging Consequences*, 29 HARV. J.L. & GENDER 151, 152 (2006). However, subsequent research has shown that these policies only nominally affect the

fertility of women on welfare. *See* Ann E. Horvath-Rose & H. Elizabeth Peters, *Welfare Waivers and Nonmarital Childbearing, in* FOR BETTER AND FOR WORSE: WELFARE REFORM AND THE WELL-BEING OF CHILDREN AND FAMILIES 222, 223 (Greg Duncan & P. Lindsay Chase-Lansdale eds., 2001). Further, research suggests that there is almost "no clear relationship" between family caps and birth rates. As evidence accumulates about such caps' lack of effect on birth rates, seven states have repealed family caps. *See* ELENA GUTIÉRREZ, CTR. ON REPROD. RIGHTS & JUSTICE, BRINGING FAMILIES OUT OF 'CAP'TIVITY: THE NEED TO REPEAL THE CALWORKS MAXIMUM FAMILY GRANT RULE 2 (2013).

2.   *TANF and the regulation of relationships.* As evidenced in *Sojourner A.*, Temporary Assistance to Needy Families (TANF), like AFDC and ADC before it, continues to regulate the relationships and family formation of recipients. As was intended in PRWORA, states are permitted wide latitude in making distinctions with respect to stepparents or adoptive parents, unmarried partners living in the home with the recipient, and blended families, where a man is a biological or adoptive father of some, but not all, of the children. Some states calculate the man's income in assessing eligibility; some do not. Some count "in kind" contributions and others do not. Still others require a partner to make a financial contribution to the household. Finally, eight states have adopted policies to reward marriage. *See* ROBERT A. MOFFITT ET AL., U.S. DEP'T OF HEALTH & HUMAN SERVS., COHABITATION AND MARRIAGE RULES IN STATE TANF PROGRAMS, at iv–v (2008). Further, the U.S. Department of Health and Human Services provides millions of dollars in grants per year to support "fatherhood initiatives," including to community and faith-based organizations working "to strengthen the role that fathers play in their families' lives," and to mentor children of prisoners. *See* U.S. DEP'T OF HEALTH & HUMAN SERVS., HHS FACT SHEET: PROMOTING RESPONSIBLE FATHERHOOD (2002), https:// www.acf.hhs.gov/ofa/programs/healthy-marriage/responsible-fatherhood. For further discussion of marriage and fatherhood promotion policies, see *supra* p. 111.

3.   *The relationship between teenage pregnancy and poverty.* Refer back to Chapter One, *supra* p. 108, where the "Findings" Section of PRWORA is excerpted. In particular, note how the discussion shifts from poor children, to unmarried mothers, to unmarried teen mothers. Teen mothers (and only occasionally fathers) are held responsible for their own—and their children's—poverty. Careful economic analysis, however, suggests that the causal link is reversed: poverty and inequality lead to the observed high levels of teenage pregnancy in the United States. Melissa Kearney & Phillip Levine, *Why Is the Teen Birth Rate in the United States So High and Why Does It Matter?*, 26 J. ECON. PERSP. 141, 142 (2012). Regardless of the causal links (or lack thereof) between teenagers, sex, and poverty; over the last fifteen years, there has been a concerted effort to promote abstinence among teenagers. As we discuss, *infra* p. 566, these efforts in the form of abstinence-only sex education programs were disproportionately implemented in schools in low-income areas.

F. ADOPTION AND FOSTER CARE

As the preceding selections suggest, one of the most common ways that the state regulates poor families is through the child welfare system, and concomitantly, the administration of foster care and adoption. The following selections explore the history of adoption as a social and legal practice, the state's regulation of adoption, the links between adoption, foster care, and the administration of the child welfare system, and the impact of the child welfare system on minority communities. This section concludes with a discussion of adoptions as a means of family formation for lesbian, gay, bisexual, and transgender persons.

Stephen B. Presser, *The Historical Background of the American Law of Adoption*
11 J. FAM. L. 443 (1972).

. . . The legally-sanctioned custom of adopting children as heirs was unknown to the common law, although it was well-known in Roman practice, and passed nearly unchanged in the civil law. No general adoption statutes were passed in America before about 1850, however, and no British statute was enacted before 1926. Once American legislatures had begun to act on the problem of adoption, however, it was not long before a host of states enacted some form of adoption law. Within twenty-five years of the passage of the first statutes, twenty-four states had adoption legislation. This chronology raises . . . intriguing questions for the legal historian: . . . Why did English and American legislatures wait so long before passing adoption laws? Since there had been virtually no law on adoption for over a thousand years in what had become the Anglo-American system of jurisprudence, why were so many adoption statutes passed in America in such a comparatively short time? . . .

. . . .

The purpose of the American adoption statutes passed in the middle of the nineteenth century was to provide for the welfare of dependent children, a purpose quite different from that of the old Roman laws. . . .

. . . .

As they had existed in the sixteenth century England, the customs of "apprenticeship" and "service" were brought to America by the New England Puritans. . . .

The practice of "putting out," [children from one "well-off" household to another] although often done voluntarily by the parent, also was done at the prompting of the state; the Laws of the Massachusetts Colony of 1648 provided that when children were allowed to become "rude, stubborn, and unruly," the state might take them from their parents and place them in another's home. . . . In short, the practice of placing a child with foster parents was hardly a new invention of nineteenth century American reformers.

. . . .

. . . [O]rphans who had no relatives were put into homes or "bound out," as it was called in the seventeenth century. This custom affected very large numbers of children, and unhappily there are indications that the custom often may have been utilized more for the economic uses of child labor than for the good of the children. . . .

. . . .

. . . Parents were often quite careless about letting their children be placed in the far-off homes of strangers. Children's societies were placing thousands of "uninvestigated children in uninvestigated homes all over the prairies." Later in the century, "there was a widespread habit of advertising children for adoption, and parents sold or gave them away." Indeed, one British adoption authority has suggested that it was this seamier side of American child-placing practice that kept Britain from passing an adoption statute until after the first World War. "It may well be that our legislators saw it as something merely wide, brash, and Yankee."

. . . .

The first comprehensive adoption statute was passed in 1851 in Massachusetts. . . .

The "avowed object" of the Massachusetts act, and presumably of the other acts that were passed over the next quarter of the century, according to one closely contemporary source, was that of "securing to adopted children a proper share in the estate of adopting parents who should die intestate." The twenty-four different statutes accomplished this object in different ways, however, although they have been conveniently classified into two broad types "based on their provision or lack of provision of republic inquiry into and control over proposed adoptions." . . .

. . . .

The available official legislative history of the adoption laws gives no indication of the motivation or the intention of the legislators who passed the first adoption statutes. . . . This lack of material has been attributed to the fact that although these statutes appear highly significant to the twentieth century observer, "the passage . . . of the first general adoption laws . . . was not one of the great issues of the day." As one commentator put it, the passage of the general adoptions laws "created little stir because they were then upon as little more than a normal and desirable next step in a development that was already taking place." . . .

. . . .

NOTES

1. *Adoption in context.* Although adoption has its roots in ancient Greece and Rome, developments in early Christian Europe discouraged its practice.

The historian Jack Goody suggests that the Catholic Church cultivated this resistance to adoption. By discouraging adoption, the Church also discouraged what Goody calls "strategies of kinship"—strategies for creating familial ties through which individuals could pass on inherited wealth and property. By discouraging the cultivation of kinship ties through adoption, the Catholic Church became the residual legatee of widows or widowers without children, thereby increasing its wealth. JACK GOODY, THE DEVELOPMENT OF THE FAMILY AND MARRIAGE IN EUROPE 99–102 (1983).

2.   *From orphanages to foster care.* The interest in adoption increased with the demise of orphanages and the rise of foster care as a means of caring for parentless children. At the 1909 White House Conference on Dependent Children, the consensus among child advocates was that dependent children should be cared for in families instead of traditional orphanages whenever possible, but orphanages remained the main haven for dependent children until the Depression. The passage of the Social Security Act of 1935 provided funds for needy children in their own homes, leaving orphanages in a financially precarious position. Marshall B. Jones, *Crisis of the American Orphanage, 1931–1940*, 63 SOC. SERV. REV. 613, 613–14, 625 (1989). By the 1960s, foster care became considerably less expensive than institutional care, and, combined with the rights movements of the 1960s, the shift from orphanages to foster care was largely complete. Marshall B. Jones, *Decline of the American Orphanage, 1941–1980*, 67 SOC. SERV. REV. 459, 471–72 (1993).

3.   *The girls who went away.* Before *Roe v. Wade* and the legalization of abortion, pregnant unmarried women had few options: get married quickly, go to a "maternity home," where a woman was effectively pressured into giving up her child for adoption and urged to move on with her life, or keep her child and accept the social stigma attached to that decision. *See* ANN FESSLER, THE GIRLS WHO WENT AWAY: THE HIDDEN HISTORY OF WOMEN WHO SURRENDERED CHILDREN FOR ADOPTION IN THE DECADES BEFORE *ROE V. WADE* 11 (2007). After *Roe v. Wade*, the number of "shotgun" marriages and children surrendered for adoption decreased. *See* RICKIE SOLINGER, WAKE UP LITTLE SUSIE: SINGLE PREGNANCY AND RACE BEFORE *ROE V. WADE* 5–7 (2000); *see also* Martin O'Connell & Maurice J. Moore, *The Legitimacy Status of First Births to U.S. Women Aged 15–24, 1939–1978*, 12 FAM. PLAN. PERSP. 16, 16–17 (1980). What does this suggest about changing attitudes regarding the stigma of unwed motherhood, and the ability of unwed mothers to make choices more broadly about whether to continue a pregnancy as well as about adoption?

4.   *Race and adoption.* In 1972, the National Association of Black Social Workers (NABSW) called for the end of transracial adoptions on the grounds that white parents could not properly prepare African-American children for the futures they would face in a prejudiced society. Child welfare agencies heeded this call. Although the effect cannot be traced directly, agencies began to prioritize intra-race adoptions. Michele Bratcher Goodwin, *Baby Markets, in* BABY MARKETS: MONEY AND THE NEW POLITICS OF CREATING FAMILIES 2, 6 (Michele Bratcher Goodwin ed., 2010); *see also* R. Richard Banks, *The Color of Desire*: *Fulfilling Adoptive Parents' Racial Preferences*

Through Discriminatory State Action, 107 YALE L.J. 875 (1998). However, in 1994 and in 1996, Congress enacted and then amended the Multi-Ethnic Placement Act, 42 U.S.C. § 622 (2014) (amended by Removal of Barriers to Interethnic Adoption Act, 42 U.S.C. § 1996b (2014)) (MEPA). Like the Adoption and Safe Families Act, *supra* p. 352, which was enacted in the same year, MEPA aimed to curb the problem of foster care drift by removing impediments—such as the need for race-matching—to adoption.

5.   *Adoption options.* The paths to the legal adoption of a child have proliferated in recent years, both for international and domestic adoptions. The Hague Convention on Protection of Children and Co-operation in Respect of Intercountry Adoption governs international adoptions of children who are from signatory countries. *See* Hague Convention on Protection of Children and Co-operation in Respect of Intercountry Adoption, May 29, 1993, 32 I.L.M. 1139. Although the United States is not a signatory to the convention, the convention nonetheless informs U.S. citizen adoptions of children from signatory countries.

6.   *The domestic adoption landscape.* In the domestic context, prospective parents can adopt from a public agency (usually these are children in foster care), from a licensed private adoption agency, from an unlicensed agency, or through an independent adoption (usually handled by an attorney). All of these domestic options may, if the parties are inclined and state law permits, entail continued contact with the child's birth parents ("open" adoption). Alternatively, such adoptions can proceed along the traditional model that maintains the anonymity of the birth parents. *See Adoption Options: A Factsheet for Families*, CHILD WELFARE INFO. GATEWAY (2010), www.child welfare.gov/pubs/f_adoptoption.cfm.

7.   *The business of adoption.* In a free market economic model, when the demand for a "product" outstrips the supply, new business opportunities arise. Today, this holds true in the adoption context. Increased interest in private adoptions, the bureaucratic difficulties of the public adoption system, as well as a focus on the "adoptability" of certain types of children, have given rise to a market model of adoption. *See* Danielle Saba Donner, *The Emerging Adoption Market: Child Welfare Agencies, Private Middlemen, and "Consumer" Remedies*, 35 U. LOUISVILLE J. FAM. L. 473, 490–91, 503–04 (1997). This increased interest in private-sector adoptions has altered the adoption landscape in important ways. For example, social workers used to control the adoption of children, even those placed through private channels. Social workers were charged with investigating prospective parents and ensuring that the placement was sound. Now, the state's oversight of private adoptions appears less robust. According to Professor Ruth-Arlene Howe, "when children are voluntarily relinquished shortly after birth, their adoption is more like a business transaction than a child welfare service." Ruth-Arlene Howe, *Adoption Laws and Practices: Serving Whose Interest?*, *in* BABY MARKETS: MONEY AND THE NEW POLITICS OF CREATING FAMILIES 86, 87 (Michele Bratcher Goodwin ed., 2010). In this age of privatization, private adoption lawyers provide services for a profit, and some states even outsource adoption and foster care to private for-profit firms.

8. *African-American children go to new homes*. In the wake of the enactment of the Multi-Ethnic Placement Act, 42 U.S.C. § 622 (2014) (amended by Removal of Barriers to Interethnic Adoption Act, 42 U.S.C. § 1996b (2014)), transracial adoptions of African-American children have increased substantially. In 2004, an estimated twenty-six percent of African-American children adopted from foster care were adopted transracially, mostly by whites. Lynette Clemetson & Ron Nixon, *Overcoming Adoption's Racial Barriers*, N.Y. TIMES, Aug. 17, 2006, at A1. Further, prospective parents from other countries have found that adopting African-American children is often faster than adopting in their home countries. Canada and the Netherlands have led the way in such adoptions. Lois M. Collins, *Black American Infants Find Homes Overseas*, DESERET NEWS (Sept. 18, 2013), https://www.deseret.com/2013/9/18/20525757/black-american-infants-find-homes-overseas. Curiously, there has been no similar increase in the adoptions of white children into African-American families. What might explain this disjunction?

Matter of Michael B.

604 N.E.2d 122 (N.Y. 1992).

■ KAYE, J.

This appeal from a custody determination, pitting a child's foster parents against his biological father, centers on the meaning of the statutory term "best interest of the child," and particularly on the weight to be given a child's bonding with his long-time foster family in deciding what placement is in his best interest. The biological father (appellant) on one side, and respondent foster parents (joined by respondent Law Guardian) on the other, each contend that a custody determination in their favor is in the best interest of the child, as that term is used in Social Services Law § 392(6), the statute governing dispositions with respect to children in foster care.

The subject of this protracted battle is Michael B., born July 29, 1985 with a positive toxicology for cocaine. Michael was voluntarily placed in foster care from the hospital by his mother, who was unmarried at the time of the birth and listed no father on the birth certificate. Michael's four siblings were then also in foster care, residing in different homes. At three months, before the identity of his father was known, Michael—needing extraordinary care—was placed in the home of intervenor Maggie W. L., a foster parent certified by respondent Catholic Child Care Society (the agency), and the child remained with the L.'s for more than five years, until December 1990. It is undisputed that the agency initially assured Mrs. L. this was a "preadoptive" placement.

Legal proceedings began in May 1987, after appellant had been identified as Michael's father. The agency sought to terminate the rights of both biological parents and free the child for adoption, alleging that for more than a year following Michael's placement the parents had failed to substantially, continuously or repeatedly maintain contact with Michael and plan for his future, although physically and financially able to do so. Michael's mother (since deceased) never appeared in the proceeding, and a finding of permanent neglect as to her was made in November 1987. Appellant did appear and in September 1987 consented to a finding of permanent neglect, and to committing custody and guardianship to the agency on condition that the children be placed with their two godmothers. That order was later vacated, on appellant's application to withdraw his pleas and obtain custody, because the agency had not in fact placed the children with their godmothers. In late 1987, appellant— a long-time alcohol and substance abuser—entered an 18-month residential drug rehabilitation program and first began to visit Michael.

In August 1988, appellant, the agency and the Law Guardian agreed to reinstatement of the permanent neglect finding, with judgment suspended for 12 months, on condition that appellant: (1) enroll in a program teaching household management and parenting skills; (2) cooperate by attending and complying with the program; (3) remain drug-free, and periodically submit to drug testing, with test results to be delivered to the agency; (4) secure and maintain employment; (5) obtain suitable housing; and (6) submit a plan for the children's care during his working day. The order recited that it was without prejudice to the agency recalendaring the case for a de novo hearing on all allegations of the petition should appellant fail to satisfy the conditions, and otherwise said nothing more of the consequences that would follow on appellant's compliance or noncompliance.

As the 12-month period neared expiration, the agency sought a hearing to help "determine the status and placement of the children." Although appellant was unemployed (he was on public assistance) and had not submitted to drug testing during the year, Family Court at the hearing held October 24, 1989 was satisfied that "there seem[ed] to be substantial compliance" with the conditions of the suspended judgment. . . .

On December 21, 1989, the Law Guardian presented a report indicating that Michael might suffer severe psychological damage if removed from his foster home, and argued for a "best interests" hearing . . . based on Michael's bonding with the L.'s and, by contrast, his lack of bonding with appellant, who had visited him infrequently. Family Court questioned whether it even had authority for such a hearing, but stayed the order directing Michael's discharge to appellant pending its determination. Michael's siblings, then approximately twelve, eight, seven and six years old, were released to appellant in January and July 1990. Litigation continued as to Michael.

In November 1990, Family Court directed Michael's discharge to appellant, concluding that it was without "authority or jurisdiction" to rehear the issue of custody based on the child's best interest, and indeed that Michael had been wrongfully held in foster care. The court noted, additionally, that the Law Guardian's arguments as to Michael's best interest went to issues of bonding with his temporary custodians rather than appellant's insufficiency as a parent—bonding that had been reinforced by the agency's failure to ensure sufficient contacts with appellant during the proceedings.

. . .

The Appellate Division reversed and remitted for a new hearing and new consideration of Michael's custody, concluding that dismissal of a permanent neglect petition cannot divest Family Court of its continuing jurisdiction over a child until there has been a "best interests" custody disposition. As for the relevance of bonding, the Appellate Division held that, given the "extraordinary circumstances"—referring particularly to Michael's long residence with his foster parents—Family Court should have conducted a hearing to consider issues such as the impact on the child of a change in custody. There having been no question of appellant's fitness, however, the Appellate Division permitted Michael to remain with his father pending the new determination.

On remittal, Family Court heard extensive testimony—including testimony from appellant, the foster parents, the agency (having changed its goal to discharge to appellant), and psychological, psychiatric and social work professionals (who overwhelmingly favored continued foster care over discharge to appellant)—but adhered to its determination that Michael should be released to his father. Family Court found appellant "fit, available and capable of adequately providing for the health, safety and welfare of the subject child, and . . . it is in the child's best interest to be returned to his father."

Again the Appellate Division reversed Family Court's order, this time itself awarding custody to the foster parents under Social Services Law § 392(6)(b), and remitting the matter to a different Family Court Judge solely to determine appellant's visitation rights. Exercising its own authority—as broad as that of the hearing court—to assess the credibility of witnesses and character and temperament of the parents, the court reviewed the evidence and, while pointing up appellant's many deficiencies, significantly stopped short of finding him an unfit parent, as it had the power to do. Rather, the court looked to Michael's lengthy stay and psychological bonding with the foster family, which it felt gave rise to extraordinary circumstances meriting an award of custody to the foster parents. According to the Appellate Division, the evidence "overwhelmingly demonstrate[d] that Michael's foster parents are better able than his natural father to provide for his physical, emotional, and intellectual needs." Since early 1992, Michael has once again resided with the L.'s.

While prolonged, inconclusive proceedings and seesawing custody of a young child—all in the name of Michael's best interest—could not conceivably serve his interest at all, we granted appellant father's motion for leave to appeal, and now reverse the Appellate Division's central holdings. The opinions of Family Court specifying deficiencies of the agency and foster parents, and the opinions of the Appellate Division specifying inadequacies of the biological parent, leave little question that the only blameless person is the child. But rather than assess fault, our review will address the legal standards that have twice divided Family Court and the Appellate Division, hopefully minimizing recurrences, for this child and others, of the tragic scenario now before us.

Appellant no longer disputes that Family Court retained jurisdiction to consider the child's best interest in connection with an award of custody even after the finding that he had substantially satisfied the conditions of the suspended judgment. All parties agree with the correctness of the Appellate Division determination that, despite appellant's apparent compliance with the conditions of the suspended judgment, Family Court retained jurisdiction to consider the best interest of the children in foster care until a final order of disposition.

What remains the bone of contention in this Court is the scope of the requisite "best interest" inquiry under Social Services Law § 392(6). Appellant urges that in cases of foster care, so long as the biological parent is not found unfit—and he underscores that neither Family Court nor the Appellate Division found him unfit—"best interest of the child" is only a limited inquiry addressed to whether the child will suffer grievous injury if transferred out of foster care to the biological parent. Respondents, by contrast, maintain that extraordinary circumstances— such as significant bonding with foster parents, after inattention and even admitted neglect by the biological parent—trigger a full inquiry into the more suitable placement as between the biological and foster parents. Subsidiarily, appellant challenges the Appellate Division's outright award of custody to the foster parents, claiming that disposition was beyond the Court's authority under Social Services Law § 392(6).

We conclude, first, that neither party advances the correct "best interest" test in the context of temporary foster care placements, but that appellant's view is more consistent with the statutory scheme than the broad-gauge inquiry advocated by respondents and applied by the Appellate Division. Second, we hold that the award of custody to the foster parents was impermissible as we interpret Social Services Law § 392(6).

This being a case of voluntary placement in foster care—a subject controlled by statute—analysis must begin with the legislative scheme, which defines and balances the parties' rights and responsibilities. An understanding of how the system is designed to operate—before the design is complicated, and even subverted, by human actors and practical realities—is essential to resolving the questions before us.

New York's foster care scheme is built around several fundamental social policy choices that have been explicitly declared by the Legislature and are binding on this Court. Under the statute, operating as written, appellant should have received the active support of both the agency in overcoming his parental deficiencies and the foster parents in solidifying his relationship with Michael, and as soon as return to the biological parent proved unrealistic, the child should have been freed for adoption.

A biological parent has a right to the care and custody of a child, superior to that of others, unless the parent has abandoned that right or is proven unfit to assume the duties and privileges of parenthood, even though the State perhaps could find "better" parents. A child is not the parent's property, but neither is a child the property of the State. Looking to the *child's* rights as well as the parents' rights to bring up their own children, the Legislature has found and declared that a child's need to grow up with a "normal family life in a permanent home" is ordinarily best met in the child's "natural home."

Parents in temporary crisis are encouraged to voluntarily place their children in foster care without fear that they will thereby forfeit their parental rights. The State's first obligation is to help the family with services to prevent its break-up, or to reunite the family if the child is out of the home. While a child is in foster care, the State must use diligent efforts to strengthen the relationship between parent and child, and work with the parent to regain custody.

Because of the statutory emphasis on the biological family as best serving a child's long-range needs, the legal rights of foster parents are necessarily limited. Legal custody of a child in foster care remains with the agency that places the child, not with the foster parents. Foster parents enter into this arrangement with the express understanding that the placement is temporary, and that the agency retains the right to remove the child upon notice at any time. As [we have] made clear . . . "foster care custodians must deliver on demand not 16 out of 17 times, but every time, or the usefulness of foster care assignments is destroyed. To the ordinary fears in placing a child in foster care should not be added the concern that the better the foster care custodians the greater the risk that they will assert, out of love and affection grown too deep, an inchoate right to adopt." Foster parents, moreover, have an affirmative obligation—similar to the obligation of the State—to attempt to solidify the relationship between biological parent and child. While foster parents may be heard on custody issues they have no standing to seek permanent custody absent termination of parental rights.

Fundamental also to the statutory scheme is the preference for providing children with stable, permanent homes as early as possible. "[W]hen it is clear that the natural parent cannot or will not provide a normal family home for the child and when continued foster care is not an appropriate plan for the child, then a permanent alternative home should be sought." Extended foster care is not in the child's best interest, because it deprives a child of a permanent, nurturing family relationship. Where it appears that the child may never be reunited with the biological parents, the responsible agency should institute a proceeding to terminate parental rights and free the child for adoption.

Parental rights may be terminated only upon clear and convincing proof of abandonment, inability to care for the child due to mental illness or retardation, permanent neglect, or severe or repeated child abuse. Of the permissible dispositions in a termination proceeding based on permanent neglect, the Legislature—consistent with its emphasis on the importance of biological ties, yet mindful of the child's need for early stability and permanence—has provided for a suspended judgment, which is a brief grace period designed to prepare the parent to be reunited with the child. Parents found to have permanently neglected a child may be given a second chance, where the court determines it is in the child's best interests, but that opportunity is strictly limited in time. Parents may have up to one year (and a second year only where there are "exceptional circumstances") during which they must comply with terms and conditions meant to ameliorate the difficulty. Noncompliance may lead to revocation of the judgment and termination of parental rights. Compliance may lead to dismissal of the termination petition with the child remaining subject to the jurisdiction of the Family Court until a determination is made as to the child's disposition pursuant to Social Services Law § 392(6).

Where parental rights have not been terminated, Social Services Law § 392 promotes the objectives of stability and permanency by requiring periodic review of foster care placements. The agency having custody must first petition for review after a child has been in continuous foster care for 18 months, and if no change is made, every 24 months thereafter. While foster parents who have been caring for such child for the prior 12 months are entitled to notice, and may also petition for review on their own initiative, a petition under section 392 (captioned "Foster care status; periodic family court review") is not an avenue to permanent custody for foster parents where the child has not been freed for adoption.

Upon such review, the court must consider the appropriateness of the agency's plan for the child, what services have been offered to strengthen and reunite the family, efforts to plan for other modes of care, and other further efforts to promote the child's welfare and in accordance with the best interest of the child, make one of the following dispositions: (1) continue the child in foster care (which may include continuation with the current foster parents); (2) direct that the child "be returned to the parent, guardian or relative, or [direct] that the child be placed in the custody of a relative or other suitable person or persons;" or (3) require the agency (or foster parents upon the agency's default) to institute a parental rights termination proceeding.

The key element in the court's disposition is the best interest of the child—the statutory term that is at the core of this appeal, and to which we now turn.

"Best interest(s) of the child" is a term that pervades the law relating to children—appearing innumerable times in the pertinent statutes, judicial decisions and literature—yet eludes ready definition. Two interpretations are advanced, each vigorously advocated.

Appellant would read the best interest standard of Social Services Law § 392 (6) narrowly, urging that Family Court should inquire only into whether the biological parent is fit, and whether the child will suffer grievous harm by being returned to the parent. Appellant urges affirmance of the Family Court orders, which (1) defined the contest as one between foster care agency and biological parent, rather than foster parent and biological parent; (2) focused first on "the ability of the father to care for the subject child," and then on whether "the child's emotional health will be so seriously impaired as to require continuance in foster care;" and (3) concluded that appellant was fit, and that Michael would not suffer irreparable emotional harm if returned to him. Wider inquiry, appellant insists, creates an "unwinnable beauty contest" the biological parent will inevitably lose where foster placement has continued for any substantial time.

Respondents take a broader view, urging that because of extraordinary circumstances largely attributable to appellant, the Appellate Division correctly compared him with the foster parents in determining Michael's custody and concluded that the child's best interest was served by the placement that better provided for his physical, emotional and intellectual needs. Respondents rely on *Matter of Bennett v. Jeffreys*, this Court's landmark decision recognizing that a child's prolonged separation from a biological parent may be considered, among other factors, to be extraordinary circumstances permitting the court to inquire into which family situation would be in the child's best interests.

In that *Matter of Bennett v. Jeffreys* concerned an unsupervised private placement, where there was no directly applicable legislation, that case is immediately distinguishable from the matter before us, which is controlled by a detailed statutory scheme. Our analysis must begin at a different point—not whether there are extraordinary circumstances, but what the Legislature intended by the words "best interest of the child" in Social Services Law § 392(6).

Necessarily, we look first to the statute itself. The question is in part answered by Social Services Law §§ 383 and 384–b, which encourage voluntary placements, with the provision that they will not result in the termination of parental rights so long as the parent is fit. To use the period during which a child lives with a foster family, and emotional ties that naturally eventuate, as a ground for comparing the biological parent with the foster parent undermines the very objective of voluntary foster care as a resource for parents in temporary crisis, who are then at risk of losing their children once a bond arises with the foster families.

. . .

Absent an explicit legislative directive . . . we are not free to overlook the legislative policies that underlie temporary foster care, including the preeminence of the biological family. Indeed, the legislative history of Social Services Law § 392(5–a), which specifies factors that must be considered in determining the child's best interests, states "this bill clearly advises the Family Court of certain considerations before making an order of disposition. These factors establish a clear policy of exploring all available means of reuniting the child with his family before the Court decides to continue his foster care or to direct a permanent adoptive placement." (Mem. Accompanying Comments on Bill, NY State Board of Social Welfare, A 12801–B, July 9, 1976, Governor's Bill Jacket, L 1976, ch. 667).

We therefore cannot endorse a pure "best interests" hearing, where biological parent and foster parents stand on equal footing and the child's interest is the sole consideration (see, Matter of People ex rel. Kropp v. Shepsky, 305 N.Y. 465, 469). In cases controlled by Social Services Law § 392(6), analysis of the child's "best interest" must begin not by measuring biological parent against foster parent but by weighing past and continued foster care against discharge to the biological parent, or other relative or suitable person within Social Services Law § 392(6)(b).

While the facts of Matter of Bennett v. Jeffreys fell outside the statute, and the Court was unrestrained by legislative prescription in defining the scope of the "best interests" inquiry, principles underlying that decision are also relevant here. It is plainly the case, for example, that a "child may be so long in the custody of the nonparent that, even though there has been no abandonment or persisting neglect by the parent, the psychological trauma of removal is grave enough to threaten destruction of the child" and we cannot discount evidence that a child may have bonded with someone other than the biological parent. In such a case, continued foster care may be appropriate although the parent has not been found unfit.

Under Social Services Law § 392, where a child has not been freed for adoption, the court must determine whether it is nonetheless appropriate to continue foster care temporarily, or whether the child should be permanently discharged to the biological parent (or a relative or "other suitable person"). In determining the best interest of a child in that situation, the fitness of the biological parent must be a primary factor. The court is also statutorily mandated to consider the agency's plan for the child, what services have been offered to strengthen and reunite the family, what reasonable efforts have been made to make it possible for the child to return to the natural home, and if return home is not likely, what efforts have been or should be made to evaluate other options. Finally, the court should consider the more intangible elements relating to the emotional well-being of the child, among them the impact on the child of immediate discharge versus an additional period of foster care.

While it is doubtful whether it could be found to be in the child's best interest to deny the parent's persistent demands for custody simply because it took so long to obtain it legally neither is a lapse of time necessarily without significance in determining custody. The child's emotional well-being must be part of the equation, parental rights notwithstanding. However, while emotional well-being may encompass bonding to someone other than the biological parent, it includes as well a recognition that, absent termination of parental rights, the nonparent cannot adopt the child, and a child in continued custody with a nonparent remains in legal—and often emotional—limbo.

The Appellate Division, applying an erroneous "best interest" test, seemingly avoided that result when it awarded legal custody to the foster parents. We next turn to why that disposition was improper.

The Appellate Division awarded legal custody of Michael to the foster parents pursuant to Social Services Law § 392(6)(b), noting that the statute "permits a court to enter an order of disposition directing, *inter alia*, that a child, whose custody and care have temporarily been transferred to an authorized agency, be placed in the custody of a suitable person or persons." The Court correctly looked to section 392 as the predicate for determining custody, but erroneously relied on paragraph (b) of subdivision (6) in awarding custody to the foster parents.

As set forth above, there are three possible dispositions after foster care review with respect to a child not freed for adoption: continued foster care; release to a parent, guardian, relative or other suitable person; and institution of parental termination proceedings.

As the first dispositional option, paragraph (a) contemplates the continuation of foster care, with the child remaining in the custody of the authorized agency, and the arrangement remaining subject to periodic review. As a result of 1989 amendments, disposition under paragraph (a) can include an order that the child be placed with (or remain with) a particular foster family until the next review. Under the statutory scheme, however, foster care is temporary, contractual and supervised.

Paragraph (b), by contrast, contemplates removal of the child from the foster care system by return to "the parent, guardian or relative, or direct[ion] that the child be placed in the custody of a relative or other suitable person or persons." The 1989 statutory revision added as a permissible disposition the placement of children with relatives or other suitable persons. The purpose of this amendment was to promote family stability by allowing placement with relatives, extended family members or persons like them, as an alternative to foster care.

Plainly, the scheme does not envision also including the foster parents—who were the subject of the amendment to paragraph (a)—as "other suitable persons." Indeed, reading paragraph (b) as the Appellate Division did, to permit removal of the child from foster care and an award of legal custody to the foster parents, exacerbates the legal limbo status.

The child is left without a placement looking to the establishment of a permanent parental relationship through adoption, or the prospect of subsequent review of foster care status with the possibility of adoption placement at that time yet has no realistic chance of return to the biological parent.

The terms of paragraph (c), providing for an order that the agency institute a parental termination proceeding, further buttress the conclusion that foster parents are not included in paragraph (b). Pursuant to paragraph (c), if the court finds reasonable cause to believe there are grounds for termination of parental rights, it may order the responsible agency to institute such proceedings. If the agency fails to do so within 90 days, the foster parents themselves may bring the proceeding, unless the court believes their subsequent petition to adopt would not be approved. Thus, in the statutory scheme the Legislature has provided a means for foster parents to secure a temporary arrangement under paragraph (a) and a permanent arrangement under paragraph (c)—both of which specifically mention foster parents. They are not also implicitly included in paragraph (b), which addresses different interests.

We therefore conclude that the Appellate Division erred in interpreting Social Services Law § 392(6) to permit the award of legal custody to respondent foster parents.

We have no occasion to apply the proper legal test to the facts at hand, as the parties urge. New circumstances require remittal to Family Court for an expedited hearing and determination of whether appellant is a fit parent and entitled to custody of Michael.

The Court has been informed that, during the pendency of the appeal, appellant was charged with—and admitted—neglect of the children in his custody (not Michael), and that those children have been removed from his home and are again in the custody of the Commissioner of the Social Services. The neglect petitions allege that appellant abused alcohol and controlled substances including cocaine, and physically abused the children. Orders of fact finding have been entered by Family Court, Queens County, recognizing appellant's admission in open court to "substance abuse, alcohol and cocaine abuse." Moreover, an Order of Protection was entered prohibiting appellant from visiting the children while under the influence of drugs or alcohol.

Appellant's request that we ignore these new developments and simply grant him custody, because matters outside the record cannot be considered by an appellate court, would exalt the procedural rule—important though it is—to a point of absurdity, and "reflect no credit on the judicial process." (Cohen and Karger, Powers of the New York Court of Appeals § 168, at 640.) Indeed, changed circumstances may have particular significance in child custody matters. This Court would therefore take notice of the new facts and allegations to the extent they indicate that the record before us is no longer sufficient for determining appellant's fitness and right to custody of Michael, and remit the matter to Family Court for a new hearing and determination of those issues. The Appellate Division concluded that the hearing should take place before a different Judge of that court, and we see no basis to disturb that determination. Pending the hearing, Michael should physically remain with his current foster parents, but legal custody should be returned to the foster care agency.

. . .

■ BELLACOSA, J., concurring.

I agree with Judge Kaye's opinion for the Court that Social Services Law § 392(6)(b) cannot be used to award permanent custody to foster parents within that statute's intended operation and integrated structure. I concur in the reversal result in this case solely for that reason, noting additionally that a contrary interpretation of that key provision, as used by the Appellate Division, would have internally contradictory implications in the field of temporary foster child placement. While I prefer an affirmance result because that might more likely conclude the litigation and allow Michael B., the 7 1/2-year-old subject of this custody battle, to get on with his life in a more settled and constructive way, I can discern no principled route to that desirable result without sacrificing the correct application of legal principles and engendering fundamentally troublesome precedential consequences.

This separate concurrence is necessary to express my difference of degree and analytical progression with respect to the best interests analysis and test, as adopted by the Court, for purposes of the remittal of this case and as the controlling guidance for countless other proceedings in the future. I would not relegate *Matter of Bennett v. Jeffreys* essentially to general relevance only, would not limit the beginning of the analysis to the statutory setting, and would allow for appropriate flexibility as to the range and manner of exercising discretion in the application of the best interests test by the Family Courts and Appellate Divisions.

I believe courts, in the fulfillment of the *parens patriae* responsibility of the State, should, as a general operating principle, have an appropriately broad range of power to act in the best interests of children. We agree that the teachings of *Matter of Bennett v. Jeffreys* are still excellent and have served the process and the affected subjects and combatants in custody disputes very well. While the common-law origination in *Bennett* is a distinguishing feature from the instant case, I do not view that aspect as subordinated to or secondary in the use of its wisdom, even in a predominantly statutory setting, where this case originates. I am not persuaded that there is any support or positive authority for the view that the Legislature meant anything different when it adopted the phrase "best interest of the child" in Social Services Law § 392(6) from the meaning of that phrase articulated in *Matter of Bennett v. Jeffreys* (*supra*). Courts must exercise common-law authority in all these circumstances, and the Legislature has not, as far as I can tell, displaced that uniquely judicial function and plenary role. Since the best of *Matter of Bennett v. Jeffreys'* best interest analysis enjoys continued vitality therefore, it should serve as a cogent, coequal common-law building block. In my view, it provides helpful understanding for and intertwined supplementation to the Social Services Law provisions as applied in these extraordinary circumstances, defined in one aspect of *Matter of Bennett v. Jeffreys* as "prolonged separation" of parent and child "for most of the child's life[.]" The child in that case was eight years of age and none of the other serious and disquieting features of this case were apparent there.

The nuances, complexity and variations of human situations make the development and application of the general axiom—best interests of the child—exceedingly difficult. As a matter of degree and perspective, however, the Court's test is concededly more limiting than *Matter of Bennett v. Jeffreys (supra)*, and therefore I believe it is more narrow than it should be in this case since I discern no compelling authority for the narrower approach. This 7 1/2-year-old child, born of a long since deceased crack-cocaine mother, has yet to be permanently placed and has suffered a continuing, lengthy, bad trip through the maze of New York's legal system. His father has an extended history of significant substance addiction and other problems, and the child has spent much of his 7 1/2 years with the same foster parents. These graphic circumstances surely present an exceptionally extraordinary and compelling case requiring significant flexibility by the courts in resolving his best interests. On this aspect of the case, therefore, I agree with the Appellate Division in its two decisions in this case, at least with respect to its best interests analysis and handling of this difficult case. On March 18, 1991, it said:

> In view of the extraordinary circumstances present in this case, the Family Court should have conducted a hearing to consider, among other things, the impact that a change of custody will have on the child in view of the bonding which has occurred between Michael and his foster parents, who have raised him since infancy. It is, therefore, necessary to remit this matter for a hearing and a custody determination to be made in accordance with Michael's best interests.

After the proper, broad, "pure" *Matter of Bennett v. Jeffreys*-type best interests hearing was held in Family Court, the Appellate Division on February 24, 1992 added in the order now before us:

> In light of the lengthy period of time during which Michael resided with and psychologically bonded to his foster parents and given the potential for emotional as well as physical harm to Michael should permanent custody be awarded to his natural father, we find that the requisite extraordinary circumstances are present and conclude that the best interests of this child will be served by allowing him to return to his foster parents.

In view of the testimony presented during the best interests hearing, this court concludes that Michael's natural father is incapable of giving him the emotional support so vital to his well-being. The testimony presented by Dr. Sullivan and Mr. Falco indicated that an emotional void still existed between Michael and his father despite the eight to nine months during which they resided together prior to the best interests hearing and that this void showed no signs of being bridged.

In sum, I cannot agree that the important and pervasive legal axiom "best interests of the child" is or was meant to be as constricted as it is in the Court's application to this case. The governing phrase and test even in this statutory scheme ought to be as all-encompassing as in *Matter of Bennett v. Jeffreys* despite the difference in the procedural origin and setting of the two cases. The approach I urge, not unlike that of the Appellate Division in this respect, better serves the objectives of finality and certainty in these matters, more realistically takes into account the widely varying human conditions, and allows the Family Courts to achieve more uniformity and evenness of application of the rules. That is a better way to promote the best interests of this youngster with reasonable finality and the best interests of all others affected by the operation of these rules.

. . .

NOTES

1.   *Domestic violence and foster care.* Studies find that children are present in an estimated thirty to sixty percent of families where domestic violence occurs. *See* Carolyn Copps Hartley, *The Co-Occurrence of Child Maltreatment and Domestic Violence: Examining Both Neglect and Child Physical Abuse*, 7 CHILD MALTREATMENT 349, 349 (2002). Domestic violence can lead to parents, including the abused parent, being charged by child-welfare authorities with failure to protect their children by having permitted the child to observe the assault. *See* H. LIEN BRAGG, U.S. DEP'T OF HEALTH & HUMAN SERVS., CHILD PROTECTION IN FAMILIES EXPERIENCING DOMESTIC VIOLENCE 12 (2003). These charges frequently stem not from physical abuse to the child, but merely from the fact that the child has witnessed the abuse. As a result, domestic violence victims face an untenable proposition. If they act to protect themselves, whether through violence or simply by leaving their batterers, they may risk further physical injury, or even death. However, if they fail to act, the law may deem them unsuitable or neglectful for failing to protect their children. In such cases, it is more likely that children will be removed from the abused parent's care and placed in foster care. Although such laws are usually gender-neutral, the majority of "failure-to-protect" cases focus on the mother, still another reason why women may fear to report domestic violence. *See* The "Failure to Protect" Working Group, *Charging Battered Mothers with "Failure to Protect": Still Blaming the Victim*, 27 FORDHAM URB. L.J. 849, 849 (2000); Audrey E. Stone & Rebecca

J. Fialk, *Criminalizing the Exposure of Children to Family Violence: Breaking the Cycle of Abuse*, 20 HARV. WOMEN'S L.J. 205, 205–06 (1997).

2. *The double-bind in real time.* When children live in homes where mothers are abused, child-welfare officials often charge the mothers with child endangerment or failure to protect. As Professor Myrna Raeder explains, the circumstances of *In re Nicholson*, 181 F. Supp. 2d 182, 185 (E.D.N.Y. 2002), provide "a classic example of the ease with which a battered woman can lose her children solely as a result of her abuse." Myrna S. Raeder, *Preserving Family Ties for Domestic Violence Survivors and Their Children by Invoking a Human Rights Approach to Avoid the Criminalization of Mothers Based on the Acts and Accusations of Their Batterers*, 17 J. GENDER RACE & JUST. 105, 117 (2014). In *Nicholson*, a class of abused mothers challenged New York City's Administration for Children Services' (ACS) practice of filing child-neglect proceedings against victims of domestic abuse. Judge Jack B. Weinstein issued a preliminary injunction to ensure that battered mothers who were fit to retain custody of their children would not face prosecution or removal of their children solely because they experienced domestic violence. *In re Nicholson*, 181 F. Supp. 2d 182, 185 (E.D.N.Y. 2002). The New York State Court of Appeals later clarified (based on a certified question from *In re Nicholson*) that, under New York law, "more is required for a showing of neglect . . . than the fact that a child was exposed to domestic abuse against the caretaker," and that removal requires additional particularized evidence of abuse and neglect. *Nicholson v. Scoppetta*, 820 N.E.2d 840, 853 (N.Y. 2004). The parties eventually settled the case, and though Judge Weinstein's injunction eventually lapsed, the court established procedures for reviewing any cases in which the *Nicholson* decision is not followed. Stipulation and Order of Settlement at 2, *Nicholson v. Williams*, 203 F. Supp. 2d 153 (E.D.N.Y. 2002).

3. *The color of child welfare.* African-American children are more likely than white children to be placed in foster care, even when controlling for family and child characteristics. *See* DOROTHY ROBERTS, SHATTERED BONDS: THE COLOR OF CHILD WELFARE 51–52 (2009). Once in foster care, African-American children stay longer, receive fewer services, and are less likely to be reunited with their parents. ROBERT B. HILL, CASEY-CSSP ALLIANCE FOR RACIAL EQUITY IN CHILD WELFARE SYS., SYNTHESIS OF RESEARCH ON DISPROPORTIONALITY IN CHILD WELFARE: AN UPDATE 17 (2006); *see also* Rebecca A. Akin, *Predictors of Foster Care Exits to Permanency: A Competing Risks Analysis of Reunification, Guardianship, and Adoption*, 33 CHILD. & YOUTH SERVICES REV. 1003 (2011). Moreover, Professor Dorothy Roberts has found that African-American mothers at risk of losing their children to foster care were more likely to be offered "soft" resources such as parenting classes and counseling, while white parents were more likely to be offered "hard" resources such as housing assistance. *See* DOROTHY ROBERTS, SHATTERED BONDS 21 (2009).

4. *Racial disparities in foster care?* The number of children in foster care exploded in the 1990s, with 8.1 children per thousand residing in foster care in 1999. However, since then, the number of children in foster care has declined. In 2011, only 5.4 children per thousand were in foster care. Of this

number, forty-seven percent were living with non-family members, twenty-seven percent were in kinship care arrangements, and the rest were housed in institutions or other settings. Despite the decline, foster care remains disproportionately racialized. African-American children make up fourteen percent of all children in the U.S., but they represent twenty-seven percent of all children in foster care. *See* CHILD TRENDS DATABANK, FOSTER CARE: INDICATORS ON CHILDREN & YOUTH 4 (2012).

5.   *Sexual abuse in foster care.* Since foster youth are by definition vulnerable, it should not be surprising that they are at an increased risk of sexual abuse, both at the hands of caregivers and by other foster children. Using data from a nationally representative sample of adolescents, the research and advocacy group Child Trends found that forty-nine percent of female adolescents in foster care reported forced sex, compared to eleven percent of young women who had never been in foster care. *See* JENNIFER MANLOVE ET AL., CHILD TRENDS, TEEN PARENTS IN FOSTER CARE: RISK FACTORS AND OUTCOMES FOR TEENS AND THEIR CHILDREN 4 (2011). Malika Saada Saar, the Director of the Human Rights Project for Girls, argues that there is a "foster care to child trafficking pipeline." Malika Saada Saar, *Stopping the Foster Care to Child Trafficking Pipeline*, HUFFINGTON POST (Oct. 29, 2013), http://www.huffingtonpost.com/malika-saada-saar/stopping-the-foster-care-_b_4170483.html. In 2013, the FBI conducted efforts to recover trafficked and sexually exploited youth in seventy cities across the United States. Of those recovered, roughly sixty percent had been residing in foster care or group homes prior to being trafficked. Similar data from other areas have led Saada Saar to claim that "the majority of trafficked youth in the United States are child welfare involved." HUMAN RIGHTS PROJECT FOR GIRLS, CHILD WELFARE AND DOMESTIC CHILD SEX TRAFFICKING 1 (2013).

6.   *Teen motherhood and pregnancy in the foster care system.* Foster children who become teen parents are likely to have unstable home environments both before and after the birth of their babies. Although they may stay in their foster families (if the family is willing and able to take in an infant), the additional money provided to foster families for the teen parent's child can be substantially less than that provided if the family had separately fostered an infant. Further, some states have additional licensing requirements when there is an infant involved. *See* Eve Stotland & Cynthia Godsoe, *The Legal Status of Pregnant and Parenting Youth in Foster Care*, 17 U. FLA. J.L. & PUB. POL'Y 1, 13 (2006). In addition to experiencing obstacles in their attempts to parent while in foster care, pregnant foster youth have encountered problems seeking abortions in states where parental consent is required. *See, e.g., In re Petition of Anonymous 5, a minor*, 838 N.W.2d 226 (Neb. 2013) (holding that a sixteen-year-old may not get an abortion without the consent of a parent, if she has not demonstrated abuse, neglect, or sufficient maturity).

7.   *LGBT youth in foster care.* Although there is little reliable data, LGBT youth are at special risk in the foster care population. In addition to the myriad reasons that propel other youth into the foster care system, LGBT youth may also experience sexual identity issues that inform their entry into

the foster care system. For example, parents may disapprove of LGBT and gender non-conforming youth and insist that they leave the family home. Indeed, in one study, about a third of gays and lesbians reported experiencing physical violence at the hands of a family member as a result of their sexual orientation. The National Network of Runaway and Youth Services has estimated that between twenty and forty percent of homeless youth are gay, lesbian, or bisexual. Once in the child welfare system, LGBT youth often face a system that has little knowledge of—or interest in accommodating—their needs. LAMBDA LEGAL DEF. & EDUC. FUND, YOUTH IN THE MARGINS: A REPORT ON THE UNMET NEEDS OF LESBIAN, GAY, BISEXUAL, AND TRANSGENDER ADOLESCENTS IN FOSTER CARE 10–12 (2001).

8.   *Kinship care.* Some states have come to rely on extended family, rather than foster families, to take care of children. Under these kinship-care arrangements, extended family members are permitted to receive subsidies from the child-welfare system for the care of children who would otherwise be admitted to the foster-care system. There are many advantages to kinship care. Extended family members are more likely to be committed to the child, to maintaining contact with the parents, and to preserving the relationship between parent and child. However, in return for financial support from the foster-care system both parents and kin must relinquish legal custody of the child to the state and submit to burdensome foster-care regulations and high levels of state surveillance. *See* Dorothy E. Roberts, *Kinship Care and the Price of State Support for Children*, 76 CHI.-KENT L. REV. 1619, 1627, 1642 (2001).

* * *

In recent years, the interaction between the child welfare system and the criminal justice system has become pronounced. As the following selections make clear, families have struggled to deal with the consequences of our increasingly carceral culture.

Adoption of Baby Boy A. v. Catholic Social Services of the Diocese of Harrisburg, Pa.

517 A.2d 1244 (Pa. 1986).

■ HUTCHINSON, J.

. . .

Baby Boy A. (child) was born on March 31, 1979. At that time appellant, who is illiterate, was serving a sentence on a rape conviction.[3] Appellant learned of the child's existence on June 28, 1979, when Kirk L. Reider, Director of Professional Services for appellee, visited him in prison. Mr. Reider visited appellant for the purpose of telling him of the birth of the child and requesting his consent to the termination of his parental rights. Mr. Reider informed appellant that the child's mother had consented to having the child adopted.

---

[3]   The child was conceived while appellant was on bail pending appeal of that conviction.

Appellee agency had placed the child in a foster home on April 4, 1979. Mr. Reider told appellant that the placement had been made, although he did not tell appellant where the child was. Appellant refused to agree to voluntary termination of his parental rights. Because he was unable at that time to care for the child himself, appellant suggested to Mr. Reider that appellant's mother might be able to care for the child for him.

From the time of Mr. Reider's visit until his release on parole on September 24, 1980, a period of fifteen months, appellant did nothing to try to find out more about the child or to have any communication with the child. Although appellant's illiteracy hindered his meaningful participation in his child's life while he was in prison, we are unwilling to hold that the law expects nothing from him at all. . . . [T]he record shows that appellant did nothing to even attempt to fulfill his parental responsibilities prior to his release on parole. Even an illiterate prisoner can show some interest in his child's well-being and we now hold the law of Pennsylvania requires him to do so if he wishes to retain an absolute right to parental status unaffected by the consideration of how ill-served the child's interest is by that tie.

Our law, in permitting termination for abandonment over the belated objections of the parent, if termination is best for the child, recognizes the occasional failure of nature's parent-child bond. It does so by a statute which provides:

Grounds for Involuntary Termination.—

The rights of a parent in regard to a child may be terminated after a petition filed pursuant to section 312, and a hearing held pursuant to section 313, on the ground that:

(1) The parent by conduct continuing for a period of at least six months either has evidenced a settled purpose of relinquishing parental claim to a child, or has refused or failed to perform parental duties; or

(2) The repeated and continued incapacity, abuse, neglect, or refusal of the parent has caused the child to be without essential parental care, control, or subsistence necessary for his physical or mental well-being and the conditions and causes of the incapacity, abuse, neglect, or refusal cannot or will not be remedied by the parent[.]

As a further protection against government interference with the family relation and the values it serves, our constitutions require clear and convincing evidence that the statute's elements exist before termination is possible. This Court has frequently held that parenthood is an active occupation. It is not enough that a parent declines to relinquish parental claim to a child; a parent must affirmatively demonstrate love, protection and concern. A parent desiring to retain parental rights must exert himself to take and maintain a place of importance in his child's life. The statute does not require a showing of both an intention to relinquish parental claim and a failure to perform parental duties. This Court will view the efforts made by a parent in light of the totality of his circumstances. Nonetheless, we cannot say that the law will excuse a total failure to act for fifteen months, even where the parent faces the obstacles which appellant faced. . . .

. . . [The court below] found that appellant's efforts in late 1980 served to defeat appellee's position and apparently excused the prior period of inaction on the basis of the obstacles facing appellant. However, "[i]t is well established that once the statutory period of abandonment has passed, mere renewal of interest and expression of desire for the return of a discarded child do not negate the abandonment." *In re In the Matter of J.F., a Minor,* 408 A.2d 1382, 1387 (1979). The wise requirement that a parent's right to a relationship with his child can only be terminated on clear and convincing evidence does not make parents owners of their children, free to cast them aside, as unwanted toys, for more than six months and then pick them up to play with again when the fancy strikes them. Instead, it arises out of our deep conviction that the bond of family love will enable most parents to give better care to their children than the best that anyone else can provide. Our confidence in that conviction is lost, however, when a parent exhibits no sign of interest in his child over extended periods. Thus, appellant's efforts during his release on parole[7] do not serve to nullify the inaction of the prior fifteen months. This is especially true because those efforts were primarily directed toward finding the child's mother, not the child.

. . . The child is now more than seven years old and there is no evidence that there has ever been any relationship between appellant and the child. Following appellant's abandonment of his child, there was, in fact, no evidence of any relationship which served the child's interest and, therefore, should be preserved. . . . [W]e conclude on this record that there is no evidence showing that the child's welfare is better served by continuing appellant's parental rights beyond the time of abandonment in light of his failure to perform his parental duties.

. . .

---

[7]   In October, 1980, appellant traveled to Red Lion, Pennsylvania, in an attempt to locate the child's mother. He also tried unsuccessfully to contact her by telephone. At about the same time he asked the public defender, who was representing him, to contact the appellee agency. The attorney did so, but no further action was taken. Appellant remained on parole until February 5, 1981, when he was recommitted for parole violation. Between September, 1980, and February, 1981, he spent thirty days in prison on a drunk and disorderly charge.

Adoption and Safe Families Act of 1997

Pub. L. No. 105–89, 111 Stat. 2115 (codified as amended
in scattered sections of 42 U.S.C.).

An Act [t]o promote the adoption of children in foster care.

. . .

TITLE I—REASONABLE EFFORTS AND SAFETY REQUIREMENTS FOR FOSTER CARE AND ADOPTION PLACEMENTS

. . .

SEC. 103. STATES REQUIRED TO INITIATE OR JOIN PROCEEDINGS TO TERMINATE PARENTAL RIGHTS FOR CERTAIN CHILDREN IN FOSTER CARE.

(a) REQUIREMENT FOR PROCEEDINGS.—Section 475(5) of the Social Security Act (42 U.S.C. 675(5)) is amended—

. . .

(3) by adding at the end the following:

"(E) in the case of a child who has been in foster care under the responsibility of the State for 15 of the most recent 22 months, or, if a court of competent jurisdiction has determined a child to be an abandoned infant (as defined under State law) or has made a determination that the parent has committed murder of another child of the parent, committed voluntary manslaughter of another child of the parent, aided or abetted, attempted, conspired, or solicited to commit such a murder or such a voluntary manslaughter, or committed a felony assault that has resulted in serious bodily injury to the child or to another child of the parent, the State shall file a petition to terminate the parental rights of the child's parents (or, if such a petition has been filed by another party, seek to be joined as a party to the petition), and, concurrently, to identify, recruit, process, and approve a qualified family for an adoption, unless—

(i) at the option of the State, the child is being cared for by a relative;

(ii) a State agency has documented in the case plan (which shall be available for court review) a compelling reason for determining that filing such a petition would not be in the best interests of the child; or

(iii) the State has not provided to the family of the child, consistent with the time period in the State case plan, such services as the State deems necessary for the safe return of the child to the child's home, if reasonable efforts of the type described in section 471(a)(15)(B)(ii) are required to be made with respect to the child." . . .

. . .

TITLE II—INCENTIVES FOR PROVIDING PERMANENT FAMILIES FOR CHILDREN

. . .

SEC. 473A. ADOPTION INCENTIVE PAYMENTS.

(a) GRANT AUTHORITY.—Subject to the availability of such amounts as may be provided in advance in appropriations Acts for this purpose, the Secretary shall make a grant to each State that is an incentive-eligible State for a fiscal year in an amount equal to the adoption incentive payment payable to the State under this section for the fiscal year, which shall be payable in the immediately succeeding fiscal year.

(b) INCENTIVE-ELIGIBLE STATE.—A State is an incentive-eligible State for a fiscal year if—

(1) the State has a plan approved under this part for the fiscal year;

(2) the number of foster child adoptions in the State during the fiscal year exceeds the base number of foster child adoptions for the State for the fiscal year;

(3) the State is in compliance with subsection (c) for the fiscal year;

(4) in the case of fiscal years 2001 and 2002, the State provides health insurance coverage to any child with special needs (as determined under section 473(c)) for whom there is in effect an adoption assistance agreement between a State and an adoptive parent or parents; and

(5) the fiscal year is any of fiscal years 1998 through 2002.

. . .

(d) ADOPTION INCENTIVE PAYMENT.—

(1) IN GENERAL.—Except as provided in paragraph (2), the adoption incentive payment payable to a State for a fiscal year under this section shall be equal to the sum of—

(A) $4,000, multiplied by the amount (if any) by which the number of foster child adoptions in the State during the fiscal year exceeds the base number of foster child adoptions for the State for the fiscal year; and

(B) $2,000, multiplied by the amount (if any) by which the number of special needs adoptions in the State during the fiscal year exceeds the base number of special needs adoptions for the State for the fiscal year.

. . .

NOTE

Good intentions gone awry. Passed in 1997, the Adoption and Safe Families Act (ASFA), was designed to keep children from languishing indefinitely in foster care. Under its terms, the parental rights of the parents of any child who has been in foster care for fifteen of the last twenty-two months will be subject to termination. Although it may not have been Congress's intent, ASFA has produced devastating consequences for incarcerated women. As Laurie Cohen has reported, about three-fourths of incarcerated women have children under eighteen, and many of them have sentences longer than the fifteen-month period allowed in ASFA. The number of cases involving termination of parental rights of incarcerated people has doubled between 1997 and 2002. Laurie Cohen, *A Law's Fallout: Women in Prison Fight for Custody*, WALL ST. J., Feb. 27, 2006, at A1.

In re R.I.S.

36 A.3d 567 (Pa. 2011).

■ McCAFFERY, J.

C.S. ("Father"), who is currently incarcerated in a State Correctional Institution in Erie County . . . is the biological father of two minor children: A.I.S. . . . and R.I.S. . . . (collectively "the children"). He appeals the Superior Court's reversal of the York County trial court's orders denying petitions for the involuntary termination of his parental rights and for changes in the placement goals for the children from reunification to adoption. . . .

Father was sentenced to serve two to four years' incarceration in June 2008. In January 2009, York County Children and Youth Services ("CYS") filed an application for protective custody of the children, based in part on a request for emergency placement made by the biological mother of the children, K.H. ("Mother"). The children were adjudicated dependent in February 2009, and were placed together in a temporary foster home. A pre-adoptive resource was identified by CYS, and in December 2009, CYS filed petitions for changes in the placement goals for the children from reunification to adoption, and for the involuntary termination of the parental rights of Father and Mother. On March 2, 2010, a hearing on the petitions was conducted.

At the hearing, it was shown that a family service plan setting forth goals for Father with respect to reunification had been created. . . . The goals set for Father included cooperating with service planning, signing necessary releases, remaining in contact with CYS through written correspondence, providing documentation upon completion of therapeutic prison programs, and maintaining a record of good prison conduct. Evidence was presented to show that Father had met each of these goals. . . .

Additionally, evidence was presented at the hearing that Father had maintained contact with the children by sending them cards on a monthly basis and by participating in a "Reading to Your Children" program sponsored by the prison whereby the children received a video of Father reading a book to them. It was shown that Father had requested visitation with the children, but the request was denied due to the time and distance that would be involved (an eleven-hour round trip by personal vehicle between the cities of York and Erie, Pennsylvania). Father's alternative request for "virtual visitation" was denied because CYS had no video-conferencing capability. It was further shown that Father purchased a pre-paid phone card and attempted several times to call the children, but the foster parents refused the calls.

. . .

. . . [T]he trial court entered orders denying the goal change petitions and the involuntary termination petitions with respect to Father.[2] It concluded that CYS had not proven any of the statutory bases for the involuntary termination of Father's rights, and characterized the CYS position as seeking termination based solely on the existence and length of Father's sentence of incarceration. CYS filed a timely appeal. . . .

The Superior Court reversed. . . . The . . . memorandum opinion . . . stated that "incarceration alone cannot constitute grounds for termination[,]" but nonetheless concluded that "Father's incarceration is evidence of his parental incapacity." On that basis, the Superior Court determined that the trial court's conclusions were not supported by the record and that the trial court had committed an abuse of discretion.

. . .

We begin our analysis by noting that the right to conceive and raise one's children has long been recognized as one of our basic civil rights. *Skinner v. Oklahoma*, 316 U.S. 535 (1942); *Meyer v. Nebraska*, 262 U.S. 390 (1923). In any context, the complete and irrevocable termination of parental rights is one of the most serious and severe steps a court can take. *In re Adoption of Sarver*, 281 A.2d 890, 891 (Pa. 1971). . . .

. . .

This Court has long held that a parent's absence or failure to support his or her child due to incarceration is not, in itself, conclusively determinative of the issue of parental abandonment. *In re Adoption of McCray*, 331 A.2d 652, 655 (Pa. 1975). Indeed, incarceration alone is not an explicit basis upon which an involuntary termination may be ordered. . . . Rather, we must inquire whether the parent has utilized those resources at his or her command while in prison to continue and pursue a close relationship with the child or children. An incarcerated parent desiring to retain parental rights must exert him- or herself to take and maintain a place of importance in the child's life. *Adoption of Baby Boy A.*, 517 A.2d 1244, 1246 (1986).

. . . In a change of goal proceeding, the best interests of the child and not the interests of the parent must guide the trial court, and the burden

---

[2] The court granted the petitions for the involuntary termination of Mother's parental rights, and there are no issues before us regarding that determination.

is on the child welfare agency involved to prove that a change in goal would be in the child's best interest.

. . .

... The trial court determined that the length of Father's sentence was not so great as to foreclose the possibility of the successful maintenance of the parent-child relationship, and that termination of Father's parental rights would not serve the best interests of the children. The Superior Court viewed the same facts, and drew the opposite conclusion. . . . [T]his Court has never adopted or countenanced a view that incarceration alone is *per se* evidence of parental incapacity or that it represents appropriate and sufficient grounds for the involuntary termination of parental rights. . . . [W]e reiterate the definitive principle that when a parent uses the opportunities that are available in prison to make sincere efforts to maintain a place of importance in the lives of his or her children, incarceration alone will not serve as grounds for the involuntary termination of his or her parental rights.[4] Accordingly, we reverse the order of the Superior Court with respect to its determination regarding the involuntary termination of Father's parental rights.

With respect to the Superior Court's reversal of the trial court's order denying the petition of CYS for a goal change from reunification to adoption, we note that the trial court concluded that reunification should remain the goal. . . . [T]he trial court stated that the challenge on appeal to that ruling was "simply another way of making the same arguments addressed in the previous five contentions [relating to the involuntary termination of parental rights] and, therefore, needs no further response." Questions regarding the propriety of an order granting or denying a goal change petition are, of course, discrete inquiries requiring an analysis of interests exquisitely separable from those interests reviewed in questions relating to the involuntary termination of parental rights. Thus, although we reverse the Superior Court's determination regarding the goal change petitions, we remand to the trial court for an examination of the merits of those petitions under the appropriate analytical model.

Reversed and remanded to the trial court for further proceedings not inconsistent with this Opinion.

■ BAER, J., concurring.

. . .

I agree with the Majority "that this Court has never adopted or countenanced a view that incarceration alone is *per se* evidence of parental incapacity." However, this statement can be misleading. There

---

[4] We make no ruling with respect to the involuntary termination of parental rights grounded on the prohibitive length of a parent's sentence of incarceration. We only note here, as the trial court properly did, that even if Father serves his maximum term of incarceration, R.I.S. and A.I.S. will still be only seven- and nine-years-old, respectively, upon his release.

is no question that the fact of incarceration, regardless of why, is not in and of itself determinative of parental incapacity. Moreover, the fact of incarceration during an ongoing dependency action will not disqualify a parent from resuming parental responsibility so long as the parent will be released quickly enough to permit the court to provide the child with timely permanency upon reunification. If, however, the length of parent's incarceration will preclude the court from unifying the (former) prisoner and the child on a timely basis in order to provide the child with the permanent home to which he or she is entitled, then the length of sentence, standing alone, should and does meet the legal criteria for involuntary termination of the incarcerated parent's parental rights. . . .

Although this Court previously stated that "incarceration is not conclusive" on issues of termination, it has not considered the relevance of parental incarceration to termination of parental rights since the enactment of the federal Adoption and Safe Families Act of 1997, which altered our national view of dependency policy. Prior to the mid-1990s, our national policy toward dependent children was to await reunification of parents and children. While undoubtedly a laudable goal, this single-minded focus on reunification led to 560,000 children in foster care as of September 1998, one-third of whom had been languishing in the foster care system for over three-years and drifting from placement to placement, while their parents were unable to remedy the problems that led to the children's placement. In reaction to this dire situation, the United States Congress enacted ASFA, thereby altering the focus of dependency proceedings to include consideration of the need to move children toward adoption in a timely manner when reunification proved unworkable. One year after ASFA, in 1998, the Pennsylvania General Assembly amended our Juvenile Act in response to the federal legislation. Our statutory scheme was modified to shift the statute's focus from a singular concern with reunification of the family to the dual purposes of preserving family unity when possible, and providing an alternative permanent family for a child when reunification of the biological parent and child could not be timely achieved.

Although the General Assembly did not amend the provisions of the Adoption Act addressing termination of parental rights following the adoption of ASFA, the Act's language has never prohibited consideration of a parent's incarceration. Significantly, the Act does not provide specific protection to incarcerated parents, even though it specifically instructs that termination cannot result "solely from environmental factors such as inadequate housing, furnishings, income, clothing and medical care if found to be beyond the control of the parent." 23 Pa.C.S. § 2511(b)[.] Accordingly, I find no statutory basis in the Adoption Act to justify ignoring the parent's incarceration generally and the length of the parent's sentence specifically in considering the propriety of termination of parental rights.

. . .

NOTE

Parenting from prison. With the vast expansion of incarceration, particularly incarceration of people of color, increasing numbers of parents face the loss of their parental rights while in prison. When fathers are incarcerated, children usually can stay in the custody of their mothers. However, when women (who now make up almost ten percent of the incarcerated population) must leave their children, fathers are far less likely to assume responsibility for the care of minor children. As a consequence, an estimated thirty-five percent of women in prison have had their children placed into foster care, and Ellen Barry argues that it is "virtually impossible" for incarcerated or formerly-incarcerated women to meet the stringent requirements of the foster care system that would enable them to regain custody of their children once they have served their sentences. The foster care system typically demands that incarcerated parents maintain contact with their children, but prisons are often located in rural areas where transportation options are meager. Even if formerly incarcerated mothers meet the time limits within which they must regain custody and maintain contact with their children despite the obstacles they face, housing, job training, and daycare can be difficult for these women to find, and hence make it even more likely they will not meet the requirements of the juvenile court. *See* Ellen Barry, *Parents in Prison, Children in Crisis, in* OUTSIDERS WITHIN: WRITING ON TRANSRACIAL ADOPTION 59, 65–67 (Jane Jeong Trenka et al. eds., 2006). In addition to these constraints, federal laws like the Adoption and Safe Families Act further exacerbate the difficulties that incarcerated mothers face. *See supra* p. 352.

* * *

The child welfare system has posed challenges for marginalized families in a variety of contexts. For example, for most of the twentieth century, government actors actively pursued the assimilation of indigenous people into mainstream Anglo culture by resorting to tactics that sought to "save" Native children by removing them from their families. Native children were forced into boarding schools (often run by religious groups), and punished for following indigenous customs. Later, Native children were often removed under the auspices of state child-welfare systems and placed in non-Native foster homes. Critically, the state often viewed the informal kinship care arrangements relied upon in Native families (as in other minority communities) as pathological and neglectful, furnishing cause for removing children from their homes. The Indian Child Welfare Act of 1978 (ICWA) sought to remedy state encroachment on Native family life and ensure the autonomy of tribal courts in child-welfare matters involving Native youth. As you read the ICWA and its subsequent interpretation in case law, consider whether it is an appropriate solution for Native American children, families, and communities. Would a version of the statute be appropriate for other minority communities in the United States as well?

Indian Child Welfare Act of 1978

Pub. L. No. 95–608, 92 Stat. 3069.

An Act to establish standards for the placement of Indian children in foster or adoptive homes, to prevent the breakup of Indian families, and for other purposes.

Be it enacted by the Senate and House of Representatives of the United States of America in Congress assembled, That this Act, 25 U.S.C. 1901, may be cited as the "Indian Child Welfare Act of 1978".

Sec. 2.   Recognizing the special relationship between the United States and the Indian tribes and their members and the Federal responsibility to Indian people, the Congress finds—

(1) that clause 3, section 8, article I of the United States Constitution provides that "The Congress shall have Power . . . To regulate Commerce . . . with Indian tribes" and, through this and other constitutional authority, Congress has plenary power over Indian affairs;

(2) that Congress, through statutes, treaties, and the general course of dealing with Indian tribes, has assumed the responsibility for the protection and preservation of Indian tribes and their resources;

(3) that there is no resource that is more vital to the continued existence and integrity of Indian tribes than their children and that the United States has a direct interest, as trustee, in protecting Indian children who are members of or are eligible for membership in an Indian tribe;

(4) that an alarmingly high percentage of Indian families are broken up by the removal, often unwarranted, of their children from them by nontribal public and private agencies and that an alarmingly high percentage of such children are placed in non-Indian foster and adoptive homes and institutions; and

(5) that the States, exercising their recognized jurisdiction over Indian child custody proceedings through administrative and judicial bodies, have often failed to recognize the essential tribal relations of Indian people and the cultural and social standards prevailing in Indian communities and families.

Sec. 3.   25 U.S.C. 1902. The Congress hereby declares that it is the policy of this Nation to protect the best interests of Indian children and to promote the stability and security of Indian tribes and families by the establishment of minimum Federal standards for the removal of Indian children from their families and the placement of such children in foster or adoptive homes which will reflect the unique values of Indian culture, and by providing for assistance to Indian tribes in the operation of child and family service programs.

. . .

Sec. 101. 25 U.S.C. 1911. (a) An Indian tribe shall have jurisdiction exclusive as to any State over any child custody proceeding involving an Indian child who resides or is domiciled within the reservation of such tribe, except where such jurisdiction is otherwise vested in the State by existing Federal law. Where an Indian child is a ward of a tribal court, the Indian tribe shall retain exclusive jurisdiction, notwithstanding the residence or domicile of the child.

(b) In any State court proceeding for the foster care placement of, or termination of parental rights to, an Indian child not domiciled or residing within the reservation of the Indian child's tribe, the court, in the absence of good cause to the contrary, shall transfer such proceeding to the jurisdiction of the tribe, absent objection by either parent, upon the petition of either parent or the Indian custodian or the Indian child's tribe: Provided, That such transfer shall be subject to declination by the tribal court of such tribe.

(c) In any State court proceeding for the foster care placement of, or termination of parental rights to, an Indian child, the Indian custodian of the child and the Indian child's tribe shall have a right to intervene at any point in the proceeding.

(d) The United States, every State, every territory or possession of the United States, and every Indian tribe shall give full faith and credit to the public acts, records, and judicial proceedings of any Indian tribe applicable to Indian child custody proceedings to the same extent that such entities give full faith and credit to the public acts, records, and judicial proceedings of any other entity.

. . .

Sec. 103. 25 U.S.C. 1913. (a) Where any parent or Indian custodian voluntarily consents to a foster care placement or to termination of parental rights, such consent shall not be valid unless executed in writing and recorded before a judge of a court of competent jurisdiction and accompanied by the presiding judge's certificate that the terms and consequences of the consent were fully explained in detail and were fully understood by the parent or Indian custodian. The court shall also certify that either the parent or Indian custodian fully understood the explanation in English or that it was interpreted into a language that the parent or Indian custodian understood. Any consent given prior to, or within ten days after, birth of the Indian child shall not be valid.

(b) Any parent or Indian custodian may withdraw consent to a foster care placement under State law at any time and, upon such withdrawal, the child shall be returned to the parent or Indian custodian.

(c) In any voluntary proceeding for termination of parental rights to, or adoptive placement of, an Indian child, the consent of the parent may be withdrawn for any reason at any time prior to the entry of a final decree of termination or adoption, as the case may be, and the child shall be returned to the parent.

(d) After the entry of a final decree of adoption of an Indian child in any State court, the parent may withdraw consent thereto upon the grounds that consent was obtained through fraud or duress and may petition the court to vacate such decree. Upon a finding that such consent was obtained through fraud or duress, the court shall vacate such decree and return the child to the parent. No adoption which has been effective for at least two years may be invalidated under the provisions of this subsection unless otherwise permitted under State law.

. . .

Sec. 105. (a) In any adoptive placement of an Indian child under State law, a preference shall be given, in the absence of good cause to the contrary, to a placement with (1) a member of the child's extended family; (2) other members of the Indian child's tribe; or (3) other Indian families.

(b) Any child accepted for foster care or preadoptive placement shall be placed in the least restrictive setting which most approximates a family and in which his special needs, if any, may be met. The child shall also be placed within reasonable proximity to his or her home, taking into account any special needs of the child. In any foster care or preadoptive placement, a preference shall be given, in the absence of good cause to the contrary, to a placement with—

(i) a member of the Indian child's extended family;

(ii) a foster home licensed, approved, or specified by the Indian child's tribe;

(iii) an Indian foster home licensed or approved by an authorized non-Indian licensing authority; or

(iv) an institution for children approved by an Indian tribe or operated by an Indian organization which has a program suitable to meet the Indian child's needs.

(c) In the case of a placement under subsection (a) or (b) of this section, if the Indian child's tribe shall establish a different order of preference by resolution, the agency or court effecting the placement shall follow such order so long as the placement is the least restrictive setting appropriate to the particular needs of the child, as provided in subsection (b) of this section. Where appropriate, the preference of the Indian child or parent shall be considered: Provided, That where a consenting parent evidences a desire for anonymity, the court or agency shall give weight to such desire in applying the preferences.

(d) The standards to be applied in meeting the preference requirements of this section shall be the prevailing social and cultural standards of the Indian community in which the parent or extended family resides or with which the parent or extended family members maintain social and cultural ties.

(e) A record of each such placement, under State law, of an Indian child shall be maintained by the State in which the placement was made, evidencing the efforts to comply with the order of preference specified in this section. Such record shall be made available at any time upon the request of the Secretary or the Indian child's tribe.

Sec. 106. 25 U.S.C. 1916. (a) Notwithstanding State law to the contrary, whenever a final decree of adoption of an Indian child has been vacated or set aside or the adoptive parents voluntarily consent to the termination of their parental rights to the child, a biological parent or prior Indian custodian may petition for return of custody and the court shall grant such petition unless there is a showing, in a proceeding subject to the provisions of section 102 of this Act, that such return of custody is not in the best interests of the child.

(b) Whenever an Indian child is removed from a foster care home or institution for the purpose of further foster care, preadoptive, or adoptive placement, such placement shall be in accordance with the provisions of this Act, except in the case where an Indian child is being returned to the parent or Indian custodian from whose custody the child was originally removed.

Sec. 107. 25 U.S.C. 1917. Upon application by an Indian individual who has reached the age of eighteen and who was the subject of an adoptive placement, the court which entered the final decree shall inform such individual of the tribal affiliation, if any, of the individual's biological parents and provide such other information as may be necessary to protect any rights flowing from the individual's tribal relationship.

. . .

Sec. 113. 25 U.S.C. 1923. None of the provisions of this title, except sections 101(a), 108, and 109, shall affect a proceeding under State law for foster care placement, termination of parental rights, preadoptive placement, or adoptive placement which was initiated or completed prior to one hundred and eighty days after the enactment of this Act, but shall apply to any subsequent proceeding in the same matter or subsequent proceedings affecting the custody or placement of the same child.

TITLE II—INDIAN CHILD AND FAMILY PROGRAMS

Sec. 201. 25 U.S.C. 1931. (a) The Secretary is authorized to make grants to Indian tribes and organizations in the establishment and operation of Indian child and family service programs on or near reservations and in the preparation and implementation of child welfare codes. The objective of every Indian child and family service program shall be to prevent the breakup of Indian families and, in particular, to insure that the permanent removal of an Indian child from the custody of his parent or Indian custodian shall be a last resort. Such child and family service programs may include, but are not limited to—

(1) a system for licensing or otherwise regulating Indian foster and adoptive homes;

(2) the operation and maintenance of facilities for the counseling and treatment of Indian families and for the temporary custody of Indian children;

(3) family assistance, including homemaker and home counselors, day care, afterschool care, and employment, recreational activities, and respite care;

(4) home improvement programs;

(5) the employment of professional and other trained personnel to assist the tribal court in the disposition of domestic relations and child welfare matters;

(6) education and training of Indians, including tribal court judges and staff, in skills relating to child and family assistance and service programs;

(7) a subsidy program under which Indian adoptive children may be provided support comparable to that for which they would be eligible as foster children, taking into account the appropriate State standards of support for maintenance and medical needs; and

(8) guidance, legal representation, and advice to Indian families involved in tribal, State, or Federal child custody proceedings.

(b) Funds appropriated for use by the Secretary in accordance with this section may be utilized as non-Federal matching share in connection with funds provided under titles IV-B and XX of the Social Security Act, 42 U.S.C. 620, 1397, or under any other Federal financial assistance programs which contribute to the purpose for which such funds are authorized to be appropriated for use under this Act. The provision or possibility of assistance under this Act shall not be a basis for the denial or reduction of any assistance otherwise authorized under titles IV-B and XX of the Social Security Act or any other federally assisted program. For purposes of qualifying for assistance under a federally assisted program, licensing or approval of foster or adoptive homes or institutions by an Indian tribe shall be deemed equivalent to licensing or approval by a State.

Sec. 202. 25 U.S.C. 1932. The Secretary is also authorized to make grants to Indian organizations to establish and operate off-reservation Indian child and family service programs which may include, but are not limited to—

(1) a system for regulating, maintaining, and supporting Indian foster and adoptive homes, including a subsidy program under which Indian adoptive children may be provided support comparable to that for which they would be eligible as Indian foster children, taking into account the appropriate State standards of support for maintenance and medical needs;

(2) the operation and maintenance of facilities and services for counseling and treatment of Indian families and Indian foster and adoptive children;

(3) family assistance, including homemaker and home counselors, day care, afterschool care, and employment, recreational activities, and respite care; and

(4) guidance, legal representation, and advice to Indian families involved in child custody proceedings.

Sec. 203. 25 U.S.C. 1933. (a) In the establishment, operation, and funding of Indian child and family service programs, both on and off reservation, the Secretary may enter into agreements with the Secretary of Health, Education, and Welfare, and the latter Secretary is hereby authorized for such purposes to use funds appropriated for similar programs of the Department of Health, Education, and welfare: Provided, That authority to make payments pursuant to such agreements shall be effective only to the extent and in such amounts as may be provided in advance by appropriation Acts.

(b) Funds for the purposes of this Act may be appropriated pursuant to the provisions of the Act of November 2, 1921, 25 U.S.C. 13 (42 Stat. 208), as amended.

. . .

Mississippi Band of Choctaw Indians v. Holyfield
490 U.S. 30 (1989).

■ BRENNAN, J.

This appeal requires us to construe the provisions of the Indian Child Welfare Act that establish exclusive tribal jurisdiction over child custody proceedings involving Indian children domiciled on the tribe's reservation.

The Indian Child Welfare Act of 1978 (ICWA), 92 Stat. 3069, was the product of rising concern in the mid-1970's over the consequences to Indian children, Indian families, and Indian tribes of abusive child welfare practices that resulted in the separation of large numbers of Indian children from their families and tribes through adoption or foster care placement, usually in non-Indian homes. Senate oversight hearings in 1974 yielded numerous examples, statistical data, and expert testimony documenting what one witness called "[t]he wholesale removal of Indian children from their homes, . . . the most tragic aspect of Indian life today." Studies undertaken by the Association on American Indian Affairs in 1969 and 1974, and presented in the Senate hearings, showed that 25 to 35% of all Indian children had been separated from their families and placed in adoptive families, foster care, or institutions. Adoptive placements counted significantly in this total: in the State of Minnesota, for example, one in eight Indian children under the age of 18 was in an adoptive home, and during the year 1971–1972 nearly one in every four infants under one year of age was placed for adoption. The adoption rate of Indian children was eight times that of non-Indian children. Approximately 90% of the Indian placements were in non-Indian homes. A number of witnesses also testified to the serious adjustment problems encountered by such children during adolescence,[1] as well as the impact of the adoptions on Indian parents and the tribes themselves.

. . .

The congressional findings that were incorporated into the ICWA reflect these sentiments. The Congress found:

(3) that there is no resource that is more vital to the continued existence and integrity of Indian tribes than their children . . . ;

(4) that an alarmingly high percentage of Indian families are broken up by the removal, often unwarranted, of their children from them by nontribal public and private agencies and that an alarmingly high percentage of such children are placed in non-Indian foster and adoptive homes and institutions; and

(5) that the States, exercising their recognized jurisdiction over Indian child custody proceedings through administrative and judicial bodies, have often failed to recognize the essential tribal relations of Indian people and the cultural and social standards prevailing in Indian communities and families." 25 U.S.C. § 1901.

At the heart of the ICWA are its provisions concerning jurisdiction over Indian child custody proceedings. Section 1911 lays out a dual jurisdictional scheme. Section 1911(a) establishes exclusive jurisdiction in the tribal courts for proceedings concerning an Indian child "who resides or is domiciled within the reservation of such tribe," as well as for wards of tribal courts regardless of domicile.[5] Section 1911(b), on the

---

[1] For example, Dr. Joseph Westermeyer, a University of Minnesota social psychiatrist, testified about his research with Indian adolescents who experienced difficulty coping in white society, despite the fact that they had been raised in a purely white environment:

[T]hey were raised with a white cultural and social identity. They are raised in a white home. They attended, predominantly white schools, and in almost all cases, attended a church that was predominantly white, and really came to understand very little about Indian culture, Indian behavior, and had virtually no viable Indian identity. They can recall such things as seeing cowboys and Indians on TV and feeling that Indians were a historical figure but were not a viable contemporary social group.

Then during adolescence, they found that society was not to grant them the white identity that they had. They began to find this out in a number of ways. For example, a universal experience was that when they began to date white children, the parents of the white youngsters were against this, and there were pressures among white children from the parents not to date these Indian children. . . .

The other experience was derogatory name calling in relation to their racial identity. . . .

[5] Section 1911(a) reads in full:

An Indian tribe shall have jurisdiction exclusive as to any State over any child custody proceeding involving an Indian child who resides or is domiciled within the reservation

other hand, creates concurrent but presumptively tribal jurisdiction in the case of children not domiciled on the reservation: on petition of either parent or the tribe, state-court proceedings for foster care placement or termination of parental rights are to be transferred to the tribal court, except in cases of "good cause," objection by either parent, or declination of jurisdiction by the tribal court.

Various other provisions of ICWA Title I set procedural and substantive standards for those child custody proceedings that do take place in state court. The procedural safeguards include requirements concerning notice and appointment of counsel; parental and tribal rights of intervention and petition for invalidation of illegal proceedings; procedures governing voluntary consent to termination of parental rights; and a full faith and credit obligation in respect to tribal court decisions. The most important substantive requirement imposed on state courts is that of § 1915(a), which, absent "good cause" to the contrary, mandates that adoptive placements be made preferentially with (1) members of the child's extended family, (2) other members of the same tribe, or (3) other Indian families.

The ICWA thus, in the words of the House Report accompanying it, "seeks to protect the rights of the Indian child as an Indian and the rights of the Indian community and tribe in retaining its children in its society." It does so by establishing "a Federal policy that, where possible, an Indian child should remain in the Indian community," *ibid.*, and by making sure that Indian child welfare determinations are not based on "a white, middle-class standard which, in many cases, forecloses placement with [an] Indian family."

This case involves the status of twin babies, known for our purposes as B.B. and G.B., who were born out of wedlock on December 29, 1985. Their mother, J.B., and father, W.J., were both enrolled members of appellant Mississippi Band of Choctaw Indians (Tribe), and were residents and domiciliaries of the Choctaw Reservation in Neshoba County, Mississippi. J.B. gave birth to the twins in Gulfport, Harrison County, Mississippi, some 200 miles from the reservation. On January 10, 1986, J.B. executed a consent-to-adoption form before the Chancery Court of Harrison County. W.J. signed a similar form. On January 16, appellees Orrey and Vivian Holyfield filed a petition for adoption in the same court, and the chancellor issued a Final Decree of Adoption on January 28. Despite the court's apparent awareness of the ICWA, the adoption decree contained no reference to it, nor to the infants' Indian background.

Two months later the Tribe moved in the Chancery Court to vacate the adoption decree on the ground that under the ICWA exclusive jurisdiction was vested in the tribal court. On July 14, 1986, the court

of such tribe, except where such jurisdiction is otherwise vested in the State by existing Federal law. Where an Indian child is a ward of a tribal court, the Indian tribe shall retain exclusive jurisdiction, notwithstanding the residence or domicile of the child.

overruled the motion, holding that the Tribe "never obtained exclusive jurisdiction over the children involved herein. . . ." The court's one-page opinion relied on two facts in reaching that conclusion. The court noted first that the twins' mother "went to some efforts to see that they were born outside the confines of the Choctaw Indian Reservation" and that the parents had promptly arranged for the adoption by the Holyfields. Second, the court stated: "At no time from the birth of these children to the present date have either of them resided on or physically been on the Choctaw Indian Reservation."

The Supreme Court of Mississippi affirmed. It rejected the Tribe's arguments that the state court lacked jurisdiction and that it, in any event, had not applied the standards laid out in the ICWA. The court recognized that the jurisdictional question turned on whether the twins were domiciled on the Choctaw Reservation. . . .

. . .

Because of the centrality of the exclusive tribal jurisdiction provision to the overall scheme of the ICWA, as well as the conflict between this decision of the Mississippi Supreme Court and those of several other state courts, we granted plenary review. We now reverse.

. . .

Tribal jurisdiction over Indian child custody proceedings is not a novelty of the ICWA. Indeed, some of the ICWA's jurisdictional provisions have a strong basis in pre-ICWA case law in the federal and state courts. . . . In enacting the ICWA Congress confirmed that, in child custody proceedings involving Indian children domiciled on the reservation, tribal jurisdiction was exclusive as to the States.

. . . The sole issue in this case is, as the Supreme Court of Mississippi recognized, whether the twins were "domiciled" on the reservation.

The meaning of "domicile" in the ICWA is, of course, a matter of Congress' intent. The ICWA itself does not define it. The initial question we must confront is whether there is any reason to believe that Congress intended the ICWA definition of "domicile" to be a matter of state law. . . .

. . .

First, and most fundamentally, the purpose of the ICWA gives no reason to believe that Congress intended to rely on state law for the definition of a critical term; quite the contrary. It is clear from the very text of the ICWA, not to mention its legislative history and the hearings that led to its enactment, that Congress was concerned with the rights of Indian families and Indian communities vis-à-vis state authorities. More specifically, its purpose was, in part, to make clear that in certain situations the state courts did *not* have jurisdiction over child custody proceedings. Indeed, the congressional findings that are a part of the statute demonstrate that Congress perceived the States and their courts as partly responsible for the problem it intended to correct. Under these circumstances it is most improbable that Congress would have intended to leave the scope of the statute's key jurisdictional provision subject to definition by state courts as a matter of state law.

Second, Congress could hardly have intended the lack of nationwide uniformity that would result from state-law definitions of domicile. . . .

We therefore think it beyond dispute that Congress intended a uniform federal law of domicile for the ICWA

It remains to give content to the term "domicile" in the circumstances of the present case. . . . The question before us, therefore, is whether under the ICWA definition of "domicile" such facts suffice to render the twins nondomiciliaries of the Reservation.

. . .

"Domicile" is, of course, a concept widely used in both federal and state courts for jurisdiction and conflict-of-laws purposes, and its meaning is generally uncontroverted. "Domicile" is not necessarily synonymous with "residence," and one can reside in one place but be domiciled in another. For adults, domicile is established by physical presence in a place in connection with a certain state of mind concerning one's intent to remain there. One acquires a "domicile of origin" at birth, and that domicile continues until a new one (a "domicile of choice") is acquired. Since most minors are legally incapable of forming the requisite intent to establish a domicile, their domicile is determined by that of their parents. In the case of an illegitimate child, that has traditionally meant the domicile of its mother. Under these principles, it is entirely logical that "[o]n occasion, a child's domicile of origin will be in a place where the child has never been."

It is undisputed in this case that the domicile of the mother (as well as the father) has been, at all relevant times, on the Choctaw Reservation. Thus, it is clear that at their birth the twin babies were also domiciled on the reservation, even though they themselves had never been there. The statement of the Supreme Court of Mississippi that "[a]t no point in time can it be said the twins . . . were domiciled within the territory set aside for the reservation," may be a correct statement of that State's law of domicile, but it is inconsistent with generally accepted doctrine in this country and cannot be what Congress had in mind when it used the term in the ICWA.

Nor can the result be any different simply because the twins were "voluntarily surrendered" by their mother. Tribal jurisdiction under § 1911(a) was not meant to be defeated by the actions of individual members of the tribe, for Congress was concerned not solely about the interests of Indian children and families, but also about the impact on the tribes themselves of the large numbers of Indian children adopted by non-Indians. The numerous prerogatives accorded the tribes through the ICWA's substantive provisions, must, accordingly, be seen as a means of protecting not only the interests of individual Indian children and families, but also of the tribes themselves.

. . .

These congressional objectives make clear that a rule of domicile that would permit individual Indian parents to defeat the ICWA's jurisdictional scheme is inconsistent with what Congress intended. The appellees in this case argue strenuously that the twins' mother went to great lengths to give birth off the reservation so that her children could be adopted by the Holyfields. But that was precisely part of Congress' concern. Permitting individual members of the tribe to avoid tribal exclusive jurisdiction by the simple expedient of giving birth off the reservation would, to a large extent, nullify the purpose the ICWA was intended to accomplish. The Supreme Court of Utah expressed this well in its scholarly and sensitive opinion in what has become a leading case on the ICWA:

> . . . The protection of this tribal interest is at the core of the ICWA, which recognizes that the tribe has an interest in the child which is distinct from but on a parity with the interest of the parents. This relationship between Indian tribes and Indian children domiciled on the reservation finds no parallel in other ethnic cultures found in the United States. It is a relationship that many non-Indians find difficult to understand and that non-Indian courts are slow to recognize. It is precisely in recognition of this relationship, however, that the ICWA designates the tribal court as the exclusive forum for the determination of custody and adoption matters for reservation-domiciled Indian children, and the preferred forum for nondomiciliary Indian children. . . . *In re Adoption of Halloway*, 732 P.2d 962, 969–970 (1986).

We agree with the Supreme Court of Utah that the law of domicile Congress used in the ICWA cannot be one that permits individual reservation-domiciled tribal members to defeat the tribe's exclusive jurisdiction by the simple expedient of giving birth and placing the child for adoption off the reservation. Since, for purposes of the ICWA, the twin babies in this case were domiciled on the reservation when adoption proceedings were begun, the Choctaw tribal court possessed exclusive jurisdiction pursuant to 25 U.S.C. § 1911(a). The Chancery Court of Harrison County was, accordingly, without jurisdiction to enter a decree of adoption; . . . its decree of January 28, 1986, must be vacated.

We are not unaware that over three years have passed since the twin babies were born and placed in the Holyfield home, and that a court deciding their fate today is not writing on a blank slate in the same way it would have in January 1986. Three years' development of family ties cannot be undone, and a separation at this point would doubtless cause considerable pain.

Whatever feelings we might have as to where the twins should live, however, it is not for us to decide that question. We have been asked to decide the legal question of *who* should make the custody determination concerning these children—not what the outcome of that determination should be. The law places that decision in the hands of the Choctaw tribal court. Had the mandate of the ICWA been followed in 1986, of course, much potential anguish might have been avoided, and in any case the law cannot be applied so as automatically to "reward those who obtain custody, whether lawfully or otherwise, and maintain it during any ensuing (and protracted) litigation." It is not ours to say whether the trauma that might result from removing these children from their adoptive family should outweigh the interest of the Tribe—and perhaps the children themselves—in having them raised as part of the Choctaw community. Rather, "we must defer to the experience, wisdom, and compassion of the [Choctaw] tribal courts to fashion an appropriate remedy."

The judgment of the Supreme Court of Mississippi is reversed, and the case is remanded for further proceedings not inconsistent with this opinion.

. . .

■ STEVENS, J., with whom THE CHIEF JUSTICE and KENNEDY, J. join, dissenting.

The parents of these twin babies unquestionably expressed their intention to have the state court exercise jurisdiction over them. J.B. gave birth to the twins at a hospital 200 miles from the reservation, even though a closer hospital was available. Both parents gave their written advance consent to the adoption and, when the adoption was later challenged by the Tribe, they reaffirmed their desire that the Holyfields adopt the two children. As the Mississippi Supreme Court found, "the parents went to some efforts to prevent the children from being placed on the reservation as the mother arranged for their birth and adoption in Gulfport Memorial Hospital, Harrison County, Mississippi." Indeed, Appellee Vivian Holyfield appears before us today, urging that she be allowed to retain custody of B.B. and G.B.

Because J.B.'s domicile is on the reservation and the children are eligible for membership in the Tribe, the Court today closes the state courthouse door to her. I agree with the Court that Congress intended a uniform federal law of domicile for the Indian Child Welfare Act of 1978 (ICWA), and that domicile should be defined with reference to the objectives of the congressional scheme. . . . I cannot agree, however, with the cramped definition the Court gives that term. To preclude parents domiciled on a reservation from deliberately invoking the adoption procedures of state court, the Court gives "domicile" a meaning that Congress could not have intended and distorts the delicate balance between individual rights and group rights recognized by the ICWA.

The ICWA was passed in 1978 in response to congressional findings that "an alarmingly high percentage of Indian families are broken up by the *removal,* often unwarranted, of their children from them by nontribal public and private agencies," . . . .

. . .

The Act gives Indian tribes certain rights, not to restrict the rights of parents of Indian children, but to complement and help effect them. The Indian tribe may petition to transfer an action in state court to the tribal court, but the Indian parent may veto the transfer. The Act provides for a tribal right of notice and intervention in involuntary proceedings but not in voluntary ones. Finally, the tribe may petition the court to set aside a parental termination action upon a showing that the provisions of the ICWA that are designed to protect parents and Indian children have been violated.

. . .

Although parents of Indian children are shielded from the exercise of state jurisdiction when they are temporarily off the reservation, the Act also reflects a recognition that allowing the tribe to defeat the parents' deliberate choice of jurisdiction would be conducive neither to the best interests of the child nor to the stability and security of Indian tribes and families. . . .

If J.B. and W.J. had established a domicile off the reservation, the state courts would have been required to give effect to their choice of jurisdiction; there should not be a different result when the parents have not changed their own domicile, but have expressed an unequivocal intent to establish a domicile for their children off the reservation. The law of abandonment, as enunciated by the Mississippi Supreme Court in this case, does not defeat, but serves the purposes, of the Act. An abandonment occurs when a parent deserts a child and places the child with another with an intent to relinquish all parental rights and obligations. . . .

When an Indian child is temporarily off the reservation, but has not been abandoned to a person off the reservation, the tribe has an interest in exclusive jurisdiction. . . . Similarly, when the child is abandoned by one parent to a person off the reservation, the tribe and the other parent domiciled on the reservation may still have an interest in the exercise of exclusive jurisdiction. That interest is protected by the rule that a child abandoned by one parent takes on the domicile of the other. But when an Indian child is deliberately abandoned by both parents to a person off the reservation, no purpose of the ICWA is served by closing the state courthouse door to them. The interests of the parents, the Indian child, and the tribe in preventing the unwarranted removal of Indian children from their families and from the reservation are protected by the Act's substantive and procedural provisions. In addition, if both parents have intentionally invoked the jurisdiction of the state court in an action involving a non-Indian, no interest in tribal self-governance is implicated.

. . .

NOTES

1.   *Whose autonomy?* Concerns about the child welfare system's removal of Native children from their parents' care prompted the enactment of the Indian Child Welfare Act of 1978. In agitating for the ICWA, Native advocates emphasized the American legal tradition of *parental* autonomy. However, as *Holyfield* makes clear, the ICWA provides for *tribal* autonomy rather than *parental* autonomy. Political scientist Sarah Song argues that in some cases tribal autonomy often means merely replicating the gender practices of the dominant culture. *See* SARAH SONG, JUSTICE, GENDER, AND THE POLITICS OF MULTICULTURALISM 132 (2007). In *Holyfield*, parental autonomy is directly in conflict with tribal autonomy. As Professor Solangel Maldonado observes, the mother in *Holyfield* went to great lengths to ensure that her twins could be adopted into the Holyfield family. Indeed, the mother went so far as to give birth to the twins off the reservation in the hope that doing so would exempt them from the ICWA's ambit. *See* Solangel Maldonado, *The Story of the Holyfield Twins:* Mississippi Band of Choctaw Indians v. Holyfield, *in* FAMILY LAW STORIES 113, 114 (Carol Sanger ed., 2008). With this critique in mind, is the ICWA the right solution to protect and promote Native-American families? When tribal and parental desires conflict, who should prevail? How should those disputes be resolved: by the state or federal government, or by the tribal government?

2.   *An African-American ICWA?* Statistics show that African-American children are more likely than white children to live among extended family. They are also more represented in the foster care system, a traditional pipeline for adoption. These realities, coupled with skepticism of transracial adoption, have led Professor Cynthia Hawkins-Leon to suggest that the ICWA's principles be applied to African-American children. Hawkins-Leon notes that the ICWA was animated by concerns regarding forced assimilation and cultural genocide—concerns that continue to undergird critiques of transracial adoption. Further, Hawkins-Leon argues that the history of abduction and enslavement of African peoples should entitle African-American children and their families to legal protection similar to that enjoyed by Native children and their families under the ICWA. Cynthia G. Hawkins-Leon, *The Indian Child Welfare Act and the African American Tribe: Facing the Adoption Crisis*, 36 BRANDEIS J. FAM. L. 201, 218 (1998). Is there cause to legally recognize the African-American community's interest in African-American children? How would this be accomplished? Would other groups be eligible for similar protections?

3.   *ICWA under attack?* In 2013, the U.S. Supreme Court granted certiorari in *Adoptive Couple v. Baby Girl*, 570 U.S. 637 (2013), a case concerning the ICWA. The case—known colloquially as the "Baby Veronica Case"—was only the second time that the Court has reviewed the ICWA (*Holyfield* was the first). In 2009, a South Carolina couple sought to adopt a child whose father,

Dusten Brown, was an enrolled member of the Cherokee Nation, and whose mother was Latina. Brown contested the adoption on the grounds that he was not properly notified in accordance with the ICWA. He was successful in the state courts, and in December 2011, was given custody of the child. The prospective adoptive parents appealed the state court ruling to the U.S. Supreme Court. There, in a 5–4 opinion, Justice Alito noted that, as a non-custodial father, Brown had no rights under the ICWA, and thus could not object to the adoption. Justice Sotomayor dissented, noting that even a non-custodial father-child relationship was a "family" for the purposes of ICWA and therefore efforts needed to be made to prevent its breakup. In failing to do so, she argued, the majority "turn[ed] [the law] upside down" and ignored the primary purpose of the ICWA. *See id.* at 2585 (Sotomayor, J., dissenting).

* * *

In recent years, LGBT persons have served as foster parents in the child welfare system. Despite their efforts as foster parents, however, gay men and women have encountered barriers to adoption. In the following selections, two courts consider challenges to Florida's ban on gay adoptions.

Lofton v. Secretary of the Department of Children and Family Services
358 F.3d 804 (11th Cir. 2004).

■ BIRCH, CIRCUIT JUDGE.

In this appeal, we decide the states' rights issue of whether Florida Statute § 63.042(3), which prevents adoption by practicing homosexuals, is constitutional as enacted by the Florida legislature and as subsequently enforced. The district court granted summary judgment to Florida over an equal protection and due process challenge by homosexual persons desiring to adopt. We affirm.

I.   BACKGROUND

A.   *The Challenged Florida Statute*

Since 1977, Florida's adoption law has contained a codified prohibition on adoption by any "homosexual" person. For purposes of this statute, Florida courts have defined the term "homosexual" as being "limited to applicants who are known to engage in current, voluntary homosexual activity," thus drawing "a distinction between homosexual orientation and homosexual activity." . . .

B.   *The Litigants*

Six plaintiffs-appellants bring this case. The first, Steven Lofton, is a registered pediatric nurse who has raised from infancy three Florida foster children, each of whom tested positive for HIV at birth. By all accounts, Lofton's efforts in caring for these children have been exemplary, and his story has been chronicled in dozens of news stories and editorials as well as on national television. We confine our discussion of that story to those facts relevant to the legal issues before us and properly before us in the record. John Doe, also named as a plaintiff-appellant in this litigation, was born on 29 April 1991. Testing positive at birth for HIV and cocaine, Doe immediately entered the Florida foster care system. Shortly thereafter, Children's Home Society, a private agency, placed Doe in foster care with Lofton, who has extensive experience treating HIV patients. At eighteen months, Doe sero-reverted and has since tested HIV negative. In September of 1994, Lofton filed an application to adopt Doe but refused to answer the application's inquiry about his sexual preference and also failed to disclose Roger Croteau, his cohabitating partner, as a member of his household. After Lofton refused requests from the Department of Children and Families ("DCF") to supply the missing information, his application was rejected pursuant to the homosexual adoption provision. . . . Two years later, in light of the length of Doe's stay in Lofton's household, DCF offered Lofton the compromise of becoming Doe's legal guardian. This arrangement would have allowed Doe to leave the foster care system and DCF supervision. However, because it would have cost Lofton over $300 a month in lost foster care subsidies and would have jeopardized Doe's Medicaid coverage, Lofton declined the guardianship option unless it was an interim stage toward adoption. Under Florida law, DCF could not accommodate this condition, and the present litigation ensued.

. . .

C. *Procedural History*

Appellants filed suit in the United States District Court for the Southern District of Florida and named as defendants Kathleen A. Kearney and Charles Auslander in their respective official capacities as DCF Secretary and DCF District Administrator for Dade and Monroe Counties. Their complaint alleged that the statute violates appellants' fundamental rights and the principles of equal protection. Jointly, appellants asked the district court to declare Fla. Stat. § 63.042(3) unconstitutional and to enjoin its enforcement. Appellants also sought class certification on behalf of two purported classes: all similarly situated adults and all similarly situated children. The district court denied the request for class certification and granted summary judgment in favor of the state on all counts, thereby upholding the statute. It is from this judgment that appellants now appeal.

. . .

II. DISCUSSION

. . .

B. *Florida's Adoption Scheme*

. . . Under Florida law, "adoption is not a right; it is a statutory privilege." . . .

In formulating its adoption policies and procedures, the State of Florida acts in the protective and provisional role of *in loco parentis* for those children who, because of various circumstances, have become wards of the state. . . . [I]n the adoption context, the state's overriding interest is the best interests of the children whom it is seeking to place with adoptive families. . . .

. . .

In short, a person who seeks to adopt is asking the state to conduct an examination into his or her background and to make a determination as to the best interests of a child in need of adoption. In doing so, the state's overriding interest is not providing individuals the opportunity to become parents, but rather identifying those individuals whom it deems most capable of parenting adoptive children and providing them with a secure family environment. . . .

C.   *Appellants' Due Process Challenges*

1.   Fundamental Right to "Family Integrity"

. . .

. . . [A]ppellants argue that, by prohibiting homosexual adoption, the state is refusing to recognize and protect constitutionally protected parent-child relationships between Lofton and Doe and between Houghton and Roe. Noting that the Supreme Court has identified "the interest of parents in the care, custody, and control of their children" as "perhaps the oldest of the fundamental liberty interests recognized by this Court," appellants argue that they are entitled to a similar constitutional liberty interest because they share deeply loving emotional bonds that are as close as those between a natural parent and child. . . .

. . . Historically, the Court's family- and parental-rights holdings have involved biological families. The Court itself has noted that "the usual understanding of 'family' implies biological relationships, and most decisions treating the relation between parent and child have stressed this element." . . .

. . .

. . . Here, we find that under Florida law neither a foster parent nor a legal guardian could have a justifiable expectation of a permanent relationship with his or her child free from state oversight or intervention. Under Florida law, foster care is designed to be a short-term arrangement while the state attempts to find a permanent adoptive home. . . Similarly, legal guardians in Florida are subject to ongoing judicial oversight, including the duty to file annual guardianship reports and annual review by the appointing court, and can be removed for a wide variety of reasons. In both cases, the state is not interfering with natural family units that exist independent of its power, but is regulating ones created by it. Lofton and Houghton entered into relationships to be a foster parent and legal guardian, respectively, with an implicit understanding that these relationships would not be immune from state oversight and would be permitted to continue only upon state approval. The emotional connections between Lofton and his foster child and between Houghton and his ward originate in arrangements that have been subject to state oversight from the outset. We conclude that Lofton, Doe, Houghton, and Roe could have no justifiable expectation of permanency in their relationships. Nor could Lofton and Houghton have developed expectations that they would be allowed to adopt, in light of the adoption provision itself.

. . .

. . . [W]e decline appellants' invitation to recognize a new fundamental right to family integrity for groups of individuals who have formed deeply loving and interdependent relationships. Under appellants' theory, any collection of individuals living together and enjoying strong emotional bonds could claim a right to legal recognition of their family unit, and every removal of a child from a long-term foster care placement—or simply the state's failure to give long-term foster parents the opportunity to adopt—would give rise to a constitutional claim. Such an expansion of the venerable right of parental control would well exceed our judicial mandate as a lower federal court.

2.   Fundamental Right to "Private Sexual Intimacy"

Laws that burden the exercise of a fundamental right require strict scrutiny and are sustained only if narrowly tailored to further a compelling government interest. Appellants argue that the Supreme Court's recent decision in *Lawrence v. Texas*, 539 U.S. 558 (2003), which struck down Texas's sodomy statute, identified a hitherto unarticulated fundamental right to private sexual intimacy. They contend that the Florida statute, by disallowing adoption to any individual who chooses to engage in homosexual conduct, impermissibly burdens the exercise of this right.

We begin with the threshold question of whether *Lawrence* identified a new fundamental right to private sexual intimacy. *Lawrence*'s holding was that substantive due process does not permit a state to impose a criminal prohibition on private consensual homosexual conduct. The effect of this holding was to establish a greater respect than previously existed in the law for the right of consenting adults to engage in private sexual conduct. Nowhere, however, did the Court characterize this right as "fundamental."

We are particularly hesitant to infer a new fundamental liberty interest from an opinion whose language and reasoning are inconsistent with standard fundamental-rights analysis. . . . Most significant . . . is the fact that the *Lawrence* Court never applied strict scrutiny, the proper standard when fundamental rights are implicated, but instead invalidated the Texas statute on rational-basis grounds, holding that it "furthers no legitimate state interest which can justify its intrusion into the personal and private life of the individual."

We conclude that it is a strained and ultimately incorrect reading of *Lawrence* to interpret it to announce a new fundamental right. . . .

Moreover, the holding of *Lawrence* does not control the present case. Apart from the shared homosexuality component, there are marked differences in the facts of the two cases. The Court itself stressed the limited factual situation it was addressing in *Lawrence*:

> The present case does not involve minors. It does not involve persons who might be injured or coerced or who are situated in relationships where consent might not easily be refused. It does not involve public conduct or prostitution. It does not involve whether the government must give formal recognition to any relationship that homosexual persons seek to enter. The case does involve two adults who, with full and mutual consent from each other, engaged in sexual practices common to a homosexual lifestyle.

Here, the involved actors are not only consenting adults, but minors as well. The relevant state action is not criminal prohibition, but grant of a statutory privilege. And the asserted liberty interest is not the negative right to engage in private conduct without facing criminal sanctions, but the affirmative right to receive official and public recognition. Hence, we conclude that the *Lawrence* decision cannot be extrapolated to create a right to adopt for homosexual persons.

. . .

NOTES

1.   *LGBT stereotypes and family law.* In an analysis of 191 child custody cases involving a gay or lesbian parent from the 1950s to the present, Clifford Rosky found that courts were likely to stereotype gay men as potentially dangerous carriers of HIV/AIDS and as child molesters. Relatedly, gay fathers and lesbian mothers were likely to be stereotyped as recruiters to the "homosexual lifestyle," and these stereotypes were more commonly invoked when the child at issue was a boy. Clifford J. Rosky, *Like Father, Like Son: Homosexuality, Parenthood, and the Gender of Homophobia*, 20 YALE J.L. & FEMINISM 257, 262–63 (2009). How might such stereotypes inform prohibitions on adoption like the one challenged (and upheld) in *Lofton*?

2.   *Same-sex parenting and adoption.* Historically, gay men and women were often allowed to foster children but not adopt them. Because adoptions by foster parents account for sixty percent of adoptions from the foster care system, the prohibition on gay adoption burdened children in foster care who were available for adoption, as well as LGBT persons who wished to adopt. It is estimated that, as of 2007, three percent of all foster children were living with gay and lesbian parents, and gay and lesbian parents had adopted four percent of all adopted children in the United States. *See* GARY J. GATES ET

AL., WILLIAMS INST. & URBAN INST., ADOPTION AND FOSTER CARE BY GAY AND LESBIAN PARENTS IN THE UNITED STATES 7, 15 (2007). Fifty percent of those LGBT individuals who adopted children adopted from the foster care system, and sixty percent of LGBT persons adopting children adopted transracially. DAVID M. BRODZINSKY, EVAN B. DONALDSON ADOPTION INST., EXPANDING RESOURCES FOR CHILDREN III: RESEARCH-BASED BEST PRACTICES IN ADOPTION BY GAYS AND LESBIANS 6 (2011).

Florida Department of Children & Families v. Adoption of X.X.G. and N.R.G.
45 So. 3d 79 (Fla. 2010).

■ COPE, J.

This is an appeal of a final judgment of adoption, under which F.G. became the adoptive father of two boys, X.X.G. and N.R.G. (collectively, "the children"). The trial court found, and all parties agree, that F.G. is a fit parent and that the adoption is in the best interest of the children.

The question in the case is whether the adoption should have been denied because F.G. is a homosexual. Under Florida law, a homosexual person is allowed to be a foster parent. F.G. has successfully served as a foster parent for the children since 2004. However, Florida law states, "No person eligible to adopt under this statute [the Florida Adoption Act] may adopt if that person is a homosexual." § 63.042(3), Fla. Stat. (2006). According to the judgment, "Florida is the only remaining state to expressly ban all gay adoptions without exception." Judge Cindy Lederman, after lengthy hearings, concluded that there is no rational basis for the statute. We agree and affirm the final judgment of adoption.

I

We begin with three observations. First, there does not appear to be any disagreement between the parties regarding the facts of the case. The parties entered into a lengthy list of stipulated facts. . . . Second, the parties agree that the father is a fit parent and that the adoption is in the best interest of the children. Third, the Department of Children and Families ["Department"] "agrees that gay people and heterosexuals make equally good parents."

. . .

Turning now to the facts of this case, in 2004 the Department removed X.X.G., then four years old, and N.R.G., then four months old, from their home based on allegations of abandonment and neglect. The Department contacted F.G., a licensed foster caregiver, and asked him to accept the children on a temporary basis until a more permanent placement could be found.[3]

---
[3]   F.G. was an experienced foster parent who had previously served as a foster parent for seven other children.

The children arrived with medical problems and other needs. X.X.G. arrived wearing a dirty adult-sized t-shirt and sneakers four sizes too small. Both children were suffering from ringworm and the four-month-old suffered from an untreated ear infection. X.X.G., the four-year-old, did not speak and his main concern was changing, feeding and caring for his baby brother.

The children thrived in F.G.'s household. "It is clear to this Court that [F.G.] is an exceptional parent to [X.X.G. and N.R.G.] who have healed in his care and are now thriving." Final Judgment at 37.

Because of the natural parents' neglect of the two children, the Department filed a petition for termination of the natural parents' parental rights. In 2006, that petition was granted and the natural parents' parental rights were terminated. X.X.G. and N.R.G. became available for adoption.

F.G. applied to adopt the children. The Center for Family and Child Enrichment, Inc. ("The Family Center"), a private nonprofit corporation, had been monitoring the two boys during foster care and was assigned the duty of evaluating F.G.'s ability to provide a satisfactory adoptive placement. The Family Center reported that F.G.'s home presented a suitable environment and that he met all the criteria required to adopt the two boys. The parties stipulated that F.G. provides a safe, healthy, stable and nurturing home for the children meeting their physical, emotional, social and educational needs. The Family Center recommended against the application, though, because F.G. is a homosexual and is prohibited from adopting children under subsection 63.042(3), Florida Statutes. The Department denied the application on that basis. The Department acknowledged that it would have approved the application if it had not been for the statute.

In 2007, F.G. filed a petition in the circuit court to adopt the children. F.G. asked the court to find subsection 63.042(3) unconstitutional because it violates his rights to equal protection, privacy, and due process. Independent counsel acting on behalf of the children asserted that the children's rights to equal protection and due process had also been violated. The Department filed a motion to dismiss, but the court only dismissed the privacy claim.

. . .

The trial court rendered a 53-page judgment declaring subsection 63.042(3) unconstitutional and granting the petition for adoption. The trial court found, among other things, that the statute violates the equal protection rights of F.G. and the children that are guaranteed by Article I, Section 2 of the Florida Constitution.

The Department has appealed.

. . .

The Department contends that the trial court erred by finding subsection 63.042(3) unconstitutional. The Department argues that there is a rational basis for the statute and that the trial court misinterpreted the law.

Under the Florida Constitution, each individual person has a right to equal protection of the laws. The constitutional provision states, in part:

> SECTION 2. Basic rights. All natural persons, female and male alike, are equal before the law and have inalienable rights, among which are the right to enjoy and defend life and liberty, to pursue happiness, to be rewarded for industry, and to acquire, possess and protect property. . . .

F.G. successfully argued in the trial court that the statute treated him unequally in violation of the constitutional provision because the statute creates an absolute prohibition on adoption by homosexual persons, while allowing all other persons—including those with criminal histories or histories of substance abuse—to be considered on a case-by-case basis.

. . .

Under the rational basis test, "a court must uphold a statute if the classification bears a rational relationship to a legitimate governmental objective." The classification must be "based *on a real difference* which is reasonably related to the subject and purpose of the regulation."

. . .

Given a total ban on adoption by homosexual persons, one might expect that this reflected a legislative judgment that homosexual persons are, as a group, unfit to be parents.

No one in this case has made, or even hinted at, any such argument. To the contrary, the parties agree "that gay people and heterosexuals make equally good parents." "The qualities that make a particular applicant the optimal match for a particular child could exist in a heterosexual or gay person."[8] Thus in this case no one attempts to justify the prohibition on homosexual adoption on any theory that homosexual persons are unfit to be parents.

Instead, the Department argues that there is a rational basis for the prohibition on homosexual adoption because children will have better role models, and face less discrimination, if they are placed in non-homosexual households, preferably with a husband and wife as the parents. But that is not what the statute does.

---

[8] There are, of course, homosexual persons who have their own biological children whom they raise. No one has suggested that such parents are unfit. As stated in the brief amicus curiae of the Family Law Section of The Florida Bar, "A parent's homosexuality is not a basis to terminate his or her parental rights. It is not a basis to deny that parent residential responsibility for his or her child or time-sharing with that child."

As previously stated, the statute specifically allows adoption by an unmarried adult. § 63.042(2)(b). Single parent adoption has been allowed under the Florida Adoption Act, enacted in 1973, and predecessor statutes. § 63.042(2)(b), Fla. Stat. (1973); ch. 73–159, § 4, Laws of Fla.; § 63.061, Fla. Stat. (1967); § 72.11, Fla. Stat. (1943). One-third of Florida's adoptions are by single adults. The Florida Statutes do not restrict adoption to heterosexual married couples.

The statute contains no prohibition on placing children with homosexual persons who are foster parents. The Department has placed children with homosexual foster parents in short-term placements, and long-term placements. The average length of stay in foster care before adoption is thirty months.

Florida also has a guardianship statute. Ch. 744, Fla. Stat. Homosexual persons "are not prohibited by any state law or regulation from being legal guardians of children in Florida." The Department has placed children in the legal guardianship of homosexual persons. This has included permanent guardianships in which the Department ceased supervision.

It is difficult to see any rational basis in utilizing homosexual persons as foster parents or guardians on a temporary or permanent basis, while imposing a blanket prohibition on adoption by those same persons. The Department contends, however, that the basis for this distinction can be found in the social science evidence.

VI.

The trial court heard extensive expert testimony in this case . . . [and concluded:] In addition to the [expert testimony], the body of research is broad; comparing children raised by lesbian couples to children raised by married heterosexual couples; children raised by lesbian parents from birth to children raised by heterosexual married couples from birth; children raised by single homosexuals to children raised by single heterosexuals; and children adopted by homosexual parents to those raised by homosexual biological parents, to name a few. *These reports and studies find that there are no differences in the parenting of homosexuals or the adjustment of their children.* These conclusions have been accepted, adopted and ratified by the American Psychological Association, the American Psychiatry Association, the American Pediatric Association, the American Academy of Pediatrics, the Child Welfare League of America and the National Association of Social Workers. As a result, based on the robust nature of the evidence available in the field, *this Court is satisfied that the issue is so far beyond dispute that it would be irrational to hold otherwise;* the best interests of children are not preserved by prohibiting homosexual adoption.

. . .This finding coincides with the Department's agreement "that gay people and heterosexuals make equally good parents."

. . .

VIII.

The Department argues that homosexuals should be barred from adopting "because the homes of homosexuals may be less stable and more prone to domestic violence." . . .

The Department says that there are disturbingly high domestic violence rates among same-sex couples. However, the Department selectively quotes the testimony by Dr. Peplau. In reality, Dr. Peplau testified that gay people or gay couples do not have higher rates of domestic violence than heterosexual couples. In the population-based study cited by Dr. Peplau, "the highest rate of domestic violence, defined as physical assault or rape . . . was 20 percent, and that was for women in heterosexual relationships being attacked by their male partner." The rates for all other groups was lower. This was consistent with a study by the Centers for Disease Control, which found that over an eighteen-year period, ninety-five percent of female homicide victims were women killed by a male domestic partner.

With regard to break-ups of relationships, the Department acknowledges Dr. Peplau's conclusion that unmarried heterosexual couples show break-up rates similar to homosexuals. The same predictors for divorce apply to evaluate the likelihood of break-up in unmarried or same-sex couples. The predictors include age at marriage, education, family income, race or ethnicity, and religion. Dr. Peplau concluded that sexual orientation is not the strongest predictor of break-up among all the different demographic characteristics. Other demographic factors "seem to have as strong or even stronger correlations with break-ups."

The Department claims that homosexual parents "support adolescent sexual activity and experimentations." The Department claims to draw this from the testimony of F.G.'s experts, but the experts did not say this. Dr. Lamb testified that research showed no difference between children of gay parents and heterosexual parents with respect to the age at which they initiated sexual activity.

Dr. Berlin testified that there is no evidence that the environment in which a child is raised, heterosexual or homosexual, would determine the sexual identity of the child who is raised in that environment. "[T]he overwhelming majority of homosexual individuals were raised in heterosexual households, suggesting that the environment in which they were raised in those instances certainly wasn't the determining factor of their development. . . ." Similarly, the overwhelming majority of those children raised in a gay environment turned out to be heterosexual, a point with which Department expert Schumm agreed.

The Department argues that placement of children with homosexuals presents a risk of discrimination and societal stigma. Here, too, the argument is misplaced. Florida already allows placement of children in foster care and guardianships with homosexual persons. This factor does not provide an argument for allowing such placements while prohibiting adoption. We reject the Department's remaining arguments for the same reason: they do not provide a reasonable basis for allowing homosexual foster parenting or guardianships while imposing a prohibition on adoption.

In conclusion on the equal protection issue, the legislature is allowed to make classifications when it enacts statutes. As a general proposition, a classification "will be upheld even if another classification or no classification might appear more reasonable." The classifications must, however, be "based on a *real* difference which is reasonably related to the subject and purpose of the regulation." "The reason for the equal protection clause was to assure that there would be no second class citizens."

Under Florida law, homosexual persons are allowed to serve as foster parents or guardians but are barred from being considered for adoptive parents. All other persons are eligible to be considered case-by-case to be adoptive parents, but not homosexual persons—even where, as here, the adoptive parent is a fit parent and the adoption is in the best interest of the children.

The Department has argued that evidence produced by its experts and F.G.'s experts supports a distinction wherein homosexual persons may serve as foster parents or guardians, but not adoptive parents. Respectfully, the portions of the record cited by the Department do not support the Department's position. We conclude that there is no rational basis for the statute. . . .

* * *

State laws limiting eligibility for adoption and foster care are not confined to those promulgated by state legislatures. In 2008, Arkansas voters passed a ballot initiative, Act 1 (also known as "The Arkansas Adoption and Foster Care Act of 2008"), which precluded unmarried couples from adopting or fostering children. The initiative was passed by fifty-seven percent of Arkansas voters.

Act 1, The Arkansas Adoption and Foster Care Act of 2008

BE IT ENACTED BY THE PEOPLE OF THE STATE OF ARKANSAS:

<u>Section 1: Adoption and foster care of minors.</u>

(a) A minor may not be adopted or placed in a foster home if the individual seeking to adopt or to serve as a foster parent is cohabiting with a sexual partner outside of a marriage which is valid under the constitution and laws of this state.

(b) The prohibition of this section applies equally to cohabiting opposite-sex and same-sex individuals.

Section 2: Guardianship of minors.

This act will not affect the guardianship of minors.

Section 3: Definition.

As used in this act, "minor" means an individual under the age of eighteen (18) years.

Section 4: Public policy.

The public policy of the state is to favor marriage, as defined by the constitution and laws of this state, over unmarried cohabitation with regard to adoption and foster care.

Section 5: Finding and declaration.

The people of Arkansas find and declare that it is in the best interest of children in need of adoption or foster care to be reared in homes in which adoptive or foster parents are not cohabiting outside of marriage.

. . .

NOTES

1.   *Adoptions, parenthood, and marriage.* It is worth noting that while Proposed Initiative Act No. 1 was aimed largely at precluding LGBT persons from adopting or serving as foster parents, the ballot initiative applied to *all* unmarried persons, whether gay or straight. With this in mind, was Act 1 primarily an anti-gay measure, or an effort to stymie all attempts to form non-traditional families?

2.   *Nonmarital families on the ballot.* In May 2012, North Carolina voters enacted Amendment 1, which amended the state constitution to preclude legal recognition of same-sex marriages. *See* Campbell Robertson, *North Carolina Voters Pass Same-Sex Marriage Ban*, N.Y. TIMES, May 9, 2012, at A15. Critically, the amendment also banned legal recognition of any other type of "domestic legal union," including civil unions and domestic partnerships. Are there connections between Act 1's limits on adoption and foster care participation and Amendment 1's limits on legal recognition of adult intimate relationships?

* * *

Efforts to curb the formation of non-traditional families have taken many forms. In the following selection, the Arkansas Supreme Court considers a ballot initiative that prohibited adoptions by persons "cohabitating outside of a valid marriage."

Arkansas Department of Human Services v. Cole

380 S.W.3d 429 (Ark. 2011).

■ BROWN, J.

Appellants, the Arkansas Department of Human Services and its Director and his successors, and the Arkansas Child Welfare Agency

Review Board and its Chairman and his successors, appeal an Order and Judgment ruling Initiated Act 1 unconstitutional as a violation of fundamental privacy rights implicit in the Arkansas Constitution. . . .

On November 4, 2008, a ballot initiative entitled "An Act Providing That an Individual Who is Cohabiting Outside of a Valid Marriage May Not Adopt or Be a Foster Parent of a Child Less Than Eighteen Years Old" was approved by fifty-seven percent of Arkansas voters. The ballot initiative is known as the Arkansas Adoption and Foster Care Act of 2008 or "Act 1." Act 1 went into effect on January 1, 2009, and is now codified at Arkansas Code Annotated sections 9–8–301 to –305.

Under Act 1, an individual is prohibited from adopting or serving as a foster parent if that individual is "cohabiting with a sexual partner outside of a marriage that is valid under the Arkansas Constitution and the laws of this state." Ark. Code Ann. § 9–8–304(a). This prohibition on adoption and foster parenting "applies equally to cohabiting opposite-sex and same-sex individuals." Act 1 further provides that the "public policy of the state is to favor marriage as defined by the constitution and laws of this state over unmarried cohabitation with regard to adoption and foster care." Act 1 also declares that "it is in the best interest of children in need of adoption or foster care to be reared in homes in which adoptive or foster parents are not cohabiting outside of marriage."

On December 30, 2008, appellees Sheila Cole and a group which includes unmarried adults who wish to foster or adopt children in Arkansas, adult parents who wish to direct the adoption of their biological children in the event of their incapacitation or death, and the biological children of those parents (collectively "Cole"), filed a complaint against the State of Arkansas, the Arkansas Attorney General, the Arkansas Department of Human Services (DHS) and its Director, and the Arkansas Child Welfare Agency Review Board (CWARB) and its Chairman (collectively "the State"). In her complaint, Cole pled . . . (10) Act 1 burdens intimate relationships and thus violates their due process, equal protection, and privacy rights under articles 8 and 21 of the Arkansas Constitution and Arkansas Code Annotated section 16–123–101; (11) the ballot title of the initiative was materially misleading in violation of amendment 7 of the Arkansas Constitution; (12) Act 1 is unconstitutionally vague in violation of the Due Process Clause of the United States Constitution and the Civil Rights Act; and (13) Act 1 is unconstitutionally vague in violation of the Due Process Clause of the Arkansas Constitution and Arkansas Code Annotated section 16–123–101.

. . .

After conducting discovery, Cole, the State, and FCAC moved for summary judgment. The circuit court conducted a hearing, and in an order dated April 16, 2010, the circuit court . . . declared Act 1 unconstitutional under the Arkansas Constitution. . . .

. . .

In *Jegley v. Picado*, this court considered a constitutional challenge to an Arkansas statute which criminalized acts of sodomy between homosexuals. The appellees in *Jegley* sought to have this sodomy statute declared unconstitutional insofar as it criminalized specific acts of private, consensual, sexual intimacy between persons of the same sex. The circuit court found the statute unconstitutional because Arkansas's fundamental right to privacy, which is implicit in the Arkansas Constitution, encompasses the right of people to engage in private, consensual, noncommercial, sexual conduct without the burden of government intrusions.

In considering the appellees' assertion in *Jegley* that the sodomy statute violated their right to privacy under the Arkansas Constitution, this court explored the rights granted to the citizens of Arkansas. We specifically found that no right to privacy is enumerated in the Arkansas Constitution. Nevertheless, we recognized that article 2, section 2 of the Arkansas Constitution does guarantee citizens certain inherent and inalienable rights, including the enjoyment of life and liberty and the pursuit of happiness, and section 15 guarantees the right of citizens to be secure in their own homes. We further noted that privacy is mentioned in more than eighty statutes enacted by the Arkansas General Assembly, thereby establishing "a public policy of the General Assembly supporting a right to privacy."

In light of the language contained in the Arkansas Constitution, our statutes and rules, and our jurisprudence, this court concluded "that Arkansas has a rich and compelling tradition of protecting individual privacy and that a fundamental right to privacy is implicit in the Arkansas Constitution." We went on to hold that "the fundamental right to privacy implicit in our law protects all private, consensual, noncommercial acts of sexual intimacy between adults." Accordingly, because the sodomy statute burdened certain sexual conduct between members of the same sex, this court found that it impinged on the fundamental right to privacy guaranteed to all citizens of Arkansas. Furthermore, because the sodomy statute burdened a fundamental right, this court concluded that the constitutionality of the statute must be analyzed under strict or heightened scrutiny. The State conceded that it could offer no compelling State interest sufficient to justify criminalizing acts of sodomy. We held that the sodomy statute was unconstitutional as applied to private, consensual, noncommercial, same-sex sodomy.

The State and FCAC now contend in the case at hand that, unlike in *Jegley,* a fundamental right is not at issue in the instant case because Act 1 only proscribes cohabitation. That argument, however, is not altogether correct. The express language of Act 1 reads that "[a] minor may not be adopted or placed in a foster home if the individual seeking to adopt or to serve as a foster parent is *cohabiting with a sexual partner* outside of a marriage that is valid under the Arkansas Constitution and the laws of this state." Ark.Code Ann. § 9–8–304(a) (emphasis added). Those words clearly make the ability to become an adoptive or foster parent conditioned on the would-be parent's sexual relationship. Hence, Act 1 does not merely prohibit cohabitation. Instead, the act expressly prohibits those persons who cohabit *with a sexual partner* from becoming adoptive or foster parents.

The State and FCAC do not really contest the fact that cohabiting adults in Arkansas have a fundamental right under *Jegley* to engage in consensual, sexual acts within the privacy of their homes without government intrusion. Their bone of contention is whether this right is indeed burdened by Act 1, and they point to the fact that adopting and fostering children are privileges bestowed by state statutes and not rights in themselves.

The problem with the argument mounted by the State and FCAC is that under Act 1 the exercise of one's fundamental right to engage in private, consensual sexual activity is conditioned on foregoing the privilege of adopting or fostering children. The choice imposed on cohabiting sexual partners, whether heterosexual or homosexual, is dramatic. They must chose [sic] either to lead a life of private, sexual intimacy with a partner without the opportunity to adopt or foster children or forego sexual cohabitation and, thereby, attain eligibility to adopt or foster.

The United States Supreme Court has rejected the concept that constitutional rights turn on whether a government benefit is characterized as a "right" or as a "privilege." *See, e.g., Shapiro v. Thompson,* 394 U.S. 618, 627 n. 6 (1969) (invalidating a law that conditioned receipt of welfare benefits on a residency requirement as an unconstitutional burden on right to interstate travel, and noting that "[t]his constitutional challenge cannot be answered by the argument that public assistance benefits are a 'privilege' and not a 'right.' "); *Sherbert v. Verner,* 374 U.S. 398, 404 (1963) ("[C]onstruction of the statute [cannot] be saved from constitutional infirmity on the ground that unemployment compensation benefits are not appellant's 'right' but merely a 'privilege.' It is too late in the day to doubt that the liberties of religion and expression may be infringed by the denial of or placing of conditions upon a benefit or privilege.").

. . .

. . . Act 1 exerts significant pressure on Cole to choose between exercising her fundamental right to engage in an intimate sexual relationship in the privacy of her home without being eligible to adopt or foster children, on the one hand, or refraining from exercising this fundamental right in order to be eligible to adopt or foster children, on the other. Similar to conditioning compensation benefits in *Sherbert* on foregoing religious rights, the condition placed on the privilege to foster or adopt thwarts the exercise of a fundamental right to sexual intimacy in the home free from government intrusion under the Arkansas Constitution.

The State and FCAC maintain that unlike the sodomy statute in *Jegley* and the DHS regulation preventing homosexuals from being foster parents in *Department of Human Services & Child Welfare Agency Review Board v. Howard*, 367 Ark. 55, 238 S.W.3d 1 (2006), Act 1 does not penalize anyone for having sexual relations. And yet, this is precisely what Act 1 does. It penalizes those couples who cohabit and engage in sexual relations by foreclosing their eligibility to have children, either through adoption or by means of foster care.

. . .

We hold that a fundamental right to privacy is at issue in this case and that, under the Arkansas Constitution, sexual cohabitors have the right to engage in private, consensual, noncommercial intimacy in the privacy of their homes. We further hold that this right is jeopardized by Act 1 which precludes all sexual cohabitors, without exception, from eligibility for parenthood, whether by means of adoption or foster care. We quickly note that in certain instances, such as in custody, visitation, or dependency-neglect matters, the State and the circuit courts of this state have a duty to protect the best interest of the child. . . .

III. *Cohabitation in Family Law Cases*

. . .

We strongly disagree with the State and FCAC's conclusion that if this court finds that the categorical ban on adoption and fostering for sexual cohabitors put in place by Act 1 violates an individual's fundamental right to sexual privacy in one's home, state courts and DHS will be prohibited henceforth from considering and enforcing non-cohabitation agreements and orders in deciding child-custody and visitation cases as well as dependency-neglect cases. That simply is not the case. The overriding concern in all of these situations is the best interest of the child. To arrive at what is in the child's best interest, the circuit courts and state agencies look at all the factors, including a non-cohabitation order if one exists, and make the best-interest determination on a case-by-case basis. Act 1's blanket ban provides for no such individualized consideration or case-by-case analysis in adoption or foster-care cases and makes the bald assumption that in *all* cases where adoption or foster care is the issue it is always against the best interest of the child to be placed in a home where an individual is cohabiting with a sexual partner outside of marriage.

But in addition to case-by-case analysis, there is another difference between cohabitation in the child-custody or dependency-neglect context and cohabiting sexual partners who wish to adopt or become foster parents. Third-party strangers who cohabit with a divorced parent are unknown in many cases to the circuit court and have not undergone the rigorous screening associated with foster care or adoption. By everyone's account, applicants for foster care must comply with a raft of DHS regulations that include criminal background checks, home studies, family histories, support systems, and the like. Adoption, under the auspices of the trial court, requires similar screening. Unsuitable and undesirable adoptive and foster parents are thereby weeded out in the screening process. The same does not pertain to a third-party stranger who cohabits with a divorced or single parent.

. . .

The State and FCAC rely on the United States Supreme Court decision in *Lyng v. Castillo*, 477 U.S. 635 (1986), for the proposition that a law does not impinge on a fundamental right to a constitutional degree unless the infringement is direct and substantial. They urge that Act 1's infringement on a non-fundamental liberty interest—the right to cohabit with a sexual partner—is not constitutionally significant because Act 1 does not prohibit Cole from residing with whomever she chooses. It merely prohibits her from being eligible to adopt or foster children, if she cohabits with a sexual partner. They conclude that this infringement, at most, is only indirect and insubstantial.

. . . We . . . disagree with the State and FCAC on the significance of the burden. The intrusion by the State into a couple's bedroom to enforce a sexual prohibition is exactly what was prohibited by this court in *Jegley v. Picado*. The same is at issue here under Act 1. State agencies must "police" couples seeking adoption or foster care to determine whether they are sexually involved in the event those couples represent that they are celibate. Compliance with Act 1 requires it. The identical threat of intrusion into the bedroom to examine sexual behavior as was involved in *Jegley* is involved in the instant case.

Thus, Act 1 directly and substantially burdens the privacy rights of "opposite-sex and same-sex individuals" who engage in private, consensual sexual conduct in the bedroom by foreclosing their eligibility to foster or adopt children, should they choose to cohabit with their sexual partner. The pressure on such couples to live apart, should they wish to foster or adopt children, is clearly significant. In *Jegley*, the burden perpetrated by the State was criminal prosecution for sodomy, although the act took place in the privacy of the bedroom. In the case before us, the burden dispensed by the State is either to remove the ability to foster or adopt children, should sexual partners live together, or to intrude into the bedroom to assure that cohabitors who adopt or foster are celibate. We conclude that, in this case as in *Jegley*, the burden is direct and substantial.

. . .

Because Act 1 burdens a fundamental right, the circuit court applied heightened scrutiny rather than a rational-basis review in its analysis. We defined heightened scrutiny in *Jegley:* "When a statute infringes upon a fundamental right, it cannot survive unless 'a compelling state interest is advanced by the statute and the statute is the least restrictive method available to carry out [the] state interest.' "

According to the circuit court's April 16, 2010 order in the instant case, when viewed under this heightened-scrutiny standard, "Initiated Act 1 is facially invalid because it casts an unreasonably broad net over more people than is needed to serve the State's compelling interest. It is not narrowly tailored to the least restrictive means necessary to serve the State's interest in determining what is in the best interest of the child."

. . .

We have held in this case that a fundamental right of privacy is at issue and that the burden imposed by the State is direct and substantial. We now hold, as an additional matter, that because of the direct and substantial burden on a fundamental right, the standard to be applied is heightened scrutiny and not a rational-basis standard. Using the heightened-scrutiny standard, because Act 1 exacts a categorical ban against all cohabiting couples engaged in sexual conduct, we hold that it is not narrowly tailored or the least restrictive means available to serve the State's compelling interest of protecting the best interest of the child.

In holding as we do, we first note that Act 1 says "[t]he people of Arkansas find and declare that it is in the best interest of children in need of adoption or foster care to be reared in homes in which adoptive or foster parents are not cohabiting outside of marriage." Ark. Code Ann. § 9–8–301. Despite this statement in Act 1, several of the State's and FCAC's own witnesses testified that they did not believe Act 1 promoted the welfare interests of the child by its categorical ban.

. . .

Furthermore, the concerns raised by the State and FCAC and used as justification for Act 1's categorical ban of cohabiting adults, such as (1) unmarried cohabiting relationships are less stable than married relationships, (2) they put children at a higher risk for domestic violence and abuse than married relationships, and (3) they have lower income levels, higher infidelity rates, and less social support than married relationships, can all be addressed by the individualized screening process currently in place in foster and adoption cases. The CWARB has Minimum Licensing Standards that require it to "select the home that is in the best interest of the child, the least restrictive possible, and is matched to the child's physical and emotional needs. The placement decision shall be based on an individualized assessment of the child's needs." Minimum Licensing Standards for Child Welfare Agencies § 200.1.

Prior to placing a child in foster care or in an adoptive home, DCFS conducts an individualized home assessment of each foster or adoptive family. The purpose of this home assessment process "is to educate prospective foster parents on the characteristics of children in out-of-home placement and evaluate their ability to meet those needs, as well as evaluate the applicants' compliance with the Minimum Licensing Standards and DFCS policy requirements for foster homes." The home assessment process is a mutual-selection process which involves several components including interviews, background checks, in-home consultation visits, preservice training, home studies, and ongoing consultations with prospective foster parents to ensure that all appropriate criteria related to compliance and quality are met. The home study, in particular, is conducted in order to evaluate the prospective foster family's dynamics, including the "motivation for wanting to foster, household composition, housing, safety hazards, income and expenses, health, education, childcare arrangements or plans, child rearing practices, daily schedules, social history, family activities, and support systems."

. . .

We conclude that the individualized assessments by DHS and our trial courts are effective in addressing issues such as relationship instability, abuse, lack of social support, and other factors that could potentially create a risk to the child or otherwise render the applicant unsuitable to be a foster or adoptive parent. These would be the least restrictive means for addressing the compelling state interest of protecting the welfare, safety, and best interest of Arkansas's children. By imposing a categorical ban on all persons who cohabit with a sexual partner, Act 1 removes the ability of the State and our courts to conduct these individualized assessments on these individuals, many of whom could qualify and be entirely suitable foster or adoptive parents. As a result, Act 1 fails to pass constitutional muster under a heightened-scrutiny analysis.

. . .

NOTES

1.   *In the shadow of sodomy.* In concluding that Act 1 violated the Arkansas Constitution, the court placed considerable reliance on an earlier precedent, *Jegley v. Picado*, 80 S.W.3d 332 (Ark. 2002). In an opinion that presaged *Lawrence v. Texas*, the Arkansas Supreme Court invalidated a state law criminalizing same-sex sodomy in *Jegley*. In doing so, the court held that "the fundamental right to privacy implicit in our law protects all private, consensual, noncommercial acts of sexual intimacy between adults." The criminal ban on same-sex sodomy, the court concluded, violated this right. In *Cole*, the court expanded upon *Jegley*'s logic, concluding that Act 1's ban on adoption by cohabiting sexual partners violated the right to privacy because it required cohabiting adults to either forego parenthood through adoption or make a dramatic change in their intimate lives.

2.   *Rights vs. privileges.* In *Cole*, the state argued that, unlike the criminal act challenged in *Jegley*, Act 1 did not implicate a fundamental right. Instead, the state simply reserved the privilege of adoption to those adults

willing to forego nonmarital cohabitation. The *Cole* court, however, noted that such a view turned on a fine distinction between rights and privileges. Relying on a line of cases involving "unconstitutional conditions," the *Cole* Court explained that, "Act 1 exerts significant pressure . . . to choose between exercising [a] fundamental right to engage in an intimate sexual relationship in the privacy of [the] home without being eligible to adopt or foster children, on the one hand, or refraining from exercising this fundamental right in order to be eligible to adopt or foster children, on the other." *Cole*, 380 S.W.3d at 437. Such conditions, the court concluded, were akin to "conditioning compensation benefits . . . on foregoing religious rights." *Id*. In so doing, Act 1 "thwart[ed] the exercise of a fundamental right to sexual intimacy in the home free from government intrusion under the Arkansas Constitution." *Id*.

G. ASSISTED REPRODUCTIVE TECHNOLOGY

As the preceding selections suggest, adoption has been a conduit to family formation for those who are unable or unwilling to have children through traditional biological means. Nevertheless, recent technological advances have created alternative ways for individuals to have children without the procedural complications of adoption. These technological changes have been particularly profound for LGBT families. However, this brave new world of reproductive technology is not without its own legal challenges, which the following materials explore.

Dorothy E. Roberts, *Privatization and Punishment in the New Era of Reprogenetics*
54 EMORY L.J. 1343 (2005).

. . . While welfare reform laws aim to deter women receiving public assistance from having even one additional healthy baby, largely unregulated fertility clinics regularly implant privileged women with multiple embryos, knowing the high risk multiple births pose for premature delivery and low birth weight. The public begrudges poor mothers a meager increase in benefits for one more child, but celebrates the birth of high-tech septuplets that require a fortune in publicly-supported hospital care.

. . . Rather than place these two categories of women in opposition, I explore how the privatization and punishment of reproduction links them together to avoid public responsibility for social inequities. Both population control programs and genetic selection technologies reinforce biological explanations for social problems and place reproductive duties on women that shift responsibility for improving social conditions away from the state. Reproductive health policies involving both categories of women play an important role in the neo-liberal state's transfer of services from the welfare state to the private realm of family and market.

Viewing new reproductive technologies as a form of private regulation of women's childbearing decisions complicates the choice-versus-regulation dichotomy that typically frames discussions of these technologies' costs and benefits.... I argue, however, that like the reproductive regulations imposed on less privileged women, use of these technologies has the potential to restrict women's control over reproduction while reinforcing social hierarchies that disadvantage women.... More importantly, recognizing the restrictive potential of reprogenetics supports greater state investment in eliminating the systemic inequities that make these technologies seem so attractive for addressing disability and illness. Rather than expand public surveillance and regulation of women's reproductive decisions, we should tackle the social conditions that limit women's options for bearing and raising healthy children who can flourish in society.

A. *Punishing Reproduction, Privatization, and Social Inequality*

The turn of the twenty-first century has ushered in an explosion of rhetoric and policies seeking to punish and regulate poor and minority women's reproductive decisions. Poor black women are especially vulnerable to proposals that punish childbearing....

. . .

These stereotypes of black female sexual and reproductive irresponsibility support welfare reform and law enforcement policies that severely regulate poor black women's sexual and child bearing decisions. Judges and legislators view poor black women as suitable subjects for harsh reproductive penalties because mainstream society does not view them as suitable mothers in the first place.

The rush to punish poor, substance-abusing mothers for their reproductive failures can be compared with the more temperate regulation of pregnant middle-class women who use risky pharmaceuticals to treat their mental health problems.... Th[e] attention to the depressed mother's perspective contrasts starkly with the typical disregard of the needs and humanity of poor black women who self-medicate with crack cocaine.

By identifying procreation as the cause of deplorable social conditions, reproductive punishments divert attention away from the need for social change....

. . .

This diversion of attention from social causes and solutions reinforces privatization, the hallmark of the neo-liberal state that pervades every aspect of public policy. In the wake of globalization, industrialized and developing states have sought to reduce the financial burden of social welfare programs while promoting the free market conditions conducive to capital accumulation.... Critical to this process of state restructuring is the transfer of services from the welfare state to the private realm of the market and family. At the same time, the state deliberately transforms its institutions to advance private sector interests in the market economy.

. . .

At the same time that the government has reduced support for families, there has been a parallel increase in state intervention in poor women's lives. Over the last two decades, the welfare system, prison system, and foster care system have clamped down on poor minority communities, especially inner-city black neighborhoods, thereby increasing many families' experience of insecurity and surveillance. Welfare is no longer a system of aid, but rather a system of behavior modification that attempts to regulate the sexual, marital, and childbearing decisions of poor unmarried mothers by placing conditions on the receipt of state assistance. The federal government encourages states to implement financial incentives that deter welfare recipients from having children and pressure them to get married.

The contraction of the U.S. welfare state, culminating in the 1996 federal welfare reform legislation, paralleled the expansion of prisons. . . . African-Americans experience a uniquely astronomical rate of imprisonment, and the social effects of imprisonment are concentrated in their communities.

. . .

The racial disparity in the child welfare system mirrors that of the prison system. Because child welfare policy relies heavily on the punitive removal of children from their homes, the largest group of the children awaiting adoption in the nation's public child welfare agencies is African-American. One year after Congress passed the welfare reform law, it enacted the Adoption and Safe Families Act of 1997 (ASFA). . . . Like welfare reform, ASFA looks to a private remedy—in this case adoption—rather than curtailing the flow of poor, minority children into foster care by providing needed resources to their families. Not only is there no guarantee that all the children awaiting adoption will be placed in adoptive homes, but adoption does nothing to address the needs of poor families who are most at risk of involvement in the child welfare system.

. . .

There is a correlation between punishment and privatization. The decrease in state responsibility for addressing poverty and social inequality has accompanied an increase in state intervention in the lives of poor-and low-income mothers, especially women of color. . . .

Private remedies for systemic inequality and punitive state regulation of the most disadvantaged communities are two sides of the same coin. Deliberate state policies and practices work affirmatively to increase economic insecurity of these communities while obscuring the state's responsibility for causing it or government's obligation to address it. Attributing social inequities to the childbearing of poor minority women and then using this attribution to justify the regulation of reproduction is a critical component of this punitive trend away from state support for families and communities.

B.   *Reproductive Genetics, Privatization, and Social Inequality*

At the other end of [the] reproductive caste system, new genetic technologies have generated greater surveillance of women, the ones primarily responsible for making the "right" genetic decisions. For decades, prenatal testing has provided the capacity to avoid bearing children with genetic disorders. Advances in reproductive-assisting technologies that create embryos in a laboratory have converged with advances in genetic testing to produce increasingly sophisticated methods to select for preferred genetic traits. Reproductive technologies like *in vitro* fertilization assist couples to have children who not only are genetically related to them but who are genetically advantaged. With preimplantation genetic diagnosis clinicians can diagnose early embryos for their chance of having over four hundred genetic conditions and implant only the ones that probably do not have these conditions. Sperm sorting allows couples to select the sex of their children with eighty-five percent accuracy. Some scientists predict that reproductive cloning and genetic engineering—actually enhancing the embryo's genetic makeup— will be developed in the near future. These cutting edge procedures that enable selection of embryos for their genetic traits are part of a new kind of reproduction-assisting science called "reprogenetics."

. . .

More generally, it is increasingly routine for pregnant woman [sic] to get prenatal diagnoses for certain genetic conditions such as Down syndrome or dwarfism. Many obstetricians provide these tests without much explanation or deliberation because they consider these screenings to be a normal part of treating their pregnant patients. The director of reproductive genetics at a large Detroit hospital reported that at least half of the women referred there with an abnormal amniocentesis result were "uncertain about why they even had the test." . . . [M]any pregnant women now view genetic testing as a requirement of responsible mothering.

. . .

Like the punishment of minority women's childbearing, reprogenetics is linked to the elimination of the welfare state and support for private remedies for illness and disease. Placing responsibility for ending health disparities on individual reproductive decisions can reduce the sense of societal obligation to address systemic inequities. Reliance on eradicating illness through genetics can divert attention and resources away from the social causes of disability and disease, as well as social norms that impair social participation by sick and disabled people. Some disability rights activists argue that genetic testing may privatize disability in the sense that availability of prenatal diagnosis for a disorder may discourage government funding for research and social services for people who have the disorder.

Genetic biotechnologies also shift responsibility for addressing disease from the government to the individual by suggesting that health disparities are a result of genetic variation rather than inequitable social structures and access to health care. . . .

. . .

Reprogenetics serves as a form of privatization that makes the individual the site of governance through the self-regulation of genetic risk. . . . The logic of reprogenetics could support the view that childhood illness and disability is the fault of mothers for not making the right genetic choices. Making the wrong genetic choices in turn disqualifies citizens from claiming public support. These women are, in effect, punished for their reproductive decision to have an ill or disabled child because they are denied the support they need to raise their child. . . .

Women bear the brunt of reprogenetics' contribution to the neoliberal restructuring of health care. Genetic technology introduces a new gendered division of reproductive labor and surveillance as women become "gatekeepers of new social order." . . .

Reprogenetics also makes eugenic thinking seem more acceptable. Sociologist Barbara Katz Rothman calls the marketing of prenatal diagnostic technologies a form of "micro-eugenics," eugenics focused on the individual . . . that values or disvalues specific characteristics believed to be inherited. Some disabilities rights advocates object to preimplantation or fetal diagnoses that lead to discarding embryos and fetuses predicted to have disabilities because they devalue people who have these disabilities, implying that they should never have been born. The quality of many disabled people's lives depends as much on social acceptance, access, and accommodation as on their physical capacities. Apart from avoiding certain fatal or severely disabling diseases . . . reprogenetics inscribes the perceived social advantage of having or not having certain abilities or traits associated with genes. . . . Unable to count on societal acceptance or support for children with disabilities . . . many women feel compelled to turn to genetic testing to ensure their children's welfare.

The role privileged women play in this integrated system of privatization and punishment is obscured by liberal notions of reproductive choice. Despite the potential for reprogenetics to diminish public health care and intensify regulation of women's reproductive decisions, its sponsors often defend the industry's immunity from state regulation in the name of women's reproductive freedom. . . . They see women's ability to select the traits of their children, including sex and other qualities unrelated to health, as an aspect of reproductive choice. Concerns about the implications for women, the disabled, racial minorities, and other disadvantaged groups are dismissed as threats to reproductive freedom.

. . .

Indeed, some clients of reprogenetics have even claimed moral superiority over women who have abortions for nonselective reasons. . . . On a website for a support group called "A Heart Breaking Choice" a mother who went to an abortion clinic complains, "I resented the fact that I had to be there with all these girls that did not want their babies." This perverse moral distinction between ordinary and so-called "medical abortion" reinforces the reproductive stratification that separates women whose childbearing is punished from those whose childbearing is technologically promoted by distinguishing even between the kinds of abortions they have.

. . .

[Prior to *Roe v. Wade*] [s]tates classified abortions as eugenic, therapeutic, or elective as a means of regulating women's access to them and limiting the potential of abortion to further women's emancipation. . . . The incorporation of eugenic values in arguments for women's reproductive freedom neglects the history of abortion regulation as well as the potential for reprogenetics to impose restrictive expectations on women to serve as genetic screeners of children.

Conclusion

The women at opposite ends of the reproductive hierarchy are part of an interlocking system of privatization and punishment. Both the punishment of marginalized women's childbearing and the promotion of reprogenetics for privileged women place reproductive duties on women that help to privatize remedies for illness and social inequities. Instead of joining together to contest the social forces that limit their reproductive freedom, including inadequate health care and the gendered division of household labor, these women are further separated by the exclusive genetic technology industry. . . . Both groups of women have an interest in halting this shift and in advocating for greater public investment in improving the social conditions that determine children's welfare.

* * *

Since the first in vitro fertilization (IVF) baby was born in 1978, assisted reproduction has become more common, and the methods more diverse. As assisted reproductive technologies have proliferated and become increasingly mainstream, they have prompted new questions regarding parenthood and the state's regulation of parents. As the following selections suggest, questions regarding who is a parent in assisted reproductive technology cases, and what features—biological, and/or social—will be used to confer parentage, have helped shape the modern legal understanding of parenthood and the relationship between parents and the state.

In re Baby M

537 A.2d 1227 (N.J. 1988).

■ WILENTZ, C.J.

In this matter the Court is asked to determine the validity of a contract that purports to provide a new way of bringing children into a family. For a fee of $10,000, a woman agrees to be artificially inseminated with the semen of another woman's husband; she is to conceive a child, carry it to term, and after its birth surrender it to the natural father and his wife. The intent of the contract is that the child's natural mother will thereafter be forever separated from her child. The wife is to adopt the child, and she and the natural father are to be regarded as its parents for all purposes. The contract providing for this is called a "surrogacy contract," the natural mother inappropriately called the "surrogate mother."

We invalidate the surrogacy contract because it conflicts with the law and public policy of this State. While we recognize the depth of the yearning of infertile couples to have their own children, we find the payment of money to a "surrogate" mother illegal, perhaps criminal, and potentially degrading to women. . . .

In February 1985, William Stern and Mary Beth Whitehead entered into a surrogacy contract. It recited that Stern's wife, Elizabeth, was infertile, that they wanted a child, and that Mrs. Whitehead was willing to provide that child as the mother with Mr. Stern as the father.

The contract provided that through artificial insemination using Mr. Stern's sperm, Mrs. Whitehead would become pregnant, carry the child to term, bear it, deliver it to the Sterns, and thereafter do whatever was necessary to terminate her maternal rights so that Mrs. Stern could thereafter adopt the child. Mrs. Whitehead's husband, Richard,[1] was also a party to the contract; Mrs. Stern was not. Mr. Whitehead promised to do all acts necessary to rebut the presumption of paternity under the Parentage Act. Although Mrs. Stern was not a party to the surrogacy agreement, the contract gave her sole custody of the child in the event of Mr. Stern's death. Mrs. Stern's status as a nonparty to the surrogate parenting agreement presumably was to avoid the application of the baby-selling statute to this arrangement.

Mr. Stern, on his part, agreed to attempt the artificial insemination and to pay Mrs. Whitehead $10,000 after the child's birth, on its delivery to him. In a separate contract, Mr. Stern agreed to pay $7,500 to the Infertility Center of New York ("ICNY"). The Center's advertising

---

[1] Subsequent to the trial court proceedings, Mr. and Mrs. Whitehead were divorced, and soon thereafter Mrs. Whitehead remarried. Nevertheless, in the course of this opinion we will make reference almost exclusively to the facts as they existed at the time of trial, the facts on which the decision we now review was reached. We note moreover that Mr. Whitehead remains a party to this dispute. For these reasons, we continue to refer to appellants as Mr. and Mrs. Whitehead.

campaigns solicit surrogate mothers and encourage infertile couples to consider surrogacy. ICNY arranged for the surrogacy contract by bringing the parties together, explaining the process to them, furnishing the contractual form, and providing legal counsel.

The history of the parties' involvement in this arrangement suggests their good faith. William and Elizabeth Stern were married in July 1974, having met at the University of Michigan, where both were Ph.D. candidates. Due to financial considerations and Mrs. Stern's pursuit of a medical degree and residency, they decided to defer starting a family until 1981. Before then, however, Mrs. Stern learned that she might have multiple sclerosis and that the disease in some cases renders pregnancy a serious health risk. Her anxiety appears to have exceeded the actual risk, which current medical authorities assess as minimal. Nonetheless that anxiety was evidently quite real, Mrs. Stern fearing that pregnancy might precipitate blindness, paraplegia, or other forms of debilitation. Based on the perceived risk, the Sterns decided to forego having their own children. The decision had special significance for Mr. Stern. Most of his family had been destroyed in the Holocaust. As the family's only survivor, he very much wanted to continue his bloodline.

Initially the Sterns considered adoption, but were discouraged by the substantial delay apparently involved and by the potential problem they saw arising from their age and their differing religious backgrounds. They were most eager for some other means to start a family.

The paths of Mrs. Whitehead and the Sterns to surrogacy were similar. Both responded to advertising by ICNY. The Sterns' response, following their inquiries into adoption, was the result of their long-standing decision to have a child. Mrs. Whitehead's response apparently resulted from her sympathy with family members and others who could have no children (she stated that she wanted to give another couple the "gift of life"); she also wanted the $10,000 to help her family.

Both parties, undoubtedly because of their own self-interest, were less sensitive to the implications of the transaction than they might otherwise have been. Mrs. Whitehead, for instance, appears not to have been concerned about whether the Sterns would make good parents for her child; the Sterns, on their part, while conscious of the obvious possibility that surrendering the child might cause grief to Mrs. Whitehead, overcame their qualms because of their desire for a child. At any rate, both the Sterns and Mrs. Whitehead were committed to the arrangement; both thought it right and constructive.

Mrs. Whitehead had reached her decision concerning surrogacy before the Sterns, and had actually been involved as a potential surrogate mother with another couple. After numerous unsuccessful artificial inseminations, that effort was abandoned. Thereafter, the Sterns learned of the Infertility Center, the possibilities of surrogacy, and of Mary Beth Whitehead. The two couples met to discuss the surrogacy arrangement and decided to go forward. On February 6, 1985, Mr. Stern and Mr. and

Mrs. Whitehead executed the surrogate parenting agreement. After several artificial inseminations over a period of months, Mrs. Whitehead became pregnant. The pregnancy was uneventful and on March 27, 1986, Baby M was born.

. . . Her birth certificate indicated her name to be Sara Elizabeth Whitehead and her father to be Richard Whitehead. In accordance with Mrs. Whitehead's request, the Sterns visited the hospital unobtrusively to see the newborn child.

Mrs. Whitehead realized, almost from the moment of birth, that she could not part with this child. She had felt a bond with it even during pregnancy. Some indication of the attachment was conveyed to the Sterns at the hospital when they told Mrs. Whitehead what they were going to name the baby. She apparently broke into tears and indicated that she did not know if she could give up the child. She talked about how the baby looked like her other daughter, and made it clear that she was experiencing great difficulty with the decision.

Nonetheless, Mrs. Whitehead was, for the moment, true to her word. Despite powerful inclinations to the contrary, she turned her child over to the Sterns on March 30 at the Whiteheads' home.

The Sterns were thrilled with their new child. They had planned extensively for its arrival, far beyond the practical furnishing of a room for her. It was a time of joyful celebration—not just for them but for their friends as well. The Sterns looked forward to raising their daughter, whom they named Melissa. While aware by then that Mrs. Whitehead was undergoing an emotional crisis, they were as yet not cognizant of the depth of that crisis and its implications for their newly-enlarged family.

Later in the evening of March 30, Mrs. Whitehead became deeply disturbed, disconsolate, stricken with unbearable sadness. She had to have her child. She could not eat, sleep, or concentrate on anything other than her need for her baby. The next day she went to the Sterns' home and told them how much she was suffering.

The depth of Mrs. Whitehead's despair surprised and frightened the Sterns. She told them that she could not live without her baby, that she must have her, even if only for one week, that thereafter she would surrender her child. The Sterns, concerned that Mrs. Whitehead might indeed commit suicide, not wanting under any circumstances to risk that, and in any event believing that Mrs. Whitehead would keep her word, turned the child over to her. It was not until four months later, after a series of attempts to regain possession of the child, that Melissa was returned to the Sterns, having been forcibly removed from the home where she was then living with Mr. and Mrs. Whitehead, the home in Florida owned by Mary Beth Whitehead's parents.

The struggle over Baby M began when it became apparent that Mrs. Whitehead could not return the child to Mr. Stern. Due to Mrs. Whitehead's refusal to relinquish the baby, Mr. Stern filed a complaint seeking enforcement of the surrogacy contract. He alleged, accurately, that Mrs. Whitehead had not only refused to comply with the surrogacy contract but had threatened to flee from New Jersey with the child in order to avoid even the possibility of his obtaining custody. The court papers asserted that if Mrs. Whitehead were to be given notice of the application for an order requiring her to relinquish custody, she would, prior to the hearing, leave the state with the baby. And that is precisely what she did. After the order was entered, *ex parte,* the process server, aided by the police, in the presence of the Sterns, entered Mrs. Whitehead's home to execute the order. Mr. Whitehead fled with the child, who had been handed to him through a window while those who came to enforce the order were thrown off balance by a dispute over the child's current name.

The Whiteheads immediately fled to Florida with Baby M. . . .

Eventually the Sterns discovered where the Whiteheads were staying, commenced supplementary proceedings in Florida, and obtained an order requiring the Whiteheads to turn over the child. Police in Florida enforced the order, forcibly removing the child from her grandparents' home. She was soon thereafter brought to New Jersey and turned over to the Sterns. The prior order of the court, issued *ex parte,* awarding custody of the child to the Sterns *pendente lite,* was reaffirmed by the trial court after consideration of the certified representations of the parties (both represented by counsel) concerning the unusual sequence of events that had unfolded. Pending final judgment, Mrs. Whitehead was awarded limited visitation with Baby M.

The Sterns' complaint, in addition to seeking possession and ultimately custody of the child, sought enforcement of the surrogacy contract. Pursuant to the contract, it asked that the child be permanently placed in their custody, that Mrs. Whitehead's parental rights be terminated, and that Mrs. Stern be allowed to adopt the child, *i.e.,* that, for all purposes, Melissa become the Sterns' child.

The trial took thirty-two days over a period of more than two months. . . . [The trial court] held that the surrogacy contract was valid; ordered that Mrs. Whitehead's parental rights be terminated and that sole custody of the child be granted to Mr. Stern; and, after hearing brief testimony from Mrs. Stern, immediately entered an order allowing the adoption of Melissa by Mrs. Stern, all in accordance with the surrogacy contract. Pending the outcome of the appeal, we granted a continuation of visitation to Mrs. Whitehead, although slightly more limited than the visitation allowed during the trial.

. . .

Considerable care was taken in this case to structure the surrogacy arrangement so as not to violate this prohibition. The arrangement was structured as follows: the adopting parent, Mrs. Stern, was not a party to the surrogacy contract; the money paid to Mrs. Whitehead was stated to be for her services—not for the adoption; the sole purpose of the contract was stated as being that "of giving a child to William Stern, its natural and biological father;" the money was purported to be "compensation for services and expenses and in no way . . . a fee for termination of parental rights or a payment in exchange for consent to surrender a child for adoption"; the fee to the Infertility Center ($7,500) was stated to be for legal representation, advice, administrative work, and other "services." Nevertheless, it seems clear that the money was paid and accepted in connection with an adoption.

. . . The payment of the $10,000 occurs only on surrender of custody of the child and "completion of the duties and obligations" of Mrs. Whitehead, including termination of her parental rights to facilitate adoption by Mrs. Stern. As for the contention that the Sterns are paying only for services and not for an adoption, we need note only that they would pay nothing in the event the child died before the fourth month of pregnancy, and only $1,000 if the child were stillborn, even though the "services" had been fully rendered. Additionally, one of Mrs. Whitehead's estimated costs, to be assumed by Mr. Stern, was an "Adoption Fee," presumably for Mrs. Whitehead's incidental costs in connection with the adoption.

Mr. Stern knew he was paying for the adoption of a child; Mrs. Whitehead knew she was accepting money so that a child might be adopted; the Infertility Center knew that it was being paid for assisting in the adoption of a child. The actions of all three worked to frustrate the goals of the statute. It strains credulity to claim that these arrangements, touted by those in the surrogacy business as an attractive alternative to the usual route leading to an adoption, really amount to something other than a private placement adoption for money.

. . . The evils inherent in baby-bartering are loathsome for a myriad of reasons. The child is sold without regard for whether the purchasers will be suitable parents. The natural mother does not receive the benefit of counseling and guidance to assist her in making a decision that may affect her for a lifetime. In fact, the monetary incentive to sell her child may, depending on her financial circumstances, make her decision less voluntary. . . .

. . . The negative consequences of baby-buying are potentially present in the surrogacy context, especially the potential for placing and adopting a child without regard to the interest of the child or the natural mother.

The termination of Mrs. Whitehead's parental rights, called for by the surrogacy contract and actually ordered by the court, fails to comply with the stringent requirements of New Jersey law. Our law, recognizing the finality of any termination of parental rights, provides for such termination only where there has been a voluntary surrender of a child to an approved agency or to the Division of Youth and Family Services ("DYFS"), accompanied by a formal document acknowledging termination of parental rights, or where there has been a showing of parental abandonment or unfitness. A termination may ordinarily take one of three forms: an action by an approved agency, an action by DYFS, or an action in connection with a private placement adoption. The three are governed by separate statutes, but the standards for termination are substantially the same, except that whereas a written surrender is effective when made to an approved agency or to DYFS, there is no provision for it in the private placement context.

. . .

Our statutes, and the cases interpreting them, leave no doubt that where there has been no written surrender to an approved agency or to DYFS, termination of parental rights will not be granted in this state absent a very strong showing of abandonment or neglect. That showing is required in every context in which termination of parental rights is sought, be it an action by an approved agency, an action by DYFS, or a private placement adoption proceeding, even where the petitioning adoptive parent is, as here, a stepparent. . . .

In this case a termination of parental rights was obtained not by proving the statutory prerequisites but by claiming the benefit of contractual provisions. From all that has been stated above, it is clear that a contractual agreement to abandon one's parental rights, or not to contest a termination action, will not be enforced in our courts. The Legislature would not have so carefully, so consistently, and so substantially restricted termination of parental rights if it had intended to allow termination to be achieved by one short sentence in a contract.

Since the termination was invalid, it follows, as noted above, that adoption of Melissa by Mrs. Stern could not properly be granted.

. . .

The surrogacy contract guarantees permanent separation of the child from one of its natural parents. Our policy, however, has long been that to the extent possible, children should remain with and be brought up by both of their natural parents. . . . This is not simply some theoretical ideal that in practice has no meaning. The impact of failure to follow that policy is nowhere better shown than in the results of this surrogacy contract. A child, instead of starting off its life with as much peace and security as possible, finds itself immediately in a tug-of-war between contending mother and father.

The surrogacy contract violates the policy of this State that the rights of natural parents are equal concerning their child, the father's right no greater than the mother's. . . . The whole purpose and effect of the surrogacy contract was to give the father the exclusive right to the child by destroying the rights of the mother.

The policies expressed in our comprehensive laws governing consent to the surrender of a child, stand in stark contrast to the surrogacy contract and what it implies. Here there is no counseling, independent or otherwise, of the natural mother, no evaluation, no warning.

The only legal advice Mary Beth Whitehead received regarding the surrogacy contract was provided in connection with the contract that she previously entered into with another couple. Mrs. Whitehead's lawyer was referred to her by the Infertility Center, with which he had an agreement to act as counsel for surrogate candidates. His services consisted of spending one hour going through the contract with the Whiteheads, section by section, and answering their questions. Mrs. Whitehead received no further legal advice prior to signing the contract with the Sterns.

Mrs. Whitehead was examined and psychologically evaluated, but if it was for her benefit, the record does not disclose that fact. The Sterns regarded the evaluation as important, particularly in connection with the question of whether she would change her mind. Yet they never asked to see it, and were content with the assumption that the Infertility Center had made an evaluation and had concluded that there was no danger that the surrogate mother would change her mind. From Mrs. Whitehead's point of view, all that she learned from the evaluation was that "she had passed." It is apparent that the profit motive got the better of the Infertility Center. Although the evaluation was made, it was not put to any use, and understandably so, for the psychologist warned that Mrs. Whitehead demonstrated certain traits that might make surrender of the child difficult and that there should be further inquiry into this issue in connection with her surrogacy. To inquire further, however, might have jeopardized the Infertility Center's fee. The record indicates that neither Mrs. Whitehead nor the Sterns were ever told of this fact, a fact that might have ended their surrogacy arrangement.

Under the contract, the natural mother is irrevocably committed before she knows the strength of her bond with her child. She never makes a totally voluntary, informed decision, for quite clearly any decision prior to the baby's birth is, in the most important sense, uninformed, and any decision after that, compelled by a pre-existing contractual commitment, the threat of a lawsuit, and the inducement of a $10,000 payment, is less than totally voluntary. Her interests are of little concern to those who controlled this transaction.

Although the interest of the natural father and adoptive mother is certainly the predominant interest, realistically the *only* interest served, even they are left with less than what public policy requires. They know little about the natural mother, her genetic makeup, and her psychological and medical history. Moreover, not even a superficial attempt is made to determine their awareness of their responsibilities as parents.

Worst of all, however, is the contract's total disregard of the best interests of the child. There is not the slightest suggestion that any inquiry will be made at any time to determine the fitness of the Sterns as custodial parents, of Mrs. Stern as an adoptive parent, their superiority to Mrs. Whitehead, or the effect on the child of not living with her natural mother.

This is the sale of a child, or, at the very least, the sale of a mother's right to her child, the only mitigating factor being that one of the purchasers is the father. Almost every evil that prompted the prohibition on the payment of money in connection with adoptions exists here.

The differences between an adoption and a surrogacy contract should be noted, since it is asserted that the use of money in connection with surrogacy does not pose the risks found where money buys an adoption.

First, and perhaps most important, all parties concede that it is unlikely that surrogacy will survive without money. Despite the alleged selfless motivation of surrogate mothers, if there is no payment, there will be no surrogates, or very few. That conclusion contrasts with adoption; for obvious reasons, there remains a steady supply, albeit insufficient, despite the prohibitions against payment. The adoption itself, relieving the natural mother of the financial burden of supporting an infant, is in some sense the equivalent of payment.

Second, the use of money in adoptions does not *produce* the problem—conception occurs, and usually the birth itself, before illicit funds are offered. With surrogacy, the "problem," if one views it as such, consisting of the purchase of a woman's procreative capacity, at the risk of her life, is caused by and originates with the offer of money.

Third, with the law prohibiting the use of money in connection with adoptions, the built-in financial pressure of the unwanted pregnancy and the consequent support obligation do not lead the mother to the highest paying, ill-suited, adoptive parents. She is just as well-off surrendering the child to an approved agency. In surrogacy, the highest bidders will presumably become the adoptive parents regardless of suitability, so long as payment of money is permitted.

Fourth, the mother's consent to surrender her child in adoptions is revocable, even after surrender of the child, unless it be to an approved agency, where by regulation there are protections against an ill-advised surrender. In surrogacy, consent occurs so early that no amount of advice would satisfy the potential mother's need, yet the consent is irrevocable.

The main difference, that the unwanted pregnancy is unintended while the situation of the surrogate mother is voluntary and intended, is really not significant. Initially, it produces stronger reactions of sympathy for the mother whose pregnancy was unwanted than for the surrogate mother, who "went into this with her eyes wide open." On reflection, however, it appears that the essential evil is the same, taking advantage of a woman's circumstances (the unwanted pregnancy or the need for money) in order to take away her child, the difference being one of degree.

In the scheme contemplated by the surrogacy contract in this case, a middle man, propelled by profit, promotes the sale. Whatever idealism may have motivated any of the participants, the profit motive predominates, permeates, and ultimately governs the transaction. The demand for children is great and the supply small. The availability of contraception, abortion, and the greater willingness of single mothers to bring up their children has led to a shortage of babies offered for adoption. The situation is ripe for the entry of the middleman who will bring some equilibrium into the market by increasing the supply through the use of money.

Intimated, but disputed, is the assertion that surrogacy will be used for the benefit of the rich at the expense of the poor. In response it is noted that the Sterns are not rich and the Whiteheads not poor. Nevertheless, it is clear to us that it is unlikely that surrogate mothers will be as proportionately numerous among those women in the top twenty percent income bracket as among those in the bottom twenty percent. Put differently, we doubt that infertile couples in the low-income bracket will find upper income surrogates.

In any event, even in this case one should not pretend that disparate wealth does not play a part simply because the contrast is not the dramatic "rich versus poor." At the time of trial, the Whiteheads' net assets were probably negative—Mrs. Whitehead's own sister was foreclosing on a second mortgage. Their income derived from Mr. Whitehead's labors. Mrs. Whitehead is a homemaker, having previously held part-time jobs. The Sterns are both professionals, she a medical doctor, he a biochemist. Their combined income when both were working was about $89,500 a year and their assets sufficient to pay for the surrogacy contract arrangements.

The point is made that Mrs. Whitehead *agreed* to the surrogacy arrangement, supposedly fully understanding the consequences. Putting aside the issue of how compelling her need for money may have been, and how significant her understanding of the consequences, we suggest that her consent is irrelevant. There are, in a civilized society, some things that money cannot buy. In America, we decided long ago that merely because conduct purchased by money was "voluntary" did not mean that it was good or beyond regulation and prohibition. Employers can no longer buy labor at the lowest price they can bargain for, even though that labor is "voluntary," or buy women's labor for less money than paid to men for the same job, or purchase the agreement of children to perform oppressive labor, or purchase the agreement of workers to subject themselves to unsafe or unhealthful working conditions. There are, in short, values that society deems more important than granting to wealth whatever it can buy, be it labor, love, or life. Whether this principle recommends prohibition of surrogacy, which presumably sometimes results in great satisfaction to all of the parties, is not for us to say. We note here only that, under existing law, the fact that Mrs. Whitehead "agreed" to the arrangement is not dispositive.

The long-term effects of surrogacy contracts are not known, but feared—the impact on the child who learns her life was bought, that she is the offspring of someone who gave birth to her only to obtain money; the impact on the natural mother as the full weight of her isolation is felt along with the full reality of the sale of her body and her child; the impact on the natural father and adoptive mother once they realize the consequences of their conduct. Literature in related areas suggests these are substantial considerations, although, given the newness of surrogacy, there is little information.

The surrogacy contract is based on[ ] principles that are directly contrary to the objectives of our laws. It guarantees the separation of a child from its mother; it looks to adoption regardless of suitability; it totally ignores the child; it takes the child from the mother regardless of her wishes and her maternal fitness; and it does all of this, it accomplishes all of its goals, through the use of money.

Beyond that is the potential degradation of some women that may result from this arrangement. In many cases, of course, surrogacy may bring satisfaction, not only to the infertile couple, but to the surrogate mother herself. The fact, however, that many women may not perceive surrogacy negatively but rather see it as an opportunity does not diminish its potential for devastation to other women.

In sum, the harmful consequences of this surrogacy arrangement appear to us all too palpable. In New Jersey the surrogate mother's agreement to sell her child is void. Its irrevocability infects the entire contract, as does the money that purports to buy it.

. . .

The right to procreate, as protected by the Constitution, has been ruled on directly only once by the United States Supreme Court. *See Skinner v. Oklahoma*, 316 U.S. 535 (1942) (forced sterilization of habitual criminals violates equal protection clause of fourteenth amendment). Although *Griswold v. Connecticut*, 381 U.S. 479 (1965), is obviously of a similar class, strictly speaking it involves the right *not* to procreate. The right to procreate very simply is the right to have natural children, whether through sexual intercourse or artificial insemination. It is no more than that. Mr. Stern has not been deprived of that right. Through artificial insemination of Mrs. Whitehead, Baby M is his child. The custody, care, companionship, and nurturing that follow birth are not parts of the right to procreation; they are rights that may also be constitutionally protected, but that involve many considerations other than the right of procreation. To assert that Mr. Stern's right of procreation gives him the right to the custody of Baby M would be to assert that Mrs. Whitehead's right of procreation does *not* give her the right to the custody of Baby M; it would be to assert that the constitutional right of procreation includes within it a constitutionally protected contractual right to destroy someone else's right of procreation.

. . .

Mr. Stern also contends that he has been denied equal protection of the laws by the State's statute granting full parental rights to a husband in relation to the child produced, with his consent, by the union of his wife with a sperm donor. The claim really is that of Mrs. Stern. It is that she is in precisely the same position as the husband in the statute: she is presumably infertile, as is the husband in the statute; her spouse by agreement with a third party procreates with the understanding that the child will be the couple's child. The alleged unequal protection is that the understanding is honored in the statute when the husband is the infertile party, but no similar understanding is honored when it is the wife who is infertile.

It is quite obvious that the situations are not parallel. A sperm donor simply cannot be equated with a surrogate mother. The State has more than a sufficient basis to distinguish the two situations—even if the only difference is between the time it takes to provide sperm for artificial insemination and the time invested in a nine-month pregnancy—so as to justify automatically divesting the sperm donor of his parental rights without automatically divesting a surrogate mother. Some basis for an equal protection argument might exist if Mary Beth Whitehead had contributed her egg to be implanted, fertilized or otherwise, in Mrs. Stern, resulting in the latter's pregnancy. That is not the case here, however.

Mrs. Whitehead, on the other hand, asserts a claim that falls within the scope of a recognized fundamental interest protected by the Constitution. As a mother, she claims the right to the companionship of her child. This is a fundamental interest, constitutionally protected. Furthermore, it was taken away from her by the action of the court below. Whether that action under these circumstances would constitute a constitutional deprivation, however, we need not and do not decide. By virtue of our decision Mrs. Whitehead's constitutional complaint—that her parental rights have been unconstitutionally terminated—is moot. We have decided that both the statutes and public policy of this state require that that termination be voided and that her parental rights be restored. It therefore becomes unnecessary to decide whether that same result would be required by virtue of the federal or state Constitutions. . . .

. . .

. . . With the surrogacy contract disposed of, the legal framework becomes a dispute between two couples over the custody of a child produced by the artificial insemination of one couple's wife by the other's husband. Under the Parentage Act the claims of the natural father and the natural mother are entitled to equal weight. . . . The applicable rule given these circumstances is clear: the child's best interests determine custody.

. . .

The Whiteheads . . . contend that the award of custody to the Sterns *pendente lite* was erroneous and that the error should not be allowed to affect the final custody decision. As noted above, at the very commencement of this action the court issued an *ex parte* order requiring Mrs. Whitehead to turn over the baby to the Sterns; Mrs. Whitehead did not comply but rather took the child to Florida. Thereafter, a similar order was enforced by the Florida authorities resulting in the transfer of possession of Baby M to the Sterns. The Sterns retained custody of the child throughout the litigation. The Whiteheads' point, assuming the *pendente* award of custody *was* erroneous, is that most of the factors arguing for awarding permanent custody to the Sterns resulted from that initial *pendente lite* order. Some of Mrs. Whitehead's alleged character failings, as testified to by experts and concurred in by the trial court, were demonstrated by her actions brought on by the custody crisis. For instance, in order to demonstrate her impulsiveness, those experts stressed the Whiteheads' flight to Florida with Baby M; to show her willingness to use her children for her own aims, they noted the telephone threats to kill Baby M and to accuse Mr. Stern of sexual abuse of her daughter; in order to show Mrs. Whitehead's manipulativeness, they pointed to her threat to kill herself; and in order to show her unsettled family life, they noted the innumerable moves from one hotel or motel to another in Florida. Furthermore, the argument continues, one of the most important factors, whether mentioned or not, in favor of custody in the Sterns is their continuing custody during the litigation, now having lasted for one-and-a-half years. The Whiteheads' conclusion is that had the trial court not given initial custody to the Sterns during the litigation, Mrs. Whitehead not only would have demonstrated her perfectly acceptable personality—the general tenor of the opinion of experts was that her personality problems surfaced primarily in crises—but would also have been able to prove better her parental skills along with an even stronger bond than may now exist between her and Baby M. Had she not been limited to custody for four months, she could have proved all of these things much more persuasively through almost two years of custody.

The argument has considerable force. It is of course possible that the trial court was wrong in its initial award of custody. It is also possible that such error, if that is what it was, may have affected the outcome. We disagree with the premise, however, that in determining custody a court should decide what the child's best interests *would be* if some hypothetical state of facts had existed. Rather, we must look to what those best interests *are, today,* even if some of the facts may have resulted in part from legal error. The child's interests come first: we will not punish it for judicial errors, assuming any were made. . . .

There were eleven experts who testified concerning the child's best interests, either directly or in connection with matters related to that issue. Our reading of the record persuades us that the trial court's decision awarding custody to the Sterns (technically to Mr. Stern) should be affirmed since "its findings . . . could reasonably have been reached on sufficient credible evidence present in the record." . . .

Our custody conclusion is based on strongly persuasive testimony contrasting both the family life of the Whiteheads and the Sterns and the personalities and characters of the individuals. The stability of the Whitehead family life was doubtful at the time of trial. Their finances were in serious trouble (foreclosure by Mrs. Whitehead's sister on a second mortgage was in process). Mr. Whitehead's employment, though relatively steady, was always at risk because of his alcoholism, a condition that he seems not to have been able to confront effectively. Mrs. Whitehead had not worked for quite some time, her last two employments having been part-time. One of the Whiteheads' positive attributes was their ability to bring up two children, and apparently well, even in so vulnerable a household. Yet substantial question was raised even about that aspect of their home life. The expert testimony contained criticism of Mrs. Whitehead's handling of her son's educational difficulties. Certain of the experts noted that Mrs. Whitehead perceived herself as omnipotent and omniscient concerning her children. She knew what they were thinking, what they wanted, and she spoke for them. As to Melissa, Mrs. Whitehead expressed the view that she alone knew what that child's cries and sounds meant. Her inconsistent stories about various things engendered grave doubts about her ability to explain honestly and sensitively to Baby M—and at the right time—the nature of her origin. Although faith in professional counseling is not a *sine qua non* of parenting, several experts believed that Mrs. Whitehead's contempt for professional help, especially professional psychological help, coincided with her feelings of omnipotence in a way that could be devastating to a child who most likely will need such help. In short, while love and affection there would be, Baby M's life with the Whiteheads promised to be too closely controlled by Mrs. Whitehead. The prospects for wholesome, independent psychological growth and development would be at serious risk.

The Sterns have no other children, but all indications are that their household and their personalities promise a much more likely foundation for Melissa to grow and thrive. There *is* a track record of sorts—during the one-and-a-half years of custody Baby M has done very well, and the relationship between both Mr. and Mrs. Stern and the baby has become very strong. The household is stable, and likely to remain so. Their finances are more than adequate, their circle of friends supportive, and their marriage happy. Most important, they are loving, giving, nurturing, and open-minded people. They have demonstrated the wish and ability to nurture and protect Melissa, yet at the same time to encourage her independence. Their lack of experience is more than made up for by a willingness to learn and to listen, a willingness that is enhanced by their professional training, especially Mrs. Stern's experience as a pediatrician. They are honest; they can recognize error, deal with it, and learn from it. They will try to determine rationally the best way to cope with problems in their relationship with Melissa. When the time comes to tell her about her origins, they will probably have found a means of doing so that accords with the best interests of Baby M. All in all, Melissa's future appears solid, happy, and promising with them.

Based on all of this we have concluded, independent of the trial court's identical conclusion, that Melissa's best interests call for custody in the Sterns. Our above-mentioned disagreements with the trial court do not, as we have noted, in any way diminish our concurrence with its conclusions. We feel, however, that those disagreements are important enough to be stated. . . .

It seems to us that given her predicament, Mrs. Whitehead was rather harshly judged—both by the trial court and by some of the experts. She was guilty of a breach of contract, and indeed, she did break a very important promise, but we think it is expecting something well beyond normal human capabilities to suggest that this mother should have parted with her newly born infant without a struggle. Other than survival, what stronger force is there? We do not know of, and cannot conceive of, any other case where a perfectly fit mother was expected to surrender her newly born infant, perhaps forever, and was then told she was a bad mother because she did not. We know of no authority suggesting that the moral quality of her act in those circumstances should be judged by referring to a contract made before she became pregnant. We do not countenance, and would never countenance, violating a court order as Mrs. Whitehead did, even a court order that is wrong; but her resistance to an order that she surrender her infant, possibly forever, merits a measure of understanding. We do not find it so clear that her efforts to keep her infant, when measured against the Sterns' efforts to take her away, make one, rather than the other, the wrongdoer. The Sterns suffered, but so did she. And if we go beyond suffering to an evaluation of the human stakes involved in the struggle, how much weight should be given to her nine months of pregnancy, the labor of childbirth, the risk to her life, compared to the payment of money, the anticipation of a child and the donation of sperm?

There has emerged a portrait of Mrs. Whitehead, exposing her children to the media, engaging in negotiations to sell a book, granting interviews that seemed helpful to her, whether hurtful to Baby M or not, that suggests a selfish, grasping woman ready to sacrifice the interests of Baby M and her other children for fame and wealth. That portrait is a half-truth, for while it may accurately reflect what ultimately occurred, its implication, that this is what Mary Beth Whitehead wanted, is totally inaccurate, at least insofar as the record before us is concerned. There is not one word in that record to support a claim that had she been allowed to continue her possession of her newly born infant, Mrs. Whitehead would have ever been heard of again; not one word in the record suggests that her change of mind and her subsequent fight for her child was motivated by anything other than love—whatever complex underlying psychological motivations may have existed.

We have a further concern regarding the trial court's emphasis on the Sterns' interest in Melissa's education as compared to the Whiteheads'. That this difference is a legitimate factor to be considered we have no doubt. But it should not be overlooked that a best-interests test is designed to create not a new member of the intelligentsia but rather a well-integrated person who might reasonably be expected to be happy with life. "Best interests" does not contain within it any idealized lifestyle; the question boils down to a judgment, consisting of many factors, about the likely future happiness of a human being. Stability, love, family happiness, tolerance, and, ultimately, support of independence—all rank much higher in predicting future happiness than the likelihood of a college education. We do not mean to suggest that the trial court would disagree. We simply want to dispel any possible misunderstanding on the issue.

Even allowing for these differences, the facts, the experts' opinions, and the trial court's analysis of both argue strongly in favor of custody in the Sterns. Mary Beth Whitehead's family life, into which Baby M would be placed, was anything but secure—the quality Melissa needs most. And today it may be even less so. Furthermore, the evidence and expert opinion based on it reveal personality characteristics, mentioned above, that might threaten the child's best development. The Sterns promise a secure home, with an understanding relationship that allows nurturing and independent growth to develop together. Although there is no substitute for reading the entire record, including the review of every word of each experts' testimony and reports, a summary of their conclusions is revealing. Six experts testified for Mrs. Whitehead: one favored joint custody, clearly unwarranted in this case; one simply rebutted an opposing expert's claim that Mary Beth Whitehead had a recognized personality disorder; one testified to the adverse impact of separation on *Mrs. Whitehead;* one testified about the evils of adoption and, to him, the probable analogous evils of surrogacy; one spoke only on the question of whether Mrs. Whitehead's consent in the surrogacy agreement was "informed consent"; and one spelled out the strong bond between mother and child. None of them unequivocally stated, or even necessarily implied, an opinion that custody in the Whiteheads was in the best interests of Melissa—the ultimate issue. The Sterns' experts, both well qualified—as were the Whiteheads'—concluded that the best interests of Melissa required custody in Mr. Stern. Most convincingly, the three experts chosen by the court-appointed guardian *ad litem* of Baby

M, each clearly free of all bias and interest, unanimously and persuasively recommended custody in the Sterns.

Some comment is required on the initial *ex parte* order awarding custody *pendente lite* to the Sterns (and the continuation of that order after a plenary hearing). The issue, although irrelevant to our disposition of this case, may recur; and when it does, it can be of crucial importance. When father and mother are separated and disagree, at birth, on custody, only in an extreme, truly rare, case should the child be taken from its mother *pendente lite, i.e.,* only in the most unusual case should the child be taken from its mother before the dispute is finally determined by the court on its merits. The probable bond between mother and child, and the child's need, not just the mother's, to strengthen that bond, along with the likelihood, in most cases, of a significantly lesser, if any, bond with the father—all counsel against temporary custody in the father. A substantial showing that the mother's continued custody would threaten the child's health or welfare would seem to be required.

In this case, the trial court, believing that the surrogacy contract might be valid, and faced with the probable flight from the jurisdiction by Mrs. Whitehead and the baby if *any* notice were served, ordered, *ex parte,* an immediate transfer of possession of the child; *i.e.,* it ordered that custody be transferred immediately to Mr. Stern, rather than order Mrs. Whitehead not to leave the State. We have ruled, however, that the surrogacy contract is unenforceable and illegal. It provides no basis for either an *ex parte,* a plenary, an interlocutory, or a final order requiring a mother to surrender custody to a father. Any application by the natural father in a surrogacy dispute for custody pending the outcome of the litigation will henceforth require proof of unfitness, of danger to the child, or the like, of so high a quality and persuasiveness as to make it unlikely that such application will succeed. Absent the required showing, all that a court should do is list the matter for argument on notice to the mother. Even her threats to flee should not suffice to warrant any other relief unless her unfitness is clearly shown. At most, it should result in an order enjoining such flight. The erroneous transfer of custody, as we view it, represents a greater risk to the child than removal to a foreign jurisdiction, unless parental unfitness is clearly proved. Furthermore, we deem it likely that, advised of the law and knowing that her custody cannot seriously be challenged at this stage of the litigation, surrogate mothers will obey any court order to remain in the jurisdiction.

... Our reversal of the trial court's order, however, requires delineation of Mrs. Whitehead's rights to visitation. It is apparent to us that this factually sensitive issue, which was never addressed below, should not be determined *de novo* by this Court. We therefore remand the visitation issue to the trial court for an abbreviated hearing and determination as set forth below.

...

We also note the following for the trial court's consideration: First, this is not a divorce case where visitation is almost invariably granted to the non-custodial spouse. To some extent the facts here resemble cases where the non-custodial spouse has had practically no relationship with the child, but it only "resembles" those cases. In the instant case, Mrs. Whitehead spent the first four months of this child's life as her mother and has regularly visited the child since then. Second, she is not only the natural mother, but also the legal mother, and is not to be penalized one iota because of the surrogacy contract. Mrs. Whitehead, as the mother (indeed, as a mother who nurtured her child for its first four months—unquestionably a relevant consideration), is entitled to have her own interest in visitation considered. . . .

In all of this, the trial court should recall the touchstones of visitation: that it is desirable for the child to have contact with both parents; that besides the child's interests, the parents' interests also must be considered; but that when all is said and done, the best interests of the child are paramount.

We have decided that Mrs. Whitehead is entitled to visitation at some point, and that question is not open to the trial court on this remand. . . . It also should be noted that the guardian's recommendation of a five-year delay is most unusual—one might argue that it begins to border on termination. Nevertheless, if the circumstances as further developed by appropriate proofs or as reconsidered on remand clearly call for that suspension under applicable legal principles of visitation, it should be so ordered.

. . .

The judgment is affirmed in part, reversed in part, and remanded for further proceedings consistent with this opinion.

NOTES

1. *Visions of motherhood. Baby M* offers two searing images of motherhood. On the one hand, the court depicted Mary Beth Whitehead's longing for her daughter as a visceral, primal—indeed animal-like—need that had to be sated. Moreover, the court suggests that the emotional connections between mother and child are first developed *in utero* during gestation. Further, the media imagery of Elizabeth "Betsy" Stern stands in stark contrast to these depictions of natural motherhood. Stern was widely castigated as a driven career woman who sought to avoid a pregnancy because of its likely impact on her career (in fact, Stern had multiple sclerosis and was told that a pregnancy might exacerbate her condition). *See, e.g.,* Yvonne Roberts, *Tuesday Women: The Woman Born to Lose Her Baby,* GUARDIAN, Feb. 13, 1990, at 17. Are either of these images an accurate—or flattering—depiction of contemporary motherhood?

2. *Love and contracts.* The media coverage of *Baby M* framed the case as one that pitted emotions against the reality of a signed contract. Elizabeth Kolbert, *In Struggle for Baby M., Fierce Emotion and Key Legal Issues,* N.Y.

TIMES, Aug. 22, 1986, at 25. The media, like the courts, struggled to square traditional notions of motherhood with the fact that Mary Beth Whitehead had executed a contract to surrender her rights to her unborn child. Indeed, the case prompted questions about whether a baby is a commodity to be purchased, or whether children and parenthood were beyond such commodification. *See, e.g.*, Margaret Jane Radin, *Market-Inalienability*, 100 HARV. L. REV. 1849, 1928–36 (1987) (positing that paid surrogacy is a commodification, and thus harmful to conceptions of personhood). Critically, the legal issues at the heart of *Baby M* were animated by the fact that Mary Beth Whitehead and William Stern both shared a genetic connection with Baby M. These concerns have altered the ways in which surrogacy is conducted today. Most surrogacies now involve a surrogate who has no genetic connection to the child. Instead, a fertilized egg is implanted into the surrogate for gestation. Accordingly, modern surrogacy most often involves "renting" a womb, rather than "buying a child." *See* Nita Bhalla & Mansi Thapliyal, *India Seeks to Regulate Its Booming 'Rent-a-Womb' Industry*, REUTERS (Sept. 30, 2013), https://www.reuters.com/article/us-india-surrogates/india-seeks-to-regulate-its-booming-rent-a-womb-industry-idUSBRE98T07F20130930.

3. *Whatever happened to Baby M?* The child at the heart of this case is now a grown woman and a college graduate. When she turned eighteen, Melissa Stern sought to terminate Whitehead's parental rights so that Elizabeth Stern might formally adopt her. *See* Allison Pries, *Whatever Happened to Baby M?*, NORTHJERSEY.COM (Jan. 5, 2010), http://www.northjersey.com/news/whatever-happened-to-baby-m-1.975840 [https://perma.cc/7SVL-8V22].

P.M. v. T.B.

907 N.W.2d 522 (Iowa 2018).

■ WATERMAN, JUSTICE.

In this appeal, we must decide a question of first impression: whether gestational surrogacy contracts are enforceable under Iowa law. The plaintiffs, the intended parents, are a married couple unable to conceive their own child. They signed a contract with the defendants, the surrogate mother and her husband, who, in exchange for future payments of up to $13,000 and medical expenses, agreed to have the surrogate mother impregnated with embryos fertilized with the plaintiff-father's sperm and the ova (eggs) of an anonymous donor. The defendants agreed to deliver the baby at birth to the intended parents. The surrogate mother became pregnant with twins, but after demanding additional payments, refused to honor the agreement. The babies were born prematurely, and one died. The intended parents sued to enforce the contract and gain custody of the surviving child.

. . . .

P.M. and C.M. were high school sweethearts but parted ways when P.M. joined the Navy upon graduation. After marrying and divorcing other spouses, they reconnected and married each other in 2013. They now live in Cedar Rapids. P.M. had two children from his first marriage, and C.M. had four children from hers. The Ms were nearing age fifty and wanted to have a child together. C.M. was no longer able to conceive, so the Ms placed an advertisement on Craigslist in 2015 seeking a woman willing to act as a surrogate mother.

T.B. and D.B. married each other in January 2009 and live in Muscatine. T.B. has four children from a prior marriage; D.B. has no children and had never been married. The Bs want to have children together. In 2010, T.B. had a tubal pregnancy which was life-threatening and incapable of leading to the birth of a viable child, so she surgically terminated the pregnancy. T.B. and D.B. continued to try to conceive without success. The Bs realized they would need the services of a reproductive endocrinologist in order to have a child. T.B. learned that the Bs' insurance would not cover infertility treatment or in vitro fertilization (IVF). They decided they needed to supplement D.B.'s income to pay for assisted reproduction procedures.

T.B. responded to the Ms' Craigslist advertisement. The four met for dinner in Coralville and got along well at first. They agreed that T.B. would gestate two embryos fertilized in vitro with P.M.'s sperm and the eggs of an anonymous donor. The Ms selected Midwest Fertility Clinic (Midwest) in Downers Grove, Illinois, to perform the IVF and embryo transfers. Midwest required a written contract between the parties, so the Ms hired a lawyer to draft the agreement. Its stated purpose was "to enable the Intended Father [P.M.] and the Intended Mother [C.M.] to have a child who is biologically related to one of them." In exchange for the gestational service, the Ms agreed to pay up to $13,000 for an IVF procedure for T.B. to enable her and D.B. to conceive their own child. This payment was conditioned upon T.B. surrendering custody of a live child upon birth.

. . . .

The contract also provided that the Ms would pay T.B.'s pregnancy-related medical expenses. At T.B.'s request, an additional term was included stating that "[i]n the event the child is miscarried or stillborn during the pregnancy, the amount of $2,000 will be paid to the Gestational Carrier." The four adults signed the final "Gestational Carrier Agreement" (the Surrogacy Agreement) on January 5, 2016.

The Surrogacy Agreement provided that . . .

T.B. and D.B. "agree[d] to surrender custody of the child to the Intended Parents immediately upon birth" and "agree[d] that the Intended Parents are the parents to be identified on the birth certificate for this child." The Surrogacy Agreement further provided,

> In the event it is required by law, the Gestational Carrier
> and her husband agree to institute and cooperate in proceedings

to terminate their respective parental rights to any child born pursuant to the terms of this agreement. . . .

The Surrogacy Agreement also stated that

each party has been given the opportunity to consult with an attorney of his or her own choice concerning the terms [and] legal significance of this agreement, and the effect it has upon any and all interests of the parties.

T.B. and D.B. did not exercise their right to consult a lawyer before the Surrogacy Agreement was signed by all four parties. But each person acknowledged in writing:

[T]hat he or she has carefully read and understood every word in this agreement and its legal effect, and each party is signing this agreement freely and voluntarily and that neither party has any reason to believe that the other party or parties did not understand fully the terms and effects of this agreement, or that the other party did not freely and voluntarily execute this agreement.

On March 27, Midwest implanted two embryos into T.B.'s uterus. The embryos were the ova of an anonymous donor fertilized with P.M.'s sperm. On April 4, blood testing confirmed T.B.'s pregnancy. The parties' relationship soon began to break down over their disagreement as to payment of medical expenses. All four attended the first ultrasound, which D.B. videotaped. The Ms later objected to his videotaping and to T.B. posting information about the baby on social media.

Their relationship worsened after the women exchanged text messages on April 13. They were discussing whether T.B. could attend a doctor's appointment scheduled by the IVF coordinator when C.M. wrote, "Well we have to go next Thursday [because the coordinator] made the [appointment] and this is our journey not anyone else's. She said you have to end with [a doctor's] exam in Chicago and [a] couple more ultrasounds. . . ." T.B. replied, "I'm not going through this with you today. She just called me." C.M. replied, "We are in charge we hired you so just let us be parents and enjoy this ok!"

A second ultrasound confirmed that T.B. was carrying viable twins. T.B. shared that news with the Ms, but the relationship remained rocky. In late April, C.M. texted this to T.B.:

Every time we question you or try to make a decision (as we should be able to) we are paying you, we hired you, and we are in charge, you get mad and upset and blow up. A carrier shouldn't act like that as the doctors told me they should be saying yes ma'am Whatever you guys want to do. But you can't stand not being in charge and you have some mental disorder for sure but yet you blame everything on us. . . . So if you wanna say u have it bad try feeling how we feel. This is our baby not yours and imagine how U would feel. I know u don't care but just for a moment stop blaming us and look what U have done to us only cuz we have ask[ed] u to do something. Compare the two and u will see we have NEVER did u wrong. This is a nightmare.

When T.B. replied, "You're crazy," C.M. wrote back, "Oh really that's what everyone says about u[.]" T.B. then stated that "everything can be handled through attorneys from here[.]" The Bs retained an attorney to speak for them and cut off direct communication with the Ms, who nevertheless persisted in trying to reach them for updates on the pregnancy.

In a May 20 letter from her attorney, T.B. sought more money from the Ms beyond the $13,000 agreed to in their contract so she could use a costlier clinic for her own IVF. . . . T.B. insisted that the Ms pay the higher cost for her to continue to serve as a gestational carrier.

On August 19, P.M. sent Facebook messages to D.B.'s sister, using racial slurs and profanity to insult D.B. D.B.'s sister shared the communication with T.B. On August 24, C.M. sent an email to T.B. and T.B.'s attorney, triggering a lengthy exchange, during which C.M. called T.B. the "N" word. That statement, along with the comments P.M. sent to D.B.'s sister, convinced T.B. that the Ms were racist. T.B. then called the Ms' attorney. When T.B. expressed concern that the Ms would not pay her, the Ms' attorney assured T.B. that the money for the Bs had already been set aside. The Ms' attorney attempted to make payment arrangements with T.B. and arrange P.M.'s listing on the birth certificate, but those matters remained unresolved. Later that day, T.B. decided that she would not turn over the babies to the Ms.

Twin babies were born thirteen weeks prematurely on August 31. T.B. did not tell the Ms about the birth. The babies were placed in the neonatal intensive care unit. One died eight days after birth. T.B. did not inform the Ms about the baby's illness or death. The Bs unilaterally arranged for the deceased baby's cremation.

. . . On October 31, the Ms filed a motion for an emergency ex parte injunction, alleging their belief that the babies had been born. The same day, the district court entered an order granting a temporary injunction that ordered T.B. and D.B. to surrender custody of "Baby H" to the Ms. . . . The Ms have had physical custody of Baby H since that date.

. . . .

. . . The Bs responded by filing an answer and counterclaim [seeking] a declaration that T.B. is the biological and legal mother of the babies and that D.B. is the legal father of the babies. The Bs also sought a declaration that P.M. has no legal right to a relationship with the surviving baby and that the Surrogacy Agreement is unenforceable under Iowa law and the United States Constitution.

. . . .

... We begin with an overview of the law governing gestational surrogacy arrangements. . . . This case involves a gestational surrogacy because T.B. is not genetically related to the child. T.B. is the surrogate mother, while P.M. and C.M. are the intended parents.

. . . .

A majority of states lack statutes addressing surrogacy. . . . In the minority of states with statutes specifically addressing surrogacy, the enactments generally impose greater restrictions on traditional surrogacies, and most of the statutes can be grouped into three categories:

> First, some states have legislatively prohibited all surrogacy contracts, declaring their terms unenforceable and, in some instances, imposing criminal penalties for those who attempt to enter into or assist in creating such a contract. . . . A second category of states prohibit only certain types of surrogacy contracts—typically those involving a traditional surrogacy. . . . Finally, states in the third category authorize both traditional and gestational surrogacy contracts, subject to regulation and specified limitations. . . .

. . . .

There are two "commonly cited model acts dealing with surrogacy agreements[:] the American Bar Association Model Act Governing Assisted Reproductive Technology (2008) and article 8 of the Uniform Parentage Act (2002), drafted by the National Conference of Commissioners on Uniform State Laws."

> Both of these model acts fall into the third category of surrogacy statutes, allowing traditional and gestational surrogacy contracts subject to extensive regulation that includes judicial pre-approval, limits on compensation, and provisions concerning the revocation rights of the parties to the agreement.

The 2017 Uniform Parentage Act (UPA) imposes greater restrictions on traditional surrogacy agreements based on the birth mother's status as a genetic parent. . . .

... Against this backdrop, we turn to the issue of whether the Surrogacy Agreement at issue is enforceable under Iowa law.

. . . .

T.B. argues the Surrogacy Agreement is unenforceable under Iowa law as inconsistent with statutory provisions and public policy. We first examine whether this contract between consenting adults is "prohibited by statute, condemned by judicial decision, [or] contrary to the public morals." We find no such statutory or judicial prohibition in our state. To the contrary, the Iowa legislature tacitly approved of surrogacy arrangements by exempting them from potential criminal liability for selling children [in Iowa Code § 710.11]. . . . This provision was enacted in 1989, one year after extensive national publicity over the decision of the New Jersey Supreme Court invalidating a surrogacy contract as contrary to that state's adoption statutes, including its "baby selling" prohibition on payment of money to adopt a child. In re Baby M, 537 A.2d at 1250 & n.10. . . .

. . . .

We conclude, based on the timing of the enactment of Iowa Code section 710.11, . . . that our state's general assembly chose in 1989 to allow surrogacy arrangements, not prohibit them. Section 710.11 specifically mentions artificial insemination of the birth mother (who is the genetic or biological mother, as in Baby M), but we decline to infer the legislature intended to allow only traditional surrogacy when the birth mother is the genetic mother and yet criminalize gestational surrogacy arrangements. IVF, allowing implantation in the surrogate mother of embryos from donor eggs, was then in its infancy and had not been the subject of a court decision of national prominence. As other courts have noted, a gestational surrogacy in which the birth mother lacks a genetic connection to the child raises fewer concerns than the traditional surrogacy expressly mentioned in section 710.11. The legislature's decision to allow traditional surrogacy arrangements can be taken as a signal that it would also allow gestational surrogacy arrangements. We conclude that neither traditional nor gestational surrogacy contracts are prohibited under section 710.11.

Our conclusion is reinforced by the regulations adopted by the [Department of Public Health] that specifically contemplate IVF gestational surrogacy agreements. The regulations are entitled "Establishment of new certificate of live birth following a birth by gestational surrogate arrangement." See Iowa Admin. Code r. 641—99.15. These regulations enjoy a presumption of validity with the force of law.

The DPH regulations provide for establishment of a new certificate of live birth following a birth by gestational surrogate arrangement [, and authorizes] court orders disestablishing the surrogate mother and her legal spouse as the legal parents and establishing the intended father and mother as the legal parents. . . .

Another reason the Surrogacy Agreement does not violate Iowa Code section 710.11 is because the Ms' payment was for T.B.'s gestational services rather than for her sale of a baby. The Surrogacy Agreement states,

> The consideration of this agreement is compensation for services and expenses as limited by law and in no way is to be construed as a fee for termination of parental rights or a payment in exchange for consent to surrender the child for adoption.

The California Supreme Court held under equivalent circumstances that the contractual payment is for gestational services, not for the sale of a baby. See Johnson v. Calvert, 851 P.2d 766, 784 (Cal. 1993) (explaining that the payments to the surrogate mother "were meant to compensate her for her services in gestating the fetus and undergoing labor"). We reach the same conclusion.

[Additionally,] T.B. relies on Iowa Code section 600A.4, which requires parents to wait seventy-two hours after a child's birth before signing a release of custody for an adoption. T.B. claims that the safeguards established in section 600A.4 are violated by the Surrogacy Agreement. We disagree because T.B. is not the genetic mother of Baby H, and section 600A.4 is therefore inapplicable. . . .

This is not a situation in which T.B. is choosing to give up her own genetically related child in order to avoid the consequences of an unwanted pregnancy or the burdens of childrearing. Instead, T.B. agreed to carry a child for the Ms after responding to their advertisement on Craigslist. But for the acted-on intention of the Ms, Baby H would not exist. The Ms would not have entrusted their embryos fertilized with P.M.'s sperm to T.B. if they thought she would attempt to raise the resulting child herself.

We hold that the adoption statute is inapplicable and the Surrogacy Agreement is not inconsistent with Iowa statutes on termination of parental rights.

. . . T.B. also claims enforcement of the Surrogacy Agreement violates Iowa's public policy. We disagree based on the freedom of contract enjoyed by consenting adults. We start with the presumption that under Iowa law a "contractual agreement is binding on the parties." "The power to invalidate a contract on public policy grounds must be used cautiously and exercised only in cases free from doubt." The party claiming the contract is contrary to public policy bears the burden of proof. We reiterate that "[t]o strike down a contract on public policy grounds, we must conclude that 'the preservation of the general public welfare . . . outweigh[s] the weighty societal interest in the freedom of contract.' "

. . . .

T.B. [further] argues a surrogacy agreement violates public policy against the exploitation of women, and contends,

> Surrogacy agreements, if enforced embody deviant societal pressures, the object of which is to use the woman, and destroy her interests as a mother to satisfy the desires of third parties. Surrogacy exploits women by treating the mother as if she is not a whole woman. It assumes she can be used much like a breeding animal and act as though she is not, in fact, a mother.

Yet T.B. entered into the Surrogacy Agreement voluntarily. She had given birth to four children of her own before signing the Surrogacy

Agreement and was no stranger to the effects of pregnancy. T.B. does not allege she signed the Surrogacy Agreement under economic duress or that its terms are unconscionable. . . .

T.B. alternatively argues the Surrogacy Agreement violates the state's public policy favoring families. We have repeatedly acknowledged Iowa's public policy "promoting the sanctity and stability of the family." T.B. characterizes surrogacy agreements as deliberately destroying the surrogate mother-child relationship (a relationship, we note, that would not exist but for the Ms' contribution of their embryos in reliance on T.B.'s willingness to serve as a gestational carrier). We conclude that gestational surrogacy agreements promote families by enabling infertile couples to raise their own children and help bring new life into this world through willing surrogate mothers. . . . T.B. has failed to show the Surrogacy Agreement violates the public policy of our state.

. . . . T.B. claims that as the birth mother she is the legal and biological mother of Baby H and that she therefore is entitled to custody of Baby H unless and until she is proven unfit by clear and convincing evidence. Iowa law establishes a rebuttable presumption that the birth mother who delivered the infant and her spouse are the legal parents of the child. . . .

. . . . Iowa Code § 232.2(39) . . . defines "parent" as "a father or mother of a child, whether by birth or adoption." . . . We hold the statutory definition of "biological parent" of Baby H does not include a surrogate birth mother who is not the genetic parent. The ordinary meaning of "biological parent" is a person who is the genetic father or mother of the child. That is also the established legal meaning of "biological parent." It makes sense that the legislature and department of health used the term "biological parent" in the commonly understood and established legal meaning of those terms.

. . . .

We next address T.B.'s constitutional claims. . . . T.B. claims that she has a fundamental liberty interest in the parent-child relationship. . . . That liberty interest belongs to P.M., the only party in this case who is a biological parent of Baby H. By contrast, T.B.'s constitutional claims rest on an incorrect premise—that she has parental rights in Baby H without being the child's genetic mother. Any constitutionally protected interest she may have as the surrogate birth mother is overcome by P.M.'s undisputed status as the biological and intended father of Baby H. . . .

. . . .

T.B. was provided sufficient procedural due process. She cannot claim lack of notice. . . . T.B. claims that enforcement of the Surrogacy Agreement would violate the substantive due process and equal protection rights of Baby H. . . . We assume without deciding that T.B., as Baby H's birth mother, would have had standing to raise constitutional claims of Baby H. But as noted above, T.B. waived her rights to assert claims on behalf of Baby H in the Surrogacy Agreement.

. . . .

For these reasons, we affirm the rulings of the district court.

NOTES

1. *Critiques of surrogacy.* One of the perennial critiques of surrogacy agreements is that they allow the wealthy to exploit the gestational labor of the less privileged. To what extent do the facts of *P.M. v. T.B.* echo these concerns?

2. *Resolving surrogacy disputes.* Courts have deployed various approaches for resolving surrogacy disputes. Originally proposed by Professor Marjorie Shultz and pioneered by the California Supreme Court in *Johnson v. Calvert*, 851 P.2d 776 (Cal. 1993), the theory resolves surrogacy disputes by looking to the parties' intentions at the time the surrogacy contract was formed and executed. In *Johnson*, for example, the court determined that legal parentage resided with the intended parents who provided the genetic material and entered into the surrogacy agreement with the intention of raising the resulting child as their own. Relying on *Johnson*, a California appellate court invoked the intent doctrine to rule that divorcing spouses were both the legal parents of a child who was created from a frozen embryo that they obtained from a fertility clinic and who was born to a gestational surrogate with whom they had contracted. *In re Marriage of Buzzanca*, 72 Cal. Rptr. 2d 280 (Ct. App. 1998).

Some states, however, have sought to codify the law of surrogacy and therefore rely on statutory approaches for resolving surrogacy disputes. Many of these states have codified provisions of the 2002 iteration Uniform Parentage Act, which permits gestational surrogacy agreements where the agreement is "validated" by a home study and judicial approval of the intended parents. If these conditions are satisfied, then then the intended parents are child's legal parents for purposes of the UPA. In 2017, in a nod to the proliferation of surrogacy use by same-sex couples, the UPA's surrogacy provisions were updated to remove gender-based language and to recognize intended parents regardless of gender or sexual orientation. The UPA also liberalized the state-level requirements for the enforcement of surrogacy contracts, including eliminating the court's role in approving gestational surrogacy agreements. Despite these changes, the UPA treats traditional surrogacy arrangements—where the surrogate has a genetic tie to the child—in the manner of an adoption, requiring judicial approval of the intended parents and allowing a period for the surrogate to change her mind post-birth.

* * *

The selection that follows highlights changes to the UPA regarding eligibility of gestational surrogates and eligibility to enter into a surrogacy agreement.

Uniform Parentage Act
(2017).

ARTICLE 8. SURROGACY AGREEMENT

§ 802. ELIGIBILITY TO ENTER GESTATIONAL OR GENETIC SURROGACY AGREEMENT

(a) To execute an agreement to act as a gestational or genetic surrogate, a woman must:

    (1) have attained 21 years of age;

    (2) previously have given birth to at least one child;

    (3) complete a medical evaluation related to the surrogacy arrangement by a licensed medical doctor;

    (4) complete a mental-health consultation by a licensed mental-health professional; and

    (5) have independent legal representation of her choice throughout the surrogacy arrangement regarding the terms of the surrogacy agreement and the potential legal consequences of the agreement.

(b) To execute a surrogacy agreement, each intended parent, whether or not genetically related to the child, must:

    (1) have attained 21 years of age;

    (2) complete a medical evaluation related to the surrogacy arrangement by a licensed medical doctor;

    (3) complete a mental-health consultation by a licensed mental health professional; and

    (4) have independent legal representation of the intended parent's choice throughout the surrogacy arrangement regarding the terms of the surrogacy agreement and the potential legal consequences of the agreement.

. . .

§ 804. REQUIREMENTS OF GESTATIONAL OR GENETIC SURROGACY AGREEMENT: CONTENT

(a) A surrogacy agreement must comply with the following requirements:

    (1) A surrogate agrees to attempt to become pregnant by means of assisted reproduction.

    (2) Except as otherwise provided in Sections 811, 814, and 815, the surrogate and the surrogate's spouse or former spouse, if any, have no claim to parentage of a child conceived by assisted reproduction under the agreement.

    (3) The surrogate's spouse, if any, must acknowledge and agree to comply with the obligations imposed on the surrogate by the agreement.

(4) Except as otherwise provided in Sections 811, 814, and 815, the intended parent or, if there are two intended parents, each one jointly and severally, immediately on birth will be the exclusive parent or parents of the child, regardless of number of children born or gender or mental or physical condition of each child.

(5) Except as otherwise provided in Sections 811, 814, and 815, the intended parent or, if there are two intended parents, each parent jointly and severally, immediately on birth will assume responsibility for the financial support of the child, regardless of number of children born or gender or mental or physical condition of each child.

(6) The agreement must include information disclosing how each intended parent will cover the surrogacy-related expenses of the surrogate and the medical expenses of the child. If health-care coverage is used to cover the medical expenses, the disclosure must include a summary of the health-care policy provisions related to coverage for surrogate pregnancy, including any possible liability of the surrogate, third-party-liability liens, other insurance coverage, and any notice requirement that could affect coverage or liability of the surrogate. Unless the agreement expressly provides otherwise, the review and disclosure do not constitute legal advice. If the extent of coverage is uncertain, a statement of that fact is sufficient to comply with this paragraph.

(7) The agreement must permit the surrogate to make all health and welfare decisions regarding herself and her pregnancy. This [act] does not enlarge or diminish the surrogate's right to terminate her pregnancy.

(8) The agreement must include information about each party's right under this [article] to terminate the surrogacy agreement.

(b) A surrogacy agreement may provide for:

(1) payment of consideration and reasonable expenses; and

(2) reimbursement of specific expenses if the agreement is terminated under this [article].

(c) A right created under a surrogacy agreement is not assignable and there is no third-party beneficiary of the agreement other than the child.

. . .

§ 809.   PARENTAGE   UNDER   GESTATIONAL   SURROGACY AGREEMENT

(a) [O]n the birth of a child conceived by assisted reproduction under a gestational surrogacy agreement, each intended parent is, by operation of law, a parent of the child.

(b)   Except as otherwise provided in subsection (c) or Section 812, neither a gestational surrogate nor the surrogate's spouse or former spouse, if any, is a parent of the child.

(c)   If a child is alleged to be a genetic child of the woman who agreed to be a gestational surrogate, the court shall order genetic testing of the child. If the child is a genetic child of the woman who agreed to be a gestational surrogate, parentage must be determined based on [Articles] 1 through 6.

(d)   Except as otherwise provided in subsection (c) or Section 810(b) or 812, if, due to a clinical or laboratory error, a child conceived by assisted reproduction under a gestational surrogacy agreement is not genetically related to an intended parent or a donor who donated to the intended parent or parents, each intended parent, and not the gestational surrogate and the surrogate's spouse or former spouse, if any, is a parent of the child, subject to any other claim of parentage.

. . .

§ 811.   GESTATIONAL SURROGACY AGREEMENT: ORDER OF PARENTAGE

(a)   Except as otherwise provided in Sections 809(c) or 812, before, on, or after the birth of a child conceived by assisted reproduction under a gestational surrogacy agreement, a party to the agreement may commence a proceeding in the [appropriate court] for an order or judgment:

> (1)   declaring that each intended parent is a parent of the child and ordering that parental rights and duties vest immediately on the birth of the child exclusively in each intended parent;

> (2)   declaring that the gestational surrogate and the surrogate's spouse or former spouse, if any, are not the parents of the child;

> (3)   designating the content of the birth record in accordance with [cite applicable law of this state other than this act] and directing the [state agency maintaining birth records] to designate each intended parent as a parent of the child;

> (4)   to protect the privacy of the child and the parties, declaring that the court record is not open to inspection [except as authorized under Section 806];

> (5)   if necessary, that the child be surrendered to the intended parent or parents; and

> (6)   for other relief the court determines necessary and proper.

(b)   The court may issue an order or judgment under subsection (a) before the birth of the child. The court shall stay enforcement of the order or judgment until the birth of the child.

(c)   Neither this state nor the [state agency maintaining birth records] is a necessary party to a proceeding under subsection (a).

§ 812.   EFFECT OF GESTATIONAL SURROGACY AGREEMENT

(a)   A gestational surrogacy agreement that complies with Sections 802, 803, and 804 is enforceable.

(b)   If a child was conceived by assisted reproduction under a gestational surrogacy agreement that does not comply with Sections 802, 803, and 804, the court shall determine the rights and duties of the parties to the agreement consistent with the intent of the parties at the time of execution of the agreement. Each party to the agreement and any individual who at the time of the execution of the agreement was a spouse of a party to the agreement has standing to maintain a proceeding to adjudicate an issue related to the enforcement of the agreement.

(c)   Except as expressly provided in a gestational surrogacy agreement or subsection (d) or (e), if the agreement is breached by the gestational surrogate or one or more intended parents, the non-breaching party is entitled to the remedies available at law or in equity.

(d)   Specific performance is not a remedy available for breach by a gestational surrogate of a provision in the agreement that the gestational surrogate be impregnated, terminate or not terminate a pregnancy, or submit to medical procedures.

(e)   Except as otherwise provided in subsection (d), if an intended parent is determined to be a parent of the child, specific performance is a remedy available for:

(1)   breach of the agreement by a gestational surrogate which prevents the intended parent from exercising immediately on birth of the child the full rights of parentage; or

(2)   breach by the intended parent which prevents the intended parent's acceptance, immediately on birth of the child conceived by assisted reproduction under the agreement, of the duties of parentage.

. . .

§ 818.   BREACH OF GENETIC SURROGACY AGREEMENT

(a)   [I]f a genetic surrogacy agreement is breached by a genetic surrogate or one or more intended parents, the non-breaching party is entitled to the remedies available at law or in equity.

(b)   Specific performance is not a remedy available for breach by a genetic surrogate of a requirement of a validated or non-validated genetic surrogacy agreement that the surrogate be impregnated, terminate or not terminate a pregnancy, or submit to medical procedures.

(c)   Except as otherwise provided in subsection (b), specific performance is a remedy available for:

(1)   breach of a validated genetic surrogacy agreement by a genetic surrogate of a requirement which prevents an intended parent from

exercising the full rights of parentage 72 hours after the birth of the child;

(2) breach by an intended parent which prevents the intended parent's acceptance of duties of parentage 72 hours after the birth of the child.

NOTES

1.   *Access to surrogacy services.* In some cases, health care providers and facilities limit access to infertility services based on certain criteria, including age and sexual orientation. For example, amidst criticism of postmenopausal women's use of donor eggs to achieve viable pregnancies, some providers have prohibited the use of ART services by older persons. Are such restrictions lawful? Ethical? Gay men, in particular, may face discrimination in seeking surrogacy services. With few conduits for genetic parenthood, many gay men explore surrogacy—and are often confronted with resistance to the prospect of gay male parenthood. As importantly, in the states that permit surrogacy, statutory law may assume that the intended parents are a heterosexual couple, further compounding the indignities to same-sex couples. *See, e.g., In re Gestational Agreement*, 449 P.3d 69 (Utah 2019).

2.   *Conscience objections to surrogacy.* Conscience objections have proliferated in the context of abortion and contraception, allowing health care professionals to refuse reproductive care on the ground that doing so violates their religious beliefs. Are similar conscience objections permissible in the context of ART?

* * *

The first generation of assisted reproductive technologies that gained popularity involved artificial insemination. In contrast to the process of surrogacy described in Baby M, *above, artificial insemination was relatively easy, and people could utilize the process without involving doctors. However, the prevalence of informal artificial insemination raised interesting legal challenges to the traditional conception of legal parenthood. The following cases raise some of the legal issues that surfaced as the law tried to account for the increased interest in artificial insemination.*

<h2 style="text-align:center">Jason P. v. Danielle S.</h2>
226 Cal. App. 4th 167 (Ct. App. 2014).

■ WILLHITE, J.

Family Code section 7613, subdivision (b) (hereafter, section 7613(b)) currently provides: "The donor of semen provided to a licensed physician and surgeon or to a licensed sperm bank for use in assisted reproduction of a woman other than the donor's spouse is treated in law as if he were not the natural parent of a child thereby conceived, unless otherwise agreed to in a writing signed by the donor and the woman prior to the conception of the child." In Steven S. v. Deborah D. (2005) 127 Cal.App.4th 319 (2005), we reversed a finding of paternity in favor of a donor of semen provided to a licensed physician, rejecting the sperm donor's argument "that we should look beyond the words of the statute to find legislative intent for a public policy favoring a finding of paternity where, as here, the mother was in an intimate relationship with a known donor and also attempted to conceive naturally, albeit unsuccessfully." In rejecting the donor's argument, we employed broad and categorical language. We declared: "There can be no paternity claim from a sperm donor who is not married to the woman who becomes pregnant with the donated semen, so long as it was provided to a licensed physician."

We should not have been so categorical, because we were not faced with a donor seeking to establish paternity under section 7611, the presumed parentage statute, and therefore had no occasion to consider whether section 7613(b) precludes any such attempt. We do so now, and conclude that section 7613(b) does not preclude a donor from establishing that he is a presumed father under section 7611.

. . . .

The parties agreed upon the following facts at the start of the trial. Jason and Danielle cohabitated for many years, but they never married. Gus was conceived through in vitro fertilization (IVF). Jason provided to a licensed fertility clinic the sperm used in the IVF procedure. Jason is not listed on Gus's birth certificate, and there is no voluntary declaration of paternity. Gus has no other natural, presumed, or potential biological father.

In addition to the agreed-upon facts, Jason presented evidence that he and Danielle tried to have a baby naturally beginning in 2006. Although Danielle became pregnant in December 2006, the pregnancy was not viable after six and a half weeks. In 2007, Danielle had two intrauterine insemination (IUI) procedures using Jason's sperm, but neither resulted in a pregnancy. In October 2007, after being advised that their inability to conceive might be due to issues regarding Jason's sperm count, Jason had a surgical procedure to address that problem. She and Jason also began to look into having an IVF procedure.

In May 2008, Danielle moved out of Jason's home and bought a home nearby. The following month she purchased sperm of an anonymous donor from a sperm bank and told Jason she was going to pursue motherhood as a single mother. At some point in the fall of 2008, she looked at a Web site for "single mothers by choice" to learn about her rights; she learned that in California, a man who gives his sperm for artificial insemination is never treated in the law as though he is the father. In September 2008, she moved back into Jason's house while the house she bought was being remodeled.

In November 2008 or January 2009, Jason gave Danielle a letter in which he wrote that he was not ready to be a father, but if Danielle wanted to use his sperm to conceive, she had his blessing as long as she did not tell others.5 Danielle chose to use Jason's sperm rather than the anonymous donor's sperm she had purchased.

After having an unsuccessful IUI procedure in January 2009 using Jason's sperm, Danielle decided to try an IVF procedure. Before the procedure, Danielle and Jason both signed a series of informed consent forms provided by California Fertility Partners. On each form, Danielle filled in both her name and Jason's name in the spaces designated for the "Intended Parent." On March 9, 2009, Jason took Danielle to California Fertility Partners for the IVF procedure. The procedure was successful, and Gus was born in December 2009.

At trial, Jason presented evidence regarding his relationship with Gus and Danielle over the next two and a half years. For example, he presented evidence that Danielle referred to Jason as "Dada" when speaking to Gus, and Gus called Jason "Dada." When Jason was working in New York for six months, Danielle and Gus flew there several times and stayed with Jason at his apartment. When Danielle and Gus were not in New York with Jason, Jason communicated with Gus over the Internet by Skype. Jason continued to maintain contact with Gus until the middle of 2012, when Danielle terminated her relationship with Jason.

[In Jason's suit to establish a parental relationship, the trial court granted Danielle's motion for a nonsuit and rejecting Jason's arguments based on estoppel and section 7611(d). The trial court's decision was based principally on *Steven S. v. Deborah D.*, 127 Cal. App. 4th 319 (Cal. App. 2005), a California intermediate appellate court decision interpreting section 7613(b) to hold that the donor of semen provided to licensed physician for use in artificial insemination of woman other than donor's wife is not the natural father of child thereby conceived, notwithstanding an intimate relationship between donor and woman who became pregnant by artificial insemination.] . . .

Finally, the trial court found that application of section 7613(b) to Jason is not unconstitutional. The court noted that "the Legislature has weighed competing public policies regarding paternity and sperm donors, and has reconciled those considerations by affording ' "to unmarried women a statutory right to bear children by artificial insemination (as well as a right of men to donate semen) without fear of a paternity claim [and] likewise provided men with a statutory vehicle for donating semen to married and unmarried women alike without fear of liability for child support." ' [Citation.] This public policy determination is within the Legislature's authority, and does not make § 7613(b) unconstitutional."

Having found that Jason did not have a parent and child relationship with Gus, the trial court found Jason was not entitled to custody of, or visitation with, Gus. . . . Judgment was entered in favor of Danielle, from which Jason appeals.

. . . .

. . . [O]ur categorical statement [in Steven S.] appears to have been undermined by an observation the California Supreme Court made in a case decided a few months after our decision in Steven S. In K.M. v. E.G., 117 P.3d 673 (Cal. 2005), the Supreme Court examined section 7613(b) in the context of a lesbian couple, where one of the women, K.M., provided ova to her partner, E.G., for use in an IVF procedure. After the relationship ended, K.M. filed an action to establish a parental relationship with the twin girls born to E.G. as a result of the IVF procedure. The trial court granted E.G.'s motion to dismiss, finding, among other things, that K.M.'s position was analogous to that of a sperm donor under section 7613(b).

The [California] Supreme Court reversed, finding that the facts "[did] not present a 'true "egg donation"' situation" because the couple lived together and intended to bring the child into their joint home, and therefore section 7613(b), assuming it applied to women who donate ova, did not apply. The court . . . noted that, while the Model UPA " 'restricts application of the nonpaternity provision of [section 7613(b)] to a "married woman other than the donor's wife[,]" ' . . . in California, [section 7613(b)] applies to all women, married or not. [¶] Thus, the California Legislature has afforded unmarried as well as married women a statutory vehicle for obtaining semen for artificial insemination without fear that the donor may claim paternity and has likewise provided men with a statutory vehicle for donating semen to married and unmarried women alike without fear of liability for child support.' " The court concluded: "It is clear, therefore, that California intended to expand the protection of the model act to include unmarried women so that unmarried women could avail themselves of artificial insemination. But there is nothing to indicate that California intended to expand the reach of this provision so far that it would apply if a man provided semen to be used to impregnate his unmarried partner in order to produce a child that would be raised in their joint home. It would be surprising, to say the least, to conclude that the Legislature intended such a result." . . . The [California] Supreme Court did not address the applicability of section 7611(d) in sperm or ova donation cases in K.M. v. E.G. . . .

[W]e hold that section 7613(b) should be interpreted only to preclude a sperm donor from establishing paternity based upon his biological connection to the child, and does not preclude him from establishing that he is a presumed parent under section 7611(d) based upon postbirth conduct.

We reach this conclusion because we must construe section 7613(b) " 'with reference to the entire scheme of law of which it is part so that the whole may be harmonized and retain effectiveness.' " [W]e choose the construction that comports most closely with the Legislature's apparent intent, endeavoring to promote rather than defeat the statute's general purpose, and avoiding a construction that would lead to absurd consequences."

Section 7613(b) and section 7611 both are part of the UPA. Section 7611 provides that "[a] person is presumed to be the natural parent of a child if the person meets the conditions provided in Chapter 1 or Chapter 3 of Part 2," or if the person meets certain other conditions set forth in the subdivisions that follow. Those conditions are: (1) the presumed parent and the mother are or have been married, and the child is born during the marriage or within 300 days after the marriage was terminated; (2) the presumed parent and the mother attempted to marry before the child's birth, but the marriage was declared invalid; (3) the presumed parent and the mother married or attempted to marry after the child's birth, and the presumed parent (with his or her consent) is named on the child's birth certificate or the presumed parent is obligated to support the child under a written agreement or court order; (4) the presumed parent receives the child into his or her home and openly holds out the child as his or her natural child; or (5) the child was conceived after the death of the presumed parent under the conditions set forth in Probate Code section 249.5.

" 'The paternity presumptions are driven by state interest in preserving the integrity of the family and legitimate concern for the welfare of the child. The state has an " 'interest in preserving and protecting the developed parent-child . . . relationships which give young children social and emotional strength and stability.' " (*In re Nicholas H.*, 46 P.3d 932 (Cal. 2002)). . . .' " " 'The statutory purpose [of section 7611] is to distinguish between those fathers who have entered into some familial relationship with the mother and child and those who have not.' " A biological connection to the child is not necessary for the presumption of paternity to arise. Nor is it necessary for the person seeking presumed parent status to have entered into the familial relationship from the time of conception or birth. "[T]he premise behind the category of presumed father is that an individual who has demonstrated a commitment to the child and the child's welfare—regardless of whether he is biologically the father—is entitled to the elevated status of presumed fatherhood." Thus, a sperm donor who has established a familial relationship with the child, and has demonstrated a commitment to the child and the child's welfare, can be found to be a presumed parent even though he could not establish paternity based upon his biological connection to the child.

By interpreting section 7613(b) only to preclude a sperm donor from establishing paternity based upon his biological connection to the child, while allowing him to establish that he is a presumed parent under section 7611 based upon a demonstrated familial relationship, we allow both statutes to retain effectiveness and promote the purpose of each. Moreover, we avoid a construction that would lead to unintended, and some might say absurd, consequences. For example, suppose an unmarried couple who had tried unsuccessfully to conceive a child naturally, finally was able to conceive through assisted reproduction. They then got married, after conception but before the birth of the child, and raised the child together. After several years, they divorced and the mother sought child support because she could not afford to care for the child on her own. Under Danielle's interpretation of section 7613(b), the mother's ex-husband would have no obligation to support the child because he was a sperm donor under section 7613(b) and could not be found to be the child's presumed father under section 7611, despite having been married to the mother at the time of the child's birth and having raised the child as his own. The Legislature could not have intended this result.

Our holding that a sperm donor is not precluded from establishing presumed parentage does not mean that a mother who conceives through assisted reproduction and allows the sperm donor to have some kind of relationship with the child necessarily loses her right to be the sole parent.

First, section 7611 requires a familial relationship. . . . A mother wishing to retain her sole right to parent her child conceived through assisted reproduction can limit the kind of contact she allows the sperm donor to have with her child to ensure that the relationship does not rise to the level of presumed parent and child.

Second, the presumption of parentage under section 7611 is, with certain exceptions, a rebuttable presumption. (§ 7612, subd. (a).) Thus, even if a sperm donor can establish that he received the child into his home and openly held out the child as his natural child, the trial court nevertheless may conclude based on other evidence that the presumption has been rebutted and the sperm donor is not the child's natural father.

In this case, Jason was denied the opportunity to present evidence to show that he is Gus's presumed father under section 7611(d). Therefore, the judgment must be reversed and the matter remanded for further proceedings.

. . . .

NOTES

1. *In the shadow of* Jhordan C. Prior to the decision in *Jason P.*, California courts relied on *Jhordan C. v. Mary K.*, 224 Cal. Rptr. 530 (Ct. App. 1986), to resolve parentage disputes between acquaintances who had availed themselves of ART. In *Jhordan C.*, Mary decided to have a child with her "close friend" Victoria and sought a sperm donor, eventually settling on Jhordan C. With Victoria's assistance, Mary inseminated herself with Jhordan's semen at home, without any physician involvement. After the child's birth, Mary allowed Jhordan monthly visitation, but terminated those visits after only five months. Jhordan then sought, over Mary's objection, to establish paternity and visitation rights in court. A California intermediate appellate court ruled in favor of Jhordan, finding that, under state law, a sperm donor's paternity rights are invalidated only if the insemination is

conducted "under the supervision of a licensed physician." *Id.* at 534. Why might the court in *Jhordan C.* have been willing to acknowledge as a father an individual who was a known sperm donor? In a later case, *Steven S. v. Deborah D.*, a California appellate court, relying on Cal. Fam. Code section 7613, refused to confer legal parentage to Steven, who had provided sperm to artificially inseminate Deborah, a woman with whom he had an on-again-off-again relationship for years. Why was the court unwilling to acknowledge as a father a man who has not only provided his sperm for insemination, but also maintained a sexual relationship with the child's mother? What distinguishes *Steven S.* from the circumstances in *Jason P.*?

2.   *Sperm donation and doctors.* The first Uniform Parentage Act, § 5(b) (1973) (UPA), noted that when a woman was inseminated by donor sperm "under the supervision of a licensed physician" and with the consent of her husband, the donor was absolved from the legal rights and obligations of paternity. However, the 2002 revision of the UPA removed the requirement of physician supervision. U.P.A. § 102, 701 (2002). Keep in mind that the UPA, like the Model Penal Code, is only advisory and states can and do continue to require a doctor's supervision as a condition for absolving the sperm donor of the rights and obligations of paternity. For example, a Kansas man donated sperm to two lesbians, who used the sperm for insemination without physician supervision. Although the donor and the intended parents signed a contract in which the donor waived all parental rights and obligations, the donor was later found liable for $4,000 in child support when one of the mothers sought public assistance. The Kansas parentage law, like the law in many states, retained the provision that, in order to absolve the donor of parental rights and obligations, sperm donation must be "provided" under the supervision of a licensed physician. Kansas Parentage Act, KAN. STAT. ANN. § 23–2208(f) (2014). According to the donor, "no one was aware of the statute." Susan Donaldson James, *Kansas Sperm Donor Ordered to Pay Child Support*, ABCNEWS.COM (Jan. 24, 2014), http://abcnews.go.com/Health/kansas-sperm-donor-ordered-pay-child-support/story?id=21657212.

3.   *Modern fatherhood.* A poll taken in 2013 found that eighty percent of men always knew they wanted to be a parent (compared with seventy percent of women). *See* Jennifer Agiesta, *Poll: Most Men Aspire to Be Dads*, AP NEWS (June 15, 2013), https://apnews.com/article/fca2ccef4c0c452c98c8f2401029106e. Further, men's attitudes toward fatherhood are changing rapidly. Men who are fathers are doing almost three times as much childcare as their fathers did. Kim Parker & Wendy Wang, *Modern Parenthood*, PEW RESEARCH: SOCIAL & DEMOGRAPHIC TRENDS (Mar. 14, 2013), http://www.pewsocialtrends.org/2013/03/14/modern-parenthood-roles-of-moms-and-dads-converge-as-they-balance-work-and-family/.

4.   *Artificial insemination in law and culture.* In the 2013 movie *Delivery Man*, Vince Vaughn portrayed a charming loser whose life changes dramatically when he discovers he has fathered 533 children over the course of two decades of regular sperm donation. DELIVERY MAN (DreamWorks 2013). *Delivery Man* may be a case of art imitating life: few regulations govern sperm donors in the United States, and only an estimated twenty percent to forty percent of users report successful pregnancies back to the

sperm bank. In the absence of regulation, web-based registries have developed to track children born from the same donor, and to connect sperm, egg, and embryo donors with the children born from these procedures. In 2011, a donor on one registry had 150 children registered. *See* Jacqueline Mroz, *From One Sperm Donor, 150 Children*, N.Y. TIMES, Sept. 5, 2011, at D1. Looking to foreign jurisdictions like Sweden, Austria, Germany, and some Australian states, which mandate sperm donor registration, Professor Naomi Cahn has advocated for a similar mandatory registration system in the United States. *See* Naomi Cahn, *The New Kinship*, 100 GEO. L.J. 367, 416, 428 (2012). While such registries may provide greater transparency for donor offspring, some scholars maintain that these gains pose too great a cost to other values that donor anonymity may foster. *See* I. Glenn Cohen, Response, *Rethinking Sperm-Donor Anonymity: Of Changed Selves, Nonidentity, and One-Night Stands*, 100 GEO. L.J. 431, 437 (2012).

* * *

As reproductive technology continued to evolve, ovum donation and gestational surrogacy became a feasible means of assisted reproductive technology for individuals seeking to expand their families. It was particularly helpful for LGBT families but was also used by heterosexual couples. The following case concerns a married couple that created a number of embryos for use in in vitro fertilization. The case grapples with the question of how to deal with unused embryos—and other genetic materials—when those preparing to use ART end their relationship.

In re Marriage of Rooks

429 P.3d 579 (Colo. 2018).

■ MARQUEZ, J.

In vitro fertilization ("IVF") has given individuals and couples who are unable to conceive conventionally the opportunity to have genetic children. [H]owever, when married couples turn to this technology and later divorce, IVF can present a host of legal dilemmas, including how to resolve disagreements over the disposition of cryogenically preserved pre-embryos that remain at the time of dissolution. [The court uses the technical term "pre-embryos" to refer to eggs that have been fertilized via IVF but not yet been implanted in the uterus.]

Petitioner Ms. Mandy Rooks and Respondent Mr. Drake Rooks married in 2002. They separated in August 2014, and Mr. Rooks filed a petition for dissolution of marriage the following month. . . . Mr. and Ms. Rooks used IVF to have their three children. [At that time, they entered into agreements with the fertility clinic that recorded the couple's decisions regarding the disposition of their frozen pre-embryos under certain scenarios. They agreed that, in the event of the husband's death, the pre-embryos would be transferred to the wife. In the event of her death, or if both parties died, the pre-embryos would be discarded. The agreements failed to specify how any remaining pre-embryos should be allocated in the event of divorce. The agreements merely provided that "the disposition of our embryos will be part of the divorce/dissolution decree paperwork."]

[At the time of the divorce, there were six remaining cryogenically preserved pre-embryos.] Ms. Rooks wished to preserve the pre-embryos for future implantation. . . . Mr. Rooks wished to thaw and discard the pre-embryos; he testified that he did not wish to have more children from his relationship with Ms. Rooks. . . .

Although this case concerns the equitable division of marital property in a divorce proceeding, we recognize that the parties' competing interests in the disputed pre-embryos derive from constitutional rights in the realm of reproductive choice. We therefore briefly discuss the governing case law in this area.

The U.S. Supreme Court has recognized the importance of individual autonomy over decisions involving reproduction. Over seventy-five years ago, the Court recognized that procreation is "one of the basic civil rights" and that marriage and procreation are fundamental to human existence and survival. As the Court considered new questions involving reproductive rights . . . , it began to articulate those rights as part of a cluster of privacy rights grounded in several fundamental constitutional guarantees. . . . "Reading [these cases together] leads to the conclusion that an individual has the fundamental right not only to bear children, but to decide not to be the source of another life as well." . . .

Having acknowledged the rights that underlie the parties' dispute here, we turn to case law from courts in other jurisdictions that have confronted similar disputes. These courts have adhered to or combined aspects of three main approaches: (1) interpreting the parties' contract or agreement regarding disposition of the pre-embryos; (2) balancing the parties' respective interests in receiving the pre-embryos; or (3) requiring the parties' mutual contemporaneous consent regarding disposition of the pre-embryos.

Many jurisdictions begin by looking for a preexisting agreement between the parties regarding disposition of remaining pre-embryos, as evidenced by consent or storage agreements between the IVF facility and the parties. . . . [T]he New York Court of Appeals determined that the IVF program consent forms signed by the couple during their marriage manifested their mutual intent that, in the event of divorce, the pre-embryos should be donated for research to the IVF program. The court thus ordered that the agreement be enforced. Similarly, in *Marriage of Dahl & Angle* [194 P.3d 834, 842 (Or. Ct. App. 2008)] and *Roman v. Roman,* [193 S.W.3d 40, 54–55 (Tex. App. 2006)], the courts resolved the dispute by interpreting the agreements the parties signed with the IVF clinics when they created the pre-embryos.

In some cases, courts have concluded that no enforceable agreement existed or that an existing agreement did not address who should receive the remaining pre-embryos in the event of divorce. For example, in *Davis v. Davis*, 842 S.W.2d 588 (Tenn. 1992), the parties did not execute a written agreement regarding the disposition of any preserved pre-embryos when they signed up for the IVF program. . . .

In cases where no enforceable agreement exists, many courts have conducted what has been termed a "balancing of interests" test to decide how to award or dispose of the pre-embryos. The Supreme Court of Tennessee employed such an approach in *Davis v. Davis*. There, the court acknowledged that the conflicting interests at stake were of "equal significance—the right to procreate and the right to avoid procreation." Given the absence of an enforceable agreement, the court resolved the dispute by considering "the positions of the parties, the significance of their interests, and the relative burdens that will be imposed by differing resolutions." In balancing these interests, the court considered several factors, including (1) the burden of unwanted parenthood on the ex-husband who wished to discard the pre-embryos, particularly in light of his own childhood experience of being separated from his parents; (2) the ex-wife's interest in donating the pre-embryos to another couple to avoid the emotional burden of knowing that the IVF procedures were futile; and (3) the ex-wife's ability to become a parent by other reasonable means in the future. Ultimately, the *Davis* court concluded that the balance of interests weighed in favor of the ex-husband's desire to discard the pre-embryos. . . .

Finally, a small minority of courts have adopted a "mutual contemporaneous consent" approach, under which the court will not award the pre-embryos over the objection of either party. Instead, "no transfer, release, disposition, or use of the [pre-]embryos can occur without the signed authorization of both donors." This approach recognizes that disputed pre-embryos are "not easily susceptible to a just division because conflicting constitutional rights are at issue." In theory, the mutual contemporaneous consent approach purportedly "subjects neither party to any unwarranted governmental intrusion but rather leaves the intimate decision of whether to potentially have more children to the parties alone."

However, the mutual contemporaneous consent approach has been criticized by other courts as being "totally unrealistic" because if the parties were capable of reaching an agreement, then they would not be in court. As both the trial court and court of appeals recognized in this case, the mutual contemporaneous consent approach gives one party a de facto veto over the other party by avoiding any resolution until the issue is eventually mooted by the passage of time. And as at least one scholar has pointed out, this de facto veto creates incentives for one party to leverage his or her power unfairly. Because the mutual contemporaneous consent approach allows one party to "change his or her mind about disposition up to the point of use or destruction of any stored [pre-]embryo," regardless of any preexisting agreement, it injects legal uncertainty into the process. Thus, this approach potentially increases litigation in already emotionally charged and fundamentally private matters.

Although these three approaches have been characterized and discussed as three different "rules" or "methods" for resolving disputes over frozen pre-embryos, we note that the approaches share conceptual underpinnings and reflect common goals. Both the contract approach and the mutual contemporaneous consent approach prioritize the parties' mutual consent and agreement. The contract approach simply encourages the parties to arrive at agreement regarding the disposition of the pre-embryos in advance of divorce. By contrast, the mutual contemporaneous consent approach requires the parties' mutual consent whenever a disposition occurs—regardless of any preexisting agreements. (Indeed, the mutual contemporaneous consent approach eliminates any incentive for parties to agree up front about what should happen with the pre-embryos in the event of divorce and thereby avoid litigation.)

Further, many courts combine one or more of the approaches in order to resolve disputes—e.g., applying the contract approach first and, if no enforceable agreement exists, then balancing the parties' competing interests.

[W]e now address how courts in Colorado should resolve disagreements over a couple's cryogenically preserved pre-embryos when that couple divorces. [C]onsidering the nature and equivalency of the underlying liberty and privacy interests at stake, we conclude that a court presiding over dissolution proceedings should strive, where possible, to honor both parties' interests in procreational autonomy when resolving these disputes. Thus, we hold that a court should look first to any existing agreement expressing the spouses' intent regarding disposition of the couple's remaining pre-embryos in the event of divorce. . . . [B]inding agreements "minimize misunderstandings and maximize procreative liberty by reserving to the progenitors [gamete donors] the authority to make what is in the first instance a quintessentially personal, private decision." We agree that, "[t]o the extent possible, it should be the progenitors—not the State and not the courts—who by their prior directive make this deeply personal life choice." . . .

However, in the absence of an enforceable agreement regarding disposition of the pre-embryos, and where the parties have turned to the courts to resolve their dispute, the dissolution court should balance the parties' respective interests and award the pre-embryos accordingly. Recognizing a couple's cryogenically preserved pre-embryos as marital property of a special character, the underlying principle that informs our balancing test is autonomy over decisions involving reproduction. Thus, the framework we adopt in this special context is [more narrow than the trial court's] consideration of various factors in determining equitable distribution of other forms of marital property. Here, underlying the court's disposition of this special form of property are the parties' individual interests in either achieving or avoiding genetic parenthood through use of the disputed pre-embryos.

We first discuss a non-exhaustive list of considerations that a court should weigh in disposing of the marital pre-embryos. . . . To begin with, courts should consider the intended use of the party seeking to preserve the disputed pre-embryos. A party who seeks to become a genetic parent through implantation of the pre-embryos, for example, has a weightier interest than one who seeks to donate the pre-embryos to another couple.

A court should also consider the demonstrated physical ability (or, conversely, inability) of the party seeking to implant the disputed pre-embryos to have biological children through other means.

Relatedly, the court should consider the parties' original reasons for pursuing IVF, which may favor preservation over disposition. For example, the couple may have turned to IVF to preserve a spouse's future ability to have biological children in the face of fertility-implicating medical treatment, such as chemotherapy.

The court's analysis should also include consideration of hardship for the person seeking to avoid becoming a genetic parent, including emotional, financial, or logistical considerations. In addition, a court should consider either spouse's demonstrated bad faith or attempt to use the pre-embryos as unfair leverage in the divorce proceedings.

Factors other than the ones described above may be relevant on a case-by-case basis. That said, we hold that the following are improper considerations in a dissolution court's allocation of a couple's cryogenically preserved pre-embryos. First, we decline to adopt a test that would allow courts to limit the size of a family based on financial and economic distinctions. Thus, a dissolution court should not assess whether the party seeking to become a genetic parent using the pre-embryos can afford another child. Nor shall the sheer number of a party's existing children, standing alone, be a reason to preclude preservation or use of the pre-embryos. Finally, we note that some courts have mentioned adoption as an alternative to biological or genetic parenthood through conventional or assisted reproduction. However, because we conclude the relevant interest at stake is the interest in achieving or avoiding genetic parenthood, courts should not consider whether a spouse seeking to use the pre-embryos to become a genetic parent could instead adopt a child or otherwise parent non-biological children.

The framework that we adopt today recognizes that both spouses have equally valid, constitutionally based interests in procreational autonomy. It encourages couples to record their mutual consent regarding the disposition of remaining pre-embryos in the event of divorce by an express agreement. [However,] where the parties' consent to disposition of the pre-embryos in the event of divorce is not memorialized in an enforceable agreement, and the parties therefore must turn to a court to resolve their dispute, [the balancing of interests approach we adopt] is consistent with Colorado law directing dissolution courts to divide marital property based on a consideration of relevant factors, while taking into account that pre-embryos are marital property of a special character.

Here, Mr. and Ms. Rooks reached agreement regarding the disposition of pre-embryos in the event of certain contingencies (such as the death of one or both of the spouses). However, they failed to agree in advance how the remaining cryogenically preserved pre-embryos should be allocated in the event of divorce. [Rather], their written agreement left it to the dissolution court to determine how to allocate the pre-embryos. Thus, awarding the pre-embryos in accordance with law governing the distribution of marital property also satisfies the expectations of the parties, who specified that in the event of divorce, the dissolution decree would address the disposition of any remaining cryogenically preserved pre-embryos. Because we announce a new framework for resolving disputes regarding the disposition of pre-embryos frozen during marriage in the event of divorce, [we reverse] and remand the case with instructions to return the matter to the trial court to balance the parties' interests under the approach we adopt today. . . .

NOTES

1.   Roe's *long shadow*. The Court's abortion jurisprudence shadows the legal status of unused embryos, raising questions as to whether embryos and pre-embryos are "human beings" or "property" or whether the right to terminate a pregnancy gestured toward a commensurate right to refuse to become a parent.

2.   *"Snowflake" adoptions*. One of the consequences of the existing forms of ART is that many more eggs are retrieved (and fertilized) than can be used in one implantation, as was the case in *Rooks*. Common practice is to cryopreserve the resulting embryos. However, the question remains: how should these frozen embryos be used? Some have argued that frozen embryos should be made available for future use by other couples. However, a survey by the Society for Assisted Reproductive Technology and the RAND Corporation in 2003 estimated that less than three percent of the approximately 400,000 frozen embryos in the United States are actually donated for use by other couples. David I. Hoffman et al., *Cryopreserved Embryos in the United States and Their Availability for Research*, 79 FERTILITY & STERILITY 1063, 1066 (2003). Those that are not donated or implanted typically are destroyed or disposed. In 1997, the Nightlight Christian Adoption Agency started the Snowflakes Frozen Embryo Adoption Program, which sought to increase donation rates of unused embryos by convincing couples to donate unused frozen embryos for "adoption" by infertile couples. Critically, the group's interest in embryo donation is shaped, in part, by their views on abortion. The campaign stresses that these embryos are unborn babies who, like snowflakes, are unique and

individualized. Pam Belluck, *From Stem Cell Opponent, an Embryo Crusade*, N.Y. TIMES, June 2, 2005, at A1.

Johnson v. Calvert

851 P.2d 776 (Cal. 1993).

■ PANELLI, J.

. . . .

Mark and Crispina Calvert are a married couple who desired to have a child. Crispina was forced to undergo a hysterectomy in 1984. Her ovaries remained capable of producing eggs, however, and the couple eventually considered surrogacy. In 1989 Anna Johnson heard about Crispina's plight from a coworker and offered to serve as a surrogate for the Calverts.

On January 15, 1990, Mark, Crispina, and Anna signed a contract providing that an embryo created by the sperm of Mark and the egg of Crispina would be implanted in Anna and the child born would be taken into Mark and Crispina's home "as their child." Anna agreed she would relinquish "all parental rights" to the child in favor of Mark and Crispina. In return, Mark and Crispina would pay Anna $10,000 in a series of installments, the last to be paid six weeks after the child's birth. Mark and Crispina were also to pay for a $200,000 life insurance policy on Anna's life.

The zygote was implanted on January 19, 1990. Less than a month later, an ultrasound test confirmed Anna was pregnant.

Unfortunately, relations deteriorated between the two sides. Mark learned that Anna had not disclosed she had suffered several stillbirths and miscarriages. Anna felt Mark and Crispina did not do enough to obtain the required insurance policy. She also felt abandoned during an onset of premature labor in June.

In July 1990, Anna sent Mark and Crispina a letter demanding the balance of the payments due her or else she would refuse to give up the child. The following month, Mark and Crispina responded with a lawsuit, seeking a declaration they were the legal parents of the unborn child. Anna filed her own action to be declared the mother of the child, and the two cases were eventually consolidated. The parties agreed to an independent *guardian ad litem* for the purposes of the suit.

The child was born on September 19, 1990, and blood samples were obtained from both Anna and the child for analysis. The blood test results excluded Anna as the genetic mother. The parties agreed to a court order providing that the child would remain with Mark and Crispina on a temporary basis with visits by Anna.

At trial in October 1990, the parties stipulated that Mark and Crispina were the child's genetic parents. After hearing evidence and arguments, the trial court ruled that Mark and Crispina were the child's "genetic, biological and natural" father and mother, that Anna had no "parental" rights to the child, and that the surrogacy contract was legal and enforceable against Anna's claims. The court also terminated the order allowing visitation. Anna appealed from the trial court's judgment. The Court of Appeal for the Fourth District, Division Three, affirmed. We granted review.

. . . .

Civil Code sections 7001 and 7002 replace the distinction between legitimate and illegitimate children with the concept of the "parent and child relationship." The "parent and child relationship" means "the legal relationship existing between a child and his natural or adoptive parents incident to which the law confers or imposes rights, privileges, duties, and obligations. It includes the mother and child relationship and the father and child relationship." (Civ. Code, § 7001.) "The parent and child relationship extends equally to every child and to every parent, regardless of the marital status of the parents." (Civ. Code, § 7002.) The "parent and child relationship" is thus a legal relationship encompassing two kinds of parents, "natural" and "adoptive."

Passage of the Act clearly was not motivated by the need to resolve surrogacy disputes, which were virtually unknown in 1975. Yet it facially applies to *any* parentage determination, including the rare case in which a child's maternity is in issue. We are invited to disregard the Act and decide this case according to other criteria, including constitutional precepts and our sense of the demands of public policy. We feel constrained, however, to decline the invitation. Not uncommonly, courts must construe statutes in factual settings not contemplated by the enacting legislature. . . . [T]he Act offers a mechanism to resolve this dispute, albeit one not specifically tooled for it. We therefore proceed to analyze the parties' contentions within the Act's framework.

These contentions are readily summarized. Anna, of course, predicates her claim of maternity on the fact that she gave birth to the child. The Calverts contend that Crispina's genetic relationship to the child establishes that she is his mother. . . .

. . . Civil Code section 7003 provides . . . that between a child and the natural mother a parent and child relationship "*may* be established by proof of her having given birth to the child, or under [the Act]." (Civ. Code, § 7003, subd. (1), emphasis added.) Apart from Civil Code section 7003, the Act sets forth no specific means by which a natural mother can establish a parent and child relationship. . . .

. . . .

Significantly for this case, Evidence Code section 892 provides that blood testing may be ordered in an action when paternity is a relevant fact. When maternity is disputed, genetic evidence derived from blood testing is likewise admissible. The Evidence Code further provides that if the court finds the conclusions of all the experts, as disclosed by the evidence based on the blood tests, are that the alleged father is not the father of the child, the question of paternity is resolved accordingly. By parity of reasoning, blood testing may also be dispositive of the question of maternity. Further, there is a rebuttable presumption of paternity (hence, maternity as well) on the finding of a certain number of genetic markers.

... [W]e are left with the undisputed evidence that Anna, not Crispina, gave birth to the child and that Crispina, not Anna, is genetically related to him. Both women thus have adduced evidence of a mother and child relationship as contemplated by the Act. Yet for any child California law recognizes only one natural mother, despite advances in reproductive technology rendering a different outcome biologically possible.[8]

We see no clear legislative preference in Civil Code section 7003 as between blood testing evidence and proof of having given birth. . . .

Because two women each have presented acceptable proof of maternity, we do not believe this case can be decided without enquiring into the parties' intentions as manifested in the surrogacy agreement. Mark and Crispina are a couple who desired to have a child of their own genes but are physically unable to do so without the help of reproductive technology. They affirmatively intended the birth of the child, and took the steps necessary to effect in vitro fertilization. But for their acted-on intention, the child would not exist. Anna agreed to facilitate the procreation of Mark's and Crispina's child. The parties' aim was to bring Mark's and Crispina's child into the world, not for Mark and Crispina to donate a zygote to Anna. Crispina from the outset intended to be the child's mother. Although the gestative function Anna performed was necessary to bring about the child's birth, it is safe to say that Anna would not have been given the opportunity to gestate or deliver the child had she, prior to implantation of the zygote, manifested her own intent to be the child's mother. No reason appears why Anna's later change of heart should vitiate the determination that Crispina is the child's natural mother.

We conclude that although the Act recognizes both genetic consanguinity and giving birth as means of establishing a mother and child relationship, when the two means do not coincide in one woman, she who intended to procreate the child—that is, she who intended to

---

[8] We decline to accept the contention of amicus curiae the American Civil Liberties Union (ACLU) that we should find the child has two mothers. Even though rising divorce rates have made multiple parent arrangements common in our society, we see no compelling reason to recognize such a situation here. The Calverts are the genetic and intending parents of their son and have provided him, by all accounts, with a stable, intact, and nurturing home. To recognize parental rights in a third party with whom the Calvert family has had little contact since shortly after the child's birth would diminish Crispina's role as mother.

bring about the birth of a child that she intended to raise as her own—is the natural mother under California law.[10]

. . . .

In deciding the issue of maternity under the Act we have felt free to take into account the parties' intentions, as expressed in the surrogacy contract, because in our view the agreement is not, on its face, inconsistent with public policy.

. . . .

Anna urges that surrogacy contracts violate several social policies. Relying on her contention that she is the child's legal, natural mother, she cites the public policy embodied in Penal Code section 273, prohibiting the payment for consent to adoption of a child. She argues further that the policies underlying the adoption laws of this state are violated by the surrogacy contract because it in effect constitutes a prebirth waiver of her parental rights.

We disagree. Gestational surrogacy differs in crucial respects from adoption and so is not subject to the adoption statutes. The parties voluntarily agreed to participate in *in vitro* fertilization and related medical procedures before the child was conceived; at the time when Anna entered into the contract, therefore, she was not vulnerable to financial inducements to part with her own expected offspring. As discussed above, Anna was not the genetic mother of the child. The payments to Anna under the contract were meant to compensate her for her services in gestating the fetus and undergoing labor, rather than for giving up "parental" rights to the child. Payments were due both during the pregnancy and after the child's birth. We are, accordingly, unpersuaded that the contract used in this case violates the public policies embodied in Penal Code section 273 and the adoption statutes. For the same reasons, we conclude these contracts do not implicate the policies underlying the statutes governing termination of parental rights.

It has been suggested that gestational surrogacy may run afoul of prohibitions on involuntary servitude. (*See* U.S. CONST., AMEND. XIII; CAL. CONST., art. I, § 6; Pen. Code, § 181.) . . . We see no potential for that

---

[10] Thus, under our analysis, in a true "egg donation" situation, where a woman gestates and gives birth to a child formed from the egg of another woman with the intent to raise the child as her own, the birth mother is the natural mother under California law.

The dissent would decide *parentage* based on the best interests of the child. Such an approach raises the repugnant specter of governmental interference in matters implicating our most fundamental notions of privacy, and confuses concepts of parentage and custody. Logically, the determination of parentage must precede, and should not be dictated by, eventual custody decisions. The implicit assumption of the dissent is that a recognition of the genetic intending mother as the natural mother may sometimes harm the child. This assumption overlooks California's dependency laws, which are designed to protect *all* children irrespective of the manner of birth or conception. Moreover, the best interests standard poorly serves the child in the present situation: it fosters instability during litigation and, if applied to recognize the gestator as the natural mother, results in a split of custody between the natural father and the gestator, an outcome not likely to benefit the child. Further, it may be argued that, by voluntarily contracting away any rights to the child, the gestator has, in effect, conceded the best interests of the child are not with her.

evil in the contract at issue here, and extrinsic evidence of coercion or duress is utterly lacking. We note that although at one point the contract purports to give Mark and Crispina the sole right to determine whether to abort the pregnancy, at another point it acknowledges: "All parties understand that a pregnant woman has the absolute right to abort or not abort any fetus she is carrying. Any promise to the contrary is unenforceable." We therefore need not determine the validity of a surrogacy contract purporting to deprive the gestator of her freedom to terminate the pregnancy.

Finally, Anna and some commentators have expressed concern that surrogacy contracts tend to exploit or dehumanize women, especially women of lower economic status. Anna's objections center around the psychological harm she asserts may result from the gestator's relinquishing the child to whom she has given birth. Some have also cautioned that the practice of surrogacy may encourage society to view children as commodities, subject to trade at their parents' will.

We are all too aware that the proper forum for resolution of this issue is the Legislature, where empirical data, largely lacking from this record, can be studied and rules of general applicability developed. However, in light of our responsibility to decide this case, we have considered as best we can its possible consequences.

We are unpersuaded that gestational surrogacy arrangements are so likely to cause the untoward results Anna cites as to demand their invalidation on public policy grounds. Although common sense suggests that women of lesser means serve as surrogate mothers more often than do wealthy women, there has been no proof that surrogacy contracts exploit poor women to any greater degree than economic necessity in general exploits them by inducing them to accept lower-paid or otherwise undesirable employment. We are likewise unpersuaded by the claim that surrogacy will foster the attitude that children are mere commodities; no evidence is offered to support it. The limited data available seem to reflect an absence of significant adverse effects of surrogacy on all participants.

The argument that a woman cannot knowingly and intelligently agree to gestate and deliver a baby for intending parents carries overtones of the reasoning that for centuries prevented women from attaining equal economic rights and professional status under the law. To resurrect this view is both to foreclose a personal and economic choice on the part of the surrogate mother, and to deny intending parents what may be their only means of procreating a child of their own genes. Certainly in the present case it cannot seriously be argued that Anna, a licensed vocational nurse who had done well in school and who had previously borne a child, lacked the intellectual wherewithal or life experience necessary to make an informed decision to enter into the surrogacy contract.

. . . .

Anna argues at length that her right to the continued companionship of the child is protected under the federal Constitution.

. . . .

Anna relies mainly on theories of substantive due process, privacy, and procreative freedom, citing a number of decisions recognizing the fundamental liberty interest of natural parents in the custody and care of their children. Most of the cases Anna cites deal with the rights of unwed fathers in the face of attempts to terminate their parental relationship to their children. These cases do not support recognition of parental rights for a gestational surrogate. Although Anna quotes language stressing the primacy of a developed parent-child relationship in assessing unwed fathers' rights certain language in the cases reinforces the importance of genetic parents' rights. (*Lehr v. Robertson, supra,* 463 U.S. at p. 262 ["The significance of the biological connection is that it offers the natural father an opportunity that no other male possesses to develop a relationship with his offspring. If he grasps that opportunity and accepts some measure of responsibility for the child's future, he may enjoy the blessings of the parent-child relationship and make uniquely valuable contributions to the child's development."]; *see also Adoption of Kelsey S.,* 1 Cal.4th 816, 838 (1992) ["The biological connection between father and child is unique and worthy of constitutional protection if the father grasps the opportunity to develop that biological connection into a full and enduring relationship."].)

Anna's argument depends on a prior determination that she is indeed the child's mother. Since Crispina is the child's mother under California law because she, not Anna, provided the ovum for the *in vitro* fertilization procedure, intending to raise the child as her own, it follows that any constitutional interests Anna possesses in this situation are something less than those of a mother. As counsel for the minor points out, the issue in this case is not whether Anna's asserted rights as a natural mother were unconstitutionally violated, but rather whether the determination that she is not the legal natural mother at all is constitutional.

Anna relies principally on the decision of the United States Supreme Court in *Michael H. v. Gerald D.,* 491 U.S. 110 (1989), to support her claim to a constitutionally protected liberty interest in the companionship of the child, based on her status as "birth mother." In that case, a plurality of the court held that a state may constitutionally deny a man parental rights with respect to a child he fathered during a liaison with the wife of another man, since it is the marital family that traditionally has been accorded a protected liberty interest, as reflected in the historic presumption of legitimacy of a child born into such a family. The reasoning of the plurality in *Michael H.* does not assist Anna. Society has not traditionally protected the right of a woman who gestates and delivers a baby pursuant to an agreement with a couple who supply the zygote from which the baby develops and who intend to raise the child as their own; such arrangements are of too recent an origin to claim the protection of tradition. To the extent that tradition has a bearing on the present case, we believe it supports the claim of the couple who exercise their right to procreate in order to form a family of their own, albeit through novel medical procedures.

Moreover, if we were to conclude that Anna enjoys some sort of liberty interest in the companionship of the child, then the liberty interests of Mark and Crispina, the child's natural parents, in their procreative choices and their relationship with the child would perforce be infringed. Any parental rights Anna might successfully assert could come only at Crispina's expense. As we have seen, Anna has no parental rights to the child under California law, and she fails to persuade us that sufficiently strong policy reasons exist to accord her a protected liberty interest in the companionship of the child when such an interest would necessarily detract from or impair the parental bond enjoyed by Mark and Crispina.

. . . .

Drawing an analogy to artificial insemination, Anna argues that Mark and Crispina were mere genetic donors who are entitled to no constitutional protection. That characterization of the facts is, however, inaccurate. Mark and Crispina never intended to "donate" genetic material to anyone. Rather, they intended to procreate a child genetically related to them by the only available means. Civil Code section 7005, governing artificial insemination, has no application here.

. . . .

The judgment of the Court of Appeal is affirmed.

■ KENNARD, J., dissenting.

. . . In my view, the woman who provided the fertilized ovum and the woman who gave birth to the child both have substantial claims to legal motherhood. Pregnancy entails a unique commitment, both psychological and emotional, to an unborn child. No less substantial, however, is the contribution of the woman from whose egg the child developed and without whose desire the child would not exist.

For each child, California law accords the legal rights and responsibilities of parenthood to only one "natural mother." When, as here, the female reproductive role is divided between two women, California law requires courts to make a decision as to which woman is the child's natural mother, but provides no standards by which to make that decision. The majority's resort to "intent" to break the "tie" between the genetic and gestational mothers is unsupported by statute, and, in the absence of appropriate protections in the law to guard against abuse of surrogacy arrangements, it is ill-advised. To determine who is the legal mother of a child born of a gestational surrogacy arrangement, I would apply the standard most protective of child welfare—the best interests of the child.

. . . .

The ethical, moral and legal implications of using gestational surrogacy for human reproduction have engendered substantial debate. . . .

Surrogacy proponents generally contend that gestational surrogacy, like the other reproductive technologies that extend the ability to procreate to persons who might not otherwise be able to have children, enhances "individual freedom, fulfillment and responsibility." . . .

. . . .

Surrogacy critics, however, maintain that the payment of money for the gestation and relinquishment of a child threatens the economic exploitation of poor women who may be induced to engage in commercial surrogacy arrangements out of financial need. Some fear the development of a "breeder" class of poor women who will be regularly employed to bear children for the economically advantaged. Others suggest that women who enter into surrogacy arrangements may underestimate the psychological impact of relinquishing a child they have nurtured in their bodies for nine months.

Gestational surrogacy is also said to be "dehumanizing" and to "commodify" women and children by treating the female reproductive capacity and the children born of gestational surrogacy arrangements as products that can be bought and sold. The commodification of women and children, it is feared, will reinforce oppressive gender stereotypes and threaten the well-being of all children. Some critics foresee promotion of an ever-expanding "business of surrogacy brokerage."

. . . .

Proponents and critics of gestational surrogacy propose widely differing approaches for deciding who should be the legal mother of a child born of a gestational surrogacy arrangement. Surrogacy advocates propose to enforce pre-conception contracts in which gestational mothers have agreed to relinquish parental rights, and, thus, would make "bargained-for intentions determinative of legal parenthood." . . .

Surrogacy critics, on the other hand, consider the unique female role in human reproduction as the determinative factor in questions of legal parentage. They reason that although males and females both contribute genetic material for the child, the act of gestating the fetus falls only on the female. Accordingly, in their view, a woman who, as the result of gestational surrogacy, is not genetically related to the child she bears is like any other woman who gives birth to a child. In either situation the woman giving birth is the child's mother. Under this approach, the laws governing adoption should govern the parental rights to a child born of gestational surrogacy. Upon the birth of the child, the gestational mother can decide whether or not to relinquish her parental rights in favor of the genetic mother.

. . . .

Faced with the failure of current statutory law to adequately address the issue of who is a child's natural mother when two women qualify under the UPA, the majority breaks the "tie" by resort to a criterion not found in the UPA—the "intent" of the genetic mother to be the child's mother.

This case presents a difficult issue. The majority's resolution of that issue deserves serious consideration. Ultimately, however, I cannot agree that "intent" is the appropriate test for resolving this case.

The majority offers four arguments in support of its conclusion to rely on the intent of the genetic mother as the exclusive determinant for deciding who is the natural mother of a child born of gestational surrogacy. Careful examination, however, demonstrates that none of the arguments mandates the majority's conclusion.

The first argument that the majority uses in support of its conclusion that the intent of the genetic mother to bear a child should be dispositive of the question of motherhood is "but-for" causation. Specifically, the majority relies on a commentator who writes that in a gestational surrogacy arrangement, "the child would not have been born *but* for the efforts of the intended parents."

. . . .

. . . Neither the "but for" nor the "substantial factor" test of causation provides any basis for preferring the genetic mother's intent as the determinative factor in gestational surrogacy cases: Both the genetic and the gestational mothers are indispensable to the birth of a child in a gestational surrogacy arrangement.

Behind the majority's reliance on "but-for" causation as justification for its intent test is a second, closely related argument. The majority draws its second rationale from a student note: " 'The mental concept of the child is a controlling factor of its creation, and the originators of that concept merit full credit as conceivers.' "

The "originators of the concept" rationale seems comfortingly familiar. The reason it seems familiar, however, is that it is a rationale that is frequently advanced as justifying the law's protection of intellectual property. As stated by one author, "an idea belongs to its creator because the idea is a manifestation of the creator's personality or self." Thus, it may be argued, just as a song or invention is protected as the property of the "originator of the concept," so too a child should be regarded as belonging to the originator of the concept of the child, the genetic mother.

The problem with this argument, of course, is that children are not property. Unlike songs or inventions, rights in children cannot be sold for consideration, or made freely available to the general public. Our most fundamental notions of personhood tell us it is inappropriate to treat children as property. Although the law may justly recognize that the originator of a concept has certain property rights in that concept, the originator of the concept of a child can have no such rights, because children cannot be owned as property. Accordingly, I cannot endorse the majority's "originators of the concept" or intellectual property rationale for employing intent to break the "tie" between the genetic mother and the gestational mother of the child.

Next, the majority offers as its third rationale the notion that bargained-for expectations support its conclusion regarding the dispositive significance of the genetic mother's intent. Specifically, the majority states that "intentions that are voluntarily chosen, deliberate, express and bargained-for ought presumptively to determine legal parenthood."

It is commonplace that, in real or personal property transactions governed by contracts, "intentions that are voluntarily chosen, deliberate, express and bargained-for" ought presumptively to be enforced and, when one party seeks to escape performance, the court may order specific performance. But the courts will not compel performance of all contract obligations. For instance, even when a party to a contract for personal services (such as employment) has wilfully breached the contract, the courts will not order specific enforcement of an obligation to perform that personal service. The unsuitability of applying the notion that, because contract intentions are "voluntarily chosen, deliberate, express and bargained-for," their performance ought to be compelled by the courts is even more clear when the concept of specific performance is used to determine the course of the life of a child. Just as children are not the intellectual property of their parents, neither are they the personal property of anyone, and their delivery cannot be ordered as a contract remedy on the same terms that a court would, for example, order a breaching party to deliver a truckload of nuts and bolts.

Thus, three of the majority's four arguments in support of its exclusive reliance on the intent of the genetic mother as determinative in gestational surrogacy cases cannot withstand analysis. And, as I shall discuss shortly, the majority's fourth rationale has merit, but does not support the majority's conclusion. But before turning to the majority's fourth rationale, I shall discuss two additional considerations, not noted by the majority, that in my view also weigh against utilizing the intent of the genetic mother as the sole determinant of the result in this case and others like it.

First, in making the intent of the genetic mother who wants to have a child the dispositive factor, the majority renders a certain result preordained and inflexible in every such case: as between an intending genetic mother and a gestational mother, the genetic mother will, under the majority's analysis, always prevail. The majority recognizes no meaningful contribution by a woman who agrees to carry a fetus to term for the genetic mother beyond that of mere employment to perform a specified biological function.

The majority's approach entirely devalues the substantial claims of motherhood by a gestational mother such as Anna. True, a woman who enters into a surrogacy arrangement intending to raise the child has by her intent manifested an assumption of parental responsibility in addition to her biological contribution of providing the genetic material. (*See Adoption of Kelsey S.*, 1 Cal.4th at pp. 838, 849.) But the gestational mother's biological contribution of carrying a child for nine months and giving birth is likewise an assumption of parental responsibility. A pregnant woman's commitment to the unborn child she carries is not just physical; it is psychological and emotional as well. . . . A pregnant woman intending to bring a child into the world is more than a mere container or breeding animal; she is a conscious agent of creation no less than the genetic mother, and her humanity is implicated on a deep level. Her role should not be devalued.

. . . .

I find the majority's reliance on "intent" unsatisfactory for yet another reason. By making intent determinative of parental rights to a child born of a gestational surrogacy arrangement, the majority would permit enforcement of a gestational surrogacy agreement without requiring any of the protections that would be afforded by the Uniform Status of Children of Assisted Conception Act[, a proposed model statute intended to deal with such issues]. Under that act, the granting of parental rights to a couple that initiates a gestational surrogacy arrangement would be conditioned upon compliance with the legislation's other provisions. They include court oversight of the gestational surrogacy arrangement before conception, legal counsel for the woman who agrees to gestate the child, a showing of need for the surrogacy, medical and mental health evaluations, and a requirement that all parties meet the standards of fitness of adoptive parents.

In my view, protective requirements such as those set forth in the USCACA are necessary to minimize any possibility in gestational surrogacy arrangements for overreaching or abuse by a party with economic advantage. . . . The model act's carefully drafted provisions would assure that the surrogacy arrangement is a matter of medical necessity on the part of the intending parents, and not merely the product of a desire to avoid the inconveniences of pregnancy, together with the financial ability to do so. Also, by requiring both pre-conception psychological counseling for all parties and judicial approval, the model act would assure that parties enter into a surrogacy arrangement only if they are legally and psychologically capable of doing so and fully understand all the risks involved, and that the surrogacy arrangement would not be substantially detrimental to the interests of any individual. Moreover, by requiring judicial approval, the model act would significantly discourage the rapid expansion of commercial surrogacy brokerage and the resulting commodification of the products of pregnancy. In contrast, here the majority's grant of parental rights to the intending mother contains no provisions for the procedural protections suggested by the commissioners who drafted the model act. The majority opinion is a sweeping endorsement of unregulated gestational surrogacy.

The majority's final argument in support of using the intent of the genetic mother as the exclusive determinant of the outcome in gestational surrogacy cases is that preferring the intending mother serves the child's interests, which are "[u]nlikely to run contrary to those of adults who choose to bring [the child] into being."

I agree with the majority that the best interests of the child is an important goal. . . . The problem with the majority's rule of intent is that application of this inflexible rule will not serve the child's best interests in every case.

. . . .

. . . In the absence of legislation that is designed to address the unique problems of gestational surrogacy, this court should look not to tort, property or contract law, but to family law, as the governing paradigm and source of a rule of decision.

The allocation of parental rights and responsibilities necessarily impacts the welfare of a minor child. And in issues of child welfare, the standard that courts frequently apply is the best interests of the child. . . . This "best interests" standard serves to assure that in the judicial resolution of disputes affecting a child's well-being, protection of the minor child is the foremost consideration. Consequently, I would apply "the best interests of the child" standard to determine who can best assume the social and legal responsibilities of motherhood for a child born of a gestational surrogacy arrangement.

. . . .

NOTES

1. *The "intentional parenthood" doctrine.* Faced with a dilemma that California law had never contemplated—that the genetic mother of a child might be a different person from the gestational mother—the California Supreme Court turned to a proposal first suggested by Professor Marjorie Shultz. Shultz argued that as assisted reproductive technology grew more common, situations such as those at issue in this case would proliferate. Accordingly, she proposed, the law should give greater respect to intention, as "purposeful affirmative commitments are deserving of societal respect and deference." On this account, since the Calverts had intended to create a family, while Johnson had not, the latter's claims should be viewed as less compelling. *See* Marjorie Maguire Shultz, *Reproductive Technology and Intent-Based Parenthood: An Opportunity for Gender Neutrality*, 1990 WIS. L. REV. 297, 308 (1990). In her dissent, Justice Kennard took a more

skeptical view of the proposal, noting the limits of "intention" as a tie-breaker in cases such as these.

2. *Social versus biological motherhood*. Feminists from the late nineteenth century onward have argued that biology is not destiny, and that there is a difference between the biological capacity to have a child and the social role that is superimposed on that biological capacity. *See* Reva Siegel, *Reasoning from the Body: A Historical Perspective on Abortion Regulation and Questions of Equal Protection*, 44 STAN. L. REV. 261, 267 (1992). In what ways does Marjorie Shultz's "intentional parenthood" model irrevocably sever social and biological motherhood?

3. *An egg donor's story*. Although Calvert was the genetic mother of the egg that produced the child at the heart of the litigation, many individuals conceive via "donated" eggs. In an account of her own experience with egg donation, writer Jen Dziura reminds potential donors of the risks associated with egg donation. Of particular concern are the physical risks of the process. As she notes, Lupron (the drug used to produce multiple eggs in a single cycle) is actually intended to treat men with prostate cancer. Lupron, she explains, is used off-label in egg donation, meaning that it is being used in a manner for which it has not been approved. The off-label use of Lupron alters hormones in donating women—the effects of which can persist well after egg retrieval. In addition to these pharmaceutical complications, the process of egg retrieval is considerably more involved than that required for sperm donation. Finally, Dziura explains that little is known about the long-term consequences—physical or psychological—of egg donation, and that there is no financial incentive to gather such data. Jen Dziura, *The Truth About Egg Donation*, CTR. FOR GENETICS & SOC'Y (2014), www.geneticsandsociety.org/article.php?id=7415. Given these concerns, should anonymous egg and sperm donors be treated the same under the law? Does the invasiveness of the egg-donation process inform the association between biological motherhood and social motherhood? Should it? In what ways do egg retrieval and donation differ from sperm donation? Should these differences inform how we view biological and social fatherhood?

Elisa B. v. Superior Court of El Dorado

117 P.3d 660 (Cal. App. 2005).

■ MORENO, J.

. . . .

In the present action for child support filed by the El Dorado County District Attorney, we conclude that a woman who agreed to raise children with her lesbian partner, supported her partner's artificial insemination using an anonymous donor, and received the resulting twin children into her home and held them out as her own, is the children's parent under the Uniform Parentage Act and has an obligation to support them.

. . . .

On June 7, 2001, the El Dorado County District Attorney filed a complaint in superior court to establish that Elisa B. is a parent of two-year-old twins Kaia B. and Ry B., who were born to Emily B.,[1] and to order Elisa to pay child support. Elisa filed an answer in which she denied being the children's parent.

A hearing was held at which Elisa testified that she entered into a lesbian relationship with Emily in 1993. They began living together six months later. Elisa obtained a tattoo that read "Emily, por vida," which in Spanish means Emily, for life. They introduced each other to friends as their "partner," exchanged rings, opened a joint bank account, and believed they were in a committed relationship.

Elisa and Emily discussed having children and decided that they both wished to give birth. Because Elisa earned more than twice as much money as Emily, they decided that Emily "would be the stay-at-home mother" and Elisa "would be the primary breadwinner for the family." At a sperm bank, they chose a donor they both would use so the children would "be biological brothers and sisters."

After several unsuccessful attempts, Elisa became pregnant in February, 1997. Emily was present when Elisa was inseminated. Emily began the insemination process in June of 1997 and became pregnant in August, 1997. Elisa was present when Emily was inseminated and, the next day, Elisa picked up additional sperm at the sperm bank and again inseminated Emily at their home to "make sure she got pregnant." They went to each other's medical appointments during pregnancy and attended childbirth classes together so that each could act as a "coach" for the other during birth, including cutting the children's umbilical cords.

Elisa gave birth to Chance in November, 1997, and Emily gave birth to Ry and Kaia prematurely in March, 1998. Ry had medical problems; he suffered from Down's Syndrome, and required heart surgery.

They jointly selected the children's names, joining their surnames with a hyphen to form the children's surname. They each breast-fed all of the children. Elisa claimed all three children as her dependents on her tax returns and obtained a life insurance policy on herself naming Emily as the beneficiary so that if "anything happened" to her, all three children would be "cared for." Elisa believed the children would be considered both of their children.

Elisa's parents referred to the twins as their grandchildren, and her sister referred to the twins as part of their family and referred to Elisa as the twins' mother. Elisa treated all of the children as hers and told a prospective employer that she had triplets. Elisa and Emily identified themselves as co-parents of Ry at an organization arranging care for his Down's Syndrome.

---

[1]   In order to protect the confidentiality of the minors, we will refer to the parties by their first names.

Elisa supported the household financially. Emily was not working. Emily testified that she would not have become pregnant if Elisa had not promised to support her financially, but Elisa denied that any financial arrangements were discussed before the birth of the children. Elisa later acknowledged in her testimony, however, that Emily "was going to be an at-home mom for maybe a couple of years and then the kids were going to go into day care and she was going to return to work."

They consulted an attorney regarding adopting "each other's child," but never did so. Nor did they register as domestic partners or execute a written agreement concerning the children. Elisa stated she later reconsidered adoption because she had misgivings about Emily adopting Chance.

Elisa and Emily separated in November, 1999. Elisa promised to support Emily and the twins "as much as I possibly could" and initially paid the mortgage payments of approximately $1,500 per month on the house in which Emily and the twins continued to live, as well as other expenses. Emily applied for aid. When they sold the house and Emily and the twins moved into an apartment in November, 2000, Elisa paid Emily $1,000 a month. In early 2001, Elisa stated she lost her position as a full-time employee and told Emily she no longer could support her and the twins. At the time of trial, Elisa was earning $95,000 a year.

The superior court rendered a written decision on July 11, 2002, finding that Elisa and Emily had rejected the option of using a private sperm donor because "[t]hey wanted the child to be raised *exclusively* by them as a couple." The court further found that they intended to create a child and "acted in all respects as a family," adding "that a person who uses reproductive technology is accountable as a de facto legal parent for the support of that child. Legal parentage is not determined exclusively by biology."

The court further found that Elisa was obligated to support the twins under the doctrine of equitable estoppel, finding Emily "agreed to have children with Respondent, and relied on her promise to raise and support her children. She would not have agreed to impregnation but for this agreement and understanding." "The need for the application of this doctrine is underscored by the fact that the decision of Respondent to create a family and desert them has caused the remaining family members to seek county assistance. One child that was created has special needs that will require the remaining parent or the County to be financially responsible for those needs. The child was deprived of the right to have a traditional father to take care of the financial needs of this child. Respondent chose to step in those shoes and assume the role and responsibility of the 'other' parent. This should be her responsibility and not the responsibility of the taxpayer." Elisa was subsequently ordered to pay child support in the amount of $907.50 per child for a total of $1815 per month.

Elisa petitioned the Court of Appeal for a writ of mandate, and the court directed the superior court to vacate its order and dismiss the action, concluding that Elisa had no obligation to pay child support because she was not a parent of the twins within the meaning of the Uniform Parentage Act (Fam. Code, § 7600 *et seq.*). We granted review.

. . . .

We must determine whether the Court of Appeal erred in ruling that Elisa could not be a parent of the twins born to her lesbian partner, and thus had no obligation to support them. This question is governed by the Uniform Parentage Act (UPA). (Fam. Code, § 7600 *et seq.*) The UPA defines the " '[p]arent and child relationship' " as "the legal relationship existing between a child and the child's natural or adoptive parents. . . . The term includes the mother and child relationship and the father and child relationship." (§ 7601.) One purpose of the UPA was to eliminate distinctions based upon whether a child was born into a marriage, and thus was "legitimate," or was born to unmarried parents, and thus was "illegitimate." Thus, the UPA provides that the parentage of a child does not depend upon " 'the marital status of the parents' " stating: "The parent and child relationship extends equally to every child and to every parent, regardless of the marital status of the parents." (§ 7602.)

The UPA contains separate provisions defining who is a "mother" and who is a "father." Section 7610 provides that "[t]he parent and child relationship may be established . . . (a) Between a child and the natural mother . . . by proof of her having given birth to the child, or under this part." Subdivision (b) of section 7610 states that the parental relationship "[b]etween a child and the natural father . . . may be established under this part."

Section 7611 provides several circumstances in which "[a] man is presumed to be the natural father of a child," including: if he is the husband of the child's mother, is not impotent or sterile, and was cohabiting with her (§ 7540); if he signs a voluntary declaration of paternity stating he is the "biological father of the child" (§ 7574, subd. (a)(6)); and if "[h]e receives the child into his home and openly holds out the child as his natural child" (§ 7611, subd. (d)).

Although, as noted above, the UPA contains separate provisions defining who is a mother and who is a father, it expressly provides that in determining the existence of a mother and child relationship, "[i]nsofar as practicable, the provisions of this part applicable to the father and child relationship apply." (§ 7650.)

The Court of Appeal correctly recognized that, under the UPA, Emily has a parent and child relationship with each of the twins because she gave birth to them. (§ 7610, subd. (a).) Thus, the Court of Appeal concluded, Emily is the twins' natural mother. Relying upon our statement in *Johnson v. Calvert*, 851 P.2d 776 (1991), that "for any child California law recognizes only one natural mother," the Court of Appeal reasoned that Elisa, therefore, could not also be the natural mother of the twins and thus "has no legal maternal relationship with the children under the UPA."

The Attorney General, appearing pursuant to section 17406 to "represent the public interest in establishing, modifying, and enforcing support obligations," argues that the Court of Appeal erred, stating: "*Johnson's* one-natural-mother comment cannot be thoughtlessly interpreted to deprive the child of same-sex couples the same opportunity as other children to two parents and to two sources of child support when only two parties are eligible for parentage." As we shall explain, the Attorney General is correct that our statement in *Johnson* that a child can have "only one natural mother" does not mean that both Elisa and Emily cannot be parents of the twins.

The issue before us in *Johnson* was whether a wife whose ovum was fertilized *in vitro* by her husband's sperm and implanted in a surrogate mother was the mother of the child so produced, rather than the surrogate. The surrogate claimed that she was the child's mother because she had given birth to the child. No provision of the UPA expressly addresses the parental rights of a woman who, like the wife in *Johnson v. Calvert*, has not given birth to a child, but has a genetic relationship because she supplied the ovum used to impregnate the birth mother. But, as noted above, the UPA does provide that provisions applicable to determining a father and child relationship shall be used to determine a mother and child relationship "[i]nsofar as practicable." Accordingly, we looked to the provisions regarding presumptions of paternity and concluded that "genetic consanguinity" could be the basis for a finding of maternity just as it is for paternity.

We concluded, therefore, that both women—the surrogate who gave birth to the child and the wife who supplied the ovum—had "adduced evidence of a mother and child relationship as contemplated by the Act." Anticipating this result, the American Civil Liberties Union appearing as amicus curiae urged this court to rule that the child, therefore, had two mothers. Because it was undisputed that the husband, who had supplied the semen used to impregnate the surrogate, was the child's father, this would have left the child with three parents. We declined the invitation, stating: "Even though rising divorce rates have made multiple parent arrangements common in our society, we see no compelling reason to recognize such a situation here. The Calverts are the genetic and intending parents of their son and have provided him, by all accounts, with a stable, intact, and nurturing home. To recognize parental rights in a third party with whom the Calvert family has had little contact since shortly after the child's birth would diminish [the wife]'s role as mother." We held instead that "for any child California law recognizes only one natural mother" and proceeded to conclude that the wife, rather than the surrogate, was the child's mother: "We conclude that although the Act recognizes both genetic consanguinity and giving birth as means of establishing a mother and child relationship, when the two means do not coincide in one woman, she who intended to procreate the child—that is, she who intended to bring about the birth of a child that she intended to raise as her own—is the natural mother under California law."

In *Johnson*, therefore, we addressed the situation in which three people claimed to be the child's parents: the husband, who undoubtedly was the child's father, and two women, who presented conflicting claims to being the child's mother. We rejected the suggestion of amicus curiae that both the wife and the surrogate could be the child's mother, stating that a child can have only one mother, but what we considered and rejected in *Johnson* was the argument that a child could have three parents: a father and two mothers.[4] We did not address the question presented in this case of whether a child could have two parents, both of whom are women.[5] The Court of Appeal in the present case erred, therefore, in concluding that our statement in *Johnson* that a child can have only one mother under California law resolved the issue presented in this case. "Language used in any opinion is of course to be understood in the light of the facts and the issue then before the court, and an opinion is not authority for a proposition not therein considered."[6]

We perceive no reason why both parents of a child cannot be women. That result now is possible under the current version of the domestic partnership statutes, which took effect this year. (§ 297 et seq.) Two women "who have chosen to share one another's lives in an intimate and committed relationship of mutual caring" and have a common residence (§ 297) can file with the Secretary of State a "Declaration of Domestic Partnership" (§ 298). Section 297.5, subdivision (d) provides, in pertinent part: "The rights and obligations of registered domestic partners with respect to a child of either of them shall be the same as those of spouses."

Prior to the effective date of the current domestic partnership statutes, we recognized in an adoption case that a child can have two parents, both of whom are women. In *Sharon S. v. Superior Court*, 73

---

[4]   We have not decided "whether there exists an overriding legislative policy limiting a child to two parents." (*Sharon S. v. Superior Court*, 73 P.3d 554 (2003)).

[5]   The situation is analogous to that in *Sharon S. v. Superior Court, supra*, 31 Cal.4th 417, 2 Cal.Rptr.3d 699, 73 P.3d 554, in which we held that a mother could consent to a "second parent" adoption by her lesbian partner despite our earlier dictum in *Estate of Jobson* (1912) 164 Cal. 312, 317, 128 P. 938, that the "duties of a child cannot be owed to two fathers at one time." We explained that this statement was "uttered in the context of concluding that a birth father who 'by virtue of the adoption proceeding [in that case], ceased to sustain the legal relation of father' could not thereafter inherit the adopted person's estate [citation], we did not consider the contingency before us today—viz., two parties who voluntarily have waived the benefit of section 8617 in order to effect a second parent adoption, where the natural parent's relationship with the child is not superseded." (*Sharon S.*, at p. 430, fn. 7, 2 Cal.Rptr.3d 699, 73 P.3d 554.)

[6]   Elisa also relies upon our observation in *Adoption of Michael H.* (1995) 10 Cal.4th 1043, 1051, 43 Cal.Rptr.2d 445, 898 P.2d 891, that "In essence, therefore, our statutory scheme creates three classes of parents: mothers, fathers who are presumed fathers, and fathers who are not presumed fathers. [Citation.]" The issue in that case was whether an unwed father was a presumed father and thus could withhold his consent to the mother's planned adoption of their child. We did not consider the questions raised in the present case.

P.3d 554 (2003), we upheld a "second parent" adoption in which the mother of a child that had been conceived by means of artificial insemination consented to adoption of the child by the mother's lesbian partner. If both parents of an adopted child can be women, we see no reason why the twins in the present case cannot have two parents, both of whom are women.

Having determined that our decision in *Johnson* does not preclude a child from having two parents both of whom are women and that no reason appears that a child's two parents cannot both be women, we proceed to examine the UPA to determine whether Elisa is a parent to the twins in addition to Emily. As noted above, section 7650 provides that provisions applicable to determining a father and child relationship shall be used to determine a mother and child relationship "insofar as practicable." (*Johnson v. Calvert, supra,* 851 P.2d 776; *In Re marriage of Buzzanca,* 61 Cal. App. 4th 1410, 1418 (1998) [the declaration in section 7613 that a husband who consents to artificial insemination is "treated in law" as the father of the child applies equally to the wife if a surrogate, rather than the wife, is artificially inseminated, making both the wife and the husband the parents of the child so produced].)

Subdivision (d) of section 7611 states that a man is presumed to be the natural father of a child if "[h]e receives the child into his home and openly holds out the child as his natural child." The Court of Appeal in *In re Karen C.,* 101 Cal.App.4th 932, 938 (2002), held that subdivision (d) of section 7611 "should apply equally to women." This conclusion was echoed by the court in *In re Salvador M.,* 111 Cal.App.4th 1353, 1357 (2003), which stated: "Though most of the decisional law has focused on the definition of the presumed father, the legal principles concerning the presumed father apply equally to a woman seeking presumed mother status."

Applying section 7611, subdivision (d), we must determine whether Elisa received the twins into her home and openly held them out as her natural children. There is no doubt that Elisa satisfied the first part of this test; it is undisputed that Elisa received the twins into her home. Our inquiry focuses, therefore, on whether she openly held out the twins as her natural children.

The circumstance that Elisa has no genetic connection to the twins does not necessarily mean that she did not hold out the twins as her "natural" children under section 7611. We held in *In re Nicholas H.,* 46 P.3d 932 (2002), that the presumption under section 7611, subdivision (d), that a man who receives a child into his home and openly holds the child out as his natural child is not necessarily rebutted when he admits he is not the child's biological father.

. . . .

The Court of Appeal in *In re Karen C.,* applied the principles discussed in *Nicholas H.* regarding presumed fathers and concluded that a woman with no biological connection to a child could be a presumed mother under section 7611, subdivision (d). Twelve-year-old Karen C. petitioned for an order determining the existence of a mother and child relationship between her and Leticia C., who had raised her from birth. Leticia admitted she was not Karen's biological mother, explaining that Karen's birth mother had tried unsuccessfully to abort her pregnancy and then agreed to give the child to Leticia. The birth mother falsely told the hospital staff that her name was Leticia C. so that Leticia's name would appear on the child's birth certificate. The birth mother gave Karen to Leticia promptly after the child was born. The juvenile court denied Karen's petition, ruling that Leticia could not be Karen's mother because she had not given birth to her and they had no genetic relationship. The Court of Appeal reversed, determining that Leticia was the child's presumed mother under section 7611 because she had taken Karen into her home and raised her as her child. The court remanded the matter to the juvenile court to apply the rule in *Nicholas H.* to determine whether this was "an appropriate action" in which to find the presumption that Leticia was Karen's mother was rebutted by the fact that she had not given birth to her.

. . . .

We conclude that the present case . . . is not "an appropriate action" in which to rebut the presumption of presumed parenthood with proof that Elisa is not the twins' biological parent. This is generally a matter within the discretion of the superior court, but we need not remand the matter to permit the superior court to exercise its discretion because it would be an abuse of discretion to conclude that the presumption may be rebutted in the present case. It is undisputed that Elisa actively consented to, and participated in, the artificial insemination of her partner with the understanding that the resulting child or children would be raised by Emily and her as coparents, and they did act as coparents for a substantial period of time. Elisa received the twins into her home and held them out to the world as her natural children. She gave the twins and the child to whom she had given birth the same surname, which was formed by joining her surname to her partner's. The twins were half siblings to the child to whom Elisa had given birth. She breast-fed all three children, claimed all three children as her dependents on her tax returns, and told a prospective employer that she had triplets. Even at the hearing before the superior court, Elisa candidly testified that she considered herself to be the twins' mother.

Declaring that Elisa cannot be the twins' parent and, thus, has no obligation to support them because she is not biologically related to them would produce a result similar to the situation we sought to avoid in *Nicholas H.* of leaving the child fatherless. The twins in the present case have no father because they were conceived by means of artificial insemination using an anonymous semen donor. Rebutting the presumption that Elisa is the twin's parent would leave them with only one parent and would deprive them of the support of their second parent. Because Emily is financially unable to support the twins, the financial burden of supporting the twins would be borne by the county, rather than Elisa.

In establishing a system for a voluntary declaration of paternity in section 7570, the Legislature declared: "There is a compelling state interest in establishing paternity for all children. Establishing paternity is the first step toward a child support award, which, in turn, provides children with equal rights and access to benefits, including, but not limited to, social security, health insurance, survivors' benefits, military benefits, and inheritance rights. . . ."

By recognizing the value of determining paternity, the Legislature implicitly recognized the value of having two parents, rather than one, as a source of both emotional and financial support, especially when the obligation to support the child would otherwise fall to the public.

We observed in dicta in *Nicholas H.* that it would be appropriate to rebut the section 7611 presumption of parentage if "a court decides that the legal rights and obligations of parenthood should devolve upon an unwilling candidate." But we decline to apply our dicta in *Nicholas H.* here, because we did not consider in *Nicholas H.* a situation like that in the present case.

Although Elisa presently is unwilling to accept the obligations of parenthood, this was not always so. She actively assisted Emily in becoming pregnant with the expressed intention of enjoying the rights and accepting the responsibilities of parenting the resulting children. She accepted those obligations and enjoyed those rights for years. Elisa's present unwillingness to accept her parental obligations does not affect her status as the children's mother based upon her conduct during the first years of their lives.

Further, our observation in *Nicholas H.* that the obligations of parenthood should not be forced upon an unwilling candidate who is not biologically related to the child must be understood in light of the circumstances before us in *Nicholas H.* In that case, as noted above, the presumed father met the child's mother when she was pregnant and voluntarily accepted the unborn child as his own. When the child later was removed from the mother's custody, the presumed father was denied custody of the child because he was not the child's biological father.

In the present case, Elisa did not meet Emily after she was pregnant, but rather was in a committed relationship with her when they decided to have children together. Elisa actively assisted Emily in becoming pregnant, with the understanding that they would raise the resulting children together. Having helped cause the children to be born, and having raised them as her own, Emily should not be permitted to later abandon the twins simply because her relationship with Emily dissolved.

As we noted in the context of a husband who consented to the artificial insemination of his wife using an anonymous sperm donor, but later denied responsibility for the resulting child: "One who consents to the production of a child cannot create a temporary relation to be assumed and disclaimed at will, but the arrangement must be of such character as to impose an obligation of supporting those for whose existence he is directly responsible." We observed that the "intent of the Legislature obviously was to include every child, legitimate or illegitimate, born or unborn, and enforce the obligation of support against the person who could be determined to be the lawful parent." Further: "a reasonable man who, because of his inability to procreate, actively participates and consents to his wife's artificial insemination in the hope that a child will be produced whom they will treat as their own, knows that such behavior carries with it the legal responsibilities of fatherhood and criminal responsibility for nonsupport. . . . [I]t is safe to assume that without defendant's active participation and consent the child would not have been procreated."

We were careful in *Nicholas H.*, therefore, not to suggest that every man who begins living with a woman when she is pregnant and continues to do so after the child is born necessarily becomes a presumed father of the child, even against his wishes. The Legislature surely did not intend to punish a man like the one in *Nicholas H.* who voluntarily provides support for a child who was conceived before he met the mother, by transforming that act of kindness into a legal obligation.

But our observation in *Nicholas H.* loses its force in a case like the one at bar in which the presumed mother under section 7611, subdivision (d), acted together with the birth mother to cause the child to be conceived. In such circumstances, unlike the situation before us in *Nicholas H.*, we believe the Legislature would have intended to impose upon the presumed father or mother the legal obligation to support the child whom she caused to be born. As stated by amicus curiae the California State Association of Counties, representing all 58 counties in California: "A person who actively participates in bringing children into the world, takes the children into her home and holds them out as her own, and receives and enjoys the benefits of parenthood, should be responsible for the support of those children—regardless of her gender or sexual orientation."

We conclude, therefore, that Elisa is a presumed mother of the twins under section 7611, subdivision (d), because she received the children into her home and openly held them out as her natural children, and that this is not an appropriate action in which to rebut the presumption that Elisa is the twins' parent with proof that she is not the children's biological mother because she actively participated in causing the children to be conceived with the understanding that she would raise the children as her own together with the birth mother, she voluntarily accepted the rights and obligations of parenthood after the children were born, and there are no competing claims to her being the children's second parent.

. . . .

The judgment of the Court of Appeal is reversed.

NOTES

1. *Two mothers, two parents. Elisa B.* represents an important departure from *Johnson v. Calvert* in that the court explicitly credits the possibility of a child having two mothers—something it would not contemplate in *Calvert*. Critically, however, the *Elisa B.* court is consistent with *Calvert* in that it limits legal parenthood to only two people. Recall the discussion of *Michael H. v. Gerald D.* in Ristroph and Murray's *Disestablishing the Family. See supra* p. 269. In that case, Carole, who was married to Gerald, gave birth to Victoria, who was the biological daughter of Carole's lover, Michael. 491 U.S. 110 (1989). In Michael's suit to protect his parental rights, Victoria also lodged a claim, arguing that she had a "due process right to maintain filial relationships with both Michael and Gerald." *Id.* at 130. The plurality flatly rejected this argument, noting "the claim that a State must recognize multiple fatherhood has no support in the history or traditions of this country." *Id.* at 131. With *Michael H.* in mind, does *Elisa B.* seem revolutionary or conventional?

2. *The female patriarch.* Note that in this case, Elisa B. is acting like a "father"—supporting the family financially while Emily stays at home to take care of the children. In fact, the court analogizes Elisa B. to a father who "receives the child into his home and openly holds out the child as his natural child." Is it meaningful that the court credits Elisa B.'s behavior as consistent with nuclear family fatherhood? Is *Elisa B.* a seachange in how the law views parenthood, or is parenthood here rendered legible because of its proximity to heterosexual parenting norms?

3. *Status and contract?* The ART cases all evince a fundamental tension between private ordering (contract) and public law (family law/status). In *Baby M*, the Sterns rely on the contract between William Stern and Mary Beth Whitehead as the basis of their claim to custody of Baby M. By contrast, Mary Beth Whitehead relies on the law of parenthood to justify her claim. Likewise, in *Elisa B.*, Emily argues that she and her former partner, Elisa B., had an agreement to get pregnant and raise the resulting children together as a family. Elisa B., however, turns to family law to argue that she is not the mother of two of the children, and thus not legally responsible for their care and upkeep. In what ways are contract and status ill-equipped to address the tensions that arise from use of these emerging reproductive technologies?

K.M. v. E.G.

117 P.3d 673 (Cal. App. 2005).

■ MORENO, J.

. . . .

In the present case, we must decide whether a woman who provided ova to her lesbian partner so that the partner could bear children by means of in vitro fertilization is a parent of those children. For the reasons that follow, we conclude that Family Code section 7613, subdivision (b), which provides that a man is not a father if he provides semen to a physician to inseminate a woman who is not his wife, does not apply when a woman provides her ova to impregnate her partner in a lesbian relationship in order to produce children who will be raised in their joint home. Accordingly, when partners in a lesbian relationship decide to produce children in this manner, both the woman who provides her ova and her partner who bears the children are the children's parents.

. . . .

On March 6, 2001, petitioner K.M.[1] filed a petition to establish a parental relationship with twin five-year-old girls born to respondent E.G., her former lesbian partner. K.M. alleged that she "is the biological parent of the minor children" because "[s]he donated her egg to respondent, the gestational mother of the children." E.G. moved to dismiss the petition on the grounds that, although K.M. and E.G. "were lesbian partners who lived together until this action was filed," K.M. "explicitly donated her ovum under a clear written agreement by which she relinquished any claim to offspring born of her donation."

On April 18, 2001, K.M. filed a motion for custody of and visitation with the twins.

A hearing was held at which E.G. testified that she first considered raising a child before she met K.M., at a time when she did not have a partner. She met K.M. in October, 1992 and they became romantically involved in June 1993. E.G. told K.M. that she planned to adopt a baby as a single mother. E.G. applied for adoption in November, 1993. K.M. and E.G. began living together in March, 1994 and registered as domestic partners in San Francisco.

E.G. visited several fertility clinics in March, 1993 to inquire about artificial insemination and she attempted artificial insemination, without success, on 13 occasions from July, 1993 through November, 1994. K.M. accompanied her to most of these appointments. K.M. testified that she and E.G. planned to raise the child together, while E.G.

---

[1]   In order to protect the confidentiality of the minors, we will refer to the parties by their initials.

insisted that, although K.M. was very supportive, E.G. made it clear that her intention was to become "a single parent."

In December, 1994, E.G. consulted with Dr. Mary Martin at the fertility practice of the University of California at San Francisco Medical Center (UCSF). E.G.'s first attempts at in vitro fertilization failed because she was unable to produce sufficient ova. In January, 1995, Dr. Martin suggested using K.M.'s ova. E.G. then asked K.M. to donate her ova, explaining that she would accept the ova only if K.M. "would really be a donor" and E.G. would "be the mother of any child," adding that she would not even consider permitting K.M. to adopt the child "for at least five years until [she] felt the relationship was stable and would endure." E.G. told K.M. that she "had seen too many lesbian relationships end quickly, and [she] did not want to be in a custody battle." E.G. and K.M. agreed they would not tell anyone that K.M. was the ova donor.

K.M. acknowledged that she agreed not to disclose to anyone that she was the ova donor, but insisted that she only agreed to provide her ova because she and E.G. had agreed to raise the child together. K.M. and E.G. selected the sperm donor together. K.M. denied that E.G. had said she wanted to be a single parent and insisted that she would not have donated her ova had she known E.G. intended to be the sole parent.

On March 8, 1995, K.M. signed a four-page form on UCSF letterhead entitled "Consent Form for Ovum Donor (Known)." The form states that K.M. agrees "to have eggs taken from my ovaries, in order that they may be donated to another woman." After explaining the medical procedures involved, the form states on the third page: "It is understood that I waive any right and relinquish any claim to the donated eggs or any pregnancy or offspring that might result from them. I agree that the recipient may regard the donated eggs and any offspring resulting therefrom as her own children." The following appears on page 4 of the form, above K.M.'s signature and the signature of a witness: "I specifically disclaim and waive any right in or any child that may be conceived as a result of the use of any ovum or egg of mine, and I agree not to attempt to discover the identity of the recipient thereof." E.G. signed a form entitled "Consent Form for Ovum Recipient" that stated, in part: "I acknowledge that the child or children produced by the IVF procedure is and shall be my own legitimate child or children and the heir or heirs of my body with all rights and privileges accompanying such status."

E.G. testified she received these two forms in a letter from UCSF dated February 2, 1995, and discussed the consent forms with K.M. during February and March. E.G. stated she would not have accepted K.M.'s ova if K.M. had not signed the consent form, because E.G. wanted to have a child on her own and believed the consent form "protected" her in this regard.

K.M. testified to the contrary that she first saw the ovum donation consent form 10 minutes before she signed it on March 8, 1995. K.M. admitted reading the form, but thought parts of the form were "odd" and did not pertain to her, such as the part stating that the donor promised not to discover the identity of the recipient. She did not intend to relinquish her rights and only signed the form so that "we could have children." Despite having signed the form, K.M. "thought [she] was going to be a parent."

Ova were withdrawn from K.M. on April 11, 1995, and embryos were implanted in E.G. on April 13, 1995. K.M. and E.G. told K. M.'s father about the resulting pregnancy by announcing that he was going to be a grandfather. The twins were born on December 7, 1995. The twins' birth certificates listed E.G. as their mother and did not reflect a father's name. As they had agreed, neither E.G. nor K.M. told anyone K.M. had donated the ova, including their friends, family and the twins' pediatrician. Soon after the twins were born, E.G. asked K.M. to marry her, and on Christmas Day, the couple exchanged rings.

Within a month of their birth, E.G. added the twins to her health insurance policy, named them as her beneficiary for all employment benefits, and increased her life insurance with the twins as the beneficiary. K.M. did not do the same.

E.G. referred to her mother, as well as K.M.'s parents, as the twins' grandparents and referred to K.M.'s sister and brother as the twins' aunt and uncle, and K.M.'s nieces as their cousins. Two school forms listed both K.M. and respondent as the twins' parents. The children's nanny testified that both K.M. and E.G. "were the babies' mother."

The relationship between K.M. and E.G. ended in March, 2001 and K.M. filed the present action. In September, 2001, E.G. and the twins moved to Massachusetts to live with E.G.'s mother.

The superior court granted E.G.'s motion to dismiss finding, in a statement of decision, "that [K.M.] ... knowingly, voluntarily and intelligently executed the ovum donor form, thereby acknowledging her understanding that, by the donation of her ova, she was relinquishing and waiving all rights to claim legal parentage of any children who might result from the *in vitro* fertilization and implantation of her ova in a recipient (in this case, a known recipient, her domestic partner [E.G.]). . . . [K.M.]'s testimony on the subject of her execution of the ovum donor form was contradictory and not always credible.

"[K.M.] and [E.G.] agreed prior to the conception of the children that [E.G.] would be the sole parent unless the children were later adopted, and [E.G.] told [K.M.] prior to her ovum donation that she ([E.G.]) would not consider an adoption by [K.M.] until some years later. [E.G.] and [K.M.] agreed in advance of the ovum donation that they would not tell others of [K.M.]'s genetic connection to the children (they also agreed that if and when it became appropriate they would consider how to inform the children); and they abided by this agreement until late 1999.

". . . By voluntarily signing the ovum donation form, [K.M.] was donating genetic material. Her position was analogous to that of a sperm donor, who is treated as a legal stranger to a child if he donates sperm through a licensed physician and surgeon under Family Code section 7613[, subdivision] (b). The Court finds no reason to treat ovum donors as having greater claims to parentage than sperm donors. . . .

The Court accepts the proposition that a child may have two legal mothers and assumed it to be the law in its analysis of the evidence herein. . . .

> [K.M.]'s claim to 'presumed' parenthood rests upon her contention that she has met the criteria of Family Code section 7611[, subdivision] (d) . . . [K.M.] . . . has failed to establish either that she received the twins into her home or that she held them out 'as [her] natural child[ren.]' Although [K.M.] *treated* the twins in all regards as though they were her own (and there can be no question but that they are fully bonded to her as such), the children were *received* into the parties' home as [E.G.]'s children and, up until late 1999, both parties scrupulously held confidential [petitioner]'s 'natural,' i.e., in this case, her genetic relationship to the children.

> [E.G.] is not estopped by her conduct. . . . The Court finds that [petitioner] was not misled by any such conduct; that she knew that [respondent] did not intend thereby to confer parental rights upon her. . . ."

The Court of Appeal affirmed the judgment, ruling that K.M. did not qualify as a parent "because substantial evidence supports the trial courts factual finding that *only* E.G. intended to bring about the birth of a child whom she intended to raise as her own." The court observed that "the status of K.M. . . . is consistent with the status of a sperm donor under the [Uniform Parentage Act], i.e., treated in law as if he were not the natural father of a child thereby conceived." Having concluded that the parties intended at the time of conception that only E.G. would be the child's mother, the court concluded that the parties['] actions following the birth did not alter this agreement. The Court of Appeal concluded that if the parties had changed their intentions and wanted K.M. to be a parent, their only option was adoption.

We granted review.

. . . .

K.M. asserts that she is a parent of the twins because she supplied the ova that were fertilized in vitro and implanted in her lesbian partner, resulting in the birth of the twins. As we will explain, we agree that K.M. is a parent of the twins because she supplied the ova that produced the children, and Family Code section 7613, subdivision (b) (hereafter section 7613(b)), which provides that a man is not a father if he provides semen to a physician to inseminate a woman who is not his wife, does not apply because K.M. supplied her ova to impregnate her lesbian partner in order to produce children who would be raised in their joint home.

The determination of parentage is governed by the Uniform Parentage Act (UPA). (§ 7600 et seq.) As we observe in the companion case of *Elisa B. v. Superior Court,* 117 P.3d at 664–665 (2005), the UPA defines the " '[p]arent and child relationship, [which] extends equally to every child and to every parent, regardless of the marital status of the parents.' (§ 7602.)"

In *Johnson v. Calvert,* 851 P.2d 776 (1993), we determined that a wife whose ovum was fertilized in vitro by her husband's sperm and implanted in a surrogate mother was the "natural mother" of the child thus produced. We noted that the UPA states that provisions applicable to determining a father and child relationship shall be used to determine a mother and child relationship "insofar as practicable." We relied, therefore, on the provisions in the UPA regarding presumptions of paternity and concluded that "genetic consanguinity" could be the basis for a finding of maternity just as it is for paternity. Under this authority, K.M.'s genetic relationship to the children in the present case constitutes "evidence of a mother and child relationship as contemplated by the Act."

The Court of Appeal in the present case concluded, however, that K.M. was not a parent of the twins, despite her genetic relationship to them, because she had the same status as a sperm donor. Section 7613(b) states: "The donor of semen provided to a licensed physician and surgeon for use in artificial insemination of a woman other than the donor's wife is treated in law as if he were not the natural father of a child thereby conceived." In *Johnson,* we considered the predecessor statute to section 7613(b), former Civil Code section 7005. We did not discuss whether this statute applied to a woman who provides ova used to impregnate another woman, but we observed that "in a true 'egg donation' situation, where a woman gestates and gives birth to a child formed from the egg of another woman with the intent to raise the child as her own, the birth mother is the natural mother under California law." We held that the statute did not apply under the circumstances in *Johnson,* because the husband and wife in *Johnson* did not intend to "donate" their sperm and ova to the surrogate mother, but rather "intended to procreate a child genetically related to them by the only available means."

The circumstances of the present case are not identical to those in *Johnson,* but they are similar in a crucial respect; both the couple in *Johnson* and the couple in the present case intended to produce a child that would be raised in their own home. In *Johnson,* it was clear that the married couple did not intend to "donate" their semen and ova to the surrogate mother, but rather permitted their semen and ova to be used to impregnate the surrogate mother in order to produce a child to be raised by them. In the present case, K.M. contends that she did not intend to donate her ova, but rather provided her ova so that E.G. could give birth to a child to be raised jointly by K.M. and E.G. E.G. hotly contests this, asserting that K.M. donated her ova to E.G., agreeing that E.G. would be the sole parent. It is undisputed, however, that the couple lived together and that they both intended to bring the child into their joint home. Thus, even accepting as true E.G.'s version of the facts (which the superior court did), the present case, like *Johnson,* does not present a "true 'egg donation' " situation. K.M. did not intend to simply donate her ova to E.G., but rather provided her ova to her lesbian partner with whom she was living so that E.G. could give birth to a child that would be raised in their joint home. Even if we assume that the provisions of section 7613(b) apply to women who donate ova, the statute does not apply under the circumstances of the present case. . . .

. . . .

As noted above, K.M.'s genetic relationship with the twins constitutes evidence of a mother and child relationship under the UPA and, as explained above, section 7613(b) does not apply to exclude K.M. as a parent of the twins. The circumstance that E.G. gave birth to the twins also constitutes evidence of a mother and child relationship. Thus, both K.M. and E.G. are mothers of the twins under the UPA.[6]

It is true we said in *Johnson* that "for any child California law recognizes only one natural mother." But as we explain in the companion case of *Elisa B. v. Superior Court,* this statement in *Johnson* must be understood in light of the issue presented in that case; "our decision in *Johnson* does not preclude a child from having two parents both of whom are women."

. . . .

Justice Werdegar's dissent states that predictability in this area is important, but relying upon a later judicial determination of the intent of the parties, as the dissent suggests, would not provide such predictability. The present case is a good example. Justice Werdegar's dissent concludes that K.M. did not intend to become a parent, because the superior court "found on the basis of conflicting evidence that she did not," noting that "[w]e must defer to the trial court's findings on this point because substantial evidence supports them." Had the superior court reached the opposite conclusion, however, the dissent presumably again would defer to the trial court's findings and reach the opposite conclusion that K.M. is a parent of the twins. Rather than provide predictability, therefore, using the intent test would rest the determination of parentage upon a later judicial determination of intent made years after the birth of the child.

Justice Werdegar's dissent cites *Troxel v. Granville,* 530 U.S. 57, 65 (2000), for the proposition that "We cannot recognize K.M. as a parent without diminishing E.G.'s existing parental rights." (Dis. opn. of Werdegar, J., *post,* 33 Cal.Rptr.3d at p. 79, 117 P.3d at p. 688.) The high

---

[6] Contrary to the suggestion in Justice Werdegar's dissent, we do not consider whether it is in the twins' best interest for the woman who supplied the ova from which they were produced, intending to raise the children in her home, to be declared their natural mother. We simply follow the dictates of the UPA.

court's decision in *Troxel* has no application here. Neither K.M.'s nor E.G.'s claim to parentage preceded the other's. K.M.'s claim to be the twins' mother because the twins were produced from her ova is equal to, and arose at the same time as, E.G.'s claim to be the twins' mother because she gave birth to them.

The superior court in the present case found that K.M. signed a waiver form, thereby "relinquishing and waiving all rights to claim legal parentage of any children who might result." But such a waiver does not affect our determination of parentage. Section 7632 provides: "Regardless of its terms, an agreement between an alleged or presumed father and the mother or child does not bar an action under this chapter." A woman who supplies ova to be used to impregnate her lesbian partner, with the understanding that the resulting child will be raised in their joint home, cannot waive her responsibility to support that child. Nor can such a purported waiver effectively cause that woman to relinquish her parental rights.

In light of our conclusion that section 7613(b) does not apply and that K.M. is the twins' parent (together with E.G.), based upon K.M.'s genetic relationship to the twins, we need not, and do not, consider whether K.M. is presumed to be a parent of the twins under section 7611, subdivision (d), which provides that a man is presumed to be a child's father if "[h]e receives the child into his home and openly holds out the child as his natural child."

DISPOSITION

The judgment of the Court of Appeal is reversed.

■ GEORGE, C.J., BAXTER and CHIN, JJ., concur.

■ KENNARD, J., dissenting.

Unlike the majority, I would apply the controlling statutes as written. The statutory scheme for determining parentage contains two provisions that resolve K.M.'s claim to be a parent of the twins born to E.G. Under one provision, a man who donates sperm for physician-assisted artificial insemination of a woman to whom he is not married is not the father of the resulting child. (Fam. Code, § 7613, subd. (b).) Under the other provision, rules for determining fatherhood are to be used for determining motherhood "[i]nsofar as practical." (*Id.*, § 7650.) Because K.M. donated her ova for physician-assisted artificial insemination and implantation in another woman, and knowingly and voluntarily signed a document declaring her intention *not* to become a parent of any resulting children, she is not a parent of the twins.

. . . .

The Court of Appeal held that K.M. had made a voluntary and informed choice to donate her ova to E.G., and that K.M.'s status with respect to any child born as a result of the ova donation was analogous to that of a sperm donor, who, by statute, is treated as if he were not the natural father of any child conceived as a result of the sperm donation. "The donor of semen provided to a licensed physician and surgeon for use in artificial insemination of a woman other than the donor's wife is treated in law as if he were not the natural father of a child thereby conceived." (§ 7613, subd. (b)). By analogy I would apply that statute here. Section 7650 states that "[i]nsofar as is practicable" the provisions "applicable" to a father and child relationship are to be used to determine a mother and child relationship.

Here it is "practicable" to treat a woman who donates ova to a licensed physician for in vitro fertilization and implantation in another woman,[3] in the same fashion as a man who donates sperm to a licensed physician for artificial insemination of a woman to whom he is not married. Treating male and female donors alike is not only practicable, but it is also consistent with the trial court's factual finding here that K.M. intended "to donate ova to E.G." so that E.G. would be the sole mother of a child born to her.

. . . .

The majority's desire to give the twins a second parent is understandable and laudable. To achieve that worthy goal, however, the majority must rewrite a statute and disregard the intentions that the parties expressed when the twins were conceived. The majority amends the sperm-donor statute by inserting a new provision making a sperm donor the legal father of a child born to a woman artificially inseminated with his sperm whenever the sperm donor and the birth mother *"intended that the resulting child would be raised in their joint home,"* even though both the donor and birth mother also intended that the donor *not* be the child's father. Finding nothing in the statutory language or history to support this construction, I reject it. Relying on the plain meaning of the statutory language, and the trial court's findings that both K.M. and E.G. intended that E.G. would be the only parent of any children resulting from the artificial insemination, I would affirm the judgment of the Court of Appeal, which in turn affirmed the trial court, rejecting K.M.'s claim to parentage of the twins born to E.G.

■ WERDEGAR, J., dissenting.

The majority determines that the twins who developed from the ova K.M. donated to E.G. have two mothers rather than one. While I disagree, as I shall explain, with that ultimate conclusion, I agree with the majority's premise that a child can have two mothers. Our previous holding that "for any child California law recognizes only one natural mother" (*Johnson v. Calvert*, 5 Cal.4th 84, 92 (1995)), must be understood

---

[3]   K.M. and E.G. were registered in San Francisco as domestic partners in 1995 at the time of the twins' birth. On March 30, 2001, E.G. filed a notice with the Clerk of the City and County of San Francisco dissolving the domestic partnership. As of January 1, 2005, domestic partners who are registered with the California Secretary of State have the same "rights and obligations" to "a child of either of them" as do spouses. (§ 297.5, subd. (d).) Obviously, this new statute has no application here.

in the context in which it arose—a married couple who intended to become parents and provided their fertilized ova to a gestational surrogate who did not intend to become a parent—and, thus understood, may properly be limited to cases in which to recognize a second mother would inject an unwanted third parent into an existing family. When, in contrast to *Johnson,* no natural[1] or adoptive father exists, two women who intend to become mothers of the same child may do so either through adoption or because both qualify as natural mothers under the Uniform Parentage Act (Fam. Code, § 7600 et seq.) (UPA), one having donated the ovum and the other having given birth.

. . . .

Precisely because predictability in this area is so important, I cannot agree with the majority that the children in this case do in fact have two mothers. Until today, when one woman has provided the ova and another has given birth, the established rule for determining disputed claims to motherhood was clear: we looked to the intent of the parties. "[I]n a true 'egg donation' situation, where a woman gestates and gives birth to a child formed from the egg of another woman with the intent to raise the child as her own, the birth mother is the natural mother under California law." Contrary to the majority's apparent assumption, to limit *Johnson*'s holding that a child can have only one mother to cases involving existing two-parent families does not require us to abandon *Johnson*'s intent test as the method for determining disputed claims of motherhood arising from the use of reproductive technology. Indeed, we have no other test sufficient to the task.

Furthermore, to apply *Johnson*'s intent test to the facts of this case necessarily leads to the conclusion that E.G. is a mother and K.M. is not. That E.G. intended to become the mother—and the only mother—of the children to whom she gave birth is unquestioned. Whether K.M. for her part also intended to become the children's mother was disputed, but the trial court found on the basis of conflicting evidence that she did not. We must defer to the trial court's findings on this point because substantial evidence supports them. K.M. represented in connection with the ovum donation process, both orally and in writing, that she did not intend to become the children's mother, and consistently with those representations subsequently held the children out to the world as E.G.'s but not her own. Thus constrained by the facts, the majority can justify its conclusion that K.M. is also the children's mother only by changing the law. This the majority does by displacing *Johnson's* intent test—at least for the purposes of this case—with the following new rule: a woman who has "supplied her ova to impregnate her lesbian partner in order to produce children who would be raised in their joint home" is a mother of

---

[1] As when an unmarried woman becomes pregnant through physician-assisted artificial insemination pursuant to Family Code section 7613, subdivision (b).

the resulting children regardless of any preconception manifestations of intent to the contrary.

. . . .

Perhaps the most serious problem with the majority's new rule is that it threatens to destabilize ovum donation and gestational surrogacy agreements. One important function of *Johnson*'s intent test was to permit persons who made use of reproductive technology to create, before conception, settled and enforceable expectations about who would and would not become parents. *Johnson*, gave E.G. a right at the time she conceived to expect that she alone would be the parent of her children— a right the majority now retrospectively abrogates. E.G.'s expectation has a constitutional dimension. We cannot recognize K.M. as a parent without diminishing E.G.'s existing parental rights. In light of the majority's abrogation of *Johnson* and apparent willingness to ignore preconception manifestations of intent, at least in some cases, women who wish to donate ova without becoming mothers, serve as gestational surrogates without becoming mothers, or accept ovum donations without also accepting the donor as a coparent would be well advised to proceed with the most extreme caution. While the majority purports to limit its holding to cohabiting lesbians, and possibly only to those cohabiting lesbians who are also domestic partners, these limitations, as I have explained, rest on questionable legal grounds and may well not stand the test of time.

. . . .

The majority seems to believe that, having concluded the sperm donation statute (Fam. Code, § 7613, subd. (b)) does not apply, one must necessarily conclude that K.M. is the mother of the children who developed from the ova she donated to E.G. This reasoning entails a non sequitur. The statute, when it applies, merely *excludes* someone as a possible parent; it does not *establish* parentage. In order to reach the further conclusion that K.M. is a parent, the majority must entertain a string of questionable assumptions: first, that we would refuse to apply the sperm donation statute (Fam. Code, § 7613, subd. (b), despite its plain language, to cut off the parental rights and responsibilities of a man who donates his sperm through a physician to a woman who is not his wife but with whom he lives, and, second, that two women who live together and divide between themselves the genetic and gestational aspects of pregnancy must be treated in exactly the same way as the man and woman just posited. The latter assumption, in turn, embodies additional, unstated assumptions about the effect of the equal protection clause. But ovum donation, which requires substantial medical and scientific assistance, is not sufficiently like sperm donation, which can easily be accomplished by unassisted laypersons, to require equal treatment under the law for all purposes. Accordingly, to recognize the sperm donation statute's inapplicability does not dispose of this case; it merely leaves us with the same question with which we began, namely, whether K.M. is a second mother of E.G.'s children. Until today, the *Johnson* intent test would have required us to answer the question in the negative. In my view, it still should.

Perhaps the best way to understand today's decision is that we appear to be moving in cases of assisted reproduction from a categorical determination of parentage based on formal, preconception manifestations of intent to a case-by-case approach implicitly motivated at least in part by our intuitions about the children's best interests. We expressly eschewed a best interests approach in *Johnson*, explaining that it "raises the repugnant specter of governmental interference in matters implicating our most fundamental notions of privacy, and confuses concepts of parentage and custody." This case, in which the majority compels E.G. to accept K.M. as an unintended parent to E.G.'s children, in part because of E.G.'s and K.M.'s sexual orientation and the character of their private relationship, shows that *Johnson*'s warning was prescient. Only legislation defining parentage in the context of assisted reproduction is likely to restore predictability and prevent further lapses into the disorder of ad hoc adjudication.

NOTE

Mothers, fathers, and (emerging) parenthood. In both *K.M. v. E.G.* and *Elisa B.*, one can see the California Supreme Court struggling to find extant templates to address the burgeoning family forms brought about by assisted reproductive technology (ART). Of particular interest here is the court's conclusion that statutes covering the earliest form of ART, artificial insemination using an anonymous sperm donor, did not apply to the situation of an egg donor in a relationship with the intended gestational mother.

Brooke S.B. v. Elizabeth A.C.C.
28 N.Y.3d 1 (2016).

■ ABDUS-SALAAM, J.

These two cases call upon us to assess the continued vitality of the rule promulgated in *Matter of Alison D. v. Virginia M.*, 572 N.E.2d 27 (1991)—namely that, in an unmarried couple, a partner without a biological or adoptive relation to a child is not that child's "parent" for purposes of standing to seek custody or visitation under Domestic Relations Law § 70(a), notwithstanding their "established relationship with the child.". . .

Petitioner and respondent entered into a relationship in 2006 and, one year later, announced their engagement. At the time, however, this was a purely symbolic gesture; same-sex couples could not legally marry in New York. Petitioner and respondent lacked the resources to travel to another jurisdiction to enter into a legal arrangement comparable to marriage, and it was then unclear whether New York would recognize an out-of-state same-sex union.

Shortly thereafter, the couple jointly decided to have a child and agreed that respondent would carry the child. In 2008, respondent became pregnant through artificial insemination. During respondent's pregnancy, petitioner regularly attended prenatal doctor's appointments, remained involved in respondent's care, and joined respondent in the emergency room when she had a complication during the pregnancy. Respondent went into labor in June 2009. Petitioner stayed by her side and, when the subject child, a baby boy, was born, petitioner cut the umbilical cord. The couple gave the child petitioner's last name.

The parties continued to live together with the child and raised him jointly, sharing in all major parental responsibilities. Petitioner stayed at home with the child for a year while respondent returned to work. The child referred to petitioner as "Mama B."

In 2010, the parties ended their relationship. Initially, respondent permitted petitioner regular visits with the child. In late 2012, however, petitioner's relationship with respondent deteriorated and, in or about July 2013, respondent effectively terminated petitioner's contact with the child.

Subsequently, petitioner commenced this proceeding seeking joint custody of the child and regular visitation.... Respondent moved to dismiss the petition, asserting that petitioner lacked standing to seek visitation or custody under Domestic Relations Law § 70 as interpreted in *Alison D.* because, in the absence of a biological or adoptive connection to the child, petitioner was not a "parent" within the meaning of the statute. Petitioner and the attorney for the child opposed the motion, contending that, in light of the legislature's enactment of the Marriage Equality Act and other changes in the law, *Alison D.* should no longer be followed. They further argued that petitioner's long-standing parental relationship with the child conferred standing to seek custody and visitation under principles of equitable estoppel.

After hearing argument on the motion, Family Court dismissed the petition. While commenting on the "heartbreaking" nature of the case, Family Court noted that petitioner did not adopt the child and therefore granted respondent's motion to dismiss on constraint of Alison D. . . .

. . . .

Domestic Relations Law § 70 provides:

"Where a minor child is residing within this state, *either parent* may apply to the supreme court for a writ of habeas corpus to have such minor child brought before such court; and on the return thereof, the court, on due consideration, may award the natural guardianship, charge and custody of such child to either parent for such time, under such regulations and restrictions, and with such provisions and directions, as the case may require, and may at any time thereafter vacate or modify such order. In all cases there shall be no prima facie right to the custody of the child in either parent, but the court shall determine solely what is for *the best interest of the child, and what will best promote its welfare and happiness, and make award accordingly*" (Domestic Relations Law § 70[a] (emphases added)).

Only a "parent" may petition for custody or visitation under Domestic Relations Law § 70, yet the statute does not define that critical term, leaving it to be defined by the courts.

In *Alison D.*, we supplied a definition. In that case, Alison D. and Virginia M. were in a long-term relationship and decided to have a child. They agreed that Virginia M. would carry the baby and that they would jointly raise the child, sharing parenting responsibilities. After the child was born, Alison D. acted as a parent in all major respects, providing financial, emotional and practical support. Even after the couple ended their relationship and moved out of their shared home, Alison D. continued to regularly visit the child until he was about six years old, at which point Virginia M. terminated contact between them.

Alison D. petitioned for visitation pursuant to Domestic Relations Law § 70. . . . The lower courts dismissed Alison D.'s petition for lack of standing, ruling that only a biological parent—and not a de facto parent—is a legal "parent" with standing to seek visitation.

We affirmed the lower courts' dismissal of Alison D.'s petition for lack of standing. . . . Specifically, we held that "a biological stranger to a child who is properly in the custody of his biological mother" has no "standing to seek visitation with the child under Domestic Relations Law § 70".

We rested our determination principally on the need to preserve the rights of biological parents. Specifically, we reasoned that, "[t]raditionally, in this State it is the child's mother and father who, assuming fitness, have the right to the care and custody of their child". We therefore determined that the statute should not be read to permit a de facto parent to seek visitation of a child in a manner that "would necessarily impair the parents' right to custody and control."

Additionally, we suggested that, because the legislature expressly allowed certain non-parents—namely, grandparents and siblings—to seek custody or visitation, it must have intended to exclude de facto parents or parents by estoppel. And so, because Alison D. had no biological or adoptive connection to the subject child, she had no standing to seek visitation and "no right to petition the court to displace the choice made by this fit parent in deciding what is in the child's best interests."

Judge [Judith] Kaye dissented on the ground that a person who "stands in loco parentis" should have standing to seek visitation under Domestic Relations Law § 70. Observing that the Court's decision would "fall[ ] hardest" on the millions of children raised in nontraditional families—including families headed by same-sex couples, unmarried opposite-sex couples, and stepparents—the dissent argued that the majority had "turn[ed] its back on a tradition of reading section 70 so as to promote the welfare of the children" The dissent asserted that, because Domestic Relations Law § 70 did not define "parent—and because the statute made express reference to the "best interest of the child"—the Court was free to craft a definition that accommodated the welfare of the child. . . .

In 1991, same-sex partners could not marry in this state. Nor could a biological parent's unmarried partner adopt the child. As a result, a partner in a same-sex relationship not biologically related to a child was entirely precluded from obtaining standing to seek custody or visitation of that child under our definition of "parent" supplied in *Alison D.*

Four years later, in *Matter of Jacob*, 660 N.E.2d 397 (1995), we had occasion to decide whether "the unmarried partner of a child's biological mother, whether heterosexual or homosexual, who is raising the child together with the biological parent, can become the child's second parent by means of adoption." We held that the adoptions sought in *Matter of Jacob*—"one by an unmarried heterosexual couple, the other by the lesbian partner of the child's mother"—were "fully consistent with the adoption statute.". We reasoned that, while the adoption statute "must be strictly construed," our "primary loyalty must be to the statute's legislative purpose—the child's best interest." The outcome in Matter of Jacob was to confer standing to seek custody or visitation upon unmarried, non-biological partners—including a partner in a same-sex relationship—who adopted the child, even under our restrictive definition of "parent" set forth in *Alison D.*

Thereafter, in *Matter of Shondel J. v. Mark D.*, 853 N.E.2d 610 (2006), we applied a similar analysis, holding that a "man who has mistakenly represented himself as a child's father may be estopped from denying paternity, and made to pay child support, when the child justifiably relied on the man's representation of paternity, to the child's detriment." We based our decision on "the best interests of the child," emphasizing "[t]he potential damage to a child's psyche caused by suddenly ending established parental support."

Despite these intervening decisions that sought a means to take into account the best interests of the child in adoption and support proceedings, we declined to revisit *Alison D.* when confronted with a nearly identical situation almost 20 years later. *Debra H. v. Janice R.*, 930 N.E.2d 184 (2010), . . . involved an unmarried same-sex couple. Petitioner alleged that they agreed to have a child, and to that end, Janice R. was artificially inseminated and bore the child. Debra H. never adopted the child. After the couple ended their relationship, Debra H. petitioned for custody and visitation. We declined to expand the definition of "parent" for purposes of Domestic Relations Law § 70, noting that "Alison D., in conjunction with second-parent adoption, creates a bright-line rule that promotes certainty in the wake of domestic breakups."

Nonetheless, in *Debra H.*, we arrived at a different result than in *Alison D.* Ultimately, we invoked the common-law doctrine of comity to rule that, because the couple had entered into a civil union in Vermont prior to the child's birth—and because the union afforded Debra H. parental status under Vermont law—her parental status should be recognized under New York law as well. . . .

In a separate discussion, we also "reaffirm[ed] our holding in *Alison D.*" We acknowledged the apparent tension in our decision to authorize parentage by estoppel in the support context and yet deny it in the visitation and custody context, but we decided that this incongruity did not fatally undermine *Alison D.*

. . . .

We must now decide whether, as respondents claim, the doctrine of stare decisis warrants retention of the rule established in *Alison D.* . . .

Long before our decision in *Alison D.*, New York courts invoked their equitable powers to ensure that matters of custody, visitation and support were resolved in a manner that served the best interests of the child. Consistent with these broad equitable powers, our courts have historically exercised their "inherent equity powers and authority" in order to determine "who is a parent and what will serve a child's best interests."

Domestic Relations Law § 70 evolved in harmony with these equitable practices. The statute expanded in scope from a law narrowly conferring standing in custody and visitation matters upon a legally separated, resident "husband and wife" pair to a broader measure granting standing to "either parent" without regard to separation. The legislature made many of these changes to conform to the courts' preexisting equitable practices. Tellingly, the statute has never mentioned, much less purported to limit, the court's equitable powers, and even after its original enactment, courts continued to employ principles of equity to grant custody, visitation or related extra-statutory relief.

Departing from this tradition of invoking equity, in *Alison D.*, we narrowly defined the term "parent," thereby foreclosing "all inquiry into the child's best interest" in custody and visitation cases involving parental figures who lacked biological or adoptive ties to the child. And, in the years that followed, lower courts applying *Alison D.* were "forced to . . . permanently sever strongly formed bonds between children and adults with whom they have parental relationships." By "limiting their opportunity to maintain bonds that may be crucial to their development," the rule of *Alison D.* has "fall[en] hardest on the children."

As a result, in the 25 years since *Alison D.* was decided, this Court has gone to great lengths to escape the inequitable results dictated by a needlessly narrow interpretation of the term "parent." Now, we find ourselves in a legal landscape wherein a non-biological, non-adoptive "parent" may be estopped from disclaiming parentage and made to pay child support in a filiation proceeding (*Shondel J.*), yet denied standing to seek custody or visitation (*Alison D.*). By creating a disparity in the support and custody contexts, *Alison D.* has created an inconsistency in the rights and obligations attendant to parenthood. Moreover, *Alison D.*'s foundational premise of heterosexual parenting and nonrecognition of same-sex couples is unsustainable, particularly in light of the enactment of same-sex marriage in New York State, and the United States Supreme Court's holding in *Obergefell v. Hodges*, 576 U.S. 644 (2015), which noted that the right to marry provides benefits not only for same-sex couples, but also the children being raised by those couples.

Under the current legal framework, which emphasizes biology, it is impossible—without marriage or adoption—for both former partners of a same-sex couple to have standing, as only one can be biologically related to the child. By contrast, where both partners in a heterosexual couple are biologically related to the child, both former partners will have standing regardless of marriage or adoption. It is this context that informs the Court's determination of a proper test for standing that ensures equality for same-sex parents and provides the opportunity for their children to have the love and support of two committed parents.

. . . By "fixing biology as the key to visitation rights," the rule of *Alison D.* has inflicted disproportionate hardship on the growing number of nontraditional families across our state. . . . [R]ecent census statistics reflect the large number of same-sex couples residing in New York, and that many of New York's same-sex couples are raising children who are related to only one partner by birth or adoption.

Relatedly, legal commentators have taken issue with *Alison D.* for its negative impact on children. A growing body of social science reveals the trauma children suffer as a result of separation from a primary attachment figure—such as a de facto parent—regardless of that figure's biological or adoptive ties to the children.

We must, however, protect the substantial and fundamental right of biological or adoptive parents to control the upbringing of their children. . . . But here we do not consider whether to allow a third party to contest or infringe on those rights; rather, the issue is who qualifies as a "parent" with coequal rights. Nevertheless, the fundamental nature of those rights mandates caution in expanding the definition of that term and makes the element of consent of the biological or adoptive parent critical.

While "parents and families have fundamental liberty interests in preserving" intimate family-like bonds, "so, too, do children have these interests," which must also inform the definition of "parent," a term so central to the life of a child. The "bright-line" rule of *Alison D.* promotes the laudable goals of certainty and predictability in the wake of domestic disruption. But bright lines cast a harsh light on any injustice. . . . We will no longer engage in the "deft legal maneuvering" necessary to read fairness into an overly-restrictive definition of "parent" that sets too high a bar for reaching a child's best interest and does not take into account equitable principles. Accordingly, we overrule *Alison D.*

. . . .

Our holding that Domestic Relations Law § 70 permits a non-biological, non-adoptive parent to achieve standing to petition for custody and visitation requires us to specify the limited circumstances in which such a person has standing as a "parent" under Domestic Relations Law § 70. Because of the fundamental rights to which biological and adoptive parents are undeniably entitled, any encroachment on the rights of such parents and, especially, any test to expand who is a parent, must be. . . appropriately narrow.

Petitioners and some of the amici urge that we endorse a functional test for standing, which has been employed in other jurisdictions that recognize parentage by estoppel in the custody and/or visitation context. The functional test considers a variety of factors, many of which relate to the post-birth relationship between the putative parent and the child. [Some amici propose] a different test that hinges on whether petitioner can prove, by clear and convincing evidence, that a couple "jointly planned and explicitly agreed to the conception of a child with the intention of raising the child as co-parents."

Although the parties and amici disagree as to what test should be applied, they generally urge us to adopt a test that will apply in determining standing as a parent for all non-biological, non-adoptive, non-marital "parents" who are raising children. We reject the premise that we must now declare that one test would be appropriate for all situations, or that the proffered tests are the only options that should be considered.

[Here, it is] alleged that the parties entered into a pre-conception agreement to conceive and raise a child as co-parents. We hold that these allegations, if proved by clear and convincing evidence, are sufficient to establish standing. Because we necessarily decide these cases based on the facts presented to us, it would be premature for us to consider adopting a test for situations in which a couple did not enter into a pre-conception agreement. Accordingly, we do not now decide whether, in a case where a biological or adoptive parent consented to the creation of a parent-like relationship between his or her partner and child after conception, the partner can establish standing to seek visitation and custody.

. . . [W]e do not opine on the proper test, if any, to be applied in situations in which a couple has not entered into a pre-conception agreement. We simply conclude that, where a petitioner proves by clear and convincing evidence that he or she has agreed with the biological parent of the child to conceive and raise the child as co-parents, the petitioner has presented sufficient evidence to achieve standing to seek custody and visitation of the child. Whether a partner without such an agreement can establish standing and, if so, what factors a petitioner must establish to achieve standing based on equitable estoppel are matters left for another day, upon a different record.

Additionally, we stress that this decision addresses only the ability of a person to establish standing as a parent to petition for custody or visitation; the ultimate determination of whether those rights shall be granted rests in the sound discretion of the court, which will determine the best interests of the child.

. . . .

■ PIGOTT, J. (concurring).

While I agree . . . that the . . . decision in *Matter of Brooke S.B. v. Elizabeth A.C.C.* should be reversed and the case remitted to Supreme Court for a hearing, I cannot join the majority's opinion overruling *Alison D. v. Virginia M.* The definition of "parent" that we applied in that case was consistent with the legislative history of Domestic Relations Law § 70 and the common law, and despite several opportunities to do so, the legislature has never altered our conclusion. Rather than craft a new definition to achieve a result the majority perceives as more just, I would retain the rule that parental status under New York law derives from marriage, biology or adoption and decide Brooke S.B. on the basis of extraordinary circumstances. As we have said before, "any change in the meaning of 'parent' under our law should come by way of legislative enactment rather than judicial revamping of precedent."

. . . .

Raymond T. v. Samantha G.

74 N.Y.S.3d 730 (2018).

■ GOLDSTEIN, J.

In the instant case, three parties—the biological mother, the biological father and the father's husband—agreed to conceive and raise a child together in a tri-parent arrangement. The question before the court is whether the father's husband has standing to seek custody and visitation with the subject child . . . even though the child already has two legal parents. . . .

The parties in the instant case, a married same-sex male couple, petitioners David S. and Raymond T., and a single woman, respondent Samantha G., were all friends. Over brunch in May 2016, the three friends discussed how each wished to be a parent and devised a plan whereby a child would be conceived and raised by the three parties in a tri-parent arrangement. While the parties agreed that the mother would continue to live in New York City and the men would continue to reside together in Jersey City, the parties agreed that they would consider themselves to be a "family." The parties then proceeded to execute their plan. For an eight-day period, Misters S. and T. alternated the daily delivery of sperm to Ms. G. for artificial insemination. On or about Labor Day weekend, 2016, Ms. G. announced that she was pregnant. The three parties publicized the impending birth on social media with a picture of all three parties dressed in T-shirts. Misters S. and T.'s shirt each said, "This guy is going to be a daddy" and Ms. G.'s shirt said, "This girl is going to be a mama." . . .

[The parties jointly chose and paid for the midwife, attended prebirth medical appointments together, were all present when the child was born, and selected a name for the child (Matthew Z. S.-G.) that recognized all three parties. Mr. T. arranged to take a 16-week paternity leave after the child was born. After a private genetic marker test determined that Mr. S. was the child's biological father, Mr. S. signed a New Jersey acknowledgement of paternity when the child was five days old. After the child's birth, Ms. G., Matthew and Ms. G.'s mother all spent a week at the home of Misters S. and T.]

At the week's conclusion, Matthew went to live with Ms. G. in New York County, where he continues to live. Misters S. and T. have regular daytime parenting time. . . . When speaking to Matthew, all parties refer to Ms. G. as "Momma," Mr. S. as "Daddy" and Mr. T. as "Papai," which is Portuguese for father. . . .

Issues arose between the two men and Ms. G. with respect to the parenting of Matthew as well as to the extent of parental access by Misters S. and T. The relationship among the parties became strained, and on November 12, 2017, Misters S. and T. filed a joint petition against Ms. G. seeking "legal custody and shared parenting time" with Matthew. [The two men contended that not only should Mr. T. be declared to have standing to seek custody and visitation as a "parent," but he should also to be declared to be the third legal parent of Matthew.]

. . . . On December 6, 2017, Ms. G. filed a cross-petition against Misters S. and T. seeking sole custody of Matthew with Misters S. and T. being granted reasonable visitation. . . . [S]he conceded that because all three parties agreed to conceive and raise a child together, Mr. T. should have standing to seek custody and visitation under DRL § 70 (a). However, she argued strenuously that the right to seek custody and visitation as a "parent" under the Domestic Relations Law does not automatically bestow parentage on the non-biological party and asked that this court not declare Mr. T. to be a third legal parent.

. . . .

The landmark Court of Appeals case [*Brooke S.B. v. Elizabeth A.C.C.*, 61 N.E.3d 488 (N.Y. 2016), changed the legal landscape regarding the rights of a partner who is not a legal parent to seek custody and visitation. *Brooke S.B.* conferred standing, under N.Y. DRL § 70, on a non-biologically related same-sex former partner to seek visitation and custody, as a parent, where a partner shows by clear and convincing evidence that the parties agreed to conceive and raise the child together.]

Domestic Relations Law § 70 (a) provides:

[T]he court . . . may award . . . custody of [a] child to either parent for such time, under such regulations and restrictions . . . as the case may require. . . . [T]here shall be no prima facie right to the custody of the child in either parent, but *the court shall determine solely what is for the best interest of the child, and what will best promote its welfare and happiness, and make award accordingly* (emphasis added).

Significantly, *Brooke S.B.* overruled the Court's ruling in *Allison D. v. Virginia M.*, 572 N.E.2d 27 (NY 1991), which denied a partner who lacked a biological or adoptive relationship with a child the right to seek visitation under DRL § 70, despite having an established "parental" type relationship with the child. In determining to break with precedent, the Brooke S.B. court gave primary consideration to the well-being of children being raised in nontraditional families and to how the *Allison D.* decision had negatively impacted those children. In making its ruling, the *Brooke S.B.* court also recognized the fundamental right of parents to control the upbringing of their children and required that the relationship between the child and the partner came into being with the consent of the legal parent.

In reaching its decision, the *Brooke S.B.* court relied heavily on the dissent of Judge Kaye in *Allison D.* Judge Kaye foresaw that the *Allison D.* ruling would " 'fall [ ] hardest' on the millions of children raised in nontraditional families—including families headed by same-sex couples, unmarried opposite-sex couples, and stepparents." "The [*Brooke S.B.*] dissent asserted that, because DRL § 70 does not define 'parent'—and because the statute made express reference to 'the best interests of the child,' the court was free to draft a definition that accommodated the welfare of the child." [T]he *Brooke S.B.* court also noted that legal commentators have "taken issue with *Allison D.* for its negative impact on children" and that "[a] growing body of social science reveals the trauma children suffer as a result of separation from a primary attachment figure—such as a de facto parent—regardless of the figure's biological or adoptive ties to the children."

Against this backdrop, this court is now called upon to determine if the ruling in *Brooke S.B.* would be applicable to the situation at hand, where three—not just two—parties agreed to a preconception plan to raise a child together. . . . The court finds that under the above circumstances where the three parties entered and followed through with a preconception plan to raise a child together in a tri-parent arrangement, the biological father's spouse has standing to seek custody and visitation as a parent pursuant to Brooke S.B. In making this decision, this court is specifically taking into consideration that the relationship between Mr. T. and Matthew came into being with the consent and blessing of the two biological parents and that both biological parents agree that Mr. T. should have standing to seek custody and visitation.

The court further finds that its ruling that Mr. T. has standing to seek custody and visitation despite the existence of two legal parents, to be consistent with the fundamental principle of *Brooke S.B.*—that DRL § 70 must be read to effectuate the welfare and best interests of children, particularly those who are being raised in a non-traditional family structure. The parent-child relationships fostered by children like Matthew, who are being raised in a tri-parent arrangement, should be entitled to no less protection than children raised by two parties.

It is worth noting that the situation before the court—where three parties are involved in raising a child—is likely to recur. Realistically, where same-sex couples seek to conceive and rear a child who is the biological child of one member of the couple, there is always a third party who provides either the egg or the sperm. While in many cases, an anonymous donor is used or all persons involved agree that the donor will not be a parent, this is not the situation in the instant case and in many other cases where the parties agree that the provider of the egg or sperm will be a parent. . . .

The situation in the instant case [is] very different from the situation where a same-sex married couple enters into an agreement with a third party to donate an egg or sperm with the understanding that the donor will not be a parent to the child who is conceived. Under such circumstances, the presumption of legitimacy—that a child born during a marriage is the legitimate child of the marriage—is of critical importance. If the presumption of legitimacy is not rebutted, the court may deem the child to be the legal child of both same-sex spouses and deny the sperm or egg donor parental status. . . .

In the instant case, although two of the parties, Misters S. and T. are married, the presumption of legitimacy is not relevant to the court's analysis. This is because the presumption that Matthew is the legitimate child of the married couple, Misters S. and T., would indisputably be rebutted by evidence that all three parties agreed that Matthew would be raised in a tri-parent arrangement and that Ms. G., the biological mother, would be a parent to Matthew.

In sum, for the reasons explained above, the court is granting Mr. T. standing to seek custody and visitation with Matthew. The court will set this matter down for a trial to determine what orders of custody and visitation are in Matthew's best interest. . . . The court is not, however, granting Mr. T. an order of parentage. That issue is not properly before the court since no petition was filed for paternity or parentage. Moreover, there is no need for the issue of parentage to be addressed since pursuant to *Brooke S.B.*, Mr. T. may seek custody and visitation as a "parent" under DRL § 70(a) without a determination that he is a legal parent. If, in the future, a proper application for a declaration of parentage is made and there is a need for a determination of parentage, for instance, to rule on a request for child support, the court may address this issue. This court, however, notes that there is not currently any New York statute which grants legal parentage to three parties, nor is there any New York case law precedent for such a determination.

NOTES

1.   *The aftermath of* Brooke S.B. As directed by the Court of Appeals, the trial court, on remand, considered whether Brooke was a parent for purposes of N.Y.D.R.L. § 70. The trial court concluded that Brooke was a parent and therefore entitled to custody.

2.   *In the shadow of marriage? Brooke S.B.* is notable on many fronts, including the New York Court of Appeals' decision to overrule an earlier case, *Alison D. v. Virginia M.* In that 1991 case, the Court of Appeals dismissed a claim for visitation on the ground that the petitioner, who lacked a legal or biological tie to the child, was not a parent for purposes of New York law. At the time the case was litigated, New York did not recognize same-sex couples in any status relationship. Is it likely that the lack of state recognition of the couple's relationship informed the court's disposition of the petitioner's claim? To what extent did the fact of marriage equality shape the court's disposition of *Brooke S.B.*—and its decision to overrule *Alison M*?

3.   *Beyond the two-parent dyad?* As *Brooke S.B.* suggests, the notion that a child should have two—and just two—parents has been remarkably durable. Even a law has evolved to recognize two legal mothers or two legal fathers, it remains stubbornly fixed on the two-parent dyad as the model for legal parentage. To what extent does *Raymond T.* suggest a softening of the two-parent dyad rule? What social changes have prompted a reappraisal of multiple parentage? What legal changes?

4.   *Privatizing dependency.* Some scholars maintain that the legal recognition of nontraditional parentage reflects law's (and society's) interest in privatizing the dependency of children within the family. On this account, the legal recognition of functional parents, multiple mothers, and intended parents is as much about ensuring two viable sources of support for a child as it is a nod to the changing nature of parenthood and family life. With this in mind, are there economic and practical concerns that might favor the legal recognition of more than two parents—or that might cut against such recognition?

* * *

The following case exemplifies concerns that have become increasingly central to issues surrounding reproduction: as new technologies and practices have expanded the ranks of people who can have babies outside of traditional marriage (lesbians, gay men, single women), medical personnel have begun to invoke "conscience clauses" in support of their contention that they have a right to withhold their medical expertise when it conflicts with their religiously-inspired beliefs surrounding sexuality and reproduction. When read carefully, this case is an early salvo in the war between those who would uphold tradition and those who wish to form families outside of the married heterosexual "charmed circle."[9]

North Coast Women's Care Medical Group v. San Diego County Superior Court

189 P.3d 959 (Cal. App. 2008).

■ KENNARD, J.

Do the rights of religious freedom and free speech, as guaranteed in both the federal and the California Constitutions, *exempt* a medical clinic's physicians from complying with the Unruh Civil Rights Act's prohibition against discrimination based on a person's sexual orientation? Our answer is no.

. . . .

Plaintiff Guadalupe T. Benitez is a lesbian who lives with her partner, Joanne Clark. . . . In 1999, after several unsuccessful efforts at pregnancy through [intravaginal self-insemination], Benitez was diagnosed with polycystic ovarian syndrome, a disorder characterized by irregular ovulation, and she was referred to defendant North Coast Women's Care Medical Group, Inc. (North Coast) for fertility treatment.

In August 1999, Benitez and Clark first met with defendant Christine Brody, an obstetrician and gynecologist employed by defendant North Coast. Benitez mentioned that she was a lesbian. Dr. Brody explained that at some point intrauterine insemination (IUI) might have to be considered. In that medical procedure, a physician threads a catheter through the patient's cervix and inserts semen through the catheter into the patient's uterus. Dr. Brody said that if IUI became necessary, her religious beliefs would preclude her from performing the procedure for Benitez.[1] According to Dr. Brody, she told Benitez and Clark at that initial meeting that her North Coast colleague, Dr. Douglas Fenton, shared her religious objection to performing IUI for an unmarried woman. . . .

---

[9]   *See* Gayle S. Rubin, *supra* p. 11.

[1]   The parties dispute the factual basis for Dr. Brody's religious objection to performing IUI for plaintiff. Dr. Brody claims that her religious beliefs preclude her from active participation in medically causing the pregnancy of *any unmarried* woman, and therefore her refusal to perform IUI for Benitez was based on Benitez's marital status, not her sexual orientation. But Benitez, whose complaint does not allege marital status discrimination, asserts that Dr. Brody objected to performing IUI for *a lesbian*, and consequently the alleged denial of the medical treatment at issue constituted sexual orientation discrimination. The trial court ruled that the factual basis for Dr. Brody's objection presented a disputed issue of material fact to be resolved at trial.

In so ruling, the trial court apparently concluded that, at the times relevant here, California's Unruh Civil Rights Act did not prohibit discrimination based on marital status. The Court of Appeal in this case expressly so held. Because Benitez's claim for relief under the Unruh Civil Rights Act is not based on marital status discrimination, we do not address that issue.

From August 1999 through June 2000, Dr. Brody treated Benitez for infertility. . . .

According to Benitez, when in April 2000 she still had not become pregnant, she decided "with the advice and consent of Dr. Brody," to try IUI. . . .

The parties agree that when Benitez told Dr. Brody she wanted to use her friend's donated fresh sperm for the IUI, Brody replied that this would pose a problem for North Coast. Its physicians had performed IUI either with fresh sperm provided by a patient's husband or sperm from a sperm bank, but never with fresh sperm donated by a patient's friend. To do the latter, Dr. Brody said, might delay the procedure as North Coast would first have to confirm that its protocols pertaining to donated fresh sperm would satisfy the requirements of North Coast's state tissue bank license and the federal Clinical Laboratory Improvement Amendment. After hearing this, Benitez opted to have the IUI with sperm from a sperm bank. Dr. Brody so noted in Benitez's medical records and then left for an out-of-state vacation.

During Dr. Brody's absence, her colleague, Dr. Douglas Fenton, took over Benitez's medical care. Dr. Fenton contends that he was unaware of Dr. Brody's record notation of Benitez's decision *not* to use her friend's fresh sperm for the IUI, because the secretary who had typed that notation in Benitez's file left it in Dr. Brody's in box awaiting her return from vacation. Therefore, according to Dr. Fenton, he mistakenly believed that Benitez intended to have IUI with fresh sperm donated by a friend. The parties agree that unlike sperm from a sperm bank, fresh sperm requires "certain preparation" before it can be used for IUI, and that "[c]ertain licensure" is necessary to do the requisite sperm preparation. Of North Coast's physicians, only Dr. Fenton was licensed to perform these tasks. But he refused to prepare donated fresh sperm for Benitez because of his religious objection. Two of his colleagues, Drs. Charles Stoopack and Ross Langley, had no such religious objection, but unlike Dr. Fenton, they were not licensed to prepare fresh sperm. Dr. Fenton then referred Benitez to a physician outside North Coast's medical practice, Dr. Michael Kettle.

The IUI performed by Dr. Kettle did not result in a pregnancy. Benitez was unable to conceive until June 2001, when Dr. Kettle performed in vitro fertilization.[3]

In August 2001, Benitez sued North Coast and its physicians, Brody and Fenton, seeking damages and injunctive relief on several theories, notably sexual orientation discrimination in violation of California's Unruh Civil Rights Act. . . .

. . . .

---

[3] In vitro fertilization is a medical procedure of assisted reproduction in which eggs and sperm are combined in a laboratory dish. When fertilization results, the embryo is transferred to the woman's uterus for development.

Benitez's claim of sexual orientation discrimination is based on California's Unruh Civil Rights Act. . . . [I]t provided: "All persons within the jurisdiction of this state are free and equal, and no matter what their sex, race, color, religion, ancestry, national origin, disability, or medical condition are entitled to the full and equal accommodations, advantages, facilities, privileges, or services in all business establishments of every kind whatsoever."

The Unruh Civil Rights Act's antidiscrimination provisions apply to business establishments that offer to the public "accommodations, advantages, facilities, privileges, or services." A medical group providing medical services to the public has been held to be a business establishment for purposes of the Act.

. . . .

The Unruh Civil Rights Act subjects to liability "[w]hoever denies, aids or incites a denial, or makes any discrimination or distinction contrary to [the Act]." Thus, liability under the Act for denying a person the "full and equal accommodations, advantages, facilities, privileges, or services" of a business establishment extends beyond the business establishment itself to the business establishment's employees responsible for the discriminatory conduct.

Below, we discuss defendant physicians' claims, first under the federal Constitution, and then under the California Constitution.

III

The First Amendment to the federal Constitution states that "Congress shall make no law respecting an establishment of religion, or prohibiting the free exercise thereof; or abridging the freedom of speech. . . ." This provision applies not only to Congress but also to the states because of its incorporation into the Fourteenth Amendment. With respect to the free exercise of religion, the First Amendment "first and foremost" protects "the right to believe and profess whatever religious doctrine one desires." Thus, it "obviously excludes all 'government regulation of religious *beliefs* as such.' " . . .

. . . .

. . . [I]n 1990, in *Employment Division v. Smith*, 494 U.S. 872 (1990), the high court . . . announced that the First Amendment's right to the free exercise of religion "does not relieve an individual of the obligation to comply with a 'valid and neutral law of general applicability on the ground that the law proscribes (or prescribes) conduct that his religion prescribes (or proscribes).' " . . .

Thus, under the United States Supreme Court's most recent holdings, a religious objector has *no federal constitutional right* to an exemption from a neutral and valid law of general applicability on the ground that compliance with that law is contrary to the objector's religious beliefs.

. . . .

    . . . [W]ith respect to defendants' reliance on the First Amendment, we apply the high court's *Smith* test. California's Unruh Civil Rights Act, from which defendant physicians seek religious exemption, is "a valid and neutral law of general applicability" As relevant in this case, it requires business establishments to provide "full and equal accommodations, advantages, facilities, privileges, or services" to all persons notwithstanding their sexual orientation. Accordingly, the First Amendment's right to the free exercise of religion does not exempt defendant physicians here from conforming their conduct to the Act's antidiscrimination requirements even if compliance poses an incidental conflict with defendants' religious beliefs.

    Defendant physicians, however, insist that the high court's decision in *Smith,* has language on "hybrid rights" that lends support to their argument that under the First Amendment they are exempt from complying with the antidiscrimination provisions of California's Unruh Civil Rights Act. The pertinent passage in *Smith* states: "The only decisions in which we have held that the First Amendment bars application of a neutral, generally applicable law to religiously motivated action have involved not the Free Exercise Clause alone, but the Free Exercise Clause in conjunction with other constitutional protections. . . ." But the facts in *Smith,* the court explained, did "not present such a hybrid situation." Defendants here contend that they do have a hybrid claim, because compliance on their part with the state's Act interferes with a combination of their First Amendment rights to free speech and to freely exercise their religion. We rejected a similar hybrid claim in *Catholic Charities*, 32 Cal.4th 527 (2004).

    In that case, we explained that "[t]he high court has not, since the decision in *Smith,* determined whether the hybrid rights theory is valid or invoked it to justify applying strict scrutiny to a free exercise claim." We added, however, that Justice Souter's concurring opinion in *Lukumi*, was critical of the idea that hybrid rights would give rise to a stricter level of scrutiny: "[I]f a hybrid claim is simply one in which another constitutional right is implicated, then the hybrid exception would probably be so vast as to swallow the *Smith* rule. . . ."

    Here, defendant physicians contend that exposing them to liability for refusing to perform the IUI medical procedure for plaintiff infringes upon their First Amendment rights to free speech and free exercise of religion. Not so. As we noted earlier, California's Unruh Civil Rights Act imposes on business establishments certain antidiscrimination obligations, thus precluding any such establishment or its agents from telling patrons that it will not comply with the Act. Notwithstanding these statutory obligations, defendant physicians remain free to voice their objections, religious or otherwise, to the Act's prohibition against sexual orientation discrimination. "For purposes of the free speech clause, simple obedience to a law that does not require one to convey a verbal or symbolic message cannot reasonably be seen as a statement of support for the law or its purpose. Such a rule would, in effect, permit each individual to choose which laws he would obey merely by declaring his agreement or opposition."

Defendant physicians also perceive a form of free speech infringement flowing from plaintiff's purported efforts "to silence the doctors at trial." But the First Amendment prohibits *government* abridgment of free speech. Here, plaintiff is a private citizen. Therefore, her conduct as complained of by defendants does not fall within the ambit of the First Amendment.

Plaintiff's motion in the trial court for summary adjudication of defendant physicians' affirmative defense claiming a religious exemption from liability under California's Unruh Civil Rights Act merely sought to preclude the presentation at trial of a defense lacking any constitutional basis. In ruling on the motion, the trial court granted summary adjudication of the defense only insofar as it applied to plaintiff's claim of sexual orientation discrimination as prohibited by the Act. Nothing in that ruling precludes defendants from later at trial offering evidence, if relevant, that their denial of the medical treatment at issue was prompted by their religious beliefs for reasons *other* than plaintiff's sexual orientation.

IV

We now turn to the California Constitution. As here relevant, it provides: "Free exercise and enjoyment of religion without discrimination or preference are guaranteed." (Cal. Const., art. I, § 4.)

. . . .

Here, defendant physicians seek a religious exemption from a state law that is " 'a valid and neutral law of general applicability' " (*Smith*, 494 U.S. at p. 879.) To date, this court has not determined the appropriate standard of review for such a challenge under the *state* Constitution's guarantee of free exercise of religion. Because construing a state constitution is a matter left exclusively to the states, the high court's *Smith* test is not controlling here. As in *Catholic Charities*, however, this case presents no need for us to determine the appropriate test. For even under a strict scrutiny standard, defendants' claim fails.

Under strict scrutiny, "a law could not be applied in a manner that substantially burden[s] a religious belief or practice unless the state show[s] that the law represent[s] the least restrictive means of achieving a compelling interest." (*Catholic Charities*, 32 Cal.4th at p. 562.) Presumably, for defendants to comply with the Unruh Civil Rights Act's prohibition against sexual orientation discrimination would substantially burden their religious beliefs. Yet that burden is insufficient to allow them to engage in such discrimination. The Act furthers California's compelling interest in ensuring full and equal access to medical treatment irrespective of sexual orientation, and there are no less restrictive means for the state to achieve that goal.

To avoid any conflict between their religious beliefs and the state Unruh Civil Rights Act's antidiscrimination provisions, defendant physicians can simply refuse to perform the IUI medical procedure at issue here for any patient of North Coast, the physicians' employer. Or, because they incur liability under the Act if they infringe upon the right to the "full and equal" services of North Coast's medical practice, defendant physicians can avoid such a conflict by ensuring that every patient requiring IUI receives "full and equal" access to that medical procedure though a North Coast physician lacking defendants' religious objections.

Both defendant physicians urge this court to adopt and apply here a standard that is significantly different than strict scrutiny. They rely on this language from our state Constitution, article I, section 4: "Free exercise and enjoyment of religion without discrimination or preference are guaranteed. *This liberty of conscience does not excuse acts that are licentious or inconsistent with the peace or safety of the State.*" (Italics added.) According to defendants, the italicized language indicates that religious objectors are free to disregard a particular state law unless doing so compromises the peace or safety of the state or is licentious— situations that are not present here. Defendants also assert that our decision in *Catholic Charities* has language, italicized here, that left open the possibility of the test proposed by defendants: "A future case might lead us to choose the rule of *Sherbert*, 374 U.S. 398, [requiring that a state law adversely affecting religious rights satisfy strict scrutiny], the rule of *Smith*, 494 U.S. 872, [recognizing no religious exemption to valid and neutral laws of general applicability], *or an as-yet unidentified rule that more precisely reflects the language and history of the California Constitution and our own understanding of its import.*" (*Catholic Charities*, 32 Cal.4th at p. 562, italics added.) We reject defendants' contention.

Our statement in *Catholic Charities*, that this court in the future might adopt some "as-yet unidentified rule" governing free exercise of religion claims under the *state* Constitution contemplated only three possible tests: (1) The strict scrutiny standard . . . established in *Sherbert* . . . (2) the high court's subsequent test established in *Smith* . . . under which religious objectors' challenges to valid and neutral laws of general applicability are rejected out of hand; or (3) an *intermediate standard*, less exacting than the rigorous first option but more so than the second. Because the standard that defendants propose would exempt a religious objector from complying with a valid and neutral law of general applicability regardless of a compelling state interest supporting the law, and regardless of the absence of lesser restrictive means for furthering that compelling state interest, their proposed standard is not an intermediate standard but rather a standard that is more stringent than strict scrutiny. Nothing in *Catholic Charities* suggests that the appropriate test for free exercise of religion claims under article I, section 4 of the California Constitution would be stricter than strict scrutiny, and we decline to adopt such a standard here.

. . . .

The judgment of the Court of Appeal is reversed.

NOTES

1.   *The role of "conscience" in the provision of medical services.* This case prompted considerable debate about whether physicians and clinics could invoke religious objections as a basis for refusing to provide ART services. Human Life International, Americans United for Life, the American Association of Pro-Life Obstetricians and Gynecologists, Physicians for Life, and the Christian Medical and Dental Association rallied to provide amicus briefs in support of North Coast Women's Care Center. Ms. Benitez likewise attracted the support of the Anti-Defamation League, Latinas for Reproductive Justice, California Women's Law Center, Lambda Legal Defense, and the Mexican American Legal Defense Fund. Is it significant that pro-life groups weighed in to support the center's right to refuse services on religious grounds? What should we make of traditional civil rights groups, like the Anti-Defamation League and the Mexican American Legal Defense Fund, intervening to support Benitez's claim? Are reproductive rights issues civil rights issues?

2.   *Lessons from the Octomom?* In January 2009, Nadya Suleman gained international celebrity when she gave birth to octuplets after in vitro fertilization. Although the initial public reaction to Suleman was favorable, it soon turned negative when it became known that Suleman was an unemployed single mother with six other children (also conceived via IVF) who was living with her parents and receiving public assistance. The "Octomom" controversy generated calls for greater regulation of ART, as many argued that people like Suleman, who were not financially independent, should not be permitted to access ART. *See* Randal C. Archibold, *Octuplets, 6 Siblings, and Many Questions*, N.Y. TIMES, Feb. 3, 2009, at A14. Does the response to the Octomom reflect a prioritization of particular family forms and norms? Are there connections that we might draw between the lesbian couple in *North Coast* and the Octomom?

3.   *Equality in ART.* Professor Radhika Rao has argued that while access to ART is currently largely unregulated in the United States, there is reason to think that such regulations are in the offing. With such regulations in mind, Rao argues that although there is no absolute right to ART grounded in a theory of reproductive *autonomy*, such a right might proceed from a theory of reproductive *equality*. In other words, while the state can ban or limit the use of reproductive technologies, it must do so across the board, rather than limiting access only to disfavored groups. *See* Radhika Rao, *Equal Liberty: Assisted Reproductive Technology and Reproductive Equality*, 76 GEO. WASH. L. REV. 1457, 1460, 1474–81 (2008).

4. *Pregnancy, oppression, and inequality.* Recall the excerpt by Professor Dorothy Roberts that introduced this section. As Roberts notes, in the United States, the reproductive choices of low-income women and women of color are often stigmatized, while white and affluent women's reproductive choices are credited and supported through costly, but perhaps risky, scientific interventions. *See* Dorothy Roberts, *Privatization and Punishment in the New Age of Reprogenetics*, 54 EMORY L. J. 1343, 1355 (2005). With all of this in mind, to what extent are women's "choices" individualized? To what extent are they responses to systemic social pressures?

5. *Choice, inequality, and reproductive tourism.* Professor Lisa Ikemoto has applied Professor Dorothy Roberts' insights regarding women's "choices" and systemic inequality to address the emerging interest in "reproductive tourism"—the "travel for ART and the practices that facilitate fertility travel." As she explains, reproductive tourism creates inequalities between and among sperm donors, egg donors, and surrogates, as well as maldistribution of resources in the countries involved in such tourism. Lisa Ikemoto, *Reproductive Tourism: Equality Concerns in the Global Market for Fertility Services*, 27 LAW & INEQ. 277, 277–79 (2009).

6. *Reproductive justice and reproductive tourism.* According to Professor Seema Mohapatra, India and the Ukraine are fast emerging as central locations for ART, especially surrogacy arrangements. In 2009, India alone had 350 facilities that offered surrogacy, as well as other fertility services. Mohapatra notes that liberal feminism, with its focus on individual autonomy, is ill-equipped to think rigorously about surrogacy arrangements in places such as these, where surrogacy is one of the few forms of unskilled labor poor women can access without competition from men. At the same time, she warns that while surrogacy can provide many benefits to poor women, it may produce pressure on other women who do not wish to engage in such labor, but are urged to do so by husbands or families. Seema Mohapatra, *Achieving Reproductive Justice in the International Surrogacy Market*, 21 ANNALS HEALTH L. 191, 192–94, 198–200 (2012).

7. *The regulated womb.* Although it is difficult to find a consistent pattern, virtually all European nations regulate the use of ART in some fashion. Regulations include those prohibiting single women from receiving artificial insemination (in Germany, Sweden, and Italy), and bans on common genetic tests (in Austria and Italy). *See* Maria Cheng, *Fertility Treatment Bans in Europe Draw Criticism*, BOS. GLOBE, Apr. 22, 2012, at A6. Many European countries also require transgender individuals who seek to change their gender on legal documents to undergo sterilization, making it practically impossible for these individuals to reproduce without access to certain forms of ART. *See* Nicole Pasulka, *17 European Countries Force Transgender Sterilization*, MOTHER JONES (Feb. 16, 2012), http://www.motherjones.com/mojo/2012/02/most-european-countries-force-sterilization-transgender-people-map. The regulation of ART in these other jurisdictions prompts several questions: Why isn't ART more heavily regulated in the United States? What are the advantages and disadvantages of the (relatively) under-regulated ART industry?

8. *ART and concerns over parental rights.* In a study of eighteen same-sex couples in gay-friendly Seattle, Professor Deirdre Bowen found that even the well-to-do and well-educated couples in her study (eight gay couples and ten lesbian couples) faced enormous insecurity about their own and their partners' legal rights as parents. What was particularly striking was that these parents, who had spent a great deal of time and money trying to secure parental rights (including completing second-parent adoptions), were anxious about the unsettled state of the law surrounding the children of same-sex couples conceived via ART, and the differing approaches to such questions depending on the jurisdiction. For example, *where* a surrogate gives birth to an ART-conceived baby, as well as where the family ultimately resides, will affect the rights of the intended parents. *See* Deirdre M. Bowen, *The Parent Trap: Differential Familial Power in Same-Sex Families*, 15 WM. & MARY J. WOMEN & L. 1, 28–38 (2008).

1. FAMILY AND REPRODUCTIVE AUTONOMY IN PUBLIC LIFE

Although most reproductive and family decisions are conceptualized as occurring within the private sphere, these decisions impact the way that individuals—and women, particularly—engage in public life. The following selections all consider the implications of reproductive decisions and family decisions on public life, particularly in the workplace and in schools. This section also surfaces the myriad ways that the expectations of public life inform individual reproductive and family choices. In the first selection, Professor Joan Williams observes the way in which workplace structures reinforce—whether consciously or not—the traditional gendered division of household labor and paid work.

Joan Williams, Unbending Gender: Why Family and Work Conflict and What to Do About It

1–9 (2001).

. . . .

The common assumption is that we are seeing the demise of domesticity in America. Domesticity is a gender system comprising most centrally of both the particular organization of market work and family work that arose around 1780, and the gender norms that justify, sustain, and reproduce that organization. Before then, market work and family work were not sharply separated in space or time. By the turn of the nineteenth century this way of life was changing, as domesticity set up the system of men working in factories and offices, while women (in theory) stayed behind to rear the children and tend the "home sweet home."

Domesticity remains the entrenched, almost unquestioned, American norm and practice. As a gender system, it has two defining characteristics. The first is its organization of market work around the ideal of a worker who works full time and overtime and takes little or no time off for childbearing or child rearing. Though this ideal-worker norm does not define all jobs today, it defines the good ones: full-time blue-collar jobs in the working-class context, and high-level executive and professional jobs for the middle class and above. When work is structured in this way, caregivers often cannot perform as ideal workers. Their inability to do so gives rise to domesticity's second defining characteristic: its system of providing for caregiving by marginalizing the caregivers, thereby cutting them off from most of the social roles that offer responsibility and authority.

Domesticity introduced not only a new structure of market work and family work but also a new description of men and women. The ideology of domesticity held that men "naturally" belong in the market because they are competitive and aggressive; women belong in the home because of their "natural" focus on relationships, children, and an ethic of care. . . .

Both the ideology and the practice of domesticity retain their hold. A recent survey found that roughly two-thirds of Americans believe it would best for women to stay home and care for family and children. Domesticity's descriptions of men and women persist in vernacular gender talk such as John Gray's *Men Are from Mars, Women Are from Venus*, as well as in the train of feminist theory that associates women with an ethic of care.

Even more important, market work continues to be structured in ways that perpetuate the economic vulnerability of caregivers. Their vulnerability stems from our definition of the ideal worker as someone who works at least forty hours a week year round. This ideal-worker norm, framed around the traditional life patterns of men, excludes most mothers of childbearing age. Nearly *two-thirds* are not ideal workers even in the minimal sense of working full time full year. One-quarter still are homemakers, and many more work part time in an economy that rigorously marginalizes part-time workers. Single as well as married mothers are affected: Never-married mothers are the group of women mostly likely to be at home.

. . . .

Our economy is divided into mothers and others. Having children has a very strong negative effect on women's income, an effect that actually increased in the 1980s despite the fact that women have become better educated. The most dramatic figure is that mothers who work full time earn only sixty cents for every dollar earned by full-time fathers. Single mothers are most severely affected, earning the lowest percentage of men's average pay. Moreover, though the wage gap between men and women has fallen, the gap between the wages of mothers and others has widened in recent years. As a result in an era when women's wages are catching up with men's, mothers lag behind. Given that nearly 90 percent of women become mothers during their working lives, this pattern is inconsistent with gender equality.

. . . .

In short, the core elements of domesticity's organization of market work and family work remain intact. . . . Women still specialize in family work. Men still specialize in market work. Market work continues to be framed around the assumption that ideal workers have access to a flow of family work few mothers enjoy. Social and cultural norms still sustain and reproduce this organization of (market and family) work.

Domesticity did not die; it mutated. In the nineteenth century most married women were marginalized outside of the economy. Although women have re-entered market work, most remain marginalized today. This is not equality.

. . . .

The commonplace observation is that women are hurt by the hard choices they face. Once the focus shifts away from women's choices to the gender system that sets the frame within which those choices occur, we can see that domesticity's peculiar structuring of market work and family work hurts not only women but also men, children, politics, and our emotional life.

. . . Mothers marry, marginalize, and then divorce in a system that typically defines women's and children's postdivorce [sic] entitlements in terms of their basic "needs," while men's entitlements reflect the assumption (derived from domesticity) that they "own" their ideal-worker wage. This double application of the ideal-worker norm, first in market work, then in family entitlements, leaves roughly 40 percent of divorced mothers in poverty. Even in families that avoid impoverishment, the children of divorce often suffer downward mobility. A disproportionate number do not attain the education level, or the class status, of their fathers.

Domesticity takes a toll in a second way: by minimizing fathers' involvement. The current pattern of fathers largely exempted from child rearing is not eternal; it arose with domesticity. Before then, child rearing was considered too important to be left to women, and child-rearing manuals addressed fathers. Men were actively involved, in part because market work and family work were not yet geographically separated, so that fathers generally worked closer to home than most do today. Fathers' involvement also was considered necessary for orderly family governance. In a society that viewed women as the "weaker vessel," intellectually and morally inferior to men, it made no sense to delegate children's health, well-being, and eternal souls to the exclusive sphere of women. Domesticity changed parental roles. Child rearing came to be viewed as mothers' work, an allocation that persists up to the present day. One study estimated that an average American father spends twelve minutes a day in solo child care. Another reported that mothers spend about three times as much time as fathers in face-to-face interaction with their children.

Domesticity also takes a toll on men by pressuring them to perform as ideal workers in an age when that often requires long hours of work; roughly one-third of fathers work forty-nine hours a week or more. The current fathers' rights and men's movements need to be seen not only as continued assertions of male privilege (which they are) but also as protests against the gender role domesticity assigns to men. That role includes both breadwinning and the narrow emotional range we associate with conventional masculinities. . . .

Domesticity also affects arenas of life we think of as unrelated to gender. It affects our politics in particularly destructive ways. Its relegation of child rearing to the private sphere intimates that the republic has no responsibility to play in raising its next generation of citizens. This is in sharp contrast to the understanding in France, for example, where child rearing is supported by generous leave policies and an extensive system of child-care centers, on the theory that the republic has an obvious interest in the health and development of its future citizens. . . . [T]he rise of domesticity accompanied an important change in the understanding of virtue. Whereas in classical republican thought virtue referred to the manly pursuit of the common good in the public sphere, under domesticity the preservation of the republic was thought to depend on the success of women in raising the next generation of citizens in the domestic sphere. Thus, with the rise of domesticity, virtues formerly thought to belong to civic life were relegated to private life. Communitarians who protest contemporary liberalism's neutral stance on issues of morality rarely recognize domesticity's role in redefining virtue as something that belonged in private as opposed to public life.

Domesticity organizes our everyday tasks, our emotions, our politics. My goal is not to advocate sameness or androgyny, but to deconstruct domesticity and encourage the development of new ways of organizing work as well as family, emotional, and political life. . . . [S]ociety needs not only market work but also family work, and . . . adults who do family work should not be marginalized.

. . . .

Several provisos are in order. Much of the discussion . . . has focused on what is usually called the "traditional" family: a mother-caregiver, a father-breadwinner, and their children. Family studies stress an age of "postmodern" families with a wide variety of family structures.

The focus on mother-caregiver, father-breadwinner families is appropriate for several reasons. First, recent data suggest that the decline in the number of married-couple families has slowed dramatically. More important is that even though the family as defined by domesticity has loosened its hold on social life, it retains a viselike grip on popular aspirations: the white picket fence in our heads is a central part of this narrative. Most important, however, is the fact that most postmodern families retain the mother-caregiver, father-breadwinner structure even if the parents are no longer married or never were. In virtually all families headed by never-married mothers, and in the nearly 90 percent of divorces where mothers retain custody, the father continues to be supported by a flow of family work from the mother of his children even if she is not his wife. In fact, domesticity's mandates affect divorced and never-married mothers even more harshly than married ones: While married mothers have access to an ideal-worker's wage, many single mothers do not. This leads to poverty in single-parents families, as women marginalized by motherhood try to perform both as ideal workers and as caregivers in a system that assumes that all ideal workers are supported by a marginalized caregiver, and that all caregivers are linked with a breadwinner. To the extent that certain racial and ethnic categories have a high percentage of single mothers, the current system penalizes them even more severely than it does the white community.

A second proviso concerns a lack of focus on gay families. This reflects the fact that the literature on the gendering of gay families is still young. From talking with divorce lawyers who specialize in gay partners, my sense is that many gay male couples often play quite traditional gender roles. In sharp contrast, the growing literature on lesbian parenting suggests that fewer lesbian couples track domesticity's gender roles than do other types of couples. The hold of domesticity's gender roles on couples that include a man reflects the powerful pull of the ideal-worker norm on men, whose self-image is so often linked with work success. It is important to remember that ideal workers and marginalized caregivers come in different body shapes; gender roles are logically independent of sexual orientation. Also, to the extent that lesbian relationships are egalitarian, they offer models of caregiving freed from the structures imposed by domesticity.

A third proviso is that although most of the discussion focuses on child rearing, it is only one type of caregiving. The focus on child rearing reflects in part its symbolic importance, for domesticity treats it as the paradigm case of caregiving. It reflects as well its practical importance: Roughly 90 percent of women will become mothers at some point during their work lives, and over 40 percent of workers are caring for children under eighteen. Nonetheless, a system that marginalizes caregivers hurts anyone with caregiving responsibilities: that includes not only parents but children. One recent survey found that more than one-quarter of workers over fifty have elder-care responsibilities, as do one-fifth of those over thirty. . . .

A final proviso is that . . . [a]lternatives [to the nuclear family household] have always existed, from monkhood to hippiedom, with many in between. Indeed, one prerequisite for healthy households is to provide alternatives for people not suited to household life. . . . [C]onventional family life does not work well for those who live it. I cannot stress enough that this is not the same as saying that everyone should live conventionally.

NOTES

1. *The burden of rights.* Although Professor Williams focuses on the workplace's role in reinscribing gendered family norms, legal historian Linda Kerber argues that this kind of reinscription is also pervasive in other aspects of public life. In particular, Kerber refers to state policies that, until quite recently, "excused" women from civic obligations such as jury service. As Kerber argues, although these exemptions were intended to allow women to continue performing their household duties, they also compromised women's civil rights. *See* LINDA K. KERBER, NO CONSTITUTIONAL RIGHT TO BE LADIES 134–36 (1999). In 1961's *Hoyt v. Florida*, 368 U.S. 57 (1961), the Supreme Court upheld a Florida policy excluding women from jury service. Such gender-based exemptions were not uncommon and they were frequently rationalized as reasonable efforts to protect women "from the filth, obscenity, and obnoxious atmosphere . . . of the courtroom." *State v. Hall*, 187 So. 2d 861 (Miss. 1966). It was not until 1975's *Taylor v. Louisiana*, 419 U.S. 522 (1975), that the Court overruled *Hoyt* and declared women's systematic exclusion from jury service unconstitutional. In reality, however, women's obligation to serve on juries was not fully enforced until *J.E.B. v. Alabama*, 511 U.S. 127 (1994), which held unconstitutional peremptory challenges based solely on a prospective juror's sex.

2. *Civic rights and family choices in the public sphere today.* Currently, sixteen states and Puerto Rico exempt breastfeeding mothers from jury service or allow women to postpone their service. *See Breastfeeding State Laws*, NAT'L CONFERENCE OF STATE LEGISLATURES (June 11, 2014), www.ncsl.org/research/health/breastfeeding-state-laws.aspx. However, it is unclear whether many states provide exemptions or postponements for *pregnant* women. Should pregnancy be accommodated in this way? Should other reproductive choices be accommodated through similar policies?

2. EMPLOYMENT

As detailed by Joan Williams, employment is one of the arenas in which the conflict between the expectations of individuals in the public and private spheres is clearest. The United States is the only industrialized democracy that does not mandate paid family leave—a choice that, for some, reflects a rigid separation between the public workplace and the private home. However, in recent years there have been attempts to remedy the injuries that arise from this public-private conflict, particularly for parenting women. The next section examines these remedial federal and state statutes, and the legal claims that have arisen in their wake.

Family and Medical Leave Act of 1993

Pub. L. No. 103–3, 107 Stat. 6 (codified as amended at 29 U.S.C. §§ 2601–2619, 6381–6387, 2631–2654 (2014)).

An Act to grant family and temporary medical leave under certain circumstances.

Be it enacted by the Senate and House of Representatives of the United States of America in Congress assembled,

. . .

29 U.S.C. § 2601

SEC. 2. FINDINGS AND PURPOSES.

(a) FINDINGS.—Congress finds that—

(1) the number of single-parent households and two-parent households in which the single parent or both parents work is increasing significantly;

(2) it is important for the development of children and the family unit that fathers and mothers be able to participate in early childrearing and the care of family members who have serious health conditions;

(3) the lack of employment policies to accommodate working parents can force individuals to choose between job security and parenting;

(4) there is inadequate job security for employees who have serious health conditions that prevent them from working for temporary periods;

(5) due to the nature of the roles of men and women in our society, the primary responsibility for family caretaking often falls on women, and such responsibility affects the working lives of women more than it affects the working lives of men; and

(6) employment standards that apply to one gender only have serious potential for encouraging employers to discriminate against employees and applicants for employment who are of that gender.

(b) PURPOSES.—It is the purpose of this Act—

(1) to balance the demands of the workplace with the needs of families, to promote the stability and economic security of families, and to promote national interests in preserving family integrity;

(2) to entitle employees to take reasonable leave for medical reasons, for the birth or adoption of a child, and for the care of a child, spouse, or parent who has a serious health condition;

(3) to accomplish the purposes described in paragraphs (1) and (2) in a manner that accommodates the legitimate interests of employers;

(4) to accomplish the purposes described in paragraphs (1) and (2) in a manner that, consistent with the Equal Protection Clause of the Fourteenth Amendment, minimizes the potential for employment discrimination on the basis of sex by ensuring generally that leave is

available for eligible medical reasons (including maternity-related disability) and for compelling family reasons, on a gender-neutral basis; and

(5) to promote the goal of equal employment opportunity for women and men, pursuant to such clause.

. . .

29 U.S.C.A. § 2614

SEC. 104.   EMPLOYMENT AND BENEFITS PROTECTION.

(a) RESTORATION TO POSITION.—

(1) IN GENERAL.—Except as provided in subsection (b), any eligible employee who takes leave under section 102 for the intended purpose of the leave shall be entitled, on return from such leave—

(A) to be restored by the employer to the position of employment held by the employee when the leave commenced; or

(B) to be restored to an equivalent position with equivalent employment benefits, pay, and other terms and conditions of employment.

(2) LOSS OF BENEFITS.—The taking of leave under section 102 shall not result in the loss of any employment benefit accrued prior to the date on which the leave commenced.

(3) LIMITATIONS.—Nothing in this section shall be construed to entitle any restored employee to—

(A) the accrual of any seniority or employment benefits during any period of leave; or

(B) any right, benefit, or position of employment other than any right, benefit, or position to which the employee would have been entitled had the employee not taken the leave.

. . .

NOTES

1.   *Where the FMLA falls short.* In its final form, the Family and Medical Leave Act (FMLA) excludes businesses that employ fewer than fifty workers, as well as workers who have worked less than twelve months and have worked less than the required 1,250 hours during those months. Critically, these provisions frequently impact low-wage workers who are often employed in jobs where high turn-over rates and part-time scheduling are common. As family-law scholar Ann O'Leary notes, the realities of low-wage work mean that low-wage workers often struggle with limited access to FMLA benefits. Ann O'Leary, *How Family Leave Laws Left out Low-Income Workers*, 28 BERKELEY J. EMP. & LAB. L. 1, 53 (2007).

2.   *Unpaid leave?* The FMLA also falls short in that it provides twelve weeks of *unpaid* leave. *See* 26 U.S.C. § 2612(c) (2014). For many low-income families, the prospect of unpaid leave makes it unlikely that they will use

the FMLA's benefits. *See, e.g.,* Robin R. Runge, *Redefining Leave from Work,* 19 GEO. J. ON POVERTY L. & POL'Y 445, 447–48 (2012) (finding that current leave policies effectively ignore the experiences of low-wage, particularly female, workers). How might unpaid leave affect the decision to take FMLA leave among moderate-income families?

3. *The motherhood penalty.* There is wide consensus in scholarly literature that mothers earn less than non-mothers. The root causes of this motherhood wage penalty, however, remain subject to debate. Is it the product of women's individual choices or is it discrimination on the part of employers? In a laboratory experiment, sociologist Shelly Correll and her colleagues gave undergraduate subjects two otherwise identical resumes. One of the resumes signaled the applicant was a mother (or in some conditions, a father). The study found that subjects deemed the mother's resume less qualified, less likely to be promoted, and entitled to less pay, relative to the other resume. These results were confirmed in an audit study, where the same procedure was used with real employers, and mothers got fewer callbacks than non-parents and fathers. Notably, parenthood for men did not lead to discrimination, and in some conditions increased how favorably prospective employers viewed male candidates. The findings suggest the mechanisms by which (often unconscious) stereotypes of the "ideal worker," see *supra* p. 495, are translated into real life discrimination. *See* Shelley J. Correll et al., *Getting a Job: Is There a Motherhood Penalty?,* 112 AM. J. SOC. 1297, 1332–33 (2007).

4. *Do rights matter?* Professor Catherine R. Albiston took on the vexing question of whether rights granted legislatively make any difference in real life. Although surveys of employers seem to suggest that the FMLA was implemented with few problems, surveys of employees reflect a very different picture. Employees often experience a range of difficulties in accessing legislatively-conferred rights, like FMLA benefits. In an empirical study, Albiston examined how this paradox developed. She found that while employers may think they are adhering to the FMLA, they often: (1) fail to publicize the FMLA's provisions to their employees, (2) cast workers who avail themselves of FMLA rights as "slackers" and disloyal workers, and (3) claim that employees cannot be spared at the time they need leave. All of this, Albiston asserts, undermines the law's reach. Albiston also notes that the existence of the law itself, and (often vague) notions of what rights it conferred, enabled women and men to challenge the employer's refrain that "that's just the way it is," and prompted them to seek outside information in order to mobilize their rights. *See* CATHERINE R. ALBISTON, INSTITUTIONAL INEQUALITY AND THE MOBILIZATION OF THE FAMILY AND MEDICAL LEAVE ACT: RIGHTS ON LEAVE 162–63 (2010).

* * *

The following cases concern claims arising under the FMLA, and in some cases, corollary state-leave statutes. When reading these cases, keep in mind the state regulation of pregnant women in workplaces and schools explored elsewhere in this book.

Nevada Department of Human Resources v. Hibbs

538 U.S. 721 (2003).

■ REHNQUIST, C.J.

The Family and Medical Leave Act of 1993 (FMLA or Act) entitles eligible employees to take up to 12 work weeks of unpaid leave annually for any of several reasons, including the onset of a "serious health condition" in an employee's spouse, child, or parent. 29 U.S.C. § 2612(a)(1)(C). The Act creates a private right of action to seek both equitable relief and money damages "against any employer (including a public agency) in any Federal or State court of competent jurisdiction," should that employer "interfere with, restrain, or deny the exercise of" FMLA rights. We hold that employees of the State of Nevada may recover money damages in the event of the State's failure to comply with the family-care provision of the Act.

Petitioners include the Nevada Department of Human Resources (Department) and two of its officers. Respondent William Hibbs (hereinafter respondent) worked for the Department's Welfare Division. In April and May 1997, he sought leave under the FMLA to care for his ailing wife, who was recovering from a car accident and neck surgery. The Department granted his request for the full 12 weeks of FMLA leave and authorized him to use the leave intermittently as needed between May and December 1997. Respondent did so until August 5, 1997, after which he did not return to work. In October 1997, the Department informed respondent that he had exhausted his FMLA leave, that no further leave would be granted, and that he must report to work by November 12, 1997. Respondent failed to do so and was terminated.

. . . The District Court awarded petitioners summary judgment on the grounds that the FMLA claim was barred by the Eleventh Amendment and that respondent's Fourteenth Amendment rights had not been violated. Respondent appealed. . . .

We granted certiorari to resolve a split among the Courts of Appeals on the question whether an individual may sue a State for money damages in federal court. . . .

For over a century now, we have made clear that the Constitution does not provide for federal jurisdiction over suits against nonconsenting States.

Congress may, however, abrogate such immunity in federal court if it makes its intention to abrogate unmistakably clear in the language of the statute and acts pursuant to a valid exercise of its power under § 5 of the Fourteenth Amendment. . . . This case turns, then, on whether Congress acted within its constitutional authority when it sought to abrogate the States' immunity for purposes of the FMLA's family-leave provision.

In enacting the FMLA, Congress relied on two of the powers vested in it by the Constitution: its Article I commerce power and its power under § 5 of the Fourteenth Amendment to enforce that Amendment's guarantees. Congress may not abrogate the States' sovereign immunity pursuant to its Article I power over commerce. *Seminole Tribe v. Florida*, 517 U.S. 44 (1994). Congress may, however, abrogate States' sovereign immunity through a valid exercise of its § 5 power, for "the Eleventh Amendment, and the principle of state sovereignty which it embodies, are necessarily limited by the enforcement provisions of § 5 of the Fourteenth Amendment."

. . . Section 5 [of the Fourteenth Amendment] grants Congress the power "to enforce" the substantive guarantees of § 1—among them, equal protection of the laws—by enacting "appropriate legislation." Congress may, in the exercise of its § 5 power, do more than simply proscribe conduct that we have held unconstitutional. . . . Congress may enact so-called prophylactic legislation that proscribes facially constitutional conduct, in order to prevent and deter unconstitutional conduct.

. . . .

The FMLA aims to protect the right to be free from gender-based discrimination in the workplace. We have held that statutory classifications that distinguish between males and females are subject to heightened scrutiny. . . .

The history of the many state laws limiting women's employment opportunities is chronicled in—and, until relatively recently, was sanctioned by—this Court's own opinions. For example, in *Bradwell v. State*, 16 Wall. 130 (1873) (Illinois), and *Goesaert v. Cleary*, 335 U.S. 464, 466 (1948) (Michigan), the Court upheld state laws prohibiting women from practicing law and tending bar, respectively. State laws frequently subjected women to distinctive restrictions, terms, conditions, and benefits for those jobs they could take. In *Muller v. Oregon*, 208 U.S. 412, 419, n. 1 (1908), for example, this Court approved a state law limiting the hours that women could work for wages, and observed that 19 States had such laws at the time. Such laws were based on the related beliefs that (1) a woman is, and should remain, "the center of home and family life," *Hoyt v. Florida*, 368 U.S. 57, 62 (1961), and (2) "a proper discharge of [a woman's] maternal functions—having in view not merely her own health, but the well-being of the race—justif[ies] legislation to protect her from the greed as well as the passion of man," *Muller*, *supra*. Until our decision in *Reed v. Reed*, 404 U.S. 71 (1971), "it remained the prevailing doctrine that government, both federal and state, could withhold from women opportunities accorded men so long as any 'basis in reason' "—such as the above beliefs—"could be conceived for the discrimination."

Congress responded to this history of discrimination by abrogating States' sovereign immunity in Title VII of the Civil Rights Act of 1964 and we sustained this abrogation. . . . But state gender discrimination did not cease. "[I]t can hardly be doubted that . . . women still face pervasive, although at times more subtle, discrimination . . . in the job market." According to evidence that was before Congress when it enacted the FMLA, States continue to rely on invalid gender stereotypes in the employment context, specifically in the administration of leave benefits. Reliance on such stereotypes cannot justify the States' gender discrimination in this area. The long and extensive history of sex discrimination prompted us to hold that measures that differentiate on the basis of gender warrant heightened scrutiny; here . . . the persistence of such unconstitutional discrimination by the States justifies Congress' passage of prophylactic § 5 legislation.

As the FMLA's legislative record reflects, a 1990 Bureau of Labor Statistics (BLS) survey stated that 37 percent of surveyed private-sector employees were covered by maternity leave policies, while only 18 percent were covered by paternity leave policies. The corresponding numbers from a similar BLS survey the previous year were 33 percent and 16 percent, respectively. While these data show an increase in the percentage of employees eligible for such leave, they also show a widening of the gender gap during the same period. Thus, stereotype-based beliefs about the allocation of family duties remained firmly rooted, and employers' reliance on them in establishing discriminatory leave policies remained widespread.

Congress also heard testimony that "[p]arental leave for fathers . . . is rare. Even . . . [w]here child-care leave policies do exist, men, *both in the public and private sectors,* receive notoriously discriminatory treatment in their requests for such leave." Many States offered women extended "maternity" leave that far exceeded the typical 4- to 8-week period of physical disability due to pregnancy and childbirth, but very few States granted men a parallel benefit: Fifteen States provided women up to one year of extended maternity leave, while only four provided men with the same. This and other differential leave policies were not attributable to any differential physical needs of men and women, but rather to the pervasive sex-role stereotype that caring for family members is women's work.

Finally, Congress had evidence that, even where state laws and policies were not facially discriminatory, they were applied in discriminatory ways. It was aware of the "serious problems with the discretionary nature of family leave," because when "the authority to grant leave and to arrange the length of that leave rests with individual supervisors," it leaves "employees open to discretionary and possibly unequal treatment." Testimony supported that conclusion, explaining that "[t]he lack of uniform parental and medical leave policies in the work place has created an environment where [sex] discrimination is rampant." 1987 Senate Labor Hearings, pt. 2, at 170 (testimony of Peggy Montes, Mayor's Commission on Women's Affairs, City of Chicago).

In spite of all of the above evidence, Justice Kennedy argues in dissent that Congress' passage of the FMLA was unnecessary because "the States appear to have been ahead of Congress in providing gender-neutral family leave benefits," and points to Nevada's leave policies in particular. However, it was only "[s]ince Federal family leave legislation was first introduced" that the States had even "begun to consider similar family leave initiatives."

Furthermore, the dissent's statement that some States "had adopted some form of family-care leave" before the FMLA's enactment glosses over important shortcomings of some state policies. First, seven States had childcare leave provisions that applied to women only. Indeed, Massachusetts required that notice of its leave provisions be posted only in "establishment[s] in which females are employed." These laws reinforced the very stereotypes that Congress sought to remedy through the FMLA. Second, 12 States provided their employees no family leave, beyond an initial childbirth or adoption, to care for a seriously ill child or family member. Third, many States provided no statutorily guaranteed right to family leave, offering instead only voluntary or discretionary leave programs. Three States left the amount of leave time primarily in employers' hands. Congress could reasonably conclude that such discretionary family-leave programs would do little to combat the stereotypes about the roles of male and female employees that Congress sought to eliminate. Finally, four States provided leave only through administrative regulations or personnel policies, which Congress could reasonably conclude offered significantly less firm protection than a federal law. Against the above backdrop of limited state leave policies, no matter how generous petitioners' own may have been, Congress was justified in enacting the FMLA as remedial legislation.

In sum, the States' record of unconstitutional participation in, and fostering of, gender-based discrimination in the administration of leave benefits is weighty enough to justify the enactment of prophylactic § 5 legislation.

. . . .

. . . Because the standard for demonstrating the constitutionality of a gender-based classification is more difficult to meet than our rational-basis test—it must "serv[e] important governmental objectives" and be "substantially related to the achievement of those objectives, . . ."—it was easier for Congress to show a pattern of state constitutional violations. Congress was similarly successful in *South Carolina v. Katzenbach*, 383 U.S. 301, 308–313 (1966), where we upheld the Voting Rights Act of 1965: Because racial classifications are presumptively invalid, most of the States' acts of race discrimination violated the Fourteenth Amendment.

The impact of the discrimination targeted by the FMLA is significant. Congress determined:

> Historically, denial or curtailment of women's employment opportunities has been traceable directly to the pervasive presumption that women are mothers first, and workers second.

This prevailing ideology about women's roles has in turn justified discrimination against women when they are mothers or mothers-to-be.

Stereotypes about women's domestic roles are reinforced by parallel stereotypes presuming a lack of domestic responsibilities for men. Because employers continued to regard the family as the woman's domain, they often denied men similar accommodations or discouraged them from taking leave. These mutually reinforcing stereotypes created a self-fulfilling cycle of discrimination that forced women to continue to assume the role of primary family caregiver, and fostered employers' stereotypical views about women's commitment to work and their value as employees. Those perceptions, in turn, Congress reasoned, lead to subtle discrimination that may be difficult to detect on a case-by-case basis.

We believe that Congress' chosen remedy, the family-care leave provision of the FMLA, is "congruent and proportional to the targeted violation." Congress had already tried unsuccessfully to address this problem through Title VII and the amendment of Title VII by the Pregnancy Discrimination Act, 42 U.S.C. § 2000e(k). Here, as in *Katzenbach*, Congress again confronted a "difficult and intractable proble[m]," where previous legislative attempts had failed. Such problems may justify added prophylactic measures in response.

By creating an across-the-board, routine employment benefit for all eligible employees, Congress sought to ensure that family-care leave would no longer be stigmatized as an inordinate drain on the workplace caused by female employees, and that employers could not evade leave obligations simply by hiring men. By setting a minimum standard of family leave for *all* eligible employees, irrespective of gender, the FMLA attacks the formerly state-sanctioned stereotype that only women are responsible for family caregiving, thereby reducing employers' incentives to engage in discrimination by basing hiring and promotion decisions on stereotypes.

The dissent characterizes the FMLA as a "substantive entitlement program" rather than a remedial statute because it establishes a floor of 12 weeks' leave. In the dissent's view, in the face of evidence of gender-based discrimination by the States in the provision of leave benefits, Congress could do no more in exercising its § 5 power than simply proscribe such discrimination. But this position cannot be squared with our recognition that Congress "is not confined to the enactment of legislation that merely parrots the precise wording of the Fourteenth Amendment," but may prohibit "a somewhat broader swath of conduct, including that which is not itself forbidden by the Amendment's text." . . .

. . . .

We also find significant the many other limitations that Congress placed on the scope of this measure. The FMLA requires only unpaid leave, and applies only to employees who have worked for the employer for at least one year and provided 1,250 hours of service within the last 12 months. Employees in high-ranking or sensitive positions are simply ineligible for FMLA leave; of particular importance to the States, the FMLA expressly excludes from coverage state elected officials, their staffs, and appointed policymakers. Employees must give advance notice of foreseeable leave, and employers may require certification by a health care provider of the need for leave. In choosing 12 weeks as the appropriate leave floor, Congress chose "a middle ground, a period long enough to serve 'the needs of families' but not so long that it would upset 'the legitimate interests of employers.' " Moreover, the cause of action under the FMLA is a restricted one: The damages recoverable are strictly defined and measured by actual monetary losses, and the accrual period for backpay is limited by the Act's 2-year statute of limitations (extended to three years only for willful violations).

For the above reasons, we conclude that § 2612(a)(1)(C) is congruent and proportional to its remedial object, and can "be understood as responsive to, or designed to prevent, unconstitutional behavior."

The judgment of the Court of Appeals is therefore *affirmed.*

■ KENNEDY, J., with whom SCALIA, J. and THOMAS, J., join, dissenting.

. . . .

The Court acknowledges that States have adopted family leave programs prior to federal intervention, but argues these policies suffered from serious imperfections. Even if correct, this observation proves, at most, that programs more generous and more effective than those operated by the States were feasible. That the States did not devise the optimal programs is not, however, evidence that the States were perpetuating unconstitutional discrimination. Given that the States assumed a pioneering role in the creation of family leave schemes, it is not surprising these early efforts may have been imperfect. This is altogether different, however, from purposeful discrimination.

. . . .

Stripped of the conduct which exhibits no constitutional infirmity, the Court's "exten[sive] and specifi[c] . . . record of unconstitutional state conduct," boils down to the fact that three States, Massachusetts, Kansas, and Tennessee, provided parenting leave only to their female employees, and had no program for granting their employees (male or female) family leave. . . . [T]he evidence related to the parenting leave is simply too attenuated to support a charge of unconstitutional discrimination in the provision of family leave. Nor, as the Court seems to acknowledge, does the Constitution require States to provide their employees with any family leave at all. A State's failure to devise a family leave program is not, then, evidence of unconstitutional behavior.

Considered in its entirety, the evidence fails to document a pattern of unconstitutional conduct sufficient to justify the abrogation of States' sovereign immunity. . . .

NOTES

1. *Remedying gender discrimination?* In upholding the FMLA, Chief Justice Rehnquist characterizes the law as remedial in nature. That is, the FMLA is an effort to remedy persistent gender discrimination and dismantle gender stereotypes regarding the provision of caregiving. But is the FMLA successful on these fronts? The fact that the FMLA provides only unpaid leave may have profound consequences for the gendered distribution of caregiving. Given the persistent wage gap between men and women, it is likely that families will conclude that it makes more sense for the (lower paid) woman to take advantage of FMLA leave, while the (better paid) man continues in his role as family breadwinner. Should we be concerned about the reality of how the FMLA is deployed, or is it enough the law reflects skepticism of these stereotypes and the gender discrimination they underwrite?

2. *The daddy double-bind.* Writer and attorney Kari Palazzari argues that the FMLA tends to reify traditional sex roles in other ways. To the extent that fathers see their main role as providing for the family (though they are increasingly becoming more involved in caretaking), elements of the FMLA—the fact that it is unpaid, that workers do not earn seniority while on leave, that the top 10% of employees are excluded—serve to make taking FMLA time seem more costly, on average, for fathers than for mothers. Because mothers are more likely to take parental leave, whether under the FMLA or any of the corollary state-leave statutes, they have a "head start" in parenting, which tends to solidify traditional caretaking roles. This structural problem, Palazzari notes, both rests on and recreates notions of what fatherhood and motherhood, as well as masculinity and femininity, mean. *See* Kari Palazzari, *The Daddy Double-Bind: How the Family and Medical Leave Act Perpetuates Sex Inequality Across All Class Levels*, 16 COLUM. J. GENDER & L. 429, 453 (2007).

Knussman v. Maryland

272 F.3d 625 (4th Cir. 2001).

■ TRAXLER, CIRCUIT JUDGE.

Howard Kevin Knussman, a trooper in the Maryland State Police, brought an action alleging that the State of Maryland and several individual employees of the Maryland State Police (collectively "the defendants") unlawfully discriminated against him on the basis of his gender, for which he sought recourse under 42 U.S.C.A. § 1983 (West Supp. 2000); and that the defendants violated his rights under the Family and Medical Leave Act of 1993 (FMLA), *see* 29 U.S.C.A. §§ 2601–2654 (West 1999), for which he sought recourse under § 1983 and directly under the FMLA. Following a jury trial and various post-trial motions, judgment in the amount of $375,000 was entered against only one of the defendants—Jill Mullineaux, a civilian employee of the Maryland State Police.

. . . .

In 1994, Knussman learned that his wife Kimberly was pregnant. At the time, Knussman held the rank of trooper first class and served as a paramedic on medevac helicopters in the Aviation Division of the Maryland State Police ("MSP"). Unfortunately, Kim's pregnancy was difficult and ultimately resulted in her confinement to bed rest in the latter stages prior to delivery. In October 1994, Knussman submitted a written request to his supervisor asking that Knussman be permitted to take four to eight weeks of paid "family sick leave" to care for his wife and spend time with his family following the birth of his child.[1] Eventually, Knussman was informed by the MSP Director of Flight Operations, First Sergeant Ronnie P. Creel, that there was "no way" that he would be allowed more than two weeks. Creel testified that, at the time of Knussman's request, the Aviation Division was understaffed. According to Knussman, Creel misinformed him that if he wanted more leave, he would be forced to take unpaid leave because the FMLA did not entitle him to further paid leave. Knussman testified that he was unfamiliar with the FMLA because the MSP had failed to provide proper notice to its employees about their rights under the FMLA.

In early December, shortly before the Knussmans' daughter was born, Jill Mullineaux, manager of the medical leave and benefit section of the MSP Personnel Management Division, notified all MSP employees of a new Maryland statutory provision that allowed the use of paid sick leave by a state employee to care for a newborn. See Md. Code Ann., *State Pers. & Pens.* §§ 7–502(b)(3), 7–508 (1994). The statute permitted "[p]rimary care givers" to "use, without certification of illness or disability, up to 30 days of accrued sick leave to care for [a] child . . . immediately following: . . . the birth of the employee's child." Md. Code Ann., *State Pers. & Pens.* § 7–508(a)(1). A "[p]rimary care giver" was defined as "an employee who is primarily responsible for the care and nurturing of a child." Md. Code Ann., *State Pers. & Pens.* § 7–508(a)(1). By contrast, a "[s]econdary care giver," *i.e.*, "an employee who is secondarily responsible for the care and nurturing of a child," might use up to 10 days of accrued sick leave without providing proof of illness or disability. Md. Code Ann., *State Pers. & Pens.* § 7–508(b)(1).[2] In contrast

---

[1]   Maryland law permitted a state employee to use paid sick leave for reasons other than the employee's own illness, including "for death, illness, or disability in the employee's immediate family." Md. Code Ann., *State Pers. & Pens.* § 7–502(b)(2) (1994). The statute was later amended and reorganized; however, Maryland law still permits this particular use of a state employee's sick leave. *See* Md. Code Ann., *State Pers. & Pens.* § 9–501(b)(2) (1996).

[2]   Section 7–508 has been amended and recodified, and it now provides for the use of up to an aggregate of 40 days of accrued sick leave if two state employees are responsible for the care of a newborn. *See* Md. Code Ann., *State Pers. & Pens.* § 9–505(b)(1) (1996). Section 7–508(b)(1), had it been in effect at the time, apparently would have applied to the Knussmans, who were both state employees.

to "family sick leave," which required an employee to provide verification of a family member's illness, the new "nurturing leave" provision permitted an employee to use paid sick leave without providing any medical documentation, since this type of leave was not actually related to the illness or disability of the employee or the employee's family.[3]

Believing that this "nurturing leave" might afford him more paid leave than he would receive from his request for "family sick leave," Knussman contacted Mullineaux for additional information about using his accrued sick leave under § 7–508. Specifically, he wanted to know whether he could qualify as a primary care giver under § 7–508(a)(1) and take 30 days of paid sick leave. According to Knussman, Mullineaux informed him that only birth mothers could qualify as primary care givers; fathers would only be permitted to take leave as secondary care givers since they "couldn't breast feed a baby." Mullineaux, who testified that she was merely passing along the Maryland Department of Personnel's (DOP) view of "primary care giver," denied adopting such a categorical interpretation.[4] In any case, Knussman's superior officers in the Aviation Division, having consulted Mullineaux about the untested nurturing leave provision, granted him 10 days of paid sick leave as the secondary care giver under § 7–508(b).

The Knussmans' daughter was born on December 9, 1994. Kimberly Knussman, however, continued to experience health problems. Before his authorized 10-day leave expired, Knussman contacted Sergeant J.C. Collins, one of his supervisors, and inquired whether his status could be changed to that of primary care giver and his paid sick leave extended to 30 days under section 7–508(a). Knussman explained to Collins that he was the primary care giver for the child because, given his wife's condition following delivery, he was performing the majority of the essential functions such as diaper changing, feeding, bathing and taking the child to the doctor.

David Czorapinski, the Assistant Commander for the Aviation Division during this time, learned of Knussman's inquiry and, unable to reach Mullineaux, gathered some preliminary information on the new law himself. Czorapinski learned that the Maryland DOP intended to take the position that the mother was the primary care giver and the father was secondary. Czorapinski passed this information down the chain-of-command and Knussman was told that it was unlikely that his paid sick leave would be extended under section 7–508(a).

On the day before Knussman was scheduled to return to work, Knussman made a final attempt at obtaining additional sick leave.

---

[3]   For ease of reference, we adopt the term "nurturing leave." This term, however, does not appear in the statute.

[4]   Mullineaux testified that she never told Knussman that fathers were, as a class, ineligible for primary care giver status. Rather, Mullineaux's version was that she told Knussman, based on information provided by the state Department of Personnel, "that the birth mother was presumed to be the primary care giver and if he wanted to qualify as the primary care giver, he could, if he could provide [supporting] information."

Sergeant Carl Lee, one of Knussman's immediate superiors, had earlier informed Knussman that although nurturing leave as a primary care giver was probably not an option, Knussman might be eligible for additional paid leave under the family sick leave provision, as long as he could demonstrate that it was medically necessary for him to care for his wife. Knussman contacted Mullineaux to find out what information he needed to supply for family sick leave.[5] During this conversation, Knussman again discussed his eligibility for nurturing leave as a primary care provider under section 7–508(a) with Mullineaux, who explained that "God made women to have babies and, unless [he] could have a baby, there is no way [he] could be primary care [giver]," and that his wife had to be "in a coma or dead," for Knussman to qualify as the primary care giver.

Mullineaux denied Knussman's request for paid sick leave under § 7–508(a) as a primary care giver. Knussman returned to work as ordered and immediately filed an administrative grievance on the grounds that he had been improperly denied primary care giver status under § 7–508(a). He did not seek review of Mullineaux's denial of his request for family sick leave under section 7–502(b)(2). Once the grievance process was underway, Knussman's claim went up the MSP chain-of-command and Mullineaux's involvement ceased.

Knussman's grievance was denied at each stage of the four-level grievance procedure. . . .

Essentially, Czorapinski believed that Kimberly Knussman, who was also a state employee, was enjoying the benefits of nurturing leave as a primary care giver because, following delivery, she took sick leave for a 30-day period—the same amount of time afforded a primary care giver under § 7–508(a). Thus, Czorapinski was concerned that both Knussmans were attempting to qualify as the primary care giver for their daughter when the statute indicated only one person could qualify. At trial, Knussman presented evidence that, prior to the step two grievance conference, Mullineaux and Czorapinski were made aware of the fact the Kimberly Knussman was, in fact, on sick leave for her own disability resulting from the difficult pregnancy. Following Czorapinski's decision, Knussman pursued his complaint through the two remaining steps of the internal grievance procedure without success.

Knussman then filed a three-count action in federal court. In Count I, Knussman sought relief under § 1983, claiming that his leave request under § 7–508(a) was denied as a result of gender discrimination in violation of the Equal Protection Clause of the Fourteenth Amendment

---

[5] Knussman subsequently submitted a letter from Kimberly Knussman's doctor in support of his request for family sick leave; however, Mullineaux concluded that the letter was insufficient to justify family sick leave because "it [did not] say what care [Knussman was] going to provide, and it [did not] say that [Knussman] need[ed] to be home . . . like it's [Knussman's] choice and not the doctor's requirement." J.A. 827. Although Czorapinski suggested to Knussman that the deficiencies could be easily corrected, Knussman refused "to pursue this option any further."

to the United States Constitution. He named as defendants the State of Maryland, the MSP, and several employees of the MSP, in both their individual and official capacities: Mullineaux, Czorapinski, Creel, and Colonel David B. Mitchell, Superintendent of the MSP.

. . . .

After a period of discovery, the defendants moved for summary judgment on the grounds that they were entitled to qualified immunity and that Knussman could not prove an equal protection violation in the first place. With respect to Knussman's equal protection claim under § 1983 (Count I), the court concluded that the facts, viewed in the light most favorable to Knussman, indicated that the defendants applied a gender-based presumption that the birth mother was the primary care giver, which would amount to an equal protection violation. The district court further concluded that the defendants were not entitled to qualified immunity because it was well-established at the time that gender discrimination in employment was prohibited under the Fourteenth Amendment:

> Although the Maryland leave law had been amended effective less than one month before [Knussman] requested leave and the DOP had not issued any guidelines regarding application of the amended law, the right to equal protection is a well-established principle. It is also clear that gender discrimination violates the equal protection clause. Discriminatory application of a gender neutral state law is patently illegal and defendants should have known at least this much.

. . . .

Thus, the case went to trial on portions of both counts in the complaint. As for Count I, Knussman's § 1983 equal protection claim remained intact against the State of Maryland (but only for declaratory and injunctive relief) and the defendants in their individual capacities. At the close of the evidence, the court submitted the question of qualified immunity to the jury as well as the ultimate question of liability. The jury concluded that each defendant denied Knussman's request for leave because of his gender; however, the jury also found that every defendant except Mullineaux was entitled to qualified immunity. Knussman does not challenge this conclusion on appeal. The jury awarded Knussman the sum of $375,000 in damages.

. . . .

On appeal, Mullineaux contends that she was entitled to qualified immunity on Knussman's equal protection claim under § 1983. She also challenges, on multiple grounds, the jury's verdict as well as the court's jury instructions.

. . . .

We first consider the issue of whether the evidence adduced at trial is sufficient to establish that Mullineaux committed a constitutional violation under the law as it currently stands. In a nutshell, Knussman's contention is that Mullineaux applied a facially neutral statute unequally solely on the basis of a gender stereotype in violation of the Equal Protection Clause of the Fourteenth Amendment. The only distinction created by the statute was between "primary care givers" and "secondary care givers," the former being entitled to 30 days of accrued sick leave to care for a newborn and the latter being entitled to 10 days of accrued sick leave. The statute made no reference to gender. Rather, the gender classification was created in the application of § 7–508. Viewed in the light most favorable to Knussman, Mullineaux, based on the comments of an administrative assistant to the DOP's Director of Legislation, took the position that only mothers could qualify for additional paid leave as primary care givers under § 7–508(a). Essentially, Mullineaux applied an irrebutable presumption that the mother is the primary care giver, and therefore entitled to greater employment benefits.

We agree with Knussman that Mullineaux's conduct violated his rights under the Equal Protection Clause. Government classifications drawn on the basis of gender have been viewed with suspicion for three decades. . . .

. . . .

In particular, justifications for gender-based distinctions that are rooted in "overbroad generalizations about the different talents, capacities, or preferences of males and females" will not suffice. . . . Thus, gender classifications that appear to rest on nothing more than conventional notions about the proper station in society for males and females have been declared invalid time and again by the Supreme Court. . . .

Gender classifications based upon generalizations about typical gender roles in the raising and nurturing of children have met a similar fate. . . .

. . . .

The defendants have not even attempted to explain how an irrebuttable presumption in favor of the mother under § 7–508 relates to an important state interest. We conclude that the presumption employed by Mullineaux here was not substantially related to an important governmental interest and, therefore, was not permissible under the Equal Protection Clause.

. . . .

We next must decide whether Mullineaux's actions contravened "clearly established statutory or constitutional rights of which a reasonable person would have known." *Harlow v. Fitzgerald*, 457 U.S. 800, 818 (1982). . . .

. . . .

Mullineaux contends that the law was not clear because the Supreme Court had determined on a number of occasions that equal protection principles permit government officials to distribute employment-related benefits pursuant to gender-based classifications. In the decisions cited by Mullineaux, however, the gender-based classification was linked to something other than a sexual stereotype. For example, Mullineaux relies on *Geduldig v. Aiello*, 417 U.S. 484 (1974). In our view, *Geduldig* does not cloud the issue. In *Geduldig*, the Court upheld a California insurance statute that excluded pregnancy-related disabilities from coverage against an equal protection challenge, observing that the exclusion of disabilities relating to normal childbirth (as well as other short-term disabilities not related to pregnancy) represented a permissible policy choice aimed at maintaining the solvency of the insurance program. . . .

. . . .

The authority cited by Mullineaux actually underscores our conclusion regarding the clarity of the law in December 1994. Mullineaux's distribution of sick leave benefits under § 7–508 was a by-product of traditional ideas about a woman's role in rearing a child, which was clearly impermissible under the Equal Protection Clause of the Fourteenth Amendment at the time in question.

. . . .

In sum, we hold that Mullineaux was not entitled to qualified immunity against Knussman's equal protection claim under § 1983 and affirm the judgment as to liability, but we conclude that the jury's award of $375,000 was excessive. Accordingly, we vacate the jury's award and remand for a new trial on damages with respect to Knussman's equal protection claim (Count I). Knussman is entitled to be compensated for emotional distress caused by Mullineaux's constitutional violation but not for any emotional distress associated with the litigation of this action or his employer's general internal grievance process.

AFFIRMED IN PART, VACATED IN PART, AND REMANDED.

■ LEE, DISTRICT JUDGE, concurring in part and dissenting in part:

. . . .

. . . I write separately to stress the fact that Mullineaux is not entitled to qualified immunity because she engaged in the discriminatory application of a gender neutral statute. . . .

Mullineaux is not entitled to qualified immunity because a reasonable personnel official in Mullineaux's position, and with her experience, would have known in 1994 that the law is clearly established that it is unlawful to administer a gender neutral leave law in a discriminatory manner and to base her decision with respect to employment benefits on an employee's gender. . . .

. . . .

The statute makes no reference to a distinction on the basis of gender. Nonetheless, in response to Knussman's request, Mullineaux told Knussman that he could not qualify as the primary care giver under the statute because he was a man. Based on these facts, it is imperative that any inquiries into the constitutional violation at issue focus on the liberties that Mullineaux took in her capacity as Manager of Medical Leave Benefits.

The Majority misplaces its focus on comparing Mullineaux's decision to that of legislators and agencies in order to determine the constitutionality of Mullineaux's decision. The Majority concludes that Mullineaux's decision is unconstitutional because she based her decision on stereotypical notions of male/female roles in society. It is true that when analyzing a legislative or state enactment on the basis of gender that the gender classification cannot be based on stereotypical notions, and must be substantially related to the achievement of an important government interest. However, this is not a situation where the state government or agency arrived at a calculated or reasoned decision to create a gender based statutory distinction to advance an important government interest. . . . Mullineaux created her own classification that primary care giver equals a woman. By comparing Mullineaux's actions to promulgated laws that make gender distinctions, the Majority mischaracterizes the gravity of Mullineaux's actions. Mullineaux engaged in the discriminatory application of Maryland's gender neutral leave statute.

The constitutional right at issue is defined in the plain text of the statute. Knussman had a right not to be discriminated against on the basis of his gender. This inquiry does not require consideration of whether the legislature drew a permissible distinction in law based on gender. The statute is completely devoid of gender classification. Significantly, the nurturing leave statute applies to adoption as well as the birth of a child; therefore, no biological gender classification is implied or inherent in the process of determining whether the leave applicant is a "primary care giver" or a "secondary care giver." In 1994, Knussman sought leave as a primary care giver pursuant to the nurturing leave statute, which provided 30 days leave for primary care givers and ten days leave for secondary care givers for parents of newborns and newly adopted children. Cloaked with the authority as the Manager of Medical Leave Benefits for the Maryland State Department of Police, Mullineaux took it upon herself to interpret this gender neutral statute in a gender specific manner. Mullineaux categorically denied Knussman's request for leave to care for his newborn daughter as a primary care giver because Knussman was a man. Knussman brought suit against Mullineaux, and others, for categorically denying him leave as a primary care giver because of his gender in violation of the Equal Protection Clause of the Fourteenth Amendment. Therefore, for the purpose of analyzing Knussman's claim, this Court must look at a person's right not to have a gender neutral statute applied in a discriminatory manner and determine if such right was clearly established at the time of Mullineaux's actions in 1994.

. . . The established Fourteenth Amendment jurisprudence in 1994 protected Knussman's right to receive nurturing leave benefits under a gender neutral leave statute without his gender effecting or impeding such decision. Therefore, the right at issue was clearly established because the contours of the right to be free from discriminatory behavior afforded Mullineaux adequate notice that her interpretation of a gender neutral leave statute, which resulted in the gender based denial of a benefit, violated the Fourteenth Amendment.

. . . .

A reasonable person in Mullineaux's position would have known that her conduct violated a person's right not to have nurturing leave benefits administered in a discriminatory manner. Mullineaux was the Manager of Medical Leave Benefits. She worked previously at the Maryland State Department of Personnel, and had approximately 15 years of experience in state employment and administrative policy matters at the time of the incident. In 1994, a person in Mullineaux's position and with her experience should have known that Maryland law prohibited her from drawing a distinction on the basis of gender when administering leave benefits to parents caring for their children. Maryland law has made it clear that gender is not a permissible factor in determining the legal rights of a woman or man. . . . Despite this unequivocal mandate, which Mullineaux should have been aware of given her experience and position, Mullineaux discriminated against Knussman by assuming that he, as a man, could not have been the primary care giver for his child.

. . . A reasonable person in Mullineaux's position would have known that they were violating Knussman's right to be free from discrimination on the basis of gender. Therefore, I concur with the Majority's conclusion that Mullineaux is not entitled to qualified immunity.

. . . .

NOTES

1. *Laboratories of democracy.* In his dissent to *Hibbs*, 538 U.S. 721, 750 (2003), Justice Kennedy credits the states as the laboratories of democracy— a concept that owes its genesis to Justice Brandeis. *See New State Ice Co. v. Leibman*, 285 U.S. 262, 311 (1952). Justice Kennedy maintains tremendous faith in the states as engines for generating progressive policies. But is this justified? Note that state control in other areas has, in some cases, resulted in the diminution of rights. For example, state control of elections and voting historically resulted in the suppression—if not disenfranchisement—of minority voters. *See* Charlie Savage, *Holder Signals Tough Review of New State Laws on Voting Rights*, N.Y. TIMES, Dec. 14, 2011, at A1. In the context

of abortion, the future-Justice Alito presciently observed that limiting abortion access (and undercutting *Roe*) could be effectively achieved by allowing the states to regulate abortion. *See infra*, p. 724. With this rich history in mind, is it preferable to have states craft their own family and medical leave policies, or should this be entirely set at the federal level?

2.   *Men and family leave.* It is assumed that family-leave policies redound to the benefit of women. However, as the facts of *Hibbs* and *Knussman* make clear, men may also participate meaningfully in family caregiving, and thus may require the accommodations that leave policies provide. This aspect of family-leave policies was not lost on Chief Justice Rehnquist, who authored the majority opinion in *Hibbs*. As Rehnquist's colleague, Justice Ruth Bader Ginsburg noted, the Court's sensitive account of gendered caregiving and the dangers of stereotyping was "a delightful surprise"—one that Ginsburg attributed to Rehnquist's own family circumstances. In an interview with the *New York Times*, Ginsburg explained that "[w]hen [Rehnquist's] daughter Janet . . . divorced, [Rehnquist] felt some kind of responsibility to be kind of a father figure to [his granddaughters]. So he became more sensitive to things that he might not have noticed." Emily Bazelon, *The Place of Women on the Court*, N.Y. TIMES, July 7, 2009, at MM22.

3.   *The beauty of male plaintiffs.* The male plaintiffs in *Hibbs* and *Knussman* are part of a broader history in which male plaintiffs have been used to press for rights typically associated with women. As part of her work with the ACLU's Women's Rights Project, Ruth Bader Ginsburg consciously selected male plaintiffs who had undertaken family caregiving responsibilities to front her challenges to gender-based classifications. By emphasizing the way in which gender-based classifications disadvantaged caregiving men, Ginsburg sought to make plain the gendered roots of state policies that stereotyped women as caregivers. *See* Cary Franklin, *Justice Ginsburg's Advocacy and the Future of Equal Protection*, 122 YALE L.J. ONLINE 227, 228–29 (2013).

Connecticut General Statutes § 31–51*ll*
(2014).

(a)(1) Subject to section 31–51mm, an eligible employee shall be entitled to a total of sixteen workweeks of leave during any twenty-four-month period. . . .

(2) Leave under this subsection may be taken for one or more of the following reasons:

(A) Upon the birth of a son or daughter of the employee;

(B) Upon the placement of a son or daughter with the employee for adoption or foster care;

(C) In order to care for the spouse, or a son, daughter, or parent of the employee, if such spouse, son, daughter or parent has a serious health condition;

(D) Because of a serious health condition of the employee; or

(E) In order to serve as an organ or bone marrow donor.

. . .

(c)(1) Leave under subparagraph (A) or (B) or subdivision (2) of subsection (a) of this section for the birth or placement of a son or daughter may not be taken by an employee intermittently or on a reduced leave schedule unless the employee and the employer agree otherwise. Subject to subdivision (2) of this subsection concerning an alternative position, subdivision (2) of subsection (f) of this section concerning the duties of the employee and subdivision (5) of subsection (b) of section 31–51mm concerning sufficient certification, leave under subparagraph (C) or (D) of subdivision (2) of subsection (a) or under subsection (i) of this section for a serious health condition may be taken intermittently or on a reduced leave schedule when medically necessary. The taking of leave intermittently or on a reduced leave schedule pursuant to this subsection shall not result in a reduction of the total amount of leave to which the employee is entitled under subsection (a) of this section beyond the amount of leave actually taken.

(2) If an employee requests intermittent leave or leave on a reduced leave schedule under subparagraph (C), (D) or (E) of subdivision (2) of subsection (a) or under subsection (i) of this section that is foreseeable based on planned medical treatment, the employer may require the employee to transfer temporarily to an available alternative position offered by the employer for which the employee is qualified and that (A) has equivalent pay and benefits, and (B) better accommodates recurring periods of leave than the regular employment position of the employee, provided the exercise of this authority shall not conflict with any provision of a collective bargaining agreement between such employer and a labor organization which is the collective bargaining representative of the unit of which the employee is a part.

(d) Except as provided in subsection (e) of this section, leave granted under subsection (a) of this section may consist of unpaid leave.

(e)(1) If an employer provides paid leave for fewer than sixteen workweeks, the additional weeks of leave necessary to attain the sixteen workweeks of leave required under sections 5–248a and 31–51kk to 31–51qq, inclusive, may be provided without compensation.

(2)(A) An eligible employee may elect, or an employer may require the employee, to substitute any of the accrued paid vacation leave, personal leave or family leave of the employee for leave provided under subparagraph (A), (B) or (C) of subdivision (2) of subsection (a) of this section for any part of the sixteen-week period of such leave under said subsection or under subsection (i) of this section for any part of the twenty-six-week period of such leave.

(B) An eligible employee may elect, or an employer may require the employee, to substitute any of the accrued paid vacation leave, personal leave, or medical or sick leave of the employee for leave provided under subparagraph (C), (D) or (E) of subdivision (2) of subsection (a) of this section for any part of the sixteen-week period of such leave under said subsection or under subsection (i) of this section for any part of the twenty-six-week period of leave, except that nothing in section 5–248a or sections 31–51kk to 31–51qq, inclusive, shall require an employer to provide paid sick leave or paid medical leave in any situation in which such employer would not normally provide any such paid leave.

(f)(1) In any case in which the necessity for leave under subparagraph (A) or (B) of subdivision (2) of subsection (a) of this section is foreseeable based on an expected birth or placement of a son or daughter, the employee shall provide the employer with not less than thirty days' notice, before the date of the leave is to begin, of the employee's intention to take leave under said subparagraph (A) or (B), except that if the date of the birth or placement of a son or daughter requires leave to begin in less than thirty days, the employee shall provide such notice as is practicable.

(2) In any case in which the necessity for leave under subparagraph (C), (D) or (E) of subdivision (2) of subsection (a) or under subsection (i) of this section is foreseeable based on planned medical treatment, the employee (A) shall make a reasonable effort to schedule the treatment so as not to disrupt unduly the operations of the employer, subject to the approval of the health care provider of the employee or the health care provider of the son, daughter, spouse or parent of the employee, as appropriate; and (B) shall provide the employer with not less than thirty days' notice, before the date the leave is to begin, of the employee's intention to take leave under said subparagraph (C), (D) or (E) or said subsection (i), except that if the date of the treatment requires leave to begin in less than thirty days, the employee shall provide such notice as is practicable.

(g) In any case in which a husband and wife entitled to leave under subsection (a) of this section are employed by the same employer, the aggregate number of workweeks of leave to which both may be entitled may be limited to sixteen workweeks during any twenty-four-month period, if such leave is taken: (1) Under subparagraph (A) or (B) of subdivision (2) of subsection (a) of this section; or (2) to care for a sick parent under subparagraph (C) of said subdivision. In any case in which a husband and wife entitled to leave under subsection (i) of this section are employed by the same employer, the aggregate number of workweeks of leave to which both may be entitled may be limited to twenty-six workweeks during any twelve-month period.

. . .

(i) Subject to section 31–51mm, an eligible employee who is the spouse, son or daughter, parent or next of kin of a current member of the armed forces, as defined in section 27–103, who is undergoing medical treatment, recuperation or therapy, is otherwise in outpatient status or is on the temporary disability retired list for a serious injury or illness incurred in the line of duty shall be entitled to a one-time benefit of twenty-six workweeks of leave during any twelve-month period for each armed forces member per serious injury or illness incurred in the line of duty. Such twelve-month period shall commence on an employee's first day of leave taken to care for a covered armed forces member and end on the date twelve months after such first day of leave. For the purposes of this subsection, (1) "next of kin" means the armed forces member's nearest blood relative, other than the covered armed forces member's spouse, parent, son or daughter, in the following order of priority: Blood relatives who have been granted legal custody of the armed forces member by court decree or statutory provisions, brothers and sisters, grandparents, aunts and uncles, and first cousins, unless the covered armed forces member has specifically designated in writing another blood relative as his or her nearest blood relative for purposes of military caregiver leave, in which case the designated individual shall be deemed to be the covered armed forces member's next of kin; and (2) "son or daughter" means a biological, adopted or foster child, stepchild, legal ward or child for whom the eligible employee or armed forces member stood in loco parentis and who is any age.

. . .

District of Columbia Code § 32–502
(2014).

(a) An employee shall be entitled to a total of 16 workweeks of family leave during any 24-month period for:

(1) The birth of a child of the employee;

(2) The placement of a child with the employee for adoption or foster care;

(3) The placement of a child with the employee for whom the employee permanently assumes and discharges parental responsibility; or

(4) The care of a family member of the employee who has a serious health condition.

(b) The entitlement to family leave under subsection (a)(1) through (3) of this section shall expire 12 months after the birth of the child or placement of the child with the employee.

(c) Subject to the requirements of subsection (h) of this section, in the case of a family member who has a serious health condition, the family leave may be taken intermittently when medically necessary.

(d) Upon agreement between the employer and the employee, family leave may be taken on a reduced leave schedule, during which the 16 workweeks of family leave may be taken over a period not to exceed 24 consecutive workweeks.

(e)(1) Except as provided in paragraphs (2) and (3) of this subsection, family leave may consist of unpaid leave.

(2) Any paid family, vacation, personal, or compensatory leave provided by an employer that the employee elects to use for family leave shall count against the 16 workweeks of allowable family leave provided in this chapter.

(3) If an employer has a program that allows an employee to use the paid leave of another employee under certain conditions, and the conditions have been met, the employee may use the paid leave as family leave and the leave shall count against the 16 workweeks of family leave provided in this chapter.

(4) Nothing in this section shall require an employer to provide paid family leave.

. . .

Massachusetts General Laws ch. 149, § 105D
(2014).

A female employee who has completed the initial probationary period set by the terms of her employment or, if there is no such probationary period, has been employed by the same employer for at least three consecutive months as a full-time employee, who is absent from such employment for a period not exceeding eight weeks for the purpose of giving birth or for adopting a child under the age of eighteen or for adopting a child under the age of twenty-three if the child is mentally or physically disabled, said period to be hereinafter called maternity leave, and who shall give at least two weeks' notice to her employer of her anticipated date of departure and intention to return, shall be restored to her previous, or a similar, position with the same status, pay, length of service credit and seniority, wherever applicable, as of the date of her leave. Said maternity leave may be with or without pay at the discretion of the employer.

Such employer shall not be required to restore an employee on maternity leave to her previous or a similar position if other employees of equal length of service credit and status in the same or similar position have been laid off due to economic conditions or other changes in operating conditions affecting employment during the period of such maternity leave; provided, however, that such employee on maternity leave shall retain any preferential consideration for another position to which she may be entitled as of the date of her leave.

Such maternity leave shall not affect the employee's right to receive vacation time, sick leave, bonuses, advancement, seniority, length of service credit, benefits, plans or programs for which she was eligible at the date of her leave, and any other advantages or rights of her employment incident to her employment position; provided, however, that such maternity leave shall not be included, when applicable, in the computation of such benefits, rights, and advantages; and provided, further, that the employer need not provide for the cost of any benefits, plans, or programs during the period of maternity leave unless such employer so provides for all employees on leave of absence. . . .

. . .

NOTE

California's Paid Family Leave. In 2002, the California legislature passed Senate Bill 1661, extending up to six weeks of paid leave for individuals to take care of ill family members (including registered domestic partners), or to bond with a new child. The program is known as Paid Family Leave (PFL) and is funded through the state disability program (SDI). *See Paid Family Leave,* STATE OF CAL. EMP'T DEV. DEP'T (2014), https://edd.ca.gov/disability/paid-family-leave/.

* * *

Paid family leave (as in California) and unpaid family leave (as in the Family and Medical Leave Act) come at the end of almost forty years of the Supreme Court struggling with the issues of pregnancy, work, and sex discrimination. In the two cases that follow, the Court examines the claims of pregnant women who sought disability payments for time lost to pregnancy. Some of these women had "normal" pregnancies; others had complications of pregnancy, such as a miscarriage or surgery following an ectopic pregnancy. For all these women, however, they were unable to work, and would have been covered by disability payments had their "disabilities" not resulted from pregnancy. Note that in many of these women's cases, the issue is not only one of principle, but also of real economic need, as the women were not paid while incapacitated.

Geduldig v. Aiello
417 U.S. 484 (1974).

For an excerpt of Geduldig v. Aiello, *please see* supra *p. 128.*

General Electric Co. v. Gilbert
429 U.S. 125 (1976).

For an excerpt of General Electric Co. v. Gilbert, *please see* supra *p. 133.*

The Pregnancy Discrimination Act of 1978 amended Title VII as Congress' direct attempt to overrule the Supreme Court's decisions in Geduldig *and* Gilbert.

Pregnancy Discrimination Act

Pub. L. No. 95–555, 92 Stat. 2076 (1978) (codified as amended at 42 U.S.C. § 2000e).

For an excerpt of the Pregnancy Discrimination Act, please see supra *p. 140.*

Although the Pregnancy Discrimination Act addressed important concerns regarding pregnancy and employment, it did not answer all questions. In the cases that follow, litigants pressed for employment accommodations for lactation under the PDA, and in so doing, sought to elaborate the scope of this anti-discrimination statute.

Fejes v. Gilpin Ventures, Inc.

960 F. Supp. 1487 (D. Colo. 1997).

■ BABCOCK, D. J.

. . . .

. . . On April 6, 1993, Gilpin Casino hired [Susan] Fejes as a full-time blackjack dealer. During her employment with Gilpin Casino, Fejes' work performance was satisfactory. On March 16, 1994, Fejes took an unpaid medical leave, pursuant to the Family and Medical Leave Act (FMLA), based on her physician's orders because of complications with her pregnancy. Her child was born on April 22, 1994. Fejes alleges that on May 27, 1994, she arranged with her supervisor, Rick Curran (Curran), to return to work two nights per week as soon as she was able to do so.

Fejes' medical leave was scheduled to end on June 8, 1994. Around June 15, 1994, Curran asked Fejes to work the weekend of June 17–18, 1994. Fejes alleges she was unable to return to work at that time because she had been unable to establish an appropriate breast-feeding schedule. Fejes also alleges that on June 20, 1994, she informed Curran that she was able to work two nights per week.

Shortly after that, Curran was made day supervisor and Fejes was referred to Gilpin Casino games manager Jerimy Fox (Fox). According to Fejes, Fox claimed to know nothing of Fejes' discussions with Curran. . . . [O]n July 8, 1994, Barbara Bennett, an administrative assistant in Gilpin Casino's human resources department, wrote Fejes a letter informing her that she was considered "self-terminated" and that her position had been filled. According to Fejes, Gilpin Casino fired her in its July 8, 1994 letter for not returning to work on June 8, 1994 and for not contacting Gilpin Casino to inform it of her intention to return to work. Defendant acknowledges that it mistakenly sent Fejes a termination letter on July 8, 1994 because the human resources department was unaware of the arrangements Fejes had made with Curran.

After Fejes "protested that she had indeed kept in contact with defendant," on July 11, 1994, Gilpin Casino offered to return her to full-time and she agreed. However, according to Fejes, when she realized that "her gaming license was about to expire and had not been renewed, Fox told her that a part-time employee would take her shift until renewal of the license, which was anticipated to occur within three weeks." On July 14, 1994, Fox wrote Fejes a letter informing her that she should "consider [her] employment with the Gilpin as terminated." Gilpin Casino states that the letter "informed [Fejes] that due to the fact that she allowed her license to expire, the Gilpin would be unable to guarantee a position for her during her renewal period and [Fejes was] therefore deemed terminated."

Fejes filed gender and pregnancy discrimination charges with the Equal Employment Opportunity Commission (EEOC) on September 1, 1994. On July 14, 1995, Fejes received a Notice of Right to Sue from the EEOC and filed this action.

Title VII discrimination

Fejes claims she was "discriminated against on the basis of her gender in terms, conditions and privileges of employment in violation of Title VII of the Civil Rights Act of 1964. . . ."

A.   *Refusal to provide an employee with a part-time schedule for breast-feeding or childrearing is not conduct protected by Title VII*

The Pregnancy Discrimination Act of 1978 (PDA) . . . is a definitional amendment to Title VII which Congress enacted to include pregnancy-based discrimination in Title VII's prohibition of gender-based employment discrimination. Section 2000e(k) provides:

> The terms "because of sex" or "on the basis of sex" include, but are not limited to, because of or on the basis of pregnancy, childbirth, or related medical conditions; and women affected by pregnancy, childbirth, or related medical conditions shall be treated the same for all employment-related purposes, including receipt of benefits under fringe benefit programs, as other persons not so affected but similar in their ability or inability to work. . . .

The Tenth Circuit has not addressed the issue whether breast-feeding or childrearing are medical conditions "related to pregnancy or childbirth," within the meaning of the PDA. Based on the language of the PDA, its legislative history, and decisions from other courts interpreting the Act, I hold that breast-feeding or childrearing are not conditions within the scope of the PDA.

. . . .

In appending the PDA amendment to Title VII, Congress considered the statement that "if a woman wants to stay home to take care of the child, no benefit must be paid because this is not a medically determined condition related to pregnancy." Nothing in the PDA, or Title VII itself, obliges an employer to accommodate the child-care concerns of breast-feeding workers. If Congress had wanted these sorts of child-care concerns to be covered in Title VII by the Pregnancy Discrimination Act, it would have said so in plain language.

. . . .

I conclude that the PDA only provides protection based on the condition of the mother—not the condition of the child. Also, I conclude that breast-feeding and child rearing concerns after pregnancy are not medical conditions related to pregnancy or childbirth within the meaning of the PDA. Accordingly, Fejes' Title VII claim is not viable.

B. *As a matter of law, Fejes is unable to establish a prima facie case of pregnancy discrimination*

To establish a *prima facie* case of pregnancy discrimination, Fejes must show that she: 1) belonged to the protected group; 2) was qualified and satisfactorily performing her job; 3) was adversely affected by the decision to terminate her; and 4) was treated less favorably than another nonpregnant employee under similar conditions. . . .

. . . .

Gilpin Casino contends that Fejes has not established a *prima facie* case of pregnancy discrimination because when she was terminated Fejes was no longer pregnant. I disagree.

Title 42 U.S.C. § 2000e–2(a), as amended by the PDA, § 2000e(k), prohibits discrimination "on the basis of pregnancy, childbirth, or related medical conditions." The statute does not specify whether the discrimination must occur during the pregnancy. However, to read Title VII so narrowly would lead to absurd results such as "prohibit[ing] an employer from firing a woman during her pregnancy but permit[ting] the employer to terminate her the day after delivery if the reason for termination was that the woman became pregnant in the first place." The plain language of the statute does not require plaintiff to be pregnant when the alleged discrimination occurs. Thus, I conclude that a plaintiff may bring a Title VII claim under the PDA even if she is not pregnant at the time of the alleged wrongdoing. However, a Title VII PDA plaintiff must nevertheless show she was pregnant at or near the time of the alleged discrimination.

In this case, on March 16, 1994, Fejes took a medical leave because of complications with her pregnancy. Her child was born on April 22, 1994. Fejes' medical leave was scheduled to end on June 8, 1994 and she was terminated on July 14, 1994. Where, as here, the termination occurred less than three months after the pregnancy ended and five weeks after her medical leave ended, for summary judgment analysis, I conclude that Fejes was a member of the protected class. Accordingly, Gilpin Casino's motion for summary judgment on this basis cannot be granted.

. . . .

Gilpin Casino contends that Fejes has not established the fourth prong of the *prima facie* case for pregnancy discrimination because she fails to proffer any evidence that other similarly situated employees (employees who have taken medical leaves) were treated differently then [sic] she. I agree.

A review of the evidence Fejes submitted ... fails to show any evidence of different treatment of males who took medical leaves. Hence, Fejes has not met her burden of showing issues of material fact to be determined on the fourth prong of her *prima facie* case. Her conclusory statements are insufficient. . . .

. . . .

... Furthermore, Fejes submits no evidence of better working conditions provided to males who took medical leaves. Accordingly, Fejes has not met her burden of showing that there are issues of material fact to be determined on this issue.

Having failed to meet her Title VII *prima facie* burden, Gilpin Casino is entitled to summary judgment on Fejes' Title VII claim in its entirety. . . .

Fejes claims that Gilpin Casino's actions in terminating her violated the Family and Medical Leave Act of 1993 (FMLA). . . .

An employer's obligation under the FMLA is to return the employee to the same or a substantially similar position. The Department of Labor, in the final rule-making phase of enacting regulations under the FMLA, stated:

> [o]n return from FMLA leave, an employee is entitled to be returned to the same position the employee held when leave commenced, or to an equivalent position with equivalent benefits, pay, and other terms and conditions of employment. . . .

Fejes argues that summary judgment should be denied because instead of being restored to her position, she was terminated in violation of the FMLA, because her gaming support license had expired. The FMLA regulations provide:

> [i]f an employee is no longer qualified for the position because of the employee's inability to ... renew a license ... as a result of the leave, the employee shall be given a reasonable opportunity to fulfill those conditions upon return to work.

29 C.F.R. § 825.215(b). Whether Fejes was unable to renew her gaming license as a result of her medical leave is genuinely disputed. . . . Because Fejes has responded with specific facts showing the existence of genuine issues of material fact on her FMLA claim, I will deny summary judgment.

. . . .

Accordingly, it is ordered that:

1.   defendant's motion for summary judgment on claim one, Title VII gender and pregnancy discrimination, is GRANTED;

2.   defendant's motion for summary judgment on claim two for violation of the FMLA is DENIED;

. . . .

NOTE

Accommodations in white- and blue-collar workplaces. Public health researcher Sylvia Guendelman and her colleagues surveyed over seven hundred working women who were new mothers in California—a state with a paid family leave policy that funds up to four weeks of leave before birth, six weeks of leave after vaginal birth, and eight weeks of leave after caesarean section. *See* CAL. WORK & FAMILY COAL., CALIFORNIA FAMILY LEAVE LAWS: KNOW YOUR RIGHTS!: A GUIDE FOR WORKERS, PARENTS AND CAREGIVERS 6 (2013). For further discussion of California's paid family leave policy, see *supra* p. 522. However, as Guendelman found, the benefits of favorable leave policies were often dwarfed by the realities of occupational conditions. According to Guendelman's study, working mothers who did not breastfeed were more likely to work in non-managerial positions, and to have inflexible work hours and limited maternal leaves. The conditions of these so-called "blue collar" workers stand in stark contrast to women in "white collar" jobs, who are more likely to have on-the-job support and flexibility to accommodate breastfeeding. Sylvia Guendelman et. al., *Juggling Work and Breastfeeding: Effects of Maternity Leave and Occupational Characteristics*, 123 PEDIATRICS e38, e45 (2009).

Falk v. City of Glendale
2012 WL 2390556 (D. Colo. June 25, 2012).

■ KANE, D.J.

. . . .

Plaintiff Katie Falk was employed by the City of Glendale Police Department as a 911 dispatcher. . . . Plaintiff held this position from approximately June 2, 2008 to approximately November 29, 2010. Plaintiff had no negative employment history before her termination. The job was demanding. During some shifts, Plaintiff was unable to take breaks and was even required to answer calls while using the restroom.

During the course of her employment, Plaintiff became pregnant and gave birth to a child. After taking her maternity leave, she returned to work on September 16, 2010. Upon her return, Plaintiff requested a space and break time so that she could pump breast milk. She was not provided with a private space and soon discovered that understaffing limited her ability to take breaks.

Nine times, Plaintiff informed her supervisors of her difficulties. Her dispatch supervisor informed Plaintiff that patrol officers would cover for Plaintiff during breaks, but patrol officers and sergeants refused to do so. Plaintiff reported the officers' unresponsiveness to her dispatch supervisor, who then reported it to [Chief of Police Victor Ross, who] informed Plaintiff that officers would provide her with two breaks per shift; Plaintiff, however, remained unable to obtain breaks. Because of this, she experienced discomfort and often had to work in a soiled bra after expressing milk on herself. This led to three separate breast infections.

Plaintiff's ongoing requests for accommodations provoked hostility from Sgt. Crystal Johnson. Johnson prohibited dispatch-trained officers from relieving Plaintiff, sending untrained officers instead. As a result, Plaintiff was frequently interrupted with questions and could not effectively express milk. Johnson prohibited Plaintiff from directly requesting patrol officers for relief.

On November 28th, 2010, Plaintiff notified Johnson three times that she needed a break, that she was experiencing discomfort, and that she had expressed milk on herself. Johnson "laughed, made a 'moo' noise, and walked away." Johnson then took a fifteen minute break. Upon returning, she continued to ignore Plaintiff, intentionally forcing Plaintiff to wait so as to make an example out of her.

Plaintiff continued to complain about her difficulties obtaining breaks as well as about Johnson's hostile behavior. The only response Plaintiff received was an e-mail stating that "the department could not accommodate her needs." Her December and January shifts were revoked. Plaintiff called Human Resources Director Polly McNeil, who confirmed that Plaintiff would not be scheduled for any hours until she weaned her daughter. . . . Plaintiff's personal items, work ID, and lockers were reassigned. Work acquaintances informed her that she was "no longer welcome at Glendale."

Plaintiff filed a complaint with the Equal Employment Opportunity Commission (E.E.O.C.). On March 12, 2012, Plaintiff received a Notice of Right to Sue from the Civil Rights Division of the United States Department of Justice. Plaintiff filed suit in this court on April 6, 2012, bringing four claims under Title VII: pregnancy discrimination, gender discrimination, gender discrimination based on hostile work environment, and retaliation.

In lieu of a response, Defendant submitted a motion to dismiss (doc. 5) pursuant to Fed. R. Civ. P. 12(b)(6).

STANDARD OF REVIEW

. . . In order to survive a Fed. R. Civ. P. 12(b)(6) motion to dismiss, a pleading must include sufficient factual allegations to state a plausible claim to relief.

Plausibility, in this sense, relates to the specificity of the allegations in the complaint; they must not be "so general that they encompass a wide swath of conduct, much of it innocent." No specific facts are required, *Khalik*, 671 F.3d at 1192, but the complaint must have sufficient factual assertions "to raise a right to relief above the speculative level. . . ."

. . . .

First and Second Claims for Relief: Pregnancy and Gender Discrimination

Title VII prohibits employment discrimination on the basis of race, color, religion, sex, or national origin. Discrimination can be shown by direct evidence or through the burden-shifting process established in *McDonnell Douglas Corp. v. Green*, 411 U.S. 792 (1973). The first step in the *McDonnell Douglas* framework requires the plaintiff to establish a prima facie case of discrimination by showing (1) that she belongs to a protected class; (2) that she was the victim of an adverse employment action; (3) that she was qualified for her job; and (4) that she was treated less favorably than similarly situated co-workers who did not belong to the protected class. A plaintiff is not required to make out all elements of a prima facie case in order to survive a 12(b)(6) motion, but considering the elements required to succeed on each claim assists in determining whether a plausible claim to relief exists.

A.   Title VII Protected Class Status

In 1976, a little over ten years after the passage of the Civil Rights Act of 1964, the Supreme Court held that pregnancy-related discrimination was not gender discrimination as prohibited by Title VII of the Act. *General Electric Co. v. Gilbert*, 429 U.S. 125, 145–146 (1976). The Court relied on the logic that even though the defendant's benefits plan did not cover pregnancy, male and female employees were eligible for the same benefits, and so no discrimination existed. . . . In response to this decision, Congress passed the Pregnancy Discrimination Act of 1978 ("PDA"), which extended Title VII's gender discrimination prohibition to include any discrimination "because of or on the basis of pregnancy, childbirth, or related medical conditions." Pregnancy Discrimination Act of 1978, 42 U.S.C. § 2000e(k) (1978). . . .

The language of the PDA focuses solely on the conditions experienced by the mother. While lactation is not *per se* excluded, Title VII does not extend to breast-feeding as a child care concern. *Fejes v. Gilpin Ventures, Inc.*, 960 F. Supp. 1487, 1492 (D.Colo.1997); *see also, e.g., Wallace v. Pyro Mining Co.*, 789 F. Supp. 867, 869 (W.D. Ky. 1990), *aff'd*, 951 F.2d 351 (6th Cir. 1991).[7] Since the complaint asserts that

---

[7]   . . . As it stands, no existing case law correctly excludes lactation or other conditions experienced by the mother as a result of breast-feeding from Title VII protection under the PDA. A plaintiff could potentially succeed on a claim if she alleged and was able to prove that lactation was a medical condition related to pregnancy, and that this condition, and not a desire to breastfeed, was the reason for the discriminatory action(s) that she suffered.

Plaintiff's desire to "continue to breast feed her infant daughter" formed the basis for the alleged discrimination, her protected status is not established. Consequently, Plaintiff does not state a claim for relief as a member of a protected class.

B. Discrimination

The Pregnancy Discrimination Act does not require any affirmative accommodations; it simply prohibits employers from treating pregnancy-related conditions "less favorably than other medical conditions." Plaintiff must show that, as a member of a protected class, she was treated differently than other co-workers not belonging to the same class. Even if Plaintiff had successfully alleged protected status, she still alleges no instances of discrimination.

It is possible that discrimination could be shown in a case involving lactation. If lactation is a natural consequence of pregnancy, then expressing milk is equivalent to any other involuntary bodily function. Therefore, if other coworkers were allowed to take breaks to use the restroom while lactating mothers were banned from pumping, discrimination might exist.

Plaintiff's complaint, however, does not allege that her non-lactating coworkers were treated more favorably. In fact, Plaintiff's complaint states that, before her pregnancy, Plaintiff "often had to use the restroom while answering radio traffic." As Plaintiff was previously not granted breaks to use the restroom, it was not discriminatory to subsequently deny her breaks to pump. This, then, appears to be a case about workplace conditions, and not about discrimination.[9]

Plaintiff's complaint does not allege sufficient facts to create a plausible inference of Title VII discrimination and must be dismissed.

Third Claim for Relief: Hostile Workplace

In order to establish a hostile work environment claim based on sex discrimination, a plaintiff must demonstrate that she was a victim of sex discrimination, and that the discrimination created an "abusive working environment" and impacted the terms of her employment. Isolated incidents of rudeness or other "ordinary tribulations of the workplace" are not sufficient to establish such an environment under Title VII.

As previously discussed, Plaintiff has not alleged sufficient facts to suggest that she was a victim of sex discrimination. Additionally, Plaintiff's hostile work environment claim rests primarily on a series of unpleasant interactions with Sgt. Johnson. Only one specific incident is cited. Plaintiff's allegations do not imply the level of severity required to

---

[9] There is also the possibility of a direct discrimination claim. If Plaintiff establishes that lactating mothers are a protected class, and her supervisor explicitly told her that the reason for lost shifts was her condition, then she may be able to assert a direct discrimination claim. Once again, the reasons for the discrimination would need to be pled in a way that invokes the protection of the PDA, as opposed to the current claim that Plaintiff was discriminated against because she wished to breastfeed her daughter.

establish a hostile workplace claim. Unpleasant or negative interactions with a co-worker are "ordinary tribulations" that are inherent when a large number of different personalities interact in an employment context. Having trouble obtaining a break in this particular position is also an ordinary tribulation that, by her own admission, Plaintiff often faced before her pregnancy. As such, Plaintiff does not state a claim to relief for sex discrimination based on a hostile work environment.

Fourth Claim for Relief: Retaliation

To succeed on a Title VII retaliation claim, Plaintiff must plead and prove (1) that she opposed some form of discrimination prohibited by Title VII, (2) that she was subject to adverse employment action, and (3) that a causal connection existed between the opposition and the adverse action. . . .

Here, Plaintiff alleges that she complained numerous times about Defendant's failure to provide her with breaks to express milk, that she lost her December and January shifts, and that this revocation was in direct response to her complaints. This is sufficient to imply opposition, adverse employment action, and a causal link between the two. Plaintiff fails to allege, however, that she believed her complaints were in opposition to the type of discrimination prohibited by Title VII. Instead, during her employment, Plaintiff repeatedly cited "[f]ederal labor law" as a way of encouraging her supervisors to accommodate her needs. Since Plaintiff does not allege that her opposition was premised on a good-faith belief that she was the victim of Title VII discrimination, Plaintiff's complaint fails to state a claim for relief for retaliation.

. . . .

Plaintiff's complaint does not state any claim upon which relief may be granted. Accordingly, Defendant's motion to dismiss is GRANTED IN PART and Plaintiff's complaint is DISMISSED WITHOUT PREJUDICE.

NOTES

1.   *Bad lawyering or bad mothering?* In *Falk*, the court repeatedly notes that the plaintiff's claims are not entitled to relief under the PDA because she did not properly plead such relief. That is, Falk's complaint never alleged that she was disadvantaged relative to her non-lactating co-workers. Accordingly, the case appeared to the court to be about the inadequacy of workplace conditions, rather than pregnancy-related discrimination. Would the court have responded differently if Falk (and her lawyers) had been more explicit about how Falk was disadvantaged relative to her colleagues?

2.   *Betwixt and between.* In observing that Falk appeared to be challenging workplace conditions, rather than pregnancy-related discrimination, the court indicated that the Fair Labor Standards Act (FLSA) might offer some relief for women who wish to have breastfeeding accommodated in the workplace. Falk, however, failed to plead a claim under the FLSA. Is lactation accommodation the kind of labor condition that the FLSA was

intended to address? Would there be a symbolic benefit in having lactation accommodated under the FLSA rather than the PDA?

Equal Employment Opportunity Commission v. Houston Funding II, Ltd.

717 F.3d 425 (5th Cir. 2013).

■ JOLLY, CIRCUIT JUDGE.

The question we must answer in this appeal is whether discharging a female employee because she is lactating or expressing breast milk constitutes sex discrimination in violation of Title VII. We hold that it does.

The Equal Employment Opportunity Commission ("EEOC"), on behalf of Donnicia Venters ("Venters"), sued Houston Funding II, Ltd. and Houston Funding Corp. ("Houston Funding"), alleging Houston Funding unlawfully discharged Venters because she was lactating and wanted to express milk at work. The district court granted summary judgment in favor of Houston Funding, finding that, as a matter of law, discharging a female employee because she is lactating or expressing milk does not constitute sex discrimination. We VACATE and REMAND. . . .

Venters worked as an account representative/collector for Houston Funding from March 2006 until she was fired in February 2009. In December 2008, she took a leave of absence to have her baby. Houston Funding has no maternity leave policy,[1] and Venters and her supervisors did not specify a date for her return. Shortly after giving birth, Venters told Harry Cagle ("Cagle"), Houston Funding's Limited Partner, that she would return to work as soon as her doctor released her. Venters suffered complications from her C-section, however, and ended up staying home through mid February.

During her absence, Venters regularly contacted her supervisor, Robert Fleming ("Fleming"), as well as other Houston Funding managers. . . . During one conversation, Venters told Fleming that she was breastfeeding her child and asked him to ask Cagle whether it might be possible for her to use a breast pump at work. Fleming stated that when he posed this question to Cagle, Cagle "responded with a strong 'NO. Maybe she needs to stay home longer.' "

On February 17, 2009, Venters called Cagle and told him her doctor had released her to return to work. Again, she mentioned she was lactating and asked whether she could use a back room to pump milk. After asking this question, Venters testified that there was a long pause, and when Cagle finally responded, he told her that they had filled her spot. . . . On February 20, Houston Funding mailed a termination letter

---

[1] Houston Funding is small enough not to be encompassed by the Family and Medical Leave Act.

dated February 16 to Venters. This letter stated Venters was discharged due to job abandonment, effective February 13.

Venters subsequently filed a charge of sex discrimination with the EEOC. . . . After investigating Venters' charge, the EEOC brought a Title VII action against Houston Funding in district court, asserting that Houston Funding unlawfully discriminated against Venters based upon her sex, including her pregnancy, childbirth, or related medical conditions, by ending her employment. . . . Houston Funding argued Title VII does not cover "breast pump discrimination" and moved for summary judgment. The district court granted the motion, finding that, even if Venters' allegations were true, "[f]iring someone because of lactation or breast-pumping is not sex discrimination," and that lactation is not a related medical condition of pregnancy. The EEOC timely appealed.

. . . .

Title VII of the Civil Rights Act "prohibits various forms of employment discrimination, including discrimination on the basis of sex." Almost immediately after the Supreme Court, in *General Electric Co. v. Gilbert*, 429 U.S. 125, 136–38 (1976), held that discrimination on the basis of pregnancy is not sex discrimination, Congress amended Title VII to include the Pregnancy Discrimination Act ("PDA"). 42 U.S.C. § 2000e–(k). The PDA provides that "[t]he terms 'because of sex' or 'on the basis of sex' include, but are not limited to, because of or on the basis of pregnancy, childbirth, or related medical conditions[.]" And the Supreme Court has recognized that this amendment "unambiguously expressed [Congress'] disapproval of both the holding and the reasoning of the Court in the *Gilbert* decision."

As such, courts have since interpreted Title VII to cover a far wider range of employment decisions entailing female physiology. . . .

In this case, the parties focus upon whether Houston Funding's conduct violated Title VII generally, as well as upon whether lactation is a related medical condition of pregnancy for purposes of the PDA. Given our precedent, we hold the EEOC's argument that Houston Funding discharged Venters because she was lactating or expressing milk states a cognizable Title VII sex discrimination claim. An adverse employment action motivated by these factors clearly imposes upon women a burden that male employees need not—indeed, could not—suffer.

Moreover, we hold that lactation is a related medical condition of pregnancy for purposes of the PDA. Lactation is the physiological process of secreting milk from mammary glands and is directly caused by hormonal changes associated with pregnancy and childbirth. It is undisputed in this appeal that lactation is a physiological result of being pregnant and bearing a child.

The PDA does not define the statutory term "medical condition" ("pregnancy, childbirth, or related medical conditions"), but "[i]t is well-settled that 'we should give words of statutes their plain meaning.' " In discerning words' plain meaning, we may consult the dictionary. The McGraw-Hill Concise Dictionary of Modern Medicine defines "medical condition" as:

> A disease, illness, or injury ... Any condition—e.g., physiological, mental, or psychologic conditions or disorders— e.g., orthopedic, visual, speech, or hearing impairments, cerebral palsy, epilepsy, muscular dystrophy, multiple sclerosis ... mental retardation, emotional or mental illness, specific learning disabilities, HIV disease, TB, drug addiction, alcoholism[.]

JOSEPH SEGEN, MCGRAW-HILL CONCISE DICTIONARY OF MODERN MEDICINE 405 (2006). This definition is consistent with those of other medical dictionaries, which also broadly construe these terms. Given that this definition includes any physiological condition, it is difficult to see how it could not encompass lactation.

. . . .

... [L]actation is a normal aspect of female physiology that is initiated by pregnancy and concludes sometime thereafter. . . . [I]t is difficult to see how an employer who makes an employment decision based upon whether a woman is lactating can avoid such unlawful sex discrimination. And as both menstruation and lactation are aspects of female physiology that are affected by pregnancy, each seems readily to fit into a reasonable definition of "pregnancy, childbirth, or related medical conditions."

. . . .

Because discriminating against a woman who is lactating or expressing breast milk violates Title VII and the PDA, we find that the EEOC has stated a *prima facie* case of sex discrimination with a showing that Houston Funding fired Venters because she was lactating and wanted to express milk at work. The EEOC has further proffered evidence showing that Houston Funding's stated reason for discharging Venters—i.e., job abandonment—was pretextual. There is, therefore, triable evidence from which a factfinder may conclude that Houston Funding violated Title VII by discharging Ms. Venters. The EEOC has thus satisfied the requirements of the *McDonnell Douglas* inferential test for Title VII discrimination such that she may proceed to trial.

For these reasons, we VACATE the judgment of the district court and REMAND for further proceedings not inconsistent with this opinion.

VACATED and REMANDED.

■ JONES, CIRCUIT JUDGE, concurring in the judgment:

... In *Urbano v. Continental Airlines, Inc.*, 138 F.3d 204 (5th Cir.1998), this court held that the PDA does not mandate special accommodations to women because of pregnancy or related conditions. It follows that if Venters intended to request special facilities or down time during work to pump or "express" breast milk, she would not have a claim under Title VII or the PDA as of the date of her lawsuit. Indeed, if providing a plaintiff with special accommodation to pump breast milk at work were required, one wonders whether a plaintiff could be denied bringing her baby to the office to breastfeed during the workday.

. . . .

NOTES

1.   *Breastfeeding as public policy.* The Healthy People Initiative has set a goal to have 81.9 percent of mothers breastfeeding by 2020. Forty-six states permit breastfeeding in any public or private place, and twenty-nine specifically exempt nursing mothers from public indecency laws. Twenty-five states have laws regarding breastfeeding in the workplace, and the Affordable Care Act amends the Fair Labor Standards Act of 1938, 29 U.S.C. § 207(v)(1) (2014), to allow for break times for nursing mothers to express milk. *See Breastfeeding State Laws*, NAT'L CONFERENCE OF STATE LEGISLATURES (June 6, 2014), http://www.ncsl.org/research/health/breast feeding-state-laws.aspx.

2.   *Culture of breastfeeding.* Public policy measures that address lactation and breastfeeding are only one part of this picture. Novelist (and Harvard Law graduate) Ayelet Waldman writes of the deeply rooted culture of breastfeeding that exists in many liberal communities. More particularly, she identifies the moral opprobrium that may attach to those who defy accepted community norms by bottle-feeding. As Waldman relates, when her son experienced difficulties breastfeeding because of a malformed palate, she made the decision to bottle-feed him formula:

> [W]henever I mixed up a bottle of formula for Abraham, I felt a sense of stabbing shame, shame I still feel, despite myself, to this day. In the park and at preschool, the other mothers—the *Good* Mothers—would cast a censorious glance at Abe's bottle and ostentatiously loose their pendulous breasts from their cow-spotted nursing bras. As they cuddled their expert nurser babies, I would blush. They, unlike me, were committed. I was a Bad Mother.

AYELET WALDMAN, BAD MOTHER: A CHRONICLE OF MATERNAL CRIMES, MINOR CALAMITIES, AND OCCASIONAL MOMENTS OF GRACE 64 (2010). Are these informal, social interactions a form of regulation?

3.   *Law school and lactation.* For many years the Law School Admission Council refused to offer accommodations for nursing mothers taking the law school admission test (LSAT) on the grounds that lactation was not a recognized disability. In 2012 this policy was changed to allow mothers to take necessary breaks to nurse or express breast milk. Further, for up to a year following the birth of her child, a mother can request a modification in test-taking procedures, such as extended breaks to express milk or nurse. Sheila Bapat, *Law School Admissions Test Makes Accommodations for Nursing Mothers*, RH REALITY CHECK (June 26, 2012), http://rhrealitycheck.org/article/2012/06/26/new-lsat-testing-policy-nursing-moms/.

4. *Legislative reform?* In May 2012, Democratic members of the House of Representatives introduced the Pregnant Workers Fairness Act (PWFA). The bill, if enacted, would guarantee pregnant women the right to reasonable accommodation when the short-term physical effects of pregnancy conflict with the demands of a particular job, as long as the accommodation does not impose an undue hardship on the employer. To date, the PWFA has not been passed. *See* Pregnant Workers Fairness Act, H.R. 1975, 113th Cong. (2013). If the act did pass, would it affect cases like those presented above?

3. FAMILY AND REPRODUCTIVE AUTONOMY IN SCHOOLS

Another critical aspect of public life is the school, where people are present both as employees and as students. Schools have always been a location for teaching morality, whether temperance in the nineteenth century or sexual abstinence in the twentieth and twenty-first centuries. As we have seen in Meyer, Pierce, *and* Prince, *supra pp. 277, 280, and 283, the education of minors puts the conflict between the state's duty to ensure the welfare of its children and citizens, and parental autonomy to raise children in the manner of their choosing, in the starkest relief.*

Cleveland Board of Education v. LaFleur
414 U.S. 632 (1974).

For an excerpt of Cleveland Board of Education v. LaFleur, *please see supra p. 141.*

Andrews v. Drew Municipal
Separate School District
507 F.2d 611 (5th Cir. 1975).

■ SIMPSON, CIRCUIT JUDGE:

. . . .

In the Spring of 1972, Superintendent Pettey learned that there were some teacher aides presently employed in the District who were parents of illegitimate children. Disturbed by this knowledge, Pettey immediately implemented an unwritten edict to the effect that parenthood of an illegitimate child would automatically disqualify an individual, whether incumbent or applicant, from employment with the school system.[2] There is no doubt that the policy is attributable solely to

---

[2] Pettey in testimony indicated confusion as to the expanse of the policy he had promulgated. He was positive that the rule should apply to all instructional personnel. Upon questioning, he expanded that list to include not only teachers and teacher aides, but also secretaries, librarians, dieticians, cafeteria operators, nurses, social workers, school principals, school volunteers and even PTA presidents. Although he was not positive, he did not think the rule should apply to bus drivers, janitors or maids.

Pettey; there was no evidence that he sought either the prior advice or the consent of the Board.[3]

Mrs. Fred McCorkle is one of the administrators responsible for implementing the unwed parent policy. As Coordinator of Elementary Instruction for the school district, she is in charge of the teacher aide program and recommends to Pettey who shall be hired to fill teacher aide vacancies. All potential teacher aides must submit an application to Mrs. McCorkle who then interviews them and investigates their applications. . . .

Both plaintiffs-appellees, Lestine Rogers and Katie Mae Andrews, were victims of the unwed parent policy. Lestine Rogers was hired as a teacher aide in the Fall preceding the initiation of the rule, although her application stated that she was single and had a child. After the Pettey policy rule was announced, Mrs. McCorkle informed Ms. Rogers that because she was the parent of an illegitimate child, she would not be re-hired for the following year. Katie Mae Andrews, on the other hand, knew about the Pettey rule prior to applying for a teacher aide position. Although she too was the mother of an illegitimate child, she did not so indicate on her application. Mrs. McCorkle learned of Ms. Andrews' illegitimate child in the course of her investigation of the application. She made a written notation of her finding on the application, and refused to consider Ms. Andrews further.

. . . .

"Traditional" equal protection analysis requires that legislative classifications must be sustained as long as the classification itself is rationally related to a legitimate governmental interest. . . . Pettey's avowed objective was to create a scholastic environment which was conducive to the moral development as well as the intellectual development of the students. Certainly this objective is not without legitimacy. . . . Schools have the right, if not the duty, to create a properly moral scholastic environment. But the issue is not simply whether the objective itself is legitimate, but rather whether the Pettey rule "advances that objective in a manner consistent with the Equal Protection Clause," *Reed v. Reed*, 404 U.S. 71, 76 (1971). We hold that it does not.

The District offers three possible rationales through which it asserts that its rule under attack furthers the creation of a properly moral scholastic environment: (1) unwed parenthood is prima facie proof of immorality; (2) unwed parents are improper communal role models, after whom students may pattern their lives; (3) employment of an unwed parent in a scholastic environment materially contributes to the problem of school-girl pregnancies.

---

[3] The Board and its individual members were unaware of the rule until the commencement of this action. The evidence indicates, however, that the Board then ratified the policy and all actions taken under it.

The first of these postulates violates not only the Equal Protection Clause, but the Due Process Clause as well. The law is clear that due process interdicts the adoption by a state of an irrebuttable presumption, as to which the presumed fact does not necessarily follow from the proven fact. *See Cleveland Board of Education v. LaFleur*, 414 U.S. 632; *Vlandis v. Kline*, 1973, 412 U.S. 441 (1973); *Stanley v. Illinois*, 405 U.S. 645 (1971). Thus, unless the presumed fact here, present immorality, necessarily follows from the proven fact, unwed parenthood, the conclusiveness inherent in the Pettey rule[7] must be held to violate due process. We agree with the district court that the one does not necessarily follow the other:

. . . .

By the rule, a parent, whether male or female, who has had such a child, would be forever precluded from employment. Thus no consideration would be given to the subsequent marriage of the parent or to the length of time elapsed since the illegitimate birth, or to a person's reputation for good character in the community. A person could live an impeccable life, yet be barred as unfit for employment for an event, whether the result of indiscretion or not, occurring at any time in the past. But human experience refutes the dogmatic attitude inherent in such a policy against unwed parents. Can it be said that an engaged woman, who has premarital sex, becomes pregnant, and whose fiance dies or is killed prior to their marriage, is morally depraved for bearing the posthumous child? The rule allows no compassion for the person who has been unwittingly subjected to sexual relations through force, deceptive design or while under the influence of drugs or alcohol, yet chooses to have the child rather than to abort it. The rule makes no distinction between the sexual neophyte and the libertine. In short, the rule leaves no consideration for the multitudinous circumstances under which illegitimate childbirth may occur and which may have little, if any, bearing on the parent's present moral worth. A past biological event like childbirth out of wedlock, even if relevant to the issue, may not be

---

[7] The conclusiveness of the Pettey rule was testified to by Superintendent Pettey himself:

Q. So I take it, Mr. Pettey, that a person who supposedly has a, quote, illegitimate child, as you put it, that fact, no matter when it took place or no matter under what circumstances it took place, is prima facie evidence of a lack of morality:

A. It would be to me, yes.

THE COURT: Mr. Pettey, you do not think the facts or circumstances under which an illegitimate birth occurred is at all relevant to the issue of good character or bad character?

A. No sir. That would be hard to get at. I think the fact that the birth occurred without the benefit of matrimony is, to me, proof enough of the . . .

THE COURT: Is conclusive?

A. Yes sir.

THE COURT: . . . Suppose a woman had an illegitimate child and then later married either the father of the child or another man. When she presented herself to you she showed she was married and had a child, one child. Would you consider her for employment?

A. No, sir, I would not.

controlling; and that it may be considered more conventional or circumspect for the infant to be surrendered to others for upbringing rather than be reared by the natural parent is hardly determinative of the matter. Furthermore, the policy, if based on moral judgment, has inherent if unintended defects or shortcomings. While obviously aimed at discouraging premarital sex relations, the policy's effect is apt to encourage abortion, which is itself staunchly opposed by some on ethical or moral grounds. It totally ignores, as a disqualification, the occurrence of extra-marital sex activity, though thought of by many as a more serious basis for moral culpability. Indeed, the superintendent's fiat, altogether unsupported by sociological data, equates the single fact of illegitimate birth with irredeemable moral disease. Such a presumption is not only patently absurd, it is mischievous and prejudicial, requiring those who administer the policy to 'investigate' the parental status of school employees and prospective applicants. Where no stigma may have existed before, such inquisitions by overzealous officialdom can rapidly create it.

We observe also that there are reasonable alternative means through which to remove or suspend teachers engaging in immoral conduct; means that guarantee the teacher a public hearing on the merits and right of appeal. 5 Miss.Code Sec. 6282–26 (1971 Supp.). By denying a public hearing to which all other teachers charged with immoral conduct are entitled, the policy denies unwed parents equal protection of the laws. Insofar as the rule inextricably binds unwed parental status to irredeemable immorality, it violates both due process and equal protection.

. . . .

> The school district urges a second rationale for its rule[:] . . .
>
> What the school board looks at is whether, moral considerations aside, proper educational growth can be furthered and respect for marriage ingrained by employing unwed parents. The question then becomes whether the open and notorious existence of the status as an unwed parent would injure the affected students.

. . . .

. . . The record before us contains no evidence of proselytizing of pupils by the plaintiffs and reveals instead that each plaintiff, along with her illegitimate offspring, is living under the same roof as her parents, brothers and sisters. It would be a wise child indeed who could infer knowledge of either plaintiff's unwed parent status based on the manner of plaintiffs' existence. As the district court observed:

> In the absence of overt, positive stimuli to which children can relate, we are convinced that the likelihood of inferred learning that unwed parenthood is necessarily good or praiseworthy, is highly improbable, if not speculative. We are not at all

persuaded by defendants' suggestions, quite implausible in our view, that students are apt to seek out knowledge of the personal and private family life-styles of teachers or other adults within a school system (i.e. whether they are divorced, separated, happily married or single, etc.), and, when known, will approve of and seek to emulate them.

In our view then, the school district's second offered justification for the unwed parent policy also falls short of equal protection requirements.

The third rationale proffered by the school district in hopes of salvaging the Pettey rule, that the presence of unwed parents in a scholastic environment materially contributes to school-girl pregnancies is without support, other than speculation and assertions of opinion, in the record before us.

Because we hold that the Board rule under attack violated traditional concepts of equal protection, we find it unnecessary to discuss numerous other issues urged on appeal by appellees or in their behalf by amici curiae; for example, whether the rule creates a suspect classification based upon race or sex, or whether it infringes upon some constitutionally protected interest such as the right to privacy or the right to procreation.

Affirmed.

NOTE

Race and unwed motherhood. Unwed motherhood is, as Professor Kristin Luker has argued, "a frontier where increasing numbers of Americans are settling." *See* KRISTIN LUKER, DUBIOUS CONCEPTIONS: THE POLITICS OF TEENAGE PREGNANCY 135 (1996). That said, nonmarital motherhood is disproportionately peopled by less educated and less affluent women. To the extent that historic discrimination against African Americans and Latinas has placed many of them in this demographic category, nonmarital childbearing has been more likely among African Americans and Latinas, although the gap between these groups and white women is narrowing. *See* STEPHANIE VENTURA & CHRISTINE BACHRACH, CTRS. FOR DISEASE CONTROL & PREVENTION, NONMARITAL CHILDBEARING IN THE UNITED STATES, 1940–99, at 5–6 (2000); *see also* JOYCE A. MARTIN ET AL., CTRS. FOR DISEASE CONTROL & PREVENTION, BIRTHS: FINAL DATA FOR 2012 (2013).

Ordway v. Hargraves

323 F. Supp. 1155 (D. Mass. 1971).

■ CAFFREY, DISTRICT JUDGE.

This is a civil action brought on behalf of an 18-year old pregnant, unmarried, senior at the North Middlesex Regional High School, Townsend, Massachusetts. . . . The matter came before the court for hearing on plaintiff's application for preliminary injunctive relief in the nature of an order requiring respondents to re-admit her to the Regional High School on a full-time, regular-class-hour, basis.

. . . On the basis of the credible evidence adduced at the hearing, I find that the minor plaintiff, Fay Ordway . . . informed Mr. Hargraves[, the principal of North Middlesex Regional High School], approximately January 28, 1971, that she was pregnant and expected to give birth to a baby in June 1971. There is outstanding a rule of the Regional school committee, numbered Rule 821, which provides: "Whenever an unmarried girl enrolled in North Middlesex Regional High School shall be known to be pregnant, her membership in the school shall be immediately terminated." . . . Mr. Hargraves informed plaintiff that she was to stop attending regular classes at the high school as of the close of school on February 12. This instruction was confirmed in writing by a letter from Mr. Hargraves to plaintiff's mother, Mrs. Iona Ordway, dated February 22, 1971, in which Mr. Hargraves stated that the following conditions would govern Fay Ordway's relations with the school for the remainder of the school year:

a)   Fay will absent herself from school during regular school hours.

b)   Fay will be allowed to make use of all school facilities such as library, guidance, administrative, teaching, etc., on any school day after the normal dismissal time of 2:16 P.M.

c)   Fay will be allowed to attend all school functions such as games, dances, plays, etc.

d)   Participation in senior activities such as class trip, reception, etc.

e)   Seek extra help from her teachers during after school help sessions when needed.

f)   Tutoring at no cost if necessary; such tutors to be approved by the administration.

g)   Her name will remain on the school register for the remainder of the 1970–71 school year (to terminate on graduation day-tentatively scheduled for June 11, 1971).

h)   Examinations will be taken periodically based upon mutual agreement between Fay and the respective teacher.

. . . .

. . . [I]n order to obtain a preliminary injunction, the plaintiff must satisfy two requirements, (1) that denial of the injunction will cause certain and irreparable injury to the plaintiff, and (2) "that there is a reasonable probability that (she) will ultimately prevail in the litigation."

At the hearing, Dr. F. Woodward Lewis testified that he is plaintiff's attending physician and that she is in excellent health to attend school. He expressed the opinion that the dangers in attending school are no worse for her than for a non-pregnant girl student, and that she can participate in all ordinary school activities with the exception of violent calisthenics. An affidavit of Dr. Charles R. Goyette, plaintiff's attending obstetrician, was admitted in evidence, in which Dr. Goyette corroborated the opinions of Dr. Lewis and added his opinion that "there is no reason that Miss Ordway could not continue to attend school until immediately before delivery."

Dr. Dorothy Jane Worth, a medical doctor, employed as Director of Family Health Services, Massachusetts Department of Public Health, testified that in her opinion exclusion of plaintiff will cause plaintiff mental anguish which will affect the course of her pregnancy. She further testified that policies relating to allowing or forbidding pregnant girls to attend high school are now widely varying within the state and throughout the United States. She testified that both Boston and New York now allow attendance of unmarried pregnant students in their high schools. She further testified that she was not aware of any reason why any health problems which arose during the day at school could not be handled by the registered nurse on duty at the high school.

Dr. Mary Jane England, a medical-doctor and psychiatrist attached to the staff of St. Elizabeth's Hospital, expressed the opinion that young girls in plaintiff's position who are required to absent themselves from school become depressed, and that the depression of the mother has an adverse effect on the child, who frequently is born depressed and lethargic. She further testified that from a psychiatric point of view it is desirable to keep a person in the position of plaintiff in as much contact with her friends and peer group as possible, and that they should not be treated as having a malady or disease.

. . . .

Plaintiff testified that her most recent grades were an A, a B-plus, and two C-pluses, and that she strongly desires to attend school with her class during regular school hours. She testified that she has not been subjected to any embarrassment by her classmates, nor has she been involved in any disruptive incidents of any kind. She further testified that she has not been aware of any resentment or any other change of attitude on the part of the other students in the school. This opinion of plaintiff as to her continuing to enjoy a good relationship with her fellow students was corroborated by the school librarian, Laura J. Connolly.

The remaining witness for plaintiff was Dr. Norman A. Sprinthall, Chairman of the Guidance Program, Harvard Graduate School of Education, who testified that in his opinion the type of program spelled out in Mr. Hargraves' letter of February 22, for after-hours instruction, was not educationally the equal of regular class attendance and participation.

It is clear . . . that no attempt is being made to stigmatize or punish plaintiff by the school principal or, for that matter, by the school committees. It is equally clear that were plaintiff married, she would be allowed to remain in class during regular school hours despite her pregnancy. . . . In response to questioning, Mr. Hargraves could not state any educational purpose to be served by excluding plaintiff from regular class hours, and he conceded that plaintiff's pregnant condition has not occasioned any disruptive incident nor has it otherwise interfered with school activities. *Cf. Tinker v. Des Moines Indep. Cmty. School Dist.*, 393 U.S. 503, 514 (1969), where the Supreme Court limited school officials' curtailment of claimed rights of students to situations involving "substantial disruption of or material interference with school activities."

Mr. Hargraves did imply, however, his opinion is that the policy of the school committee might well be keyed to a desire on the part of the school committee not to appear to condone conduct on the part of unmarried students of a nature to cause pregnancy. The thrust of his testimony seems to be: the regional school has both junior and senior high school students in its student population; he finds the twelve-to-fourteen age group to be still flexible in their attitudes; they might be led to believe that the school authorities are condoning premarital relations if they were to allow girl students in plaintiff's situation to remain in school.

It should be noted that if concerns of this nature were a valid ground for the school committee regulation, the contents of paragraph b), c) and d) of Mr. Hargraves' letter of February 22 to plaintiff's mother substantially undercut those considerations.

In summary, no danger to petitioner's physical or mental health resultant from her attending classes during regular school hours has been shown; no likelihood that her presence will cause any disruption of or interference with school activities or pose a threat of harm to others has been shown; and no valid educational or other reason to justify her segregation and to require her to receive a type of educational treatment which is not the equal of that given to all others in her class has been shown.

It would seem beyond argument that the right to receive a public school education is a basic personal right or liberty. Consequently, the burden of justifying any school rule or regulation limiting or terminating that right is on the school authorities. . . .

On the record before me, respondents have failed to carry this burden.

. . . .

NOTES

1.   *Policies for parenting youth.* Abstinence-only education fails to consider the experiences of students who are already pregnant or parenting. Other aspects of school programming also fail to account for the needs of pregnant and parenting students. Because of the extreme stigma attached to young women (but not men) who experience out-of-wedlock pregnancies, schools

routinely expelled pregnant unmarried school girls, lest they provide unseemly examples for non-pregnant youth. Although Fay Ordway successfully sued to be able to take classes alongside her non-pregnant classmates, thirty years later similar policies that disadvantage and discriminate against pregnant students persist. In 1998, two pregnant and unmarried high school honor students were denied admission to the National Honor Society, on the ground that the students' exclusion would further "the public school's efforts to encourage high morals and strong character as part of the educational process." William H. Honan, *Honor Society Ordered to Admit Pregnant Girls*, N.Y. TIMES, Dec. 30, 1998, at A15. Although Title IX prohibits discrimination against pregnant or parenting teens, it is not vigorously enforced unless a student complains. Further, de facto policies (including those prohibiting excessive absences and providing no opportunities to express breast milk), school administrators' attitudes towards pregnant and parenting youth, as well as the other troubles that teenaged parents face often prompt this population to leave school. *See* THE NAT'L WOMEN'S LAW CTR., A PREGNANCY TEST FOR SCHOOLS: THE IMPACT OF EDUCATION LAWS ON PREGNANT AND PARENTING STUDENTS 3–6 (2012).

2.   *Teen pregnancy and high school graduation rates.* High school graduation rates are low among pregnant and parenting teens. In a recent survey, more than one-quarter of all respondents who dropped out indicated that parenthood was a factor in their decision to do so; more than one-third of young women surveyed indicated that it was a major factor. *See* JOHN M. BRIDGELAND, JOHN J. DILULIO, JR. AND KAREN BURKE MORISON, THE SILENT EPIDEMIC: PERSPECTIVES OF HIGH SCHOOL DROPOUTS 6 (2006). However, careful research on the matter suggests that many teens are already disengaged from school before a pregnancy occurs. Thus young people who find school unrewarding may initiate a pregnancy as a step towards adult autonomy. *See* Jennifer Manlove, *The Influence of High School Dropout and School Disengagement on the Risk of School-Age Pregnancy*, 8 J. RES. ON ADOLESCENCE 201, 202 (1998).

3.   *Racial disparities.* Teen pregnancy rates are higher among African Americans and Latinas, a factor that contributes to racial disparities in high school graduation rates. *See* NAT'L CAMPAIGN TO PREVENT TEEN & UNPLANNED PREGNANCY, POLICY BRIEF: RACIAL AND ETHNIC DISPARITIES IN TEEN PREGNANCY 1 (2010).

4.   *Obstacles to graduation.* Pregnant and parenting teens face various obstacles to completing high school. These obstacles include: stigma, inadequate postpartum recovery time, limited opportunity or support for making up missed work, lack of child care, prohibition on participation in extracurricular activities, and, in some cases, the school's refusal to let them participate in the graduation ceremony with their class. *See* NAT'L WOMEN'S LAW CTR., EXECUTIVE SUMMARY: A PREGNANCY TEST FOR SCHOOLS: THE IMPACT OF EDUCATION LAWS ON PREGNANT AND PARENTING STUDENTS 2–3 (2012).

5.   *Title IX and teen pregnancy.* Discrimination against pregnant or parenting teens is illegal. Title IX of the Education Amendments of 1972 (as amended) prohibits gender discrimination in education, and this includes

students who are, might be, or have been pregnant. Specifically, Title IX requires that any school that receives federal funds "shall not discriminate against any student, or exclude any student from its education program or activity, including any class or extracurricular activity, on the basis of such student's pregnancy, childbirth, false pregnancy, termination of pregnancy or recovery therefrom, unless the student requests voluntarily to participate in a separate portion of the program or activity of the recipient." 20 U.S.C. § 1681 (1972); 34 C.F.R. § 106.40(b)(1) (2014). With this in mind, do school policies that penalize or otherwise negatively impact pregnant and parenting teens violate Title IX?

* * *

Religious schools that function both as sites for the education of children and the employment of adults raise important questions regarding exemptions from the ambit of anti-discrimination law. In Hosanna-Tabor Evangelical Lutheran Church & School v. Equal Employment Opportunity Commission, *565 U.S. 171 (2012), Cheryl Perich filed a complaint with the EEOC against her employer, an evangelical school, on the ground that the school violated her rights under the Americans with Disabilities Act. Upon being diagnosed with narcolepsy, Perich took disability leave to complete treatment. After concluding treatment, she returned to work, only to find that her employer had hired someone else to fill her position. When Perich threatened to sue, the school fired her for "insubordination and disruptive behavior." Perich's employer argued that, as a church-sponsored school, they enjoyed a "ministerial exemption" from anti-discrimination laws. According to the employer, the ministerial exemption, which is derived from the First Amendment, allowed it to make employment decisions without state interference—including operation of the ADA. Perich argued that the ministerial exemption was intended to allow religious institutions to make decisions regarding the employment of clergy. Because she was a teacher, and not a clergyperson, she argued that the exemption did not apply in her situation. On appeal, the Supreme Court determined that the ministerial exemption applied. The Court noted that Perich was not simply a teacher, but also a "commissioned minister" who taught religion classes and led students in prayer. While* Hosannah-Tabor *did not involve an employee trying to exercise her reproductive rights, as the following selections make clear, the Court's reasoning shadows such cases.*

Dias v. Archdiocese of Cincinnati

2013 WL 360355 (S.D. Ohio Jan. 30, 2013).

■ SPIEGEL, S.D.J.

. . . .

I.   Background

. . . .

. . . Plaintiff was an employee, a computer technology coordinator, at two of Defendant Archdiocese schools, Defendants Holy Family and St. Lawrence. She became pregnant through artificial insemination. She was unmarried. When she told her principal, Jennifer O'Brien, at Holy Family that she was pregnant, O'Brien . . . informed her that she would probably lose her job because she was pregnant and unmarried.

At that point, Plaintiff informed O'Brien, that, in fact, she had become pregnant not through premarital sex but through artificial insemination. Defendants then offered a second reason, stating she was terminated for being pregnant by means of artificial insemination. . . .

After her termination Plaintiff [alleged] that Defendants' actions amounted to pregnancy discrimination under federal and state law, and that Defendants breached her employment contracts without good cause. Defendants initially moved to dismiss the complaint, invoking the "ministerial exception" to Title VII, as well as contending Plaintiff violated a "morals clause"[1] in her contract and thus could not sue to enforce it. The Court denied Defendants' motion, finding the facts as alleged showed Plaintiff was not a minister, and in fact, that as a non-Catholic, she was not even permitted to teach Catholic doctrine. As such, the Court found Plaintiff had protections under state and federal law against pregnancy discrimination. However, the Court found the facts as alleged further showed a lack of "meeting of the minds" as to the contract, because the "morals clause" did not address artificial insemination, and there was a question of fact as to whether Plaintiff knew she was barred from such action.

Defendants now move for summary judgment contending under the McDonnell-Douglas burden-shifting analysis, that conceding Plaintiff has a *prima facie* case of pregnancy discrimination, she cannot rebut their proffered legitimate non-discriminatory justification for her termination, their morals clause. They further argue discovery yielded new facts that show Plaintiff should be considered a "minister" and thus the ministerial exception should apply to this case. Defendants further contend new facts show Plaintiff violated the contract in other ways that show as a matter of law, she has "unclean hands" so as to be unable to enforce the contract against them. Finally, Defendants argue the Archdiocese should not be a Defendant in this case because the Defendant schools "enjoy a unique level of independence from centralized Archdiocese operations," and that "[e]ach parish hires and fires employees, owns its own land and generally manages its affairs."

Plaintiff similarly moves for summary judgment, on her claims of pregnancy discrimination and on the Archdiocese's status as her employer. In her view, facts revealed in discovery in no way change the Court's determination that she was not a ministerial employee. Plaintiff

---

[1] Such clause stated generally that Plaintiff would "comply with and act consistently in accordance with the stated philosophy and teaching of the Roman Catholic Church."

claims it does not really matter whether the morals clause encompasses her pregnancy, because as a non-ministerial employee, her Title VII rights trump any illegal anti-pregnancy provision in a contract. Because there is no dispute that Defendants either terminated her for being pregnant and unwed, or being pregnant by artificial insemination, Plaintiff contends she should prevail on her pregnancy discrimination claims as a matter of law. Finally, Plaintiff offers an extensive analysis based on the integrated enterprise doctrine, showing the Archdiocese and the schools had interrelated operations, common management, and shared centralized control of labor relations and personnel.

. . . .

III. Discussion

A. The Ministerial Exception and the Integrated Employer Doctrine.

As an initial matter, Defendants argued at the hearing and in their briefing that based on new discovery the Court should revisit its analysis of the ministerial exception, and also, it should find the Archdiocese is not a proper party to this litigation. The Court rejects both arguments. . . . First, Defendants attempt to swallow up the ministerial exception by characterizing teachers generally as role models and therefore "ministers." . . . [B]ecause Plaintiff, as a non-Catholic, was not permitted to teach Catholic doctrine, she cannot genuinely be considered a "minister" of the Catholic faith. Plaintiff therefore retains her Title VII protection against pregnancy discrimination.

Second, . . . the Archdiocese is a proper party to this litigation. Facts show the Archdiocese is involved in setting uniform employment contracts, performing background checks on new employees, and evaluating job performance of school employees. The Archdiocese sets policies for the schools—and its overall relationship with the schools shows an interrelation of operations, common management, centralized control of labor relations, and that it can exercise a meaningful degree of financial control over its parishes.

B. Pregnancy Discrimination

The Court therefore proceeds to the heart of the matter, Plaintiff's pregnancy discrimination claims. Plaintiff brings such claims pursuant to Title VII and Ohio Revised Code Chapter 4112.[2] Under these provisions, Plaintiffs may assert a *prima facie* case of pregnancy discrimination through the presentation of either direct or indirect evidence. . . .

. . . .

---

[2] The Pregnancy Discrimination Act, 42 U.S.C. § 2000e(k), amended Title VII in 1978 so as to prohibit discrimination on the basis of pregnancy, childbirth, or related medical conditions. Pregnancy discrimination claims under Ohio Rev.Code § 4112.01 *et seq.* are analyzed pursuant to federal case law involving 42 U.S.C. § 2000e.

... Defendant concedes that Plaintiff can establish a *prima facie* case of pregnancy discrimination, such that the analysis turns on whether its proffered legitimate non-discriminatory justification for its action, its morals clause in the contract, is a pretext for pregnancy discrimination.

Defendants argued at the hearing and in their papers that because Plaintiff cannot show Defendants' reliance on the morals clause was not the real reason for her termination, they should be entitled to summary judgment in their favor. Plaintiff responds that the morals clause in this case is an illegal provision because it prohibits being unwed and pregnant and being pregnant by artificial insemination, two conditions she claims are squarely protected by Title VII.

The Court finds it appropriate to revisit the Sixth Circuit's decision in *Boyd v. Harding Academy of Memphis, Inc.*, 88 F.3d 410, 414–15 (6th Cir.1996), in which the court upheld the termination of a teacher at a religious school based on the school's proffered legitimate justification that it had a policy against its teachers engaging in sex outside marriage. The Sixth Circuit found that so long as such a code of conduct was applied equally to both genders, it could be upheld as valid and nonpretextual. The Court noted that though the defendant in *Boyd* used the phrase "pregnant and unwed" in conversations with the plaintiff, the real reason behind such statement, and consistent with the school's policy, was a prohibition against engaging in extramarital sex. The Sixth Circuit repeated in *Cline v. Catholic Diocese*, 206 F.3d 651, 658 (6th Cir.1999) that a policy against premarital sex can be upheld so long as it is enforced in a gender-neutral fashion.

In the light of *Boyd* and *Cline* the Court cannot adopt Plaintiff's view that terminating an employee for being "pregnant and unwed" automatically amounts to a violation of Title VII.[3] The morals clause in this case lacks specificity such that only an evaluation of the decision-makers' testimony can show whether their initial reason for terminating Plaintiff was simply enforcement of a policy against premarital sex. This in the Court's view is a factual determination for a jury: to answer why Defendant really terminated Plaintiff.

Even should a jury find Defendant initially terminated Plaintiff based on its view that she engaged in premarital sex, Plaintiff could still prevail should the jury find the policy was not enforced in a gender-neutral manner. Taking all inferences in Plaintiff's favor ... it finds a genuine issue of material fact as to whether the policy was only enforced against women. Plaintiff's discovery has shown that only female employees of the Archdiocese have been terminated due to the "morals

---

[3] Plaintiff cited *Jacobs v. Martin Sweets Co., Inc.*, 550 F.2d 364 (6th Cir.1977) at oral argument in support of her view, but such case noted that "Jacobs' employment was terminated because she was pregnant and unmarried-not because of her premarital sexual activity." The Sixth Circuit appears to have consistently made a distinction between policies targeting sexual activity as opposed to illegal policies against pregnancy.

clause," such that a jury might conclude the proffered reason is pretextual. *Cline*, 206 F.3d 651, 667 (where a pregnancy alone signaled teacher engaged in premarital sex and school did not otherwise inquire of male teachers regarding premarital sex, a genuine issue is raised whether defendant only enforces its policy against pregnant female teachers, which is a form of pregnancy discrimination).

This case offers the further twist of a second proffered reason for Plaintiff's termination. After Plaintiff informed Defendants she was pregnant through the means of artificial insemination, they responded that such means of becoming pregnant was also justification for her termination.

The Court already noted in its decision on Defendant's motion to dismiss that the Sixth Circuit suggested in *Boyd* that a pregnancy by artificial insemination might be viewed differently than a pregnancy due to extra-marital intercourse. It appears the Sixth Circuit may have been signaling that a pregnancy by artificial insemination might fall outside a policy prohibiting extra-marital intercourse. Should that be the case, the Court nonetheless finds no reason that a policy against artificial insemination, like a policy against extra-marital sex, could be upheld so long as it would be enforced in a gender-neutral manner. As such, the Court rejects Plaintiff's views, as expressed in her motion for summary judgment, that being terminated for being "pregnant by artificial insemination" is a per se violation of Title VII.

However, as above, the Court finds the Plaintiff has raised a genuine issue of material fact as to whether Defendant has enforced its policy as to men. Although no men have been fired due to engaging in artificial insemination, this is no indication that male employees have or have not engaged in such a procedure. There is admittedly a difficulty to enforcement of such a policy. Defendant indicates its decision-makers would enforce such policy when violations were self-reported or became evident, for example, through child support orders. The parties dispute whether a former male employee of a parish within the Archdiocese, who testified he engaged in artificial insemination without being fired, serves as evidence of disparate treatment. In the Court's view, under these circumstances, it is a jury question to evaluate the credibility of Defendants' decision-makers as to enforcement of such policy. Should the jury conclude after hearing the testimony of the decision-makers that the policy has been enforced unequally as to men and women, they could find Defendants' reason pretext for pregnancy discrimination.

C.   Plaintiff's Contract Claim

Defendants also move for summary judgment as to Plaintiff's contract claim. . . . [T]here were factual questions relating to whether the parties ever arrived at a "meeting of the minds" as to the meaning of the "morals clause," which did not specifically prohibit artificial insemination. Discovery has only confirmed that Plaintiff did not know such procedure was prohibited. However, discovery also yielded facts that Plaintiff admitted she was in a long-term homosexual relationship during her employment, and that she kept such fact secret from Defendants as she knew Defendants would view her relationship as a violation of the morals clause. Under such circumstances, the Court finds Plaintiff, with "unclean hands," cannot invoke a cause of action based on a contract she knew she was breaching. A party that breaches a contract cannot scrupulously enforce the contract against the other contracting party. *Midwest Payment Systems, Inc. v. Citibank Federal Savings Bank*, 801 F.Supp. 9 (S.D.Ohio, 1992). Having concluded as such, however, the Court finds the contract issue distinct from that of Plaintiff's potential Title VII rights, and that her breach of such contract in no way absolves Defendants[ ] of any responsibility to conform to the requirements of law against pregnancy discrimination.

. . . .

NOTES

1. *Morality clauses and parochial schools.* As the facts of *Dias* suggest, in recent years, employees of parochial schools have been under increasing pressure to conform their professional and *private* lives to church doctrine. In May 2014, Michael Barber, the bishop of the Catholic Church's Oakland diocese, ordered a morality clause inserted into the employment contracts of all Catholic school employees in the diocese. Under the morality clause, educators were required to obey Catholic teachings in their private, as well as professional lives. Educators who refused to submit to the clause were to be terminated. Roughly twenty percent of the diocese's teachers are not Catholic. Joe Garofoli, *Oakland Bishop Softens on Controversial Morality Clause in Catholic Teacher Contract*, S.F. CHRON. (May 28, 2014), http://blog. sfgate.com/stew/2014/05/28/oakland-bishop-softens-on-controversial-morality-clause-in-catholic-teacher-contract/. Although the Oakland bishop is reconsidering the clause, such clauses are commonplace in many dioceses. *Id.* Do these morality clauses offend anti-discrimination principles? Should churches be permitted to impose such requirements on their employees?

2. *Pregnant role models.* As we have seen, schools traditionally placed pregnant married women on leave until surprisingly recently, presumably on the grounds that a swelling belly would prompt students to think about sex. More recently, schools and youth-serving groups have focused on unmarried pregnant women, on the grounds that they are poor role models for young people. In 1986, for example, the Girls Clubs of America fired an African-American woman for being pregnant and unwed. *Chambers v. Omaha Girls Club*, 629 F. Supp. 925 (D. Neb. 1986). In 2012, a Christian church in Texas fired teacher and volleyball coach Cathy Samford for the same reason. Rheana Murray, *Religious School Fires Teacher for Getting Pregnant out of Wedlock*, N.Y. DAILY NEWS (Apr. 11, 2012), http://www. nydailynews.com/news/national/religious-school-fires-teacher-pregnant-wed lock-bad-christian-role-model-article-1.1060205.

* * *

Within the public school system, the conflicts between state duties to educate students and parental autonomy in how children are raised can also be seen in the fight over sex education. As the following cases suggest, sex education in public schools is particularly contentious today, as sexual patterns, including rates of marriage, change. How should a just society reconcile the need for family autonomy with the need to expose children to a wide range of ideas?

Smith v. Ricci
446 A.2d 501 (N.J. 1982).

■ CLIFFORD, J.

Appellants challenge a regulation of the State Board of Education (Board) that requires each local school district to develop and implement a family life education program in the public elementary and secondary curricula. *N.J.A.C.* 6:29–7.1. Appellants contend that such a program impinges upon the free exercise of their religion and constitutes an establishment of religion in violation of the United States Constitution. U.S. Const. amend. I. . . .

. . . .

Appellants' principal objection to the regulation is that it violates both the Free Exercise and Establishment clauses of the First Amendment.

. . . .

Appellants assert that by teaching about human reproduction, sexuality, and the development of personal and social values, the schools will "inhibit the moral concepts held by those students who have received them through their Judeo-Christian and other home teaching." As a result, children will be exposed to attitudes, goals, and values that are contrary to their own and to those of their parents, and will thereby be inhibited in the practice of their religion. We do not question that this argument is sincerely made. Whether or not it is well reasoned we need not now decide, for we believe that the simple fact that parents can remove their children from any objectionable part of the program is dispositive. If the program violates a person's beliefs, that person is not required to participate. Where there is no compulsion to participate in this program, there can be no infringement upon appellants' rights freely to exercise their religion. . . .

Even though the program permits excusal, appellants argue that it nonetheless inhibits the free exercise of their religion. They assert that requiring pupils affirmatively to assert their objection to the program in front of teachers and peers exerts an intolerable pressure on those pupils such that they may be compelled to abandon their beliefs and to choose not to exercise their option to be excused. [T]hey argue that such pressure is constitutionally unacceptable.

We do not doubt that the exercise of the right to be excluded may be difficult for some. The constitution does not guarantee, however, that the exercise of religion will be without difficulty. The Supreme Court repeatedly has upheld neutral laws of general applicability even though such laws have somehow burdened the exercise of some religions. *See, e.g., United States v. Lee,* [455 U.S. 252] (1982) (social security taxes); *Gillette v. United States,* 401 U.S. 437 (1971) (selective service laws); *Braunfeld v. Brown,* 366 U.S. 599 (1961) (Sunday closing laws); *Prince v. Massachusetts,* 321 U.S. 158 (1943) (child labor laws); *Reynolds v. United States,* 98 U.S. 145 (1879) (polygamy laws).

. . . .

Courts in at least two states have addressed the validity of sex education curricula in light of free exercise considerations. In both instances the courts held that where there was adequate provision for excusal on the grounds of conscientiously-held belief, sex education or family life education programs did not offend the Free Exercise Clause. . . .

Indeed, both the Hawaii and California courts pointed out that accepting the argument that public schools may not offer curricula that offend the religious or moral views of a particular group would be tantamount to enshrining that group's views as state policy, thereby violating the Establishment Clause. *Medeiros v. Kiyosaki, supra,* 478 P.2d at 318–19; *Citizens for Parental Rights v. San Mateo County Bd. of Ed., supra,* 51 Cal. App.3d at 18. In *Epperson v. Arkansas,* 393 U.S. 97 (1968) the Supreme Court said, "There is and can be no doubt that the First Amendment does not permit the State to require that teaching and learning must be tailored to the principles or prohibitions of any religious sect or dogma." *Id.* at 106, 89 *S.Ct.* at 271. The Court in *Epperson* held that the prohibition of teaching one point of view (evolution) because it was contrary to the religious views of some constituted an impermissible establishment of religion. Appellants' argument is essentially the same as the one rejected in *Epperson.*

Thus, appellants' argument based on the Free Exercise Clause is flawed in two ways. First, the regulation, because of the excusal clause, does not inhibit the free exercise of religion. Second, to permit the appellants to control what others may study because the subject may be offensive to appellants' religious or moral scruples would violate the Establishment Clause.

Establishment Clause

Appellants contend that the regulation violates the Establishment Clause in that the family life education program will establish secularism (or "Secular Humanism") as a religion and inhibit all traditional religions to the point of establishing secularism as a religion. . . .

Appellants do not contend that the regulation is nonsecular; their argument assumes its secularity. Nor do they present a valid argument that the regulation fosters excessive governmental entanglement with religion. The gravamen of their Establishment Clause argument is that the regulation, because it is secular, will in its primary effect inhibit religion.

This argument is unpersuasive. There is absolutely nothing in the regulation or in the curriculum guidelines that gives even the slightest indication that the program favors a "secular" view of its subject matter over a "religious" one. The program is, as it must be, neither antagonistic toward religion nor supportive of non-religion. The mention of religion in the classroom is not forbidden. Indeed, it might be entirely appropriate in the context of discussing sexuality for a teacher to mention that different religions have different views as to the morality of certain aspects of sexual behavior and to encourage the students to seek guidance from their parents and clergymen. As one writer has stated,

> As long as the state does not unfairly represent any moral views that might undercut the teaching of a child's religion, sex is as unobjectionable a classroom subject as lyric passages from the Bible. Further, such a course need not be "dehumanizing," or constitute a "religion of secularism". Competing moral interpretations of sex may still be discussed, provided that one particular interpretation is not stressed to the exclusion of others. . . .

The regulation is barren of any requirement that a point of view, be it secular or religious, must be stressed to the exclusion of others. We therefore hold that this program does not . . . constitute an establishment of religion.

III

Appellants argue that the Board's action in adopting *N.J.A.C.* 6:29–7.1 violates the Due Process Clause of the Fourteenth Amendment because the Board did not show a reasonable relationship between the goals of the family life education program and the means adopted.

The Board, on the other hand, maintains that the Family Life Committee Report, as well as the testimony of knowledgeable people such as the Commissioner of the Department of Health and the Commissioner of Human Services, supports the view that not only is there a relationship between the program and the reduction of teenage pregnancy, venereal disease, and other social problems, but also the program is necessary if these problems are to be ameliorated.

It is well established that a presumption of reasonableness attaches to the actions of an administrative agency and that the burden of proving unreasonableness falls upon those who challenge the validity of the action. . . . Appellants have offered no evidence to meet that burden but instead merely assert that there are no data that prove that the program will have any effect on the societal ills that it attacks. This bare assertion does not satisfy appellants' burden of proving that the regulation is unreasonable.

In addition, the record reveals a sufficient factual basis for the Board's conclusion that the family life education program is a reasonable, desirable, and necessary method of dealing with readily identifiable educational and social problems. If the Board were required to prove the efficacy of each curricular program before implementing it, the Board's ability to operate would be severely and unnecessarily encumbered. No such proof is required.

. . . .

Affirmed.

NOTES

1. *When sex goes to school.* In her book, *When Sex Goes to School*, Professor Kristin Luker argues that the debate over sex education in schools boils down to two tensions: first, who should be the source of information about sexuality for children—parents or schools? And second, which forms of sexuality are acceptable and which are not? KRISTIN LUKER, WHEN SEX GOES TO SCHOOL: WARRING VIEWS ON SEX—AND SEX EDUCATION—SINCE THE SIXTIES 184 (2007). In what other debates are these tensions present?

2. *Illiberal values in liberal society.* In the section that opened this chapter, Professors Alice Ristroph and Melissa Murray argue that a liberal society should tolerate a great deal of family autonomy, even when some families use that autonomy to teach their children values that contradict liberal values. However, Professor Kimberly Yuracko invites us to contemplate the case of home-schooling families who teach only the Bible (or the Koran, or the Torah), eschewing all other instruction. Yuracko reminds us that home-schooling in the United States is proliferating, and that there is virtually no regulation as to the content or competence of those doing the schooling. Critically, she notes that some home-schooling families have chosen to home school in order to avoid values they find threatening—for example, gender equality. *See* Kimberly Yuracko, *Education Off the Grid: Constitutional Constraints on Home Schooling*, 96 CALIF. L. REV. 123, 123–24 (2008).

Brown v. Hot, Sexy, and Safer

68 F.3d 525 (1st Cir. 1995).

■ TORRUELLA, C.J.

BACKGROUND

On April 8, 1992, [plaintiffs] Mesiti and Silva attended a mandatory, school-wide "assembly" at Chelmsford High School. Both students were fifteen years old at the time. The assembly consisted of a ninety-minute presentation characterized by the defendants as an AIDS awareness program (the "Program"). The Program was staged by defendant Suzi

Landolphi ("Landolphi"), contracting through defendant Hot, Sexy, and Safer, Inc., a corporation wholly owned by Landolphi.

Plaintiffs allege that Landolphi gave sexually explicit monologues and participated in sexually suggestive skits with several minors chosen from the audience. Specifically, the complaint alleges that Landolphi: 1) told the students that they were going to have a "group sexual experience, with audience participation"; 2) used profane, lewd, and lascivious language to describe body parts and excretory functions; 3) advocated and approved oral sex, masturbation, homosexual sexual activity, and condom use during promiscuous premarital sex; 4) simulated masturbation; 5) characterized the loose pants worn by one minor as "erection wear"; 6) referred to being in "deep sh—" after anal sex; 7) had a male minor lick an oversized condom with her, after which she had a female minor pull it over the male minor's entire head and blow it up; 8) encouraged a male minor to display his "orgasm face" with her for the camera; 9) informed a male minor that he was not having enough orgasms; 10) closely inspected a minor and told him he had a "nice butt"; and 11) made eighteen references to orgasms, six references to male genitals, and eight references to female genitals.

Plaintiffs maintain that the sexually explicit nature of Landolphi's speech and behavior humiliated and intimidated Mesiti and Silva. Moreover, many students copied Landolphi's routines and generally displayed overtly sexual behavior in the weeks following the Program, allegedly exacerbating the minors' harassment. The complaint does not allege that either of the minor plaintiffs actually participated in any of the skits, or were the direct objects of any of Landolphi's comments.

The complaint names eight co-defendants along with Hot, Sexy, and Safer, and Landolphi, alleging that each played some role in planning, sponsoring, producing, and compelling the minor plaintiffs' attendance at the Program. In March 1992, defendant Judith Hass ("Hass"), then chairperson of the Chelmsford Parent Teacher Organization (the "PTO"), initiated negotiations with Hot, Sexy, and Safer. Hass and defendant Michael Gilchrist, M.D., also a member of the PTO, as well as the school physician, viewed a promotional videotape of segments of Landolphi's past performances and then recommended the Program to the school administration. On behalf of defendant Chelmsford School Committee (the "School Committee"), Hass executed an agreement with Hot, Sexy, and Safer, and authorized the release of $1,000 of Chelmsford school funds to pay Landolphi's fee.

The complaint also names as defendants two other members of the School Committee, Wendy Marcks and Mary E. Frantz, as well as the Superintendent and Assistant Superintendent of the Chelmsford Public Schools, Richard H. Moser, and David S. Troughton, and the Principal of Chelmsford High School, George J. Betses. Plaintiffs allege that all the defendants participated in the decisions to hire Landolphi, and to compel the students to attend the Program. All the defendants were physically present during the Program.

A school policy adopted by the School Committee required "[p]ositive subscription, with written parental permission" as a prerequisite to "instruction in human sexuality." The plaintiffs allege, however, that the parents were not given advance notice of the content of the Program or an opportunity to excuse their children from attendance at the assembly.

. . . .

The plaintiffs seek both declaratory and monetary relief, alleging that the school sponsored program deprived the minor plaintiffs of: . . . their privacy rights under the First and Fourteenth Amendments; . . . their First Amendment rights under the Free Exercise Clause (in conjunction with a deprivation of the parent plaintiffs' right to direct and control the upbringing of their children). Plaintiffs also allege that the Program created a sexually hostile educational environment in violation of Title IX of the Education Amendments of 1972, 20 U.S.C. § 1681 *et seq.*

. . . .

The Supreme Court has held that the Fourteenth Amendment encompasses a privacy right that protects against significant government intrusions into certain personal decisions. *See Roe v. Wade,* 410 U.S. 113, 152 (1973). This right of privacy "has some extension to activities relating to marriage, procreation, contraception, family relationships, and child rearing and education." *Id.* Nevertheless, the Supreme Court has explained that only those rights that "can be deemed 'fundamental' or 'implicit in the concept of ordered liberty' are included in this guarantee of personal privacy." *Id.* . . . Regulations limiting these "fundamental rights" may be justified "only by a 'compelling state interest' . . . [and] must be narrowly drawn to express only the legitimate interests at stake." *Id.* (citations omitted).

. . . .

Parent-plaintiffs allege that the defendants violated their privacy right to direct the upbringing of their children and educate them in accord with their own views. This, they maintain, is a constitutionally protected "fundamental right" and thus can only be infringed upon a showing of a "compelling state interest" that cannot be achieved by any less restrictive means.

The genesis of the right claimed here can be found in *Meyer v. Nebraska,* 262 U.S. 390 (1923), and *Pierce v. Society of Sisters,* 268 U.S. 510, 535 (1925). . . .

. . . .

The *Meyer* and *Pierce* decisions have since been interpreted by the Court as recognizing that, under our Constitutional scheme, "the custody, care and nurture of the child reside first in the parents." *Prince v. Massachusetts,* 321 U.S. 158, 166 (1944). . . .

. . . .

The *Meyer* and *Pierce* cases, we think, evince the principle that the state cannot prevent parents from choosing a specific educational program—whether it be religious instruction at a private school or instruction in a foreign language. That is, the state does not have the power to "standardize its children" or "foster a homogenous people" by completely foreclosing the opportunity of individuals and groups to choose a different path of education. *Meyer*, 262 U.S. at 402. We do not think, however, that this freedom encompasses a fundamental constitutional right to dictate the curriculum at the public school to which they have chosen to send their children. . . . We think it is fundamentally different for the state to say to a parent, "You can't teach your child German or send him to a parochial school," than for the parent to say to the state, "You can't teach my child subjects that are morally offensive to me." The first instance involves the state proscribing parents from educating their children, while the second involves parents prescribing what the state shall teach their children. If all parents had a fundamental constitutional right to dictate individually what the schools teach their children, the schools would be forced to cater a curriculum for each student whose parents had genuine moral disagreements with the school's choice of subject matter. We cannot see that the Constitution imposes such a burden on state educational systems, and accordingly find that the rights of parents as described by *Meyer* and *Pierce* do not encompass a broad-based right to restrict the flow of information in the public schools.

. . . .

. . . [P]laintiffs allege that their case falls within the "hybrid" exception recognized by *Smith* for cases that involve "the Free Exercise Clause in conjunction with other constitutional protections." [*Employment Div., Dept. of Human Resources of Ore. v.*] *Smith*, 494 U.S. [872,] 881. The most relevant of the so-called hybrid cases is *Wisconsin v. Yoder*, 406 U.S. 205, 232–33 (1972), in which the Court invalidated a compulsory school attendance law as applied to Amish parents who refused on religious grounds to send their children to school. In so holding, the Court explained that

> *Pierce* stands as a charter of the rights of parents to direct the religious upbringing of their children. And, when combined with a free exercise claim of the nature revealed by this record, more than merely a "reasonable relation to some purpose within the competency of the State" is required to sustain the validity of the State's requirement under the First Amendment.

Id. at 232–32 (discussing *Pierce*, 268 U.S. 510). We find that the plaintiffs['] allegations do not bring them within the sweep of *Yoder* for two distinct reasons.

First, as we explained, the plaintiffs' allegations of interference with family relations and parental prerogatives do not state a privacy or substantive due process claim. Their free exercise challenge is thus not conjoined with an independently protected constitutional protection. Second, their free exercise claim is qualitatively distinguishable from that alleged in *Yoder*. As the Court in *Yoder* emphasized:

> the Amish in this case have convincingly demonstrated the sincerity of their religious beliefs, the interrelationship of belief with their mode of life, the vital role that belief and daily conduct play in the continued survival of Old Order Amish communities and their religious organization, and the hazards presented by the State's enforcement of a Statute generally valid as to others.

Id. at 235. Here, the plaintiffs do not allege that the one-time compulsory attendance at the Program threatened their entire way of life. Accordingly, the plaintiffs' free exercise claim for damages was properly dismissed.

. . . .

The plaintiffs' [final] claim alleges that the defendants engaged in sexual harassment by creating a sexually hostile environment, in violation of Title IX of the Education Amendments of 1972. Title IX provides in relevant part:

. . . .

Title IX is violated "[w]hen the [educational environment] is permeated with 'discriminatory intimidation, ridicule, and insult' that is 'sufficiently severe or pervasive to alter the conditions of the victim's employment and create an abusive . . . environment.'" *Harris*, 510 U.S. at [20] (quoting *Meritor* [*Sav. Bank, FSB v. Vinson*], 477 U.S. at 64–65 (1986)); *Lipsett*, 864 F.2d at 898. While a court must consider all of the circumstances in determining whether a plaintiff has established that an environment is hostile or abusive, it must be particularly concerned with (1) the frequency of the discriminatory conduct; (2) its severity; (3) whether it is physically threatening or humiliating rather than a mere offensive utterance; and (4) whether it unreasonably interferes with an employee's work performance. . . . Although the presence or absence of psychological harm or an unreasonable effect on work performance [is] relevant, no single factor is required. . . .

The Court has explained that the relevant factors must be viewed both objectively and subjectively. . . . If the conduct is not so severe or pervasive that a reasonable person would find it hostile or abusive, it is beyond Title IX's purview. *See id.* Similarly, if the plaintiff does not subjectively perceive the environment to be abusive, the conduct has not actually altered the conditions of her employment, and there is no Title IX violation. . . .

[W]e find that the facts alleged here are insufficient to state a claim for sexual harassment under a hostile environment theory. The plaintiffs' allegations are weak on every one of the *Harris* factors, and when considered in sum, are clearly insufficient to establish the existence of an objectively hostile or abusive environment. First, plaintiffs cannot claim that the offensive speech occurred frequently, as they allege only a one-time exposure to the comments.

We also think that the plaintiffs' allegations do not establish that Landolphi's comments were so severe as to create an objectively hostile environment. . . . The remarks were given to the entire ninth and tenth grades at what the defendants labelled an "AIDS awareness program." Significantly, the plaintiffs do not allege that they were required to participate in any of the offensive skits or that they were the direct objects of Landolphi's sexual comments.

. . . .

Similarly, Landolphi stated in her opening remarks that "[w]e're going to talk about AIDS, but not in the usual way." These prefaces framed the Program in such a way that an objective person would understand that Landolphi's allegedly vulgar sexual commentary was intended to educate the students about the AIDS virus rather than to create a sexually hostile environment.

These introductions also belie the plaintiffs' claim that Landolphi's speech was physically threatening and humiliating, rather than a mere offensive utterance. Landolphi's remarks were not directed specifically at the plaintiffs and were couched in an attempt to use humor to educate the students on sex and the AIDS virus. In this context, while average high school students might have been offended by the graphic sexual discussions alleged here, Landolphi's remarks could not reasonably be considered physically threatening or humiliating so as to create a hostile environment.

Similarly, the plaintiffs' allegations establish that the Program did not significantly alter their educational environment from an objective standpoint. The Program consisted of two ninety-minute sex-education presentations, and although the plaintiffs allege that "coarse jesting, sexual innuendo, and overtly sexual behavior took place for the weeks following the Program," they fail to explain how the coarse jesting and overtly sexual behavior "create[d] an atmosphere so infused with hostility toward members of one sex that [it] alter[ed] the [educational environment] for them." *Lipsett*, 864 F.2d at 897. In fact, they allege that the offensive behavior was visited on "those students," regardless of gender, "who were not inclined to accept 'the message' about human sexuality." If anything, then, they allege discrimination based upon the basis of viewpoint, rather than on the basis of gender, as required by Title IX. We therefore find that their claim under Title IX fails.

. . . .

Affirmed.

NOTE

LGBT youth and sex education. Sex education programs have generally presumed students' heterosexuality, thus excluding information about non-heterosexual sexual activity. The consequences of these assumptions can be profound. LGBT youth are often more vulnerable to issues of sexual health, and many struggle with attitudes that stigmatize or dismiss such young people. For an overview, see Hannah Slater, *LGBT-Inclusive Sex Education Means Healthier Youth and Safer Schools*, CTR. FOR AM. PROGRESS (June 21, 2013), http://www.americanprogress.org/issues/lgbt/news/2013/06/21/67411/ lgbt-inclusive-sex-education-means-healthier-youth-and-safer-schools/. In 2013, the late Senator Frank Lautenberg proposed the Real Education for Healthy Youth Act of 2013, H.R. 725, 113th Cong. (2013). If enacted, the "REAL" Act would provide grants for schools to develop comprehensive sex education curricula sensitive to sexual orientation, gender, and gender identity. To date, Congress has not enacted the REAL Act.

Minority Staff Special Investigations Division, U.S. House of Representatives Committee on Government Reform, 108th Cong., Report on the Content of Federally Funded Abstinence-Only Education Programs (2004) ["The Waxman Report"]

. . . .

One recent study of abstinence-only programs found that they may actually increase participants' risk. . . . [R]esearchers found the while virginity "pledge" programs helped some participants to delay sex, 88% still had premarital sex, and their rates of sexually transmitted diseases showed no statistically significant difference from those of non-pledgers. Virginity pledgers were also less likely to use contraception when they did have sex and were less likely to seek STD testing despite comparable infection rates.

In contrast, comprehensive sex education that both encourages abstinence and teaches about effective contraceptive use has been shown in many studies to delay sex, reduce the frequency of sex, and increase the use of condoms and other contraceptives.

. . . .

While there have been evaluations of the effectiveness of abstinence-only education programs, the content of the curricula taught in these programs has received little attention. The federal government does not review or approve the accuracy of the information presented in abstinence-only programs. SPRANS applicants, for example, are required to submit only the table of contents or a brief summary of the curricula they plan to use.

At the request of Rep. Henry Waxman, this report is a comprehensive evaluation of the content of the curricula used in federally funded abstinence-only education programs. It is based on a review of the most popular abstinence-only curricula used by grantees in the SPRANS program.

To conduct this evaluation, the Special Investigations Division obtained from the Health Resources and Services Administration the program summaries of the 100 organizations that received SPRANS abstinence funding during fiscal year 2003. Each summary contains a proposal listing the curricula that the program intends to use. The Special Investigations Division then acquired each curriculum that was listed by at least five funding recipients. Thirteen curricula met this criterion.

The 13 curricula were reviewed for scientific accuracy. For several curricula with a separate teacher's guide, both the student and teacher manuals were included. The review was intended to provide an overall assessment of the accuracy of the curricula, not to identify all potential errors.

. . . .

Eleven of the thirteen curricula most common used by SPRANS programs contain major errors and distortions of public health information. . . .

. . . .

The eleven curricula are used in 25 states by 69 grantees, including state health departments, school districts, and hospitals, as well as religious organizations and pro-life organizations. These 69 grantees received over $32 million in SPRANS abstinence-only funding in fiscal year 2003, the year examined in this report. In total, the 69 grantees have received over $90 million in federal funding since fiscal year 2001.

. . . .

Under the SPRANS requirements, abstinence-only education programs are not allowed to teach their participants any methods to reduce the risk of pregnancy other than abstaining until marriage. They are allowed to mention contraceptives only to describe their failure rates. Although the curricula purport to provide scientifically accurate information about contraceptive failure rates, many exaggerate these failure rates, providing affirmatively false or misleading information that misstates the effectiveness of various contraceptive methods in preventing disease transmission or pregnancy.

. . . .

One curriculum draws an analogy between the HIV virus and a penny and compares it to a sperm cell ("Speedy the Sperm"), which on the same scale would be almost 19 feet long. The curriculum asks, "If the condom has a failure rate of 14% in preventing 'Speedy' from getting through to create a new life, what happens if this guy (penny) gets through? You have a death: your own."

. . . .

None of the curricula provides information on how to select a birth control method and use it effectively. However, several curricula exaggerate condom failure rates in preventing pregnancy.

. . . .

. . . [One] curriculum presents misleading information about the risk of pregnancy from sexual activity other than intercourse. The curriculum erroneously states that touching another person's genitals "can result in pregnancy." In fact, the source cited for this contention specifically states that "remaining a virgin all but eliminates the possibility of becoming pregnant."

. . . .

A high number of the programs receiving SPRANS funding are formally opposed to abortion access. . . . Several of the curricula used by these and other recipients give misleading information about the physical and psychological effects of legal abortions.

. . . [A]ccording to the American Medical Association Council on Scientific Affairs, "[t]he risk of major complications from abortion-related procedures declined dramatically between 1970 and 1990." The curriculum inaccurately describes the risks of sterility, premature birth and mental retardation, and ectopic pregnancies:

> The curriculum states, "Sterility: Studies show that five to ten percent of women will never again be pregnant after having a legal abortion." In fact, obstetrics textbooks teach that "[f]ertility is not altered by an elective abortion."

. . . .

By their nature, abstinence-only curricula teach moral judgments alongside scientific facts. The SPRANS program mandates, for example, that programs teach that having sex only within marriage "is the expected standard of human sexual activity." In some of the curricula, the moral judgments are explicitly religious. For example, in a newsletter accompanying one popular curriculum, the author laments that as a result of societal change, "No longer were we valued as spiritual beings made by a loving Creator." The curriculum's author closes the section by signing, "In His Service."

. . . .

One curriculum that describes fetuses as "babies" describes the blastocyst, technically a ball of 107 to 256 cells at the beginning of uterine implantation, as "snuggling" into the uterus. . . .

. . . .

Many abstinence-only curricula begin with a detailed discussion of differences between boys and girls. . . . [and several] present stereotypes as scientific fact.

. . . .

Several curricula teach that girls care less about achievement and their futures than do boys.

One curriculum instructs: "Women gauge their happiness and judge their success by their relationships. Men's happiness and success hinge on their accomplishments." . . .

. . . .

A third curriculum depicts emotions as limiting girls' ability to focus. It states: "Generally, guys are able to focus better on one activity at a time and may not connect feelings with actions. Girls access both sides of the brain at once, so they often experience feelings and emotions as part of every situation."

. . . .

Some of the curricula describe girls as helpless or dependent upon men.

. . . .

[One] curriculum . . . teaches: "The father gives the bride to the groom because he is the one man who has had the responsibility of protecting her throughout her life. He is now giving his daughter to the only other man who will take over this protective role."

. . . The curriculum concludes:

Moral of the story: Occasional suggestions and assistance may be alright, but too much of it will lessen a man's confidence or even turn him away from his princess.

. . . .

[Another curriculum teaches:] "A male is usually less discriminating about those to whom he is sexually attracted. . . . Women usually have great intuitive awareness of how to develop a loving relationship."

The same curriculum tells participants: "While a man needs little or no preparation for sex, a woman often needs hours of emotional and mental preparation."

. . . .

Many of the curricula distort information about the risks of sexual activity. In the case of cervical cancer, the risk of disease is stressed, but simple prevention measures often go unmentioned. HIV exposure risks are discussed in confusing terms, and risks of substances and activities are exaggerated. Several curricula also present misleading information about the relationship between sexual activity and mental health, inaccurately suggesting that abstinence can solve all psychological problems.

. . . .

Several of the curricula that mention mental health concerns depict them as simple problems that can be fixed by abstaining from sexual activity. There does not appear to be scientific support for these assertions, however. . . .

. . . [O]ne curriculum tells youth that a long list of personal problems—including isolation, jealousy, poverty, heartbreak, substance abuse, unstable longterm commitments, sexual violence, embarrassment, depression, personal disappointment, feelings of being used, loss of honesty, loneliness, and suicide—"can be eliminated by being abstinent until marriage." . . .

. . . .

In addition to the inaccurate and misleading information discussed above, a number of the abstinence-only curricula contain erroneous information about basic scientific facts. . . .

. . . One curriculum states: "Twenty-four chromosomes from the mother and twenty-four chromosomes from the father join to create this new individual." In fact, human cells have 23 chromosomes from each parent, for a total of 46 in each body cell. . . .

. . . [Another] defines "sexually transmitted infections" as "bacterial infections that are acute and usually can be cured" and defines "sexually transmitted diseases" as "infections that are viral in nature, chronic, and usually can not be cured, but rather controlled through treatment." In fact, these terms are used interchangeably in medicine, and the program's definitions are not widely accepted.

. . . .

. . . Another curriculum erroneously includes "tears" and "sweat" in a column titled "At risk" for HIV transmission. In fact, according to the CDC, "[c]ontact with saliva, tears, or sweat has never been shown to result in transmission of HIV."

. . . This report finds that over two-thirds of abstinence-only education programs funded by the largest federal abstinence initiative are using curricula with multiple scientific and medical inaccuracies. These curricula contain misinformation about condoms, abortion, and basic scientific facts. They also blur religion and science and present gender stereotypes as fact.

NOTES

1. *Funding abstinence.* Federal funding to encourage adolescents to abstain from sex before marriage emerged on the national policy scene in 1981 with the Adolescent Family Life Act, 42 U.S.C. § 300z *et seq.* (1981) (AFLA). The passage of PRWORA substantially increased the amount of

funding dedicated to these programs, carving out fifty million dollars a year from existing maternal- and child-health programs. Matching grants from the states raised this amount to $87.5 million annually. Additionally, President George W. Bush signed a federal earmark known as Community-Based Abstinence Education (CBAE), which granted additional funding directly to community- and faith-based organizations, therefore bypassing states. *See* ALESHA E. DOAN & JEAN CALTERONE WILLIAMS, THE POLITICS OF VIRGINITY: ABSTINENCE IN SEX EDUCATION 510 (2008). CBAE reached its peak in funding in 2006, at $113 million. Since 2010, however, CBAE has been defunded in favor of grants to organizations that provide more comprehensive sex education.

2.   *Cultivating acceptable sexual practices?* Critically, the abstinence-promotion efforts described above were complemented with policies that pressured mothers receiving public assistance to identify the fathers of their children, as well as the increased policing of statutory rape. 42 U.S.C. § 602(a)(1)(A)(i)–(vi). What messages do these public policy efforts send about the expected sexual behaviors of public assistance recipients? Of the federal government's view of appropriate sexual behavior of its citizens more generally?

3.   *Effectiveness of abstinence-only sex education.* Confirming the findings of the Waxman Report, the U.S. General Accounting Office commissioned Mathematica Policy Research to empirically review the impact of abstinence-only sex education. Drawing on four programs that were the best-designed, longest, and most comprehensive, investigators randomly assigned students to abstinence-only sex education programs or to no sex education at all. Results suggested that abstinence-only programs had virtually no impact on behavior, but it did make program participants more skeptical of the effectiveness of condoms. *See* CHRISTOPHER TRENHOLM ET AL., MATHEMATICA POL. RESEARCH, IMPACTS OF FOUR TITLE V, SECTION 510 ABSTINENCE EDUCATION PROGRAMS: FINAL REPORT 41–57 (2007). Reviewing a wider range of programs, Douglas Kirby, a social science expert in adolescent behavior, came to the same conclusion, and contrasted these results with positive results found in the majority of comprehensive sex education programs. *See* DOUGLAS KIRBY, NAT'L CAMPAIGN TO PREVENT TEEN & UNPLANNED PREGNANCY, EMERGING ANSWERS 2007: RESEARCH FINDINGS ON PROGRAMS TO REDUCE TEEN PREGNANCY AND SEXUALLY TRANSMITTED DISEASES 15 (2007).

4.   *Sex education and sexual assault.* The Waxman Report was particularly concerned that some abstinence-only sex education curricula reinforced stereotypical beliefs about male and female sexuality. Such views, the Report worried, could subtly encourage sexual coercion or sexual violence. To the extent that some of these curricula portray men as inherently sexually aggressive, and assign women responsibility to control male sexuality, the Report expressed concern that these lessons may have divested young men of the responsibility to ensure that all sexual activity is consensual.

5.   *Disparate impact of abstinence-only sex education programs.* Risha Foulkes of the ACLU Women's Rights Project notes that the impact of abstinence-only education policies fall disproportionately on young people of

color. She argues that communities of color are less likely to have parent-child discussions about sex, and young people of color are more likely to have their sex education limited to abstinence-only programs because they are more likely to be in the low-income schools targeted by Title V abstinence-only legislation. At the same time, these young people are at higher risk of sexually transmitted infections and unintended pregnancy. These effects are compounded by the barriers to access to medical care (and especially to abortion services) in communities of color. Risha K. Foulkes, *Abstinence-Only Education and Minority Teenagers: The Importance of Race in a Question of Constitutionality*, 10 BERKELEY J. AFR.-AM. L. & POL'Y 3, 4–5 (2013). For a discussion of abstinence-only education and minors' access to comprehensive health care, see *infra* pp. 561–566.

6.   *Patriarchal proms.* Echoing the historical forms of sexual control of women examined in Chapter 1, a new product of the abstinence-only movement is the "purity prom." During these proms (which include vows, a white cake, and a first dance) fathers pledge to protect their daughters' chastity, and daughters pledge to remain abstinent. *See* Gigi Stone, *Teen Girls 'Date' Dad, Pledge Purity*, ABC NEWS (Mar. 12, 2007), http://abcnews.go.com/WNT/teen-girls-date-dad-pledge-purity/story?id=2928607. A variation on this theme is the "purity pledge" where students pledge to remain virgins until marriage. Sociologists Peter Bearman and Hannah Brückner found that eighty-eight percent of those who have pledged to remain virgins until marriage had sex before marriage and were as likely as non-pledgers to have sexually transmitted infections (STI). Hannah Brückner & Peter Bearman, *After the Promise: The STD Consequences of Adolescent Virginity Pledges*, 36 J. ADOLESCENT HEALTH 271, 275, 277 (2005).

CHAPTER 4

REGULATING REPRODUCTION

A. INTRODUCTION

Previous sections have illustrated how gender roles based on reproduction were naturalized by reference to divine creation, nature, and/or the need to regulate families. In this chapter, we trace what happens when declining infant mortality, industrialization, changing reproductive technologies, and agitation for women's equality challenge the "natural" order of things. We begin with a selection from Reva Siegel, who demonstrates that as modern life gave rise to new ideas about gender in the United States, physicians reinscribed gender roles—this time based on biology rather than divine will. More tellingly, Siegel argues that the terms of the argument, as articulated by nineteenth-century physicians, continue to dominate our thinking (and regulation) of sexuality and reproduction to this day.

Reva Siegel, *Reasoning from the Body: A Historical Perspective on Abortion Regulation and Questions of Equal Protection*
44 STAN. L. REV. 261 (1992).

[I]t was the medical profession that led the nineteenth century campaign to criminalize abortion. The doctors who advocated criminalizing abortion quite openly argued that regulating women's reproductive conduct was necessary, not merely to protect potential life, but also to ensure women's performance of marital and maternal obligations and to preserve the ethnic character of the nation. . . .

. . . .

At the opening of the nineteenth century, abortion was governed by common law, and was not a criminal offense if performed before quickening—the point at which a pregnant woman perceived fetal movement, typically late in the fourth month or early in the fifth month of gestation. During the ensuing decades, especially in the years following the Civil War, states began to enact legislative restrictions on abortion. . . .

This transformation in the law of abortion occurred at the behest of the nation's physicians—at once the architects and exponents of legal reform. In the early decades of the nineteenth century, when America's politicians, clergy, and press were silent on the question of abortion, the doctors began a concerted campaign, directed at fellow practitioners, legislators, religious leaders, and the public at large, to put abortion on the national political agenda.

. . . Doctors premised their campaign on a scientific understanding of human development as continuous from the point of conception, a scheme in which "quickening" had no special significance. With this understanding of human development and certain judgments about the nature of family life, doctors began to articulate strong moral objections to the practice of abortion, contending, as a matter of professional ethics, that abortion at any stage of pregnancy was an unwarranted destruction of human life.

. . . The obstetricians and gynecologists who led the mid-century campaign against abortion were attempting to build a professional practice in a field traditionally dominated by women. . . . By opposing abortion, gynecologists and obstetricians hoped to establish their authority in matters of birthing, and so improve their status in the eyes of the profession and the public at large. At a time when medical practitioners could do little to prolong life, the doctors' efforts to assert scientific authority over the inception of life enhanced the stature of the profession as a whole.

The doctors began their campaign quietly, working with legislators engaged in reforming state codes. It was not until the middle of the century that they took their campaign to the public. Until then, abortion had been considered the last resort of the desperate single woman. By mid-century, however, abortion was commonly perceived as a practice of married women seeking to avoid dangerous pregnancies and to control family size—a matter of special concern to middle-class families in the new industrial order. . . .

Doctors advocating criminalization of abortion thus seized an issue of intersecting professional, familial, and societal significance and made it a text of America's future. . . .

. . . .

In arguing that life begins at conception, physicians . . . sought to define life from the standpoint of medical science, in purely biological terms. Their arguments against abortion emphasized that the fertilized egg had a physiological capacity for growth, and derived from this capacity for growth the embryo's status as an autonomous life form. Thus, in defending the claim that life begins at conception, physicians redefined the maternal/fetal relation, offering a physiological account of human development that treated women's role in reproduction as a matter of minor consequence—from the point of conception onwards.

Yet, the doctors' most powerful strategy for demonstrating the autonomy of unborn life did not require confusing the facts of human development; it worked by focusing upon them selectively. The doctors rested their case that life begins at conception on "objective," but objectively incomplete, facts about human development, depicting the developmental process in ways that obscured the physical and social work of reproduction women perform. . . .

While the account of human genesis the doctors presented was internally coherent, it was dramatically at odds with the norms and practices of childrearing prevailing in mid-nineteenth century America. During this era, the parent who served as primary childrearer shifted from father to mother, and methods of childrearing shifted from discipline to character formation, a process which required meticulous maternal supervision of child development. By mid-century these changes in family norms assumed the pronounced forms popularly associated with the "cult of domesticity" or "separate spheres tradition." Thus, doctors justifying the conception standard emphasized the developmental autonomy of the unborn at a time when cultural authorities, including the medical profession itself, insisted that women's conduct in gestating and nurturing a child was the single most important determinant of its welfare. . . . In short, their account of human genesis contradicted, almost point for point, the norms and practices of reproduction prevailing during the era of the antiabortion campaign. In retrospect, it appears that if the medical profession did persuade nineteenth century audiences to think of the embryo/fetus as an autonomous life form, it was by encouraging Americans to take for granted the work of gestation and nurturance women perform—work which the "cult of domesticity" defined as a woman's duty to perform.

. . . .

The doctors made little effort to conceal the religious sources of this pronatalist ethic. Yet, while physicians freely invoked biblical authority to condemn nonprocreative sexuality as sin, they most frequently spoke as physiologists, emphasizing the many diseases which issued from any effort to defeat the procreative purposes of marital sexuality. Thus, doctors elaborated a norm of marital sexuality in therapeutic terms, and in doing so, they defined women's health as a condition of continuous reproductive activity.

. . . .

Laws that forbid or impair women's access to abortion in fact have many effects on women's lives. Restrictions on abortion affect not only pregnant women, but all women who believe they are capable of conceiving, whether or not they are presently sexually active, whether or not they engage in some form of contraceptive practice. Because such laws deprive women of means to determine whether or not they will become mothers should they become pregnant, they impair the possibility of sexual pleasure for women, and aggravate the force of sexual fear. Abortion-restrictive regulation does not of course prevent all pregnant women who seek abortions from obtaining them; rather, it subjects all pregnant women seeking abortions to social indignity, some to illicit procedures fraught with fear and physical hazard, and the rest to the burden of state-coerced pregnancy.

. . . .

For too long this nation has regulated women's status through the institution of motherhood. Its judgments about the ways in which it is reasonable to impose on women as mothers are deeply distorted by a long history of denigrating, controlling, and using women as mothers. For this reason, the physiological paradigms that currently dominate review of reproductive regulation are deeply pernicious. They invite public actors to use state power against women without the minimal forms of self-scrutiny that requirements of equal protection normally impose. They invite abusive exercise of public power against women because they suspend rudimentary safeguards on the exercise of such power in precisely those circumstances where safeguards are most needed. Before this society rushes to judge women's conduct toward the unborn, it ought to reflect upon its own conduct toward women. Instead of devising new ways to control women as mothers, it needs to promote the welfare of future generations by means that respect and support women in their work as mothers. Only then will the story of the nineteenth century criminal abortion campaign be a closed chapter in American history—and not a continuing part of American life.

* * *

Like Siegel, historian Linda Gordon notes the opposition to various forms of birth control in the nineteenth century. However, as Gordon observes, women, perhaps paradoxically, were opposed to the effort to expand access to contraception. As Gordon explains, although nineteenth-century feminists were favorably inclined toward contraception, they hoped that its use would be linked to a broader campaign for women's liberation and equality.

Linda Gordon, *Why Nineteenth-Century Feminists Did Not Support "Birth Control" and Twentieth-Century Feminists Do: Feminism, Reproduction, and the Family, in* Rethinking the Family: Some Feminist Questions

40–52 (Barrie Thorne & Marie Yalom eds. 1982).

. . . The abortion struggle today is in part an updated version of a birth-control struggle at least 150 years old. No issue of women's liberation has ever been as hotly contested; no conflict in industrial society, with the exception of the social relations of labor itself, has been as bitter; and there may be no social issue that is more passionately debated.

Let me introduce a brief historical summary. Between earliest recorded history, and even as far back as some prehistoric archeological evidence, until the 1870s, there were no significant technological advances in birth control whatever. All the basic forms of birth control—abortions, douches, condoms, and devices to cover the cervix—are ancient. The social regulation of the use of these techniques changed in various historical eras and places in the context of power relations and economic needs. By and large, birth control was uncontroversial and widely practiced in preagricultural societies; by contrast, in peasant societies large families were an asset, continuing high infant mortality necessitated many pregnancies, and birth control was suppressed.

. . . [F]rom the 1840s there appeared the first American birth-control movement within the women's rights movement, in the form of a demand for "voluntary motherhood." The meaning of that phrase should be evident. It had no antimotherhood implications; in fact, Voluntary Motherhood advocates argued that willing mothers would be better mothers.

. . . Voluntary Motherhood was a campaign exclusively focused on women. It must be distinguished from two other, separate streams in the historical movement for contraception. The first was neo-Malthusianism, or population control, a plan to ameliorate social problems by reducing the size of populations on a large scale.

. . . The second movement, eugenics, was really a subcategory of neo-Malthusianism, an effort to apply population control differentially and thus to reduce the size of certain unwanted human "types". . . . The upper-class WASP elite of the industrial North became increasingly aware of its own small-family pattern, in contrast to the continuing large-family preferences of immigrants and the rural poor. From as early as the 1860s the fear of so-called race suicide emerged. In that phrase, race was used ambiguously: to equate the "human race" with WASPs. Out of fears of a loss of political (and social and economic) dominance to an expanding population of "inferiors" grew a plan for reestablishing social stability through differential breeding: The superior should have more children, the inferior fewer. (In the twentieth century blacks and the welfare poor replaced immigrants and sharecroppers as the primary targets of eugenical policies. But that is getting ahead of our story.)

. . . By the end of the century, then, there were three separate reproduction control movements—Voluntary Motherhood, population control, and eugenics. All three were to some extent responses to the fact that birth control was being widely used . . . [but] there was a sharp difference among them: The eugenicists and population controllers supported the legalization of contraception, but the Voluntary Motherhood advocates opposed it. For birth control, they proposed abstinence—either periodic, based on an incorrect rhythm method, or long-term, allowing for intercourse only when a conception was desired. . . .

. . . .

The Voluntary Motherhood advocates . . . realized that while women needed freedom from excessive childbearing, they also needed the respect and self-respect motherhood brought. By and large, motherhood then was the only challenging, dignified, and rewarding work that women could get (it still is, for the majority of women). Second, they understood that while women needed freedom from pregnancy, they also needed freedom from male sexual tyranny, especially in a society that had almost completely suppressed accurate information about female sexuality and replaced it with information and attitudes so false as to virtually guarantee that women would not enjoy sex. Abstinence as a form of birth control may well have been the solution that made most sense in the particular historical circumstance. Abstinence helped women strengthen their ability to say no to their husbands' sexual demands, for example, while contraception and abortion would have weakened it.

... The Voluntary Motherhood advocates faced a second set of contradictions in their ambivalent attitude toward individualism. The essence of their feminism was their anger at the suppression of the capabilities and aspirations of individual women. They envisaged a public sphere of adults equal in rights, though unequal in native abilities, each individual guaranteed maximum opportunity for self-development.... [W]hat civilization *meant* to nineteenth-century feminists was the tempering of the individual struggle for survival by greater social values and aspirations that, they believed, women supported through their nurturing role in the division of labor....

...They argued that more respect for women should be used to reinforce motherhood, to give it more freedom, respect, and self-respect. Hence their reluctance to accept a form of birth control that could exempt women from motherhood.

... When socialist feminists first adopted pro-birth-control positions in the early twentieth century, nonfeminist socialists had divided reactions. The majority of the U.S. Socialist Party, for example, believed that, at best, birth control was a dangerous distraction from the class struggle.... Some Socialists, however, supported the birth-control movement, if weakly, because they believed it could reduce women's domestic burdens and free them for greater political activity in support of their class interests.

By contrast, black radicals in the United States in the 1910s tended to support birth control far more frequently. They saw it as a tool for the self-determination of black Americans. In the 1920s and afterward, however, birth control was increasingly absorbed into programs aimed not at self-determination but at social control by the elite. Eugenics became a dominant motif in the effort to legalize contraception and sterilization, and even birth controllers from the socialist-feminist tradition, such as Margaret Sanger, made accommodations with the eugenicists. These policies cost the birth controllers most of their black support—and many of their white radical supporters as well.

... Thus the cry of genocide that began to be raised against reproductive-control campaigns in the 1930s, and continues today, is not wrong. It is only too simple. It arises from at least three sources. First, the tensions between white feminism and black liberation movements that arose in the struggle over the Fourteenth Amendment underlie this problem and have virtually blotted out the contribution of black feminists (not only today but historically). . . .

Second, beyond this general distrust is the actual racism of the white-dominated women's movement, which was clearly manifested in the birth-control movement as much by socialist as by liberal feminists. . . .

Third, and most pertinent, is the dominance of the relatively conservative population-control and eugenics programs over the feminist birth-control program. Planned Parenthood's use of small-family ideology and its international emphasis on sterilization rather than safe and controllable contraception have far overshadowed its feminist program for women's self-determination. . . .

The[se] distinctions started to reappear in the 1960s with the emergence of abortion as the key reproductive-control issue. In the early twentieth century, most feminists did not support abortion for several reasons: reluctance to take on too much of a backlash at once; their own conviction that sex belonged primarily in marriage, where contraceptive use was more likely to be systematic and where an unplanned child was not usually the total disaster it might be for an unmarried woman; and the fact that most poor women still had no access to decent medical care. The contemporary drive for abortion rights was a response to several factors that developed gradually in the 1920–60 period. First, there was a great increase in teen-age sexual activity without contraceptive use— in other words, it was not technology that increased sexual activity but the behavior that increased the demand. Second, there was a great increase in the number of families absolutely dependent on two incomes and an increase in women-headed families, thus making it no longer possible for mothers to stay home with an unplanned baby; this spurred the demand for abortion among married women for whom contraception had failed. The third and perhaps more surprising factor behind the movement for abortion rights was the relative underdevelopment of contraception. In this factor we see yet another flaw in the technological-determinist explanation of birth control. Far from being an area of great progress, the field of contraception today lags far behind our need for it. Women must still do almost all the contracepting, and they are forced to choose among unwieldy, dangerous, or irreversible methods.

The changes in the dominant feminist positions about birth control should now be clearer. For feminists, the issue of reproductive control is a part of an overall calculus of how to improve women's situation. The birth-control campaign of the late 1960s and '70s was not a single-issue reform campaign, such as that of the population controllers and eugenists who had dominated in the 1920s through '50s. Feminists always have to balance the gains and losses from contraception and abortion against the other problems women face, such as unequal employment opportunity, unequal wealth, unequal education, and unequal domestic responsibilities. . . .

. . . In thinking about the family, contemporary feminism, like feminism a century ago, contains an ambivalence between individualism and its critique. The individualism has reached a much higher development with the challenge to gender definitions. Few modern feminists would argue that women are innately suited to domestic activity and unsuited to public activity. The rejection of gender is an ultimate commitment to the right of all individuals to develop to their highest potential. . . . But parts of the feminist movement identify with this ideal. Those parts of the movement have deemphasized the other side of the feminist tradition: the critique of the man-made society, the refusal to accept merely integration of female individuals into a competition whose rules we did not define and do not endorse. There is, in fact, a tradition of feminist criticism of capitalism itself, representing it as the opposite of the nurturing values of motherhood. Without weakening our support of the rights of individual women to seek achievement, it is important to keep both sides of this ambivalence in view. Feminists have conducted a close scrutiny of the family in the last years and have seen how oppressive it can be for women. But undermining the family has costs, for women as well as men, in the form of isolation and the further deterioration of child raising, general unhappiness, social distrust and, solipsism; and sensitivity to these problems is also part of the feminist heritage.

The feminist critique of individualism should give us some insight into the opposition. What are the abortion opponents afraid of? I do not think it is the loss of fetuses, for most. . . . The abortion opponents today, like those of a hundred years ago, are afraid of a loss of mothering, in the symbolic sense. They fear a completely individualized society with all services based on cash nexus relationships, without the influence of nurturing women counteracting the completely egoistic principles of the economy, and without any forms in which children can learn about lasting human commitments to other people.

. . . The problem is to develop a feminist program and philosophy that defends individual rights and also builds constructive bonds between individuals. . . . The truth is that feminism has undermined the family as it once existed faster than it has been able to substitute more egalitarian communities. This is not a criticism of the women's movement. Perhaps families held together by domination, fear, violence, squelched talents, and resignation should not survive. Furthermore, the women's movement has already done a great deal toward building supportive institutions that prefigure a better society: day-care centers, shelters, women's centers, communes, gay bars and bars where women feel comfortable, publications, women's studies programs, and health clinics.

. . . [But t]hese very successes have created problems. Clearly the successes created a backlash. More complicated, the successes in consciousness changing outstripped successes in community and institution building. The nuclear, male-dominated family remains for the vast majority the only experience of permanent, noninstrumental personal commitments. Within the family, motherhood still is—and may forever be—one of the most challenging and rewarding emotional and work experiences people can have. The feminist reproductive rights movement faces the task of finding a program that equally defends women's individual rights to freedom, including sexual freedom, *and* the dignity of women's need and capacity for nurturance and being nurtured, with or without biological motherhood. This is but the application to one issue—reproduction—of the general task of feminism: to defend all the gains of bourgeois individualism and feminism while transcending the capitalist-competitive aspects of individualism with a vision of loving, egalitarian communities.

NOTES

1.   *The social meaning of contraception.* Linda Gordon paints a complicated picture of the social impulses surrounding contraceptive use during the nineteenth century. In your view, are the current debates around contraceptive use, abortion, and sterilization also informed by similar impulses? Are they as complicated as the picture Gordon paints?

2.   *Race and contraception.* Gordon notes the racial dynamics of birth control movements, specifically identifying the tensions between white feminism and black liberation movements. Is the current debate around contraception also inflected with notions of race?

3.   *Abstinence then and now.* Gordon observes that abstinence as a form of birth control may well have been the most desirable solution for early feminists with respect to reproductive control. Today, however, abstinence has become the core of conservative responses to efforts to educate adolescents about abortion and sexual intercourse. What social dynamics, if any, explain the shift in understanding abstinence as a method of contraception rather than as the antithesis of contraception?

B. THE REGULATION OF CONTRACEPTION

1. TECHNOLOGICAL CHANGE AND BIRTH CONTROL

Historians have noted that use of contraception has been around as long as civilization, and that the debates around its use have been around for almost as long. In the following excerpts, historians detail the progress of contraception, from primitive methods to methods more familiar to modern readers as a result of technological advances that accompanied industrialization. Below, historian Norman Himes translates Egyptian papyri that detail various methods that the ancient Egyptians used to prevent conception.

Norman Himes, Medical History of Contraception

59–64 (1970) (excerpted from Boston Medical Library in the
Francis A. Countway Library of Medicine).

If our prehistoric ancestors knew something of contraceptive technique, we shall not be surprised to learn that in the civilizations of antiquity such knowledge was great in extent than heretofore supposed. The antique peoples studied in this Part are the Egyptians, ancient Hebrews and early Christians, as well as certain writers representing the thought of Greece and Rome. Attention will first be directed to contraceptive technique as reported in Egyptian papyri.

§ 1   Petri or Kahun Papyrus (1850 B.C.)

The oldest medical prescriptions for the prevention of conception still extant in writing are to be found in certain Egyptian papyri. The Petri Papyrus . . . dating from the reign of Amenemhat III of the Twelfth Dynasty (c. 1850 B.C.), is a medical papyrus consisting of gynecological instructions and prescriptions. . . . [I]t is by no means certain that the contraception practices recommended were sheer quackery. . . .

Dawson has well summarized the purport of these prescriptions in saying that "The first consists of crocodile's dung mixed with a paste-like vehicle, and is probably a pessary for insertion in the vagina; the second consists of irrigating [or plugging?] the vagina with honey and natron [native sodium carbonate], and the third mentions a gum-like substance for insertion in the vagina."

We may not consider whether the use of these substances was exclusively magical or whether perchance their use, empirically determined in the first instance, was not also based upon some appreciation of their physiological properties. . . . [H]oney, like oil, has a physical clogging capacity; and that greasy substances form the base of many modern contraceptive suppositories. . . . [T]he use of crocodile's dung inserted as a pessary in the vagina 'is not essentially unlike a sponge soak in some weak acid,' a contraceptive more or less effectively employed in our time. . . .

. . . The motility of spermatazoa is arrested at a pH of 6.0 or below . . . crocodile dung, in most instances, would increase alkalinity and promote conception. . . . The use of dung in contraceptive pessary can be traced in the literature for over 3,000 years. After the Kahun papyrus (1850 B.C.) it reappeared in various works produced in the ninth, eleventh, and thirteenth centuries. Of course, the prescriptions varied somewhat; but their continuity is the significant feature.

§ 2   Ebers (1550 B.C.)

The Ebers papyrus . . . from 1550 B.C. . . . contains perhaps the first reference in writing to a medicated lint tampon designed to prevent conception. The original prescription reads as follows: "Beginning of the recipes made for women in order to cause that a woman should cease to conceive for one year, two years, or three years: Tips (?) of acacia. D' r. t' Triturate with a measure of honey, moisten lint therewith and place in her vulva."

The remarkable nature of this recipe, dating from 1550 B.C., is apparent when it is recalled that jellies in which lactic acid is the active agent are used by most of the birth-control clinics in England and the U.S.A., sometimes alone (being smeared on the cervix and into the fornices by turning a key on a tube which expels the jelly or paste through a nozzle previously inserted), sometimes as a smear on cervical rubber caps or vaginal diaphragms to prevent spermatozoa from swimming around the edge. Gum Arabic, or gum acacia, is also generally used in the production of modern contraceptive jellies as vehicle or medium.

* * *

The advent of the industrial age brought considerable changes in all aspects of nineteenth-century life. Among those changes were technological advancements that led to improvements in sexual aids, contraceptives, and prophylactics. As John D'Emilio and Estelle Freedman note in the following excerpt, Charles Goodyear's 1844 patent to "vulcanize" rubber transformed the manufacture of contraceptives and sexual aids by permitting the creation of inexpensive, durable and flexible products.

John D'Emilio and Estelle Freedman, Intimate Matters: A History of Sexuality in America
60, 130–32 (1988).

In 1846, a diaphragm was patented under the title "The Wife's Protector." Pessaries, which were sold in drugstores to help correct prolapsed (fallen) uterus, came in over a hundred varieties—wood, cotton, and sponge. By the late nineteenth century, devices made of India rubber could be used like vaginal diaphragms, while rubber condoms joined the contraceptive market. Even books that recommended the "natural mode," or rhythm, included detailed information on sponges, condoms, and syringes for douching.

Not only middle-class readers of marital advice guides had access to contraceptive information. Advertisements in newspapers and almanacs reached a wider audience, especially in cities, while declining prices made contraceptives available for workers as well as members of the middle class. . . . An 1861 *New York Times* advertisement revealed that Dr. Power's French Preventives (condoms) sold for five dollars per dozen. By the 1870s, the price of these and other contraceptives had fallen, so that most couples could afford to purchase condoms for six to twelve cents each, diaphragms for a dollar, or syringes for forty cents. . . . In addition to the emergence of new types of intimate relationships, the social spaces in which the expression of sexuality took place expanded over the course of the nineteenth century. Although the middle-class family valued sexual privacy and called for public reticence, within working-class neighborhoods, sex retained its public presence, and the growing world of commerce increasingly incorporated sexuality within its nexus. Beginning in port cities of the late eighteenth century, certain urban districts catered to sexual commerce.

. . . In addition to the lure of dance halls and houses of assignation, by midcentury sex for sale took the form of cheap "licentious" literature, or what would later be termed pornography. Prior to the 1840s, Americans could procure only limited reprints of erotic classics published in Europe. . . . The production of an indigenous American pornography began after 1846, when William Haynes . . . took the money he had made by publishing *Fanny Hill* in the United States and reinvested it into the production of cheap erotic novels. Titles such as *Confessions of a Lady's Waiting Maid* (1848), *Amours of an American Adventurer in the New World and Old* (1865), and *The Merry Order of St. Bridget* (a flagellation novel, 1857) rolled off American presses.

. . . Titillating pictures and literature continued to circulate during the late nineteenth century. In the newly popular pool halls, working-class men exchanged obscene postcards and books, while images of semiclothed women adorned the wall. . . . [At] Saloons . . . men could drink, talk, and glance through the scandalous *Police Gazette*. This popular crime and sports newspaper, which often portrayed women of the "demimonde," carried ads for patent medicines promising to cure syphilis and gonorrhea or to enlarge "certain parts" of the body.

* * *

The previous selection suggests a social milieu rife with sexual influences and impulses. For many, this frankly sexual culture was threatening to marriage, the family, and society as a whole. It was not long before the state—here, the U.S. government—took strong steps to curb this perceived culture of licentiousness.

The Comstock Act of 1873
ch. 258, 18 Stat. 598 (codified as amended at 18 U.S.C. § 1461 (2014)).

An Act for the Suppression of Trade in, and Circulation of, obscene Literature and Articles of Immoral Use

Be it enacted by the Senate and House of Representatives in the United States of America in Congress assembled, That whoever, within the District of Columbia or any of the Territories of the United States, or other place within the exclusive jurisdiction of the United States, shall sell, or lend, or give away, or in many manner exhibit, or shall offer to sell, or to lend, or to give away, or in any manner to exhibit, or shall otherwise publish or offer to publish in any manner, or shall have in his possession, for any such purpose or purposes, an obscene book, pamphlet, paper, writing, advertisement, circular, print, picture, drawing or other representation, figure, or image on or of paper or other material, or any cast instrument, or other article of an immoral nature, or any drug or medicine, or any article whatever, for the prevention of conception, or for causing unlawful abortion, or shall advertise the same for sale, or shall write or print, or cause to be written or printed, any card, circular, book, pamphlet, advertisement, or notice of any kind, stating when, where, how, or of whom, or by what means, any of the articles in this section hereinbefore mentioned, can be purchased or obtained, or shall manufacture, draw, or print, or in any wise make any of such articles, shall be deemed guilty of a misdemeanor, and on conviction thereof in any court of the United States having criminal jurisdiction in the District of Columbia, or in any Territory or place within the exclusive jurisdiction in the District of Columbia, or in any Territory or place within the exclusive jurisdiction of the United States, where such misdemeanor shall have been committed; and on conviction thereof, he shall be imprisoned at hard labor in the penitentiary for not less than six months nor more than five years for each offense, or fined not less than one hundred dollars nor more than two thousand dollars, with costs of court.

Sec. 2.   That section one hundred and forty-eight of the act to revise consolidate and amend the statutes relating to the Post-office Department approved June eighth, eighteen hundred and seventy-two, be amended to read as follows:

"Sec. 148. That no obscene, lewd, or lascivious book, pamphlet, picture, paper, print, or other publication of an indecent character, or any article or thing designed or intended for the prevented of conception or procuring of abortion, nor any article or thing intended or adapted for any indecent or immoral use or nature, nor any written or printed card, circular, book, pamphlet, advertisement or notice of any kind giving information, directly or indirectly, where, or how, or of whom, or by what means either of the things before mentioned may be obtained or made, nor any letter upon the envelope of which, or postal-card upon which indecent or scurrilous epithets may be written or printed, shall be carried in the mail, and any person who shall knowingly deposit, or cause to be deposited, for mailing or delivery, any of the hereinbefore-mentioned articles or things, or any notice, or paper containing any advertisement relating to the aforesaid articles or things, and any person who, in pursuance of any plan or scheme for disposing of any of the hereinbefore-mentioned articles or things, shall take, or cause to be taken, from the mail any such letter or package, shall be deemed guilty of a misdemeanor, and on conviction thereof, shall, for every offense, be fined not less than one hundred dollars nor more than five thousand dollars, or imprisoned at hard labor not less than one year nor more than ten years, or both, in the discretion of the judge."

erotic prints or advertisment of contraception not allowed

charges for violation

Sec. 3.   That all persons are prohibited from importing into the United States, from any foreign country, any of the hereinbefore-mentioned articles or things, except the drugs hereinbefore-mentioned when imported in bulk, and not put up for any of the purposes before mentioned; and all such prohibited articles in the course of importation shall be detained by the officer of customs, and proceedings taken against the same under section five of this act.

Sec. 4.   That whoever, being an officer, agent, or employee of the government of the United States, shall knowingly aid or abet any person engaged in any violation of this act, shall be deemed guilty of a misdemeanor, and, on conviction thereof, shall, for every offense, be punished as provided in section two of this act.

Sec. 5.   That any judge of any district or circuit court of the United States, within the proper district, before whom complaint in writing of any violation of this act shall be made, to the satisfaction of such judge, and founded on knowledge or belief, and, if upon belief, setting forth the ground of such belief, and supported by oath or affirmation of the complainant, may issue, conformably to the Constitution, a warrant directing him to search for, seize, and take possession of any such article or thing herein-before mentioned, and to make due and immediate return thereof, to the end that the same may be condemned and destroyed by proceedings, which shall be conducted in the same manner as other proceedings in case of municipal seizure, and with the same right of appeal or writ of error: Provided, That nothing in this section shall be construed as repealing the one hundred and forty-eighth section of the act of which this act is amendatory, or to affect any indictments heretofore found for offenses against the same, but the said indictments may be prosecuted to judgment as if this section had not been enacted.

APPROVED, March 3, 1873.

NOTES

1.   *Origins of the Comstock Act.* Although the Comstock Act has come to occupy an important position in the history of sexual regulation, its origins were more ambiguous. Indeed, historian Andrea Tone remarks that "[i]n the final hours of the term, [the Forty-second] Congress passed some 260 acts, the precise provisions of which remained unknown to many members." One of these measures, passed in a "last-minute frenzy" was an anti-obscenity bill that defined contraceptives as obscene materials. The statute was called the Comstock Act after its chief proponent, the morals crusader and United States Postal Inspector Anthony Comstock. It was "embedded in a broader postal act, passed after little political debate and was signed into law along with 117 other bills." ANDREA TONE, DEVICES AND DESIRES: A HISTORY OF CONTRACEPTIVES IN AMERICA 3–4 (2002).

2.   *Condoms in the courts.* In a 1930 case, Youngs Rubber Corporation, the manufacturer of the popular Trojan brand condoms, sued competitor C.I. Lee & Company for trademark infringement. Youngs Rubber claimed to have

trademarked the Trojan name for its products. C.I. Lee, it alleged, had improperly appropriated the Trojan name for its own competing products. Youngs Rubber admitted that it had sold and distributed its products in interstate commerce. C.I. Lee seized upon this information to claim that Youngs Rubber had violated the Comstock Act. According to C.I. Lee, because it illegally distributed its products, Youngs Rubber was precluded under the Trademark Act from bringing a trademark suit. The United States Court of Appeals for the Second Circuit observed that the sale and manufacture of contraceptives was not absolutely prohibited by federal statute. And under New York law, it continued, "such articles" may be provided to patients by "lawfully practicing physicians, or by their direction." With this in mind, "it cannot be held under either federal or state law that all sales of the plaintiff's article are illegal. Since the article may be legally sold under some circumstances, we see no reason to doubt the validity of the trade-mark." *Youngs Rubber Corp. v. C.I. Lee & Co.*, 45 F.2d 103, 107–08 (2d Cir. 1930).

United States v. One Package
86 F.2d 737 (2d Cir. 1936).

■ A. HAND, J.

The United States filed this libel against a package containing 120 vaginal pessaries . . ., alleged to be imported contrary to section 305(a) of the Tariff Act of 1930. From the decree dismissing the libel the United States has appealed. In our opinion the decree should be affirmed.

The claimant Dr. Stone is a New York physician who has been licensed to practice for sixteen years and has specialized in gynecology. The package containing pessaries was sent to her by a physician in Japan for the purpose of trying them in her practice and giving her opinion as to their usefulness for contraceptive purposes. She testified that she prescribes the use of pessaries in cases where it would not be desirable for a patient to undertake a pregnancy. . . . The New York Penal Law which makes it in general a misdemeanor to sell or give away or to advertise or offer for sale any articles for the prevention of conception excepts furnishing such articles to physicians who may in good faith prescribe their use for the cure or prevention of disease. *People v. Sanger*, 118 N.E. 637 (N.Y. 1917). The witnesses for both the government and the claimant testified that the use of contraceptives was in many cases necessary for the health of women and that they employed articles of the general nature of the pessaries in their practice. . . .

Section 305(a) of the Tariff Act of 1930 provides that: "All persons are prohibited from importing into the United States from any foreign country . . . any article whatever for the prevention of conception or for causing unlawful abortion."

The question is whether physicians who import such articles as those involved in the present case in order to use them for the health of their patients are excepted by implication from the literal terms of the statute. Certainly they are excepted in the case of an abortive which is prescribed to save life, for section 305(a) of the Tariff Act only prohibits the importation of articles for causing "unlawful abortion." . . .

Section 305(a) of the Tariff Act of 1930, as well as title 18, section 334, of the U.S. Code, prohibiting the mailing, and title 18, section 396 of the U.S. Code, prohibiting the importing or transporting in interstate commerce of articles "designed, adapted, or intended for preventing conception, or producing abortion," all originated from the so-called Comstock Act of 1873, which was entitled, "An Act for the Suppression of Trade in, and Circulation of, obscene Literature and Articles of immoral Use."

Section 1 of the act of 1873 made it a crime to sell, lend or give away, "any drug or medicine, or any article whatever, for the prevention of conception, or for causing unlawful abortion." Section 2 prohibited sending through the mails "any article or thing designed or intended for the prevention of conception or procuring of abortion." Section 3 forbade the importation of "any of the hereinbefore-mentioned articles or things, except the drugs hereinbefore-mentioned when imported in bulk, and not put up for any of the purposes before mentioned." All the statutes we have referred to were part of a continuous scheme to suppress immoral articles and obscene literature and should so far as possible be construed together and consistently. If this be done, the articles here in question ought not to be forfeited when not intended for an immoral purpose. . . .

It is argued that section 305(a) of the Tariff Act of 1930 differs from the statutes prohibiting carriage by mail and in interstate commerce of articles "intended for preventing conception or producing abortion" because in section 305(a) the adjective "unlawful" is coupled with the word "abortion," but not with the words "prevention of conception." But in the Comstock Act, from which the others are derived, the word "unlawful" was sometimes inserted to qualify the word "abortion," and sometimes omitted. It seems hard to suppose that under the second and third sections articles intended for use in procuring abortions were prohibited in all cases while, under the first section, they were only prohibited when intended for use in an "unlawful abortion." Nor can we see why the statute should, at least in section 1, except articles for producing abortions if used to safeguard life, and bar articles for preventing conception though employed by a physician in the practice of his profession in order to protect the health of his patients or to save them from infection.

It is true that in 1873, when the Comstock Act was passed, information now available as to the evils resulting in many cases from conception was most limited, and accordingly it is argued that the language prohibiting the sale or mailing of contraceptives should be taken literally and that Congress intended to bar the use of such articles completely. While we may assume that section 305(a) of the Tariff Act of

1930 exempts only such articles as the act of 1873 excepted, yet we are satisfied that this statute, as well as all the acts we have referred to, embraced only such articles as Congress would have denounced as immoral if it had understood all the conditions under which they were to be used. Its design, in our opinion, was not to prevent the importation, sale, or carriage by mail of things which might intelligently be employed by conscientious and competent physicians for the purpose of saving life or promoting the well being of their patients. The word "unlawful" would make this clear as to articles for producing abortion, and the courts have read an exemption into the act covering such articles even where the word "unlawful" is not used. The same exception should apply to articles for preventing conception. . . . It seems unreasonable to suppose that the national scheme of legislation involves such inconsistencies and requires the complete suppression of articles, the use of which in many cases is advocated by such a weight of authority in the medical world. . . .

NOTES

1.   *(Re-)linking contraception and obscenity.* In the late nineteenth century, a growing consumer culture rooted in male sexual pleasure made the once-tenuous link between contraception and obscenity more concrete. Concern about men's widespread access to condoms, pornography, and dance halls melded these discrete items into a single, troublesome whole: the new obscenity. The new obscenity was particularly threatening because of the kinds of men imagined to be using these affordable condoms, pictures, and dance halls. The low prices for these products meant that working men and immigrants, who did not need to be literate to avail themselves of cheap erotica, might engage in forms of sexual pleasure (including masturbation) that elites and middle-class people saw as threatening to the family. *See* JOHN D'EMILIO AND ESTELLE FREEDMAN, INTIMATE MATTERS: A HISTORY OF SEXUALITY IN AMERICA 130–31, 156–60 (1988). What sexual anxieties have the new technologies of our own era produced?

2.   *Moving from obscenity to contraception.* As we have just seen, the connection between sex and normative values about marriage and the family rendered abortion and contraception obscene in and of themselves. However, historian Leigh Ann Wheeler goes further, making a more provocative claim. As she notes, the ACLU's efforts to secure First Amendment rights eventually evolved to include access to information regarding contraception and abortion. The expansion of "free speech," Wheeler argues, was the result of a paradigm shift in which the ACLU came to understand free speech as, "not only the right to speak but also the right to *consume* speech," including information about sex and contraception. LEIGH ANN WHEELER, HOW SEX BECAME A CIVIL LIBERTY 6 (2012) (emphasis added).

3.   *Sex and civil liberties.* Legal historian Laura Weinrib has also documented the links between the ACLU's First Amendment advocacy and the organization's entry into obscenity litigation. The catalyst for this change, she argues, was a postal censorship dispute involving Mary Ware Dennett's sex education pamphlet, *The Sex Side of Life: An Explanation for*

Young People. Despite its many endorsements from medical practitioners, religious groups, and government agencies, postal authorities declared the pamphlet obscene. The ACLU defended Dennett and *The Sex Side of Life* because it believed that liberalizing access to scientific knowledge promoted the public interest, while also highlighting the dangers of suppressing subversive ideas. However, as Weinrib recounts, *United States v. Dennett* underwrote a more sweeping anti-censorship campaign. Dennett's heavily publicized conviction generated popular hostility toward obscenity laws and convinced ACLU attorneys that speech should be protected regardless of its social value. In this way, *Dennett* laid the foundation for the ACLU's focus on civil liberties premised on individual expressive freedom. *See* Laura Weinrib, *The Sex Side of Civil Liberties:* United States v. Dennett *and the Changing Face of Free Speech*, 30 LAW & HIST. REV. 325, 326–27 (2012).

4.   *Origins of the modern birth-control movement.* Margaret Sanger is credited with founding the modern birth control movement. In 1916, Sanger opened her first birth control clinic in the Brownsville neighborhood of Brooklyn, New York. Her actions led to her arrest and conviction, which she challenged in *People v. Sanger*, 118 N.E. 637 (N.Y. 1918). There, the New York Court of Appeals affirmed Sanger's conviction, while also identifying an exception to state obscenity laws for lawfully practicing physicians and those operating at a physician's direction. Sanger then went on to found the American Birth Control League (ABCL) in 1921. The ABCL represented a more conservative, natalist turn in Sanger's contraceptive philosophies. In its mission statement, the ABCL held "that children should be (1) Conceived in love; (2) Born of the mother's conscious desire; (3) And only begotten under conditions which render possible the heritage of health." MARGARET SANGER, THE PIVOT OF CIVILIZATION 280 (1922). The organization pursued greater access to contraception on the ground that "every woman must possess the power and freedom to prevent conception except when these conditions can be satisfied." *Id.* In 1939, the ABCL absorbed its more radical competitor, Mary Ware Dennett's Voluntary Parenthood League, and Sanger assumed leadership of the newly-formed organization—the Birth Control Federation of America (BCFA). *See Biographical Sketch*, N.Y. UNIV.: MARGARET SANGER PAPERS PROJECT (2014), https://sanger.hosting.nyu.edu/aboutms/msbio/. In 1942, BCFA changed its name to Planned Parenthood Federation of America. *See id.*

5.   *The family as social policy.* As the trajectory of Sanger's career suggests, the fight for birth control became increasingly professionalized and less radical. Historian Linda Gordon notes that while earlier organizations (and Sanger herself) saw birth control as a tool for social justice and the liberation of women, over time, the interest in access to birth control became grounded in efforts to strengthen the family—and society—through "family planning." *See* LINDA GORDON, THE MORAL PROPERTY OF WOMEN: A HISTORY OF BIRTH CONTROL POLITICS IN AMERICA 171–72, 242 (1974) (2002).

6.   *Sanger and eugenics.* The history of the birth-control movement must grapple with its association with the rise of the eugenics movement in the United States. In the nineteenth and early twentieth centuries, eugenicists advocated "rational control" of reproduction as a means of improving society.

On this account, reproduction by "unfit" persons should be curtailed, whether through sterilization or less invasive means of contraception. Whether Margaret Sanger herself was a eugenicist—and an adherent to the more racially-charged strains of eugenics—is a matter of some debate. Ellen Chesler's voluminous biography of Sanger argues that although Sanger used eugenic rhetoric in the service of her cause, by the standards of the time, Sanger was remarkably non-racist. As Chesler explains, "Margaret Sanger was never herself a racist, but she lived in a profoundly bigoted society, and her failure to repudiate prejudice unequivocally—especially when it was manifest among proponents of her cause—has haunted her ever since." ELLEN CHESLER, WOMAN OF VALOR: MARGARET SANGER AND THE BIRTH CONTROL MOVEMENT IN AMERICA 15 (2007). That said, some might read the third item in ABCL's founding statement—that children should be "only begotten under conditions which render possible the heritage of health"—as reflecting eugenicist impulses. Historian Daniel Kevles notes that there were both left-wing and right-wing eugenicists. While the left wing aspired to change the social conditions under which women became pregnant and gave birth, the right wing assumed that poverty and other human troubles were the effect of inherited characteristics that were immutable. DANIEL J. KEVLES, IN THE NAME OF EUGENICS: GENETICS AND THE USES OF HUMAN HEREDITY 63–66 (1995).

7. *Race, eugenics, and family planning.* Legal scholar Dorothy E. Roberts has noted the many links between eugenics, racism, and the birth-control movement. As Roberts explains, "[b]irth control policy put into practice an explanation for racial inequality that was rooted in nature rather than power." Further, Roberts notes that black women did not always welcome access to contraception:

> Black people's ambivalence about birth control adds an important dimension to the contemporary understanding of reproductive freedom as a woman's right to choose contraception and abortion. We must acknowledge the justice of ensuring equal access to birth control for poor and minority women without denying the injustice of imposing birth control as a means of reducing their fertility.

DOROTHY E. ROBERTS, KILLING THE BLACK BODY 56–57 (1997).

2. A RIGHT TO BIRTH CONTROL?

Poe v. Ullman
367 U.S. 497 (1961).

■ FRANKFURTER, J.

These appeals challenge the constitutionality, under the Fourteenth Amendment, of Connecticut statutes which, as authoritatively construed by the Connecticut Supreme Court of Errors, prohibit the use of contraceptive devices and the giving of medical advice in the use of such devices. In proceedings seeking declarations of law, not on review of convictions for violation of the statutes, that court has ruled that these statutes would be applicable in the case of married couples and even under claim that conception would constitute a serious threat to the health or life of the female spouse.

. . . .

The Connecticut law prohibiting the use of contraceptives has been on the State's books since 1879. During the more than three-quarters of a century since its enactment, a prosecution for its violation seems never to have been initiated, save in *State v. Nelson*, 126 Conn. 412 (1940). The circumstances of that case . . . only prove the abstract character of what is before us. There, a test case was brought to determine the constitutionality of the Act as applied against two doctors and a nurse who had allegedly disseminated contraceptive information. After the Supreme Court of Errors sustained the legislation on appeal from a demurrer to the information, the State moved to dismiss the information. Neither counsel nor our own researches [sic] have discovered any other attempt to enforce the prohibition of distribution or use of contraceptive devices by criminal process. The unreality of these law suits is illumined by another circumstance. We were advised by counsel for appellants that contraceptives are commonly and notoriously sold in Connecticut drug stores. Yet no prosecutions are recorded; and certainly such ubiquitous, open, public sales would more quickly invite the attention of enforcement officials than the conduct in which the present appellants wish to engage—the giving of private medical advice by a doctor to his individual patients, and their private use of the devices prescribed. The undeviating policy of nullification by Connecticut of its anti-contraceptive laws throughout all the long years that they have been on the statute books bespeaks more than prosecutorial paralysis. What was said in another context is relevant here. "Deeply embedded traditional ways of carrying out state policy . . ."—or not carrying it out—"are often tougher and truer law than the dead words of the written text." *Nashville, C. & St. L.R. Co. v. Browning*, 310 U.S. 362, 369 (1940).

The restriction of our jurisdiction to cases and controversies within the meaning of Article III of the Constitution, is not the sole limitation on the exercise of our appellate powers, especially in cases raising constitutional questions. The policy reflected in numerous cases and over a long period was thus summarized in the oft-quoted statement of Mr. Justice Brandeis: "The Court [has] developed, for its own governance in the cases confessedly within its jurisdiction, a series of rules under which it has avoided passing upon a large part of all the constitutional questions pressed upon it for decision." . . . [These] rules . . . have derived from the historically defined, limited nature and function of courts and from the recognition that, within the framework of our adversary system, the adjudicatory process is most securely founded when it is exercised under the impact of a lively conflict between antagonistic demands, actively pressed, which make resolution of the controverted issue a practical necessity. In part they derive from the fundamental federal and tripartite character of our National Government and from the role—restricted by its very responsibility—of the federal courts, and particularly this Court, within that structure.

These considerations press with special urgency in cases challenging legislative action or state judicial action as repugnant to the Constitution. "The best teaching of this Court's experience admonishes us not to entertain constitutional questions in advance of the strictest necessity." . . .

. . . .

. . . It is clear that the mere existence of a state penal statute would constitute insufficient grounds to support a federal court's adjudication of its constitutionality in proceedings brought against the State's prosecuting officials if real threat of enforcement is wanting. . . . The fact that Connecticut has not chosen to press the enforcement of this statute deprives these controversies of the immediacy which is an indispensable condition of constitutional adjudication. This Court cannot be umpire to debates concerning harmless, empty shadows. To find it necessary to pass on these statutes now, in order to protect appellants from the hazards of prosecution, would be to close our eyes to reality.

. . . .

Dismissed.

. . . .

■ BRENNAN, J., concurring.

. . . I am not convinced, on this skimpy record, that these appellants as individuals are truly caught in an inescapable dilemma. The true controversy in this case is over the opening of birth-control clinics on a large scale; it is that which the State has prevented in the past, not the use of contraceptives by isolated and individual married couples. It will be time enough to decide the constitutional questions urged upon us when, if ever, that real controversy flares up again. Until it does, or until the State makes a definite and concrete threat to enforce these laws against individual married couples—a threat which it has never made in the past except under the provocation of litigation—this Court may not be compelled to exercise its most delicate power of constitutional adjudication.

■ DOUGLAS, J., dissenting.

. . . .

If there is a case where the need for this remedy in the shadow of a criminal prosecution is shown, it is this one. . . . Plaintiffs . . . are two sets of husband and wife. One wife is pathetically ill, having delivered a stillborn fetus. If she becomes pregnant again, her life will be gravely jeopardized. This couple have been unable to get medical advice concerning the 'best and safest' means to avoid pregnancy from their physician . . . because if he gave it he would commit a crime. The use of contraceptive devices would also constitute a crime. And it is alleged—and admitted by the State—that the State's Attorney intends to enforce the law by prosecuting offenses under the laws.

A public clinic dispensing birth-control information has indeed been closed by the State. Doctors and a nurse working in that clinic were arrested by the police and charged with advising married women on the use of contraceptives. That litigation produced *State v. Nelson*, which upheld these statutes. That same police raid on the clinic resulted in the seizure of a quantity of the clinic's contraception literature and medical equipment and supplies. . . .

The Court refers to the *Nelson* prosecution as a "test case" and implies that it had little impact. Yet its impact was described differently by a contemporary observer who concluded his comment with this sentence: "This serious setback to the birth control movement (the *Nelson* case) led to the closing of all the clinics in the state, just as they had been previously closed in the state of Massachusetts." At oral argument, counsel for appellants confirmed that the clinics are still closed. . . .

These, then, are the circumstances in which the Court feels that it can, contrary to every principle of American or English common law, go outside the record to conclude that there exists a "tacit agreement" that these statutes will not be enforced. No lawyer, I think, would advise his clients to rely on that "tacit agreement." No police official, I think, would feel himself bound by that "tacit agreement." After our national experience during the prohibition era, it would be absurd to pretend that all criminal statutes are adequately enforced. But that does not mean that bootlegging was the less a crime. In fact, an arbitrary administrative pattern of non-enforcement may increase the hardships of those subject to the law.

When the Court goes outside the record to determine that Connecticut has adopted "The undeviating policy of nullification . . . of its anti-contraceptive laws," it selects a particularly poor case in which to exercise such a novel power. This is not a law which is a dead letter. Twice since 1940, Connecticut has reenacted these laws as part of general statutory revisions. Consistently, bills to remove the statutes from the books have been rejected by the legislature. In short, the statutes—far from being the accidental left-overs of another era—are the center of a continuing controversy in the State.

. . . .

NOTES

1. *Availability of contraception and clinics in Connecticut.* In concluding that the case was not ripe for review, the *Poe* majority emphasized that because the challenged law was unlikely to be enforced, and contraceptives were available throughout Connecticut, there was no justiciable case or controversy. In an impassioned dissent, Justice Douglas provided a counter-

narrative. As he argued, state officials were actively enforcing the challenged law; more troublingly, this enforcement had led to the shuttering of the state's lone remaining contraceptive clinic. More recently, legal historian Mary Dudziak has argued that the burden of the contraceptive crisis to which Douglas adverted in his dissent was borne almost exclusively by "lower-income women who needed the free or low-cost services birth control clinics provided." Mary L. Dudziak, *Just Say No: Birth Control in the Connecticut Supreme Court Before* Griswold v. Connecticut, 75 IOWA L. REV 915, 917 (1990). In light of this evidence of enforcement and its consequences, why did the *Poe* majority insist that there was no justiciable case or controversy?

2.   *A footnote to a footnote? Poe v. Ullman* was litigated alongside another challenge to the Connecticut contraceptive ban. The case, *Trubek v. Ullman*, has been overlooked by many, and to the extent it is acknowledged, it is as a footnote to *Poe*, which in turn became a footnote to *Griswold*. As legal scholar Melissa Murray maintains, *Trubek* is worthy of attention in its own right. At the center of the case were two married Yale Law students, David and Louise Trubek. If the couples in *Poe* reflected a more traditional understanding of marriage, with breadwinning husbands and homemaker wives, the Trubeks represented a new reality—one in which both spouses pursued careers. In this regard, the Trubeks' interest in contraception was rooted in their desire to plan their family in a manner that made sense for their marriage, and, just as importantly, allowed both of them to work as practicing lawyers. As Murray notes, "[i]f the *Poe* plaintiffs reflected contraception's benign potential—saving lives in the face of pregnancy-related health risks—then the Trubeks represented something more alarming." By facilitating more egalitarian marriages and liberating wives to pursue careers—contraception "threatened the disruption of marriage and the family, the foundations of civil society." In the end, the Court never explored the connections between contraception, egalitarian marriage, and women's liberation and equality. *Poe* and *Trubek* were dismissed on jurisdictional grounds, setting the stage for *Griswold*. *See* Melissa Murray, *Overlooking Equality on the Road to* Griswold, 124 YALE L.J. F. 324 (2015).

3.   *The Catholic Church and contraception in Connecticut.* Professor Gene Burns argues that by presenting itself as a moral arbiter for all Connecticut citizens and not just Catholics, the Catholic Church exercised a "moral veto" on the issue of contraceptive access during the period when *Poe* was litigated. In this way, while the Church successfully forestalled legal change on contraception in Connecticut, it could not stanch the rising tide of changing public opinion on the issue of contraception. When public sentiment regarding the propriety of contraceptive use began to shift, the Church's capacity to block legal change dissolved. *See* GENE BURNS, THE MORAL VETO: FRAMING CONTRACEPTION, ABORTION, AND CULTURAL PLURALISM IN THE UNITED STATES 106–07 (2005). In light of the recent actions of the Catholic Church with respect to federal policies mandating contraceptive coverage in employee health plans, see *infra* pp. 684–685, does Burns' claim about the Catholic Church's inability to promote legal change still hold true?

4. *Presaging privacy.* The connections between obscenity and privacy are often overlooked. However, as Leigh Ann Wheeler explains, ACLU lawyers came to see a link between government searches in pursuit of obscene materials and an unarticulated interest in a sphere of liberty beyond government reach. Indeed, they sought to make these connections clear in the landmark Fourth Amendment case, *Mapp v. Ohio*, 367 U.S. 643 (1961). In 1957, three Cleveland police officers forcibly entered Dollree Mapp's home "searching for evidence that Mapp was harboring a bombing suspect[.]" The officers had no warrant. Although they found no such evidence, the officers did find pamphlets, books, and pictures that they considered obscene under Ohio's obscenity law. Mapp sued, ultimately appealing her conviction to the United States Supreme Court, where the case attracted the ACLU's attention. Instead of focusing narrowly on overturning Ohio's obscenity law, ACLU lawyers noted:

> [We] saw great promise in *Mapp v. Ohio* for persuading the Court to prohibit the use of illegally seized evidence in federal cases through the exclusionary rule of the Fourth and Fourteenth Amendments. The same amendments protected Mapp's right to privacy, [we] argued.

LEIGH ANN WHEELER, HOW SEX BECAME A CIVIL LIBERTY 103 (2012). This history illuminates *Poe*'s tentative discussion of a right to privacy. In his dissent, Justice Harlan noted that "the most substantial claim which these married persons press is their right to enjoy the privacy of their marital relations free of the enquiry of the criminal law, whether it be in a prosecution of them or of a doctor whom they have consulted." *Poe*, 367 U.S. at 536 (1961) (J. Harlan, dissenting). Although constitutional protections for the marital relationship were not explicitly articulated in the text of the Constitution, Harlan observed that an interest in such protections was evident in the spirit of other constitutional provisions, like the Fourth Amendment. *Id.* at 552. As we shall see, these observations formed the basis of the Court's landmark decision in *Griswold v. Connecticut*.

5. *Setting the stage for* Griswold. Despite the setback in *Poe v. Ullman*, Planned Parenthood continued to devise ways to challenge the Connecticut statutes prohibiting contraceptive use. As Mary Dudziak describes, on November 1, 1961, Planned Parenthood opened a new birth control clinic in New Haven, Connecticut. The group hoped that the clinic's operation would prompt a criminal inquiry and prosecution, thereby providing the basis for a constitutional challenge. On November 3, two detectives visited the clinic, acting on a complaint they had received from James G. Morris of West Haven, an ardent Catholic who believed that "a Planned Parenthood Center is like a house of prostitution. It is against the natural law which says marital relations are for procreation and not entertainment." A week later, police returned to arrest Estelle Griswold and Lee Buxton, the clinic's Executive Director and Medical Director. Griswold and Buxton were charged with violating the state birth-control ban. Mary L. Dudziak, *Just Say No: Birth Control in the Connecticut Supreme Court Before* Griswold v. Connecticut, 75 IOWA L. REV. 915, 937 (1990).

Griswold v. Connecticut

381 U.S. 479 (1965).

■ DOUGLAS, J.

Appellant Griswold is Executive Director of the Planned Parenthood League of Connecticut. Appellant Buxton is a licensed physician and a professor at the Yale Medical School who served as Medical Director for the League at its Center in New Haven—a center open and operating from November 1 to November 10, 1961, when appellants were arrested.

They gave information, instruction, and medical advice to *married persons* as to the means of preventing conception.... Fees were usually charged, although some couples were serviced free.

The statutes whose constitutionality is involved in this appeal are §§ 53–32 and 54–196 of the General Statutes of Connecticut (1958 rev.). The former provides:

> Any person who uses any drug, medicinal article or instrument for the purpose of preventing conception shall be fined not less than fifty dollars or imprisoned not less than sixty days nor more than one year or be both fined and imprisoned.

Section 54–196 provides:

> Any person who assists, abets, counsels, causes, hires or commands another to commit any offense may be prosecuted and punished as if he were the principal offender.

The appellants were found guilty as accessories and fined $100 each, against the claim that the accessory statute as so applied violated the Fourteenth Amendment....

. . . .

Coming to the merits, we are met with a wide range of questions that implicate the Due Process Clause of the Fourteenth Amendment. Overtones of some arguments suggest that *Lochner v. New York*, 198 U.S. 45 [(1905)], should be our guide. But we decline that invitation.... We do not sit as a super-legislature to determine the wisdom, need, and propriety of laws that touch economic problems, business affairs, or social conditions. This law, however, operates directly on an intimate relation of husband and wife and their physician's role in one aspect of that relation.

The association of people is not mentioned in the Constitution nor in the Bill of Rights. The right to educate a child in a school of the parents' choice—whether public or private or parochial—is also not mentioned. Nor is the right to study any particular subject or any foreign language. Yet the First Amendment has been construed to include certain of those rights.

By *Pierce v. Society of Sisters*, 268 U.S. 510 (1925), the right to educate one's children as one chooses is made applicable to the States by the force of the First and Fourteenth Amendments. By *Meyer v. State of Nebraska*, 262 U.S. 390 (1923), the same dignity is given the right to study the German language in a private school. In other words, the State may not, consistently with the spirit of the First Amendment, contract the spectrum of available knowledge. . . . Without those peripheral rights the specific rights would be less secure. And so we reaffirm the principle of the *Pierce* and the *Meyer* cases.

In *NAACP v. Alabama*, 357 U.S. 449 (1958), we protected the "freedom to associate and privacy in one's associations," noting that freedom of association was a peripheral First Amendment right. . . . In other words, the First Amendment has a penumbra where privacy is protected from governmental intrusion. In like context, we have protected forms of "association" that are not political in the customary sense but pertain to the social, legal, and economic benefit of the members. *NAACP v. Button*, 371 U.S. 415, 430–31 (1963). . . .

. . . .

The foregoing cases suggest that specific guarantees in the Bill of Rights have penumbras, formed by emanations from those guarantees that help give them life and substance. Various guarantees create zones of privacy. The right of association contained in the penumbra of the First Amendment is one, as we have seen. The Third Amendment in its prohibition against the quartering of soldiers "in any house" in time of peace without the consent of the owner is another facet of that privacy. The Fourth Amendment explicitly affirms the "right of the people to be secure in their persons, houses, papers, and effects, against unreasonable searches and seizures." The Fifth Amendment in its Self-Incrimination Clause enables the citizen to create a zone of privacy which government may not force him to surrender to his detriment. The Ninth Amendment provides: "The enumeration in the Constitution, of certain rights, shall not be construed to deny or disparage others retained by the people."

. . . .

The present case, then, concerns a relationship lying within the zone of privacy created by several fundamental constitutional guarantees. And it concerns a law which, in forbidding the *use* of contraceptives rather than regulating their manufacture or sale, seeks to achieve its goals by means having a maximum destructive impact upon that relationship. Such a law cannot stand in light of the familiar principle . . . that a "governmental purpose to control or prevent activities constitutionally subject to state regulation may not be achieved by means which sweep unnecessarily broadly and thereby invade the area of protected freedoms." Would we allow the police to search the sacred precincts of marital bedrooms for telltale signs of the use of contraceptives? The very idea is repulsive to the notions of privacy surrounding the marriage relationship.

We deal with a right of privacy older than the Bill of Rights—older than our political parties, older than our school system. Marriage is a coming together for better or for worse, hopefully enduring, and intimate to the degree of being sacred. It is an association that promotes a way of life, not causes; a harmony in living, not political faiths; a bilateral loyalty, not commercial or social projects. Yet it is an association for as noble a purpose as any involved in our prior decisions.

Reversed.

■ GOLDBERG, J., with whom THE CHIEF JUSTICE and BRENNAN, J., join, concurring.

... I do agree that the concept of liberty protects those personal rights that are fundamental, and is not confined to the specific terms of the Bill of Rights. My conclusion ... is supported both by numerous decisions of this Court, referred to in the Court's opinion, and by the language and history of the Ninth Amendment. ...

. . . .

This Court, in a series of decisions, has held that the Fourteenth Amendment absorbs and applies to the States those specifics of the first eight amendments which express fundamental personal rights. The language and history of the Ninth Amendment reveal that the Framers of the Constitution believed that there are additional fundamental rights, protected from governmental infringement, which exist alongside those fundamental rights specifically mentioned in the first eight constitutional amendments.

The Ninth Amendment reads, "The enumeration in the Constitution, of certain rights, shall not be construed to deny or disparage others retained by the people." The Amendment is almost entirely the work of James Madison. It was introduced in Congress by him and passed the House and Senate with little or no debate and virtually no change in language. It was proffered to quiet expressed fears that a bill of specifically enumerated rights could not be sufficiently broad to cover all essential rights and that the specific mention of certain rights would be interpreted as a denial that others were protected.

. . . .

... To hold that a right so basic and fundamental and so deep-rooted in our society as the right of privacy in marriage may be infringed because that right is not guaranteed in so many words by the first eight amendments to the Constitution is to ignore the Ninth Amendment and to give it no effect whatsoever. ...

. . . .

■ WHITE, J., concurring in the judgment.

In my view this Connecticut law as applied to married couples deprives them of "liberty" without due process of law. ...

. . . .

. . . [T]he statute is said to serve the State's policy against all forms of promiscuous or illicit sexual relationships, be they premarital or extramarital, concededly a permissible and legitimate legislative goal.

Without taking issue with the premise that the fear of conception operates as a deterrent to such relationships in addition to the criminal proscriptions Connecticut has against such conduct, I wholly fail to see how the ban on the use of contraceptives by married couples in any way reinforces the State's ban on illicit sexual relationships. . . .

. . . .

. . . A statute limiting its prohibition on use to persons engaging in the prohibited relationship would serve the end posited by Connecticut in the same way, and with the same effectiveness, or ineffectiveness, as the broad anti-use statute under attack in this case. I find nothing in this record justifying the sweeping scope of this statute, with its telling effect on the freedoms of married persons, and therefore conclude that it deprives such persons of liberty without due process of law.

■ BLACK, J., with whom STEWART, J., joins, dissenting.

. . . I do not to any extent whatever base my view that this Connecticut law is constitutional on a belief that the law is wise or that its policy is a good one. In order that there may be no room at all to doubt why I vote as I do, I feel constrained to add that the law is every bit as offensive to me as it is my Brethren of the majority . . . who . . . hold it unconstitutional. There is no single one of the graphic and eloquent strictures and criticisms fired at the policy of this Connecticut law either by the Court's opinion or by those of my concurring Brethren to which I cannot subscribe—except their conclusion that the evil qualities they see in the law make it unconstitutional.

. . . .

The Court talks about a constitutional "right of privacy" as though there is some constitutional provision or provisions forbidding any law ever to be passed which might abridge the "privacy" of individuals. But there is not. There are, of course, guarantees in certain specific constitutional provisions which are designed in part to protect privacy at certain times and places with respect to certain activities. . . .

. . . For these reasons I get nowhere in this case by talk about a constitutional "right of privacy" as an emanation from one or more constitutional provisions.[1] I like my privacy as well as the next one, but

---

[1] The phrase "right to privacy" appears first to have gained currency from an article written by Messrs. Warren and (later Mr. Justice) Brandeis in 1890 which urged that States should give some form of tort relief to persons whose private affairs were exploited by others. *The Right to Privacy*, 4 HARV. L. REV. 193 [1890]. Largely as a result of this article, some States have passed statutes creating such a cause of action, and in others state courts have done the same thing by exercising their powers as courts of common law. . . . Observing that "the right of privacy . . . presses for recognition here," today this Court, which I did not understand to have power to sit as a court of common law, now appears to be exalting a phrase which Warren and

I am nevertheless compelled to admit that government has a right to invade it unless prohibited by some specific constitutional provision. . . .

This brings me to the arguments [that] . . . would invalidate it by reliance on the Due Process Clause of the Fourteenth Amendment, [or] . . . also [by reliance] on the Ninth Amendment. . . . [N]either the Due Process Clause nor the Ninth Amendment, nor both together, could under any circumstances be a proper basis for invalidating the Connecticut law. . . .

The due process argument . . . is based . . . on the premise that this Court is vested with power to invalidate all state laws that it consider to be arbitrary, capricious, unreasonable, or oppressive, or this Court's belief that a particular state law under scrutiny has no "rational or justifying" purpose, or is offensive to a "sense of fairness and justice." . . . While I completely subscribe to the holding of *Marbury v. Madison*, 1 Cranch 137, 2 L.Ed. 60, and subsequent cases, that our Court has constitutional power to strike down statutes, state or federal, that violate commands of the Federal Constitution, I do not believe that we are granted power by the Due Process Clause or any other constitutional provision or provisions to measure constitutionality by our belief that legislation is arbitrary, capricious or unreasonable, or accomplishes no justifiable purpose, or is offensive to our own notions of "civilized standards of conduct." Such an appraisal of the wisdom of legislation is an attribute of the power to make laws, not of the power to interpret them. The use by federal courts of such a formula or doctrine or whatnot to veto federal or state laws simply takes away from Congress and States the power to make laws based on their own judgment of fairness and wisdom and transfers that power to this Court for ultimate determination—a power which was specifically denied to federal courts by the convention that framed the Constitution.

. . . .

. . . [In order to consider the Ninth Amendment] as authority to strike down all state legislation which this Court thinks violates "fundamental principles of liberty and justice," or is contrary to the "traditions and (collective) conscience of our people[,]" . . . one would certainly have to look far beyond the language of the Ninth Amendment to find that the Framers vested in this Court any such awesome veto powers over lawmaking, either by the States or by the Congress. Nor does anything in the history of the Amendment offer any support for such a shocking doctrine. The whole history of the adoption of the Constitution and Bill of Rights points the other way. . . . [T]he Ninth Amendment was intended to protect against the idea that "by enumerating particular exceptions to the grant of power" to the Federal Government, "those rights which were not singled out, were intended to be assigned into the

---

Brandeis used in discussing grounds for tort relief, to the level of a constitutional rule which prevents state legislatures from passing any law deemed by this Court to interfere with "privacy."

hands of the General Government (the United States), and were consequently insecure." That Amendment was passed, not to broaden the powers of this Court or any other department of "the General Government," but, as every student of history knows, to assure the people that the Constitution in all its provisions was intended to limit the Federal Government to the powers granted expressly or by necessary implication. If any broad, unlimited power to hold laws unconstitutional because they offend what this Court conceives to be the "(collective) conscience of our people" is vested in this Court by the Ninth Amendment, the Fourteenth Amendment, or any other provision of the Constitution, it was not given by the Framers, but rather has been bestowed on the Court by the Court. . . .

I repeat so as not to be misunderstood that this Court does have power, which it should exercise, to hold laws unconstitutional where they are forbidden by the Federal Constitution. My point is that there is no provision of the Constitution which either expressly or impliedly vests power in this Court to sit as a supervisory agency over acts of duly constituted legislative bodies and set aside their laws because of the Court's belief that the legislative policies adopted are unreasonable, unwise, arbitrary, capricious or irrational. The adoption of such a loose, flexible, uncontrolled standard for holding laws unconstitutional, if ever it is finally achieved, will amount to a great unconstitutional shift of power to the courts which I believe and am constrained to say will be bad for the courts and worse for the country. Subjecting federal and state laws to such an unrestrained and unrestrainable judicial control as to the wisdom of legislative enactments would, I fear, jeopardize the separation of governmental powers that the Framers set up and at the same time threaten to take away much of the power of States to govern themselves which the Constitution plainly intended them to have.

. . . .

So far as I am concerned, Connecticut's law as applied here is not forbidden by any provision of the Federal Constitution as that Constitution was written, and I would therefore affirm.

■ STEWART, J., whom BLACK, J., joins, dissenting.

Since 1879 Connecticut has had on its books a law which forbids the use of contraceptives by anyone. I think this is an uncommonly silly law. As a practical matter, the law is obviously unenforceable, except in the oblique context of the present case. As a philosophical matter, I believe the use of contraceptives in the relationship of marriage should be left to personal and private choice, based upon each individual's moral, ethical, and religious beliefs. As a matter of social policy, I think professional counsel about methods of birth control should be available to all, so that each individual's choice can be meaningfully made. But we are not asked in this case to say whether we think this law is unwise, or even asinine. We are asked to hold that it violates the United States Constitution. And that I cannot do.

In the course of its opinion the Court refers to no less than six Amendments to the Constitution: the First, the Third, the Fourth, the Fifth, the Ninth, and the Fourteenth. But the Court does not say which of these Amendments, if any, it thinks is infringed by this Connecticut law.

. . . .

The Court also quotes the Ninth Amendment, and my Brother Goldberg's concurring opinion relies heavily upon it. But to say that the Ninth Amendment has anything to do with this case is to turn somersaults with history. The Ninth Amendment, like its companion the Tenth . . . was framed by James Madison and adopted by the States simply to make clear that the adoption of the Bill of Rights did not alter the plan that the Federal Government was to be a government of express and limited powers, and that all rights and powers not delegated to it were retained by the people and the individual States. Until today no member of this Court has ever suggested that the Ninth Amendment meant anything else, and the idea that a federal court could ever use the Ninth Amendment to annul a law passed by the elected representatives of the people of the State of Connecticut would have caused James Madison no little wonder.

What provision of the Constitution, then, does make this state law invalid? The Court says it is the right of privacy "created by several fundamental constitutional guarantees." With all deference, I can find no such general right of privacy in the Bill of Rights, in any other part of the Constitution, or in any case ever before decided by this Court.

At the oral argument in this case we were told that the Connecticut law does not "conform to current community standards." But it is not the function of this Court to decide cases on the basis of community standards. We are here to decide cases "agreeably to the Constitution and laws of the United States." . . . If, as I should surely hope, the law before us does not reflect the standards of the people of Connecticut, the people of Connecticut can freely exercise their true Ninth and Tenth Amendment rights to persuade their elected representatives to repeal it. That is the constitutional way to take this law off the books.[8]

NOTES

1.   Griswold's *Criminal Law Antecedents*. *Griswold* is a stalwart of the constitutional law and reproductive rights canon; but, as Melissa Murray argues, it should also be considered part of the criminal law canon. The contraceptive ban challenged in *Griswold* carried a criminal penalty; and, critically, Estelle Griswold and Lee Buxton were arraigned, charged, and tried before a court for violating the Connecticut law. As importantly,

---

[8]   . . . The Connecticut House of Representatives recently passed a bill (House Bill No. 2462) repealing the birth control law. The State Senate has apparently not yet acted on the measure, and today is relieved of that responsibility by the Court. New Haven Journal-Courier, Wed., May 19, 1965, p. 1, col. 4, and p. 13, col. 7.

Griswold was part of a broader criminal law reform project that was taking place in the 1950s and 1960s—one that sought to limit the state's use of criminal law as a means of policing and enforcing compliance with majoritarian sexual mores. With this history in mind, *Griswold* was not simply about birth control, but rather, about designing limits on the state. As Murray explains, recuperating *Griswold*'s place in the criminal law reform debate brings these interests into focus—and makes it easier to discern the notion of privacy as a bulwark against the state's efforts to compel moral conformity. Melissa Murray, *Sexual Liberty and Criminal Law Reform: The Story of* Griswold v. Connecticut *in* REPRODUCTIVE RIGHTS AND JUSTICE STORIES (Murray, Shaw & Siegel, eds. 2019).

2. *The dark side of privacy. Griswold*'s articulation of the "sanctity of the marital bedroom" evokes the long-standing principle of marital privacy, which limited governmental intrusion into private family matters, such as those involving sexual relations between married persons. However, the concept of marital privacy can be both liberating and confining. As Professor Elizabeth Schneider observes, "[t]he concept of marital privacy, established as a constitutional principle in *Griswold*, historically has been the key ideological rationale for state refusal to intervene to protect battered women within ongoing intimate relationships." She cautions that even as we celebrate *Griswold*, "we also must examine its underside: the dark and violent side of privacy." Elizabeth M. Schneider, *The Violence of Privacy*, 23 CONN. L. REV. 973, 974 (1991).

3. *The Public Dimension of Privacy.* As Professor Cary Franklin argues, *Griswold* was as much about class and poverty as it was about access to birth control and reproductive rights. The true impact of the Connecticut birth control ban, Franklin explains, was in preventing the operation of public birth control clinics that could dispense contraception to the poor, who lacked access to private medical care. In striking down the law, Griswold did more than secure a right to contraception—it made it possible for birth control clinics to operate publicly and to serve those who had previously lacked access to contraception because of their socio-economic status. On this account, the right to privacy that *Griswold* announced was not solely about the right to be left alone to make intimate choices, but rather, about the state's obligation to provide—or at the very least, to not withhold—a public infrastructure that allowed everyone, regardless of class status, to exercise the right to contraception. Cary Franklin, Griswold *and the Public Dimension of the Right to Privacy*, 124 YALE L.J. F. 332 (2015).

4. *In the shadow of* Lochner v. New York. The ghost of *Lochner v. New York*, 198 U.S. 45 (1905), and the tainted doctrine of substantive due process, haunt *Griswold*. In *Lochner*, the Supreme Court famously struck down a New York law that, in the interest of safeguarding public health, mandated maximum hours for the employment of bakers. According to the Court, the challenged Bakeshop Act imposed upon an individual's "general right to make a contract in relation to his business." *Id.* at 53. The Court went on to hold that although the state retained the police power to legislate on behalf of the general welfare, it was the court's duty to determine whether legislation is "a fair, reasonable, and appropriate exercise of the police power

of the State, or . . . an unreasonable, unnecessary and arbitrary interference with the right of the individual . . . to enter into those contracts in relation to labor which may seem to him appropriate." *Id.* at 56. Until it was discredited in 1937's *West Coast Hotel v. Parrish*, 300 U.S. 379 (1937), *Lochner* thwarted a variety of legislation during the Progressive Era.

With this history in mind, it is unsurprising that some saw shades of *Lochner* in the *Griswold* Court's invalidation of the Connecticut anti-contraception statute. Indeed, in the text of the opinion, Justice Douglas valiantly tried to distinguish *Griswold* from the discredited *Lochner* doctrine:

> [S]ome . . . suggest that *Lochner v. State of New York*, 198 U.S. 45 (1905) should be our guide. But we decline that invitation. . . . We do not sit as a super-legislature to determine the wisdom, need, and propriety of laws that touch economic problems, business affairs, or social conditions. This law, however, operates directly on an intimate relation of husband and wife and their physician's role in one aspect of that relation.

Griswold, 381 U.S. at 481–82. Is Douglas's effort to distinguish the right to privacy from *Lochner*-ian substantive due process convincing?

5. *Public response to* Griswold. A content analysis of California newspapers conducted in 1983 and an analysis of national newspapers conducted for this publication, indicated that the response to *Griswold* was both mild and factual, with few writers at the time seeing it as a moral issue. Given the controversy later created by *Roe v. Wade*, see *infra* p. 709, why was *Griswold* not more controversial?

6. *The debate over incorporation.* One of the subtexts in *Griswold*, which may not be immediately apparent, is a debate about the extent to which the Fourteenth Amendment makes binding on the states the Bill of Rights' protections for fundamental rights "implicit in the concept of ordered liberty." *Palko v. Connecticut*, 302 U.S. 319, 325 (1937). Although incorporation was a relatively recent constitutional development, the majority opinion in *Griswold* assumes that states must observe the Fourteenth Amendment's protections for individual liberty.

7. *Ménage à trois?* Griswold reprises a consistent theme in the regulation of contraception and reproduction: that the control of reproduction is properly vested in the hands of physicians. Even as the *Griswold* Court located the right to privacy in the marital relationship, it also noted that the challenged Connecticut statute "operates directly on an intimate relation of husband and wife *and their physician's role* in one aspect of that relation." 381 U.S. at 482 (emphasis added).

8. *The invention of the birth control pill.* In 1960, the Food and Drug Administration (FDA) approved the first birth control pill for public use. According to historian Elaine Tyler May, the introduction of "the pill" unleashed a host of Cold War metaphors. The pill, she writes, was seen as a "magic bullet" that would avert the explosion of the dreaded "population bomb." "By reducing the population, [the pill] would alleviate the conditions of poverty and unrest that might lead developing nations to embrace

communism, and instead promote the growth of markets for consumer goods and the embrace of capitalism." As importantly, the pill would also "bolster the 'nuclear' family," "[b]y freeing married couples from fears of unwanted pregnancy" and promoting the "planned and happy families" that were viewed as "the key to social order." ELAINE TYLER MAY, AMERICA AND THE PILL: A HISTORY OF PROMISE, PERIL, AND LIBERATION 3 (2010).

9. *Testing the pill.* The first large-scale clinical trials of the pill were conducted on women in Puerto Rico. These women, most of whom were poor, may have been particularly susceptible to the allure of contraceptive trials, as the trials included free medical care and access to contraception at a time when sterilization was the only available contraceptive option. Some scholars, such as Angela Davis, have argued that these trials exploited their impoverished subjects. *See* ANGELA DAVIS, WOMEN, RACE, AND CLASS 219 (1981). Elaine Tyler May, whose father was involved in the trials, however, qualifies this argument, explaining that "by the standards of the day, the studies were scrupulously conducted." ELAINE TYLER MAY, AMERICA AND THE PILL: A HISTORY OF PROMISE, PERIL, AND LIBERATION 31 (2010).

Eisenstadt v. Baird

405 U.S. 438 (1972).

■ BRENNAN, J.

Appellee William Baird was convicted at a bench trial in the Massachusetts Superior Court . . . for exhibiting contraceptive articles in the course of delivering a lecture on contraception to a group of students at Boston University and . . . for giving a young woman a package of Emko vaginal foam at the close of his address. The Massachusetts Supreme Judicial Court unanimously set aside the conviction for exhibiting contraceptives on the ground that it violated Baird's First Amendment rights, but by a four-to-three vote sustained the conviction for giving away the foam. . . .

Massachusetts General Laws Ann., c. 272, § 21, under which Baird was convicted, provides a maximum five-year term of imprisonment for "whoever . . . gives away . . . any drug, medicine, instrument or article whatever for the prevention of conception," except as authorized in § 21A. Under § 21A, "(a) registered physician may administer to or prescribe for any married person drugs or articles intended for the prevention of pregnancy or conception. (And a) registered pharmacist actually engaged in the business of pharmacy may furnish such drugs or articles to any married person presenting a prescription from a registered physician." . . .

. . . The question for our determination in this case is whether there is some ground of difference that rationally explains the different treatment accorded married and unmarried persons under Massachusetts General Laws Ann., c. 272, § 21 and § 21A. For the reasons that follow, we conclude that no such ground exists.

First... It would be plainly unreasonable to assume that Massachusetts has prescribed pregnancy and the birth of an unwanted child as punishment for fornication, which is a misdemeanor under Massachusetts General Laws Ann., c. 272, § 18. Aside from the scheme of values that assumption would attribute to the State, it is abundantly clear that the effect of the ban on distribution of contraceptives to unmarried persons has at best a marginal relation to the proffered objective....

. . .

Second.... If health were the rationale of § 21A, the statute would be both discriminatory and overbroad ... in view of the federal and state laws already regulating the distribution of harmful drugs. See Federal Food, Drug, and Cosmetic Act, § 503, 52 Stat. 1051, as amended, 21 U.S.C. s 353; Mass. Gen. Laws Ann., c. 94, § 187A, as amended. We conclude, accordingly, that, despite the statute's superficial earmarks as a health measure, health, on the face of the statute, may no more reasonably be regarded as its purpose than the deterrence of premarital sexual relations.

Third. If the Massachusetts statute cannot be upheld as a deterrent to fornication or as a health measure, may it, nevertheless, be sustained simply as a prohibition on contraception? ...

. . .

We need not and do not, however, decide that important question in this case because, whatever the rights of the individual to access to contraceptives may be, the rights must be the same for the unmarried and the married alike.

If under *Griswold* the distribution of contraceptives to married persons cannot be prohibited, a ban on distribution to unmarried persons would be equally impermissible. It is true that in *Griswold* the right of privacy in question inhered in the marital relationship. Yet the marital couple is not an independent entity with a mind and heart of its own, but an association of two individuals each with a separate intellectual and emotional makeup. If the right of privacy means anything, it is the right of the individual, married or single, to be free from unwarranted governmental intrusion into matters so fundamentally affecting a person as the decision whether to bear or beget a child. *See Stanley v. Georgia,* 394 U.S. 557 (1969).

On the other hand, if *Griswold* is no bar to a prohibition on the distribution of contraceptives, the State could not, consistently with the Equal Protection Clause, outlaw distribution to unmarried but not to married persons. In each case the evil, as perceived by the State, would be identical, and the underinclusion would be invidious....

. . .

. . . We hold that by providing dissimilar treatment for married and unmarried persons who are similarly situated, Massachusetts General Laws Ann., c. 272, § 21 and 21A, violate the Equal Protection Clause. The judgment of the Court of Appeals is . . . [a]ffirmed.

. . .

NOTES

1. *Extending the right of privacy.* Perhaps the most cited aspect of *Eisenstadt* is the Court's conclusion that "the marital couple is not an independent entity with a mind and heart of its own, but an association of two individuals each with a separate intellectual and emotional makeup." Thus, "[i]f the right of privacy means anything, it is the right of the individual, married or single, to be free from unwarranted governmental intrusion into matters so fundamentally affecting a person as the decision whether to bear or beget a child." 405 U.S. at 453. With this, the *Eisenstadt* Court elaborated *Griswold*'s logic, extending the right of privacy beyond the marital couple to the individual.

2. *Equality vs. liberty.* Although *Eisenstadt* extends *Griswold*'s logic to unmarried persons, it does not rely on substantive due process doctrine as *Griswold* does. Instead, *Eisenstadt* is rooted in equal protection doctrine. According to the Court, "whatever the rights of the individual to access to contraceptives may be, the rights must be the same for the unmarried and the married alike." 405 U.S. at 453. What explains the Court's choice to ground the decision in equality, rather than liberty? What are the implications of this doctrinal choice?

3. *A new family law?* Professor Susan Frelich Appleton maintains that "[i]n extending constitutional protection to unmarried persons' access to birth control, *Eisenstadt* heralded a new family law that would be more inclusive, liberatory, sex-positive, and feminist than its predecessors." As Appleton explains, *Eisenstadt* "offers an illuminating point of departure for examining family law because it defies the field's traditional boundaries: *Eisenstadt* concerns sex but has nothing to do with domesticity. It makes marriage beside the point, thus ignoring a central pillar of traditional family law. And while collectives—whether the couple, parents and children, or even communes and extended families—provide the typical focus of family law, *Eisenstadt* on its face emphasizes the individual." Regrettably, *Eisenstadt*'s full transformative potential has been forgotten, if not co-opted, in service of a narrower vision of family law—one that is focused on marriage and the marital family. Susan Frelich Appleton, *The Forgotten Family Law of* Eisenstadt v. Baird, 28 YALE J.L. & FEMINISM 1, 1–2 (2016).

4. *New sexual patterns.* In the period in which *Eisenstadt* was decided, there were dramatic changes in the sexual and reproductive lives of Americans. Premarital sex was becoming increasingly common. In keeping with this trend, Americans were more likely to have had multiple sexual partners, and to delay marriage. Changes in sexual practices were particularly pronounced among adolescents. Only forty-eight percent of people who turned fifteen between 1954 and 1963 had premarital sex by age

twenty. Lawrence B. Finer, *Trends in Premarital Sex in the United States, 1954–2003*, 122 PUB. HEALTH REP. 73, 76 (2007). By the early 1980s, however, over seventy percent of American nineteen-year-olds had premarital sex. *See* Sandra L. Hofferth et al., *Premarital Sexual Activity among U.S. Teenage Women over the Past Three Decades*, 19 FAM. PLAN. PERSP. 46, 47 (1987). Among unmarried couples, cohabitation rates were also on the rise—increasing three hundred percent between 1970 and 1980. *See* Graham B. Spanier, *Cohabitation in the 1980s: Recent Changes in the United States, in* CONTEMPORARY MARRIAGE: COMPARATIVE PERSPECTIVES ON A CHANGING INSTITUTION 91, 92 (Kingsley Davis ed., 1985).

5.   *The rise of non-prescription contraceptives.* As we have seen, the practice of putting preparations in the vagina to avoid conception is over four thousand years old. *See supra* p. 578. The *efficacy* of these concoctions increased substantially with the 1950 invention of the non-prescription spermicide nonoxynol-9, which was added to contraceptive foams, jellies, gels, films, and suppositories. Starting with Emko foam in 1961 (William Baird, the defendant in *Eisenstadt*, was Emko's clinical director), the range of effective over-the-counter contraceptives expanded. *See* Raymond Belsky, *Vaginal Contraceptives: A Time for Reappraisal*, 3 POPULATION REP. H–37, H–40 (1975).

6.   *Fighting poverty with the pill.* In 1964, as part of the War on Poverty, the federal government began to fund birth control for poor women. Over the next four years, the federal government expanded both funding and eligibility for birth control for low-income women. Indeed, in 1970 the Senate unanimously passed Title X of the Public Health Service, which provided the largest single source of funding for birth control for over two decades. The legislation also enjoyed overwhelming support in the House. *See* KRISTIN LUKER, DUBIOUS CONCEPTIONS: THE POLITICS OF TEENAGE PREGNANCY 55–60 (1996). Contrast this legislative milieu with the current controversies over federal health care coverage of contraception. *See infra* p. 651.

7.   *The pill and women's progress.* The last half century has seen unprecedented changes in the status of women, including a massive expansion of women into professional occupations. Economists Claudia Goldin and Lawrence Katz argue that these developments can be directly attributed to the use of the pill, and perhaps legalized abortion as well. According to Goldin and Katz, when women have complete control over their fertility, it becomes both less risky to invest in higher education and more problematic for other people to discriminate against them on the grounds that they might get pregnant. With this in mind, Goldin and Katz attribute the rise in women's enrollment in graduate and professional school (below) to increased access to contraception and abortion.

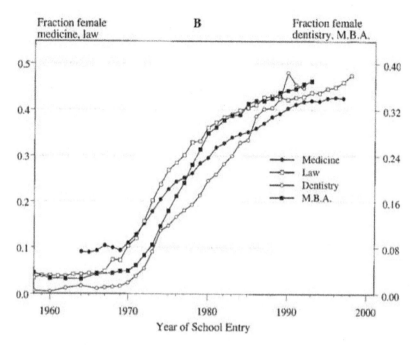

Fraction female medicine, law — B — Fraction female dentistry, M.B.A.

Year of School Entry

Claudia Goldin & Lawrence F. Katz, *The Power of the Pill: Oral Contraceptives and Women's Career and Marriage Decisions*, 110 J. POL. ECON. 730, 750 (2002).

8.   *A male pill?* Since World War II, thirteen new contraceptives for women have been released for consumer use, and none for men. While various technical reasons have been given for this inequity, (e.g., sperm vastly outnumber eggs and therefore are more difficult to contracept), it is not hard to imagine a cultural reason for this disparity: women have historically been seen as the ones responsible for contraception. *See* ELAINE TYLER MAY, AMERICA AND THE PILL: A HISTORY OF PROMISE, PERIL, AND LIBERATION 93, 95 (2010). Related to this idea of women as the keepers of contraception and reproduction, many women say that they would not trust a man who *says* he's "on the pill," but bears no responsibility for reproduction. *Id.* at 114–15.

* * *

Enacted in 1970, Title X of the Public Health Service Act, Public Law 91–572, is the only federal grant program dedicated to providing individuals with comprehensive family planning and related preventive health services.

Title X

Pub. L. No. 91–572 (1970) (codified as amended at 42 U.S.C. §§ 300 *et seq.*)

AN ACT to promote public health and welfare by expanding, improving, and better coordinating the family planning services and population research activities of the Federal Government, and for other purposes.

Be it enacted by the Senate and House of Representatives of the United States of America in Congress assembled,

Sec. 1.   This Act may be cited as the "Family Planning Services and Population Research Act of 1970"

Declaration of Purpose

Sec. 2.   It is the purpose of this Act—

(1) to assist in making comprehensive voluntary family planning services readily available to all persons desiring such services;

(2) to coordinate domestic population and family planning research with the present and future needs of family planning programs;

(3) to improve administrative and operational supervision of domestic family planning services and of population research programs related to such services;

(4) to enable public and nonprofits entities to plan and develop comprehensive programs of family planning services;

(5) to develop and make readily available information (including educational materials) on family planning and population growth to all persons desiring such information;

(6) to evaluation and improve the effectiveness of family planning service programs and of population research;

(7) to assist in providing trained manpower needed to effectively carry out programs of population research and family planning services; and

(8) to establish an Office of Population Affairs in the Department of Health, Education, and Welfare as a primary focus within the Federal Government on matters pertaining to population research and family planning, through which the Secretary of Health, Education, and Welfare (hereafter in this Act referred to as the "Secretary") shall carry out the purposes of this act.

Office of Population Affairs

Sec. 3(a) There is established within the Department of Health, Education, and Welfare an Office of Population Affairs to be directed by a Deputy Assistant Secretary for Population Affairs under the direct supervision of the Assistant Secretary for Health and Scientific Affairs. The Deputy Assistant Secretary for Population Affairs shall be appointed by the Secretary.

. . .

Functions of the Deputy Assistant Secretary for Population Affairs

Sec. 4.   The Secretary shall utilize the Deputy Assistant Secretary for Population Affairs—

(1) to administer all Federal laws for which the Secretary has administrative responsibility and which provide for or authorize the making of grants or contracts related to population research and family planning programs;

(2) to administer and be responsible for all population and family planning research carried on directly by the Department of Health, Education, and Welfare or supported by the Department through grants to, or contracts with, entities and individuals;

(3) to act as a clearinghouse for information pertaining to domestic and international population research and family planning programs for use by all interested persons and public and private entities;

(4) to provide a liaison with the activities carried on by other agencies and instrumentalities of the Federal Government relating to population research and family planning;

(5) to provide or support training for necessary manpower for domestic programs of population research and family planning programs of service and research; and

(6) to coordinate and be responsible for the evaluation of the other Department of Health, Education, and Welfare programs related to population research and family planning and to make periodic recommendations to the Secretary.

Plans and Reports

Sec. 5.   (a) Not later than six months after the date of enactment this Act the Secretary shall make a report to the Congress setting forth a plan, to be carried out over a period of five years, for extension of family planning services to all persons desiring such services, for family planning and population research programs, for training of necessary manpower for the programs authorized by title X of the Public Health Service Act and other Federal laws for which the Secretary has responsibility, and for carrying out the other purposes set forth in this Act and in such title X.

(b) Such a plan shall, at a minimum, indicate on phased basis—

(1) the number of individuals to be served by family planning programs under title X of the Public Health Service Act and other Federal laws for which the Secretary has responsibility, the types of family planning and population growth information and educational materials to be developed under such laws and how they will be made available, the research goals to be reached under such laws, and the manpower to be trained under such laws;

(2) an estimate of the costs and personnel requirements needed to meet these objectives; and

(3) the steps to be taken to establish a systematic reporting system capable of yielding the comprehensive data on which service figures and program evaluations for the Department of Health, Education, and Welfare shall be based.

. . .

Sec. 6 . . . (c) The Public Health Service Act . . . is further amended by adding after title IX the following new title:

Title X—Population Research and Voluntary Family Planning Programs

Project Grants and Contracts for Family Planning Services

Sec. 1001. (a) The Secretary is authorized to make grants to and enter into contracts with public or nonprofit private entities to assist in the establishment and operation of voluntary family planning projects.

(b) The sums appropriated to carry out the provisions of this section shall be allotted to the States by the Secretary on the basis of the population and the financial need of the respective States.

(c) For the purposes of this section, the term 'State' includes the Commonwealth of Puerto Rico, Guam, American Samoa, the Virgin Islands, the District of Columbia, and the Trust Territory of the Pacific Islands.

(d) For the purpose of making grants under this section, there are authorized to be appropriated $10,000,000 for the fiscal year ending June 30, 1971; $15,000,000 for the fiscal year ending June 30, 1972; and $20,000,000 for the fiscal year ending June 30, 1973.

. . .

Training Grants and Contracts

Sec. 1003 (a) The Secretary is authorized to make grants to public or nonprofit private entities and to enter into contracts with public or private entities and individuals to provide the training for personnel to carry out family planning service programs described in section 1001 or 1002.

(b) For the purpose of making payments pursuant to grants and contracts under this section, there are authorized to be appropriated $2,000,000 for the fiscal year ending June 30, 1971; $3,000,000 for the fiscal year ending June 30, 1972; and $4,000,000 for the fiscal year ending June 30, 1973.

. . .

Informational and Educational Materials

Sec. 1005. (a) The Secretary is authorized to make grants to public or nonprofit private entities and to enter into contracts with public or private entities and individuals to assist in developing and making available family planning and population growth information (including educational materials) to all persons desiring such information (or materials).

(b) For the purpose of making payments pursuant to grants and contracts under this section, there are authorized to be appropriated $750,000 for the fiscal year ending June 30, 1971; $1,000,000 for the fiscal year ending June 30, 1972; and $1,250,000 for the fiscal year ending June 30, 1973.

Regulations and Payments

Sec. 1006. (a) Grants and contracts made under this title shall be made in accordance with such regulations as the Secretary may promulgate.

(b) Grants under this title shall be payable in such installments and subject to such conditions as the Secretary may determine to be appropriate to assure that such grants will be effectively utilized for the purposed for which made.

(c) A grant may be made or contract entered into under section 1001 or 1002 for a family planning service project or program only upon assurances satisfactory to the Secretary that—

(1) priority will be given in such project or program to the furnishing of such service to persons from low-income families; and

(2) no charge will be made in such project or program for services provide to any person from a low-income family except to the extent that payment will be made by a third party (including a government agency) which is authorized or is under legal obligation to pay such charge.

For purposed of this subsection, the term 'low-income family' shall be defined by the Secretary in accordance with such criteria as he may prescribe.

Voluntary Participation

Sec. 1007. The acceptance by any individual of family planning services or family planning or population growth information (including educational materials) provided through financial assistance under this title (whether by grant or contract) shall be voluntary and shall not be a prerequisite to eligibility for or receipt of any other service or assistance from, or to participation in, any other program of the entity or individual that provided such a service or information.

Prohibition of Abortion

Sec. 1008. None of the funds appropriate under this title shall be used in programs where abortion is a method of family planning.

Approved December 24, 1970.

NOTES

1. *Abortion and the "Gag Rule".* In 1991, federal regulations governing the operation of Title X-funded clinics limited physicians' capacity to inform, counsel, or refer pregnant women about abortion. These regulations specified that no Title X funds "shall be used in programs where abortion is a method of family planning." Note that the term "family planning" is an ambiguous one, developed by Margaret Sanger to make birth control more mainstream. In *Rust v. Sullivan*, 500 U.S. 173 (1991), *infra* p. 787, the Court upheld these regulations. Using a frame of negative rights that has characterized its jurisprudence on abortion, as well as many other social and economic issues, the Court held that while abortion may be a protected right, the government has no obligation to subsidize that right. For further discussion of Title X's prohibition of funding to "programs where abortion is a method of family planning," see *infra* p. 610.

2. *President Clinton and the "Gag Rule."* As one of his very first acts of his presidency, and on the twentieth anniversary of *Roe v. Wade*, President William J. Clinton sent a memo to the Secretary of Health and Human Services, repealing the "gag rule." President Clinton noted that this memo would permit counseling and referrals and would also permit clinics accepting Title X money to perform abortions with non-Title X funds. *See* Memorandum on the Title X "Gag Rule", 39 WEEKLY COMP. PRES. DOC. 87 (Jan. 22, 1993).

3. *Trump Administration "Gag Rule."* In early 2019, the Trump Administration reinstated the gag rule, prohibiting Title X providers to provide abortion counseling to their patients. The administration went further to require providers to formally separate, for funding purposes, their abortion provision operations from operations associated with the provision of other health care. The new rule change was part of an effort to make good on a campaign promise to "defund Planned Parenthood," which, at the time, served 41 percent of Title X patients. Women's health advocates argued that these policy changes "limit[ed] patients' access to medically accurate family planning information by banning abortion referrals and force[d] abortion providers to physically and financially separate abortion services from family planning services in order to receive Title X funding." Katelyn Burns, *Trump Administration Releases Final Text of Domestic 'Gag Rule' Restriction on Title X*, REWIRE NEWS, Feb. 22, 2019.

4. *Planned Parenthood's response.* Hamstrung by the Trump Administration's conditions on Title X funding, in August 2019, Planned Parenthood, which served 40% of Title X patients across the country, announced that it would withdraw from the Title X program. Other, smaller family planning providers also announced that they would be withdrawing from Title X. This development signaled a significant change in how Title X operates—and indeed, in how contraceptive services and health care are administered and provided to low-income persons. Abortion opponents cheered Planned Parenthood's withdrawal, noting that it would likely provide an opening for other groups, including religiously based organizations and crisis pregnancy centers that counsel women against

abortions, to obtain federal funding for their operations. Sarah McCammon, *Planned Parenthood Withdraws from Title X Program over Trump Abortion Rule*, NPR, Aug. 19, 2019.

Carey v. Population Services International
431 U.S. 678 (1977).

■ BRENNAN, J. delivered the opinion of the Court (Parts I, II, III, and V), together with an opinion (Part IV), in which STEWART, J., MARSHALL, J., and BLACKMUN, J., joined.

Under New York Ed[ucation] Law § 6811(8) (McKinney 1972) it is a crime (1) for any person to sell or distribute any contraceptive of any kind to a minor under the age of 16 years; (2) for anyone other than a licensed pharmacist to distribute contraceptives to persons 16 or over; and (3) for anyone, including licensed pharmacists, to advertise or display contraceptives.[1] . . .

The definition of "drugs" in Education Law § 6802(7) (McKinney 1972) apparently includes any contraceptive drug or device.

. . . .

Although "(t)he Constitution does not explicitly mention any right of privacy," the Court has recognized that one aspect of the "liberty" protected by the Due Process Clause of the Fourteenth Amendment is "a right of personal privacy, or a guarantee of certain areas or zones of privacy." *Roe v. Wade*, 410 U.S. 113, 152 (1973). This right of personal privacy includes "the interest in independence in making certain kinds of important decisions." *Whalen v. Roe*, 429 U.S. 589, 599–600 (1977). . . .

The decision whether or not to beget or bear a child is at the very heart of this cluster of constitutionally protected choices. . . .

That the constitutionally protected right of privacy extends to an individual's liberty to make choices regarding contraception does not, however, automatically invalidate every state regulation in this area. The business of manufacturing and selling contraceptives may be regulated in ways that do not infringe protected individual choices. And even a burdensome regulation may be validated by a sufficiently compelling state interest. . . . "Compelling" is of course the key word; where a decision as fundamental as that whether to bear or beget a child is involved, regulations imposing a burden on it may be justified only by compelling state interests, and must be narrowly drawn to express only those interests.

---

[1] . . . After some dispute in the District Court the parties apparently now agree that Education Law § 6807(b) (McKinney 1972) constitutes an exception to the distribution prohibitions of § 6811(8). Section 6807 (b) provides:

This article shall not be construed to affect or prevent:

(b) Any physician . . . who is not the owner of a pharmacy, or registered store, or who is not in the employ of such owner, from supplying his patients with such drugs as the physician . . . deems proper in connection with his practice. . . .

. . . .

Restrictions on the distribution of contraceptives clearly burden the freedom to make such decisions [about reproduction]. A total prohibition against sale of contraceptives, for example, would intrude upon individual decisions in matters of procreation and contraception as harshly as a direct ban on their use. Indeed, in practice, a prohibition against all sales, since more easily and less offensively enforced, might have an even more devastating effect upon the freedom to choose contraception. . . .

Limiting the distribution of nonprescription contraceptives to licensed pharmacists clearly imposes a significant burden on the right of the individuals to use contraceptives if they choose to do so. The burden is, of course, not as great as that under a total ban on distribution. Nevertheless, the restriction of distribution channels to a small fraction of the total number of possible retail outlets renders contraceptive devices considerably less accessible to the public, reduces the opportunity for privacy of selection and purchase, and lessens the possibility of price competition. . . .

There remains the inquiry whether the provision serves a compelling state interest. Clearly "interests . . . in maintaining medical standards, and in protecting potential life," *Roe v. Wade*, 410 U.S. at 154, cannot be invoked to justify this statute. Insofar as § 6811(8) applies to nonhazardous contraceptives, it bears no relation to the State's interest in protecting health. Nor is the interest in protecting potential life implicated in state regulation of contraceptives.

Appellants therefore suggest that § 6811(8) furthers other state interests. But none of them is comparable to those the Court has heretofore recognized as compelling. Appellants argue that the limitation of retail sales of nonmedical contraceptives to pharmacists (1) expresses "a proper concern that young people not sell contraceptives"; (2) "allows purchasers to inquire as to the relative qualities of the varying products and prevents anyone from tampering with them"; and (3) facilitates enforcement of the other provisions of the statute. The first hardly can justify the statute's incursion into constitutionally protected rights, and in any event the statute is obviously not substantially related to any goal of preventing young people from selling contraceptives. Nor is the statute designed to serve as a quality control device. Nothing in the record suggests that pharmacists are particularly qualified to give advice on the merits of different nonmedical contraceptives, or that such advice is more necessary to the purchaser of contraceptive products than to consumers of other nonprescription items. Why pharmacists are better able or more inclined than other retailers to prevent tampering with prepackaged products, or, if they are, why contraceptives are singled out for this special protection, is also unexplained. As to ease of enforcement, the prospect of additional administrative inconvenience has not been thought to justify invasion of fundamental constitutional rights.

. . . .

The District Court also held unconstitutional, as applied to nonprescription contraceptives, the provision of § 6811(8) prohibiting the distribution of contraceptives to those under 16 years of age.[13] Appellants contend that this provision of the statute is constitutionally permissible as a regulation of the morality of minors, in furtherance of the State's policy against promiscuous sexual intercourse among the young. . . .

Of particular significance to the decision of this case, the right to privacy in connection with decisions affecting procreation extends to minors as well as to adults. *Planned Parenthood of Central Missouri v. Danforth* held that a State "may not impose a blanket provision . . . requiring the consent of a parent or person *in loco parentis* as a condition for abortion of an unmarried minor during the first 12 weeks of her pregnancy." State restrictions inhibiting privacy rights of minors are valid only if they serve "any significant state interest . . . that is not present in the case of an adult."[15] *Planned Parenthood* found that no such interest justified a state requirement of parental consent.

Since the State may not impose a blanket prohibition, or even a blanket requirement of parental consent, on the choice of a minor to terminate her pregnancy, the constitutionality of a blanket prohibition of the distribution of contraceptives to minors is a fortiori foreclosed. The State's interests in protection of the mental and physical health of the pregnant minor, and in protection of potential life are clearly more implicated by the abortion decision than by the decision to use a nonhazardous contraceptive.

Appellants argue, however, that significant state interests are served by restricting minors' access to contraceptives, because free availability to minors of contraceptives would lead to increased sexual activity among the young, in violation of the policy of New York to discourage such behavior.[17] The argument is that minors' sexual activity may be deterred by increasing the hazards attendant on it. The same argument, however, would support a ban on abortions for minors, or

---

[13] Subject to an apparent exception for distribution by physicians in the course of their practice.

[15] This test is apparently less rigorous than the "compelling state interest" test applied to restrictions on the privacy rights of adults. Such lesser scrutiny is appropriate both because of the States' greater latitude to regulate the conduct of children, and because the right of privacy implicated here is "the interest in independence in making certain kinds of important decisions," *Whalen v. Roe*, 429 U.S. 589, 599–600 (1977), and the law has generally regarded minors as having a lesser capability for making important decisions.

[17] Appellees argue that the State's policy to discourage sexual activity of minors is itself unconstitutional, for the reason that the right to privacy comprehends a right of minors as well as adults to engage in private consensual sexual behavior. We observe that the Court has not definitively answered the difficult question whether and to what extent the Constitution prohibits state statutes regulating such behavior among adults. But whatever the answer to that question . . . in the area of sexual mores, as in other areas, the scope of permissible state regulation is broader as to minors than as to adults. In any event, it is unnecessary to pass upon this contention of appellees, and our decision proceeds on the assumption that the Constitution does not bar state regulation of the sexual behavior of minors.

indeed support a prohibition on abortions, or access to contraceptives, for the unmarried, whose sexual activity is also against the public policy of many States. Yet, in each of these areas, the Court has rejected the argument, noting in *Roe v. Wade*, that "no court or commentator has taken the argument seriously." The reason for this unanimous rejection was stated in *Eisenstadt v. Baird*: "It would be plainly unreasonable to assume that (the State) has prescribed pregnancy and the birth of an unwanted child (or the physical and psychological dangers of an abortion) as punishment for fornication." We remain reluctant to attribute any such "scheme of values" to the State.[18]

Moreover, there is substantial reason for doubt whether limiting access to contraceptives will in fact substantially discourage early sexual behavior. . . . Although we take judicial notice . . . that with or without access to contraceptives, the incidence of sexual activity among minors is high, and the consequences of such activity are frequently devastating,[21] the studies cited by appellees play no part in our decision. It is enough that we again confirm the principle that when a State, as here, burdens the exercise of a fundamental right, its attempt to justify that burden as a rational means for the accomplishment of some significant state policy requires more than a bare assertion, based on a conceded complete absence of supporting evidence, that the burden is connected to such a policy. . . .

Appellants argue that New York does not totally prohibit distribution of contraceptives to minors under 16, and that accordingly § 6811(8) cannot be held unconstitutional. Although § 6811(8) on its [face] is a flat unqualified prohibition, . . . § 6807(b) provides that nothing in Education Law §§ 6800–6826 shall be construed to prevent "(a)ny physician . . . from supplying his patients with such drugs as (he) . . . deems proper in connection with his practice." This narrow exception, however, does not save the statute. As we have held above as to limitations upon distribution to adults, less than total restrictions on access to contraceptives that significantly burden the right to decide

---

[18] We note, moreover, that other provisions of New York law argue strongly against any conclusion that the deterrence of illegal sexual conduct among minors was an objective of § 6811(8). First, a girl in New York may marry as young as 14, with the consent of her parents and a family court judge. Yet although sexual intercourse by a married woman of that age violates no state law, § 6811(8) prohibits distribution of contraceptives to her. Second, New York requires that birth control information and services be provided to recipients of certain welfare programs, provided only that they are "of childbearing age, including children who can be considered sexually active." Although extramarital intercourse is presumably as contrary to state policy among minors covered by those programs as among others, state law requires distribution of contraceptives to them and prohibits their distribution to all others.

[21] Although this is not the occasion for a full examination of these problems, the following data sketchily indicate their extent. According to New York City Department of Health statistics, . . . in New York City alone there were over 6,000 live births to girls under the age of 17 in 1975, as well as nearly 11,000 abortions. Moreover, "(t)eenage motherhood involves a host of problems, including adverse physical and psychological effects upon the minor and her baby, the continuous stigma associated with unwed motherhood, the need to drop out of school with the accompanying impairment of educational opportunities, and other dislocations (including) forced marriage of immature couples and the often acute anxieties involved in deciding whether to secure an abortion."

whether to bear children must also pass constitutional scrutiny. Appellants assert no medical necessity for imposing a medical limitation on the distribution of nonprescription contraceptives to minors. Rather, they argue that such a restriction serves to emphasize to young people the seriousness with which the State views the decision to engage in sexual intercourse at an early stage. But this is only another form of the argument that juvenile sexual conduct will be deterred by making contraceptives more difficult to obtain. Moreover, that argument is particularly poorly suited to the restriction appellants are attempting to justify, which on appellants' construction delegates the State's authority to disapprove of minors' sexual behavior to physicians, who may exercise it arbitrarily, either to deny contraceptives to young people, or to undermine the State's policy of discouraging illicit early sexual behavior. This the State may not do.

. . . .

Affirmed.

. . . .

■ POWELL, J., concurring in part and concurring in the judgment.

. . . Court quite unnecessarily extends the reach of cases like *Griswold* and *Roe*. Neither our precedents nor sound principles of constitutional analysis require state legislation to meet the exacting "compelling state interest" standard whenever it implicates sexual freedom. In my view, those cases make clear that that standard has been invoked only when the state regulation entirely frustrates or heavily burdens the exercise of constitutional rights in this area. This is not to say that other state regulation is free from judicial review. But a test so severe that legislation rarely can meet it should be imposed by courts with deliberate restraint in view of the respect that properly should be accorded legislative judgments.

. . . .

There is also no justification for subjecting restrictions on the sexual activity of the young to heightened judicial review. Under our prior cases, the States have broad latitude to legislate with respect to adolescents. The principle is well settled that "a State may permissibly determine that, at least in some precisely delineated areas, a child . . . is not possessed of that full capacity for individual choice" which is essential to the exercise of various constitutionally protected interests. This principle is the premise of our prior decisions . . . holding that "the power of the state to control the conduct of children reaches beyond the scope of its authority over adults." *Prince v. Massachusetts*, 321 U.S. 158 (1944). Restraints on the freedom of minors may be justified "even though comparable restraints on adults would be constitutionally impermissible."

. . . .

[I]n my view there is considerably more room for state regulation in this area than would be permissible under the plurality's opinion. It seems clear to me, for example, that the State would further a constitutionally permissible end if it encouraged adolescents to seek the advice and guidance of their parents before deciding whether to engage in sexual intercourse. The State justifiably may take note of the psychological pressures that might influence children at a time in their lives when they generally do not possess the maturity necessary to understand and control their responses. Participation in sexual intercourse at an early age may have both physical and psychological consequences. These include the risks of venereal disease and pregnancy, and the less obvious mental and emotional problems that may result from sexual activity by children. Moreover, society has long adhered to the view that sexual intercourse should not be engaged in promiscuously, a judgment that an adolescent may be less likely to heed than an adult.

. . . .

A requirement of prior parental consultation is merely one illustration of permissible regulation in this area. As long as parental distribution is permitted, a State should have substantial latitude in regulating the distribution of contraceptives to minors. . . .

But even if New York were to enact constitutionally permissible limitations on access for children, I doubt that it could justify the present pharmacy restriction as an enforcement measure. Restricting the kinds of retail outlets that may distribute contraceptives may well be justified, but the present statute even prohibits distribution by mail to adults. In this respect, the statute works a significant invasion of the constitutionally protected privacy in decisions concerning sexual relations. By requiring individuals to buy contraceptives over the counter, the statute heavily burdens constitutionally protected freedom.

. . . .

■ REHNQUIST, J., dissenting.

Those who valiantly but vainly defended the heights of Bunker Hill in 1775 made it possible that men such as James Madison might later sit in the first Congress and draft the Bill of Rights to the Constitution. The post-Civil War Congresses which drafted the Civil War Amendments to the Constitution could not have accomplished their task without the blood of brave men on both sides which was shed at Shiloh, Gettysburg, and Cold Harbor. If those responsible for these Amendments, by feats of valor or efforts of draftsmanship, could have lived to know that their efforts had enshrined in the Constitution the right of commercial vendors of contraceptives to peddle them to unmarried minors through such means as window displays and vending machines located in the men's room of truck stops, notwithstanding the considered judgment of the New York Legislature to the contrary, it is not difficult to imagine their reaction.

. . . .

No questions of religious belief, compelled allegiance to a secular creed, or decisions on the part of married couples as to procreation, are involved here. New York has simply decided that it wishes to discourage unmarried minors under 16 from having promiscuous sexual intercourse with one another. Even the Court would scarcely go so far as to say that this is not a subject with which the New York Legislature may properly concern itself.

That legislature has not chosen to deny to a pregnant woman, after the *fait accompli* of pregnancy, the one remedy which would enable her to terminate an unwanted pregnancy. It has instead sought to deter the conduct which will produce such *faits accomplis*. The majority of New York's citizens are in effect told that however deeply they may be concerned about the problem of promiscuous sex and intercourse among unmarried teenagers, they may not adopt this means of dealing with it. The Court holds that New York may not use its police power to legislate in the interests of its concept of the public morality as it pertains to minors. . . . I would reverse . . . .

NOTES

1. *Changing views of teenage sexuality.* Over the past century, the Court (and the American public) has struggled to come to terms with the sexual and reproductive changes in the lives of American teens. *Eisenstadt* made contraceptives available to the unmarried in 1972, and *Carey* extended this access to unmarried minors in 1977. In 1981, the Court upheld a gendered statutory rape law in *Michael M. v. Superior Court of Sonoma County*, 450 U.S. 464 (1981), on the ground that although pregnancy deterred young women from sex, no such deterrent was available for young men, who needed the additional deterrent of criminal prosecution. *Michael M.* reflected a view of sexually active young women as victims faced with the threat of teen pregnancy. However, by 1981 this view of young women was in flux. Under the Adolescent Family Life Act, sexually active teenage women were no longer victims in need of legislative protection, but rather were promiscuous rebels threatening the traditional family and the structure of society. Opposition to teen sexuality hardened after Ronald Reagan's election in 1980, with both the Republican party and Congress trying to create policies that would deter teen sexual activity. *See* Kristin Luker, Dubious Conceptions: The Politics of Teenage Pregnancy 67–78 (1996). Why were sexually active teenagers seen as threatening?

2. *A right to sexual privacy?* Together, *Eisenstadt*, *Roe*, and *Carey* have been interpreted as establishing a right to engage in sex outside of marriage. *See* David B. Cruz, *"The Sexual Freedom Cases"? Contraception, Abortion, Abstinence, and the Constitution*, 35 Harv. C.R.-C.L. L. Rev. 299 (2000) (discussing reactions to this suite of cases). Others have interpreted these cases in a more limited fashion. According to privacy-law scholar Jed Rubenfeld, although "[t]he laws struck down under the rubric of privacy have had a peculiar tendency to gravitate around sexuality," they do not offer an

explicit right to engage in sex as such. Instead, these decisions refer to "the network of decisions and conduct relating to the conditions under which sex is permissible, the social institutions surrounding sexual relationships, and the procreative consequences of sex." Jed Rubenfeld, *The Right of Privacy*, 102 HARV. L. REV. 737, 738–44 (1989). Notably, in *Doe v. Commonwealth's Attorney*, 403 F. Supp. 1199 (E.D. Va. 1975), a district court rejected a constitutional challenge to a state law prohibiting same-sex sodomy. The law, the court noted, "has a rational basis of State interest demonstrably legitimate and mirrored in the cited decisional law of the Supreme Court." *Id.* at 1203. The Supreme Court affirmed the district court's judgment summarily, although three members of the Court "would [have] note[d] probable jurisdiction and set [the] case for oral argument." *Doe v. Commonwealth's Attorney*, 425 U.S. 901 (1976).

3.   *Changing views of "family planning."* In the 1960s, federal funding was designed to help poor women and/or women of color avoid "excess fertility"— the phenomenon of having additional children after one had borne her desired number of children. With the advent of sexually active teens and the increasing age of first marriage, contraception is now a means of *postponing* family formation, rather than a means of tailoring the size of an already-established family. How does this change in the cultural understanding of contraception help explain the increasingly militant opposition to contraceptive use?

3.   TESTING AND REGULATING BIRTH CONTROL

Richard B. Sobol, Bending the Law: The Story of the Dalkon Shield Bankruptcy
1–11 (1991).

The Dalkon Shield . . . is a piece of flexible plastic, about three-quarters of an inch across, shaped like a shield. . . . The device has four or five prongs jutting out of each side at a downward angle. Because of their direction the prongs resisted the expulsion of the device. As it turned out, however, the prongs often made insertion or removal painful and difficult, and they were responsible for the tendency of the device to embed itself in the uterine wall or to perforate the uterus.

A more serious design problem of the Dalkon Shield [is] related to its string. . . . [O]n IUDs other than the Dalkon Shield the tailstring is made of a single plastic filament—a "monofilament"—in order to avoid the absorption of moisture, and with it bacteria, . . . a major cause of dangerous and potentially life-threatening infections, known as pelvic inflammatory disease, or PID. Frequently, a hysterectomy must be performed to overcome PID, and even when hysterectomy is not necessary, infertility often results.

Davis and Lerner did not use a monofilament string on their new Dalkon Shield. The monofilament strings they tested either were too weak and would break during removal because of the resistance offered by the prongs, or were too stiff and would cause discomfort to the man during intercourse. Instead, Davis and Lerner used a multifilament string . . . encased in a nylon sheath. . . .

For two reasons the sheath did not do its job. First, inexplicably, Davis and Lerner failed to seal its ends. Fluid from the vagina could enter the open end at the bottom of the sheath and wick up . . . to the open end . . . inside the uterus. [T]he nylon sheath made the problem of wicking worse because it shielded the bacteria inside the sheath from the antibacterial action . . . [of] the cervical plug. Second, the sheath developed holes either in the initial tying process or as a result of decomposition after the IUD was in place. These holes allowed the bacteria to escape into the uterus without even reaching the top of the string.

. . . .

During the years that [A.H.] Robins[, the producer of the Shield] marketed the Dalkon Shield, the company [received] information reporting high pregnancy rates with the Dalkon Shield and information indicating the hazards of the product. . . . [T]he two problems intersected, because the first reports of serious injuries associated with the Dalkon Shield concerned women who had become pregnant with the device in place and had suffered septic abortions. A septic abortion is a spontaneous termination of a pregnancy resulting from an infection of the reproductive system.

. . . .

During 1972 and 1973 Robins received a stream of other reports of spontaneous septic abortions, as well as reports of uterine infections among nonpregnant women using the Dalkon Shield. In several instances women had almost died as a result of virulent infections. Robins deflected these as isolated or insufficiently documented incidents and did nothing to address the problem.

The matter took on a critical dimension in May 1973, when Robins received reports of the deaths of two young women who had become pregnant while wearing the Dalkon Shield. . . . Robins's only reaction to these reports came five months and several hundred thousand Dalkon Shield sales later, when, in October 1973, the company printed new labels that acknowledged the risk of "severe sepsis with fatal outcome, most often associated with spontaneous abortion following pregnancy with the Dalkon Shield *in situ.*"

. . . .

Within weeks Robins was forced by the momentum of negative developments to withdraw the Dalkon Shield from the domestic market. On May 28, 1974, the Planned Parenthood Federation instructed its 183 clinics around the country to stop using the Dalkon Shield. . . .

. . . .

In July 1974 the Centers for Disease Control in Atlanta issued a report that singled out the Dalkon Shield as being associated with septic abortions. . . .

. . . In April 1975, with 15 fatal and 245 nonfatal septic abortions now reported, Robins announced the cessation of foreign sales.

Robins's decision to discontinue sales of the Dalkon Shield did nothing to reduce the threat of injury to the women who were still using the device. Some 3.6 million Dalkon Shields had been implanted in women all over the world, and many, if not most, of these devices were still in place. Robins had the choice of acknowledging the Dalkon Shield was unsafe and recalling the product, thereby limiting the number of further injuries and the number of future claims, or not recalling the Dalkon Shield and continuing to proclaim its safety in defense of the claims for injuries that had already occurred. Robins chose the latter course. When it announced the final cessation of sales, the company blamed negative publicity and stated that it "remains firm in the belief that the Dalkon Shield, when properly used, is a safe and effective IUD." Robins never deviated from that position.

NOTES

1.   *"Testing" the Dalkon Shield.* In 1970, the Dalkon Shield was acquired by the pharmaceutical company A.H. Robins from its developer, Hugh J. Davis, M.D., then a faculty member at the Johns Hopkins University School of Medicine. Davis claimed he had tested the Shield extensively and found low rates of pregnancy (just over one percent). However, Davis never publicly disclosed that he had a conflict of interest (he was the developer of the device and owned substantial shares in the company). Nor did he disclose that his trials had been of a small group of women over a fairly short period of time, and that he had advised his patients to use contraceptive foam for the first few months after insertion. Finally, Davis had calculated failure rates so quickly after the end of the study that additional pregnancies resulting from the failure of the Shield were not tabulated in his published results. Although Davis' experimental oversights are stunning to modern readers, they are more comprehensible in light of the fact that in 1970, IUDs were regulated as "devices" rather than drugs, thereby requiring no testing of safety or effectiveness. RICHARD B. SOBOL, BENDING THE LAW: THE STORY OF THE DALKON SHIELD BANKRUPTCY 2–5 (1991).

2.   *International IUD usage.* In the wake of the well-publicized problems associated with the Dalkon Shield, American women abandoned the IUD as a contraceptive device. Recent years, however, have seen the invention of newer and allegedly safer IUDs, including hormonal and copper IUDS. But the results of the Dalkon Shield debacle—in which seventeen women died and an estimated two hundred thousand suffered complications—have left their mark. Although IUD use in the United States is increasing, only about five percent of contracepting women use one, compared to eighteen percent in Denmark, seventeen percent in France, twenty-one percent in Sweden, and twenty-seven percent in Norway. *See* Adam Sonfield, *Popularity*

Disparity: Attitudes About the IUD in Europe and the United States, 10 GUTTMACHER POL. REV. 4 (2007).

3.   *Risks vs. benefits.* With the recent development of two new IUDs, the copper-containing ParaGard, and the hormone-containing Mirena, IUDs seem poised to make a comeback. Anna Bahr, *As Memories of Dalkon Shield Fade, Women Embrace IUDs Again*, MS. MAG. (Aug. 29, 2012), http:// msmagazine.com/blog/2012/08/29/as-memories-of-dalkon-shield-fade-women-embrace-iuds-again/. Yet concerns about coercion continue, particularly in the context of public assistance. *See infra* p. 72. Moreover, some worry that IUDs do not protect against sexually transmitted infections or Pelvic Inflammatory Disease (PID) (although IUD users have lower reported rates of PID than those who use no contraception). How should sound policy weigh the costs and benefits of these new IUDs?

4.   *Advances in woman-controlled contraception.* The last two decades have seen only modest increases in woman-controlled (rather than physician-controlled) contraception. In addition to the spermicides that became available in the 1970s (and which now exist in a variety of forms), women can now use a female condom and the contraceptive sponge. Public health expert Bethany Young Holt notes that despite these advances, what is needed are multipurpose methods that both prevent pregnancy and protect against HIV and AIDS. On the horizon are a one-size cervical barrier that contains a microbicide, a vaginal ring that prevents pregnancy, HIV and herpes, and new ways of delivering microbicides, including nanoparticles and body-responsive gels. *See* PUB. HEALTH INST., SAVING LIVES WITH MULTIPURPOSE PREVENTION TECHNOLOGIES: TURNING IDEAS INTO SOLUTIONS FOR SEXUAL AND REPRODUCTIVE HEALTH (FACT SHEET) (2010).

5.   *Contraception and intimate partner abuse.* The American College of Obstetricians and Gynecologists (ACOG) has noted that contraceptive sabotage can often be a part of Intimate Partner Violence (IPV). Destroying birth control pills, poking holes in condoms, and coercively removing diaphragms and cervical caps are all ways that abusive men attempt to force pregnancy on their partners, often in the belief that a pregnancy will bind women more closely to them. In light of this, ACOG has suggested that health care providers consider offering vulnerable women the IUD as a form of contraception, as this form of contraception does not require regular ingestion of pills or pre-coital insertion of a device. ACOG has further recommended that physicians take the additional step of trimming the IUD strings so that IUD use will be less noticeable. AM. COLL. OF OBSTETRICIANS & GYNECOLOGISTS, COMMITTEE OPINION NO. 554: REPRODUCTIVE AND SEXUAL COERCION 1–2 (2013).

Dorothy Roberts, Killing the Black Body: Race Reproduction, and the Meaning of Liberty
105–06, 108–09, 111–12 (1997).

Norplant consists of six silicone capsules, each about the size of a matchstick, filled with a synthetic hormone called levonorgestral (that same type of progestin used in some birth control pills.). . . . Once the tubes are inserted, a woman is protected against pregnancy for five years without any further hassle. . . .

Norplant's potential to enhance women's reproductive freedom was quickly overshadowed by its potential for reproductive abuse. The new contraceptive was instantly embraced by policymakers, legislators, and social pundits as a way of curbing the birthrate of poor Black women.

. . . What appeared to be an expensive contraceptive marketed to affluent women through private physicians soon became the focus of government programs for poor women. . . . At a time when legislatures nationwide are slashing social programs for the poor, public aid for Norplant became a popular budget item. . . . Every state and the District of Columbia almost immediately made Norplant available to poor women through Medicaid. . . . By 1994, states had already spent $34 million on Norplant-related benefits. As a result, as least of half the women in the United States who have used Norplant are Medicaid recipients.

. . . Simply making Norplant more accessible to indigent women was not enough for some lawmakers. Within two years thirteen state legislatures had proposed some twenty measures to implant poor women with Norplant. A number of these bills would pressure women on welfare to use the device either by offering them a financial bonus or by requiring implantation as a condition of receiving benefits.

. . . [R]ace lurks behind proposals to induce poor women in general to use Norplant. Not only will these incentives disproportionately affect Black women, but they may be covertly targeted at these women as well. . . . Although most families on welfare are not Black, Blacks disproportionately rely on welfare to support their children. Black women are only 6 percent of the population, but they represent a third of AFDC [Aid to Families with Dependent Children] recipients. The concentration of Black welfare recipients is even greater in the nation's inner cities, where Norplant has primarily been dispensed. . . . "[W]elfare" has become a code word for "race." People can avoid the charge of racism by directing their vitriol at the welfare system instead of explicitly assailing Black people.

. . . Contemporary welfare rhetoric blames Black single mothers for transmitting a deviant lifestyle to their children, a lifestyle marked not only by persistent welfare dependency but also by moral degeneracy and criminality.

White Americans resent the welfare queen who rips off their tax dollars, but even more they fear the Willie Horton she gives birth to. These images are distinctly Black; they have no white counterparts.

NOTES

1. *Maximum family grant and "Welfare Caps."* Proceeding under the assumption that women on public assistance have additional children in order to increase their welfare subsidy, California implemented a maximum

family grant policy in 1994 whereby any child born into a household already in receipt of cash aid would be ineligible for cash aid. *See* CAL. WELF. & INST. CODE § 11450.04 (2014). In 2016, California repealed the policy. Shortly thereafter, Massachusetts and New Jersey also repealed their family welfare caps. Teresa Wiltz, *Family Welfare Caps Lose Favor in More States*, Pew Research Center (May 3, 2019). Currently, thirteen states—Arizona, Arkansas, Connecticut, Delaware, Florida, Georgia, Indiana, Mississippi, North Carolina, North Dakota, South Carolina, Tennessee, and Virginia maintain family welfare caps. Critically, there is no convincing evidence that welfare family caps impact childbearing by welfare recipients. On the contrary, considerable evidence suggests that these policies inflict additional hardships on poor women and their families. Further, the negative view of welfare recipients that this policy implies is evident in the exemption California provides to women who conceive a child as a result of rape, incest, or the failure of an IUD, Norplant, Depo-Provera, or sterilization (provided that these circumstances are reported to the relevant agency within a specific period of time). *See* ELENA GUTIÉRREZ, CTR. ON REPROD. RIGHTS & JUSTICE, BRINGING FAMILIES OUT OF 'CAP'TIVITY: THE NEED TO REPEAL THE CALWORKS MAXIMUM FAMILY GRANT RULE 1, 3 (2013).

2. *Race, welfare, and the elusive safety net.* According to Roberts, African Americans "disproportionately rely on welfare to support their children." This empirical observation is perhaps ironic in light of the history of public assistance. When the Social Security Act of 1935 was first passed, African-American women were largely unaffected by its provisions. The Act made domestic and agricultural workers, whose ranks were disproportionately populated by African Americans, ineligible to participate in the Old Age Insurance program, unemployment program, and the programs aimed at providing support for the elderly. Derived from state-based "mothers' pensions," the Act's Aid to Dependent Children (ADC) program provided some assistance to "worthy" single mothers—that is, women who had been widowed or abandoned by their husbands. However, at least initially, African-American women were largely excluded from participation in the program because of a provision that allowed states to limit ADC benefits to women residing in "suitable homes."

The exclusion of African Americans and "unworthy" single mothers from the ADC program ended in the 1970s, when the National Welfare Rights Organization (NWRO) launched a litigation effort to strike down the state-level restrictions that were used to exclude African-American women—and other unworthy single mothers—from participation in the program. *See* JILL S. QUADAGNO, THE COLOR OF WELFARE: HOW RACISM UNDERMINED THE WAR ON POVERTY 157–8 (1996). For more information on mobilization by the NWRO, see FELICIA KORNBLUH, THE BATTLE FOR WELFARE RIGHTS: POLITICS AND POVERTY IN MODERN AMERICA (2007).

In reflecting on this history, some have argued that racial discrimination played no role in the initial decision to exclude agricultural and domestic workers from eligibility for key Social Security Act programs. *See* U.S. SOC. SECURITY ADMIN., SOC. SECURITY BULLETIN NO. 70–4, THE DECISION TO EXCLUDE AGRICULTURAL AND DOMESTIC WORKERS FROM THE

1935 SOCIAL SECURITY (2010). Others contend that although race was not a direct factor in this decision, it nonetheless played a mediating role in limiting eligibility. *See* CYBELLE FOX, THREE WORLDS OF RELIEF: RACE, IMMIGRATION, AND THE AMERICAN WELFARE STATE FROM THE PROGRESSIVE ERA TO THE NEW DEAL (2012).

3.   *Contraception as a condition of parole.* Judges have been placing limits on the right of women, and some men, to procreate for over seventy-five years, offering those convicted of certain kinds of crimes the "choice" of limiting reproductive autonomy or enduring extended periods of incarceration. Some of these reproductive limits take the form of permanent sterilization, discussed *infra* p. 1055. However, Norplant has also figured prominently in the effort to limit the reproductive capacities of criminal defendants. As prison rights scholar Rachel Roth has observed, judges have offered defendants the "choice" of using Norplant or (more recently) similar long-acting and removable contraceptives ("LARC"), or of facing more severe criminal penalties. "With their freedom on the line, defendants in criminal cases are extremely vulnerable to 'suggestions' that they sacrifice their sexuality, bodily integrity, and reproductive intentions for the future, allowing judges to structure defendants' lives under the guise of 'voluntary' decisions." *See* Rachel Roth, *No New Babies? Gender Inequality and Reproductive Control in the Criminal Justice and Prison Systems*, 12 AM. U. J. GENDER SOC. POL'Y & L. 391, 408 (2004).

4.   ACCESS TO CONTRACEPTION TODAY: A CULTURAL CONFLICT REVISITED

R. Alta Charo, American Constitution Society, Issue Brief: Health Care Provider Refusals to Treat, Prescribe, Refer or Inform: Professionalism and Conscience
(2007).

I.   INTRODUCTION

A woman who has been raped is refused emergency contraception by a pharmacist. Another who wants a child is refused fertility services by a physician because she is gay. Another is refused a prescription for a drug needed for the aftermath of a miscarriage, because the pharmacist thinks it may be used for an abortion. A physician refuses to forward medical records for a patient who had an abortion after the fetus was diagnosed with severe deformities. Another physician refuses to perform a routine physical as part of an adoption procedure, because the woman is single.

Largely as artifacts of the abortion wars, almost every state has some form of a "conscience clause" on its books. . . . Traditionally, these laws referred to physician obligations to provide abortion services and, in most cases, the provision of a referral satisfied one's professional obligations. But in recent years . . . nurses and pharmacists have begun demanding the same right of refusal. Even more expansively, some professionals are claiming that even a referral or the provision of information makes one complicit in the objectionable act, and therefore are asserting a much broader freedom to avoid facilitating a patient's health care needs.

The debate surrounding health care provider ("HCP") right of conscience has emerged with fresh force in the last few years, embedded in a larger national debate about the role of religion in public and professional lives. . . .

. . . .

Shortly after the U.S. Supreme Court's decision in *Roe v. Wade* in 1973, Congress passed [t]he federal abortion conscience clause, called the Church Amendment, [which] amended the Public Health and Welfare Act and protects federally funded individuals and entities that refuse to provide sterilization or abortion services. . . . The protection takes two forms—institutions may not be denied eligibility for federal grants, and they are prohibited from taking action against personnel because of their participation, nonparticipation or beliefs about abortion and sterilization. The Church Amendment concerned provision of services only, and did not address refusals to make referrals or to provide information about legal options for care, as part of the informed consent process. Forty-five states followed suit and passed laws to allow certain healthcare providers to refuse to provide abortion services.

. . . [Subsequently], Congress passed the Weldon Amendment, prohibiting state and local authorities from "discriminating" against any health care entity that will not "pay for, provide coverage for or refer for abortions." It also allows a hospital to refuse care to a woman who is in need of an emergency abortion, even if the state law requires abortion coverage in such an emergency situation.

. . . .

While conscience clauses originated with an emphasis on physicians, recent legislative efforts have broadened to include pharmacists, nurses or even all persons connected with health care delivery. . . . The most expansive bills would also extend refusal privileges to ancillary personnel, theoretically encompassing medical assistants or even orderlies and clerical workers.

In addition, while earlier conscience clauses focused on abortion and sterilization, the newer proposals include other reproductive services, such as traditional contraception, emergency contraception, and IVF or other fertility services. They also include non-reproductive services, such as end of life care . . . or any therapy derived from fetal tissue or embryonic stem cell research (including, for example, some childhood vaccinations).

Further, the range of refusals now includes not only a refusal to perform a procedure, but also the refusal to provide a referral, to offer information or counseling . . . or to do anything that the HCP regards as "participating" in the service in any way.

Finally, protections in some of the newer proposals recite an expansive list of actions that can no longer be taken against professionals who refuse to provide health care services. These protections include immunity from medical or other professional malpractice liability; protection from state licensing board disciplinary action, and protection from employment practices that might put those who assert a right of conscience at a disadvantage in hiring, retention and promotion.

. . . But at the same time that proposals to expand the scope of permitted refusals are proliferating, some actions have been taken to limit refusals, especially by pharmacists. Policies by statute, regulation or administrative interpretation in a number of states attempt to ensure that patients have access to legally prescribed medications, often by requiring a pharmacy to meet this need even if an individual pharmacist it employs refuses. Several proposals forbid pharmacists from refusing to refer or transfer prescriptions, verbally abusing patients, and threatening to breach patients' confidentiality. Moreover, the AMA adopted a resolution supporting legislative efforts that require pharmacists and pharmacies to fill valid prescriptions or "provide immediate referral to an appropriate alternative dispensing pharmacy without interference."

The North Carolina and Massachusetts pharmacy boards . . . have issued statements indicating that pharmacists who impede patients' access to prescription medications will be met with disciplinary action under existing state laws and regulations. According to the National Women's Law Center, pharmacy boards in Delaware, New York, Oregon and Texas have also issued policies so that when a pharmacist refuses to fill a prescription or provide medication, the pharmacy nonetheless ensures delivery of services to the patient.

And state professional licensing boards have on occasion proceeded to discipline their members for failure to provide services. For example, in one of the country's most egregious cases, a Wisconsin pharmacist not only refused to fill a prescription for birth control, but also refused to transfer it to another pharmacy or to return it to the patient, thus leaving her unable to seek services elsewhere. The pharmacist was eventually disciplined by the state licensing board, although the case turned in large part upon his untruthful claims to his employer that he was prepared to provide a full range of services, rather than upon a finding that such actions are impermissible as a matter of professional obligation and the terms of the license to be a pharmacist.

. . . .

While not addressing the broader class of health care providers, nor the broader range of services now being refused, in recent years a number of states have passed legislation or issued regulations to ensure that women seeking medications are not disadvantaged by pharmacists who refuse to fill their prescriptions. As of early 2007, five states explicitly require pharmacists or pharmacies to ensure that valid prescriptions are filled: California, Illinois, Massachusetts, Maine, and Nevada. California's law prohibits pharmacist refusals except when the patient can nonetheless receive her services in a timely manner, the employer has been notified in writing, and the employer can make an accommodation without hardship. Maine pharmacy law and regulations restrict pharmacist refusals to professional and medical reasons. Religious or personal convictions do not justify refusals.

. . . [R]efusals continue to be a problem in states without applicable legislation or regulation, even if pharmacy policies require that patients be given service. In Ohio, for example, a woman and her boyfriend requested Plan B, a form of emergency contraception, but the pharmacist "shook his head and laughed," according to the woman. The pharmacist, she reports, told her that he stocked Plan B but would not sell it to her because he believed it to be a form of abortion. Wal-Mart, in whose pharmacy this occurred, has a corporate policy to stock Plan B, and allows any Wal-Mart worker who does not feel comfortable dispensing a product to refuse service, but also directs such employees to refer customers to another pharmacist, pharmacy worker or sales associate.

. . . .

IV. ETHICAL ARGUMENTS FOR AND AGAINST THE PERMISSIBILITY OF PROVIDER REFUSALS TO PROVIDE SERVICES

In a 2005 article entitled "Dispensing With Liberty," philosophers Elizabeth Fenton and Loran Lomasky delineate the major lines of traditional argumentation concerning provider refusals on the grounds of religious belief or personal conscience. Their conclusion . . . is that traditional arguments are undermined by their primary focus on a contest between the moral claims of individual patients and providers. . . . [A]ttention to the power imbalance between the parties, and the special obligations placed upon professionals as a group due to their privileged, quasi-monopoly status as health care providers, form the basis for what is arguably a collective obligation of the profession to provide non-discriminatory access to all lawful services.

Fenton and Lomasky begin by noting that "obligations to perform typically have to meet a higher burden of justification than do obligations to desist." . . .

Following this line of analysis, one can argue that failure to perform a service, whether performing an abortion, filling a contraceptive prescription, or informing a parent of the timeliness of a childhood varicella vaccine, simply constitutes a refusal to act, and that forcing a professional to act in such circumstances requires a high level of justification. . . . "By refusing to enter into a transaction that the other party desires, one thereby *fails to provide a benefit* but not to *inflict a liability*." . . .

Responses to this argument are several-fold. First, it clearly separates out the calls for right to conscience that encompass forcibly imposing unwanted medical interventions . . . [I]n this case, at least, it is a provider's actions, not inactions, that are at issue. And of course, such actions would also constitute a common-law battery. Further, state legislation protecting HCPs who inflict such unwanted care on competent patients would run afoul of constitutional protections for patient autonomy.

Second . . . it is suggestive of an as-yet undiscussed aspect of the refusal clause debate. Specifically, the so-called "right of conscience" may be far easier to defend in the case of the non-professional than in the case of the professional. A clothing store salesperson who refuses to assist a single woman shopping for maternity clothes may indeed be leaving her no better or worse off than before she entered the store, and be under no ethical duty to do more than this. But where an affirmative duty to provide a service does exist, then failure to act is not merely nonfeasance, but rather is an active form of misfeasance. Thus, refusal by a licensed taxi driver to pick up an African-American man is more than nonfeasance; due to legal obligations to provide non-discriminatory service, this failure to act is a form of active misfeasance.

Thus, whether the refusal to provide a service should be regarded as mere nonfeasance or as a more serious problem of misfeasance turns, somewhat tautologically, on whether there is a duty to provide service. But on this, there is indeed some guidance, as the statements of the relevant professional societies suggest that just such a duty does indeed exist. . . .

. . . By failing to abide by the standards set by their own professions, those practicing refusal of informing patients of their options and providing referrals or other alternatives are not merely denying a discretionary benefit to the consumer but rather are affirmatively violating a duty to their patients.

A rejoinder might be that these professional standards are wrongheaded, because they deny to HCPs the opportunity to avoid being transformed into mere purveyors of goods and services. The essence of professionalism, the argument goes, involves discretion and judgment, which is why the physician ought to have more authority over patient choices than a candy seller has over consumer purchases. To do otherwise is to render medical services no different than gumballs. . . . ["]It is not inconsistent with professional practice to limit one's clientele. Indeed, just the reverse; one attribute of professionalism is an entitlement to employ one's own judgment concerning which associations to enter."

Two responses to this argument are in order. . . . Refusals based on moral disapprobation . . . are not typical of medical ethics. Thus, the physician is trained to heal the criminal, regardless of personal feelings about the criminal's moral culpability, and leaves to the criminal justice system the task of working to ensure that the now-healed criminal will not use his good health to engage in further criminal acts. This is as true of the thief shot by the homeowner as it is of the battering spouse who presents for repair of his broken knuckles. Even knowing that the act of healing may result in further abusive and criminal acts does not yield a medical ethic that calls for refusing care lest one become complicit in those acts. Instead, the prevailing medical ethic is one of universal care.

Second, the choice of refusals follows a pattern that suggests a discriminatory effect, whether direct or indirect. The argument from complicity, that is, the argument that one ought not be forced to become complicit in an immoral act, is not frequently raised in the context of setting the broken hand bones of the wife-beating husband who might then batter again. Instead, it is raised most frequently in the context of refusing to be complicit with acts that form families with single or gay mothers or with acts that prevent conception or gestation of a child. These are settings in which the parties most frequently affected are women. . . .

Actions that have a disparate impact on one class of persons—here, on women—are not necessarily unethically or illegally discriminatory (although they may be in some circumstances). But the disparate impact does raise legitimate questions about the underlying motivations of the actors, and the sufficiency of their justifications. This is especially true when those actions impinge upon protected classes of persons, that is, those whom we have historically disadvantaged in law and practice and for whom court now offer [sic] more protection from discriminatory state action. It is also true when those actions impinge upon protected classes of rights, of which reproductive choice is one. Some protections are offered by the courts only in the context of state action, but it is illuminating even in a non-legal and purely ethical context to note the intersection of protected class and protected rights at the center of the category of people and services most typically denied on the basis of a right of conscience. One might ask whether the current debate over refusal clauses would sound any different if it were more baldly framed as the asserted right of health care providers to refuse service to "bad women."

A last major source of argument in favor of the right to exercise conscientious objection is the assertion that in most cases the services requested are not really medical services. . . . They do not cure a disease, the argument goes, but rather use drugs and medical techniques to accomplish a lifestyle goal.

Again, the argument has multiple responses. First, medical professionals consider these services, at least in most circumstances, to be an important part of good health care. For example, given that pregnancy is a condition with significant medical consequences and a risk of both morbidity and mortality, contraception constitutes preventive health care. To trivialize these services as "lifestyle" issues is to ignore women's health care needs.

Second, to the extent these may in some circumstances be viewed as choices dictated more by lifestyle than by medical necessity, they are nonetheless choices that are constrained by the state-created limits on consumer access to the products and services needed to accomplish these goals. . . . Even beyond the practical constraints of insurance coverage (which often directs patients to a limited range of physicians and pharmacies lest coverage be denied), the very products and services themselves cannot be sold except by those who are members of a special collective, that is, licensed health care providers.

. . . If these professionals, who have a state-created and state-maintained collective monopoly on these products and services, will not provide service, the patients have nowhere to turn. Thus, what might otherwise be an issue of lifestyle choices is transformed by state action into an issue of medical choice, in which patient and provider stand not as equals with competing moral compasses but rather as petitioner and grantor in a regulated relationship.

. . . There is ample precedent for limiting the range of conscientious objection for professionals who operate as state actors. The question arises, then, whether such limitations might appropriately be extended to . . . private actors . . . in possession of unique privileges by virtue of state licensing schemes that grant them, as a professional group, a monopoly on a public service.

In *Endres v. Indiana State Police*, for example, the Seventh Circuit considered a case arising from a religious objection on the part of a state trooper who claimed that his assignment to work as a Gaming Commission agent—an assignment that would require him to assist in the management of the casino industry—would violate his religious beliefs concerning the immorality of gambling. . . .

Judge Easterbrook, writing for court, held that the relevant provision of Title VII did not oblige states "to afford the sort of accommodation that Endres requested . . ." as, otherwise, "law enforcement personnel [would have] a right to choose which laws they will enforce, and whom they will protect from crime."

. . . But the *Endres'* court's opinion went further, stating that accommodation would be unreasonable even in the absence of hardship. Agencies "designed to protect the public from danger may insist that all of their personnel protect all members of the public—that they leave their religious (and other) views behind so that they may serve all without favor on religious grounds."

. . . .

A natural result of such an analysis might well be that, at the very least, a profession in possession of a state-created right to be the sole purveyor of products and services must ensure that every member of the public have non-discriminatory access to its products and services. That is, the profession as a collective unit takes upon itself a collective obligation to the patients it serves. . . . In the early era of the AIDS crisis, for example, some HCPs resisted treating HIV-positive patients for fear of becoming infected themselves. Yet as professional groups, HCPs recognized the obligation to provide care. In some settings . . . only volunteer HCPs treat[ed] the infected patients, while other HCPs opted out. In other settings, the obligation to treat was shared by every member of the profession and no opt-out provisions were made. In all cases, though, there was a shared agreement that there was indeed an obligation to provide care, because no other market for care existed outside the profession.

In the context of today's debates, one means of meeting a collective obligation is to require every individual HCP to provide all products and services, thus denying the legitimacy of even the narrowest conscientious refusal laws of the 1970s, which focused almost exclusively on the actual performance of abortions and sterilizations. This could be accomplished at the state level either by establishing such a duty as a condition of licensing, or by enshrining such a duty in state law such that violation rendered the HCP vulnerable to medical malpractice litigation. Another approach would be to modify employment discrimination laws to make it more difficult for employees in health care professions to sustain religious discrimination claims when they are penalized for failing to perform their duties to their patients. . . . [P]rofessional societies can [also] continue to articulate their own ethical standards, and in this way lay the groundwork both for individual HCPs to see their way clear to serving patients even in ways that violate their own preferences and beliefs, as well as to assist courts in determining the customary and standard practice in medical malpractice cases based on refusal of service or medical abandonment.

A less extreme means for achieving a reasonable result for patients is to accept a collective responsibility to make all legal products and services reasonably available. This is the tactic taken by those laws that focus on establishments rather than individual professionals. Thus, such laws may require that all licensed pharmacies have at least one pharmacist on hand during business hours who can fill all prescriptions, without requiring that each and every pharmacist at the establishment actually fill the prescriptions. While potentially burdensome for small pharmacy practices, it is manageable for larger establishments and most chains. (And indeed, many public accommodation laws make some exception for small family-owned businesses where compliance would be unusually burdensome.)

This approach still requires the refusing provider to inform patients of their legal options and to make a referral (or pass along a prescription) where necessary. . . . For many who assert a right of refusal, such a solution still fails to meet their objection to being made complicit in the patient's choices. . . . [S]ome professionals are now arguing that the right to practice their religion requires that they not be made complicit in any practice to which they object on religious or moral grounds, even if their concerns about complicity do not extend to the situations of criminals (discussed above) nor comport with modern notions of non-discrimination against women.

. . . .

More ominously, some establishments are seeking to avoid these battles entirely by simply choosing not to stock the products that are the most contentious. In the most well-known example of this tactic, Wal-Mart made the decision to avoid stocking emergency contraception, thus eliminating the problem of managing individual pharmacist refusals . . .

While Wal-Mart subsequently reversed this policy, it was an object lesson for other businesses that may be considering a wholesale withdrawal from the field of selling contraceptives or providing reproductive care. The reversal of the Wal-Mart policy followed a very vocal public campaign, but smaller businesses—which may nonetheless be significant factors in their local markets—may choose the same strategy, with little risk of generating a national outcry sufficient to trigger a reversal of their policy.

NOTES

1. *Conscientious objection, reproductive justice.* Public policy has long permitted individuals whose religion demands pacifism to refrain from (i.e. "object to") carrying arms in time of war. This practice became codified after 1917, with the institutionalization of a national draft. *See* Kent Greenawalt, *All or Nothing at All: The Defeat of Selective Conscientious Objection*, 1971 SUP. CT. REV. 31, 35. In the wake of *Roe v. Wade*, the concept of conscientious objection expanded beyond the martial context to the abortion context. In 1973, Congress passed Senator Frank Church's amendment to the Public Health Service Act. The Church Amendment allows individuals or entities who receive certain public funds to decline to perform abortion or sterilization procedures, or to decline to make facilities or personnel available for the performance of such procedures if such performance "would be contrary to [the individual or entity's] religious beliefs or moral convictions." *See* 42 U.S.C. § 300a–7 (2014).

2. *Complicity-based conscience claims.* In a 2015 article, Professors Douglas NeJaime and Reva Siegel document the rise of that they term "complicity-based conscience claims." As they explain, persons of faith now seek religious exemptions from laws concerning sex, reproduction, and marriage on the ground that the law in question makes the religious objector complicit in the sinful conduct of others. What makes complicity-based

claims distinct from traditional conscience exemptions is that accommodating claims of this kind risks inflicting "material and dignitary harms" on third parties. Because "complicity claims focus on the conduct of others outside the faith community, their accommodation therefore has potential to harm those whom the claimants view as sinning." And while conscience exemptions have traditionally been touted as a means of resolving conflict over fraught social issues, NeJaime and Siegel maintain that in implicitly condemning the "sinful" conduct of third parties, complicity-based conscience exemption may "extend, rather than settle, conflict." Douglas NeJaime & Reva B. Siegel, *Conscience Wars: Complicity-Based Conscience Claims in Religion and Politics*, 124 YALE L.J. 2516 (2015).

3. *Conscience clauses' expanse.* The case of Edwin Graning suggests the almost unlimited reach of conscience clauses. Graning, a bus driver for the Texas Capital Area Rural Transportation System (CARTS), refused to take two women to a Planned Parenthood Clinic, on the ground that to do so might involve him (albeit indirectly) in an abortion, which conflicted with his religious beliefs. He was fired. With legal representation from the American Center for Law & Justice, a conservative legal aid service founded by Christian media mogul Pat Robertson, he argued that his termination constituted discrimination on the basis of religion. On the advice of counsel, CARTS settled the case for $21,000 dollars. As part of the settlement, Graning agreed never to seek employment from CARTS. *See* Steven Kreytak, *Fired bus driver gets $21,000 settlement after refusing ride to Planned Parenthood*, AUSTIN AM. STATESMAN (Apr. 26, 2011, 12:01 AM), https://www.statesman.com/story/news/local/2011/04/26/fired-bus-driver-gets-21/6683474007/. Might CARTS's response to Graning's suit have been different if it had sought counsel and advice from a reproductive rights organization? If providers do have a right to refuse to perform a service on the basis of religious objection, how far should this right extend? Whose interests should the right cover?

* * *

Since their development in the 1990s, emergency contraception pills have been controversial—sparring over their availability has occurred in political, administrative, and judicial arenas. In 1999 the FDA approved Plan B emergency-contraception pills for prescription-only use. In 2006, the FDA approved over-the-counter (OTC) sales of the Plan B pill for women eighteen and older. In so doing, the FDA rejected a citizen petition that would have made Plan B available to women of all ages without a prescription. In Tummino v. Torti, *603 F. Supp. 2d 519 (E.D.N.Y. 2009), a group of individuals and organizations advocating wider distribution of and access to emergency contraceptives challenged the FDA's action in court, alleging that the agency's decision was unduly influenced by political concerns. A district court agreed, remanding the citizen petition to the FDA for reconsideration. In 2011, relying on scientific evidence, the FDA concluded that Plan B was safe for sale without restrictions. Nevertheless, Health and Human Services Secretary Kathleen Sebelius overruled the agency's decision, citing concerns that "the product would be available, without a prescription or other point-of-sale restrictions, even to the youngest girls of reproductive age." The agency's action generated another courtroom clash over access to emergency contraception.*

Tummino v. Hamburg

936 F. Supp. 2d 198 (E.D.N.Y. 2013).

■ KORMAN, J.

... This case involved Plan B and Plan B One-Step, emergency contraceptives that can be taken to reduce the risk of pregnancy after unprotected intercourse. They must, however, be taken as soon as possible after unprotected intercourse. The longer the delay, the less effective they become. The effort to convert these levonorgestrel-based contraceptives from prescription to over-the-counter status has gone on for over twelve years, even though they would be among the safest drugs available to children and adults on any drugstore shelf.

The FDA, responding to unjustified political interference, delayed as long as it possibly could before it took even one incremental step in the process. Ultimately, on December 7, 2011, in response to an application filed by Teva Women's Health ("Teva"), the FDA concluded that Plan B One-Step—the one-pill version of the drug—could be sold over-the-counter and without a prescription or age restriction. The FDA was reversed by the Secretary of Health and Human Services on the same day in a decision that was politically motivated and that, even without regard to the Secretary's motives, was so unpersuasive as to call into question her good faith. Some five days later, the FDA rejected a Citizen Petition that sought unrestricted over-the-counter status for Plan B—the original two-pill emergency contraceptive product—and all drugs that are "equivalent" to Plan B. This decision was compelled by Secretary's reasoning in ordering the FDA to reject Teva's application. Specifically, the Secretary found that information that she deemed essential was not provided by Teva. The Citizen Petition lacked the same information. The Citizen Petition Denial Letter, which came five days after the denial of Teva's Plan B One-Step application, was clearly prompted by the Secretary's action despite the FDA's fanciful effort to make it appear that it undertook an independent review of the Citizen Petition.

On April 5, 2013, I issued an order directing the defendants—the Commissioner of Food and Drugs and the Secretary of Health and Human Services—to grant the Citizen Petition filed by the plaintiffs and make levonorgestrel-based emergency contraceptives available over-the-counter and without point-of-sale or age restrictions. I did so because the Secretary's action was politically motivated, scientifically unjustified, and contrary to agency precedent, and because it could not provide a basis to sustain the denial of the Citizen Petition. ...

... [T]he effect of my decision was to make levonorgestrel-based emergency contraceptives available without a prescription and without any point-of-sale or age restrictions. The only practical difference between my decision and the decision of the FDA that the Secretary reversed was that the FDA's decision was arguably directed towards the one-pill version of the drug, and my decision applied to both versions. Nevertheless, responding to farfetched concerns ultimately voiced in response to the prospect of making the two-pill version available without a prescription, I advised the FDA that if it actually believed there was a significant difference between the one-and two-pill products, it was free to limit the relief on the Citizen Petition to the one-pill product.

With this concession to the FDA's concerns, my decision was entirely consistent with the initial decision of the FDA. I adopted and completely agreed with Commissioner Hamburg's conclusion that "there is adequate and reasonable, well-supported, and science-based evidence that Plan B One-Step is safe and effective and should be approved for nonprescription use for all females of child-bearing potential"—a conclusion that she reached after she had "reviewed and thoughtfully considered the data, clinical information, and analysis provided by" the FDA's Center for Drug Evaluation and Research. Notwithstanding my deference to the Commissioner and the scientists at the FDA, the defendants have filed a notice of appeal and a motion to stay my decision as they continue their administrative agency filibuster through the appellate process.

I pause here before proceeding to a discussion of the merits of the motion to comment on the defendants' analysis of the manner in which drug approval applications should be made. Thus, they tell me that "[a] drug approval decision involves scientific judgments as to whether statutory and regulatory factors are met that warrant deference to those charged with the statutory responsibility to make those decisions. The agency alone has the necessary information and scientific expertise to assess the data and information required to make a determination that a drug is safe and effective." This salutary principle was flagrantly violated by Secretary Sebelius, who completely lacks the "necessary information and scientific expertise to assess the data and information required to make a determination that a drug is safe and effective," and whose role in the process has been circumscribed by Congress as well as by the delegation to the Commissioner of any authority that the Secretary may have—a clear recognition by Congress and the Secretary of her lack of competence in this area. Yet, in something out of an alternate reality, the defendants seek a stay to pursue an appeal that would vindicate the Secretary's disregard of the very principle they advocate.

DISCUSSION

There are four factors to be considered before granting a stay pending appeal: (1) whether a party will suffer irreparable injury if a stay is issued, (2) whether the movant will suffer irreparable injury absent a stay, (3) whether the movant has demonstrated a substantial possibility, although less than a likelihood, of success on appeal, and (4) the public interests that may be affected. . . . "[T]he necessary 'level' or 'degree' of possibility of success will vary according to the Court's assessment of the other [stay] factors." *Mohammed v. Reno*, 309 F. 3d 101 (2d Cir. 2002). [As the Second Circuit has] observed: "[t]he probability of success that must be demonstrated is inversely proportional to the amount of irreparable injury plaintiff will suffer absent the stay. Simply stated, more of one excuses less of the other." Against this backdrop, I turn to a discussion of the relevant factors.

Irreparable Injury to the Plaintiffs

The defendants' argument that the plaintiffs will not suffer any harm if a stay is granted is based solely on an agreement they reached with Teva the day before they filed their notice of appeal. . . . On March 9, 2012, three months after the Secretary overruled the FDA and directed the denial of Teva's application to make Plan B One-Step available over-the-counter without a prescription to all women, Teva filed a letter with the FDA seeking to make Plan B One-Step available for sale to women 15 years of age and over without a prescription and to eliminate the sale of Plan B One-Step by prescription for women under 15 years of age. Under this proposal, the drug would be stocked on the shelves of any retail establishment with an on-site pharmacy, and customers would be required to prove their age by providing photo identification to the cashier of the retail establishment as opposed to the pharmacist.

Teva and the FDA exchanged correspondence regarding this proposal through June 2012. After an eight-month hiatus, they resumed communication in March 2013, shortly after I indicated my intention to rule on the plaintiffs' Citizen Petition by the end of March—a decision which the defendants had to have known from oral argument would strike down the order of the Secretary and the FDA's action which was dictated by it. My decision was filed on April 5, 2013. Teva's application was approved on April 30, 2013, the day before defendants in this case filed their notice of appeal. The FDA has provided for no reason for the delay in ruling on Teva's application. Indeed, as I observed at oral argument, the approval—when it finally came—was intended to provide a sugarcoating for the FDA's appeal.

Nevertheless, there was something in it for Teva as well. The benefits the proposal would confer on Teva were not insignificant. Because . . . 99% of Plan B One-Step consumers are aged 15 and above, Teva would lose next to nothing in the way of revenue by limiting sales to those women. On the other hand, Teva's proposal would enable it to have its product, and its product alone, displayed on the shelves in the family planning area of stores with an on-site pharmacy. Thus, a consumer looking for an emergency contraceptive would only find Plan B One-Step on the shelves, and if she came in after the pharmacy counter was closed, her only option would be Plan B One-Step. If she were under the age of 15, she would have no option, because she could only obtain levonorgestrel-based emergency contraceptives with a prescription.

Moreover, because the FDA claimed that one of the studies conducted by Teva—the so-called "actual use" study—was essential to the approval of Teva's proposal, Teva enjoys three years of marketing exclusivity to the 15 and 16 year old consumers. The pharmaceutical companies that sell "brand X" versions of Plan B One-Step as well as the two-pill package of the drug could not display their products on the shelf because the old marketing regime remains in effect for them, and their products can only be sold from behind the pharmacy counter. Anyone under the age of 17 needs a prescription to obtain these products, and anyone over the age of 17 can only obtain them from the pharmacy by showing proof-of-age identification.

While this proposal was a boon to Teva, it did little to eliminate the practical obstructions in obtaining emergency contraception to women of child-bearing age whether over or under age 15. On the contrary, Teva will use its privileged marketing status and exclusivity to increase the cost of the drug. The price of Plan B One-Step under the new marketing regime is expected to be $60, significantly more than the one-or two-pill generic version, and could conceivably go higher, if only to accommodate the more expensive packing, age-verification tags, and anti-theft technology that the new marketing arrangement would require. The cost of all emergency contraception, particularly Plan B One-Step, which is the most expensive, is already an impediment to access for many women and adolescents.

Nevertheless, the Secretary of Health and Human Services and the Commissioner of Food and Drugs argue that a stay of my order to make levonorgestrel-based emergency contraceptives available without a prescription and without point-of-sale and age restrictions "will not harm plaintiffs." This argument is based on the premise that the plaintiffs "are all over age 15 and therefore will soon be able to obtain at least one emergency contraceptive containing levonorgestrel ... without a prescription at retail establishments that have a pharmacy counter." Thus, the order that I entered and they seek to appeal "is not required to afford relief to any of the plaintiffs. They can purchase the product whenever the store is open (regardless of whether the pharmacy is open) by showing proof of age."

... [T]he defendants' argument ignores (1) the fact that "showing proof of age," which means government-issued photo identification, constitutes a substantial impediment to obtaining emergency contraception, particularly for young women of reproductive age, and (2) that emergency contraception can only be obtained at retail establishments with on-site pharmacies. Moreover, while there are some retail establishments that are open for longer hours than their pharmacy counters, the unjustifiable point-of-sale restrictions left in place under the Teva-FDA agreement will continue to present barriers to all women.

Many women do not live near a store with an on-site pharmacy, and even when the drugstore or comparable facility has an on-site pharmacy, the difference between the hours of the pharmacy and the store itself is often significant. Indeed, a research letter published in the journal of the American Medical Association found that "of the 943 pharmacies called" in a survey of emergency contraceptive availability in five geographically diverse cities, "only 4.7% were open 24 hours." Tracey A. Wilkinson et al., *Research Letter: Access to Emergency Contraception for Adolescents*, 307 J. AM. MED. ASS'N 362 (January 25, 2012).

Significantly, a study conducted by the Brennan Center for the purpose of showing the extent to which photo identification requirements throw roadblocks in the way of voters found that African-American citizens disproportionately lack photo identification. Specifically, "[t]wenty-five percent of African-American voting-age citizens have no current government-issued photo ID, compared to eight percent of white voting-age citizens." Using 2000 census figures, the Brennan Center concluded that "this amounts to more than 5.5 million adult African-American citizens without photo identification." Similarly, "[c]itizens earning less than $35,000 per year are more than twice as likely to lack current government-issued photo identification as those earning more than $35,000. Indeed, the survey indicates that at least 15 percent of voting-age American citizens earning less than $35,000 per year do not have a valid government-issued photo ID." Indeed, [one of the] proposed findings of fact submitted by the Department of Justice in [an unrelated case,] *South Carolina v. Holder*, . . . is that "[m]inority voters in [South Carolina] are disproportionately less likely than white voters to possess any of the currently available, acceptable forms of [photographic voter identification]. . . . This conclusion holds true for black voters, Native American voters, and Hispanic voters, all of whom are significantly less likely than white voters to possess an allowable [photograph voter identification]. . . . These disparities are statistically significant." United States' Proposed Findings of Fact and Conclusions of Law at 8, *South Carolina v. Holder*, No. 12–cv–203 (D.D.C.).

These statistics do not necessarily correlate with women of reproductive age. Nevertheless, they indicate the disproportionate burden that the Teva-FDA agreement places on African-American and poor adults over age 18. Moreover, it can reasonably be assumed that the proportion of women between 15 and 18 who lack government-issued photo identification is much higher, with a similar disparate impact on African-Americans and the poor. Nor does the nature of the age identification required under Teva's proposal make any concession to the difficulties they face. Thus, in response to a question posed by the FDA, Teva responded that "[t]he age verification system is based on federal and state guidelines for the sale of tobacco and alcohol and as such requires a government-issued photo ID (including driver's license, military card, immigration card, or passport) with date of birth." Letter from Valerie M. Mulligan, Senior Dir. of Reg. Affairs, Teva Women's Health, to Andrea Leonard-Segal, Center for Drug Evaluation and Research, FDA at 2 (June 27, 2012). Teva also observed that "a school-issued ID and birth certificate would not be considered acceptable age-verification." And, "for consumers age 15, there are some states that issue a driver's permit at age 15, or a consumer may use one of the other types of ID listed above, *if available.*" *Id.* (emphasis added).

Moreover, the Teva-FDA agreement does nothing to relieve the burden on younger adolescents who still require a prescription from a physician in order to obtain an emergency contraceptive. Indeed, because the Teva-FDA agreement provides that Teva will no longer market Plan B One-Step as a prescription product, younger adolescents receive no benefit from the new marketing agreement. Instead, the requirement of a prescription only adds the additional cost of a doctor's visit and delay to obtaining a time-sensitive emergency contraceptive that is more effective the sooner it is taken after unprotected intercourse. . . . I do not dwell on this aspect of the prejudice suffered by the population of the youngest adolescents, although it should not be ignored, because the number of these adolescents who actually use levonorgestrel-based emergency contraceptives is miniscule, and they have been invoked in the debate over access to these contraceptives mostly as a red herring to justify the continued burdens suffered by older women who seek access to the drug.

Irreparable Injury to the Defendants and the Public Interest

The defendants argue that they "and the public interest" will suffer irreparable harm absent a stay for a number of reasons. Thus, they argue that the FDA and the public will be irreparably and immediately harmed "if a drug product that purported to be 'FDA approved' were approved instead at the direction of a court." This is so because, they suggest, "[t]he public properly relies upon FDA classification of drugs as non-prescription as a reflection of the agency's judgment regarding the safety and proper use of a drug without a doctor's prescription. Thus, the public interest will not be served by reclassification of drugs as non-prescription without agency approval." This argument ignores the fact that the FDA found that the drug was safe and could be used properly without a doctor's prescription, and was prepared to make it available over-the-counter for all ages. As Commissioner Hamburg observed, "there is adequate and reasonable, well-supported, and science-based evidence that Plan B One-Step is safe and effective and should be approved for nonprescription use for all females of child-bearing potential." Thus, if a stay is denied, the public can have confidence that the FDA's judgment is being vindicated, and if a stay is granted, it will allow the bad-faith, politically motivated decision of Secretary Sebelius, who lacks any medical or scientific expertise, to prevail—thus justifiably undermining the public's confidence in the drug approval process.

Nor is there any merit to the related argument that a stay will "prevent public uncertainty regarding the status of the drugs at issue here pending the government's appeal to the Second Circuit." This silly argument ignores the fact it is the government's appeal from the order that sustained the judgment of the Commissioner of the FDA that is the cause of any uncertainty, and that that appeal is taken solely to vindicate the improper conduct of the Secretary and possibly for the purpose of further delaying greater access to emergency contraceptives for purely political reasons. Whether my order is stayed or not will not resolve any uncertainty.

The defendants also argue that "if the status of these drugs is changed and later reversed, it can lead to situations in which women mistakenly believe that they can obtain the drug without a prescription or at certain locations where it used to be available, but is no longer." This argument assumes that defendants have a likelihood of success on the merits, an issue that I will shortly address, and is largely an insult to the intelligence of women. If women can no longer obtain Plan B without a prescription at certain locations, they will go to locations where it is available. On the other hand, if a stay is granted, the prejudice to those who need ready access to emergency contraceptives is a certainty, and is likely to continue until the resolution of the appeal—a period of time which is difficult to predict.

Moreover, this argument comes with ill grace from the defendants, who have added significant confusion by putting in place a convoluted triple-tiered marketing scheme that will only increase the confusion that already prevents women from obtaining timely access to emergency contraceptives. Specifically, women and retailers across the country will be forced to operate under the following set of nonsensical rules: (1) women 15 years of age or older with adequate proof of age will be permitted to purchase Plan B One-Step, which will only be available on the shelves in stores with on-site pharmacies; (2) other levonorgestrel-based products will remain behind the counter, but will be available without a prescription to women over 17 years of age who have government issued proof of age; and, (3) women who lack adequate proof of age or are under the age of 15 will not have access to Plan B One-Step and must obtain a prescription for another levonorgestrel-based contraceptive product. The confusion caused by this system, the only purpose of which is to sugarcoat the defendants' appeal, is much greater than any potential confusion that could result from simply returning a product to prescription status.

The defendants' last argument is that the government interest in conferring marketing exclusivity will be irreparably harmed absent a stay. I do not question the validity of the policies underlying the statutes and regulations conferring marketing exclusivity on pharmaceutical companies that perform needed research to make drugs available and obtain approval to market drugs as a result. Nevertheless, at the time of my decision there was no issue of market exclusivity, because Teva's previous applications to expand access to Plan B One-Step had been denied, and it had not appealed. . . .

Moreover, if I was operating in ignorance of the fact that Teva was negotiating a sweetheart agreement with the FDA, it was because nothing happened in this regard from December 2011 until April 30, 2013, 25 days after I issued my opinion in this case. Indeed, it would not have been unreasonable for me to assume that after 16 months of silence, the verdict of the quiescent years—to borrow a phrase from Brainerd Currie—was that nothing happened. Nevertheless, I acknowledge that I ordered the Citizen Petition be granted in part because it was my view that the plaintiffs were entitled to the relief they sought even without the actual use study paid for by Teva. Indeed, the 2003 FDA advisory committee formed to consider the first application for over-the-counter access to levonorgestrel-based emergency contraceptives voted by the most overwhelming of margins to approve it, without the benefit of the actual use study that Teva submitted with its more recent application, and it was only the political interference by the Bush White House that prevented their recommendation from being adopted. If Teva could somehow benefit from the relief sought by the Citizen Petition, it was simply because the relief it sought from the FDA overlapped to a degree with the Citizen Petition.

Defendants' Likelihood of Success on the Merits

The defendants offer two arguments in support of their claim that they have "a substantial likelihood of success on appeal." The first argument is that I was without subject matter jurisdiction to review the denial of Teva's petition. This argument is frivolous. I repeatedly recognized in my opinion, as the defendants acknowledged in their memorandum in support of their motion for a stay, that I did not have the authority to review the denial of Teva's petition for the purpose of granting relief. Nor did I direct the defendants to grant Teva's petition. I need not burden this opinion with a further discussion of this claim, because it is belied by what has actually happened since my opinion. Specifically, Teva is not making any effort to take advantage of my decision. Instead, it has entered into an agreement with the FDA, which I previously described. Since Teva has acquiesced in the denial of its petition, and entered into an agreement designed to "address the Secretary's stated concerns," there is nothing for the Court of Appeals to review, even if my decision had affected Teva's petition. Indeed, this issue could be said to be moot.

The defendants' next argument in support of their claim that they have a substantial likelihood of success on appeal is that I exceeded my authority in ordering a change of Plan B for prescription to over-the-counter instead of remanding to the agency. Specifically, the defendants argue that "[r]ather than issuing a directive to the agency as to what specific action to take, the Court should have remanded to the agency for compliance with its legal ruling." Quoting from a decision of the Supreme Court, they argue that "the proper course, *except in rare circumstances*, is to remand to the agency for additional investigation or explanation. The reviewing court is not *generally* empowered to conduct a *de novo* inquiry into the matter being reviewed and to reach its own conclusions based on such an inquiry."

The defendants' own admission that they could not continue to reach the same decision . . . after remand and claim that the only remedy was yet another remand clearly establishes that the question is not whether I have authority to grant relief. So too does a careful study of the language of the Supreme Court decision on which they rely, and which recognizes that there are "rare circumstances" in which remand is not necessary. This case presents the kind of "rare circumstances" where a remand to the agency is not only unnecessary but would constitute an abuse of discretion. First, the FDA is not the problem. The cause of the rejection of over-the-counter sale of levonorgestrel-based emergency contraceptives was the Secretary of Health and Human Services. She has not changed her position. A remand would thus be futile.

More significantly, I have been there and done that. In my 2009 opinion, [in *Tummino v. Torti*, 603 F. Supp. 2d 519 (E.D.N.Y. 2009)] after concluding that the administrative agency process was corrupted by political interference, I declined the plaintiffs' request to avoid a remand and simply direct that the FDA award them the relief that they sought. I did so for two reasons. First, it was my view that a decision on whether Plan B "may be used safely without a prescription by children as young as 11 or 12, is best left to the expertise of the FDA, to which Congress has entrusted this responsibility; it should not be made by a federal district court judge." *Tummino v. Torti*, 603 F. Supp. 2d at 549. Second, a new FDA Commissioner, Deputy Commissioner, and President had come into office since the agency's decision on Plan B had been made, who I thought could be "trusted to conduct a fair assessment of the scientific evidence." Neither of these grounds is applicable here.

On remand, defendants engaged in the same bad faith that resulted in my initial remand. They delayed the decision for three years and, ultimately, improper political influence prevented the FDA from granting the petition. Nor do they claim a reasonable probability of success on appeal in challenging my analysis of their flagrant misconduct. Indeed, I traced the numerous departures from agency policy and defects in the proceedings for yet a second time. Significantly, defendants do not take any issue with any of my substantive conclusions. Instead, they seek another remand, without any assurance that the result would be any different. On the contrary, the defendants assert that, even if the Secretary changed her mind and the FDA agreed that the Citizen Petition contained sufficient data to support an over-the-counter switch, the FDA would be obligated to conduct what could be described as a national referendum: "[A] rule making proceeding [in] which the public and all stakeholders would have an opportunity to participate and share their views including Teva, including plaintiffs, including the petitioners, including anybody else who has an interest in the issue would be able to submit their views." I need not here deal with the argument that such a rulemaking procedure would be required in the ordinary case. As I noted . . . earlier . . . :

> [T]he bad faith that has permeated consideration of the Citizen Petition, not to speak of the Plan B sponsor's applications, should rule out such relief here. More than twelve years have passed since the Citizen Petition was filed and eight years since this lawsuit commenced. The FDA has engaged in intolerable delays in processing the petition. Indeed, it could accurately be described as an administrative agency filibuster. Moreover, one of the devices the FDA has employed to stall proceedings was to seek public comment on whether or not it needed to engage in rulemaking in order to adopt an age-restricted marketing regime. After eating up eleven months, 47,000 public comments, and hundreds of thousands, if not millions, of dollars, it decided that it did not need rulemaking after all. The plaintiffs should not be forced to endure, nor should the agency's misconduct be rewarded by, an exercise that permits the FDA to engage in further delay and obstruction.

CONCLUSION

The motion for a stay pending the appeal is denied. Indeed, in my view, the defendants' appeal is frivolous and is taken for the purpose of delay. Nevertheless, as a courtesy to the Court of Appeals, and to enable it to schedule the motion in the ordinary course, I grant a stay pending the hearing or submission of the defendants' motion for a stay in the Court of Appeals. . . .

SO ORDERED.

Erickson v. Bartell Drugs

141 F. Supp. 2d 1266 (W.D. Wash. 2001).

■ LASNIK, DISTRICT JUDGE.

The parties' cross-motions for summary judgment in this case raise an issue of first impression in the federal courts' whether the selective exclusion of prescription contraceptives from defendant's generally comprehensive prescription plan constitutes discrimination on the basis of sex.[1] In particular, plaintiffs assert that Bartell's decision not to cover

---

[1] Bartell's benefit plan is self-insured and covers all prescription drugs, including a number of preventative drugs and devices, such as blood-pressure and cholesterol-lowering drugs, hormone replacement therapies, prenatal vitamins, and drugs to prevent allergic reactions, breast cancer, and blood clotting. The plan specifically excludes from coverage a handful of products, including contraceptive devices, drugs prescribed for weight reduction,

prescription contraceptives such as birth control pills, Norplant, Depo-Provera, intra-uterine devices, and diaphragms under its Prescription Benefit Plan for non-union employees violates Title VII, 42 U.S.C. § 2000e *et seq.*, as amended by the Pregnancy Discrimination Act, 42 U.S.C. § 2000e(k).[2]

A. APPLICATION OF TITLE VII

Title VII makes it unlawful for an employer "to fail or refuse to hire or to discharge any individual, or otherwise to discriminate against any individual with respect to his compensation, terms, conditions, or privileges of employment, because of such individual's race, color, religion, sex, or national origin," 42 U.S.C. § 2000e–2(a)(1). Unfortunately, the legislative history of the Civil Rights Act of 1964, of which Title VII is a part, is not particularly helpful in determining what Congress had in mind when it added protection from discrimination based on sex. The 1964 law, coming in the midst of the Civil Rights movement and the turmoil in the South, was predominately about racial fairness for blacks, not gender equity for women. In fact, the late amendment that added "sex" to one portion of the proposed civil rights law came from a powerful Congressman from Virginia who may have been attempting to derail the proposed law by adding a classification that would be seen as controversial. . . . Yet whatever the motivation . . . once sex was added to Title VII, all future attempts to remove it or limit it were defeated.

. . . .

In 1978, Congress had the opportunity to expound on its view of sex discrimination by amending Title VII to make clear that discrimination because of "pregnancy, childbirth, or related medical conditions" is discrimination on the basis of sex. The amendment, known as the Pregnancy Discrimination Act ("PDA"), was not meant to alter the contours of Title VII: rather, Congress intended to correct what it felt was an erroneous interpretation of Title VII by the United States Supreme Court in *General Electric Co. v. Gilbert*, 429 U.S. 125 (1976). In *Gilbert*, the Supreme Court held that an otherwise comprehensive short-term disability policy that excluded pregnancy-related disabilities from coverage did not discriminate on the basis of sex. The *Gilbert* majority based its decision on two findings: (a) pregnancy discrimination does not adversely impact all women and therefore is not the same thing as gender discrimination; and (b) disability insurance which covers the same illnesses and conditions for both men and women is equal coverage. To the *Gilbert* majority, the fact that pregnancy-related disabilities were an uncovered risk unique to women did not destroy the facial parity of the

---

infertility drugs, smoking cessation drugs, dermatologicals for cosmetic purposes, growth hormones, and experimental drugs.

   [2] . . . This matter is proceeding as a class action on behalf of "[a]ll female employees of Bartell who at any time after December 29, 1997, were enrolled in Bartell's Prescription Benefit Plan for non-union employees while using prescription contraceptives."

coverage. The dissenting justices, Justice Brennan, Justice Marshall, and Justice Stevens, took issue with these findings, arguing that: (a) women, as the only sex at risk for pregnancy, were being subjected to unlawful discrimination; and (b) in determining whether an employment policy treats the sexes equally, the court must look at the comprehensiveness of the coverage provided to each sex. It was the dissenters' interpretation of Title VII which ultimately prevailed in Congress. . . .

The language of the PDA was chosen in response to the factual situation presented in *Gilbert,* namely a case of overt discrimination toward pregnant employees. Not surprisingly, the amendment makes no reference whatsoever to prescription contraceptives. Of critical importance to this case, however, is the fact that, in enacting the PDA, Congress embraced the dissent's broader interpretation of Title VII which not only recognized that there are sex-based differences between men and women employees, but also required employers to provide women-only benefits or otherwise incur additional expenses on behalf of women in order to treat the sexes the same.

Although this litigation involves an exclusion for prescription contraceptives rather than an exclusion for pregnancy-related disability costs, the legal principles established by *Gilbert* and its legislative reversal govern the outcome of this case. An employer has chosen to offer an employment benefit which excludes from its scope of coverage services which are available only to women. All of the services covered by the policy are available to both men and women, so, as was the case in *Gilbert,* "[t]here is no risk from which men are protected and women are not. Likewise, there is no risk from which women are protected and men are not." Nevertheless, the intent of Congress in enacting the PDA, even if not the exact language used in the amendment, shows that mere facial parity of coverage does not excuse or justify an exclusion which carves out benefits that are uniquely designed for women.

. . . .

Having reviewed the legislative history of Title VII and the PDA, the language of the statute itself, and the relevant case law, the Court finds that Bartell's exclusion of prescription contraception from its prescription plan is inconsistent with the requirements of federal law. The PDA is not a begrudging recognition of a limited grant of rights to a strictly defined group of women who happen to be pregnant. Read in the context of Title VII as a whole, it is a broad acknowledgment of the intent of Congress to outlaw any and all discrimination against any and all women in the terms and conditions of their employment, including the benefits an employer provides to its employees. Male and female employees have different, sex-based disability and healthcare needs, and the law is no longer blind to the fact that only women can get pregnant, bear children, or use prescription contraception. The special or increased healthcare needs associated with a woman's unique sex-based characteristics must be met to the same extent, and on the same terms, as other healthcare needs. Even if one were to assume that Bartell's prescription plan was not the result of intentional discrimination,[7] the exclusion of women-only benefits from a generally comprehensive prescription plan is sex discrimination under Title VII.

Title VII does not require employers to offer any particular type or category of benefit. However, when an employer decides to offer a prescription plan covering everything except a few specifically excluded drugs and devices, it has a legal obligation to make sure that the resulting plan does not discriminate based on sex-based characteristics and that it provides equally comprehensive coverage for both sexes. In light of the fact that prescription contraceptives are used only by women, Bartell's choice to exclude that particular benefit from its generally applicable benefit plan is discriminatory.[8]

B. SPECIFIC ARGUMENTS RAISED BY DEFENDANT-EMPLOYER

. . . .

(1) *Contraceptives as a health care need.*

An underlying theme in Bartell's argument is that a woman's ability to control her fertility differs from the type of illness and disease normally treated with prescription drugs in such significant respects that it is permissible to treat prescription contraceptives differently than all other prescription medicines. The evidence submitted by plaintiffs shows, however, that the availability of affordable and effective contraceptives is of great importance to the health of women and children because it can help to prevent a litany of physical, emotional, economic, and social consequences.

Unintended pregnancies, the condition which prescription contraceptives are designed to prevent, are shockingly common in the United States and carry enormous costs and health consequences for the mother, the child, and society as a whole. Over half of all pregnancies in this country are unintended. A woman with an unintended pregnancy is less likely to seek prenatal care, more likely to engage in unhealthy activities, more likely to have an abortion, and more likely to deliver a low birth weight, ill, or unwanted baby. Unintended pregnancies impose

---

[7] There is no evidence or indication that Bartell's coverage decisions were intended to hinder women in their ability to participate in the workforce or to deprive them of equal treatment in employment or benefits. The most reasonable explanation for the current state of affairs is that the exclusion of women-only benefits is merely an unquestioned holdover from a time when employment-related benefits were doled out less equitably than they are today. The lack of evidence of bad faith or malice toward women does not affect the validity of plaintiffs' Title VII claim. Where a benefit plan is discriminatory on its face, no inquiry into subjective intent is necessary.

[8] Bartell's argument that its prescription plan is not discriminatory because the female dependents of male employees are subject to the same exclusions as are female employees is unavailing. First, discriminating against a protected class cannot be justified through consistency. Second, Bartell ignores the clear import of Congress' repudiation of *Gilbert*: a policy which uses sex-based characteristics to limit benefits, thereby creating a plan which is less comprehensive for one sex than the other, violates Title VII.

significant financial burdens on the parents in the best of circumstances. If the pregnancy results in a distressed newborn, the costs increase by tens of thousands of dollars. In addition, the adverse economic and social consequences of unintended pregnancies fall most harshly on women and interfere with their choice to participate fully and equally in the "marketplace and the world of ideas."

The availability of a reliable, affordable way to prevent unintended pregnancies would go a long way toward ameliorating the ills described above. . . . Insurance policies and employee benefit plans which exclude coverage for effective forms of contraception contribute to the failure of at-risk women to seek a physician's assistance in avoiding unwanted pregnancies.

. . . .

(3) *Business Decision to Control Costs*

Bartell also suggests that it should be permitted to limit the scope of its employee benefit programs in order to control costs. Cost is not, however, a defense to allegations of discrimination under Title VII. While it is undoubtedly true that employers may cut benefits, raise deductibles, or otherwise alter coverage options to comply with budgetary constraints, the method by which the employer seeks to curb costs must not be discriminatory. Bartell offers its employees an admittedly generous package of healthcare benefits, including both third-party healthcare plans and an in-house prescription program. It cannot, however, penalize female employees in an effort to keep its benefit costs low. . . .

(4) *Neutrality of Exclusions*

Prescription contraceptives are not the only drugs or devices excluded from coverage under Bartell's benefit plan. Bartell argues that it has chosen to exclude from coverage all drugs for "family planning," and that this exclusion is neutral and non-discriminatory. There is no "family planning" exclusion in the benefit plan, however, and the contours of such a theoretical exclusion are not clear. . . .

Even if the Court were able to identify a consistent theory to explain the various exclusions and inclusions in Bartell's plan, the exclusion of prescription contraceptives, alone or in combination with the exclusion of infertility drugs, is in no way neutral or equal. . . . The additional exclusion of prescription contraceptives . . . reduces the comprehensiveness of the coverage offered to female employees while leaving the coverage offered to male employees unchanged. As discussed above, such inequities are discriminatory and violate Title VII.

(5) *New Interpretation of an Old Law*

. . . .

Although the Court's decision is a matter of first impression for the judiciary, it is not the first tribunal to consider the lawfulness of a contraception exclusion. On December 14, 2000, the EEOC made a finding of reasonable cause on the same issue which is entitled to some deference. *See, e.g., EEOC v. Commercial Office Products Co.*, 486 U.S. 107 (1988) ("[I]t is axiomatic that the EEOC's interpretation of Title VII, for which it has primary enforcement responsibility ... need only be reasonable to be entitled to deference."). Although the Commission's analysis focused primarily on the PDA, it considered some of the arguments raised by Bartell in this case (such as the alleged distinctions between contraceptives and other drugs and the appropriateness of limiting coverage in order to contain costs). Most importantly, however, the enforcing agency's overall interpretation of Title VII comports with this Court's construction of the Act and led the Commission to the same conclusion reached by this Court. As the Commission found, the exclusion of prescription contraceptives from a generally comprehensive insurance policy constitutes sex discrimination under Title VII because the employers "have circumscribed the treatment options available to women, but not to men." This unequal treatment is an unlawful employment practice under Title VII of the Civil Rights Act of 1964.

(6)   *Legislative Issue*

Although this litigation involves politically charged issues with far-reaching social consequences, the parties' dispute turns on the interpretation of an existing federal statute.... Contrary to defendant's suggestion, it is the role of the judiciary, not the legislature, to interpret existing laws and determine whether they apply to a particular set of facts. ...

C.   CONCLUSION

... For all of the foregoing reasons, the Court finds that Bartell's prescription drug plan discriminates against Bartell's female employees by providing less complete coverage than that offered to male employees. Although the plan covers almost all drugs and devices used by men, the exclusion of prescription contraceptives creates a gaping hole in the coverage offered to female employees, leaving a fundamental and immediate healthcare need uncovered. Pursuant to the analysis in the *Gilbert* dissents, *Newport News*, and *Johnson Controls*, Title VII requires employers to recognize the differences between the sexes and provide equally comprehensive coverage, even if that means providing additional benefits to cover women-only expenses. ...

NOTES

1.   *"Sex" as clutter.* The *Erickson* court revisits a familiar narrative in American political lore—that "sex" was added to the Civil Rights Act of 1964 in an effort to "clutter up" the bill, thereby preventing its passage. However, women's rights scholar Jo Freeman argues that this narrative conveniently ignores the considerable political agency that women exercised during this period. As she recounts, women activists lobbied for the inclusion of sex as a category in Title VII. Because the bill's Southern opponents had already conceded defeat and gone home, attempts to sway their votes by stripping

"sex" from the bill were irrelevant. More revealingly, the addition of sex as a category survived other attempts to "declutter" the bill. *See* Jo Freeman, *How Sex Got into Title VII: Persistent Opportunism as a Maker of Public Policy*, 9 LAW & INEQ. 163, 164 (1991).

2.   *Pragmatism or discrimination?* The fight to have contraceptives covered in employee health care plans has a long history as a core part of antidiscrimination efforts. Indeed, Title VII of the Civil Rights Act of 1964 specifically noted that disparities in pay and benefits constituted an important aspect of discrimination. This view of discrimination, however, was complicated in the wake of a series of critical Supreme Court decisions. In *General Electric Co. v. Gilbert* and *Geduldig v. Aiello*, *supra* pp. 133 and 128, the Court declared that discrimination against pregnant women was not discrimination on the basis of "sex." Instead, the Court reasoned, these policies simply reflected biological differences between men and women. In response, in 1978, Congress passed the Pregnancy Discrimination Act, *supra* p. 140, to specifically include pregnancy within the ambit of Title VII. In 2000, the Equal Employment Opportunity Commission ("EEOC") concluded that exclusion of contraceptives from covered health benefits was, in fact, a form of "sex" discrimination. *See* EEOC Decision on Coverage of Contraception (Dec. 14, 2000), https://www.eeoc.gov/commission-decision-coverage-contraception. Subsequently, the EEOC held that this guidance applied to religious employers as well. *See* EEOC Compliance Manual No. 915.003: Section 12 Religious Discrimination (July 22, 2008), http://www.eeoc.gov/policy/docs/religion.html.

3.   *Conflicting views.* Although the district court in *Erickson* concluded that Bartell Drugs violated the PDA, other lower courts have upheld employer programs that do not subsidize women's contraception. In *In re Union Pacific Railroad Employment Practices Litigation*, 479 F. 3d 436 (8th Cir. 2007), a series of consolidated cases in which female employees claimed that the exclusion of contraception from Union Pacific Railroad's employee health insurance plan violated the PDA, the Eighth Circuit concluded otherwise. Specifically, the court determined that although contraception or lack thereof could affect the causal chain leading to pregnancy, it was not a medical treatment necessary in the event of pregnancy, and thus was not "related to" pregnancy for purposes of the PDA. In so doing, the court referenced its earlier decision in *Krauel v. Iowa Methodist Medical Center*, 95 F.3d 674 (8th Cir. 1996), in which the court, relying on *Johnson Controls*, concluded that the phrase "related medical conditions" in the PDA refers only to medical conditions associated with "pregnancy" and "childbirth," and thus, does not include infertility treatments. *Id.* at 679.

4.   *Objecting to contraception as a matter of conscience.* Although Bartell Drugs objected to contraceptive coverage on secular grounds, many other employers object to such coverage as a matter of religious conscience. As of April 2014, six states permit pharmacists to exercise conscience clauses with respect to contraception, and two states explicitly exclude emergency contraception from their contraceptive coverage mandate. *See* GUTTMACHER INST., STATE POLICIES IN BRIEF: EMERGENCY CONTRACEPTION 1 (2014).

5.   *Accessibility of contraception.* Employer efforts to limit contraceptive coverage do not occur in a vacuum, but instead should be understood in the context of a broader effort to reduce access to contraceptives more generally. For example, Texas has reduced its funding for family planning—including contraceptive coverage—by two-thirds, New Hampshire by sixty percent, while New Jersey and Montana have eliminated their family planning programs entirely. Stephanie Simon, *States Slash Birth Control Subsidies as Federal Debate Rages*, REUTERS (Mar. 2, 2012), https://www.reuters.com/article/us-states-slash-birth-control/states-slash-birth-control-subsidies-as-federal-debate-rages-idUKTRE8240Z020120305.   These developments suggest that even though efforts to legalize contraceptives have succeeded, actual *access* to contraceptives continues to be uneven—among more marginalized populations, and as a result of employer objections among the middle class. Should our understanding of the legal right to use contraceptives account for the ability to access and exercise that right? While the Supreme Court has repeatedly refused to frame a right to contraception as a positive right, how would framing it in this way transform the government's role in providing meaningful access to contraception?

* * *

Starting with debates on health insurance reform under President Bill Clinton, women's health advocates documented that substantial numbers of insurers excluded contraceptives from coverage. The passage of the Health Insurance Portability and Accountability Act of 1996 (HIPAA) moved at least some regulation of health insurance from the state level to the federal government and, importantly, covered self-insured programs which historically were not covered by state regulation. In the following four years, at least twenty states passed their own contraceptive equity laws. These contraceptive equity laws were passed in part based on evidence that, even as they refused to cover contraception, insurance plans had hastened to cover the cost of Viagra, and routinely covered hair transplants. Further, data showed that the increased cost of covering contraceptives was minimal. In 2012, the debates over "Obamacare" resurfaced these issues surrounding insurance providers and contraceptive coverage. Initially, the Patient Protection and Affordable Care Act (ACA) required insurance providers to cover contraception. However, upon vigorous objections from, among others, religiously-affiliated employers, the Obama Administration introduced an exemption to the contraception mandate for "religious employers." The section that follows provides the administrative regulations used to implement the ACA. Note the definition of the term "religious employer."

Coverage of Preventive Health Services
45 C.F.R. § 147.130 (2013).

The following is an excerpt from the Department of Health and Human Services' Regulation regarding preventive health services under the Affordable Care Act.

(a) Services—

(1) In general. Beginning at the time described in paragraph (b) of this section and subject to § 147.131, a group health plan, or a health insurance issuer offering group or individual health insurance coverage, must provide coverage for all of the following items and services, and may not impose any cost-sharing requirements (such as a copayment, coinsurance, or a deductible) with respect to those items and services:

. . .

(iv) With respect to women, to the extent not described in paragraph (a)(1)(i) of this section, preventive care and screenings provided for in binding comprehensive health plan coverage guidelines supported by the Health Resources and Services Administration.

(A) In developing the binding health plan coverage guidelines specified in this paragraph (a)(1)(iv), the Health Resources and Services Administration shall be informed by evidence and may establish exemptions from such guidelines with respect to group health plans established or maintained by religious employers and health insurance coverage provided in connection with group health plans established or maintained by religious employers with respect to any requirement to cover contraceptive services under such guidelines.

(B) For purposes of this subsection, a "religious employer" is an organization that meets all of the following criteria:

(1) The inculcation of religious values is the purpose of the organization.

(2) The organization primarily employs persons who share the religious tenets of the organization.

(3) The organization serves primarily persons who share the religious tenets of the organization.

(4) The organization is a nonprofit organization as described in section 6033(a)(1) and section 6033(a)(3)(A)(i) or (iii) of the Internal Revenue Code of 1986, as amended.

NOTES

1. *"Obamacare" and the contraceptive mandate.* The Obama Administration asked the prestigious Institute of Medicine ("IOM") to devise guidelines for the Department of Health and Human Services ("HHS") with respect to the Affordable Care Act's coverage of services for women. The IOM called for the provision of: all FDA-approved contraceptives, prenatal care, postnatal care, and screening and treatment for sexually transmitted infections (STIs). *See* INST. OF MED., CLINICAL PREVENTIVE SERVICES FOR WOMEN: CLOSING THE GAPS 56–57 (2011). According to the IOM's recommendations, both individual and group plans must provide these services unless the plans are "grandfathered" in, meaning that they were in existence in March 2010, *and have not changed in any significant way*. In

addition, such plans must disclose to women if they do not offer the covered services. Under the religious exemption, churches may be exempted from the regulations, but other religiously-affiliated institutions such as schools and nonprofit organizations are not. In response to the concerns of social conservatives and religiously-affiliated employers, HHS created a one-year "safe harbor," delaying enforcement of the provisions to nonexempt, non-grandfathered group health plans established and maintained by nonprofit organizations with religious objections to contraceptive coverage. *See* 45 C.F.R. 147.140(g) (2013).

2.   *Who falls through the gaps?* Under the ACA, insurance providers are required to cover all FDA-approved contraceptives. Since the ACA's passage, the proportion of privately insured women who paid no out-of-pocket costs for contraception surged from fifteen percent to forty percent. *See* Lawrence B. Finer et al., *Changes in Out-of-Pocket Payments for Contraception by Privately Insured Women During Implementation of the Federal Contraceptive Care Coverage Requirement*, 89 CONTRACEPTION 97, 100 (2014). However, even in the face of these significant gains, the ACA falls short of making contraception easily available to all individuals at risk of unintended pregnancy. For example, as of October 2013, twenty-six states refused to expand Medicaid coverage, leaving an estimated eight million low-income Americans ineligible for either Medicaid or subsidies that could be used to participate in state-insurance exchanges. In addition, undocumented immigrants and some legal permanent residents ("green card holders") may not qualify for Medicaid coverage. Even those individuals covered by Medicaid or insurance may face issues of transportation, stigmatization, lack of knowledge about medical access, and providers who lack either the language skills or the cultural competence to provide contraceptive care and other medical services. *See* Sabrina Tavernise & Robert Gebeloff, *Millions of Poor Are Left Uncovered by Health Law*, N.Y. TIMES, Oct. 2, 2013, at A1; *see also* Frances Casey & Veronica Gomez-Lobo, *Disparities in Contraceptive Access and Provision*, 31 SEMINARS REPROD. MED. 347 (2013) (listing challenges to access of contraceptive care and recommendations to improve disparities).

3.   *Objections to contraception in Obamacare.* The HHS regulations on contraceptive coverage under the ACA prompted over seventy lawsuits in almost every federal circuit. Many of these lawsuits seek religious exemptions from the contraceptive mandate for businesses and religious institutions (not churches) on the ground that contraceptive use contradicts these employers' religious beliefs. *See* Elizabeth Sepper, *Contraception and the Birth of Corporate Conscience*, 22 AM. U. J. GENDER SOC. POL'Y & L. 303, 304 (2014). In *Burwell v. Hobby Lobby*, 573 U.S. 682 (2014), *infra* p. 654, the United States Supreme Court determined that, under the Religious Freedom Restoration Act, closely-held corporations could avoid complying with the contraception mandate by registering their religious objections. However, questions remain as to whether non-profits and larger corporations may also do so. In your view, should companies be permitted to claim religious exemptions?

4. *Rush Limbaugh and Sandra Fluke.* In February 2011, the Committee on Oversight and Government Reform conducted hearings on the ACA's contraceptive mandate. Democrats proposed that Sandra Fluke, a student at Georgetown University Law Center and a member of Law Students for Reproductive Justice, provide testimony on the hardships that women students faced because Georgetown—a Jesuit-affiliated institution—refused to cover contraception. Congressman Darrell Issa, who chaired the committee, rejected Fluke's proposed testimony, explaining that Fluke was ill-equipped to testify before Congress because the issue was not contraceptive coverage, but rather religious freedom. Instead, Fluke provided her statements to Congressional Democrats. Six days later, conservative radio host Rush Limbaugh called Fluke a "slut" and a "prostitute" on his radio show. Limbaugh went on to suggest that if the public was obliged to pay for Fluke's birth control, then it had the right to obtain videos of Fluke having sex. In the resulting media firestorm, Limbaugh apologized, and Fluke received a supportive call from President Obama. Fluke has since graduated from law school and has gone on to be a prominent voice for reproductive justice and women's rights. *See* Jonathan Weisman, *Obama Backs Student in Furor with Limbaugh on Birth Control*, N.Y. TIMES: THE CAUCUS (Mar. 2, 2012, 12:55 PM), https://archive.nytimes.com/thecaucus.blogs.nytimes.com/2012/03/02/boehner-condemns-limbaughs-comments/.

Burwell v. Hobby Lobby Stores, Inc.
573 U.S. 682 (2014).

■ ALITO, J.

We must decide in these cases whether the Religious Freedom Restoration Act of 1993 (RFRA), . . . 42 U. S. C. § 2000bb *et seq.*, permits the United States Department of Health and Human Services (HHS) to demand that three closely held corporations provide health-insurance coverage for methods of contraception that violate the sincerely held religious beliefs of the companies' owners. We hold that the regulations that impose this obligation violate RFRA, which prohibits the Federal Government from taking any action that substantially burdens the exercise of religion unless that action constitutes the least restrictive means of serving a compelling government interest.

. . . .

I

A

Congress enacted RFRA in 1993 in order to provide very broad protection for religious liberty. RFRA's enactment came three years after this Court's decision in *Employment Div., Dept. of Human Resources of Ore. v. Smith*, 494 U.S. 872 (1990), which largely repudiated the method of analyzing free-exercise claims that had been used in cases like *Sherbert v. Verner*, 374 U.S. 398 (1963), and *Wisconsin v. Yoder*, 406 U.S.

205 (1972). In determining whether challenged government actions violated the Free Exercise Clause of the First Amendment, those decisions used a balancing test that took into account whether the challenged action imposed a substantial burden on the practice of religion, and if it did, whether it was needed to serve a compelling government interest. . . .

In *Smith*, . . . the Court rejected "the balancing test set forth in *Sherbert*." . . .

. . .The Court . . . held that, under the First Amendment, "neutral, generally applicable laws may be applied to religious practices even when not supported by a compelling governmental interest."

Congress responded to *Smith* by enacting RFRA. . . . In order to ensure broad protection for religious liberty, RFRA provides that "Government shall not substantially burden a person's exercise of religion even if the burden results from a rule of general applicability." § 2000bb–1(a). If the Government substantially burdens a person's exercise of religion, under the Act that person is entitled to an exemption from the rule unless the Government "demonstrates that application of the burden to the person—(1) is in furtherance of a compelling governmental interest; and (2) is the least restrictive means of furthering that compelling governmental interest." § 2000bb–1(b).[3]

Effectively Sherbert

As enacted in 1993, RFRA applied to both the Federal Government and the States, but the constitutional authority invoked for regulating federal and state agencies differed. As applied to a federal agency, RFRA is based on the enumerated power that supports the particular agency's work, but in attempting to regulate the States and their subdivisions, Congress relied on its power under Section 5 of the Fourteenth Amendment to enforce the First Amendment. . . . In *City of Boerne*, however, we held that Congress had overstepped its Section 5 authority because "[t]he stringent test RFRA demands" "far exceed[ed] any pattern or practice of unconstitutional conduct under the Free Exercise Clause as interpreted in *Smith*." *Id.*, at 533–534. . . .

Following our decision in *City of Boerne*, Congress passed the Religious Land Use and Institutionalized Persons Act of 2000 (RLUIPA), 114 Stat. 803, 42 U.S.C. § 2000cc *et seq*. That statute, enacted under Congress's Commerce and Spending Clause powers, imposes the same general test as RFRA but on a more limited category of governmental actions. . . . And, what is most relevant for present purposes, RLUIPA amended RFRA's definition of the "exercise of religion." See § 2000bb–2(4) (importing RLUIPA definition). Before RLUIPA, RFRA's definition made reference to the First Amendment. See § 2000bb–2(4) (1994 ed.)

---

[3]   In *City of Boerne v. Flores*, 521 U.S., 507 (1997), we wrote that RFRA's "least restrictive means requirement was not used in the pre-*Smith* jurisprudence RFRA purported to codify." *Id.*, at 509. On this understanding of our pre-*Smith* cases, RFRA did more than merely restore the balancing test used in the *Sherbert* line of cases; it provided even broader protection for religious liberty than was available under those decisions.

(defining "exercise of religion" as "the exercise of religion under the First Amendment"). In RLUIPA, in an obvious effort to effect a complete separation from First Amendment case law, Congress deleted the reference to the First Amendment and defined the "exercise of religion" to include "any exercise of religion, whether or not compelled by, or central to, a system of religious belief." § 2000cc–5(7)(A). And Congress mandated that this concept "be construed in favor of a broad protection of religious exercise, to the maximum extent permitted by the terms of this chapter and the Constitution." § 2000cc–3(g).

encompasses more benefit?

B

At issue in these cases are HHS regulations promulgated under the Patient Protection and Affordable Care Act of 2010 (ACA). . . . [The] ACA generally requires employers with 50 or more full-time employees to offer "a group health plan or group health insurance coverage" that provides "minimum essential coverage." 26 U.S.C. § 5000A(f)(2); §§ 4980H(a), (c)(2). Any covered employer that does not provide such coverage must pay a substantial price. Specifically, if a covered employer provides group health insurance but its plan fails to comply with ACA's group-health-plan requirements, the employer may be required to pay $100 per day for each affected "individual." §§ 4980D(a)–(b). And if the employer decides to stop providing health insurance altogether and at least one full-time employee enrolls in a health plan and qualifies for a subsidy on one of the government-run ACA exchanges, the employer must pay $2,000 per year for each of its full-time employees. §§ 4980H(a), (c)(1).

Unless an exception applies, ACA requires an employer's group health plan or group-health-insurance coverage to furnish "preventive care and screenings" for women without "any cost sharing requirements." 42 U.S.C. § 300gg–13(a)(4). Congress itself, however, did not specify what types of preventive care must be covered. Instead, Congress authorized the Health Resources and Services Administration (HRSA), a component of HHS, to make that important and sensitive decision. . . .

covered contraception

In August 2011, . . . the HRSA promulgated the Women's Preventive Services Guidelines. . . . The Guidelines provide that nonexempt employers are generally required to provide "coverage, without cost sharing" for "[a]ll Food and Drug Administration [(FDA)] approved contraceptive methods, sterilization procedures, and patient education and counseling." 77 Fed. Reg. 8725 (internal quotation marks omitted). Although many of the required, FDA-approved methods of contraception work by preventing the fertilization of an egg, four of those methods (those specifically at issue in these cases) may have the effect of preventing an already fertilized egg from developing any further by inhibiting its attachment to the uterus. . . .

religious exemption for churches

HHS also authorized the HRSA to establish exemptions from the contraceptive mandate for "religious employers." 45 CFR § 147.131(a). That category encompasses "churches, their integrated auxiliaries, and conventions or associations of churches," as well as "the exclusively religious activities of any religious order." . . . In its Guidelines, HRSA exempted these organizations from the requirement to cover contraceptive services. . . .

In addition, HHS has effectively exempted certain religious nonprofit organizations, described under HHS regulations as "eligible organizations," from the contraceptive mandate. . . . An "eligible organization" means a nonprofit organization that "holds itself out as a religious organization" and "opposes providing coverage for some or all of any contraceptive services required to be covered . . . on account of religious objections." 45 CFR § 147.131(b). To qualify for this accommodation, an employer must certify that it is such an organization. § 147.131(b)(4). . . .

In addition to these exemptions for religious organizations, ACA exempts a great many employers from most of its coverage requirements. Employers providing "grandfathered health plans"—those that existed prior to March 23, 2010, and that have not made specified changes after that date—need not comply with many of the Act's requirements, including the contraceptive mandate. 42 U.S.C. §§ 18011(a), (e). And employers with fewer than 50 employees are not required to provide health insurance at all. 26 U.S.C. § 4980H(c)(2).

. . . .

[The Plaintiffs, Norman and Elizabeth Hahn and David and Barbara Green own and operate closely-held corporations. The Hahns own and operate Conestoga Wood Specialities and Mardel Corporation and the Greens own and operate Hobby Lobby craft stores. The Hahns are devout Mennonites and the Greens are Christians. Both sets of plaintiffs] believe that life begins at conception and that it would violate their religion to facilitate access to contraceptive drugs or devices that operate after that point. 723 F.3d, at 1122. They specifically object to four contraceptive methods [that act after fertilization of an egg—namely, two forms of the "morning after" pill and two intrauterine devices—]they have no objection to the other 16 FDA-approved methods of birth control. *Id.*, at 1125. . . .

. . . .

III
A

RFRA prohibits the "Government [from] substantially burden[ing] *a person's* exercise of religion even if the burden results from a rule of general applicability" unless the Government "demonstrates that application of the burden to *the person*—(1) is in furtherance of a compelling governmental interest; and (2) is the least restrictive means of furthering that compelling governmental interest." 42 U.S.C. §§ 2000bb–1(a), (b) (emphasis added). The first question that we must address is whether this provision applies to regulations that govern the activities of for-profit corporations like Hobby Lobby, Conestoga, and Mardel.

. . . .

. . . RFRA applies to "a person's" exercise of religion, 42 U.S.C. §§ 2000bb–1(a), (b), and RFRA itself does not define the term "person." We therefore look to the Dictionary Act, which we must consult "[i]n determining the meaning of any Act of Congress, unless the context indicates otherwise." 1 U.S.C. § 1.

Under the Dictionary Act, "the wor[d] 'person' . . . include[s] corporations, companies, associations, firms, partnerships, societies, and joint stock companies, as well as individuals." . . .

. . . We have entertained RFRA and free-exercise claims brought by nonprofit corporations, see *Gonzales v. O Centro Espírita Beneficiente União do Vegetal*, 546 U.S. 418 (2006) (RFRA); *Hosanna-Tabor Evangelical Lutheran Church and School v. EEOC*, 565 U.S. 171 (2012) (Free Exercise); *Church of the Lukumi Babalu Aye, Inc. v. Hialeah*, 508 U.S. 520 (1993) (Free Exercise), and HHS concedes that a nonprofit corporation can be a "person" within the meaning of RFRA. See Brief for HHS in No. 13–354, at 17. . . .

. . . .

The principal argument advanced by HHS and the principal dissent regarding RFRA protection for Hobby Lobby, Conestoga, and Mardel focuses . . . on the phrase "exercise of religion." According to HHS and the dissent, these corporations are not protected by RFRA because they cannot exercise religion. Neither HHS nor the dissent, however, provides any persuasive explanation for this conclusion.

Is it because of the corporate form? The corporate form alone cannot provide the explanation because . . . HHS concedes that nonprofit corporations can be protected by RFRA. The dissent suggests that nonprofit corporations are special because furthering their religious "autonomy . . . often furthers individual religious freedom as well." *Post*, at 15 (quoting *Corporation of Presiding Bishop of Church of Jesus Christ of Latter-day Saints v. Amos*, 483 U.S. 327, 342 (1987) (Brennan, J., concurring in judgment)). But this principle applies equally to for-profit corporations: Furthering their religious freedom also "furthers individual religious freedom." In these cases, for example, allowing Hobby Lobby, Conestoga, and Mardel to assert RFRA claims protects the religious liberty of the Greens and the Hahns.

If the corporate form is not enough, what about the profit-making objective? In *Braunfeld [v. Brown]*, 366 U.S. 599 (1961), we entertained the free-exercise claims of individuals who were attempting to make a profit as retail merchants, and the Court never even hinted that this objective precluded their claims. . . . Business practices that are compelled or limited by the tenets of a religious doctrine fall comfortably within that definition. Thus, a law that "operates so as to make the practice of . . . religious beliefs more expensive" in the context of business activities imposes a burden on the exercise of religion. . . .

If, as *Braunfeld* recognized, a sole proprietorship that seeks to make a profit may assert a free-exercise claim, why can't Hobby Lobby, Conestoga, and Mardel do the same?

Some lower court judges have suggested that RFRA does not protect for-profit corporations because the purpose of such corporations is simply to make money.[23] . . . While it is certainly true that a central objective of for-profit corporations is to make money, modern corporate law does not require for-profit corporations to pursue profit at the expense of everything else, and many do not do so. For-profit corporations, with ownership approval, support a wide variety of charitable causes, and it is not at all uncommon for such corporations to further humanitarian and other altruistic objectives. . . .

HHS would draw a sharp line between nonprofit corporations (which, HHS concedes, are protected by RFRA) and for-profit corporations (which HHS would leave unprotected), but the actual picture is less clear-cut. Not all corporations that decline to organize as nonprofits do so in order to maximize profit. For example, organizations with religious and charitable aims might organize as for-profit corporations because of the potential advantages of that corporate form,

---

[23] See, *e.g.*, 724 F.3d, at 385 ("We do not see how a for-profit, 'artificial being,' . . . that was created to make money" could exercise religion); *Grote v. Sebelius*, 708 F.3d 850, 857 (C.A.7 2013) (Rovner, J. dissenting) ("So far as it appears, the mission of Grote Industries, like that of any other for-profit, secular business, is to make money in the commercial sphere"); *Autocam Corp. v. Sebelius*, 730 F.3d 618, 626 (C.A.7 2013) ("Congress did not intend to include corporations primarily organized for secular, profit-seeking purposes as 'persons' under RFRA"); see also 723 F.3d, at 1171–1172 (Briscoe, C. J., dissenting) ("[T]he specific purpose for which [a corporation] is created matters greatly to how it will be categorized and treated under the law" and "it is undisputed that Hobby Lobby and Mardel are for-profit corporations focused on selling merchandise to consumers").

The principal dissent makes a similar point, stating that "[f]or-profit corporations are different from religious nonprofits in that they use labor to make a profit, rather than to perpetuate the religious values shared by a community of believers." *Post*, at 2797 (internal quotation marks omitted). The first half of this statement is a tautology; for-profit corporations do indeed differ from nonprofits insofar as they seek to make a profit for their owners, but the second part is factually untrue. As the activities of the for-profit corporations involved in these cases show, some for-profit corporations do seek "to perpetuate the religious values shared," in these cases, by their owners. Conestoga's Vision and Values Statement declares that the company is dedicated to operating "in [a] manner that reflects our Christian heritage and the highest ethical and moral principles of business." App. In No. 13–356, p. 94. Similarly, Hobby Lobby's statement of purpose proclaims that the company "is committed to . . . Honoring the Lord in all we do by operating . . . in a manner consistent with Biblical principles." App. in No. 13–354, p. 135. The dissent also believes that history is not on our side because even Blackstone recognized the distinction between "ecclesiastical and lay" corporations. *Post*, at 18. What Blackstone illustrates, however, is that dating back to 1765, there was no sharp divide among corporations in their capacity to exercise religion; Blackstone recognized that even what he termed "lay" corporations might serve "the promotion of piety." 1 W. Blackstone, Commentaries on the Law of England 458–459 (1765). And whatever may have been the case at the time of Blackstone, modern corporate law (and the law of the States in which these three companies are incorporated) allows for-profit corporations to "perpetuat[e] religious values."

such as the freedom to participate in lobbying for legislation or campaigning for political candidates who promote their religious or charitable goals. In fact, recognizing the inherent compatibility between establishing a for-profit corporation and pursuing nonprofit goals, States have increasingly adopted laws formally recognizing hybrid corporate forms. Over half of the States, for instance, now recognize the "benefit corporation," a dual-purpose entity that seeks to achieve both a benefit for the public and a profit for its owners.[25]

In any event, the objectives that may properly be pursued by the companies in these cases are governed by the laws of the States in which they were incorporated—Pennsylvania and Oklahoma—and the laws of those States permit for-profit corporations to pursue "any lawful purpose" or "act," including the pursuit of profit in conformity with the owners' religious principles. 15 Pa. Cons. Stat. § 1301 (2001) ("Corporations may be incorporated under this subpart for any lawful purpose or purposes"); Okla. Stat., Tit. 18, §§ 1002, 1005 (West 2012) ("[E]very corporation, whether profit or not for profit" may "be incorporated or organized . . . to conduct or promote any lawful business or purposes"). . . .

3

HHS and the principal dissent make one additional argument in an effort to show that a for-profit corporation cannot engage in the "exercise of religion" within the meaning of RFRA: HHS argues that RFRA did no more than codify this Court's pre-*Smith* Free Exercise Clause precedents, and because none of those cases squarely held that a for-profit corporation has free-exercise rights, RFRA does not confer such protection. This argument has many flaws.

First, nothing in the text of RFRA as originally enacted suggested that the statutory phrase "exercise of religion under the First Amendment" was meant to be tied to this Court's pre-*Smith* interpretation of that Amendment. When first enacted, RFRA defined the "exercise of religion" to mean "the exercise of religion under the First Amendment"—not the exercise of religion as recognized only by then-existing Supreme Court precedents. 42 U.S.C. § 2000bb–2(4) (1994 ed.). When Congress wants to link the meaning of a statutory provision to a body of this Court's case law, it knows how to do so. See, *e.g.,* Antiterrorism and Effective Death Penalty Act of 1996, 28 U.S.C. § 2254(d)(1) (authorizing habeas relief from a state-court decision that

---

[25] See Benefit Corp. Information Center, online at http://www.benefitcorp.net/state-by-state-legislative-status; *e.g.,* Va. Code Ann. §§ 13.1–787, 13.1–626, 13.1–782 (Lexis 2011) ("A benefit corporation shall have as one of its purposes the purpose of creating a general public benefit," and "may identify one or more specific public benefits that it is the purpose of the benefit corporation to create. . . . This purpose is in addition to [the purpose of engaging in any lawful business]." " 'Specific public benefit' means a benefit that serves one or more public welfare, religious, charitable, scientific, literary, or educational purposes, or other purpose or benefit beyond the strict interest of the shareholders of the benefit corporation. . . ."); S.C. Code Ann. §§ 33–38–300 (2012 Cum. Supp.), 33–3–101 (2006), 33–38–130 (2012 Cum. Supp.) (similar).

"was contrary to, or involved an unreasonable application of, clearly established Federal law, as determined by the Supreme Court of the United States").

Second, if the original text of RFRA was not clear enough on this point—and we think it was—the amendment of RFRA through RLUIPA surely dispels any doubt. That amendment deleted the prior reference to the First Amendment . . . and neither HHS nor the principal dissent can explain why Congress did this if it wanted to tie RFRA coverage tightly to the specific holdings of our pre-*Smith* free-exercise cases. Moreover, as discussed, the amendment went further, providing that the exercise of religion "shall be construed in favor of a broad protection of religious exercise, to the maximum extent permitted by the terms of this chapter and the Constitution." § 2000cc–3(g). It is simply not possible to read these provisions as restricting the concept of the "exercise of religion" to those practices specifically addressed in our pre-*Smith* decisions.

. . . .

Finally, the results would be absurd if RFRA merely restored this Court's pre-*Smith* decisions in ossified form and did not allow a plaintiff to raise a RFRA claim unless that plaintiff fell within a category of plaintiffs one of whom had brought a free-exercise claim that this Court entertained in the years before *Smith*. For example, we are not aware of any pre-*Smith* case in which this Court entertained a free-exercise claim brought by a resident noncitizen. Are such persons also beyond RFRA's protective reach simply because the Court never addressed their rights before *Smith*?

Presumably in recognition of the weakness of this argument, both HHS and the principal dissent fall back on the broader contention that the Nation lacks a tradition of exempting for-profit corporations from generally applicable laws. By contrast, HHS contends, statutes like Title VII, 42 U.S.C. § 2000e–19(A), expressly exempt churches and other nonprofit religious institutions but not for-profit corporations. See Brief for HHS in No. 13–356, p. 26. In making this argument, however, HHS did not call to our attention the fact that some federal statutes *do* exempt categories of entities that include for-profit corporations from laws that would otherwise require these entities to engage in activities to which they object on grounds of conscience. See, *e.g.*, 42 U.S.C. § 300a–7(b)(2); § 238n(a). If Title VII and similar laws show anything, it is that Congress speaks with specificity when it intends a religious accommodation not to extend to for-profit corporations.

4

Finally, HHS contends that Congress could not have wanted RFRA to apply to for-profit corporations because it is difficult as a practical matter to ascertain the sincere "beliefs" of a corporation. HHS goes so far as to raise the specter of "divisive, polarizing proxy battles over the religious identity of large, publicly traded corporations such as IBM or General Electric." Brief for HHS in No. 13–356, at 30.

These cases, however, do not involve publicly traded corporations, and it seems unlikely that the sort of corporate giants to which HHS refers will often assert RFRA claims. . . . The companies in the cases before us are closely held corporations, each owned and controlled by members of a single family, and no one has disputed the sincerity of their religious beliefs.

HHS has also provided no evidence that the purported problem of determining the sincerity of an asserted religious belief moved Congress to exclude for-profit corporations from RFRA's protection. On the contrary, the scope of RLUIPA shows that Congress was confident of the ability of the federal courts to weed out insincere claims. RLUIPA applies to "institutionalized persons," a category that consists primarily of prisoners, and by the time of RLUIPA's enactment, the propensity of some prisoners to assert claims of dubious sincerity was well documented. Nevertheless, after our decision in *City of Boerne*, Congress enacted RLUIPA to preserve the right of prisoners to raise religious liberty claims. If Congress thought that the federal courts were up to the job of dealing with insincere prisoner claims, there is no reason to believe that Congress limited RFRA's reach out of concern for the seemingly less difficult task of doing the same in corporate cases. And if, as HHS seems to concede, Congress wanted RFRA to apply to nonprofit corporations, see, Reply Brief in No. 13–354, at 7–8, what reason is there to think that Congress believed that spotting insincere claims would be tougher in cases involving for-profits?

. . . .

IV *Mandate "substantially burdens" religion?*

Because RFRA applies in these cases, we must next ask whether the HHS contraceptive mandate "substantially burden[s]" the exercise of religion. 42 U.S.C. § 2000bb–1(a). We have little trouble concluding that it does.

A

As we have noted, the Hahns and Greens have a sincere religious belief that life begins at conception. They therefore object on religious grounds to providing health insurance that covers methods of birth control that, as HHS acknowledges, see Brief for HHS in No. 13–354, at 9, n. 4, may result in the destruction of an embryo. By requiring the Hahns and Greens and their companies to arrange for such coverage, the HHS mandate demands that they engage in conduct that seriously violates their religious beliefs.

If the Hahns and Greens and their companies do not yield to this demand, the economic consequences will be severe. If the companies continue to offer group health plans that do not cover the contraceptives at issue, they will be taxed $100 per day for each affected individual. 26

U.S.C. § 4980D. For Hobby Lobby, the bill could amount to $1.3 million per day or about $475 million per year; for Conestoga, the assessment could be $90,000 per day or $33 million per year; and for Mardel, it could be $40,000 per day or about $15 million per year. These sums are surely substantial.

It is true that the plaintiffs could avoid these assessments by dropping insurance coverage altogether and thus forcing their employees to obtain health insurance on one of the exchanges established under ACA. But if at least one of their full-time employees were to qualify for a subsidy on one of the government-run exchanges, this course would also entail substantial economic consequences. The companies could face penalties of $2,000 per employee each year. § 4980H. These penalties would amount to roughly $26 million for Hobby Lobby, $1.8 million for Conestoga, and $800,000 for Mardel.

B

Although these totals are high, *amici* supporting HHS have suggested that the $2,000 per-employee penalty is actually less than the average cost of providing health insurance, see Brief for Religious Organizations 22, and therefore, they claim, the companies could readily eliminate any substantial burden by forcing their employees to obtain insurance in the government exchanges. . . .

Even if we were to reach this argument, we would find it unpersuasive. As an initial matter, it entirely ignores the fact that the Hahns and Greens and their companies have religious reasons for providing health-insurance coverage for their employees. Before the advent of ACA, they were not legally compelled to provide insurance, but they nevertheless did so—in part, no doubt, for conventional business reasons, but also in part because their religious beliefs govern their relations with their employees. . . .

Putting aside the religious dimension of the decision to provide insurance, moreover, it is far from clear that the net cost to the companies of providing insurance is more than the cost of dropping their insurance plans and paying the ACA penalty. Health insurance is a benefit that employees value. If the companies simply eliminated that benefit and forced employees to purchase their own insurance on the exchanges, without offering additional compensation, it is predictable that the companies would face a competitive disadvantage in retaining and attracting skilled workers. . . .

The companies could attempt to make up for the elimination of a group health plan by increasing wages, but this would be costly. Group health insurance is generally less expensive than comparable individual coverage, so the amount of the salary increase needed to fully compensate for the termination of insurance coverage may well exceed the cost to the companies of providing the insurance. In addition, any salary increase would have to take into account the fact that employees must pay income taxes on wages but not on the value of employer-provided health insurance. 26 U.S.C. § 106(a). Likewise, employers can deduct the cost of providing health insurance, see § 162(a)(1), but apparently cannot deduct the amount of the penalty that they must pay if insurance is not provided; that difference also must be taken into account. Given these economic incentives, it is far from clear that it would be financially advantageous for an employer to drop coverage and pay the penalty.

In sum, we refuse to sustain the challenged regulations on the ground—never maintained by the Government—that dropping insurance coverage eliminates the substantial burden that the HHS mandate imposes. We doubt that the Congress that enacted RFRA—or, for that matter, ACA—would have believed it a tolerable result to put family-run businesses to the choice of violating their sincerely held religious beliefs or making all of their employees lose their existing healthcare plans.

C

In taking the position that the HHS mandate does not impose a substantial burden on the exercise of religion, HHS's main argument (echoed by the principal dissent) is basically that the connection between what the objecting parties must do (provide health-insurance coverage for four methods of contraception that may operate after the fertilization of an egg) and the end that they find to be morally wrong (destruction of an embryo) is simply too attenuated. . . . HHS and the dissent note that providing the coverage would not itself result in the destruction of an embryo; that would occur only if an employee chose to take advantage of the coverage and to use one of the four methods at issue. . . .

This argument dodges the question that RFRA presents (whether the HHS mandate imposes a substantial burden on the ability of the objecting parties to conduct business in accordance with *their religious beliefs*) and instead addresses a very different question that the federal courts have no business addressing (whether the religious belief asserted in a RFRA case is reasonable). The Hahns and Greens believe that providing the coverage demanded by the HHS regulations is connected to the destruction of an embryo in a way that is sufficient to make it immoral for them to provide the coverage. This belief implicates a difficult and important question of religion and moral philosophy, namely, the circumstances under which it is wrong for a person to perform an act that is innocent in itself but that has the effect of enabling or facilitating the commission of an immoral act by another. Arrogating the authority to provide a binding national answer to this religious and philosophical question, HHS and the principal dissent in effect tell the plaintiffs that their beliefs are flawed. For good reason, we have repeatedly refused to take such a step. . . .

. . . .

[handwritten margin note:] Alleges that above argument shouldn't be examined based on whether it's reasonable but from perspective of petitioners' religious beliefs

. . . [T]he Hahns and Greens and their companies sincerely believe that providing the insurance coverage demanded by the HHS regulations lies on the forbidden side of the line, and it is not for us to say that their religious beliefs are mistaken or insubstantial. Instead, our "narrow function . . . in this context is to determine" whether the line drawn reflects "an honest conviction," . . . and there is no dispute that it does.

. . . .

[handwritten: ✓ compelling gov interest AND least restrictive means?]

Since the HHS contraceptive mandate imposes a substantial burden on the exercise of religion, we must move on and decide whether HHS has shown that the mandate both "(1) is in furtherance of a compelling governmental interest; and (2) is the least restrictive means of furthering that compelling governmental interest." 42 U.S.C. § 2000bb–1(b).

A

HHS asserts that the contraceptive mandate serves a variety of important interests, but many of these are couched in very broad terms, such as promoting "public health" and "gender equality." . . . RFRA, however, contemplates a "more focused" inquiry: It "requires the Government to demonstrate that the compelling interest test is satisfied through application of the challenged law 'to the person'—the particular *[handwritten: look @ particular claimant]* claimant whose sincere exercise of religion is being substantially burdened." *O Centro*, 546 U.S., at 430–431 (quoting § 2000bb–1(b)). This requires us to "loo[k] beyond broadly formulated interests" and to "scrutiniz[e] the asserted harm of granting specific exemptions to particular religious claimants"—in other words, to look to the marginal interest in enforcing the contraceptive mandate in these cases. *O Centro, supra*, at 431.

In addition to asserting these very broadly framed interests, HHS maintains that the mandate serves a compelling interest in ensuring that all women have access to all FDA-approved contraceptives without cost sharing. . . . Under our cases, women (and men) have a constitutional right to obtain contraceptives, see *Griswold v. Connecticut*, 381 U.S. 479, 485–486 (1965), and HHS tells us that "[s]tudies have demonstrated that even moderate copayments for preventive services can deter patients from receiving those services." . . .

The objecting parties contend that HHS has not shown that the mandate serves a compelling government interest, and it is arguable that there are features of ACA that support that view. As we have noted, many employees—those covered by grandfathered plans and those who work for employers with fewer than 50 employees—may have no contraceptive coverage without cost sharing at all.

. . . .

We find it unnecessary to adjudicate this issue. We will assume that the interest in guaranteeing cost-free access to the four challenged contraceptive methods is compelling within the meaning of RFRA, and we will proceed to consider the final prong of the RFRA test. . . .

[handwritten: might be compelling ← B]

[handwritten: interest, but not]

[handwritten: least restrictive means]

The least-restrictive-means standard is exceptionally demanding . . . and it is not satisfied here. HHS has not shown that it lacks other means of achieving its desired goal without imposing a substantial burden on the exercise of religion by the objecting parties in these cases. See §§ 2000bb–1(a), (b) (requiring the Government to "demonstrat[e] that application of [a substantial] burden to *the person* . . . is the least restrictive means of furthering [a] compelling governmental interest" (emphasis added)).

[handwritten: gov should just pay!]

The most straightforward way of doing this would be for the Government to assume the cost of providing the four contraceptives at issue to any women who are unable to obtain them under their health-insurance policies due to their employers' religious objections. This would certainly be less restrictive of the plaintiffs' religious liberty, and HHS has not shown, see § 2000bb–1(b)(2), that this is not a viable alternative. HHS has not provided any estimate of the average cost per employee of providing access to these contraceptives, two of which, according to the FDA, are designed primarily for emergency use. . . . Nor has HHS provided any statistics regarding the number of employees who might be affected because they work for corporations like Hobby Lobby, Conestoga, and Mardel. Nor has HHS told us that it is unable to provide such statistics. It seems likely, however, that the cost of providing the forms of contraceptives at issue in these cases (if not all FDA-approved contraceptives) would be minor when compared with the overall cost of ACA. According to one of the Congressional Budget Office's most recent forecasts, ACA's insurance-coverage provisions will cost the Federal Government more than $1.3 trillion through the next decade. . . . If, as HHS tells us, providing all women with cost-free access to all FDA-approved methods of contraception is a Government interest of the highest order, it is hard to understand HHS's argument that it cannot be required under RFRA to pay *anything* in order to achieve this important goal.

HHS contends that RFRA does not permit us to take this option into account because "RFRA cannot be used to require creation of entirely new programs." Brief for HHS in 13–354, at 15. But we see nothing in RFRA that supports this argument, and drawing the line between the "creation of an entirely new program" and the modification of an existing program (which RFRA surely allows) would be fraught with problems. We do not doubt that cost may be an important factor in the least-restrictive-means analysis, but both RFRA and its sister statute, RLUIPA, may in some circumstances require the Government to expend additional funds to accommodate citizens' religious beliefs. Cf. § 2000cc–3(c) (RLUIPA: "[T]his chapter may require a government to incur expenses in its own operations to avoid imposing a substantial burden on religious exercise."). HHS's view that RFRA can never require the Government to spend even a small amount reflects a judgment about the importance of religious liberty that was not shared by the Congress that enacted that law.

In the end, however, we need not rely on the option of a new, government-funded program in order to conclude that the HHS regulations fail the least-restrictive-means test. HHS itself has demonstrated that it has at its disposal an approach that is less restrictive than requiring employers to fund contraceptive methods that violate their religious beliefs. As we explained above, HHS has already established an accommodation for nonprofit organizations with religious objections. . . . Under that accommodation, the organization can self-certify that it opposes providing coverage for particular contraceptive services. See 45 CFR §§ 147.131(b)(4), (c)(1); 26 CFR §§ 54.9815–2713A(a)(4), (b). If the organization makes such a certification, the organization's insurance issuer or third-party administrator must "[e]xpressly exclude contraceptive coverage from the group health insurance coverage provided in connection with the group health plan" and "[p]rovide separate payments for any contraceptive services required to be covered" without imposing "any cost-sharing requirements . . . on the eligible organization, the group health plan, or plan participants or beneficiaries." 45 CFR § 147.131(c)(2); 26 CFR § 54.9815–2713A(c)(2).

We do not decide today whether an approach of this type complies with RFRA for purposes of all religious claims. At a minimum, however, it does not impinge on the plaintiffs' religious belief that providing insurance coverage for the contraceptives at issue here violates their religion, and it serves HHS's stated interests equally well.

. . . Under the accommodation, the plaintiffs' female employees would continue to receive contraceptive coverage without cost sharing for all FDA-approved contraceptives, and they would continue to "face minimal logistical and administrative obstacles," . . . because their employers' insurers would be responsible for providing information and coverage, see, *e.g.*, 45 CFR §§ 147.131(c)–(d); cf. 26 CFR §§ 54.9815–2713A(b), (d). . . .

C

HHS and the principal dissent argue that a ruling in favor of the objecting parties in these cases will lead to a flood of religious objections regarding a wide variety of medical procedures and drugs, such as vaccinations and blood transfusions, but HHS has made no effort to substantiate this prediction. HHS points to no evidence that insurance plans in existence prior to the enactment of ACA excluded coverage for such items. Nor has HHS provided evidence that any significant number of employers sought exemption, on religious grounds, from any of ACA's coverage requirements other than the contraceptive mandate.

It is HHS's apparent belief that no insurance-coverage mandate would violate RFRA—no matter how significantly it impinges on the religious liberties of employers—that would lead to intolerable consequences. Under HHS's view, RFRA would permit the Government to require all employers to provide coverage for any medical procedure allowed by law in the jurisdiction in question—for instance, third-trimester abortions or assisted suicide. The owners of many closely held corporations could not in good conscience provide such coverage, and thus HHS would effectively exclude these people from full participation in the economic life of the Nation. RFRA was enacted to prevent such an outcome.

In any event, our decision in these cases is concerned solely with the contraceptive mandate. Our decision should not be understood to hold that an insurance-coverage mandate must necessarily fail if it conflicts with an employer's religious beliefs. Other coverage requirements, such as immunizations, may be supported by different interests (for example, the need to combat the spread of infectious diseases) and may involve different arguments about the least restrictive means of providing them.

. . . .

* * *

The contraceptive mandate, as applied to closely held corporations, violates RFRA. Our decision on that statutory question makes it unnecessary to reach the First Amendment claim raised by Conestoga and the Hahns.

The judgment of the Tenth Circuit in No. 13–354 is affirmed; the judgment of the Third Circuit in No. 13–356 is reversed, and that case is remanded for further proceedings consistent with this opinion.

It is so ordered.

. . . .

■ GINSBURG, J., with whom SOTOMAYOR, J. joins, and with whom BREYER, J. and KAGAN, J. join as to all but Part III-C-1, dissenting.

. . . .

I

"The ability of women to participate equally in the economic and social life of the Nation has been facilitated by their ability to control their reproductive lives." *Planned Parenthood of Southeastern Pa. v. Casey*, 505 U.S. 833, 856 (1992). Congress acted on that understanding when, as part of a nationwide insurance program intended to be comprehensive, it called for coverage of preventive care responsive to women's needs. Carrying out Congress' direction, the Department of Health and Human Services (HHS), in consultation with public health experts, promulgated regulations requiring group health plans to cover all forms of contraception approved by the Food and Drug Administration

(FDA). The genesis of this coverage should enlighten the Court's resolution of these cases.

A

The Affordable Care Act (ACA), in its initial form, specified three categories of preventive care that health plans must cover at no added cost to the plan participant or beneficiary. Particular services were to be recommended by the U.S. Preventive Services Task Force, an independent panel of experts. The scheme had a large gap, however; it left out preventive services that "many women's health advocates and medical professionals believe are critically important." 155 Cong. Rec. 28841 (2009) (statement of Sen. Boxer). To correct this oversight, Senator Barbara Mikulski introduced the Women's Health Amendment, which added to the ACA's minimum coverage requirements a new category of preventive services specific to women's health.

Women paid significantly more than men for preventive care, the amendment's proponents noted; in fact, cost barriers operated to block many women from obtaining needed care at all. See, e.g., id., at 29070 (statement of Sen. Feinstein) ("Women of childbearing age spend 68 percent more in out-of-pocket health care costs than men."); id., at 29302 (statement of Sen. Mikulski) ("co-payments are [often] so high that [women] avoid getting [preventive and screening services] in the first place"). And increased access to contraceptive services, the sponsors comprehended, would yield important public health gains. See, e.g., id., at 29768 (statement of Sen. Durbin) ("This bill will expand health insurance coverage to the vast majority of [the 17 million women of reproductive age in the United States who are uninsured]. . . . This expanded access will reduce unintended pregnancies.").

As altered by the Women's Health Amendment's passage, the ACA requires new insurance plans to include coverage without cost sharing of "such additional preventive care and screenings . . . as provided for in comprehensive guidelines supported by the Health Resources and Services Administration [(HRSA)]," a unit of HHS. 42 U.S.C. § 300gg–13(a)(4). Thus charged, the HRSA developed recommendations in consultation with the Institute of Medicine (IOM). See 77 Fed. Reg. 8725–8726 (2012).[3] The IOM convened a group of independent experts, including "specialists in disease prevention [and] women's health"; those experts prepared a report evaluating the efficacy of a number of preventive services. IOM, Clinical Prevention Services for Women: Closing the Gaps 2 (2011) (hereinafter IOM Report). Consistent with the findings of "[n]umerous health professional associations" and other organizations, the IOM experts determined that preventive coverage

---

[3]   The IOM is an arm of the National Academy of Sciences, an organization Congress established "for the explicit purpose of furnishing advice to the Government." *Public Citizen v. Department of Justice*, 491 U.S. 440, 460, n. 11 (1989) (internal quotation marks omitted).

should include the "full range" of FDA-approved contraceptive methods. *Id.*, at 10. . . .

In line with the IOM's suggestions, the HRSA adopted guidelines recommending coverage of "[a]ll [FDA-] approved contraceptive methods, sterilization procedures, and patient education and counseling for all women with reproductive capacity." Thereafter, HHS, the Department of Labor, and the Department of Treasury promulgated regulations requiring group health plans to include coverage of the contraceptive services recommended in the HRSA guidelines, subject to certain exceptions. . . . This opinion refers to these regulations as the contraceptive coverage requirement.

B

While the Women's Health Amendment succeeded, a countermove proved unavailing. The Senate voted down the so-called "conscience amendment," which would have enabled any employer or insurance provider to deny coverage based on its asserted "religious beliefs or moral convictions." 158 Cong. Rec. S539 (Feb. 9, 2012); see *id.*, at S1162–S1173 (Mar. 1, 2012) (debate and vote). That amendment, Senator Mikulski observed, would have "pu[t] the personal opinion of employers and insurers over the practice of medicine." *Id.*, at S1127 (Feb. 29, 2012). Rejecting the "conscience amendment," Congress left health care decisions—including the choice among contraceptive methods—in the hands of women, with the aid of their health care providers. . . .

Congress left health care choices in hands of women ←

III

A

. . . Hobby Lobby and Conestoga rely on RFRA, a statute instructing that "[g]overnment shall not substantially burden a person's exercise of religion even if the burden results from a rule of general applicability" unless the government shows that application of the burden is "the least restrictive means" to further a "compelling governmental interest." 42 U.S.C. § 2000bb–1(a), (b)(2). . . .

RFRA's purpose is specific and written into the statute itself. The Act was crafted to "restore the compelling interest test as set forth in *Sherbert v. Verner*, 374 U.S. 398 (1963) and *Wisconsin v. Yoder*, 406 U.S. 205 (1972) and to guarantee its application in all cases where free exercise of religion is substantially burdened." § 2000bb(b)(1).[9] See also § 2000bb(a)(5) ("[T]he compelling interest test as set forth in prior Federal court rulings is a workable test for striking sensible balances between religious liberty and competing prior governmental interests.");

---

[9]   Under *Sherbert* and *Yoder*, the Court "requir[ed] the government to justify any substantial burden on religiously motivated conduct by a compelling state interest and by means narrowly tailored to achieve that interest." *Employment Div., Dept. of Human Resources of Ore. v. Smith*, 494 U.S. 872, 894 (1990) (O'Connor, J., concurring in judgment).

ante, at 2785 (agreeing that the pre-*Smith* compelling interest test is "workable" and "strike[s] sensible balances").

. . . .

B *Congress intended to restore*
Pre - Smith 1A test

. . . [T]he Court sees RFRA as a bold initiative departing from, rather than restoring, pre-*Smith* jurisprudence. To support its conception of RFRA as a measure detached from this Court's decisions, one that sets a new course, the Court points first to the Religious Land Use and Institutionalized Persons Act of 2000 (RLUIPA), 42 U.S.C. § 2000cc *et seq.*, which altered RFRA's definition of the term "exercise of religion." RFRA, as originally enacted, defined that term to mean "the exercise of religion under the First Amendment to the Constitution." § 2000bb–2(4) (1994 ed.). . . . As amended by RLUIPA, RFRA's definition now includes "any exercise of religion, whether or not compelled by, or central to, a system of religious belief." § 2000bb–2(4) (2012 ed.) (cross-referencing § 2000cc–5). That definitional change, according to the Court, reflects "an obvious effort to effect a complete separation from First Amendment case law." . . .

The Court's reading is not plausible. RLUIPA's alteration clarifies that courts should not question the centrality of a particular religious exercise. But the amendment in no way suggests that Congress meant to expand the class of entities qualified to mount religious accommodation claims, nor does it relieve courts of the obligation to inquire whether a government action substantially burdens a religious exercise. See *Rasul v. Myers*, 563 F.3d 527, 535 (C.A.D.C.2009) (Brown, J., concurring) ("There is no doubt that RLUIPA's drafters, in changing the definition of 'exercise of religion,' wanted to broaden the scope of the kinds of practices protected by RFRA, not increase the universe of individuals protected by RFRA."); H.R.Rep. No. 106–219, p. 30 (1999). See also *Gilardi v. United States Dept. of Health and Human Servs.*, 733 F.3d 1208, 1211 (C.A.D.C.2013) (RFRA, as amended, "provides us with no helpful definition of 'exercise of religion.' "); *Henderson v. Kennedy*, 265 F.3d 1072, 1073 (C.A.D.C.2001) ("The [RLUIPA] amendments did not alter RFRA's basic prohibition that the '[g]overnment shall not substantially burden a person's exercise of religion.' ").

Next, the Court highlights RFRA's requirement that the government, if its action substantially burdens a person's religious observance, must demonstrate that it chose the least restrictive means for furthering a compelling interest. "[B]y imposing a least-restrictive-means test," the Court suggests, RFRA "went beyond what was required by our pre-*Smith* decisions." . . . But as RFRA's statements of purpose and legislative history make clear, Congress intended only to restore, not to scrap or alter, the balancing test as this Court had applied it pre-*Smith*. . . .

The Congress that passed RFRA correctly read this Court's pre-*Smith* case law as including within the "compelling interest test" a "least restrictive means" requirement. See, *e.g.*, Senate Report 5 ("Where [a substantial] burden is placed upon the free exercise of religion, the Court ruled [in *Sherbert*], the Government must demonstrate that it is the least restrictive means to achieve a compelling governmental interest."). . . .

Our decision in *City of Boerne*, it is true, states that the least restrictive means requirement "was not used in the pre-*Smith* jurisprudence RFRA purported to codify." . . . As just indicated, however, that statement does not accurately convey the Court's pre-*Smith* jurisprudence. See *Sherbert*, 374 U.S., at 407 ("[I]t would plainly be incumbent upon the [government] to demonstrate that no alternative forms of regulation would combat [the problem] without infringing First Amendment rights."); *Thomas v. Review Bd. of Indiana Employment Security Div.*, 450 U.S. 707, 718 (1981) ("The state may justify an inroad on religious liberty by showing that it is the least restrictive means of achieving some compelling state interest."). See also Berg, *The New Attacks on Religious Freedom Legislation and Why They Are Wrong*, 21 Cardozo L. Rev. 415, 424 (1999) ("In *Boerne*, the Court erroneously said that the least restrictive means test 'was not used in the pre-*Smith* jurisprudence.' ").[11]

C

With RFRA's restorative purpose in mind, I turn to the Act's application to the instant lawsuits. That task, in view of the positions taken by the Court, requires consideration of several questions, each potentially dispositive of Hobby Lobby's and Conestoga's claims: Do for-profit corporations rank among "person[s]" who "exercise . . . religion"? Assuming that they do, does the contraceptive coverage requirement "substantially burden" their religious exercise? If so, is the requirement "in furtherance of a compelling government interest"? And last, does the requirement represent the least restrictive means for furthering that interest?

Misguided by its errant premise that RFRA moved beyond the pre-*Smith* case law, the Court falters at each step of its analysis.

1

RFRA's compelling interest test, as noted, see *supra*, at 2790, applies to government actions that "substantially burden *a person's exercise of religion.*" 42 U.S.C. § 2000bb–1(a) (emphasis added). This reference, the Court submits, incorporates the definition of "person" found in the Dictionary Act, 1 U.S.C. § 1, which extends to "corporations, companies,

---

[11] The Court points out that I joined the majority opinion in *City of Boerne* and did not then question the statement that "least restrictive means . . . was not used [pre-*Smith*]." *Ante*, at 2767, n. 18. Concerning that observation, I remind my colleagues of Justice Jackson's sage comment: "I see no reason why I should be consciously wrong today because I was unconsciously wrong yesterday." *Massachusetts v. United States*, 333 U.S. 611, 639–640 (1948) (dissenting opinion).

associations, firms, partnerships, societies, and joint stock companies, as well as individuals." See *ante,* at 2768. The Dictionary Act's definition, however, controls only where "context" does not "indicat[e] otherwise." § 1. Here, context does so indicate. RFRA speaks of "a person's *exercise of religion*." 42 U.S.C. § 2000bb–1(a) (emphasis added). See also §§ 2000bb–2(4), 2000cc–5(7)(a). Whether a corporation qualifies as a "person" capable of exercising religion is an inquiry one cannot answer without reference to the "full body" of pre-*Smith* "free-exercise caselaw." *Gilardi,* 733 F.3d, at 1212. There is in that case law no support for the notion that free exercise rights pertain to for-profit corporations.

[handwritten margin note: RFRA protects people]

Until this litigation, no decision of this Court recognized a for-profit corporation's qualification for a religious exemption from a generally applicable law, whether under the Free Exercise Clause or RFRA. The absence of such precedent is just what one would expect, for the exercise of religion is characteristic of natural persons, not artificial legal entities. As Chief Justice Marshall observed nearly two centuries ago, a corporation is "an artificial being, invisible, intangible, and existing only in contemplation of law." *Trustees of Dartmouth College v. Woodward,* 4 Wheat. 518, 636 (1819). Corporations, Justice Stevens more recently reminded, "have no consciences, no beliefs, no feelings, no thoughts, no desires." *Citizens United v. Federal Election Comm'n,* 558 U.S. 310, 466 (2010) (opinion concurring in part and dissenting in part).

The First Amendment's free exercise protections, the Court has indeed recognized, shelter churches and other nonprofit religion-based organizations. "For many individuals, religious activity derives meaning in large measure from participation in a larger religious community," and "furtherance of the autonomy of religious organizations often furthers individual religious freedom as well." *Corporation of Presiding Bishop of Church of Jesus Christ of Latter-day Saints v. Amos,* 483 U.S. 327, 342 (1987) (Brennan, J., concurring in judgment). The Court's "special solicitude to the rights of religious organizations," *Hosanna-Tabor Evangelical Lutheran Church and School v. EEOC,* 565 U.S. 171, 189, 132 S.Ct. 694, 706 (2012), however, is just that. No such solicitude is traditional for commercial organizations. Indeed, until today, religious exemptions had never been extended to any entity operating in "the commercial, profit-making world." *Amos,* 483 U.S., at 337.

The reason why is hardly obscure. Religious organizations exist to foster the interests of persons subscribing to the same religious faith. Not so of for-profit corporations. Workers who sustain the operations of those corporations commonly are not drawn from one religious community. Indeed, by law, no religion-based criterion can restrict the work force of for-profit corporations. See 42 U.S.C. §§ 2000e(b), 2000e–1(a), 2000e–2(a); cf. *Trans World Airlines, Inc. v. Hardison,* 432 U.S. 63, 80–81 (1977) (Title VII requires reasonable accommodation of an employee's religious exercise, but such accommodation must not come "at the expense of other[employees]"). The distinction between a community made up of believers in the same religion and one embracing persons of diverse beliefs, clear as it is, constantly escapes the Court's attention. . . .

Reading RFRA, as the Court does, to require extension of religion-based exemptions to for-profit corporations surely is not grounded in the pre-*Smith* precedent Congress sought to preserve. Had Congress intended RFRA to initiate a change so huge, a clarion statement to that effect likely would have been made in the legislation. . . . The text of RFRA makes no such statement and the legislative history does not so much as mention for-profit corporations. . . .

The Court notes that for-profit corporations may support charitable causes and use their funds for religious ends, and therefore questions the distinction between such corporations and religious nonprofit organizations. . . . Again, the Court forgets that religious organizations exist to serve a community of believers. For-profit corporations do not fit that bill. Moreover, history is not on the Court's side. Recognition of the discrete characters of "ecclesiastical and lay" corporations dates back to Blackstone, see 1 W. Blackstone, Commentaries on the Laws of England 458 (1765), and was reiterated by this Court centuries before the enactment of the Internal Revenue Code. See *Terrett v. Taylor*, 9 Cranch 43, 49 (1815) (describing religious corporations); *Trustees of Dartmouth College*, 4 Wheat., at 645 (discussing "eleemosynary" corporations, including those "created for the promotion of religion"). To reiterate, "for-profit corporations are different from religious non-profits in that they use labor to make a profit, rather than to perpetuate [the] religious value[s] [shared by a community of believers]." . . .

Citing *Braunfeld v. Brown*, 366 U.S. 599 (1961), the Court questions why, if "a sole proprietorship that seeks to make a profit may assert a free-exercise claim, [Hobby Lobby and Conestoga] can't . . . do the same?" . . . But even accepting, *arguendo*, the premise that unincorporated business enterprises may gain religious accommodations under the Free Exercise Clause, the Court's conclusion is unsound. In a sole proprietorship, the business and its owner are one and the same. By incorporating a business, however, an individual separates herself from the entity and escapes personal responsibility for the entity's obligations. One might ask why the separation should hold only when it serves the interest of those who control the corporation. In any event, *Braunfeld* is hardly impressive authority for the entitlement Hobby Lobby and Conestoga seek. The free exercise claim asserted there was promptly rejected on the merits.

The Court's determination that RFRA extends to for-profit corporations is bound to have untoward effects. Although the Court attempts to cabin its language to closely held corporations, its logic extends to corporations of any size, public or private.[19] Little doubt that

---

[19] The Court does not even begin to explain how one might go about ascertaining the religious scruples of a corporation where shares are sold to the public. No need to speculate on that, the Court says, for "it seems unlikely" that large corporations "will often assert RFRA

RFRA claims will proliferate, for the Court's expansive notion of corporate personhood—combined with its other errors in construing RFRA—invites for-profit entities to seek religion-based exemptions from regulations they deem offensive to their faith.

2 doesn't substantially burden religious exercise

Even if Hobby Lobby and Conestoga were deemed RFRA "person[s]," to gain an exemption, they must demonstrate that the contraceptive coverage requirement "substantially burden[s] [their] exercise of religion." 42 U.S.C. § 2000bb–1(a). Congress no doubt meant the modifier "substantially" to carry weight. In the original draft of RFRA, the word "burden" appeared unmodified. The word "substantially" was inserted pursuant to a clarifying amendment offered by Senators Kennedy and Hatch. See 139 Cong. Rec. 26180. In proposing the amendment, Senator Kennedy stated that RFRA, in accord with the Court's pre-*Smith* case law, "does not require the Government to justify every action that has some effect on religious exercise." *Ibid.*

The Court barely pauses to inquire whether any burden imposed by the contraceptive coverage requirement is substantial. Instead, it rests on the Greens' and Hahns' "belie[f] that providing the coverage demanded by the HHS regulations is connected to the destruction of an embryo in a way that is sufficient to make it immoral for them to provide the coverage." . . .[20] I agree with the Court that the Green and Hahn families' religious convictions regarding contraception are sincerely held. . . . But those beliefs, however deeply held, do not suffice to sustain a RFRA claim. RFRA, properly understood, distinguishes between "factual allegations that [plaintiffs'] beliefs are sincere and of a religious nature," which a court must accept as true, and the "legal conclusion . . . that [plaintiffs'] religious exercise is substantially burdened," an inquiry the court must undertake. . . .

Sincere vs substantially burdened

---

claims." *Ante,* at 2774. Perhaps so, but as Hobby Lobby's case demonstrates, such claims are indeed pursued by large corporations, employing thousands of persons of different faiths, whose ownership is not diffuse. "Closely held" is not synonymous with "small." Hobby Lobby is hardly the only enterprise of sizable scale that is family owned or closely held. For example, the family-owned candy giant Mars, Inc., takes in $33 billion in revenues and has some 72,000 employees, and closely held Cargill, Inc., takes in more than $136 billion in revenues and employs some 140,000 persons. See Forbes, America's Largest Private Companies 2013, available at http://www.forbes.com/largest-private-companies/.

Nor does the Court offer any instruction on how to resolve the disputes that may crop up among corporate owners over religious values and accommodations. The Court is satisfied that "[s]tate corporate law provides a ready means for resolving any conflicts[.]" . . .

[20] The Court dismisses the argument, advanced by some *amici,* that the $2,000-per-employee tax charged to certain employers that fail to provide health insurance is less than the average cost of offering health insurance, noting that the Government has not provided the statistics that could support such an argument. See *ante* at 2775–2777. The Court overlooks, however, that it is not the Government's obligation to prove that an asserted burden is *in*substantial. Instead, it is incumbent upon plaintiffs to demonstrate, in support of a RFRA claim, the substantiality of the alleged burden.

. . . Inattentive to this guidance, today's decision elides entirely the distinction between the sincerity of a challenger's religious belief and the substantiality of the burden placed on the challenger.

Undertaking the inquiry that the Court forgoes, I would conclude that the connection between the families' religious objections and the contraceptive coverage requirement is too attenuated to rank as substantial. The requirement carries no command that Hobby Lobby or Conestoga purchase or provide the contraceptives they find objectionable. Instead, it calls on the companies covered by the requirement to direct money into undifferentiated funds that finance a wide variety of benefits under comprehensive health plans. Those plans, in order to comply with the ACA, . . . must offer contraceptive coverage without cost sharing, just as they must cover an array of other preventive services.

Importantly, the decisions whether to claim benefits under the plans are made not by Hobby Lobby or Conestoga, but by the covered employees and dependents, in consultation with their health care providers. Should an employee of Hobby Lobby or Conestoga share the religious beliefs of the Greens and Hahns, she is of course under no compulsion to use the contraceptives in question. But "[n]o individual decision by an employee and her physician—be it to use contraception, treat an infection, or have a hip replaced—is in any meaningful sense [her employer's] decision or action." *Grote v. Sebelius*, 708 F.3d 850, 865 (C.A.7 2013) (Rovner, J., dissenting). It is doubtful that Congress, when it specified that burdens must be "substantia[l]," had in mind a linkage thus interrupted by independent decisionmakers (the woman and her health counselor) standing between the challenged government action and the religious exercise claimed to be infringed. Any decision to use contraceptives made by a woman covered under Hobby Lobby's or Conestoga's plan will not be propelled by the Government, it will be the woman's autonomous choice, informed by the physician she consults.

3 *compelling gov interests*

Even if one were to conclude that Hobby Lobby and Conestoga meet the substantial burden requirement, the Government has shown that the contraceptive coverage for which the ACA provides furthers compelling interests in public health and women's well being. Those interests are concrete, specific, and demonstrated by a wealth of empirical evidence. To recapitulate, the mandated contraception coverage enables women to avoid the health problems unintended pregnancies may visit on them and their children. . . . The coverage helps safeguard the health of women for whom pregnancy may be hazardous, even life threatening. . . . And the mandate secures benefits wholly unrelated to pregnancy, preventing certain cancers, menstrual disorders, and pelvic pain. . . .

That Hobby Lobby and Conestoga resist coverage for only 4 of the 20 FDA-approved contraceptives does not lessen these compelling interests. Notably, the corporations exclude intrauterine devices (IUDs), devices significantly more effective, and significantly more expensive than other contraceptive methods. . . .[22] Moreover, the Court's reasoning appears to permit commercial enterprises like Hobby Lobby and Conestoga to exclude from their group health plans all forms of contraceptives. See Tr. of Oral Arg. 38–39 (counsel for Hobby Lobby acknowledged that his "argument . . . would apply just as well if the employer said 'no contraceptives' " (internal quotation marks added)).

Perhaps the gravity of the interests at stake has led the Court to assume, for purposes of its RFRA analysis, that the compelling interest criterion is met in these cases. . . . It bears note in this regard that the cost of an IUD is nearly equivalent to a month's full-time pay for workers earning the minimum wage . . . that almost one-third of women would change their contraceptive method if costs were not a factor, Frost & Darroch, *Factors Associated With Contraceptive Choice and Inconsistent Method Use*, United States, 2004, 40 Perspectives on Sexual & Reproductive Health 94, 98 (2008); and that only one-fourth of women who request an IUD actually have one inserted after finding out how expensive it would be, Gariepy, Simon, Patel, Creinin, & Schwarz, *The Impact of Out-of-Pocket Expense on IUD Utilization Among Women With Private Insurance*, 84 Contraception e39, e40 (2011). See also Eisenberg, *supra*, at S60 (recent study found that women who face out-of-pocket IUD costs in excess of $50 were "11-times less likely to obtain an IUD than women who had to pay less than $50"); Postlethwaite, Trussell, Zoolakis, Shabear, & Petitti, *A Comparison of Contraceptive Procurement Pre-and Post-Benefit Change*, 76 Contraception 360, 361–362 (2007) (when one health system eliminated patient cost sharing for IUDs, use of this form of contraception more than doubled).

Stepping back from its assumption that compelling interests support the contraceptive coverage requirement, the Court notes that small employers and grandfathered plans are not subject to the requirement. If there is a compelling interest in contraceptive coverage, the Court suggests, Congress would not have created these exclusions. . . .

Federal statutes often include exemptions for small employers, and such provisions have never been held to undermine the interests served by these statutes. See, *e.g.*, Family and Medical Leave Act of 1993, 29 U.S.C. § 2611(4)(A)(i) (applicable to employers with 50 or more employees); Age Discrimination in Employment Act of 1967, 29 U.S.C. § 630(b) (originally exempting employers with fewer than 50 employees, 81 Stat. 605, the statute now governs employers with 20 or more employees); Americans With Disabilities Act, 42 U.S.C. § 12111(5)(A) (applicable to employers with 15 or more employees); Title VII, 42 U.S.C. § 2000e(b) (originally exempting employers with fewer than 25

[handwritten margin note: Some exemptions dont eliminate all claims of compelling gov interests]

---

[22] IUDs, which are among the most reliable forms of contraception, generally cost women more than $1,000 when the expenses of the office visit and insertion procedure are taken into account. See Eisenberg, McNicholas, & Peipert, Cost as a Barrier to Long-Acting Reversible Contraceptive (LARC) Use in Adolescents, 52 J. Adolescent Health S59, S60 (2013). See also Winner et al., Effectiveness of Long-Acting Reversible Contraception, 366 New Eng. J. Medicine 1998, 1999 (2012).

employees, see *Arbaugh* v. *Y & H Corp.*, 546 U.S. 500, 505, n. 2 (2006), the statute now governs employers with 15 or more employees).

The ACA's grandfathering provision, 42 U.S.C. § 18011, allows a phasing-in period for compliance with a number of the Act's requirements (not just the contraceptive coverage or other preventive services provisions). Once specified changes are made, grandfathered status ceases. See 45 CFR § 147.140(g). Hobby Lobby's own situation is illustrative. By the time this litigation commenced, Hobby Lobby did not have grandfathered status. Asked why by the District Court, Hobby Lobby's counsel explained that the "grandfathering requirements mean that you can't make a whole menu of changes to your plan that involve things like the amount of co-pays, the amount of co-insurance, deductibles, that sort of thing." App. in No. 13–354, pp. 39–40. Counsel acknowledged that, "just because of economic realities, our plan has to shift over time. I mean, insurance plans, as everyone knows, shif[t] over time." *Id.*, at 40.[24] The percentage of employees in grandfathered plans is steadily declining, having dropped from 56% in 2011 to 48% in 2012 to 36% in 2013. Kaiser Family Foundation & Health Research & Educ. Trust, Employer Benefits 2013 Annual Survey 7, 196. In short, far from ranking as a categorical exemption, the grandfathering provision is "temporary, intended to be a means for gradually transitioning employers into mandatory coverage." *Gilardi*, 733 F.3d, at 1241 (Edwards, J., concurring in part and dissenting in part).

The Court ultimately acknowledges a critical point: RFRA's application "*must* take adequate account of the burdens a requested accommodation may impose on non-beneficiaries." *Ante*, at 2781, n. 37 (quoting *Cutter v. Wilkinson*, 544 U.S. 709, 720 (2005); emphasis added). No tradition, and no prior decision under RFRA, allows a religion-based exemption when the accommodation would be harmful to others—here, the very persons the contraceptive coverage requirement was designed to protect. . . .

After assuming the existence of compelling government interests, the Court holds that the contraceptive coverage requirement fails to satisfy RFRA's least restrictive means test. But the Government has shown that there is no less restrictive, equally effective means that would both (1) satisfy the challengers' religious objections to providing insurance coverage for certain contraceptives (which they believe cause abortions); and (2) carry out the objective of the ACA's contraceptive coverage requirement, to ensure that women employees receive, at no cost to them, the preventive care needed to safeguard their health and

---

[24] Hobby Lobby's *amicus* National Religious Broadcasters similarly states that, "[g]iven the nature of employers' needs to meet changing economic and staffing circumstances, and to adjust insurance coverage accordingly, the actual benefit of the 'grandfather' exclusion is *de minimis* and transitory at best." Brief for National Religious Broadcasters as *Amicus Curiae* in No. 13–354, p. 28.

well being. A "least restrictive means" cannot require employees to relinquish benefits accorded them by federal law in order to ensure that their commercial employers can adhere unreservedly to their religious tenets. . . .

Then let the government pay (rather than the employees who do not share their employer's faith), the Court suggests. "The most straightforward [alternative]," the Court asserts, "would be for the Government to assume the cost of providing . . . contraceptives . . . to any women who are unable to obtain them under their health-insurance policies due to their employers' religious objections." *Ante*, at 2780. The ACA, however, requires coverage of preventive services through the existing employer-based system of health insurance "so that [employees] face minimal logistical and administrative obstacles." 78 Fed.Reg. 39888. Impeding women's receipt of benefits "by requiring them to take steps to learn about, and to sign up for, a new [government funded and administered] health benefit" was scarcely what Congress contemplated. *Ibid.* Moreover, Title X of the Public Health Service Act, 42 U.S.C. § 300 *et seq.*, "is the nation's only dedicated source of federal funding for safety net family planning services." Brief for National Health Law Program et al. as *Amici Curiae* 23. "Safety net programs like Title X are not designed to absorb the unmet needs of . . . insured individuals." . . .

And where is the stopping point to the "let the government pay" alternative? Suppose an employer's sincerely held religious belief is offended by health coverage of vaccines, or paying the minimum wage, see *Tony and Susan Alamo Foundation v. Secretary of Labor*, 471 U.S. 290, 303 (1985), or according women equal pay for substantially similar work, see *Dole v. Shenandoah Baptist Church*, 899 F.2d 1389, 1392 (C.A.4 1990)? Does it rank as a less restrictive alternative to require the government to provide the money or benefit to which the employer has a religion-based objection? Because the Court cannot easily answer that question, it proposes something else: Extension to commercial enterprises of the accommodation already afforded to nonprofit religion-based organizations. . . . "At a minimum," according to the Court, such an approach would not "impinge on [Hobby Lobby's and Conestoga's] religious belief." . . . I have already discussed the "special solicitude" generally accorded nonprofit religion-based organizations that exist to serve a community of believers, solicitude never before accorded to commercial enterprises comprising employees of diverse faiths. . . .

. . . .

In sum, in view of what Congress sought to accomplish, *i.e.*, comprehensive preventive care for women furnished through employer-based health plans, none of the proffered alternatives would satisfactorily serve the compelling interests to which Congress responded.

IV

Among the pathmarking pre-*Smith* decisions RFRA preserved is *United States v. Lee*, 455 U.S. 252 (1982). Lee, a sole proprietor engaged in farming and carpentry, was a member of the Old Order Amish. He sincerely believed that withholding Social Security taxes from his employees or paying the employer's share of such taxes would violate the Amish faith. This Court held that, although the obligations imposed by the Social Security system conflicted with Lee's religious beliefs, the burden was not unconstitutional. *Id.*, at 260–261. See also *id.*, at 258 (recognizing the important governmental interest in providing a "nationwide . . . comprehensive insurance system with a variety of benefits available to all participants, with costs shared by employers and employees").[28] . . . [T]oday's Court dismisses *Lee* as a tax case. . . .

But the *Lee* Court made two key points one cannot confine to tax cases. "When followers of a particular sect enter into commercial activity as a matter of choice," the Court observed, "the limits they accept on their own conduct as a matter of conscience and faith are not to be superimposed on statutory schemes which are binding on others in that activity." *Id.*, at 261. The statutory scheme of employer-based comprehensive health coverage involved in these cases is surely binding on others engaged in the same trade or business as the corporate challengers here, Hobby Lobby and Conestoga. Further, the Court recognized in *Lee* that allowing a religion-based exemption to a commercial employer would "operat[e] to impose the employer's religious faith on the employees." *Ibid.*[29] No doubt the Greens and Hahns and all who share their beliefs may decline to acquire for themselves the contraceptives in question. But that choice may not be imposed on employees who hold other beliefs. Working for Hobby Lobby or Conestoga, in other words, should not deprive employees of the preventive care available to workers at the shop next door,[30] at least in the absence of directions from the Legislature or Administration to do so.

Why should decisions of this order be made by Congress or the regulatory authority, and not this Court? Hobby Lobby and Conestoga surely do not stand alone as commercial enterprises seeking exemptions from generally applicable laws on the basis of their religious beliefs. See,

---

[28] As a sole proprietor, Lee was subject to personal liability for violating the law of general application he opposed. His claim to a religion-based exemption would have been even thinner had he conducted his business as a corporation, thus avoiding personal liability.

[29] Congress amended the Social Security Act in response to *Lee*. The amended statute permits Amish sole proprietors and partnerships (but not Amish-owned corporations) to obtain an exemption from the obligation to pay Social Security taxes only for employees who are co-religionists and who likewise seek an exemption and agree to give up their Social Security benefits. See 26 U.S.C. § 3127(a)(2), (b)(1). Thus, employers with sincere religious beliefs have no right to a religion-based exemption that would deprive employees of Social Security benefits without the employee's consent—an exemption analogous to the one Hobby Lobby and Conestoga seek here.

[30] Cf. *Tony and Susan Alamo Foundation v. Secretary of Labor*, 471 U.S. 290, 299 (1985) (disallowing religion-based exemption that "would undoubtedly give [the commercial enterprise seeking the exemption] and similar organizations an advantage over their competitors").

e.g., Newman v. Piggie Park Enterprises, Inc., 256 F. Supp. 941, 945 (D.S.C. 1966) (owner of restaurant chain refused to serve black patrons based on his religious beliefs opposing racial integration), aff'd in relevant part and rev'd in part on other grounds, 377 F.2d 433 (C.A.4 1967), aff'd and modified on other grounds, 390 U.S. 400 (1968); *In re Minnesota ex rel. McClure*, 370 N.W.2d 844, 847 (Minn.1985) (born-again Christians who owned closely held, for-profit health clubs believed that the Bible proscribed hiring or retaining an "individua[l] living with but not married to a person of the opposite sex," "a young, single woman working without her father's consent or a married woman working without her husband's consent," and any person "antagonistic to the Bible," including "fornicators and homosexuals" (internal quotation marks omitted)), appeal dismissed, 478 U.S. 1015 (1986); *Elane Photography, LLC v. Willock*, 2013–NMSC–040, N.M., 309 P.3d 53 (for-profit photography business owned by a husband and wife refused to photograph a lesbian couple's commitment ceremony based on the religious beliefs of the company's owners), cert. denied, 572 U.S. 1046 (2014). Would RFRA require exemptions in cases of this ilk? And if not, how does the Court divine which religious beliefs are worthy of accommodation, and which are not? Isn't the Court disarmed from making such a judgment given its recognition that "courts must not presume to determine . . . the plausibility of a religious claim"? . . .

Would the exemption the Court holds RFRA demands for employers with religiously grounded objections to the use of certain contraceptives extend to employers with religiously grounded objections to blood transfusions (Jehovah's Witnesses); antidepressants (Scientologists); medications derived from pigs, including anesthesia, intravenous fluids, and pills coated with gelatin (certain Muslims, Jews, and Hindus); and vaccinations (Christian Scientists, among others)?[31] . . .

Slippery slope — how far?

The Court, however, sees nothing to worry about. Today's cases, the Court concludes, are "concerned solely with the contraceptive mandate. Our decision should not be understood to hold that an insurance-coverage mandate must necessarily fall if it conflicts with an employer's religious beliefs. Other coverage requirements, such as immunizations, may be supported by different interests (for example, the need to combat the spread of infectious diseases) and may involve different arguments about the least restrictive means of providing them." *Ante*, at 2783. But the Court has assumed, for RFRA purposes, that the interest in women's health and well being is compelling and has come up with no means adequate to serve that interest, the one motivating Congress to adopt the Women's Health Amendment.

---

[31] Religious objections to immunization programs are not hypothetical. See *Phillips v. New York*, 27 F. Supp. 3d 310, 2014 WL 2547584 (E.D.N.Y., June 5, 2014) (dismissing free exercise challenges to New York's vaccination practices); Liberty Counsel, Compulsory Vaccinations Threaten Religious Freedom (2007), available at http://www.lc.org/media/9980/attachments/memo_vaccination.pdf.

There is an overriding interest, I believe, in keeping the courts "out of the business of evaluating the relative merits of differing religious claims," *Lee*, 455 U.S., at 263, n. 2 (Stevens, J., concurring in judgment), or the sincerity with which an asserted religious belief is held. Indeed, approving some religious claims while deeming others unworthy of accommodation could be "perceived as favoring one religion over another," the very "risk the Establishment Clause was designed to preclude." *Ibid.* The Court, I fear, has ventured into a minefield . . . by its immoderate reading of RFRA. I would confine religious exemptions under that Act to organizations formed "for a religious purpose," "engage[d] primarily in carrying out that religious purpose," and not "engaged . . . substantially in the exchange of goods or services for money beyond nominal amounts." . . .

[handwritten margin note: exceptions here should be limited to religious non profits]

* * *

For the reasons stated, I would reverse the judgment of the Court of Appeals for the Tenth Circuit and affirm the judgment of the Court of Appeals for the Third Circuit.

. . . .

NOTES

1.   *RFRA in context.* The Religious Freedom Restoration Act of 1993 (RFRA) was enacted in response to the Supreme Court's decision in *Employment Division v. Smith*, 494 U.S. 872 (1990). In *Smith*, the state of Oregon refused unemployment benefits to two Native Americans on the ground that they had been fired from their positions at a drug rehabilitation center because they had tested positive for mescaline, the main psychoactive compound in the peyote cactus. The two men argued that because they had used peyote in the context of a Native-American religious ceremony, the state's refusal to issue them unemployment benefits violated their First Amendment rights to free exercise of religion. In a controversial decision, the Court upheld the state's actions, concluding that Oregon's ban on peyote use was a "neutral law of general applicability" that was not intended to impede religious exercise. Accordingly, the Court used a lower standard of review, rather than the more rigorous strict scrutiny standard that traditionally is used to review laws that implicate religious exercise.

In an effort to counteract the Court's decision in *Smith*, and reinstate strict scrutiny as the appropriate standard of review for laws that implicate religious exercise, even where those laws apply generally and do not target a particular religious group, Congress passed RFRA. Critically, the law enjoyed bipartisan support. It passed unanimously in the House of Representatives, and garnered ninety-seven (out of one hundred) votes in the Senate.

Ultimately, the constitutionality of RFRA's application to state actors was challenged in *City of Boerne v. Flores*, 521 U.S. 507 (1997). There, the Court held that, in enacting RFRA, Congress had exceeded its authority under § 5 of the Fourteenth Amendment. In response to *Boerne*, some individual states passed state-level Religious Freedom Restoration Acts that apply to state governments and local municipalities. The Court confirmed RFRA's constitutionality as applied to the federal government in *Gonzales v. O Centro Espírita Beneficente União do Vegetal*, 546 U.S. 418 (2006).

2.   *When does "life" actually begin?* As technologies improve, the questions raised in *Hobby Lobby* turn in part upon complex philosophical and medical issues. The establishment of pregnancy is traditionally defined as the moment when a fertilized egg implants in the wall of the uterus. *See, e.g.*, Additional Protections for Pregnant Women, Human Fetuses and Neonates Involved in Research, 45 C.F.R. § 46.202 (2014) (defining pregnancy as the implantation of a fertilized egg in the context of pregnant women as research subjects). However, Hobby Lobby and similar proponents argue that contraception, and in particular emergency contraception, prevents a fertilized egg from implanting in the uterus, in their view causing a very early abortion. The situation is made even more confusing because there is little consensus about how emergency contraception works. Emergency contraception could prevent pregnancy by several plausible mechanisms: affecting sperm motility, ovulation, changes in the lining of the uterus, changes in hormonal environment, and/or by affecting the cervical mucus. Still more confusing, emergency contraception may operate through different mechanisms depending upon at what point in the ovulation cycle it is taken. The available evidence, however, both biochemical and epidemiological, suggests that it is unlikely to prevent pregnancy post-fertilization, thus undercutting the corporations' claim in *Hobby Lobby*. *See* Frank Davidoff & James Trussell, *Plan B and the Politics of Doubt*, 296 J. AM. MED. ASS'N 1775, 1776–77 (2006).

3.   *Corporations as believers.* Traditionally, the First Amendment has protected the *individual's* right of religious free exercise. However, *Hobby Lobby* and similar cases do not raise individual objections to the contraceptive mandate. Instead, these cases reflect the view that religious-affiliated *corporations* enjoy First Amendment protections. Professor Elizabeth Sepper cautions that if courts recognize conscience—an "inherently human" trait—of corporations, employees, and particularly female employees, would become especially vulnerable to health and labor rights violations. "Religiously affiliated commercial actors," Sepper notes, "already assert rights to defy health and safety laws, pay women less, and fire pregnant women." If secular employers were allowed similar exemptions, women workers would doubly experience the hurdles to gender equality in the workplace. Elizabeth Sepper, *Contraception and the Birth of Corporate Conscience*, 22 AM. U. J. GENDER SOC. POL'Y & L. 303, 304–05 (2014). Should a for-profit corporation be entitled to the protection that individuals have to freely exercise their religion? Do corporations have a religious identity that is compromised by subsidizing contraception as part of employer-provided health care plans?

4.   Wheaton College v. Burwell. The *Hobby Lobby* majority emphasized that the opinion was narrow and limited to the question of whether RFRA exempted closely-held, private corporations from complying with the contraceptive mandate. Nevertheless, on July 3, 2014, the Court issued a

provisional order exempting—at least temporarily until lower courts decide the issue—Wheaton College, a Christian college in Illinois, from complying with the administrative procedures for accommodating the religious views of religious non-profit organizations. *See Wheaton College v. Burwell*, 573 U.S. 958 (2014). Under a religious accommodation provision of the ACA, religious non-profit organizations may be exempted from the contraceptive mandate by completing a form and registering their religious objections. Compliance with these administrative procedures allows the non-profit's insurers or government administrators to take on the responsibility of paying for the birth control, relieving the non-profit of the cost of coverage. Wheaton College, however, objected to these administrative measures, arguing that completing the form simply transferred the burden of providing contraception to other parties, making Wheaton complicit in actions that offended its religious beliefs. Under the Court's order, Wheaton need not comply with the administrative procedures. It need only file a letter with the federal government stating its religious objections, and the government then would notify the third party to provide the contraceptives.

Notably, the three female members of the Court (Justices Ginsburg, Kagan, and Sotomayor) registered their disagreement with what they perceived as an expansion of *Hobby Lobby*'s religious accommodation logic. In a vigorous dissent in which Justices Ginsburg and Kagan joined, Justice Sotomayor questioned whether the obligation to complete and file a one-page form truly constituted an impermissible imposition on Wheaton College's religious beliefs. *Id.* at 2815. (Sotomayor, J., dissenting). As she observed, "the Court's grant of an injunction in this case allows Wheaton's beliefs about the effects of its actions to trump the democratic interest in allowing the Government to enforce the law." *Id.*

Critically, in January 2014, the Court issued a similar provisional ruling in *Little Sisters of the Poor v. Sebelius*, 571 U.S. 1171 (2014). As with *Wheaton College v. Burwell*, a legal challenge was pending in the lower courts as to whether religious non-profit organizations were required to comply with the accommodation procedures in order to be exempt from the ACA's contraceptive mandate. Notwithstanding this, the Court's order relieved the Little Sisters of the Poor, an order of Catholic nuns, from completing the required form to register its religious objections to the contraceptive mandate.

In her dissent in *Wheaton College*, Justice Sotomayor distinguished the Court's order in *Little Sisters of the Poor* from the case at hand. In her view, there, the court order in *Little Sisters of the Poor* was " 'based on all the circumstances of the case'—in particular, the fact that the applicants' third-party administrator was a 'church plan' that had no legal obligation or intention to provide contraceptive coverage." *Id.* at 2814, n.6. As such, the order "did not affect any individual's access to contraceptive coverage." *Id.* By contrast, because "Wheaton's third-party administrator bears the legal obligation to provide contraceptive coverage only upon receipt of a valid self-certification," the Court's injunction "risks depriving hundreds of Wheaton's employees and students of their legal entitlement to contraceptive coverage." *Id.* As importantly, "because Wheaton is materially indistinguishable from other nonprofits that object to the Government's accommodation, the issuance of an injunction in this case will presumably entitle hundreds or thousands of other objectors to the same remedy." *Id.*

5.   *Anticipating* Hobby Lobby. The California Legislature enacted the Women's Contraceptive Equity Act (WCEA) in 1999 in order to improve access to prescription contraceptives. In a preview of issues raised by *Hobby Lobby*, the Catholic Charities of Sacramento, Inc. sued the California Department of Managed Health Care to be relieved of its obligations under WCEA. Critically, WCEA exempted "religious employers," which it defined as "those that have as their purpose the inculcation of religious values and primarily employ and serve persons who share their religious tenets." Catholic Charities did not meet the criteria for exemption as "the vast majority of its employees and beneficiaries are not Catholic," it accepted substantial public funding, was independently incorporated, and entered into contracts with public agencies. Nevertheless, Catholic Charities argued it should be exempted under the Free Exercise and Establishment Clauses of both the federal and California constitutions. The California Supreme Court disagreed, holding that WCEA was a "neutral and generally applicable" statute that did not impose a substantial burden on the exercise of religion. Moreover, the court concluded that, even if WCEA imposed a burden on religious exercise, the burden was justified on the ground that the statute served the compelling state interest in eliminating gender discrimination in prescription drug coverage. *See Catholic Charities of Sacramento, Inc. v. Superior Court of Sacramento Cnty.*, 85 P.3d 67, 82–83 (Cal. 2004).

6.   *Low-wage workers.* The issues in *Hobby Lobby* are anything but theoretical for low-wage workers. As the National Women's Law Center's research shows, women make up three-quarters of the lowest wage workers. *See* Joan Entmacher, et al., Nat'l Women's Law Ctr., Women are 76 Percent of Workers in the 10 Largest Low-Wage Jobs and Suffer a 10 Percent Wage Gap (2014), https://nwlc.org/wp-content/uploads/2015/08/women_are_76_percent_of_workers_in_the_10_largest_low-wage_jobs_and_suffer_a_10_percent_wage_gap_april_2014.pdf. In graphic terms, the following infographic demonstrates the real costs in terms of wages for common contraceptives.

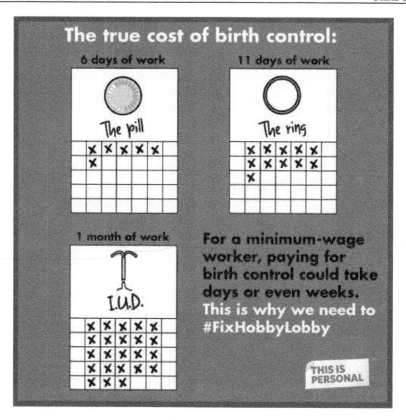

7.   *Federal funding in an earlier age.* In contrast to current debates, when President Richard M. Nixon expanded Medicaid in 1972, he required that contraception be a "mandatory service" for which all health care providers must offer or provide referrals. Astonishingly, this mandate prompted no objection from the Catholic Church. Moreover, the Nixon Administration reimbursed these services at ninety percent in contrast to the fifty- to eighty-percent reimbursement rate then in effect for other services. There is little evidence that this funding policy was controversial. *See* THOMAS B. LITTLEWOOD, THE POLITICS OF POPULATION CONTROL 53–57 (1977). Indeed, by 1969, Catholic bishops had even tacitly agreed to support federal family planning. DONALD T. CRITCHLOW, INTENDED CONSEQUENCES: BIRTH CONTROL, ABORTION, AND THE FEDERAL GOVERNMENT IN MODERN AMERICA 83 (2001). With this history in mind, why is federally-mandated contraceptive coverage such a fraught issue among religious institutions and religiously-affiliated institutions today?

8.   *New administration, new rules.* In May 2017, the Trump Administration issued an executive order rolling back the Affordable Care Act's contraceptive mandate. The executive order, titled "Promoting Free Speech and Religious Liberty," directed the Secretaries of the Treasury, Labor, Health and Human Services to "[issue] amended regulations . . . to address conscience-based objections to the preventive-care mandate promulgated under [the ACA]." In response, the Department of Health and Human Services issued two interim final rules that offered an exemption to any

nonprofit, educational, and for-profit employer with religious or moral objections to contraception. Moreover, the new rules made compliance with the much-debated accommodation process optional. The rules took effect immediately, without prior notice or opportunity for comment. Several states, including Pennsylvania, sued to block enforcement. Federal courts in California and Pennsylvania issued nationwide injunctions on the grounds that the rules likely violated the Administrative Procedure Act.

In November 2018, while this litigation was pending, the Administration issued two final rules that were "virtually identical" to the interim final rules that had been enjoined by the courts. Like their 2017 predecessors, the 2018 final rules expanded the scope of entities permitted to invoke the exemptions, offered the same exemptions to entities with moral objections, and made the accommodation process optional. Again, numerous states challenged the rules and federal courts in California and Pennsylvania blocked their enforcement. In upholding the Pennsylvania court's injunction, the Third Circuit emphasized that neither RFRA nor *Hobby Lobby* required the agencies to permit objectors to ignore the accommodation process. The court also concluded that the rules "would impose an undue burden" on female employees, noting that thousands of women were at risk of losing contraceptive coverage if the rules were to be enforced. The Trump Administration and Little Sisters of the Poor, an order of nuns that intervened in the litigation, petitioned for certiorari and the Supreme Court granted review.

9.   Hobby Lobby *redux?* On July 8, 2020, the Supreme Court upheld the challenged Trump Administration rules in a fractured 7–2 decision. Reversing and remanding the Third Circuit's judgment, the Court held that the agencies had statutory authority under the ACA to provide and create exemptions for employers with religious and moral objections. Justice Clarence Thomas, writing for the Court and joined by Chief Justice John Roberts and Justices Alito, Gorsuch, and Kavanaugh, noted that the ACA gave the Health Resources and Services Administration (HRSA) "virtually unbridled discretion to decide what counts as preventative care and screenings." *Little Sisters of the Poor Saints Peter & Paul Home v. Pennsylvania*, 140 S. Ct. 2367, 2380 (2020). Justice Thomas explained that this "same capacious grant of authority that empowers HRSA to make these determinations leaves its discretion equally unchecked in other areas, including the ability to identify and create exemptions." *Id*. Although the Court did not technically reach the RFRA claim, Justice Thomas clarified that it was appropriate for the agencies to consider RFRA and even required by the Court's decisions in *Hobby Lobby* and *Zubik*. *Id*. at 2383. The Court also rejected the states' procedural claims regarding the agencies' failure to provide appropriate notice and keep an open mind throughout the promulgation process. *Id*. at 2385.

Justices Elena Kagan and Samuel Alito wrote concurring opinions. Deferring to the agencies' interpretation, Justice Kagan, joined by Justice Stephen Breyer, joined the Court's judgment, but cautioned that additional issues, including the possibility of the rules being overbroad, warranted further consideration from the lower courts. *Id*. at 2397–98. In contrast,

Justice Alito would have gone further than the majority to hold that RFRA required the exemptions. *Id.* at 2387.

In a scathing dissent, Justice Ruth Bader Ginsburg, joined by Justice Sonia Sotomayor, criticized the majority for "[casting] totally aside countervailing rights and interests in its zeal to secure religious rights to the nth degree." *Id.* at 2400. Emphasizing that access to contraception "safeguards women's health and enables women to chart their life course," Justice Ginsburg bemoaned the decision's impact on women, noting between a minimum of between 70,500 and 126,400 women would lose access to contraceptive coverage through their employer-provided insurance plans. *Id.* at 2408. Ginsburg passed away on September 18, 2020. This was her last separate writing as a Justice.

C. REGULATION OF ABORTION

Much controversy surrounds the history of abortion with present-day commentators who oppose it arguing that prohibition of abortion was "an almost absolute value in history," while those who support it point to the long history of both techniques and recipes to produce it. Both sides quote Hippocrates, with some pointing to the prohibition of abortifacient pessaries in the Hippocratic Oath (which Hippocrates may or may not have written), and others pointing to his suggestion that vigorous leaping was an effective means of producing an abortion. As historian Janet Farrell Brodie recounts, in the Colonial and early Republic period, women could obtain information about bringing on "delayed menses" from herbalists, midwives, "Indian doctors," and each other. Even Thomas Jefferson observed the practice of abortion. In his Notes on the State of Virginia, *Jefferson documented that indigenous women had "learnt the practice of procuring abortion by the use of some vegetable." Indeed, herbs used by indigenous women were highly valued as abortifacients among colonists and during the first half of the nineteenth century. What probably is true, however, is that herbal abortions (likely the primary way of obtaining abortion until recently) were not very effective and using an instrument to enter the uterus in the days before antibiotics was quite dangerous. This background, discussed further below, led to a movement by physicians and others to criminalize abortions.*

1. THE PROFESSIONALIZATION OF MEDICINE AND THE CRIMINALIZATION OF ABORTION

Starting in the second half of the nineteenth century, "regular" physicians (those trained in the emerging medical science) began to press state legislatures to pass laws against abortion. In so doing, they made two claims: first, that they knew that a pregnancy represented a full human being from conception onwards, and second, that physicians were professionals vested with "moral authority" in this realm. However, physicians' claims to be protectors of fetal life were called into question by the fact that almost all state laws passed at the urging of physicians contained a clause indicating that otherwise illegal abortions could be legal if undertaken by a physician. The following selection is an excerpt from the American Medical Association's 1859 Report on Abortion, detailing the newly formed organization's attack on abortion.

Horatio R. Storer et al., *Report on Criminal Abortion*

12 TRANSACTIONS AM. MED. ASS'N 75 (1859).

The heinous guilt of criminal abortion, however viewed by the community, is everywhere acknowledged by medical men. Its frequency—among all classes of society, rich and poor, single and married—most physicians have been led to suspect.... Were [there] any doubt ... it is at once removed by comparisons of the present with our past rates of increase in population, the size of our families, the statistics of our foetal deaths.... The evidence from these sources is too constant and too overwhelming to be explained on the ground that pregnancies are merely prevented; or on any other supposition than that of fearfully extended crime.

The causes of [abortion] are manifold. There are three of them, however ... with which the medical profession have especially to do.

The first of these causes is a wide-spread popular ... belief, even among mothers themselves, that the foetus is not alive till after the period of quickening.

The second ... is the fact that the profession themselves are frequently supposed careless of foetal life; not that its respectable members are ever knowingly ... accessory to the unjustifiable commission of abortion, but that they are thought at times to omit precautions ... that might prevent the occurrence of so unfortunate an event.

The third reason ... is found in the grave defects of our laws, both common and statute, as regards the independent and actual existence of the child before birth, as a living being. These errors, which are sufficient in most instances to prevent conviction, are based ... upon mistaken and exploded medical dogmas. With strange inconsistency, the law fully acknowledges the foetus in utero ... for civil purposes; while ... as criminally affected, it fails to recognize it, and to its life as yet denies all protection.

* * *

As Reva Siegel notes, supra p. *569, the medical profession's crusade in the nineteenth century essentialized pregnancy as an inherent product of female nature. In doing so, it obfuscated the social and political aspects of pregnancy. Consider how this effect can be traced throughout the development of abortion jurisprudence, as well as the jurisprudence concerning sterilization and contraception, from the days of* Commonwealth v. Bangs, *excerpted below, through today.*

Commonwealth v. Bangs
9 Mass. 387 (1812).

The defendant was indicted, October term, 1810, for assaulting and beating one Lucy Holman, and administering to her a certain dangerous and deleterious draught or potion, against her will, with intent to procure the abortion and premature birth of a bastard child, of which she was then pregnant, and which the defendant had before that time begotten of her body . . . to the great damage of said Lucy, against good morals and mood manners, in evil example to others in like case to offend. . . .

. . . A verdict was found . . . that the defendant was guilty of all the several matters charged in the indictment, excepting that the said potion was taken by the said Lucy voluntarily.

After the verdict was returned, the defendant moved the Court to arrest the judgment, on the ground that no indictable offence was described in the indictment except the [assault and battery charges].

. . . Fay [defendant's counsel], in support of the motion, contended that . . . there remained nothing against the defendant but the administering, with the patient's consent, some potion, with intent that the same should produce an abortion. No abortion was produced; and if there had been, there is no averment that the woman was quick with child; both which circumstances are necessary ingredients in the offence intended to be charged in the indictment.

The Solicitor-General argued that any overt act, perpetrated with the intent to procure a misdemeanor to be committed, was itself a misdemeanor, and the patient's consent to take the deleterious draught did not make the administering of it lawful.

By the Court.

There can be no sentence upon this verdict. . . . [N]o abortion is alleged to have followed the taking of the potion; and if an abortion had been alleged and proved to have ensured, the averment that the woman was quick with child at the time is a necessary part of the indictment.

Judgment arrested.

NOTES

1.   *Quickening in context.* Note that the trimester framework proposed in *Roe v. Wade, infra* p. 709, echoes the ancient belief that a very early pregnancy represents something categorically different from a newborn baby. In the absence of reliable pregnancy tests (which did not exist until the 1930s) the subjective difference between a late period and a pregnancy was not obvious until the woman felt fetal movement. Critically, under this logic, the only reliable informant as to whether or not the pregnancy had

"quickened" was the woman herself, which surely precluded prosecution in many cases. KRISTIN LUKER, ABORTION AND THE POLITICS OF MOTHERHOOD 14–15 (1984).

2. *Abortion in the early republic. Bangs* reflects the common law view that, until "quickening," terminating an early pregnancy was neither morally nor legally troubling. Interestingly, the term "quick" is an archaic term for "alive." The Bible, for example speaks of the "quick and the dead," comparing the living to the dead. While quickening—the point at which fetal movement can be detected—may differ among women and among pregnancies, almost all of what we moderns would call first-trimester (and some second-trimester) abortions would have been legally unproblematic in the eighteenth and early nineteenth centuries. *See* JAMES MOHR, ABORTION IN AMERICA 4–5 (1978).

2. STATUTES CRIMINALIZING ABORTION

The statutes that follow reflect two distinct approaches for regulating abortion. The Texas statute reflects the earliest efforts to criminalize abortion in the United States. Although the Texas statute was codified in 1961, it is substantively unchanged from Texas's initial effort— undertaken in the mid-nineteenth century—to regulate abortion. By contrast, the 1968 Georgia statute reflects efforts to reform abortion law. Based on the Model Penal Code, the Georgia statute provides for an exception to the criminal ban on abortion in certain circumstances.

2A Texas Penal Code, Arts. 1191, 1196
(1961).

Article 1191. ABORTION

If any person shall designedly administer to a pregnant woman or knowingly procure to be administered with her consent any drug or medicine, or shall use toward her any violence or means whatsoever externally or internally applied, and thereby procure an abortion, he shall be confined in the penitentiary for not less than two nor more than five years; if it be done without her consent, the punishment shall be doubled. By "abortion" is meant that the life of the fetus or embryo shall be destroyed in the woman's womb or that a premature birth shall be caused.

Art. 1196. BY MEDICAL ADVICE

Nothing in this chapter applies to an abortion procured or attempted by medical advice for the purpose of saving the life of the mother.

Georgia Criminal Code, §§ 26–1201–1203
(1968).

26–1201. Criminal Abortion. Except as otherwise provided in section 26–1202, a person commits criminal abortion when he administers any medicine, drug or other substance whatever to any woman or when he uses any instrument or other means whatever upon any woman with intent to produce a miscarriage or abortion.

26–1202. Exception.

(a) Section 26–1201 shall not apply to an abortion performed by a physician duly licensed to practice medicine and surgery pursuant to Chapter 84–9 or 84–12 of the Code of Georgia of 1933, as amended, based upon his best clinical judgment that an abortion is necessary because:

(1) A continuation of the pregnancy would endanger the life of the pregnant woman or would seriously and permanently injure her health; or

(2) The fetus would very likely be born with a grave, permanent, and irremediable mental or physical defect; or

(3) The pregnancy resulted from forcible or statutory rape.

(b) No abortion is authorized or shall be performed under this section unless each of the following conditions is met:

(1) The pregnant woman requesting the abortion certifies in writing under oath and subject to the penalties . . . of false swearing to the physician who proposes to perform the abortion that she is a bona fide legal resident of the State of Georgia.

(2) The physician certifies that he believes the woman is a bona fide resident of this State and that he has no information which should lead him to believe otherwise.

(3) Such physician's judgment is reduced to writing and concurred in by at least two other physicians duly licensed to practice medicine and surgery pursuant to Chapter 84–9 of the Code of Georgia of 1933, as amended, who certify in writing that, based upon their separate personal medical examinations of the pregnant woman, the abortion is, in their judgment, necessary because of one or more of the reasons enumerated above.

(4) Such abortion is performed in a hospital licensed by the State Board of Health and accredited by the Joint Commission on Accreditation of Hospitals.

(5) The performance of the abortion has been approved in advance by a committee of the medical staff of the hospital in which the operation is to be performed. This committee must be one established and maintained in accordance with the standards promulgated by the Joint Commission on the Accreditation of Hospitals, and its approval must be by a majority vote of a membership of not less than three members of the hospital's staff; the physician proposing to perform the operation may not be counted as a member of the committee for this purpose.

(6) If the proposed abortion is considered necessary because the woman has been raped, the woman makes a written statement under oath, and subject to the penalties of false swearing, of the date, time and place of the rape and the name of the rapist, if known. There must be attached to this statement a certified copy of any report of the rape made by any law enforcement officer or agency and a statement by the solicitor general of the judicial circuit where the rape occurred or allegedly occurred that, according to his best information, there is probable cause to believe that the rape did occur.

(7) Such written opinions, statements, certificates, and concurrences are maintained in the permanent files of such hospital and are available at all reasonable times to the solicitor general of the judicial circuit in which the hospital is located.

(8) A copy of such written opinions, statements, certificates, and concurrences is filed with the Director of the State Department of Public Health within 10 days after such operation is performed.

(9) All written opinions, statements, certificates, and concurrences filed and maintained pursuant to paragraphs (7) and (8) of this subsection shall be confidential record and shall not be made available for public inspection at any time.

(c) Any solicitor General of the judicial circuit in which an abortion is to be performed under this section, or any person who would be a relative of the child within the second degree of consanguinity, may petition the superior court of the county in which the abortion is to be performed for a declaratory judgment whether the performance of such abortion would violate any constitutional or other legal rights of the fetus. Such solicitor General may also petition such court for the purpose of taking issue with compliance with the requirements of this section. The physician who proposes to perform the abortion and the pregnant woman shall be respondents. The petition shall be heard expeditiously, and if the court adjudges that such abortion would violate the constitutional or other legal rights of the fetus, the court shall so declare and shall restrain the physician from performing the abortion.

(d) If an abortion is performed in compliance with this section, the death of the fetus shall not give rise to any claim for wrongful death.

(e) Nothing in this section shall require a hospital to admit any patient under the provisions hereof for the purpose of performing an abortion, nor shall any hospital be required to appoint a committee such as contemplated under subsection (b)(5). A physician, or any other person who is a member of or associated with the staff of a hospital, or any employee of a hospital in which an abortion has been authorized, who shall state in writing an objection to such abortion on moral or religious grounds shall not be required to participate in the medical procedures which will result in the abortion, and the refusal of any such person to participate therein shall not form the basis of any claim for damages on account of such refusal or for any disciplinary or recriminatory action against such person.

26–1203. Punishment. A person convicted of criminal abortion shall be punished by imprisonment for not less than one nor more than 10 years.

NOTES

1. *Earliest abortion statutes.* Following physician mobilization for stricter abortion laws, at least forty laws criminalizing abortion were passed in states and territories between 1860 and 1880. Virtually all such laws contained an explicit exemption for abortions performed by doctors; by 1900, only six states lacked protections for physicians who undertook "therapeutic" abortions. *See* JAMES MOHR, ABORTION IN AMERICA 200–02 (1978); KRISTIN LUKER, ABORTION AND THE POLITICS OF MOTHERHOOD 32–33 (1984).

2. *"Race suicide" and abortion.* New historical research using the pronouncements of nineteenth-century anti-abortion physicians themselves has shown that physician activism on abortion was a product both of concerns over "race suicide" (native born white women were having fewer children than were immigrants and women of color) and worries about changing gender roles. For an overview, see Reva Siegel, *Reasoning from the Body: A Historical Perspective on Abortion Regulation and Questions of Equal Protection*, 44 STAN. L. REV. 261 (1992).

3. *Domestic abortion before World War II.* Until World War II, most Americans received medical care—including most obstetric and gynecological care—in the home. Frederick Taussig, writing in the early twentieth century (a time when most states had criminal abortion statutes on the books), provided detailed instructions on how to perform an abortion on a kitchen table. Although the context makes clear that Taussig envisioned interventions in the wake of a miscarriage, the rest of the volume suggests that Taussig thought medical abortion was a standard and necessary part of medical practice. *See* FREDERICK J. TAUSSIG, THE PREVENTION AND TREATMENT OF ABORTION 34, 98 (1910).

4. *Abortion regulation, old and new.* The two abortion statutes above reflect two very different eras in abortion regulation. The Texas statute is consistent with nineteenth-century abortion regulations, which criminalized abortion except when it was necessary to preserve the woman's life. Although the Texas legislature reissued the statute in 1961, its substance remained fundamentally unchanged. By contrast, the Georgia statute, which was enacted in 1968, reflected the modern impulse toward abortion liberalization. Modeled after the Model Penal Code's provisions on abortion, *infra* p. 695, the Georgia law permitted abortion when it was deemed necessary by a physician to preserve the woman's health, or where the fetus would be born with physical or mental defects, or where the pregnancy was the result of forcible or statutory rape. Georgia built upon the Model Penal Code's reforms by imposing a number of additional restrictions on the performance of abortion.

5. *Abortion at the high court.* As you may have surmised, the constitutionality of the Texas and Georgia statutes provided here were ultimately challenged in federal court. In 1973, the Supreme Court took up the question of whether these statutes violated the Constitution in *Roe v. Wade* (Texas), *infra* p. 709 and *Doe v. Bolton* (Georgia).

* * *

As noted in Chapter 1, the Model Penal Code was an attempt to modernize and rationalize American criminal law. Of particular relevance to this chapter, the Model Penal Code proposed guidelines for "therapeutic" abortions. These provisions were intended to rationalize the hodgepodge criminal-abortion statutes that existed across the various states. More particularly, the MPC's abortion statute responded to concerns that criminal regulation of abortion should be liberalized to allow abortion in certain contexts.

American Law Institute, Model Penal Code § 230.3

(1962).

§ 230.3. Abortion

(1) Unjustified Abortion. A person who purposely and unjustifiably terminates the pregnancy of another otherwise than by a live birth commits a felony of the third degree or, where the pregnancy has continued beyond the twenty-sixth week, a felony of the second degree.

(2) Justifiable Abortion. A licensed physician is justified in terminating a pregnancy if he believes there is substantial risk that continuance of the pregnancy would gravely impair the physical or mental health of the mother or that the child would be born with grave physical or mental defect, or that the pregnancy resulted from rape, incest, or other felonious intercourse. All illicit intercourse with a girl below the age of 16 shall be deemed felonious for purposes of this subsection. Justifiable abortions shall be performed only in a licensed hospital except in case of emergency when hospital facilities are unavailable. [Additional exceptions from the requirement of hospitalization may be incorporated here to take account of situations in sparsely settled areas where hospitals are not generally accessible.]

(3) Physicians' Certificates; Presumption from Non-Compliance. No abortion shall be performed unless two physicians, one of whom may be the person performing the abortion, shall have certified in writing the circumstances which they believe to justify the abortion. Such certificate shall be submitted before the abortion to the hospital where it is to be performed and, in the case of abortion following felonious intercourse, to the prosecuting attorney or the police. Failure to comply with any of the requirements of this Subsection gives rise to a presumption that the abortion was unjustified.

(4) Self-Abortion. A woman whose pregnancy has continued beyond the twenty-sixth week commits a felony of the third degree if she purposely terminates her own pregnancy otherwise than by a live birth, or if she uses instruments, drugs or violence upon herself for that purpose. Except as justified under Subsection (2), a person who induces or knowingly aids a woman to use instruments, drugs or violence upon herself for the purpose of terminating her pregnancy otherwise than by a live birth commits a felony of the third degree whether or not the pregnancy has continued beyond the twenty-sixth week.

(5) Pretended Abortion. A person commits a felony of the third degree if, representing that it is his purpose to perform an abortion, he does an act adapted to cause abortion in a pregnant woman although the woman is in fact not pregnant, or the actor does not believe she is. A person charged with unjustified abortion under Subsection (1) or an attempt to commit that offense may be convicted thereof upon proof of conduct prohibited by this Subsection.

(6) Distribution of Abortifacients. A person who sells, offers to sell, possesses with intent to sell, advertises, or displays for sale anything specially designed to terminate a pregnancy, or held out by the actor as useful for that purpose, commits a misdemeanor, unless:

(a) the sale, offer or display is to a physician or druggist or to an intermediary in a chain of distribution to physicians or druggists; or

(b) the sale is made upon prescription or order of a physician; or

(c) the possession is with intent to sell as authorized in paragraphs (a) and (b); or

(d) the advertising is addressed to persons named in paragraph (a) and confined to trade or professional channels not likely to reach the general public.

(7) Section Inapplicable to Prevention of Pregnancy. Nothing in this Section shall be deemed applicable to the prescription, administration or distribution of drugs or other substances for avoiding pregnancy, whether by preventing implantation of a fertilized ovum or by any other method that operates before, at or immediately after fertilization.

NOTES

1. *The MPC and abortion liberalization before* Roe v. Wade. In a footnote to *Roe v. Wade,* the Supreme Court listed the fourteen states that adopted some form of the Model Penal Code's provisions on abortion: Arkansas, California, Colorado, Delaware, Florida, Georgia, Kansas, Maryland, New Mexico, Mississippi, North Carolina, Oregon, South Carolina, and Virginia. In addition, by 1973, four other states—Alaska, Hawaii, New York, and Washington—had essentially repealed their abortion laws. Reflecting the rapid changes in this area, the *Roe* Court noted, "[t]he precise status of criminal abortion laws in some States is made unclear by recent decisions in

state and federal courts striking down existing state laws, in whole or in part." *Roe v. Wade*, 410 U.S. 113, 140 n.37 (1973).

2.   *The paradox of the South*. As noted above, fourteen states adopted some version of the American Law Institute ("ALI")'s model abortion law prior to *Roe*. Intriguingly, five of the adopting states were in the South, now a center of contemporary anti-abortion activity. Professor Gene Burns' review of historical evidence suggests that the South's receptivity to the more liberal ALI model was due to the medical profession's strength (and the small Catholic population) in those states. GENE BURNS, THE MORAL VETO: FRAMING CONTRACEPTION, ABORTION, AND CULTURAL PLURALISM IN THE UNITED STATES 185–96 (2005).

3.   *Access to abortion after criminalization and before* Roe. As historian Leslie Reagan reminds us, the criminal enforcement of abortion laws had a disproportionate impact on the lives of working-class women and women of color. In the early twentieth century, affluent women seeking abortions were more likely to go to physicians, while less well-to-do women and immigrants went to midwives. After 1940, when the practice of "therapeutic" abortions in hospitals—and the concomitant effort to enforce laws against "illegal abortions"—began, well-to-do women were better equipped than their poorer, darker sisters to navigate the terrain of "official" abortions. *See* LESLIE J. REAGAN, WHEN ABORTION WAS A CRIME: WOMEN, MEDICINE, AND LAW IN THE UNITED STATES, 1867–1973, at 137 (1997).

4.   *Reform and repeal*. Physicians welcomed the ALI effort to liberalize abortion laws because such reforms helped to clarify the legal status of the abortions that physicians were already performing (e.g., many physicians performed abortions in cases where a woman had been exposed to rubella). Because of the medical profession's support, these legislative reform efforts were usually uncontroversial. However, as the women's movement gathered momentum, the limits of the ALI reforms became obvious. In particular, women activists observed that, regardless of the reforms, women still had to seek physician "approval" for an abortion—a requirement that many saw as unduly burdensome and patriarchal. Frustrated with the limits of the reform effort, women activists began to press for the *repeal* of abortion laws. *See* LINDA GREENHOUSE & REVA SIEGEL, BEFORE *ROE V. WADE*: VOICES THAT SHAPED THE ABORTION DEBATE BEFORE THE SUPREME COURT'S RULING 35 (2010).

3.   CHALLENGES TO THE CRIMINALIZATION OF ABORTION

In the years leading up to Roe v. Wade, *many states liberalized their abortion statutes in the direction suggested by the Model Penal Code. On the eve of* Roe, *fourteen states had laws modeled on the Model Penal Code and four others had repealed criminal penalties for abortion. A challenge to one such abortion law is excerpted below. As you read this case, consider the values and issues raised by the court, as well as whether or not the statute challenged is a traditional abortion ban, or a more modern abortion statute that tracks the reformed Model Penal Code. Critically, note the shift from the argument that abortion reform is needed in order to give physicians clear indications as to which abortions are legal and to safeguard maternal health, to an emerging discourse about privacy and equal protection.*

People v. Belous

458 P.2d 194 (Cal. 1969).

■ PETERS, J.

Dr. Leon Phillip Belous was convicted in January 1967, after a jury trial, of abortion, in violation of section 274 of the Penal Code, and conspiracy to commit an abortion, in violation of section 182 of the Penal Code, both felonies. The court suspended proceedings, imposed a fine of $5,000, and placed Dr. Belous on probation for two years. He appeals.

Dr. Belous is a physician and surgeon, licensed since 1931 to practice medicine in the State of California, and specializing in obstetrics and gynecology. . . . He is considered by his associates to be an eminent physician in his field.

The prosecution's witnesses, a young woman and her husband, Cheryl and Clifton, testified to the following:

In 1966, Cheryl, then unmarried, believed she was pregnant. A family physician had given her pills which would induce menstruation if she were not pregnant, but the pills did not work. She and Clifton had sometime earlier seen Dr. Belous on television, advocating a change in the California abortion laws. They had never heard of Dr. Belous before. Clifton obtained the doctor's phone number from the television station and . . . asked for Dr. Belous' help. Dr. Belous told him there was nothing he could do, but Clifton 'continued pleading,' and threatened that Cheryl would go to Tijuana for an abortion. Finally, the doctor agreed to see them at his office.

Dr. Belous examined Cheryl at his Beverly Hills office and confirmed that she was possibly pregnant. . . . The visit lasted about 45 minutes and was very emotional. Both Clifton and Cheryl pleaded for help, cried, insisted they were going to have an abortion "one way or another." The doctor lectured them on the dangers of criminal abortions, and Tijuana abortions in particular, and suggested that they get married. He insisted he did not perform abortions. . . . Finally, in response to their pleadings, Dr. Belous gave them a piece of paper with a Chula Vista phone number. He told them an abortion would cost about $500. He gave Cheryl a prescription for some antibiotics and instructed her to return for an examination.

Dr. Belous testified that he was very familiar with the abortion business in Tijuana. He had visited the clinics there to learn about conditions and knew that women who went to Tijuana were taking their lives in their hands. He met Karl Lairtus while in Tijuana and knew from personal observation that Lairtus, licensed to practice in Mexico but not in California, was performing skilled and safe abortions in Mexico. . . . It was Lairtus' number that Belous gave to Cheryl and Clifton. . . .

Cheryl and Clifton made arrangements with Lairtus, and went to the address which Lairtus gave them on the phone. After the abortion was performed, while Cheryl was resting, the police, having been advised by another woman that Lairtus was performing abortions at that address, came to his apartment, followed another couple into the apartment and arrested Lairtus. They found two notebooks, containing women's names, ages, dates of last menstruation, and physician's names, including Dr. Belous' name, which the police interpreted as the referring doctor with whom Lairtus was to split his fees. On the basis of this information, Dr. Belous was arrested at his office. Lairtus pleaded guilty. . . .

The substance of Dr. Belous' defense was that he gave Lairtus' phone number to Cheryl and Clifton only because he believed that they would, in fact, do anything to terminate the pregnancy, which might involve butchery in Tijuana or self-mutilation; that in face of their pleading and tears, he gave out the phone number of someone whom he knew to be a competent doctor, although unlicensed in this state. The doctor believed that if the young couple carried out their threats, Cheryl's very life was in danger.

Section 274 of the Penal Code, when the conduct herein involved occurred, read: "Every person who provides, supplies, or administers to any woman, or procures any woman to take any medicine, drug, or substance, or uses or employs any instrument or other means whatever, with intent thereby to procure the miscarriage of such woman, unless the same is necessary to preserve her life, is punishable by imprisonment in the State prison not less than two nor more than five years."

The statute was substantially unchanged since it was originally enacted in 1850. In 1967, the statute was amended and sections 25950 through 25954 ("Therapeutic Abortion Act") added to the Health and Safety Code. The act extends the lawful grounds for obtaining an abortion.[2] . . . .

We have concluded that the term "necessary to preserve" in section 274 of the Penal Code is not susceptible of a construction that does not violate legislative intent and that is sufficiently certain to satisfy due

---

[2] Penal Code, section 274 as amended reads: "Every person who provides, supplies, or administers to any woman, or procures any woman to take any medicine, drug, or substance, or uses or employs any instrument or other means whatever, with intent thereby to procure the miscarriage of such woman, *except as provided in the Therapeutic Abortion Act . . . of the Health and Safety Code*, is punishable by imprisonment in the state prison. . . ."

The Therapeutic Abortion Act (Health & Saf. Code, §§ 25950–25954) authorizes abortions 'only' if the abortion takes place in an accredited hospital; the abortion is approved by a hospital staff committee consisting of at least three licensed physicians and surgeons . . . ; and there is "substantial risk that continuance of the pregnancy would gravely impair the physical or mental health of the mother" . . . ; the pregnancy resulted from rape or incest . . . ; or the woman is under 15 years of age . . .

process requirements without improperly infringing on fundamental constitutional rights.

"The requirement of a reasonable degree of certainty in legislation, especially in the criminal law, is a well established element of the guarantee of due process of law.["] "No one may be required at peril of life, liberty or property to speculate as to the meaning of penal statutes. All are entitled to be informed as to what the State commands or forbids. . . . '[A] statute which either forbids or requires the doing of an act in terms so vague that men of common intelligence must necessarily guess at its meaning and differ as to its application, violates the first essential of due process of law.[' "]

. . . The requirement of certainty in legislation is greater where the criminal statute is a limitation on constitutional rights. On the other hand, mathematical certainty is not required; "some matter of degree" is involved in most penal statutes.

Dictionary definitions and judicial interpretations fail to provide a clear meaning for the words, "necessary" or "preserve". There is, of course, no standard definition of "necessary to preserve," and taking the words separately, no clear meaning emerges. "Necessary" is defined as: "1. Essential to a desirable or projected end or condition; not to be dispensed with without loss, damage, inefficiency, or the like; . . ." (Webster's New International Dictionary (2d ed.), unabridged.) The courts have recognized that "[']necessary' has not a fixed meaning, but is flexible and relative."

The definition of "preserve" is even less enlightening. It is defined as: "1. To keep or save from injury or destruction; to guard or defend from evil; to protect; save. 2. To keep in existence or intact; . . . To save from decomposition, . . . 3. To maintain; to keep up; . . ." (Webster's New International Dictionary, *supra*.) The meanings for "preserve" range from the concept of maintaining the status quo—that is, the woman's condition of life at the time of pregnancy—to maintaining the biological or medical definition of "life"—that is, as opposed to the biological or medical definition of "death".

Since abortion before quickening was not a crime at common law we cannot rely on common law meanings or common law referents.

Various possible meanings of "necessary to preserve . . . life" have been suggested. However, none of the proposed definitions will sustain the statute.

Respondent asserts: "If medical science feels the abortion should be performed as it is necessary to preserve her life, then it may be performed; that is, unless it is performed the patient will die."

Our courts, however, have rejected an interpretation of "necessary to preserve" which requires certainty or immediacy of death. . . .

In *People v. Ballard,* the evidence established that the woman was "extremely nervous . . . upset, had headaches, was unable to sleep, and thought that she was pregnant. She was agitated, disturbed and had many problems." In *People v. Ballard,* it was established that at the time each of the women went to the defendant doctor she was in a "bad state of health" because of self-imposed abortive practices. And in *People v. Abarbanel,* the obstetrician performed the abortion after receiving letters from two psychiatrists to the effect that abortion was indicated as necessary to save the woman's life from the "possibility" of suicide. In each of the cases the conviction was reversed.

If the fact of ill health or the mere "possibility" of suicide is sufficient to meet the test of "necessary to preserve her life," it is clear that a showing of immediacy or certainty of death is not essential for a lawful abortion. . . .

After the decision in *Ballard,* the Legislature did not amend the statute to repudiate the rule suggested by that case and to establish a definition requiring certainty of death.

It would be anomalous to uphold a criminal statute against a charge of vagueness by adopting a construction of the statute rejected by the courts of this state as not reflecting legislative intent unless there was a clear showing of a strong public policy or legislative intent requiring adoption of the rejected construction. No such showing has been made with regard to the construction urged by respondent.

Moreover, a definition requiring certainty of death would work an invalid abridgment of the woman's constitutional rights. . . .

The fundamental right of the woman to choose whether to bear children follows from the Supreme Court's and this court's repeated acknowledgment of a "right of privacy" or "liberty" in matters related to marriage, family, and sex. That such a right is not enumerated in either the United States or California Constitutions is no impediment to the existence of the right. . . .

The critical issue is not whether such rights exist, but whether the state has a compelling interest in the regulation of a subject which is within the police powers of the state whether the regulation is "necessary . . . to the accomplishment of a permissible state policy", and whether legislation impinging on constitutionally protected areas is narrowly drawn and not of "unlimited and indiscriminate sweep."

It is possible that the definition suggested by respondent, requiring that death be certain, was that intended by the Legislature when the first abortion law was adopted in 1850 and that, in the light of the then existing medical and surgical science, the great and direct interference with a woman's constitutional rights was warranted by considerations of the woman's health. When California's first anti-abortion statute was enacted, any surgical procedure which entered a body cavity was extremely dangerous. . . .

... In due course safe procedures were developed for specific operations. Curettage, used for abortion in the first trimester, became a safe, accepted and routinely employed medical technique, especially after antibiotics were developed in the early 1940's. It is now safer for a woman to have a hospital therapeutic abortion during the first trimester than to bear a child.

Although abortions early in pregnancy, and properly performed present minimal danger to the woman, criminal abortions are "the most common single cause of maternal deaths in California." In California, it is estimated that 35,000 to 100,000 such abortions occur each year. (Fox, *supra*, at p. 645.)

The incidence of severe infection from criminal abortion is very much greater than the incidence of death. The Los Angeles County Hospital alone, for example, in 1961 admitted over 3,500 patients treated for such abortions. Possibly more significant than the mere incidence of infection caused by criminal abortions is the result of such infection. "Induced Illegal Abortion ... is one of the important causes of subsequent infertility and pelvic disease." (Kleegman & Kaufman, Infertility in Women (1966) p. 301.)[9]

Amici for appellant, 178 deans of medical schools, including the deans of all California medical schools, chairmen of medical school departments, and professors of medical schools state: "These recorded facts bring one face-to-face with the hard, shocking—almost brutal—reality that our statute designed in 1850 to protect women from serious risks to life and health has in modern times become a scourge."

Although we may assume that the law was valid when first enacted, the validity of the law in 1850 does not resolve the issue of whether the law is constitutionally valid today.

Constitutional concepts are not static.... ["]Likewise, the Equal Protection Clause is not shackled to the political theory of a particular era. In determining what lines are unconstitutionally discriminatory, we have never been confined to historic notions of equality, any more than we have restricted due process to a fixed catalogue of what was at a given time deemed to be the limits of fundamental rights.["] ...

In the light of modern medical surgical practice, the great and direct infringement of constitutional rights which would result from a definition requiring certainty of death may not be justified on the basis of considerations of the woman's health where, as here, abortion is sought during the first trimester.

---

[9] There is considerable literature describing the experience of various hospitals with infected abortion. Hospital experience, however, can be assumed to be only the tip of the iceberg. Many badly infected women will be treated at home or in a doctor's office.

It is next urged that the state has a compelling interest in the protection of the embryo and fetus[11] and that such interest warrants the limitation on the woman's constitutional rights. Reliance is placed upon several statutes and court rules which assertedly show that the embryo or fetus is equivalent to a born child. However, all of the statutes and rules relied upon require a live birth or reflect the interest of the parents.

... [T]here are major and decisive areas where the embryo and fetus are not treated as equivalent to the born child. Probably the most important is reflected by the statute before us. The intentional destruction of the born child is murder or manslaughter. The intentional destruction of the embryo or fetus is never treated as murder, and only rarely as manslaughter but rather as the lesser offense of abortion.

Furthermore, the law has always recognized that the pregnant woman's right to life takes precedence over any interest the state may have in the unborn. The California abortion statutes, as do the abortion laws of all 51 United States jurisdictions, make an exception in favor of the life of the prospective mother. Although there may be doubts as to whether the state's interest may ever justify requiring a woman to risk death, it is clear that the state could not forbid a woman to procure an abortion where, to a medical certainty, the result of childbirth would be death. We are also satisfied that the state may not require that degree of risk involved in respondent's definition, which would prohibit an abortion, where death from childbirth although not medically certain, would be substantially certain or more likely than not. Accordingly, the definition of the statute suggested by respondent must be rejected as an invalid infringement upon the woman's constitutional rights.

Another definition of the term "necessary to preserve" is suggested by *People v. Abarbanel*, where the court held that an abortion was not unlawful where the obstetrician performed the abortion based on the "possibility" of suicide. *Abarbanel* might be understood as meaning that "necessary to preserve" refers to a possibility of death different from or greater than the ordinary risk of childbirth. To so interpret "necessary to preserve" would mean that in nearly every case, if not all, a woman who wished an abortion could have one. A woman who is denied a desired lawful abortion and forced to continue an unwanted pregnancy would seem to face a greater risk of death, because of psychological factors, than the average woman, because the average includes all those women who wish to bear the child to term. The psychological factor alone, which under *Abarbanel* is a proper consideration, would seem to be decisive. Such a construction of the statute permitting voluntary abortions would render the statute virtually meaningless. Moreover to determine the right to an abortion solely on the basis of the dangers of childbirth

---

[11] It has been pointed out that "embryo" is more accurately descriptive than "fetus" in the instant case. Webster's New International Dictionary, *supra*, states: "... In mammals ... *embryo* is applied only to early stages passed within the mother's body; later (in human embryology, usually after the third month of development) the young is called a *fetus*...." (Italics in original.)

without regard to the relative dangers of the abortion would be contrary to good medical practice.

. . . .

There is one suggested test which is based on a policy underlying the statute and which would serve to make the statute certain. The test is probably in accord with the legislative intent at the time the statute was adopted. The Legislature may have intended in adopting the statute that abortion was permitted when the risk of death due to the abortion was less than the risk of death in childbirth and that otherwise abortion should be denied. As we have seen, at the time of the adoption of the statute abortion was a highly dangerous procedure, and under the relative safety test abortion would be permissible only where childbirth would be even more dangerous. In light of the test and the then existing medical practice, the question whether abortion should be limited to protect the embryo or fetus may have been immaterial because any such interest would be effectuated by limiting abortions to the rare cases where they were safer than childbirth.

. . . .

Although the suggested construction of former section 274, making abortion lawful where it is safer than childbirth and unlawful where abortion is more dangerous, may have been in accord with legislative intent, the statute may not be upheld against a claim of vagueness on the basis of such a construction. The language of the statute, "unless the same is necessary to preserve her life," does not suggest a relative safety test, and no case interpreting the statute has suggested that the statute be so construed. . . .

The problem caused by the vagueness of the statute is accentuated because under the statute the doctor is, in effect, delegated the duty to determine whether a pregnant woman has the right to an abortion and the physician acts at his peril if he determines that the woman is entitled to an abortion. He is subject to prosecution for a felony and to deprivation of his right to practice medicine if his decision is wrong. Rather than being impartial, the physician has a "direct, personal, substantial, pecuniary interest in reaching a conclusion" that the woman should not have an abortion. The delegation of decision-making power to a directly involved individual violates the Fourteenth Amendment.

The inevitable effect of such delegation may be to deprive a woman of an abortion when under any definition of section 274 of the Penal Code, she would be entitled to such an operation, because the state, in delegating the power to decide when an abortion is necessary, has skewed the penalties in one direction: *no* criminal penalties are imposed where the doctor refuses to perform a necessary operation, even if the woman should in fact die because the operation was not performed.

The pressures on a physician to decide not to perform an absolutely necessary abortion are, under section 274 of the Penal Code, enormous, and because section 274 authorizes—and requires—the doctor to decide, at his peril, whether an abortion is necessary, a woman whose life is at stake may be as effectively condemned to death as if the law flatly prohibited all abortions.

To some extent the Therapeutic Abortion Act reduces these pressures. The act specifically authorizes an abortion by a licensed physician in an accredited hospital where the abortion is approved in advance by a committee of the medical staff of the hospital, applying medical standards. (Health & Saf. Code, § 25951.) At least in cases where there has been adherence to the procedural requirements of the statute, physicians may not be held criminally responsible, and a jury may not subsequently determine that the abortion was not authorized by statute.

We conclude that the validity of section 274 of the Penal Code before amendment cannot be sustained.

Since section 274 is invalid, Dr. Belous' conviction for violation of section 182 of the Penal Code, conspiracy to commit abortion, must likewise fall. . . .

■ BURKE, J., dissenting.

. . . .

The defendant was found guilty by jury trial of a wilful violation of the abortion statute as it existed at the time of the offense. That he violated the statute is all but conceded in the briefs filed in his behalf. Although he testified that he directed the young couple to a doctor, unlicensed in California, because he believed that if they carried out their threats of going to Tijuana to procure an abortion the young woman's life would be in danger, he acknowledged upon cross-examination that her life would not have been endangered if she were not aborted. His assertions that he acted in good faith and out of compassion are tainted somewhat by the evidence which showed that he had referred other women to the same unlicensed physician on a number of occasions and that he had participated on at least one-half of those occasions in the fee paid the abortionist.

Had the doctor truly believed that the young woman's life was in danger he could have done what was the common practice of taking the patient to one of the several hospitals in which therapeutic abortions were being performed. To my knowledge there is not one single instance of a decision of the appellate courts of this state in which a doctor or a hospital has been prosecuted for the performance of an abortion where an independent hospital committee deemed the abortion to be necessary to preserve the woman's life. The plain fact is, as the jury found it to be, that this doctor, whatever his motive, possessed the intent to assist in procuring the miscarriage of the woman for reasons other than to preserve her life. This is the specific intent which the law requires for conviction.

. . . .

The majority would reverse the conviction by declaring the statute unconstitutional because of asserted uncertainty in the phrase, "necessary to preserve [the woman's] life." This phrase has been an integral part of the California law against illegal abortions from the time of its enactment in 1872 until the 1967 amendment to the section, and similar language was in the original statute adopted in 1850. Thus for over a hundred years in this state doctors, hospital committees, judges, lawyers and juries have been called upon to give the phrase the common sense interpretation which the words appear to me to suggest. For this court over a hundred years later to find the language unconstitutionally vague and uncertain is a "negation of experience and common sense."

. . . .

Several statutes show that the California law has been in accord in regarding the unborn child as a human being for various purposes. . . .

It is reasonable to believe that section 274, as it read at the time in question, was not an exception to the law's attitude respecting the unborn child as a human being and that it was designed to protect not only the mother's life but also that of the child. In view of that purpose it would appear that the Legislature intended that the child would be deprived of his right to life only if in the absence of an abortion there was a danger of the mother's death—not merely of injury to her.

" '[T]he Constitution does not require impossible standards'; all that is required is that the language 'conveys sufficiently definite warning as to the proscribed conduct when measured by common understanding and practices. . . .' " The phrase in question, when applied according to the standard heretofore stated (namely, whether persons reasonably skilled in their profession practicing in the same community recognized and approved the act as being required to save the patient from dying) clearly gives such warning.

Furthermore, section 274 punishes only those who act with " '. . . the intent to commit a criminal abortion, that is, an abortion for a purpose other than to preserve (i.e. save from destruction) the life of the mother.' " The requirement of such an intent eviscerates much of the majority's claim that the section is impermissibly vague. A person who performs an abortion with such an intent has fair warning that his conduct may violate the law even though he may not be certain where the jury will draw the line on the matter of necessity.

. . . .

■ SULLIVAN, J., dissenting.

. . . The statute plainly prohibits an abortion unless it is necessary to save the mother's life. It strains reason to say that this crystal-clear exception to the law is "so vague that men of common intelligence must necessarily guess at its meaning. . . ." And it strains credulity to assume that this defendant, who under the evidence wilfully violated the statute, had to engage in any such guesswork with respect to the law governing his conduct. . . .

NOTES

1. *When abortion was a crime. Belous* paints a searing portrait of the period before *Roe v. Wade* when therapeutic abortions—abortions performed for the sake of a woman's mental or physical health, or a fetus's physical health—were incredibly rare, and in this case, illegal. It is striking that the couple in *Belous* was so desperate to obtain an abortion that they were willing to consult with a physician they had only seen on television. The fact that the couple was willing to risk the dangers associated with a "Tijuana abortion" in order to terminate the pregnancy further suggests their desperation. It is worth noting that after his efforts to dissuade the young couple from having an abortion failed, Dr. Belous eventually prescribed antibiotics and referred the couple to Lairtus, an unlicensed physician who would be willing to perform the desired abortion.

2. *The social construction of "criminal" abortion.* The court in *Belous* struggles to define the boundaries between "therapeutic" and "criminal" abortion in the wake of California's new Therapeutic Abortion Act of 1967. Previously, there had been a tacit consensus among physicians that an abortion performed openly by a licensed doctor in good standing, who consulted colleagues, was a therapeutic abortion. In those days, doctors were extremely reluctant to judge each other's clinical decisions. Accordingly, conflicts over whether an abortion was "therapeutic" were rare, whether or not a physician supported "therapeutic" abortions in principle. In *Belous* however, the couple seeking an abortion was unmarried, which raised the question of whether Dr. Belous was aiding and abetting sexual immorality. Note also that Belous referred the couple to an *unlicensed* physician and may have engaged in fee-splitting. These facts, and the fact that he was actively involved in supporting the passage of Therapeutic Abortion Act of 1967, may have made Belous a very tempting target for those opposed to broadening the grounds of legal abortion. *See* KRISTIN LUKER, ABORTION AND THE POLITICS OF MOTHERHOOD 83–86 (1984).

3. *The genesis of California's Therapeutic Abortion Act.* California experienced a serious outbreak of rubella (German measles) in 1964–1965. Critically, when contracted by a pregnant woman, rubella can cause serious harm to the fetus. Accordingly, many physicians routinely performed abortions on women who had credible proof that they had been exposed to rubella. But while an abortion to prevent the birth of a handicapped child might well protect a woman's "life" in the sense of her mental, social, and emotional life, it was in no way necessary to protect her life in a physical sense. For this reason, an anti-abortion advocate who also served as a member of the State Board of Medical Examiners, publicly threatened to "get" any physician who performed an abortion for rubella. True to his word, seven physicians who were among the profession's elite were accused of committing "criminal" abortions because they had performed abortions on women who had been exposed to rubella. The accusations mobilized over 2,000 physicians around the country to support these doctors and created

momentum to encourage the State Assembly to codify an abortion law that would permit them to continue performing the abortions that, in their judgment, were therapeutic. *See* KRISTIN LUKER, ABORTION AND THE POLITICS OF MOTHERHOOD 86–87 (1984). In 1967, Governor Ronald Reagan signed the California Therapeutic Abortion Act into law.

4.   *Patchwork progress.* The interest in liberalizing abortion laws, coupled with judicial review of existing statutes, meant that in the period before *Roe v. Wade* there was a significant state-level effort to consider extant and prospective abortion regulation. However, these efforts were not uniform. Pre-*Roe* abortion reform took on a patchwork character in that it involved both repeal and liberalization, some of it through judicial review, and some of it through legislative and popular activity, as described below. *See* Ruth Roemer, *Abortion Law Reform and Repeal: Legislative and Judicial Developments*, 61 AM. J. PUB. HEALTH 500, 500–03 (1971)

5.   *Legislative and popular repeal of abortion laws.* During the late 1960s and early 1970s, legislatures that were considering abortion regulation were largely occupied with liberalizing extant abortion laws. However, in a minority of states, legislatures went further to repeal criminal abortion statutes entirely. Four states—New York, Hawaii, Alaska, and Washington—passed laws that were essentially repeal bills. In Washington, the legislature passed a repeal law that required public approval in a referendum. When put to a public vote, the repeal law passed. *See* Ruth Roemer, *Abortion Law Reform and Repeal: Legislative and Judicial Developments*, 61 AM. J. PUB. HEALTH 500, 500 (1971).

6.   *The turn from legislative reform to the courts.* Physicians welcomed the legislative reform efforts of the late 1960s and early 1970s because they clarified the rights of doctors to perform abortions in certain circumstances. Due to this broad support from physicians, the reform efforts were relatively uncontroversial, passing by strong margins in most state legislatures. Feminists, however, were skeptical of legislative reform, noting that, even after liberalization, women still had to convince doctors that the abortions they sought were medically necessary. Accordingly, feminist reformers advocated for the total repeal of abortion laws. Once abortion became defined as a women's rights issue, it became more controversial and the legislative liberalization effort stalled. Critically, no state legislatures liberalized their abortion laws after 1970, causing supporters of abortion access to turn to the courts. *See* GENE BURNS, THE MORAL VETO: FRAMING CONTRACEPTION, ABORTION, AND CULTURAL PLURALISM IN THE UNITED STATES 207–43 (2005).

Clergy Statement on Abortion Law Reform and Consultation Service on Abortion (1967), *reprinted in* Linda Greenhouse & Reva Siegel, Before *Roe v. Wade*: The Voices That Shaped the Abortion Debate

30–31 (2010), *available at* http://documents.law.yale.edu/before-roe.

The present abortion laws require over a million women in the United States each year to seek illegal abortions which often cause severe mental anguish, physical suffering, and unnecessary death of women. These laws also compel the birth of unwanted, unloved, and often deformed children; yet a truly human society is one in which the birth of a child is an occasion for genuine celebration, not the imposition of a penalty or punishment upon the mother. . . .

. . . .

Therefore we pledge ourselves as clergymen to a continuing effort to educate and inform the public to the end that a more liberal abortion law in this state and throughout the nation be enacted. . . . Therefore believing as clergymen that there are higher laws and moral obligations transcending legal codes, we believe that it is our pastoral responsibility and religious duty to give aid and assistance to all women with problem pregnancies. To that end, we are establishing a Clergymen's Consultation Service on Abortion which will include referral to the best available medical advice and aid to women in need.

NOTE

Contradicting the conventional wisdom. As the preceding statement makes clear, prior to *Roe v. Wade*, abortion reform enjoyed popular support, even among the clergy. How does this source complicate or elaborate the prevailing narrative surrounding the years preceding *Roe*? How does the clergy statement complicate current narratives that position abortion access and religiosity as in conflict?

Roe v. Wade
410 U.S. 113 (1973).

■ BLACKMUN, J.

. . . .

We forthwith acknowledge our awareness of the sensitive and emotional nature of the abortion controversy, of the vigorous opposing views, even among physicians, and of the deep and seemingly absolute convictions that the subject inspires. One's philosophy, one's experiences, one's exposure to the raw edges of human existence, one's religious training, one's attitudes toward life and family and their values, and the moral standards one establishes and seeks to observe, are all likely to influence and to color one's thinking and conclusions about abortion.

In addition, population growth, pollution, poverty, and racial overtones tend to complicate and not to simplify the problem.

Our task, of course, is to resolve the issue by constitutional measurement, free of emotion and of predilection. We seek earnestly to do this, and, because we do, we have inquired into, and in this opinion place some emphasis upon, medical and medical-legal history and what that history reveals about man's attitudes toward the abortion procedure over the centuries. . . .

I

The Texas statutes that concern us here . . . make it a crime to "procure an abortion," as therein defined, or to attempt one, except with respect to "an abortion procured or attempted by medical advice for the purpose of saving the life of the mother." Similar statutes are in existence in a majority of the States.

. . . .

. . . The final article in each of these compilations provided the same exception, as does the present Article 1196, for an abortion by "medical advice for the purpose of saving the life of the mother."[3]

II

Jane Roe, a single woman who was residing in Dallas County, Texas . . . alleged that she was unmarried and pregnant; that she wished to terminate her pregnancy by an abortion "performed by a competent, licensed physician, under safe, clinical conditions"; that she was unable to get a "legal" abortion in Texas because her life did not appear to be threatened by the continuation of her pregnancy; and that she could not afford to travel to another jurisdiction in order to secure a legal abortion under safe conditions. She claimed that the Texas statutes were unconstitutionally vague and that they abridged her right of personal privacy, protected by the First, Fourth, Fifth, Ninth, and Fourteenth Amendments.

. . . .

VI

It perhaps is not generally appreciated that the restrictive criminal abortion laws in effect in a majority of States today are of relatively recent vintage. Those laws, generally proscribing abortion or its attempt at any time during pregnancy except when necessary to preserve the pregnant woman's life, are not of ancient or even of common-law origin.

---

[3] Long ago, a suggestion was made that the Texas statutes were unconstitutionally vague because of definitional deficiencies. The Texas Court of Criminal Appeals disposed of that suggestion peremptorily, saying only,

"It is also insisted in the motion in arrest of judgment that the statute is unconstitutional and void, in that it does not sufficiently define or describe the offense of abortion. We do not concur with counsel in respect to this question." *Jackson v. State*, 115 S.W. 262, 268 (1908).

The same court recently has held again that the State's abortion statutes are not unconstitutionally vague or overbroad. *Thompson v. State*, 493 S.W.2d 913 (1971), appeal docketed, No. 71–1200. The court held that "the State of Texas has a compelling interest to protect fetal life"; that Art. 1191 "is designed to protect fetal life"; that the Texas homicide statutes, particularly Act. 1205 of the Penal Code, are intended to protect a person "in existence by actual birth" and thereby implicitly recognize other human life that is not "in existence by actual birth"; that the definition of human life is for the legislature and not the courts; that Art. 11196 "is more definite that the District of Columbia statute upheld in *United States v. Vuitch*, 402 U.S. 62 (1971)"; and that the Texas statute "is not vague and indefinite or overbroad." A physician's abortion conviction was affirmed.

In 493 S.W.2d, at 920 n. 2, the court observed that any issue as to the burden of proof under the exemption of Art. 1196 "is not before us." *But see Veevers v. State*, 354 S.W.2d 161, 166–167 (1962). *Cf. United States v. Vuitch*, 402 U.S. 62, 69–71 (1971).

Instead, they derive from statutory changes effected, for the most part, in the latter half of the 19th century.

1.   Ancient   attitudes.   These   are   not   capable   of   precise determination. We are told that at the time of the Persian Empire abortifacients were known and that criminal abortions were severely punished. We are also told, however, that abortion was practiced in Greek times as well as in the Roman Era, and that "it was resorted to without scruple." The Ephesian, Soranos, often described as the greatest of the ancient gynecologists, appears to have been generally opposed to Rome's prevailing free-abortion practices. He found it necessary to think first of the life of the mother, and he resorted to abortion when, upon this standard, he felt the procedure advisable. Greek and Roman law afforded little protection to the unborn. If abortion was prosecuted in some places, it seems to have been based on a concept of a violation of the father's right to his offspring. Ancient religion did not bar abortion.

2.   The Hippocratic Oath. What then of the famous Oath that has stood so long as the ethical guide of the medical profession and that bears the name of the great Greek (460(?)–377(?) B.C.), who has been described as the Father of Medicine, the "wisest and the greatest practitioner of his art," and the "most important and most complete medical personality of antiquity," who dominated the medical schools of his time, and who typified the sum of the medical knowledge of the past? The Oath varies somewhat according to the particular translation, but in any translation the content is clear: "I will give no deadly medicine to anyone if asked, nor suggest any such counsel; and in like manner I will not give to a woman a pessary to produce abortion," . . . .

. . . Why did not the authority of Hippocrates dissuade abortion practice in his time and that of Rome? The late Dr. Edelstein provides us with a theory: The Oath was not uncontested even in Hippocrates' day; only the Pythagorean school of philosophers frowned upon the related act of suicide. Most Greek thinkers, on the other hand, commended abortion, at least prior to viability. . . .

Dr. Edelstein then concludes that the Oath originated in a group representing only a small segment of Greek opinion and that it certainly was not accepted by all ancient physicians. . . .

3.   The common law. It is undisputed that at common law, abortion performed before "quickening"—the first recognizable movement of the fetus in utero, appearing usually from the 16th to the 18th week of pregnancy—was not an indictable offense. The absence of a common-law crime for pre-quickening abortion appears to have developed from a confluence of earlier philosophical, theological, and civil and canon law concepts of when life begins. . . .

Whether abortion of a quick fetus was a felony at common law, or even a lesser crime, is still disputed. . . .

. . . .

5.   The American law. In this country, the law in effect in all but a few States until mid-19th century was the pre-existing English common law. Connecticut, the first State to enact abortion legislation, adopted in 1821 that part of Lord Ellenborough's Act that related to a woman "quick with child." The death penalty was not imposed. Abortion before quickening was made a crime in that State only in 1860. . . . It was not until after the War Between the States that legislation began generally to replace the common law. . . .

Gradually, in the middle and late 19th century the quickening distinction disappeared from the statutory law of most States and the degree of the offense and the penalties were increased. By the end of the 1950's a large majority of the jurisdictions banned abortion, however and whenever performed, unless done to save or preserve the life of the mother. . . . In the past several years, however, a trend toward liberalization of abortion statutes has resulted in adoption, by about one-third of the States, of less stringent laws, most of them patterned after the ALI Model Penal Code. . . . It is thus apparent that at common law, at the time of the adoption of our Constitution, and throughout the major portion of the 19th century, abortion was viewed with less disfavor than under most American statutes currently in effect. . . .

6.   The position of the American Medical Association. The anti-abortion mood prevalent in this country in the late 19th century was shared by the medical profession. Indeed, the attitude of the profession may have played a significant role in the enactment of stringent criminal abortion legislation during that period.

. . . .

In 1871 a long and vivid report was submitted by the [American Medical Association's] Committee on Criminal Abortion . . . recommending, among other things, that it "be unlawful and unprofessional for any physician to induce abortion or premature labor, without the concurrent opinion of at least one respectable consulting physician, and then always with a view to the safety of the child—if that be possible," and calling "the attention of the clergy of all denominations to the perverted views of morality entertained by a large class of females—aye, and men also, on this important question."

Except for periodic condemnation of the criminal abortionist, no further formal AMA action took place until 1967. In that year, the Committee on Human Reproduction urged the adoption of a stated policy of opposition to induced abortion, except when there is "documented medical evidence" of a threat to the health or life of the mother, or that the child "may be born with incapacitating physical deformity or mental deficiency," or that a pregnancy "resulting from legally established statutory or forcible rape or incest may constitute a threat to the mental or physical health of the patient," two other physicians "chosen because of their recognized professional competency have examined the patient and have concurred in writing," and the procedure "is performed in a hospital accredited by the Joint Commission on Accreditation of Hospitals." . . . This recommendation was adopted by the House of Delegates.

In 1970, after the introduction of a variety of proposed resolutions, and of a report from its Board of Trustees, a reference committee noted "polarization of the medical profession on this controversial issue"; division among those who had testified; a difference of opinion among AMA councils and committees; "the remarkable shift in testimony" in six months, felt to be influenced "by the rapid changes in state laws and by the judicial decisions which tend to make abortion more freely available;" and a feeling "that this trend will continue." On June 25, 1970, the House of Delegates adopted preambles and most of the resolutions proposed by the reference committee. The preambles emphasized "the best interests of the patient," "sound clinical judgment," and "informed patient consent," in contrast to "mere acquiescence to the patient's demand." The resolutions asserted that abortion is a medical procedure that should be performed by a licensed physician in an accredited hospital only after consultation with two other physicians and in conformity with state law, and that no party to the procedure should be required to violate personally held moral principles.

. . . .

VII

Three reasons have been advanced to explain historically the enactment of criminal abortion laws in the 19th century and to justify their continued existence.

It has been argued occasionally that these laws were the product of a Victorian social concern to discourage illicit sexual conduct. Texas, however, does not advance this justification in the present case, and it appears that no court or commentator has taken the argument seriously. . . .

A second reason is concerned with abortion as a medical procedure. When most criminal abortion laws were first enacted, the procedure was a hazardous one for the woman. This was particularly true prior to the development of antisepsis. Antiseptic techniques, of course, were based on discoveries by Lister, Pasteur, and others first announced in 1867, but were not generally accepted and employed until about the turn of the century. Abortion mortality was high. Even after 1900, and perhaps until as late as the development of antibiotics in the 1940's, standard modern techniques such as dilation and curettage were not nearly so safe as they are today. Thus, it has been argued that a State's real concern in enacting a criminal abortion law was to protect the pregnant woman, that is, to restrain her from submitting to a procedure that placed her life in serious jeopardy.

. . . Appellants and various amici refer to medical data indicating that abortion in early pregnancy, that is, prior to the end of the first trimester, although not without its risk, is now relatively safe. Mortality rates for women undergoing early abortions, where the procedure is legal, appear to be as low as or lower than the rates for normal childbirth. Consequently, any interest of the State in protecting the woman from an inherently hazardous procedure, except when it would be equally dangerous for her to forgo it, has largely disappeared. Of course, important state interests in the areas of health and medical standards do remain. The State has a legitimate interest in seeing to it that abortion, like any other medical procedure, is performed under circumstances that insure maximum safety for the patient. This interest obviously extends at least to the performing physician and his staff, to the facilities involved, to the availability of after-care, and to adequate provision for any complication or emergency that might arise. The prevalence of high mortality rates at illegal 'abortion mills' strengthens, rather than weakens, the State's interest in regulating the conditions under which abortions are performed. Moreover, the risk to the woman increases as her pregnancy continues. Thus, the State retains a definite interest in protecting the woman's own health and safety when an abortion is proposed at a late stage of pregnancy.

The third reason is the State's interest—some phrase it in terms of duty—in protecting prenatal life. Some of the argument for this justification rests on the theory that a new human life is present from the moment of conception. The State's interest and general obligation to protect life then extends, it is argued, to prenatal life. Only when the life of the pregnant mother herself is at stake, balanced against the life she carries within her, should the interest of the embryo or fetus not prevail. Logically, of course, a legitimate state interest in this area need not stand or fall on acceptance of the belief that life begins at conception or at some other point prior to life birth. In assessing the State's interest, recognition may be given to the less rigid claim that as long as at least potential life is involved, the State may assert interests beyond the protection of the pregnant woman alone.

. . . .

It is with these interests, and the weight to be attached to them, that this case is concerned.

VIII

The Constitution does not explicitly mention any right of privacy. In a line of decisions, however, going back perhaps as far as *Union Pacific R. Co. v. Botsford*, 141 U.S. 250, 251 (1891), the Court has recognized that a right of personal privacy, or a guarantee of certain areas or zones of privacy, does exist under the Constitution. . . .

This right of privacy, whether it be founded in the Fourteenth Amendment's concept of personal liberty and restrictions upon state action, as we feel it is, or, as the District Court determined, in the Ninth Amendment's reservation of rights to the people, is broad enough to encompass a woman's decision whether or not to terminate her pregnancy. The detriment that the State would impose upon the pregnant woman by denying this choice altogether is apparent. Specific and direct harm medically diagnosable even in early pregnancy may be involved. Maternity, or additional offspring, may force upon the woman a distressful life and future. Psychological harm may be imminent. Mental and physical health may be taxed by child care. There is also the distress, for all concerned, associated with the unwanted child, and there is the problem of bringing a child into a family already unable, psychologically and otherwise, to care for it. In other cases, as in this one, the additional difficulties and continuing stigma of unwed motherhood may be involved. All these are factors the woman and her responsible physician necessarily will consider in consultation.

On the basis of elements such as these, appellant and some amici argue that the woman's right is absolute and that she is entitled to terminate her pregnancy at whatever time, in whatever way, and for whatever reason she alone chooses. With this we do not agree. Appellant's arguments that Texas either has no valid interest at all in regulating the abortion decision, or no interest strong enough to support any limitation upon the woman's sole determination, are unpersuasive. The Court's decisions recognizing a right of privacy also acknowledge that some state regulation in areas protected by that right is appropriate. As noted above, a State may properly assert important interests in safeguarding health, in maintaining medical standards, and in protecting potential life. At some point in pregnancy, these respective interests become sufficiently compelling to sustain regulation of the factors that govern the abortion decision. The privacy right involved, therefore, cannot be said to be absolute. . . .

We, therefore, conclude that the right of personal privacy includes the abortion decision, but that this right is not unqualified and must be considered against important state interests in regulation.

. . . .

IX

. . . .

A.   The appellee and certain amici argue that the fetus is a "person" within the language and meaning of the Fourteenth Amendment. In support of this, they outline at length and in detail the well-known facts of fetal development. If this suggestion of personhood is established, the appellant's case, of course, collapses, for the fetus' right to life would then be guaranteed specifically by the Amendment. . . .

The Constitution does not define "person" in so many words. . . .

. . . .

. . . [T]his, together with our observation, that throughout the major portion of the 19th century prevailing legal abortion practices were far freer than they are today, persuades us that the word "person," as used in the Fourteenth Amendment, does not include the unborn. . . .

B. The pregnant woman cannot be isolated in her privacy. She carries an embryo and, later, a fetus, if one accepts the medical definitions of the developing young in the human uterus. The situation therefore is inherently different from marital intimacy, or bedroom possession of obscene material, or marriage, or procreation, or education, with which *Eisenstadt* and *Griswold, Stanley, Loving, Skinner* and *Pierce* and *Meyer* were respectively concerned. As we have intimated above, it is reasonable and appropriate for a State to decide that at some point in time another interest, that of health of the mother or that of potential human life, becomes significantly involved. The woman's privacy is no longer sole and any right of privacy she possesses must be measured accordingly.

Texas urges that, apart from the Fourteenth Amendment, life begins at conception and is present throughout pregnancy, and that, therefore, the State has a compelling interest in protecting that life from and after conception. We need not resolve the difficult question of when life begins. When those trained in the respective disciplines of medicine, philosophy, and theology are unable to arrive at any consensus, the judiciary, at this point in the development of man's knowledge, is not in a position to speculate as to the answer.

It should be sufficient to note briefly the wide divergence of thinking on this most sensitive and difficult question. There has always been strong support for the view that life does not begin until live birth. This was the belief of the Stoics. It appears to be the predominant, though not the unanimous, attitude of the Jewish faith. It may be taken to represent also the position of a large segment of the Protestant community, insofar as that can be ascertained; organized groups that have taken a formal position on the abortion issue have generally regarded abortion as a matter for the conscience of the individual and her family. As we have noted, the common law found greater significance in quickening. Physicians and their scientific colleagues have regarded that event with less interest and have tended to focus either upon conception, upon live birth, or upon the interim point at which the fetus becomes "viable," that is, potentially able to live outside the mother's womb, albeit with artificial aid. Viability is usually placed at about seven months (28 weeks) but may occur earlier, even at 24 weeks. . . . [T]hose in the Church . . . would recognize the existence of life from the moment of conception. The latter is now, of course, the official belief of the Catholic Church. As one brief amicus discloses, this is a view strongly held by many non-Catholics as well, and by many physicians. Substantial problems for precise definition of this view are posed, however, by new embryological data that purport to indicate that conception is a "process" over time, rather than an event, and by new medical techniques such as menstrual extraction, the "morning-after" pill, implantation of embryos, artificial insemination, and even artificial wombs.

. . . .

X

In view of all this, we do not agree that, by adopting one theory of life, Texas may override the rights of the pregnant woman that are at stake. We repeat, however, that the State does have an important and legitimate interest in preserving and protecting the health of the pregnant woman, whether she be a resident of the State or a non-resident who seeks medical consultation and treatment there, and that it has still another important and legitimate interest in protecting the potentiality of human life. These interests are separate and distinct. Each grows in substantiality as the woman approaches term and, at a point during pregnancy, each becomes "compelling."

With respect to the State's important and legitimate interest in the health of the mother, the "compelling" point, in the light of present medical knowledge, is at approximately the end of the first trimester. This is so because of the now-established medical fact, referred to above, that until the end of the first trimester mortality in abortion may be less than mortality in normal childbirth. It follows that, from and after this point, a State may regulate the abortion procedure to the extent that the regulation reasonably relates to the preservation and protection of maternal health. Examples of permissible state regulation in this area are requirements as to the qualifications of the person who is to perform the abortion; as to the licensure of that person; as to the facility in which the procedure is to be performed, that is, whether it must be a hospital or may be a clinic or some other place of less-than-hospital status; as to the licensing of the facility; and the like.

This means, on the other hand, that, for the period of pregnancy prior to this "compelling" point, the attending physician, in consultation with his patient, is free to determine, without regulation by the State, that, in his medical judgment, the patient's pregnancy should be terminated. If that decision is reached, the judgment may be effectuated by an abortion free of interference by the State.

With respect to the State's important and legitimate interest in potential life, the "compelling" point is at viability. This is so because the fetus then presumably has the capability of meaningful life outside the mother's womb. State regulation protective of fetal life after viability thus has both logical and biological justifications. If the State is interested in protecting fetal life after viability, it may go so far as to proscribe abortion during that period, except when it is necessary to preserve the life or health of the mother.

Measured against these standards, Art. 1196 of the Texas Penal Code, in restricting legal abortions to those "procured or attempted by medical advice for the purpose of saving the life of the mother," sweeps too broadly. The statute makes no distinction between abortions performed early in pregnancy and those performed later, and it limits to a single reason, "saving" the mother's life, the legal justification for the procedure. The statute, therefore, cannot survive the constitutional attack made upon it here.

. . . .

XI

To summarize and to repeat:

1.   A state criminal abortion statute of the current Texas type, that excepts from criminality only a life-saving procedure on behalf of the mother, without regard to pregnancy stage and without recognition of the other interests involved, is violative of the Due Process Clause of the Fourteenth Amendment.

(a)   For the stage prior to approximately the end of the first trimester, the abortion decision and its effectuation must be left to the medical judgment of the pregnant woman's attending physician.

(b)   For the stage subsequent to approximately the end of the first trimester, the State, in promoting its interest in the health of the mother, may, if it chooses, regulate the abortion procedure in ways that are reasonably related to maternal health.

(c)   For the stage subsequent to viability, the State in promoting its interest in the potentiality of human life may, if it chooses, regulate, and even proscribe, abortion except where it is necessary, in appropriate medical judgment, for the preservation of the life or health of the mother.

2.   The State may define the term "physician," as it has been employed in the preceding paragraphs of this Part XI of this opinion, to mean only a physician currently licensed by the State, and may proscribe any abortion by a person who is not a physician as so defined.

. . . .

■ REHNQUIST, J., dissenting.

. . . I have difficulty in concluding, as the Court does, that the right of "privacy" is involved in this case. Texas, by the statute here challenged, bars the performance of a medical abortion by a licensed physician on a plaintiff such as Roe. A transaction resulting in an operation such as this is not 'private' in the ordinary usage of that word. Nor is the "privacy" that the Court finds here even a distant relative of the freedom from searches and seizures protected by the Fourth Amendment to the Constitution, which the Court has referred to as embodying a right to privacy. *Katz v. United States*, 389 U.S. 347 (1967).

If the Court means by the term "privacy" no more than that the claim of a person to be free from unwanted state regulation of consensual transactions may be a form of "liberty" protected by the Fourteenth Amendment, there is no doubt that similar claims have been upheld in our earlier decisions on the basis of that liberty . . . But that liberty is not guaranteed absolutely against deprivation, only against deprivation without due process of law. The test traditionally applied in the area of social and economic legislation is whether or not a law such as that challenged has a rational relation to a valid state objective. *Williamson v. Lee Optical Inc.*, 348 U.S. 483, 491 (1955). The Due Process Clause of the Fourteenth Amendment undoubtedly does place a limit, albeit a broad one, on legislative power to enact laws such as this. If the Texas statute were to prohibit an abortion even where the mother's life is in jeopardy, I have little doubt that such a statute would lack a rational relation to a valid state objective under the test stated in *Williamson*. But the Court's sweeping invalidation of any restrictions on abortion during the first trimester is impossible to justify under that standard, and the conscious weighing of competing factors that the Court's opinion apparently substitutes for the established test is far more appropriate to a legislative judgment than to a judicial one.

. . . The decision here to break pregnancy into three distinct terms and to outline the permissible restrictions the State may impose in each one, for example, partakes more of judicial legislation than it does of a determination of the intent of the drafters of the Fourteenth Amendment.

The fact that a majority of the States reflecting, after all the majority sentiment in those States, have had restrictions on abortions for at least a century is a strong indication, it seems to me, that the asserted right to an abortion is not "so rooted in the traditions and conscience of our people as to be ranked as fundamental," *Snyder v. Massachusetts*, 291 U.S. 97, 105 (1934). Even today, when society's views on abortion are changing, the very existence of the debate is evidence that the "right" to an abortion is not so universally accepted as the appellant would have us believe.

To reach its result, the Court necessarily has had to find within the Scope of the Fourteenth Amendment a right that was apparently completely unknown to the drafters of the Amendment. As early as 1821, the first state law dealing directly with abortion was enacted by the Connecticut Legislature. By the time of the adoption of the Fourteenth Amendment in 1868, there were at least 36 laws enacted by state or territorial legislatures limiting abortion. While many States have amended or updated their laws, 21 of the laws on the books in 1868 remain in effect today. Indeed, the Texas statute struck down today was, as the majority notes, first enacted in 1857 and "has remained substantially unchanged to the present time."

There apparently was no question concerning the validity of this provision or of any of the other state statutes when the Fourteenth Amendment was adopted. The only conclusion possible from this history is that the drafters did not intend to have the Fourteenth Amendment withdraw from the States the power to legislate with respect to this matter.

. . . .

NOTES

1.   *A companion case.* It is important to remember that, in addition to *Roe v. Wade*, the Court heard and reported a companion case, *Doe v. Bolton*, 410 U.S. 179 (1973). Unlike *Roe*, which challenged a Texas abortion statute based on a nineteenth-century law criminalizing abortion, *Doe* challenged Georgia's ALI-inspired reform law, which was passed in 1968, see *supra* p. 691. In addition to codifying the ALI guidelines for permitting abortion, the Georgia law imposed additional conditions on those seeking an abortion. Specifically, the challenged law restricted abortion to Georgia residents, required a written physician's note explaining why an abortion was indicated, as well as the approval of two other Georgia-licensed physicians. It further mandated that all abortions be performed in an accredited hospital. In striking down the Georgia statute *and* the Texas statute, the Court signaled that *neither* the nineteenth-century abortion laws, *nor* the more liberal twentieth-century abortion laws passed constitutional muster. *Id.* at 201–02.

2.   *A road not taken?* According to legal scholar Linda Greenhouse, there was a great deal of discussion as to which abortion case (*Roe* or *Doe*) should be the lead case. Justice Blackmun, who had been counsel to the Mayo Clinic, favored making *Doe* the lead case, and he wanted to treat abortion primarily as a health care issue. *See* LINDA GREENHOUSE, BECOMING JUSTICE BLACKMUN: HARRY BLACKMUN'S SUPREME COURT JOURNEY 93 (2006). What if *Doe* had been the lead case, as Justice Blackmun suggested? What if the right to abortion had been framed as a health care decision?

3.   *Doe vs. Roe?* As Linda Greenhouse recounts, the two cases *Roe* and *Doe* "each represented a point on the evolving spectrum of the abortion debate." LINDA GREENHOUSE, BECOMING JUSTICE BLACKMUN 78 (2006). Behind the two cases lurked a definitional fight, one that had begun to ensnare "reputable" physicians in its web, as changes in medical technology and practice forced professionals to define the precise nature of the "life" of the woman. The Texas law in *Roe* represented the view that "life" was a biological state, and that abortions could be performed only in cases where the woman's death was imminent. The Georgia law in *Doe*, however, recognized that a problematic pregnancy not only could endanger biological life but also could affect "life" in the broader sense of the word, by "seriously and permanently injur[ing] [the woman's] health." *Doe v. Bolton*, 410 U.S. 179, 183 (1973). For how these conflicting meanings of "life" played out in one state, see KRISTIN LUKER, ABORTION AND THE POLITICS OF MOTHERHOOD 60–65 (1984).

4.   *Void for vagueness?* An early draft of *Roe* reveals that Justice Blackmun initially relied on void-for-vagueness doctrine to invalidate the Texas law criminalizing abortion. According to legal historian Risa Goluboff, Justice Blackmun was sympathetic to the doctors' argument that "[u]nder laws prohibiting all abortions but those necessary for the 'life' or 'health' of the mother, doctors argued that they chanced a felony every time they guessed that a particular abortion came within such exceptions." Risa L. Goluboff, *Dispatch from the Supreme Court Archives: Vagrancy, Abortion, and What*

the Links Between Them Reveal About the History of Fundamental Rights, 62 STAN. L. REV. 1361, 1379 (citing Justice Harry A. Blackmun, First Draft, Roe v. Wade, No. 70–18, at 13–14 (May 18, 1972) (Blackmun Papers, Box 151) (2010)). Moreover, focusing on vagueness allowed Justice Blackmun to avoid the fraught issue of when life began. *Id*. Justices Brennan and Douglas, however, urged Blackmun "to reach 'the core issue' of privacy" instead. *Id*. (citing Memorandum from Justice William J. Brennan to Justice Harry A. Blackmun, Re: Roe v. Wade, No. 70–18 (May 18, 1972) (Brennan Papers, Box I-285); Memorandum from Justice William O. Douglas to Justice Harry A. Blackmun, Re: Roe v. Wade, No. 70–18 (May 19, 1972) (Douglas Papers, Box 1589)). Goluboff notes that the evolution of *Roe*'s doctrinal underpinnings serves as a reminder that *Roe* was a case "in which the Court was placing substantive limits on the extent to which the criminal law could be used as a mechanism of morals regulation." *Id*. at 1384.

5.   *Courting controversy.* According to Linda Greenhouse, the Court was unprepared for the controversy that followed in *Roe*'s wake. Indeed, as memoranda and draft opinions circulated among the Justices' chambers make clear, the Court grappled with *Roe* and *Doe* without grasping the full extent of the political firestorm the decisions would unleash. Astonishingly, memos suggest that some Justices were willing to hear the cases as a seven-person court (Justices Black and Harlan had recently retired for health reasons), rather than wait for Justices Powell and Rehnquist, both of whom had recently been appointed, to take their seats. In the end, the cases were argued once before the seven-member court, and then again, after Powell and Rehnquist had been seated. In all, it seems the social and political dimension of the abortion debate may have escaped the Justices, many of whom regarded abortion primarily as a medical decision within the ambit of physician discretion. *See* LINDA GREENHOUSE, BECOMING JUSTICE BLACKMUN: HARRY BLACKMUN'S SUPREME COURT JOURNEY 72–101 (2006).

6.   *The personal side of* Roe. Prior to joining the Court, Harry Blackmun, who authored the majority opinion in *Roe*, served for nine years as resident counsel to the Mayo Clinic. In her biography of Blackmun, Linda Greenhouse suggests that this professional experience informed Blackmun's understanding of the relationship between a pregnant woman and her physician, as well as the medical issues surrounding the abortion decision. Greenhouse also notes that Blackmun's daughter Sally had experienced an unintended pregnancy while a sophomore in college. She married the man involved but suffered a miscarriage. Like many marriages begun under these inauspicious beginnings, Sally Blackmun's marriage did not survive. Finally, when the issue was discussed at the Blackmuns' dinner table, all three of the Justice's daughters supported greater access to abortion. LINDA GREENHOUSE, BECOMING JUSTICE BLACKMUN 72–101 (2006).

7.   *Cyril Means and* Roe. In *Roe v. Wade*, the Supreme Court relied heavily on the work of Cyril Means, then a law professor at New York University. In 1968, Governor Nelson Rockefeller appointed Means to review New York's abortion law. In his research, Means argued that nineteenth-century abortion laws were animated by an interest in protecting women's lives as instrument abortions, which carried a greater risk of infection and death,

replaced earlier herbal abortions. Glimmers of Means's research can be glimpsed throughout *Roe*—particularly in the Court's reasoning that criminal abortion statutes were not a long-standing part of the Anglo-American legal tradition apart from context-specific justifications, such as medical practices, of a time period. *Roe v. Wade*, 410 U.S. 113, 133–35 nn.21, 22 & 26 (1973).

8.   *Rethinking the Means thesis.* While the *Roe* Court relied heavily on Cyril Means's work arguing that nineteenth-century abortion laws were rooted in an interest in preserving women's health in the face of the risk of surgical infection, more recently legal scholars and historians have argued that the interest in women's health does not fully explain the nineteenth-century effort to criminalize abortion. According to these scholars, changing women's roles, the first-wave feminist movement, and physicians' desires to professionalize and control reproduction, among other things, were also factors in the effort to criminalize abortion. Reva B. Siegel, *Reasoning from the Body: A Historical Perspective on Abortion Regulation and Questions of Equal Protection*, 44 STAN. L. REV. 261, 281–87 (1992).

9.   *Sodomy and abortion.* Legal historian David Garrow documents the close—but largely unacknowledged—connections between the efforts to invalidate laws criminalizing abortion and sodomy. In 1969, Dallas lawyer Henry McCluskey filed a lawsuit challenging Texas' sodomy statute, which prohibited sodomy, even when practiced by married couples. In bringing the suit, McCluskey sought assistance and advice from other local lawyers, including Linda Coffee, who was trying to launch a challenge to Texas's abortion law. On the advice of Coffee and others, McCluskey filed *Buchanan v. Batchelor*, claiming that the sweeping Texas sodomy statute violated the principle of marital privacy articulated in *Griswold v. Connecticut*. A three-judge panel of the Northern District of Texas agreed, concluding that traditional moral disapproval of sodomy was "not sufficient reason for the State to encroach upon the liberty of married persons in their private conduct." *Buchanan v. Batchelor*, 308 F. Supp. 729, 733 (N.D. Tex. 1970); DAVID GARROW, LIBERTY AND SEXUALITY: THE RIGHT TO PRIVACY AND THE MAKING OF *ROE V. WADE* 400–07 (1994). The panel studiously avoided the question of whether the statute was unconstitutional with regard to homosexual intimacy.

In the months before the district court announced its decision in *Buchanan v. Batchelor*, McCluskey, whose practice often involved more routine legal matters, received a visit from a young woman. Having failed in her search to secure a safe abortion, Norma McCorvey hoped to resolve her unwanted pregnancy through adoption. McCluskey, however, thought McCorvey would be an ideal client for Coffee, who, in order to avoid mooting a challenge to the abortion statute, was searching for a plaintiff who would still be pregnant at the time the case was filed. McCluskey introduced McCorvey to Coffee, setting the stage for *Roe v. Wade*. GARROW, *supra* at 402–04. *Buchanan* was appealed to the U.S. Supreme Court, which vacated the judgment and remanded for reconsideration in light of two recently decided cases concerning standing. *See Buchanan v. Wade*, 401 U.S. 989 (1971).

10. *Alternative doctrinal grounds for a right to abortion*. In a brief submitted in *Struck v. Secretary of Defense*, 409 U.S. 1071 (1972), Ruth Bader Ginsburg, then of the American Civil Liberties Union (ACLU) Women's Rights Project, offered an alternative intellectual framing for abortion rights. In 1970, Susan Struck, a devout Catholic and career Air Force officer who served in Vietnam, found herself pregnant and unmarried. Struck planned to use her accrued leave to give birth, after which she would place the child for adoption. The Air Force insisted that she either have an abortion or be discharged. Critically, the Air Force did not require male officers facing physical incapacitation—or impending fatherhood—to make the same choice. Struck sued the Air Force, but in the end, the Air Force relented and waived her discharge, mooting the case. In the *Struck* brief, Ginsburg argued that the regulation of pregnancy and abortion subordinated women by compelling them to adopt social norms prescribing "proper" motherhood, thus reinforcing classic sex stereotypes. Although Ginsburg argued that the legal regulation of pregnancy and abortion reinforced sex role stereotypes, thereby implicating women's equality, she did not discredit the attendant liberty and autonomy concerns surrounding the case. Even before the *Roe* Court decisively linked abortion rights with the right to privacy, Ginsburg argued that the military's desire to determine the outcome of Captain Struck's pregnancy was an impermissible intrusion into her private life. *See* Brief for Petitioner at 7–12, *Struck v. Secretary of Defense*, 409 U.S. 1071 (1972) (No. 72–178).

However, thirteen years after *Struck*, Ginsburg continued to press for framing abortion rights in the context of equality, rather than substantive due process. In 1985, Ginsburg, then a judge on the U.S. Court of Appeals for the District of Columbia, argued that *Roe* should have located its reasoning in equal protection, rather than rooting it solely in autonomy. According to Ginsburg, women needed to control their fertility in order "to participate as men's full partners in the nation's social, political and economic life." Moreover, Ginsburg noted that, as a practical matter, there was wide public acceptance of sex-based equal protection, while constitutional protections for privacy and autonomy continued to be controversial. Ruth Bader Ginsburg, *Some Thoughts on Autonomy and Equality in Relation to* Roe v. Wade, 63 N.C. L. REV. 375, 375, 382–83 (1985). Do you agree with Ginsburg that equal protection would provide a better doctrinal home for the abortion right than privacy and substantive due process? If *Struck* had reached the court before *Roe*, how might the right to abortion have developed differently?

11. Roe *and right-wing backlash*. In recent years, it has become *au courant* among legal scholars and abortion opponents to say that the Court "overreached" in *Roe*, deciding a contentious issue that should have been left to legislatures. Indeed, some scholars (including Justice Ruth Bader Ginsburg) have argued that *Roe* was decided at a time when abortion liberalization was proceeding slowly but surely through state legislatures. On this account, *Roe* caused a backlash that arrested legislative progress and, more troublingly, led to anti-abortion mobilization. As such, *Roe*, and the reaction to it, have become part of a long-standing debate about the role

of courts, and how and when they should defer to the popular will. Scholars such as Michael Klarman and Cass Sunstein have urged the Supreme Court (and courts in general) to be wary of deciding divisive social issues for fear that such "judicial activism" will prompt backlash. *See* Michael J. Klarman, *How* Brown *Changed Race Relations: The Backlash Thesis*, 81 J. AM. HIST. 81, 82 (1994); Cass R. Sunstein, *Foreword: Leaving Things Undecided*, 110 HARV. L. REV. 4, 33 (1996).

12. *Pushback on backlash*. Professors Robert Post and Reva Siegel have challenged the backlash thesis, arguing that the prospect of pre-*Roe* legislative liberalization was overstated and that legislative efforts to repeal abortion laws had stalled at the state level at the time *Roe* was decided. Moreover, they show that conservative opposition to abortion (and other civil rights) was well underway by 1973, when *Roe* was decided. Post and Siegel further note that proponents of "judicial minimalism," who want the court to avoid deciding controversial issues and defer to the democratic process, risk ignoring the needs of emerging groups (minorities, including sexual minorities and women), whose exclusion calls that democratic process into question. Robert Post & Reva Siegel, Roe *Rage: Democratic Constitutionalism and Backlash*, 42 HARV. C.R.-C.L. L. REV. 373, 410–12, 425–27 (2007).

4.   ABORTION JURISPRUDENCE AND DEBATE POST-*ROE V. WADE*

As opposition to abortion hardened along partisan lines, the Reagan Administration began to support the rights of states to regulate key aspects of abortion. Samuel Alito, (now Justice Alito) an Assistant to the Solicitor General, wrote a memorandum urging the Solicitor General to support the restoration of state regulations on abortion that had been struck down in lower courts. Among the cases to which Alito was responding in his memorandum were American College of Obstetrics & Gynecology v. Thornburgh, *737 F.2d 283 (3d Cir. 1984),* Diamond v. Charles, *749 F.2d 452 (7th Cir. 1984), and* City of Akron v. Akron Center for Reproductive Health, *462 U.S. 416 (1983). In his memorandum, Alito argued that, in line with the Court's evolving jurisprudence on abortion, state restrictions on abortion were reasonable measures aimed at protecting health and the potentiality of life, and thus were constitutional.*

Memorandum From Samuel Alito, Assistant to the Solicitor General, to Charles Fried, Solicitor General
(May 30, 1985).

Our point is that, even after *Akron*, abortion is not unregulable. There may be an opportunity to nudge the Court toward the principles in Justice O'Connor's *Akron* dissent, to provide greater recognition of the states' interest in protecting the unborn through pregnancy, or to dispel in part the mystical faith in the attending physician that supports *Roe* and the subsequent cases.

I find this approach preferable to a frontal assault on *Roe v. Wade*.[1] It has most of the advantages of a brief devoted to the overruling of *Roe v. Wade*: it makes our position clear, does not even tacitly concede *Roe's* legitimacy, and signals that we regard the question as live and open. At the same time, it is free of many of the disadvantages that would accompany a major effort to overturn *Roe*. When the Court hands down its decision and *Roe* is not overruled, the decision will not be portrayed as a stinging rebuke.

NOTES

1. *A new game plan?* In his memorandum to the Solicitor General, Alito prescribes a course of action that seems aimed at incrementally chipping away at the abortion right through iterative state regulation, rather than a full-scale effort to overrule *Roe*. Has this strategy been implemented? If so, how have abortion regulations evolved to limit, without obviously challenging the constitutionality of, the abortion right?

2. *Abortion and party politics.* Prior to the late twentieth century, Republicans historically were more liberal on reproductive issues, as the Democratic Party was associated with urban Catholic constituencies. It is not until 1980, seven years after *Roe v. Wade* that opposition to abortion became a Republican issue and support for it a Democratic issue. Political scientists describe this as "issue evolution"—the process by which controversial issues lead to party realignment. *See generally* Greg Adams, *Abortion: Evidence of an Issue Evolution*, 41 AM. J. POL. SCI. 718 (1997).

* * *

In keeping with the Alito memo's guidance, abortion opponents shifted their efforts from court challenges that sought to overrule Roe *to state-level legislation to limit abortion rights. Critically, a series of Supreme Court decisions—some of them cited in the Alito memo as laying a foundation for appropriate state-level regulation of abortion—has facilitated the shift toward state legislatures as a vehicle for restricting abortion rights. As the following cases make clear, even as post-*Roe *decisions have preserved the right to abortion, they have also provided the states with a broader platform to limit, contain, or reduce abortion through "reasonable" legislation.*

---

[1] The case against *Roe v. Wade* has been fully and publicly made. *See, e.g.*, A. Bickel, *The Morality of Consent*, 27–29 (1975); A. COX, THE ROLE OF THE SUPREME COURT IN AMERICA Government 112–114 (1976); Epstein, *Substantive Due Process by Any Other Name*, 1973 SUP. CT. REV. 167–185; Ely, *The Wages of Crying Wolf: A Comment on Roe v. Wade*, 82 YALE L.J. 920 (1973). In *Akron*, the Court's response was stare decisis and the "rule of law."

Bellotti v. Baird
443 U.S. 622 (1979).

■ POWELL, J. announced the judgment of the Court and delivered an opinion, in which THE CHIEF JUSTICE, STEWART, J., and REHNQUIST, J., joined.

These appeals present a challenge to the constitutionality of a state statute regulating the access of minors to abortions. . . .

On August 2, 1974, the Legislature of the Commonwealth of Massachusetts passed, over the Governor's veto, an Act pertaining to abortions performed within the State . . . Shortly before the Act was to go into effect, the class action from which these appeals arise was commenced in the District Court to enjoin, as unconstitutional, the provision of the Act now codified as Mass. Gen. Laws Ann., ch. 112, § 12S

Section 12S provides in part:

> If the mother is less than eighteen years of age and has not married, the consent of both the mother and her parents [to an abortion to be performed on the mother] is required. If one or both of the mother's parents refuse such consent, consent may be obtained by order of a judge of the superior court for good cause shown, after such hearing as he deems necessary. Such a hearing will not require the appointment of a guardian for the mother. If one of the parents has died or has deserted his or her family, consent by the remaining parent is sufficient. If both parents have died or have deserted their family, consent of the mother's guardian or other person having duties similar to a guardian, or any person who had assumed the care and custody of the mother is sufficient. The commissioner of public health shall prescribe a written form for such consent. Such form shall be signed by the proper person or persons and given to the physician performing the abortion who shall maintain it in his permanent files.

Physicians performing abortions in the absence of the consent required by § 12S are subject to injunctions and criminal penalties.

. . . .

Appellants sought review in this Court, and we noted probable jurisdiction. After briefing and oral argument, it became apparent that § 12S was susceptible of a construction that "would avoid or substantially modify the federal constitutional challenge to the statute." We therefore vacated the judgment of the District Court, concluding that it should have abstained and certified to the Supreme Judicial Court of Massachusetts appropriate questions concerning the meaning of § 12S, pursuant to existing procedure in that State.

On remand, the District Court certified nine questions to the Supreme Judicial Court.[9] These were answered in an opinion styled *Baird v. Attorney General*, 360 N.E.2d 288 (Mass. 1977) (*Attorney General*). Among the more important aspects of § 12S, as authoritatively construed by the Supreme Judicial Court, are the following:

1. In deciding whether to grant consent to their daughter's abortion, parents are required by § 12S to consider exclusively what will serve her best interests.

2. The provision in § 12S that judicial consent for an abortion shall be granted, parental objections notwithstanding, "for good cause shown" means that such consent shall be granted if found to be in the minor's best interests. The judge "must disregard all parental objections, and other considerations, which are not based exclusively" on that standard.

3. Even if the judge in a § 12S proceeding finds "that the minor is capable of making, and has made, an informed and reasonable decision to have an abortion," he is entitled to withhold consent "in circumstances where he determines that the best interests of the minor will not be served by an abortion."

4. As a general rule, a minor who desires an abortion may not obtain judicial consent without first seeking both parents' consent. Exceptions to the rule exist when a parent is not available or when the need for the abortion constitutes " 'an emergency requiring immediate

---

[9] The nine questions certified by the District Court, with footnotes omitted, are as follows:

1. What standards, if any, does the statute establish for a parent to apply when considering whether or not to grant consent?

a) Is the parent to consider "exclusively . . . what will serve the child's best interest"?

b) If the parent is not limited to considering exclusively the minor's best interests, can the parent take into consideration the "long-term consequences to the family and her parents' marriage relationship"?

c) Other?

2. What standard or standards is the superior court to apply?

a) Is the superior court to disregard all parental objections that are not based exclusively on what would serve the minor's best interests?

b) If the superior court finds that the minor is capable, and has, in fact, made and adhered to, an informed and reasonable decision to have an abortion, may the court refuse its consent based on a finding that a parent's, or its own, contrary decision is a better one?

c) Other?

3. Does the Massachusetts law permit a minor (a) "capable of giving informed consent," or (b) "incapable of giving informed consent," "to obtain [a court] order without parental consultation"?

4. If the court answers any of question 3 in the affirmative, may the superior court, for good cause shown, enter an order authorizing an abortion, (a), without prior notification to the parents, and (b), without subsequent notification?

5. Will the Supreme Judicial Court prescribe a set of procedures to implement c. 112, [§ 12S] which will expedite the application, hearing, and decision phases of the superior court proceeding provided thereunder? Appeal?

6. To what degree do the standards and procedures set forth in c. 112, § 12F (Stat.1975, c. 564), authorizing minors to give consent to medical and dental care in specified circumstances, parallel the grounds and procedures for showing good cause under c. 112, [§ 12S]? . . .

action.' " Unless a parent is not available, he must be notified of any judicial proceedings brought under § 12S.

5.   The resolution of § 12S cases and any appeals that follow can be expected to be prompt. The name of the minor and her parents may be held in confidence. If need be, the Supreme Judicial Court and the superior courts can promulgate rules or issue orders to ensure that such proceedings are handled expeditiously.

6.   Massachusetts Gen. Laws Ann., ch. 112, § 12F, which provides, *inter alia*, that certain classes of minors may consent to most kinds of medical care without parental approval, does not apply to abortions, except as to minors who are married, widowed, or divorced. Nor does the State's common-law "mature minor rule" create an exception to § 12S.

. . . .

Following the judgment of the Supreme Judicial Court, appellees returned to the District Court and obtained a stay of the enforcement of § 12S until its constitutionality could be determined. After permitting discovery by both sides, holding a pretrial conference, and conducting further hearings, the District Court again declared § 12S unconstitutional and enjoined its enforcement. The court identified three particular aspects of the statute which, in its view, rendered it unconstitutional.

First, as construed by the Supreme Judicial Court, § 12S requires parental notice in virtually every case where the parent is available. The court believed that the evidence warranted a finding "that many, perhaps a large majority of 17-year olds are capable of informed consent, as are a not insubstantial number of 16-year olds, and some even younger." In addition, the court concluded that it would not be in the best interests of some "immature" minors—those incapable of giving informed consent— even to inform their parents of their intended abortions. . . . [I]t concluded that Massachusetts could not constitutionally insist that parental permission be sought or notice given "in those cases where a court, if given free rein, would find that it was to the minor's best interests that one or both of her parents not be informed. . . ."

Second, the District Court held that § 12S was defective in permitting a judge to veto the abortion decision of a minor found to be capable of giving informed consent. The court reasoned that upon a finding of maturity and informed consent, the State no longer was entitled to impose legal restrictions upon this decision. Given such a finding, the court could see "no reasonable basis" for distinguishing between a minor and an adult, and it therefore concluded that § 12S was not only "an undue burden in the due process sense, [but] a discriminatory denial of equal protection [as well]."

Finally, the court decided that § 12S suffered from what it termed "formal overbreadth" because the statute failed explicitly to inform parents that they must consider only the minor's best interests in deciding whether to grant consent. The court believed that, despite the Supreme Judicial Court's construction of § 12S, parents naturally would infer from the statute that they were entitled to withhold consent for other, impermissible reasons. This was thought to create a "chilling effect" by enhancing the possibility that parental consent would be denied wrongfully and that the minor would have to proceed in court.

Having identified these flaws in § 12S, the District Court considered whether it should engage in "judicial repair." It declined either to sever the statute or to give it a construction different from that set out by the Supreme Judicial Court, as that tribunal arguably had invited it to do. The District Court therefore adhered to its previous position, declaring § 12S unconstitutional and permanently enjoining its enforcement. . . .

A child, merely on account of his minority, is not beyond the protection of the Constitution. "[W]hatever may be their precise impact, neither the Fourteenth Amendment nor the Bill of Rights is for adults alone."[12] This observation, of course, is but the beginning of the analysis. The Court long has recognized that the status of minors under the law is unique in many respects. As Mr. Justice Frankfurter aptly put it: "[C]hildren have a very special place in life which law should reflect. Legal theories and their phrasing in other cases readily lead to fallacious reasoning if uncritically transferred to determination of a State's duty towards children." The unique role in our society of the family, the institution by which "we inculcate and pass down many of our most cherished values, moral and cultural," requires that constitutional principles be applied with sensitivity and flexibility to the special needs of parents and children. We have recognized three reasons justifying the conclusion that the constitutional rights of children cannot be equated with those of adults: the peculiar vulnerability of children; their inability to make critical decisions in an informed, mature manner; and the importance of the parental role in child rearing.

A

The Court's concern for the vulnerability of children is demonstrated in its decisions dealing with minors' claims to constitutional protection against deprivations of liberty or property interests by the State. With respect to many of these claims, we have concluded that the child's right is virtually coextensive with that of an adult. For example, the Court has held that the Fourteenth Amendment's guarantee against the deprivation of liberty without due process of law is applicable to children in juvenile delinquency proceedings. *In re Gault*, 387 U.S. 1 (1967). In particular, minors involved in such proceedings are entitled to adequate notice, the assistance of counsel, and the opportunity to confront their

---

[12] Similarly, the Court said in *Planned Parenthood of Central Missouri v. Danforth*, 428 U.S. 52, 74 (1976):

"Constitutional rights do not mature and come into being magically only when one attains the state-defined age of majority. Minors, as well as adults, are protected by the Constitution and possess constitutional rights."

accusers. They can be found guilty only upon proof beyond a reasonable doubt, and they may assert the privilege against compulsory self-incrimination. . . .

. . . Viewed together, our cases show that although children generally are protected by the same constitutional guarantees against governmental deprivations as are adults, the State is entitled to adjust its legal system to account for children's vulnerability and their needs for "concern, . . . sympathy, and . . . paternal attention."

. . . .

Second, the Court has held that the States validly may limit the freedom of children to choose for themselves in the making of important, affirmative choices with potentially serious consequences. These rulings have been grounded in the recognition that, during the formative years of childhood and adolescence, minors often lack the experience, perspective, and judgment to recognize and avoid choices that could be detrimental to them.

Ginsberg v. New York, 390 U.S. 629 (1968), illustrates well the Court's concern over the inability of children to make mature choices, as the First Amendment rights involved are clear examples of constitutionally protected freedoms of choice. At issue was a criminal conviction for selling sexually oriented magazines to a minor under the age of 17 in violation of a New York state law. It was conceded that the conviction could not have stood under the First Amendment if based upon a sale of the same material to an adult. Notwithstanding the importance the Court always has attached to First Amendment rights, it concluded that "even where there is an invasion of protected freedoms 'the power of the state to control the conduct of children reaches beyond the scope of its authority over adults . . . .'" The Court was convinced that the New York Legislature rationally could conclude that the sale to children of the magazines in question presented a danger against which they should be guarded. It therefore rejected the argument that the New York law violated the constitutional rights of minors.

. . . .

Third, the guiding role of parents in the upbringing of their children justifies limitations on the freedoms of minors. The State commonly protects its youth from adverse governmental action and from their own immaturity by requiring parental consent to or involvement in important decisions by minors. But an additional and more important justification for state deference to parental control over children is that "[t]he child is not the mere creature of the state; those who nurture him and direct his destiny have the right, coupled with the high duty, to recognize and prepare him for additional obligations." "The duty to prepare the child for 'additional obligations' . . . must be read to include the inculcation of moral standards, religious beliefs, and elements of good citizenship." This affirmative process of teaching, guiding, and inspiring by precept and example is essential to the growth of young people into mature, socially responsible citizens.

We have believed in this country that this process, in large part, is beyond the competence of impersonal political institutions. Indeed, affirmative sponsorship of particular ethical, religious, or political beliefs is something we expect the State *not* to attempt in a society constitutionally committed to the ideal of individual liberty and freedom of choice. . . .

Unquestionably, there are many competing theories about the most effective way for parents to fulfill their central role in assisting their children on the way to responsible adulthood. While we do not pretend any special wisdom on this subject, we cannot ignore that central to many of these theories, and deeply rooted in our Nation's history and tradition, is the belief that the parental role implies a substantial measure of authority over one's children. . . .

Properly understood, then, the tradition of parental authority is not inconsistent with our tradition of individual liberty; rather, the former is one of the basic presuppositions of the latter. Legal restrictions on minors, especially those supportive of the parental role, may be important to the child's chances for the full growth and maturity that make eventual participation in a free society meaningful and rewarding. Under the Constitution, the State can "properly conclude that parents and others, teachers for example, who have [the] primary responsibility for children's well-being are entitled to the support of laws designed to aid discharge of that responsibility."

With these principles in mind, we consider the specific constitutional questions presented by these appeals. In § 12S, Massachusetts has attempted to reconcile the constitutional right of a woman, in consultation with her physician, to choose to terminate her pregnancy . . . with the special interest of the State in encouraging an unmarried pregnant minor to seek the advice of her parents in making the important decision whether or not to bear a child. . . . The question before us . . . is whether § 12S, as authoritatively interpreted by the Supreme Judicial Court, provides for parental notice and consent in a manner that does not unduly burden the right to seek an abortion.

Appellees and intervenors contend that even as interpreted by the Supreme Judicial Court of Massachusetts, § 12S does unduly burden this right. They suggest, for example, that the mere requirement of parental notice constitutes such a burden. . . . As Mr. Justice STEWART wrote in concurrence in *Planned Parenthood of Central Missouri v. Danforth*, 428 U.S. 52 (1976):

> There can be little doubt that the State furthers a constitutionally permissible end by encouraging an unmarried pregnant minor to seek the help and advice of her parents in making the very important decision whether or not to bear a

child. That is a grave decision, and a girl of tender years, under emotional stress, may be ill-equipped to make it without mature advice and emotional support. It seems unlikely that she will obtain adequate counsel and support from the attending physician at an abortion clinic, where abortions for pregnant minors frequently take place. (Footnote omitted.)[21]

. . . The abortion decision differs in important ways from other decisions that may be made during minority. The need to preserve the constitutional right and the unique nature of the abortion decision, especially when made by a minor, require a State to act with particular sensitivity when it legislates to foster parental involvement in this matter.

. . . .

The pregnant minor's options are much different from those facing a minor in other situations, such as deciding whether to marry. A minor not permitted to marry before the age of majority is required simply to postpone her decision. She and her intended spouse may preserve the opportunity for later marriage should they continue to desire it. A pregnant adolescent, however, cannot preserve for long the possibility of aborting, which effectively expires in a matter of weeks from the onset of pregnancy.

Moreover, the potentially severe detriment facing a pregnant woman is not mitigated by her minority. Indeed, considering her probable education, employment skills, financial resources, and emotional maturity, unwanted motherhood may be exceptionally burdensome for a minor. In addition, the fact of having a child brings with it adult legal responsibility, for parenthood, like attainment of the age of majority, is one of the traditional criteria for the termination of the legal disabilities of minority. In sum, there are few situations in which denying a minor the right to make an important decision will have consequences so grave and indelible.

Yet, an abortion may not be the best choice for the minor. The circumstances in which this issue arises will vary widely. In a given case, alternatives to abortion, such as marriage to the father of the child, arranging for its adoption, or assuming the responsibilities of motherhood with the assured support of family, may be feasible and relevant to the minor's best interests. Nonetheless, the abortion decision

---

[21] . . . In *Roe v. Wade* . . . we emphasized the importance of the role of the attending physician. Those cases involved adult women presumably capable of selecting and obtaining a competent physician. In this case, however, we are concerned only with minors who, according to the record, may range in age from children of 12 years to 17-year-old teenagers. Even the latter are less likely than adults to know or be able to recognize ethical, qualified physicians, or to have the means to engage such professionals. Many minors who bypass their parents probably will resort to an abortion clinic, without being able to distinguish the competent and ethical from those that are incompetent or unethical.

is one that simply cannot be postponed, or it will be made by default with far-reaching consequences.

For these reasons . . . "the State may not impose a blanket provision . . . requiring the consent of a parent or person *in loco parentis* as a condition for abortion of an unmarried minor during the first 12 weeks of her pregnancy." Although . . . such deference to parents may be permissible with respect to other choices facing a minor, the unique nature and consequences of the abortion decision make it inappropriate "to give a third party an absolute, and possibly arbitrary, veto over the decision of the physician and his patient to terminate the patient's pregnancy, regardless of the reason for withholding the consent." We therefore conclude that if the State decides to require a pregnant minor to obtain one or both parents' consent to an abortion, it also must provide an alternative procedure whereby authorization for the abortion can be obtained.

A pregnant minor is entitled in such a proceeding to show either: (1) that she is mature enough and well enough informed to make her abortion decision, in consultation with her physician, independently of her parents' wishes;[23] or [(]2) that even if she is not able to make this decision independently, the desired abortion would be in her best interests. The proceeding in which this showing is made must assure that a resolution of the issue, and any appeals that may follow, will be completed with anonymity and sufficient expedition to provide an effective opportunity for an abortion to be obtained. In sum, the procedure must ensure that the provision requiring parental consent does not in fact amount to the "absolute, and possibly arbitrary, veto." . . .

It is against these requirements that § 12S must be tested. We observe initially that as authoritatively construed by the highest court of the State, the statute satisfies some of the concerns that require special treatment of a minor's abortion decision. It provides that if parental consent is refused, authorization may be "obtained by order of a judge of the superior court for good cause shown, after such hearing as he deems necessary." A superior court judge presiding over a § 12S proceeding "must disregard all parental objections, and other considerations, which are not based exclusively on what would serve the minor's best interests." The Supreme Judicial Court also stated: "Prompt resolution of a [§ 12S] proceeding may be expected. . . . The proceeding need not be brought in the minor's name and steps may be taken, by impoundment or otherwise,

---

[23] The nature of both the State's interest in fostering parental authority and the problem of determining "maturity" makes clear why the State generally may resort to objective, though inevitably arbitrary, criteria such as age limits, marital status, or membership in the Armed Forces for lifting some or all of the legal disabilities of minority. Not only is it difficult to define, let alone determine, maturity, but also the fact that a minor may be very much an adult in some respects does not mean that his or her need and opportunity for growth under parental guidance and discipline have ended. As discussed in the text, however, the peculiar nature of the abortion decision requires the opportunity for case-by-case evaluations of the maturity of pregnant minors.

to preserve confidentiality as to the minor and her parents.... [W]e believe that an early hearing and decision on appeal from a judgment of a Superior Court judge may also be achieved." ...

Despite these safeguards ... § 12S falls short of constitutional standards in certain respects. We now consider these.

Among the questions certified to the Supreme Judicial Court was whether § 12S permits any minors—mature or immature—to obtain judicial consent to an abortion without any parental consultation whatsoever. The state court answered that, in general, it does not. "[T]he consent required by [§ 12S must] be obtained for every nonemergency abortion where the mother is less than eighteen years of age and unmarried." The text of § 12S itself states an exception to this rule, making consent unnecessary from any parent who has "died or has deserted his or her family." The Supreme Judicial Court construed the statute as containing an additional exception: Consent need not be obtained "where no parent (or statutory substitute) is available." The court also ruled that an available parent must be given notice of any judicial proceedings brought by a minor to obtain consent for an abortion.

We think that, construed in this manner, § 12S would impose an undue burden upon the exercise by minors of the right to seek an abortion. As the District Court recognized, "there are parents who would obstruct, and perhaps altogether prevent, the minor's right to go to court." ... [M]any parents hold strong views on the subject of abortion, and young pregnant minors, especially those living at home, are particularly vulnerable to their parents' efforts to obstruct both an abortion and their access to court. It would be unrealistic, therefore, to assume that the mere existence of a legal right to seek relief in superior court provides an effective avenue of relief for some of those who need it the most.

We conclude, therefore, that under state regulation such as that undertaken by Massachusetts, every minor must have the opportunity—if she so desires—to go directly to a court without first consulting or notifying her parents. If she satisfies the court that she is mature and well enough informed to make intelligently the abortion decision on her own, the court must authorize her to act without parental consultation or consent. If she fails to satisfy the court that she is competent to make this decision independently, she must be permitted to show that an abortion nevertheless would be in her best interests. If the court is persuaded that it is, the court must authorize the abortion. If, however, the court is not persuaded by the minor that she is mature or that the abortion would be in her best interests, it may decline to sanction the operation.

There is, however, an important state interest in encouraging a family rather than a judicial resolution of a minor's abortion decision. Also, as we have observed above, parents naturally take an interest in the welfare of their children—an interest that is particularly strong where a normal family relationship exists and where the child is living with one or both parents. These factors properly may be taken into account by a court called upon to determine whether an abortion in fact is in a minor's best interests. If, all things considered, the court determines that an abortion is in the minor's best interests, she is entitled to court authorization without any parental involvement. On the other hand, the court may deny the abortion request of an immature minor in the absence of parental consultation if it concludes that her best interests would be served thereby, or the court may in such a case defer decision until there is parental consultation in which the court may participate. But this is the full extent to which parental involvement may be required.[28] For the reasons stated above, the constitutional right to seek an abortion may not be unduly burdened by state-imposed conditions upon initial access to court.

Section 12S requires that both parents consent to a minor's abortion. The District Court found it to be "custom" to perform other medical and surgical procedures on minors with the consent of only one parent, and it concluded that "nothing about abortions . . . requires the minor's interest to be treated differently."

We are not persuaded that, as a general rule, the requirement of obtaining both parents' consent unconstitutionally burdens a minor's right to seek an abortion. The abortion decision has implications far broader than those associated with most other kinds of medical treatment. At least when the parents are together and the pregnant minor is living at home, both the father and mother have an interest— one normally supportive—in helping to determine the course that is in the best interests of a daughter. Consent and involvement by parents in important decisions by minors long have been recognized as protective of their immaturity. In the case of the abortion decision, for reasons we have stated, the focus of the parents' inquiry should be the best interests of their daughter. As every pregnant minor is entitled in the first instance to go directly to the court for a judicial determination without prior parental notice, consultation, or consent, the general rule with respect to parental consent does not unduly burden the constitutional right. Moreover, where the pregnant minor goes to her parents and consent is denied, she still must have recourse to a prompt judicial determination of her maturity or best interests.[29]

Another of the questions certified by the District Court to the Supreme Judicial Court was the following: "If the superior court finds that the minor is capable [of making], and has, in fact, made and adhered to, an informed and reasonable decision to have an abortion, may the

---

[28] Of course, if the minor consults with her parents voluntarily and they withhold consent, she is free to seek judicial authorization for the abortion immediately.

[29] There will be cases where the pregnant minor has received approval of the abortion decision by one parent. In that event, the parent can support the daughter's request for a prompt judicial determination, and the parent's support should be given great, if not dispositive, weight.

court refuse its consent based on a finding that a parent's, or its own, contrary decision is a better one?" To this the state court answered:

> [W]e do not view the judge's role as limited to a determination that the minor is capable of making, and has made, an informed and reasonable decision to have an abortion. Certainly the judge must make a determination of those circumstances, but, if the statutory role of the judge to determine the best interests of the minor is to be carried out, he must make a finding on the basis of all relevant views presented to him. We suspect that the judge will give great weight to the minor's determination, if informed and reasonable, but in circumstances where he determines that the best interests of the minor will not be served by an abortion, the judge's determination should prevail, assuming that his conclusion is supported by the evidence and adequate findings of fact.

The Supreme Judicial Court's statement reflects the general rule that a State may require a minor to wait until the age of majority before being permitted to exercise legal rights independently. But we are concerned here with the exercise of a constitutional right of unique character. As stated above, if the minor satisfies a court that she has attained sufficient maturity to make a fully informed decision, she then is entitled to make her abortion decision independently. We therefore agree with the District Court that § 12S cannot constitutionally permit judicial disregard of the abortion decision of a minor who has been determined to be mature and fully competent to assess the implications of the choice she has made.

. . . .

Although it satisfies constitutional standards in large part, § 12S falls short of them in two respects: First, it permits judicial authorization for an abortion to be withheld from a minor who is found by the superior court to be mature and fully competent to make this decision independently. Second, it requires parental consultation or notification in every instance, without affording the pregnant minor an opportunity to receive an independent judicial determination that she is mature enough to consent or that an abortion would be in her best interests. Accordingly, we affirm the judgment of the District Court insofar as it invalidates this statute and enjoins its enforcement.

Affirmed.

. . . .

■ STEVENS, J., with whom BRENNAN, J., MARSHALL, J., and BLACKMUN, J. join, concurring in the judgment.

In *Roe v. Wade* the Court held that a woman's right to decide whether to terminate a pregnancy is entitled to constitutional protection. In *Planned Parenthood of Central Missouri v. Danforth*, 428 U.S. 52 (1976), the Court held that a pregnant minor's right to make the abortion decision may not be conditioned on the consent of one parent. I am persuaded that these decisions require affirmance of the District Court's holding that the Massachusetts statute is unconstitutional.

The Massachusetts statute is, on its face, simple and straightforward. It provides that every woman under 18 who has not married must secure the consent of both her parents before receiving an abortion. "If one or both of the mother's parents refuse such consent, consent may be obtained by order of a judge of the Superior Court for good cause shown."

Whatever confusion or uncertainty might have existed as to how this statute was to operate, has been eliminated by the authoritative construction of its provisions by the Massachusetts Supreme Judicial Court. The statute was construed to require that every minor who wishes an abortion must first seek the consent of both parents, unless a parent is not available or unless the need for the abortion constitutes " 'an emergency requiring immediate action.' " Both parents, so long as they are available, must also receive notice of judicial proceedings brought under the statute by the minor. In those proceedings, the task of the judge is to determine whether the best interests of the minor will be served by an abortion. The decision is his to make, even if he finds "that the minor is capable of making, and has made, an informed and reasonable decision to have an abortion." Thus, no minor in Massachusetts, no matter how mature and capable of informed decisionmaking, may receive an abortion without the consent of either both her parents or a superior court judge. In every instance, the minor's decision to secure an abortion is subject to an absolute third-party veto.

In *Planned Parenthood of Central Missouri v. Danforth*, this Court invalidated statutory provisions requiring the consent of the husband of a married woman and of one parent of a pregnant minor to an abortion. As to the spousal consent, the Court concluded that "we cannot hold that the State has the constitutional authority to give the spouse unilaterally the ability to prohibit the wife from terminating her pregnancy, when the State itself lacks that right." as to the parental consent, the Court held that "[j]ust as with the requirement of consent from the spouse, so here, the State does not have the constitutional authority to give a third party an absolute, and possibly arbitrary, veto over the decision of the physician and his patient to terminate the patient's pregnancy, regardless of the reason for withholding the consent." These holdings, I think, equally apply to the Massachusetts statute. The differences between the two statutes are few. Unlike the Missouri statute, Massachusetts requires the consent of both of the woman's parents. It does, of course, provide an alternative in the form of a suit initiated by the woman in superior court. But in that proceeding, the judge is afforded an absolute veto over the minor's decisions, based on his judgment of her best interests. In Massachusetts, then, as in Missouri, the State has imposed an "absolute limitation on the minor's right to obtain an abortion," applicable to every pregnant minor in the State who has not married.

The provision of an absolute veto to a judge—or, potentially, to an appointed administrator—is to me particularly troubling.... It is inherent in the right to make the abortion decision that the right may be exercised without public scrutiny and in defiance of the contrary opinion of the sovereign or other third parties. In Massachusetts, however, every minor who cannot secure the consent of both her parents—which under *Danforth* cannot be an absolute prerequisite to an abortion—is required to secure the consent of the sovereign. As a practical matter, I would suppose that the need to commence judicial proceedings in order to obtain a legal abortion would impose a burden at least as great as, and probably greater than, that imposed on the minor child by the need to obtain the consent of a parent. Moreover, once this burden is met, the only standard provided for the judge's decision is the best interest of the minor. That standard provides little real guidance to the judge, and his decision must necessarily reflect personal and societal values and mores whose enforcement upon the minor—particularly when contrary to her own informed and reasonable decision—is fundamentally at odds with privacy interests underlying the constitutional protection afforded to her decision.

In short, it seems to me that this litigation is governed by *Danforth*; to the extent this statute differs from that in *Danforth*, it is potentially even more restrictive of the constitutional right to decide whether or not to terminate a pregnancy. Because the statute has been once authoritatively construed by the Massachusetts Supreme Judicial Court, and because it is clear that the statute as written and construed is not constitutional, I agree with Mr. Justice Powell that the District Court's judgment should be affirmed. Because his opinion goes further, however, and addresses the constitutionality of an abortion statute that Massachusetts has not enacted, I decline to join his opinion.

■ WHITE, J., dissenting.

I was in dissent in *Planned Parenthood of Central Missouri v. Danforth*, 428 U.S. 52, 94–95 (1976), on the issue of the validity of requiring the consent of a parent when an unmarried woman under 18 years of age seeks an abortion. I continue to have the views I expressed there.... I would not, therefore, strike down this Massachusetts law.

But even if a parental consent requirement of the kind involved in *Danforth* must be deemed invalid, that does not condemn the Massachusetts law, which, when the parents object, authorizes a judge to permit an abortion if he concludes that an abortion is in the best interests of the child. Going beyond *Danforth*, the Court now holds it unconstitutional for a State to require that in all cases parents receive notice that their daughter seeks an abortion and, if they object to the abortion, an opportunity to participate in a hearing that will determine whether it is in the "best interests" of the child to undergo the surgery.

Until now, I would have thought inconceivable a holding that the United States Constitution forbids even notice to parents when their minor child who seeks surgery objects to such notice and is able to convince a judge that the parents should be denied participation in the decision.

With all due respect, I dissent.

NOTES

1.   *Teen sexuality and parental consent.* For further discussion of the tensions between minors' reproductive and sexual rights and parental autonomy, see discussion of sex education *supra* p. 552.

2.   *Teen pregnancy at the border.* In September 2017, Jane Doe, an undocumented teenager, came to the United States without her parents and was detained and placed into care of the Office of Refugee Resettlement (ORR) at a Texas detention center. Doe, who was then eight weeks pregnant, decided to terminate her pregnancy. Because Texas requires minors seeking an abortion to either secure parental consent or a judicial waiver, Doe, with the assistance of counsel and an appointed guardian, petitioned a Texas court for a judicial waiver. On September 25, 2017, a Texas judge granted Doe's petition, however, ORR refused to allow Doe to leave the detention center to obtain an abortion. ORR officials were acting pursuant to guidance from ORR Director Scott Lloyd, which, in March 2017, forbid federally funded shelters from taking "any action that facilitates" an abortion without his express approval. Doe's guardian ad litem, Rochelle Garza, then sued the Acting United States Secretary of Health and Human Services in the United States District Court for the District of Columbia, on the ground that the government's position violated Doe's constitutional right to obtain an abortion.

On October 18, 2017, a federal district court granted Doe's request for a temporary restraining order, ordering the government to allow Doe to leave the shelter to attend the pre-abortion counseling required by Texas law and to undergo the abortion. *Garza v. Hargan*, 2017 WL 4707287 (D.D.C. Oct. 18, 2017). Two days later, a panel of the United States Court of Appeals for the District of Columbia Circuit granted the government's emergency motion to stay the district court's order. In an unsigned order by Circuit Judges Brett Kavanaugh and Karen LeCraft Henderson, the court allowed ORR to prevent Doe from leaving its shelter to undergo an abortion until October 31, provided that the government sought to "expeditiously" place Doe in the custody of a sponsor. *Garza v. Hargan*, 2017 WL 4707112 (D.C. Cir. Oct. 19, 2017). One member of the panel, Judge Patricia Millett, dissented on the ground that the majority was imposing an undue burden on abortion in violation of *Whole Woman's Health v. Hellerstedt* (2016), the Supreme Court's most recent abortion decision. *Garza v. Hargan*, 2017 WL 9854555 (D.C. Cir. Oct. 20, 2017) (Millett, *J.*, dissenting).

On October 24, 2017, the D.C. Circuit, sitting *en banc*, reversed the panel's decision, reinstating the district court order requiring the government to grant Jane access to an abortion. *Garza v. Hargan*, 874 F.3d 735 (D.C. Cir. 2017). Judge Kavanaugh, joined by Judges Henderson and

Thomas B. Griffith, dissented, defending the panel decision. 874 F.3d at 752 (Kavanaugh, *J.*, dissenting). That day, the district court amended its order to allow Doe's abortion to proceed "promptly and without delay." A year later, the case was again in the spotlight in conjunction with Judge Kavanaugh's nomination to replace Justice Anthony Kennedy on the U.S. Supreme Court.

Harris v. McRae
448 U.S. 297 (1980).

■ STEWART, J.

This case presents statutory and constitutional questions concerning the public funding of abortions under Title XIX of the Social Security Act, commonly known as the "Medicaid" Act, and recent annual Appropriations Acts containing the so-called "Hyde Amendment." The statutory question is whether Title XIX requires a State that participates in the Medicaid program to fund the cost of medically necessary abortions for which federal reimbursement is unavailable under the Hyde Amendment. The constitutional question, which arises only if Title XIX imposes no such requirement, is whether the Hyde Amendment, by denying public funding for certain medically necessary abortions, contravenes the liberty or equal protection guarantees of the Due Process Clause of the Fifth Amendment. . . .

. . . .

Since September 1976, Congress has prohibited . . . the use of any federal funds to reimburse the cost of abortions under the Medicaid program except under certain specified circumstances. This funding restriction is commonly known as the "Hyde Amendment". . . . The current version of the Hyde Amendment . . . provides:

> [N]one of the funds provided by this joint resolution shall be used to perform abortions except where the life of the mother would be endangered if the fetus were carried to term; or except for such medical procedures necessary for the victims of rape or incest when such rape or incest has been reported promptly to a law enforcement agency or public health service.

. . . The plaintiffs . . . sought to enjoin the enforcement of the funding restriction on abortions. They alleged that the Hyde Amendment violated the First, Fourth, Fifth, and Ninth Amendments of the Constitution insofar as it limited the funding of abortions to those necessary to save the life of the mother, while permitting the funding of costs associated with childbirth. . . .

. . . .

The appellees assert that a participating State has an independent funding obligation under Title XIX because (1) the Hyde Amendment is, by its own terms, only a limitation on federal reimbursement for certain medically necessary abortions, and (2) Title XIX does not permit a participating State to exclude from its Medicaid plan any medically necessary service solely on the basis of diagnosis or condition, even if federal reimbursement is unavailable for that service. It is thus the appellees' view that the effect of the Hyde Amendment is to withhold federal reimbursement for certain medically necessary abortions, but not to relieve a participating State of its duty under Title XIX to provide for such abortions in its Medicaid plan.

The District Court rejected this argument. It concluded that, although Title XIX would otherwise have required a participating State to include medically necessary abortions in its Medicaid program, the Hyde Amendment substantively amended Title XIX so as to relieve a State of that obligation. . . .

We agree with the District Court, but for somewhat different reasons . . . The cornerstone of Medicaid is financial contribution by both the Federal Government and the participating State. Nothing in Title XIX as originally enacted, or in its legislative history, suggests that Congress intended to require a participating State to assume the full costs of providing any health services in its Medicaid plan. . . .

Since the Congress that enacted Title XIX did not intend a participating State to assume a unilateral funding obligation for any health service in an approved Medicaid plan, it follows that Title XIX does not require a participating State to include in its plan any services for which a subsequent Congress has withheld federal funding. . . .

. . . [E]ven if a State were otherwise required to include medically necessary abortions in its Medicaid plan, the withdrawal of federal funding under the Hyde Amendment would operate to relieve the State of that obligation for those abortions for which federal reimbursement is unavailable. . . .

Having determined that Title XIX does not obligate a participating State to pay for those medically necessary abortions for which Congress has withheld federal funding, we must consider the constitutional validity of the Hyde Amendment. The appellees assert that the funding restrictions of the Hyde Amendment violate several rights secured by the Constitution—(1) the right of a woman, implicit in the Due Process Clause of the Fifth Amendment, to decide whether to terminate a pregnancy, (2) the prohibition under the Establishment Clause of the First Amendment against any "law respecting an establishment of religion," and (3) the right to freedom of religion protected by the Free Exercise Clause of the First Amendment. The appellees also contend that, quite apart from substantive constitutional rights, the Hyde Amendment violates the equal protection component of the Fifth Amendment.

. . . .

We address first the appellees' argument that the Hyde Amendment, by restricting the availability of certain medically necessary abortions under Medicaid, impinges on the "liberty" protected by the Due Process Clause as recognized in *Roe v. Wade*, 410 U.S. 113 (1973), and its progeny.

. . . The constitutional underpinning of *Wade* was a recognition that the "liberty" protected by the Due Process Clause of the Fourteenth Amendment includes not only the freedoms explicitly mentioned in the Bill of Rights, but also a freedom of personal choice in certain matters of marriage and family life.[18] This implicit constitutional liberty, the Court in *Wade* held, includes the freedom of a woman to decide whether to terminate a pregnancy.

But the Court in *Wade* also recognized that a State has legitimate interests during a pregnancy in both ensuring the health of the mother and protecting potential human life. These state interests, which were found to be "separate and distinct" and to "gro[w] in substantiality as the woman approaches term," pose a conflict with a woman's untrammeled freedom of choice. In resolving this conflict, the Court held that before the end of the first trimester of pregnancy, neither state interest is sufficiently substantial to justify any intrusion on the woman's freedom of choice. In the second trimester, the state interest in maternal health was found to be sufficiently substantial to justify regulation reasonably related to that concern. And at viability, usually in the third trimester, the state interest in protecting the potential life of the fetus was found to justify a criminal prohibition against abortions, except where necessary for the preservation of the life or health of the mother. Thus, inasmuch as the Texas criminal statute allowed abortions only where necessary to save the life of the mother and without regard to the stage of the pregnancy, the Court held in *Wade* that the statute violated the Due Process Clause of the Fourteenth Amendment.

In *Maher v. Roe*, 432 U.S. 464 (1977), the Court was presented with the question whether the scope of personal constitutional freedom recognized in *Roe v. Wade* included an entitlement to Medicaid payments for abortions that are not medically necessary. . . .

. . . The doctrine of *Roe v. Wade*, the Court held in *Maher*, "protects the woman from unduly burdensome interference with her freedom to decide whether to terminate her pregnancy." . . .

But the constitutional freedom recognized in *Wade* and its progeny, the *Maher* Court explained, did not prevent Connecticut from making "a value judgment favoring childbirth over abortion, and . . . implement[ing] that judgment by the allocation of public funds." . . .

---

[18] The Court in *Wade* observed that previous decisions of this Court had recognized that the liberty protected by the Due Process Clause "has some extension to activities relating to marriage, *Loving v. Virginia*, 388 U.S. 1, 12 (1967); procreation, *Skinner v. Oklahoma*, 316 U.S. 535, 541–542 (1942); contraception, *Eisenstadt v. Baird*, 405 U.S., [438,] at 453–454; *id.*, at 460, 463–465 (White, J., concurring in result); family relationships, *Prince v. Massachusetts*, 321 U.S. 158, 166 (1944); and child rearing and education, *Pierce v. Society of Sisters*, 268 U.S. 510, 535 (1925); *Meyer v. Nebraska* [262 U.S. 390, 399 (1923)]." 410 U.S., at 152–153.

... In explaining why the constitutional principle recognized in *Wade* and later cases—protecting a woman's freedom of choice—did not translate into a constitutional obligation of Connecticut to subsidize abortions, the Court cited the "basic difference between direct state interference with a protected activity and state encouragement of an alternative activity consonant with legislative policy. Constitutional concerns are greatest when the State attempts to impose its will by force of law; the State's power to encourage actions deemed to be in the public interest is necessarily far broader." ...

The Hyde Amendment, like the Connecticut welfare regulation at issue in *Maher*, places no governmental obstacle in the path of a woman who chooses to terminate her pregnancy, but rather, by means of unequal subsidization of abortion and other medical services, encourages alternative activity deemed in the public interest. The present case does differ factually from *Maher* insofar as that case involved a failure to fund nontherapeutic abortions, whereas the Hyde Amendment withholds funding of certain medically necessary abortions ... It is the appellees' view that to the extent that the Hyde Amendment withholds funding for certain medically necessary abortions, it clearly impinges on the constitutional principle recognized in *Wade*.

... [I]t simply does not follow that a woman's freedom of choice carries with it a constitutional entitlement to the financial resources to avail herself of the full range of protected choices. ... [A]lthough government may not place obstacles in the path of a woman's exercise of her freedom of choice, it need not remove those not of its own creation. Indigency falls in the latter category. The financial constraints that restrict an indigent woman's ability to enjoy the full range of constitutionally protected freedom of choice are the product not of governmental restrictions on access to abortions, but rather of her indigency. Although Congress has opted to subsidize medically necessary services generally, but not certain medically necessary abortions, the fact remains that the Hyde Amendment leaves an indigent woman with at least the same range of choice in deciding whether to obtain a medically necessary abortion as she would have had if Congress had chosen to subsidize no health care costs at all. We are thus not persuaded that the Hyde Amendment impinges on the constitutionally protected freedom of choice recognized in *Wade*.

... It cannot be that because government may not prohibit the use of contraceptives, *Griswold v. Connecticut*, 381 U.S. 479 (1965), or prevent parents from sending their child to a private school, *Pierce v. Society of Sisters*, 268 U.S. 510 (1925), government, therefore, has an affirmative constitutional obligation to ensure that all persons have the financial resources to obtain contraceptives or send their children to private schools. To translate the limitation on governmental power implicit in the Due Process Clause into an affirmative funding obligation would require Congress to subsidize the medically necessary abortion of an indigent woman even if Congress had not enacted a Medicaid program to subsidize other medically necessary services. Nothing in the Due Process Clause supports such an extraordinary result. . . .

. . . .

It remains to be determined whether the Hyde Amendment violates the equal protection component of the Fifth Amendment. This challenge is premised on the fact that, although federal reimbursement is available under Medicaid for medically necessary services generally, the Hyde Amendment does not permit federal reimbursement of all medically necessary abortions. . . . [A]ppellees argue here, that this selective subsidization violates the constitutional guarantee of equal protection.

The guarantee of equal protection under the Fifth Amendment is not a source of substantive rights or liberties, but rather a right to be free from invidious discrimination in statutory classifications and other governmental activity. It is well settled that where a statutory classification does not itself impinge on a right or liberty protected by the Constitution, the validity of classification must be sustained unless "the classification rests on grounds wholly irrelevant to the achievement of [any legitimate governmental] objective." This presumption of constitutional validity, however, disappears if a statutory classification is predicated on criteria that are, in a constitutional sense, "suspect," the principal example of which is a classification based on race.

For the reasons stated above, we have already concluded that the Hyde Amendment violates no constitutionally protected substantive rights. We now conclude as well that it is not predicated on a constitutionally suspect classification. In reaching this conclusion, we again draw guidance from the Court's decision in *Maher v. Roe*. . . .

. . . Here, as in *Maher*, the principal impact of the Hyde Amendment falls on the indigent. But that fact does not itself render the funding restriction constitutionally invalid, for this Court has held repeatedly that poverty, standing alone is not a suspect classification. That *Maher* involved the refusal to fund nontherapeutic abortions, whereas the present case involves the refusal to fund medically necessary abortions, has no bearing on the factors that render a classification "suspect" within the meaning of the constitutional guarantee of equal protection.

The remaining question then is whether the Hyde Amendment is rationally related to a legitimate governmental objective. It is the Government's position that the Hyde Amendment bears a rational relationship to its legitimate interest in protecting the potential life of the fetus. We agree.

In *Wade*, the Court recognized that the State has an "important and legitimate interest in protecting the potentiality of human life." That interest was found to exist throughout a pregnancy, "grow[ing] in substantiality as the woman approaches term." . . .

It follows that the Hyde Amendment, by encouraging childbirth except in the most urgent circumstances, is rationally related to the legitimate governmental objective of protecting potential life. By subsidizing the medical expenses of indigent women who carry their pregnancies to term while not subsidizing the comparable expenses of women who undergo abortions (except those whose lives are threatened), Congress has established incentives that make childbirth a more attractive alternative than abortion for persons eligible for Medicaid. These incentives bear a direct relationship to the legitimate congressional interest in protecting potential life. Nor is it irrational that Congress has authorized federal reimbursement for medically necessary services generally, but not for certain medically necessary abortions. Abortion is inherently different from other medical procedures, because no other procedure involves the purposeful termination of a potential life.

. . . .

Where, as here, the Congress has neither invaded a substantive constitutional right or freedom, nor enacted legislation that purposefully operates to the detriment of a suspect class, the only requirement of equal protection is that congressional action be rationally related to a legitimate governmental interest. The Hyde Amendment satisfies that standard. It is not the mission of this Court or any other to decide whether the balance of competing interests reflected in the Hyde Amendment is wise social policy. If that were our mission, not every Justice who has subscribed to the judgment of the Court today could have done so. But we cannot, in the name of the Constitution, overturn duly enacted statutes simply "because they may be unwise, improvident, or out of harmony with a particular school of thought." Rather, "when an issue involves policy choices as sensitive as those implicated [here] . . . the appropriate forum for their resolution in a democracy is the legislature."

For the reasons stated in this opinion, we hold that a State that participates in the Medicaid program is not obligated under Title XIX to continue to fund those medically necessary abortions for which federal reimbursement is unavailable under the Hyde Amendment. We further hold that the funding restrictions of the Hyde Amendment violate . . . the Fifth Amendment. . . .

It is so ordered.

NOTES

1. *The battle over funding.* Medicaid, a 1965 expansion of the Social Security Act, provides federal funds to reimburse states for medical care to the poor. In the aftermath of *Roe*, states used Medicaid funds to pay for abortions. However, as opposition to abortion hardened, states began to place restrictions on the use of Medicaid funds. The issue of federal funding of abortion was litigated in *Beal v. Doe*, 432 U.S. 438 (1977) and *Maher v. Roe*, 432 U.S. 464 (1977). Both *Beal* and *Maher* involved state statutes that

restricted "Medicaid-funded abortions." In both cases, the Court affirmed a constitutional right to an abortion. Nevertheless, the Court upheld both state statutes, concluding that recognizing a constitutionally-protected right of abortion does not require the state to publicly fund or otherwise subsidize abortions.

2.   *McRae's backstory. McRae* represented another iteration of the Medicaid-funding wars. On behalf of Cora McRae and other indigent women otherwise eligible for Medicaid, women's rights advocates filed suit in the Eastern District of New York to enjoin implementation of the Hyde Amendment. *McRae v. Mathews*, 421 F. Supp. 533 (E.D.N.Y. 1976). Rhonda Copelon and Sylvia Law, two pioneering feminist legal scholars and activists, litigated the case. Initially, their efforts were successful. Judge John Dooling granted the injunction, finding that the Hyde Amendment's restrictions violated both the Fifth Amendment's Due Process Clause and the First Amendment's Establishment Clause. In 1977, however, Judge Dooling lifted the injunction, setting the stage for *Harris v. McRae. See* Rhonda Copelon & Sylvia Law, *"Nearly Allied to Her Right to Be"—Medicaid Funding for Abortion: The Story of* Harris v. McRae, *in* ELIZABETH M. SCHNEIDER & STEPHANIE M. WILDMAN, WOMEN AND THE LAW: STORIES 207 (2010).

3.   *Race, gender, and class arguments in* Harris v. McRae. From the start, many recognized that the *McRae* lawsuit implicated issues of race, gender, and class, as the Hyde Amendment would have a disproportionate impact on poor women of color. And yet, in their briefs, Copelon and Law did not foreground these intersecting concerns. Some have suggested that the prioritization of gender over class reflected the narrow concerns of second wave feminism. However, as Professor Khiara Bridges observes, this choice was likely more strategic than neglectful. In the years preceding *McRae*, the Court had issued a number of unfavorable decisions that made it harder for plaintiffs to prevail on constitutional disparate impact claims, claims of discrimination on the basis of socio-economic status, and discrimination on the basis of pregnancy. "[B]y the time the Court heard *McRae* in 1980, the Court's prior precedents had foreclosed avenues that would have made claims rooted in race, class, and gender more obviously cognizable." Further, constitutional developments outside of the courts also shaped the arguments in *McRae*. As Bridges notes, "[t]he politics swirling around the Equal Rights Amendment ("ERA"), and the effort to ratify it, also dissuaded Copelon and her team from arguing that the Hyde Amendment was sex discrimination prohibited by the equal protection clause." Concerned that a link between abortion rights and equal protection would jeopardize support for the ERA, ERA proponents were skeptical of arguments that restrictions on abortion and abortion funding amounted to sex discrimination. Khiara M. Bridges, *Elision and Erasure: Race, Class, and Gender in* Harris v. McRae, *in* REPRODUCTIVE RIGHTS AND JUSTICE STORIES (Murray, Shaw & Siegel, eds. 2019).

4.   *The Hyde Amendment.* Enacted in 1976, the Hyde Amendment is not a stand-alone statute, but a rider that, in various forms, may be attached to annual appropriations bills. Named for its sponsor, Illinois representative Henry Hyde, the 1976 version of the Hyde Amendment placed strict

limitations on Medicaid-funded abortions. Since its initial incarnation in 1976, the Hyde Amendment has been altered several times. The version in force from 1981 until 1993 prohibited the use of federal funds for abortions "except where the life of the mother would be endangered if the fetus were carried to term." A 1993 version of the Amendment expanded the category of abortions for which Medicaid funds may be used to include abortions in cases of rape and incest. *See* 42 U.S.C. § 300a–6 (1993).

Thornburgh v. American College of Obstetricians & Gynecologists

476 U.S. 747 (1986).

■ BLACKMUN, J.

This is an appeal from a judgment of the United States Court of Appeals for the Third Circuit reviewing the District Court's rulings upon a motion for a preliminary injunction. The Court of Appeals held unconstitutional several provisions of Pennsylvania's current Abortion Control Act, 1982 Pa.Laws, Act No. 138, now codified as 18 Pa.Cons.Stat. § 3201 *et seq.* (1982). Among the provisions ruled invalid by the Court of Appeals were portions of § 3205, relating to "informed consent"; § 3208, concerning "printed information"; §§ 3210(b) and (c), having to do with postviability abortions; and § 3211(a) and § 3214(a) and (h), regarding reporting requirements.

I

The Abortion Control Act was approved by the Governor of the Commonwealth on June 11, 1982. By its own terms, however, see § 7 of the Act, it was to become effective only 180 days thereafter, that is, on the following December 8. . . .

. . . .

After the passage of the Act, but before its effective date, the present litigation was instituted in the United States District Court for the Eastern District of Pennsylvania. The plaintiffs, who are the appellees here, were the American College of Obstetricians and Gynecologists, Pennsylvania Section; certain physicians licensed in Pennsylvania; clergymen; an individual who purchases from a Pennsylvania insurer health-care and disability insurance extending to abortions; and Pennsylvania abortion counselors and providers. Alleging that the Act violated the United States Constitution, the plaintiffs, pursuant to 42 U.S.C. § 1983, sought declaratory and injunctive relief. The defendants named in the complaint were the Governor of the Commonwealth, other Commonwealth officials, and the District Attorney for Montgomery County, Pa.

. . . .

IV

This case, as it comes to us, concerns the constitutionality of six provisions of the Pennsylvania Act that the Court of Appeals struck down as facially invalid: § 3205 ("informed consent"); § 3208 ("printed information"); § 3214(a) and (h) (reporting requirements); § 3211(a) (determination of viability); § 3210(b) (degree of care required in postviability abortions); and § 3210(c) (second-physician requirement). We have no reason to address the validity of the other sections of the Act challenged in the District Court.

A

... The States are not free, under the guise of protecting maternal health or potential life, to intimidate women into continuing pregnancies. Appellants claim that the statutory provisions before us today further legitimate compelling interests of the Commonwealth. Close analysis of those provisions, however, shows that they wholly subordinate constitutional privacy interests and concerns with maternal health in an effort to deter a woman from making a decision that, with her physician, is hers to make.

B

We turn to the challenged statutes:

1.   Section 3205 ("informed consent") and § 3208 ("printed information"). Section 3205(a) requires that the woman give her "voluntary and informed consent" to an abortion. Failure to observe the provisions of § 3205 subjects the physician to suspension or revocation of his license, and subjects any other person obligated to provide information relating to informed consent to criminal penalties. ...

... We conclude that, like Akron's ordinance, §§ 3205 and 3208 fail the *Akron* measurement. The two sections prescribe in detail the method for securing "informed consent." Seven explicit kinds of information must be delivered to the woman at least 24 hours before her consent is given, and five of these must be presented by the woman's physician. The five are: (a) the name of the physician who will perform the abortion, (b) the "fact that there may be detrimental physical and psychological effects which are not accurately foreseeable," (c) the "particular medical risks associated with the particular abortion procedure to be employed," (d) the probable gestational age, and (e) the "medical risks associated with carrying her child to term." The remaining two categories are (f) the "fact that medical assistance benefits may be available for prenatal care, childbirth and neonatal care," and (g) the "fact that the father is liable to assist" in the child's support, "even in instances where the father has offered to pay for the abortion." §§ 3205(a)(1) and (2). The woman also must be informed that materials printed and supplied by the Commonwealth that describe the fetus and that list agencies offering alternatives to abortion are available for her review. If she chooses to review the materials but is unable to read, the materials "shall be read to her," and any answer she seeks must be "provided her in her own language." § 3205(a)(2)(iii). She must certify in writing, prior to the abortion, that all this has been done. § 3205(a)(3). The printed materials "shall include the following statement":

> " 'There are many public and private agencies willing and able to help you to carry your child to term, and to assist you and your child after your child is born, whether you choose to keep your child or place her or him for adoption. The Commonwealth of Pennsylvania strongly urges you to contact them before making a final decision about abortion. The law requires that your physician or his agent give you the opportunity to call agencies like these before you undergo an abortion.' " § 3208(a)(1).

The materials must describe the "probable anatomical and physiological characteristics of the unborn child at two-week gestational increments from fertilization to full term, including any relevant information on the possibility of the unborn child's survival." § 3208(a)(2).

. . . .

. . . The printed materials required by §§ 3205 and 3208 seem to us to be nothing less than an outright attempt to wedge the Commonwealth's message discouraging abortion into the privacy of the informed-consent dialogue between the woman and her physician. . . .

. . . .

2. Sections 3214(a) and (h) (reporting) and § 3211(a) (determination of viability). Section 3214(a)(8), part of the general reporting section, incorporates § 3211(a). Section 3211(a) requires the physician to report the basis for his determination "that a child is not viable." It applies only after the first trimester. The report required by § 3214(a) and (h) is detailed and must include, among other things, identification of the performing and referring physicians and of the facility or agency; information as to the woman's political subdivision and State of residence, age, race, marital status, and number of prior pregnancies; the date of her last menstrual period and the probable gestational age; the basis for any judgment that a medical emergency existed; the basis for any determination of nonviability; and the method of payment for the abortion. The report is to be signed by the attending physician. § 3214(b).

Despite the fact that § 3214(e)(2) provides that such reports "shall not be deemed public records," within the meaning of the Commonwealth's "Right-to-Know Law," Pa. Stat. Ann., Tit. 65, § 66.1 *et seq.* (Purdon 1959 and Supp.1985), each report "shall be made available for public inspection and copying within 15 days of receipt in a form which will not lead to the disclosure of the identity of any person filing a report." Similarly, the report of complications, required by § 3214(h), "shall be open to public inspection and copying." A willful failure to file a report required under § 3214 is "unprofessional conduct" and the noncomplying physician's license "shall be subject to suspension or revocation." § 3214(i)(1).

. . . .

A woman and her physician will necessarily be more reluctant to choose an abortion if there exists a possibility that her decision and her identity will become known publicly. Although the statute does not specifically require the reporting of the woman's name, the amount of information about her and the circumstances under which she had an abortion are so detailed that identification is likely. Identification is the obvious purpose of these extreme reporting requirements. . . .

. . . Pennsylvania's reporting requirements raise the specter of public exposure and harassment of women who choose to exercise their personal, intensely private, right, with their physician, to end a pregnancy. Thus, they pose an unacceptable danger of deterring the exercise of that right, and must be invalidated.

3.   Section 3210(b) (degree of care for postviability abortions) and § 3210(c) (second-physician requirement when the fetus is possibly viable). Section 3210(b) sets forth two independent requirements for a postviability abortion. First, it demands the exercise of that degree of care "which such person would be required to exercise in order to preserve the life and health of any unborn child intended to be born and not aborted." Second, "the abortion technique employed shall be that which would provide the best opportunity for the unborn child to be aborted alive unless," in the physician's good-faith judgment, that technique "would present a significantly greater medical risk to the life or health of the pregnant woman." An intentional, knowing, or reckless violation of this standard is a felony of the third degree, and subjects the violator to the possibility of imprisonment for not more than seven years and to a fine of not more than $15,000. See 18 Pa. Cons. Stat. §§ 1101(2) and 1103(3) (1982).

The Court of Appeals ruled that § 3210(b) was unconstitutional because it required a "trade-off" between the woman's health and fetal survival, and failed to require that maternal health be the physician's paramount consideration. 737 F.2d, at 300, citing *Colautti v. Franklin*, 439 U.S. 379, 397–401 (1979) (where Pennsylvania's 1974 Abortion Control Act was reviewed). . . .

. . . We agree with the Court of Appeals and therefore find the statute to be facially invalid.

Section 3210(c) requires that a second physician be present during an abortion performed when viability is possible. The second physician is to "take control of the child and . . . provide immediate medical care for the child, taking all reasonable steps necessary, in his judgment, to preserve the child's life and health." Violation of this requirement is a felony of the third degree.

In *Planned Parenthood Assn. of Kansas City, Mo. v. Ashcroft*, 462 U.S. 476 (1983), the Court, by a 5–4 vote, but not by a controlling single opinion, ruled that a Missouri statute requiring the presence of a second physician during an abortion performed after viability was constitutional. Justice POWELL, joined by THE CHIEF JUSTICE, concluded that the State had a compelling interest in protecting the life of a viable fetus and that the second physician's presence provided assurance that the State's interest was protected more fully than with only one physician in attendance. *Id.*, at 482–486. Justice POWELL recognized that, to pass constitutional muster, the statute must contain an exception for the situation where the health of the mother was endangered by delay in the arrival of the second physician. Recognizing that there was "no clearly expressed exception" on the face of the Missouri statute for the emergency situation, Justice POWELL found the exception implicit in the statutory requirement that action be taken to preserve the fetus "provided it does not pose an increased risk to the life or health of the woman." *Id.* at 485, n. 8.

Like the Missouri statute, § 3210(c) of the Pennsylvania statute contains no express exception for an emergency situation. While the Missouri statute, in the view of Justice POWELL, was worded sufficiently to imply an emergency exception, Pennsylvania's statute contains no such comforting or helpful language and evinces no intent to protect a woman whose life may be at risk. Section 3210(a) provides only a defense to criminal liability for a physician who concluded, in good faith, that a fetus was nonviable "or that the abortion was necessary to preserve maternal life or health." It does not relate to the second-physician requirement and its words are not words of emergency.

It is clear that the Pennsylvania Legislature knows how to provide a medical-emergency exception when it chooses to do so. It defined "[m]edical emergency" in general terms in § 3203, and it specifically provided a medical-emergency exception with respect to informational requirements, § 3205(b); for parental consent, § 3206; for post-first-trimester hospitalization, § 3209; and for a public official's issuance of an order for an abortion without the express voluntary consent of the woman, § 3215(f). We necessarily conclude that the legislature's failure to provide a medical-emergency exception in § 3210(c) was intentional. All the factors are here for chilling the performance of a late abortion, which, more than one performed at an earlier date, perhaps tends to be under emergency conditions.

V

Constitutional rights do not always have easily ascertainable boundaries, and controversy over the meaning of our Nation's most majestic guarantees frequently has been turbulent. As judges, however, we are sworn to uphold the law even when its content gives rise to bitter dispute. See *Cooper v. Aaron*, 358 U.S. 1. We recognized at the very beginning of our opinion in *Roe,* 410 U.S., at 116, that abortion raises moral and spiritual questions over which honorable persons can disagree sincerely and profoundly. But those disagreements did not then and do not now relieve us of our duty to apply the Constitution faithfully.

Our cases long have recognized that the Constitution embodies a promise that a certain private sphere of individual liberty will be kept largely beyond the reach of government.... That promise extends to women as well as to men. Few decisions are more personal and intimate, more properly private, or more basic to individual dignity and autonomy, than a woman's decision—with the guidance of her physician and within the limits specified in *Roe*—whether to end her pregnancy. A woman's right to make that choice freely is fundamental. Any other result, in our view, would protect inadequately a central part of the sphere of liberty that our law guarantees equally to all.

The Court of Appeals correctly invalidated the specified provisions of Pennsylvania's 1982 Abortion Control Act. Its judgment is affirmed.

It is so ordered.

. . . .

■ BURGER, C.J., dissenting.

. . . .

The Court in *Roe* further recognized that the State "has still *another* important and legitimate interest" which is "separate and distinct" from the interest in protecting maternal health, *i.e.,* an interest in "protecting the potentiality of human life." *Ibid.* The point at which these interests become "compelling" under *Roe* is at viability of the fetus. *Id.,* at 163. Today, however, the Court abandons that standard and renders the solemnly stated concerns of the 1973 *Roe* opinion for the interests of the states mere shallow rhetoric. The statute at issue in this case requires that a second physician be present during an abortion performed after viability, so that the second physician can "take control of the child and ... provide immediate medical care ... taking all reasonable steps necessary, in his judgment, to preserve the child's life and health." 18 Pa.Cons.Stat. § 3210(c) (1982).

Essentially this provision simply states that a viable fetus is to be cared for, not destroyed. No governmental power exists to say that a viable fetus should not have every protection required to preserve its life. Undoubtedly the Pennsylvania Legislature added the second-physician requirement on the mistaken assumption that this Court meant what it said in *Roe* concerning the "compelling interest" of the states in potential life after viability.

. . . .

■ WHITE, J., with whom REHNQUIST, J., joins, dissenting.

. . . .

If the woman's liberty to choose an abortion is fundamental, then, it is not because any of our precedents (aside from *Roe* itself) command or justify that result; it can only be because protection for this unique choice is itself "implicit in the concept of ordered liberty" or, perhaps, "deeply rooted in this Nation's history and tradition." It seems clear to me that it is neither. The Court's opinion in *Roe* itself convincingly refutes the notion that the abortion liberty is deeply rooted in the history or tradition of our people, as does the continuing and deep division of the people themselves over the question of abortion. As for the notion that choice in the matter of abortion is implicit in the concept of ordered liberty, it seems apparent to me that a free, egalitarian, and democratic society does not presuppose any particular rule or set of rules with respect to abortion. And again, the fact that many men and women of good will and high commitment to constitutional government place themselves on both sides of the abortion controversy strengthens my own conviction that the values animating the Constitution do not compel recognition of the abortion liberty as fundamental. In so denominating that liberty, the Court engages not in constitutional interpretation, but in the unrestrained imposition of its own, extra-constitutional value preferences.

. . . .

. . . Abortion is a hotly contested moral and political issue. Such issues, in our society, are to be resolved by the will of the people, either as expressed through legislation or through the general principles they have already incorporated into the Constitution they have adopted. *Roe v. Wade* implies that the people have already resolved the debate by weaving into the Constitution the values and principles that answer the issue. As I have argued, I believe it is clear that the people have never— not in 1787, 1791, 1868, or at any time since—done any such thing. I would return the issue to the people by overruling *Roe v. Wade.*

. . . .

The decision today appears symptomatic of the Court's own insecurity over its handiwork in *Roe v. Wade* and the cases following that decision. Aware that in *Roe* it essentially created something out of nothing and that there are many in this country who hold that decision to be basically illegitimate, the Court responds defensively. Perceiving, in a statute implementing the State's legitimate policy of preferring childbirth to abortion, a threat to or criticism of the decision in *Roe v. Wade,* the majority indiscriminately strikes down statutory provisions that in no way contravene the right recognized in *Roe.* I do not share the warped point of view of the majority, nor can I follow the tortuous path the majority treads in proceeding to strike down the statute before us. I dissent.

■ O'CONNOR, J., with whom REHNQUIST, J., joins, dissenting.

This Court's abortion decisions have already worked a major distortion in the Court's constitutional jurisprudence. See *Akron v. Akron Center for Reproductive Health, Inc.*, 462 U.S. 416, 4527 (1983) (O'CONNOR, J., dissenting). Today's decision goes further, and makes it painfully clear that no legal rule or doctrine is safe from ad hoc nullification by this Court when an occasion for its application arises in a case involving state regulation of abortion. The permissible scope of abortion regulation is not the only constitutional issue on which this Court is divided, but—except when it comes to abortion—the Court has generally refused to let such disagreements, however longstanding or deeply felt, prevent it from evenhandedly applying uncontroversial legal doctrines to cases that come before it. . . .

The Court today holds that "[t]he Court of Appeals correctly invalidated the specified provisions of Pennsylvania's 1982 Abortion Control Act." *Ante,* at 2185. In so doing, the Court prematurely decides serious constitutional questions on an inadequate record, in contravention of settled principles of constitutional adjudication and procedural fairness. The constitutionality of the challenged provisions was not properly before the Court of Appeals, and is not properly before this Court. There has been no trial on the merits, and appellants have had no opportunity to develop facts that might have a bearing on the constitutionality of the statute. The only question properly before the Court is whether or not a preliminary injunction should have been issued to restrain enforcement of the challenged provisions pending trial on the merits. . . .

. . . .

. . . By holding that each of the challenged provisions is facially unconstitutional as a matter of law, and that no conceivable facts appellants might offer could alter this result, the Court appears to adopt as its new test a *per se* rule under which any regulation touching on abortion must be invalidated if it poses "an unacceptable danger of deterring the exercise of that right." *Ante,* at 2182. Under this prophylactic test, it seems that the mere possibility that some women will be less likely to choose to have an abortion by virtue of the presence of a particular state regulation suffices to invalidate it. Simultaneously, the Court strains to discover "the anti-abortion character of the statute," *ante,* at 2180, and, as Justice WHITE points out, invents an unprecedented canon of construction under which "in cases involving abortion, a permissible reading of a statute is to be avoided at all costs." *Ante,* at 2205 (dissenting). I shall not belabor the dangerous extravagance of this dual approach, because I hope it represents merely a temporary aberration rather than a portent of lasting change in settled principles of constitutional law. Suffice it to say that I dispute not only the wisdom but also the legitimacy of the Court's attempt to discredit and pre-empt state abortion regulation regardless of the interests it serves and the impact it has.

. . . .

NOTE

Post-Roe *retrenchment. Thornburgh* reflects the emerging battle lines in the abortion debate, and the changing nature of the Court's jurisprudential approach to abortion litigation. Indeed, one might conclude that *Thornburgh* evinces the emergence of the strategy that Samuel Alito outlined in his memorandum to Solicitor General Charles Fried in 1985, *supra* p. 724. Instead of a frontal assault designed to overrule and repudiate *Roe*, abortion opponents would seek state-level regulations that incrementally restricted abortion access. While Justice Blackmun clearly recognized that such regulations would likely deter women from seeking abortions, Chief Justice Burger articulated the growing concern over viewing abortion as a woman's right, noting, "[w]e have apparently already passed the point at which abortion is available merely on demand. If the statute at issue here is to be invalidated, the 'demand' will not even have to be the result of an informed choice." *Thornburgh*, 476 U.S. at 783–84.

Akron v. Akron Center for Reproductive Health
462 U.S. 416 (1983).

■ POWELL, J.

In this litigation we must decide the constitutionality of several provisions of an ordinance enacted by the city of Akron, Ohio, to regulate the performance of abortions. Today we also review abortion regulations enacted by the State of Missouri. . . .

These cases come to us a decade after we held in *Roe v. Wade,* 410 U.S. 113 (1973), that the right of privacy, grounded in the concept of personal liberty guaranteed by the Constitution, encompasses a woman's right to decide whether to terminate her pregnancy. Legislative responses to the Court's decision have required us on several occasions, and again today, to define the limits of a State's authority to regulate the performance of abortions. And arguments continue to be made, in these cases as well, that we erred in interpreting the Constitution. Nonetheless, the doctrine of *stare decisis,* while perhaps never entirely persuasive on a constitutional question, is a doctrine that demands respect in a society governed by the rule of law. We respect it today, and reaffirm *Roe v. Wade.*

I

In February 1978 the city council of Akron enacted Ordinance No. 160–1978, entitled "Regulation of Abortions." The ordinance sets forth 17 provisions that regulate the performance of abortions, see Akron Codified Ordinances ch. 1870, five of which are at issue in this case:

(i)   Section 1870.03 requires that all abortions performed after the first trimester of pregnancy be performed in a hospital.

(ii) Section 1870.05 sets forth requirements for notification of and consent by parents before abortions may be performed on unmarried minors.

(iii) Section 1870.06 requires that the attending physician make certain specified statements to the patient "to insure that the consent for an abortion is truly informed consent."

(iv) Section 1870.07 requires a 24-hour waiting period between the time the woman signs a consent form and the time the abortion is performed.

(v) Section 1870.16 requires that fetal remains be "disposed of in a humane and sanitary manner."

A violation of any section of the ordinance is punishable as a criminal misdemeanor. . . .

On April 19, 1978, a lawsuit challenging virtually all of the ordinance's provisions was filed in the District Court for the Northern District of Ohio. . . .

In August 1979, after hearing evidence, the . . . District Court invalidated four provisions, including § 1870.05 (parental notice and consent), § 1870.06(B) (requiring disclosure of facts concerning the woman's pregnancy, fetal development, the complications of abortion, and agencies available to assist the woman), and § 1870.16 (disposal of fetal remains). The court upheld the constitutionality of the remainder of the ordinance, including § 1870.03 (hospitalization for abortions after the first trimester), § 1870.06(C) (requiring disclosure of the particular risks of the woman's pregnancy and the abortion technique to be employed), and § 1870.07 (24-hour waiting period).

All parties appealed some portion of the District Court's judgment. The Court of Appeals for the Sixth Circuit . . . affirmed the District Court's decision that § 1870.03's hospitalization requirement is constitutional. It also affirmed the ruling that §§ 1870.05, 1870.06(B), and 1870.16 are unconstitutional. The Court of Appeals reversed the District Court's decision on §§ 1870.06(C) and 1870.07, finding these provisions to be unconstitutional.

. . . We now reverse the judgment of the Court of Appeals upholding Akron's hospitalization requirement, but affirm the remainder of the decision invalidating the provisions on parental consent, informed consent, waiting period, and disposal of fetal remains.

II

In *Roe v. Wade,* the Court held that the "right of privacy, . . . founded in the Fourteenth Amendment's concept of personal liberty and restrictions upon state action, . . . is broad enough to encompass a woman's decision whether or not to terminate her pregnancy." Although the Constitution does not specifically identify this right, the history of this Court's constitutional adjudication leaves no doubt that "the full scope of the liberty guaranteed by the Due Process Clause cannot be found in or limited by the precise terms of the specific guarantees elsewhere provided in the Constitution." Central among these protected liberties is an individual's "freedom of personal choice in matters of marriage and family life." The decision in *Roe* was based firmly on this long-recognized and essential element of personal liberty.

The Court also has recognized, because abortion is a medical procedure, that the full vindication of the woman's fundamental right necessarily requires that her physician be given "the room he needs to make his best medical judgment." The physician's exercise of this medical judgment encompasses both assisting the woman in the decisionmaking process and implementing her decision should she choose abortion.

At the same time, the Court in *Roe* acknowledged that the woman's fundamental right "is not unqualified and must be considered against important state interests in abortion." But restrictive state regulation of the right to choose abortion, as with other fundamental rights subject to searching judicial examination, must be supported by a compelling state interest. We have recognized two such interests that may justify state regulation of abortions.

First, a State has an "important and legitimate interest in protecting the potentiality of human life." Although this interest exists "throughout the course of the woman's pregnancy," it becomes compelling only at viability, the point at which the fetus "has the capability of meaningful life outside the mother's womb." At viability this interest in protecting the potential life of the unborn child is so important that the State may proscribe abortions altogether, "except when it is necessary to preserve the life or health of the mother."

Second, because a State has a legitimate concern with the health of women who undergo abortions, "a State may properly assert important interests in safeguarding health [and] in maintaining medical standards." We held in *Roe*, however, that this health interest does not become compelling until "approximately the end of the first trimester" of pregnancy. Until that time, a pregnant woman must be permitted, in consultation with her physician, to decide to have an abortion and to effectuate that decision "free of interference by the State."

This does not mean that a State never may enact a regulation touching on the woman's abortion right during the first weeks of pregnancy. Certain regulations that have no significant impact on the woman's exercise of her right may be permissible where justified by important state health objectives. In *Planned Parenthood of Central Missouri v. Danforth*, 428 U.S. 52 (1976), we unanimously upheld two Missouri statutory provisions, applicable to the first trimester, requiring the woman to provide her informed written consent to the abortion and the physician to keep certain records, even though comparable requirements were not imposed on most other medical procedures. The decisive factor was that the State met its burden of demonstrating that these regulations furthered important health-related State concerns. But even these minor regulations on the abortion procedure during the first trimester may not interfere with physician-patient consultation or with the woman's choice between abortion and childbirth.

From approximately the end of the first trimester of pregnancy, the State "may regulate the abortion procedure to the extent that the regulation reasonably relates to the preservation and protection of maternal health." The State's discretion to regulate on this basis does not, however, permit it to adopt abortion regulations that depart from accepted medical practice. We have rejected a State's attempt to ban a particular second-trimester abortion procedure, where the ban would have increased the costs and limited the availability of abortions without promoting important health benefits. If a State requires licensing or undertakes to regulate the performance of abortions during this period, the health standards adopted must be "legitimately related to the objective the State seeks to accomplish."

Section 1870.03 of the Akron ordinance requires that any abortion performed "upon a pregnant woman subsequent to the end of the first trimester of her pregnancy" must be "performed in a hospital." A "hospital" is "a general hospital or special hospital devoted to gynecology or obstetrics which is accredited by the Joint Commission on Accreditation of Hospitals or by the American Osteopathic Association." Accreditation by these organizations requires compliance with comprehensive standards governing a wide variety of health and surgical services. The ordinance thus prevents the performance of abortions in outpatient facilities that are not part of an acute-care, full-service hospital.

. . . .

In *Roe v. Wade* the Court held that after the end of the first trimester of pregnancy the State's interest becomes compelling, and it may "regulate the abortion procedure to the extent that the regulation reasonably relates to the preservation and protection of maternal health." We noted, for example, that States could establish requirements relating "to the facility in which the procedure is to be performed, that is, whether it must be in a hospital or may be a clinic or some other place of less-than-hospital status." In the companion case of *Doe v. Bolton* the Court invalidated a Georgia requirement that all abortions be performed in a hospital licensed by the State Board of Health and accredited by the Joint Commission on Accreditation of Hospitals. We recognized the State's legitimate health interests in establishing, for second-trimester abortions, "standards for licensing all facilities where abortions may be performed." We found, however, that "the State must show more than [was shown in *Doe*] in order to prove that only the full resources of a licensed hospital, rather than those of some other appropriately licensed institution, satisfy these health interests."

. . . .

There can be no doubt that § 1870.03's second-trimester hospitalization requirement places a significant obstacle in the path of women seeking an abortion. A primary burden created by the requirement is additional cost to the woman. The Court of Appeals noted that there was testimony that a second-trimester abortion costs more than twice as much in a hospital as in a clinic. Moreover, the court indicated that second-trimester abortions were rarely performed in Akron hospitals. Thus, a second-trimester hospitalization requirement may force women to travel to find available facilities, resulting in both financial expense and additional health risk. It therefore is apparent that a second-trimester hospitalization requirement may significantly limit a woman's ability to obtain an abortion.

Akron does not contend that § 1870.03 imposes only an insignificant burden on women's access to abortion, but rather defends it as a reasonable health regulation. This position had strong support at the time of *Roe v. Wade,* as hospitalization for second-trimester abortions was recommended by the American Public Health Association and the American College of Obstetricians and Gynecologists (ACOG), see Standards for Obstetric-Gynecologic Services 65 (4th ed. 1974). Since then, however, the safety of second-trimester abortions has increased dramatically. The principal reason is that the D & E procedure is now widely and successfully used for second-trimester abortions. . . .

For our purposes, an even more significant factor is that experience indicates that D & E may be performed safely on an outpatient basis in appropriate nonhospital facilities. The evidence is strong enough to have convinced the APHA to abandon its prior recommendation of hospitalization for all second-trimester abortions. . . .

Similarly, the ACOG no longer suggests that all second-trimester abortions be performed in a hospital. . . .

These developments . . . constitute impressive evidence that—at least during the early weeks of the second trimester—D & E abortions may be performed as safely in an outpatient clinic as in a full-service hospital. We conclude, therefore, that "present medical knowledge," convincingly undercuts Akron's justification for requiring that *all* second-trimester abortions be performed in a hospital.

. . . By preventing the performance of D & E abortions in an appropriate nonhospital setting, Akron has imposed a heavy, and unnecessary, burden on women's access to a relatively inexpensive, otherwise accessible, and safe abortion procedure. Section 1870.03 has "the effect of inhibiting . . . the vast majority of abortions after the first 12 weeks," and therefore unreasonably infringes upon a woman's constitutional right to obtain an abortion.

We turn next to § 1870.05(B), the provision prohibiting a physician from performing an abortion on a minor pregnant woman under the age of 15 unless he obtains "the informed written consent of one of her parents or her legal guardian" or unless the minor obtains "an order from a court having jurisdiction over her that the abortion be performed or induced." . . .

The relevant legal standards are not in dispute. The Court has held that "the State may not impose a blanket provision . . . requiring the consent of a parent or person *in loco parentis* as a condition for abortion of an unmarried minor." In *Bellotti v. Baird,* 443 U.S. 622 (1979) (*Bellotti II*), a majority of the Court indicated that a State's interest in protecting immature minors will sustain a requirement of a consent substitute, either parental or judicial. The *Bellotti II* plurality cautioned, however, that the State must provide an alternative procedure whereby a pregnant minor may demonstrate that she is sufficiently mature to make the abortion decision herself or that, despite her immaturity, an abortion would be in her best interests. . . .

Akron's ordinance does not create expressly the alternative procedure required by *Bellotti II*. But Akron contends that the Ohio Juvenile Court will qualify as a "court having jurisdiction" within the meaning of § 1870.05(B), and that "it is not to be assumed that during the course of the juvenile proceedings the Court will not construe the ordinance in a manner consistent with the constitutional requirement of a determination of the minor's ability to make an informed consent." Akron concludes that the courts below should not have invalidated § 1870.05(B) on its face. The city relies on *Bellotti v. Baird,* 428 U.S. 132 (1976) (*Bellotti I*), in which the Court did not decide whether a State's parental consent provisions were unconstitutional as applied to mature minors, holding instead that "abstention is appropriate where an unconstrued state statute is susceptible of a construction by the state judiciary 'which might avoid in whole or in part the necessity for federal constitutional adjudication, or at least materially change the nature of the problem.' "

We do not think that the abstention principle should have been applied here. It is reasonable to assume, as we did in *Bellotti I* . . . that a state court presented with a state statute specifically governing abortion consent procedures for pregnant minors will attempt to construe the statute consistently with constitutional requirements. This suit, however, concerns a municipal ordinance that creates no procedures for making the necessary determinations. Akron seeks to invoke the Ohio statute governing juvenile proceedings, but that statute neither mentions minors' abortions nor suggests that the Ohio Juvenile Court has authority to inquire into a minor's maturity or emancipation. In these circumstances, we do not think that the Akron ordinance, as applied in Ohio juvenile proceedings, is reasonably susceptible of being construed to create an "opportunity for case-by-case evaluations of the maturity of pregnant minors." We therefore affirm the Court of Appeals' judgment that § 1870.05(B) is unconstitutional.

The Akron ordinance provides that no abortion shall be performed except "with the informed written consent of the pregnant woman, . . . given freely and without coercion." § 1870.06(A). Furthermore, "in order to insure that the consent for an abortion is truly informed consent," the woman must be "orally informed by her attending physician" of the status of her pregnancy, the development of her fetus, the date of possible viability, the physical and emotional complications that may result from an abortion, and the availability of agencies to provide her with assistance and information with respect to birth control, adoption, and childbirth. § 1870.06(B). In addition, the attending physician must inform her "of the particular risks associated with her own pregnancy and the abortion technique to be employed . . . [and] other information which in his own medical judgment is relevant to her decision as to whether to have an abortion or carry her pregnancy to term." § 1870.06(C).

. . . The Court of Appeals concluded that both provisions were unconstitutional. We affirm.

. . . .

The validity of an informed consent requirement thus rests on the State's interest in protecting the health of the pregnant woman. The decision to have an abortion has "implications far broader than those associated with most other kinds of medical treatment," and thus the State legitimately may seek to ensure that it has been made "in the light of all attendant circumstances—psychological and emotional as well as physical—that might be relevant to the well-being of the patient." This does not mean, however, that a State has unreviewable authority to decide what information a woman must be given before she chooses to have an abortion. It remains primarily the responsibility of the physician to ensure that appropriate information is conveyed to his patient, depending on her particular circumstances. *Danforth's* recognition of the State's interest in ensuring that this information be given will not justify abortion regulations designed to influence the woman's informed choice between abortion or childbirth.

. . . [W]e believe that § 1870.06(B) attempts to extend the State's interest in ensuring "informed consent" beyond permissible limits. First, it is fair to say that much of the information required is designed not to inform the woman's consent but rather to persuade her to withhold it altogether. Subsection (3) requires the physician to inform his patient that "the unborn child is a human life from the moment of conception," a requirement inconsistent with the Court's holding in *Roe v. Wade* that a State may not adopt one theory of when life begins to justify its regulation of abortions. Moreover, much of the detailed description of "the anatomical and physiological characteristics of the particular unborn child" required by subsection (3) would involve at best speculation by the physician. And subsection (5), that begins with the dubious statement that "abortion is a major surgical procedure" and proceeds to describe numerous possible physical and pyschological complications of abortion, is a "parade of horribles" intended to suggest that abortion is a particularly dangerous procedure.

An additional, and equally decisive, objection to § 1870.06(B) is its intrusion upon the discretion of the pregnant woman's physician. This provision specifies a litany of information that the physician must recite to each woman regardless of whether in his judgment the information is relevant to her personal decision. For example, even if the physician believes that some of the risks outlined in subsection (5) are nonexistent for a particular patient, he remains obligated to describe them to her. . . . Consistent with its interest in ensuring informed consent, a State may require that a physician make certain that his patient understands the physical and emotional implications of having an abortion. But Akron has gone far beyond merely describing the general subject matter relevant to informed consent. By insisting upon recitation of a lengthy and inflexible list of information, Akron unreasonably has placed "obstacles in the path of the doctor upon whom [the woman is] entitled to rely for advice in connection with her decision."

Section 1870.06(C) presents a different question. Under this provision, the "attending physician" must inform the woman of the particular risks associated with her own pregnancy and the abortion technique to be employed including providing her with at least a general description of the medical instructions to be followed subsequent to the abortion in order to insure her safe recovery, and shall in addition provide her with such other information which in his own medical judgment is relevant to her decision as to whether to have an abortion or carry her pregnancy to term.

The information required clearly is related to maternal health and to the State's legitimate purpose in requiring informed consent. Nonetheless, the Court of Appeals determined that it interfered with the physician's medical judgment "in exactly the same way as section 1870.06(B). It requires the doctor to make certain disclosures in all cases, regardless of his own professional judgment as to the desirability of doing so." This was a misapplication of *Danforth*. There we construed "informed consent" to mean "the giving of information to the patient as to just what would be done and as to its consequences." We see no significant difference in Akron's requirement that the woman be told of the particular risks of her pregnancy and the abortion technique to be used, and be given general instructions on proper post-abortion care. Moreover, in contrast to subsection (B), § 1870.06(C) merely describes in general terms the information to be disclosed. It properly leaves the precise nature and amount of this disclosure to the physician's discretion and "medical judgment."

The Court of Appeals also held, however, that § 1870.06(C) was invalid because it required that the disclosure be made by the "attending physician." The court found that "the practice of all three plaintiff clinics has been for the counseling to be conducted by persons other than the doctor who performs the abortion," and determined that Akron had not justified requiring the physician personally to describe the health risks. Akron challenges this holding as contrary to our cases that emphasize the importance of the physician-patient relationship. In Akron's view . . . the "attending physician" requirement "does no more than seek to ensure that there is in fact a true physician-patient relationship even for the woman who goes to an abortion clinic."

Requiring physicians personally to discuss the abortion decision, its health risks, and consequences with each patient may in some cases add to the cost of providing abortions, though the record here does not suggest that ethical physicians will charge more for adhering to this typical element of the physician-patient relationship. Yet in *Roe* and subsequent cases we have "stressed repeatedly the central role of the physician, both in consulting with the woman about whether or not to have an abortion, and in determining how any abortion was to be carried out." Moreover, we have left no doubt that, to ensure the safety of the abortion procedure, the States may mandate that only physicians perform abortions.

We are not convinced, however, that there is as vital a state need for insisting that the physician performing the abortion, or for that matter any physician, personally counsel the patient in the absence of a request. The State's interest is in ensuring that the woman's consent is informed and unpressured; the critical factor is whether she obtains the necessary information and counseling from a qualified person, not the identity of the person from whom she obtains it. . . . [O]n the record before us we cannot say that the woman's consent to the abortion will not be informed if a physician delegates the counseling task to another qualified individual.

In so holding, we do not suggest that the State is powerless to vindicate its interest in making certain the "important" and "stressful" decision to abort "is made with full knowledge of its nature and consequences." Nor do we imply that a physician may abdicate his essential role as the person ultimately responsible for the medical aspects of the decision to perform the abortion. A State may define the physician's responsibility to include verification that adequate counseling has been provided and that the woman's consent is informed. In addition, the State may establish reasonable minimum qualifications for those people who perform the primary counseling function. In light of these alternatives, we believe that it is unreasonable for a State to insist that only a physician is competent to provide the information and counseling relevant to informed consent. We affirm the judgment of the Court of Appeals that § 1870.06(C) is invalid.

The Akron ordinance prohibits a physician from performing an abortion until 24 hours after the pregnant woman signs a consent form. § 1870.07. The District Court upheld this provision on the ground that it furthered Akron's interest in ensuring "that a woman's abortion decision is made after careful consideration of all the facts applicable to her particular situation." The Court of Appeals reversed, finding that the inflexible waiting period had "no medical basis," and that careful consideration of the abortion decision by the woman "is beyond the state's power to require." We affirm the Court of Appeals' judgment.

The District Court found that the mandatory 24-hour waiting period increases the cost of obtaining an abortion by requiring the woman to make two separate trips to the abortion facility. Plaintiffs also contend that because of scheduling difficulties the effective delay may be longer than 24 hours, and that such a delay in some cases could increase the risk of an abortion. Akron denies that any significant health risk is created by a 24-hour waiting period, and argues that a brief period of delay-with the opportunity for reflection on the counseling received-often will be beneficial to the pregnant woman.

We find that Akron has failed to demonstrate that any legitimate state interest is furthered by an arbitrary and inflexible waiting period. There is no evidence suggesting that the abortion procedure will be performed more safely. Nor are we convinced that the State's legitimate concern that the woman's decision be informed is reasonably served by requiring a 24-hour delay as a matter of course. The decision whether to proceed with an abortion is one as to which it is important to "affor[d] the physician adequate discretion in the exercise of his medical judgment." In accordance with the ethical standards of the profession, a physician will advise the patient to defer the abortion when he thinks this will be beneficial to her. But if a woman, after appropriate counseling, is prepared to give her written informed consent and proceed with the abortion, a State may not demand that she delay the effectuation of that decision.

Section 1870.16 of the Akron ordinance requires physicians performing abortions to "insure that the remains of the unborn child are disposed of in a humane and sanitary manner." The Court of Appeals found that the word "humane" was impermissibly vague as a definition of conduct subject to criminal prosecution. The court invalidated the entire provision, declining to sever the word "humane" in order to uphold the requirement that disposal be "sanitary." We affirm this judgment.

Akron contends that the purpose of § 1870.16 is simply " 'to preclude the mindless dumping of aborted fetuses on garbage piles.' " It is far from clear, however, that this provision has such a limited intent. The phrase "humane and sanitary" does, as the Court of Appeals noted, suggest a possible intent to "mandate some sort of 'decent burial' of an embryo at the earliest stages of formation." This level of uncertainty is fatal where criminal liability is imposed. Because § 1870.16 fails to give a physician "fair notice that his contemplated conduct is forbidden," we agree that it violates the Due Process Clause.

VIII

We affirm the judgment of the Court of Appeals invalidating those sections of Akron's "Regulations of Abortions" ordinance that deal with parental consent, informed consent, a 24-hour waiting period, and the disposal of fetal remains. The remaining portion of the judgment, sustaining Akron's requirement that all second-trimester abortions be performed in a hospital, is reversed.

It is so ordered.

■ O'CONNOR, J., with whom WHITE, J., and REHNQUIST, J. join, dissenting.

In *Roe v. Wade,* 410 U.S. 113 (1973), the Court held that the "right of privacy . . . founded in the Fourteenth Amendment's concept of personal liberty and restrictions upon state action . . . is broad enough to encompass a woman's decision whether or not to terminate her pregnancy." The parties in these cases have not asked the Court to reexamine the validity of that holding and the court below did not address it. Accordingly, the Court does not re-examine its previous holding. Nonetheless, it is apparent from the Court's opinion that neither sound constitutional theory nor our need to decide cases based on the application of neutral principles can accommodate an analytical framework that varies according to the "stages" of pregnancy, where those stages, and their concomitant standards of review, differ according to the level of medical technology available when a particular challenge to state regulation occurs. The Court's analysis of the Akron regulations is inconsistent both with the methods of analysis employed in previous cases dealing with abortion, and with the Court's approach to fundamental rights in other areas.

Our recent cases indicate that a regulation imposed on "a lawful abortion 'is not unconstitutional unless it unduly burdens the right to seek an abortion.' " In my view, this "unduly burdensome" standard should be applied to the challenged regulations throughout the entire pregnancy without reference to the particular "stage" of pregnancy involved. If the particular regulation does not "unduly burden[ ]" the fundamental right, then our evaluation of that regulation is limited to our determination that the regulation rationally relates to a legitimate state purpose. . . .

The trimester or "three-stage" approach adopted by the Court in *Roe*, and, in a modified form, employed by the Court to analyze the state regulations in these cases, cannot be supported as a legitimate or useful framework for accommodating the woman's right and the State's interests. The decision of the Court today graphically illustrates why the trimester approach is a completely unworkable method of accommodating the conflicting personal rights and compelling state interests that are involved in the abortion context.

As the Court indicates today, the State's compelling interest in maternal health changes as medical technology changes, and any health regulation must not "depart from accepted medical practice." . . .

It is not difficult to see that despite the Court's purported adherence to the trimester approach adopted in *Roe,* the lines drawn in that decision have now been "blurred" because of what the Court accepts as technological advancement in the safety of abortion procedure. The State may no longer rely on a "bright line" that separates permissible from impermissible regulation, and it is no longer free to consider the second trimester as a unit and weigh the risks posed by all abortion procedures throughout that trimester. Rather, the State must continuously and conscientiously study contemporary medical and scientific literature in order to determine whether the effect of a particular regulation is to "depart from accepted medical practice" insofar as particular procedures and particular periods within the trimester are concerned. Assuming that legislative bodies are able to engage in this exacting task, it is difficult to believe that our Constitution *requires* that they do it as a prelude to protecting the health of their citizens. It is even more difficult to believe that this Court, without the resources available to those bodies entrusted with making legislative choices, believes itself competent to make these inquiries and to revise these standards every time the American College of Obstetricians and Gynecologists (ACOG) or similar group revises its views about what is and what is not appropriate medical procedure in this area. Indeed, the ACOG standards on which the Court relies were changed in 1982 after trial in the present cases. Before ACOG changed its standards in 1982, it recommended that all mid-trimester abortions be performed in a hospital. As today's decision indicates, medical technology is changing, and this change will necessitate our continued functioning as the nation's "*ex officio* medical board with powers to approve or disapprove medical and operative practices and standards throughout the United States."

Just as improvements in medical technology inevitably will move *forward* the point at which the State may regulate for reasons of maternal health, different technological improvements will move *backward* the point of viability at which the State may proscribe abortions except when necessary to preserve the life and health of the mother.

In 1973, viability before 28 weeks was considered unusual. . . . However, recent studies have demonstrated increasingly earlier fetal viability. It is certainly reasonable to believe that fetal viability in the first trimester of pregnancy may be possible in the not too distant future. . . .

The *Roe* framework, then, is clearly on a collision course with itself. As the medical risks of various abortion procedures decrease, the point at which the State may regulate for reasons of maternal health is moved further forward to actual childbirth. As medical science becomes better able to provide for the separate existence of the fetus, the point of viability is moved further back toward conception. . . . The *Roe* framework is inherently tied to the state of medical technology that exists whenever particular litigation ensues. Although legislatures are better suited to make the necessary factual judgments in this area, the Court's framework forces legislatures, as a matter of constitutional law, to speculate about what constitutes "accepted medical practice" at any given time. Without the necessary expertise or ability, courts must then pretend to act as science review boards and examine those legislative judgments.

The Court adheres to the *Roe* framework because the doctrine of *stare decisis* "demands respect in a society governed by the rule of law." Although respect for *stare decisis* cannot be challenged, "this Court's considered practice [is] not to apply *stare decisis* as rigidly in constitutional as in nonconstitutional cases." Although we must be mindful of the "desirability of continuity of decision in constitutional questions . . . when convinced of former error, this Court has never felt constrained to follow precedent. In constitutional questions, when correction depends on amendment and not upon legislative action this Court throughout its history has freely exercised its power to reexamine the basis of its constitutional decisions."

Even assuming that there is a fundamental right to terminate pregnancy in some situations, there is no justification in law or logic for the trimester framework adopted in *Roe* and employed by the Court today on the basis of *stare decisis*. For the reasons stated above, that framework is clearly an unworkable means of balancing the fundamental right and the compelling state interests that are indisputably implicated.

The Court in *Roe* correctly realized that the State has important interests "in the areas of health and medical standards" and that "[t]he State has a legitimate interest in seeing to it that abortion, like any other medical procedure, is performed under circumstances that insure maximum safety for the patient." The Court also recognized that the State has "*another* important and legitimate interest in protecting the potentiality of human life." I agree completely that the State has these interests, but in my view, the point at which these interests become compelling does not depend on the trimester of pregnancy. Rather, these interests are present *throughout* pregnancy.

. . . Under the *Roe* framework, however, the state interest in maternal health cannot become compelling until the onset of the second trimester of pregnancy because "until the end of the first trimester mortality in abortion may be less than mortality in normal childbirth." Before the second trimester, the decision to perform an abortion "must be left to the medical judgment of the pregnant woman's attending physician."

The fallacy inherent in the *Roe* framework is apparent: just because the State has a compelling interest in ensuring maternal safety once an abortion may be more dangerous in childbirth, it simply does not follow that the State has *no* interest before that point that justifies state regulation to ensure that first-trimester abortions are performed as safely as possible.

The state interest in potential human life is likewise extant throughout pregnancy. In *Roe,* the Court held that although the State had an important and legitimate interest in protecting potential life, that interest could not become compelling until the point at which the fetus was viable. The difficulty with this analysis is clear: *potential* life is no less potential in the first weeks of pregnancy than it is at viability or afterward. At any stage in pregnancy, there is the *potential* for human life. . . . The choice of viability as the point at which the state interest in *potential* life becomes compelling is no less arbitrary than choosing any point before viability or any point afterward. Accordingly, I believe that the State's interest in protecting potential human life exists throughout the pregnancy.

Although the State possesses compelling interests in the protection of potential human life and in maternal health throughout pregnancy, not every regulation that the State imposes must be measured against the State's compelling interests and examined with strict scrutiny. ". . . *Roe* did not declare an unqualified 'constitutional right to an abortion,'. . . . Rather, the right protects the woman from unduly burdensome interference with her freedom to decide whether to terminate her pregnancy." The Court and its individual Justices have repeatedly utilized the "unduly burdensome" standard in abortion cases.

. . . .

Indeed, the Court today follows this approach. Although the Court does not use the expression "undue burden," the Court recognizes that even a "significant obstacle" can be justified by a "reasonable" regulation.

. . . .

The "unduly burdensome" standard is particularly appropriate in the abortion context because of the *nature* and *scope* of the right that is involved. The privacy right involved in the abortion context "cannot be said to be absolute. . . . Rather, the *Roe* right is intended to protect against state action "drastically limiting the availability and safety of the desired service," against the imposition of an "absolute obstacle" on the abortion decision, or against "official interference" and "coercive restraint" imposed on the abortion decision. That a state regulation may "inhibit" abortions to some degree does not require that we find that the regulation is invalid.

The abortion cases demonstrate that an "undue burden" has been found for the most part in situations involving absolute obstacles or severe limitations on the abortion decision. In *Roe,* the Court invalidated a Texas statute that criminalized *all* abortions except those necessary to save the life of the mother. In *Danforth,* the Court invalidated a state prohibition of abortion by saline amniocentesis because the ban had "the effect of inhibiting ... the vast majority of abortions after the first 12 weeks." ...

In determining whether the State imposes an "undue burden," we must keep in mind that when we are concerned with extremely sensitive issues, such as the one involved here, "the appropriate forum for their resolution in a democracy is the legislature. We should not forget that "legislatures are ultimate guardians of the liberties and welfare of the people in quite as great a degree as the courts." This does not mean that in determining whether a regulation imposes an "undue burden" on the *Roe* right that we defer to the judgments made by state legislatures. "The point is, rather, that when we face a complex problem with many hard questions and few easy answers we do well to pay careful attention to how the other branches of Government have addressed the same problem."

. . . .

Section 1870.03 of the Akron ordinance requires that second-trimester abortions be performed in hospitals. The Court holds that this requirement imposes a "significant obstacle" in the form of increased cost and decreased availability of abortions, *ante,* at 2495, and the Court rejects the argument offered by the State that the requirement is a reasonable health regulation under *Roe.*

For the reasons stated above, I find no justification for the trimester approach used by the Court to analyze this restriction. I would apply the "unduly burdensome" test and find that the hospitalization requirement does not impose an undue burden on that decision.

. . . .

The hospitalization requirement does not impose an undue burden, and it is not necessary to apply an exacting standard of review. Further, the regulation has a "rational relation" to a valid state objective of ensuring the health and welfare of its citizens.

B

Section 1870.05(B) of the Akron ordinance provides that no physician shall perform an abortion on a minor under 15 years of age unless the minor gives written consent, and the physician first obtains the informed written consent of a parent or guardian, or unless the minor first obtains "an order from a court having jurisdiction over her that the abortion be performed or induced." Despite the fact that this regulation has yet to be construed in the state courts, the Court holds that the regulation is unconstitutional because it is not "reasonably susceptible of being construed to create an 'opportunity for case-by-case evaluations of the maturity of pregnant minors.' " I believe that the Court should have abstained from declaring the ordinance unconstitutional.

In *Bellotti I, supra,* the Court abstained from deciding whether a state parental consent provision was unconstitutional as applied to mature minors. The Court recognized and respected the well-settled rule that abstention is proper "where an unconstrued state statute is susceptible of a construction by the state judiciary 'which might avoid in whole or in part the necessity for federal constitutional adjudication, or at least materially change the nature of the problem.'" While acknowledging the force of the abstention doctrine, . . . the Court nevertheless declines to apply it. Instead, it speculates that a state juvenile court *might* inquire into a minor's maturity and ability to decide to have an abortion in deciding whether the minor is being provided "'surgical care . . . necessary for his health, morals, or well being.'" The Court ultimately rejects this possible interpretation of state law, however, because filing a petition in juvenile court requires parental notification, an unconstitutional condition insofar as mature minors are concerned.

Assuming *arguendo* that the Court is correct in holding that a parental notification requirement would be unconstitutional as applied to mature minors, I see no reason to assume that the Akron ordinance and the state juvenile court statute compel state judges to notify the parents of a mature minor if such notification was contrary to the minor's best interests. Further, there is no reason to believe that the state courts would construe the consent requirement to impose any type of parental or judicial veto on the abortion decisions of mature minors. In light of the Court's complete lack of knowledge about how the Akron ordinance will operate, and how the Akron ordinance and the state juvenile court statute interact, our "'scrupulous regard for the rightful independence of state governments'" counsels against "unnecessary interference by the federal courts with proper and validly administered state concerns, a course so essential to the balanced working of our federal system."

The Court invalidates the informed consent provisions of § 1870.06(B) and § 1870.06(C) of the Akron ordinance. . . .

The validity of subsections (3), (4), and (5) are not before the Court because it appears that the City of Akron conceded their unconstitutionality before the court below. In my view, the remaining subsections of § 1870.06(B) are separable from the subsections conceded to be unconstitutional. Section 1870.19 contains a separability clause which creates a "'presumption of divisibility'" and places "the burden . . . on the litigant who would escape its operation." Akron Center has failed to show that severance of subsections (3), (4), and (5) would "create a program quite different from the one the legislature actually adopted."

The remainder of § 1870.06(B), and § 1870.06(C), impose no undue burden or drastic limitation on the abortion decision. The City of Akron is merely attempting to ensure that the decision to abort is made in light of that knowledge that the City deems relevant to informed choice. As such, these regulations do not impermissibly affect any privacy right under the Fourteenth Amendment.

Section 1870.07 of the Akron ordinance requires a 24-hour waiting period between the signing of a consent form and the actual performance of the abortion, except in cases of emergency. The court below invalidated this requirement because it affected abortion decisions during the first trimester of pregnancy. The Court affirms the decision below, not on the ground that it affects early abortions, but because "Akron has failed to demonstrate that any legitimate state interest is furthered by an arbitrary and inflexible waiting period." . . .

. . . .

Assuming *arguendo* that any additional costs are such as to impose an undue burden on the abortion decision, the State's compelling interests in maternal physical and mental health and protection of fetal life clearly justify the waiting period. As we acknowledged in *Danforth,* the decision to abort is "a stressful one," and the waiting period reasonably relates to the State's interest in ensuring that a woman does not make this serious decision in undue haste. The decision also has grave consequences for the fetus, whose life the State has a compelling interest to protect and preserve. "No other [medical] procedure involves the purposeful termination of a potential life." The waiting period is surely a small cost to impose to ensure that the woman's decision is well-considered in light of its certain and irreparable consequences on fetal life, and the possible effects on her own.

Finally, § 1870.16 of the Akron ordinance requires that "[a]ny physician who shall perform or induce an abortion upon a pregnant woman shall insure that the remains of the unborn child are disposed of in a humane and sanitary manner." The Court finds this provision void-for-vagueness. I disagree.

. . . In the present case, the City of Akron has informed this Court that the intent of the "humane" portion of its statute, as distinguished from the "sanitary" portion, is merely to ensure that fetuses will not be " 'dump[ed] . . . on garbage piles.' " In light of the fact that the City of Akron indicates no intent to require that physicians provide "decent burials" for fetuses, and that "humane" is no more vague than the term "sanitary," the vagueness of which Akron Center does not question, I cannot conclude that the statute is void for vagueness.

For the reasons set forth above, I dissent from the judgment of the Court in these cases.

NOTES

1. *Rejecting the trimester framework.* Justice O'Connor's dissent in *Akron* presages the Court's 1992 decision in *Planned Parenthood of Southeastern Pennsylvania v. Casey* in important ways. As an initial matter, O'Connor's dissent registers intense skepticism of *Roe*'s trimester framework as an

appropriate means of determining when the state can and cannot regulate abortion. *City of Akron v. Akron Center for Reproductive Health, Inc.*, 462 U.S. 416, 453–57 (1983) (O'Connor, J., dissenting). Technological advances in medical practice, O'Connor observes, had complicated the question of viability, making it an unstable marker for abortion regulation. *Id.* at 455–57 (O'Connor, J., dissenting). Further, as O'Connor notes, the state's interest in assuring maternal health, as well as the potentiality for life "are present *throughout* pregnancy," not just in the second and third trimesters of pregnancy, as *Roe* prescribed. *Id.* at 459 (O'Connor, J., dissenting).

2.   *The roots of the undue burden test.* O'Connor's dissent is also noteworthy in that it reveals an interest in reducing the standard of review for legal challenges to abortion laws. In an earlier abortion challenge, *Carey v. Population Services*, 431 U.S. 678 (1977), the Court reviewed the challenged New York statutes under strict scrutiny—the traditional standard of review for laws that implicate the exercise of a fundamental right. The *Carey* Court held that, "[r]egulations imposing a burden on a decision as fundamental as whether to bear or beget a child may be justified only by compelling state interests, and must be narrowly drawn to express those interests." *Id.* at 684–86. By contrast, in *Akron*, O'Connor makes clear, "not every regulation that the State imposes must be measured against the State's compelling interests and examined with strict scrutiny." *Akron*, 462 U.S. at 461. On this account, "*Roe* did not declare an unqualified 'constitutional right to an abortion,'. . . Rather, the right protects the woman from unduly burdensome interference with her freedom to decide whether to terminate her pregnancy." *Id.* As we will see, O'Connor's logic reaches fruition in 1992's *Planned Parenthood of Southeastern Pennsylvania v. Casey*, 505 U.S. 833 (1992), *infra* p. 797, in which the Court rejected *Roe*'s trimester framework *and* articulated a new standard of review for laws that challenged the abortion right—the undue burden standard.

Webster v. Reproductive Health Services
492 U.S. 490 (1989).

■ REHNQUIST, J., announced the judgment of the Court and delivered the opinion of the Court with respect to Parts I, II-A, II-B, and II-C, and an opinion with respect to Parts II-D and III, in which WHITE, J., and KENNEDY, J., join.

This appeal concerns the constitutionality of a Missouri statute regulating the performance of abortions. The United States Court of Appeals for the Eighth Circuit struck down several provisions of the statute on the ground that they violated this Court's decision in *Roe v. Wade*, 410 U.S. 113 (1973), and cases following it. We . . . now reverse.

. . . .

II

. . . [T]his case requires us to address four sections of the Missouri Act: (a) the preamble; (b) the prohibition on the use of public facilities or employees to perform abortions; (c) the prohibition on public funding of abortion counseling; and (d) the requirement that physicians conduct viability tests prior to performing abortions. We address these *seriatim*.

A

The Act's preamble ... sets forth "findings" by the Missouri Legislature that "[t]he life of each human being begins at conception," and that "[u]nborn children have protectable interests in life, health, and well-being." The Act then mandates that state laws be interpreted to provide unborn children with "all the rights, privileges, and immunities available to other persons, citizens, and residents of this state," subject to the Constitution and this Court's precedents. In invalidating the preamble, the Court of Appeals relied on this Court's dictum that " 'a State may not adopt one theory of when life begins to justify its regulation of abortions.' " 851 F.2d, at 1075–1076, quoting *Akron v. Akron Center for Reproductive Health, Inc.*, 462 U.S. 416, 444 (1983). . .

The State contends that the preamble itself is precatory and imposes no substantive restrictions on abortions. . . . Appellees, on the other hand, insist that the preamble is an operative part of the Act intended to guide the interpretation of other provisions of the Act. They maintain, for example, that the preamble's definition of life may prevent physicians in public hospitals from dispensing certain forms of contraceptives, such as the intrauterine device.

In our view, the Court of Appeals misconceived the meaning of the *Akron* dictum, which was only that a State could not "justify" an abortion regulation otherwise invalid under *Roe v. Wade* on the ground that it embodied the State's view about when life begins. Certainly the preamble does not by its terms regulate abortion or any other aspect of appellees' medical practice. The Court has emphasized that *Roe v. Wade* "implies no limitation on the authority of a State to make a value judgment favoring childbirth over abortion." The preamble can be read simply to express that sort of value judgment.

. . . .

It will be time enough for federal courts to address the meaning of the preamble should it be applied to restrict the activities of appellees in some concrete way. Until then, this Court "is not empowered to decide ... abstract propositions, or to declare, for the government of future cases, principles or rules of law which cannot affect the result as to the thing in issue in the case before it." We therefore need not pass on the constitutionality of the Act's preamble.

B

Section 188.210 provides that "[i]t shall be unlawful for any public employee within the scope of his employment to perform or assist an abortion, not necessary to save the life of the mother," while § 188.215 makes it "unlawful for any public facility to be used for the purpose of performing or assisting an abortion not necessary to save the life of the mother." The Court of Appeals held that these provisions contravened this Court's abortion decisions. We take the contrary view.

As we said earlier this Term in *DeShaney v. Winnebago County Dept. of Social Services*, 489 U.S. 189, 196 (1989); "[O]ur cases have recognized that the Due Process Clauses generally confer no affirmative right to governmental aid, even where such aid may be necessary to secure life, liberty, or property interests of which the government itself may not deprive the individual." In *Maher v. Roe*, the Court upheld a Connecticut welfare regulation under which Medicaid recipients received payments for medical services related to childbirth, but not for nontherapeutic abortions. The Court rejected the claim that this unequal subsidization of childbirth and abortion was impermissible under *Roe v. Wade*. . . .

Relying on *Maher*, the Court in *Poelker v. Doe*, 432 U.S. 519, 521 (1977), held that the city of St. Louis committed "no constitutional violation . . . in electing, as a policy choice, to provide publicly financed hospital Services for childbirth without providing corresponding services for nontherapeutic abortions."

More recently, in *Harris v. McRae*, 448 U.S. 297 (1980), the Court upheld "the most restrictive version of the Hyde Amendment," which withheld from States federal funds under the Medicaid program to reimburse the costs of abortions, " 'except where the life of the mother would be endangered if the fetus were carried to term.' " As in *Maher* and *Poelker*, the Court required only a showing that Congress' authorization of "reimbursement for medically necessary services generally, but not for certain medically necessary abortions" was rationally related to the legitimate governmental goal of encouraging childbirth.

The Court of Appeals distinguished these cases on the ground that "[t]o prevent access to a public facility does more than demonstrate a political choice in favor of childbirth; it clearly narrows and in some cases forecloses the availability of abortion to women." . . .

We think that this analysis is much like that which we rejected in *Maher*, *Poelker*, and *McRae*. . . . Missouri's refusal to allow public employees to perform abortions in public hospitals leaves a pregnant woman with the same choices as if the State had chosen not to operate any public hospitals at all. The challenged provisions only restrict a woman's ability to obtain an abortion to the extent that she chooses to use a physician affiliated with a public hospital. . . . Having held that the State's refusal to fund abortions does not violate *Roe v. Wade*, it strains logic to reach a contrary result for the use of public facilities and employees. If the State may "make a value judgment favoring childbirth over abortion and . . . implement that judgment by the allocation of public funds," surely it may do so through the allocation of other public resources, such as hospitals and medical staff.

. . . .

. . . Thus we uphold the Act's restrictions on the use of public employees and facilities for the performance or assistance of nontherapeutic abortions.

. . . .

D

Section 188.029 of the Missouri Act provides:

Before a physician performs an abortion on a woman he has reason to believe is carrying an unborn child of twenty or more weeks gestational age, the physician shall first determine if the unborn child is viable by using and exercising that degree of care, skill, and proficiency commonly exercised by the ordinarily skillful, careful, and prudent physician engaged in similar practice under the same or similar conditions. In making this determination of viability, the physician shall perform or cause to be performed such medical examinations and tests as are necessary to make a finding of the gestational age, weight, and lung maturity of the unborn child and shall enter such findings and determination of viability in the medical record of the mother.

As with the preamble, the parties disagree over the meaning of this statutory provision. The State emphasizes the language of the first sentence, which speaks in terms of the physician's determination of viability being made by the standards of ordinary skill in the medical profession. Appellees stress the language of the second sentence, which prescribes such "tests as are necessary" to make a finding of gestational age, fetal weight, and lung maturity.

. . . .

We think the viability-testing provision makes sense only if the second sentence is read to require only those tests that are useful to making subsidiary findings as to viability. If we construe this provision to require a physician to perform those tests needed to make the three specified findings *in all circumstances,* including when the physician's reasonable professional judgment indicates that the tests would be irrelevant to determining viability or even dangerous to the mother and the fetus, the second sentence of § 188.029 would conflict with the first sentence's *requirement* that a physician apply his reasonable professional skill and judgment. It would also be incongruous to read this provision, especially the word "necessary," to require the performance of tests irrelevant to the expressed statutory purpose of determining viability. . . .

The viability-testing provision of the Missouri Act is concerned with promoting the State's interest in potential human life rather than in maternal health. Section 188.029 creates what is essentially a presumption of viability at 20 weeks, which the physician must rebut with tests indicating that the fetus is not viable prior to performing an abortion. It also directs the physician's determination as to viability by specifying consideration, if feasible, of gestational age, fetal weight, and lung capacity. . . .

In *Roe v. Wade*, the Court recognized that the State has "important and legitimate" interests in protecting maternal health and in the potentiality of human life. During the second trimester, the State "may, if it chooses, regulate the abortion procedure in ways that are reasonably related to maternal health." After viability, when the State's interest in potential human life was held to become compelling, the State "may, if it chooses, regulate, and even proscribe, abortion except where it is necessary, in appropriate medical judgment, for the preservation of the life or health of the mother."

. . . To the extent that § 188.029 regulates the method for determining viability, it undoubtedly does superimpose state regulation on the medical determination whether a particular fetus is viable. The Court of Appeals and the District Court thought it unconstitutional for this reason. To the extent that the viability tests increase the cost of what are in fact second-trimester abortions, their validity may also be questioned under *Akron,* where the Court held that a requirement that second-trimester abortions must be performed in hospitals was invalid because it substantially increased the expense of those procedures.

We think that the doubt cast upon the Missouri statute by these cases is not so much a flaw in the statute as it is a reflection of the fact that the rigid trimester analysis of the course of a pregnancy enunciated in *Roe* has resulted in . . . making constitutional law in this area a virtual Procrustean bed. Statutes specifying elements of informed consent to be provided abortion patients, for example, were invalidated if they were thought to "structur[e] . . . the dialogue between the woman and her physician." *Thornburgh v. American College of Obstetricians and Gynecologists*, 476 U.S. 747, 763 (1986). As the dissenters in *Thornburgh* pointed out, such a statute would have been sustained under any traditional standard of judicial review, or for any other surgical procedure except abortion.

Stare decisis is a cornerstone of our legal system, but it has less power in constitutional cases, where, save for constitutional amendments, this Court is the only body able to make needed changes. We have not refrained from reconsideration of a prior construction of the Constitution that has proved "unsound in principle and unworkable in practice." We think the *Roe* trimester framework falls into that category.

In the first place, the rigid *Roe* framework is hardly consistent with the notion of a Constitution cast in general terms, as ours is, and usually speaking in general principles, as ours does. The key elements of the *Roe* framework—trimesters and viability—are not found in the text of the Constitution or in any place else one would expect to find a constitutional principle. Since the bounds of the inquiry are essentially indeterminate, the result has been a web of legal rules that have become increasingly intricate, resembling a code of regulations rather than a body of constitutional doctrine. . . .

In the second place, we do not see why the State's interest in protecting potential human life should come into existence only at the point of viability, and that there should therefore be a rigid line allowing state regulation after viability but prohibiting it before viability. . . .

The tests that § 188.029 requires the physician to perform are designed to determine viability. . . . It is true that the tests in question increase the expense of abortion, and regulate the discretion of the physician in determining the viability of the fetus. Since the tests will undoubtedly show in many cases that the fetus is not viable, the tests will have been performed for what were in fact second-trimester abortions. But we are satisfied that the requirement of these tests permissibly furthers the State's interest in protecting potential human life, and we therefore believe § 188.029 to be constitutional.

. . . .

Because none of the challenged provisions of the Missouri Act properly before us conflict with the Constitution, the judgment of the Court of Appeals is

Reversed.

■ O'CONNOR, J., concurring in part and concurring in the judgment.

I concur in Parts I, II-A, II-B, and II-C of the Court's opinion.

. . . .

In its interpretation of Missouri's "determination of viability" provision, the plurality has proceeded in a manner unnecessary to deciding the question at hand. I agree with the plurality that it was plain error for the Court of Appeals to interpret the second sentence of § 188.029 as meaning that "doctors *must* perform tests to find gestational age, fetal weight and lung maturity." When read together with the first sentence of § 188.029—which requires a physician to "determine if the unborn child is viable by using and exercising that degree of care, skill, and proficiency commonly exercised by the ordinary skillful, careful, and prudent physician engaged in similar practice under the same or similar conditions"—it would be contradictory nonsense to read the second sentence as requiring a physician to perform viability examinations and tests in situations where it would be careless and imprudent to do so. The plurality is quite correct: "the viability-testing provision makes sense only if the second sentence is read to require only those tests that are useful to making subsidiary findings as to viability," and, I would add, only those examinations and tests that it would not be imprudent or careless to perform in the particular medical situation before the physician.

Unlike the plurality, I do not understand these viability testing requirements to conflict with any of the Court's past decisions concerning state regulation of abortion. Therefore, there is no necessity to accept the State's invitation to reexamine the constitutional validity of *Roe v. Wade*, 410 U.S. 113 (1973). Where there is no need to decide a constitutional question, it is a venerable principle of this Court's adjudicatory processes not to do so. . . . Quite simply, "[i]t is not the habit of the court to decide questions of a constitutional nature unless absolutely necessary to a decision of the case." The Court today has accepted the State's every interpretation of its abortion statute and has upheld, under our existing precedents, every provision of that statute which is properly before us. Precisely for this reason reconsideration of *Roe* falls not into any "good-cause exception" to this "fundamental rule of judicial restraint. . . ." When the constitutional invalidity of a State's abortion statute actually turns on the constitutional validity of *Roe v. Wade*, there will be time enough to reexamine *Roe*. And to do so carefully.

. . . .

I do not think the second sentence of § 188.029, as interpreted by the Court, imposes a degree of state regulation on the medical determination of viability that in any way conflicts with prior decisions of this Court. As the plurality recognizes, the requirement that, where not imprudent, physicians perform examinations and tests useful to making subsidiary findings to determine viability "promot[es] the State's interest in potential human life rather than in maternal health." No decision of this Court has held that the State may not directly promote its interest in potential life when viability is possible. Quite the contrary. In *Thornburgh v. American College of Obstetricians and Gynecologists*, 476 U.S. 747 (1986), the Court considered a constitutional challenge to a Pennsylvania statute requiring that a second physician be present during an abortion performed "when viability is possible." . . . The *Thornburgh* majority struck down the Pennsylvania statute merely because the statute had no exception for emergency situations and not because it found a constitutional difference between the State's promotion of its interest in potential life when viability is possible and when viability is certain. . . .

. . . .

It is clear to me that requiring the performance of examinations and tests useful to determining whether a fetus is viable, when viability is possible, and when it would not be medically imprudent to do so, does not impose an undue burden on a woman's abortion decision. On this ground alone I would reject the suggestion that § 188.029 as interpreted is unconstitutional. More to the point . . . I see no conflict between § 188.029 and the Court's opinion in *Akron*. The second-trimester hospitalization requirement struck down in *Akron* imposed, in the majority's view, "a heavy, and unnecessary, burden," more than doubling the cost of "women's access to a relatively inexpensive, otherwise accessible, and safe abortion procedure." By contrast, the cost of examinations and tests that could usefully and prudently be performed when a woman is 20–24 weeks pregnant to determine whether the fetus is viable would only marginally, if at all, increase the cost of an abortion. . . .

Moreover, the examinations and tests required by § 188.029 are to be performed when viability is possible. This feature of § 188.029 distinguishes it from the second-trimester hospitalization requirement struck down by the *Akron* majority. As the Court recognized in *Thornburgh*, the State's compelling interest in potential life postviability renders its interest in determining the critical point of viability equally compelling. Under the Court's precedents, the same cannot be said for the *Akron* second-trimester hospitalization requirement. As I understand the Court's opinion in *Akron*, therefore, the plurality's suggestion today that *Akron* casts doubt on the validity of § 188.029, even as the Court has interpreted it, is without foundation and cannot provide a basis for reevaluating *Roe*. . . .

■ SCALIA, J., concurring in part and concurring in the judgment.

. . . As to Part II-D, I share Justice BLACKMUN's view . . . that it effectively would overrule *Roe v. Wade*, 410 U.S. 113 (1973). I think that should be done, but would do it more explicitly. . . .

Justice O'Connor's assertion that a " 'fundamental rule of judicial restraint' " requires us to avoid reconsidering *Roe*, cannot be taken seriously. By finessing *Roe* we do not, as she suggests, adhere to the strict and venerable rule that we should avoid " 'decid[ing] questions of a constitutional nature.' " We have not disposed of this case on some statutory or procedural ground, but have decided, and could not avoid deciding, whether the Missouri statute meets the requirements of the United States Constitution. The only choice available is whether, in deciding that constitutional question, we should use *Roe v. Wade* as the benchmark, or something else. What is involved, therefore, is not the rule of avoiding constitutional issues where possible, but the quite separate principle that we will not " 'formulate a rule of constitutional law broader than is required by the precise facts to which it is to be applied.' " The latter is a sound general principle, but one often departed from when good reason exists. . . .

. . . .

The real question, then, is whether there are valid reasons to go beyond the most stingy possible holding today. It seems to me there are not only valid but compelling ones. Ordinarily, speaking no more broadly than is absolutely required avoids throwing settled law into confusion; doing so today preserves a chaos that is evident to anyone who can read and count. Alone sufficient to justify a broad holding is the fact that our retaining control, through *Roe*, of what I believe to be, and many of our citizens recognize to be, a political issue, continuously distorts the public perception of the role of this Court. We can now look forward to at least another Term with carts full of mail from the public, and streets full of demonstrators, urging us—their unelected and life-tenured judges who have been awarded those extraordinary, undemocratic characteristics precisely in order that we might follow the law despite the popular will—to follow the popular will. Indeed, I expect we can look forward to even more of that than before, given our indecisive decision today. And if these reasons for taking the unexceptional course of reaching a broader holding are not enough, then consider the nature of the constitutional question we avoid: In most cases, we do no harm by not speaking more broadly than the decision requires. Anyone affected by the conduct that the avoided holding would have prohibited will be able to challenge it himself and have his day in court to make the argument. Not so with respect to the harm that many States believed, pre-*Roe*, and many may continue to believe, is caused by largely unrestricted abortion. That will continue to occur if the States have the constitutional power to prohibit it, and would do so, but we skillfully avoid telling them so. Perhaps those abortions cannot constitutionally be proscribed. That is surely an arguable question, the question that reconsideration of *Roe v. Wade* entails. But what is not at all arguable, it seems to me, is that we should decide now and not insist that we be run into a corner before we grudgingly yield up our judgment. The only sound reason for the latter course is to prevent a change in the law—but to think that desirable begs the question to be decided.

It was an arguable question today whether § 188.029 of the Missouri law contravened this Court's understanding of *Roe v. Wade*, and I would have examined *Roe* rather than examining the contravention. Given the Court's newly contracted abstemiousness, what will it take, one must wonder, to permit us to reach that fundamental question? The result of our vote today is that we will not reconsider that prior opinion, even if most of the Justices think it is wrong, unless we have before us a statute that in fact contradicts it—and even then (under our newly discovered "no-broader-then-necessary" requirement) only minor problematical aspects of *Roe* will be reconsidered, unless one expects state legislatures to adopt provisions whose compliance with *Roe* cannot even be argued with a straight face. It thus appears that the mansion of constitutionalized abortion law, constructed overnight in *Roe v. Wade*, must be disassembled doorjamb by doorjamb, and never entirely brought down, no matter how wrong it may be.

. . . .

■ BLACKMUN, J., with whom BRENNAN, J., and MARSHALL, J. join, concurring in part and dissenting in part.

Today, *Roe v. Wade*, 410 U.S. 113 (1973), and the fundamental constitutional right of women to decide whether to terminate a pregnancy, survive but are not secure. Although the Court extricates itself from this case without making a single, even incremental, change in the law of abortion, the plurality and Justice Scalia would overrule *Roe* (the first silently, the other explicitly) and would return to the States virtually unfettered authority to control the quintessentially intimate, personal, and life-directing decision whether to carry a fetus to term. Although today, no less than yesterday, the Constitution and the decisions of this Court prohibit a State from enacting laws that inhibit women from the meaningful exercise of that right, a plurality of this Court implicitly invites every state legislature to enact more and more restrictive abortion regulations in order to provoke more and more test cases, in the hope that sometime down the line the Court will return the law of procreative freedom to the severe limitations that generally prevailed in this country before January 22, 1973. Never in my memory has a plurality announced a judgment of this Court that so foments disregard for the law and for our standing decisions.

. . . With feigned restraint, the plurality announces that its analysis leaves *Roe* "undisturbed," albeit "modif[ied] and narrow[ed]." But this disclaimer is totally meaningless. The plurality opinion is filled with winks, and nods, and knowing glances to those who would do away with *Roe* explicitly, but turns a stone face to anyone in search of what the plurality conceives as the scope of a woman's right under the Due Process Clause to terminate a pregnancy free from the coercive and brooding influence of the State. The simple truth is that *Roe* would not survive the plurality's analysis, and that the plurality provides no substitute for *Roe*'s protective umbrella.

I fear for the future. I fear for the liberty and equality of the millions of women who have lived and come of age in the 16 years since *Roe* was decided. I fear for the integrity of, and public esteem for, this Court.

I dissent.

. . . .

Having set up the conflict between § 188.029 and the *Roe* trimester framework, the plurality summarily discards *Roe*'s analytic core as "'unsound in principle and unworkable in practice.'" This is so, the plurality claims, because the key elements of the framework do not appear in the text of the Constitution, because the framework more closely resembles a regulatory code than a body of constitutional doctrine, and because under the framework the State's interest in potential human life is considered compelling only after viability, when, in fact, that interest is equally compelling throughout pregnancy. The plurality does not bother to explain these alleged flaws in *Roe*. Bald assertion masquerades as reasoning. The object, quite clearly, is not to persuade, but to prevail.

1

The plurality opinion is far more remarkable for the arguments that it does not advance than for those that it does. The plurality does not even mention, much less join, the true jurisprudential debate underlying this case: whether the Constitution includes an "unenumerated" general right to privacy as recognized in many of our decisions, most notably *Griswold v. Connecticut*, 381 U.S. 479 (1965), and *Roe*, and, more specifically, whether, and to what extent, such a right to privacy extends to matters of childbearing and family life, including abortion. These are questions of unsurpassed significance in this Court's interpretation of the Constitution, and mark the battleground upon which this case was fought, by the parties, by the United States as *amicus* on behalf of petitioners, and by an unprecedented number of *amici*. On these grounds, abandoned by the plurality, the Court should decide this case.

But rather than arguing that the text of the Constitution makes no mention of the right to privacy, the plurality complains that the critical elements of the *Roe* framework—trimesters and viability—do not appear in the Constitution and are, therefore, somehow inconsistent with a Constitution cast in general terms. Were this a true concern, we would have to abandon most of our constitutional jurisprudence. As the plurality well knows, or should know, the "critical elements" of countless constitutional doctrines nowhere appear in the Constitution's text. . . . Similarly, the Constitution makes no mention of the rational-basis test, or the specific verbal formulations of intermediate and strict scrutiny by which this Court evaluates claims under the Equal Protection Clause. The reason is simple. Like the *Roe* framework, these tests or standards are not, and do not purport to be, rights protected by the Constitution. Rather, they are judge-made methods for evaluating and measuring the strength and scope of constitutional rights or for balancing the constitutional rights of individuals against the competing interests of government.

With respect to the *Roe* framework, the general constitutional principle, indeed the fundamental constitutional right, for which it was developed is the right to privacy, a species of "liberty" protected by the Due Process Clause, which under our past decisions safeguards the right of women to exercise some control over their own role in procreation. As we recently reaffirmed in *Thornburgh v. American College of Obstetricians and Gynecologists*, 476 U.S. 747 (1986), few decisions are "more basic to individual dignity and autonomy" or more appropriate to that "certain private sphere of individual liberty" that the Constitution reserves from the intrusive reach of government than the right to make the uniquely personal, intimate, and self-defining decision whether to end a pregnancy. It is this general principle, the " 'moral fact that a person belongs to himself and not others nor to society as a whole,' " that is found in the Constitution. The trimester framework simply defines and limits that right to privacy in the abortion context to accommodate, not destroy, a State's legitimate interest in protecting the health of pregnant women and in preserving potential human life. Fashioning such accommodations between individual rights and the legitimate interests of government, establishing benchmarks and standards with which to evaluate the competing claims of individuals and government, lies at the very heart of constitutional adjudication. To the extent that the trimester framework is useful in this enterprise, it is not only consistent with constitutional interpretation, but necessary to the wise and just exercise of this Court's paramount authority to define the scope of constitutional rights.

2

The plurality next alleges that the result of the trimester framework has "been a web of legal rules that have become increasingly intricate, resembling a code of regulations rather than a body of constitutional doctrine." Again, if this were a true and genuine concern, we would have to abandon vast areas of our constitutional jurisprudence. The plurality complains that under the trimester framework the Court has distinguished between a city ordinance requiring that second-trimester abortions be performed in clinics and a state law requiring that these abortions be performed in hospitals, or between laws requiring that certain information be furnished to a woman by a physician or his assistant and those requiring that such information be furnished by the physician exclusively. . . .

That numerous constitutional doctrines result in narrow differentiations between similar circumstances does not mean that this Court has abandoned adjudication in favor of regulation. Rather, these careful distinctions reflect the process of constitutional adjudication itself, which is often highly fact specific, requiring such determinations as whether state laws are "unduly burdensome" or "reasonable" or bear a "rational" or "necessary" relation to asserted state interests. . . .

. . . If, in delicate and complicated areas of constitutional law, our legal judgments "have become increasingly intricate," it is not, as the plurality contends, because we have overstepped our judicial role. Quite the opposite: the rules are intricate because we have remained conscientious in our duty to do justice carefully, especially when fundamental rights rise or fall with our decisions.

3

Finally, the plurality asserts that the trimester framework cannot stand because the State's interest in potential life is compelling throughout pregnancy, not merely after viability. *Ante*, at 3057. The opinion contains not one word of rationale for its view of the State's interest. This "it-is-so-because-we-say-so" jurisprudence constitutes nothing other than an attempted exercise of brute force; reason, much less persuasion, has no place.

. . . .

. . . I remain convinced, as six other Members of this Court 16 years ago were convinced, that the *Roe* framework, and the viability standard in particular, fairly, sensibly, and effectively functions to safeguard the constitutional liberties of pregnant women while recognizing and accommodating the State's interest in potential human life. The viability line reflects the biological facts and truths of fetal development; it marks that threshold moment prior to which a fetus cannot survive separate from the woman and cannot reasonably and objectively be regarded as a subject of rights or interests distinct from, or paramount to, those of the pregnant woman. At the same time, the viability standard takes account of the undeniable fact that as the fetus evolves into its postnatal form, and as it loses its dependence on the uterine environment, the State's interest in the fetus' potential human life, and in fostering a regard for human life in general, becomes compelling. As a practical matter, because viability follows "quickening"—the point at which a woman feels movement in her womb—and because viability occurs no earlier than 23 weeks gestational age, it establishes an easily applicable standard for regulating abortion while providing a pregnant woman ample time to exercise her fundamental right with her responsible physician to terminate her pregnancy. Although I have stated previously for a majority of this Court that "[c]onstitutional rights do not always have easily ascertainable boundaries," to seek and establish those boundaries remains the special responsibility of this Court. In *Roe*, we discharged that responsibility as logic and science compelled. The plurality today advances not one reasonable argument as to why our judgment in that case was wrong and should be abandoned.

C

Having contrived an opportunity to reconsider the *Roe* framework, and then having discarded that framework, the plurality finds the testing provision unobjectionable because it "permissibly furthers the State's interest in protecting potential human life." This newly minted standard is circular and totally meaningless. Whether a challenged abortion regulation "permissibly furthers" a legitimate state interest is the *question* that courts must answer in abortion cases, not the standard for courts to apply. In keeping with the rest of its opinion, the plurality makes no attempt to explain or to justify its new standard, either in the abstract or as applied in this case. Nor could it. The "permissibly furthers" standard has no independent meaning, and consists of nothing other than what a majority of this Court may believe at any given moment in any given case. The plurality's novel test appears to be nothing more than a dressed-up version of rational-basis review, this Court's most lenient level of scrutiny. One thing is clear, however: were the plurality's "permissibly furthers" standard adopted by the Court, for all practical purposes, *Roe* would be overruled.

. . . .

The plurality pretends that *Roe* survives, explaining that the facts of this case differ from those in *Roe:* here, Missouri has chosen to assert its interest in potential life only at the point of viability, whereas, in *Roe*, Texas had asserted that interest from the point of conception, criminalizing all abortions, except where the life of the mother was at stake. This, of course, is a distinction without a difference. The plurality repudiates every principle for which *Roe* stands; in good conscience, it cannot possibly believe that *Roe* lies "undisturbed" merely because this case does not call upon the Court to reconsider the Texas statute, or one like it. . . . It is impossible to read the plurality opinion and especially its final paragraph, without recognizing its implicit invitation to every State to enact more and more restrictive abortion laws, and to assert their interest in potential life as of the moment of conception. All these laws will satisfy the plurality's non-scrutiny, until sometime, a new regime of old dissenters and new appointees will declare what the plurality intends: that *Roe* is no longer good law.

D

Thus, "not with a bang, but a whimper," the plurality discards a landmark case of the last generation, and casts into darkness the hopes and visions of every woman in this country who had come to believe that the Constitution guaranteed her the right to exercise some control over her unique ability to bear children. The plurality does so either oblivious or insensitive to the fact that millions of women, and their families, have ordered their lives around the right to reproductive choice, and that this right has become vital to the full participation of women in the economic and political walks of American life. The plurality would clear the way once again for government to force upon women the physical labor and specific and direct medical and psychological harms that may accompany carrying a fetus to term. The plurality would clear the way again for the State to conscript a woman's body and to force upon her a "distressful life and future."

. . . .

For today, at least, the law of abortion stands undisturbed. For today, the women of this Nation still retain the liberty to control their destinies. But the signs are evident and very ominous, and a chill wind blows.

NOTES

1. *Legal "personhood" of the unborn.* Note that the Missouri law overturned in *Webster* included a preamble finding that the "life of each human being begins at conception" and that the state has an interest in the "life, health and well-being" of unborn children. MO. REV. STAT. § 1.205(1) (1986). The preamble granted "unborn children" "all the rights, privileges, and immunities available to other persons, citizens, and residents of this state, subject only to the Constitution of the United States." *Id.* Even as the Supreme Court invalidated the statute's operative provisions, it allowed this section to stand because it was not being used to directly regulate abortion access in any way. *Webster*, 492 U.S. at 490–91. Do you agree? Social scientists have argued that the manner in which an issue is "framed" is a powerful force in how it is legitimated. *See* Robert D. Benford & David A. Snow, *Framing Processes and Social Movements: An Overview and Assessment*, 26 ANN. REV. SOC. 611, 614, 627 (2000). On this account, if the abortion debate turns on whether the entity involved is a "baby" or a "fetus,"

does allowing the preamble to stand accept one side's framing over the other's? Does the framing matter in the long run?

2.   *When life begins.* Relying upon *Akron*'s admonition that "a State may not adopt one theory of when life begins to justify its regulation of abortions," 462 U.S. at 444 (internal citations and quotations omitted), the Eighth Circuit invalidated the Missouri statute's preamble because it was "an impermissible state adoption of a theory of when life begins to justify its abortion regulations." *Reproductive Health Service v. Webster*, 851 F.2d 1071, 1076 (8th Cir. 1988). However, on appeal, the Supreme Court held that such language was merely "precatory," expressing an opinion, rather than creating law. *Webster*, 492 U.S. at 505. Do you agree?

3.   *Personalizing the fetus. Webster* represents a shift in the rhetoric surrounding abortion, leaving unchallenged the Missouri statute's characterization of the fetus as an "unborn child," the preferred nomenclature of abortion opponents. In the period leading up to *Webster*, abortion opponents had begun to characterize the fetus visually, as well as rhetorically, as a baby. Indeed, the 1984 documentary *The Silent Scream* purported to show an abortion from the vantage point of the fetus, using ultrasound technology to claim that the "agitated movements" of the "child" were (silent) cries of pain, although many neurologists and neuroembryologists contested this characterization. The National Right to Life Committee distributed 10,000 copies of *The Silent Scream* to the public, including members of Congress and the Supreme Court. *See* SARA DUBOW, OURSELVES UNBORN: A HISTORY OF THE FETUS IN MODERN AMERICA 159 (2011).

4.   *The reprise of legal "personhood."* The challenged Missouri statutory provision granting fetuses the status of legal persons was by no means the first or last legislative attempt to define legal personhood as beginning at conception. Most recently, ballot initiatives in Colorado and Mississippi would have granted legal personhood at the point of conception. Both initiatives failed, but the question will return to Colorado's ballot in 2014. Critically, the effects of such a law would stretch beyond the question of the legality of abortion to implicate the use of assisted reproductive technologies and some forms of birth control. Organizations such as Personhood USA (http://www.personhoodusa.com/), along with other pro-life organizations, have pressed for such statutes. In addition to their implications for abortion rights, will such laws prompt questions about maternal behavior during pregnancy, such as drinking, smoking, using drugs, or refusing to comply with medically-ordered interventions?

5.   *Overruling* Roe? According to Professor Sylvia Law, the Court's holding in *Webster* "effectively overruled *Roe*." Specifically, "Justices Rehnquist, White, Kennedy, and Scalia rejected *Roe*'s core holding that a woman's right to choose abortion is a fundamental constitutionally protected right," while also rejecting "*Roe*'s rule that the state cannot act to protect fetal life prior to viability . . . allow[ing] the state to protect fetal life from the moment of conception." And meaningfully, in a separate concurrence, "Justice Scalia . . . urged open recognition that [*Webster*] overruled *Roe* and seemed to deny that the Constitution had any bearing on laws controlling a woman's reproductive

capacity." Sylvia A. Law, *Abortion Compromise—Inevitable and Impossible*, 1992 U. ILL. L. REV. 921, 925. Do you agree with this assessment?

Rust v. Sullivan
500 U.S. 173 (1991).

■ REHNQUIST, C.J.

These cases concern a facial challenge to Department of Health and Human Services (HHS) regulations which limit the ability of Title X fund recipients to engage in abortion-related activities.

. . . .

In 1970, Congress enacted Title X of the Public Health Service Act (Act), which provides federal funding for family-planning services. The Act authorizes the Secretary to "make grants to and enter into contracts with public or nonprofit private entities to assist in the establishment and operation of voluntary family planning projects which shall offer a broad range of acceptable and effective family planning methods and services." Grants and contracts under Title X must "be made in accordance with such regulations as the Secretary may promulgate." Section 1008 of the Act, however, provides that "[n]one of the funds appropriated under this subchapter shall be used in programs where abortion is a method of family planning." That restriction was intended to ensure that Title X funds would "be used only to support preventive family planning services, population research, infertility services, and other related medical, informational, and educational activities."

In 1988, the Secretary promulgated new regulations designed to provide " 'clear and operational guidance' to grantees about how to preserve the distinction between Title X programs and abortion as a method of family planning." The regulations clarify, through the definition of the term "family planning," that Congress intended Title X funds "to be used only to support *preventive* family planning services." Accordingly, Title X services are limited to "preconceptional counseling, education, and general reproductive health care," and expressly exclude "pregnancy care (including obstetric or prenatal care)." . . .

The regulations attach three principal conditions on the grant of federal funds for Title X projects. First, the regulations specify that a "Title X project may not provide counseling concerning the use of abortion as a method of family planning or provide referral for abortion as a method of family planning." . . .

Second, the regulations broadly prohibit a Title X project from engaging in activities that "encourage, promote or advocate abortion as a method of family planning." § 59.10(a). Forbidden activities include lobbying for legislation that would increase the availability of abortion as a method of family planning, developing or disseminating materials advocating abortion as a method of family planning, providing speakers to promote abortion as a method of family planning, using legal action to make abortion available in any way as a method of family planning, and paying dues to any group that advocates abortion as a method of family planning as a substantial part of its activities.

Third, the regulations require that Title X projects be organized so that they are "physically and financially separate" from prohibited abortion activities. To be deemed physically and financially separate, "a Title X project must have an objective integrity and independence from prohibited activities. Mere bookkeeping separation of Title X funds from other monies is not sufficient." . . .

Petitioners contend that the regulations violate the First Amendment by impermissibly discriminating based on viewpoint because they prohibit "all discussion about abortion as a lawful option—including counseling, referral, and the provision of neutral and accurate information about ending a pregnancy—while compelling the clinic or counselor to provide information that promotes continuing a pregnancy to term." They assert that the regulations violate the "free speech rights of private health care organizations that receive Title X funds, of their staff, and of their patients" by impermissibly imposing "viewpoint-discriminatory conditions on government subsidies" and thus "penaliz[e] speech funded with non-Title X monies." Because "Title X continues to fund speech ancillary to pregnancy testing in a manner that is not evenhanded with respect to views and information about abortion, it invidiously discriminates on the basis of viewpoint." . . .

There is no question but that the statutory prohibition contained in § 1008 is constitutional. In *Maher v. Roe*, 432 U.S. 464 (1977), we upheld a state welfare regulation under which Medicaid recipients received payments for services related to childbirth, but not for nontherapeutic abortions. The Court rejected the claim that this unequal subsidization worked a violation of the Constitution. We held that the government may "make a value judgment favoring childbirth over abortion, and . . . implement that judgment by the allocation of public funds." . . .

. . . The Government can, without violating the Constitution, selectively fund a program to encourage certain activities it believes to be in the public interest, without at the same time funding an alternative program which seeks to deal with the problem in another way. In so doing, the Government has not discriminated on the basis of viewpoint; it has merely chosen to fund one activity to the exclusion of the other. "[A] legislature's decision not to subsidize the exercise of a fundamental right does not infringe the right." A refusal to fund protected activity, without more, cannot be equated with the imposition of a "penalty" on that activity. "There is a basic difference between direct state interference with a protected activity and state encouragement of an alternative activity consonant with legislative policy."

The challenged regulations implement the statutory prohibition by prohibiting counseling, referral, and the provision of information regarding abortion as a method of family planning. They are designed to ensure that the limits of the federal program are observed. The Title X program is designed not for prenatal care, but to encourage family planning. A doctor who wished to offer prenatal care to a project patient who became pregnant could properly be prohibited from doing so because such service is outside the scope of the federally funded program. The regulations prohibiting abortion counseling and referral are of the same ilk; "no funds appropriated for the project may be used in programs where abortion is a method of family planning," and a doctor employed by the project may be prohibited in the course of his project duties from counseling abortion or referring for abortion. This is not a case of the Government "suppressing a dangerous idea," but of a prohibition on a project grantee or its employees from engaging in activities outside of the project's scope.

To hold that the Government unconstitutionally discriminates on the basis of viewpoint when it chooses to fund a program dedicated to advance certain permissible goals, because the program in advancing those goals necessarily discourages alternative goals, would render numerous Government programs constitutionally suspect.... Petitioners' assertions ultimately boil down to the position that if the government chooses to subsidize one protected right, it must subsidize analogous counterpart rights. But the Court has soundly rejected that proposition. Within far broader limits than the petitioners are willing to concede, when the Government appropriates public funds to establish a program it is entitled to define the limits of that program.

. . . .

Petitioners also contend that the restrictions on the subsidization of abortion-related speech contained in the regulations are impermissible because they condition the receipt of a benefit, in these cases Title X funding, on the relinquishment of a constitutional right, the right to engage in abortion advocacy and counseling. . . .

Petitioners' reliance on these cases is unavailing, however, because here the Government is not denying a benefit to anyone, but is instead simply insisting that public funds be spent for the purposes for which they were authorized. The Secretary's regulations do not force the Title X grantee to give up abortion-related speech; they merely require that the grantee keep such activities separate and distinct from Title X activities. . . .The grantee receives Title X funds, however, for the specific and limited purpose of establishing and operating a Title X project. The regulations govern the scope of the Title X *project's* activities, and leave the grantee unfettered in its other activities. The Title X *grantee* can continue to perform abortions, provide abortion-related services, and engage in abortion advocacy; it simply is required to conduct those activities through programs that are separate and independent from the project that receives Title X funds.

In contrast, our "unconstitutional conditions" cases involve situations in which the Government has placed a condition on the *recipient* of the subsidy rather than on a particular program or service, thus effectively prohibiting the recipient from engaging in the protected conduct outside the scope of the federally funded program. . . .

. . . .

By requiring that the Title X grantee engage in abortion-related activity separately from activity receiving federal funding, Congress has . . . not denied it the right to engage in abortion-related activities. Congress has merely refused to fund such activities out of the public fisc, and the Secretary has simply required a certain degree of separation from the Title X project in order to ensure the integrity of the federally funded program.

The same principles apply to petitioners' claim that the regulations abridge the free speech rights of the grantee's staff. Individuals who are voluntarily employed for a Title X project must perform their duties in accordance with the regulation's restrictions on abortion counseling and referral. The employees remain free, however, to pursue abortion-related activities when they are not acting under the auspices of the Title X project. The regulations, which govern solely the scope of the Title X project's activities, do not in any way restrict the activities of those persons acting as private individuals. The employees' freedom of expression is limited during the time that they actually work for the project; but this limitation is a consequence of their decision to accept employment in a project, the scope of which is permissibly restricted by the funding authority.

This is not to suggest that funding by the Government, even when coupled with the freedom of the fund recipients to speak outside the scope of the Government-funded project, is invariably sufficient to justify Government control over the content of expression. For example, this Court has recognized that the existence of a Government "subsidy," in the form of Government-owned property, does not justify the restriction of speech in areas that have "been traditionally open to the public for expressive activity." Similarly, we have recognized that the university is a traditional sphere of free expression so fundamental to the functioning of our society that the Government's ability to control speech within that sphere by means of conditions attached to the expenditure of Government funds is restricted by the vagueness and overbreadth doctrines of the First Amendment. It could be argued by analogy that traditional relationships such as that between doctor and patient should enjoy protection under the First Amendment from Government regulation, even when subsidized by the Government. We need not resolve that question here, however, because the Title X program regulations do not significantly impinge upon the doctor-patient relationship. Nothing in them requires a doctor to represent as his own any opinion that he does not in fact hold. Nor is the doctor-patient relationship established by the Title X program sufficiently all encompassing so as to justify an expectation on the part of the patient of comprehensive medical advice. The program does not provide post conception medical care, and therefore a doctor's silence with regard to abortion cannot reasonably be thought to mislead a client into thinking that the doctor does not consider abortion an appropriate option for her. The doctor is always free to make clear that advice regarding abortion is simply beyond the scope of the program. In these circumstances, the general rule that the Government may choose not to subsidize speech applies with full force.

We turn now to petitioners' argument that the regulations violate a woman's Fifth Amendment right to choose whether to terminate her pregnancy. We recently reaffirmed the long-recognized principle that " 'the Due Process Clauses generally confer no affirmative right to governmental aid, even where such aid may be necessary to secure life, liberty, or property interests of which the government itself may not deprive the individual.' " The Government has no constitutional duty to subsidize an activity merely because the activity is constitutionally protected and may validly choose to fund childbirth over abortion and " 'implement that judgment by the allocation of public funds' " for medical services relating to childbirth but not to those relating to abortion. The Government has no affirmative duty to "commit any resources to facilitating abortions," and its decision to fund childbirth but not abortion "places no governmental obstacle in the path of a woman who chooses to terminate her pregnancy, but rather, by means of unequal subsidization of abortion and other medical services, encourages alternative activity deemed in the public interest."

That the regulations do not impermissibly burden a woman's Fifth Amendment rights is evident from the line of cases beginning with *Maher* and *McRae* and culminating in our most recent decision in *Webster*. Just as Congress' refusal to fund abortions in *McRae* left "an indigent woman with at least the same range of choice in deciding whether to obtain a medically necessary abortion as she would have had if Congress had chosen to subsidize no health care costs at all," and "Missouri's refusal to allow public employees to perform abortions in public hospitals leaves a pregnant woman with the same choices as if the State had chosen not to operate any public hospitals," Congress' refusal to fund abortion counseling and advocacy leaves a pregnant woman with the same choices as if the Government had chosen not to fund family-planning services at all. The difficulty that a woman encounters when a Title X project does not provide abortion counseling or referral leaves her in no different position than she would have been if the Government had not enacted Title X.

. . . .

Petitioners also argue that by impermissibly infringing on the doctor-patient relationship and depriving a Title X client of information concerning abortion as a method of family planning, the regulations violate a woman's Fifth Amendment right to medical self-determination and to make informed medical decisions free of government-imposed harm. They argue that under our decisions in *Akron v. Akron Center for Reproductive Health, Inc.*, 462 U.S. 416 (1983), and *Thornburgh v. American College of Obstetricians and Gynecologists*, 476 U.S. 747 (1986), the Government cannot interfere with a woman's right to make an informed and voluntary choice by placing restrictions on the patient-doctor dialogue.

. . . Critical to our decisions in *Akron* and *Thornburgh* to invalidate a governmental intrusion into the patient-doctor dialogue was the fact that the laws in both cases required *all* doctors within their respective jurisdictions to provide *all* pregnant patients contemplating an abortion a litany of information, regardless of whether the patient sought the information or whether the doctor thought the information necessary to the patient's decision. Under the Secretary's regulations, however, a doctor's ability to provide, and a woman's right to receive, information concerning abortion and abortion-related services outside the context of the Title X project remains unfettered. It would undoubtedly be easier for a woman seeking an abortion if she could receive information about abortion from a Title X project, but the Constitution does not require that the Government distort the scope of its mandated program in order to provide that information.

Petitioners contend, however, that most Title X clients are effectively precluded by indigency and poverty from seeing a health-care provider who will provide abortion-related services. But once again, even these Title X clients are in no worse position than if Congress had never enacted Title X. "The financial constraints that restrict an indigent woman's ability to enjoy the full range of constitutionally protected freedom of choice are the product not of governmental restrictions on access to abortion, but rather of her indigency."

The Secretary's regulations are a permissible construction of Title X and do not violate either the First or Fifth Amendments to the Constitution. Accordingly, the judgment of the Court of Appeals is

Affirmed.

■ BLACKMUN, J., with whom MARSHALL, J., joins, with whom STEVENS, J., joins as to Parts II and III, and with whom O'CONNOR, J., joins as to Part I, dissenting.

. . . .

Until today, the Court never has upheld viewpoint-based suppression of speech simply because that suppression was a condition upon the acceptance of public funds. Whatever may be the Government's power to condition the receipt of its largess upon the relinquishment of constitutional rights, it surely does not extend to a condition that suppresses the recipient's cherished freedom of speech based solely upon the content or viewpoint of that speech. This rule is a sound one, for, as the Court often has noted: " 'A regulation of speech that is motivated by nothing more than a desire to curtail expression of a particular point of view on controversial issues of general interest is the purest example of a "law . . . abridging the freedom of speech, or of the press." ' " . . .

. . . .

It cannot seriously be disputed that the counseling and referral provisions at issue in the present cases constitute content-based regulation of speech. Title X grantees may provide counseling and referral regarding any of a wide range of family planning and other topics, save abortion.

The regulations are also clearly viewpoint based. While suppressing speech favorable to abortion with one hand, the Secretary compels antiabortion speech with the other. For example, the Department of Health and Human Services' own description of the regulations makes plain that "Title X projects are *required* to facilitate access to prenatal care and social services, including adoption services, that might be needed by the pregnant client to promote her well-being and that of her child, while making it abundantly clear that the project is not permitted to promote abortion by facilitating access to abortion through the referral process."

Moreover, the regulations command that a project refer for prenatal care each woman diagnosed as pregnant, irrespective of the woman's expressed desire to continue or terminate her pregnancy. If a client asks directly about abortion, a Title X physician or counselor is required to say, in essence, that the project does not consider abortion to be an appropriate method of family planning. Both requirements are antithetical to the First Amendment.

The regulations pertaining to "advocacy" are even more explicitly viewpoint based. These provide: "A Title X project may not *encourage, promote or advocate* abortion as a method of family planning." They explain: "This requirement prohibits actions to *assist* women to obtain abortions or *increase* the availability or accessibility of abortion for family planning purposes." The regulations do not, however, proscribe or even regulate anti-abortion advocacy. These are clearly restrictions aimed at the suppression of "dangerous ideas."

Remarkably, the majority concludes that "the Government has not discriminated on the basis of viewpoint; it has merely chosen to fund one activity to the exclusion of the other." But the majority's claim that the regulations merely limit a Title X project's speech to preventive or preconceptional services, rings hollow in light of the broad range of nonpreventive services that the regulations authorize Title X projects to provide. By refusing to fund those family-planning projects that advocate abortion *because* they advocate abortion, the Government plainly has targeted a particular viewpoint. . . .

The Court concludes that the challenged regulations do not violate the First Amendment rights of Title X staff members because any limitation of the employees' freedom of expression is simply a consequence of their decision to accept employment at a federally funded project. But it has never been sufficient to justify an otherwise unconstitutional condition upon public employment that the employee may escape the condition by relinquishing his or her job. It is beyond question "that a government may not require an individual to relinquish rights guaranteed him by the First Amendment as a condition of public employment."

. . . .

The majority attempts to circumvent this principle by emphasizing that Title X physicians and counselors "remain free . . . to pursue abortion-related activities when they are not acting under the auspices of the Title X project." "The regulations," the majority explains, "do not in any way restrict the activities of those persons acting as private individuals." Under the majority's reasoning, the First Amendment could be read to tolerate *any* governmental restriction upon an employee's speech so long as that restriction is limited to the funded workplace. This is a dangerous proposition, and one the Court has rightly rejected in the past.

. . . .

By far the most disturbing aspect of today's ruling is the effect it will have on the Fifth Amendment rights of the women who, supposedly, are beneficiaries of Title X programs. The majority rejects petitioners' Fifth Amendment claims summarily. It relies primarily upon the decisions in *Harris v. McRae*, 448 U.S. 297 (1980), and *Webster v. Reproductive Health Services*, 492 U.S. 490 (1989). There were dissents in those cases, and we continue to believe that they were wrongly and unfortunately decided. Be that as it may, even if one accepts as valid the Court's theorizing in those cases, the majority's reasoning in the present cases is flawed.

Until today, the Court has allowed to stand only those restrictions upon reproductive freedom that, while limiting the availability of abortion, have left intact a woman's ability to decide without coercion whether she will continue her pregnancy to term. *McRae* and *Webster* are all to this effect. Today's decision abandons that principle, and with disastrous results.

Contrary to the majority's characterization, this is not a situation in which individuals seek Government aid in exercising their fundamental rights. The Fifth Amendment right asserted by petitioners is the right of a pregnant woman to be free from affirmative governmental *interference* in her decision. *Roe v. Wade*, 410 U.S. 113 (1973), and its progeny are not so much about a medical procedure as they are about a woman's fundamental right to self-determination. Those cases serve to vindicate the idea that "liberty," if it means anything, must entail freedom from governmental domination in making the most intimate and personal of decisions. By suppressing medically pertinent information and injecting a restrictive ideological message unrelated to considerations of maternal health, the Government places formidable obstacles in the path of Title X clients' freedom of choice and thereby violates their Fifth Amendment rights.

It is crystal clear that the aim of the challenged provisions—an aim the majority cannot escape noticing—is not simply to ensure that federal funds are not used to perform abortions, but to "reduce the incidence of abortion." As recounted above, the regulations require Title X physicians and counselors to provide information pertaining only to childbirth, to refer a pregnant woman for prenatal care irrespective of her medical situation, and, upon direct inquiry, to respond that abortion is not an "appropriate method" of family planning.

The undeniable message conveyed by this forced speech, and the one that the Title X client will draw from it, is that abortion nearly always is an improper medical option. Although her physician's words, in fact, are strictly controlled by the Government and wholly unrelated to her particular medical situation, the Title X client will reasonably construe them as professional advice to forgo her right to obtain an abortion. As would most rational patients, many of these women will follow that perceived advice and carry their pregnancy to term, despite their needs to the contrary and despite the safety of the abortion procedure for the vast majority of them. Others, delayed by the regulations' mandatory prenatal referral, will be prevented from acquiring abortions during the period in which the process is medically sound and constitutionally protected.

In view of the inevitable effect of the regulations, the majority's conclusion that "[t]he difficulty that a woman encounters when a Title X project does not provide abortion counseling or referral leaves her in no different position than she would have been if the Government had not enacted Title X," is insensitive and contrary to common human experience. Both the purpose and result of the challenged regulations are to deny women the ability voluntarily to decide their procreative destiny. For these women, the Government will have obliterated the freedom to choose as surely as if it had banned abortions outright. The denial of this freedom is not a consequence of poverty but of the Government's ill-intentioned distortion of information it has chosen to provide.

The substantial obstacles to bodily self-determination that the regulations impose are doubly offensive because they are effected by manipulating the very words spoken by physicians and counselors to their patients. In our society, the doctor-patient dialogue embodies a unique relationship of trust. The specialized nature of medical science and the emotional distress often attendant to health-related decisions requires that patients place their complete confidence, and often their very lives, in the hands of medical professionals. One seeks a physician's aid not only for medication or diagnosis, but also for guidance, professional judgment, and vital emotional support. Accordingly, each of us attaches profound importance and authority to the words of advice spoken by the physician.

. . . .

The majority attempts to distinguish our holdings in *Akron* and *Thornburgh* on the *post hoc* basis that the governmental intrusions into the doctor-patient dialogue invalidated in those cases applied to *all* physicians within a jurisdiction while the regulations now before the Court pertain to the narrow class of healthcare professionals employed at Title X projects. But the rights protected by the Constitution are *personal* rights. And for the individual woman, the deprivation of liberty by the Government is no less substantial because it affects few rather than many. It cannot be that an otherwise unconstitutional infringement of choice is made lawful because it touches only some of the Nation's pregnant women and not all of them.

The manipulation of the doctor-patient dialogue achieved through the Secretary's regulations is clearly an effort "to deter a woman from making a decision that, with her physician, is hers to make." As such, it violates the Fifth Amendment.

In its haste further to restrict the right of every woman to control her reproductive freedom and bodily integrity, the majority disregards established principles of law and contorts this Court's decided cases to arrive at its preordained result. The majority professes to leave undisturbed the free speech protections upon which our society has come to rely, but one must wonder what force the First Amendment retains if it is read to countenance the deliberate manipulation by the Government of the dialogue between a woman and her physician. While technically leaving intact the fundamental right protected by *Roe v. Wade*, the Court, "through a relentlessly formalistic catechism" . . . once again has rendered the right's substance nugatory. This is a course nearly as noxious as overruling *Roe* directly, for if a right is found to be unenforceable, even against flagrant attempts by government to circumvent it, then it ceases to be a right at all. This, I fear, may be the effect of today's decision.

NOTES

1. *Private and public services.* The *Rust* Court argues that restrictions on the provision of abortion services in public facilities leave women no worse off than they would be absent such services. After all, women can seek abortion counseling and provision from private providers. However, this argument overlooks the degree to which many women are unable to afford—or access—private health care, requiring them to rely on public services for their health care needs. Does this reality alter your views of the Court's conclusions in *Rust*?

2.   *The end of the "gag" rule.* As discussed above, *supra* p. 611, upon assuming office in 1993, President Bill Clinton issued a memorandum rescinding the regulations upheld in *Rust v. Sullivan*, including the "gag rule" that prevented Title X recipients from counseling patients on abortion. An international analogue of the gag rule, which prohibited recipients of U.S. international aid from providing abortion counseling was instituted under Presidents Ronald Reagan, George H.W. Bush, and George W. Bush. Presidents Clinton and Obama rescinded these international gag-rule regulations, as President Clinton had.

5.   NEW LIMITS ON THE RIGHT TO ACCESS ABORTION

As the preceding cases make clear, the introduction of the abortion right vexed the Court in the years after Roe v. Wade. *As an initial matter, some members of the Court were deeply troubled that the trimester framework imposed rigid limits on when the state's interest in health and the potentiality of life could be vindicated. Other members of the Court appeared concerned that technological advances had radically altered the concept of viability, again calling into question the trimester framework. In addition, the Court also grappled with the difficult question of whether the right to an abortion also required the state to provide public support for abortion services. These doctrinal concerns arose amidst a heady political climate in which opposition to* Roe *and abortion had steadily galvanized. All of these factors came to a head in a 1992 challenge to Pennsylvania's Abortion Control Act of 1982.*

Planned Parenthood of Southeastern Pennsylvania v. Casey
505 U.S. 833 (1992).

■ O'CONNOR, J., KENNEDY, J., and SOUTER, J., announced the judgment of the Court and delivered the opinion of the Court with respect to Parts I, II, III, V-A, V-C, and VI, an opinion with respect to Part V-E, in which STEVENS, J., joins, and an opinion with respect to Parts IV, V-B, and V-D.

I

Liberty finds no refuge in a jurisprudence of doubt. Yet 19 years after our holding that the Constitution protects a woman's right to terminate her pregnancy in its early stages, that definition of liberty is still questioned. Joining the respondents as *amicus curiae*, the United States, as it has done in five other cases in the last decade, again asks us to overrule *Roe*.

At issue in these cases are five provisions of the Pennsylvania Abortion Control Act of 1982, as amended in 1988 and 1989. . . . The Act requires that a woman seeking an abortion give her informed consent prior to the abortion procedure, and specifies that she be provided with certain information at least 24 hours before the abortion is performed.

For a minor to obtain an abortion, the Act requires the informed consent of one of her parents, but provides for a judicial bypass option if the minor does not wish to or cannot obtain a parent's consent. Another provision of the Act requires that, unless certain exceptions apply, a married woman seeking an abortion must sign a statement indicating that she has notified her husband of her intended abortion. The Act exempts compliance with these three requirements in the event of a "medical emergency[.]" . . . In addition to the above provisions regulating the performance of abortions, the Act imposes certain reporting requirements on facilities that provide abortion services.

. . . .

After considering the fundamental constitutional questions resolved by *Roe*, principles of institutional integrity, and the rule of *stare decisis*, we are led to conclude this: the essential holding of *Roe v. Wade* should be retained and once again reaffirmed.

It must be stated at the outset and with clarity that *Roe*'s essential holding, the holding we reaffirm, has three parts. First is a recognition of the right of the woman to choose to have an abortion before viability and to obtain it without undue interference from the State. Before viability, the State's interests are not strong enough to support a prohibition of abortion or the imposition of a substantial obstacle to the woman's effective right to elect the procedure. Second is a confirmation of the State's power to restrict abortions after fetal viability, if the law contains exceptions for pregnancies which endanger the woman's life or health. And third is the principle that the State has legitimate interests from the outset of the pregnancy in protecting the health of the woman and the life of the fetus that may become a child. . . .

II

Constitutional protection of the woman's decision to terminate her pregnancy derives from the Due Process Clause of the Fourteenth Amendment. . . . Although a literal reading of the Clause might suggest that it governs only the procedures by which a State may deprive persons of liberty, for at least 105 years . . . the Clause has been understood to contain a substantive component as well. . . .

It is also tempting . . . to suppose that the Due Process Clause protects only those practices, defined at the most specific level, that were protected against government interference by other rules of law when the Fourteenth Amendment was ratified. But such a view would be inconsistent with our law. It is a promise of the Constitution that there is a realm of personal liberty which the government may not enter. We have vindicated this principle before. Marriage is mentioned nowhere in the Bill of Rights and interracial marriage was illegal in most States in the 19th century, but the Court was no doubt correct in finding it to be an aspect of liberty protected against state interference by the substantive component of the Due Process Clause in *Loving v. Virginia*, 388 U.S. 1, 12 (1967). . . .

Neither the Bill of Rights nor the specific practices of States at the time of the adoption of the Fourteenth Amendment marks the outer limits of the substantive sphere of liberty which the Fourteenth Amendment protects. See U.S. Const., Amdt. 9. . . .

. . . .

. . . Abortion is a unique act. It is an act fraught with consequences for others: for the woman who must live with the implications of her decision; for the persons who perform and assist in the procedure; for the spouse, family, and society which must confront the knowledge that these procedures exist, procedures some deem nothing short of an act of violence against innocent human life; and, depending on one's beliefs, for the life or potential life that is aborted. Though abortion is conduct, it does not follow that the State is entitled to proscribe it in all instances. That is because the liberty of the woman is at stake in a sense unique to the human condition and so unique to the law. The mother who carries a child to full term is subject to anxieties, to physical constraints, to pain that only she must bear. That these sacrifices have from the beginning of the human race been endured by woman with a pride that ennobles her in the eyes of others and gives to the infant a bond of love cannot alone be grounds for the State to insist she make the sacrifice. Her suffering is too intimate and personal for the State to insist, without more, upon its own vision of the woman's role, however dominant that vision has been in the course of our history and our culture. The destiny of the woman must be shaped to a large extent on her own conception of her spiritual imperatives and her place in society.

It should be recognized, moreover, that in some critical respects the abortion decision is of the same character as the decision to use contraception, to which *Griswold v. Connecticut, Eisenstadt v. Baird*, and *Carey v. Population Services International* afford constitutional protection. We have no doubt as to the correctness of those decisions. They support the reasoning in *Roe* relating to the woman's liberty because they involve personal decisions concerning not only the meaning of procreation but also human responsibility and respect for it. . . .

III

A

. . . [I]n this case we may enquire whether *Roe*'s central rule has been found unworkable; whether the rule's limitation on state power could be removed without serious inequity to those who have relied upon it or significant damage to the stability of the society governed by it; whether the law's growth in the intervening years has left *Roe*'s central rule a doctrinal anachronism discounted by society; and whether *Roe*'s premises of fact have so far changed in the ensuing two decades as to render its central holding somehow irrelevant or unjustifiable in dealing with the issue it addressed.

1

Although *Roe* has engendered opposition, it has in no sense proven "unworkable," representing as it does a simple limitation beyond which a state law is unenforceable. While *Roe* has, of course, required judicial assessment of state laws affecting the exercise of the choice guaranteed against government infringement, and although the need for such review will remain as a consequence of today's decision, the required determinations fall within judicial competence.

2

The inquiry into reliance counts the cost of a rule's repudiation as it would fall on those who have relied reasonably on the rule's continued application. . . .

While neither respondents nor their *amici* in so many words deny that the abortion right invites some reliance prior to its actual exercise, one can readily imagine an argument stressing the dissimilarity of this case to one involving property or contract. Abortion is customarily chosen as an unplanned response to the consequence of unplanned activity or to the failure of conventional birth control, and except on the assumption that no intercourse would have occurred but for *Roe*'s holding, such behavior may appear to justify no reliance claim. . . .

To eliminate the issue of reliance that easily, however, one would need to limit cognizable reliance to specific instances of sexual activity. But to do this would be simply to refuse to face the fact that for two decades of economic and social developments, people have organized intimate relationships and made choices that define their views of themselves and their places in society, in reliance on the availability of abortion in the event that contraception should fail. The ability of women to participate equally in the economic and social life of the Nation has been facilitated by their ability to control their reproductive lives. The Constitution serves human values, and while the effect of reliance on *Roe* cannot be exactly measured, neither can the certain cost of overruling *Roe* for people who have ordered their thinking and living around that case be dismissed.

3

No evolution of legal principle has left *Roe*'s doctrinal footings weaker than they were in 1973. No development of constitutional law since the case was decided has implicitly or explicitly left *Roe* behind as a mere survivor of obsolete constitutional thinking.

It will be recognized, of course, that *Roe* stands at an intersection of two lines of decisions, but in whichever doctrinal category one reads the case, the result for present purposes will be the same. The *Roe* Court itself placed its holding in the succession of cases most prominently exemplified by *Griswold v. Connecticut*, 381 U.S. 479 (1965). . . .

Roe, however, may be seen not only as an exemplar of *Griswold* liberty but as a rule (whether or not mistaken) of personal autonomy and bodily integrity, with doctrinal affinity to cases recognizing limits on governmental power to mandate medical treatment or to bar its rejection. If so, our cases since *Roe* accord with *Roe*'s view that a State's interest in the protection of life falls short of justifying any plenary override of individual liberty claims.

Finally, one could classify *Roe* as *sui generis.* If the case is so viewed, then there clearly has been no erosion of its central determination. . . .

. . . .

The soundness of this prong of the *Roe* analysis is apparent from a consideration of the alternative. If indeed the woman's interest in deciding whether to bear and beget a child had not been recognized as in *Roe,* the State might as readily restrict a woman's right to choose to carry a pregnancy to term as to terminate it, to further asserted state interests in population control, or eugenics, for example. Yet *Roe* has been sensibly relied upon to counter any such suggestions. *E.g., Arnold v. Board of Education of Escambia County, Ala.,* 880 F.2d 305, 311 (CA11 1989) (relying upon *Roe* and concluding that government officials violate the Constitution by coercing a minor to have an abortion); *Avery v. County of Burke,* 660 F.2d 111, 115 (CA4 1981) (county agency inducing teenage girl to undergo unwanted sterilization on the basis of misrepresentation that she had sickle cell trait); see also *In re Quinlan,* 70 N.J. 10, 355 A.2d 647 (relying on *Roe* in finding a right to terminate medical treatment). . . .

4

. . . [T]ime has overtaken some of *Roe*'s factual assumptions: advances in maternal health care allow for abortions safe to the mother later in pregnancy than was true in 1973 and advances in neonatal care have advanced viability to a point somewhat earlier. But these facts go only to the scheme of time limits on the realization of competing interests, and the divergences from the factual premises of 1973 have no bearing on the validity of *Roe*'s central holding, that viability marks the earliest point at which the State's interest in fetal life is constitutionally adequate to justify a legislative ban on nontherapeutic abortions. . . .

5

The sum of the precedential enquiry to this point shows *Roe*'s underpinnings unweakened in any way affecting its central holding. . . .

B

In a less significant case, *stare decisis* analysis could, and would, stop at the point we have reached. But the sustained and widespread debate *Roe* has provoked calls for some comparison between that case and others of comparable dimension that have responded to national controversies and taken on the impress of the controversies addressed. Only two such decisional lines from the past century present themselves for examination, and in each instance the result reached by the Court accorded with the principles we apply today.

The first example is that line of cases identified with *Lochner v. New York*, 198 U.S. 45 (1905), which imposed substantive limitations on legislation limiting economic autonomy in favor of health and welfare regulation ... in which this Court held it to be an infringement of constitutionally protected liberty of contract to require the employers of adult women to satisfy minimum wage standards. *West Coast Hotel Co. v. Parrish*, 300 U.S. 379 (1937), signaled the demise of *Lochner* by overruling *Adkins*. In the meantime, the Depression had come and, with it, the lesson that seemed unmistakable to most people by 1937, that the interpretation of contractual freedom protected in *Adkins* rested on fundamentally false factual assumptions about the capacity of a relatively unregulated market to satisfy minimal levels of human welfare.... The facts upon which the earlier case had premised a constitutional resolution of social controversy had proven to be untrue, and history's demonstration of their untruth not only justified but required the new choice of constitutional principle that *West Coast Hotel* announced. Of course, it was true that the Court lost something by its misperception, or its lack of prescience, and the Court-packing crisis only magnified the loss; but the clear demonstration that the facts of economic life were different from those previously assumed warranted the repudiation of the old law.

The second comparison that 20th century history invites is with the cases employing the separate-but-equal rule for applying the Fourteenth Amendment's equal protection guarantee. They began with *Plessy v. Ferguson*, 163 U.S. 537 (1896).... The *Plessy* Court considered "the underlying fallacy of the plaintiff's argument to consist in the assumption that the enforced separation of the two races stamps the colored race with a badge of inferiority. If this be so, it is not by reason of anything found in the act, but solely because the colored race chooses to put that construction upon it."... But this understanding of the facts and the rule it was stated to justify were repudiated in *Brown v. Board of Education*, 347 U.S. 483 (1954)....

The Court in *Brown* addressed these facts of life by observing that whatever may have been the understanding in *Plessy*'s time of the power of segregation to stigmatize those who were segregated with a "badge of inferiority," it was clear by 1954 that legally sanctioned segregation had just such an effect, to the point that racially separate public educational facilities were deemed inherently unequal. 347 U.S., at 494–495. Society's understanding of the facts upon which a constitutional ruling was sought in 1954 was thus fundamentally different from the basis claimed for the decision in 1896. While we think *Plessy* was wrong the day it was decided, we must also recognize that the *Plessy* Court's explanation for its decision was so clearly at odds with the facts apparent to the Court in 1954 that the decision to reexamine *Plessy* was on this ground alone not only justified but required.

West Coast Hotel and *Brown* each rested on facts, or an understanding of facts, changed from those which furnished the claimed justifications for the earlier constitutional resolutions. Each case was comprehensible as the Court's response to facts that the country could understand, or had come to understand already, but which the Court of an earlier day, as its own declarations disclosed, had not been able to perceive. As the decisions were thus comprehensible they were also defensible, not merely as the victories of one doctrinal school over another by dint of numbers (victories though they were), but as applications of constitutional principle to facts as they had not been seen by the Court before. In constitutional adjudication as elsewhere in life, changed circumstances may impose new obligations, and the thoughtful part of the Nation could accept each decision to overrule a prior case as a response to the Court's constitutional duty.

Because the cases before us present no such occasion it could be seen as no such response. Because neither the factual underpinnings of *Roe*'s central holding nor our understanding of it has changed (and because no other indication of weakened precedent has been shown), the Court could not pretend to be reexamining the prior law with any justification beyond a present doctrinal disposition to come out differently from the Court of 1973. To overrule prior law for no other reason than that would run counter to the view repeated in our cases, that a decision to overrule should rest on some special reason over and above the belief that a prior case was wrongly decided.

C

The examination of the conditions justifying the repudiation of *Adkins* by *West Coast Hotel* and *Plessy* by *Brown* is enough to suggest the terrible price that would have been paid if the Court had not overruled as it did. In the present cases, however, as our analysis to this point makes clear, the terrible price would be paid for overruling. Our analysis would not be complete, however, without explaining why overruling *Roe*'s central holding would not only reach an unjustifiable result under principles of *stare decisis*, but would seriously weaken the Court's capacity to exercise the judicial power and to function as the Supreme Court of a Nation dedicated to the rule of law. . . .

. . . .

The need for principled action to be perceived as such is implicated to some degree whenever this, or any other appellate court, overrules a prior case. . . .

In two circumstances, however, the Court would almost certainly fail to receive the benefit of the doubt in overruling prior cases. There is, first, a point beyond which frequent overruling would overtax the country's belief in the Court's good faith. . . .

That first circumstance can be described as hypothetical; the second is to the point here and now. Where, in the performance of its judicial duties, the Court decides a case in such a way as to resolve the sort of intensely divisive controversy reflected in *Roe* and those rare, comparable cases, its decision has a dimension that the resolution of the normal case does not carry. It is the dimension present whenever the Court's interpretation of the Constitution calls the contending sides of a national controversy to end their national division by accepting a common mandate rooted in the Constitution.

. . . [T]o overrule under fire in the absence of the most compelling reason to reexamine a watershed decision would subvert the Court's legitimacy beyond any serious question.

. . . .

. . . A decision to overrule *Roe*'s essential holding under the existing circumstances would address error, if error there was, at the cost of both profound and unnecessary damage to the Court's legitimacy, and to the Nation's commitment to the rule of law. It is therefore imperative to adhere to the essence of *Roe*'s original decision, and we do so today.

IV

. . . The woman's liberty is not so unlimited, however, that from the outset the State cannot show its concern for the life of the unborn, and at a later point in fetal development the State's interest in life has sufficient force so that the right of the woman to terminate the pregnancy can be restricted.

. . . .

We conclude the line should be drawn at viability, so that before that time the woman has a right to choose to terminate her pregnancy. We adhere to this principle for two reasons. First, as we have said, is the doctrine of *stare decisis*. . . .

The second reason is that the concept of viability, as we noted in *Roe,* is the time at which there is a realistic possibility of maintaining and nourishing a life outside the womb, so that the independent existence of the second life can in reason and all fairness be the object of state protection that now overrides the rights of the woman. . . .

On the other side of the equation is the interest of the State in the protection of potential life. . . .

. . . [I]t must be remembered that *Roe v. Wade* speaks with clarity in establishing not only the woman's liberty but also the State's "important and legitimate interest in potential life." That portion of the decision in *Roe* has been given too little acknowledgment and implementation by the Court in its subsequent cases. . . .

Roe established a trimester framework to govern abortion regulations. Under this elaborate but rigid construct, almost no regulation at all is permitted during the first trimester of pregnancy; regulations designed to protect the woman's health, but not to further the State's interest in potential life, are permitted during the second trimester; and during the third trimester, when the fetus is viable, prohibitions are permitted provided the life or health of the mother is not at stake. . . .

The trimester framework no doubt was erected to ensure that the woman's right to choose not become so subordinate to the State's interest in promoting fetal life that her choice exists in theory but not in fact. We do not agree, however, that the trimester approach is necessary to accomplish this objective. A framework of this rigidity was unnecessary and in its later interpretation sometimes contradicted the State's permissible exercise of its powers.

. . . .

We reject the trimester framework, which we do not consider to be part of the essential holding of *Roe*. . . . The trimester framework suffers from these basic flaws: in its formulation it misconceives the nature of the pregnant woman's interest; and in practice it undervalues the State's interest in potential life, as recognized in *Roe*.

. . . .

These considerations of the nature of the abortion right illustrate that it is an overstatement to describe it as a right to decide whether to have an abortion "without interference from the State." . . . Not all governmental intrusion is of necessity unwarranted; and that brings us to the other basic flaw in the trimester framework: even in *Roe*'s terms, in practice it undervalues the State's interest in the potential life within the woman.

. . . .

The very notion that the State has a substantial interest in potential life leads to the conclusion that not all regulations must be deemed unwarranted. Not all burdens on the right to decide whether to terminate a pregnancy will be undue. In our view, the undue burden standard is the appropriate means of reconciling the State's interest with the woman's constitutionally protected liberty.

. . . .

A finding of an undue burden is a shorthand for the conclusion that a state regulation has the purpose or effect of placing a substantial obstacle in the path of a woman seeking an abortion of a nonviable fetus. A statute with this purpose is invalid because the means chosen by the State to further the interest in potential life must be calculated to inform the woman's free choice, not hinder it. And a statute which, while furthering the interest in potential life or some other valid state interest, has the effect of placing a substantial obstacle in the path of a woman's choice cannot be considered a permissible means of serving its legitimate ends. . . . Understood another way, we answer the question, left open in previous opinions discussing the undue burden formulation, whether a law designed to further the State's interest in fetal life which imposes an undue burden on the woman's decision before fetal viability could be constitutional. The answer is no.

Some guiding principles should emerge. What is at stake is the woman's right to make the ultimate decision, not a right to be insulated from all others in doing so. Regulations which do no more than create a structural mechanism by which the State, or the parent or guardian of a minor, may express profound respect for the life of the unborn are permitted, if they are not a substantial obstacle to the woman's exercise of the right to choose. Unless it has that effect on her right of choice, a state measure designed to persuade her to choose childbirth over abortion will be upheld if reasonably related to that goal. Regulations designed to foster the health of a woman seeking an abortion are valid if they do not constitute an undue burden.

. . . We give this summary:

(a) To protect the central right recognized by *Roe v. Wade* while at the same time accommodating the State's profound interest in potential life, we will employ the undue burden analysis as explained in this opinion. An undue burden exists, and therefore a provision of law is invalid, if its purpose or effect is to place a substantial obstacle in the path of a woman seeking an abortion before the fetus attains viability.

(b) We reject the rigid trimester framework of *Roe v. Wade.* To promote the State's profound interest in potential life, throughout pregnancy the State may take measures to ensure that the woman's choice is informed, and measures designed to advance this interest will not be invalidated as long as their purpose is to persuade the woman to choose childbirth over abortion. These measures must not be an undue burden on the right.

(c) As with any medical procedure, the State may enact regulations to further the health or safety of a woman seeking an abortion. Unnecessary health regulations that have the purpose or effect of presenting a substantial obstacle to a woman seeking an abortion impose an undue burden on the right.

(d) Our adoption of the undue burden analysis does not disturb the central holding of *Roe v. Wade,* and we reaffirm that holding. Regardless of whether exceptions are made for particular circumstances, a State may not prohibit any woman from making the ultimate decision to terminate her pregnancy before viability.

(e) We also reaffirm *Roe*'s holding that "subsequent to viability, the State in promoting its interest in the potentiality of human life may, if it chooses, regulate, and even proscribe, abortion except where it is necessary, in appropriate medical judgment, for the preservation of the life or health of the mother."

These principles control our assessment of the Pennsylvania statute, and we now turn to the issue of the validity of its challenged provisions.

V

. . . .

A

Because it is central to the operation of various other requirements, we begin with the statute's definition of medical emergency. Under the statute, a medical emergency is

"[t]hat condition which, on the basis of the physician's good faith clinical judgment, so complicates the medical condition of a pregnant woman as to necessitate the immediate abortion of her pregnancy to avert her death or for which a delay will create serious risk of substantial and irreversible impairment of a major bodily function."

. . . .

The District Court found that there were three serious conditions which would not be covered by the statute: preeclampsia, inevitable abortion, and premature ruptured membrane. Yet, as the Court of Appeals observed, it is undisputed that under some circumstances each of these conditions could lead to an illness with substantial and irreversible consequences. While the definition could be interpreted in an unconstitutional manner, the Court of Appeals construed the phrase "serious risk" to include those circumstances. . . . We adhere to that course today, and conclude that, as construed by the Court of Appeals, the medical emergency definition imposes no undue burden on a woman's abortion right.

B

We next consider the informed consent requirement. Except in a medical emergency, the statute requires that at least 24 hours before performing an abortion a physician inform the woman of the nature of the procedure, the health risks of the abortion and of childbirth, and the "probable gestational age of the unborn child." The physician or a qualified nonphysician must inform the woman of the availability of printed materials published by the State describing the fetus and providing information about medical assistance for childbirth, information about child support from the father, and a list of agencies which provide adoption and other services as alternatives to abortion. An abortion may not be performed unless the woman certifies in writing that she has been informed of the availability of these printed materials and has been provided them if she chooses to view them.

. . . .

To the extent [our prior decisions in *Akron*] and *Thornburgh* find a constitutional violation when the government requires, as it does here, the giving of truthful, nonmisleading information about the nature of the procedure, the attendant health risks and those of childbirth, and the "probable gestational age" of the fetus, those cases go too far, are inconsistent with *Roe*'s acknowledgment of an important interest in potential life, and are overruled.... In attempting to ensure that a woman apprehend the full consequences of her decision, the State furthers the legitimate purpose of reducing the risk that a woman may elect an abortion, only to discover later, with devastating psychological consequences, that her decision was not fully informed. If the information the State requires to be made available to the woman is truthful and not misleading, the requirement may be permissible.

We also see no reason why the State may not require doctors to inform a woman seeking an abortion of the availability of materials relating to the consequences to the fetus, even when those consequences have no direct relation to her health....

. . . .

All that is left of petitioners' argument is an asserted First Amendment right of a physician not to provide information about the risks of abortion, and childbirth, in a manner mandated by the State. To be sure, the physician's First Amendment rights not to speak are implicated, but only as part of the practice of medicine, subject to reasonable licensing and regulation by the State. We see no constitutional infirmity in the requirement that the physician provide the information mandated by the State here.

The Pennsylvania statute also requires us to reconsider the holding in [*Akron*] that the State may not require that a physician, as opposed to a qualified assistant, provide information relevant to a woman's informed consent. Since there is no evidence on this record that requiring a doctor to give the information as provided by the statute would amount in practical terms to a substantial obstacle to a woman seeking an abortion, we conclude that it is not an undue burden....

... In [*Akron*] we said: "Nor are we convinced that the State's legitimate concern that the woman's decision be informed is reasonably served by requiring a 24-hour delay as a matter of course." We consider that conclusion to be wrong. The idea that important decisions will be more informed and deliberate if they follow some period of reflection does not strike us as unreasonable, particularly where the statute directs that important information become part of the background of the decision....

Whether the mandatory 24-hour waiting period is nonetheless invalid because in practice it is a substantial obstacle to a woman's choice to terminate her pregnancy is a closer question. The findings of fact by the District Court indicate that because of the distances many women must travel to reach an abortion provider, the practical effect will often be a delay of much more than a day because the waiting period requires that a woman seeking an abortion make at least two visits to the doctor. The District Court also found that in many instances this will increase the exposure of women seeking abortions to "the harassment and hostility of anti-abortion protestors demonstrating outside a clinic." As a result, the District Court found that for those women who have the fewest financial resources, those who must travel long distances, and those who have difficulty explaining their whereabouts to husbands, employers, or others, the 24-hour waiting period will be "particularly burdensome."

These findings are troubling in some respects, but they do not demonstrate that the waiting period constitutes an undue burden.... [A]s we have stated, under the undue burden standard a State is permitted to enact persuasive measures which favor childbirth over abortion, even if those measures do not further a health interest. And while the waiting period does limit a physician's discretion, that is not, standing alone, a reason to invalidate it....

. . . .

We are left with the argument that the various aspects of the informed consent requirement are unconstitutional because they place barriers in the way of abortion on demand. Even the broadest reading of *Roe*, however, has not suggested that there is a constitutional right to abortion on demand. Rather, the right protected by *Roe* is a right to decide to terminate a pregnancy free of undue interference by the State. Because the informed consent requirement facilitates the wise exercise of that right, it cannot be classified as an interference with the right *Roe* protects. The informed consent requirement is not an undue burden on that right.

C

Section 3209 of Pennsylvania's abortion law provides, except in cases of medical emergency, that no physician shall perform an abortion on a married woman without receiving a signed statement from the woman that she has notified her spouse that she is about to undergo an abortion. The woman has the option of providing an alternative signed statement certifying that her husband is not the man who impregnated her; that her husband could not be located; that the pregnancy is the result of spousal sexual assault which she has reported; or that the woman believes that notifying her husband will cause him or someone else to inflict bodily injury upon her. A physician who performs an abortion on a married woman without receiving the appropriate signed statement will have his or her license revoked, and is liable to the husband for damages.

The District Court heard the testimony of numerous expert witnesses, and made detailed findings of fact regarding the effect of this statute. These included:

. . . .

279.   The 'bodily injury' exception could not be invoked by a married woman whose husband, if notified, would, in her reasonable belief, threaten to (a) publicize her intent to have an abortion to family, friends or acquaintances; (b) retaliate against her in future child custody or divorce proceedings; (c) inflict psychological intimidation or emotional harm upon her, her children or other persons; (d) inflict bodily harm on other persons such as children, family members or other loved ones; or (e) use his control over finances to deprive of necessary monies for herself or her children. . . .

. . .

281.   Studies reveal that family violence occurs in two million families in the United States. This figure, however, is a conservative one that substantially understates (because battering is usually not reported until it reaches life-threatening proportions) the actual number of families affected by domestic violence. In fact, researchers estimate that one of every two women will be battered at some time in their life. . . .

282.   A wife may not elect to notify her husband of her intention to have an abortion for a variety of reasons, including the husband's illness, concern about her own health, the imminent failure of the marriage, or the husband's absolute opposition to the abortion. . . .

. . .

289.   Mere notification of pregnancy is frequently a flashpoint for battering and violence within the family. The number of battering incidents is high during the pregnancy and often the worst abuse can be associated with pregnancy. . . . The battering husband may deny parentage and use the pregnancy as an excuse for abuse. . . .

290.   Secrecy typically shrouds abusive families. Family members are instructed not to tell anyone, especially police or doctors, about the abuse and violence. Battering husbands often threaten their wives or her children with further abuse if she tells an outsider of the violence and tells her that nobody will believe her. A battered woman, therefore, is highly unlikely to disclose the violence against her for fear of retaliation by the abuser. . . .

. . .

298.   Because of the nature of the battering relationship, battered women are unlikely to avail themselves of the exceptions to section 3209 of the Act, regardless of whether the section applies to them.

These findings are supported by studies of domestic violence. . . .

. . . [T]here are millions of women in this country who are the victims of regular physical and psychological abuse at the hands of their husbands. Should these women become pregnant, they may have very good reasons for not wishing to inform their husbands of their decision to obtain an abortion. Many may have justifiable fears of physical abuse, but may be no less fearful of the consequences of reporting prior abuse to the Commonwealth of Pennsylvania. . . .

Respondents attempt to avoid the conclusion that § 3209 is invalid by pointing out that . . . the effects of § 3209 are felt by only one percent of the women who obtain abortions. . . . We disagree with respondents' basic method of analysis.

The analysis does not end with the one percent of women upon whom the statute operates; it begins there. Legislation is measured for consistency with the Constitution by its impact on those whose conduct it affects. . . .

. . . The unfortunate yet persisting conditions we document above will mean that in a large fraction of the cases in which § 3209 is relevant, it will operate as a substantial obstacle to a woman's choice to undergo an abortion. It is an undue burden, and therefore invalid.

This conclusion is in no way inconsistent with our decisions upholding parental notification or consent requirements. Those enactments, and our judgment that they are constitutional, are based on the quite reasonable assumption that minors will benefit from consultation with their parents and that children will often not realize that their parents have their best interests at heart. We cannot adopt a parallel assumption about adult women.

. . . .

. . . It is an inescapable biological fact that state regulation with respect to the child a woman is carrying will have a far greater impact on the mother's liberty than on the father's. The effect of state regulation on a woman's protected liberty is doubly deserving of scrutiny in such a case, as the State has touched not only upon the private sphere of the family but upon the very bodily integrity of the pregnant woman. The Court has held that "when the wife and the husband disagree on this decision, the view of only one of the two marriage partners can prevail. Inasmuch as it is the woman who physically bears the child and who is the more directly and immediately affected by the pregnancy, as between the two, the balance weighs in her favor." . . . The Constitution protects individuals, men and women alike, from unjustified state interference, even when that interference is enacted into law for the benefit of their spouses.

. . . .

The husband's interest in the life of the child his wife is carrying does not permit the State to empower him with this troubling degree of authority over his wife. The contrary view leads to consequences reminiscent of the common law. A husband has no enforceable right to require a wife to advise him before she exercises her personal choices. . . . A State may not give to a man the kind of dominion over his wife that parents exercise over their children.

Section 3209 embodies a view of marriage consonant with the common-law status of married women but repugnant to our present understanding of marriage and of the nature of the rights secured by the Constitution. Women do not lose their constitutionally protected liberty when they marry. . . .

D

We next consider the parental consent provision. Except in a medical emergency, an unemancipated young woman under 18 may not obtain an abortion unless she and one of her parents (or guardian) provides informed consent as defined above. If neither a parent nor a guardian provides consent, a court may authorize the performance of an abortion upon a determination that the young woman is mature and capable of giving informed consent and has in fact given her informed consent, or that an abortion would be in her best interests.

. . . .

The only argument made by petitioners respecting this provision and to which our prior decisions do not speak is the contention that the parental consent requirement is invalid because it requires informed parental consent. For the most part, petitioners' argument is a reprise of their argument with respect to the informed consent requirement in general, and we reject it for the reasons given above. . . .

E

Under the recordkeeping and reporting requirements of the statute, every facility which performs abortions is required to file a report stating its name and address as well as the name and address of any related entity, such as a controlling or subsidiary organization. In the case of state-funded institutions, the information becomes public.

. . . .

In *Danforth*, we held that recordkeeping and reporting provisions "that are reasonably directed to the preservation of maternal health and that properly respect a patient's confidentiality and privacy are permissible." We think that under this standard, all the provisions at issue here, except that relating to spousal notice, are constitutional. Although they do not relate to the State's interest in informing the woman's choice, they do relate to health. The collection of information with respect to actual patients is a vital element of medical research, and so it cannot be said that the requirements serve no purpose other than to make abortions more difficult. Nor do we find that the requirements impose a substantial obstacle to a woman's choice. At most they might increase the cost of some abortions by a slight amount. While at some point increased cost could become a substantial obstacle, there is no such showing on the record before us.

. . . .

VI

Our Constitution is a covenant running from the first generation of Americans to us and then to future generations. It is a coherent succession. Each generation must learn anew that the Constitution's written terms embody ideas and aspirations that must survive more ages than one. We accept our responsibility not to retreat from interpreting the full meaning of the covenant in light of all of our precedents. We invoke it once again to define the freedom guaranteed by the Constitution's own promise, the promise of liberty.

. . . .

It is so ordered.

■ STEVENS, J., concurring in part and dissenting in part.

. . . .

I

. . . The societal costs of overruling *Roe* at this late date would be enormous. *Roe* is an integral part of a correct understanding of both the concept of liberty and the basic equality of men and women.

. . . .

II

My disagreement with the joint opinion begins with its understanding of the trimester framework established in *Roe*. . . . [I]t is not a "contradiction" to recognize that the State may have a legitimate interest in potential human life and, at the same time, to conclude that that interest does not justify the regulation of abortion before viability (although other interests, such as maternal health, may). The fact that the State's interest is legitimate does not tell us when, if ever, that interest outweighs the pregnant woman's interest in personal liberty. It is appropriate, therefore, to consider more carefully the nature of the interests at stake.

First, it is clear that, in order to be legitimate, the State's interest must be secular; consistent with the First Amendment the State may not promote a theological or sectarian interest. . . .

Identifying the State's interests—which the States rarely articulate with any precision—makes clear that the interest in protecting potential life is not grounded in the Constitution. It is, instead, an indirect interest supported by both humanitarian and pragmatic concerns. Many of our citizens believe that any abortion reflects an unacceptable disrespect for potential human life and that the performance of more than a million abortions each year is intolerable; many find third-trimester abortions performed when the fetus is approaching personhood particularly offensive. The State has a legitimate interest in minimizing such offense. The State may also have a broader interest in expanding the population, believing society would benefit from the services of additional productive citizens—or that the potential human lives might include the occasional Mozart or Curie. . . .

In counterpoise is the woman's constitutional interest in liberty. One aspect of this liberty is a right to bodily integrity, a right to control one's person. This right is neutral on the question of abortion: The Constitution would be equally offended by an absolute requirement that all women undergo abortions as by an absolute prohibition on abortions. "Our whole constitutional heritage rebels at the thought of giving government the power to control men's minds." The same holds true for the power to control women's bodies.

. . . .

Weighing the State's interest in potential life and the woman's liberty interest, I agree with the joint opinion that the State may " 'expres[s] a preference for normal childbirth,' " that the State may take steps to ensure that a woman's choice "is thoughtful and informed," and that "States are free to enact laws to provide a reasonable framework for a woman to make a decision that has such profound and lasting meaning." questions arise, however, when a State attempts to "persuade the woman to choose childbirth over abortion." Decisional autonomy must limit the State's power to inject into a woman's most personal deliberations its own views of what is best. . . .

. . . .

. . . Under these principles, Pa. Cons. Stat. §§ 3205(a)(2)(i)–(iii) (1990) of the Pennsylvania statute are unconstitutional. Those sections require a physician or counselor to provide the woman with a range of materials clearly designed to persuade her to choose not to undergo the abortion. While the Commonwealth is free, pursuant to § 3208 of the Pennsylvania law, to produce and disseminate such material, the Commonwealth may not inject such information into the woman's deliberations just as she is weighing such an important choice.

Under this same analysis, §§ 3205(a)(1)(i) and (iii) of the Pennsylvania statute are constitutional. Those sections, which require the physician to inform a woman of the nature and risks of the abortion procedure and the medical risks of carrying to term, are neutral requirements comparable to those imposed in other medical procedures. Those sections indicate no effort by the Commonwealth to influence the woman's choice in any way. If anything, such requirements *enhance*, rather than skew, the woman's decisionmaking.

The 24-hour waiting period required by §§ 3205(a)(1)–(2) of the Pennsylvania statute raises even more serious concerns. Such a requirement arguably furthers the Commonwealth's interests in two ways, neither of which is constitutionally permissible.

. . . .

In my opinion, a correct application of the "undue burden" standard leads to the same conclusion concerning the constitutionality of these requirements. A state-imposed burden on the exercise of a constitutional right is measured both by its effects and by its character: A burden may be "undue" either because the burden is too severe or because it lacks a legitimate, rational justification.

The 24-hour delay requirement fails both parts of this test. . . .

The counseling provisions are similarly infirm. Whenever government commands private citizens to speak or to listen, careful review of the justification for that command is particularly appropriate. In these cases, the Pennsylvania statute directs that counselors provide women seeking abortions with information concerning alternatives to abortion, the availability of medical assistance benefits, and the possibility of child-support payments. The statute requires that this information be given to *all* women seeking abortions, including those for whom such information is clearly useless, such as those who are married, those who have undergone the procedure in the past and are fully aware of the options, and those who are fully convinced that abortion is their only reasonable option. Moreover, the statute requires physicians to inform all of their patients of "[t]he probable gestational age of the unborn child." This information is of little decisional value in most cases, because 90% of all abortions are performed during the first trimester when fetal age has less relevance than when the fetus nears viability. . . .

■ BLACKMUN, J., concurring in part, concurring in the judgment in part, and dissenting in part.

. . . .

State restrictions on abortion violate a woman's right of privacy in two ways. First, compelled continuation of a pregnancy infringes upon a woman's right to bodily integrity by imposing substantial physical intrusions and significant risks of physical harm. During pregnancy, women experience dramatic physical changes and a wide range of health consequences. Labor and delivery pose additional health risks and physical demands. In short, restrictive abortion laws force women to endure physical invasions far more substantial than those this Court has held to violate the constitutional principle of bodily integrity in other contexts. *See, e.g., Winston v. Lee*, 470 U.S. 753 (1985) (invalidating surgical removal of bullet from murder suspect); *Rochin v. California*, 342 U.S. 165 (1952) (invalidating stomach pumping).

Further, when the State restricts a woman's right to terminate her pregnancy, it deprives a woman of the right to make her own decision about reproduction and family planning—critical life choices that this Court long has deemed central to the right to privacy. . . .

A State's restrictions on a woman's right to terminate her pregnancy also implicate constitutional guarantees of gender equality. State restrictions on abortion compel women to continue pregnancies they otherwise might terminate. By restricting the right to terminate pregnancies, the State conscripts women's bodies into its service, forcing women to continue their pregnancies, suffer the pains of childbirth, and in most instances, provide years of maternal care. The State does not compensate women for their services; instead, it assumes that they owe this duty as a matter of course. This assumption—that women can simply be forced to accept the "natural" status and incidents of motherhood—appears to rest upon a conception of women's role that has triggered the protection of the Equal Protection Clause. The joint opinion recognizes that these assumptions about women's place in society "are no longer consistent with our understanding of the family, the individual, or the Constitution."

. . . .

The 24-hour waiting period following the provision of the foregoing information is . . . clearly unconstitutional. . . .

. . . .

. . . [T]he Pennsylvania statute requires every facility performing abortions to report its activities to the Commonwealth. . . . The Commonwealth attempts to justify its required reports on the ground that the public has a right to know how its tax dollars are spent. A regulation designed to inform the public about public expenditures does not further the Commonwealth's interest in protecting maternal health. Accordingly, such a regulation cannot justify a legally significant burden on a woman's right to obtain an abortion.

. . . .

■ REHNQUIST, C.J, with whom WHITE, J., SCALIA, J., and THOMAS, J., join, concurring in the judgment in part and dissenting in part.

The joint opinion, following its newly minted variation on *stare decisis*, retains the outer shell of *Roe v. Wade*, 410 U.S. 113 (1973), but beats a wholesale retreat from the substance of that case. We believe that *Roe* was wrongly decided, and that it can and should be overruled consistently with our traditional approach to *stare decisis* in constitutional cases. We would adopt the approach of the plurality in *Webster v. Reproductive Health Services*, 492 U.S. 490 (1989), and uphold the challenged provisions of the Pennsylvania statute in their entirety.

I

. . . .

. . . Unlike marriage, procreation, and contraception, abortion "involves the purposeful termination of a potential life." . . . One cannot ignore the fact that a woman is not isolated in her pregnancy, and that the decision to abort necessarily involves the destruction of a fetus.

Nor do the historical traditions of the American people support the view that the right to terminate one's pregnancy is "fundamental." The common law which we inherited from England made abortion after "quickening" an offense. At the time of the adoption of the Fourteenth Amendment, statutory prohibitions or restrictions on abortion were commonplace; in 1868, at least 28 of the then-37 States and 8 Territories had statutes banning or limiting abortion. By the turn of the century virtually every State had a law prohibiting or restricting abortion on its books. By the middle of the present century, a liberalization trend had set in. But 21 of the restrictive abortion laws in effect in 1868 were still in effect in 1973 when *Roe* was decided, and an overwhelming majority of the States prohibited abortion unless necessary to preserve the life or health of the mother. On this record, it can scarcely be said that any deeply rooted tradition of relatively unrestricted abortion in our history supported the classification of the right to abortion as "fundamental" under the Due Process Clause of the Fourteenth Amendment.

We think, therefore, both in view of this history and of our decided cases dealing with substantive liberty under the Due Process Clause, that the Court was mistaken in *Roe* when it classified a woman's decision to terminate her pregnancy as a "fundamental right" that could be abridged only in a manner which withstood "strict scrutiny." . . .

II

The joint opinion . . . cannot bring itself to say that *Roe* was correct as an original matter, but the authors are of the view that "the immediate question is not the soundness of *Roe*'s resolution of the issue, but the precedential force that must be accorded to its holding." Instead of claiming that *Roe* was correct as a matter of original constitutional interpretation, the opinion therefore contains an elaborate discussion of *stare decisis*. This discussion of the principle of *stare decisis* appears to be almost entirely dicta, because the joint opinion does not apply that principle in dealing with *Roe*. *Roe* decided that a woman had a fundamental right to an abortion. The joint opinion rejects that view. *Roe* decided that abortion regulations were to be subjected to "strict scrutiny" and could be justified only in the light of "compelling state interests." The joint opinion rejects that view. *Roe* analyzed abortion regulation under a rigid trimester framework, a framework which has guided this Court's decisionmaking for 19 years. The joint opinion rejects that framework.

. . . .

In our view, authentic principles of *stare decisis* do not require that any portion of the reasoning in *Roe* be kept intact. . . . Erroneous decisions in such constitutional cases are uniquely durable, because correction through legislative action, save for constitutional amendment, is impossible. . . .

The joint opinion discusses several *stare decisis* factors which, it asserts, point toward retaining a portion of *Roe*. Two of these factors are that the main "factual underpinning" of *Roe* has remained the same, and that its doctrinal foundation is no weaker now than it was in 1973. Of course, what might be called the basic facts which gave rise to *Roe* have remained the same—women become pregnant, there is a point somewhere, depending on medical technology, where a fetus becomes viable, and women give birth to children. But this is only to say that the same facts which gave rise to *Roe* will continue to give rise to similar cases. It is not a reason, in and of itself, why those cases must be decided in the same incorrect manner as was the first case to deal with the question. . . .

. . . .

The joint opinion also points to the reliance interests involved in this context in its effort to explain why precedent must be followed for precedent's sake. Certainly it is true that where reliance is truly at issue, as in the case of judicial decisions that have formed the basis for private decisions, "[c]onsiderations in favor of *stare decisis* are at their acme." But, as the joint opinion apparently agrees, *ante*, at 2809, any traditional notion of reliance is not applicable here. . . .

. . . .

Apparently realizing that conventional *stare decisis* principles do not support its position, the joint opinion advances a belief that retaining a portion of *Roe* is necessary to protect the "legitimacy" of this Court. Because the Court must take care to render decisions "grounded truly in principle," and not simply as political and social compromises, the joint opinion properly declares it to be this Court's duty to ignore the public criticism and protest that may arise as a result of a decision. . . .

But the joint opinion goes on to state that when the Court "resolve[s] the sort of intensely divisive controversy reflected in *Roe* and those rare, comparable cases," its decision is exempt from reconsideration under established principles of *stare decisis* in constitutional cases. . . .

The first difficulty with this principle lies in its assumption that cases that are "intensely divisive" can be readily distinguished from those that are not. The question of whether a particular issue is "intensely divisive" enough to qualify for special protection is entirely subjective and dependent on the individual assumptions of the Members of this Court. . . .

The joint opinion picks out and discusses two prior Court rulings that it believes are of the "intensely divisive" variety, and concludes that they are of comparable dimension to *Roe*. It appears to us very odd indeed that the joint opinion chooses as benchmarks two cases in which the Court chose *not* to adhere to erroneous constitutional precedent, but instead enhanced its stature by acknowledging and correcting its error, apparently in violation of the joint opinion's "legitimacy" principle. . . .

. . . .

The joint opinion agrees that the Court's stature would have been seriously damaged if in *Brown* and *West Coast Hotel* it had dug in its heels and refused to apply normal principles of *stare decisis* to the earlier decisions. But the opinion contends that the Court was entitled to overrule *Plessy* and *Lochner* in those cases, despite the existence of opposition to the original decisions, only because both the Nation and the Court had learned new lessons in the interim. This is at best a feebly supported, *post hoc* rationalization for those decisions.

For example, the opinion asserts that the Court could justifiably overrule its decision in *Lochner* only because the Depression had convinced "most people" that constitutional protection of contractual freedom contributed to an economy that failed to protect the welfare of all. Surely the joint opinion does not mean to suggest that people saw this Court's failure to uphold minimum wage statutes as the cause of the Great Depression! In any event, the *Lochner* Court did not base its rule upon the policy judgment that an unregulated market was fundamental to a stable economy; it simply believed, erroneously, that "liberty" under the Due Process Clause protected the "right to make a contract." . . .

When the Court finally recognized its error in *West Coast Hotel*, it did not engage in the *post hoc* rationalization that the joint opinion attributes to it today; it did not state that *Lochner* had been based on an economic view that had fallen into disfavor, and that it therefore should be overruled. Chief Justice Hughes in his opinion for the Court simply recognized what Justice Holmes had previously recognized in his *Lochner* dissent, that "[t]he Constitution does not speak of freedom of contract." . . . .

. . . The Court in *Brown* simply recognized, as Justice Harlan had recognized beforehand, that the Fourteenth Amendment does not permit racial segregation. The rule of *Brown* is not tied to popular opinion about the evils of segregation; it is a judgment that the Equal Protection Clause does not permit racial segregation, no matter whether the public might come to believe that it is beneficial. . . .

. . . .

. . . That is, quite simply, the issue in these cases: not whether the power of a woman to abort her unborn child is a "liberty" in the absolute sense; or even whether it is a liberty of great importance to many women. Of course it is both. The issue is whether it is a liberty protected by the Constitution of the United States. I am sure it is not. I reach that conclusion not because of anything so exalted as my views concerning the "concept of existence, of meaning, of the universe, and of the mystery of human life." Rather, I reach it for the same reason I reach the conclusion that bigamy is not constitutionally protected—because of two simple facts: (1) the Constitution says absolutely nothing about it, and (2) the longstanding traditions of American society have permitted it to be legally proscribed.

. . . .

... [A]pplying the rational basis test, I would uphold the Pennsylvania statute in its entirety. I must, however, respond to a few of the more outrageous arguments in today's opinion, which it is beyond human nature to leave unanswered. . . .

. . . .

The Court's description of the place of *Roe* in the social history of the United States is unrecognizable. Not only did *Roe* not, as the Court suggests, *resolve* the deeply divisive issue of abortion; it did more than anything else to nourish it, by elevating it to the national level where it is infinitely more difficult to resolve. National politics were not plagued by abortion protests, national abortion lobbying, or abortion marches on Congress before *Roe v. Wade* was decided. Profound disagreement existed among our citizens over the issue—as it does over other issues, such as the death penalty—but that disagreement was being worked out at the state level. As with many other issues, the division of sentiment within each State was not as closely balanced as it was among the population of the Nation as a whole, meaning not only that more people would be satisfied with the results of state-by-state resolution, but also that those results would be more stable. Pre-*Roe,* moreover, political compromise was possible.

Roe's mandate for abortion on demand destroyed the compromises of the past, rendered compromise impossible for the future, and required the entire issue to be resolved uniformly, at the national level. At the same time, *Roe* created a vast new class of abortion consumers and abortion proponents by eliminating the moral opprobrium that had attached to the act. ("If the Constitution *guarantees* abortion, how can it be bad?"—not an accurate line of thought, but a natural one.) Many favor all of those developments, and it is not for me to say that they are wrong. But to portray *Roe* as the statesmanlike "settlement" of a divisive issue, a jurisprudential Peace of Westphalia that is worth preserving, is nothing less than Orwellian. *Roe* fanned into life an issue that has inflamed our national politics in general, and has obscured with its smoke the selection of Justices to this Court in particular, ever since. . . .

. . . .

What makes all this relevant to the bothersome application of "political pressure" against the Court are the twin facts that the American people love democracy and the American people are not fools. As long as this Court thought (and the people thought) that we Justices were doing essentially lawyers' work up here—reading text and discerning our society's traditional understanding of that text—the public pretty much left us alone. Texts and traditions are facts to study, not convictions to demonstrate about. . . .

There is a poignant aspect to today's opinion. Its length, and what might be called its epic tone, suggest that its authors believe they are bringing to an end a troublesome era in the history of our Nation and of our Court. "It is the dimension" of authority, they say, to "cal[l] the contending sides of national controversy to end their national division by accepting a common mandate rooted in the Constitution."

There comes vividly to mind a portrait by Emanuel Leutze that hangs in the Harvard Law School: Roger Brooke Taney, painted in 1859, the 82d year of his life, the 24th of his Chief Justiceship, the second after his opinion in *Dred Scott*. He is all in black, sitting in a shadowed red armchair, left hand resting upon a pad of paper in his lap, right hand hanging limply, almost lifelessly, beside the inner arm of the chair. He sits facing the viewer and staring straight out. There seems to be on his face, and in his deep-set eyes, an expression of profound sadness and disillusionment. Perhaps he always looked that way, even when dwelling upon the happiest of thoughts. But those of us who know how the lustre of his great Chief Justiceship came to be eclipsed by *Dred Scott* cannot help believing that he had that case—its already apparent consequences for the Court and its soon-to-be-played-out consequences for the Nation—burning on his mind. I expect that two years earlier he, too, had thought himself "call[ing] the contending sides of national controversy to end their national division by accepting a common mandate rooted in the Constitution."

It is no more realistic for us in this litigation, than it was for him in that, to think that an issue of the sort they both involved—an issue involving life and death, freedom and subjugation—can be "speedily and finally settled" by the Supreme Court, as President James Buchanan in his inaugural address said the issue of slavery in the territories would be. Quite to the contrary, by foreclosing all democratic outlet for the deep passions this issue arouses, by banishing the issue from the political forum that gives all participants, even the losers, the satisfaction of a fair hearing and an honest fight, by continuing the imposition of a rigid national rule instead of allowing for regional differences, the Court merely prolongs and intensifies the anguish.

We should get out of this area, where we have no right to be, and where we do neither ourselves nor the country any good by remaining.

NOTES

1.   *Dreading* Casey. When the Court granted certiorari in *Casey*, many abortion-rights advocates feared that the case would be a vehicle for overturning *Roe v. Wade*. As legal historian David Garrow notes, after oral arguments in *Casey*, "few observers saw any prospects for *Roe* beyond a further *Webster*-style slide into feeble irrelevancy." DAVID J. GARROW, LIBERTY AND SEXUALITY: THE RIGHT TO PRIVACY AND THE MAKING OF *ROE V. WADE* 692 (1998). While the Court declined to overturn *Roe* explicitly, it did grant far more latitude to the states to regulate abortion, signaling a more restrictive approach than that offered in *Roe*.

2.   *A powerful friend of the Court.* Acting on behalf of the Bush Administration, Solicitor General Kenneth Starr submitted an amicus brief

defending the Pennsylvania law challenged in *Casey*, and urging the court to analyze abortion restrictions using a rational basis standard of review, rather than strict scrutiny. Starr also took part in oral arguments, arguing on behalf of the United States as *amicus curiae. See* Brief for the United States as Amicus Curiae Supporting Respondents, *Planned Parenthood v. Casey*, 505 U.S. 833 (1993) (Nos. 91–744, 91–902).

3.   *Death by a thousand cuts?* Although the majority opinion in *Casey* professed to preserve *Roe v. Wade*'s essential holding, the decision nonetheless did away with *Roe*'s trimester framework and permitted state regulation of abortion, so long as it was not unduly burdensome. Do these changes preserve *Roe*'s legacy, or do they incrementally chip away at the rights that *Roe* articulated, as some have suggested?

4.   *Technology and viability.* In *Casey*, some of the justices seem convinced that technological advances have altered—or will alter—the point of viability. However, "[w]hile there have been significant developments in the care of infants born prematurely, the rate of survival for infants born at or before 24 weeks has not changed and is well below 50 percent." ADVANCING NEW STANDARDS IN REPROD. HEALTH, ISSUE BRIEF 4: THE SCIENCE OF "VIABILITY" 2 (2010). Does this misperception of the effect of technological advances on viability play a role in the Court's rejection of the trimester framework in *Casey*?

5.   *The evolution of abortion and equality.* When deciding *Roe v. Wade*, the Supreme Court's majority made a conscious decision to root abortion rights in substantive due process and the right to privacy. Nan D. Hunter, *Justice Blackmun, Abortion, and the Myth of Medical Independence*, 72 BROOK. L. REV. 147, 187–88 (2006). However, over time, glimmers of an equality framework for abortion rights emerged in Justice Blackmun's writings. In his dissent to *Webster v. Reproductive Health Services*, Blackmun explicitly linked the concepts of liberty and equality in the context of abortion rights, writing that he "fear[ed] for the liberty and equality of the millions of women who have lived and come of age in the 16 years since *Roe* was decided." 492 U.S. at 538. Three years later in his opinion in *Planned Parenthood of Southeastern Pennsylvania v. Casey*, Blackmun went even further, elaborating the intersecting claims of liberty and equality at stake in abortion discourse. As Blackmun explained:

> By restricting the right to terminate pregnancies, the State conscripts women's bodies into its service, forcing women to continue their pregnancies, suffer the pains of childbirth, and in most instances, provide years of maternal care. The State does not compensate women for their services; instead, it assumes that they owe this duty as a matter of course. This assumption—that women can simply be forced to accept the "natural" status and incidents of motherhood—appears to rest upon a conception of women's role that has triggered the protection of the Equal Protection Clause.

505 U.S. at 928 (Blackmun, J., concurring in part and dissenting in part). To support his view that abortion rights implicated women's equality, Blackmun cited *Mississippi University for Women v. Hogan*, a decision in

which the Court held that Mississippi University for Women's single-sex admissions policy violated the Equal Protection Clause. Critically, in that case, Blackmun filed a dissenting opinion bemoaning that "it is easy to go too far with rigid rules in this area of claimed sex discrimination, and to lose—indeed destroy—values that mean much to some people. . . ." 458 U.S. at 734 (1982) (Blackmun, J., dissenting). As abortion discourse evolved to embrace equality, it seemed that Justice Blackmun's views evolved as well.

Gonzales v. Carhart
550 U.S. 124 (2007).

■ KENNEDY, J.

These cases require us to consider the validity of the Partial-Birth Abortion Ban Act of 2003(Act), a federal statute regulating abortion procedures. In recitations preceding its operative provisions the Act refers to the Court's opinion in *Stenberg v. Carhart* (2000), which also addressed the subject of abortion procedures used in the later stages of pregnancy. Compared to the state statute at issue in *Stenberg*, the Act is more specific concerning the instances to which it applies and in this respect more precise in its coverage. We conclude the Act should be sustained against the objections lodged by the broad, facial attack brought against it.

. . . .

The Act proscribes a particular manner of ending fetal life, so it is necessary here, as it was in *Stenberg*, to discuss abortion procedures in some detail. . . .

Abortion methods vary depending to some extent on the preferences of the physician and, of course, on the term of the pregnancy and the resulting stage of the unborn child's development. Between 85 and 90 percent of the approximately 1.3 million abortions performed each year in the United States take place in the first three months of pregnancy, which is to say in the first trimester. The most common first-trimester abortion method is vacuum aspiration (otherwise known as suction curettage) in which the physician vacuums out the embryonic tissue. Early in this trimester an alternative is to use medication, such as mifepristone (commonly known as RU–486), to terminate the pregnancy. The Act does not regulate these procedures.

Of the remaining abortions that take place each year, most occur in the second trimester. The surgical procedure referred to as "dilation and evacuation" or "D & E" is the usual abortion method in this trimester. Although individual techniques for performing D & E differ, the general steps are the same.

A doctor must first dilate the cervix at least to the extent needed to insert surgical instruments into the uterus and to maneuver them to evacuate the fetus. The steps taken to cause dilation differ by physician and gestational age of the fetus. . . .

After sufficient dilation the surgical operation can commence. The woman is placed under general anesthesia or conscious sedation. The doctor, often guided by ultrasound, inserts grasping forceps through the woman's cervix and into the uterus to grab the fetus. The doctor grips a fetal part with the forceps and pulls it back through the cervix and vagina, continuing to pull even after meeting resistance from the cervix. The friction causes the fetus to tear apart. For example, a leg might be ripped off the fetus as it is pulled through the cervix and out of the woman. The process of evacuating the fetus piece by piece continues until it has been completely removed. A doctor may make 10 to 15 passes with the forceps to evacuate the fetus in its entirety, though sometimes removal is completed with fewer passes. Once the fetus has been evacuated, the placenta and any remaining fetal material are suctioned or scraped out of the uterus. The doctor examines the different parts to ensure the entire fetal body has been removed.

Some doctors, especially later in the second trimester, may kill the fetus a day or two before performing the surgical evacuation. They inject digoxin or potassium chloride into the fetus, the umbilical cord, or the amniotic fluid. Fetal demise may cause contractions and make greater dilation possible. Once dead, moreover, the fetus' body will soften, and its removal will be easier. Other doctors refrain from injecting chemical agents, believing it adds risk with little or no medical benefit.

The abortion procedure that was the impetus for the numerous bans on "partial-birth abortion," including the Act, is a variation of this standard D & E. The medical community has not reached unanimity on the appropriate name for this D & E variation. It has been referred to as "intact D & E," "dilation and extraction" (D & X), and "intact D & X." For discussion purposes this D & E variation will be referred to as intact D & E. The main difference between the two procedures is that in intact D & E a doctor extracts the fetus intact or largely intact with only a few passes. There are no comprehensive statistics indicating what percentage of all D & Es are performed in this manner.

Intact D & E, like regular D & E, begins with dilation of the cervix. Sufficient dilation is essential for the procedure. . . .

In an intact D & E procedure the doctor extracts the fetus in a way conducive to pulling out its entire body, instead of ripping it apart. One doctor, [Martin Haskell], testified:

. . . .

> [T]he surgeon then forces the scissors into the base of the skull or into the foramen magnum. Having safely entered the skull, he spreads the scissors to enlarge the opening.

> The surgeon removes the scissors and introduces a suction catheter into this hole and evacuates the skull contents. With

the catheter still in place, he applies traction to the fetus, removing it completely from the patient.

This is an abortion doctor's clinical description. Here is another description from a nurse who witnessed the same method performed on a 26½-week fetus and who testified before the Senate Judiciary Committee:

> Dr. Haskell went in with forceps and grabbed the baby's legs and pulled them down into the birth canal. Then he delivered the baby's body and the arms—everything but the head. The doctor kept the head right inside the uterus.

> The baby's little fingers were clasping and unclasping, and his little feet were kicking. Then the doctor stuck the scissors in the back of his head, and the baby's arms jerked out, like a startle reaction, like a flinch, like a baby does when he thinks he is going to fall.

> The doctor opened up the scissors, stuck a high-powered suction tube into the opening, and sucked the baby's brains out. Now the baby went completely limp.

> He cut the umbilical cord and delivered the placenta. He threw the baby in a pan, along with the placenta and the instruments he had just used.

Dr. Haskell's approach is not the only method of killing the fetus once its head lodges in the cervix, and "the process has evolved" since his presentation. Another doctor, for example, squeezes the skull after it has been pierced "so that enough brain tissue exudes to allow the head to pass through." Still other physicians reach into the cervix with their forceps and crush the fetus' skull. Others continue to pull the fetus out of the woman until it disarticulates at the neck, in effect decapitating it. These doctors then grasp the head with forceps, crush it, and remove it.

. . . .

D & E and intact D & E are not the only second-trimester abortion methods. Doctors also may abort a fetus through medical induction. The doctor medicates the woman to induce labor, and contractions occur to deliver the fetus. Induction, which unlike D & E should occur in a hospital, can last as little as 6 hours but can take longer than 48. It accounts for about 5 percent of second-trimester abortions before 20 weeks of gestation and 15 percent of those after 20 weeks. Doctors turn to two other methods of second-trimester abortion, hysterotomy and hysterectomy, only in emergency situations because they carry increased risk of complications. In a hysterotomy, as in a cesarean section, the doctor removes the fetus by making an incision through the abdomen and uterine wall to gain access to the uterine cavity. A hysterectomy requires the removal of the entire uterus. These two procedures represent about 0.07 percent of second-trimester abortions.

After Dr. Haskell's procedure received public attention, with ensuing and increasing public concern, bans on " 'partial birth abortion' " proliferated. By the time of the *Stenberg* decision, about 30 States had enacted bans designed to prohibit the procedure. In 1996, Congress also acted to ban partial-birth abortion. President Clinton vetoed the congressional legislation, and the Senate failed to override the veto. Congress approved another bill banning the procedure in 1997, but President Clinton again vetoed it. In 2003, after this Court's decision in *Stenberg*, Congress passed the Act at issue here. On November 5, 2003, President Bush signed the Act into law. It was to take effect the following day.

The Act responded to *Stenberg* in two ways. First, Congress made factual findings. . . . Congress found, among other things, that "[a] moral, medical, and ethical consensus exists that the practice of performing a partial-birth abortion . . . is a gruesome and inhumane procedure that is never medically necessary and should be prohibited."

Second, and more relevant here, the Act's language differs from that of the Nebraska statute struck down in *Stenberg*. The operative provisions of the Act provide in relevant part:

(a) Any physician who, in or affecting interstate or foreign commerce, knowingly performs a partial-birth abortion and thereby kills a human fetus shall be fined under this title or imprisoned not more than 2 years, or both. This subsection does not apply to a partial-birth abortion that is necessary to save the life of a mother whose life is endangered by a physical disorder, physical illness, or physical injury, including a life-endangering physical condition caused by or arising from the pregnancy itself. This subsection takes effect 1 day after the enactment.

(b) As used in this section—

(1) the term 'partial-birth abortion' means an abortion in which the person performing the abortion—

(A) deliberately and intentionally vaginally delivers a living fetus until, in the case of a head-first presentation, the entire fetal head is outside the body of the mother, or, in the case of breech presentation, any part of the fetal trunk past the navel is outside the body of the mother, for the purpose of performing an overt act that the person knows will kill the partially delivered living fetus; and

(B) performs the overt act, other than completion of delivery, that kills the partially delivered living fetus; and

. . . (d)(1) A defendant accused of an offense under this section may seek a hearing before the State Medical Board on whether the physician's conduct was necessary to save the life of the mother whose life was endangered by a physical disorder, physical illness, or physical injury, including a life-endangering physical condition caused by or arising from the pregnancy itself.

... (e) A woman upon whom a partial-birth abortion is performed may not be prosecuted under this section, for a conspiracy to violate this section, or for an offense under section 2, 3, or 4 of this title based on a violation of this section.

. . . .

We assume the following principles for the purposes of this opinion. Before viability, a State "may not prohibit any woman from making the ultimate decision to terminate her pregnancy." It also may not impose upon this right an undue burden, which exists if a regulation's "purpose or effect is to place a substantial obstacle in the path of a woman seeking an abortion before the fetus attains viability." On the other hand, "[r]egulations which do no more than create a structural mechanism by which the State, or the parent or guardian of a minor, may express profound respect for the life of the unborn are permitted, if they are not a substantial obstacle to the woman's exercise of the right to choose." *Casey v. Planned Parenthood*, in short, struck a balance. The balance was central to its holding. We now apply its standard to the cases at bar.

. . . .

Respondents agree the Act encompasses intact D & E, but they contend its additional reach is both unclear and excessive. Respondents assert that, at the least, the Act is void for vagueness because its scope is indefinite. In the alternative, respondents argue the Act's text proscribes all D & Es. Because D & E is the most common second-trimester abortion method, respondents suggest the Act imposes an undue burden. In this litigation the Attorney General does not dispute that the Act would impose an undue burden if it covered standard D & E.

We conclude that the Act is not void for vagueness, does not impose an undue burden from any overbreadth, and is not invalid on its face.

A

The Act punishes "knowingly perform[ing]" a "partial-birth abortion. It defines the unlawful abortion in explicit terms.

First, the person performing the abortion must "vaginally delive[r] a living fetus." § 1531(b)(1)(A). The Act does not restrict an abortion procedure involving the delivery of an expired fetus. The Act, furthermore, is inapplicable to abortions that do not involve vaginal delivery (for instance, hysterotomy or hysterectomy). The Act does apply both previability and postviability because, by common understanding and scientific terminology, a fetus is a living organism while within the womb, whether or not it is viable outside the womb. . . .

Second, the Act's definition of partial-birth abortion requires the fetus to be delivered "until, in the case of a head-first presentation, the entire fetal head is outside the body of the mother, or, in the case of breech presentation, any part of the fetal trunk past the navel is outside the body of the mother." The Attorney General concedes, and we agree, that if an abortion procedure does not involve the delivery of a living fetus to one of these "anatomical 'landmarks' "—where, depending on the presentation, either the fetal head or the fetal trunk past the navel is outside the body of the mother—the prohibitions of the Act do not apply.

Third, to fall within the Act, a doctor must perform an "overt act, other than completion of delivery, that kills the partially delivered living fetus." For purposes of criminal liability, the overt act causing the fetus' death must be separate from delivery. And the overt act must occur after the delivery to an anatomical landmark. . . .

Fourth, the Act contains scienter requirements concerning all the actions involved in the prohibited abortion. To begin with, the physician must have "deliberately and intentionally" delivered the fetus to one of the Act's anatomical landmarks. If a living fetus is delivered past the critical point by accident or inadvertence, the Act is inapplicable. In addition, the fetus must have been delivered "for the purpose of performing an overt act that the [doctor] knows will kill [it]." If either intent is absent, no crime has occurred. This follows from the general principle that where scienter is required no crime is committed absent the requisite state of mind.

Respondents contend the language described above is indeterminate, and they thus argue the Act is unconstitutionally vague on its face. "As generally stated, the void-for-vagueness doctrine requires that a penal statute define the criminal offense with sufficient definiteness that ordinary people can understand what conduct is prohibited and in a manner that does not encourage arbitrary and discriminatory enforcement." The Act satisfies both requirements.

The Act provides doctors "of ordinary intelligence a reasonable opportunity to know what is prohibited." Indeed, it sets forth "relatively clear guidelines as to prohibited conduct" and provides "objective criteria" to evaluate whether a doctor has performed a prohibited procedure. Unlike the statutory language in *Stenberg* that prohibited the delivery of a " 'substantial portion' " of the fetus—where a doctor might question how much of the fetus is a substantial portion—the Act defines the line between potentially criminal conduct on the one hand and lawful abortion on the other. Doctors performing D & E will know that if they do not deliver a living fetus to an anatomical landmark they will not face criminal liability.

This conclusion is buttressed by the intent that must be proved to impose liability. The Court has made clear that scienter requirements alleviate vagueness concerns. The Act requires the doctor deliberately to have delivered the fetus to an anatomical landmark. Because a doctor performing a D & E will not face criminal liability if he or she delivers a fetus beyond the prohibited point by mistake, the Act cannot be described as "a trap for those who act in good faith."

Respondents likewise have failed to show that the Act should be invalidated on its face because it encourages arbitrary or discriminatory enforcement. Just as the Act's anatomical landmarks provide doctors with objective standards, they also "establish minimal guidelines to govern law enforcement." The scienter requirements narrow the scope of the Act's prohibition and limit prosecutorial discretion. It cannot be said that the Act "vests virtually complete discretion in the hands of [law enforcement] to determine whether the [doctor] has satisfied [its provisions]." Respondents' arguments concerning arbitrary enforcement, furthermore, are somewhat speculative. This is a preenforcement challenge, where "no evidence has been, or could be, introduced to indicate whether the [Act] has been enforced in a discriminatory manner or with the aim of inhibiting [constitutionally protected conduct]." The Act is not vague.

We next determine whether the Act imposes an undue burden, as a facial matter, because its restrictions on second-trimester abortions are too broad. A review of the statutory text discloses the limits of its reach. The Act prohibits intact D & E; and, notwithstanding respondents' arguments, it does not prohibit the D & E procedure in which the fetus is removed in parts.

The Act prohibits a doctor from intentionally performing an intact D & E. . . .

The Act excludes most D & Es in which the fetus is removed in pieces, not intact. If the doctor intends to remove the fetus in parts from the outset, the doctor will not have the requisite intent to incur criminal liability. . . . Removing the fetus in this manner does not violate the Act because the doctor will not have delivered the living fetus to one of the anatomical landmarks or committed an additional overt act that kills the fetus after partial delivery.

A comparison of the Act with the Nebraska statute struck down in *Stenberg* confirms this point. The statute in *Stenberg* prohibited " 'deliberately and intentionally delivering into the vagina a living unborn child, or a substantial portion thereof, for the purpose of performing a procedure that the person performing such procedure knows will kill the unborn child and does kill the unborn child.' " The Court concluded that this statute encompassed D & E because "D & E will often involve a physician pulling a 'substantial portion' of a still living fetus, say, an arm or leg, into the vagina prior to the death of the fetus". . . .

Congress, it is apparent, responded to these concerns because the Act departs in material ways from the statute in *Stenberg*. It adopts the phrase "delivers a living fetus," instead of " 'delivering . . . a living unborn child, or a substantial portion thereof' ". . . .

The identification of specific anatomical landmarks to which the fetus must be partially delivered also differentiates the Act from the statute at issue in *Stenberg*. The Court in *Stenberg* interpreted " 'substantial portion' " of the fetus to include an arm or a leg. The Act's anatomical landmarks, by contrast, clarify that the removal of a small portion of the fetus is not prohibited. The landmarks also require the fetus to be delivered so that it is partially "outside the body of the mother." To come within the ambit of the Nebraska statute, on the other hand, a substantial portion of the fetus only had to be delivered into the vagina; no part of the fetus had to be outside the body of the mother before a doctor could face criminal sanctions.

By adding an overt-act requirement Congress sought further to meet the Court's objections to the state statute considered in *Stenberg*. The Act makes the distinction the Nebraska statute failed to draw (but the Nebraska Attorney General advanced) by differentiating between the overall partial-birth abortion and the distinct overt act that kills the fetus. The fatal overt act must occur after delivery to an anatomical landmark, and it must be something "other than [the] completion of delivery." This distinction matters because, unlike intact D & E, standard D & E does not involve a delivery followed by a fatal act.

. . . .

Under the principles accepted as controlling here, the Act, as we have interpreted it, would be unconstitutional "if its purpose or effect is to place a substantial obstacle in the path of a woman seeking an abortion before the fetus attains viability." The abortions affected by the Act's regulations take place both previability and postviability; so the quoted language and the undue burden analysis it relies upon are applicable. The question is whether the Act, measured by its text in this facial attack, imposes a substantial obstacle to late-term, but previability, abortions. The Act does not on its face impose a substantial obstacle, and we reject this further facial challenge to its validity.

The Act's purposes are set forth in recitals preceding its operative provisions. A description of the prohibited abortion procedure demonstrates the rationale for the congressional enactment. The Act proscribes a method of abortion in which a fetus is killed just inches before completion of the birth process. Congress stated as follows: "Implicitly approving such a brutal and inhumane procedure by choosing not to prohibit it will further coarsen society to the humanity of not only newborns, but all vulnerable and innocent human life, making it increasingly difficult to protect such life." The Act expresses respect for the dignity of human life.

Congress was concerned, furthermore, with the effects on the medical community and on its reputation caused by the practice of partial-birth abortion. . . .

There can be no doubt the government "has an interest in protecting the integrity and ethics of the medical profession." *Washington v. Glucksberg*, 521 U.S. 702, 731 (1997). Under our precedents it is clear the State has a significant role to play in regulating the medical profession.

. . . .

The Act's ban on abortions that involve partial delivery of a living fetus furthers the Government's objectives. No one would dispute that, for many, D & E is a procedure itself laden with the power to devalue human life. Congress could nonetheless conclude that the type of abortion proscribed by the Act requires specific regulation because it implicates additional ethical and moral concerns that justify a special prohibition. Congress determined that the abortion methods it proscribed had a "disturbing similarity to the killing of a newborn infant," and thus it was concerned with "draw[ing] a bright line that clearly distinguishes abortion and infanticide." The Court has in the past confirmed the validity of drawing boundaries to prevent certain practices that extinguish life and are close to actions that are condemned. *Glucksberg* found reasonable the State's "fear that permitting assisted suicide will start it down the path to voluntary and perhaps even involuntary euthanasia."

Respect for human life finds an ultimate expression in the bond of love the mother has for her child. The Act recognizes this reality as well. Whether to have an abortion requires a difficult and painful moral decision. While we find no reliable data to measure the phenomenon, it seems unexceptionable to conclude some women come to regret their choice to abort the infant life they once created and sustained. Severe depression and loss of esteem can follow.

In a decision so fraught with emotional consequence some doctors may prefer not to disclose precise details of the means that will be used, confining themselves to the required statement of risks the procedure entails. . . .

It is, however, precisely this lack of information concerning the way in which the fetus will be killed that is of legitimate concern to the State. *Casey*, 505 U.S. 833, 873 (1992) (plurality opinion) ("States are free to enact laws to provide a reasonable framework for a woman to make a decision that has such profound and lasting meaning"). The State has an interest in ensuring so grave a choice is well informed. It is self-evident that a mother who comes to regret her choice to abort must struggle with grief more anguished and sorrow more profound when she learns, only after the event, what she once did not know: that she allowed a doctor to pierce the skull and vacuum the fast-developing brain of her unborn child, a child assuming the human form.

It is a reasonable inference that a necessary effect of the regulation and the knowledge it conveys will be to encourage some women to carry the infant to full term, thus reducing the absolute number of late-term abortions. The medical profession, furthermore, may find different and less shocking methods to abort the fetus in the second trimester, thereby accommodating legislative demand. The State's interest in respect for life is advanced by the dialogue that better informs the political and legal systems, the medical profession, expectant mothers, and society as a whole of the consequences that follow from a decision to elect a late-term abortion.

It is objected that the standard D & E is in some respects as brutal, if not more, than the intact D & E, so that the legislation accomplishes little. What we have already said, however, shows ample justification for the regulation. Partial-birth abortion, as defined by the Act, differs from a standard D & E because the former occurs when the fetus is partially outside the mother to the point of one of the Act's anatomical landmarks. It was reasonable for Congress to think that partial-birth abortion, more than standard D & E, "undermines the public's perception of the appropriate role of a physician during the delivery process, and perverts a process during which life is brought into the world." ... In sum, we reject the contention that the congressional purpose of the Act was "to place a substantial obstacle in the path of a woman seeking an abortion." *Casey*, 505 U.S. at 878 (plurality opinion).

The Act's furtherance of legitimate government interests bears upon, but does not resolve, the next question: whether the Act has the effect of imposing an unconstitutional burden on the abortion right because it does not allow use of the barred procedure where " 'necessary, in appropriate medical judgment, for the preservation of the . . . health of the mother.' " The prohibition in the Act would be unconstitutional, under precedents we here assume to be controlling, if it "subject[ed] [women] to significant health risks." ... [W]hether the Act creates significant health risks for women has been a contested factual question. The evidence presented in the trial courts and before Congress demonstrates both sides have medical support for their position.

Respondents presented evidence that intact D & E may be the safest method of abortion, for reasons similar to those adduced in *Stenberg*. Abortion doctors testified, for example, that intact D & E decreases the risk of cervical laceration or uterine perforation because it requires fewer passes into the uterus with surgical instruments and does not require the removal of bony fragments of the dismembered fetus, fragments that may be sharp. Respondents also presented evidence that intact D & E was safer both because it reduces the risks that fetal parts will remain in the uterus and because it takes less time to complete. Respondents, in addition, proffered evidence that intact D & E was safer for women with certain medical conditions or women with fetuses that had certain anomalies.

These contentions were contradicted by other doctors who testified in the District Courts and before Congress. They concluded that the alleged health advantages were based on speculation without scientific studies to support them. They considered D & E always to be a safe alternative.

There is documented medical disagreement whether the Act's prohibition would ever impose significant health risks on women. . . .

This traditional rule is consistent with *Casey*, which confirms the State's interest in promoting respect for human life at all stages in the pregnancy. Physicians are not entitled to ignore regulations that direct them to use reasonable alternative procedures. The law need not give abortion doctors unfettered choice in the course of their medical practice, nor should it elevate their status above other physicians in the medical community. . . .

Medical uncertainty does not foreclose the exercise of legislative power in the abortion context any more than it does in other contexts. The medical uncertainty over whether the Act's prohibition creates significant health risks provides a sufficient basis to conclude in this facial attack that the Act does not impose an undue burden.

The conclusion that the Act does not impose an undue burden is supported by other considerations. Alternatives are available to the prohibited procedure. As we have noted, the Act does not proscribe D & E. . . . If the intact D & E procedure is truly necessary in some circumstances, it appears likely an injection that kills the fetus is an alternative under the Act that allows the doctor to perform the procedure.

. . . .

In reaching the conclusion the Act does not require a health exception we reject certain arguments made by the parties on both sides of these cases. On the one hand, the Attorney General urges us to uphold the Act on the basis of the congressional findings alone. Although we review congressional factfinding under a deferential standard, we do not in the circumstances here place dispositive weight on Congress' findings. The Court retains an independent constitutional duty to review factual findings where constitutional rights are at stake.

As respondents have noted, and the District Courts recognized, some recitations in the Act are factually incorrect . . . Uncritical deference to Congress' factual findings in these cases is inappropriate.

On the other hand, relying on the Court's opinion in *Stenberg*, respondents contend that an abortion regulation must contain a health exception "if 'substantial medical authority supports the proposition that banning a particular procedure could endanger women's health.' " . . .

A zero tolerance policy would strike down legitimate abortion regulations, like the present one, if some part of the medical community were disinclined to follow the proscription. This is too exacting a standard to impose on the legislative power, exercised in this instance under the Commerce Clause, to regulate the medical profession. Considerations of marginal safety, including the balance of risks, are within the legislative competence when the regulation is rational and in pursuit of legitimate ends. When standard medical options are available, mere convenience does not suffice to displace them; and if some procedures have different risks than others, it does not follow that the State is altogether barred from imposing reasonable regulations. The Act is not invalid on its face where there is uncertainty over whether the barred procedure is ever necessary to preserve a woman's health, given the availability of other abortion procedures that are considered to be safe alternatives.

The considerations we have discussed support our further determination that these facial attacks should not have been entertained in the first instance. In these circumstances the proper means to consider exceptions is by as-applied challenge. The Government has acknowledged that preenforcement, as-applied challenges to the Act can be maintained. This is the proper manner to protect the health of the woman if it can be shown that in discrete and well-defined instances a particular condition has or is likely to occur in which the procedure prohibited by the Act must be used. In an as-applied challenge the nature of the medical risk can be better quantified and balanced than in a facial attack.

The latitude given facial challenges in the First Amendment context is inapplicable here. Broad challenges of this type impose "a heavy burden" upon the parties maintaining the suit.

. . . .

As the previous sections of this opinion explain, respondents have not demonstrated that the Act would be unconstitutional in a large fraction of relevant cases. . . .

The Act is open to a proper as-applied challenge in a discrete case. No as-applied challenge need be brought if the prohibition in the Act threatens a woman's life because the Act already contains a life exception.

Respondents have not demonstrated that the Act, as a facial matter, is void for vagueness, or that it imposes an undue burden on a woman's right to abortion based on its overbreadth or lack of a health exception. For these reasons the judgments of the Courts of Appeals for the Eighth and Ninth Circuits are reversed.

It is so ordered.

■ THOMAS, J., with whom SCALIA, J., joins, concurring.

I join the Court's opinion because it accurately applies current jurisprudence, including *Planned Parenthood of Southeastern Pa. v. Casey*, 505 U.S. 833 (1992). I write separately to reiterate my view that the Court's abortion jurisprudence, including *Casey* and *Roe v. Wade*, 410 U.S. 113 (1973), has no basis in the Constitution. I also note that whether the Partial-Birth Abortion Ban Act of 2013 constitutes a permissible exercise of Congress' power under the Commerce Clause is not before the

Court. The parties did not raise or brief that issue; it is outside the question presented; and the lower courts did not address it.

■ GINSBURG, J., with whom STEVENS, J., SOUTER, J., and BREYER, J., join, dissenting.

. . . .

Today's decision is alarming. It refuses to take *Casey* and *Stenberg* seriously. It tolerates, indeed applauds, federal intervention to ban nationwide a procedure found necessary and proper in certain cases by the American College of Obstetricians and Gynecologists (ACOG). It blurs the line, firmly drawn in *Casey*, between previability and postviability abortions. And, for the first time since *Roe*, the Court blesses a prohibition with no exception safeguarding a woman's health.

. . . .

As *Casey* comprehended, at stake in cases challenging abortion restrictions is a woman's "control over her [own] destiny." "There was a time, not so long ago," when women were "regarded as the center of home and family life, with attendant special responsibilities that precluded full and independent legal status under the Constitution." Those views, this Court made clear in *Casey*, "are no longer consistent with our understanding of the family, the individual, or the Constitution." Women, it is now acknowledged, have the talent, capacity, and right "to participate equally in the economic and social life of the Nation." Their ability to realize their full potential, the Court recognized, is intimately connected to "their ability to control their reproductive lives." Thus, legal challenges to undue restrictions on abortion procedures do not seek to vindicate some generalized notion of privacy; rather, they center on a woman's autonomy to determine her life's course, and thus to enjoy equal citizenship stature.

In keeping with this comprehension of the right to reproductive choice, the Court has consistently required that laws regulating abortion, at any stage of pregnancy and in all cases, safeguard a woman's health.

We have thus ruled that a State must avoid subjecting women to health risks not only where the pregnancy itself creates danger, but also where state regulation forces women to resort to less safe methods of abortion. . . .

In *Stenberg*, we expressly held that a statute banning intact D & E was unconstitutional in part because it lacked a health exception. We noted that there existed a "division of medical opinion" about the relative safety of intact D & E, but we made clear that as long as "substantial medical authority supports the proposition that banning a particular abortion procedure could endanger women's health," a health exception is required. . . .

In 2003, a few years after our ruling in *Stenberg*, Congress passed the Partial-Birth Abortion Ban Act—without an exception for women's health. The congressional findings on which the Partial-Birth Abortion Ban Act rests do not withstand inspection, as the lower courts have determined and this Court is obliged to concede.

. . . .

More important, Congress claimed there was a medical consensus that the banned procedure is never necessary. But the evidence "very clearly demonstrate[d] the opposite."

Similarly, Congress found that "[t]here is no credible medical evidence that partial-birth abortions are safe or are safer than other abortion procedures." But the congressional record includes letters from numerous individual physicians stating that pregnant women's health would be jeopardized under the Act, as well as statements from nine professional associations, including ACOG, the American Public Health Association, and the California Medical Association, attesting that intact D & E carries meaningful safety advantages over other methods. . . .

In contrast to Congress, the District Courts made findings after full trials at which all parties had the opportunity to present their best evidence. The courts had the benefit of "much more extensive medical and scientific evidence . . . concerning the safety and necessity of intact D & Es."

During the District Court trials, "numerous" "extraordinarily accomplished" and "very experienced" medical experts explained that, in certain circumstances and for certain women, intact D & E is safer than alternative procedures and necessary to protect women's health.

According to the expert testimony plaintiffs introduced, the safety advantages of intact D & E are marked for women with certain medical conditions, for example, uterine scarring, bleeding disorders, heart disease, or compromised immune systems. Further, plaintiffs' experts testified that intact D & E is significantly safer for women with certain pregnancy-related conditions, such as placenta previa and accreta, and for women carrying fetuses with certain abnormalities, such as severe hydrocephalus.

Intact D & E, plaintiffs' experts explained, provides safety benefits over D & E by dismemberment for several reasons: *First*, intact D & E minimizes the number of times a physician must insert instruments through the cervix and into the uterus, and thereby reduces the risk of trauma to, and perforation of, the cervix and uterus—the most serious complication associated with nonintact D & E. *Second*, removing the fetus intact, instead of dismembering it *in utero,* decreases the likelihood that fetal tissue will be retained in the uterus, a condition that can cause infection, hemorrhage, and infertility. *Third*, intact D & E diminishes the chances of exposing the patient's tissues to sharp bony fragments sometimes resulting from dismemberment of the fetus. *Fourth*, intact D & E takes less operating time than D & E by dismemberment, and thus may reduce bleeding, the risk of infection, and complications relating to anesthesia.

Based on thoroughgoing review of the trial evidence and the congressional record, each of the District Courts to consider the issue rejected Congress' findings as unreasonable and not supported by the evidence. The trial courts concluded, in contrast to Congress' findings, that "significant medical authority supports the proposition that in some circumstances, [intact D & E] is the safest procedure.

The District Courts' findings merit this Court's respect. Today's opinion supplies no reason to reject those findings. Nevertheless, despite the District Courts' appraisal of the weight of the evidence, and in undisguised conflict with *Stenberg*, the Court asserts that the Partial-Birth Abortion Ban Act can survive "when ... medical uncertainty persists." This assertion is bewildering. Not only does it defy the Court's longstanding precedent affirming the necessity of a health exception, with no carve-out for circumstances of medical uncertainty; it gives short shrift to the records before us, carefully canvassed by the District Courts. Those records indicate that "the majority of highly-qualified experts on the subject believe intact D & E to be the safest, most appropriate procedure under certain circumstances."

. . . .

The Court offers flimsy and transparent justifications for upholding a nationwide ban on intact D & E *sans* any exception to safeguard a woman's health. Today's ruling, the Court declares, advances "a premise central to [*Casey's*] conclusion"—*i.e.*, the Government's "legitimate and substantial interest in preserving and promoting fetal life." But the Act scarcely furthers that interest: The law saves not a single fetus from destruction, for it targets only a *method* of performing abortion. And surely the statute was not designed to protect the lives or health of pregnant women. In short, the Court upholds a law that, while doing nothing to "preserv[e] ... fetal life," *ante*, at 1626, bars a woman from choosing intact D & E although her doctor "reasonably believes [that procedure] will best protect [her]."

As another reason for upholding the ban, the Court emphasizes that the Act does not proscribe the nonintact D & E procedure. But why not, one might ask. Nonintact D & E could equally be characterized as "brutal," *ante*, at 1633, involving as it does "tear[ing] [a fetus] apart" and "rip[ing] off" its limbs. "[T]he notion that either of these two equally gruesome procedures ... is more akin to infanticide than the other, or that the State furthers any legitimate interest by banning one but not the other, is simply irrational."

. . . .

Ultimately, the Court admits that "moral concerns" are at work, concerns that could yield prohibitions on any abortion. Notably, the concerns expressed are untethered to any ground genuinely serving the

Government's interest in preserving life. By allowing such concerns to carry the day and case, overriding fundamental rights, the Court dishonors our precedent.

Revealing in this regard, the Court invokes an antiabortion shibboleth for which it concededly has no reliable evidence: Women who have abortions come to regret their choices, and consequently suffer from "[s]evere depression and loss of esteem." Because of women's fragile emotional state and because of the "bond of love the mother has for her child," the Court worries, doctors may withhold information about the nature of the intact D & E procedure. The solution the Court approves, then, is *not* to require doctors to inform women, accurately and adequately, of the different procedures and their attendant risks. Instead, the Court deprives women of the right to make an autonomous choice, even at the expense of their safety.

This way of thinking reflects ancient notions about women's place in the family and under the Constitution—ideas that have long since been discredited. . . .

Though today's majority may regard women's feelings on the matter as "self-evident," this Court has repeatedly confirmed that "[t]he destiny of the woman must be shaped . . . on her own conception of her spiritual imperatives and her place in society."

In cases on a "woman's liberty to determine whether to [continue] her pregnancy," this Court has identified viability as a critical consideration. "[T]here is no line [more workable] than viability," the Court explained in *Casey*, for viability is "the time at which there is a realistic possibility of maintaining and nourishing a life outside the womb, so that the independent existence of the second life can in reason and all fairness be the object of state protection that now overrides the rights of the woman. . . . In some broad sense it might be said that a woman who fails to act before viability has consented to the State's intervention on behalf of the developing child."

Today, the Court blurs that line, maintaining that "[t]he Act [legitimately] appl[ies] both previability and postviability because . . . a fetus is a living organism while within the womb, whether or not it is viable outside the womb." Instead of drawing the line at viability, the Court refers to Congress' purpose to differentiate "abortion and infanticide" based not on whether a fetus can survive outside the womb, but on where a fetus is anatomically located when a particular medical procedure is performed.

One wonders how long a line that saves no fetus from destruction will hold in face of the Court's "moral concerns." The Court's hostility to the right *Roe* and *Casey* secured is not concealed. Throughout, the opinion refers to obstetrician-gynecologists and surgeons who perform abortions not by the titles of their medical specialties, but by the pejorative label "abortion doctor." A fetus is described as an "unborn child," and as a "baby;" second-trimester, previability abortions are referred to as "late-term;" and the reasoned medical judgments of highly trained doctors are dismissed as "preferences" motivated by "mere convenience." Instead of the heightened scrutiny we have previously applied, the Court determines that a "rational" ground is enough to uphold the Act. And, most troubling, *Casey's* principles, confirming the continuing vitality of "the essential holding of *Roe*," are merely "assume[d]" for the moment, rather than "retained" or "reaffirmed."

The Court further confuses our jurisprudence when it declares that "facial attacks" are not permissible in "these circumstances," *i.e.*, where medical uncertainty exists. This holding is perplexing given that, in materially identical circumstances we held that a statute lacking a health exception was unconstitutional on its face.

Without attempting to distinguish *Stenberg* and earlier decisions, the majority asserts that the Act survives review because respondents have not shown that the ban on intact D & E would be unconstitutional "in a large fraction of [relevant] cases." But *Casey* makes clear that, in determining whether any restriction poses an undue burden on a "large fraction" of women, the relevant class is *not* "all women," nor "all pregnant women," nor even all women "seeking abortions." Rather, a provision restricting access to abortion "must be judged by reference to those [women] for whom it is an actual rather than an irrelevant restriction." Thus the absence of a health exception burdens *all* women for whom it is relevant—women who, in the judgment of their doctors, require an intact D & E because other procedures would place their health at risk. It makes no sense to conclude that this facial challenge fails because respondents have not shown that a health exception is necessary for a large fraction of second-trimester abortions, including those for which a health exception is unnecessary: The very purpose of a health *exception* is to protect women in *exceptional* cases.

If there is anything at all redemptive to be said of today's opinion, it is that the Court is not willing to foreclose entirely a constitutional challenge to the Act. "The Act is open," the Court states, "to a proper as-applied challenge in a discrete case." But the Court offers no clue on what a "proper" lawsuit might look like. Nor does the Court explain why the injunctions ordered by the District Courts should not remain in place, trimmed only to exclude instances in which another procedure would safeguard a woman's health at least equally well. Surely the Court cannot mean that no suit may be brought until a woman's health is immediately jeopardized by the ban on intact D & E. A woman "suffer[ing] from medical complications," needs access to the medical procedure at once and cannot wait for the judicial process to unfold.

The Court appears, then, to contemplate another lawsuit by the initiators of the instant actions. In such a second round, the Court suggests, the challengers could succeed upon demonstrating that "in discrete and well-defined instances a particular condition has or is likely to occur in which the procedure prohibited by the Act must be used." One may anticipate that such a preenforcement challenge will be mounted swiftly, to ward off serious, sometimes irremediable harm, to women whose health would be endangered by the intact D & E prohibition.

. . . .

The Court's allowance only of an "as-applied challenge in a discrete case," jeopardizes women's health and places doctors in an untenable position. Even if courts were able to carve out exceptions through piecemeal litigation for "discrete and well-defined instances," women whose circumstances have not been anticipated by prior litigation could well be left unprotected. In treating those women, physicians would risk criminal prosecution, conviction, and imprisonment if they exercise their best judgment as to the safest medical procedure for their patients. The Court is thus gravely mistaken to conclude that narrow as-applied challenges are "the proper manner to protect the health of the woman."

. . . .

In sum, the notion that the Partial-Birth Abortion Ban Act furthers any legitimate governmental interest is, quite simply, irrational. The Court's defense of the statute provides no saving explanation. In candor, the Act, and the Court's defense of it, cannot be understood as anything other than an effort to chip away at a right declared again and again by this Court—and with increasing comprehension of its centrality to women's lives. When "a statute burdens constitutional rights and all that can be said on its behalf is that it is the vehicle that legislators have chosen for expressing their hostility to those rights, the burden is undue."

NOTES

1. *"Life" in context.* Abortion opponents hailed *Carhart* as a step forward in articulating and protecting a "culture of life"—and specifically, the view that life begins upon conception. However, the question of when life begins was not always so settled. In October 1973, Dr. Kenneth Edelin performed an abortion on a seventeen-year-old unmarried woman. The procedure was undertaken with the consent of the patient and her mother. After performing the abortion, Edelin was indicted and convicted on manslaughter charges. He challenged his conviction, which was eventually overturned by the Massachusetts Supreme Judicial Court in 1976. Decided soon after *Roe v. Wade*, the conflict in *Commonwealth v. Edelin* centered on whether or not the non-viable fetus *in utero* was a "living" being. The Massachusetts Supreme Judicial Court held that "[i]n order for a person to exist, he or she must be born." *Commonwealth v. Edelin*, 359 N.E.2d 4, 10 (Mass. 1976). In 1976, this understanding of birth as the determinative marker for personhood was a commonplace view. By the time that *Gonzales v. Carhart* was decided, however, the political terrain had shifted considerably. When the *Carhart* Court endorsed Congress' view that late term abortions are "similar to the killing of a newborn infant," and repeated its dicta in *Casey* that "respect for human life finds an ultimate expression in a mother's love

for her child," it endorsed a view of the fetus as a person and proclaimed the essential nature of maternal love.

2.   *Fetal pain and junk science.* Many states have passed "fetal pain" statutes forbidding abortion at twenty weeks after fertilization on the alleged ground that, at this point, the fetus can feel pain. Indeed, in 2013, even the U.S. House of Representatives took up the issue of fetal pain, passing H.R. 1797, colloquially known as the Pain-Capable Unborn Child Protection Act. *See Blackburn: We Have a Moral Obligation to Protect Women and Babies from Dangerous Late-Term Abortions*, NAT'L RIGHT TO LIFE NEWS TODAY (June 18, 2014), http://www.nationalrighttolifenews.org/news/2014/06/blackburn-we-have-a-moral-obligation-to-protect-women-and-babies-from-dangerous-late-term-abortions/#.U7OlbI1dWYk. The issue of fetal pain, however, is not clearly established by scientific evidence. A careful multidisciplinary review of all available studies on fetal pain noted that pain is not easily measured. However, electroencephalography (EEG) on premature babies "suggests the capacity for functional pain perception . . . probably does not exist before 29 or 30 weeks." *See* Susan J. Lee et al., *Fetal Pain: A Systematic Multidisciplinary Review of the Evidence*, 294 J. AM. MED. ASS'N 947, 947 (2005). A more recent report from the United Kingdom's Royal College of Obstetricians and Gynaecologists (RCOG) came to essentially the same conclusion: "Interpretation of existing data suggests that cortical processing and therefore fetal perception of pain cannot occur before 24 weeks of gestation." ROYAL COLL. OF OBSTETRICIANS & GYNAECOLOGISTS, FETAL AWARENESS: REVIEW OF RESEARCH AND RECOMMENDATIONS FOR PRACTICE: REPORT OF A WORKING PARTY (2010). Even in the face of a medical and scientific consensus, state and national legislators seem to rely on dubious research, often called "junk science," to support the theory of fetal pain.

3.   *The changing composition of the Court.* In a stinging dissent, Justice Ruth Bader Ginsburg observed that "[t]hough today's opinion does not go so far as to discard *Roe* or *Casey*, the Court, differently composed than it was when we last considered a restrictive abortion regulation, is hardly faithful to our earlier invocations of 'the rule of law' and the 'principles of stare decisis.' " *Gonzales v. Carhart*, 550 U.S. 124, 191 (2007). In both *Casey* (1992) and *Stenberg* (1999), a 5–4 majority of the Court struck down laws that would have limited abortion, and in so doing, professed fidelity to *Roe*'s essential holding. Critically, in *Carhart*, Justice Sandra Day O'Connor, one of the five justices in the *Casey* and *Stenberg* majorities, had retired from the Court. *See New Justices, Old Issue*, L.A. TIMES, Nov. 6, 2006, at A16. President George W. Bush initially appointed Judge John G. Roberts of the D.C. Circuit to fill O'Connor's seat. However, on September 3, 2005, the Court unexpectedly lost its leader when Chief Justice William Rehnquist died. President Bush nominated Roberts, who had served as a law clerk to Rehnquist, to the position of Chief Justice. Bush then nominated Judge Samuel Alito of the Third Circuit to fill O'Connor's seat. *See* Linda Greenhouse, *With O'Connor Retirement and a New Chief Justice Comes an Awareness of Change*, N.Y. TIMES, Jan. 28, 2006, at A10.

4. *Equality ascendant again?* In her stinging dissent in *Gonzalez v. Carhart*, Justice Ruth Bader Ginsburg sought to yoke the abortion right explicitly to women's equality, noting that "legal challenges to undue restrictions on abortion procedures do not seek to vindicate some generalized notion of privacy; rather, they center on a woman's autonomy to determine her life's course, and thus to enjoy equal citizenship stature." *Gonzales v. Carhart*, 550 U.S. at 172 (Ginsburg, *J.*, dissenting). As Professor Reva Siegel observes, Ginsburg's nod to equality recalled arguments that feminists had made in pre-*Roe* challenges to abortion, including *Abele v. Markle*, 342 F. Supp. 800 (D. Conn. 1972). *See* Reva B. Siegel, *Roe's Roots: The Women's Rights Claims that Engendered* Roe, 90 BOS. U. L. REV. 1875 (2010).

5. *Biological and social motherhood.* Reva Siegel has observed that debates over abortion are embedded in what she terms "physiological naturalism"—a view of reproduction that focuses exclusively on physiological aspects of reproduction and women's bodies. In so doing, she maintains, these arguments conflate women's social roles as mothers to their physiological capacity to bear children, naturalizing motherhood as women's inevitable destiny. *See* Reva Siegel, *Reasoning from the Body: A Historical Perspective on Abortion Regulation and Questions of Equal Protection*, 44 STAN. L. REV. 261, 267–68 (1992). In many respects, the Court's decision in *Gonzales v. Carhart* reflects a similar conflation of biological and social motherhood in its veneration of maternal love and its emphasis on the physiological personhood of the fetus. This is particularly evident in the Court's discussion of post-abortion stress syndrome, and its view of abortion regulation as necessary for protecting women from the mental and physical consequences of an abortion. If you credit this view of *Carhart*, how should feminists respond to the decision?

6. *Ultrasound: the fetus as fetish. Carhart*'s interest in protecting the fetus as a prospective person may be connected to other cultural trends regarding birth. In a prescient article now more than a quarter-century old, Professor Rosalind Petchesky reminds us that no visual image comes to us objectively; all images are mediated by cultural assumptions and power relations. Rosalind Petchesky, *Fetal Images: The Power of Visual Culture in the Politics of Reproduction*, 13 FEMINIST STUD. 263, 277 (1987). With this caveat in mind, Professor Carol Sanger argues that mandatory ultrasound legislation, which requires ultrasounds as a precondition of abortion, is intended to entrench a cultural view of the fetus as a person and make the abortion decision more difficult for women. "Fetal imagery, or even the word fetus, alerts us to the presence of abortion politics. . . . [Mandatory ultrasound is] a fortuitous combination of imagery, imagination, and ideology . . . harassment masquerading as information." Carol Sanger, *Seeing and Believing: Mandatory Ultrasound and the Path to a Protected Choice*, 56 UCLA L. REV. 351, 358, 370 (2008). Sanger goes further to argue that mandatory ultrasounds create the impression of the fetus as disconnected from the woman—that is, as an astronaut in (unoccupied) space. In this way, mandatory ultrasounds not only complicate the decision-making process for women, they also erase women from the picture, putting the focus on the fetus as an independent being with rights and interests. Are Petchesky and

Sanger correct? What role do fetal ultrasounds play in cultivating a culture of life?

7.   *The culture of life, Catholic hospitals, and the future of reproductive care.* The phrase "culture of life" is common in moral theology. However, the phrase did not become part of the popular lexicon until Pope John Paul II used it in a 1993 speech. Since then, the term has been closely associated with Catholicism and Catholic doctrine. In this way, adherence to a culture of life—with its opposition to abortion, sterilization, and euthanasia—has become an issue in the operation of hospitals affiliated with the Catholic Church. As women's health advocates Susan Berke Fogel and Lourdes Rivera explain, religiously-controlled hospitals are the fastest growing sector of the national hospital system, and the bulk of non-profit hospitals operate under the auspices of Catholic institutions. Because of their core religious beliefs, such institutions often refuse to prescribe contraception or sterilization, offer abortions, permit oocyte cryopreservation (egg freezing) before chemotherapy, or permit in vitro fertilization. In addition to refusing services, such hospitals often forbid physicians from providing referrals—or even information—about other institutions and physicians that would provide such services. *See* Susan Berke Fogel & Lourdes A. River, *Saving Roe Is Not Enough: When Religion Controls Healthcare*, 31 FORDHAM URB. L.J. 725, 727–29 (2003). In recent years, a number of Catholic hospitals have merged, while others have acquired secular hospitals. These developments have further limited access to certain reproductive services because they have increased the likelihood that, for many Americans, the nearest (or only) hospital will be operated under the auspices of the Catholic Church. Is there a meaningful difference between conscience clauses allowing individuals to refrain from providing certain reproductive services on the ground that they contradict religious beliefs and institutional policies that prohibit provision of services by employees for the same reason? Given that they control an increasing share of the health care market, and receive substantial public funding, should the law treat Catholic hospitals as places of public accommodation?

8.   *Do anti-abortion policies risk women's health?* In December 2013, the American Civil Liberties Union sued the Unites States Conference of Catholic Bishops ("USCCB"), arguing that their anti-abortion policies, codified in the Religious and Ethical Directives to Catholic Hospitals, risked a pregnant woman's health and possibly her life. Tamesha Means was eighteen weeks pregnant when her water broke, a routine but potentially life-threatening event due to the possibility of infection. Means went to Mercy Health Partners in Muskegon, Michigan, a Catholic hospital and the only hospital in her county. Means alleges that the hospital sent her home twice and did not advise her of the risks of infection. On her third visit she was admitted, feverish and bleeding. She ultimately miscarried. Means contends that her treatment was the product of the Catholic hospital's anti-abortion policies, rather than sound medical practice. Critically, she is suing the USCCB, which promulgated the policy and directed its implementation, rather than the hospital itself. *See* Erik Eckholm, *Bishops Sued Over Anti-Abortion Policies at Catholic Hospitals*, N.Y. TIMES, Dec. 2, 2013, at A12. To

date, the case is still pending. *See Means v. United States Conference of Catholic Bishops et al.*, No. 2:13–CV–14916 (E.D. Mich. Filed Nov. 29, 2013).

9. *The color of religious health care.* In the 2018 report, "Bearing Faith: The Limits of Catholic Health Care for Women of Color," Columbia Law School's Law, Rights, and Religion Project, in partnership with Public Health Solutions, presented data showing that in many states, women of color disproportionately give birth in Catholic hospitals that place religious restrictions on care—even during medical emergencies. As the report explains, such restrictions may exacerbate the existing disparities women of color already face in accessing quality reproductive health care. *See* Law, Rights, and Religion Project & Public Health Solutions, *Bearing Faith: The Limits of Catholic Health Care for Women of Color* (2018) (available at https://lawrightsreligion.law.columbia.edu/bearingfaith).

10. *The success of the culture of life.* Perhaps the Americans United for Life document "Defending Life" says it best:

> [M]ore pro-life laws are in effect than ever before, life-affirming legislation continues to be introduced in record numbers in a majority of the states, and there is increasing public recognition of the negative impact of abortion on women. . . . AUL actively pursues a strategy of accumulated victories, advocating the systematic and persistent adoption and implementation of life-affirming laws in the states. We provide . . . lawmakers . . . proven legal strategies and tools that will . . . state-by-state, lead to a more pro-life America and help set the stage for the state-by-state battle that will follow *Roe*'s ultimate reversal.

AMERICANS UNITED FOR LIFE, DEFENDING LIFE 55–56 (2013).

11. *The culture of life and contraception.* One might be forgiven for thinking that the issue of contraception was settled in the 1960s, in the era of *Griswold* and *Eisenstadt*, but that would not be the case. Buoyed by their success in opposing abortion, conservative groups have put opposing contraception on their agendas, as well. Russell Shorto, *Contra-Contraception*, N.Y. TIMES MAG., May 7, 2006, at 48. Those who believe that life begins upon the fertilization of an ovum oppose specific contraceptives, like the "morning after pill," the pill, and the IUD on the ground that these contraceptives may in fact prevent fertilized eggs from implanting, thus qualifying as abortifacients. AMERICANS UNITED FOR LIFE, DEFENDING LIFE 134–136 (2013). Critically, contraception, unlike abortion, does not involve issues regarding the personhood of ova or other genetic material. Nevertheless, the characterization of contraception as akin to abortion seems rooted in a common discomfort with the idea of women's sexuality disconnected from procreation. In this vein, calls to defund Planned Parenthood and to ban public funding of any contraceptive devices suggest that broader issues of sexual regulation and gender roles continue to fuel opposition to abortion and contraception alike.

12. *A strategic shift in anti-abortion discourse.* David C. Reardon is the creator of a rhetorical shift in anti-abortion discourse. Traditionally, anti-abortion discourse focused on characterizing the fetus as a person and

emphasizing the loss of an innocent life. Under Reardon's direction, anti-abortion rhetoric has shifted from the emphasis on the fetus to one that Reardon has dubbed "pro-life and pro-woman." The new rhetoric, which emphasizes abortion's alleged harms—physical and psychological—to women, is intended to counter the pro-choice rhetoric that depicts the right to an abortion as an essential aspect of women's empowerment and autonomy. Although this rhetorical shift has been well-received in some quarters—note Justice Kennedy's nod to this rhetoric in *Gonzales v. Carhart*—it has been divisive among anti-abortion advocates and activists, many of whom find the new rhetoric a distraction to the underlying issues of fetal personhood and the preservation of life. *See* David C. Reardon, *A Defense of the Neglected Rhetorical Strategy (NRS)*, 18 ETHICS & MED. 23 (2002).

13. *The effects of* Casey *and* Carhart. The following chart, prepared by the Guttmacher Institute, a reproductive rights and health research group, documents the rapid increase of state-level legislation affecting abortion. In 2011, for example, ninety-two different provisions were passed in state legislatures, nearly three times the previous level of thirty-four in 2005.

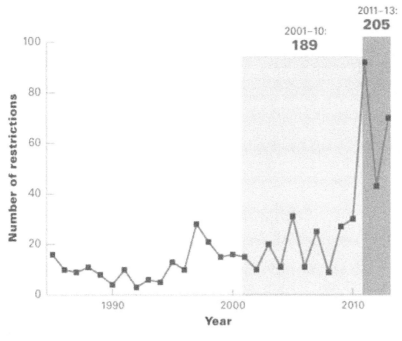

© 2014 Guttmacher Institute | guttmacher.org

More State Abortion Restrictions Were Enacted in 2011–2013 than in the Entire Previous Decade, GUTTMACHER INST. (Jan. 2, 2014), https://

www.guttmacher.org/article/2014/01/more-state-abortion-restrictions-were-enacted-2011-2013-entire-previous-decade.

6.　IN THE WAKE OF *CASEY* AND *CARHART*

Casey proved a turning point in abortion litigation. The Court overruled the Pennsylvania Abortion Control Act's provision requiring spousal consent to abortion, but accepted the law's provisions mandating informed consent, parental consent, a twenty-four hour waiting period, and new reporting requirements for facilities providing abortions. More importantly, the standard for judicial review of abortion regulations was downgraded from the strict scrutiny review used in earlier cases, which regarded abortion as a fundamental right, to the undue burden standard originally proposed by Justice O'Connor in her dissent to Thornburgh v. American College of Obstetricians and Gynecologists, *476 U.S. 747 (1986),* supra *p. 747.*

Below we have provided examples of state-level statutory and regulatory restrictions on the provision of abortion and related services. Such laws and regulations have become increasingly common since Casey *and* Carhart. *Some of these restrictions explicitly regulate a woman's right to obtain an abortion by requiring counseling, waiting periods, and ultrasounds. By contrast, other restrictions focus on other aspects of the provision of abortion. For example, some states have revised their building codes to require particular standards for facilities that provide abortions. Others have required abortion-services providers to have admitting privileges at local hospitals. Do such restrictions impair the abortion right by raising the cost of abortions, or limiting access to abortion? Do these requirements have the effect of increasing the costs associated with operating abortion clinics? If so, do they contribute to the diminishing number of facilities available to provide abortion? Finally, with these concerns in mind, do these restrictions comport with* Casey's *undue burden test? Would they have survived the strict scrutiny standard used in* Roe v. Wade?

Idaho Code § 18–608A

(2013).

SEC. 8A.　*Persons authorized to perform abortions*

It is unlawful for any person other than a physician to cause or perform an abortion.

Massachusetts General Laws, ch. 112, § 12S

(2013).

SEC. 12S. *Consent to abortion; form; persons less than eighteen years of age*

No physician may perform an abortion upon a pregnant woman without first obtaining her written informed consent. The commissioner of public health shall prescribe a form for physicians to use in obtaining such consent. This form shall be written in a manner designed to permit a person unfamiliar with medical terminology to understand its purpose and content, and shall include the following information: a description of the stage of development of the unborn child; the type of procedure which the physician intends to use to perform the abortion; and the possible complications associated with the use of the procedure and with the performance of the abortion itself; the availability of alternatives to abortion; and a statement that, under the law of the commonwealth, a person's refusal to undergo an abortion does not constitute grounds for the denial of public assistance. A pregnant woman seeking an abortion shall sign the consent form described above at least twenty-four hours in advance of the time for which the abortion is scheduled, except in an emergency requiring immediate action. She shall then return it to the physician performing the abortion who shall maintain it in his files and destroy it seven years after the date upon which the abortion is performed.

The said consent form and any other forms, transcript of evidence, or written findings and conclusions of a court, shall be confidential and may not be released to any person except by the pregnant woman's written informed consent or by a proper judicial order, other than to the pregnant woman herself, to whom such documents relate, the operating physician, or any person whose consent is required pursuant to this section, or under the law. If a pregnant woman is less than eighteen years of age and has not married, a physician shall not perform an abortion upon her unless he first obtains both the consent of the pregnant woman and that of her parents, except as hereinafter provided. In deciding whether to grant such consent, a pregnant woman's parents shall consider only their child's best interests. If one of the pregnant woman's parents has died or is unavailable to the physician within a reasonable time and in a reasonable manner, consent of the remaining parent shall be sufficient. If both parents have died or are otherwise unavailable to the physician within a reasonable time and in a reasonable manner, consent of the pregnant woman's guardian or guardians shall be sufficient. If the pregnant woman's parents are divorced, consent of the parent having custody shall be sufficient. If a pregnant woman less than eighteen years of age has not married and if one or both of her parents or guardians refuse to consent to the performance of an abortion, or if she elects not to seek the consent of one or both of her parents or guardians, a judge of the superior court department of the trial court shall, upon petition, or motion, and after an appropriate hearing, authorize a physician to perform the abortion if said judge determines that the pregnant woman is mature and capable of giving informed consent to the proposed abortion or, if said judge determines that she is not mature, that the performance of an abortion upon her would be in her best interests. A pregnant woman less than eighteen years of age may participate in proceedings in the superior court department of the trial court on her own behalf, and the court may appoint a guardian ad litem for her. The court shall, however, advise her that she has a right to court appointed counsel, and shall, upon her request, provide her with such counsel. Proceedings in the superior court department of the trial court under this section shall be confidential and shall be given such precedence over other pending matters that the court may reach a decision promptly and without delay so as to serve the best interests of the pregnant woman. A judge of the superior court department of the trial court who conducts proceedings under this section shall make in writing specific factual findings and legal conclusions supporting his decision and shall order a record of the evidence to be maintained including his own findings and conclusions.

South Dakota Codified Laws § 34–23A–10.1
(2013).

SEC. 10.1. *Voluntary and informed consent required; Medical emergency exception; Information provided*

No abortion may be performed unless the physician first obtains a voluntary and informed written consent of the pregnant woman upon whom the physician intends to perform the abortion, unless the physician determines that obtaining an informed consent is impossible due to a medical emergency and further determines that delaying in performing the procedure until an informed consent can be obtained from the pregnant woman or her next of kin in accordance with chapter 34–12C is impossible due to the medical emergency, which determinations shall then be documented in the medical records of the patient. A consent to an abortion is not voluntary and informed, unless, in addition to any other information that must be disclosed under the common law doctrine, the physician provides that pregnant woman with the following information:

(1)   A statement in writing providing the following information:

(a)   The name of the physician who will perform the abortion;

(b)   That the abortion will terminate the life of a whole, separate, unique, living human being;

(c)   That the pregnant woman has an existing relationship with that unborn human being and that the relationship enjoys protection under the United States Constitution and under the laws of South Dakota;

(d) That by having an abortion, her existing relationship and her existing constitutional rights with regards to that relationship will be terminated;

(e) A description of all known medical risks of the procedure and statistically significant risk factors to which the pregnant woman would be subjected, including:

(i) Depression and related psychological distress;

(ii) Increased risk of suicide ideation and suicide;

(iii) A statement setting forth an accurate rate of deaths due to abortions, including all deaths in which the abortion procedure was a substantial contributing factor;

(iv) All other known medical risks to the physical health of the woman, including the risk of infection, hemorrhage, danger to subsequent pregnancies, and infertility;

(f) The probable gestational age of the unborn child at the time the abortion is to be performed, and a scientifically accurate statement describing the development of the unborn child at that age; and

(g) The statistically significant medical risks associated with carrying her child to term compared to undergoing an induced abortion. The disclosures set forth above shall be provided to the pregnant woman in writing and in person no later than two hours before the procedure is to be performed. The physician shall ensure that the pregnant woman signs each page of the written disclosure with the certification that she has read and understands all of the disclosures, prior to the patient signing a consent for the procedure. If the pregnant woman asks for a clarification or explanation of any particular disclosure, or asks any other question about a matter of significance to her, the explanation or answer shall be made in writing and be given to the pregnant woman before signing a consent for the procedure and shall be made part of the permanent medical record of the patient;

(2) A statement by telephone or in person, by the physician who is to perform the abortion, or by the referring physician, or by an agent of both, at least twenty-four hours before the abortion, providing the following information:

(a) That medical assistance benefits may be available for prenatal care, childbirth, and neonatal care;

(b) That the father of the unborn child is legally responsible to provide financial support for her child following birth, and that this legal obligation of the father exists in all instances, even in instances in which the father has offered to pay for the abortion;

(c)   The name, address, and telephone number of a pregnancy help center in reasonable proximity of the abortion facility where the abortion will be performed; and

. . .

Prior to the pregnant woman signing a consent to the abortion, she shall sign a written statement that indicates that the requirements of this section have been complied with. Prior to the performance of the abortion, the physician who is to perform the abortion shall receive a copy of the written disclosure documents required by this section, and shall certify in writing that all of the information described in those subdivisions has been provided to the pregnant woman, that the physician is, to the best of his or her ability, satisfied that the pregnant woman has read the materials which are required to be disclosed, and that the physician believes she understands the information imparted.

South Dakota Codified Laws § 34–23A–56
(2013).

SEC. 56.   *Scheduling of abortion—Prior requirements.*

No surgical or medical abortion may be scheduled except by a licensed physician and only after the physician physically and personally meets with the pregnant mother, consults with her, and performs an assessment of her medical and personal circumstances. Only after the physician completes the consultation and assessment . . . inclusive, may the physician schedule a surgical or medical abortion, but in no instance may the physician schedule such surgical or medical abortion to take place in less than seventy-two hours from the completion of such consultation and assessment except in a medical emergency as set forth in § 34–23A–10.1 and subdivision 34–23A–1(5). No Saturday, Sunday, or annually recurring holiday . . . may be included or counted in the calculation of the seventy-two hour minimum time period between the initial physician consultation and assessment and the time of the scheduled abortion procedure. No physician may have the pregnant mother sign a consent for the abortion on the day of this initial consultation. No physician may take a signed consent from the pregnant mother unless the pregnant mother is in the physical presence of the physician and except on the day the abortion is scheduled. . . . During the initial consultation between the physician and the pregnant mother, prior to scheduling a surgical or medical abortion, the physician shall:

(1)   Do an assessment of the pregnant mother's circumstances to make a reasonable determination whether the pregnant mother's decision to submit to an abortion is the result of any coercion or pressure from other persons. In conducting that assessment, the physician shall obtain from the pregnant mother the age or approximate age of the father of the unborn child, and the physician

shall consider whether any disparity in age between the mother and father is a factor when determining whether the pregnant mother has been subjected to pressure, undue influence, or coercion;

(2) Provide the written disclosure required by subdivision 34–23A–10.1(1) and discuss them with her to determine that she understands them;

(3) Provide the pregnant mother with the names, addresses, and telephone numbers of all pregnancy help centers that are registered with the South Dakota Department of Health ... inclusive, and provide her with written instructions that set forth the following:

(a) That prior to the day of any scheduled abortion the pregnant mother must have a consultation at a pregnancy help center at which the pregnancy help center shall inform her about what education, counseling, and other assistance is available to help the pregnant mother keep and care for her child, and have a private interview to discuss her circumstances that may subject her decision to coercion;

(b) That prior to signing a consent to an abortion, the physician shall first obtain from the pregnant mother, a written statement that she obtained a consultation with a pregnancy help center, which sets forth the name and address of the pregnancy help center, the date and time of the consultation, and the name of the counselor at the pregnancy help center with whom she consulted;

(4) Conduct an assessment of the pregnant mother's health and circumstances to determine if any of the following preexisting risk factors associated with adverse psychological outcomes following an abortion are present in her case:

(a) Coercion;

(b) Pressure from others to have an abortion;

(c) The pregnant mother views an abortion to be in conflict with her personal or religious values;

(d) The pregnant mother is ambivalent about her decision to have an abortion, or finds the decision of whether to have an abortion difficult and she has a high degree of decisional distress;

(e) That the pregnant mother has a commitment to the pregnancy or prefers to carry the child to term;

(f) The pregnant mother has a medical history that includes a pre-abortion mental health or psychiatric problem; and

(g) The pregnant mother is twenty-two years old or younger.

The physician making the assessment shall record in the pregnant mother's medical records, on a form created for such purpose, each of the risk factors associated with adverse psychological outcomes following an abortion listed in this subdivision that are present in her case and which are not present in her case;

(5) The physician shall identify for the pregnant mother and explain each of the risk factors associated with adverse psychological outcomes following an abortion listed in subdivision (4) which are present in her case;

(6) The physician shall advise the pregnant mother of each risk factor associated with adverse psychological outcomes following an abortion . . . which the physician determines are present in her case and shall discuss with the pregnant mother, in such a manner and detail as is appropriate, so that the physician can certify that the physician has made a reasonable determination that the pregnant mother understands the information imparted, all material information about the risk of adverse psychological outcomes known to be associated with each of the risk factors found to be present;

(7) In the event that no risk factor is determined to be present, the physician shall include in the patient's records a statement that the physician has discussed the information required by the other parts of this section and that the physician has made a reasonable determination that the mother understands the information in question;

(8) Records of the assessments, forms, disclosures, and instructions performed and given pursuant to this section shall be prepared by the physician and maintained as a permanent part of the pregnant mother's medical records.

Tennessee Code § 39–15–202
(2013).

SEC. 2. *Informed consent; children and minors*

(a)(1) An abortion otherwise permitted by law shall be performed or induced only with the informed written consent of the pregnant woman, given freely and without coercion. Such consent shall be treated as confidential.

(2)(A) Any private physician's office, ambulatory surgical treatment center or other facility or clinic in which abortions, other than abortions necessary to prevent the death of the pregnant female, are performed shall conspicuously post a sign in a location defined in subdivision (a)(2)(C) so as to be clearly visible to patients, which reads:

Notice: It is against the law for anyone, regardless of the person's relationship to you, to coerce you into having or to force you to have an abortion. By law, we cannot perform an abortion on you unless we have your freely given and voluntary consent.

It is against the law to perform an abortion on you against your will. You have the right to contact any local or state law enforcement agency to receive protection from any actual or threatened criminal offense to coerce an abortion.

(B) The sign required pursuant to subdivision (a)(2)(A) shall be printed in languages appropriate for the majority of clients of the facility with lettering that is legible and that is Arial font, at least 40-point bold-faced type.

(C) A facility in which abortions are performed that is a private physician's office or an ambulatory surgical treatment center shall post the required sign in each patient waiting room and patient consultation room used by patients on whom abortions are performed. A hospital or any other facility in which abortions are performed that is not a private physician's office or ambulatory surgical treatment center shall post the required sign in the admissions or registration department used by patients on whom abortions are performed.

(3)(A) An ambulatory surgical treatment center or other licensed facility shall be assessed a civil penalty by the board for licensing health care facilities of two thousand five hundred dollars ($2,500) for each day of violation in which:

(i)   The sign required in subdivision (a)(2)(A) was not posted during business hours when patients or prospective patients are present; and

(ii) An abortion other than an abortion necessary to prevent the death of the pregnant female was performed in the ambulatory surgical treatment center or other licensed facility.

(B) A licensed physician shall be assessed a civil penalty by the physician's title 63 medical licensing board of one thousand dollars ($1,000) for each day of violation in which:

(i)   The sign required in subdivision (a)(2)(A) was not posted during business hours when patients or prospective patients are present at the private physician's office or clinic; and

(ii) The physician performed an abortion in the private physician's office.

(4) The penalty provided for in subdivision (a)(3) is in addition to any other remedies applicable under other law, and subdivision (a)(3) does not preclude prosecution and conviction under any applicable criminal law.

(b) In order to ensure that a consent for an abortion is truly informed consent, an abortion shall be performed or induced upon a pregnant woman only after she has been orally informed by her attending physician of the following facts and has signed a consent form acknowledging that she has been informed as follows:

(1) That according to the best judgment of her attending physician she is pregnant;

(2) The number of weeks elapsed from the probable time of the conception of her unborn child, based upon the information provided by her as to the time of her last menstrual period or after a history, physical examination, and appropriate laboratory tests;

(3) That if more than twenty-four (24) weeks have elapsed from the time of conception, her child may be viable, that is, capable of surviving outside of the womb, and that if the child is prematurely born alive in the course of an abortion her attending physician has a legal obligation to take steps to preserve the life and health of the child;

(4) That abortion in a considerable number of cases constitutes a major surgical procedure;

(5) That numerous public and private agencies and services are available to assist her during her pregnancy and after the birth of her child, if she chooses not to have the abortion, whether she wishes to keep her child or place the child for adoption, and that her physician will provide her with a list of the agencies and the services available if she so requests; or

(6) Numerous benefits and risks are attendant either to continued pregnancy and childbirth or to abortion depending upon the circumstances in which the patient might find herself. The physician shall explain these benefits and risks to the best of the physician's ability and knowledge of the circumstances involved.

(c) At the same time the attending physician provides the information required by subsection (b), the physician shall inform the pregnant woman of the particular risks associated with her pregnancy and childbirth and the abortion or child delivery technique to be employed, including providing her with at least a general description of the medical instructions to be followed subsequent to the abortion or childbirth in order to ensure her safe recovery.

(d)(1) There shall be a two-day waiting period after the physician provides the required information, excluding the day on which the information was given. On the third day following the day the information was given, the patient may return to the physician and sign a consent form.

(2) A violation of this subsection (d) by a physician is a Class E felony.

(3) This subsection (d) shall not apply when the attending physician, utilizing experience, judgment or professional competence, determines that a two-day waiting period or any waiting period would endanger the life of the pregnant woman. The determination made by the attending physician shall be in writing and shall state the physician's medical reasons upon which the physician bases the opinion that the

waiting period would endanger the life of the pregnant woman. This provision shall not relieve the attending physician of the duty to the pregnant woman to inform her of the facts under subsection (b).

(e) The attending physician performing or inducing the abortion shall provide the pregnant woman with a duplicate copy of the consent form signed by her.

(f) "The physician" or "the attending physician," as used in this section, means any licensed physician on the service treating the pregnant woman.

(g) The provisions of this section shall not apply in those situations where an abortion is certified by a licensed physician as necessary to preserve the life of the pregnant woman.

(h)(1) A physician may not perform an abortion unless the physician has admitting privileges at a hospital licensed under title 68 that is located:

(A) In the county in which the abortion is performed; or

(B) In a county adjacent to the county in which the abortion is performed.

(2) The physician who performs an abortion or a health care provider licensed pursuant to title 63 under the supervision of the physician shall notify the patient of the location of the hospital at which the physician has privileges and where the patient may receive follow-up care by the physician if complications arise.

Texas Health & Safety Code § 171.0031

(2013).

SEC. 031. *Requirements of Physician; Offense*

(a) A physician performing or inducing an abortion:

(1) must, on the date the abortion is performed or induced, have active admitting privileges at a hospital that:

(A) is located not further than 30 miles from the location at which the abortion is performed or induced; and

(B) provides obstetrical or gynecological health care services; and

(2) shall provide the pregnant woman with:

(A) a telephone number by which the pregnant woman may reach the physician, or other health care personnel employed by the physician or by the facility at which the abortion was performed or induced with access to the woman's relevant medical records, 24 hours a day to request assistance for any complications that arise from the performance or induction of the abortion or ask health-related questions regarding the abortion; and

(B) the name and telephone number of the nearest hospital to the home of the pregnant woman at which an emergency arising from the abortion would be treated.

(b) A physician who violates Subsection (a) commits an offense. An offense under this section is a Class A misdemeanor punishable by a fine only, not to exceed $4,000.

Texas Health & Safety Code § 171.012
(2013).

SEC. 012. *Voluntary and Informed Consent*

(a) Consent to an abortion is voluntary and informed only if:

(1) the physician who is to perform the abortion informs the pregnant woman on whom the abortion is to be performed of:

(A) the physician's name;

(B) the particular medical risks associated with the particular abortion procedure to be employed, including, when medically accurate:

(i) the risks of infection and hemorrhage;

(ii) the potential danger to a subsequent pregnancy and of infertility; and

(iii) the possibility of increased risk of breast cancer following an induced abortion and the natural protective effect of a completed pregnancy in avoiding breast cancer;

(C) the probable gestational age of the unborn child at the time the abortion is to be performed; and

(D) the medical risks associated with carrying the child to term;

(2) the physician who is to perform the abortion or the physician's agent informs the pregnant woman that:

(A) medical assistance benefits may be available for prenatal care, childbirth, and neonatal care;

(B) the father is liable for assistance in the support of the child without regard to whether the father has offered to pay for the abortion; and

(C) public and private agencies provide pregnancy prevention counseling and medical referrals for obtaining pregnancy prevention medications or devices, including emergency contraception for victims of rape or incest;

(3) the physician who is to perform the abortion or the physician's agent:

(A) provides the pregnant woman with the printed materials [required under Texas law] and

(B) informs the pregnant woman that those materials:

(i)   have been provided by the Department of State Health Services;

(ii) are accessible on an Internet website sponsored by the department;

(iii) describe the unborn child and list agencies that offer alternatives to abortion; and

(iv) include a list of agencies that offer sonogram services at no cost to the pregnant woman;

(4) before any sedative or anesthesia is administered to the pregnant woman and at least 24 hours before the abortion or at least two hours before the abortion if the pregnant woman waives this requirement by certifying that she currently lives 100 miles or more from the nearest abortion provider that is a facility licensed under Chapter 245 or a facility that performs more than 50 abortions in any 12-month period:

(A) the physician who is to perform the abortion or an agent of the physician who is also a sonographer certified by a national registry of medical sonographers performs a sonogram on the pregnant woman on whom the abortion is to be performed;

(B) the physician who is to perform the abortion displays the sonogram images in a quality consistent with current medical practice in a manner that the pregnant woman may view them;

(C) the physician who is to perform the abortion provides, in a manner understandable to a layperson, a verbal explanation of the results of the sonogram images, including a medical description of the dimensions of the embryo or fetus, the presence of cardiac activity, and the presence of external members and internal organs; and

(D) the physician who is to perform the abortion or an agent of the physician who is also a sonographer certified by a national registry of medical sonographers makes audible the heart auscultation for the pregnant woman to hear, if present, in a quality consistent with current medical practice and provides, in a manner understandable to a layperson, a simultaneous verbal explanation of the heart auscultation;

(5) before receiving a sonogram under Subdivision (4)(A) and before the abortion is performed and before any sedative or anesthesia is administered, the pregnant woman completes and certifies with her signature an election form that states as follows:

"ABORTION AND SONOGRAM ELECTION

(1) THE INFORMATION AND PRINTED MATERIALS DESCRIBED BY SECTIONS 171.012(a)(1)–(3), TEXAS HEALTH AND SAFETY CODE, HAVE BEEN PROVIDED AND EXPLAINED TO ME.

(2) I UNDERSTAND THE NATURE AND CONSEQUENCES OF AN ABORTION.

(3) TEXAS LAW REQUIRES THAT I RECEIVE A SONOGRAM PRIOR TO RECEIVING AN ABORTION.

(4) I UNDERSTAND THAT I HAVE THE OPTION TO VIEW THE SONOGRAM IMAGES.

(5) I UNDERSTAND THAT I HAVE THE OPTION TO HEAR THE HEARTBEAT.

(6) I UNDERSTAND THAT I AM REQUIRED BY LAW TO HEAR AN EXPLANATION OF THE SONOGRAM IMAGES UNLESS I CERTIFY IN WRITING TO ONE OF THE FOLLOWING:

_____ I AM PREGNANT AS A RESULT OF A SEXUAL ASSAULT, INCEST, OR OTHER VIOLATION OF THE TEXAS PENAL CODE THAT HAS BEEN REPORTED TO LAW ENFORCEMENT AUTHORITIES OR THAT HAS NOT BEEN REPORTED BECAUSE I REASONABLY BELIEVE THAT DOING SO WOULD PUT ME AT RISK OF RETALIATION RESULTING IN SERIOUS BODILY INJURY.

_____ I AM A MINOR AND OBTAINING AN ABORTION IN ACCORDANCE WITH JUDICIAL BYPASS PROCEDURES UNDER CHAPTER 33, TEXAS FAMILY CODE.

_____ MY FETUS HAS AN IRREVERSIBLE MEDICAL CONDITION OR ABNORMALITY, AS IDENTIFIED BY RELIABLE DIAGNOSTIC PROCEDURES AND DOCUMENTED IN MY MEDICAL FILE.

(7) I AM MAKING THIS ELECTION OF MY OWN FREE WILL AND WITHOUT COERCION.

(8) FOR A WOMAN WHO LIVES 100 MILES OR MORE FROM THE NEAREST ABORTION PROVIDER THAT IS A FACILITY LICENSED UNDER CHAPTER 245 OR A FACILITY THAT PERFORMS MORE THAN 50 ABORTIONS IN ANY 12-MONTH PERIOD ONLY:

I CERTIFY THAT, BECAUSE I CURRENTLY LIVE 100 MILES OR MORE FROM THE NEAREST ABORTION PROVIDER THAT IS A FACILITY LICENSED UNDER CHAPTER 245 OR A FACILITY THAT PERFORMS MORE THAN 50 ABORTIONS IN ANY 12-MONTH PERIOD, I WAIVE THE REQUIREMENT TO WAIT 24 HOURS AFTER THE SONOGRAM IS PERFORMED BEFORE

RECEIVING THE ABORTION PROCEDURE. MY PLACE OF RESIDENCE IS: _____ .

_____   _____

SIGNATURE   DATE"

(6) before the abortion is performed, the physician who is to perform the abortion receives a copy of the signed, written certification required by Subdivision (5); and

(7) the pregnant woman is provided the name of each person who provides or explains the information required under this subsection.

(a–1) During a visit made to a facility to fulfill the requirements of Subsection (a), the facility and any person at the facility may not accept any form of payment, deposit, or exchange or make any financial agreement for an abortion or abortion-related services other than for payment of a service required by Subsection (a). The amount charged for a service required by Subsection (a) may not exceed the reimbursement rate established for the service by the Health and Human Services Commission for statewide medical reimbursement programs.

(b) The information required to be provided under Subsections (a)(1) and (2) may not be provided by audio or video recording and must be provided at least 24 hours before the abortion is to be performed:

(1) orally and in person in a private and confidential setting if the pregnant woman currently lives less than 100 miles from the nearest abortion provider that is a facility licensed under Chapter 245 or a facility that performs more than 50 abortions in any 12-month period; or

(2) orally by telephone or in person in a private and confidential setting if the pregnant woman certifies that the woman currently lives 100 miles or more from the nearest abortion provider that is a facility licensed under Chapter 245 or a facility that performs more than 50 abortions in any 12-month period.

(c) When providing the information under Subsection (a)(3), the physician or the physician's agent must provide the pregnant woman with the address of the Internet website on which the printed materials described by Section 171.014 may be viewed as required by Section 171.014(e).

(d) The information provided to the woman under Subsection (a)(2)(B) must include, based on information available from the Office of the Attorney General and the United States Department of Health and Human Services Office of Child Support Enforcement for the three-year period preceding the publication of the information, information regarding the statistical likelihood of collecting child support.

(e) The department is not required to republish informational materials described by Subsection (a)(2)(B) because of a change in information described by Subsection (d) unless the statistical information in the materials changes by five percent or more.

NOTES

1. *Abortion regulation via TRAP laws.* Many state laws enacted to restrict abortion access do not explicitly restrict abortion services themselves, but instead take the form of regulations on facilities and doctors that perform abortions. These laws, often known as TRAP ("Targeted Regulation of Abortion Providers") laws, range from regulations requiring certain building structures for facilities in which abortions are performed, to onerous recordkeeping and reporting requirements, to requiring doctors who perform abortions to have admitting privileges at local hospitals. Critically, these regulations are generally not imposed on other ambulatory surgery centers. Do these regulations serve to distinguish the provision of abortion care from the provision of other medical care? If so, how does this distinction affect the accessibility of abortion? Do these laws create an "undue burden" on the right to abortion?

2. *A paucity of providers.* Beyond mounting legal restrictions, one of the biggest challenges faced by patients needing abortions is a dearth of providers. Eighty-nine percent of all counties in the U.S., and ninety-seven percent of rural counties, do not have a single abortion provider. Between 1982 and 2005, the number of abortion providers declined by thirty-eight percent to its lowest point. In recent years, however, this steady slide has leveled off. Rachel K. Jones & Kathryn Kooistra, *Abortion Incidence and Access to Services in the United States, 2008*, 43 PERSP. ON SEXUAL & REPROD. HEALTH 41, 46, 49 (2011). This development is due in large part to the efforts of Medical Students for Choice, a group that has organized and advocated for medical school curriculum reform, as well as increased opportunities for clinical exposure to, and training in, abortion care. Even with the organization's successes, which include successfully lobbying the Accrediting Council for Graduate Medical Education to require abortion's inclusion in OB-GYN residency training, only fourteen percent of OB-GYNs provided abortion care in 2011. Critically, ninety-seven percent of OB-GYNs encountered patients seeking abortions. Debra B. Stulberg et al., *Abortion Provision Among Practicing Obstetrician-Gynecologists*, 118 OBSTETRICS & GYNECOLOGY 609, 612 (2011).

3. *Abortion and the administrative state.* The regulation of abortion services is no longer limited to statutory law. Increasingly, abortion regulation occurs via administrative codes, shifting the debate over abortion access to the administrative state. Critically, court review of these regulations is guided not only by the extant abortion jurisprudence, but also administrative law principles. For example, courts reviewing administrative regulations concerning abortion will often defer to the expertise of administrative agencies, upholding the challenged regulation. Abortion regulation's migration to the administrative state has also meant that the regulations, which are often promulgated by state agencies, will be reviewed by state courts, rather than federal courts. For a further discussion of the interaction between administrative law and abortion jurisprudence, see

Gillian E. Metzger, *Abortion, Equality, and Administrative Regulation*, 56 EMORY L. J. 865 (2007).

4. *Aggregate burden.* Individually, many abortion regulations appear straightforward and unobjectionable. However, when these regulations are considered in the aggregate, they may have the effect of imposing substantial obstacles to the provision of abortion. Increased regulation, including laws prescribing hospital admitting privileges, facilities licensing requirements—and even the size of hallways and closets in health care facilities—may limit the number of providers available to perform abortions, while also increasing the costs—financial and personal—of seeking an abortion or serving as an abortion provider. In this way, the cumulative effect of such regulations may be to foreclose abortion access entirely. And the foreclosure of access has burdensome consequences. An ongoing study by the University of California San Francisco's medical school has been examining the lives of almost a thousand women seeking abortion. In research covering thirty abortion facilities, Advancing New Standards in Reproductive Health (ANSIRH) interviewed 231 women who were just over the gestational limit for an abortion, and compared them to 452 women who sought abortions just under gestational limits. (273 women having first-trimester abortions were included as a third comparison group.) Interviewed every six months for five years, the women denied abortion had either found abortions elsewhere (about twenty percent), given their child up for adoption (nine percent), or their child. While many of the women came to bond with their children, preliminary results suggest that women unable to obtain abortions suffered significant economic and health consequences. *See* Joshua Lang, *Unintentional Motherhood*, N.Y. TIMES, June 12, 2013, at MM42; *Turnaway Study*, ADVANCING NEW STANDARDS IN REPROD. HEALTH (2014), http://www.ansirh.org/research/turnaway.php.

5. *The difficulty of accessing abortion in the age of TRAP laws.* On July 13, 2013, the Texas legislature passed a law requiring, among other things, that a physician performing or inducing an abortion have admitting privileges on the date of the abortion at a hospital no more than thirty miles from the location where the abortion is provided. *See* TEX. HEALTH & SAFETY CODE § 171.0031(a)(1) (2013). Arguing that the law would drastically reduce the number of abortion providers in Texas, and especially the Rio Grande Valley, an expansive area with only two clinics that provided abortion services, Planned Parenthood of Greater Texas filed suit to declare the law unconstitutional, and to enjoin its implementation and enforcement. In March 2014, the Fifth Circuit rejected these claims, upholding the law and paving the way for its implementation. *See Planned Parenthood of Greater Texas v. Abbott*, 748 F.3d 583 (5th Cir. 2014). Chief Judge Edith Jones found the claim that the admitting privileges requirement would further diminish the availability of abortion services in the Rio Grande Valley, forcing women to travel great distances to obtain abortion services, especially unconvincing. As she observed, "travel between [the Rio Grande Valley] and Corpus Christi, where abortion services are still provided, takes less than three hours on Texas highways (distances up to 150 miles maximum and most far less)." *Id.* at 597. What kinds of assumptions is Chief Judge Jones making

about these women and their circumstances? Do you agree that the burden imposed by the Texas law was minimal?

* * *

The following case from the United States Court of Appeals for the Ninth Circuit makes clear the degree to which the cumulative effects of abortion restrictions may result in burdens for women, and particularly for poor and rural women, seeking abortion services.

McCormack v. Hiedeman

694 F.3d 1004 (9th Cir. 2012).

■ PREGERSON, CIRCUIT JUDGE.

On May 18, 2011, Mark Hiedeman, the Bannock County, Idaho prosecuting attorney, filed a felony criminal complaint . . . against Jennie Linn McCormack. The complaint charged McCormack with "the public offense of Unlawful Abortion, Idaho Code § 18–606," which makes it a felony for any woman to undergo an abortion in a manner not authorized by statute. As a result, McCormack faced the possibility of up to five years imprisonment. . . .

On September 24, 2011, McCormack filed in the U.S. District Court for the District of Idaho a class action lawsuit . . . charg[ing], among other things, that Idaho Code § 18–606 violates various provisions of the United States Constitution. The district court issued a preliminary injunction, restraining Hiedeman from enforcing Idaho Code §§ 18–606 and 18–608(1). Hiedeman appeals. . . . Additionally, McCormack argues that she has standing to challenge the enforcement of Chapter 5, the Pain-Capable Unborn Child Protection Act (including Idaho Code §§ 18–505—18–507).

For the reasons set forth below, we affirm in part and reverse in part the district court's grant of a preliminary injunction.

. . . .

In the fall of 2010, McCormack was pregnant and sought an abortion. She knew that abortions were not available in southeast Idaho. In fact, there are no licensed health care providers offering abortion services in the eight southeastern Idaho counties. McCormack knew that abortions are available in Salt Lake City, Utah, but at costs between $400–$2,000 depending on how far along the pregnancy is.

But McCormack found out that abortions could be performed in Idaho using medications, rather than surgery and that the cost of such medical abortions was significantly less than the cost of a surgical abortion like those offered in Salt Lake City, Utah. She further learned that medications inducing abortions had been approved for use in the U.S. and could be purchased over the internet.

In McCormack's complaint, she states that she "considered terminating her pregnancy . . . by ingesting one or more medications she reasonably believed to have been prescribed by a health care provider practicing outside Bannock County, Idaho." . . .

On May 18, 2011, Hiedeman, in his capacity as Bannock County prosecuting attorney, filed a criminal complaint . . . charging McCormack with the felony of "the public offense of Unlawful Abortion, Idaho Code § 18–606." The criminal complaint alleged:

> That the said Jennie Lynn McCormack, in the County of Bannock, State of Idaho, on the 24th day of December, 2010, did induce or knowingly aid in the production or performance of an abortion by knowingly submitting to an abortion and/or soliciting of another, for herself, the production of an abortion; and/or who purposely terminated her own pregnancy other than by live birth.

A magistrate judge dismissed the criminal complaint without prejudice on September 7, 2011. Hiedeman has not determined whether to re-file the criminal complaint.

McCormack does not want to have additional children. If she became pregnant, she would seek an abortion again. Because there are no providers of medical abortions in southeast Idaho, McCormack would need to seek the assistance of providers of abortion services outside of southeast Idaho.

This case requires the interpretation of three Idaho abortion statutes: Idaho Code § 18–606, Idaho Code § 18–608, and Idaho Code § 18–505. We summarize the substance of each statute.

Idaho Code § 18–606(2) makes it a felony, except as permitted by the remainder of Title 8, Chapter 6 of the Idaho Code, for "[e]very woman who knowingly submits to an abortion or solicits of another, for herself, the production of an abortion, or who purposely terminates her own pregnancy otherwise than by a live birth. . . ." Anyone deemed guilty of violating § 18–606 "shall be fined not to exceed five thousand dollars ($5,000) and/or imprisoned in the state prison for not less than one (1) and not more than five (5) years."

Idaho Code § 18–608, entitled "Certain abortions permitted— Conditions and guidelines" provides the statutory content for the limitation on the applicability of Idaho Code § 18–606.

Under § 18–608(1), a woman may terminate her pregnancy during the first trimester if the abortion is performed by a physician:

> in a hospital or in a physician's regular office or a clinic which office or clinic is properly staffed and equipped for the performance of such procedures and respecting which the responsible physician or physicians have made satisfactory arrangements with one or more acute care hospitals within

reasonable proximity thereof providing for the prompt availability of hospital care as may be required due to complications or emergencies that might arise.

Under § 18–608(2), a woman may terminate her pregnancy during the second trimester of pregnancy, but the abortion must be "performed in a hospital and [must be], in the judgment of the attending physician, in the best medical interest of such pregnant woman."

Idaho Code § 18–505, or the Pain-Capable Unborn Child Protection Act ("PUCPA"), categorically bans non-therapeutic abortions at and after twenty weeks. "Any person who intentionally or recklessly performs or attempts to perform an abortion in violation of the provisions of section 18–505, Idaho Code, is guilty of a felony." The Act further states "No penalty shall be assessed against the woman upon whom the abortion is performed or attempted to be performed." *Id.*

The Act also provides civil remedies in the form of actual damages to "[a]ny woman upon whom an abortion has been performed in violation of the pain-capable unborn child protection act or the father of the unborn child. . . ." Idaho Code § 18–508(1). The Act also permits certain persons, including a prosecuting attorney, to file an action for injunctive relief against an abortion provider who violates § 18–505.

. . . .

We review the district court's grant of a preliminary injunction for abuse of discretion. A district court abuses its discretion if it bases its decision on an erroneous legal standard or clearly erroneous findings of fact. Application of an incorrect legal standard for preliminary relief or with regard to the underlying issues in the case are grounds for reversal. *See Earth Island Inst. v. U.S. Forest Serv.*, 351 F.3d 1291, 1298 (9th Cir. 2003); *Sports Form, Inc. v. United Press Int'l, Inc.*, 686 F.2d 750, 752 (9th Cir. 1982). The district court's interpretation of underlying legal principles is subject to *de novo* review. *Sw. Voter Reg. Educ. Project v. Shelley*, 344 F.3d 914, 918 (9th Cir. 2003).

. . . "A plaintiff seeking a preliminary injunction must establish that [s]he is likely to succeed on the merits, that [s]he is likely to suffer irreparable harm in the absence of preliminary relief, that the balance of equities tips in [her] favor, and that an injunction is in the public interest." *Winter v. Natural Resources Defense Council, Inc.*, 555 U.S. 7, 20 (2008).

This case turns on the first factor—whether McCormack established that she was likely to succeed on the merits. Hiedeman contends that the U.S. District Court's conclusion concerning the probability of success is based on incorrect legal analysis and unsupported factual determinations. Hiedeman is wrong on both counts.

. . . The district court rested its decision to grant the preliminary injunction on the "undue burden test" set out in *Planned Parenthood v. Casey*, 505 U.S. 833 (1992). Prosecuting attorney Hiedeman does not argue that the U.S. District Court's use of *Casey* is an erroneous legal standard. Instead, Hiedeman argues that "[t]he rationale for [abortion] statutes—the woman's health and safety—applies with no less force where the woman rather than another person performs the abortion." Thus, he argues that the U.S. District Court erred in determining that McCormack was likely to succeed on the merits. We disagree.

. . . Historically, laws regulating abortion have sought to further the state's interest in protecting the health and welfare of pregnant women, who alone bear the burden and risks of pregnancies. With this interest in mind, abortion statutes were first enacted to protect pregnant females from third parties providing dangerous abortions. . . .

As a result, abortion statutes have traditionally criminalized the behavior of third parties to protect the health of pregnant women. . . .

Most modern state criminal statutes continue to apply criminal liability to third parties who perform abortion in a manner not proscribed by the statute. These statutes, known as physician-only statutes, impose criminal liability on anyone other than a licensed physician from performing abortions. But many of these same criminal statutes expressly exempt women from criminal liability for obtaining an abortion and do not hold them liable for actions or inactions that affect their pregnancy outcomes.[3] When state statutes do not expressly exempt pregnant women, state courts interpreting them have concluded that pregnant women are exempt from criminal prosecution.

. . . Consistent with this history, there is no Supreme Court precedent that recognizes or suggests that third party criminal liability may extend to pregnant women who obtain an abortion in a manner inconsistent with state abortion statutes. Nevertheless, prosecuting attorney Hiedeman asserts that under current precedent physician-only

---

[3]   *See, e.g.,* Alaska Stat. § 11.41.289 (liability for "assault of an unborn child" does not apply to actions "committed by a pregnant woman against herself and her own unborn child"); Ark. Code Ann. §§ 5–61–101(c), 5–61–102(c) ("Nothing in this section shall be construed to allow the charging or conviction of a woman with any criminal offense in the death of her own unborn child in utero"); Fla. Stat. § 782.36("A patient receiving a partial-birth-abortion procedure may not be prosecuted under this act."); 720 Ill. Comp. Stat. 5/9–1.2(b)(criminal liability for intentional homicide of an unborn child does not apply to "the pregnant woman whose unborn child is killed"); Kan. Stat. Ann. § 65–6703(e) ("A woman upon whom an abortion is performed shall not be prosecuted under this section. . . ."); Ky. Rev. Stat. Ann. § 507A.010(3) ("nothing in this chapter shall apply to any acts of a pregnant woman that caused the death of her unborn child"); La.Rev. Stat. Ann. § 14:87(A)(2) (penalties for criminalized abortions not applicable to pregnant women having abortions); Minn. Stat. § 609.266 (excluding the "pregnant woman" from liability for "crimes against unborn children"); Neb. Rev. Stat. § 28–335 (providing "[n]o civil or criminal penalty . . . against the patient upon whom the abortion is performed"); Ohio Rev. Code Ann. § 2919.17(I)(expressly excluding women from liability for post-viability abortions); 18 Pa. Cons. Stat. Ann. § 2608 (exempting pregnant women from liability "in regards to crimes against her unborn child"); Tex. Penal Code Ann. § 19.06(1) (exempting the woman from liability for "death of an unborn child"); Utah Code Ann. § 76–7–314.5(2) ("A woman is not criminally liable for (a) seeking to obtain, or obtaining, an abortion that is permitted by this part; or (b) a physician's failure to comply [with specified statutes.]"); Vt. Stat. Ann. tit. 13 § 101 ("However, the woman whose miscarriage is caused or attempted shall not be liable to the penalties prescribed by this section."); Wis. Stat. Ann. § 940.13 (providing no fine or imprisonment for a woman who obtains an abortion or violates any provision of an abortion statute).

provisions in abortion statutes can be applied with equal force to pregnant women who fail to comply with state abortion statutes. He argues that "[a] State . . . has an interest in strict adherence to physician-only requirements and need not, as a constitutional matter, carve out an enforcement exception for women who take it upon themselves to self-abort."

. . . .

. . . Hiedeman asserts that under *Roe*, a state may constitutionally prohibit anyone other than a licensed physician from performing an abortion . . . Hiedeman cites the following passage from *Roe* to support his argument that McCormack can be held criminally liable for failing to comply with Idaho's abortion statutes:

> The State has a legitimate interest in seeing to it that abortion, like any other medical procedure, is performed *under circumstances that insure maximum safety for the patient.* This interest obviously extends at least to the performing physician and his staff, to the facilities involved, to the availability of aftercare, and to adequate provision for any complication or emergency that might arise.

Id. at 150 (emphasis added). Further, Hiedeman notes that *Roe* held that "[t]he State may define the term 'physician' . . . to mean only a physician currently licensed by the State, and may proscribe any abortion by a person who is not a physician as so defined." *Id.* at 165. Hiedeman further argues that *Casey* did not disturb this long-standing Supreme Court precedent.

Hiedeman's attempt to equate these Supreme Court principles with the Idaho statute at issue in this case is unpersuasive. These principles, embraced by the Supreme Court, recognize that women's health is an important interest for the state and one that is considered in crafting abortion statutes. These principles, however, in no way recognize, permit, or stand for the proposition that a state may prosecute a pregnant woman who seeks an abortion in a manner that may not be authorized by the state's statute, including when a pregnant woman receives physician-prescribed medication to terminate her pregnancy. Hiedeman's reading of *Roe* and *Casey* expands these Supreme Court holdings to reach an unintended result.

Hiedeman's reliance on *Connecticut v. Menillo* is equally unpersuasive. In *Menillo*, the Supreme Court reinstated the conviction of Patrick Menillo for attempting to procure an abortion. *Menillo*, 423 U.S. 9 (1975). "Menillo, a nonphysician with no medical training, performed an abortion upon a female in normal good health for a $400 fee." *State v. Menillo*, 171 Conn. 141 (1976). A jury found Menillo guilty under a Connecticut statute, which prescribes that "any person who gives or administers to any woman, or advises or causes her to take or use anything . . . with the intent to procure upon her a miscarriage or abortion, unless the same is necessary to preserve her life or that of her unborn child, shall be fined . . . or imprisoned." *Menillo*, 423 U.S. at 10 n. 1. The Connecticut Supreme Court overturned Menillo's conviction, holding that the statute was "null and void" under federal law. The U.S. Supreme Court vacated and reinstated Menillo's conviction. *Id.* The U.S. Supreme Court stated that *Roe* supported the "continued enforceability of criminal abortion statutes against nonphysicians." . . .

Like *Roe*, *Menillo* also does not discuss the issue presented here: whether the state can impose criminal liability on pregnant women for failing to abide by the state's abortion statutes. . . . The statute at issue in *Menillo* was directed only against the person who commits or attempts to commit the act on the pregnant woman (i.e., it criminalized the actions of a third party—a nonphysician). Thus, *Menillo* stands for the unremarkable proposition that states may prosecute unlicensed providers of unsafe, "back-alley" abortions.

. . . Hiedeman also erroneously relies on the more recent case of *Mazurek v. Armstrong*, 520 U.S. 968 (1997) (per curiam). The Montana statute at issue in *Mazurek* was aimed at stopping a physician assistant, who had legally provided abortion services under the supervision of a physician, from continuing to provide that care. . . . The question before the Supreme Court in *Mazurek* was whether a state could bar *medical professionals* other than physicians from providing abortion services. *Mazurek* did not involve an attempt to prosecute a woman for seeking a pre-viability abortion. Consequently, like Hiedeman's reliance on *Menillo*, Hiedeman's reliance on *Mazurek* is unavailing.

. . . Idaho Code § 18–606(2), which criminalizes the conduct of pregnant women—as opposed to the conduct of a third-party performing the abortion—is, as described above, different from any matter the U.S. Supreme Court or this court has considered since *Roe* was handed down. For the reasons explained below, it is likely that McCormack will succeed on the merits because § 18–606(2) imposes an undue burden on a woman's ability to terminate her pregnancy.

. . . .

Under *Casey*, the challenged Idaho abortion statute, § 18–606, constitutes a substantial obstacle in the path of women seeking an abortion of a nonviable fetus. Under Idaho Code § 18–606, "[e]very woman who knowingly submits to an abortion or solicits of another, for herself, the production of an abortion, or who purposely terminates her own pregnancy otherwise than by a live birth" is subject to felony charges, unless the abortion was performed as permitted by the remainder of Title 8, Chapter 6 of the Idaho Code. A pregnant woman who violates this statute is subject to the possibility of up to five years imprisonment. The remainder of Chapter 6 details the manner in which a woman in Idaho may obtain a lawful abortion.

Chapter 6 puts an undue burden on women seeking abortions by requiring them to police their provider's compliance with Idaho's regulations. If a woman terminates her pregnancy during the first trimester but fails to ask the physician whether the office has made "satisfactory arrangements with one or more acute care hospitals within reasonable proximity thereof providing for the prompt availability of hospital care as may be required due to complications or emergencies that might arise," she would be subject to a felony charge if the physician has not made such arrangements. If a woman finds a doctor who provides abortions during the second trimester of a woman's pregnancy, but the doctor fails to tell the pregnant woman that the abortion will be performed in a clinic as opposed to a hospital, the pregnant woman would be subject to felony charges. Or, as is the case here, if a woman elects to take physician prescribed pills obtained over the internet to end her pregnancy, which is not authorized by statute, she is subject to felony charges.

There can be no doubt that requiring women to explore the intricacies of state abortion statutes to ensure that they and their provider act within the Idaho abortion statute framework, results in an "undue burden" on a woman seeking an abortion of a nonviable fetus. Under this Idaho statute, a pregnant woman in McCormack's position has three options: (1) carefully read the Idaho abortion statutes to ensure that she and her provider are in compliance with the Idaho laws to avoid felony prosecution; (2) violate the law either knowingly or unknowingly in an attempt to obtain an abortion; or (3) refrain altogether from exercising her right to choose an abortion.

This Idaho statute heaps yet another substantial obstacle in the already overburdened path that McCormack and pregnant women like her face when deciding whether to obtain an abortion. For many women, the decision whether to have an abortion is a difficult one involving the consideration of weighty ethical, moral, financial, and other considerations. . . .

Further, McCormack and other women in her position, have to grapple with the cost of the abortion itself as well as the long-term financial implications of not having one. Because they do not have the financial wherewithal to confirm suspected pregnancies, low-income women are often forced to wait until later in their pregnancies to obtain an abortion. Delayed confirmation compounds the financial difficulties, as the cost of abortion services increases throughout the gestational period.

Many women, like McCormack, must travel long distances to the closest abortion provider. This requires a pregnant woman take time to miss work, find childcare, make arrangements for travel to and from the hospital and/or clinic, and to possibly make arrangements to stay overnight to satisfy the 24-hour requirement. In fact, this has been shown to be a significant factor when a woman delays an abortion, and low-income women are more likely to have this problem. Once at the clinic, pregnant women may have to further manage "the harassment and hostility of antiabortion protestors demonstrating outside a clinic."

While the Supreme Court has permitted many restrictions that make obtaining an abortion more difficult, particularly for low-income women, it has not authorized the criminal prosecution of women seeking abortion care. Imposing criminal liability upon women for their providers' purported failure to comply with state abortion regulations places a substantial obstacle in the path of women seeking an abortion. Accordingly, McCormack is likely to succeed on her claim that Chapter 6 constitutes an undue burden on a woman's constitutional right to terminate her pregnancy before viability.

. . . .

The district court's findings of fact, namely that McCormack received from a physician FDA-approved medication used to induce an abortion, were not clearly erroneous . . . McCormack stated in her declaration that the medication was "approved for use in the United States" and that these medications "are currently offered for sale over the internet by abortion providers outside southeast Idaho." In her complaint, McCormack stated that "physicians providing abortion services in the United States often prescribe medications approved by the U.S. Federal Drug Agency ("FDA") to cause women to abort their pregnancies medically, i.e., non-surgically." She also stated in her complaint that she considered "ingesting one or more medications she reasonably believed to have been prescribed by a health care provider practicing outside Bannock County, Idaho to induce [her] abortion." There is no disputing that an affidavit and a complaint may be the basis for a preliminary injunction unless the facts are substantially controverted by counter-affidavits. . . . Hiedeman did not offer any controverted affidavits as to whether the pills were obtained from a physician over the internet or whether they were FDA-approved. Additionally, the district court merely commented that oral argument provided clarity to the extent that the complaint and affidavit had to be carefully worded because of the potential for McCormack's prosecution.

These factual findings cannot be said to be "clearly erroneous" such that the court is left with a definite and firm conviction that the district court committed a clear error of judgment. . . .

The scope of a preliminary injunction is generally reviewed for abuse of discretion. *SEC v. Interlink Data Network of Los Angeles, Inc.*, 77 F.3d 1201, 1204 (9th Cir. 1996).

The district court's preliminary injunction states that prosecuting attorney Hiedeman "is restrained from enforcing Idaho Code §§ 18–606 and 18–608(1)." Hiedeman argues that the district court's preliminary injunction is overbroad to the extent that it grants relief beyond McCormack herself. For the reasons set forth below, we conclude that the preliminary injunction is overbroad and should be limited to enforcement of the applicable code sections against McCormack only.

. . . .

At least one Supreme Court decision suggests that federal courts should only enjoin enforcement of criminal statutes against the plaintiffs before the court. In *Doran v. Salem Inn, Inc.*, the Court said "neither declaratory nor injunctive relief can directly interfere with enforcement of contested statutes or ordinances except with respect to the particular federal plaintiffs, and the State is free to prosecute others who may violate the statute." . . .

There is no need for the preliminary injunction in this case to bar enforcement of § 18–606 against anyone except McCormack in order to preserve the status quo between the parties. The fact that McCormack may ultimately be entitled to a declaratory judgment stating that § 18–606 is unconstitutional on its face (which would clearly bar prosecution of any pregnant woman under the statute) does not mean that the *preliminary* injunction should apply so broadly, at least in the absence of class certification.

Accordingly, we conclude that the district court's preliminary injunction should be narrowed so that it enjoins only future prosecution of McCormack.

In her cross-appeal, McCormack makes two arguments: (1) that the district court should have enjoined enforcement of Idaho Code § 18–606 in conjunction with both §§ 18–608(1) *and 18–608(2)*; and (2) that she has standing to challenge the enforcement of Chapter 5, the Pain-Capable Unborn Child Protection Act ("PUCPA").

. . . In granting McCormack's motion for a preliminary injunction, the district court limited the injunction to § 18–608(1), which is the code section governing abortions during the first trimester of pregnancy. The district court refused to extend the preliminary injunction to cover § 18–608(2), which is the code section governing abortions during the second trimester of pregnancy. . . . The district court found that "[b]ased on the facts alleged, there can be no argument that [McCormack] violated either § 18–608(2) or § 18–608(3)." Thus, the court found that McCormack "does not face any threat of prosecution under these subsections." Accordingly, the court found that there was not a case or controversy as to § 18–608(2) or § 18–608(3).

McCormack alleges that the district court erred because the basis for the district court's injunction against enforcement of Idaho Code § 18–608(1) applies with equal force to § 18608(2). . . . [W]e agree with McCormack that the district court erred in failing to extend the preliminary injunction to § 18–608(2) because McCormack faces a genuine threat of prosecution under this subsection of the statute.

. . . McCormack faced prosecution and continues to be threatened with prosecution as a result of her alleged violation of Idaho Code § 18–

606, in conjunction with either § 18–608(1) or § 18–608(2). First, McCormack has allegedly already violated Idaho Code § 18–606, which makes it a felony to obtain an abortion in a manner not authorized by the Idaho abortion statutes. There is no question that prosecuting attorney Hiedeman filed felony charges against McCormack for allegedly violating Idaho Code § 18–606. But, the criminal complaint fails to specify whether in conjunction with § 18–606 Hiedeman brought charges under § 18–608(1), regulating abortions during the first trimester, or § 18–608(2), regulating abortions during the second trimester. Further, there is nothing in the criminal complaint that states the gestational age of the fetus or the trimester that McCormack was in when the alleged abortion occurred. It is also undisputed that the state court dismissed these charges without prejudice and Hiedeman has not decided whether to re-file the charges against McCormack. Thus, McCormack is susceptible to Hiedeman recommencing the criminal charges against McCormack under § 18–606 in conjunction with either § 18–608(1) *or § 18–608(2)*. Second, Hiedeman, in his capacity as county prosecutor, has communicated a specific threat on two occasions to bring felony charges against McCormack, when he: (1) actually brought a criminal complaint against McCormack, and (2) filed a declaration stating that he may still re-file the complaint. Finally, this history of past prosecution, in the form of an actual criminal complaint being filed against McCormack under Idaho Code § 18–606, weighs in favor of a preliminary injunction for McCormack with regard to § 18–606 in conjunction with both § 18–608(1) and § 18–608(2).

Thus the possibility exists that Hiedeman was going to (and may still) bring criminal charges against McCormack based on her alleged violation of either § 18–608(1) *or* § 18–608(2). Accordingly, we conclude that the district court erred in failing to extend the preliminary injunction to § 18–608(2) in conjunction with § 18–606.

. . . .

In her cross-appeal, McCormack also argues that she has standing to challenge the enforcement of Chapter 5, the "PUCPA." PUCPA categorically bans non-therapeutic abortions at and after twenty weeks. "Any person who intentionally or recklessly performs or attempts to perform an abortion in violation of the provisions of section 18–505, Idaho Code, is guilty of a felony." Idaho Code § 18–507. PUCPA further states: "No penalty shall be assessed against the woman upon whom the abortion is performed or attempted to be performed." *Id.* PUCPA also provides civil remedies in the form of actual damages to "[a]ny woman upon whom an abortion has been performed in violation of the [PUCPA] or the father of the unborn child." Idaho Code § 18–508(1). PUCPA further permits certain persons, including a prosecuting attorney, to file an action for injunctive relief against an abortion provider who violates § 18–505 by performing an abortion at or after twenty weeks. Idaho Code § 18–508(2).

. . . .

The district court determined that McCormack lacked standing to challenge enforcement of PUCPA and, for that reason, refused to issue a preliminary injunction enjoining Hiedeman from criminally prosecuting or bringing any civil action for injunctive relief against abortion providers. The district court concluded that McCormack does not allege that she was pregnant when she filed this action nor does she allege that her past conduct in purchasing medication to induce an abortion would fall within the proscription of PUCPA. Further, the court found that her testimony that she would seek an abortion if she became pregnant did not suffice to give her standing.

. . . Although McCormack was prosecuted for submitting to a pre-viability abortion, PUCPA was not even enacted at the time the criminal complaint was filed.

McCormack argues, however, that she remains threatened with prosecution under PUCPA based on the prior Chapter 6 criminal case being dismissed without prejudice and Hiedeman's declaration that he may re-commence a prosecution. . . .

She asserts that to determine issues of standing, the court must look to the facts as they existed at the time the complaint was filed. Here, when McCormack filed her civil complaint on September 16, 2011, PUCPA was enacted. Thus, she asserts that the court can consider the effect that PUCPA has on McCormack's *prospective* chance of being criminally charged.

McCormack cannot satisfy [the] three-part test . . . for determining whether a plaintiff faces a "genuine threat of prosecution" under PUCPA. First, McCormack does not have a "concrete plan" to violate PUCPA. PUCPA explicitly excludes women from criminal liability. Idaho Code § 18–507 ("No penalty shall be assessed against the woman upon whom the abortion is performed or attempted to be performed."). Therefore, there is no "concrete" way for McCormack to violate the law as an individual pregnant woman because PUCPA specifically excludes women from criminal liability. Second, the "prosecuting authorities have [not] communicated a specific warning or threat to initiate proceedings" under PUCPA. Hiedeman's declaration specifically states: "My office has not determined as of this date whether new or additional evidence is or may become available to warrant recommencing a prosecution under § 18–606." Thus, the only threat of future prosecution is under Chapter 6, not Chapter 5 (PUCPA). Finally, the third . . . factor does not tilt in her favor because there is no history of past prosecution or enforcement under PUCPA. McCormack was prosecuted under Chapter 6, not Chapter 5 (PUCPA).

In short, McCormack does not face a genuine threat of prosecution under PUCPA sufficient to confer standing to challenge the statute.

. . . .

McCormack's testimony that she would seek an abortion if she became pregnant does not suffice to give her standing. It is undisputed that McCormack was not pregnant when she filed this lawsuit. As a result, she does not have standing under any theory articulated in *Roe*.

In contrast with Jane Roe and akin to McCormack's position, the *Roe* Court found that John and Mary Doe, a married couple who filed a companion complaint along with Roe's, did not have standing. *Roe*, 410 U.S. at 127–129. The Does alleged that they were childless, that Mrs. Doe was not pregnant, and that they had been advised that Mrs. Doe should avoid pregnancy for medical and "other highly personal reasons." *Id.* at 127. They alleged that if Mrs. Doe became pregnant, they would want to terminate the pregnancy by abortion. *Id.* at 128. They also alleged that they were injured because they were forced to choose between abstaining from normal sexual relations or putting Mrs. Doe's health at risk through a possible pregnancy. The Court said, "[t]heir claim is that sometime in the future Mrs. Doe might become pregnant because of possible failure of contraceptive measures, and at that time in the future she might want an abortion that might then be illegal under the Texas statutes." The Court concluded that the Does did not have standing:

> Their alleged injury rests on possible future contraceptive failure, possible future pregnancy, possible future unpreparedness for parenthood, and possible future impairment of health. . . . [W]e are not prepared to say that the bare allegation of so indirect an injury is sufficient to present an actual case or controversy.

. . . .

As with the Does, in McCormack's case there are too many "possibilities that may not take place and all may not combine." *Roe*, 410 U.S. at 128. Therefore, McCormack does not have standing to challenge PUCPA based on the fact that she was pregnant before filing her civil complaint or based on a possible future pregnancy.

. . . Even if a doctor could bring a challenge to PUCPA on the basis of potential prosecution, McCormack cannot do so on behalf of an unnamed provider. Accordingly, the district court did not err in determining that McCormack lacked standing to challenge PUCPA.

For the reasons discussed above . . . we AFFIRM the district court's determination that McCormack will likely succeed with her facial constitutional challenges to Idaho Code §§ 18–606 and 18–608(1) and; AFFIRM the district court's conclusion that McCormack lacked standing to seek pre-enforcement relief against the enforcement of PUCPA.

We REVERSE the scope of the injunction to the extent that it grants relief beyond McCormack. We also REVERSE the district court's determination that McCormack did not have standing to enjoin enforcement of Idaho Code § 18–608(2) in conjunction with § 18–606.

AFFIRMED in part, REVERSED in part, and REMANDED.

NOTE

Abortion restrictions and the criminalization of pregnant women. Jennie Lynn McCormack, unable to access abortion services, was criminally charged for ending her own pregnancy. Recall the discussion in Chapter 2, *supra* p. 164, about the ongoing and growing efforts to criminalize pregnant women's conduct as child endangerment. How are these efforts related? How does regulation of pregnant women's conduct interact with regulation of access to abortion? What messages do these sets of regulations send about the appropriate role of women when it comes to procreation?

7. ABORTION AND THE CULTURE OF LIFE

Law not only regulates behavior, but also instantiates ways of thinking. Roe v. Wade, *and the cultural conflict it produced, have fundamentally changed the status of pregnancy and birth. The availability of abortion also fundamentally altered the legal and social status of women. Once confined almost exclusively to the roles of mothers or potential mothers, women may now treat motherhood as a choice. As Justice O'Connor observed in* Planned Parenthood of Southeastern Pennsylvania v. Casey, *505 U.S. 833 (1992), the prospect of voluntary motherhood made it possible for women "to participate equally in the economic and social life of the Nation." However, for those women who value motherhood as the most socially and economically rewarding role a woman can play, greater availability of abortion may portend great loss— the loss of the child and the lost veneration of motherhood. For these women, greater access to abortion has transformed a sacred calling into a voluntary lifestyle choice. At the same time as the status of mothers has changed, the fetus/baby has become an object of cultural attention, both by those who oppose abortion, and by those who proudly display the ultrasound as "Baby's First Picture." Below, we explore some of the social and legal consequences of this cultural shift.*

Carol Sanger, *M Is for the Many Things*
1 S. CAL. REV. L. & WOMEN'S STUD. 15 (1992).

People have gotten quite a few things about mothers and motherhood wrong over the last 700 or so years. Educators, historians, jurists, philosophers, physicians, social workers, and theologians have been telling us what mothers are like: what they need, how they feel, what pleases them, how and how well they think. . . .

This essay is not an attempt to set the record straight. That massive task is being undertaken by others whose dissatisfactions with established medical, historical, and social facts have led them to uncover a different record with a truer ring. . . .

. . . .

My basic argument is this: Motherhood is a central but confusing icon within our social structure. It is at once dominating and dominated, much as mothers are both revered and regulated. The reverence and regulation are not so much in conflict as in league. The rules remind women of how to behave in order to stay revered. This reverence is something more than a fan club for mothers. It matters in such practical and concrete ways as keeping one's children, having credibility in court, getting promoted at work, and so on.

The connection between maternal reverence and reward is possible because of an understanding within American culture that there is a way that mothers are supposed to be. . . . [M]uch thinking about mothers starts from an adherence to an ideal model of motherhood which, even adjusted for the late twentieth century, few mothers match. The ideal model is used to determine what conduct by mothers is in some official sense "motherly;" that model then becomes the essence of what mothers are about, an unstated reference point in the formation of public policy and the application of legal rules. For most of this century, the dominant model of motherhood has meant something closer to "housewife"—a married, nonworking, inherently selfless, largely nonsexual, white woman with children.[16]

But (some) things change. Mothers are now too varied to satisfy the model and too alert to want to. . . .

. . . [W]hat motherhood means—as an icon, an institution, a role or a status—is no longer certain. Mothers themselves are now startlingly different and more varied than the institution of motherhood—which once would have offered them immediate complimentary membership— has been able to acknowledge. Even a simple question like who *is* a mother no longer has a simple answer, now that genetic contribution, gestation, and stroller pushing may each be provided by a different woman. Different kinds of mothers and their supporters now claim not only membership in the institution of modem motherhood but participatory drafting rights in its terms. Motherhood has become what philosophers call an "essentially contested concept," as competing claims about its nature, essence, and obligations are urged and defended.

. . . [M]uch rests on who "counts" as a mother and who does not. An array of interests and concerns about personal worth, social status, legal entitlements, public morality, public costs, children's welfare, and family preservation are now at stake. To receive the good-housekeeping stamp of approval for one's relationship with a child secures privileges, respect,

---

[16] For the origins of the transcendent mother, *see* Ruth H. Bloch, *American Feminine Ideals in Transition: The Rise of the Moral Mother, 1785–1815*, 4 FEM. STUD. 101 (1978). As Eileen Boris has observed, by the late 19th century African-American women's organizations and white women's organizations invoked a discourse that "relied on the same central image— the altruistic, protective, and nurturing mother. . . . [Yet w]ithin the word 'mother,' as used by many reformers and makers of public policy, lurked the referent 'white.' " Eileen Boris, *The Power of Motherhood: Black and White Activist Women Redefine the "Political"*, 2 YALE J. L. & FEMINISM 25, 26–27 (1989).

and support (such as it exists) from the rest of the community. On the other side, the tangible and the symbolic deprivations are equally powerful. Excluding certain women with children from the status of mother or regarding them as marginal or deviant cases serves to deny them some or all of the actual and symbolic power that maternity sometimes confers.

. . . .

South Dakota Codified Laws, ch. 34–23A–10.1, Performance of Abortions

(2014).

34–23A–10.1.   Voluntary and informed consent required—Medical emergency exception—Information provided

No abortion may be performed unless the physician first obtains a voluntary and informed written consent of the pregnant woman upon whom the physician intends to perform the abortion, unless the physician determines that obtaining an informed consent is impossible due to a medical emergency and further determines that delaying in performing the procedure until an informed consent can be obtained from the pregnant woman or her next of kin in accordance with chapter 34–12C is impossible due to the medical emergency, which determinations shall then be documented in the medical records of the patient. A consent to an abortion is not voluntary and informed, unless, in addition to any other information that must be disclosed under the common law doctrine, the physician provides that pregnant woman with the following information:

(1)   A statement in writing providing the following information:

(a)   The name of the physician who will perform the abortion;

(b)   That the abortion will terminate the life of a whole, separate, unique, living human being;

(c)   That the pregnant woman has an existing relationship with that unborn human being and that the relationship enjoys protection under the United States Constitution and under the laws of South Dakota;

(d)   That by having an abortion, her existing relationship and her existing constitutional rights with regards to that relationship will be terminated;

(e)   A description of all known medical risks of the procedure and statistically significant risk factors to which the pregnant woman would be subjected, including:

(i)   Depression and related psychological distress;

(ii)   Increased risk of suicide ideation and suicide;

(iii) A statement setting forth an accurate rate of deaths due to abortions, including all deaths in which the abortion procedure was a substantial contributing factor;

(iv) All other known medical risks to the physical health of the woman, including the risk of infection, hemorrhage, danger to subsequent pregnancies, and infertility;

(f)   The probable gestational age of the unborn child at the time the abortion is to be performed, and a scientifically accurate statement describing the development of the unborn child at that age; and

(g)   The statistically significant medical risks associated with carrying her child to term compared to undergoing an induced abortion.

. . .

The disclosures set forth above shall be provided to the pregnant woman in writing and in person no later than two hours before the procedure is to be performed. The physician shall ensure that the pregnant woman signs each page of the written disclosure with the certification that she has read and understands all of the disclosures, prior to the patient signing a consent for the procedure. If the pregnant woman asks for a clarification or explanation of any particular disclosure, or asks any other question about a matter of significance to her, the explanation or answer shall be made in writing and be given to the pregnant woman before signing a consent for the procedure and shall be made part of the permanent medical record of the patient;

(2)   A statement by telephone or in person, by the physician who is to perform the abortion, or by the referring physician, or by an agent of both, at least twenty-four hours before the abortion, providing the following information:

(a)   That medical assistance benefits may be available for prenatal care, childbirth, and neonatal care;

(b)   That the father of the unborn child is legally responsible to provide financial support for her child following birth, and that this legal obligation of the father exists in all instances, even in instances in which the father has offered to pay for the abortion;

(c)   The name, address, and telephone number of a pregnancy help center in reasonable proximity of the abortion facility where the abortion will be performed; and

. . .

(3)   A written statement that sex-selective abortions are illegal in the State of South Dakota and that a pregnant mother cannot have an abortion, either solely or partly, due to the unborn child's sex, regardless of whether that unborn child is a girl or a boy or whether it is of the

pregnant mother's free will or the result of the use of pressure and coercion.

Prior to the pregnant woman signing a consent to the abortion, she shall sign a written statement that indicates that the requirements of this section have been complied with. Prior to the performance of the abortion, the physician who is to perform the abortion shall receive a copy of the written disclosure documents required by this section, and shall certify in writing that all of the information described in those subdivisions has been provided to the pregnant woman, that the physician is, to the best of his or her ability, satisfied that the pregnant woman has read the materials which are required to be disclosed, and that the physician believes she understands the information imparted.

NOTES

1.   *An invitation to the legislature?* In *Gonzales v. Carhart*, Justice Anthony Kennedy observed that "some women come to regret their choice to abort the infant life they once created and sustained." 550 U.S. 124, 159 (2007). Kennedy suggests that if women were better informed about the nature of the abortion procedure and the risks and consequences associated with it, they may elect not to abort, sparing themselves "grief more anguished and sorrow more profound" caused by discovering how their pregnancy had been terminated. Many interpreted Kennedy's observations as an invitation to state legislatures to revise existing abortion statutes to include more rigorous informed consent standards.

2.   *Sticking to the (statutory) script.* The text of this South Dakota informed consent statute is so detailed and specific in its requirements that physicians often comport with its terms by simply reading its text to their patients. In this way, the statute has become "a script" that physicians, regardless of their views, must read in the performance of their practical duties. *See* Zita Lazzarini, *South Dakota's Abortion Script—Threatening the Physician-Patient Relationship*, 359 NEW ENG. J. MED 2189, 2189 (2008).

3.   *Hamstringing doctors?* Some physicians have responded negatively to the emerging informed consent standards. These new requirements, they argue, force them to espouse the state's position on abortion, even where it conflicts with their own views, infringing upon their First Amendment rights. As importantly, they maintain that the standards compromise the patient-physician relationship by requiring doctors to provide their patients with information about the emotional and psychological risks of abortion that is not supported by scientific research. Patients expect that physicians:

> will provide them with accurate and complete medical information that will guide them in making medical decisions. . . . By requiring physicians to deliver such misinformation and discouraging them from providing alternative accurate information, the statute forces physicians to violate their obligation to solicit truly informed consent—and thereby detracts from the essential trust between patients and their physicians.

Zita Lazzarini, *South Dakota's Abortion Script—Threatening the Physician-Patient Relationship*, 359 NEW ENG. J. MED 2189, 2191 (2008).

4. *Informed consent in context.* It is worth noting that when South Dakota passed this law in 2005, there was (and still is) only a single operating abortion clinic in the state. *See* GUTTMACHER INST., STATE FACTS ABOUT ABORTION: SOUTH DAKOTA (2014). Further, the informed consent law came in the midst of three separate attempts to implement broad bans on abortion. *See* Gretchen Ruethling, *National Briefing: Plains: South Dakota: Bills on Abortion Signed*, N.Y. TIMES, Mar. 18, 2005, at A18. Although the informed consent statute does not ban abortion outright, some have argued that it poses serious obstacles to women seeking an abortion and physicians willing to provide abortion services. *See* Maya Manian, *Perverting Informed Consent: The South Dakota Court Decision*, RH REALITY CHECK (Aug. 1, 2012), http://rhrealitycheck.org/article/2012/08/01/perverting-informed-consent-south-dakota/.

5. *You say person, I say human being.* The South Dakota statute also reflects a strategic choice of words. Recall that the statute requires physicians to inform women that the abortion that they seek "will terminate the life of a whole, separate, unique, living *human being*." (emphasis added). According to legal commentator Emily Bazelon, the use of the term "human being" is purposeful:

> In *Roe v. Wade*, the Supreme Court ruled that a fetus is not a person, in the legal sense of the word, which is to say it doesn't have the same rights [as a person]. So South Dakota couldn't order doctors to tell women that to have an abortion is to kill a person. But human being is a different term that's up for grabs, the drafters of the legislation decided.

Emily Bazelon, *Telling Doctors What to Think*, SLATE (July 2, 2008), http://www.slate.com/articles/news_and_politics/jurisprudence/2008/07/telling_doctors_what_to_think.html.

Planned Parenthood v. Rounds
686 F.3d 889 (8th Cir. 2012).

■ GRUENDER, CIRCUIT JUDGE.

. . . .

In 2005, South Dakota enacted House Bill 1166 ("the Act"), amending the requirements for obtaining informed consent to an abortion as codified in S.D.C.L. § 34–23A–10.1. Section 7 of the Act requires physicians, in the course of obtaining informed consent, to provide certain information to the patient seeking an abortion. In June 2005, Planned Parenthood sued to prevent the Act from taking effect, contending that several of its provisions constituted an undue burden on abortion rights and facially violated patients' and physicians' free speech rights, while other provisions were unconstitutionally vague. After the district court preliminarily enjoined the Act and a divided panel of this court affirmed, this court sitting en banc vacated the preliminary injunction and remanded for further proceedings.

On remand, the parties filed cross-motions for summary judgment with respect to the challenged provisions. The district court ruled that a biological disclosure, and a medical emergency exception, were facially sound with respect to the First Amendment and imposed no undue burden, while disclosures regarding the protected relationship between the patient and the unborn child, and the suicide advisory, failed to meet both constitutional requirements. The district court also held that a requirement to disclose "all known medical risks of the procedure," was not unconstitutionally vague, but that a requirement to disclose "statistically significant risk factors," was.

Planned Parenthood appealed the district court's decision on the biological disclosure and the "all known medical risks" disclosure, while the State and Intervenors appealed the district court's decision on the relationship disclosures and the suicide advisory. A panel of this court affirmed unanimously with respect to the biological disclosure and the "all known medical risks" disclosure, reversed unanimously with respect to the relationship disclosures, and affirmed in a divided decision as to the suicide advisory. We granted this rehearing en banc solely on the issue of the suicide advisory.

. . . .

[T]o succeed on either its undue burden or compelled speech claims, Planned Parenthood must show that the disclosure at issue "is either untruthful, misleading or not relevant to the patient's decision to have an abortion." To evaluate the constitutional merits of the suicide advisory, we will examine first what disclosure actually is required, second whether that disclosure is truthful, and third whether it is non-misleading and relevant to the patient's decision to have an abortion.

Section 34–23A–10.1 requires a physician seeking to perform an abortion to present to the patient:

> (1) A statement in writing providing the following information:
>
> (e) A description of all known medical risks of the procedure and statistically significant risk factors to which the pregnant woman would be subjected, including:
>
> > (i)   Depression and related psychological distress;
> >
> > (ii) Increased risk of suicide ideation and suicide;
>
> * * *

Planned Parenthood argues, and the district court agreed, that subsection (ii) must be construed to require a disclosure of a conclusive causal link between abortion and suicide. However, no language in subsection (ii), or in the heading of section 10.1(1)(e), refers to such a causal link. "The intent of a statute is determined from what the legislature said, rather than what the courts think it should have said, and the court must confine itself to the language used."

Here, the language actually used by the legislature—"medical risks," "statistically significant risk factors," "[i]ncreased risk"—denotes risk in a medical context. Moreover, while the heading of subsection (e) refers broadly to "all known medical risks of the [abortion] procedure . . . including" those listed in its subsections, the suicide advisory is the only subsection to further incorporate the more precise phrase "[i]ncreased risk." *See* § 34–23A–10.1(1)(e)(ii). Therefore, we must presume that the term "increased risk" has a more precise meaning than the umbrella term "risk" by itself. The term "increased risk" is not defined in the statute, and it has more than one reasonable definition in the medical field. South Dakota law requires that such a term "must be construed according to its accepted usage, and a strained, unpractical or absurd result is to be avoided." *Peters v. Spearfish ETJ Planning Comm'n*, 567 N.W.2d 880, 885 (S.D.1997).

As a result, the disclosure actually required by the suicide advisory depends upon the accepted usage of the term "increased risk" in the relevant medical field. . . .

The peer-reviewed medical literature in the record on the topic of suicide and abortion consistently uses the term "increased risk" to refer to a relatively higher probability of an adverse outcome in one group compared to other groups—that is, to "relative risk." *See* Stedman's Medical Dictionary 1701 (28th ed. 2006) (defining relative risk as "the ratio of the r[isk] of disease among those exposed to a r[isk] factor to the r[isk] among those not exposed"). For example, one study compared the rate of suicide for women who had received an induced abortion with the rates of suicide for two other groups, women who had given birth and women who had miscarried. *See* Ex. 60, Mika Gissler et al., *Suicides After Pregnancy in Finland*, 1987–94, 313 Brit. Med. J. 1431, 1432 (1996). That study characterized its finding of a vastly higher suicide rate for women who received an induced abortion as "an increased risk of suicide." *Id.* at 1434. Another study compared the rate of, *inter alia*, suicide ideation in women who had received an induced abortion with the rates for women who had given birth and for women who had not become pregnant. *See* David M. Fergusson et al., *Abortion in Young Women and Subsequent Mental Health*, 47 J. Child Psychol. & Psychiatry 16, 19 (2006). That study concluded, "Certainly in this study, those young women who had abortions appeared to be at moderately *increased risk* of both concurrent and subsequent mental health problems when compared with equivalent groups of pregnant or non-pregnant peers." *Id.* at 23 (emphasis added).

. . . .

Even the evidence upon which Planned Parenthood heavily relies is consistent with the "relative risk" definition of "increased risk," with no requirement for proof of causation. For example, the report of the American Psychological Association's ("APA") Task Force on Mental

Health and Abortion, Branson Decl., decries the "tendency to confuse a risk and a cause" as a "logical fallacy." APA Report at 31. As another example, Planned Parenthood submitted into the record a letter to a medical journal from one of the researchers mentioned above. While the researcher emphasized that his studies linking suicide and abortion did not prove causation, he resolutely reiterated his finding of "increased risk." Mika Gissler et al., *Letter to the Editor: Pregnancy-Related Violent Deaths*, 27 Scand. J. Pub. Health 1:54, 55 (1999). It would be nonsensical for those in the field to distinguish a relationship of "increased risk" from one of causation if the term "risk" itself was equivalent to causation.

In the face of this extensive evidence of the accepted usage of the term "increased risk," Planned Parenthood makes two arguments as to why the suicide advisory should be read to require a disclosure of proof of causation. First, it argues that the statute refers to the "increased risk of suicide ideation and suicide" as a risk "to which the pregnant woman *would be subjected*" by the abortion procedure implying that the abortion procedure directly subjects the patient to, or causes, the result. A relevant rule of statutory construction, however, holds that "a limiting clause or phrase . . . should ordinarily be read as modifying only the noun or phrase that it immediately follows." *Barnhart v. Thomas*, 540 U.S. 20, 26 (2003). Under that rule, the phrase "to which the pregnant woman would be subjected" modifies only the immediately preceding phrase "statistically significant risk factors" (which is not at issue here), not the phrase "all known medical risks of the procedure" (of which the "increased risk of suicide ideation and suicide" is a listed example). *See* § 34–23A–10.1(1)(e).

Moreover, even if the phrase "to which the pregnant woman would be subjected" is construed to modify the "increased risk" language, it would not advance Planned Parenthood's argument because the result to which the pregnant woman would be subjected is the *increased risk*. In other words, the abortion procedure causes the patient to become a member of a group for which an increased risk is documented relative to other groups. This does not imply proof that the abortion procedure directly causes the adverse outcome in those cases where the risk materializes. There is a very real difference between (1) a statement that an action places an individual at an increased risk for an adverse outcome, and (2) a statement that, if the individual experiences the adverse outcome, the action will have been the direct cause.

Second, Planned Parenthood relies on the "established principle of statutory construction that, where the wording of an act is changed by amendment, it is evidential of an intent that the words shall have a different construction." *Lewis & Clark Rural Water Sys., Inc. v. Seeba*, 709 N.W.2d 824, 831 (S.D. 2006). The informed-consent statute in effect prior to the Act required the disclosure of "[t]he particular medical risks associated with the particular abortion procedure to be employed including, when medically accurate, the risks of infection, hemorrhage, danger to subsequent pregnancies, and infertility." S.D.C.L. § 34–23A–10.1(1)(b) (2004). The Act expanded this subject matter into a new, four-part subsection:

(e) A description of all known medical risks of the procedure and statistically significant risk factors to which the pregnant woman would be subjected, including:

(i) Depression and related psychological distress;

(ii) Increased risk of suicide ideation and suicide;

(iii) A statement setting forth an accurate rate of deaths due to abortions, including all deaths in which the abortion procedure was a substantial contributing factor;

(iv) All other known medical risks to the physical health of the woman, including the risk of infection, hemorrhage, danger to subsequent pregnancies, and infertility[.]

§ 34–23A–10.1(1)(e) (2005). Because this provision as amended by the Act no longer includes the word "associated," Planned Parenthood asks us to conclude that the legislature intended the term "increased risk" to imply proof of causation, rather than that the procedure and the adverse outcome are merely "associated" by a correlative relationship such as relative risk.

We certainly agree that the amendments to the medical-risks provision are "evidential of an intent that the words shall have a different construction," but in this case that different construction does not hinge on the removal of one word. Instead, the Act effects essentially a complete rewriting of the former § 34–23A–10.1(1)(b) (2004), removing thirteen of the original twenty-eight words and adding seventy new words, including an entirely new introduction requiring a description of "all known medical risks" and a listing of three new specific areas of concern in subsections (i)–(iii). Taken as a whole, these sweeping changes to the language of the provision express the legislature's intent to address a much broader range of specific medical risks in the required disclosure, not to implicitly sever the term "increased risk" from its accepted usage in the medical field. Indeed, where only fifteen words of original language remain in an amended provision of eighty-five words, ascribing such an effect to the removal of a single word would go far beyond any use of the cited rule of statutory construction of which we are aware.

. . . .

[I]n subsection (ii), the legislature expressly required the disclosure of an "increased risk," not a causal link. Based on the accepted usage of the term "increased risk" in the relevant medical field, the usage of that term in the context of § 34–23A–10.1(1)(e)(ii) does not imply a disclosure of a causal relationship. Instead, subsection (ii) requires a disclosure simply that the risk of suicide and suicide ideation is higher among women who abort compared to women in other relevant groups, such as women who give birth or do not become pregnant.

. . . With regard to whether the required disclosure is truthful, the State submitted into the record numerous studies published in peer-reviewed medical journals that demonstrate a statistically significant correlation between abortion and suicide. The studies were published in respected, peer-reviewed journals . . . and there is no indication that the peer-review process was compromised for the studies at issue.

Planned Parenthood argues that these studies do not examine the correlation between abortion and suicide in sufficient detail to prove a causal link . . . but, as we concluded above, the suicide advisory does not require disclosure of a causal link. With regard to the accuracy of the correlation itself, there is nothing in the record to suggest that the underlying data or calculations in any of these studies are flawed. For example, Planned Parenthood's own expert, Dr. Nada Stotland, admitted that one of the studies . . . "indicates an association; not causation, but an association" between abortion and suicide. . . .

Based on the record, the studies submitted by the State are sufficiently reliable to support the truth of the proposition that the relative risk of suicide and suicide ideation is higher for women who abort their pregnancies compared to women who give birth or have not become pregnant. It also is worth noting that Planned Parenthood does not challenge the disclosure that "[d]epression and related psychological distress" is a "known medical risk [ ] of the [abortion] procedure." As a matter of common sense, the onset of depression and psychological distress also would increase one's risk of suicide and suicide ideation. Thus, there appears to be little dispute about the truthfulness of the required disclosure.

Finally, Planned Parenthood contends that the suicide advisory is not truthful because an increased risk of suicide after abortion is not "known" as required by the statute. Once again, however, this contention is premised on Planned Parenthood's argument that the term "increased risk" implies a *causal link* that is not generally "known." Because the statute does not require the disclosure of any causal link, Planned Parenthood's argument on this point is misdirected. The record indicates that the disclosure actually required—that the relative risk of suicide and suicide ideation is higher for women who abort compared to women in other relevant groups—is generally "known." . . .

As a result, we hold that the disclosure facially mandated by the suicide advisory is truthful.

. . . .

Despite the extensive evidence in the record of an "increased risk" of suicide, Planned Parenthood contends that disclosure of the increased risk would be misleading and irrelevant to a patient seeking an abortion, because some authorities have indicated that there is no direct causal link. In particular, Planned Parenthood argues that it is more plausible that certain underlying factors, such as pre-existing mental health problems, predispose some women both to have unwanted pregnancies and to have suicidal tendencies, resulting in a misleading correlation between abortion and suicide that has no direct causal component. Under this view, the required disclosure would be misleading or irrelevant to the decision to have an abortion because the patient's decision would not alter the underlying factors that actually cause the observed increased risk of suicide.

As an initial matter, the standard medical practice, as reflected in the record, is to *recognize* a strongly correlated adverse outcome as a "risk" while further studies are conducted to clarify whether various underlying factors play causal roles. . . .

. . . [T]he truthful disclosure regarding increased risk cannot be unconstitutionally misleading or irrelevant simply because of some degree of "medical and scientific uncertainty," *Gonzales*, 550 U.S. 124, 163 (2007), as to whether abortion plays a causal role in the observed correlation between abortion and suicide. Instead, Planned Parenthood would have to show that any "medical and scientific uncertainty" has been resolved into a certainty *against* a causal role for abortion. In other words, in order to render the suicide advisory unconstitutionally misleading or irrelevant, Planned Parenthood would have to show that abortion has been ruled out, to a degree of scientifically accepted certainty, as a statistically significant causal factor in post-abortion suicides. An examination of Planned Parenthood's evidence reveals that it has not met this burden.

First, Planned Parenthood points out that the label approved by the Food and Drug Administration ("FDA") for the abortion-inducing drug Mifeprex (mifepristone, also known as RU–486) does not list suicide or suicide ideation as a risk of using the drug, despite FDA labeling regulations requiring the listing of, *inter alia,* all "clinically significant adverse reactions" and "other potential safety hazards." However, an FDA-approved label does not represent the definitive or exclusive list of risks associated with a drug. The record before us does not show whether any evidence of the link between abortion and suicide was submitted to the FDA, nor does it provide details of the FDA's analysis, if any, of the link. Thus, the FDA-approved label for Mifeprex yields no information as to whether abortion has been ruled out as a statistically significant causal factor in post-abortion suicides.

Second, Planned Parenthood argues, and the district court found, that the American College of Obstetricians and Gynecologists ("ACOG") . . . "rejects any suggestion that increased risk of suicide and suicide ideation are known risks of abortion." Unfortunately, there was no evidence from ACOG in the record for the district court to consider. The only evidence in the record pertaining to ACOG's position is a second-hand reference in a 2005 report by the State's expert . . . that quoted two sentences from a single ACOG Practice Bulletin: "Long-term risks sometimes attributed to surgical abortion include potential effects on . . . psychological sequelae. However, the medical literature, when carefully evaluated, clearly demonstrates no significant negative impact on any of these factors with surgical abortion." Elizabeth M. Shadigian, Report to the S.D. Task Force to Study Abortion 4, Sept. 21, 2005. Dr. Shadigian further reported her opinion that ACOG's statement was erroneous and that "ACOG seems to claim that they have adequately evaluated the medical literature, but they do not consider our study or the many other studies we evaluated." Shadigian Report at 5. . . . The two unsupported sentences from an ACOG Practice Bulletin lend no credence to the argument that abortion has been ruled out as a statistically significant causal factor in post-abortion suicides.

Third, Planned Parenthood cites the previously mentioned APA Report. . . . [T]he APA Report reviewed "50 papers published in peer-reviewed journals between 1990 and 2007 that analyzed empirical data of a quantitative nature on psychological experiences associated with induced abortion, compared to an alternative." For some of the studies that found increased mental health risks associated with abortion, the APA Report identifies perceived methodological deficiencies, including an inability to limit the comparison group to women who carried unplanned or unwanted pregnancies to term. Based on one study that attempted to account for that variable, the report states that "the *best* scientific evidence indicates that the relative risk of mental health problems among adult women who have an *unplanned pregnancy* is no greater if they have an elective first-trimester abortion than if they deliver that pregnancy." In the very same sentence, however, the report states that the published literature could not provide "unequivocal evidence regarding the relative mental health risks associated with abortion per se compared to its alternatives (childbirth of an unplanned pregnancy)."

The State and Intervenors argue that the APA Report is deficient in several respects. While the APA Report alleges methodological flaws in all of the studies that found a strong link between abortion and adverse mental health outcomes, it does not systematically list or analyze those flaws for each study considered. Instead, the report uses a handful of studies as illustrative examples. The State and Intervenors contend that this lack of rigor allowed the APA Report to analyze studies that found abortion to be "a benign experience for most women" less stringently than studies that found abortion to cause adverse effects . . . The APA Report also does not acknowledge that some of the studies showing increased risk did statistically control for other potential causal factors such as history of depression, anxiety, suicide ideation, childhood sexual abuse, physical abuse, child neuroticism, and low self-esteem. As another example, although a high rate of attrition (i.e., the loss of subjects from a long-term study before the study is complete) is typically regarded as a methodological weakness, the APA Report downplays the significance of attrition, possibly because "the studies with the highest attrition rates . . . are also the ones that provide little evidence of negative effects" of abortion. A number of published authors in the field contacted the APA to point out these problems and ask that the APA Report be retracted.

At a minimum, it appears that many published authors in the field do not accept the opinion of the APA's six-person task force that the "best evidence" suggests that there is no real significance to the link between abortion and suicide. Even if one accepts the findings in the APA Report at face value, however, the crux of the matter is that while the APA Report states that the evidence available at the time of its review is not "sufficient to support the claim that an observed association between abortion history and mental health was *caused* by the abortion," it also concludes that the published literature is inconclusive and more research is needed "to disentangle confounding factors and establish relative risks of abortion compared to its alternatives." . . . Thus, the APA Report provides no support for the proposition that abortion has been ruled out as a statistically significant causal factor in post-abortion suicides.

Finally, the dissent relies on six recent publications submitted to this Court by Planned Parenthood as a supplement to the district court record. . . .

. . . .

We acknowledge that these studies, like the studies relied upon by the State and Intervenors, have strengths as well as weaknesses. Like all studies on the topic, they must make use of imperfect data that typically was collected for entirely different purposes, and they must attempt to glean some insight through the application of sophisticated statistical techniques and informed assumptions. While the studies all agree that the relative risk of suicide is higher among women who abort compared to women who give birth or do not become pregnant, they diverge as to the extent to which other underlying factors account for that link. We express no opinion as to whether some of the studies are more reliable than others; instead, we hold only that the state legislature, rather than a federal court, is in the best position to weigh the divergent results and come to a conclusion about the best way to protect its populace. So long as the means chosen by the state does not impose an unconstitutional burden on women seeking abortions or their physicians, we have no basis to interfere.

In summary, although the record reflects "medical and scientific uncertainty," as to whether abortion itself is a causal factor in the observed correlation between abortion and suicide, there is nothing in the record to suggest that abortion as a cause *per se* has been ruled out with certainty. As a result, the disclosure of the observed correlation as an "increased risk" is not unconstitutionally misleading or irrelevant under *Casey* and *Gonzales*. . . .

In conclusion, we hold that the requirements of S.D.C.L. § 34–23A–10.1(1)(e)(ii) are satisfied by a disclosure that the relative risk of suicide and suicide ideation is higher for women who abort compared to women in other relevant groups, as described in the relevant medical research. The statute does not require the physician to disclose that a causal link between abortion and suicide has been proved. The disclosure is truthful, as evidenced by a multitude of studies published in peer-reviewed medical journals that found an increased risk of suicide for women who had received abortions compared to women who gave birth, miscarried, or never became pregnant . . .

Moreover, the suicide advisory is non-misleading and relevant to the patient's decision to have an abortion, as required by *Casey*. It is a typical medical practice to inform patients of statistically significant risks that have been associated with a procedure through medical research, even if causation has not been proved definitively . . . Thus, a truthful disclosure cannot be unconstitutionally misleading or irrelevant simply because some degree of medical and scientific uncertainty persists . . .

On its face, the suicide advisory presents neither an undue burden on abortion rights nor a violation of physicians' free speech rights. Accordingly, we reverse the district court's grant of summary judgment to Planned Parenthood. . . .

. . . .

■ MURPHY, CIRCUIT JUDGE, with whom WOLLMAN, BYE, and MELLOY, CIRCUIT JUDGES, join, dissenting.

. . . .

In order to be constitutional an informed consent requirement must be truthful, non-misleading, and relevant. Requiring physicians to provide their patients with information that does not meet this standard violates the physicians' First Amendment right against compelled speech.

The content of the 2005 suicide advisory raises constitutional problems which the prior version of the South Dakota statute did not. The previous provision required a physician to advise a patient about the "particular medical risks *associated with* the particular abortion procedure to be employed, including *when medically accurate,* the risks of infection, hemorrhage, danger to subsequent pregnancies, and infertility." S.D.C.L. § 34–23A–10.1(1)(b) (2003) (emphasis added). In contrast, the statute before the court requires doctors to tell a pregnant woman that a greater likelihood of suicide and suicide ideation is a "*known medical risk* [ ]" to which she "*would be subjected*" by having an abortion. S.D.C.L. § 34–23A–10.1(1)(e) (2005) (emphasis added).

The record clearly demonstrates, however, that suicide is not a known medical risk of abortion and that suicide is caused instead by factors preexisting an abortion such as a history of mental illness, domestic violence, and young age at the time of pregnancy.

As can be seen, the prior version of the South Dakota law did not carry the fatal flaw embodied in the statute now being considered. The wording of the statute under consideration conveys a causal relationship between abortion and the risk of suicide "to which the pregnant woman *would be subjected.*" The phrase to subject someone to something means "to cause to undergo or submit to." *Webster's Third New Int'l Dictionary* 2275 (2002). In contrast, the wording in the prior state legislation spoke of the "risks *associated with* . . . abortion." An association is defined as "the relationship of the occurrence of two events, without evidence that the event being investigated actually causes the second condition." *Taber's Cyclopaedic Med. Dictionary* 201 (21st ed. 2009). Legislative findings show that the statutory drafters intended that the advisory under review convey causality, for they stated that women must be informed that "procedures terminating the life of an unborn child *impose* risks to the life and health of the pregnant woman." S.D.C.L. § 34–23A–1.4 (emphasis added).

The majority concedes that there is no proof in the medical literature that abortion causes suicide and it recognizes that an advisory telling a woman that abortion causes an increased risk of suicide would be untruthful. It seeks to avoid the constitutional problem created by the current statutory text by suggesting that the legislature's amendment substituting subjected to for "associated with" should not be understood to mean causality since nearly all of the words in the advisory were changed. The new language is explained as merely informing women that their decision to have an abortion would "cause[ ] [them] to become a member of a group" with a statistically higher rate of suicide. That is not what the plain language of the statute says, however, and the medical evidence shows that women sharing certain factors may have a higher rate of suicide but not that abortion causes suicide.

The evidence considered by the district court shows that an advisory informing women that abortion *causes* them to be more likely to commit suicide is untruthful and misleading. That record made clear that abortion does not *cause* a "known" risk of suicide or suicide ideation. The record included volumes of deposition testimony, published medical research, and legislative reports supporting the district court's conclusion that the suicide advisory is unconstitutional.

. . . .

Since the district court enjoined the suicide advisory and a panel of this court affirmed that decision, the United Kingdom's Royal College of Obstetricians and Gynaecologists (RCOG) has issued recommendations that women "be informed that the evidence suggests that they are no more or less likely to suffer adverse psychological sequelae whether they have an abortion or continue with the pregnancy and have the baby." The United Kingdom's National Collaborating Centre for Mental Health arrived at the same conclusion in its report to the Academy of Medical Royal Colleges.

These conclusions are based on numerous studies which strengthen the evidence on which the district court relied. The studies establish that post abortion suicide rates are linked to preexisting mental illness and domestic violence, not to the decision to undergo an abortion. If, as the majority points out, "the standard medical practice . . . is to recognize a strongly correlated adverse outcome as a 'risk' while further studies are conducted to clarify whether various underlying factors play causal roles," must not research conducted by experts in the field after the district court's decision be considered as corroboration of its findings and conclusions?

. . . .

The majority concedes though that if the correlation between abortion and suicide were not due to a causal relationship, then the advisory "would be misleading or irrelevant to the decision to have an abortion because the patient's decision would not alter the underlying factors that actually cause the observed increased risk of suicide." The vast majority of researchers, however, assert that this is precisely the case. Those studies in the record show that other independent factors which co-occur with both abortion and suicide, such as prepregnancy mental health problems, domestic violence, and youth, account for the correlation between abortion and suicide risk.

To overcome this evidentiary problem a new standard for informed consent advisories is offered. Under this proposed test, so long as a causal link between abortion and suicide would be theoretically possible, an advisory is truthful, non-misleading, and relevant unless Planned Parenthood can prove the absence of a causal link with "scientifically accepted certainty." In support the court turns to *Gonzales*, 550 U.S. at 163–67, to rely on its discussion of medical uncertainty. The Court there was not considering a *Casey* issue about informed consent, however. . . . The Court concluded only that Congress, which was fully informed of the contradicting medical opinions, could balance the need to protect the state's interests in the "ethics of the medical profession" and "respect for dignity of human life" against the uncertain risks to women's health resulting from the ban. *Gonzales*, 550 U.S. at 157, 166.

The state's interest in this case is to promote a "wise," "mature [,] and informed" decision by women considering abortion. *Casey*, 505 U.S. at 883, 887. Here, any medical uncertainty as to whether abortion causes an increased risk of suicide undermines the advisory's constitutionality because a woman's ability to make a wise, mature, and informed choice is hindered by being told that the increased risk of suicide is a "known medical risk[ ]" "to which . . . [she] would be subjected" by having an abortion when the weight of the medical research indicates the opposite and she is not informed of the debate. The state's interest is thus not furthered by such an advisory.

. . . .

... [I]nstead of recognizing that medical research has shown that South Dakota's suicide advisory is untruthful, misleading, and irrelevant, the majority tries to shift the responsibility to attending physicians to "review[ ] the research in the field, understand[ ] the difference between relative risk and proof of causation, and explain[ ] it correctly to their patients." The statute provides only for a written transaction between doctor and patient in which explanation and clarification occur if a woman requests it, *see* S.D.C.L. § 34–23A–10.1 ¶¶ 2, 3, but no judicial attempt to direct the content of the conversation between a patient and her doctor can remedy the advisory's constitutional shortcomings.

By forcing doctors to inform women that abortion subjects them to a risk which the record medical evidence refutes, the suicide advisory places an undue burden on a pregnant woman's due process rights and violates a doctor's First Amendment right against compelled speech. The district court's order enjoining the suicide advisory should therefore be affirmed.

NOTES

1.   *Informed consent and speech.* First Amendment scholar Robert Post argues that there is a fundamental difference between regulating the speech of professionals and regulating professional speech. A physician may give a speech denouncing (or supporting) the Affordable Care Act in public without fear of regulation. Such speech is considered the speech of professionals, and thus, is beyond the scope of government regulation. However, in the context of the patient-doctor relationship, the state can and does regulate speech, in particular, insisting on informed consent. Such speech, the state argues, is *professional speech*—and as such, is well within the ambit of state regulation. Drawing on jurisprudence concerning the regulation of commercial speech, Post argues that state regulation of professional speech should be limited to requiring that such speech be "accurate and not misleading," according to the preponderance of the evidence. As Post contends, the danger of state regulation of professional speech is that it risks making the physician party to an ideological conflict. In so doing, state regulation threatens the integrity of the doctor-patient relationship as a source of accurate and trustworthy information, precisely the kind of relationship that the First Amendment seeks to protect as an essential component of a democratic society. *See* Robert Post, *Informed Consent to Abortion: A First Amendment Analysis of Compelled Physician Speech*, 2007 U. ILL. L. REV. 939, 981.

2.   *Post-abortion stress and women's nature? Rounds*, like *Carhart* before it, surfaces the concern that there is a "post-abortion stress syndrome"—akin to Post Traumatic Stress Disorder ("PTSD")—whereby women may experience intense depression, anxiety, and guilt after having an abortion. Some might argue that post-abortion stress syndrome is rooted in what Reva Siegel has termed "physiological naturalism"—the belief that women experience an inherent maternal attachment that is rooted in biology, as opposed to being socially constructed. On this account, abortion is traumatic

because it goes against women's essential nature. *See* Reva Siegel, *Reasoning from the Body: A Historical Perspective on Abortion Regulation and Questions of Equal Protection*, 44 STAN. L. REV. 261, 377–78 (1992).

3.   *Contesting post-abortion stress syndrome.* Although in *Rounds* the Eighth Circuit was persuaded by the logic of post-abortion stress syndrome, others are less convinced. A task force appointed by the American Psychological Association ("APA") conducted a careful examination of the most methodologically rigorous studies, noting that "[t]he strongest comparison-group studies based on U.S. samples found no differences in the mental health of women who terminated a single unintended pregnancy compared with other groups of women once [other variables] were controlled." The APA report stresses that the appropriate comparison group is women who have an unintended pregnancy and do not have an abortion, rather than women who give birth after a planned and wanted pregnancy. *See* Brenda Major et al., *Abortion and Mental Health: Evaluating the Evidence*, 64 AM. PSYCHOLOGIST 863, 884 (2009).

4.   *Protecting women?* In recent years the pro-life movement has moved away from the argument that abortion kills a baby, and towards the argument that abortion harms women both physically and psychologically. Although the studies cited in this discourse are controversial among mainstream medical and health experts, it is now a common part of anti-abortion rhetoric. *See* Byron C. Calhoun & Mailee Smith, *Significant Potential for Harm: Growing Medical Evidence of Abortion's Negative Impact on Women, in* DENISE M. BURKE, DEFENDING LIFE: DECONSTRUCTING *ROE*: ABORTION'S NEGATIVE IMPACT ON WOMEN 25–36 (2013). *Casey* and its progeny show clearly that this discourse has been adopted by at least some members of the Court. *See* Reva Siegel, *The Right's Reasons: Constitutional Conflict and the Spread of Woman-Protective Anti-Abortion Argument*, 57 DUKE L.J. 1641, 1691 (2008) (tracing the origins of this discourse to *Casey*).

5.   *The genesis of woman-protective arguments.* In a cover story for the *New York Times*, journalist Emily Bazelon traces the history of "woman-protective" anti-abortion activists to one David Reardon, whom she calls the "Moses" of this line of argument. She quotes Reardon as saying, "[w]e must change the abortion debate so that we are arguing with our opponents on their own turf, on the issue of defending the interests of women." She also provides a careful review of the contested social science data on which the argument is premised. Emily Bazelon, *Is There a Post-Abortion Syndrome?*, N.Y. TIMES MAG., Jan. 21, 2007, at 41.

6.   *Feminism and trauma.* Professor Jeannie Suk argues that the emergence of abortion-trauma discourse is not only an outgrowth of anti-abortion rhetoric, but can be linked to a larger feminist effort that emphasizes trauma to women as part of a rights-expanding project. Suk warns us, however, that embedding women's rights in trauma may underscore the view of women as passive and in need of the law's protection, posing challenges to the larger project of women's equality. *See* Jeannie Suk, *The Trajectory of Trauma: Bodies and Minds of Abortion Discourse*, 110 COLUM. L. REV. 1193, 1251 (2010).

8. THE ROLE OF SPEECH IN ABORTION JURISPRUDENCE

In Rust v. Sullivan, supra *p. 787, the Supreme Court determined that regulations limiting the speech rights of health care providers receiving Title X funding were constitutional. Since* Rust, *courts have found that the scope of the state's authority to regulate provider speech extends beyond those providers who receive federal funds. An example can be seen in* Planned Parenthood v. Casey, supra *p. 797, where the Supreme Court upheld Pennsylvania's "informed consent" provision requiring doctors to provide certain information to patients prior to abortions. More recently, courts have focused on protester speech outside of abortion clinics.*

Rust v. Sullivan
500 U.S. 173 (1991).

For an excerpt of Rust v. Sullivan, *please see* supra *p. 787.*

NOTE

Characterizing speech. One of the key insights from the Supreme Court decision in *Rust* is that the speech of medical practitioners who receive federal funding can be regulated as government speech without running afoul of the First Amendment. If government speech can be regulated in this way, what other types of speech can be? Can the speech of medical practitioners constitutionally be regulated as commercial speech?

* * *

A second line of case law concerning state regulation of abortion-related speech focuses on anti-abortion protestors and activists. Most of these cases consider the degree to which the First Amendment limits the state's ability to restrict or regulate protesting outside abortion clinics. The Supreme Court has examined this issue several times, mostly recently in Hill v. Colorado *(2000), and* McCullen v. Coakley *(2014)—both cases involved the constitutionality of state "buffer zone" laws.*

Hill v. Colorado
530 U.S. 703 (2000).

■ STEVENS, J.

At issue is the constitutionality of a 1993 Colorado statute Colo.Rev.Stat. § 18–9–122(3) (1999), that . . . makes it unlawful within the regulated areas for any person to "knowingly approach" within eight feet of another person, without that person's consent, "for the purpose of passing a leaflet or handbill to, displaying a sign to, or engaging in oral protest, education, or counseling with such other person. . . ." Although the statute prohibits speakers from approaching unwilling listeners, it does not require a standing speaker to move away from anyone passing by. Nor does it place any restriction on the content of any message that anyone may wish to communicate to anyone else, either inside or outside the regulated areas. It does, however, make it more difficult to give unwanted advice, particularly in the form of a handbill or leaflet, to persons entering or leaving medical facilities.

The question is whether the First Amendment rights of the speaker are abridged by the protection the statute provides for the unwilling listener.

Five months after the statute was enacted, petitioners filed a complaint . . . praying for a declaration that § 18–9–122(3) was facially invalid and seeking an injunction against its enforcement. They stated that prior to the enactment of the statute, they had engaged in "sidewalk counseling" on the public ways and sidewalks within 100 feet of the entrances to facilities where human abortion is practiced or where medical personnel refer women to other facilities for abortions. "Sidewalk counseling" consists of efforts "to educate, counsel, persuade, or inform passersby about abortion and abortion alternatives by means of verbal or written speech, including conversation and/or display of signs and/or distribution of literature." They further alleged that such activities frequently entail being within eight feet of other persons and that their fear of prosecution under the new statute caused them "to be chilled in the exercise of fundamental constitutional rights."

. . . It is apparent from the testimony of both supporters and opponents of the statute that demonstrations in front of abortion clinics impeded access to those clinics and were often confrontational. Indeed, it was a common practice to provide escorts for persons entering and leaving the clinics both to ensure their access and to provide protection from aggressive counselors who sometimes used strong and abusive language in face-to-face encounters. There was also evidence that emotional confrontations may adversely affect a patient's medical care. There was no evidence, however, that the "sidewalk counseling" conducted by petitioners in this case was ever abusive or confrontational.

. . . We now [uphold this statute].

. . . The right to free speech, of course, includes the right to attempt to persuade others to change their views, and may not be curtailed simply because the speaker's message may be offensive to his audience. But the protection afforded to offensive messages does not always embrace offensive speech that is so intrusive that the unwilling audience cannot avoid it. Indeed, "[i]t may not be the content of the speech, as much as the deliberate 'verbal or visual assault,' that justifies proscription." Even in a public forum, one of the reasons we tolerate a protester's right to wear a jacket expressing his opposition to government policy in vulgar language is because offended viewers can "effectively avoid further bombardment of their sensibilities simply by averting their eyes."

The recognizable privacy interest in avoiding unwanted communication varies widely in different settings. It is far less important when "strolling through Central Park" than when "in the confines of one's own home," or when persons are "powerless to avoid" it . . . More specific to the facts of this case, we have recognized that "[t]he First Amendment does not demand that patients at a medical facility undertake Herculean efforts to escape the cacophony of political protests."

The unwilling listener's interest in avoiding unwanted communication has been repeatedly identified in our cases. It is an aspect of the broader "right to be let alone" that one of our wisest Justices characterized as "the most comprehensive of rights and the right most valued by civilized men." The right to avoid unwelcome speech has special force in the privacy of the home, and its immediate surroundings, but can also be protected in confrontational settings. . . .

. . . .

The dissenters argue that we depart from precedent by recognizing a "right to avoid unpopular speech in a public forum." Rather, we are merely noting that our cases have repeatedly recognized the interests of unwilling listeners in situations where "the degree of captivity makes it impractical for the unwilling viewer or auditor to avoid exposure . . . The dissenters, however, appear to consider recognizing any of the interests of unwilling listeners—let alone balancing those interests against the rights of speakers—to be unconstitutional. Our cases do not support this view.

All four of the state court opinions upholding the validity of this statute concluded that it is a content-neutral time, place, and manner regulation . . . It is therefore appropriate to comment on the "content neutrality" of the statute. As we explained in *Ward v. Rock Against Racism*, 491 U.S. 781 (1989):

> The principal inquiry in determining content neutrality, in speech cases generally and in time, place, or manner cases in particular, is whether the government has adopted a regulation of speech because of disagreement with the message it conveys.

The Colorado statute passes that test for three independent reasons. First, it is not a "regulation of speech." Rather, it is a regulation of the places where some speech may occur. Second, it was not adopted "because of disagreement with the message it conveys." This conclusion is supported not just by the Colorado courts' interpretation of legislative history, but more importantly by the State Supreme Court's unequivocal holding that the statute's "restrictions apply equally to all demonstrators, regardless of viewpoint, and the statutory language makes no reference to the content of the speech."[27] Third, the State's interests in protecting access and privacy, and providing the police with

---

[27] . . . This observation in *Madsen* is equally applicable here: "There is no suggestion in this record that Florida law would not equally restrain similar conduct directed at a target having nothing to do with abortion; none of the restrictions imposed by the court were directed at the contents of petitioner's message." 512 U.S., at 762–763.

clear guidelines, are unrelated to the content of the demonstrators' speech. As we have repeatedly explained, government regulation of expressive activity is "content neutral" if it is justified without reference to the content of regulated speech.

Petitioners nevertheless argue that the statute is not content neutral insofar as it applies to some oral communication. The statute applies to all persons who "knowingly approach" within eight feet of another for the purpose of leafletting or displaying signs; for such persons, the content of their oral statements is irrelevant. With respect to persons who are neither leafletters nor sign carriers, however, the statute does not apply unless their approach is "for the purpose of . . . engaging in oral protest, education, or counseling." Petitioners contend that an individual near a health care facility who knowingly approaches a pedestrian to say "good morning" or to randomly recite lines from a novel would not be subject to the statute's restrictions. Because the content of the oral statements made by an approaching speaker must sometimes be examined to determine whether the knowing approach is covered by the statute, petitioners argue that the law is "content-based" under our reasoning in *Carey v. Brown*, 447 U.S. 455, 462 (1980).

Although this theory was identified in the complaint, it is not mentioned in any of the four Colorado opinions, all of which concluded that the statute was content neutral. For that reason, it is likely that the argument has been waived. Additionally, the Colorado attorney general argues that we should assume that the state courts tacitly construed the terms "protest, education, or counseling" to encompass "all communication." Instead of relying on those arguments, however, we shall explain why petitioners' contention is without merit and why their reliance on *Carey v. Brown* is misplaced.

It is common in the law to examine the content of a communication to determine the speaker's purpose. Whether a particular statement constitutes a threat, blackmail, an agreement to fix prices, a copyright violation, a public offering of securities, or an offer to sell goods often depends on the precise content of the statement. We have never held, or suggested, that it is improper to look at the content of an oral or written statement in order to determine whether a rule of law applies to a course of conduct. With respect to the conduct that is the focus of the Colorado statute, it is unlikely that there would often be any need to know exactly what words were spoken in order to determine whether "sidewalk counselors" are engaging in "oral protest, education, or counseling" rather than pure social or random conversation.

Theoretically, of course, cases may arise in which it is necessary to review the content of the statements made by a person approaching within eight feet of an unwilling listener to determine whether the approach is covered by the statute. But that review need be no more extensive than a determination whether a general prohibition of "picketing" or "demonstrating" applies to innocuous speech. The regulation of such expressive activities, by definition, does not cover social, random, or other everyday communications. *See* Webster's Third New International Dictionary 600, 1710 (1993) (defining "demonstrate" as "to make a public display of sentiment for or against a person or cause" and "picket" as an effort "to persuade or otherwise influence"). Nevertheless, we have never suggested that the kind of cursory examination that might be required to exclude casual conversation from the coverage of a regulation of picketing would be problematic.

In *Carey v. Brown* we examined a general prohibition of peaceful picketing that contained an exemption for picketing a place of employment involved in a labor dispute. We concluded that this statute violated the Equal Protection Clause of the Fourteenth Amendment, because it discriminated between lawful and unlawful conduct based on the content of the picketers' messages. That discrimination was impermissible because it accorded preferential treatment to expression concerning one particular subject matter—labor disputes—while prohibiting discussion of all other issues. Although our opinion stressed that "it is the content of the speech that determines whether it is within or without the statute's blunt prohibition," we appended a footnote to that sentence explaining that it was the fact that the statute placed a prohibition on discussion of particular topics, while others were allowed, that was constitutionally repugnant. Regulation of the subject matter of messages, though not as obnoxious as viewpoint-based regulation, is also an objectionable form of content-based regulation.

The Colorado statute's regulation of the location of protests, education, and counseling is easily distinguishable from *Carey*. It places no restrictions on—and clearly does not prohibit—either a particular viewpoint or any subject matter that may be discussed by a speaker. Rather, it simply establishes a minor place restriction on an extremely broad category of communications with unwilling listeners. Instead of drawing distinctions based on the subject that the approaching speaker may wish to address, the statute applies equally to used car salesmen, animal rights activists, fundraisers, environmentalists, and missionaries. Each can attempt to educate unwilling listeners on any subject, but without consent may not approach within eight feet to do so.

The dissenters, nonetheless, contend that the statute is not "content neutral." As Justice Scalia points out, the vice of content-based legislation in this context is that "it lends itself" to being " 'used for invidious thought-control purposes.' " But a statute that restricts certain categories of speech only lends itself to invidious use if there is a significant number of communications, raising the same problem that the statute was enacted to solve, that fall outside the statute's scope, while others fall inside. Here, the statute's restriction seeks to protect those who enter a health care facility from the harassment, the nuisance, the persistent importuning, the following, the dogging, and the implied threat of physical touching that can accompany an unwelcome approach within eight feet of a patient by a person wishing to argue vociferously face-to-face and perhaps thrust an undesired handbill upon her. The statutory phrases, "oral protest, education, or counseling," distinguish speech activities likely to have those consequences from speech activities . . . that are most unlikely to have those consequences. The statute does not distinguish among speech instances that are similarly likely to raise the legitimate concerns to which it responds. Hence, the statute cannot be struck down for failure to maintain "content neutrality," or for "underbreadth."

Also flawed is Justice Kennedy's theory that a statute restricting speech becomes unconstitutionally content based because of its application "to the specific locations where [that] discourse occurs." A statute prohibiting solicitation in airports that was motivated by the aggressive approaches of Hare Krishnas does not become content based solely because its application is confined to airports—"the specific locations where [that] discourse occurs." A statute making it a misdemeanor to sit at a lunch counter for an hour without ordering any food would also not be "content based" even if it were enacted by a racist legislature that hated civil rights protesters (although it might raise separate questions about the State's legitimate interest at issue).

Similarly, the contention that a statute is "viewpoint based" simply because its enactment was motivated by the conduct of the partisans on one side of a debate is without support. The antipicketing ordinance upheld in *Frisby v. Schultz*, 487 U.S. 474 (1988), a decision in which both of today's dissenters joined, was obviously enacted in response to the activities of antiabortion protesters who wanted to protest at the home of a particular doctor to persuade him and others that they viewed his practice of performing abortions to be murder. We nonetheless summarily concluded that the statute was content neutral.

Justice Kennedy further suggests that a speaker who approaches a patient and "chants in praise of the Supreme Court and its abortion decisions," or hands out a simple leaflet saying, " 'We are for abortion rights,' " would not be subject to the statute. But what reason is there to believe the statute would not apply to that individual? She would be engaged in "oral protest" and "education," just as the abortion opponent who expresses her view that the Supreme Court decisions were incorrect would be "protest[ing]" the decisions and "educat[ing]" the patient on the issue. The close approach of the latter, more hostile, demonstrator may be more likely to risk being perceived as a form of physical harassment; but the relevant First Amendment point is that the statute would prevent both speakers, unless welcome, from entering the 8-foot zone. The statute is not limited to those who oppose abortion. It applies to the demonstrator in Justice Kennedy's example. It applies to all "protest," to all "counseling," and to all demonstrators whether or not the demonstration concerns abortion, and whether they oppose or support the woman who has made an abortion decision. That is the level of neutrality that the Constitution demands.

The Colorado courts correctly concluded that § 18–9–122(3) is content neutral.

We also agree with the state courts' conclusion that § 18–9–122(3) is a valid time, place, and manner regulation under the test applied in *Ward* because it is "narrowly tailored." We already have noted that the statute serves governmental interests that are significant and legitimate and that the restrictions are content neutral. We are likewise persuaded that the statute is "narrowly tailored" to serve those interests and that it leaves open ample alternative channels for communication. As we have emphasized on more than one occasion, when a content-neutral regulation does not entirely foreclose any means of communication, it may satisfy the tailoring requirement even though it is not the least restrictive or least intrusive means of serving the statutory goal.

The three types of communication regulated by § 18–9–122(3) are the display of signs, leafletting, and oral speech. The 8-foot separation between the speaker and the audience should not have any adverse impact on the readers' ability to read signs displayed by demonstrators. In fact, the separation might actually aid the pedestrians' ability to see the signs by preventing others from surrounding them and impeding their view. Furthermore, the statute places no limitations on the number, size, text, or images of the placards. And, as with all of the restrictions, the 8-foot zone does not affect demonstrators with signs who remain in place.

With respect to oral statements, the distance certainly can make it more difficult for a speaker to be heard, particularly if the level of background noise is high and other speakers are competing for the pedestrian's attention. Notably, the statute places no limitation on the number of speakers or the noise level, including the use of amplification equipment, although we have upheld such restrictions in past cases. More significantly, this statute does not suffer from the failings that compelled us to reject the "floating buffer zone" in *Schenck*, 519 U.S., at 377. Unlike the 15-foot zone in *Schenck*, this 8-foot zone allows the speaker to communicate at a "normal conversational distance." Additionally, the statute allows the speaker to remain in one place, and other individuals can pass within eight feet of the protester without causing the protester to violate the statute. Finally, here there is a "knowing" requirement that protects speakers "who thought they were keeping pace with the targeted individual" at the proscribed distance from inadvertently violating the statute.

It is also not clear that the statute's restrictions will necessarily impede, rather than assist, the speakers' efforts to communicate their messages. The statute might encourage the most aggressive and vociferous protesters to moderate their confrontational and harassing conduct, and thereby make it easier for thoughtful and law-abiding sidewalk counselors like petitioners to make themselves heard. But whether or not the 8-foot interval is the best possible accommodation of the competing interests at stake, we must accord a measure of deference to the judgment of the Colorado Legislature. Once again, it is worth reiterating that only attempts to address unwilling listeners are affected.

The burden on the ability to distribute handbills is more serious because it seems possible that an 8-foot interval could hinder the ability of a leafletter to deliver handbills to some unwilling recipients. The statute does not, however, prevent a leafletter from simply standing near the path of oncoming pedestrians and proffering his or her material, which the pedestrians can easily accept. And, as in all leafletting situations, pedestrians continue to be free to decline the tender. . . . [T]he First Amendment protects the right of every citizen to " 'reach the minds of willing listeners and to do so there must be opportunity to win their attention.' " The Colorado statute adequately protects those rights.

Finally, in determining whether a statute is narrowly tailored, we have noted that "[w]e must, of course, take account of the place to which the regulations apply in determining whether these restrictions burden more speech than necessary." States and municipalities plainly have a substantial interest in controlling the activity around certain public and private places. For example, we have recognized the special governmental interests surrounding schools, courthouses, polling places, and private homes. Additionally, we previously have noted the unique concerns that surround health care facilities:

> " 'Hospitals, after all, are not factories or mines or assembly plants. They are hospitals, where human ailments are treated, where patients and relatives alike often are under emotional strain and worry, where pleasing and comforting patients are principal facets of the day's activity, and where the patient and [her] family . . . need a restful, uncluttered, relaxing, and helpful atmosphere.' "

Persons who are attempting to enter health care facilities—for any purpose—are often in particularly vulnerable physical and emotional conditions. The State of Colorado has responded to its substantial and legitimate interest in protecting these persons from unwanted encounters, confrontations, and even assaults by enacting an exceedingly modest restriction on the speakers' ability to approach.

Justice Kennedy, however, argues that the statute leaves petitioners without adequate means of communication. This is a considerable overstatement. The statute seeks to protect those who wish to enter health care facilities, many of whom may be under special physical or emotional stress, from close physical approaches by demonstrators. In doing so, the statute takes a prophylactic approach; it forbids all unwelcome demonstrators to come closer than eight feet. We recognize that by doing so, it will sometimes inhibit a demonstrator whose approach in fact would have proved harmless. But the statute's prophylactic aspect is justified by the great difficulty of protecting, say, a pregnant woman from physical harassment with legal rules that focus exclusively on the individual impact of each instance of behavior, demanding in each case an accurate characterization (as harassing or not harassing) of each individual movement within the 8-foot boundary. Such individualized characterization of each individual movement is often difficult to make accurately. A bright-line prophylactic rule may be the best way to provide protection, and, at the same time, by offering clear guidance and avoiding subjectivity, to protect speech itself.

As we explained above, the 8-foot restriction on an unwanted physical approach leaves ample room to communicate a message through speech. Signs, pictures, and voice itself can cross an 8-foot gap with ease. If the clinics in Colorado resemble those in *Schenck*, demonstrators with leaflets might easily stand on the sidewalk at entrances (without blocking the entrance) and, without physically approaching those who are entering the clinic, peacefully hand them leaflets as they pass by.

Finally, the 8-foot restriction occurs only within 100 feet of a health care facility—the place where the restriction is most needed. . . .

This restriction is thus reasonable and narrowly tailored.

Petitioners argue that § 18–9–122(3) is invalid because it is "overbroad." There are two parts to petitioners' "overbreadth" argument. On the one hand, they argue that the statute is too broad because it protects too many people in too many places, rather than just the patients at the facilities where confrontational speech had occurred. Similarly, it burdens all speakers, rather than just persons with a history of bad conduct. On the other hand, petitioners also contend that the statute is overbroad because it "bans virtually the universe of protected expression, including displays of signs, distribution of literature, and mere verbal statements."

The first part of the argument does not identify a constitutional defect. The fact that the coverage of a statute is broader than the specific concern that led to its enactment is of no constitutional significance. What is important is that all persons entering or leaving health care facilities share the interests served by the statute. It is precisely because the Colorado Legislature made a general policy choice that the statute is assessed under the constitutional standard set forth in *Ward*, 491 U.S., at 791, rather than a more strict standard. The cases cited by petitioners are distinguishable from this statute. In those cases, the government attempted to regulate nonprotected activity, yet because the statute was overbroad, protected speech was also implicated. In this case, it is not disputed that the regulation affects protected speech activity; the question is thus whether it is a "reasonable restrictio[n] on the time, place, or manner of protected speech." Here, the comprehensiveness of the statute is a virtue, not a vice, because it is evidence against there being a discriminatory governmental motive. . . .

The second part of the argument is based on a misreading of the statute and an incorrect understanding of the overbreadth doctrine. As we have already noted, § 18–9–122(3) simply does not "ban" any messages, and likewise it does not "ban" any signs, literature, or oral statements. It merely regulates the places where communications may occur ... [T]he overbreadth doctrine enables litigants "to challenge a statute not because their own rights of free expression are violated, but because of a judicial prediction or assumption that the statute's very existence may cause others not before the court to refrain from constitutionally protected speech or expression." Moreover, "particularly where conduct and not merely speech is involved, we believe that the overbreadth of a statute must not only be real, but substantial as well, judged in relation to the statute's plainly legitimate sweep." Petitioners have not persuaded us that the impact of the statute on the conduct of other speakers will differ from its impact on their own sidewalk counseling. Like petitioners' own activities, the conduct of other protesters and counselors at all health care facilities are encompassed within the statute's "legitimate sweep." Therefore, the statute is not overly broad.

Petitioners also claim that § 18–9–122(3) is unconstitutionally vague. They find a lack of clarity in three parts of the section: the meaning of "protest, education, or counseling"; the "consent" requirement; and the determination whether one is "approaching" within eight feet of another.

A statute can be impermissibly vague for either of two independent reasons. First, if it fails to provide people of ordinary intelligence a reasonable opportunity to understand what conduct it prohibits. Second, if it authorizes or even encourages arbitrary and discriminatory enforcement.

In this case, the first concern is ameliorated by the fact that § 18–9–122(3) contains a scienter requirement. The statute only applies to a person who "knowingly" approaches within eight feet of another, without that person's consent, for the purpose of engaging in oral protest, education, or counseling. The likelihood that anyone would not understand any of those common words seems quite remote.

Petitioners proffer hypertechnical theories as to what the statute covers, such as whether an outstretched arm constitutes "approaching." And while "[t]here is little doubt that imagination can conjure up hypothetical cases in which the meaning of these terms will be in nice question," because we are "[c]ondemned to the use of words, we can never expect mathematical certainty from our language." ... We thus conclude that "it is clear what the ordinance as a whole prohibits." More importantly, speculation about possible vagueness in hypothetical situations not before the Court will not support a facial attack on a statute when it is surely valid "in the vast majority of its intended applications."

For the same reason, we are similarly unpersuaded by the suggestion that § 18–9–122(3) fails to give adequate guidance to law enforcement authorities. Indeed, it seems to us that one of the section's virtues is the specificity of the definitions of the zones described in the statute. "As always, enforcement requires the exercise of some degree of police judgment," and the degree of judgment involved here is acceptable.

Finally, petitioners argue that § 18–9–122(3)'s consent requirement is invalid because it imposes an unconstitutional "prior restraint" on speech . . . Under this statute, absolutely no channel of communication is foreclosed. No speaker is silenced. And no message is prohibited. Petitioners are simply wrong when they assert that "[t]he statute compels speakers to obtain consent to speak and it authorizes private citizens to deny petitioners' requests to engage in expressive activities." To the contrary, this statute does not provide for a "heckler's veto" but rather allows every speaker to engage freely in any expressive activity communicating all messages and viewpoints subject only to the narrow place requirement imbedded within the "approach" restriction.

Furthermore, our concerns about "prior restraints" relate to restrictions imposed by official censorship. The regulations in this case, however, only apply if the pedestrian does not consent to the approach. Private citizens have always retained the power to decide for themselves what they wish to read, and within limits, what oral messages they want to consider. This statute simply empowers private citizens entering a health care facility with the ability to prevent a speaker, who is within eight feet and advancing, from communicating a message they do not wish to hear. Further, the statute does not authorize the pedestrian to affect any other activity at any other location or relating to any other person. These restrictions thus do not constitute an unlawful prior restraint.

The judgment of the Colorado Supreme Court is affirmed.

It is so ordered.

. . . .

■ SCALIA, J., with whom THOMAS, J., joins, dissenting.

. . . .

Colorado's statute makes it a criminal act knowingly to approach within 8 feet of another person on the public way or sidewalk area within 100 feet of the entrance door of a health care facility for the purpose of passing a leaflet to, displaying a sign to, or engaging in oral protest, education, or counseling with such person. Whatever may be said about the restrictions on the other types of expressive activity, the regulation as it applies to oral communications is obviously and undeniably content based. A speaker wishing to approach another for the purpose of communicating *any* message except one of protest, education, or counseling may do so without first securing the other's consent. Whether a speaker must obtain permission before approaching within eight feet—

and whether he will be sent to prison for failing to do so—depends entirely on *what he intends to say* when he gets there. I have no doubt that this regulation would be deemed content based *in an instant* if the case before us involved antiwar protesters, or union members seeking to "educate" the public about the reasons for their strike. "[I]t is," we would say, "the content of the speech that determines whether it is within or without the statute's blunt prohibition." But the jurisprudence of this Court has a way of changing when abortion is involved.

The Court asserts that this statute is not content based for purposes of our First Amendment analysis because it neither (1) discriminates among viewpoints nor (2) places restrictions on "any subject matter that may be discussed by a speaker." But we have never held that the universe of content-based regulations is limited to those two categories, and such a holding would be absurd . . .

"The vice of content-based legislation—what renders it deserving of the high standard of strict scrutiny—is not that it is always used for invidious, thought-control purposes, but that it lends itself to use for those purposes." A restriction that operates only on speech that communicates a message of protest, education, or counseling presents exactly this risk. When applied, as it is here, at the entrance to medical facilities, it is a means of impeding speech against abortion. . . .

. . . .

[T]he Court is not correct in its assertion that the restriction here is content neutral because it is "*justified* without reference to the content of regulated speech," in the sense that "the State's interests in protecting access and privacy, and providing the police with clear guidelines, are unrelated to the content of the demonstrators' speech." That is not an accurate statement of our law. The Court makes too much of the statement in *Ward v. Rock Against Racism*, 491 U.S. 781 (1989), that "[t]he principal inquiry in determining content neutrality . . . is whether the government has adopted a regulation of speech because of disagreement with the message it conveys." That is indeed "the *principal* inquiry"—suppression of uncongenial ideas is the worst offense against the First Amendment—but it is not the *only* inquiry. Even a law that has as its purpose something unrelated to the suppression of particular content cannot irrationally single out that content for its prohibition. An ordinance directed at the suppression of noise (and therefore "justified without reference to the content of regulated speech") cannot be applied only to sound trucks delivering messages of "protest." . . .

But in any event, if one accepts the Court's description of the interest served by this regulation, it is clear that the regulation is *both* based on content *and* justified by reference to content. Constitutionally proscribable "secondary effects" of speech are directly addressed in subsection (2) of the statute, which makes it unlawful to obstruct, hinder, impede, or block access to a health care facility—a prohibition broad enough to include all physical threats and all physically threatening approaches. The purpose of subsection (3), however (according to the Court), is to protect "[t]he unwilling listener's interest in avoiding unwanted communication," *ante*, at 2489. On this analysis, Colorado has restricted certain categories of speech—protest, counseling, and education—out of an apparent belief that only speech with this content is sufficiently likely to be annoying or upsetting as to require consent before it may be engaged in at close range. It is reasonable enough to conclude that even the most gentle and peaceful close approach by a so-called "sidewalk counselor"—who wishes to "educate" the woman entering an abortion clinic about the nature of the procedure, to "counsel" against it and in favor of other alternatives, and perhaps even (though less likely if the approach is to be successful) to "protest" her taking of a human life—will often, indeed usually, have what might be termed the "secondary effect" of annoying or deeply upsetting the woman who is planning the abortion. *But that is not an effect which occurs "without reference to the content" of the speech.* This singling out of presumptively "unwelcome" communications fits precisely the description of prohibited regulation set forth in *Boos v. Barry*, 485 U.S. 312, 321 (1988): It "targets the *direct impact* of a particular category of speech, not a secondary feature that happens to be associated with that type of speech." (Emphasis added.)

In sum, it blinks reality to regard this statute, in its application to oral communications, as anything other than a content-based restriction upon speech in the public forum. As such, it must survive that stringent mode of constitutional analysis our cases refer to as "strict scrutiny," which requires that the restriction be narrowly tailored to serve a compelling state interest. Since the Court does not even attempt to support the regulation under this standard, I shall discuss it only briefly. Suffice it to say that if protecting people from unwelcome communications (the governmental interest the Court posits) is a compelling state interest, the First Amendment is a dead letter. And if (as I shall discuss at greater length below) forbidding peaceful, nonthreatening, but uninvited speech from a distance closer than eight feet is a "narrowly tailored" means of preventing the obstruction of entrance to medical facilities (the governmental interest the State asserts), narrow tailoring must refer not to the standards of Versace, but to those of Omar the tentmaker. In the last analysis all of this does not matter, however, since as I proceed to discuss neither the restrictions upon oral communications nor those upon handbilling can withstand a proper application of even the less demanding scrutiny we apply to truly content-neutral regulations of speech in a traditional public forum.

As the Court explains, under our precedents even a content-neutral, time, place, and manner restriction must be narrowly tailored to advance a significant state interest, and must leave open ample alternative means of communication. It cannot be sustained if it "burden[s] substantially more speech than is necessary to further the government's legitimate interests."

This requires us to determine, first, what *is* the significant interest the State seeks to advance? Here there appears to be a bit of a disagreement between the State of Colorado (which should know) and the Court (which is eager to speculate). Colorado has identified in the text of the statute itself the interest it sought to advance: to ensure that the State's citizens may "obtain medical counseling and treatment in an unobstructed manner" by "preventing the willful obstruction of a person's access to medical counseling and treatment at a health care facility." In its brief here, the State repeatedly confirms the interest squarely identified in the statute under review. *See, e.g.*, Brief for Respondents 15 ("Each provision of the statute was chosen to precisely address crowding and physical intimidation: conduct shown to impede access, endanger safety and health, and strangle effective law enforcement"); *id.*, at 14 ("[T]his provision narrowly addresses the conduct shown to interfere with access through crowding and physical threats"). The Court nevertheless concludes that the Colorado provision is narrowly tailored to serve . . . the State's interest in protecting its citizens' rights to be let alone from unwanted speech.

. . . .

To support the legitimacy of its self-invented state interest, the Court relies upon a *bon mot* in a 1928 dissent (which we evidently overlooked in *Schenck*). It characterizes the "unwilling listener's interest in avoiding unwanted communication" as an "aspect of the broader 'right to be let alone'" Justice Brandeis coined in his dissent in *Olmstead v. United States*, 277 U.S. 438, 478. The amusing feature is that even this slim reed contradicts rather than supports the Court's position. The right to be let alone that Justice Brandeis identified was a right the Constitution "conferred, *as against the government*"; it was *that* right, not some generalized "common-law right" or "interest" to be free from hearing the unwanted opinions of one's fellow citizens, which he called the "most comprehensive" and "most valued by civilized men." *Id.* (emphasis added). To the extent that there can be gleaned from our cases a "right to be let alone" in the sense that Justice Brandeis intended, it is the right of the *speaker* in the public forum to be free from government interference of the sort Colorado has imposed here.

In any event, the Court's attempt to disguise the "right to be let alone" as a "governmental interest in protecting the right to be let alone" is unavailing for the simple reason that this is not an interest that may be legitimately weighed against the speakers' First Amendment rights. . . . We have consistently held that "the Constitution does not *permit* government to decide which types of otherwise protected speech are sufficiently offensive to require protection *for the unwilling listener or viewer*." *Erznoznik v. Jacksonville*, 422 U.S. 205, 210 (1975) (emphasis added). And as recently as in *Schenck*, the Court reiterated that "[a]s a general matter, we have indicated that in public debate our own citizens must tolerate insulting, and even outrageous, speech in order to provide adequate breathing space to the freedoms protected by the First Amendment."

The Court nonetheless purports to derive from our cases a principle limiting the protection the Constitution affords the speaker's right to direct "offensive messages" at "unwilling" audiences in the public forum. There is no such principle. We have upheld limitations on a speaker's exercise of his right to speak on the public streets *when that speech intrudes into the privacy of the home. Frisby*, 487 U.S., at 483, upheld a content-neutral municipal ordinance prohibiting picketing outside a residence or dwelling. The ordinance, we concluded, was justified by, and narrowly tailored to advance, the government's interest in the "protection of residential privacy." *Id.*, at 484. Our opinion rested upon the "unique nature of the home"; "the home," we said, "is different." *Ibid.* The reasoning of the case plainly assumed the *nonexistence* of the right— common law or otherwise—that the Court relies on today, the right to be free from unwanted speech when on the public streets and sidewalks. The home, we noted, was " 'the one retreat to which men and women can repair to escape from the tribulations of their daily pursuits.' " . . . The Court today elevates the abortion clinic to the status of the home.

. . . .

. . . Preserving the "right to be free" from "persisten[t] importunity, following and dogging" does not remotely require imposing upon all speakers who wish to protest, educate, or counsel a duty to request permission to approach closer than eight feet. The only way the narrow-tailoring objection can be eliminated is to posit a state-created, First-Amendment-trumping "right to be let alone" as broad and undefined as Brandeis's *Olmstead* dictum, which may well (why not, if the Court wishes it?) embrace a right not to be spoken to without permission from a distance closer than eight feet. Nothing stands in the way of *that* solution to the narrow-tailoring problem—except, of course, its utter absurdity, which is no obstacle in abortion cases.

I turn now to the real state interest at issue here—the one set forth in the statute and asserted in Colorado's brief: the preservation of unimpeded access to health care facilities. We need look no further than subsection (2) of the statute to see what a provision would look like that is narrowly tailored to serve *that* interest. Under the terms of that subsection, any person who "knowingly obstructs, detains, hinders, impedes, or blocks another person's entry to or exit from a health care facility" is subject to criminal and civil liability. It is possible, I suppose, that subsection (2) of the Colorado statute will leave unrestricted some expressive activity that, if engaged in from within eight feet, may be sufficiently harassing as to have the effect of impeding access to health care facilities. In subsection (3), however, the State of Colorado has prohibited a vast amount of speech that cannot possibly be thought to correspond to that evil.

To begin with, the 8-foot buffer zone attaches to *every* person on the public way or sidewalk within 100 feet of the entrance of a medical facility, regardless of whether that person is seeking to enter or exit the facility. . . . And even with respect to those who *are* seeking to enter or exit the facilities, the statute does not protect them only from speech that is so intimidating or threatening as to impede access. Rather, it covers *all* unconsented-to approaches for the purpose of oral protest, education, or counseling (including those made for the purpose of the most peaceful appeals) and, perhaps even more significantly, *every* approach made for the purposes of leafletting or handbilling, which we have never considered, standing alone, obstructive or unduly intrusive. The sweep of this prohibition is breathtaking.

. . . I scarcely know how to respond to such an unabashed repudiation of our First Amendment doctrine. Prophylaxis is the antithesis of narrow tailoring. . . . If the Court were going to make this concession, it could simply have dispensed with its earlier (unpersuasive) attempt to show that the statute *was* narrowly tailored. So one can add to the casualties of our whatever-it-takes proabortion jurisprudence the First Amendment doctrine of narrow tailoring and overbreadth. R.I.P.

Before it effectively threw in the towel on the narrow-tailoring point, the Court asserted the importance of taking into account " 'the place to which the regulations apply in determining whether these restrictions burden more speech than necessary.' " A proper regard for the "place" involved in this case should result in, if anything, a commitment by this Court to adhere to and rigorously enforce our speech-protective standards. The public forum involved here—the public spaces outside of health care facilities—has become, by necessity and by virtue of this Court's decisions, a forum of last resort for those who oppose abortion. The possibility of limiting abortion by legislative means—even abortion of a live-and-kicking child that is almost entirely out of the womb—has been rendered impossible by our decisions. . . . For those who share an abiding moral or religious conviction (or, for that matter, simply a biological appreciation) that abortion is the taking of a human life, there is no option but to persuade women, one by one, not to make that choice. And as a general matter, the most effective place, if not the only place, where that persuasion can occur is outside the entrances to abortion facilities. By upholding these restrictions on speech in this place the Court ratifies the State's attempt to make even that task an impossible one.

Those whose concern is for the physical safety and security of clinic patients, workers, and doctors should take no comfort from today's decision. Individuals or groups intent on bullying or frightening women out of an abortion, or doctors out of performing that procedure, will not be deterred by Colorado's statute; bullhorns and screaming from eight feet away will serve their purposes well. But those who would accomplish their moral and religious objectives by peaceful and civil means, by trying to persuade individual women of the rightness of their cause, will be deterred; and that is not a good thing in a democracy. This Court once recognized, as the Framers surely did, that the freedom to speak and persuade is inseparable from, and antecedent to, the survival of self-government. The Court today rotates that essential safety valve on our democracy one-half turn to the right, and no one who seeks safe access to health care facilities in Colorado or elsewhere should feel that her security has by this decision been enhanced.

. . . As I have suggested throughout this opinion, today's decision is not an isolated distortion of our traditional constitutional principles, but is one of many aggressively proabortion novelties announced by the Court in recent years. Today's distortions, however, are particularly blatant. Restrictive views of the First Amendment that have been in dissent since the 1930's suddenly find themselves in the majority. "Uninhibited, robust, and wide open" debate is replaced by the power of the State to protect an unheard-of "right to be let alone" on the public streets. I dissent.

■ KENNEDY, J., dissenting.

The Court's holding contradicts more than a half century of well-established First Amendment principles. For the first time, the Court approves a law which bars a private citizen from passing a message, in a peaceful manner and on a profound moral issue, to a fellow citizen on a public sidewalk. If from this time forward the Court repeats its grave errors of analysis, we shall have no longer the proud tradition of free and open discourse in a public forum. . . .

. . . .

. . . The law imposes content-based restrictions on speech by reason of the terms it uses, the categories it employs, and the conditions for its enforcement. It is content based, too, by its predictable and intended operation. Whether particular messages violate the statute is determined by their substance. The law is a prime example of a statute inviting screening and censoring of individual speech; and it is serious error to hold otherwise.

The Court errs in asserting the Colorado statute is no different from laws sustained as content neutral in earlier cases. . . . Under the Colorado enactment, however, the State must review content to determine whether a person has engaged in criminal "protest, education, or counseling." When a citizen approaches another on the sidewalk in a disfavored-speech zone, an officer of the State must listen to what the speaker says. If, in the officer's judgment, the speaker's words stray too far toward "protest, education, or counseling"—the boundaries of which are far from clear—the officer may decide the speech has moved from the permissible to the criminal. The First Amendment does not give the government such power.

The statute is content based for an additional reason: It restricts speech on particular topics. Of course, the enactment restricts "oral protest, education, or counseling" on any subject; but a statute of broad application is not content neutral if its terms control the substance of a speaker's message. If oral protest, education, or counseling on every subject within an 8-foot zone present a danger to the public, the statute should apply to every building entrance in the State. It does not. It applies only to a special class of locations: entrances to buildings with health care facilities. We would close our eyes to reality were we to deny that "oral protest, education, or counseling" outside the entrances to medical facilities concern a narrow range of topics—indeed, one topic in particular. By confining the law's application to the specific locations where the prohibited discourse occurs, the State has made a content-based determination. The Court ought to so acknowledge. Clever content-based restrictions are no less offensive than censoring on the basis of content. . . .

. . . The purpose and design of the statute—as everyone ought to know and as its own defenders urge in attempted justification—are to restrict speakers on one side of the debate: those who protest abortions. The statute applies only to medical facilities, a convenient yet obvious mask for the legislature's true purpose and for the prohibition's true effect. One need read no further than the statute's preamble to remove any doubt about the question. The Colorado Legislature sought to restrict "a person's right to protest or counsel against certain medical procedures." Colo. Rev. Stat. § 18–9–122(1) (1999). The word "against" reveals the legislature's desire to restrict discourse on one side of the issue regarding "certain medical procedures." The testimony to the Colorado Legislature consisted, almost in its entirety, of debates and controversies with respect to abortion. . . . The legislature's purpose to restrict unpopular speech should be beyond dispute.

The statute's operation reflects its objective. Under the most reasonable interpretation of Colorado's law, if a speaker approaches a fellow citizen within any one of Colorado's thousands of disfavored-speech zones and chants in praise of the Supreme Court and its abortion decisions, I should think there is neither protest, nor education, nor counseling. If the opposite message is communicated, however, a prosecution to punish protest is warranted. The antispeech distinction also pertains if a citizen approaches a public official visiting a health care facility to make a point in favor of abortion rights. If she says, "Good job, Governor," there is no violation; if she says, "Shame on you, Governor," there is. Furthermore, if the speaker addresses a woman who is considering an abortion and says, "Please take just a moment to read these brochures and call our support line to talk with women who have been in your situation," the speaker would face criminal penalties for counseling. Yet if the speaker simply says, "We are for abortion rights," I should think this is neither education nor counseling. Thus does the Court today ensure its own decisions can be praised but not condemned. Thus does it restrict speech designed to teach that the exercise of a constitutional right is not necessarily concomitant with making a sound moral choice. Nothing in our law or our enviable free speech tradition sustains this self-serving rule. Colorado is now allowed to punish speech because of its content and viewpoint.

. . . .

The Colorado statute offends settled First Amendment principles in another fundamental respect. It violates the constitutional prohibitions against vague or overly broad criminal statutes regulating speech. The enactment's fatal ambiguities are multiple and interact to create further imprecisions. The result is a law more vague and overly broad than any criminal statute the Court has sustained as a permissible regulation of speech. The statute's imprecisions are so evident that this, too, ought to have ended the case without further discussion.

The law makes it a criminal offense to "knowingly approach another person within eight feet of such person, unless such other person consents, for the purpose of passing a leaflet or handbill to, displaying a sign to, or engaging in oral protest, education, or counseling with such other person in the public way or sidewalk area within a radius of one hundred feet from any entrance door to a health care facility." Colo. Rev. Stat. § 18–9–122(3) (1999). The operative terms and phrases of the statute are not defined. The case comes to us from the state court system; and as the Colorado courts did not give the statute a sufficient narrowing construction, questions of vagueness and overbreadth should be addressed by this Court in the first instance.

In the context of a law imposing criminal penalties for pure speech, "protest" is an imprecise word; "counseling" is an imprecise word; "education" is an imprecise word. No custom, tradition, or legal authority gives these terms the specificity required to sustain a criminal prohibition on speech. I simply disagree with the majority's estimation that it is "quite remote" that "anyone would not understand any of those common words." The criminal statute is subject to manipulation by police, prosecutors, and juries. Its substantial imprecisions will chill speech, so the statute violates the First Amendment.

In operation the statute's inevitable arbitrary effects create vagueness problems of their own. The 8-foot no-approach zone is so unworkable it will chill speech. Assume persons are about to enter a building from different points and a protester is walking back and forth with a sign or attempting to hand out leaflets. If she stops to create the 8-foot zone for one pedestrian, she cannot reach other persons with her message; yet if she moves to maintain the 8-foot zone while trying to talk to one patron she may move knowingly closer to a patron attempting to enter the facility from a different direction. In addition, the statute requires a citizen to give affirmative consent before the exhibitor of a sign or the bearer of a leaflet can approach. When dealing with strangers walking fast toward a building's entrance, there is a middle ground of ambiguous answers and mixed signals in which misinterpretation can subject a good-faith speaker to criminal liability. The mere failure to give a reaction, for instance, is a failure to give consent. These elements of ambiguity compound the others. Finally, as we all know, the identity or enterprise of the occupants of a building which fronts on a public street is not always known to the public. Health care providers may occupy but a single office in a large building. The Colorado citizen may walk from a disfavored-speech zone to a free zone with little or no ability to discern when one ends and the other begins. The statute's vagueness thus becomes as well one source of its overbreadth. The only sure way to avoid violating the law is to refrain from picketing, leafletting, or oral advocacy altogether. Scienter cannot save so vague a statute as this.

A statute is vague when the conduct it forbids is not ascertainable. . . . The terms "oral protest, education, or counseling" are at least as imprecise as criminal prohibitions on speech the Court has declared void for vagueness in past decades. . . .

. . . .

Rather than adhere to this rule, the Court turns it on its head, stating the statute's overbreadth is "a virtue, not a vice." The Court goes even further, praising the statute's "prophylactic approach; it forbids all unwelcome demonstrators to come closer than eight feet." Indeed, in the Court's view, "bright-line prophylactic rule[s] may be the best way to provide protection" to those individuals unwilling to hear a fellow citizen's message in a public forum. The Court is quite wrong. Overbreadth is a constitutional flaw, not a saving feature. Sweeping within its ambit even more protected speech does not save a criminal statute invalid in its essential reach and design. The Court, moreover, cannot meet the concern that the statute is vague; for neither the Colorado courts nor established legal principles offer satisfactory guidance in interpreting the statute's imprecisions.

Even aside from the erroneous, most disturbing assumptions that the statute is content neutral, viewpoint neutral, and neither vague nor overbroad, the Court falls into further serious error when it turns to the time, place, and manner rules set forth in *Ward*.

An essential requirement under *Ward* is that the regulation in question not "burden substantially more speech than is necessary to further the government's legitimate interests." As we have seen, however, Colorado and the Court attempt to justify the law on just the opposite assumption.

. . . .

The whimsical, arbitrary nature of the statute's operation is further demonstration of a restriction upon more speech than necessary. The happenstance of a dental office being located in a building brings the restricted-speech zone into play. If the same building also houses an organization dedicated, say, to environmental issues, a protest against the group's policies would be barred. Yet if, on the next block there were a public interest enterprise in a building with no health care facility, the speech would be unrestricted. The statute is a classic example of a proscription not narrowly tailored and resulting in restrictions of far more speech than necessary to achieve the legislature's object. The first time, place, and manner requirement of *Ward* cannot be satisfied.

. . . .

The majority insists the statute aims to protect distraught women who are embarrassed, vexed, or harassed as they attempt to enter abortion clinics. If these are punishable acts, they should be prohibited in those terms. In the course of praising Colorado's approach, the majority does not pause to tell us why, in its view, substantially less restrictive means cannot be employed to ensure citizens access to health care facilities or to prevent physical contact between citizens. The Court's approach is at odds with the rigor demanded by *Ward*.

. . . .

The statute fails a further test under *Ward*, for it does not " 'leave open ample alternative channels for communication of the information.' "

. . . .

In addition to leaving petitioners without adequate means of communication, the law forecloses peaceful leafletting, a mode of speech with deep roots in our Nation's history and traditions. In an age when vast resources and talents are commanded by a sophisticated media to shape opinions on limitless subjects and ideas, the distribution of leaflets on a sidewalk may seem a bit antiquated. This case proves the necessity for the traditional mode of speech. It must be remembered that the whole course of our free speech jurisprudence, sustaining the idea of open public discourse which is the hallmark of the American constitutional system, rests to a significant extent on cases involving picketing and leafletting. Our foundational First Amendment cases are based on the recognition that citizens, subject to rare exceptions, must be able to discuss issues, great or small, through the means of expression they deem best suited to their purpose. It is for the speaker, not the government, to choose the best means of expressing a message. . . .

. . . .

In *Planned Parenthood of Southeastern Pa. v. Casey*, the Court reaffirmed its prior holding that the Constitution protects a woman's right to terminate her pregnancy in its early stages. The majority opinion in *Casey* considered the woman's liberty interest and principles of *stare decisis*, but took care to recognize the gravity of the personal decision: "[Abortion] is an act fraught with consequences for others: for the woman who must live with the implications of her decision; for the persons who perform and assist in the procedure; for the spouse, family, and society which must confront the knowledge that these procedures exist, procedures some deem nothing short of an act of violence against innocent human life; and, depending on one's beliefs, for the life or potential life that is aborted."

The Court now strikes at the heart of the reasoned, careful balance I had believed was the basis for the opinion in *Casey*. The vital principle of the opinion was that in defined instances the woman's decision whether to abort her child was in its essence a moral one, a choice the State could not dictate. Foreclosed from using the machinery of government to ban abortions in early term, those who oppose it are remitted to debate the issue in its moral dimensions. In a cruel way, the Court today turns its back on that balance. It in effect tells us the moral debate is not so important after all and can be conducted just as well through a bullhorn from an 8-foot distance as it can through a peaceful, face-to-face exchange of a leaflet. The lack of care with which the Court sustains the Colorado statute reflects a most troubling abdication of our responsibility to enforce the First Amendment.

There runs through our First Amendment theory a concept of immediacy, the idea that thoughts and pleas and petitions must not be lost with the passage of time. In a fleeting existence we have but little time to find truth through discourse. No better illustration of the immediacy of speech, of the urgency of persuasion, of the preciousness of time, is presented than in this case. Here the citizens who claim First Amendment protection seek it for speech which, if it is to be effective, must take place at the very time and place a grievous moral wrong, in their view, is about to occur. The Court tears away from the protesters the guarantees of the First Amendment when they most need it. So committed is the Court to its course that it denies these protesters, in the face of what they consider to be one of life's gravest moral crises, even the opportunity to try to offer a fellow citizen a little pamphlet, a handheld paper seeking to reach a higher law.

. . . .

NOTES

1. *Abortion protests in jurisprudential context.* Critically, *Hill v. Colorado* was not the Court's first foray into the vexed collision of First Amendment and abortion rights. In *Madsen v. Women's Health Center, Inc.*, 512 U.S. 753 (1994), a health clinic that performed abortions sought to broaden a previously entered injunction against Operation Rescue anti-abortion protestors. According to the clinic, the existing injunction had been ineffective and the protestors' activities continued to impede access to the clinic, discouraging some potential patients from entering the clinic, and having deleterious physical effects on other prospective patients. A Florida court granted the request for an expanded injunction, and the protestors filed suit. Ultimately, the U.S. Supreme Court upheld the injunction in part and

invalidated it in part. The Court concluded that the fact that the injunction restricted only anti-abortion protestors' speech did not make it an impermissible content-based restriction. The Court went on to uphold those provisions of the content-neutral injunction establishing a thirty-six-foot buffer zone around clinic entrances and driveways and imposing limited noise restrictions. However, the Court invalidated the injunction's provision establishing a thirty-six-foot buffer zone on private property, banning observable images, establishing a 300-foot no-approach zone around the clinic, and establishing a 300-foot buffer zone around staff residences on the ground that these restrictions burdened more speech than necessary to serve the government's interests in public safety and noise control.

2.   *Abortion counseling in the public sphere.* One anti-abortion tactic that emerged in the 1980s and 1990s was "sidewalk counseling," whereby abortion opponents speak, or distribute leaflets, to women entering abortion facilities in the hope of deterring abortions. *See* Joe Scheidler & Ann Scheidler, *Controversy in the Activist Movement*, PROLIFE ACTION LEAGUE (Aug., 2002), https://prolifeaction.org/2002/2002v21n2controversy/. Initially, abortion-rights groups sought relief from the courts in the form of court-ordered injunctions imposing "buffer zones" separating anti-abortion counselors from clinic patients and staff. In 1997's *Schenck v. Pro-Choice Network of Western New York*, 519 U.S. 357 (1997), the Court considered the constitutionality of a court-imposed injunction restricting anti-abortion sidewalk counselors from approaching abortion-clinic patients and others with Bibles, tracts, and pro-life messages. In an 8–1 decision, the Court invalidated the provisions of the injunction creating "floating buffer zones" to prevent protesters approaching people entering or leaving abortion clinics. According to the Court, the indefinite and movable nature of the floating buffer zones made them difficult to administer and risked overly restricting free speech. By contrast, the Court upheld the provisions of the injunction creating "fixed buffer zones" around the clinics. As Professor Serena Mayeri observes, both sides framed *Schenck* as a civil rights case. Serena Mayeri, *Civil Rights on Both Sides: Reproductive Rights and Free Speech in* Schenck v. Pro-Choice Network of Western New York, *in* CIVIL RIGHTS STORIES 293, 318 (Myriam E. Gilles & Risa L. Goluboff eds., 2008). For women's rights advocates, the injunction was necessary to preserve for women the fundamental right to an abortion. For anti-abortion activists, the injunctions impermissibly infringed upon their First Amendment rights to counsel young women about the risks and dangers—moral, emotional, and physical—of abortion. Regardless of the framing, *Schenck*'s legacy is perhaps best reflected in state and local legislation, like the kind seen in *Hill*, establishing buffer zones in the vicinity of abortion clinics.

McCullen v. Coakley

573 U.S. 464 (2014).

■ ROBERTS, C.J.

A Massachusetts statute makes it a crime to knowingly stand on a "public way or sidewalk" within 35 feet of an entrance or driveway to any place, other than a hospital, where abortions are performed. Mass. Gen. Laws, ch. 266, §§ 120E½(a), (b) (West 2012). Petitioners are individuals who approach and talk to women outside such facilities, attempting to dissuade them from having abortions. The statute prevents petitioners from doing so near the facilities' entrances. The question presented is whether the statute violates the First Amendment.

A

. . . .

. . . The [challenged] statute . . . provides:

"No person shall knowingly enter or remain on a public way or sidewalk adjacent to a reproductive health care facility within a radius of 35 feet of any portion of an entrance, exit or driveway of a reproductive health care facility or within the area within a rectangle created by extending the outside boundaries of any entrance, exit or driveway of a reproductive health care facility in straight lines to the point where such lines intersect the sideline of the street in front of such entrance, exit or driveway." Mass. Gen. Laws, ch. 266, § 120E½(b) (West 2012). . . .

The 35-foot buffer zone applies only "during a facility's business hours," and the area must be "clearly marked and posted." § 120E½(c). In practice, facilities typically mark the zones with painted arcs and posted signs on adjacent sidewalks and streets. . . .

The Act exempts four classes of individuals: (1) "persons entering or leaving such facility"; (2) "employees or agents of such facility acting within the scope of their employment"; (3) "law enforcement, ambulance, firefighting, construction, utilities, public works and other municipal agents acting within the scope of their employment"; and (4) "persons using the public sidewalk or street right-of-way adjacent to such facility solely for the purpose of reaching a destination other than such facility." § 120E½(b)(1)–(4). . . .

B

Some of the individuals who stand outside Massachusetts abortion clinics are fairly described as protestors, who express their moral or religious opposition to abortion through signs and chants or, in some cases, more aggressive methods such as face-to-face confrontation. Petitioners take a different tack. They attempt to engage women approaching the clinics in what they call "sidewalk counseling," which involves offering information about alternatives to abortion and help pursuing those options. . . . Such interactions, petitioners believe, are a much more effective means of dissuading women from having abortions than confrontational methods such as shouting or brandishing signs, which in petitioners' view tend only to antagonize their intended audience.

In unrefuted testimony, petitioners say they have collectively persuaded hundreds of women to forgo abortions.

. . . .

Petitioners . . . claim that the buffer zones have significantly hampered their counseling efforts. Although they have managed to conduct some counseling and to distribute some literature outside the buffer zones . . . they say they have had many fewer conversations and distributed many fewer leaflets since the zones went into effect. . . .

The . . . statutory exemption allows clinic employees and agents acting within the scope of their employment to enter the buffer zones. Relying on this exemption, [one] clinic uses "escorts" to greet women as they approach the clinic, accompanying them through the zones to the clinic entrance. Petitioners claim that the escorts sometimes thwart petitioners' attempts to communicate with patients by blocking petitioners from handing literature to patients, telling patients not to "pay any attention" or "listen to" petitioners, and disparaging petitioners as "crazy." . . .

C

In January 2008, petitioners sued Attorney General Coakley and other Commonwealth officials. They sought to enjoin enforcement of the Act, alleging that it violates the First and Fourteenth Amendments, both on its face and as applied to them. . . .

. . . .

II

By its very terms, the Massachusetts Act regulates access to "public way[s]" and "sidewalk[s]." . . . Such areas occupy a "special position in terms of First Amendment protection" because of their historic role as sites for discussion and debate. *United States v. Grace*, 461 U.S. 171, 180 (1983). These places—which we have labeled "traditional public fora"— " 'have immemorially been held in trust for the use of the public and, time out of mind, have been used for purposes of assembly, communicating thoughts between citizens, and discussing public questions.' " *Pleasant Grove City v. Summum*, 555 U.S. 460, 469 (2009) (quoting *Perry Ed. Assn. v. Perry Local Educators' Assn.*, 460 U.S. 37, 45 (1983)).

It is no accident that public streets and sidewalks have developed as venues for the exchange of ideas. Even today, they remain one of the few places where a speaker can be confident that he is not simply preaching to the choir. With respect to other means of communication, an individual confronted with an uncomfortable message can always turn the page, change the channel, or leave the Web site. Not so on public streets and sidewalks. There, a listener often encounters speech he might otherwise tune out. In light of the First Amendment's purpose "to preserve an uninhibited marketplace of ideas in which truth will ultimately prevail," *FCC v. League of Women Voters of Cal.*, 468 U.S. 364, 377 (1984) (internal quotation marks omitted), this aspect of traditional public fora is a virtue, not a vice.

. . . Thus, even though the Act says nothing about speech on its face, there is no doubt—and respondents do not dispute—that it restricts access to traditional public fora and is therefore subject to First Amendment scrutiny. . . .

Consistent with the traditionally open character of public streets and sidewalks, we have held that the government's ability to restrict speech in such locations is "very limited." . . . In particular, the guiding First Amendment principle that the "government has no power to restrict expression because of its message, its ideas, its subject matter, or its content" applies with full force in a traditional public forum. *Police Dept. of Chicago v. Mosley*, 408 U.S. 92, 95 (1972). As a general rule, in such a forum the government may not "selectively . . . shield the public from some kinds of speech on the ground that they are more offensive than others." *Erznoznik v. Jacksonville*, 422 U.S. 205, 209 (1975).

We have, however, afforded the government somewhat wider leeway to regulate features of speech unrelated to its content. "[E]ven in a public forum the government may impose reasonable restrictions on the time, place, or manner of protected speech, provided the restrictions 'are justified without reference to the content of the regulated speech, that they are narrowly tailored to serve a significant governmental interest, and that they leave open ample alternative channels for communication of the information.'" *Ward* [*v. Rock against Racism*] 491 U.S. [781], 791 (quoting *Clark v. Community for Creative Non-Violence*, 468 U.S. 288, 293 (1984)).[2]

. . . .

III

Petitioners contend that the Act is not content neutral for two independent reasons: First, they argue that it discriminates against abortion-related speech because it establishes buffer zones only at clinics that perform abortions. Second, petitioners contend that the Act, by exempting clinic employees and agents, favors one viewpoint about abortion over the other. If either of these arguments is correct, then the Act must satisfy strict scrutiny—that is, it must be the least restrictive means of achieving a compelling state interest. See *United States v. Playboy Entertainment Group, Inc.*, 529 U.S. 803, 813 (2000). . . .

A

The Act applies only at a "reproductive health care facility," defined as "a place, other than within or upon the grounds of a hospital, where abortions are offered or performed." Mass. Gen. Laws, ch. 266,

---

[2] A different analysis would of course be required if the government property at issue were not a traditional public forum but instead "a forum that is limited to use by certain groups or dedicated solely to the discussion of certain subjects." *Pleasant Grove City v. Summum*, 555 U.S. 460, 470 (2009).

§ 120E½(a). Given this definition, petitioners argue, "virtually all speech affected by the Act is speech concerning abortion," thus rendering the Act content based. . . .

We disagree. To begin, the Act does not draw content-based distinctions on its face. . . . The Act would be content based if it required "enforcement authorities" to "examine the content of the message that is conveyed to determine whether" a violation has occurred. . . . But it does not. Whether petitioners violate the Act "depends" not "on what they say," . . . but simply on where they say it. Indeed, petitioners can violate the Act merely by standing in a buffer zone, without displaying a sign or uttering a word.

It is true, of course, that by limiting the buffer zones to abortion clinics, the Act has the "inevitable effect" of restricting abortion-related speech more than speech on other subjects. . . . But a facially neutral law does not become content based simply because it may disproportionately affect speech on certain topics. On the contrary, "[a] regulation that serves purposes unrelated to the content of expression is deemed neutral, even if it has an incidental effect on some speakers or messages but not others." *Ward, supra,* at 791. The question in such a case is whether the law is " 'justified without reference to the content of the regulated speech.' " *Renton v. Playtime Theatres, Inc.,* 475 U.S. 41, 48 (1986) (quoting *Virginia Pharmacy Board v. Virginia Citizens Consumer Council, Inc.,* 425 U.S. 748, 771 (1976); emphasis deleted).

The Massachusetts Act is. Its stated purpose is to "increase forthwith public safety at reproductive health care facilities." 2007 Mass. Acts p. 660. Respondents have articulated similar purposes before this Court—namely, "public safety, patient access to healthcare, and the unobstructed use of public sidewalks and roadways." . . .

We have previously deemed the foregoing concerns to be content neutral. . . . Obstructed access and congested sidewalks are problems no matter what caused them. A group of individuals can obstruct clinic access and clog sidewalks just as much when they loiter as when they protest abortion or counsel patients.

To be clear, the Act would not be content neutral if it were concerned with undesirable effects that arise from "the direct impact of speech on its audience" or "[l]isteners' reactions to speech." . . . If, for example, the speech outside Massachusetts abortion clinics caused offense or made listeners uncomfortable, such offense or discomfort would not give the Commonwealth a content-neutral justification to restrict the speech. All of the problems identified by the Commonwealth here, however, arise irrespective of any listener's reactions. . . . [L]arge crowds outside abortion clinics can still compromise public safety, impede access, and obstruct sidewalks.

Petitioners do not really dispute that the Commonwealth's interests in ensuring safety and preventing obstruction are, as a general matter, content neutral. But petitioners note that these interests "apply outside every building in the State that hosts any activity that might occasion protest or comment," not just abortion clinics. . . . By choosing to pursue these interests only at abortion clinics, petitioners argue, the Massachusetts Legislature evinced a purpose to "single[ ] out for regulation speech about one particular topic: abortion." . . .

We cannot infer such a purpose from the Act's limited scope. The broad reach of a statute can help confirm that it was not enacted to burden a narrower category of disfavored speech. . . . The Massachusetts Legislature amended the Act in 2007 in response to a problem that was, in its experience, limited to abortion clinics. There was a record of crowding, obstruction, and even violence outside such clinics. There were apparently no similar recurring problems associated with other kinds of healthcare facilities. . . . In light of the limited nature of the problem, it was reasonable for the Massachusetts Legislature to enact a limited solution. When selecting among various options for combating a particular problem, legislatures should be encouraged to choose the one that restricts less speech, not more.

. . . .

B

Petitioners also argue that the Act is content based because it exempts four classes of individuals, . . . one of which comprises "employees or agents of [a reproductive healthcare] facility acting within the scope of their employment." § 120E½(b)(2). This exemption, petitioners say, favors one side in the abortion debate and thus constitutes viewpoint discrimination—an "egregious form of content discrimination," *Rosenberger v. Rector and Visitors of Univ. of Va.*, 515 U.S. 819, 829 (1995). In particular, petitioners argue that the exemption allows clinic employees and agents—including the volunteers who "escort" patients arriving at the Boston clinic—to speak inside the buffer zones.

. . . .

There is nothing inherently suspect about providing some kind of exemption to allow individuals who work at the clinics to enter or remain within the buffer zones. In particular, the exemption cannot be regarded as simply a carve-out for the clinic escorts; it also covers employees such as the maintenance worker shoveling a snowy sidewalk or the security guard patrolling a clinic entrance. . . . Given the need for an exemption for clinic employees, the "scope of their employment" qualification simply ensures that the exemption is limited to its purpose of allowing the employees to do their jobs. . . . There is no suggestion in the record that any of the clinics authorize their employees to speak about abortion in the buffer zones. The "scope of their employment" limitation thus seems designed to protect against exactly the sort of conduct that petitioners . . . fear.

. . . .

We thus conclude that the Act is neither content nor viewpoint based and therefore need not be analyzed under strict scrutiny.

IV

Even though the Act is content neutral, it still must be "narrowly tailored to serve a significant governmental interest." *Ward*, 491 U.S., at 796 (internal quotation marks omitted). . . .

For a content-neutral time, place, or manner regulation to be narrowly tailored, it must not "burden substantially more speech than is necessary to further the government's legitimate interests." *Ward*, 491 U.S., at 799. Such a regulation, unlike a content-based restriction of speech, "need not be the least restrictive or least intrusive means of" serving the government's interests. *Id.*, at 798. But the government still "may not regulate expression in such a manner that a substantial portion of the burden on speech does not serve to advance its goals." *Id.*, at 799.

A

As noted, respondents claim that the Act promotes "public safety, patient access to healthcare, and the unobstructed use of public sidewalks and roadways. We have, moreover, previously recognized the legitimacy of the government's interests in "ensuring public safety and order, promoting the free flow of traffic on streets and sidewalks, protecting property rights, and protecting a woman's freedom to seek pregnancy-related services." *Schenck v. Pro-Choice Network of Western N.Y.*, 519 U.S. 357, 376 (1997). . . . The buffer zones clearly serve these interests.

At the same time, the buffer zones impose serious burdens on petitioners' speech. At each of the three Planned Parenthood clinics where petitioners attempt to counsel patients, the zones carve out a significant portion of the adjacent public sidewalks, pushing petitioners well back from the clinics' entrances and driveways. The zones thereby compromise petitioners' ability to initiate the close, personal conversations that they view as essential to "sidewalk counseling."

. . . .

These burdens on petitioners' speech have clearly taken their toll. . . .

The buffer zones have also made it substantially more difficult for petitioners to distribute literature to arriving patients. As explained, because petitioners in Boston cannot readily identify patients before they enter the zone, they often cannot approach them in time to place literature near their hands—the most effective means of getting the patients to accept it. . . . In short, the Act operates to deprive petitioners of their two primary methods of communicating with patients.

. . . [W]hile the First Amendment does not guarantee a speaker the right to any particular form of expression, some forms—such as normal conversation and leafletting on a public sidewalk—have historically been more closely associated with the transmission of ideas than others.

In the context of petition campaigns, we have observed that "one-on-one communication" is "the most effective, fundamental, and perhaps economical avenue of political discourse." *Meyer v. Grant*, 486 U.S. 414, 424 (1988). . . . And "handing out leaflets in the advocacy of a politically controversial viewpoint . . . is the essence of First Amendment expression"; "[n]o form of speech is entitled to greater constitutional protection." *McIntyre v. Ohio Elections Comm'n*, 514 U.S. 334, 347 (1995) . . . When the government makes it more difficult to engage in these modes of communication, it imposes an especially significant First Amendment burden.[5]

Respondents also emphasize that the Act does not prevent petitioners from engaging in various forms of "protest"—such as chanting slogans and displaying signs—outside the buffer zones . . . That misses the point. Petitioners are not protestors. They seek not merely to express their opposition to abortion, but to inform women of various alternatives and to provide help in pursuing them. Petitioners believe that they can accomplish this objective only through personal, caring, consensual conversations. And for good reason: It is easier to ignore a strained voice or a waving hand than a direct greeting or an outstretched arm. While the record indicates that petitioners have been able to have a number of quiet conversations outside the buffer zones, respondents have not refuted petitioners' testimony that the conversations have been far less frequent and far less successful since the buffer zones were instituted. It is thus no answer to say that petitioners can still be "seen and heard" by women within the buffer zones. *Id.*, at 51–53. If all that the women can see and hear are vociferous opponents of abortion, then the buffer zones have effectively stifled petitioners' message.

. . . .

B

1

The buffer zones burden substantially more speech than necessary to achieve the Commonwealth's asserted interests. At the outset, we note that the Act is truly exceptional: Respondents and their *amici* identify no other State with a law that creates fixed buffer zones around abortion clinics.[6] That of course does not mean that the law is invalid. It does,

---

[5]   As a leading historian has noted:

"It was in this form—as pamphlets—that much of the most important and characteristic writing of the American Revolution appeared. For the Revolutionary generation, as for its predecessors back to the early sixteenth century, the pamphlet had peculiar virtues as a medium of communication. Then, as now, it was seen that the pamphlet allowed one to do things that were not possible in any other form." B. Bailyn, The Ideological Origins of the American Revolution 2 (1967).

[6]   *Amici* do identify five localities with laws similar to the Act here. Brief for State of New York et al. as *Amici Curiae* 14, n. 7.

however, raise concern that the Commonwealth has too readily forgone options that could serve its interests just as well, without substantially burdening the kind of speech in which petitioners wish to engage.

That is the case here. The Commonwealth's interests include ensuring public safety outside abortion clinics, preventing harassment and intimidation of patients and clinic staff, and combating deliberate obstruction of clinic entrances. The Act itself contains a separate provision, subsection (e)—unchallenged by petitioners—that prohibits much of this conduct. That provision subjects to criminal punishment "[a]ny person who knowingly obstructs, detains, hinders, impedes or blocks another person's entry to or exit from a reproductive health care facility." Mass. Gen. Laws, ch. 266, § 120E½(e). If Massachusetts determines that broader prohibitions along the same lines are necessary, it could enact legislation similar to the federal Freedom of Access to Clinic Entrances Act of 1994 (FACE Act), 18 U.S.C. § 248(a)(1), which subjects to both criminal and civil penalties anyone who "by force or threat of force or by physical obstruction, intentionally injures, intimidates or interferes with or attempts to injure, intimidate or interfere with any person because that person is or has been, or in order to intimidate such person or any other person or any class of persons from, obtaining or providing reproductive health services." ... If the Commonwealth is particularly concerned about harassment, it could also consider an ordinance such as the one adopted in New York City that not only prohibits obstructing access to a clinic, but also makes it a crime "to follow and harass another person within 15 feet of the premises of a reproductive health care facility." N.Y.C. Admin. Code § 8–803(a)(3) (2014).

The Commonwealth points to a substantial public safety risk created when protestors obstruct driveways leading to the clinics. . . . That is, however, an example of its failure to look to less intrusive means of addressing its concerns. Any such obstruction can readily be addressed through existing local ordinances. See, *e.g.*, Worcester, Mass., Revised Ordinances of 2008, ch. 12, § 25(b) ("No person shall stand, or place any obstruction of any kind, upon any street, sidewalk or crosswalk in such a manner as to obstruct a free passage for travelers thereon"); Boston, Mass., Municipal Code, ch. 16–41.2(d) (2013) ("No person shall solicit while walking on, standing on or going into any street or highway used for motor vehicle travel, or any area appurtenant thereto (including medians, shoulder areas, bicycle lanes, ramps and exit ramps)").

All of the foregoing measures are, of course, in addition to available generic criminal statutes forbidding assault, breach of the peace, trespass, vandalism, and the like.

In addition, subsection (e) of the Act, the FACE Act, and the New York City anti-harassment ordinance are all enforceable not only through criminal prosecutions but also through public and private civil actions for injunctions and other equitable relief. See Mass. Gen. Laws

§ 120E½(f); 18 U.S.C. § 248(c)(1); N.Y.C. Admin. Code §§ 8–804, 8–805. We have previously noted the First Amendment virtues of targeted injunctions as alternatives to broad, prophylactic measures. Such an injunction "regulates the activities, and perhaps the speech, of a group," but only "because of the group's past *actions* in the context of a specific dispute between real parties." *Madsen*, 512 U.S., at 762 (emphasis added). Moreover, given the equitable nature of injunctive relief, courts can tailor a remedy to ensure that it restricts no more speech than necessary. . . . In short, injunctive relief focuses on the precise individuals and the precise conduct causing a particular problem. The Act, by contrast, categorically excludes non-exempt individuals from the buffer zones, unnecessarily sweeping in innocent individuals and their speech.

The Commonwealth also asserts an interest in preventing congestion in front of abortion clinics. According to respondents, even when individuals do not deliberately obstruct access to clinics, they can inadvertently do so simply by gathering in large numbers. But the Commonwealth could address that problem through more targeted means. Some localities, for example, have ordinances that require crowds blocking a clinic entrance to disperse when ordered to do so by the police, and that forbid the individuals to reassemble within a certain distance of the clinic for a certain period. . . .

And to the extent the Commonwealth argues that even these types of laws are ineffective, it has another problem. The portions of the record that respondents cite to support the anticongestion interest pertain mainly to one place at one time: the Boston Planned Parenthood clinic on Saturday mornings. . . . Respondents point us to no evidence that individuals regularly gather at other clinics, or at other times in Boston, in sufficiently large groups to obstruct access. For a problem shown to arise only once a week in one city at one clinic, creating 35-foot buffer zones at every clinic across the Commonwealth is hardly a narrowly tailored solution.

The point is not that Massachusetts must enact all or even any of the proposed measures discussed above. The point is instead that the Commonwealth has available to it a variety of approaches that appear capable of serving its interests, without excluding individuals from areas historically open for speech and debate.

2

. . . Respondents emphasize the history in Massachusetts of obstruction at abortion clinics, and the Commonwealth's allegedly failed attempts to combat such obstruction with injunctions and individual prosecutions. . . . According to respondents, this history shows that Massachusetts has tried less restrictive alternatives to the buffer zones, to no avail.

We cannot accept that contention. Although respondents claim that Massachusetts "tried other laws already on the books," *id.*, at 41, they identify not a single prosecution brought under those laws within at least the last 17 years. And while they also claim that the Commonwealth "tried injunctions," . . . the last injunctions they cite date to the 1990s. . . . In short, the Commonwealth has not shown that it seriously undertook to address the problem with less intrusive tools readily available to it. Nor has it shown that it considered different methods that other jurisdictions have found effective.

. . . .

Given the vital First Amendment interests at stake, it is not enough for Massachusetts simply to say that other approaches have not worked.[9]

Petitioners wish to converse with their fellow citizens about an important subject on the public streets and sidewalks—sites that have hosted discussions about the issues of the day throughout history. Respondents assert undeniably significant interests in maintaining public safety on those same streets and sidewalks, as well as in preserving access to adjacent healthcare facilities. But here the Commonwealth has pursued those interests by the extreme step of closing a substantial portion of a traditional public forum to all speakers. It has done so without seriously addressing the problem through alternatives that leave the forum open for its time-honored purposes. The Commonwealth may not do that consistent with the First Amendment.

The judgment of the Court of Appeals for the First Circuit is reversed, and the case is remanded for further proceedings consistent with this opinion.

It is so ordered.

■ SCALIA, J., with whom KENNEDY, J., and THOMAS, J., join, concurring in the judgment.

. . . .

First, petitioners maintain that the Act targets abortion-related— for practical purposes, abortion-opposing—speech because it applies outside abortion clinics only (rather than outside other buildings as well).

Public streets and sidewalks are traditional forums for speech on matters of public concern. . . . It blinks reality to say, as the majority does, that a blanket prohibition on the use of streets and sidewalks where speech on only one politically controversial topic is likely to occur—and where that speech can most effectively be communicated—is not content based. Would the Court exempt from strict scrutiny a law banning access to the streets and sidewalks surrounding the site of the Republican National Convention? Or those used annually to commemorate the 1965

---

[9]   Because we find that the Act is not narrowly tailored, we need not consider whether the Act leaves open ample alternative channels of communication. Nor need we consider petitioners' overbreadth challenge.

Selma-to-Montgomery civil rights marches? Or those outside the Internal Revenue Service? Surely not.

The majority says, correctly enough, that a facially neutral speech restriction escapes strict scrutiny, even when it "may disproportionately affect speech on certain topics," so long as it is "justified without reference to the content of the regulated speech." . . . But the cases in which the Court has previously found that standard satisfied—in particular, *Renton v. Playtime Theatres, Inc.*, 475 U.S. 41 (1986), and *Ward v. Rock Against Racism*, 491 U.S. 781 (1989), both of which the majority cites—are a far cry from what confronts us here.

Renton upheld a zoning ordinance prohibiting adult motion-picture theaters within 1,000 feet of residential neighborhoods, churches, parks, and schools. The ordinance was content neutral, the Court held, because its purpose was not to suppress pornographic speech *qua* speech but, rather, to mitigate the "secondary effects" of adult theaters—including by "prevent[ing] crime, protect[ing] the city's retail trade, [and] maintain[ing] property values." 475 U.S., at 47, 48. The Court reasoned that if the city " 'had been concerned with restricting the message purveyed by adult theaters, it would have tried to close them or restrict their number rather than circumscribe their choice as to location.' " . . . *Ward*, in turn, involved a New York City regulation requiring the use of the city's own sound equipment and technician for events at a bandshell in Central Park. The Court held the regulation content neutral because its "principal justification [was] the city's desire to control noise levels," a justification that " 'ha[d] nothing to do with [the] content' " of respondent's rock concerts or of music more generally. 491 U.S., at 792. The regulation "ha[d] no material impact on any performer's ability to exercise complete artistic control over sound quality." *Id.*, at 802. . . .

Compare these cases' reasons for concluding that the regulations in question were "justified without reference to the content of the regulated speech" with the feeble reasons for the majority's adoption of that conclusion in the present case. The majority points only to the statute's stated purpose of increasing " 'public safety' " at abortion clinics . . . and to the additional aims articulated by respondents before this Court— namely, protecting " 'patient access to healthcare . . . and the unobstructed use of public sidewalks and roadways,' " *ante*, at 13 (quoting Brief for Respondents 27). Really? Does a statute become "justified without reference to the content of the regulated speech" simply because the statute itself and those defending it in court *say* that it is? Every objective indication shows that the provision's primary purpose is to restrict speech that opposes abortion.

I begin, as suggested above, with the fact that the Act burdens only the public spaces outside abortion clinics. One might have expected the majority to defend the statute's peculiar targeting by arguing that those locations regularly face the safety and access problems that it says the Act was designed to solve. But the majority does not make that argument because it would be untrue. As the Court belatedly discovers in Part IV of its opinion, although the statute applies to all abortion clinics in Massachusetts, only one is known to have been beset by the problems that the statute supposedly addresses. . . . The Court uses this striking fact (a smoking gun, so to speak) as a basis for concluding that the law is insufficiently "tailored" to safety and access concerns . . . rather than as a basis for concluding that it is not *directed* to those concerns at all, but to the suppression of antiabortion speech. That is rather like invoking the eight missed human targets of a shooter who has killed one victim to prove, not that he is guilty of attempted mass murder, but that *he has bad aim.*

Whether the statute "restrict[s] more speech than necessary" in light of the problems that it allegedly addresses . . . is, to be sure, relevant to the tailoring component of the First Amendment analysis (the shooter doubtless did have bad aim), but it is also relevant—powerfully relevant—to whether the law is really directed to safety and access concerns or rather to the suppression of a particular type of speech. Showing that a law that suppresses speech on a specific subject is so far-reaching that it applies even when the asserted non-speech-related problems are not present is persuasive evidence that the law is content based. In its zeal to treat abortion-related speech as a special category, the majority distorts not only the First Amendment but also the ordinary logic of probative inferences.

. . . .

Further contradicting the Court's fanciful defense of the Act is the fact that subsection (b) was enacted as a more easily enforceable substitute for a prior provision. That provision did not exclude people entirely from the restricted areas around abortion clinics; rather, it forbade people in those areas to approach within six feet of another person *without that person's consent* "for the purpose of passing a leaflet or handbill to, displaying a sign to, or engaging in oral protest, education or counseling with such other person." § 120E½(b) (West 2000). . . . [T]hat provision was "modeled on a . . . Colorado law that this Court had upheld in *Hill*." . . . And in that case, the Court recognized that the statute in question was directed at the suppression of unwelcome speech, vindicating what *Hill* called "[t]he unwilling listener's interest in avoiding unwanted communication." 530 U.S., at 716. The Court held that interest to be content neutral. . . .

The provision at issue here was indisputably meant to serve the same interest in protecting citizens' supposed right to avoid speech that they would rather not hear. For that reason, we granted a second question for review in this case (though one would not know that from the Court's opinion, which fails to mention it): whether *Hill* should be cut back or cast aside. . . . The majority avoids that question by declaring the Act content neutral on other (entirely unpersuasive) grounds. In concluding that the statute is content based and therefore subject to strict scrutiny, I necessarily conclude that *Hill* should be overruled. . . . Protecting people from speech they do not want to hear is not a function that the First Amendment allows the government to undertake in the public streets and sidewalks.

. . . .

B.   Exemption for Abortion-Clinic Employees or Agents

Petitioners contend that the Act targets speech opposing abortion (and thus constitutes a presumptively invalid viewpoint-discriminatory restriction) for another reason as well: It exempts "employees or agents" of an abortion clinic "acting within the scope of their employment," § 120E½(b)(2).

. . . The majority opinion sets forth a two-part inquiry for assessing whether a regulation is content based, but when it comes to assessing the exemption for abortion-clinic employees or agents, the Court forgets its own teaching. Its opinion jumps right over the prong that asks whether the provision "draw[s] . . . distinctions on its face," *ante*, at 12, and instead proceeds directly to the purpose-related prong, see *ibid.*, asking whether the exemption "represent[s] a governmental attempt to give one side of a debatable public question an advantage in expressing its views to the people[.]" . . .

Is there any serious doubt that *abortion-clinic employees or agents* "acting within the scope of their employment" near clinic entrances may—indeed, often will—speak in favor of abortion ("You are doing the right thing")? Or speak in opposition to the message of abortion opponents—saying, for example, that "this is a safe facility" to rebut the statement that it is not? . . . The Court's contrary assumption is simply incredible. And the majority makes no attempt to establish the further necessary proposition that abortion-clinic employees and agents do not engage in nonspeech activities directed to the suppression of antiabortion speech by hampering the efforts of counselors to speak to prospective clients. Are we to believe that a clinic employee sent out to "escort" prospective clients into the building would not seek to prevent a counselor like Eleanor McCullen from communicating with them? . . .

The Court points out that the exemption may allow into the speech-free zones clinic employees other than escorts, such as "the maintenance worker shoveling a snowy sidewalk or the security guard patrolling a clinic entrance." . . . I doubt that Massachusetts legislators had those people in mind, but whether they did is in any event irrelevant. Whatever other activity is permitted, so long as the statute permits speech favorable to abortion rights while excluding antiabortion speech, it discriminates on the basis of viewpoint.

. . . .

In sum, the Act should be reviewed under the strict-scrutiny standard applicable to content-based legislation. That standard requires that a regulation represent "the least restrictive means" of furthering "a compelling Government interest." *United States v. Playboy Entertainment Group, Inc.*, 529 U.S. 803, 813 (2000) (internal quotation marks omitted). Respondents do not even attempt to argue that subsection (b) survives this test. See *ante*, at 10. "Suffice it to say that if protecting people from unwelcome communications"—the actual purpose of the provision—"is a compelling state interest, the First Amendment is a dead letter." *Hill*, 530 U.S., at 748–749 (SCALIA, J., dissenting).

. . . .

Having determined that the Act is content based and does not withstand strict scrutiny, I need not pursue the inquiry conducted in Part IV of the Court's opinion—whether the statute is " 'narrowly tailored to serve a significant governmental interest[.]' " . . . I suppose I *could* do so, taking as a given the Court's erroneous content-neutrality conclusion in Part III; and if I did, I suspect I would agree with the majority that the legislation is not narrowly tailored to advance the interests asserted by respondents. But I prefer not to take part in the assembling of an apparent but specious unanimity. I leave both the plainly unnecessary and erroneous half and the arguably correct half of the court's analysis to the majority.

. . .

The obvious purpose of the challenged portion of the Massachusetts Reproductive Health Care Facilities Act is to "protect" prospective clients of abortion clinics from having to hear abortion-opposing speech on public streets and sidewalks. The provision is thus unconstitutional root and branch and cannot be saved, as the majority suggests, by limiting its application to the single facility that has experienced the safety and access problems to which it is quite obviously not addressed. I concur only in the judgment that the statute is unconstitutional under the First Amendment.

■ ALITO, J., concurring in the judgment.

I agree that the Massachusetts statute at issue in this case, Mass. Gen. Laws, ch. 266, § 120E½(b) (West 2012), violates the First Amendment. As the Court recognizes, if the Massachusetts law discriminates on the basis of view-point, it is unconstitutional, see *ante*, at 10, and I believe the law clearly discriminates on this ground.

The Massachusetts statute generally prohibits any person from entering a buffer zone around an abortion clinic during the clinic's business hours, § 120E½(c), but the law contains an exemption for "employees or agents of such facility acting within the scope of their employment." § 120E½(b)(2). Thus, during business hours, individuals who wish to counsel against abortion or to criticize the particular clinic may not do so within the buffer zone. If they engage in such conduct, they commit a crime. See § 120E½(d). By contrast, employees and agents of the clinic may enter the zone and engage in any conduct that falls within the scope of their employment. A clinic may direct or authorize an employee or agent, while within the zone, to express favorable views about abortion or the clinic, and if the employee exercises that authority, the employee's conduct is perfectly lawful. In short, petitioners and other critics of a clinic are silenced, while the clinic may authorize its employees to express speech in support of the clinic and its work.

Consider this entirely realistic situation. A woman enters a buffer zone and heads haltingly toward the entrance. A sidewalk counselor, such as petitioners, enters the buffer zone, approaches the woman and says, "If you have doubts about an abortion, let me try to answer any questions you may have. The clinic will not give you good information." At the same time, a clinic employee, as instructed by the management, approaches the same woman and says, "Come inside and we will give you honest answers to all your questions." The sidewalk counselor and the clinic employee expressed opposing viewpoints, but only the first violated the statute.

Or suppose that the issue is not abortion but the safety of a particular facility. Suppose that there was a recent report of a botched abortion at the clinic. A nonemployee may not enter the buffer zone to warn about the clinic's health record, but an employee may enter and tell prospective clients that the clinic is safe.

It is clear on the face of the Massachusetts law that it discriminates based on viewpoint. Speech in favor of the clinic and its work by employees and agents is permitted; speech criticizing the clinic and its work is a crime. This is blatant viewpoint discrimination.

The Court holds not only that the Massachusetts law is viewpoint neutral but also that it does not discriminate based on content. See *ante*, at 11–15. The Court treats the Massachusetts law like one that bans all speech within the buffer zone. While such a law would be content neutral on its face, there are circumstances in which a law forbidding all speech at a particular location would not be content neutral in fact. Suppose, for example, that a facially content-neutral law is enacted for the purpose of suppressing speech on a particular topic. Such a law would not be content neutral. *See, e.g., Turner Broadcasting System, Inc. v. FCC,* 512 U.S. 622, 645–46 (1994).

In this case, I do not think that it is possible to reach a judgment about the intent of the Massachusetts Legislature without taking into account the fact that the law that the legislature enacted blatantly discriminates based on viewpoint. In light of this feature, as well as the overbreadth that the Court identifies, see *ante*, at 23–27, it cannot be said, based on the present record, that the law would be content neutral even if the exemption for clinic employees and agents were excised. However, if the law were truly content neutral, I would agree with the Court that the law would still be unconstitutional on the ground that it burdens more speech than is necessary to serve the Commonwealth's asserted interests.

NOTES

1.   *Who is Eleanor McCullen?* A 77-year old life-long Catholic from Newton, Massachusetts, Eleanor McCullen had a "spiritual awakening" that, over the years, prompted her to devote countless hours to "sidewalk counseling" in front of a Boston abortion clinic. Indeed, according to McCullen, her grandmotherly air and gentle manner, made her unusually effective as an anti-abortion counselor. As she put it, her approach to "counseling" prospective abortion patients departs sharply from the shrill tones often associated with anti-abortion protesters. Instead of screaming and shouting, McCullen simply approached the woman seeking an abortion with a quiet "hello" and an offer to answer any questions the woman might have. *See* Karla Dail, *More than Words*, CITIZEN LINK: A PUB. POLICY PARTNER OF FOCUS ON THE FAMILY (Oct. 27, 2011), http://www.citizenlink.com/2011/10/27/more-than-words/. The Court seemed particularly impressed with McCullen's demeanor, observing that "McCullen and the other petitioners consider it essential to maintain a caring demeanor, a calm tone of voice, and direct eye contact during the exchange." *McCullen*, 573 U.S. 464, 472–73 (2014). Recall the discussion of plaintiff selection in marriage-equality litigation, see *supra* p. 81. To what extent do similar concerns guide the selection of plaintiffs in both of these contexts?

2.   *Consent in context.* The *McCullen* majority imagined pro-life advocates engaging in "personal, caring, consensual conversations" with women entering abortion clinics. *McCullen*, 573 U.S. 464, 489 (2014). At oral argument, however, Massachusetts argued that such conversations were hardly consensual, as the petitioners' actions had an edge of violence and intimidation. Transcript of Oral Argument, *McCullen v. Coakley*, 2014 WL 144977, at *29, *44 (No. 12–1168) (Jan. 15, 2014). Given the fraught context in which these conversations take place, is it likely that such conversations comport with traditional understandings of consent?

3.   *How much does history count?* Notwithstanding the amiable demeanor of Mrs. McCullen and her colleagues, peaceful counseling has not always characterized anti-abortion activism. As constitutional law scholar Walter Dellinger noted in an amicus brief filed on behalf of the Planned Parenthood League of Massachusetts (PPLM) and the Planned Parenthood Federation of America (PPFA), "the [challenged Massachusetts] Act followed thirty years of violent protests and patient harassment. Previous legislation, criminal prosecution, and injunctions all failed to keep the peace at PPLM's Facilities. Amici support the rights of protesters to be present and communicate their messages, but they also seek to ensure the safety of PPLM's patients and staff and maintain access to PPLM's health centers." Brief of Amici Curiae Planned Parenthood League of Massachusetts & Planned Parenthood Federation of America in Support of Respondents at 1, *McCullen v. Coakley*, 2014 WL 2882079 (2014) (No. 12–1168). Dellinger also documented the pattern of violent protests that had confronted PPLM's abortion clinics and reminded the Court of the murder of two clinic employees at a PPLM facility in 1994. *See id.* at 6–8. Does the Court engage this history directly in its opinion?

4. *Abortion exceptionalism.* As Professor Caitlin Borgmann explains, " 'Abortion exceptionalism' is a term that has been used to describe the tendency of legislatures and courts to subject abortion to unique, and uniquely burdensome, rules," as compared to other procedures. Caitlin E. Borgmann, *Abortion Exceptionalism and Undue Burden Preemption*, 71 WASH. & LEE L. REV. 1047, 1048 (2012). As with so many things in the abortion debate, even the term "abortion exceptionalism" is subject to contest. Abortion opponents have appropriated the term to suggest that courts have privileged abortion over competing constitutional rights. *See "Abortion Exceptionalism" to Be Reviewed by U.S. Supreme Court*, LIFE LEGAL DEF. FUND (Sept. 12, 2013), http://lldf.org/abortion-exceptionalism-to-be-reviewed-by-u-s-supreme-court/. Indeed, as Justice Scalia argues in his concurrence to *McCullen*, "[t]here is an entirely separate, abridged edition of the First Amendment applicable to speech against abortion." *McCullen*, 573 U.S. at 497 (Scalia, J., concurring).

5. *Law vs. practice?* Massachusetts had attempted earlier to deal with abortion protesting by establishing a defined area with an 18-foot radius around the entrances and driveways of such facilities. Although anyone could enter that area, once within it, no one (other than certain exempt individuals) could knowingly approach within six feet of another person—without that person's consent. As Massachusetts argued, this "floating" buffer zone proved difficult to police and enforce. In 2007, the state enacted the law challenged in *McCullen*, which established a fixed 35-foot buffer zone. According to the state, this new law was much easier to enforce and police. In its opinion, the Court adverted to these concerns regarding enforceability, but nevertheless struck down the fixed buffer-zone law on the ground that there were other, less burdensome, alternatives that Massachusetts might have pursued. Did the Court give short shrift to these practical concerns?

6. *Residential picketing.* As *McCullen* suggests, abortion protesting often takes place in the vicinity of abortion clinics. However, this has not been the *only* location for protests. In 1985, Sandra C. Schultz and Robert C. Braun protested abortion by picketing outside the Brookfield, Wisconsin home of Dr. Benjamin Victoria, a physician who performed abortions. On some occasions, the protests amassed as many as forty protestors. In response, the town of Brookfield, emphasizing the need for "the protection and preservation of the home," enacted an ordinance that banned all residential picketing. The protestors challenged the ordinance all the way to the U.S. Supreme Court. There, in a 6–3 opinion authored by Justice Sandra Day O'Connor, the Court upheld the ordinance on the ground that it was content neutral, "preserve[d] ample alternative channels of communication," served a "significant government interest," and was narrowly tailored to achieve that interest. In this vein, the majority underscored the narrowness of the ordinance, which the Court interpreted to limit picketing in front of a single residence—indeed, the Court suggested that limiting picketing on a larger scale would be unconstitutional and would prove to interfere with the First Amendment rights of the people. *Frisby v. Schultz*, 487 U.S. 474, 477, 482 (1988).

* * *

An emerging area of anti-abortion speech involves state regulation of "crisis pregnancy centers," free prenatal centers run by anti-abortion advocates that, in the manner of medical clinics, provide pregnancy tests and counseling, but which also provide particular information about pregnancy and abortion. States and localities have sought to deal with the proliferation of these centers through resort to consumer protection measures, like the California FACT Act, which was challenged on First Amendment grounds in NIFLA v. Becerra.

National Institute of Family and Life Advocates v. Becerra

138 S. Ct. 2361 (2018).

■ THOMAS, J.

The California Reproductive Freedom, Accountability, Comprehensive Care, and Transparency Act (FACT Act) requires clinics that primarily serve pregnant women to provide certain notices. Licensed clinics must notify women that California provides free or low-cost services, including abortions, and give them a phone number to call. Unlicensed clinics must notify women that California has not licensed the clinics to provide medical services. The question in this case is whether these notice requirements violate the First Amendment.

I

The California State Legislature enacted the FACT Act to regulate crisis pregnancy centers. Crisis pregnancy centers—according to a report commissioned by the California State Assembly, App. 86—are "pro-life (largely Christian belief-based) organizations that offer a limited range of free pregnancy options, counseling, and other services to individuals that visit a center." "[U]nfortunately," the author of the FACT Act stated, "there are nearly 200 licensed and unlicensed" crisis pregnancy centers in California. These centers "aim to discourage and prevent women from seeking abortions." The author of the FACT Act observed that crisis pregnancy centers "are commonly affiliated with, or run by organizations whose stated goal" is to oppose abortion—including "the National Institute of Family and Life Advocates," one of the petitioners here. To address this perceived problem, the FACT Act imposes two notice requirements on facilities that provide pregnancy-related services—one for licensed facilities and one for unlicensed facilities.

The first notice requirement applies to "licensed covered facilit[ies]." To fall under the definition of "licensed covered facility," a clinic must be a licensed primary care or specialty clinic or qualify as an intermittent clinic under California law. A licensed covered facility also must have the "primary purpose" of "providing family planning or pregnancy-related services." And it must satisfy at least two of the following six requirements:

(1) The facility offers obstetric ultrasounds, obstetric sonograms, or prenatal care to pregnant women.

(2) The facility provides, or offers counseling about, contraception or contraceptive methods.

(3) The facility offers pregnancy testing or pregnancy diagnosis.

(4) The facility advertises or solicits patrons with offers to provide prenatal sonography, pregnancy tests, or pregnancy options counseling.

(5) The facility offers abortion services.

(6) The facility has staff or volunteers who collect health information from clients.

The FACT Act exempts several categories of clinics that would otherwise qualify as licensed covered facilities. Clinics operated by the United States or a federal agency are excluded, as are clinics that are "enrolled as a Medi-Cal provider" and participate in "the Family Planning, Access, Care, and Treatment Program" (Family PACT program). § 123471(c). To participate in the Family PACT program, a clinic must provide "the full scope of family planning ... services specified for the program," including sterilization and emergency contraceptive pills.

If a clinic is a licensed covered facility, the FACT Act requires it to disseminate a government-drafted notice on site. The notice states that "California has public programs that provide immediate free or low-cost access to comprehensive family planning services (including all FDA-approved methods of contraception), prenatal care, and abortion for eligible women. To determine whether you qualify, contact the county social services office at [insert the telephone number]." This notice must be posted in the waiting room, printed and distributed to all clients, or provided digitally at check-in. The notice must be in English and any additional languages identified by state law. In some counties, that means the notice must be spelled out in 13 different languages.

The stated purpose of the FACT Act, including its licensed notice requirement, is to "ensure that California residents make their personal reproductive health care decisions knowing their rights and the health care services available to them." The Legislature posited that "thousands of women remain unaware of the public programs available to provide them with contraception, health education and counseling, family planning, prenatal care, abortion, or delivery." Citing the "time sensitive" nature of pregnancy-related decisions, the Legislature concluded that requiring licensed facilities to inform patients themselves would be "[t]he most effective" way to convey this information.

The second notice requirement in the FACT Act applies to "unlicensed covered facilit[ies]." To fall under the definition of "unlicensed covered facility," a facility must not be licensed by the State, not have a licensed medical provider on staff or under contract, and have the "primary purpose" of "providing pregnancy-related services." An unlicensed covered facility also must satisfy at least two of the following four requirements:

(1) The facility offers obstetric ultrasounds, obstetric sonograms, or prenatal care to pregnant women.

(2) The facility offers pregnancy testing or pregnancy diagnosis.

(3) The facility advertises or solicits patrons with offers to provide prenatal sonography, pregnancy tests, or pregnancy options counseling.

(4) The facility has staff or volunteers who collect health information from clients.

Clinics operated by the United States and licensed primary care clinics enrolled in Medi-Cal and Family PACT are excluded.

Unlicensed covered facilities must provide a government-drafted notice stating that "[t]his facility is not licensed as a medical facility by the State of California and has no licensed medical provider who provides or directly supervises the provision of services." This notice must be provided on site and in all advertising materials. Onsite, the notice must be posted "conspicuously" at the entrance of the facility and in at least one waiting area. It must be "at least 8.5 inches by 11 inches and written in no less than 48-point type." In advertisements, the notice must be in the same size or larger font than the surrounding text, or otherwise set off in a way that draws attention to it. Like the licensed notice, the unlicensed notice must be in English and any additional languages specified by state law. Its stated purpose is to ensure "that pregnant women in California know when they are getting medical care from licensed professionals."

After the Governor of California signed the FACT Act, petitioners—a licensed pregnancy center, an unlicensed pregnancy center, and an organization composed of crisis pregnancy centers—filed this suit. Petitioners alleged that the licensed and unlicensed notices abridge the freedom of speech protected by the First Amendment. The District Court denied their motion for a preliminary injunction. . . . The Court of Appeals for the Ninth Circuit affirmed. . . . We reverse with respect to both notice requirements.

II

We first address the licensed notice. . . . The First Amendment, applicable to the States through the Fourteenth Amendment, prohibits laws that abridge the freedom of speech. When enforcing this prohibition, our precedents distinguish between content-based and content-neutral regulations of speech. Content-based regulations "target speech based on its communicative content." As a general matter, such laws "are presumptively unconstitutional and may be justified only if the government proves that they are narrowly tailored to serve compelling state interests." This stringent standard reflects the fundamental principle that governments have " 'no power to restrict expression because of its message, its ideas, its subject matter, or its content.' "

The licensed notice is a content-based regulation of speech. By compelling individuals to speak a particular message, such notices "alte[r] the content of [their] speech." Here, for example, licensed clinics must provide a government-drafted script about the availability of state-sponsored services, as well as contact information for how to obtain them. One of those services is abortion—the very practice that petitioners are devoted to opposing. By requiring petitioners to inform women how they can obtain state-subsidized abortions—at the same time petitioners try to dissuade women from choosing that option—the licensed notice plainly "alters the content" of petitioners' speech.

Although the licensed notice is content based, the Ninth Circuit did not apply strict scrutiny because it concluded that the notice regulates "professional speech. Some Courts of Appeals have recognized "professional speech" as a separate category of speech that is subject to different rules. These courts define "professionals" as individuals who provide personalized services to clients and who are subject to "a generally applicable licensing and regulatory regime." "Professional speech" is then defined as any speech by these individuals that is based on "[their] expert knowledge and judgment," or that is "within the confines of [the] professional relationship." So defined, these courts except professional speech from the rule that content-based regulations of speech are subject to strict scrutiny.

But this Court has not recognized "professional speech" as a separate category of speech. Speech is not unprotected merely because it is uttered by "professionals." This Court has "been reluctant to mark off new categories of speech for diminished constitutional protection." And it has been especially reluctant to "exemp[t] a category of speech from the normal prohibition on content-based restrictions." This Court's precedents do not permit governments to impose content-based restrictions on speech without " 'persuasive evidence . . . of a long (if heretofore unrecognized) tradition' " to that effect.

This Court's precedents do not recognize such a tradition for a category called "professional speech." This Court has afforded less protection for professional speech in two circumstances—neither of which turned on the fact that professionals were speaking. First, our precedents have applied more deferential review to some laws that require professionals to disclose factual, noncontroversial information in their "commercial speech." Second, under our precedents, States may regulate professional conduct, even though that conduct incidentally involves speech. But neither line of precedents is implicated here.

This Court's precedents have applied a lower level of scrutiny to laws that compel disclosures in certain contexts. . . . Most obviously, the licensed notice is not limited to "purely factual and uncontroversial information about the terms under which . . . services will be available. . . .

In addition . . ., this Court has upheld regulations of professional conduct that incidentally burden speech. . . .

In *Planned Parenthood of Southeastern Pa. v. Casey*, for example, this Court upheld a law requiring physicians to obtain informed consent before they could perform an abortion. Pennsylvania law required physicians to inform their patients of "the nature of the procedure, the health risks of the abortion and childbirth, and the 'probable gestational age of the unborn child.' " . . . .

The joint opinion in *Casey* rejected a free-speech challenge to this informed-consent requirement. It described the Pennsylvania law as "a requirement that a doctor give a woman certain information as part of obtaining her consent to an abortion," which "for constitutional purposes, [was] no different from a requirement that a doctor give certain specific information about any medical procedure." The joint opinion explained that the law regulated speech only "as part of the practice of medicine, subject to reasonable licensing and regulation by the State." Indeed, the requirement that a doctor obtain informed consent to perform an operation is "firmly entrenched in American tort law."

The licensed notice at issue here is not an informed-consent requirement or any other regulation of professional conduct. The notice does not facilitate informed consent to a medical procedure. In fact, it is not tied to a procedure at all. It applies to all interactions between a covered facility and its clients, regardless of whether a medical procedure is ever sought, offered, or performed. If a covered facility does provide medical procedures, the notice provides no information about the risks or benefits of those procedures. . . .

The dangers associated with content-based regulations of speech are also present in the context of professional speech. As with other kinds of speech, regulating the content of professionals' speech "pose[s] the inherent risk that the Government seeks not to advance a legitimate regulatory goal, but to suppress unpopular ideas or information." Take medicine, for example. "Doctors help patients make deeply personal decisions, and their candor is crucial." Throughout history, governments have "manipulat[ed] the content of doctor-patient discourse" to increase state power and suppress minorities. . . .

Further, when the government polices the content of professional speech, it can fail to " 'preserve an uninhibited marketplace of ideas in which truth will ultimately prevail.' " . . .

"Professional speech" is also a difficult category to define with precision. As defined by the courts of appeals, the professional-speech doctrine would cover a wide array of individuals—doctors, lawyers, nurses, physical therapists, truck drivers, bartenders, barbers, and many others. One court of appeals has even applied it to fortune tellers. See All that is required to make something a "profession," according to these courts, is that it involves personalized services and requires a professional license from the State. But that gives the States unfettered power to reduce a group's First Amendment rights by simply imposing a licensing requirement. States cannot choose the protection that speech receives under the First Amendment, as that would give them a powerful tool to impose "invidious discrimination of disfavored subjects."

In sum, neither California nor the Ninth Circuit has identified a persuasive reason for treating professional speech as a unique category that is exempt from ordinary First Amendment principles. We do not foreclose the possibility that some such reason exists. We need not do so because the licensed notice cannot survive even intermediate scrutiny. California asserts a single interest to justify the licensed notice: providing low-income women with information about state-sponsored services. Assuming that this is a substantial state interest, the licensed notice is not sufficiently drawn to achieve it.

If California's goal is to educate low-income women about the services it provides, then the licensed notice is "wildly underinclusive." The notice applies only to clinics that have a "primary purpose" of "providing family planning or pregnancy-related services" and that provide two of six categories of specific services. Other clinics that have another primary purpose, or that provide only one category of those services, also serve low-income women and could educate them about the State's services. According to the legislative record, California has "nearly 1,000 community clinics"—including "federally designated community health centers, migrant health centers, rural health centers, and frontier health centers"—that "serv[e] more than 5.6 million patients . . . annually through over 17 million patient encounters." But most of those clinics are excluded from the licensed notice requirement without explanation. Such "[u]nderinclusiveness raises serious doubts about whether the government is in fact pursuing the interest it invokes, rather than disfavoring a particular speaker or viewpoint."

The FACT Act also excludes, without explanation, federal clinics and Family PACT providers from the licensed-notice requirement. . . . The FACT Act's exemption for these clinics, which serve many women who are pregnant or could become pregnant in the future, demonstrates the disconnect between its stated purpose and its actual scope. Yet "[p]recision . . . must be the touchstone" when it comes to regulations of speech, which "so closely touc[h] our most precious freedoms."

Further, California could inform low-income women about its services "without burdening a speaker with unwanted speech." Most obviously, it could inform the women itself with a public-information campaign. California could even post the information on public property near crisis pregnancy centers. California argues that it has already tried an advertising campaign, and that many women who are eligible for publicly-funded healthcare have not enrolled. But California has identified no evidence to that effect. And regardless, a "tepid response" does not prove that an advertising campaign is not a sufficient alternative. Here, for example, individuals might not have enrolled in California's services because they do not want them, or because California spent insufficient resources on the advertising campaign. Either way, California cannot co-opt the licensed facilities to deliver its message for it. "[T]he First Amendment does not permit the State to sacrifice speech for efficiency."

In short, petitioners are likely to succeed on the merits of their challenge to the licensed notice. Contrary to the suggestion in the dissent, we do not question the legality of health and safety warnings long considered permissible, or purely factual and uncontroversial disclosures about commercial products.

III

. . . .

We need not decide what type of state interest is sufficient to sustain a disclosure requirement like the unlicensed notice. California has not demonstrated any justification for the unlicensed notice that is more than "purely hypothetical." The only justification that the California Legislature put forward was ensuring that "pregnant women in California know when they are getting medical care from licensed professionals." At oral argument, however, California denied that the justification for the FACT Act was that women "go into [crisis pregnancy centers] and they don't realize what they are." Indeed, California points to nothing suggesting that pregnant women do not already know that the covered facilities are staffed by unlicensed medical professionals. The services that trigger the unlicensed notice—such as having "volunteers who collect health information from clients," "advertis[ing] . . . pregnancy options counseling," and offering over-the-counter "pregnancy testing"— do not require a medical license. And California already makes it a crime for individuals without a medical license to practice medicine. At this preliminary stage of the litigation, we agree that petitioners are likely to prevail on the question whether California has proved a justification for the unlicensed notice.

Even if California had presented a nonhypothetical justification for the unlicensed notice, the FACT Act unduly burdens protected speech. The unlicensed notice imposes a government-scripted, speaker-based disclosure requirement that is wholly disconnected from California's informational interest. It requires covered facilities to post California's precise notice, no matter what the facilities say on site or in their advertisements. And it covers a curiously narrow subset of speakers.

While the licensed notice applies to facilities that provide "family planning" services and "contraception or contraceptive methods," the California Legislature dropped these triggering conditions for the unlicensed notice. The unlicensed notice applies only to facilities that primarily provide "pregnancy-related" services. Thus, a facility that advertises and provides pregnancy tests is covered by the unlicensed notice, but a facility across the street that advertises and provides nonprescription contraceptives is excluded—even though the latter is no less likely to make women think it is licensed. This Court's precedents are deeply skeptical of laws that "distinguis[h] among different speakers, allowing speech by some but not others." Speaker-based laws run the risk that "the State has left unburdened those speakers whose messages are in accord with its own views."

The application of the unlicensed notice to advertisements demonstrates just how burdensome it is. The notice applies to all "print and digital advertising materials" by an unlicensed covered facility. These materials must include a government-drafted statement that "[t]his facility is not licensed as a medical facility by the State of California and has no licensed medical provider who provides or directly supervises the provision of services." An unlicensed facility must call attention to the notice, instead of its own message, by some method such as larger text or contrasting type or color. This scripted language must be posted in English and as many other languages as California chooses to require. As California conceded at oral argument, a billboard for an unlicensed facility that says "Choose Life" would have to surround that two-word statement with a 29-word statement from the government, in as many as 13 different languages. In this way, the unlicensed notice drowns out the facility's own message. More likely, the "detail required" by the unlicensed notice "effectively rules out" the possibility of having such a billboard in the first place.

.... We express no view on the legality of a similar disclosure requirement that is better supported or less burdensome.

We hold that petitioners are likely to succeed on the merits of their claim that the FACT Act violates the First Amendment. . . .

■ JUSTICE KENNEDY, with whom THE CHIEF JUSTICE, JUSTICE ALITO, and JUSTICE GORSUCH join, concurring.

. . . .

This separate writing seeks to underscore that the apparent viewpoint discrimination here is a matter of serious constitutional concern. The Court, in my view, is correct not to reach this question. It was not sufficiently developed, and the rationale for the Court's decision today suffices to resolve the case. . . .

It does appear that viewpoint discrimination is inherent in the design and structure of this Act. This law is a paradigmatic example of the serious threat presented when government seeks to impose its own message in the place of individual speech, thought, and expression. For here the State requires primarily pro-life pregnancy centers to promote the State's own preferred message advertising abortions. This compels individuals to contradict their most deeply held beliefs, beliefs grounded in basic philosophical, ethical, or religious precepts, or all of these. And the history of the Act's passage and its underinclusive application suggest a real possibility that these individuals were targeted because of their beliefs.

The California Legislature included in its official history the congratulatory statement that the Act was part of California's legacy of "forward thinking." But it is not forward thinking to force individuals to "be an instrument for fostering public adherence to an ideological point of view [they] fin[d] unacceptable." It is forward thinking to begin by reading the First Amendment as ratified in 1791; to understand the history of authoritarian government as the Founders then knew it; to confirm that history since then shows how relentless authoritarian regimes are in their attempts to stifle free speech; and to carry those lessons onward as we seek to preserve and teach the necessity of freedom of speech for the generations to come. Governments must not be allowed to force persons to express a message contrary to their deepest convictions. Freedom of speech secures freedom of thought and belief. This law imperils those liberties.

■ JUSTICE BREYER, with whom JUSTICE GINSBURG, JUSTICE SOTOMAYOR, and JUSTICE KAGAN join, dissenting.

The petitioners ask us to consider whether two sections of a California statute violate the First Amendment. The first section requires licensed medical facilities (that provide women with assistance involving pregnancy or family planning) to tell those women where they might obtain help, including financial help, with comprehensive family planning services, prenatal care, and abortion. The second requires un licensed facilities offering somewhat similar services to make clear that they are unlicensed. In my view both statutory sections are likely constitutional, and I dissent from the Court's contrary conclusions.

. . . .

Before turning to the specific law before us, I focus upon the general interpretation of the First Amendment that the majority says it applies. It applies heightened scrutiny to the Act because the Act, in its view, is "content based." "By compelling individuals to speak a particular message," it adds, "such notices 'alte[r] the content of [their] speech.'" "As a general matter," the majority concludes, such laws are "presumptively unconstitutional" and are subject to "stringent" review.

. . . .

This constitutional approach threatens to create serious problems. Because much, perhaps most, human behavior takes place through speech and because much, perhaps most, law regulates that speech in terms of its content, the majority's approach at the least threatens considerable litigation over the constitutional validity of much, perhaps most, government regulation. Virtually every disclosure law could be considered "content based," for virtually every disclosure law requires individuals "to speak a particular message." Thus, the majority's view, if taken literally, could radically change prior law, perhaps placing much securities law or consumer protection law at constitutional risk, depending on how broadly its exceptions are interpreted.

. . . .

The majority, at the end of Part II of its opinion, perhaps recognizing this problem, adds a general disclaimer. It says that it does not "question the legality of health and safety warnings long considered permissible, or purely factual and uncontroversial disclosures about commercial products." But this generally phrased disclaimer would seem more likely to invite litigation than to provide needed limitation and clarification. The majority, for example, does not explain why the Act here, which is justified in part by health and safety considerations, does not fall within its "health" category. Nor does the majority opinion offer any reasoned basis that might help apply its disclaimer for distinguishing lawful from unlawful disclosures. In the absence of a reasoned explanation of the disclaimer's meaning and rationale, the disclaimer is unlikely to withdraw the invitation to litigation that the majority's general broad "content-based" test issues. That test invites courts around the Nation to apply an unpredictable First Amendment to ordinary social and economic regulation, striking down disclosure laws that judges may disfavor, while upholding others, all without grounding their decisions in reasoned principle.

. . . .

Precedent does not require a test such as the majority's. Rather, in saying the Act is not a longstanding health and safety law, the Court substitutes its own approach—without a defining standard—for an approach that was reasonably clear. Historically, the Court has been wary of claims that regulation of business activity, particularly health-related activity, violates the Constitution. Ever since this Court departed from the approach it set forth in Lochner v. New York (1905), ordinary economic and social legislation has been thought to raise little constitutional concern. . . .

. . . . I, too, value this role that the First Amendment plays—in an appropriate case. But here, the majority enunciates a general test that reaches far beyond the area where this Court has examined laws closely in the service of those goals. And, in suggesting that heightened scrutiny applies to much economic and social legislation, the majority pays those First Amendment goals a serious disservice through dilution. Using the First Amendment to strike down economic and social laws that legislatures long would have thought themselves free to enact will, for the American public, obscure, not clarify, the true value of protecting freedom of speech.

Still, what about this specific case? The disclosure at issue here concerns speech related to abortion. It involves health, differing moral values, and differing points of view. Thus, rather than set forth broad, new, First Amendment principles, I believe that we should focus more directly upon precedent more closely related to the case at hand. This Court has more than once considered disclosure laws relating to reproductive health. Though those rules or holdings have changed over time, they should govern our disposition of this case.

. . . . In *Planned Parenthood of Southeastern Pennsylvania v. Casey* (1992), the Court again considered a state law that required doctors to provide information to a woman deciding whether to proceed with an abortion. That law required the doctor to tell the woman about the nature of the abortion procedure, the health risks of abortion and of childbirth, the " 'probable gestational age of the unborn child,' " and the availability of printed materials describing the fetus, medical assistance for childbirth, potential child support, and the agencies that would provide adoption services (or other alternatives to abortion).

. . . .

The joint opinion specifically discussed the First Amendment, the constitutional provision now directly before us. It concluded that the statute did not violate the First Amendment. It wrote:

> "All that is left of petitioners' argument is an asserted First Amendment right of a physician not to provide information about the risks of abortion, and childbirth, in a manner mandated by the State. To be sure, the physician's First Amendment rights not to speak are implicated, but only as part of the practice of medicine, subject to reasonable licensing and regulation by the State. We see no constitutional infirmity in the requirement that the physician provide the information mandated by the State here."

Thus, the Court considered the State's statutory requirements, including the requirement that the doctor must inform his patient about where she could learn how to have the newborn child adopted (if carried to term) and how she could find related financial assistance. To repeat the point, the Court then held that the State's requirements did not violate either the Constitution's protection of free speech or its protection of a woman's right to choose to have an abortion.

. . . . If a State can lawfully require a doctor to tell a woman seeking an abortion about adoption services, why should it not be able, as here, to require a medical counselor to tell a woman seeking prenatal care or other reproductive healthcare about childbirth and abortion services? As the question suggests, there is no convincing reason to distinguish between information about adoption and information about abortion in this context. After all, the rule of law embodies evenhandedness, and "what is sauce for the goose is normally sauce for the gander."

. . . .

The majority also finds it "[t]ellin[g]" that general practice clinics— i.e., paid clinics—are not required to provide the licensed notice. But the lack-of-information problem that the statute seeks to ameliorate is a problem that the State explains is commonly found among low-income women. That those with low income might lack the time to become fully informed and that this circumstance might prove disproportionately correlated with income is not intuitively surprising. Nor is it surprising that those with low income, whatever they choose in respect to pregnancy, might find information about financial assistance particularly useful. There is "nothing inherently suspect" about this distinction, which is not "based on the content of [the advocacy] each group offers," but upon the patients the group generally serves and the needs of that population.

. . . .

Accordingly, the majority's reliance on cases that prohibit rather than require speech is misplaced. I agree that " 'in the fields of medicine and public heath, . . . information can save lives,' " but the licensed disclosure serves that informational interest by requiring clinics to notify patients of the availability of state resources for family planning services, prenatal care, and abortion, which—unlike the majority's examples of normative statements—is truthful and nonmisleading information. Abortion is a controversial topic and a source of normative debate, but the availability of state resources is not a normative statement or a fact of debatable truth. The disclosure includes information about resources available should a woman seek to continue her pregnancy or terminate it, and it expresses no official preference for one choice over the other. Similarly, the majority highlights an interest that often underlies our decisions in respect to speech prohibitions—the marketplace of ideas. But that marketplace is fostered, not hindered, by providing information to patients to enable them to make fully informed medical decisions in respect to their pregnancies.

Of course, one might take the majority's decision to mean that speech about abortion is special, that it involves in this case not only professional medical matters, but also views based on deeply held religious and moral beliefs about the nature of the practice. . . . But assuming that is so, the law's insistence upon treating like cases alike should lead us to reject the petitioners' arguments that I have discussed. This insistence, the need for evenhandedness, should prove particularly weighty in a case involving abortion rights. That is because Americans hold strong, and differing, views about the matter. Some Americans believe that abortion involves the death of a live and innocent human being. Others believe that the ability to choose an abortion is "central to personal dignity and autonomy," and note that the failure to allow women to choose an abortion involves the deaths of innocent women. We have previously noted that we cannot try to adjudicate who is right and who is wrong in this moral debate. But we can do our best to interpret American constitutional law so that it applies fairly within a Nation whose citizens strongly hold these different points of view. That is one reason why it is particularly important to interpret the First Amendment so that it applies evenhandedly as between those who disagree so strongly. For this reason too a Constitution that allows States to insist that medical providers tell women about the possibility of adoption should also allow States similarly to insist that medical providers tell women about the possibility of abortion.

. . . .

The second statutory provision covers pregnancy-related facilities that provide women with certain medical-type services (such as obstetric ultrasounds or sonograms, pregnancy diagnosis, counseling about pregnancy options, or prenatal care), are not licensed as medical facilities by the State, and do not have a licensed medical provider on site. The statute says that such a facility must disclose that it is not "licensed as a medical facility." And it must make this disclosure in a posted notice and in advertising.

The majority does not question that the State's interest (ensuring that "pregnant women in California know when they are getting medical care from licensed professionals") is the type of informational interest that [prior decisions encompass]. . . .

There is no basis for finding the State's interest "hypothetical." The legislature heard that information-related delays in qualified healthcare negatively affect women seeking to terminate their pregnancies as well as women carrying their pregnancies to term, with delays in qualified prenatal care causing life-long health problems for infants. Even without such testimony, it is "self-evident" that patients might think they are receiving qualified medical care when they enter facilities that collect health information, perform obstetric ultrasounds or sonograms, diagnose pregnancy, and provide counseling about pregnancy options or other prenatal care. The State's conclusion to that effect is certainly reasonable.

. . . .

Relatedly, the majority suggests that the Act is suspect because it covers some speakers but not others. . . .

There is no cause for such concern here. The Act does not, on its face, distinguish between facilities that favor pro-life and those that favor pro-choice points of view. Nor is there any convincing evidence before us or in the courts below that discrimination was the purpose or the effect of the statute. Notably, California does not single out pregnancy-related facilities for this type of disclosure requirement. And it is unremarkable that the State excluded the provision of family planning and contraceptive services as triggering conditions. After all, the State was seeking to ensure that "pregnant women in California know when they are getting medical care from licensed professionals," and pregnant women generally do not need contraceptive services.

Finally, the majority concludes that the Act is overly burdensome.... But these and similar claims are claims that the statute could be applied unconstitutionally, not that it is unconstitutional on its face....

... As I understand the Act, it would require disclosure in no more than two languages—English and Spanish—in the vast majority of California's 58 counties. The exception is Los Angeles County, where, given the large number of different-language speaking groups, expression in many languages may prove necessary to communicate the message to those whom that message will help. Whether the requirement of 13 different languages goes too far and is unnecessarily burdensome in light of the need to secure the statutory objectives is a matter that concerns Los Angeles County alone, and it is a proper subject for a Los Angeles-based as applied challenge in light of whatever facts a plaintiff finds relevant. At most, such facts might show a need for fewer languages, not invalidation of the statute.

. . . .

NOTES

1.   *Abandoning precedent?* In an attempt to distinguish the facts of *NIFLA* from those in *Planned Parenthood v. Casey*, 505 U.S. 833 (1992), Justice Thomas narrowly characterizes the disclosure requirements challenged in *Casey* as informed consent requirements related to medical procedures that may impact a patient's health, as opposed to disclosures aimed at providing information to consumers about particular services. *Nat'l Inst. of Family & Life Advocates v. Becerra*, 138 S. Ct. 2361, 2373 (2018). In a dissenting opinion, Justice Breyer rejects this characterization, arguing that, like *Casey*, *NIFLA* also concerns "medical personnel engaging in activities that directly affect a woman's health." 138 S. Ct. at 2387 (Breyer, J., dissenting). Justice Breyer suggests that, by allowing the state to require doctors to inform patients about alternatives to abortion in *Casey* but prohibiting the state from requiring crisis pregnancy centers to inform patients about the availability of legal abortion services in *NIFLA*, the majority creates an unfortunate double standard. Some scholars have gone further, maintaining that *NIFLA* was erroneously decided, and that the Court's selective abandonment of the precedent established in *Casey* reflects its general animus toward abortion rights. *See* Erwin Chemerinsky & Michele Goodwin, *Constitutional Gerrymandering Against Abortion Rights:* NIFLA v. Becerra, 94 N.Y.U. L. REV. 61, 108–110 (2019).

2.   *Doctrinal incoherence?* Professors Erwin Chemerinsky and Michele Goodwin maintain that the Court's decision in *NIFLA v. Becerra* "is inconsistent with other Supreme Court precedents concerning notice

requirements, including decisions upholding requirements that lawyers disclose pertinent information to potential clients and that mandate doctors provide information to women seeking abortions. In *Planned Parenthood of Southeastern Pennsylvania v. Casey*, the Court upheld a law that required doctors to provide information to a woman deciding whether to proceed with an abortion." *See* Erwin Chemerinsky & Michele Goodwin, *Constitutional Gerrymandering Against Abortion Rights: NIFLA v. Becerra*, 94 N.Y.U. L. REV. 61, 66 (2019). In *Casey*, the Court saw "no reason why the State may not require doctors to inform a woman seeking an abortion of the availability of materials," including those related to consequences of the pregnancy such as fetal development, "even when those consequences have no direct relation to her health." *Planned Parenthood of Southeastern Pennsylvania v. Casey*, 505 U.S. 833, 882 (1992). As Chemerinsky and Goodwin note, "Justice Thomas did not apply the Court's Casey standard and by failing to do so, he ensured an outcome consistent with antiabortion ideological leanings of the majority." Chemerinsky & Goodwin, *supra* at 66.

3. *Consequences for commercial disclosure regulations.* In *NIFLA*, the Court utilized the traditional test for determining whether regulations mandating certain commercial disclosures violate the First Amendment. The test, which was first announced in *Zauderer v. Office of Disciplinary Counsel of Supreme Court of Ohio*, 471 U.S. 626 (1985), considers whether the commercial speech in question is limited to "purely factual and uncontroversial information." In *NIFLA*, the majority concluded that the FACT Act's required disclosures went beyond "purely factual and uncontroversial information." And even if the disclosures were permissible under the *Zauderer* test, they would be "unjustified or unduly burdensome" because they were simultaneously overinclusive in covering facilities regardless of the content of their advertisements, and underinclusive by applying to a very "narrow subset of speakers." The majority's application of the *Zauderer* test raises questions about how to evaluate future disclosure requirements in traditional commercial contexts and can be read to require a higher level of scrutiny than is ordinarily required for commercial speech- a standard that would likely invalidate a broad range of existing disclosure requirements. *See* Andra Lim, Note, *Limiting* NIFLA, 72 STAN. L. REV. 127, 129–141 (2020).

4. *Deception by crisis pregnancy centers.* Crisis pregnancy centers have been criticized for engaging in deceptive marketing practices, including representing themselves as full-service abortion clinics while hiding their anti-choice views, and offering patients misleading and incorrect information about abortion services. Additionally, crisis pregnancy centers are often located near abortion providers, and even engage in online advertising targeted toward those seeking information about abortion services. *See* Sasha M. Raab, *Playing Doctor: When Crisis Pregnancy Centers and States Blur the Line of Informed Consent*, 68 U. KAN. L. REV. 829, 829 (2020). Given these concerns, are states and localities justified in intervening to protect consumers? Or do such centers provide a necessary counterpoint to pro-choice views in the marketplace?

5.   *Targeting religion?* In a concurrence to the *NIFLA* majority opinion, Justice Kennedy expresses concern about the prospect of religious discrimination. Specifically, he maintains that the California FACT Act at issue in *NIFLA* deliberately targeted crisis pregnancy centers "because of their [religious] beliefs." Dahlia Lithwick, *Supreme Court Rules That California Can't Make Crisis Pregnancy Centers Reveal What They Are*, SLATE (June 26, 2018). The day after the Court handed down *NIFLA* decision, Kennedy announced his retirement from the Court.

6.   *A silver lining?* In his dissent, Justice Breyer suggests a silver lining for *NIFLA*. Under the majority's logic, he argues, the many state-level "script" laws that require physicians, even over their own objections and medical reality, to warn women that abortion increases the risk of suicide, breast cancer, and depression also should be invalidated. As Breyer explains, "if a State can lawfully require a doctor to tell a woman seeking an abortion about adoption services, why should it not be able, as here, to require a medical counselor to tell a woman seeking prenatal care or other reproductive healthcare about childbirth and abortion services?" *Nat'l Inst. of Family & Life Advocates v. Becerra*, 138 S. Ct. 2361, 2385 (2018) (Breyer, J. dissenting). As he noted at the *NIFLA* oral argument, "the rule of law embodies evenhandedness, and 'what is sauce for the goose is normally sauce for the gander.'" *Id.*

9.   REVISITING LEGAL STANDARDS GOVERNING THE ABORTION RIGHT

Since Casey *was decided in 1992, lower courts have struggled with applying its nebulous "undue burden" standard. In 2007's* Gonzales v. Carhart, *some members of the Court argued that the majority's decision to uphold the Partial Birth Abortion Ban misapplied the* Casey *standard, deferring unduly to the legislature's proffered rationales for the challenged law. In 2016, the Court again took up a challenge to various abortion restrictions, and in so doing, appeared to inject some rigor into* Casey's *undue burden standard.*

Whole Woman's Health v. Hellerstedt

579 U.S. 582 (2016).

■ BREYER, J.

In *Planned Parenthood of Southeastern Pa. v. Casey*, 505 U.S. 833, 878 (1992), a plurality of the Court concluded that there "exists" an "undue burden" on a woman's right to decide to have an abortion, and consequently a provision of law is constitutionally invalid, if the "*purpose or effect*" of the provision "*is to place a substantial obstacle* in the path of a woman seeking an abortion before the fetus attains viability." (Emphasis added.) The plurality added that "[u]nnecessary health regulations that have the purpose or effect of presenting a substantial obstacle to a woman seeking an abortion impose an undue burden on the right."

We must here decide whether two provisions of Texas' House Bill 2 violate the Federal Constitution as interpreted in *Casey*. The first provision, which we shall call the *"admitting-privileges requirement,"* says that

> "[a] physician performing or inducing an abortion . . . must, on the date the abortion is performed or induced, have active admitting privileges at a hospital that . . . is located not further than 30 miles from the location at which the abortion is performed or induced."

. . . .

The second provision, which we shall call the *"surgical-center requirement,"* says that

> "the minimum standards for an abortion facility must be equivalent to the minimum standards adopted under [the Texas Health and Safety Code section] for ambulatory surgical centers."

We conclude that neither of these provisions confers medical benefits sufficient to justify the burdens upon access that each imposes. Each places a substantial obstacle in the path of women seeking a previability abortion, each constitutes an undue burden on abortion access, and each violates the Federal Constitution.

I

. . . .

The District Court . . . received stipulations from the parties and depositions from the parties' experts. The court conducted a 4-day bench trial. It heard, among other testimony, the opinions from expert witnesses for both sides. On the basis of the stipulations, depositions, and testimony, that court reached the following conclusions:

1. Of Texas' population of more than 25 million people, "approximately 5.4 million" are "women" of "reproductive age," living within a geographical area of "nearly 280,000 square miles."

2. "In recent years, the number of abortions reported in Texas has stayed fairly consistent at approximately 15–16% of the reported pregnancy rate, for a total number of approximately 60,000–72,000 legal abortions performed annually."

3. Prior to the enactment of H.B. 2, there were more than 40 licensed abortion facilities in Texas, which "number dropped by almost half leading up to and in the wake of enforcement of the admitting-privileges requirement that went into effect in late-October 2013."

4. If the surgical-center provision were allowed to take effect, the number of abortion facilities, after September 1, 2014, would be reduced further, so that "only seven facilities and a potential eighth will exist in Texas.

5. Abortion facilities "will remain only in Houston, Austin, San Antonio, and the Dallas/Fort Worth metropolitan region." These include "one facility in Austin, two in Dallas, one in Fort Worth, two in Houston, and either one or two in San Antonio."

6. "Based on historical data pertaining to Texas's average number of abortions, and assuming perfectly equal distribution among the remaining seven or eight providers, this would result in each facility serving between 7,500 and 10,000 patients per year. Accounting for the seasonal variations in pregnancy rates and a slightly unequal distribution of patients at each clinic, it is foreseeable that over 1,200 women per month could be vying for counseling, appointments, and follow-up visits at some of these facilities."

7. The suggestion "that these seven or eight providers could meet the demand of the entire state stretches credulity."

8. "Between November 1, 2012 and May 1, 2014," that is, before and after enforcement of the admitting-privileges requirement, "the decrease in geographical distribution of abortion facilities" has meant that the number of women of reproductive age living more than 50 miles from a clinic has doubled (from 800,000 to over 1.6 million); those living more than 100 miles has increased by 150% (from 400,000 to 1 million); those living more than 150 miles has increased by more than 350% (from 86,000 to 400,000); and those living more than 200 miles has increased by about 2,800% (from 10,000 to 290,000). After September 2014, should the surgical-center requirement go into effect, the number of women of reproductive age living significant distances from an abortion provider will increase as follows: 2 million women of reproductive age will live more than 50 miles from an abortion provider; 1.3 million will live more than 100 miles from an abortion provider; 900,000 will live more than 150 miles from an abortion provider; and 750,000 more than 200 miles from an abortion provider.

9. The "two requirements erect a particularly high barrier for poor, rural, or disadvantaged women."

10. "The great weight of evidence demonstrates that, before the act's passage, abortion in Texas was extremely safe with

particularly low rates of serious complications and virtually no deaths occurring on account of the procedure."

11. "Abortion, as regulated by the State before the enactment of House Bill 2, has been shown to be much safer, in terms of minor and serious complications, than many common medical procedures not subject to such intense regulation and scrutiny."

12. "Additionally, risks are not appreciably lowered for patients who undergo abortions at ambulatory surgical centers as compared to nonsurgical-center facilities."

13. "[W]omen will not obtain better care or experience more frequent positive outcomes at an ambulatory surgical center as compared to a previously licensed facility."

14. "[T]here are 433 licensed ambulatory surgical centers in Texas," of which "336 ... are apparently either 'grandfathered' or enjo[y] the benefit of a waiver of some or all" of the surgical-center "requirements."

15. The "cost of coming into compliance" with the surgical-center requirement "for existing clinics is significant," "undisputedly approach[ing] 1 million dollars," and "most likely exceed[ing] 1.5 million dollars," with "[s]ome ... clinics" unable to "comply due to physical size limitations of their sites." The "cost of acquiring land and constructing a new compliant clinic will likely exceed three million dollars."

On the basis of these and other related findings, the District Court determined that the surgical-center requirement "imposes an undue burden on the right of women throughout Texas to seek a previability abortion," and that the "admitting-privileges requirement, ... in conjunction with the ambulatory-surgical-center requirement, imposes an undue burden on the right of women in the Rio Grande Valley, El Paso, and West Texas to seek a previability abortion." The District Court concluded that the "two provisions" would cause "the closing of almost all abortion clinics in Texas that were operating legally in the fall of 2013," and thereby create a constitutionally "impermissible obstacle as applied to all women seeking a previability abortion" by "restricting access to previously available legal facilities."

. . . .

III

Undue Burden—Legal Standard

We begin with the standard, as described in *Casey*. We recognize that the "State has a legitimate interest in seeing to it that abortion, like any other medical procedure, is performed under circumstances that insure maximum safety for the patient." But, we added, "a statute which, while furthering [a] valid state interest, has the effect of placing a substantial obstacle in the path of a woman's choice cannot be considered a permissible means of serving its legitimate ends." Moreover, "[u]nnecessary health regulations that have the purpose or effect of presenting a substantial obstacle to a woman seeking an abortion impose an undue burden on the right."

The Court of Appeals wrote that a state law is "constitutional if: (1) it does not have the purpose or effect of placing a substantial obstacle in the path of a woman seeking an abortion of a nonviable fetus; and (2) it is reasonably related to (or designed to further) a legitimate state interest." The Court of Appeals went on to hold that "the district court erred by substituting its own judgment for that of the legislature" when it conducted its "undue burden inquiry," in part because "medical uncertainty underlying a statute is for resolution by legislatures, not the courts."

The Court of Appeals' articulation of the relevant standard is incorrect. The first part of the Court of Appeals' test may be read to imply that a district court should not consider the existence or nonexistence of medical benefits when considering whether a regulation of abortion constitutes an undue burden. The rule announced in *Casey,* however, requires that courts consider the burdens a law imposes on abortion access together with the benefits those laws confer. And the second part of the test is wrong to equate the judicial review applicable to the regulation of a constitutionally protected personal liberty with the less strict review applicable where, for example, economic legislation is at issue. . . .

The statement that legislatures, and not courts, must resolve questions of medical uncertainty is also inconsistent with this Court's case law. Instead, the Court, when determining the constitutionality of laws regulating abortion procedures, has placed considerable weight upon evidence and argument presented in judicial proceedings. . . .

. . . For a district court to give significant weight to evidence in the judicial record in these circumstances is consistent with this Court's case law. As we shall describe, the District Court did so here. It did not simply substitute its own judgment for that of the legislature. It considered the evidence in the record—including expert evidence, presented in stipulations, depositions, and testimony. It then weighed the asserted benefits against the burdens. We hold that, in so doing, the District Court applied the correct legal standard.

IV

Undue Burden—Admitting-Privileges Requirement

Turning to the lower courts' evaluation of the evidence, we first consider the admitting-privileges requirement. . . .

The purpose of the admitting-privileges requirement is to help ensure that women have easy access to a hospital should complications arise during an abortion procedure. Brief for Respondents 32–37. But the District Court found that it brought about no such health-related benefit. The court found that "[t]he great weight of evidence demonstrates that, before the act's passage, abortion in Texas was extremely safe with particularly low rates of serious complications and virtually no deaths occurring on account of the procedure." Thus, there was no significant health-related problem that the new law helped to cure.

. . . .

We add that, when directly asked at oral argument whether Texas knew of a single instance in which the new requirement would have helped even one woman obtain better treatment, Texas admitted that there was no evidence in the record of such a case. This answer is consistent with the findings of the other Federal District Courts that have considered the health benefits of other States' similar admitting-privileges laws.

At the same time, the record evidence indicates that the admitting-privileges requirement places a "substantial obstacle in the path of a woman's choice." The District Court found, as of the time the admitting-privileges requirement began to be enforced, the number of facilities providing abortions dropped in half, from about 40 to about 20. Eight abortion clinics closed in the months leading up to the requirement's effective date. Eleven more closed on the day the admitting-privileges requirement took effect.

Other evidence helps to explain why the new requirement led to the closure of clinics. We read that other evidence in light of a brief filed in this Court by the Society of Hospital Medicine. That brief describes the undisputed general fact that "hospitals often condition admitting privileges on reaching a certain number of admissions per year." . . . In a word, doctors would be unable to maintain admitting privileges or obtain those privileges for the future, because the fact that abortions are so safe meant that providers were unlikely to have any patients to admit.

. . . .

In our view, the record contains sufficient evidence that the admitting-privileges requirement led to the closure of half of Texas' clinics, or thereabouts. Those closures meant fewer doctors, longer waiting times, and increased crowding. . . .

V

Undue Burden—Surgical-Center Requirement

The second challenged provision of Texas' new law sets forth the surgical-center requirement. Prior to enactment of the new requirement, Texas law required abortion facilities to meet a host of health and safety requirements. . . .

There is considerable evidence in the record supporting the District Court's findings indicating that the statutory provision requiring all abortion facilities to meet all surgical-center standards does not benefit patients and is not necessary. The District Court found that "risks are not appreciably lowered for patients who undergo abortions at ambulatory surgical centers as compared to nonsurgical-center facilities." The court added that women "will not obtain better care or experience more frequent positive outcomes at an ambulatory surgical center as compared to a previously licensed facility." And these findings are well supported.

. . . .

The upshot is that this record evidence, along with the absence of any evidence to the contrary, provides ample support for the District Court's conclusion that "[m]any of the building standards mandated by the act and its implementing rules have such a tangential relationship to patient safety in the context of abortion as to be nearly arbitrary." That conclusion, along with the supporting evidence, provides sufficient support for the more general conclusion that the surgical-center requirement "will not [provide] better care or . . . more frequent positive outcomes." The record evidence thus supports the ultimate legal conclusion that the surgical-center requirement is not necessary.

At the same time, the record provides adequate evidentiary support for the District Court's conclusion that the surgical-center requirement places a substantial obstacle in the path of women seeking an abortion. The parties stipulated that the requirement would further reduce the number of abortion facilities available to seven or eight facilities, located in Houston, Austin, San Antonio, and Dallas/Fort Worth. In the District Court's view, the proposition that these "seven or eight providers could meet the demand of the entire State stretches credulity." We take this statement as a finding that these few facilities could not "meet" that "demand."

. . . .

. . . [T]he challenged provisions of H.B. 2 close most of the abortion facilities in Texas and place added stress on those facilities able to remain open. They vastly increase the obstacles confronting women seeking abortions in Texas without providing any benefit to women's health capable of withstanding any meaningful scrutiny. The provisions are unconstitutional on their face. . . .

* * *

For these reasons the judgment of the Court of Appeals is reversed, and the case is remanded for further proceedings consistent with this opinion.

■ JUSTICE GINSBURG, concurring.

The Texas law called H.B. 2 inevitably will reduce the number of clinics and doctors allowed to provide abortion services. Texas argues that H.B. 2's restrictions are constitutional because they protect the health of women who experience complications from abortions. In truth, "complications from an abortion are both rare and rarely dangerous." Many medical procedures, including childbirth, are far more dangerous to patients, yet are not subject to ambulatory-surgical-center or hospital admitting-privileges requirements. Given those realities, it is beyond rational belief that H.B. 2 could genuinely protect the health of women, and certain that the law "would simply make it more difficult for them to obtain abortions." When a State severely limits access to safe and legal procedures, women in desperate circumstances may resort to unlicensed rogue practitioners, *faute de mieux,* at great risk to their health and safety. So long as this Court adheres to *Roe v. Wade* (1973) and *Planned Parenthood of Southeastern Pennsylvania v. Casey* (1992), Targeted Regulation of Abortion Providers laws like H.B. 2 that "do little or nothing for health, but rather strew impediments to abortion," cannot survive judicial inspection.

■ JUSTICE THOMAS, dissenting.

Today the Court strikes down two state statutory provisions in all of their applications, at the behest of abortion clinics and doctors. That decision exemplifies the Court's troubling tendency "to bend the rules when any effort to limit abortion, or even to speak in opposition to abortion, is at issue." . . . I write separately to emphasize how today's decision perpetuates the Court's habit of applying different rules to different constitutional rights—especially the putative right to abortion.

To begin, the very existence of this suit is a jurisprudential oddity. Ordinarily, plaintiffs cannot file suits to vindicate the constitutional rights of others. But the Court employs a different approach to rights that it favors. So in this case and many others, the Court has erroneously allowed doctors and clinics to vicariously vindicate the putative constitutional right of women seeking abortions.

This case also underscores the Court's increasingly common practice of invoking a given level of scrutiny—here, the abortion-specific undue burden standard—while applying a different standard of review entirely. . . .

I remain fundamentally opposed to the Court's abortion jurisprudence. Even taking *Casey* as the baseline, however, the majority radically rewrites the undue-burden test in three ways. First, today's decision requires courts to "consider the burdens a law imposes on abortion access together with the benefits those laws confer." Second, today's opinion tells the courts that, when the law's justifications are medically uncertain, they need not defer to the legislature, and must instead assess medical justifications for abortion restrictions by scrutinizing the record themselves. Finally, even if a law imposes no "substantial obstacle" to women's access to abortions, the law now must have more than a "reasonabl[e] relat[ion] to . . . a legitimate state interest." These precepts are nowhere to be found in *Casey* or its successors, and transform the undue-burden test to something much more akin to strict scrutiny.

. . . .

Today's decision will prompt some to claim victory, just as it will stiffen opponents' will to object. But the entire Nation has lost something essential. The majority's embrace of a jurisprudence of rights-specific exceptions and balancing tests is "a regrettable concession of defeat—an acknowledgement that we have passed the point where 'law,' properly speaking, has any further application." Scalia, *The Rule of Law as a Law of Rules*, 56 U. CHI. L. REV. 1175, 1182 (1989). I respectfully dissent.

June Medical Services v. Russo
140 S. Ct. 2103 (2020).

■ JUSTICE BREYER announced the judgment of the Court and delivered an opinion, in which JUSTICE GINSBURG, JUSTICE SOTOMAYOR, and JUSTICE KAGAN join.

. . . .

In this case, we consider the constitutionality of a Louisiana statute, Act 620, that is almost word-for-word identical to Texas' admitting-privileges law. As in *Whole Woman's Health*, the District Court found that the statute offers no significant health benefit. It found that conditions on admitting privileges common to hospitals throughout the State have made and will continue to make it impossible for abortion providers to obtain conforming privileges for reasons that have nothing to do with the State's asserted interests in promoting women's health and safety. And it found that this inability places a substantial obstacle in the path of women seeking an abortion. As in *Whole Woman's Health*, the substantial obstacle the Act imposes, and the absence of any health-related benefit, led the District Court to conclude that the law imposes an undue burden and is therefore unconstitutional.

The Court of Appeals agreed with the District Court's interpretation of the standards we have said apply to regulations on abortion. It thought, however, that the District Court was mistaken on the facts. We disagree. We have examined the extensive record carefully and conclude that it supports the District Court's findings of fact. Those findings mirror those made in *Whole Woman's Health* in every relevant respect and require the same result. We consequently hold that the Louisiana statute is unconstitutional.

. . . .

In March 2014, five months after Texas' admitting-privileges requirement forced the closure of half of that State's abortion clinics, Louisiana's Legislature began to hold hearings to consider a substantially identical proposal. The proposal became law in mid-June 2014.

... Act 620 requires any doctor who performs abortions to hold "active admitting privileges at a hospital that is located not further than thirty miles from the location at which the abortion is performed or induced and that provides obstetrical or gynecological health care services."

. . . .

A few weeks before Act 620 was to take effect in September 2014, three abortion clinics and two abortion providers filed a lawsuit in Federal District Court. They alleged that Act 620 was unconstitutional because (among other things) it imposed an undue burden on the right of their patients to obtain an abortion. . . .

. . . .

Because the issues before us in this case primarily focus upon the factual findings (and fact-related determinations) of the District Court, we set forth only the essential findings here, giving greater detail in the analysis that follows.

With respect to the Act's asserted benefits, the District Court found that:

- "[A]bortion in Louisiana has been extremely safe, with particularly low rates of serious complications." The "testimony of clinic staff and physicians demonstrated" that it "rarely . . . is necessary to transfer patients to a hospital: far less than once a year, or less than one per several thousand patients." And "[w]hether or not a patient's treating physician has admitting privileges is not relevant to the patient's care."

- There was accordingly " 'no significant health-related problem that the new law helped to cure.' The record does not contain any evidence that complications from abortion were being treated improperly, nor any evidence that any negative outcomes could have been avoided if the abortion provider had admitting privileges at a local hospital."

- There was also "no credible evidence in the record that Act 620 would further the State's interest in women's health beyond that which is already insured under existing Louisiana law."

Turning to Act 620's impact on women's access to abortion, the District Court found that:

- Approximately 10,000 women obtain abortions in Louisiana each year. At the outset of this litigation, those women were served by six doctors at five abortion clinics. By the time the court rendered its decision, two of those clinics had closed, and one of the doctors (Doe 4) had retired, leaving only Does 1, 2, 3, 5, and 6.

- "[N]otwithstanding the good faith efforts of Does 1, 2, 4, 5 and 6 to comply with the Act by getting active admitting privileges at a hospital within 30 miles of where they perform abortions, they have had very limited success for reasons related to Act 620 and not related to their competence."

- These doctors' inability to secure privileges was "caused by Act 620 working in concert with existing laws and practices," including hospital bylaws and criteria that "preclude or, at least greatly discourage, the granting of privileges to abortion providers."

- These requirements establish that admitting privileges serve no " 'relevant credentialing function' " because physicians may be denied privileges "for reasons unrelated to competency."

- They also make it "unlikely that the [a]ffected clinics will be able to comply with the Act by recruiting new physicians who have or can obtain admitting privileges."

- Doe 3 testified credibly "that, as a result of his fears, and the demands of his private OB/GYN practice, if he is the last physician performing abortion in either the entire state or in the northern part of the state, he will not continue to perform abortions."

- Enforcing the admitting-privileges requirement would therefore "result in a drastic reduction in the number and geographic distribution of abortion providers, reducing the number of clinics to one, or at most two, and leaving only one, or at most two, physicians providing abortions in the entire state," Does 3 and 5, who would only be allowed to practice in Shreveport and New Orleans. Depending on whether Doe 3 stopped practicing, or whether his retirement was treated as legally relevant, the impact would be a 55%–70% reduction in capacity.

- "The result of these burdens on women and providers, taken together and in context, is that many women seeking a safe, legal abortion in Louisiana will be unable to obtain one. Those who can will face substantial obstacles in exercising their constitutional right to choose abortion due to the dramatic reduction in abortion services."

- In sum, "Act 620 does not advance Louisiana's legitimate interest in protecting the health of women seeking abortions. Instead, Act 620 would increase the risk of harm to women's health by dramatically reducing the availability of safe abortion in Louisiana."

The District Court added that

"there is no legally significant distinction between this case and [*Whole Woman's Health*]: Act 620 was modeled after the Texas admitting privileges requirement, and it functions in the same manner, imposing significant obstacles to abortion access with no countervailing benefits."

On the basis of these findings, the court held that Act 620 and its implementing regulations are unconstitutional. It entered an injunction permanently forbidding their enforcement.

. . . .

The State appealed. A divided panel of the Court of Appeals reversed the District Court's judgment. The panel majority concluded that Act 620's impact was "dramatically less" than that of the Texas law invalidated in *Whole Woman's Health*. . . . Rejecting the District Court's contrary finding, it concluded that the admitting-privileges requirement "performs a real, and previously unaddressed, credentialing function that promotes the wellbeing of women seeking abortion." . . .

Moving on to Act 620's burdens, the appeals court wrote that "everything turns on whether the privileges requirement actually would prevent doctors from practicing in Louisiana. . . . The court noted that "[a]t least three hospitals have proven willing to extend privileges." It thought that "only Doe 1 has put forth a good-faith effort to get admitting privileges," while "Doe 2, Doe 5, and Doe 6 could likely obtain privileges," and "Doe 3's personal choice to stop practicing cannot be legally attributed to Act 620."

. . . .

On the basis of these findings, the panel majority concluded that Louisiana's admitting-privileges requirement would impose no "substantial burden at all" on Louisiana women seeking an abortion, "much less a substantial burden on a large fraction of women . . . ."

. . . .

Turning to the merits, we apply the constitutional standards set forth in our earlier abortion-related cases, and in particular in *Casey* and *Whole Woman's Health*. At the risk of repetition, we remind the reader of the standards we described above. In *Whole Woman's Health*, we quoted *Casey* in explaining that " 'a statute which, while furthering [a] valid state interest has the effect of placing a substantial obstacle in the path of a woman's choice cannot be considered a permissible means of serving its legitimate ends.' " We added that " '[u]nnecessary health regulations' " impose an unconstitutional " 'undue burden' " if they have " 'the purpose or effect of presenting a substantial obstacle to a woman seeking an abortion.' "

We went on to explain that, in applying these standards, courts must "consider the burdens a law imposes on abortion access together with the benefits those laws confer." We cautioned that courts "must review legislative 'factfinding under a deferential standard.' But they "must not 'place dispositive weight' on those 'findings,' " for the courts " 'retai[n] an independent constitutional duty to review factual findings where constitutional rights are at stake.' "

We held in *Whole Woman's Health* that the trial court faithfully applied these standards. It "considered the evidence in the record— including expert evidence, presented in stipulations, depositions, and testimony." It "then weighed the asserted benefits" of the law "against the burdens" it imposed on abortion access. And it concluded that the balance tipped against the statute's constitutionality. The District Court in this suit did the same.

. . . .

We start from the premise that a district court's findings of fact, "whether based on oral or other evidence, must not be set aside unless clearly erroneous, and the reviewing court must give due regard to the trial court's opportunity to judge the witnesses' credibility." In " 'applying [this] standard to the findings of a district court sitting without a jury, appellate courts must constantly have in mind that their function is not to decide factual issues de novo.' " Where "the district court's account of the evidence is plausible in light of the record viewed in its entirety, the court of appeals may not reverse it even though convinced that had it been sitting as the trier of fact, it would have weighed the evidence differently." . . .

. . . .

Under that familiar standard, we find that the testimony and other evidence contained in the extensive record developed over the 6-day trial support the District Court's ultimate conclusion that, "[e]ven if Act 620 could be said to further women's health to some marginal degree, the burdens it imposes far outweigh any such benefit, and thus the Act imposes an unconstitutional undue burden."

The District Court found that enforcing the admitting-privileges requirement would "result in a drastic reduction in the number and geographic distribution of abortion providers." In light of demographic, economic, and other evidence, the court concluded that this reduction would make it impossible for "many women seeking a safe, legal abortion in Louisiana . . . to obtain one" and that it would impose "substantial obstacles" on those who could. We consider each of these findings in turn.

Act 620's Effect on Abortion Providers

. . . [The district] court found that the Act would prevent Does 1, 2, and 6 from providing abortions. And it found that the Act would bar Doe 5 from working in his Baton Rouge-based clinic, relegating him to New Orleans.

In *Whole Woman's Health*, we said that, by presenting "direct testimony" from doctors who had been unable to secure privileges, and "plausible inferences to be drawn from the timing of the clinic closures" around the law's effective date, the plaintiffs had "satisfied their burden" to establish that the Texas admitting-privileges requirement caused the closure of those clinics.

We wrote that these inferences were bolstered by the submissions of amici in the medical profession, which "describe[d] the undisputed general fact that hospitals often" will restrict admitting privileges to doctors likely to seek a "certain number of admissions per year." The likely effect of such requirements was that abortion providers "would be unable to maintain admitting privileges or obtain those privileges for the future, because the fact that abortions are so safe meant that providers were unlikely to have any patients to admit." . . .

To illustrate how these criteria impacted abortion providers, we noted the example of an obstetrician with 38 years' experience who had been denied admitting privileges for reasons " 'not based on clinical competence considerations.' " This, we said, showed that the law served no "relevant credentialing function," but prevented qualified providers from serving women who seek an abortion. And that, in turn, "help[ed] to explain why the new [law's admitting-privileges] requirement led to the closure of " so many Texas clinics.

The evidence on which the District Court relied in this case is even stronger and more detailed. The District Court supervised Does 1, 2, 5, and 6 for over a year and a half as they tried, and largely failed, to obtain conforming privileges from 13 relevant hospitals. The court heard direct evidence that some of the doctors' applications were denied for reasons that had nothing to do with their ability to perform abortions safely. . . .

The evidence shows, among other things, that the fact that hospital admissions for abortion are vanishingly rare means that, unless they also maintain active OB/GYN practices, abortion providers in Louisiana are unlikely to have any recent in-hospital experience. Yet such experience can well be a precondition to obtaining privileges. . . .

The evidence also shows that many providers, even if they could initially obtain admitting privileges, would be unable to keep them. That is because, unless they have a practice that requires regular in-hospital care, they will lose the privileges for failing to use them. . . .

The evidence also shows that opposition to abortion played a significant role in some hospitals' decisions to deny admitting privileges. Some hospitals expressly bar anyone with privileges from performing abortions. Others are unwilling to extend privileges to abortion providers as a matter of discretion. . . .

Still other hospitals have requirements that abortion providers cannot satisfy because of the hostility they face in Louisiana. Many Louisiana hospitals require applicants to identify a doctor (called a "covering physician") willing to serve as a backup should the applicant admit a patient and then for some reason become unavailable. The District Court found "that opposition to abortion can present a major, if not insurmountable hurdle, for an applicant getting the required covering physician." . . .

Just as in *Whole Woman's Health*, the experiences of the individual doctors in this case support the District Court's factual finding that Louisiana's admitting-privileges requirement, like that in Texas' law, serves no " 'relevant credentialing function.' "

. . . .

Act 620's Impact on Abortion Access

The District Court drew from the record evidence, including the factual findings we have just discussed, several conclusions in respect to the burden that Act 620 is likely to impose upon women's ability to access abortions in Louisiana. To better understand the significance of these conclusions, the reader should keep in mind the geographic distribution of the doctors and their clinics. . . .

. . . .

Those women not altogether prevented from obtaining an abortion would face other burdens. As in *Whole Woman's Health*, the reduction in abortion providers caused by Act 620 would inevitably mean "longer waiting times, and increased crowding." The District Court heard testimony that delays in obtaining an abortion increase the risk that a woman will experience complications from the procedure and may make it impossible for her to choose a noninvasive medication abortion.

Even if they obtain an appointment at a clinic, women who might previously have gone to a clinic in Baton Rouge or Shreveport would face increased driving distances. New Orleans is nearly a five hour drive from Shreveport; it is over an hour from Baton Rouge; and Baton Rouge is more than four hours from Shreveport. The impact of those increases would be magnified by Louisiana's requirement that every woman undergo an ultrasound and receive mandatory counseling at least 24 hours before an abortion. . . .

Taken together, we think that these findings and the evidence that underlies them are sufficient to support the District Court's conclusion that Act 620 would place substantial obstacles in the path of women seeking an abortion in Louisiana.

Benefits

We turn finally to the law's asserted benefits. The District Court found that there was " 'no significant health-related problem that the new law helped to cure.' " It found that the admitting-privileges requirement "[d]oes [n]ot [p]rotect [w]omen's [h]ealth," provides "no significant health benefits," and makes no improvement to women's health "compared to prior law." Our examination of the record convinces us that these findings are not "clearly erroneous."

. . . .

As in *Whole Woman's Health*, the State introduced no evidence "showing that patients have better outcomes when their physicians have admitting privileges" or "of any instance in which an admitting privileges requirement would have helped even one woman obtain better treatment." . . .

Conclusion

We conclude, in light of the record, that the District Court's significant factual findings—both as to burdens and as to benefits—have ample evidentiary support. None is "clearly erroneous." Given the facts found, we must also uphold the District Court's related factual and legal determinations. These include its determination that Louisiana's law poses a "substantial obstacle" to women seeking an abortion; its determination that the law offers no significant health-related benefits; and its determination that the law consequently imposes an "undue burden" on a woman's constitutional right to choose to have an abortion. We also agree with its ultimate legal conclusion that, in light of these findings and our precedents, Act 620 violates the Constitution.

As a postscript, we explain why we have found unconvincing several further arguments that the State has made. First, the State suggests that the record supports the Court of Appeals' conclusion that Act 620 poses no substantial obstacle to the abortion decision. This argument misconceives the question before us. "The question we must answer" is "not whether the [Fifth] Circuit's interpretation of the facts was clearly erroneous, but whether the District Court's finding[s were] clearly erroneous." As we have explained, we think the District Court's factual findings here are plausible in light of the record as a whole. Nothing in the State's briefing furnishes a basis to disturb that conclusion.

Second, the State says that the record does not show that Act 620 will burden every woman in Louisiana who seeks an abortion. True, but beside the point. As we stated in *Casey*, a State's abortion-related law is unconstitutional on its face if "it will operate as a substantial obstacle to a woman's choice to undergo an abortion" in "a large fraction of the cases in which [it] is relevant." In *Whole Woman's Health*, we reaffirmed that standard. We made clear that the phrase refers to a large fraction of "those women for whom the provision is an actual rather than an irrelevant restriction." That standard, not an "every woman" standard, is the standard that must govern in this case.

Third, the State argues that Act 620 would not make it "nearly impossible" for a woman to obtain an abortion. But, again, the words "nearly impossible" do not describe the legal standard that governs here. Since *Casey*, we have repeatedly reiterated that the plaintiff's burden in a challenge to an abortion regulation is to show that the regulation's "purpose or effect" is to "plac[e] a substantial obstacle in the path of a woman seeking an abortion of a nonviable fetus."

. . . .

This case is similar to, nearly identical with, *Whole Woman's Health*. And the law must consequently reach a similar conclusion. Act 620 is unconstitutional. . . .

■ CHIEF JUSTICE ROBERTS, concurring in the judgment.

. . . .

The legal doctrine of stare decisis requires us, absent special circumstances, to treat like cases alike. The Louisiana law imposes a burden on access to abortion just as severe as that imposed by the Texas law, for the same reasons. Therefore Louisiana's law cannot stand under our precedents.

Stare decisis ("to stand by things decided") is the legal term for fidelity to precedent. It has long been "an established rule to abide by former precedents, where the same points come again in litigation; as well to keep the scale of justice even and steady, and not liable to waver with every new judge's opinion." 1 W. BLACKSTONE, COMMENTARIES ON THE LAWS OF ENGLAND 69 (1765). This principle is grounded in a basic humility that recognizes today's legal issues are often not so different from the questions of yesterday and that we are not the first ones to try to answer them. . . .

Adherence to precedent is necessary to "avoid an arbitrary discretion in the courts." THE FEDERALIST NO. 78, p. 529 (J. Cooke ed. 1961) (A. Hamilton). The constraint of precedent distinguishes the judicial "method and philosophy from those of the political and legislative process." Jackson, *Decisional Law and Stare Decisis*, 30 A. B. A. J. 334 (1944).

The doctrine also brings pragmatic benefits. Respect for precedent "promotes the evenhanded, predictable, and consistent development of legal principles, fosters reliance on judicial decisions, and contributes to the actual and perceived integrity of the judicial process." It is the "means by which we ensure that the law will not merely change erratically, but will develop in a principled and intelligible fashion." In that way, "stare decisis is an old friend of the common lawyer."

Stare decisis is not an "inexorable command." But for precedent to mean anything, the doctrine must give way only to a rationale that goes beyond whether the case was decided correctly. The Court accordingly considers additional factors before overruling a precedent, such as its administrability, its fit with subsequent factual and legal developments, and the reliance interests that the precedent has engendered.

Stare decisis principles also determine how we handle a decision that itself departed from the cases that came before it. In those instances, "[r]emaining true to an 'intrinsically sounder' doctrine established in prior cases better serves the values of stare decisis than would following" the recent departure. Stare decisis is pragmatic and contextual, not "a mechanical formula of adherence to the latest decision."

Both Louisiana and the providers agree that the undue burden standard announced in *Casey* provides the appropriate framework to analyze Louisiana's law. Neither party has asked us to reassess the constitutional validity of that standard.

Casey reaffirmed "the most central principle of *Roe v. Wade*," "a woman's right to terminate her pregnancy before viability." At the same time, it recognized that the State has "important and legitimate interests in . . . protecting the health of the pregnant woman and in protecting the potentiality of human life."

. . . .

Under *Casey*, the State may not impose an undue burden on the woman's ability to obtain an abortion. "A finding of an undue burden is a shorthand for the conclusion that a state regulation has the purpose or effect of placing a substantial obstacle in the path of a woman seeking an abortion of a nonviable fetus." Laws that do not pose a substantial obstacle to abortion access are permissible, so long as they are "reasonably related" to a legitimate state interest.

After faithfully reciting this standard, the Court in *Whole Woman's Health* added the following observation: "The rule announced in *Casey* . . . requires that courts consider the burdens a law imposes on abortion access together with the benefits those laws confer." The plurality repeats today that the undue burden standard requires courts "to weigh the law's asserted benefits against the burdens it imposes on abortion access."

Read in isolation from *Casey*, such an inquiry could invite a grand "balancing test in which unweighted factors mysteriously are weighed." Under such tests, "equality of treatment is . . . impossible to achieve; predictability is destroyed; judicial arbitrariness is facilitated; judicial courage is impaired." Scalia, *The Rule of Law as a Law of Rules*, 56 U. CHI. L. REV. 1175, 1182 (1989).

In this context, courts applying a balancing test would be asked in essence to weigh the State's interests in "protecting the potentiality of human life" and the health of the woman, on the one hand, against the woman's liberty interest in defining her "own concept of existence, of meaning, of the universe, and of the mystery of human life" on the other. There is no plausible sense in which anyone, let alone this Court, could objectively assign weight to such imponderable values and no meaningful way to compare them if there were. Attempting to do so would be like "judging whether a particular line is longer than a particular rock is heavy." Pretending that we could pull that off would require us to act as legislators, not judges, and would result in nothing other than an "unanalyzed exercise of judicial will" in the guise of a "neutral utilitarian calculus."

Nothing about *Casey* suggested that a weighing of costs and benefits of an abortion regulation was a job for the courts.... *Casey* instead focuses on the existence of a substantial obstacle, the sort of inquiry familiar to judges across a variety of contexts.

. . . .

Whole Woman's Health held that Texas's admitting privileges requirement placed "a substantial obstacle in the path of women seeking a previability abortion," independent of its discussion of benefits. Because Louisiana's admitting privileges requirement would restrict women's access to abortion to the same degree as Texas's law, it also cannot stand under our precedent.

. . . .

Stare decisis instructs us to treat like cases alike. The result in this case is controlled by our decision four years ago invalidating a nearly identical Texas law. The Louisiana law burdens women seeking previability abortions to the same extent as the Texas law, according to factual findings that are not clearly erroneous. For that reason, I concur in the judgment of the Court that the Louisiana law is unconstitutional.

■ JUSTICE THOMAS, dissenting.

Today a majority of the Court perpetuates its ill-founded abortion jurisprudence by enjoining a perfectly legitimate state law and doing so without jurisdiction. As is often the case with legal challenges to abortion regulations, this suit was brought by abortionists and abortion clinics. . . .

. . . The plurality and the Chief Justice ultimately cast aside this jurisdictional barrier to conclude that Louisiana's law is unconstitutional under our precedents. But those decisions created the right to abortion out of whole cloth, without a shred of support from the Constitution's text. Our abortion precedents are grievously wrong and should be overruled. Because we have neither jurisdiction nor constitutional authority to declare Louisiana's duly enacted law unconstitutional, I respectfully dissent.

. . . .

. . . [The challenged Louisiana law] represents a constitutionally valid exercise of the State's traditional police powers. The plurality and the Chief Justice claim that the Court's judgment is dictated by "our precedents," particularly *Whole Woman's Health.*

But today's decision is wrong for a far simpler reason: The Constitution does not constrain the States' ability to regulate or even prohibit abortion. This Court created the right to abortion based on an amorphous, unwritten right to privacy, which it grounded in the "legal fiction" of substantive due process. As the origins of this jurisprudence readily demonstrate, the putative right to abortion is a creation that should be undone.

The Court first conceived a free-floating constitutional right to privacy in *Griswold v. Connecticut*, 381 U.S. 479 (1965). . . . The Court explained that this right could be found in the "penumbras" of five different Amendments to the Constitution—the First, Third, Fourth, Fifth, and Ninth. Rather than explain what free speech or the quartering of troops had to do with contraception, the Court simply declared that these rights had created "zones of privacy" with their "penumbras," which were "formed by emanations from those guarantees that help give them life and substance." This reasoning is as mystifying as it is baseless.

. . . .

Just eight years later, the Court utilized its newfound power in *Roe v. Wade*, 410 U.S. 113 (1973). There, the Court struck down a Texas law restricting abortion as a violation of a woman's constitutional "right of privacy," which it grounded in the "concept of personal liberty" purportedly protected by the Due Process Clause of the Fourteenth Amendment. . . . Without any legal explanation, the Court simply concluded that this unwritten right to privacy was "broad enough to encompass a woman's [abortion] decision."

Roe is grievously wrong for many reasons, but the most fundamental is that its core holding—that the Constitution protects a woman's right to abort her unborn child—finds no support in the text of the Fourteenth Amendment. *Roe* suggests that the Due Process Clause's reference to "liberty" could provide a textual basis for its novel privacy right. But that Clause does not guarantee liberty *qua* liberty. Rather, it expressly contemplates the deprivation of liberty and requires only that such deprivations occur through "due process of law." As I have previously explained, there is " 'considerable historical evidence support[ing] the position that "due process of law" was [originally understood as] a separation-of-powers concept . . . forbidding only deprivations not authorized by legislation or common law.' " Others claim that the original understanding of this Clause requires that "statutes that purported to empower the other branches to deprive persons of rights without adequate procedural guarantees [be] subject to judicial review." But, whatever the precise requirements of the Due Process Clause, "the notion that a constitutional provision that guarantees only 'process' before a person is deprived of life, liberty, or property could define the substance of those rights strains credulity for even the most casual user of words."

More specifically, the idea that the Framers of the Fourteenth Amendment understood the Due Process Clause to protect a right to abortion is farcical. In 1868, when the Fourteenth Amendment was ratified, a majority of the States and numerous Territories had laws on the books that limited (and in many cases nearly prohibited) abortion. It would no doubt shock the public at that time to learn that one of the new constitutional Amendments contained hidden within the interstices of its text a right to abortion. The fact that it took this Court over a century to find that right all but proves that it was more than hidden—it simply was not (and is not) there.

. . . .

JUSTICE ALITO, with whom JUSTICE GORSUCH joins, with whom JUSTICE THOMAS joins except as to Parts III-C and IV-F, and with whom JUSTICE KAVANAUGH joins as to Parts I, II, and III, dissenting.

The majority bills today's decision as a facsimile of *Whole Woman's Health v. Hellerstedt* and it's true they have something in common. In both, the abortion right recognized in this Court's decisions is used like a bulldozer to flatten legal rules that stand in the way.

. . . .

Today's decision claims new victims. The divided majority cannot agree on what the abortion right requires, but it nevertheless strikes down a Louisiana law, Act 620, that the legislature enacted for the asserted purpose of protecting women's health. To achieve this end, the majority misuses the doctrine of stare decisis, invokes an inapplicable standard of appellate review, and distorts the record.

The plurality eschews the constitutional test set out in *Casey* and instead employs the balancing test adopted in *Whole Woman's Health*. The plurality concludes that the Louisiana law does nothing to protect the health of women, but that is disproved by substantial evidence in the record. And the plurality upholds the District Court's finding that the Louisiana law would cause a drastic reduction in the number of abortion providers in the State even though this finding was based on an erroneous legal standard and a thoroughly inadequate factual inquiry.

The Chief Justice stresses the importance of stare decisis and thinks that precedent, namely *Whole Woman's Health*, dooms the Louisiana law. But at the same time, he votes to overrule *Whole Woman's Health* insofar as it changed the *Casey* test.

. . . .

For these reasons, I cannot join the decision of the Court. I would remand the case to the District Court and instruct that court, before proceeding any further, to require the joinder of a plaintiff with standing. If a proper plaintiff is added, the District Court should conduct a new trial and determine, based on proper evidence, whether enforcement of Act 620 would diminish the number of abortion providers in the State to such a degree that women's access to abortions would be substantially impaired. In making that determination, the court should jettison the nebulous "good faith" test that it used in judging whether the physicians who currently lack admitting privileges would be able to obtain privileges and thus continue to perform abortions if Act 620 were permitted to take effect. Because the doctors in question (many of whom are or were plaintiffs in this case) stand to lose, not gain, by obtaining privileges, the court should require the plaintiffs to show that these doctors sought admitting privileges with the degree of effort that they would expend if their personal interests were at stake.

. . . .

■ JUSTICE GORSUCH, dissenting.

The judicial power is constrained by an array of rules. Rules about the deference due the legislative process, the standing of the parties before us, the use of facial challenges to invalidate democratically enacted statutes, and the award of prospective relief. Still more rules seek to ensure that any legal tests judges may devise are capable of neutral and principled administration. Individually, these rules may seem prosaic. But, collectively, they help keep us in our constitutionally assigned lane, sure that we are in the business of saying what the law is, not what we wish it to be.

Today's decision doesn't just overlook one of these rules. It overlooks one after another. And it does so in a case touching on one of the most controversial topics in contemporary politics and law, exactly the context where this Court should be leaning most heavily on the rules of the judicial process. In truth, *Roe v. Wade* is not even at issue here. The real question we face concerns our willingness to follow the traditional constraints of the judicial process when a case touching on abortion enters the courtroom.

When confronting a constitutional challenge to a law, this Court ordinarily reviews the legislature's factual findings under a "deferential" if not "[u]ncritical" standard. When facing such a challenge, too, this Court usually accepts that "the public interest has been declared in terms well-nigh conclusive" by the legislature's adoption of the law—so we may review the law only for its constitutionality, not its wisdom. Today, however, the plurality declares that the law before us holds no benefits for the public and bears too many social costs. All while sharing virtually nothing about the facts that led the legislature to conclude otherwise. The law might as well have fallen from the sky.

Of course, that's hardly the case. In Act 620, Louisiana's legislature found that requiring abortion providers to hold admitting privileges at a hospital within 30 miles of the clinic where they perform abortions would serve the public interest by protecting women's health and safety. Those in today's majority never bother to say so, but it turns out that Act 620's admitting privileges requirement for abortion providers tracks longstanding state laws governing physicians who perform relatively low-risk procedures like colonoscopies, Lasik eye surgeries, and steroid injections at ambulatory surgical centers. In fact, the Louisiana legislature passed Act 620 only after extensive hearings at which experts detailed how the Act would promote safer abortion treatment—by providing "a more thorough evaluation mechanism of physician competency," promoting "continuity of care" following abortion, enhancing inter-physician communication, and preventing patient abandonment.

Testifying physicians explained, for example, that abortions carry inherent risks including uterine perforation, hemorrhage, cervical laceration, infection, retained fetal body parts, and missed ectopic pregnancy. Unsurprisingly, those risks are minimized when the physician providing the abortion is competent. Yet, unlike hospitals which undertake rigorous credentialing processes, Louisiana's abortion clinics historically have done little to ensure provider competence. Clinics have failed to perform background checks or to inquire into the training of doctors they brought on board. Clinics have even hired physicians whose specialties were unrelated to abortion—including a radiologist and an ophthalmologist. Requiring hospital admitting privileges, witnesses testified, would help ensure that clinics hire competent professionals and provide a mechanism for ongoing peer review of physician proficiency. Loss of admitting privileges, as well, might signal a problem meriting further investigation by state officials. At least one Louisiana abortion provider's loss of admitting privileges following a patient's death alerted the state licensing board to questions about his competence, and ultimately resulted in restrictions on his practice.

The legislature also heard testimony that Louisiana's clinics and the physicians who work in them have racked up dozens of citations for safety and ethical violations in recent years. Violations have included failing to use sterile equipment, maintaining unsanitary conditions, failing to monitor patients' vital signs, permitting improper administration of medications by unauthorized persons, and neglecting to obtain informed consent from patients. Some clinics have failed to maintain supplies of emergency medications and medical equipment for treating surgical complications. One clinic used single-use hoses and tubes on multiple patients, and the solution needed to sterilize instruments was changed so infrequently that it often had pieces of tissue floating in it. Hospital credentialing processes, witnesses suggested, could help prevent such violations. In the course of the credentialing process, physicians' prior safety lapses, including criminal violations and medical malpractice suits, would be revealed and investigated, and incompetent doctors might be weeded out.

The legislature heard, too, from affected women and emergency room physicians about clinic doctors' record of abandoning their patients. One woman testified that, while she was hemorrhaging, her abortion provider told her, " 'You're on your own. Get out.' " Eventually, the woman went to a hospital where an emergency room physician removed fetal body parts that the abortion provider had left in her body. Another patient who complained of severe pain following her abortion was told simply to go home and lie down. When she decided for herself to go to the emergency room, physicians discovered a tear in her uterus and a large hematoma containing a fetal head. The woman required an emergency hysterectomy. In another case, a clinic physician allowed a patient to bleed for three hours, yet a clinic employee testified that the physician would not let her call 911 because of possible media involvement. In the end, the employee called anyway and emergency room personnel discovered that the woman had a perforated uterus and a needed a hysterectomy. A different physician explained that she routinely treats abortion complications in the emergency room when the physician who performed the abortion lacks admitting privileges. In her experience, that situation "puts a woman's health at an unnecessary, unacceptable risk that results from a delay of care . . . and a lack of continuity of care." Admitting privileges would mitigate these risks, she testified, because "the physician who performed the procedure would be the one best equipped to evaluate and treat the patient."

Nor did the legislature neglect to consider the law's potential burdens. As witnesses explained, the admitting privileges requirement in Act 620 for abortion clinic providers would parallel existing requirements for many physicians who work at ambulatory surgical centers. And there is no indication this parallel admitting privileges requirement has led to the closing of any surgical centers or otherwise presented obstacles to quality care in Louisiana. Further, legislators learned that at least one Louisiana abortion provider already had qualifying admitting privileges, suggesting other competent abortion providers would be able to comply with the new regulation as well.

> . . . .

. . . From beginning to end, the plurality treats *Whole Woman's Health*'s fact-laden predictions about how a Texas law would impact the availability of abortion in that State in 2016 as if they obviously and necessarily applied to Louisiana in 2020. Most notably, the plurality cites Whole Woman's Health for the proposition that admitting privileges requirements offer no benefit when it comes to patient safety or otherwise. But *Whole Woman's Health* found an absence of benefit based only on the particular factual record before it. Nothing in the decision suggested that its conclusions about the costs and benefits of the Texas statute were universal principles of law, medicine, or economics true in all places and at all times. . . .

Not only does today's decision treat factual questions as if they were legal ones, it treats legal questions as if they were facts. . . . The plurality defers not only to the district court's findings about the extent of the law's benefits, but also to the lower court's judgment that the benefits are so limited that the law's burden on abortion access is "undue." . . .

. . . [A]s today's concurrence recognizes, the legal standard the plurality applies when it comes to admitting privileges for abortion clinics turns out to be exactly the sort of all-things-considered balancing of benefits and burdens this Court has long rejected. Really, it's little more than the judicial version of a hunter's stew: Throw in anything that looks interesting, stir, and season to taste. In another context, this Court has described the sort of decisionmaking on display today as "inherently, and therefore permanently, unpredictable." Under its terms, "[w]hether a [burden] is deemed [undue] depends heavily on which factors the judge considers and how much weight he accords each of them."

. . . .

When judges take it upon themselves to assess the raw costs and benefits of a new law or regulation, it can come as no surprise that "[s]ome courts wind up attaching the same significance to opposite facts," and even attaching the opposite significance to the same facts. It can come as no surprise, either, that judges retreat to their underlying assumptions or moral intuitions when deciding whether a burden is undue. For what else is left?

. . . The lament is understandable. Missing here is exactly what judges usually depend on when asked to make tough calls: an administrable legal rule to follow, a neutral principle, something outside themselves to guide their decision.

. . . A deeper respect for stare decisis and existing precedents, the concurrence assures us, supplies the key to a safe way out. Unfortunately, however, the reality proves more complicated.

Start with the concurrence's discussion of *Whole Woman's Health*. Immediately after paying homage to stare decisis, the concurrence refuses to follow the all-things-considered balancing test that decision employed when striking down Texas's admitting privileges law. In the process, the concurrence rightly recounts many of the problems with raw balancing tests. But then, switching directions again, ... the concurrence concludes, because the facts of this suit look like those in *Whole Woman's Health*, we must find an impermissible substantial obstacle here too.

But . . . the facts of this suit cannot be so neatly reduced to *Whole Woman's Health* redux. . . . At no point did the Court hold that the burdens imposed by the Texas law alone—divorced from any consideration of the law's benefits—could suffice to establish a substantial obstacle. To the contrary, *Whole Woman's Health* insisted that the substantial obstacle test "requires that courts consider the burdens a law imposes on abortion access together with the benefits th[e] la[w] confer[s]." And whatever else respect for stare decisis might suggest, it cannot demand allegiance to a nonexistent ruling inconsistent with the approach actually taken by the Court.

The concurrence's fallback argument doesn't solve the problem either. So what if *Whole Woman's Health* rejected the benefits-free version of the "substantial obstacle" test the concurrence endorses? The concurrence assures us that *Planned Parenthood of Southeastern Pa. v. Casey* specified this form of the test, so we must (or at least may) do the same, whatever *Whole Woman's Health* says.

But . . . [i]n the context of medical regulations, too, the concurrence's new test might even prove stricter than strict scrutiny. After all, it's possible for a regulation to survive strict scrutiny if it is narrowly tailored to advance a compelling state interest. And no one doubts that women's health can be such an interest. Yet, under the concurrence's test it seems possible that even the most compelling and narrowly tailored medical regulation would have to fail if it placed a substantial obstacle in the way of abortion access. Such a result would appear to create yet another discontinuity with *Casey*, which expressly disavowed any test as strict as strict scrutiny.

To arrive at today's result, rules must be brushed aside and shortcuts taken. While the concurrence parts ways with the plurality at the last turn, the road both travel leads us to a strangely open space, unconstrained by many of the neutral principles that normally govern the judicial process. The temptation to proceed this direction, closer with each step toward an unobstructed exercise of will, may be always with us, a danger inherent in judicial review. But it is an impulse this Court normally strives mightily to resist. Today, in a highly politicized and contentious arena, we prove unwilling, or perhaps unable, to resist that temptation. Either way, respectfully, it is a sign we have lost our way.

■ JUSTICE KAVANAUGH, dissenting.

. . . . A threshold question in this case concerns the proper standard for evaluating state abortion laws. . . .

Today, five Members of the Court reject the *Whole Woman's Health* cost-benefit standard. A different five Members of the Court conclude that Louisiana's admitting-privileges law is unconstitutional because it "would restrict women's access to abortion to the same degree as" the Texas law in *Whole Woman's Health*.

I agree with the first of those two conclusions. But I respectfully dissent from the second because, in my view, additional factfinding is necessary to properly evaluate Louisiana's law. . . . [T]he factual record at this stage of plaintiffs' facial, pre-enforcement challenge does not adequately demonstrate that the three relevant doctors . . . cannot obtain admitting privileges or, therefore, that any of the three Louisiana abortion clinics would close as a result of the admitting-privileges law. . . . In short, I agree with Justice Alito that the Court should remand the case for a new trial and additional factfinding under the appropriate legal standards.

NOTES

1.   *Giving the undue burden standard teeth?* Commentators maintain that *Whole Woman's Health v. Hellerstedt* puts teeth into the undue burden requirement that will constrain courts from unscientific speculation in the future. Linda Greenhouse & Reva Siegel, *The Difference a Whole Woman*

Makes: Protection for the Abortion Right After Whole Woman's Health, 126 YALE L.J. FORUM 149, 149–50 (2016).

2.   *Reneging on* Whole Woman's Health? *Abortion* rights advocates praised *Whole Woman's Health* for settling, once and for all, a contentious debate about the appropriate level of scrutiny and judicial review for abortion regulations. However, as Professor Leah Litman explains, "states and the federal courts of appeals do not seem to have gotten the message," relying on various approaches, including recycling arguments the Court rejected in *Whole Woman's Health*, to limit the decision's force. Leah Litman, *Unduly Burdening Women's Health: How Lower Courts Are Undermining* Whole Women's Health v. Hellerstedt, 116 MICH. L. REV. ONLINE 50, 51 (2017). Specifically, state legislatures have defended new abortion restrictions on the ground that, *Whole Woman's Health* applies only to laws aimed at promoting maternal health. On this account, new laws that aim to protect fetal life, as opposed to maternal health, are beyond the ambit of *Whole Woman's Health*. But it is not just that lower courts have narrowly interpreted *Whole Woman's Health*'s mandate to apply only to those measures aimed at promoting maternal health; lower courts have also interpreted the decision to require courts to engage in extensive—and quite specific—fact-finding before invalidating—or even enjoining—a challenged restriction. For example, in *Planned Parenthood of Arkansas & Eastern Oklahoma v. Jegley*, 2018 WL 3029104 (E.D. Ark. W.D. 2018), a federal district court issued a preliminary injunction preventing the state from enforcing a law requiring medication-abortion providers to have a contract with a physician with hospital admitting privileges. The district court noted that, like Texas admitting the privileges requirement invalidated in *Whole Woman's Health*, the Arkansas restriction, if it were to take effect, would result in the shuttering of abortion clinics in that state. Nevertheless, on appeal, the Eighth Circuit vacated the preliminary injunction on the ground that the district court "did not define or estimate the number of women who would be unduly burdened" by the requirement because it "did not determine how many women would face increased travel distances." 864 F.3d 953 (8th Cir. 2017). Further, the district court failed to "estimate the number of women who would forgo abortions" or "estimate the number of women who would postpone their abortions" because of the restriction. Does *Whole Woman's Health* require such detailed and extensive fact-finding in order to determine that a restriction poses an undue burden?

In addition to employing interpretive tactics designed to limit *Whole Woman's Health*'s reach, some lower courts have been more upfront about their opposition to the precedent, explicitly urging the Supreme Court to "reevaluate" its abortion jurisprudence. *See* Litman, *supra* at 58.

3.   *Defanging the undue burden standard?* If *Whole Woman's Health* injected some teeth into *Casey*'s undue burden standard, does *June Medical Services v. Russo* extract these teeth, returning the jurisprudence to the *Casey* status quo? Is it an effective overruling of *Whole Woman's Health*? As Melissa Murray notes, Chief Justice Roberts's concurrence emphasizes the importance of precedent, but insists that *Whole Woman's Health* is not the relevant precedent to be followed—*Casey* is. "[I]n the name of stare decisis

and restraint, Chief Justice Roberts at once adhered to *Whole Woman's Health* and simultaneously denounced the decision as a departure from past precedent (*Casey*). *See* Melissa Murray, *The Symbiosis of Abortion and Precedent*, 134 HARV. L. REV. 308, 325 (2020). Do you agree with this account of *June Medical Services*?

4.   *What opinion controls?* How should we understand Chief Justice Roberts's concurrence in *June Medical Services*? Does it control, or does Justice Breyer's plurality opinion, reiterating the *Whole Woman's Health* balancing test, control? Under *Marks v. United States*, 430 U.S. 188 (1977), "[w]hen a fragmented Court decides a case and no single rationale explaining the result enjoys the assent of five Justices, 'the holding of the Court may be viewed as that position taken by those Members who concurred in the judgments on the narrowest grounds.'" *Id*. at 193. With this in mind, what is the applicable standard that emerges from *June Medical Services*?

5.   *Lower courts respond to* June Medical Services. Some lower courts have regarded the Chief Justice's concurrence in *June Medical Services* as controlling precedent. In *Hopkins v. Jegley*, 968 F.3d 912 (8th Cir. 2020), the Eighth Circuit relied on *Marks* in concluding that the Chief Justice's "separate opinion is controlling." *Id*. at 915. The court went on to conclude that "the appropriate inquiry under *Casey*" required only determining "whether the law poses 'a substantial obstacle' or 'substantial burden, not whether benefits outweighed burdens.'" *Id*. Likewise, in *EMW Women's Surgical Center, P.S.C. v. Friedlander*, 978 F.3d 418 (6th Cir. 2020), the Sixth Circuit regarded the Chief Justice's concurrence as the controlling opinion, noting that it "clarified that the undue burden standard is not a balancing test." *Id*. at 437.

6.   *Abortion rights head back to the Court*. On May 17, 2021, just one year after its decision in *June Medical Services*, the United States Supreme Court granted Mississippi's petition for a writ of certiorari in *Dobbs v. Jackson Women's Health Organization*, a challenge to HB 1510, a 15-week abortion ban. Although Mississippi presented three questions for review, the Court agreed to review only one: Whether all pre-viability prohibitions on elective abortions are unconstitutional?

7.   *Shifting priorities*. In its initial petition for a writ of certiorari in *Dobbs v. Jackson Women's Health Organization*, Mississippi assured the Court that its request for review was quite modest and need not require a complete reappraisal of the Court's extant abortion jurisprudence. However, when Mississippi filed its brief before the Court on July 22, 2021, it explicitly invited the Court to reconsider—and overrule—*Roe v. Wade* and *Planned Parenthood v. Casey*, stating that "*Roe* and *Casey* are egregiously wrong."

What happened in the space of thirteen months that would prompt such a shift? A great deal, it would seem. Perhaps most importantly, the Court's composition changed. Justice Ruth Bader Ginsburg passed away on September 18, 2020, and Trump appointee Amy Coney Barrett was confirmed on October 26, 2020. Justice Ginsburg was a reliable vote in favor of abortion rights, whereas Justice Barrett is a member of a conservative Catholic group that publicly opposes abortion and has said that abortion is "always immoral." Justice Barrett's confirmation installed a 6–3 conservative super-majority at the Court—and perhaps explains Mississippi's more aggressive litigation posture.

8. *Destabilizing privacy?* Although the *Dobbs* challenge is narrowly focused on the constitutionality of HB 1510, the Mississippi law that prohibits abortion at 15 weeks of pregnancy, the case has implications for other rights involving intimate life. In their brief on behalf of Texas Right for Life, amici Jonathan Mitchell, the architect of Texas's SB 8, and Adam Mortara invited the Court to not only overrule *Roe* and *Casey*, but to also exercise its duty to destabilize, or even overturn, "court-invented rights to homosexual behavior and same-sex marriage." *See* Brief of Texas Right to Life as Amicus Curiae in Support of the Petitioners, No. 19–1392, at *24 (citing *Lawrence v. Texas*, 539 U.S. 558 (2003) and *Obergefell v. Hodges*, 576 U.S. 644 (2015)). Mitchell and Mortara maintain that the rights to same-sex sexual conduct and marriage equality recognized in *Lawrence* and *Obergefell* are, "like the right to abortion[,] . . . judicial concoctions, and there is no other source of law that can be invoked to salvage their existence." *Id.* If overruling *Roe* and *Casey* destabilizes *Lawrence* and *Obergefell*, does it also destabilize the right to privacy recognized in *Griswold v. Connecticut*, 381 U.S. 479 (1965)?

Dobbs v. Jackson Women's Health Organization
142 S. Ct. 2228 (2022).

■ JUSTICE ALITO delivered the opinion of the Court.

Abortion presents a profound moral issue on which Americans hold sharply conflicting views. . . .

For the first 185 years after the adoption of the Constitution, each State was permitted to address this issue in accordance with the views of its citizens. Then, in 1973, this Court decided. Even though the Constitution makes no mention of abortion, the Court held that it confers a broad right to obtain one. It did not claim that American law or the common law had ever recognized such a right, and its survey of history ranged from the constitutionally irrelevant (e.g., its discussion of abortion in antiquity) to the plainly incorrect (e.g., its assertion that abortion was probably never a crime under the common law). After cataloging a wealth of other information having no bearing on the meaning of the Constitution, the opinion concluded with a numbered set of rules much like those that might be found in a statute enacted by a legislature.

Under this scheme, each trimester of pregnancy was regulated differently, but the most critical line was drawn at roughly the end of the second trimester, which, at the time, corresponded to the point at which a fetus was thought to achieve "viability," i.e., the ability to survive outside the womb. Although the Court acknowledged that States had a legitimate interest in protecting "potential life,"[1] it found that this interest could not justify any restriction on pre-viability abortions. The

Court did not explain the basis for this line, and even abortion supporters have found it hard to defend *Roe*'s reasoning. . . .

At the time of *Roe*, 30 States still prohibited abortion at all stages. In the years prior to that decision, about a third of the States had liberalized their laws, but *Roe* abruptly ended that political process. It imposed the same highly restrictive regime on the entire Nation, and it effectively struck down the abortion laws of every single State. As Justice Byron White aptly put it in his dissent, the decision represented the "exercise of raw judicial power," and it sparked a national controversy that has embittered our political culture for a half century.[4]

Eventually, in *Planned Parenthood of Southeastern Pa. v. Casey*, the Court revisited *Roe*, but the Members of the Court split three ways. Two Justices expressed no desire to change *Roe* in any way. Four others wanted to overrule the decision in its entirety. And the three remaining Justices, who jointly signed the controlling opinion, took a third position. Their opinion did not endorse *Roe*'s reasoning, and it even hinted that one or more of its authors might have "reservations" about whether the Constitution protects a right to abortion. But the opinion concluded that stare decisis, which calls for prior decisions to be followed in most instances, required adherence to what it called *Roe*'s "central holding"— that a State may not constitutionally protect fetal life before "viability"— even if that holding was wrong. Anything less, the opinion claimed, would undermine respect for this Court and the rule of law.

Paradoxically, the judgment in *Casey* did a fair amount of overruling. Several important abortion decisions were overruled in toto, and *Roe* itself was overruled in part. *Casey* threw out *Roe*'s trimester scheme and substituted a new rule of uncertain origin under which States were forbidden to adopt any regulation that imposed an "undue burden" on a woman's right to have an abortion. The decision provided no clear guidance about the difference between a "due" and an "undue" burden. But the three Justices who authored the controlling opinion "call[ed] the contending sides of a national controversy to end their national division" by treating the Court's decision as the final settlement of the question of the constitutional right to abortion.

As has become increasingly apparent in the intervening years, *Casey* did not achieve that goal. Americans continue to hold passionate and widely divergent views on abortion, and state legislatures have acted accordingly.

. . . . The State of Mississippi asks us to uphold the constitutionality of a law that generally prohibits an abortion after the 15th week of pregnancy—several weeks before the point at which a fetus is now regarded as "viable" outside the womb. In defending this law, the State's

---

[4] *See* R. Ginsburg, *Speaking in a Judicial Voice*, 67 N. Y. U. L. REV. 1185, 1208 (1992) ("*Roe* . . . halted a political process that was moving in a reform direction and thereby, I believed, prolonged divisiveness and deferred stable settlement of the issue").

primary argument is that we should reconsider and overrule *Roe* and *Casey* and once again allow each State to regulate abortion as its citizens wish. On the other side, respondents and the Solicitor General ask us to reaffirm *Roe* and *Casey,* and they contend that the Mississippi law cannot stand if we do so. Allowing Mississippi to prohibit abortions after 15 weeks of pregnancy, they argue, "would be no different than overruling *Casey* and *Roe* entirely." They contend that "no half-measures" are available and that we must either reaffirm or overrule *Roe* and *Casey.*

We hold that *Roe* and *Casey* must be overruled. The Constitution makes no reference to abortion, and no such right is implicitly protected by any constitutional provision, including the one on which the defenders of *Roe* and *Casey* now chiefly rely—the Due Process Clause of the Fourteenth Amendment. That provision has been held to guarantee some rights that are not mentioned in the Constitution, but any such right must be "deeply rooted in this Nation's history and tradition" and "implicit in the concept of ordered liberty."

The right to abortion does not fall within this category. Until the latter part of the 20th century, such a right was entirely unknown in American law. Indeed, when the Fourteenth Amendment was adopted, three quarters of the States made abortion a crime at all stages of pregnancy. The abortion right is also critically different from any other right that this Court has held to fall within the Fourteenth Amendment's protection of "liberty." *Roe*'s defenders characterize the abortion right as similar to the rights recognized in past decisions involving matters such as intimate sexual relations, contraception, and marriage, but abortion is fundamentally different . . . because it destroys what those decisions called "fetal life" and what the law now before us describes as an "unborn human being."

Stare decisis . . . does not compel unending adherence to *Roe*'s abuse of judicial authority. *Roe* was egregiously wrong from the start. Its reasoning was exceptionally weak, and the decision has had damaging consequences. And far from bringing about a national settlement of the abortion issue, *Roe* and *Casey* have enflamed debate and deepened division.

It is time to heed the Constitution and return the issue of abortion to the people's elected representatives. . . .

We begin by considering the critical question whether the Constitution, properly understood, confers a right to obtain an abortion. . . .

. . . . The Constitution makes no express reference to a right to obtain an abortion, and therefore those who claim that it protects such a right must show that the right is somehow implicit in the constitutional text.

Roe, however, was remarkably loose in its treatment of the constitutional text. It held that the abortion right, which is not mentioned in the Constitution, is part of a right to privacy, which is also not mentioned. And that privacy right, *Roe* observed, had been found to spring from no fewer than five different constitutional provisions—the First, Fourth, Fifth, Ninth, and Fourteenth Amendments.

. . . .

We discuss this theory in depth below, but before doing so, we briefly address one additional constitutional provision that some of respondents' amici have now offered as yet another potential home for the abortion right: the Fourteenth Amendment's Equal Protection Clause. Neither *Roe* nor *Casey* saw fit to invoke this theory, and it is squarely foreclosed by our precedents, which establish that a State's regulation of abortion is not a sex-based classification and is thus not subject to the "heightened scrutiny" that applies to such classifications. The regulation of a medical procedure that only one sex can undergo does not trigger heightened constitutional scrutiny unless the regulation is a "mere pretex[t] designed to effect an invidious discrimination against members of one sex or the other." And as the Court has stated, the "goal of preventing abortion" does not constitute "invidiously discriminatory animus" against women. Accordingly, laws regulating or prohibiting abortion are not subject to heightened scrutiny. Rather, they are governed by the same standard of review as other health and safety measures.

With this new theory addressed, we turn to *Casey*'s bold assertion that the abortion right is an aspect of the "liberty" protected by the Due Process Clause of the Fourteenth Amendment.

. . . [O]ur decisions have held that the Due Process Clause protects two categories of substantive rights.

The first consists of rights guaranteed by the first eight Amendments. Those Amendments originally applied only to the Federal Government, but this Court has held that the Due Process Clause of the Fourteenth Amendment "incorporates" the great majority of those rights and thus makes them equally applicable to the States. The second category—which is the one in question here—comprises a select list of fundamental rights that are not mentioned anywhere in the Constitution.

In deciding whether a right falls into either of these categories, the Court has long asked whether the right is "deeply rooted in [our] history and tradition" and whether it is essential to our Nation's "scheme of ordered liberty." And in conducting this inquiry, we have engaged in a careful analysis of the history of the right at issue.

. . . .

Historical inquiries of this nature are essential whenever we are asked to recognize a new component of the "liberty" protected by the Due Process Clause because the term "liberty" alone provides little guidance. "Liberty" is a capacious term. . . .

In interpreting what is meant by the Fourteenth Amendment's reference to "liberty," we must guard against the natural human tendency to confuse what that Amendment protects with our own ardent views about the liberty that Americans should enjoy.... As the Court cautioned in *Glucksberg v. Washington*, "[w]e must ... exercise the utmost care whenever we are asked to break new ground in this field, lest the liberty protected by the Due Process Clause be subtly transformed into the policy preferences of the Members of this Court."

.... Instead, guided by the history and tradition that map the essential components of our Nation's concept of ordered liberty, we must ask what the Fourteenth Amendment means by the term "liberty." When we engage in that inquiry in the present case, the clear answer is that the Fourteenth Amendment does not protect the right to an abortion.

Until the latter part of the 20th century, there was no support in American law for a constitutional right to obtain an abortion. No state constitutional provision had recognized such a right. Until a few years before *Roe* was handed down, no federal or state court had recognized such a right....

Not only was there no support for such a constitutional right until shortly before *Roe*, but abortion had long been a crime in every single State. At common law, abortion was criminal in at least some stages of pregnancy and was regarded as unlawful and could have very serious consequences at all stages. American law followed the common law until a wave of statutory restrictions in the 1800s expanded criminal liability for abortions. By the time of the adoption of the Fourteenth Amendment, three-quarters of the States had made abortion a crime at any stage of pregnancy, and the remaining States would soon follow.

Roe either ignored or misstated this history, and Casey declined to reconsider *Roe*'s faulty historical analysis. It is therefore important to set the record straight.

We begin with the common law, under which abortion was a crime at least after "quickening"—i.e., the first felt movement of the fetus in the womb, which usually occurs between the 16th and 18th week of pregnancy.

. . . .

Sir Edward Coke's 17th-century treatise ... asserted that abortion of a quick child was "murder" if the "childe be born alive" and a "great misprision" if the "childe dieth in her body." Two treatises by Sir Matthew Hale likewise described abortion of a quick child who died in the womb as a "great crime" and a "great misprision." And writing near the time of the adoption of our Constitution, William Blackstone explained that abortion of a "quick" child was "by the ancient law homicide or manslaughter" and at least a very "heinous misdemeanor."

Although a pre-quickening abortion was not itself considered homicide, it does not follow that abortion was permissible at common law—much less that abortion was a legal right. . . . That the common law did not condone even prequickening abortions is confirmed by what one might call a proto-felony-murder rule. Hale and Blackstone explained a way in which a pre-quickening abortion could rise to the level of a homicide. Hale wrote that if a physician gave a woman "with child" a "potion" to cause an abortion, and the woman died, it was "murder" because the potion was given "unlawfully to destroy her child within her."

. . .

Notably, Blackstone, like Hale, did not state that this proto-felony-murder rule required that the woman be "with quick child"—only that she be "with child." And it is revealing that Hale and Blackstone treated abortionists differently from other physicians or surgeons who caused the death of a patient "without any intent of doing [the patient] any bodily hurt." These other physicians—even if "unlicensed"—would not be "guilty of murder or manslaughter." But a physician performing an abortion would, precisely because his aim was an "unlawful" one.

In sum, although common-law authorities differed on the severity of punishment for abortions committed at different points in pregnancy, none endorsed the practice. Moreover, we are aware of no common-law case or authority, and the parties have not pointed to any, that remotely suggests a positive right to procure an abortion at any stage of pregnancy.

Just said was a crime at certain level, but didn't condone it

In this country, the historical record is similar. The "most important early American edition of Blackstone's Commentaries," reported Blackstone's statement that abortion of a quick child was at least "a heinous misdemeanor," and that edition also included Blackstone's discussion of the proto-felony-murder rule. Manuals for justices of the peace printed in the Colonies in the 18th century typically restated the common-law rule on abortion, and some manuals repeated Hale's and Blackstone's statements that anyone who prescribed medication "unlawfully to destroy the child" would be guilty of murder if the woman died.

The few cases available from the early colonial period corroborate that abortion was a crime. . . . And by the 19th century, courts frequently explained that the common law made abortion of a quick child a crime.

The original ground for drawing a distinction between pre- and post-quickening abortions is not entirely clear, but some have attributed the rule to the difficulty of proving that a pre-quickening fetus was alive. At that time, there were no scientific methods for detecting pregnancy in its early stages, and thus, as one court put it in 1872: "[U]ntil the period of quickening there is no evidence of life; and whatever may be said of the feotus, the law has fixed upon this period of gestation as the time when the child is endowed with life" because "foetal movements are the first clearly marked and well defined evidences of life."

The Solicitor General offers a different explanation of the basis for the quickening rule, namely, that before quickening the common law did not regard a fetus "as having a 'separate and independent existence.'" But the case on which the Solicitor General relies for this proposition also suggested that the criminal law's quickening rule was out of step with the treatment of prenatal life in other areas of law, noting that "to many purposes, in reference to civil rights, an infant *in ventre sa mere* is regarded as a person in being."

At any rate, the original ground for the quickening rule is of little importance for present purposes because the rule was abandoned in the 19th century. During that period, treatise writers and commentators criticized the quickening distinction as "neither in accordance with the result of medical experience, nor with the principles of the common law."

. . . .

19th c criminalization

In this country during the 19th century, the vast majority of the States enacted statutes criminalizing abortion at all stages of pregnancy. By 1868, the year when the Fourteenth Amendment was ratified, three-quarters of the States, 28 out of 37, had enacted statutes making abortion a crime even if it was performed before quickening. Of the nine States that had not yet criminalized abortion at all stages, all but one did so by 1910.

The trend in the Territories that would become the last 13 States was similar: All of them criminalized abortion at all stages of pregnancy between 1850 (the Kingdom of Hawaii) and 1919 (New Mexico). By the end of the 1950s, according to the Roe Court's own count, statutes in all but four States and the District of Columbia prohibited abortion "however and whenever performed, unless done to save or preserve the life of the mother."

This overwhelming consensus endured until the day *Roe* was decided. . . . And though *Roe* discerned a "trend toward liberalization" in about "one-third of the States," those States still criminalized some abortions and regulated them more stringently than *Roe* would allow. In short, the "Court's opinion in *Roe* itself convincingly refutes the notion that the abortion liberty is deeply rooted in the history or tradition of our people."

The inescapable conclusion is that a right to abortion is not deeply rooted in the Nation's history and traditions. On the contrary, an unbroken tradition of prohibiting abortion on pain of criminal punishment persisted from the earliest days of the common law until 1973. . . .

Respondents can't find 14A nor hx history before Roe

. . . .

Not only are respondents and their amici unable to show that a constitutional right to abortion was established when the Fourteenth Amendment was adopted, but they have found no support for the existence of an abortion right that predates the latter part of the 20th century—no state constitutional provision, no statute, no judicial decision, no learned treatise. The earliest sources called to our attention are a few district court and state court decisions decided shortly before Roe and a small number of law review articles from the same time period.

. . . .

The Solicitor General next suggests that history supports an abortion right because the common law's failure to criminalize abortion before quickening means that "at the Founding and for decades thereafter, women generally could terminate a pregnancy, at least in its early stages." But the insistence on quickening was not universal, and regardless, the fact that many States in the late 18th and early 19th century did not criminalize pre-quickening abortions does not mean that anyone thought the States lacked the authority to do so. When legislatures began to exercise that authority as the century wore on, no one, as far as we are aware, argued that the laws they enacted violated a fundamental right. That is not surprising since common-law authorities had repeatedly condemned abortion and described it as an "unlawful" act without regard to whether it occurred before or after quickening.

Another amicus brief relied upon by respondents tries to dismiss the significance of the state criminal statutes that were in effect when the Fourteenth Amendment was adopted by suggesting that they were enacted for illegitimate reasons. According to this account, which is based almost entirely on statements made by one prominent proponent of the statutes, important motives for the laws were the fear that Catholic immigrants were having more babies than Protestants and that the availability of abortion was leading White Protestant women to "shir[k their] maternal duties." Brief for American Historical Association et al. as Amici Curiae 20.

Resort to this argument is a testament to the lack of any real historical support for the right that Roe and Casey recognized. This Court has long disfavored arguments based on alleged legislative motives. . . .

Here, the argument about legislative motive is not even based on statements by legislators, but on statements made by a few supporters of the new 19th-century abortion laws, and it is quite a leap to attribute these motives to all the legislators whose votes were responsible for the enactment of those laws. Recall that at the time of the adoption of the Fourteenth Amendment, over three-quarters of the States had adopted statutes criminalizing abortion (usually at all stages of pregnancy), and that from the early 20th century until the day Roe was handed down, every single State had such a law on its books. Are we to believe that the hundreds of lawmakers whose votes were needed to enact these laws were motivated by hostility to Catholics and women?

There is ample evidence that the passage of these laws was instead spurred by a sincere belief that abortion kills a human being. . . .

One may disagree with this belief (and our decision is not based on any view about when a State should regard prenatal life as having rights or legally cognizable interests), but even *Roe* and *Casey* did not question the good faith of abortion opponents. And we see no reason to discount the significance of the state laws in question based on these amici's suggestions about legislative motive.[41]

Instead of seriously pressing the argument that the abortion right itself has deep roots, supporters of *Roe* and *Casey* contend that the abortion right is an integral part of a broader entrenched right. *Roe* termed this a right to privacy, and *Casey* described it as the freedom to make "intimate and personal choices" that are "central to personal dignity and autonomy." *Casey* elaborated: "At the heart of liberty is the right to define one's own concept of existence, of meaning, of the universe, and of the mystery of human life."

The Court did not claim that this broadly framed right is absolute, and no such claim would be plausible. While individuals are certainly free to think and to say what they wish about "existence," "meaning," the "universe," and "the mystery of human life," they are not always free to act in accordance with those thoughts. License to act on the basis of such beliefs may correspond to one of the many understandings of "liberty," but it is certainly not "ordered liberty."

Ordered liberty sets limits and defines the boundary between competing interests. *Roe* and *Casey* each struck a particular balance between the interests of a woman who wants an abortion and the interests of what they termed "potential life." But the people of the various States may evaluate those interests differently. . . . Our Nation's historical understanding of ordered liberty does not prevent the people's elected representatives from deciding how abortion should be regulated.

Nor does the right to obtain an abortion have a sound basis in precedent. *Casey* relied on cases involving the right to marry a person of a different race, the right to marry while in prison, the right to obtain contraceptives, the right to reside with relatives, the right to make decisions about the education of one's children, the right not to be sterilized without consent, and the right in certain circumstances not to undergo involuntary surgery, forced administration of drugs, or other substantially similar procedures. Respondents and the Solicitor General also rely on post-*Casey* decisions like *Lawrence v. Texas*, (right to engage

---

[41] Other amicus briefs present arguments about the motives of proponents of liberal access to abortion. They note that some such supporters have been motivated by a desire to suppress the size of the African-American population. *See* Brief for African-American Organization et al. as Amici Curiae 14–21; *see also* Box v. Planned Parenthood of Ind. and Ky., Inc., 587 U.S. ___, ___–___, 139 S.Ct. 1780, 1782–1784 (2019) (Thomas, J., concurring). And it is beyond dispute that *Roe* has had that demographic effect. A highly disproportionate percentage of aborted fetuses are Black. *See, e.g.*, Dept. of Health and Human Servs., Centers for Disease Control and Prevention (CDC), K. Kortsmit et al., Abortion Surveillance—United States, 2019, 70 Morbidity and Mortality Report, Surveillance Summaries, p. 20 (Nov. 26, 2021) (Table 6). For our part, we do not question the motives of either those who have supported or those who have opposed laws restricting abortions.

in private, consensual sexual acts), and *Obergefell v. Hodges*, (right to marry a person of the same sex).

These attempts to justify abortion through appeals to a broader right to autonomy and to define one's "concept of existence" prove too much. Those criteria, at a high level of generality, could license fundamental rights to illicit drug use, prostitution, and the like. None of these rights has any claim to being deeply rooted in history.

What sharply distinguishes the abortion right from the rights recognized in the cases on which *Roe* and *Casey* rely is something that both those decisions acknowledged: Abortion destroys what those decisions call "potential life" and what the law at issue in this case regards as the life of an "unborn human being." None of the other decisions cited by *Roe* and *Casey* involved the critical moral question posed by abortion. They are therefore inapposite. They do not support the right to obtain an abortion, and by the same token, our conclusion that the Constitution does not confer such a right does not undermine them in any way.

. . . .

The dissent is very candid that it cannot show that a constitutional right to abortion has any foundation, let alone a "deeply rooted" one, "in this Nation's history and tradition." The dissent does not identify any pre-*Roe* authority that supports such a right—no state constitutional provision or statute, no federal or state judicial precedent, not even a scholarly treatise. Nor does the dissent dispute the fact that abortion was illegal at common law at least after quickening; that the 19th century saw a trend toward criminalization of pre-quickening abortions; that by 1868, a supermajority of States (at least 26 of 37) had enacted statutes criminalizing abortion at all stages of pregnancy; that by the late 1950s at least 46 States prohibited abortion "however and whenever performed" except if necessary to save "the life of the mother," and that when *Roe* was decided in 1973 similar statutes were still in effect in 30 States.

The dissent's failure to engage with this long tradition is devastating to its position. We . . . held [in *Glucksburg v. Washington*] that the "established method of substantive-due-process analysis" requires that an unenumerated right be "deeply rooted in this Nation's history and tradition" before it can be recognized as a component of the "liberty" protected in the Due Process Clause. But despite the dissent's professed fidelity to stare decisis, it fails to seriously engage with that important precedent—which it cannot possibly satisfy.

. . . .

Because the dissent cannot argue that the abortion right is rooted in this Nation's history and tradition, it contends that the "constitutional tradition" is "not captured whole at a single moment," and that its "meaning gains content from the long sweep of our history and from successive judicial precedents." This vague formulation imposes no clear restraints on what Justice White called the "exercise of raw judicial power," and while the dissent claims that its standard "does not mean anything goes," any real restraints are hard to discern.

. . . .

So without support in history or relevant precedent, *Roe*'s reasoning cannot be defended even under the dissent's proposed test, and the dissent is forced to rely solely on the fact that a constitutional right to abortion was recognized in *Roe* and later decisions that accepted *Roe*'s interpretation. Under the doctrine of stare decisis, those precedents are entitled to careful and respectful consideration, and we engage in that analysis below. But as the Court has reiterated time and time again, adherence to precedent is not "'an inexorable command.'" There are occasions when past decisions should be overruled. . . .

The most striking feature of the dissent is the absence of any serious discussion of the legitimacy of the States' interest in protecting fetal life. . . .

. . . The dissent has much to say about the effects of pregnancy on women, the burdens of motherhood, and the difficulties faced by poor women. These are important concerns. However, the dissent evinces no similar regard for a State's interest in protecting prenatal life. The dissent repeatedly praises the "balance" that the viability line strikes between a woman's liberty interest and the State's interest in prenatal life. But . . . the viability line makes no sense. It was not adequately justified in *Roe*, and the dissent does not even try to defend it today. Nor does it identify any other point in a pregnancy after which a State is permitted to prohibit the destruction of a fetus.

Our opinion is not based on any view about if and when prenatal life is entitled to any of the rights enjoyed after birth. The dissent, by contrast, would impose on the people a particular theory about when the rights of personhood begin. According to the dissent, the Constitution requires the States to regard a fetus as lacking even the most basic human right—to live—at least until an arbitrary point in a pregnancy has passed. Nothing in the Constitution or in our Nation's legal traditions authorizes the Court to adopt that "'theory of life.'"

We next consider whether the doctrine of stare decisis counsels continued acceptance of *Roe* and *Casey*. Stare decisis plays an important role in our case law, and we have explained that it serves many valuable ends. It protects the interests of those who have taken action in reliance on a past decision. It "reduces incentives for challenging settled precedents, saving parties and courts the expense of endless relitigation." It fosters "evenhanded" decisionmaking by requiring that like cases be decided in a like manner. It "contributes to the actual and perceived integrity of the judicial process." And it restrains judicial hubris and reminds us to respect the judgment of those who have grappled with important questions in the past. . . .

We have long recognized, however, that stare decisis is "not an inexorable command," and it "is at its weakest when we interpret the Constitution." . . .

Some of our most important constitutional decisions have overruled prior precedents. We mention three. In *Brown v. Board of Education*, the Court repudiated the "separate but equal" doctrine, which had allowed States to maintain racially segregated schools and other facilities. In so doing, the Court overruled the infamous decision in *Plessy v. Ferguson*, along with six other Supreme Court precedents that had applied the separate-but-equal rule.

examples of overturning precedent

In *West Coast Hotel Co. v. Parrish*, the Court overruled *Adkins v. Children's Hospital of D.C.*, which had held that a law setting minimum wages for women violated the "liberty" protected by the Fifth Amendment's Due Process Clause. *West Coast Hotel* signaled the demise of an entire line of important precedents that had protected an individual liberty right against state and federal health and welfare legislation.

Finally, in *West Virginia Bd. of Ed. v. Barnette*, after the lapse of only three years, the Court overruled *Minersville School Dist. v. Gobitis*, and held that public school students could not be compelled to salute the flag in violation of their sincere beliefs. *Barnette* stands out because nothing had changed during the intervening period other than the Court's belated recognition that its earlier decision had been seriously wrong.

On many other occasions, this Court has overruled important constitutional decisions. Without these decisions, American constitutional law as we know it would be unrecognizable, and this would be a different country.

. . . [O]verruling a precedent is a serious matter. It is not a step that should be taken lightly. Our cases have attempted to provide a framework for deciding when a precedent should be overruled, and they have identified factors that should be considered in making such a decision.

In this case, five factors weigh strongly in favor of overruling *Roe* and *Casey*: the nature of their error, the quality of their reasoning, the "workability" of the rules they imposed on the country, their disruptive effect on other areas of the law, and the absence of concrete reliance.

factors when considering overturning precedent

The nature of the Court's error. An erroneous interpretation of the Constitution is always important, but some are more damaging than others.

The infamous decision in *Plessy v. Ferguson*, was one such decision. It betrayed our commitment to "equality before the law." It was "egregiously wrong" on the day it was decided, and as the Solicitor General agreed at oral argument, it should have been overruled at the earliest opportunity.

Roe was also egregiously wrong and deeply damaging. For reasons already explained, *Roe*'s constitutional analysis was far outside the bounds of any reasonable interpretation of the various constitutional provisions to which it vaguely pointed.

Roe was on a collision course with the Constitution from the day it was decided, *Casey* perpetuated its errors, and those errors do not concern some arcane corner of the law of little importance to the American people. Rather, wielding nothing but "raw judicial power," the Court usurped the power to address a question of profound moral and social importance that the Constitution unequivocally leaves for the people. *Casey* described itself as calling both sides of the national controversy to resolve their debate, but in doing so, *Casey* necessarily declared a winning side. Those on the losing side—those who sought to advance the State's interest in fetal life—could no longer seek to persuade their elected representatives to adopt policies consistent with their views. The Court short-circuited the democratic process by closing it to the large number of Americans who dissented in any respect from *Roe*. "*Roe* fanned into life an issue that has inflamed our national politics in general, and has obscured with its smoke the selection of Justices to this Court in particular, ever since." Together, *Roe* and *Casey* represent an error that cannot be allowed to stand.

As the Court's landmark decision in *West Coast Hotel* illustrates, the Court has previously overruled decisions that wrongly removed an issue from the people and the democratic process. As Justice White later explained, "decisions that find in the Constitution principles or values that cannot fairly be read into that document usurp the people's authority, for such decisions represent choices that the people have never made and that they cannot disavow through corrective legislation. For this reason, it is essential that this Court maintain the power to restore authority to its proper possessors by correcting constitutional decisions that, on reconsideration, are found to be mistaken."

. . . . Under our precedents, the quality of the reasoning in a prior case has an important bearing on whether it should be reconsidered. . . .

Roe found that the Constitution implicitly conferred a right to obtain an abortion, but it failed to ground its decision in text, history, or precedent. It relied on an erroneous historical narrative; it devoted great attention to and presumably relied on matters that have no bearing on the meaning of the Constitution; it disregarded the fundamental difference between the precedents on which it relied and the question before the Court; it concocted an elaborate set of rules, with different restrictions for each trimester of pregnancy, but it did not explain how this veritable code could be teased out of anything in the Constitution, the history of abortion laws, prior precedent, or any other cited source; and its most important rule (that States cannot protect fetal life prior to "viability") was never raised by any party and has never been plausibly explained. *Roe*'s reasoning quickly drew scathing scholarly criticism, even from supporters of broad access to abortion.

The weaknesses in *Roe*'s reasoning are well-known. Without any grounding in the constitutional text, history, or precedent, it imposed on the entire country a detailed set of rules much like those that one might expect to find in a statute or regulation. Dividing pregnancy into three trimesters, the Court imposed special rules for each. During the first trimester, the Court announced, "the abortion decision and its effectuation must be left to the medical judgment of the pregnant woman's attending physician." After that point, a State's interest in regulating abortion for the sake of a woman's health became compelling, and accordingly, a State could "regulate the abortion procedure in ways that are reasonably related to maternal health." Finally, in "the stage subsequent to viability," which in 1973 roughly coincided with the beginning of the third trimester, the State's interest in "the potentiality of human life" became compelling, and therefore a State could "regulate, and even proscribe, abortion except where it is necessary, in appropriate medical judgment, for the preservation of the life or health of the mother."

This elaborate scheme was the Court's own brainchild. Neither party advocated the trimester framework; nor did either party or any amicus argue that "viability" should mark the point at which the scope of the abortion right and a State's regulatory authority should be substantially transformed.

Not only did this scheme resemble the work of a legislature, but the Court made little effort to explain how these rules could be deduced from any of the sources on which constitutional decisions are usually based. . . .

. . . *Roe* did not provide was any cogent justification for the lines it drew. Why, for example, does a State have no authority to regulate first trimester abortions for the purpose of protecting a woman's health? The Court's only explanation was that mortality rates for abortion at that stage were lower than the mortality rates for childbirth. But the Court did not explain why mortality rates were the only factor that a State could legitimately consider. Many health and safety regulations aim to avoid adverse health consequences short of death. And the Court did not explain why it departed from the normal rule that courts defer to the judgments of legislatures "in areas fraught with medical and scientific uncertainties."

An even more glaring deficiency was *Roe*'s failure to justify the critical distinction it drew between pre- and post-viability abortions. . . .

This arbitrary line has not found much support among philosophers and ethicists who have attempted to justify a right to abortion. Some have argued that a fetus should not be entitled to legal protection until it acquires the characteristics that they regard as defining what it means to be a "person." Among the characteristics that have been offered as essential attributes of "personhood" are sentience, self-awareness, the ability to reason, or some combination thereof. By this logic, it would be an open question whether even born individuals, including young children or those afflicted with certain developmental or medical conditions, merit protection as "persons." But even if one takes the view that "personhood" begins when a certain attribute or combination of attributes is acquired, it is very hard to see why viability should mark the point where "personhood" begins.

Criticity legal personhood

The most obvious problem with any such argument is that viability is heavily dependent on factors that have nothing to do with the characteristics of a fetus. One is the state of neonatal care at a particular point in time. Due to the development of new equipment and improved practices, the viability line has changed over the years. In the 19th century, a fetus may not have been viable until the 32d or 33d week of pregnancy or even later. When *Roe* was decided, viability was gauged at roughly 28 weeks. Today, respondents draw the line at 23 or 24 weeks. So, according to *Roe*'s logic, States now have a compelling interest in protecting a fetus with a gestational age of, say, 26 weeks, but in 1973 States did not have an interest in protecting an identical fetus. How can that be?

Viability also depends on the "quality of the available medical facilities." Thus, a 24-week-old fetus may be viable if a woman gives birth in a city with hospitals that provide advanced care for very premature babies, but if the woman travels to a remote area far from any such hospital, the fetus may no longer be viable. On what ground could the constitutional status of a fetus depend on the pregnant woman's location? And if viability is meant to mark a line having universal moral significance, can it be that a fetus that is viable in a big city in the United States has a privileged moral status not enjoyed by an identical fetus in a remote area of a poor country?

In addition, as the Court once explained, viability is not really a hard-and-fast line. A physician determining a particular fetus's odds of surviving outside the womb must consider "a number of variables," including "gestational age," "fetal weight," a woman's "general health and nutrition," the "quality of the available medical facilities," and other factors. It is thus "only with difficulty" that a physician can estimate the "probability" of a particular fetus's survival. And even if each fetus's probability of survival could be ascertained with certainty, settling on a "probabilit[y] of survival" that should count as "viability" is another matter. Is a fetus viable with a 10 percent chance of survival? 25 percent? 50 percent? Can such a judgment be made by a State? And can a State specify a gestational age limit that applies in all cases? Or must these difficult questions be left entirely to the individual "attending physician on the particular facts of the case before him"?

The viability line, which *Casey* termed *Roe*'s central rule, makes no sense, and it is telling that other countries almost uniformly eschew such a line. The Court thus asserted raw judicial power to impose, as a matter of constitutional law, a uniform viability rule that allowed the States less freedom to regulate abortion than the majority of western democracies enjoy.

All in all, *Roe*'s reasoning was exceedingly weak, and academic commentators, including those who agreed with the decision as a matter of policy, were unsparing in their criticism. . . .

Casey . . . either refused to reaffirm or rejected important aspects of *Roe*'s analysis, failed to remedy glaring deficiencies in *Roe*'s reasoning, endorsed what it termed *Roe*'s central holding while suggesting that a majority might not have thought it was correct, provided no new support for the abortion right other than *Roe*'s status as precedent, and imposed a new and problematic test with no firm grounding in constitutional text, history, or precedent.

As discussed below, *Casey* also deployed a novel version of the doctrine of stare decisis. This new doctrine did not account for the profound wrongness of the decision in *Roe*, and placed great weight on an intangible form of reliance with little if any basis in prior case law. Stare decisis does not command the preservation of such a decision.

. . . . Our precedents counsel that another important consideration in deciding whether a precedent should be overruled is whether the rule it imposes is workable—that is, whether it can be understood and applied in a consistent and predictable manner. *Casey*'s "undue burden" test has scored poorly on the workability scale.

Problems begin with the very concept of an "undue burden." As Justice Scalia noted in his *Casey* partial dissent, determining whether a burden is "due" or "undue" is "inherently standardless."

The *Casey* plurality tried to put meaning into the "undue burden" test by setting out three subsidiary rules, but these rules created their own problems. The first rule is that "a provision of law is invalid, if its purpose or effect is to place a substantial obstacle in the path of a woman seeking an abortion before the fetus attains viability." But whether a particular obstacle qualifies as "substantial" is often open to reasonable debate. In the sense relevant here, "substantial" means "of ample or considerable amount, quantity, or size." Random House Webster's Unabridged Dictionary 1897 (2d ed. 2001). Huge burdens are plainly "substantial," and trivial ones are not, but in between these extremes, there is a wide gray area.

This ambiguity is a problem, and the second rule, which applies at all stages of a pregnancy, muddies things further. It states that measures designed "to ensure that the woman's choice is informed" are constitutional so long as they do not impose "an undue burden on the right." To the extent that this rule applies to pre-viability abortions, it overlaps with the first rule and appears to impose a different standard. Consider a law that imposes an insubstantial obstacle but serves little purpose. As applied to a pre-viability abortion, would such a regulation be constitutional on the ground that it does not impose a "substantial obstacle"? Or would it be unconstitutional on the ground that it creates an "undue burden" because the burden it imposes, though slight, outweighs its negligible benefits? *Casey* does not say, and this ambiguity would lead to confusion down the line.

The third rule complicates the picture even more. Under that rule, "[u]nnecessary health regulations that have the purpose or effect of presenting a substantial obstacle to a woman seeking an abortion impose an undue burden on the right." This rule contains no fewer than three vague terms. It includes the two already discussed—"undue burden" and "substantial obstacle"—even though they are inconsistent. And it adds a third ambiguous term when it refers to "unnecessary health regulations." The term "necessary" has a range of meanings—from "essential" to merely "useful." *Casey* did not explain the sense in which the term is used in this rule.

In addition to these problems, one more applies to all three rules. They all call on courts to examine a law's effect on women, but a regulation may have a very different impact on different women for a variety of reasons, including their places of residence, financial resources, family situations, work and personal obligations, knowledge about fetal development and abortion, psychological and emotional disposition and condition, and the firmness of their desire to obtain abortions. In order to determine whether a regulation presents a substantial obstacle to women, a court needs to know which set of women it should have in mind and how many of the women in this set must find that an obstacle is "substantial."

Casey provided no clear answer to these questions. It said that a regulation is unconstitutional if it imposes a substantial obstacle "in a large fraction of cases in which [it] is relevant," but there is obviously no clear line between a fraction that is "large" and one that is not. Nor is it clear what the Court meant by "cases in which" a regulation is "relevant." These ambiguities have caused confusion and disagreement.

. . . . *Roe* and *Casey* have led to the distortion of many important but unrelated legal doctrines, and that effect provides further support for overruling those decisions.

. . . .

The Court's abortion cases have diluted the strict standard for facial constitutional challenges. They have ignored the Court's third-party standing doctrine. They have disregarded standard res judicata principles. They have flouted the ordinary rules on the severability of unconstitutional provisions, as well as the rule that statutes should be read where possible to avoid unconstitutionality. And they have distorted First Amendment doctrines.

When vindicating a doctrinal innovation requires courts to engineer exceptions to longstanding background rules, the doctrine "has failed to deliver the 'principled and intelligible' development of the law that stare decisis purports to secure."

. . . . We last consider whether overruling *Roe and Casey* will upend substantial reliance interests.

Traditional reliance interests arise "where advance planning of great precision is most obviously a necessity." In *Casey*, the controlling opinion conceded that those traditional reliance interests were not implicated because getting an abortion is generally "unplanned activity," and "reproductive planning could take virtually immediate account of any sudden restoration of state authority to ban abortions." For these reasons, we agree with the *Casey* plurality that conventional, concrete reliance interests are not present here.

Unable to find reliance in the conventional sense, the controlling opinion in *Casey* perceived a more intangible form of reliance. It wrote that "people [had] organized intimate relationships and made choices that define their views of themselves and their places in society . . . in reliance on the availability of abortion in the event that contraception should fail" and that "[t]he ability of women to participate equally in the economic and social life of the Nation has been facilitated by their ability to control their reproductive lives." But this Court is ill-equipped to assess "generalized assertions about the national psyche." *Casey*'s notion of reliance thus finds little support in our cases, which instead emphasize very concrete reliance interests, like those that develop in "cases involving property and contract rights."

When a concrete reliance interest is asserted, courts are equipped to evaluate the claim, but assessing the novel and intangible form of reliance endorsed by the *Casey* plurality is another matter. That form of reliance depends on an empirical question that is hard for anyone—and in particular, for a court—to assess, namely, the effect of the abortion right on society and in particular on the lives of women. The contending sides in this case make impassioned and conflicting arguments about the effects of the abortion right on the lives of women. The contending sides also make conflicting arguments about the status of the fetus. This Court has neither the authority nor the expertise to adjudicate those disputes, and the *Casey* plurality's speculations and weighing of the relative importance of the fetus and mother represent a departure from the "original constitutional proposition" that "courts do not substitute their social and economic beliefs for the judgment of legislative bodies."

Our decision returns the issue of abortion to those legislative bodies, and it allows women on both sides of the abortion issue to seek to affect the legislative process by influencing public opinion, lobbying legislators, voting, and running for office. Women are not without electoral or political power. It is noteworthy that the percentage of women who register to vote and cast ballots is consistently higher than the percentage of men who do so. In the last election in November 2020, women, who make up around 51.5 percent of the population of Mississippi, constituted 55.5 percent of the voters who cast ballots.

. . . .

Having shown that traditional stare decisis factors do not weigh in favor of retaining *Roe* or *Casey*, we must address one final argument that featured prominently in the *Casey* plurality opinion.

The argument was cast in different terms, but stated simply, it was essentially as follows. The American people's belief in the rule of law would be shaken if they lost respect for this Court as an institution that decides important cases based on principle, not "social and political pressures." There is a special danger that the public will perceive a decision as having been made for unprincipled reasons when the Court overrules a controversial "watershed" decision, such as *Roe*. A decision overruling *Roe* would be perceived as having been made "under fire" and as a "surrender to political pressure," and therefore the preservation of public approval of the Court weighs heavily in favor of retaining *Roe*.

. . . . The *Casey* plurality was certainly right that it is important for the public to perceive that our decisions are based on principle, and we should make every effort to achieve that objective by issuing opinions that carefully show how a proper understanding of the law leads to the results we reach. But we cannot exceed the scope of our authority under the Constitution, and we cannot allow our decisions to be affected by any extraneous influences such as concern about the public's reaction to our work. That is true both when we initially decide a constitutional issue and when we consider whether to overrule a prior decision. As Chief Justice Rehnquist explained, "The Judicial Branch derives its legitimacy, not from following public opinion, but from deciding by its best lights whether legislative enactments of the popular branches of Government comport with the Constitution. The doctrine of stare decisis is an adjunct of this duty, and should be no more subject to the vagaries of public opinion than is the basic judicial task." In suggesting otherwise, the *Casey* plurality went beyond this Court's role in our constitutional system.

The *Casey* plurality "call[ed] the contending sides of a national controversy to end their national division," and claimed the authority to impose a permanent settlement of the issue of a constitutional abortion right simply by saying that the matter was closed. . . .

The *Casey* plurality . . . misjudged the practical limits of this Court's influence. *Roe* certainly did not succeed in ending division on the issue of abortion. On the contrary, *Roe* "inflamed" a national issue that has remained bitterly divisive for the past half century. And for the past 30 years, *Casey* has done the same.

. . . . This Court's inability to end debate on the issue should not have been surprising. This Court cannot bring about the permanent resolution of a rancorous national controversy simply by dictating a settlement and telling the people to move on. Whatever influence the Court may have on public attitudes must stem from the strength of our opinions, not an attempt to exercise "raw judicial power."

We do not pretend to know how our political system or society will respond to today's decision overruling *Roe and Casey*. And even if we could foresee what will happen, we would have no authority to let that knowledge influence our decision. We can only do our job, which is to interpret the law, apply longstanding principles of stare decisis, and decide this case accordingly.

We therefore hold that the Constitution does not confer a right to abortion. *Roe and Casey* must be overruled, and the authority to regulate abortion must be returned to the people and their elected representatives.

The dissent argues that we have "abandon[ed]" stare decisis, but we have done no such thing, and it is the dissent's understanding of stare decisis that breaks with tradition. The dissent's foundational contention is that the Court should never (or perhaps almost never) overrule an egregiously wrong constitutional precedent unless the Court can "poin[t] to major legal or factual changes undermining [the] decision's original basis." To support this contention, the dissent claims that *Brown v. Board of Education*, and other landmark cases overruling prior precedents "responded to changed law and to changed facts and attitudes that had taken hold throughout society." The unmistakable implication of this argument is that only the passage of time and new developments justified those decisions. Recognition that the cases they overruled were egregiously wrong on the day they were handed down was not enough.

The Court has never adopted this strange new version of stare decisis—and with good reason. Does the dissent really maintain that overruling Plessy was not justified until the country had experienced more than a half-century of state-sanctioned segregation and generations of Black school children had suffered all its effects?

Here is another example. On the dissent's view, it must have been wrong for *West Virginia Bd. of Ed. v. Barnette* to overrule *Minersville School Dist. v. Gobitis*, a bare three years after it was handed down. In both cases, children who were Jehovah's Witnesses refused on religious grounds to salute the flag or recite the pledge of allegiance. The *Barnette* Court did not claim that its reexamination of the issue was prompted by any intervening legal or factual developments, so if the Court had followed the dissent's new version of stare decisis, it would have been compelled to adhere to Gobitis and countenance continued First Amendment violations for some unspecified period.

Precedents should be respected, but sometimes the Court errs, and occasionally the Court issues an important decision that is egregiously wrong. When that happens, stare decisis is not a straitjacket. And indeed, the dissent eventually admits that a decision could "be overruled just because it is terribly wrong," though the dissent does not explain when that would be so.

. . . .

The dissent, however, is undeterred. It contends that the "very controversy surrounding *Roe* and *Casey*" is an important stare decisis consideration that requires upholding those precedents. The dissent characterizes *Casey* as a "precedent about precedent" that is permanently shielded from further evaluation under traditional stare decisis principles. But as we have explained, *Casey* broke new ground when it treated the national controversy provoked by *Roe* as a ground for refusing to reconsider that decision, and no subsequent case has relied on that factor. Our decision today simply applies longstanding stare decisis factors instead of applying a version of the doctrine that seems to apply only in abortion cases.

Finally, the dissent suggests that our decision calls into question *Griswold* [*v. Connecticut*], *Eisenstadt* [*v. Baird*], *Lawrence* [*v. Texas*], and *Obergefell* [*v. Hodges*]. But we have stated unequivocally that "[n]othing in this opinion should be understood to cast doubt on precedents that do not concern abortion." We have also explained why that is so: rights regarding contraception and same-sex relationships are inherently different from the right to abortion because the latter (as we have stressed) uniquely involves what *Roe and Casey* termed "potential life." Therefore, a right to abortion cannot be justified by a purported analogy to the rights recognized in those other cases or by "appeals to a broader right to autonomy." It is hard to see how we could be clearer. Moreover, even putting aside that these cases are distinguishable, there is a further point that the dissent ignores: Each precedent is subject to its own stare decisis analysis, and the factors that our doctrine instructs us to consider like reliance and workability are different for these cases than for our abortion jurisprudence.

We now turn to the [Chief Justice's] concurrence in the judgment, which reproves us for deciding whether *Roe and Casey* should be retained or overruled. That opinion . . . recommends a "more measured course," which it defends based on what it claims is "a straightforward stare decisis analysis." The concurrence would "leave for another day whether to reject any right to an abortion at all," and would hold only that if the Constitution protects any such right, the right ends once women have had "a reasonable opportunity" to obtain an abortion. The concurrence does not specify what period of time is sufficient to provide such an opportunity, but it would hold that 15 weeks, the period allowed under Mississippi's law, is enough—at least "absent rare circumstances."

. . . .

The concurrence's most fundamental defect is its failure to offer any principled basis for its approach. The concurrence would "discar[d]" "the rule from *Roe and Casey* that a woman's right to terminate her pregnancy extends up to the point that the fetus is regarded as 'viable' outside the womb." But this rule was a critical component of the holdings in *Roe and Casey*, and stare decisis is "a doctrine of preservation, not transformation," Citizens United v. Federal Election Comm'n, 558 U.S. 310, 384 (2010) (Roberts, C. J., concurring). Therefore, a new rule that discards the viability rule cannot be defended on stare decisis grounds.

The concurrence concedes that its approach would "not be available" if "the rationale of *Roe and Casey* were inextricably entangled with and dependent upon the viability standard." But the concurrence asserts that the viability line is separable from the constitutional right they recognized, and can therefore be "discarded" without disturbing any past precedent. That is simply incorrect.

Roe's trimester rule was expressly tied to viability, and viability played a critical role in later abortion decisions. . . .

When the Court reconsidered *Roe* in *Casey*, it left no doubt about the importance of the viability rule. It described the rule as *Roe*'s "central holding," and repeatedly stated that the right it reaffirmed was "the right of the woman to choose to have an abortion before viability." Our subsequent cases have continued to recognize the centrality of the viability rule. . . .

Not only is the new rule proposed by the concurrence inconsistent with *Casey*'s unambiguous "language," it is also contrary to the judgment in that case and later abortion cases. . . .

For all these reasons, stare decisis cannot justify the new "reasonable opportunity" rule propounded by the concurrence. If that rule is to become the law of the land, it must stand on its own, but the concurrence makes no attempt to show that this rule represents a correct interpretation of the Constitution. The concurrence does not claim that the right to a reasonable opportunity to obtain an abortion is "deeply rooted in this Nation's history and tradition" and "implicit in the concept of ordered liberty." Nor does it propound any other theory that could show that the Constitution supports its new rule. And if the Constitution protects a woman's right to obtain an abortion, the opinion does not explain why that right should end after the point at which all "reasonable" women will have decided whether to seek an abortion. While the concurrence is moved by a desire for judicial minimalism, "we cannot embrace a narrow ground of decision simply because it is narrow; it must also be right.". . .

. . . [T]he concurrence's quest for a middle way would only put off the day when we would be forced to confront the question we now decide. The turmoil wrought by *Roe* and *Casey* would be prolonged. It is far better—for this Court and the country—to face up to the real issue without further delay.

We must now decide what standard will govern if state abortion regulations undergo constitutional challenge and whether the law before us satisfies the appropriate standard.

Under our precedents, rational-basis review is the appropriate standard for such challenges. As we have explained, procuring an abortion is not a fundamental constitutional right because such a right has no basis in the Constitution's text or in our Nation's history.

It follows that the States may regulate abortion for legitimate reasons, and when such regulations are challenged under the Constitution, courts cannot "substitute their social and economic beliefs for the judgment of legislative bodies." That respect for a legislature's judgment applies even when the laws at issue concern matters of great social significance and moral substance.

A law regulating abortion, like other health and welfare laws, is entitled to a "strong presumption of validity." It must be sustained if there is a rational basis on which the legislature could have thought that it would serve legitimate state interests. These legitimate interests include respect for and preservation of prenatal life at all stages of development, the protection of maternal health and safety; the elimination of particularly gruesome or barbaric medical procedures; the preservation of the integrity of the medical profession; the mitigation of fetal pain; and the prevention of discrimination on the basis of race, sex, or disability.

These legitimate interests justify Mississippi's Gestational Age Act. Except "in a medical emergency or in the case of a severe fetal abnormality," the statute prohibits abortion "if the probable gestational age of the unborn human being has been determined to be greater than fifteen (15) weeks." The Mississippi Legislature's findings recount the stages of "human prenatal development" and assert the State's interest in "protecting the life of the unborn." § 2(b)(i). The legislature also found that abortions performed after 15 weeks typically use the dilation and evacuation procedure, and the legislature found the use of this procedure "for nontherapeutic or elective reasons [to be] a barbaric practice, dangerous for the maternal patient, and demeaning to the medical profession." These legitimate interests provide a rational basis for the Gestational Age Act, and it follows that respondents' constitutional challenge must fail.

We end this opinion where we began. Abortion presents a profound moral question. The Constitution does not prohibit the citizens of each State from regulating or prohibiting abortion. *Roe and Casey* arrogated that authority. We now overrule those decisions and return that authority to the people and their elected representatives.

. . . .

It is so ordered.

. . . .

■ JUSTICE THOMAS, concurring.

I join the opinion of the Court because it correctly holds that there is no constitutional right to abortion. Respondents invoke one source for that right: the Fourteenth Amendment's guarantee that no State shall "deprive any person of life, liberty, or property without due process of law." The Court well explains why, under our substantive due process precedents, the purported right to abortion is not a form of "liberty" protected by the Due Process Clause. Such a right is neither "deeply rooted in this Nation's history and tradition" nor "implicit in the concept of ordered liberty." . . .

I write separately to emphasize a second, more fundamental reason why there is no abortion guarantee lurking in the Due Process Clause. . . . [T]he Due Process Clause at most guarantees process. It does not, as the Court's substantive due process cases suppose, "forbi[d] the government to infringe certain 'fundamental' liberty interests at all, no matter what process is provided."

As I have previously explained, "substantive due process" is an oxymoron that "lack[s] any basis in the Constitution." "The notion that a constitutional provision that guarantees only 'process' before a person is deprived of life, liberty, or property could define the substance of those rights strains credulity for even the most casual user of words." The resolution of this case is thus straightforward. Because the Due Process Clause does not secure any substantive rights, it does not secure a right to abortion.

The Court today declines to disturb substantive due process jurisprudence generally or the doctrine's application in other, specific contexts. Cases like *Griswold v. Connecticut* (right of married persons to obtain contraceptives),* *Lawrence v. Texas* (right to engage in private, consensual sexual acts), and *Obergefell v. Hodges* (right to same-sex marriage), are not at issue. The Court's abortion cases are unique, and no party has asked us to decide "whether our entire Fourteenth Amendment jurisprudence must be preserved or revised." Thus, I agree that "[n]othing in [the Court's] opinion should be understood to cast doubt on precedents that do not concern abortion."

---

* *Griswold v. Connecticut* purported not to rely on the Due Process Clause, but rather reasoned "that specific guarantees in the Bill of Rights"—including rights enumerated in the First, Third, Fourth, Fifth, and Ninth Amendments—"have penumbras, formed by emanations," that create "zones of privacy." Since *Griswold*, the Court, perhaps recognizing the facial absurdity of *Griswold*'s penumbral argument, has characterized the decision as one rooted in substantive due process.

For that reason, in future cases, we should reconsider all of this Court's substantive due process precedents, including *Griswold*, *Lawrence*, and *Obergefell*. Because any substantive due process decision is "demonstrably erroneous," we have a duty to "correct the error" established in those precedents. After overruling these demonstrably erroneous decisions, the question would remain whether other constitutional provisions guarantee the myriad rights that our substantive due process cases have generated. For example, we could consider whether any of the rights announced in this Court's substantive due process cases are "privileges or immunities of citizens of the United States" protected by the Fourteenth Amendment. Amdt. 14, § 1. To answer that question, we would need to decide important antecedent questions, including whether the Privileges or Immunities Clause protects any rights that are not enumerated in the Constitution and, if so, how to identify those rights. That said, even if the Clause does protect unenumerated rights, the Court conclusively demonstrates that abortion is not one of them under any plausible interpretive approach.

Moreover, apart from being a demonstrably incorrect reading of the Due Process Clause, the "legal fiction" of substantive due process is "particularly dangerous." At least three dangers favor jettisoning the doctrine entirely.

First, "substantive due process exalts judges at the expense of the People from whom they derive their authority." Because the Due Process Clause "speaks only to 'process,' the Court has long struggled to define what substantive rights it protects." In practice, the Court's approach for identifying those "fundamental" rights "unquestionably involves policymaking rather than neutral legal analysis." The Court divines new rights in line with "its own, extraconstitutional value preferences" and nullifies state laws that do not align with the judicially created guarantees.

. . . .

Second, substantive due process distorts other areas of constitutional law. For example, once this Court identifies a "fundamental" right for one class of individuals, it invokes the Equal Protection Clause to demand exacting scrutiny of statutes that deny the right to others. Statutory classifications implicating certain "nonfundamental" rights, meanwhile, receive only cursory review. Similarly, this Court deems unconstitutionally "vague" or "overbroad" those laws that impinge on its preferred rights, while letting slide those laws that implicate supposedly lesser values. . . . Therefore, regardless of the doctrinal context, the Court often "demand[s] extra justifications for encroachments" on "preferred rights" while "relax[ing] purportedly higher standards of review for lesspreferred rights." Substantive due process is the core inspiration for many of the Court's constitutionally unmoored policy judgments.

Third, substantive due process is often wielded to "disastrous ends." For instance, in *Dred Scott v. Sandford*, the Court invoked a species of substantive due process to announce that Congress was powerless to emancipate slaves brought into the federal territories. While *Dred Scott* "was overruled on the battlefields of the Civil War and by constitutional amendment after Appomattox," that overruling was "[p]urchased at the price of immeasurable human suffering." Now today, the Court rightly overrules *Roe* and *Casey*—two of this Court's "most notoriously incorrect" substantive due process decisions—after more than 63 million abortions have been performed, see National Right to Life Committee, Abortion Statistics (Jan. 2022), https://www.nrlc.org/uploads/factsheets/FS01 AbortionintheUS.pdf. The harm caused by this Court's forays into substantive due process remains immeasurable.

* * *

Because the Court properly applies our substantive due process precedents to reject the fabrication of a constitutional right to abortion, and because this case does not present the opportunity to reject substantive due process entirely, I join the Court's opinion. But, in future cases, we should "follow the text of the Constitution, which sets forth certain substantive rights that cannot be taken away, and adds, beyond that, a right to due process when life, liberty, or property is to be taken away." Substantive due process conflicts with that textual command and has harmed our country in many ways. Accordingly, we should eliminate it from our jurisprudence at the earliest opportunity.

■ JUSTICE KAVANAUGH, concurring.

I write separately to explain my additional views about why *Roe* was wrongly decided, why *Roe* should be overruled at this time, and the future implications of today's decision.

Abortion is a profoundly difficult and contentious issue because it presents an irreconcilable conflict between the interests of a pregnant woman who seeks an abortion and the interests in protecting fetal life. The interests on both sides of the abortion issue are extraordinarily weighty.

. . . .

The issue before this Court, however, is not the policy or morality of abortion. The issue before this Court is what the Constitution says about abortion. The Constitution does not take sides on the issue of abortion. The text of the Constitution does not refer to or encompass abortion. To be sure, this Court has held that the Constitution protects unenumerated rights that are deeply rooted in this Nation's history and tradition, and implicit in the concept of ordered liberty. But a right to abortion is not deeply rooted in American history and tradition, as the Court today thoroughly explains.

The Court's opinion today also recounts the pre-constitutional common-law history in England. That English history supplies background information on the issue of abortion. As I see it, the dispositive point in analyzing American history and tradition for purposes of the Fourteenth Amendment inquiry is that abortion was largely prohibited in most American States as of 1868 when the Fourteenth Amendment was ratified, and that abortion remained largely prohibited in most American States until Roe was decided in 1973.

On the question of abortion, the Constitution is therefore neither pro-life nor pro-choice. The Constitution is neutral and leaves the issue for the people and their elected representatives to resolve through the democratic process in the States or Congress—like the numerous other difficult questions of American social and economic policy that the Constitution does not address.

Because the Constitution is neutral on the issue of abortion, this Court also must be scrupulously neutral. The nine unelected Members of this Court do not possess the constitutional authority to override the democratic process and to decree either a pro-life or a pro-choice abortion policy for all 330 million people in the United States.

. . . . The Court's decision today properly returns the Court to a position of neutrality and restores the people's authority to address the issue of abortion through the processes of democratic self-government established by the Constitution.

. . . .

To be clear, then, the Court's decision today does not outlaw abortion throughout the United States. On the contrary, the Court's decision properly leaves the question of abortion for the people and their elected representatives in the democratic process. Through that democratic process, the people and their representatives may decide to allow or limit abortion. As Justice Scalia stated, the "States may, if they wish, permit abortion on demand, but the Constitution does not require them to do so."

Today's decision therefore does not prevent the numerous States that readily allow abortion from continuing to readily allow abortion. . . . By contrast, other States may maintain laws that more strictly limit abortion. After today's decision, all of the States may evaluate the competing interests and decide how to address this consequential issue.

. . . .

After today's decision, the nine Members of this Court will no longer decide the basic legality of pre-viability abortion for all 330 million Americans. That issue will be resolved by the people and their representatives in the democratic process in the States or Congress. But the parties' arguments have raised other related questions, and I address some of them here.

First is the question of how this decision will affect other precedents involving issues such as contraception and marriage—in particular, the decisions in *Griswold v. Connecticut, Eisenstadt v. Baird, Loving v. Virginia,* and *Obergefell v. Hodges.* I emphasize what the Court today states: Overruling *Roe* does not mean the overruling of those precedents, and does not threaten or cast doubt on those precedents.

Second, as I see it, some of the other abortion-related legal questions raised by today's decision are not especially difficult as a constitutional matter. For example, may a State bar a resident of that State from traveling to another State to obtain an abortion? In my view, the answer is no based on the constitutional right to interstate travel. May a State retroactively impose liability or punishment for an abortion that occurred before today's decision takes effect? In my view, the answer is no based on the Due Process Clause or the Ex Post Facto Clause.

Other abortion-related legal questions may emerge in the future. But this Court will no longer decide the fundamental question of whether abortion must be allowed throughout the United States through 6 weeks, or 12 weeks, or 15 weeks, or 24 weeks, or some other line. The Court will no longer decide how to evaluate the interests of the pregnant woman and the interests in protecting fetal life throughout pregnancy. Instead, those difficult moral and policy questions will be decided, as the Constitution dictates, by the people and their elected representatives through the constitutional processes of democratic self-government.

. . . .

■ CHIEF JUSTICE ROBERTS, concurring in the judgment.

We granted certiorari to decide one question: "Whether all pre-viability prohibitions on elective abortions are unconstitutional." That question is directly implicated here: Mississippi's Gestational Age Act generally prohibits abortion after the fifteenth week of pregnancy—several weeks before a fetus is regarded as "viable" outside the womb. In urging our review, Mississippi stated that its case was "an ideal vehicle" to "reconsider the bright-line viability rule," and that a judgment in its favor would "not require the Court to overturn" *Roe v. Wade* and *Planned Parenthood of Southeastern Pa. v. Casey.*

Today, the Court nonetheless rules for Mississippi by doing just that. I would take a more measured course. I agree with the Court that the viability line established by *Roe* and *Casey* should be discarded under a straightforward stare decisis analysis. That line never made any sense. Our abortion precedents describe the right at issue as a woman's right to choose to terminate her pregnancy. That right should therefore extend far enough to ensure a reasonable opportunity to choose, but need not extend any further—certainly not all the way to viability. . . .

Surely we should adhere closely to principles of judicial restraint here, where the broader path the Court chooses entails repudiating a constitutional right we have not only previously recognized, but also expressly reaffirmed applying the doctrine of stare decisis. The Court's opinion is thoughtful and thorough, but those virtues cannot compensate for the fact that its dramatic and consequential ruling is unnecessary to decide the case before us.

. . . .

. . . . A thoughtful Member of this Court once counseled that the difficulty of a question "admonishes us to observe the wise limitations on our function and to confine ourselves to deciding only what is necessary to the disposition of the immediate case." *Whitehouse v. Illinois Central R. Co.*, 349 U.S. 366 (1955) (Frankfurter, J., for the Court). I would decide the question we granted review to answer—whether the previously recognized abortion right bars all abortion restrictions prior to viability, such that a ban on abortions after fifteen weeks of pregnancy is necessarily unlawful. The answer to that question is no, and there is no need to go further to decide this case.

I therefore concur only in the judgment.

■ JUSTICE BREYER, JUSTICE SOTOMAYOR, and JUSTICE KAGAN, dissenting.

For half a century, *Roe v. Wade* and *Planned Parenthood of Southeastern Pa. v. Casey* have protected the liberty and equality of women. Roe held, and Casey reaffirmed, that the Constitution safeguards a woman's right to decide for herself whether to bear a child. *Roe* held, and *Casey* reaffirmed, that in the first stages of pregnancy, the government could not make that choice for women. The government could not control a woman's body or the course of a woman's life: It could not determine what the woman's future would be. Respecting a woman as an autonomous being, and granting her full equality, meant giving her substantial choice over this most personal and most consequential of all life decisions.

Roe and *Casey* well understood the difficulty and divisiveness of the abortion issue. . . . So the Court struck a balance, as it often does when values and goals compete. It held that the State could prohibit abortions after fetal viability, so long as the ban contained exceptions to safeguard a woman's life or health. It held that even before viability, the State could regulate the abortion procedure in multiple and meaningful ways. But until the viability line was crossed, the Court held, a State could not impose a "substantial obstacle" on a woman's "right to elect the procedure" as she (not the government) thought proper, in light of all the circumstances and complexities of her own life.

Today, the Court discards that balance. It says that from the very moment of fertilization, a woman has no rights to speak of. A State can force her to bring a pregnancy to term, even at the steepest personal and familial costs. An abortion restriction, the majority holds, is permissible whenever rational, the lowest level of scrutiny known to the law. And because, as the Court has often stated, protecting fetal life is rational,

States will feel free to enact all manner of restrictions. The Mississippi law at issue here bars abortions after the 15th week of pregnancy. Under the majority's ruling, though, another State's law could do so after ten weeks, or five or three or one—or, again, from the moment of fertilization. States have already passed such laws, in anticipation of today's ruling. More will follow. Some States have enacted laws extending to all forms of abortion procedure, including taking medication in one's own home. They have passed laws without any exceptions for when the woman is the victim of rape or incest. Under those laws, a woman will have to bear her rapist's child or a young girl her father's—no matter if doing so will destroy her life. So too, after today's ruling, some States may compel women to carry to term a fetus with severe physical anomalies—for example, one afflicted with Tay-Sachs disease, sure to die within a few years of birth. States may even argue that a prohibition on abortion need make no provision for protecting a woman from risk of death or physical harm. Across a vast array of circumstances, a State will be able to impose its moral choice on a woman and coerce her to give birth to a child.

Enforcement of all these draconian restrictions will also be left largely to the States' devices. A State can of course impose criminal penalties on abortion providers, including lengthy prison sentences. But some States will not stop there. Perhaps, in the wake of today's decision, a state law will criminalize the woman's conduct too, incarcerating or fining her for daring to seek or obtain an abortion. And as Texas has recently shown [through the enactment of S.B. 8], a State can turn neighbor against neighbor, enlisting fellow citizens in the effort to root out anyone who tries to get an abortion, or to assist another in doing so.

The majority tries to hide the geographically expansive effects of its holding. Today's decision, the majority says, permits "each State" to address abortion as it pleases. That is cold comfort, of course, for the poor woman who cannot get the money to fly to a distant State for a procedure. Above all others, women lacking financial resources will suffer from today's decision. In any event, interstate restrictions will also soon be in the offing. After this decision, some States may block women from traveling out of State to obtain abortions, or even from receiving abortion medications from out of State. Some may criminalize efforts, including the provision of information or funding, to help women gain access to other States' abortion services. Most threatening of all, no language in today's decision stops the Federal Government from prohibiting abortions nationwide, once again from the moment of conception and without exceptions for rape or incest. If that happens, "the views of [an individual State's] citizens" will not matter.

Whatever the exact scope of the coming laws, one result of today's decision is certain: the curtailment of women's rights, and of their status as free and equal citizens. Yesterday, the Constitution guaranteed that a woman confronted with an unplanned pregnancy could (within reasonable limits) make her own decision about whether to bear a child, with all the life-transforming consequences that act involves. And in thus safeguarding each woman's reproductive freedom, the Constitution also protected "[t]he ability of women to participate equally in [this Nation's] economic and social life." But no longer. . . . The Constitution will, today's majority holds, provide no shield, despite its guarantees of liberty and equality for all.

And no one should be confident that this majority is done with its work. The right *Roe* and *Casey* recognized does not stand alone. To the contrary, the Court has linked it for decades to other settled freedoms involving bodily integrity, familial relationships, and procreation. Most obviously, the right to terminate a pregnancy arose straight out of the right to purchase and use contraception. They are all part of the same constitutional fabric, protecting autonomous decisionmaking over the most personal of life decisions. The majority (or to be more accurate, most of it) is eager to tell us today that nothing it does "cast[s] doubt on precedents that do not concern abortion." But how could that be? The lone rationale for what the majority does today is that the right to elect an abortion is not "deeply rooted in history": Not until *Roe*, the majority argues, did people think abortion fell within the Constitution's guarantee of liberty. The same could be said, though, of most of the rights the majority claims it is not tampering with. The majority could write just as long an opinion showing, for example, that until the mid-20th century, "there was no support in American law for a constitutional right to obtain [contraceptives]." So one of two things must be true. Either the majority does not really believe in its own reasoning. Or if it does, all rights that have no history stretching back to the mid-19th century are insecure. Either the mass of the majority's opinion is hypocrisy, or additional constitutional rights are under threat. It is one or the other.

One piece of evidence on that score seems especially salient: The majority's cavalier approach to overturning this Court's precedents. Stare decisis is the Latin phrase for a foundation stone of the rule of law: that things decided should stay decided unless there is a very good reason for change. It is a doctrine of judicial modesty and humility. Those qualities are not evident in today's opinion. The majority has no good reason for the upheaval in law and society it sets off. *Roe* and *Casey* have been the law of the land for decades, shaping women's expectations of their choices when an unplanned pregnancy occurs. Women have relied on the availability of abortion both in structuring their relationships and in planning their lives. The legal framework *Roe* and *Casey* developed to balance the competing interests in this sphere has proved workable in courts across the country. No recent developments, in either law or fact, have eroded or cast doubt on those precedents. Nothing, in short, has changed. Indeed, the Court in *Casey* already found all of that to be true. *Casey* is a precedent about precedent. It reviewed the same arguments made here in support of overruling *Roe*, and it found that doing so was not warranted. The Court reverses course today for one reason and one reason only: because the composition of this Court has changed. Stare decisis, this Court has often said, "contributes to the actual and perceived integrity of the judicial process" by ensuring that decisions are "founded in the law rather than in the proclivities of individuals." Today, the proclivities of individuals rule. The Court departs from its obligation to faithfully and impartially apply the law. We dissent.

We start with *Roe* and *Casey*, and with their deep connections to a broad swath of this Court's precedents. To hear the majority tell the tale, *Roe* and *Casey* are aberrations: They came from nowhere, went nowhere—and so are easy to excise from this Nation's constitutional law. That is not true. After describing the decisions themselves, we explain how they are rooted in—and themselves led to—other rights giving individuals control over their bodies and their most personal and intimate associations. The majority does not wish to talk about these matters for obvious reasons; to do so would both ground *Roe* and *Casey* in this Court's precedents and reveal the broad implications of today's decision. But the facts will not so handily disappear. *Roe* and *Casey* were from the beginning, and are even more now, embedded in core constitutional concepts of individual freedom, and of the equal rights of citizens to decide on the shape of their lives. Those legal concepts, one might even say, have gone far toward defining what it means to be an American. For in this Nation, we do not believe that a government controlling all private choices is compatible with a free people. So we do not (as the majority insists today) place everything within "the reach of majorities and [government] officials." We believe in a Constitution that puts some issues off limits to majority rule. Even in the face of public opposition, we uphold the right of individuals—yes, including women—to make their own choices and chart their own futures. Or at least, we did once.

Some half-century ago, *Roe* struck down a state law making it a crime to perform an abortion unless its purpose was to save a woman's life. The *Roe* Court knew it was treading on difficult and disputed ground. It understood that different people's "experiences," "values," and "religious training" and beliefs led to "opposing views" about abortion. But by a 7-to-2 vote, the Court held that in the earlier stages of pregnancy, that contested and contestable choice must belong to a woman, in consultation with her family and doctor. The Court explained that a long line of precedents, "founded in the Fourteenth Amendment's concept of personal liberty," protected individual decisionmaking related to "marriage, procreation, contraception, family relationships, and child rearing and education." For the same reasons, the Court held, the Constitution must protect "a woman's decision whether or not to terminate her pregnancy." The Court recognized the myriad ways bearing a child can alter the "life and future" of a woman and other members of her family. A State could not, "by adopting one theory of life," override all "rights of the pregnant woman."

At the same time, though, the Court recognized "valid interest[s]" of the State "in regulating the abortion decision." The Court noted in particular "important interests" in "protecting potential life," "maintaining medical standards," and "safeguarding [the]" health of the woman. No "absolut[ist]" account of the woman's right could wipe away those significant state claims.

The Court therefore struck a balance, turning on the stage of the pregnancy at which the abortion would occur. . . .

In the 20 years between *Roe and Casey*, the Court expressly reaffirmed *Roe* on two occasions, and applied it on many more. Then, in *Casey*, the Court considered the matter anew, and again upheld *Roe's* core precepts. . . .

Central to that conclusion was a full-throated restatement of a woman's right to choose. Like *Roe*, *Casey* grounded that right in the Fourteenth Amendment's guarantee of "liberty." That guarantee encompasses realms of conduct not specifically referenced in the Constitution: "Marriage is mentioned nowhere" in that document, yet the Court was "no doubt correct" to protect the freedom to marry "against state interference." And the guarantee of liberty encompasses conduct today that was not protected at the time of the Fourteenth Amendment. "It is settled now," the Court said—though it was not always so—that "the Constitution places limits on a State's right to interfere with a person's most basic decisions about family and parenthood, as well as bodily integrity." . . .

In reaffirming the right *Roe* recognized, the [*Casey*] Court took full account of the diversity of views on abortion, and the importance of various competing state interests. . . . So *Casey* again struck a balance, differing from *Roe's* in only incremental ways. It retained *Roe's* "central holding" that the State could bar abortion only after viability. The viability line, *Casey* thought, was "more workable" than any other in marking the place where the woman's liberty interest gave way to a State's efforts to preserve potential life. At that point, a "second life" was capable of "independent existence." If the woman even by then had not acted, she lacked adequate grounds to object to "the State's intervention on [the developing child's] behalf." At the same time, *Casey* decided, based on two decades of experience, that the *Roe* framework did not give States sufficient ability to regulate abortion prior to viability. In that period, *Casey* now made clear, the State could regulate not only to protect the woman's health but also to "promot[e] prenatal life." In particular, the State could ensure informed choice and could try to promote childbirth. But the State still could not place an "undue burden"—or "substantial obstacle"—"in the path of a woman seeking an abortion." Prior to viability, the woman, consistent with the constitutional "meaning of liberty," must "retain the ultimate control over her destiny and her body."

.... As just described, *Roe* and *Casey* invoked powerful state interests in that protection, operative at every stage of the pregnancy and overriding the woman's liberty after viability. The strength of those state interests is exactly why the Court allowed greater restrictions on the abortion right than on other rights deriving from the Fourteenth Amendment.[1] But what *Roe* and *Casey* also recognized—which today's majority does not—is that a woman's freedom and equality are likewise involved. That fact—the presence of countervailing interests—is what made the abortion question hard, and what necessitated balancing. The majority scoffs at that idea, castigating us for "repeatedly prais[ing] the 'balance'" the two cases arrived at (with the word "balance" in scare quotes). To the majority "balance" is a dirty word, as moderation is a foreign concept. The majority would allow States to ban abortion from conception onward because it does not think forced childbirth at all implicates a woman's rights to equality and freedom. Today's Court, that is, does not think there is anything of constitutional significance attached to a woman's control of her body and the path of her life. *Roe* and *Casey* thought that one-sided view misguided. In some sense, that is the difference in a nutshell between our precedents and the majority opinion. The constitutional regime we have lived in for the last 50 years recognized competing interests, and sought a balance between them. The constitutional regime we enter today erases the woman's interest and recognizes only the State's (or the Federal Government's).

The majority makes this change based on a single question: Did the reproductive right recognized in *Roe* and *Casey* exist in "1868, the year when the Fourteenth Amendment was ratified"? The majority says (and with this much we agree) that the answer to this question is no: In 1868, there was no nationwide right to end a pregnancy, and no thought that the Fourteenth Amendment provided one.

Of course, the majority opinion refers as well to some later and earlier history. On the one side of 1868, it goes back as far as the 13th (the 13th!) century. But that turns out to be wheel-spinning. First, it is not clear what relevance such early history should have, even to the majority. If the early history obviously supported abortion rights, the majority would no doubt say that only the views of the Fourteenth Amendment's ratifiers are germane. Second—and embarrassingly for the majority—early law in fact does provide some support for abortion rights. Common-law authorities did not treat abortion as a crime before

---

[1] For this reason, we do not understand the majority's view that our analogy between the right to an abortion and the rights to contraception and same-sex marriage shows that we think "[t]he Constitution does not permit the States to regard the destruction of a 'potential life' as a matter of any significance." To the contrary. The liberty interests underlying those rights are, as we will describe, quite similar. But only in the sphere of abortion is the state interest in protecting potential life involved. So only in that sphere, as both *Roe* and *Casey* recognized, may a State impinge so far on the liberty interest (barring abortion after viability and discouraging it before). The majority's failure to understand this fairly obvious point stems from its rejection of the idea of balancing interests in this (or maybe in any) constitutional context. The majority thinks that a woman has no liberty or equality interest in the decision to bear a child, so a State's interest in protecting fetal life necessarily prevails.

"quickening"—the point when the fetus moved in the womb.[2] And early American law followed the common-law rule.[3] So the criminal law of that early time might be taken as roughly consonant with *Roe*'s and *Casey*'s different treatment of early and late abortions. Better, then, to move forward in time. On the other side of 1868, the majority occasionally notes that many States barred abortion up to the time of *Roe*. That is convenient for the majority, but it is window dressing. As the same majority (plus one) just informed us, "post-ratification adoption or acceptance of laws that are inconsistent with the original meaning of the constitutional text obviously cannot overcome or alter that text." *New York State Rifle & Pistol Assn., Inc. v. Bruen*, 597 U.S., at ___ (2022). Had the pre-Roe liberalization of abortion laws occurred more quickly and more widely in the 20th century, the majority would say (once again) that only the ratifiers' views are germane.

The majority's core legal postulate, then, is that we in the 21st century must read the Fourteenth Amendment just as its ratifiers did. And that is indeed what the majority emphasizes over and over again. If the ratifiers did not understand something as central to freedom, then neither can we. Or said more particularly: If those people did not understand reproductive rights as part of the guarantee of liberty conferred in the Fourteenth Amendment, then those rights do not exist.

As an initial matter, note a mistake in the just preceding sentence. We referred there to the "people" who ratified the Fourteenth Amendment: What rights did those "people" have in their heads at the time? But, of course, "people" did not ratify the Fourteenth Amendment. Men did. So it is perhaps not so surprising that the ratifiers were not perfectly attuned to the importance of reproductive rights for women's liberty, or for their capacity to participate as equal members of our Nation. Indeed, the ratifiers—both in 1868 and when the original Constitution was approved in 1788—did not understand women as full members of the community embraced by the phrase "We the People." In 1868, the first wave of American feminists were explicitly told—of course by men—that it was not their time to seek constitutional protections. (Women would not get even the vote for another half-century.) To be sure, most women in 1868 also had a foreshortened view of their rights: If most men could not then imagine giving women control over their bodies, most women could not imagine having that kind of autonomy. But that takes away nothing from the core point. Those responsible for the original Constitution, including the Fourteenth Amendment, did not perceive women as equals, and did not recognize women's rights. When the

---

[2] *See, e.g.*, 1 W. Blackstone, Commentaries on the Laws of England 129–130 (7th ed. 1775) (Blackstone); E. Coke, Institutes of the Laws of England 50 (1644).

[3] *See* J. MOHR, ABORTION IN AMERICA: THE ORIGINS AND EVOLUTION OF NATIONAL POLICY, 1800–1900, pp. 3–4 (1978). The majority offers no evidence to the contrary—no example of a founding-era law making prequickening abortion a crime (except when a woman died). And even in the mid-19th century, more than 10 States continued to allow pre-quickening abortions. *See* Brief for American Historical Association et al. as Amici Curiae 27, and n. 14.

majority says that we must read our foundational charter as viewed at the time of ratification (except that we may also check it against the Dark Ages), it consigns women to second-class citizenship.

Casey itself understood this point, as will become clear. It recollected with dismay a decision this Court issued just five years after the Fourteenth Amendment's ratification, approving a State's decision to deny a law license to a woman and suggesting as well that a woman had no legal status apart from her husband. "There was a time," *Casey* explained, when the Constitution did not protect "men and women alike." But times had changed. A woman's place in society had changed, and constitutional law had changed along with it. The relegation of women to inferior status in either the public sphere or the family was "no longer consistent with our understanding" of the Constitution. Now, "[t]he Constitution protects all individuals, male or female," from "the abuse of governmental power" or "unjustified state interference."

So how is it that, as *Casey* said, our Constitution, read now, grants rights to women, though it did not in 1868? How is it that our Constitution subjects discrimination against them to heightened judicial scrutiny? How is it that our Constitution, through the Fourteenth Amendment's liberty clause, guarantees access to contraception (also not legally protected in 1868) so that women can decide for themselves whether and when to bear a child? How is it that until today, that same constitutional clause protected a woman's right, in the event contraception failed, to end a pregnancy in its earlier stages?

The answer is that this Court has rejected the majority's pinched view of how to read our Constitution. "The Founders," we recently wrote, "knew they were writing a document designed to apply to ever-changing circumstances over centuries." Or in the words of the great Chief Justice John Marshall, our Constitution is "intended to endure for ages to come," and must adapt itself to a future "seen dimly," if at all. That is indeed why our Constitution is written as it is. The Framers (both in 1788 and 1868) understood that the world changes. So they did not define rights by reference to the specific practices existing at the time. Instead, the Framers defined rights in general terms, to permit future evolution in their scope and meaning. And over the course of our history, this Court has taken up the Framers' invitation. It has kept true to the Framers' principles by applying them in new ways, responsive to new societal understandings and conditions.

Nowhere has that approach been more prevalent than in construing the majestic but open-ended words of the Fourteenth Amendment—the guarantees of "liberty" and "equality" for all. And nowhere has that approach produced prouder moments, for this country and the Court. Consider an example *Obergefell* used a few years ago. The Court there confronted a claim, based on *Washington v. Glucksberg*, 521 U.S. 702 (1997), that the Fourteenth Amendment "must be defined in a most circumscribed manner, with central reference to specific historical

practices"—exactly the view today's majority follows. And the Court
specifically rejected that view.[4] In doing so, the Court reflected on what
the proposed, historically circumscribed approach would have meant for
interracial marriage. The Fourteenth Amendment's ratifiers did not
think it gave black and white people a right to marry each other. To the
contrary, contemporaneous practice deemed that act quite as
unprotected as abortion. Yet the Court in *Loving v. Virginia*, 388 U.S. 1
(1967), read the Fourteenth Amendment to embrace the Lovings' union.
If, *Obergefell* explained, "rights were defined by who exercised them in
the past, then received practices could serve as their own continued
justification"—even when they conflict with "liberty" and "equality" as
later and more broadly understood. The Constitution does not freeze for
all time the original view of what those rights guarantee, or how they
apply.

   That does not mean anything goes. The majority wishes people to
think there are but two alternatives: (1) accept the original applications
of the Fourteenth Amendment and no others, or (2) surrender to judges'
"own ardent views," ungrounded in law, about the "liberty that
Americans should enjoy." At least, that idea is what the majority
sometimes tries to convey. At other times, the majority (or, rather, most
of it) tries to assure the public that it has no designs on rights (for
example, to contraception) that arose only in the back half of the 20th
century—in other words, that it is happy to pick and choose, in accord
with individual preferences. . . . [A]pplications of liberty and equality can
evolve while remaining grounded in constitutional principles,
constitutional history, and constitutional precedents. The second Justice
Harlan discussed how to strike the right balance when he explained why
he would have invalidated a State's ban on contraceptive use. Judges, he
said, are not "free to roam where unguided speculation might take them."
Yet they also must recognize that the constitutional "tradition" of this
country is not captured whole at a single moment. Rather, its meaning
gains content from the long sweep of our history and from successive
judicial precedents—each looking to the last and each seeking to apply
the Constitution's most fundamental commitments to new conditions.
That is why Americans, to go back to *Obergefell*'s example, have a right
to marry across racial lines. And it is why, to go back to Justice Harlan's
case, Americans have a right to use contraceptives so they can choose for
themselves whether to have children.

   . . . .

   And that conclusion still held good, until the Court's intervention
here. It was settled at the time of *Roe*, settled at the time of *Casey*, and
settled yesterday that the Constitution places limits on a State's power

---

   [4] The majority ignores that rejection. But it is unequivocal: The Glucksberg test,
Obergefell said, "may have been appropriate" in considering physician-assisted suicide, but "is
inconsistent with the approach this Court has used in discussing other fundamental rights,
including marriage and intimacy."

to assert control over an individual's body and most personal decisionmaking. A multitude of decisions supporting that principle led to *Roe*'s recognition and *Casey*'s reaffirmation of the right to choose; and *Roe* and *Casey* in turn supported additional protections for intimate and familial relations. The majority has embarrassingly little to say about those precedents. It (literally) rattles them off in a single paragraph; and it implies that they have nothing to do with each other, or with the right to terminate an early pregnancy. But that is flat wrong. The Court's precedents about bodily autonomy, sexual and familial relations, and procreation are all interwoven—all part of the fabric of our constitutional law, and because that is so, of our lives. Especially women's lives, where they safeguard a right to self-determination.

And eliminating that right, we need to say before further describing our precedents, is not taking a "neutral" position, as Justice Kavanaugh tries to argue. His idea is that neutrality lies in giving the abortion issue to the States, where some can go one way and some another. But would he say that the Court is being "scrupulously neutral" if it allowed New York and California to ban all the guns they want? If the Court allowed some States to use unanimous juries and others not? If the Court told the States: Decide for yourselves whether to put restrictions on church attendance? We could go on—and in fact we will. Suppose Justice Kavanaugh were to say (in line with the majority opinion) that the rights we just listed are more textually or historically grounded than the right to choose. What, then, of the right to contraception or same-sex marriage? Would it be "scrupulously neutral" for the Court to eliminate those rights too? The point of all these examples is that when it comes to rights, the Court does not act "neutrally" when it leaves everything up to the States. Rather, the Court acts neutrally when it protects the right against all comers. And to apply that point to the case here: When the Court decimates a right women have held for 50 years, the Court is not being "scrupulously neutral." It is instead taking sides: against women who wish to exercise the right, and for States (like Mississippi) that want to bar them from doing so. . . .

. . . .

. . . *Roe* and *Casey* fit neatly into a long line of decisions protecting from government intrusion a wealth of private choices about family matters, child rearing, intimate relationships, and procreation. Those cases safeguard particular choices about whom to marry; whom to have sex with; what family members to live with; how to raise children—and crucially, whether and when to have children. In varied cases, the Court explained that those choices—"the most intimate and personal" a person can make—reflect fundamental aspects of personal identity; they define the very "attributes of personhood." And they inevitably shape the nature and future course of a person's life (and often the lives of those closest to her). So, the Court held, those choices belong to the individual, and not the government. That is the essence of what liberty requires.

And liberty may require it, this Court has repeatedly said, even when those living in 1868 would not have recognized the claim—because they would not have seen the person making it as a full-fledged member of the community. Throughout our history, the sphere of protected liberty has expanded, bringing in individuals formerly excluded. In that way, the constitutional values of liberty and equality go hand in hand; they do not inhabit the hermetically sealed containers the majority portrays. So before *Roe* and *Casey*, the Court expanded in successive cases those who could claim the right to marry—though their relationships would have been outside the law's protection in the mid-19th century. And after *Roe* and *Casey*, of course, the Court continued in that vein. With a critical stop to hold that the Fourteenth Amendment protected same-sex intimacy, the Court resolved that the Amendment also conferred on same-sex couples the right to marry. In considering that question, the Court held, "[h]istory and tradition," especially as reflected in the course of our precedent, "guide and discipline [the] inquiry." But the sentiments of 1868 alone do not and cannot "rule the present."

. . . .

Faced with all these connections between *Roe/Casey* and judicial decisions recognizing other constitutional rights, the majority tells everyone not to worry. It can (so it says) neatly extract the right to choose from the constitutional edifice without affecting any associated rights. (Think of someone telling you that the Jenga tower simply will not collapse.) Today's decision, the majority first says, "does not undermine" the decisions cited by *Roe* and *Casey*—the ones involving "marriage, procreation, contraception, [and] family relationships"—"in any way." . . . So the majority depicts today's decision as "a restricted railroad ticket, good for this day and train only." Should the audience for these too-much-repeated protestations be duly satisfied? We think not.

The first problem with the majority's account comes from Justice Thomas's concurrence—which makes clear he is not with the program. In saying that nothing in today's opinion casts doubt on non-abortion precedents, Justice Thomas explains, he means only that they are not at issue in this very case. But he lets us know what he wants to do when they are. "[I]n future cases," he says, "we should reconsider all of this Court's substantive due process precedents, including *Griswold*, *Lawrence*, and *Obergefell*." And when we reconsider them? Then "we have a duty" to "overrul[e] these demonstrably erroneous decisions." So at least one Justice is planning to use the ticket of today's decision again and again and again.

Even placing the concurrence to the side, the assurance in today's opinion still does not work. Or at least that is so if the majority is serious about its sole reason for overturning *Roe and Casey*: the legal status of abortion in the 19th century. Except in the places quoted above, the state interest in protecting fetal life plays no part in the majority's analysis. To the contrary, the majority takes pride in not expressing a view "about the status of the fetus." The majority's departure from *Roe and Casey* rests instead—and only—on whether a woman's decision to end a pregnancy involves any Fourteenth Amendment liberty interest (against which *Roe and Casey* balanced the state interest in preserving fetal life). According to the majority, no liberty interest is present—because (and only because) the law offered no protection to the woman's choice in the 19th century. But here is the rub. The law also did not then (and would not for ages) protect a wealth of other things. It did not protect the rights recognized in *Lawrence* and *Obergefell* to same-sex intimacy and marriage. It did not protect the right recognized in *Loving* to marry across racial lines. It did not protect the right recognized in *Griswold* to contraceptive use. For that matter, it did not protect the right recognized in *Skinner v. Oklahoma ex rel. Williamson*, not to be sterilized without consent. So if the majority is right in its legal analysis, all those decisions were wrong, and all those matters properly belong to the States too— whatever the particular state interests involved. And if that is true, it is impossible to understand (as a matter of logic and principle) how the majority can say that its opinion today does not threaten—does not even "undermine"—any number of other constitutional rights.

Nor does it even help just to take the majority at its word. Assume the majority is sincere in saying, for whatever reason, that it will go so far and no further. Scout's honor. Still, the future significance of today's opinion will be decided in the future. And law often has a way of evolving without regard to original intentions—a way of actually following where logic leads, rather than tolerating hard-to-explain lines. Rights can expand in that way. . . . Rights can contract in the same way and for the same reason—because whatever today's majority might say, one thing really does lead to another. We fervently hope that does not happen because of today's decision. . . . But we cannot understand how anyone can be confident that today's opinion will be the last of its kind.

. . . .

Anyway, today's decision, taken on its own, is catastrophic enough. As a matter of constitutional method, the majority's commitment to replicate in 2022 every view about the meaning of liberty held in 1868 has precious little to recommend it. Our law in this constitutional sphere, as in most, has for decades upon decades proceeded differently. It has considered fundamental constitutional principles, the whole course of the Nation's history and traditions, and the step-by-step evolution of the Court's precedents. It is disciplined but not static. It relies on accumulated judgments, not just the sentiments of one long-ago generation of men (who themselves believed, and drafted the Constitution to reflect, that the world progresses). And by doing so, it includes those excluded from that olden conversation, rather than perpetuating its bounds.

As a matter of constitutional substance, the majority's opinion has all the flaws its method would suggest. Because laws in 1868 deprived women of any control over their bodies, the majority approves States doing so today. Because those laws prevented women from charting the course of their own lives, the majority says States can do the same again. Because in 1868, the government could tell a pregnant woman—even in the first days of her pregnancy—that she could do nothing but bear a child, it can once more impose that command. Today's decision strips women of agency over what even the majority agrees is a contested and contestable moral issue. It forces her to carry out the State's will, whatever the circumstances and whatever the harm it will wreak on her and her family. In the Fourteenth Amendment's terms, it takes away her liberty. . . . [W]e dissent.

By overruling *Roe*, *Casey*, and more than 20 cases reaffirming or applying the constitutional right to abortion, the majority abandons stare decisis, a principle central to the rule of law. . . .

Stare decisis also "contributes to the integrity of our constitutional system of government" by ensuring that decisions "are founded in the law rather than in the proclivities of individuals." . . .

That means the Court may not overrule a decision, even a constitutional one, without a "special justification." Stare decisis is, of course, not an "inexorable command"; it is sometimes appropriate to overrule an earlier decision. But the Court must have a good reason to do so over and above the belief "that the precedent was wrongly decided." "[I]t is not alone sufficient that we would decide a case differently now than we did then."

. . . . Nothing—and in particular, no significant legal or factual change—supports overturning a half-century of settled law giving women control over their reproductive lives. First, for all the reasons we have given, *Roe* and *Casey* were correct. In holding that a State could not "resolve" the debate about abortion "in such a definitive way that a woman lacks all choice in the matter," the Court protected women's liberty and women's equality in a way comporting with our Fourteenth Amendment precedents. Contrary to the majority's view, the legal status of abortion in the 19th century does not weaken those decisions. And the majority's repeated refrain about "usurp[ing]" state legislatures' "power to address" a publicly contested question does not help it on the key issue here. To repeat: The point of a right is to shield individual actions and decisions "from the vicissitudes of political controversy, to place them beyond the reach of majorities and officials and to establish them as legal principles to be applied by the courts." However divisive, a right is not at the people's mercy.

In any event "[w]hether or not we . . . agree" with a prior precedent is the beginning, not the end, of our analysis—and the remaining "principles of stare decisis weigh heavily against overruling" *Roe and Casey*. *Casey* itself applied those principles, in one of this Court's most important precedents about precedent. After assessing the traditional stare decisis factors, *Casey* reached the only conclusion possible—that stare decisis operates powerfully here. It still does. The standards *Roe and Casey* set out are perfectly workable. No changes in either law or fact have eroded the two decisions. And tens of millions of American women have relied, and continue to rely, on the right to choose. So under traditional stare decisis principles, the majority has no special justification for the harm it causes.

And indeed, the majority comes close to conceding that point. The majority barely mentions any legal or factual changes that have occurred since *Roe and Casey*. It suggests that the two decisions are hard for courts to implement, but cannot prove its case. In the end, the majority says, all it must say to override stare decisis is one thing: that it believes *Roe and Casey* "egregiously wrong." That rule could equally spell the end of any precedent with which a bare majority of the present Court disagrees. So how does that approach prevent the "scale of justice" from "waver[ing] with every new judge's opinion"? 1 BLACKSTONE 69. It does not. It makes radical change too easy and too fast, based on nothing more than the new views of new judges. The majority has overruled *Roe and Casey* for one and only one reason: because it has always despised them, and now it has the votes to discard them. The majority thereby substitutes a rule by judges for the rule of law.

Contrary to the majority's view, there is nothing unworkable about *Casey's* "undue burden" standard. Its primary focus on whether a State has placed a "substantial obstacle" on a woman seeking an abortion is "the sort of inquiry familiar to judges across a variety of contexts." And it has given rise to no more conflict in application than many standards this Court and others unhesitatingly apply every day.

General standards, like the undue burden standard, are ubiquitous in the law, and particularly in constitutional adjudication. When called on to give effect to the Constitution's broad principles, this Court often crafts flexible standards that can be applied case-by-case to a myriad of unforeseeable circumstances. The *Casey* undue burden standard is the same. It also resembles general standards that courts work with daily in other legal spheres—like the "rule of reason" in antitrust law or the "arbitrary and capricious" standard for agency decisionmaking. Applying general standards to particular cases is, in many contexts, just what it means to do law.

And the undue burden standard has given rise to no unusual difficulties. Of course, it has provoked some disagreement among judges. *Casey* knew it would: That much "is to be expected in the application of any legal standard which must accommodate life's complexity." Which is to say: That much is to be expected in the application of any legal standard. . . .

Anyone concerned about workability should consider the majority's substitute standard. The majority says a law regulating or banning abortion "must be sustained if there is a rational basis on which the legislature could have thought that it would serve legitimate state interests." And the majority lists interests like "respect for and preservation of prenatal life," "protection of maternal health," elimination of certain "medical procedures," "mitigation of fetal pain," and others. This Court will surely face critical questions about how that test applies. Must a state law allow abortions when necessary to protect a woman's life and health? And if so, exactly when? How much risk to a woman's life can a State force her to incur, before the Fourteenth Amendment's protection of life kicks in? . . . Further, the Court may face questions about the application of abortion regulations to medical care most people view as quite different from abortion. What about the morning-after pill? IUDs? In vitro fertilization? And how about the use of dilation and evacuation or medication for miscarriage management?[12]

Finally, the majority's ruling today invites a host of questions about interstate conflicts. Can a State bar women from traveling to another State to obtain an abortion? Can a State prohibit advertising out-of-state abortions or helping women get to out-of-state providers? Can a State interfere with the mailing of drugs used for medication abortions? The Constitution protects travel and speech and interstate commerce, so today's ruling will give rise to a host of new constitutional questions. Far from removing the Court from the abortion issue, the majority puts the Court at the center of the coming "interjurisdictional abortion wars."

In short, the majority does not save judges from unwieldy tests or extricate them from the sphere of controversy. To the contrary, it discards a known, workable, and predictable standard in favor of something novel and probably far more complicated. It forces the Court to wade further into hotly contested issues, including moral and philosophical ones, that the majority criticizes *Roe* and *Casey* for addressing.

When overruling constitutional precedent, the Court has almost always pointed to major legal or factual changes undermining a decision's original basis. . . . But . . . not so today. Although nodding to some arguments others have made about "modern developments," the majority does not really rely on them, no doubt seeing their slimness. The majority briefly invokes the current controversy over abortion. But it has to acknowledge that the same dispute has existed for decades: Conflict over abortion is not a change but a constant. . . . In the end, the majority throws longstanding precedent to the winds without showing that anything significant has changed to justify its radical reshaping of the law.

Subsequent legal developments have only reinforced *Roe* and *Casey*. The Court has continued to embrace all the decisions *Roe* and *Casey* cited, decisions which recognize a constitutional right for an individual to make

---

[12] To take just the last, most medical treatments for miscarriage are identical to those used in abortions. Blanket restrictions on "abortion" procedures and medications therefore may be understood to deprive women of effective treatment for miscarriages, which occur in about 10 to 30 percent of pregnancies.

her own choices about "intimate relationships, the family," and contraception. . . .

Moreover, no subsequent factual developments have undermined *Roe* and *Casey*. Women continue to experience unplanned pregnancies and unexpected developments in pregnancies. Pregnancies continue to have enormous physical, social, and economic consequences. Even an uncomplicated pregnancy imposes significant strain on the body, unavoidably involving significant physiological change and excruciating pain. For some women, pregnancy and childbirth can mean life-altering physical ailments or even death. Today, as noted earlier, the risks of carrying a pregnancy to term dwarf those of having an abortion. Experts estimate that a ban on abortions increases maternal mortality by 21 percent, with white women facing a 13 percent increase in maternal mortality while black women face a 33 percent increase. Pregnancy and childbirth may also impose large-scale financial costs. The majority briefly refers to arguments about changes in laws relating to healthcare coverage, pregnancy discrimination, and family leave. Many women, however, still do not have adequate healthcare coverage before and after pregnancy; and, even when insurance coverage is available, healthcare services may be far away. Women also continue to face pregnancy discrimination that interferes with their ability to earn a living. Paid family leave remains inaccessible to many who need it most. Only 20 percent of private-sector workers have access to paid family leave, including a mere 8 percent of workers in the bottom quartile of wage earners.

The . . . growing prevalence of safe haven laws and demand for adoption [has been noted], but, to the degree that these are changes at all, they too are irrelevant. Neither reduces the health risks or financial costs of going through pregnancy and childbirth. Moreover, the choice to give up parental rights after giving birth is altogether different from the choice not to carry a pregnancy to term. The reality is that few women denied an abortion will choose adoption. The vast majority will continue, just as in *Roe* and *Casey*'s time, to shoulder the costs of childrearing. Whether or not they choose to parent, they will experience the profound loss of autonomy and dignity that coerced pregnancy and birth always impose.

. . . .

The only notable change we can see since *Roe* and *Casey* cuts in favor of adhering to precedent: It is that American abortion law has become more and more aligned with other nations. The majority . . . claims that the United States is an extreme outlier when it comes to abortion regulation. The global trend, however, has been toward increased provision of legal and safe abortion care. A number of countries, including New Zealand, the Netherlands, and Iceland, permit abortions up to a roughly similar time as Roe and Casey set. Canada has decriminalized abortion at any point in a pregnancy. Most Western European countries impose restrictions on abortion after 12 to 14 weeks, but they often have liberal exceptions to those time limits, including to prevent harm to a woman's physical or mental health. They also typically make access to early abortion easier, for example, by helping cover its cost. Perhaps most notable, more than 50 countries around the world—in Asia, Latin America, Africa, and Europe—have expanded access to abortion in the past 25 years. In light of that worldwide liberalization of abortion laws, it is American States that will become international outliers after today.

In sum, the majority can point to neither legal nor factual developments in support of its decision. Nothing that has happened in this country or the world in recent decades undermines the core insight of Roe and Casey. It continues to be true that, within the constraints those decisions established, a woman, not the government, should choose whether she will bear the burdens of pregnancy, childbirth, and parenting.

In support of its holding, the majority invokes two watershed cases overruling prior constitutional precedents: *West Coast Hotel Co. v. Parrish* and *Brown v. Board of Education*. But those decisions, unlike today's, responded to changed law and to changed facts and attitudes that had taken hold throughout society. As *Casey* recognized, the two cases are relevant only to show—by stark contrast—how unjustified overturning the right to choose is.

West Coast Hotel overruled *Adkins v. Children's Hospital of D. C.*, and a whole line of cases beginning with *Lochner v. New York*. *Adkins* had found a state minimum-wage law unconstitutional because, in the Court's view, the law interfered with a constitutional right to contract. But then the Great Depression hit, bringing with it unparalleled economic despair. The experience undermined—in fact, it disproved— *Adkins*'s assumption that a wholly unregulated market could meet basic human needs. As Justice [Robert] Jackson (before becoming a Justice) wrote of that time: "The older world of laissez faire was recognized everywhere outside the Court to be dead." In *West Coast Hotel*, the Court caught up, recognizing through the lens of experience the flaws of existing legal doctrine. The havoc the Depression had worked on ordinary Americans, the Court noted, was "common knowledge through the length and breadth of the land." . . . There was no escaping the need for *Adkins* to go.

Brown v. Board of Education overruled *Plessy v. Ferguson*, along with its doctrine of "separate but equal." By 1954, decades of Jim Crow had made clear what *Plessy*'s turn of phrase actually meant: "inherent[ ] [in]equal[ity]." Segregation was not, and could not ever be, consistent with the Reconstruction Amendments, ratified to give the former slaves full citizenship. Whatever might have been thought in *Plessy*'s time, the *Brown* Court explained, both experience and "modern authority" showed the "detrimental effect[s]" of state-sanctioned segregation: It "affect[ed] [children's] hearts and minds in a way unlikely ever to be undone." By that point, too, the law had begun to reflect that understanding. In a series of decisions, the Court had held unconstitutional public graduate schools' exclusion of black students. The logic of those cases, *Brown* held, "appl[ied] with added force to children in grade and high schools." Changed facts and changed law required *Plessy*'s end.

. . . .

Casey itself addressed both *West Coast Hotel* and *Brown*, and found that neither supported *Roe*'s overruling. In *West Coast Hotel*, *Casey* explained, "the facts of economic life" had proved "different from those previously assumed." And even though "*Plessy* was wrong the day it was decided," the passage of time had made that ever more clear to ever more citizens: "Society's understanding of the facts" in 1954 was "fundamentally different" than in 1896. So the Court needed to reverse course. "In constitutional adjudication as elsewhere in life, changed circumstances may impose new obligations." And because such dramatic change had occurred, the public could understand why the Court was acting. . . . But that would not be true of a reversal of *Roe*—"[b]ecause neither the factual underpinnings of *Roe*'s central holding nor our understanding of it has changed."

That is just as much so today, because *Roe* and *Casey* continue to reflect, not diverge from, broad trends in American society. It is, of course, true that many Americans, including many women, opposed those decisions when issued and do so now as well. Yet the fact remains: *Roe* and *Casey* were the product of a profound and ongoing change in women's roles in the latter part of the 20th century. Only a dozen years before *Roe*, the Court described women as "the center of home and family life," with "special responsibilities" that precluded their full legal status under the Constitution. By 1973, when the Court decided *Roe*, fundamental social change was underway regarding the place of women—and the law had begun to follow. By 1992, when the Court decided *Casey*, the traditional view of a woman's role as only a wife and mother was "no longer consistent with our understanding of the family, the individual, or the Constitution." Under that charter, *Casey* understood, women must take their place as full and equal citizens. And for that to happen, women must have control over their reproductive decisions. Nothing since *Casey*—no changed law, no changed fact—has undermined that promise.

The reasons for retaining *Roe* and *Casey* gain further strength from the overwhelming reliance interests those decisions have created. The Court adheres to precedent not just for institutional reasons, but because it recognizes that stability in the law is "an essential thread in the mantle of protection that the law affords the individual." So when overruling precedent "would dislodge [individuals'] settled rights and expectations," stare decisis has "added force." *Casey* understood that to deny individuals' reliance on *Roe* was to "refuse to face the fact[s]." Today the majority refuses to face the facts. "The most striking feature of the [majority] is the absence of any serious discussion" of how its ruling will affect women. By characterizing *Casey*'s reliance arguments as "generalized assertions about the national psyche," it reveals how little it knows or cares about women's lives or about the suffering its decision will cause.

In *Casey*, the Court observed that for two decades individuals "have organized intimate relationships and made" significant life choices "in reliance on the availability of abortion in the event that contraception should fail." Over another 30 years, that reliance has solidified. For half a century now, in *Casey*'s words, "[t]he ability of women to participate equally in the economic and social life of the Nation has been facilitated by their ability to control their reproductive lives." Indeed, all women now of childbearing age have grown up expecting that they would be able to avail themselves of *Roe*'s and *Casey*'s protections.

The disruption of overturning *Roe* and *Casey* will therefore be profound. Abortion is a common medical procedure and a familiar experience in women's lives. About 18 percent of pregnancies in this country end in abortion, and about one quarter of American women will have an abortion before the age of 45. Those numbers reflect the predictable and life-changing effects of carrying a pregnancy, giving birth, and becoming a parent. As *Casey* understood, people today rely on their ability to control and time pregnancies when making countless life decisions: where to live, whether and how to invest in education or careers, how to allocate financial resources, and how to approach intimate and family relationships. Women may count on abortion access for when contraception fails. They may count on abortion access for when contraception cannot be used, for example, if they were raped. They may count on abortion for when something changes in the midst of a pregnancy, whether it involves family or financial circumstances, unanticipated medical complications, or heartbreaking fetal diagnoses. Taking away the right to abortion, as the majority does today, destroys all those individual plans and expectations. . . .

The majority's response to these obvious points exists far from the reality American women actually live. The majority proclaims that "'reproductive planning could take virtually immediate account of any sudden restoration of state authority to ban abortions.'" . . . For those who will now have to undergo [a] pregnancy, the loss of Roe and Casey could be disastrous.

That is especially so for women without money. When we "count[ ] the cost of [*Roe*'s] repudiation" on women who once relied on that decision, it is not hard to see where the greatest burden will fall. In States that bar abortion, women of means will still be able to travel to obtain the services they need. It is women who cannot afford to do so who will suffer most. . . . After today, in States where legal abortions are not available, they will lose any ability to obtain safe, legal abortion care. They will not have the money to make the trip necessary; or to obtain childcare for that time; or to take time off work. Many will endure the costs and risks of pregnancy and giving birth against their wishes. Others will turn in desperation to illegal and unsafe abortions. They may lose not just their freedom, but their lives.[27]

Finally, the expectation of reproductive control is integral to many women's identity and their place in the Nation. That expectation helps define a woman as an "equal citizen[ ]," with all the rights, privileges, and obligations that status entails. It reflects that she is an autonomous person, and that society and the law recognize her as such. Like many constitutional rights, the right to choose situates a woman in relationship to others and to the government. It helps define a sphere of freedom, in which a person has the capacity to make choices free of government control. . . .

Withdrawing a woman's right to choose whether to continue a pregnancy does not mean that no choice is being made. It means that a majority of today's Court has wrenched this choice from women and given it to the States. To allow a State to exert control over one of "the most intimate and personal choices" a woman may make is not only to affect the course of her life, monumental as those effects might be. It is to alter her "views of [herself]" and her understanding of her "place[ ] in society" as someone with the recognized dignity and authority to make these choices. Women have relied on *Roe* and *Casey* in this way for 50 years. Many have never known anything else. When *Roe* and *Casey* disappear, the loss of power, control, and dignity will be immense.

The Court's failure to perceive the whole swath of expectations *Roe* and *Casey* created reflects an impoverished view of reliance. . . . While many of this Court's cases addressing reliance have been in the "commercial context," none holds that interests must be analogous to commercial ones to warrant stare decisis protection. This unprecedented assertion is, at bottom, a radical claim to power. By disclaiming any need to consider broad swaths of individuals' interests, the Court arrogates to itself the authority to overrule established legal principles without even acknowledging the costs of its decisions for the individuals who live under the law, costs that this Court's stare decisis doctrine instructs us to privilege when deciding whether to change course.

The majority claims that the reliance interests women have in *Roe* and *Casey* are too "intangible" for the Court to consider, even if it were inclined to do so. This is to ignore as judges what we know as men and

---

[27] Mississippi is likely to be one of the States where these costs are highest, though history shows that it will have company. As described above, Mississippi provides only the barest financial support to pregnant women. The State will greatly restrict abortion care without addressing any of the financial, health, and family needs that motivate many women to seek it. The effects will be felt most severely, as they always have been, on the bodies of the poor. The history of state abortion restrictions is a history of heavy costs exacted from the most vulnerable women. It is a history of women seeking illegal abortions in hotel rooms and home kitchens; of women trying to self-induce abortions by douching with bleach, injecting lye, and penetrating themselves with knitting needles, scissors, and coat hangers. It is a history of women dying.

women. The interests women have in *Roe* and *Casey* are perfectly, viscerally concrete. . . . For millions of women, *Roe* and *Casey* have been critical in giving them control of their bodies and their lives. Closing our eyes to the suffering today's decision will impose will not make that suffering disappear. . . . Stare decisis requires that the Court calculate the costs of a decision's repudiation on those who have relied on the decision, not on those who have disavowed it.

More broadly, the majority's approach to reliance cannot be reconciled with our Nation's understanding of constitutional rights. The majority's insistence on a "concrete," economic showing would preclude a finding of reliance on a wide variety of decisions recognizing constitutional rights—such as the right to express opinions, or choose whom to marry, or decide how to educate children. The Court, on the majority's logic, could transfer those choices to the State without having to consider a person's settled understanding that the law makes them hers. That must be wrong. All those rights, like the right to obtain an abortion, profoundly affect and, indeed, anchor individual lives. To recognize that people have relied on these rights is not to dabble in abstractions, but to acknowledge some of the most "concrete" and familiar aspects of human life and liberty.

. . . . Rescinding an individual right in its entirety and conferring it on the State, an action the Court takes today for the first time in history, affects all who have relied on our constitutional system of government and its structure of individual liberties protected from state oversight. *Roe* and *Casey* have of course aroused controversy and provoked disagreement. But the right those decisions conferred and reaffirmed is part of society's understanding of constitutional law and of how the Court has defined the liberty and equality that women are entitled to claim.

After today, young women will come of age with fewer rights than their mothers and grandmothers had. The majority accomplishes that result without so much as considering how women have relied on the right to choose or what it means to take that right away. The majority's refusal even to consider the life-altering consequences of reversing *Roe* and *Casey* is a stunning indictment of its decision.

One last consideration counsels against the majority's ruling: the very controversy surrounding *Roe and Casey*. The majority accuses *Casey* of acting outside the bounds of the law to quell the conflict over abortion—of imposing an unprincipled "settlement" of the issue in an effort to end "national division." But that is not what *Casey* did. As shown above, *Casey* applied traditional principles of stare decisis—which the majority today ignores—in reaffirming *Roe*. *Casey* carefully assessed changed circumstances (none) and reliance interests (profound). It considered every aspect of how Roe's framework operated. It adhered to the law in its analysis, and it reached the conclusion that the law required. True enough that *Casey* took notice of the "national controversy" about abortion. . . . But *Casey*'s reason for acknowledging public conflict was the exact opposite of what the majority insinuates. *Casey* addressed the national controversy in order to emphasize how important it was, in that case of all cases, for the Court to stick to the law. Would that today's majority had done likewise.

. . . .

"Power, not reason, is the new currency of this Court's decisionmaking." *Payne v. Tennessee*, 501 U.S. 808, 844 (1991). *Roe* has stood for fifty years. *Casey*, a precedent about precedent specifically confirming *Roe*, has stood for thirty. And the doctrine of stare decisis—a critical element of the rule of law—stands foursquare behind their continued existence. The right those decisions established and preserved is embedded in our constitutional law, both originating in and leading to other rights protecting bodily integrity, personal autonomy, and family relationships. The abortion right is also embedded in the lives of women—shaping their expectations, influencing their choices about relationships and work, supporting (as all reproductive rights do) their social and economic equality. Since the right's recognition (and affirmation), nothing has changed to support what the majority does today. Neither law nor facts nor attitudes have provided any new reasons to reach a different result than *Roe* and *Casey* did. All that has changed is this Court.

. . . . Now a new and bare majority of this Court—acting at practically the first moment possible—overrules *Roe* and *Casey*. It converts a series of dissenting opinions expressing antipathy toward *Roe* and *Casey* into a decision greenlighting even total abortion bans. It eliminates a 50-year-old constitutional right that safeguards women's freedom and equal station. It breaches a core rule-of-law principle, designed to promote constancy in the law. In doing all of that, it places in jeopardy other rights, from contraception to same-sex intimacy and marriage. And finally, it undermines the Court's legitimacy.

Casey itself made the last point in explaining why it would not overrule *Roe*—though some members of its majority might not have joined *Roe* in the first instance. . . . "[T]he Court," *Casey* explained, "could not pretend" that overruling *Roe* had any "justification beyond a present doctrinal disposition to come out differently from the Court of 1973." And to overrule for that reason? . . . *Casey* explained that to do so—to reverse prior law "upon a ground no firmer than a change in [the Court's] membership"—would invite the view that "this institution is little different from the two political branches of the Government." No view, *Casey* thought, could do "more lasting injury to this Court and to the system of law which it is our abiding mission to serve." For overruling *Roe*, *Casey* concluded, the Court would pay a "terrible price."

The Justices who wrote those words—O'Connor, Kennedy, and Souter—they were judges of wisdom. They would not have won any contests for the kind of ideological purity some court watchers want Justices to deliver. But if there were awards for Justices who left this

Court better than they found it? And who for that reason left this country better? And the rule of law stronger? Sign those Justices up.

They knew that "the legitimacy of the Court [is] earned over time." They also would have recognized that it can be destroyed much more quickly. They worked hard to avert that outcome in *Casey*. The American public, they thought, should never conclude that its constitutional protections hung by a thread—that a new majority, adhering to a new "doctrinal school," could "by dint of numbers" alone expunge their rights. It is hard—no, it is impossible—to conclude that anything else has happened here. One of us once said that "[i]t is not often in the law that so few have so quickly changed so much." S. Breyer, *Breaking the Promise of Brown: The Resegregation of America's Schools* 30 (2022). For all of us, in our time on this Court, that has never been more true than today. In overruling *Roe* and *Casey*, this Court betrays its guiding principles.

With sorrow—for this Court, but more, for the many millions of American women who have today lost a fundamental constitutional protection—we dissent.

NOTES

1. *The leaked draft opinion.* In an unusual turn of events, on Monday, May 2, 2022, Politico published a leaked draft majority opinion in *Dobbs v. Jackson Women's Health Organization.* Written by Justice Alito for a majority of the Court, the leaked draft opinion upheld by a 6–3 vote, Mississippi's 15-week abortion ban. However, the draft went further to overrule, by a 5–4 majority, *Roe v. Wade* and *Planned Parenthood v. Casey*, the two pillars of the Court's abortion jurisprudence. Though it was not the Court's final opinion in *Dobbs*, the leaked draft sparked nationwide debate about the future of abortion access and called into question the institutional legitimacy of the Supreme Court. After confirming the draft's authenticity, Chief Justice John Roberts directed the Marshal of the Court to launch a formal investigation to determine the source of the leak. Press Release, The Supreme Court of the United States, (May 3, 2022). Acknowledging that while members of the Court routinely circulate opinion drafts in advance of a final announcement, the Chief Justice made clear that a disclosure to the public of such a high-profile draft opinion was highly unorthodox and "a singular and egregious breach of . . . trust that is an affront to the Court and the community of public servants who work here." *Id.* To date, the source of the leak, if known, has not been made public.

2. *Trigger laws and "zombie" laws.* The Court's final decision in *Dobbs* was released on June 24, 2022, upholding the Mississippi 15-week ban and overruling *Roe* and *Casey*. The Court's decision "triggered" laws in thirteen states (Arkansas, Idaho, Kentucky, Louisiana, Mississippi, Missouri, North Dakota, Oklahoma, South Dakota, Tennessee, Texas, Utah and Wyoming) that would ban abortion upon the overruling of *Roe v. Wade. See* Elizabeth Nash & Isabel Guarnieri, *13 States Have Abortion Trigger Bans—Here's What Happens When* Roe *Is Overturned*, Guttmacher Institute (June 6,

2022), https://www.guttmacher.org/article/2022/06/13-states-have-abortion-trigger-bans-heres-what-happens-when-roe-overturned.

There are three types of trigger bans—those that immediately go into effect without any further action required, those that have a 30-day grace period, and those that require additional procedural steps, like certifying whether the central holding of *Roe* was overturned, to implement the new ban. *Id*. All thirteen state trigger bans criminalize abortion with limited exceptions for when the pregnant person's life is in danger and only four states make allowances for when the pregnant person is the victim of rape or incest. *Id*.

Trigger bans are not the only feature of the post-*Dobbs* landscape. Some states have bans passed after *Roe* was decided that have been blocked by court orders. The overruling of *Roe* means that these bans may now be lawfully enforced. Other states have so-called "zombie" bans enacted before *Roe* was decided that have never been repealed but remain unenforced—at least until the Court overruled *Roe*. *Abortion Policy in the Absence of* Roe, Guttmacher Institute (June 1, 2022), https://www.guttmacher.org/state-policy/explore/abortion-policy-absence-roe. The *Dobbs* opinion will allow state attorney generals to either enforce these laws or obtain a court order upholding the enjoined restrictions.

3.   *New interjurisdictional conflicts*. Although the *Dobbs* majority insisted that returning the abortion question to the states would help to settle conflict, in fact, its decision is likely to provoke interjurisdictional conflicts that have never been seen before. According to legal scholars Greer Donley, David Cohen, and Rachel Rebouché, the *Dobbs* decision is likely to "trigger new kinds of battles—among the states, and between states and the federal government" straining the United States federalist system. Rachel Rebouché, Greer Donley, & David S. Cohen, *Four Collisions to Expect if* Roe *is Repealed*, Politico (May 5, 2022, 4:30 AM), https://www.politico.com/news/magazine/2022/05/05/leave-abortion-to-states-not-easy-00029978. For example, providers in "safe haven" states, where abortion remains legal, could be at risk of prosecution for providing abortion services to a resident of a state where abortion is criminalized. In December 2021, Missouri legislator, Mary Elizabeth Coleman, proposed a law modeled after Texas S.B. 8 that would allow private citizens to sue anyone who helps a pregnant person obtain an abortion, even if it occurred out-of-state. Lydia Wheeler & Patricia Hurtado, *Abortion-Travel Bans Are 'Next Frontier' With* Roe *Set to Topple*, Bloomberg Law (May 4, 2022, 5:35 AM), https://news.bloomberglaw.com/health-law-and-business/abortion-travel-bans-emerge-as-next-frontier-after-roes-end. Though the proposal did not become law, it makes clear the lengths that anti-abortion advocates and legislators are prepared to go to prohibit abortion across the country. As Conley, Cohen, and Rebouché argue, these kinds of laws implicate constitutional protections, like the right to travel, the full-faith and credit clause, due process of law, and the Dormant Commerce Clause, which prohibits states from unduly burdening interstate commerce. *Id*.

4.   *Blue state response*. In the face of losing the federal constitutional protection for abortion, more progressive states have taken affirmative steps

to protect reproductive rights, including invoking state constitutions, codifying *Roe* into state law, and passing legislation protecting out-of-state abortion seekers. Four states and Washington, D.C. have protected the right to abortion at all stages of pregnancy without state interference, while twelve states have opted to permit abortion prior to viability, with post-viability exceptions for the life or health of the pregnant person. Some states, like Maryland, have expanded access to abortion by allowing midwives, physician assistants, and nurse practitioners to perform abortion procedures. Other states, like California, Oregon, Illinois and New York, have sought to expand financial support for abortion access by passing laws eliminating out-of-pocket insurance fees for abortions. Jaclyn Diaz & James Doubek, *How blue states are preparing if* Roe v. Wade *is overturned*, NPR (May 3, 2022, 10:18 PM), https://www.npr.org/2022/03/28/1088238619/legislation-abortion-bans.

Other blue states have focused on the prospect of interstate conflict over abortion rights. For example, Connecticut and New York enacted laws that would bar the state from assisting in interstate investigations and limit the governor's extradition power over abortion providers who have served out-of-state patients. Veronica Stracqualursi, *New York governor signs legislative package aimed at protecting patients and abortion providers from our of state legal action*, CNN (June 13, 2022, 7:54 PM), https://www.cnn.com/2022/06/13/politics/kathy-hochul-abortion-new-york/index.html; Veronica Stracqualursi & Paul LeBlanc, *Connecticut governor signs law protecting abortion seekers and providers from out-of-state lawsuits*, CNN (May 5, 2022, 6:01 PM), https://www.cnn.com/2022/05/05/politics/connecticut-abortion-protection-law-out-of-state-lawsuits/index.html. These kinds of protective measures are at odds with the cooperation and respect that sister states typically extend to one another. Addressing states' ability to exercise their jurisdiction beyond their borders or prevent anti-abortion states from investigating resident abortion seekers will likely lead to fierce legal battles in state and federal court.

5.   *Executive action?* When President Biden was campaigning for the presidency in 2020, he vowed to "codify *Roe v. Wade*, and [direct the] Justice Department [to] do everything in its power to stop the rash state laws that so blatantly violate the constitutional right to an abortion." Healthcare Plan for Biden Presidential Campaign, Biden Harris, https://joebiden.com/healthcare/# (last visited June 19, 2022). Indeed, on the day the *Dobbs* opinion was released, Attorney General Merrick Garland released a statement about the Federal Drug Administration's preemption of conflicting state laws concerning medication abortion. Press Release, The United States Department of Justice, Attorney General Merrick B. Garland Statement on Supreme Court Ruling in *Dobbs v. Jackson Women's Health Organization*, (June 24, 2022), https://www.justice.gov/opa/pr/attorney-general-merrick-b-garland-statement-supreme-court-ruling-dobbs-v-jackson-women-s. As the Attorney General explained, states cannot "ban Mifepristone, [one of the drugs in the two-drug protocol for medication abortion] based on disagreement with the FDA's expert judgement about its safety and efficacy." *Id*. Despite these efforts, the Biden Administration has been criticized for not having a more robust response to *Dobbs* and its

overruling of *Roe*. On July 8, 2022, three weeks after the *Dobbs* decision was released, President Biden signed an executive order aimed at ensuring access to abortion medication and emergency contraception. *See* Executive Order 14076, Protecting Access to Reproductive Healthcare Services (July 8, 2022). On August 3, 2022, he issued a second executive order to create an inter-agency task force aimed at ensuring the right to travel between states for abortion care. *See* Fact Sheet: President Biden Issues Executive Order at the First Meeting of the Task Force on Reproductive Healthcare Access (Aug. 3, 2022) https://www.whitehouse.gov/briefing-room/statements-releases/2022/08/03/fact-sheet-president-biden-issues-executive-order-at-the-first-meeting-of-the-task-force-on-reproductive-healthcare-access-2/ (last visited Aug. 3, 2022).

Some have argued that these steps are toothless to disrupt the increasing limits on abortion access across the country and have urged the Administration to do more. For example, some pro-choice advocates have suggested leasing federal property to abortion clinics and limiting the scope of state criminal and civil law that would apply on federal lands. Others have argued that the Administration should declare a national public health emergency to help abortion seekers in restrictive states. Andrea Grimes, *Biden's Troubling Response to* "*Dobbs*", The Nation (July 9, 2022), https://www.thenation.com/article/politics/biden-response-dobbs-abortion/ (last visited Aug. 3, 2022).

6. *Other fundamental rights.* Despite Justice Alito's assurance that "Nothing in this opinion should be understood to cast doubt on precedents that do not concern abortion," the Court's decision in *Dobbs* implicates other fundamental rights, including rights to contraception, interracial and same-sex marriage, and sexual intimacy, and parental rights. According to Justice Alito, there is no constitutional protection for abortion rights because the right to an abortion is not explicitly enumerated in the Constitution and is not "deeply rooted" in the history and traditions of the United States. However, the same could be said for contraception, interracial and same-sex marriage, sexual intimacy, and parental rights. In his concurrence, Justice Thomas acknowledges the implications for other fundamental rights—and indeed, calls upon the Court to reconsider and "correct the error" of its substantive due process precedents, including *Griswold v. Connecticut* (right to contraception), *Lawrence v. Texas* (sexual intimacy), and *Obergefell v. Hodges* (same-sex marriage). A number of states and legislators seem eager to take up this invitation. Texas Attorney General Ken Paxton has indicated that he would welcome reconsideration of *Lawrence v. Texas*, the 2003 decision that invalidated a Texas prohibition on same-sex sodomy. *See* Timothy Bella, *Texas AG says he'd defend sodomy law if Supreme Court revisits ruling*, WASH. POST, June 29, 2022, https://www.washingtonpost.com/politics/2022/06/29/texas-sodomy-supreme-court-lawrence-paxton-lgbtq/ (last visited Aug. 3, 2022).

7. *I don't think we're in Kansas anymore?* On August 2, 2022, voters in red-state Kansas headed to the polls to vote on a state constitutional amendment that would remove abortion rights protections from the Kansas Constitution. If successful, the measure could pave the way for state lawmakers to pass

far-reaching abortion restrictions, or even to pursue a ban on abortion. Ultimately, the measure was defeated by a vote of 58.8% against to 41.2% in favor. *See Kansas Abortion Amendment Election Results*, N.Y. TIMES, Aug. 3, 2022, https://www.nytimes.com/interactive/2022/08/02/us/elections/results-kansas-abortion-amendment.html (last visited Aug. 3, 2022). The vote was widely viewed as a bellwether of public reaction to the *Dobbs* decision. *See* Katie Glueck and Shane Goldmacher, *'Your bedroom is on the ballot:' How Democrats see shifting abortion politics after Kansas*, N.Y. TIMES, Aug. 3, 2022, https://www.nytimes.com/live/2022/08/03/us/elections-primary-midterms-kansas-az?action=click&pgtype=Article&state=default&module=styln-elections-2022&region=TOP_BANNER&context=election_recirc#democrats-abortion-kansas (last visited Aug. 3, 2022).

10. EMERGING ISSUES IN ABORTION REGULATION

As the preceding material suggests, the terrain of abortion restriction has shifted dramatically over time. Critically, landscape continues to be dynamic as new venues and arguments for challenging the availability and accessibility of abortion develop and emerge. To be clear, the following two selections are not meant to be exhaustive of these shifts. Rather, they give a flavor for the shifting terrain and discourse of abortion regulation.

Indiana Code § 16–34–3
(2019).

CHAPTER 3.   TREATMENT OF ABORTION REMAINS

SEC. 2.   (a) A pregnant woman who has an abortion under this article has the right to determine the final disposition of the aborted fetus.

(b)   After receiving the notification and information required by Indiana Code 16–34–2–1.1(a)(2)(H) and Indiana Code 16–34–2–1.1(a)(2)(I), the pregnant woman shall inform the abortion clinic or the health care facility:

(1)   in writing; and

(2)   on a form prescribed by the state department;

of the pregnant woman's decision for final disposition of the aborted fetus before the aborted fetus may be discharged from the abortion clinic or the health care facility.

(c)   If the pregnant woman is a minor, the abortion clinic or health care facility shall obtain parental consent in the disposition of the aborted fetus unless the minor has received a waiver of parental consent under Indiana Code 16–34–2–4 .

(d)   The abortion clinic or the health care facility shall document the pregnant woman's decision concerning disposition of the aborted fetus in the pregnant woman's medical record.

SEC. 3.   If the pregnant woman chooses a location for final disposition other than the location of final disposition that is usual and customary for an abortion clinic or a health care facility, the pregnant woman is responsible for the costs related to the final disposition of the aborted fetus at the chosen location.

SEC. 4. (a) An abortion clinic or health care facility having possession of an aborted fetus shall provide for the final disposition of the aborted fetus. The burial transit permit requirements of Indiana Code 16–37–3 apply to the final disposition of an aborted fetus, which must be interred or cremated. However:

> (1) a person is not required to designate a name for the aborted fetus on the burial transit permit and the space for a name may remain blank; and
>
> (2) any information submitted under this section that may be used to identify the pregnant woman is confidential and must be redacted from any public records maintained under Indiana Code 16–37–3.

Aborted fetuses may be cremated by simultaneous cremation.

(b) The local health officer shall issue a permit for the disposition of the aborted fetus to the person in charge of interment for the interment of the aborted fetus. A certificate of stillbirth is not required to be issued for an aborted fetus with a gestational age of less than twenty (20) weeks of age.

(c) Indiana Code 23–14–31–26, Indiana Code 23–14–55–2, IC 25–15–9–18, and Indiana Code 29–2–19–17 concerning the authorization of disposition of human remains apply to this section.

NOTES

1. *Common origins.* Fetal disposal restrictions gained popularity in 2016 after an anti-abortion organization, the Center for Medical Progress, released a series of highly-edited videos accusing abortion providers, and Planned Parenthood in particular, of selling fetal remains. Although none of the ensuing investigations found any evidence of wrongdoing on the part of Planned Parenthood, the videos sparked significant controversy and numerous states, including Alabama, Arizona, Idaho, Indiana, Louisiana, South Dakota, Tennessee, and Texas, responded by imposing new restrictions on the use and disposal of fetal tissue. Indiana, Louisiana, and Texas all passed laws mandating the interment (or burial) or cremation of fetal remains, joining Arkansas and Georgia who already had similar laws on the books. *See* Elizabeth Kimball Key, Note, *The Forced Choice of Dignified Disposal: Government Mandate of Interment or Cremation of Fetal Remains*, 51 U.C. DAVIS L. REV. 305, 309–10 (2017). The new laws were based on model legislation drafted by the anti-abortion advocacy group Americans United for Life to "assist states in ensuring that every mother of a deceased unborn infant is given the opportunity to ensure that her infant is treated with dignity and respect." *Id.* at 319.

2. *Pandora's* Box. Planned Parenthood of Indiana and Kentucky (PPINKY) challenged the constitutionality of an Indiana fetal disposal law. Rather than arguing that the law implicated the fundamental right to abortion, PPINKY instead argued that the disposal requirements violated due process by being irrational. Applying rational basis review, the district court struck down the law, concluding that "if the law does not recognize a fetus as a person, there can be no legitimate state interest in requiring an entity to treat an aborted fetus the same as a deceased human." *Planned Parenthood of Ind. & Ky. v. Comm'r*, 265 F. Supp. 3d 859, 870 (S.D. Ind. 2017). The Seventh Circuit affirmed, noting that even if the state's interest in the dignified disposal of fetal remains were legitimate, the law was not rationally related to that interest because it permitted patients to dispose of fetal material without restriction and allowed for mass cremation—neither of which are consistent with disposal requirements for human remains. *Planned Parenthood of Ind. & Ky. v. Comm'r*, 888 F.3d 300, 309 (7th Cir. 2018). In *Box v. Planned Parenthood of Indiana and Kentucky*, the Supreme Court reversed the Seventh Circuit's decision, explaining that it had "already acknowledged that a State has a 'legitimate interest in proper disposal of fetal remains,' " and concluded that the Indiana law was rationally related to that interest, "even if it is not perfectly tailored to that end." 139 S. Ct. 1780, 1782 (2019) (quoting *City of Akron v. Akron Ctr. for Reproductive Health*, 462 U.S. 416, 452 n.45 (1983)). Perhaps emboldened by the Court's decision, Indiana passed a new law in 2020 that clarified that patients who choose to personally dispose of fetal tissue must also do so by way of interment or cremation. Act of Mar. 18, 2020, 2020 Ind. Legis. Serv. P.L. 77–2020 (West) (codified at Ind. Code § 16–34–2–1.1). The new law also requires abortion providers to inform patients undergoing medical abortions that they may return any fetal material passed at home to the clinic for disposal. *See id.*

3. *The government's interest in "proper disposal."* In *Box*, the Supreme Court referenced its decision in *City of Akron v. Akron Center for Reproductive Health, Inc.*, for the proposition that a state has a legitimate interest in the proper disposal of fetal remains. 139 S. Ct. at 1782 (quoting *City of Akron*, 462 U.S. at 452 n.45). In *City of Akron*, the Court struck down as unconstitutionally vague an ordinance that required abortion providers to dispose of fetal remains in a "humane and sanitary manner." *City of Akron*, 462 U.S. at 451. Critically, the ordinance gave no guidance on which disposal methods met the "humane and sanitary" standard, prompting the Court to hold "that the ordinance violated the Due Process Clause of the Fourteenth Amendment because it failed to give appropriate notice to abortion providers as to whether and when their actions triggered criminal liability." *Id.* at 452. Despite striking down the ordinance, the Court explicitly recognized a state's legitimate interest in ensuring the "proper disposal of fetal remains." *Id.* at 452 n.45. Does *Box* provide a standard for what constitutes "proper disposal" in this context? Is the government's interest in ensuring "proper disposal" based on public health, morals, or something else?

4. *Regulating medical and pathological waste.* Most states treat fetal tissue similarly to other forms of medical or pathological waste. Pathological waste is a type of medical waste and consists of recognizable human or

animal body parts or tissue. *See* Elizabeth Kimball Key, Note, *The Forced Choice of Dignified Disposal: Government Mandate of Interment or Cremation of Fetal Remains*, 51 U.C. DAVIS L. REV. 305, 313 (2017). The medical community, including organizations such as the World Health Organization and the Red Cross, defines pathological waste as encompassing fetal matter. *Id.* at 324. Typically, medical facilities, including those that provide abortion care, contract with private medical waste services to dispose of fetal tissue alongside other pathological waste in accordance with state and local laws. *Id.* 315. Prior to 2016, even Indiana allowed abortion clinics to dispose of fetal tissue alongside other pathological materials. *Id.* at 324.

5.   *Disposal laws and fetal personhood*. Fetal disposal laws are predicated on the concept of "fetal personhood, or the idea that zygotes and embryos are legal persons subject to protections and benefits of the law . . . ." *See* Elizabeth Kimball Key, Note, *The Forced Choice of Dignified Disposal: Government Mandate of Interment or Cremation of Fetal Remains*, 51 U.C. DAVIS L. REV. 305, 320 (2017). As an example, Indiana defended its disposal law on the ground that it furthered the state's interest in "treating fetal remains the same as other human remains . . . ." *Planned Parenthood of Ind. & Ky. v. Comm'r*, 265 F. Supp. 3d 859, 870 (S.D. Ind. 2017). Is such a premise consistent with the Court's jurisprudence on the matter? Recall that in *Roe v. Wade*, the Court explicitly rejected the notion that a fetus is person under the Constitution. 410 U.S. 113, 157 (1973). Can a state have a legitimate interest in ensuring that fetal tissue is disposed of in the same manner of as human remains despite the fact that fetuses are not recognized as persons under the law? Notably, in *Planned Parenthood v. Commissioner*, the district court concluded that there can be no legitimate state interest in treating an aborted fetus as if it were a deceased human because the law does not recognize a fetus as a person. 265 F. Supp. 3d at 870.

6.   *Fetal tissue disposal and medical abortions*. The abortion providers that challenged Louisiana's fetal disposal law argued that it imposed an undue burden on a woman's right to terminate a pregnancy by banning medical abortions, a nonsurgical method of terminating a pregnancy up to ten weeks. During a medical abortion, a patient is given a dose of an abortion-inducing medication at the clinic, but must take a second dose later at home. The resulting fetal material "is typically collected by a sanitary pad and is physically indistinguishable from menstruation." Elizabeth Kimball Key, Note, *The Forced Choice of Dignified Disposal: Government Mandate of Interment or Cremation of Fetal Remains*, 51 U.C. DAVIS L. REV. 305, 332 (2017). The providers argued that because medical abortions are completed at home, any resulting fetal material "cannot in practice be interred or cremated." *June Med. Servs. v. Gee*, 280 F. Supp. 3d 849, 857 (M.D. La. 2017).

7.   *An undue burden?* Interment and cremation are "considerably more expensive" than other disposal methods. Elizabeth Kimball Key, Note, *The Forced Choice of Dignified Disposal: Government Mandate of Interment or Cremation of Fetal Remains*, 51 U.C. DAVIS L. REV. 305, 329 (2017). Because "abortion clinics already operate under slim margins," compliance with disposal laws means that providers will likely have to increase the cost of the procedure just to stay in business." *Id.* at 330. If providers choose to pass the

increased costs on to patients, it is likely to push affordable abortion care out of reach for many women, exacerbating the impact of other measures, like the Hyde Amendment. *See* Stanley K. Henshaw, et. al., Guttmacher Inst., *Restrictions on Medicaid Funding for Abortions: A Literature Review* 27 (2009) ("[A] reasonable estimate is that lack of funding influences about a quarter of Medicaid eligible women to continue unwanted pregnancies."). Given the impact of compliance on abortion access, could fetal tissue disposal laws be challenged under the undue burden standard on the grounds that they make abortion unaffordable and/or lead to clinic closures? *See Whole Woman's Health v. Smith*, 338 F. Supp. 3d 606, 636–37 (W.D. Tex. 2018) ("The lack of capable and reliable options to dispose of embryonic and fetal remains in compliance with the challenged laws would likely cripple the ability of healthcare providers to offer surgical abortions and thus is a substantial obstacle in the path of women seeking a previability abortion.").

Indiana Code § 16–34–4
(2019).

CHAPTER 4.   SEX-SELECTIVE AND DISABILITY ABORTION BAN

SEC. 1.   (a) As used in this chapter, "any other disability" means any disease, defect, or disorder that is genetically inherited. The term includes the following:

    (1)   A physical disability.

    (2)   A mental or intellectual disability.

    (3)   A physical disfigurement.

    (4)   Scoliosis.

    (5)   Dwarfism.

    (6)   Down syndrome.

    (7)   Albinism.

    (8)   Amelia.

    (9)   A physical or mental disease.

    (b)   The term does not include a lethal fetal anomaly.

SEC. 2. As used in this chapter, "Down syndrome" means a chromosomal disorder associated with an extra chromosome 21 or an effective trisomy for chromosome 21.

SEC. 3. As used in this chapter, "potential diagnosis" refers to the presence of some risk factors that indicate that a health problem may occur.

SEC. 4. As used in this chapter, "sex selective abortion" means an abortion that is performed solely because of the sex of the fetus.

SEC. 5. (a) A person may not intentionally perform or attempt to perform an abortion before the earlier of viability of the fetus or twenty

(20) weeks of postfertilization age if the person knows that the pregnant woman is seeking a sex selective abortion.

. . .

SEC. 6. (a) A person may not intentionally perform or attempt to perform an abortion before the earlier of viability of the fetus or twenty (20) weeks of postfertilization age if the person knows that the pregnant woman is seeking the abortion solely because the fetus has been diagnosed with Down syndrome or has a potential diagnosis of Down syndrome.

    (b) A person may not intentionally perform or attempt to perform an abortion after viability of the fetus or twenty (20) weeks of postfertilization age if the person knows that the pregnant woman is seeking the abortion solely because the fetus has been diagnosed with Down syndrome or has a potential diagnosis of Down syndrome.

. . .

SEC. 7. (a) A person may not intentionally perform or attempt to perform an abortion before the earlier of viability of the fetus or twenty (20) weeks of postfertilization age if the person knows that the pregnant woman is seeking the abortion solely because the fetus has been diagnosed with any other disability or has a potential diagnosis of any other disability.

    (b) A person may not intentionally perform or attempt to perform an abortion after viability of the fetus or twenty (20) weeks of postfertilization age if the person knows that the pregnant woman is seeking the abortion solely because the fetus has been diagnosed with any other disability or has a potential diagnosis of any other disability.

. . .

SEC. 8. (a) A person may not intentionally perform or attempt to perform an abortion before the earlier of viability of the fetus or twenty (20) weeks of postfertilization age if the person knows that the pregnant woman is seeking the abortion solely because of the race, color, national origin, or ancestry of the fetus.

    (b) A person may not intentionally perform or attempt to perform an abortion after viability of the fetus or twenty (20) weeks of postfertilization age if the person knows that the pregnant woman is seeking the abortion solely because of the race, color, national origin, or ancestry of the fetus.

. . .

SEC. 9. (a) A person who knowingly or intentionally performs an abortion in violation of this chapter may be subject to:

    (1) disciplinary sanctions under Indiana Code 25–1–9; and

    (2) civil liability for wrongful death.

(b) A pregnant woman upon whom an abortion is performed in violation of this chapter may not be prosecuted for violating or conspiring to violate this chapter.

NOTES

1. *Protecting the fetus from discrimination.* The Arizona statute excerpted above reflects a national trend toward laws that prohibit abortion, if undertaken for the purposes of sex selection, race selection or addressing a genetic anomaly. These bans ostensibly seek to eliminate discrimination on the basis of race, sex, and disability. However, they are often based on inconclusive and incomplete evidence that sex selection is being practiced among some Asian communities in the United States, and that Black women are specifically targeted by abortion providers. In addition to these concerns about the basis for such legislation, reproductive rights proponents maintain that these bans suggest that pregnant persons, and especially those of color, cannot be trusted to make their own medical decisions. Further, by inviting additional scrutiny of women's motivations for choosing an abortion, these bans facilitate additional discrimination against and racial profiling of persons of color and immigrants, and discourage honest, confidential conversations between patients and physicians. As a result of the bans, patients may withhold information or be dissuaded from seeking care from providers altogether.

2. *Sex selection in context.* Because sex selection has occurred most frequently in countries where there is a strong gender bias that manifests in a preference for sons, reproductive rights advocates argue that bans on sex selective abortion do not work to prevent sex selection, because they do nothing to challenge the phenomenon of son preference or its root causes. Moreover, such bans are difficult to enforce. There is broad international consensus that the most effective way to combat sex selection is to implement policies that promote gender equity.

3. *Sex-selection, abortion, and women's autonomy in global perspective.* While it is often assumed that East and South Asian communities both in the United States and in their native countries readily resort to sex-selective abortion because of "son preference," reproductive health scholar Sujatha Jesudason points out that the reality is far more complex than this simplistic vision suggests. Parents in many countries, including the United States, have a preference for "sex balancing." That is, they have no sex preference for the first child, but they do subsequently prefer a child of the opposite sex. *See* SUJATHA JESUDASON, GENERATIONS AHEAD, ATTITUDES TOWARDS AND PREVALENCE OF SON PREFERENCE AND SEX SELECTION IN SOUTH ASIAN AMERICAN COMMUNITIES IN THE UNITED STATES 2–4 (2012). Moreover, demographer Monica Das Gupta persuasively argues that son preference is common only where rulers used rigid gender hierarchies to "organize and administer their citizens" (hierarchies like those in premodern China, Korea, and Northwest India). Modern states, however, unleash forces undermining these gender hierarchies, and although the timing is uncertain, Das Gupta confidently predicts the inevitable "unraveling" of son preferences, something already seen in some Asian and South Asian countries. *See*

MONICA DAS GUTPA, THE WORLD BANK, FAMILY SYSTEMS, POLITICAL SYSTEMS, AND ASIA'S 'MISSING GIRLS': POLICY RESEARCH WORKING PAPER NO. 5148, at 17–20 (2009).

4.   *Trait selection in context.* As the prior notes suggest, race-selective abortion bans are based on the idea that abortion providers coerce women of color into abortions or that people of color are willingly participating in the deracination of their communities. Despite these assumptions, there is little evidence that people of color seek abortions because of race or that a ban on race-selective abortions would decrease abortions among this group. Guttmacher Institute, *Banning Abortions in Cases of Race or Sex Selection or Fetal Anomaly* (January 2020). Indeed, among racial minorities, economic insecurity is more likely to be a driver of the decision to choose an abortion. *Id.*

Efforts to limit abortion in cases of fetal genetic abnormalities are ostensibly animated by an interest in reducing the stigmatization of disability. According to the proponents of these laws, abortion has enabled the elimination of entire populations of disabled persons. Specifically, they point to Iceland, where the population of individuals with Down's Syndrome has been reduced dramatically. Still, in the United States, the decision to choose an abortion in the wake of a genetic abnormality diagnosis is often animated by concerns about the ability to provide for and raise a child with special needs in a society with limited social supports for families. In this vein, reproductive rights advocates argue that these bans severely limit the ability of pregnant persons and their families to make decisions that are best for them.

5.   *The Tea Party and abortion politics.* State-level legislation aimed at deterring race and sex-selective abortions was successful in part due to the mobilization of the Tea Party movement. The Tea Party movement is made up of people who not only want to reduce the size of government, but who are also notably conservative on social issues such as same-sex marriage and abortion. Tea Partyers are also likely to say that their religion is very important to them. *See* Religion & Pub. Life Project, *The Tea Party and Religion*, PEW RESEARCH (Feb. 23, 2011), http://www.pewforum.org/2011/02/23/tea-party-and-religion/. The Tea Party is not known for being particularly race-conscious, so their interest in deterring race-selective abortions may seem curious. The position is perhaps more readily comprehensible if one considers that interest in these laws stems from antipathy to the perceived practice of sex-selective abortions in South Asia, and in India, in particular. In what ways are race politics and immigration politics shaping and complicating the emerging interest in sex- and race-selective abortion?

6.   *A federal analogue?* Animated by reports that sex-selective abortions were taking place in Asia, abortion opponents have introduced four different versions of a bill prohibiting sex-selective abortions since 2011. None of these bills was successfully enacted. Most recently, the "Prenatal Nondiscrimination Act of 2019" ("PRENDA") was introduced into the House of Representatives, while a companion bill was introduced into the Senate. Prenatal Nondiscrimination Act of 2019, H.R. 2373 (116th Cong. 2019–20); S. 182 (116th Cong. 2019–20). Both bills create new federal crimes related to

the performance of sex-selection abortions, and subject violators to criminal penalties—a fine, a prison term of up to five years, or both. *Id.* Intriguingly, this latest iteration of PRENDA focuses solely on sex-selective abortions. By contrast, earlier iterations prioritized sex- *and* race-selective abortions.

* * *

An earlier incarnation of PRENDA was introduced into the House of Representatives in 2011. As the excerpted testimony from the Congressional hearings on the bill suggest, race and race politics played an important role in shaping the bill. The selection that follows excerpts the testimony of a reproductive justice group that was opposed to the bill. As you read the testimony, consider the following questions: to what are the bill's opponents responding? How did the drafters of the bill frame its content? Is it framed as an abortion regulation or as an anti-discrimination measure or both? What work is race, the history of race, and contemporary racial politics doing in shaping this bill and the response of its opponents?

Written Testimony from the Reproductive Justice Community, Hearing on H.R. 3541, The Susan B. Anthony and Frederick Douglass Prenatal Nondiscrimination Act (PRENDA) of 2011

(Dec. 6, 2011).

We write to you as organizations concerned with protecting the rights and ensuring the wellbeing of women of color. We are organizations dedicated to reproductive justice, women's empowerment, racial justice, and human rights, and we are outraged by the introduction of H.R. 3541, the "Prenatal Nondiscrimination Act." This bill is a deceptive attempt to limit abortion access for women of color, and it targets Black, Latina and Asian American and Pacific Islander communities. We write to go on record with our opposition to this legislation.

. . . .

This bill places an unfair burden on women of color that other women do not have to face—increased scrutiny around our motives for seeking abortion care. This scrutiny promotes racial profiling by pushing doctors to assume Black, Latina, and Asian women are seeking abortions because of the race or sex of the fetus.

Moreover, making abortion harder to obtain will exacerbate the health disparities women of color already face. For example, Black women are already three to four times more likely to die from pregnancy related causes than white women, and the unintended pregnancy rate is 67% compared to 40% for white women. This bill would encourage unsafe practices that put women's lives at risk. Family planning programs allow women of color to access contraceptives, prevent unplanned pregnancies, and improve healthcare outcomes for themselves and their children. Yet, the proponents of this bill, who claim they are concerned about women of color, want to introduce another barrier to access and have repeatedly proposed legislation to cut funding for family planning and women's healthcare programs.

. . . .

This anti-choice measure dressed as an anti-discrimination bill is not a way to promote racial and gender inequality. Instead, it further exacerbates inequities and diminishes the health, well-being, and dignity of women and girls by restricting their access to reproductive health care.

NOTES

1.   *What's in a name?* As the excerpted testimony makes clear, the 2011 incarnation of PRENDA was introduced as the Susan B. Anthony and Frederick Douglass Prenatal Nondiscrimination Act of 2011. Why did the bill's drafters choose this name?

2.   *The new (old) race suicide?* As discussed elsewhere, earlier efforts to regulate reproductive rights were often animated by concerns that racial minorities were overpopulating, while whites were not. In this way, fears of "race suicide" underwrote initial efforts to curb abortion and contraceptive use. In recent years, a new rhetoric of race suicide has emerged—one that feeds on age-old fears of government-sponsored deracination. In a new tactic, anti-abortion activists have focused on abortion in minority communities. For example, the following billboard was displayed in Harlem, an historically Black neighborhood in New York City:

The billboard is said to respond to empirical evidence regarding the rate of African Americans having abortions. Is this new race consciousness consistent with the earlier arguments that link abortion to "race suicide" among whites? In what ways does this new rhetoric challenge the reproductive choices of women of color?

3.   *Whose decision?* This new wave of regulation being created at the state level, including those banning sex- and race-selective abortion, has prompted concerns that abortion decision-making will once again be consolidated in the hands of doctors. Doctors would then have primary authority to determine whether the desired abortion is permissible under the extant regulations. Some have argued that the shift in decision-making power from women back to their physicians will lead to fewer abortions, as doctors will err on the side of caution in approving requests for abortion.

4.   *A Justice enters the debate.* Most of the debate concerning prenatal nondiscrimination laws has occurred outside of the U.S. Supreme Court. However, in May 2019, the Court considered a petition for certiorari challenging an Indiana law that prohibited abortions performed solely because of the fetus's gender, race, ethnicity, or disabilities. *Box v. Planned Parenthood of Indiana and Kentucky*, 139 S. Ct. 1780 (2019) (per curiam). A majority of the Court declined to hear the case, prompting Justice Clarence Thomas to issue his own separate opinion. According to Justice Thomas, the challenged Indiana law "and other laws like it promote a State's compelling interest in preventing abortion from becoming a tool of modern-day eugenics." 139 S. Ct. at 1782 (Thomas, J., concurring). In making this claim, Thomas invoked a selective history of reproductive rights. As he explained, the modern birth control movement "developed alongside the American eugenics movement," which was preoccupied with both "inhibiting reproduction of the unfit" and preventing the white race from being "overtaken by inferior races." *Id.* at 3, 4, 6. Although Thomas conceded that the birth control movement was distinct from the movement to legalize abortion, he maintained that the arguments lodged in favor of expanding access to contraception "apply with even greater force to abortion, making it significantly more effective as a tool of eugenics." *Id.* at 3. Throughout, Thomas invoked Margaret Sanger, the founder of Planned Parenthood and the modern birth control movement. Sanger, Thomas recounts, was an unrepentant eugenicist whose interest in eugenics often tilted toward the elimination of the "unfit," a group that often included non-whites.

Historians, including those relied upon by Thomas in his unusual concurrence, dispute the veracity of his historical account. Adam Cohen, whose book *Imbeciles: The Supreme Court, American Eugenics, and the Sterilization of Carrie Buck* (2017), Thomas cited repeatedly, noted that Thomas's invocation of Margaret Sanger's ties to eugenics "is not particularly relevant to abortion." Adam Cohen, *Clarence Thomas Knows Nothing of My Work*, THE ATLANTIC, May 29, 2019. The most prominent eugenicists of the day did not support abortion. *Id.* As importantly, eugenics and abortion raise markedly different issues of state control over reproduction and individual autonomy. According to Cohen, "between eugenic sterilization and abortion lie two crucial differences: who is making the decision, and why they are making it." *Id*. Unlike eugenic sterilization, in which "the state decides who may not reproduce and acts with the goal of 'improving' the population," abortion involves an individual making the decision "not to reproduce, for personal reasons related to a specific pregnancy." *Id*. decisions, while abortion involves an exercise of individual autonomy.

5. *Abortion, eugenics, and* Roe v. Wade. Professor Melissa Murray argues that Justice Thomas's aspirations for his concurrence in *Box v. Planned Parenthood of Indiana and Kentucky* are likely twofold: to provide a short-term defense of trait-selection laws and to seed new ground for overruling *Roe v. Wade*. As Murray explains, the *Box* concurrence trades on the recent success of the reproductive justice movement, which "has surfaced the myriad ways in which race, class, and other forms of marginalization shape women's experiences with, and the state's efforts to regulate, reproduction. Melissa Murray, *Race-ing* Roe: *Reproductive Justice, Racial Justice, and the Battle for* Roe v. Wade, 134 HARV. L. REV. 2025 (2021). But rather than surfacing race as a means of promoting greater reproductive autonomy and access in service of *Roe v. Wade*, as the reproductive justice movement does, the *Box* concurrence integrates racial injustice into the history of abortion for the purpose of destabilizing abortion rights." *Id*.

6. *Race, racism, and abortion*. Justice Thomas's concurrence in *Box* is not the only abortion decision to invoke the specter of race and racial injustice. In *Jackson Women's Health Organization v. Currier*, 349 F. Supp. 3d 536 (S.D. Miss. 2018) *aff'd sub nom. Jackson Women's Health Org. v. Dobbs*, 945 F.3d 265 (5th Cir. 2019), a challenge to Mississippi HB 1510, a ban on abortion at 15 weeks, ostensibly for the purpose of promoting and protecting women's health, United States District Judge Carlton Reeves invokes race to link abortion restrictions to a broader history of state control and subordination of Black and Brown bodies. *Id*. at 540 n. 22. According to Judge Reeves, the Mississippi legislature's "professed interest in 'women's health' is pure gaslighting" from a state that has "not to lift a finger to address the tragedies lurking on the other side of the delivery room: our alarming infant and maternal mortality rates." *Id*. According to Judge Reeves, "legislation like H.B. 1510 is closer to the old Mississippi—the Mississippi bent on controlling women and minorities. . . . The Mississippi that, in Fannie Lou Hamer's reporting, sterilized six out of ten black women in Sunflower County at the local hospital—against their will." *Id*.

Meaningfully, much of Judge Reeves's critique of Mississippi's history and its present-day inattention to issues of maternal and infant mortality and access to healthcare occurs in footnotes, while the body of the opinion is devoted to a straight-forward discussion of the unconstitutionality of pre-viability bans on abortion. Why do you think this is the case? Is it relevant that Judge Reeves's footnote text is explicitly intersectional in its account of the costs and consequences of the abortion debate?

7. *A Fifth Circuit judge responds*. Mississippi appealed the district court's decision in *Jackson Women's Health Organization v. Currier* to the United States Court of Appeals for the Fifth Circuit. Although a panel of the Fifth Circuit affirmed the lower court's ruling, Circuit Judge James Ho concurred

separately—and in doing so, chided Judge Reeves for "disparag[ing] the Mississippi legislation as 'pure gaslighting,'" "equat[ing] a belief in the sanctity of life with sexism," "disregarding the millions of women who strongly oppose abortion," and smear[ing] Mississippi legislators by linking House Bill 1510 to the state's tragic history of race relations, while ignoring abortion's own checkered racial past." *Jackson Women's Health Org. v. Dobbs*, 945 F.3d 265, 278 (5th Cir. 2019), *cert. granted in part*, 141 S. Ct. 2619 (May 17, 2021). Judge Ho then proceeded to cite the *Box* concurrence— and reiterated its logic—noting "the racial history of abortion advocacy as a tool of the eugenics movement." As Judge Ho reasoned, "[g]iven the links between abortion and eugenics, accepting the district court's logic— connecting Mississippi's own tragic racial history with the recent enactment of HB 1510—means that the history of abortion advocacy must likewise haunt modern proponents of permissive abortion policies, and infect them with the taint of racism as well." *Id.* at 285.

8.   *Building a narrative?* As Judge Ho's concurrence in *Dobbs* suggests, although no other members of the Court joined Justice Thomas's concurrence in *Box*, in a relatively short period of time, its logic has found a receptive audience among lower federal courts. In a dissent from the majority opinion in *Preterm-Cleveland v. Himes*, 940 F.3d 318 (6th Cir. 2019), a challenge to an Ohio law that prohibited abortion if undertaken to avoid a disability or fetal abnormality, Judge Alice Batchelder reiterated the concurrence's logic, noting that the law "promote[d] a State's compelling interest in preventing abortion from becoming a tool of modern-day eugenics." *Id.* at 325. That decision was later vacated and the challenge reheard *en banc* by the full Sixth Circuit, which upheld the challenged law. Writing for the majority, Judge Batchelder again cited the *Box* concurrence to credit state's interest in preventing "eugenic abortion." *Preterm-Cleveland v. McCloud*, 994 F.3d 512, 517 (6th Cir. 2021). More importantly, three of the four separate concurrences cited the *Box* concurrence and prospect of "eugenic" abortion. *Id.*

Similarly, in *Reproductive Health Services of Planned Parenthood of St. Louis Region, Inc. v. Parson*, 389 F. Supp. 3d 631 (W.D. Mo.), *modified*, 408 F. Supp. 3d 1049 (W.D. Mo. 2019), a district court concluded that the challenged reason ban was dangerously close to an unconstitutional previability abortion ban. Nevertheless, it further noted that while "[t]he Supreme Court has not dealt with the merits of this question," Justice Thomas has "demonstrated great interest in the ultimate question of a State's authority . . . to prevent 'abortion from becoming a tool of modern-day eugenics.'" *Id.* at 634.

Indiana Code § 16–25–4.5

(2018).

CHAPTER 4.5 PERINATAL HOSPICE

SEC. 1. The purpose of this chapter is to ensure that:

(1) women considering abortion after receiving a diagnosis of a lethal fetal anomaly are informed of the availability of perinatal hospice care; and

(2) women choosing abortion after receiving a diagnosis of a lethal fetal anomaly are making a fully informed decision.

SEC. 2. As used in this chapter, "lethal fetal anomaly" means a fetal condition diagnosed before birth that, if the pregnancy results in a live birth, will with reasonable certainty result in the death of the child not more than three (3) months after the child's birth.

SEC. 3. As used in this chapter, "perinatal hospice" means the provision of comprehensive, supportive care to a pregnant woman and her family beginning with the diagnosis of a lethal fetal anomaly and continuing through the live birth and death of the woman's child as a result of the lethal fetal anomaly. The term includes counseling and medical care provided by maternal-fetal medical specialists, obstetricians, neonatologists, anesthesia specialists, specialty nurses, clergy, social workers, and others that are focused on alleviating fear and ensuring that the woman and her family experience the life and death of the child in a comfortable and supportive environment.

SEC. 4. (a) The state department shall develop a perinatal hospice brochure and post the perinatal hospice brochure on the state department's Internet web site.

(b) The perinatal brochure developed under this section must include the following:

(1) A description of the health care and other services available from perinatal hospice.

(2) Information that medical assistance benefits may be available for prenatal care, childbirth, and perinatal hospice.

(3) Information regarding telephone 211 dialing code services for accessing grief counseling and other human services as described in Indiana Code 8–1–19.5, and the types of services that are available through this service.

SEC. 5. The state department shall develop and regularly update a list of all perinatal hospice providers and programs in Indiana. The state department may include on the list perinatal hospice providers and programs in other states that provide care to Indiana residents. The state department shall post the list of perinatal hospice providers and programs on the state department's Internet web site.

SEC. 6. (a) The state department shall develop a form on which a pregnant woman certifies, at the time of receiving a diagnosis that the pregnant woman's unborn child has a lethal fetal anomaly, that the pregnant woman has received the following:

(1) A copy of the perinatal hospice brochure developed under this chapter.

(2) A list of the perinatal hospice providers and programs developed under section 5 of this chapter.

(b) The provider diagnosing the pregnant woman's unborn child with the lethal fetal anomaly shall, at the time of diagnosis:

(1) provide the pregnant woman with a written copy of:

(A) the perinatal brochure developed under this chapter; and

(B) the certification form developed by the state department under subsection (a); and

(2) have the pregnant woman complete the certification form.

NOTES

1. *History of perinatal hospice counseling laws.* In 2006, Minnesota enacted the first mandatory perinatal hospice counseling law, requiring abortion providers to provide women with information on perinatal hospice care before permitting them to proceed with an abortion. When Indiana enacted its perinatal hospice counseling legislation in 2016, it was the sixth state to do so. Other states with perinatal hospice counseling requirements are Arizona, Kansas, Mississippi, and Oklahoma. *See* Danielle Paquette, *Perinatal Hospice Care Prepares Parents for the End, at Life's Beginning,* WASH. POST, Apr. 16, 2016. In 2019, Arkansas passed several bills to restrict access to abortion, which included a requirement that anyone whose fetus is diagnosed with a lethal fatal anomaly receive information about perinatal palliative care. Linda Satter, *New Restrictions Put on Abortions in Arkansas Part of Wave in U.S.,* ARK. DEMOCRAT GAZETTE, Apr. 22, 2019.

2. *Legitimate service or limiting choice?* Perinatal hospice facilities emerged decades before mandatory counseling laws requiring existed. The primary goal of those perinatal hospice facilities and programs was to provide comfort, support and information for those who chose to continue their pregnancies while knowing that the fetus was unlikely to survive, or that, once born, their child would almost certainly die within hours or days after delivery. *See* Neela Banerjee, *A Place to Turn When a Newborn is Fated to Die,* N.Y. TIMES, Mar. 13, 2007. Critics of mandatory perinatal hospice counseling do not necessarily oppose the existence of perinatal hospice facilities or services, but instead take issue with legislation that mandates specific counseling. They argue that such legislation is similar to other informed consent laws that pressure patients to continue their pregnancies and undermine or stigmatize those who have already chosen to terminate a

pregnancy. *See* s.e. smith, *Disabled People are Tired of Being a Talking Point in the Abortion Debate*, VOX, May 29, 2019; Emily Crockett, *Indiana Crammed as Many Anti-Abortion Bills as It Could into This Horrifying New Law*, VOX, Mar. 26, 2019. Given that perinatal hospice facilities may offer beneficial services, is there a reasonable justification for such mandatory counseling laws? Are there alternatives to these mandatory counseling laws that would provide pregnant women with information about such perinatal hospice care, without restricting their freedom to make independent reproductive health decisions?

* * *

In March 2020, the United States joined the global community in battling COVID-19, a highly communicable virus with no known cure. As the pandemic raged, many states and localities implemented shelter-in-place orders that required residents to remain in their homes and shuttered non-essential businesses. Further, in an effort to preserve hospital capacity and personal protective equipment, some state and local governments prohibited the performance of elective and non-essential medical procedures. In most cases, these orders were interpreted to include abortions.

Texas Executive Order GA-09
March 22, 2020.

WHEREAS, I, Greg Abbott, Governor of Texas, issued a disaster proclamation on March 13, 2020, certifying under Section 418.014 of the Texas Government Code that the novel coronavirus (COVID-19) poses an imminent threat of disaster for all counties in the State of Texas; and

WHEREAS, the Texas Department of State Health Services has determined that, as of March 19, 2020, COVID-19 represents a public health disaster within the meaning of Chapter 81 of the Texas Health and Safety Code; and

WHEREAS, on March 19, 2020, I issued an executive order in accordance with the President's Coronavirus Guidelines for America, as promulgated by President Donald J. Trump and the Centers for Disease Control and Prevention (CDC), and mandated certain obligations for Texans that are aimed at slowing the spread of COVID-19; and

WHEREAS, a shortage of hospital capacity or personal protective equipment would hinder efforts to cope with the COVID-19 disaster; and

WHEREAS, hospital capacity and personal protective equipment are being depleted by surgeries and procedures that are not medically necessary to correct a serious medical condition or to preserve the life of a patient, contrary to recommendations from the President's Coronavirus Task Force, the CDC, the U.S. Surgeon General, and the Centers for Medicare and Medicaid Services; and

WHEREAS, various hospital licensing requirements would stand in the way of implementing increased occupancy in the event of surge needs for hospital capacity due to COVID-19; and

WHEREAS, the "governor is responsible for meeting. . . the dangers to the state and people presented by disasters" under Section 418.011 of the Texas Government Code, and the legislature has given the governor broad authority to fulfill that responsibility; and

WHEREAS, under Section 418.0 12, the "governor may issue executive orders. . . hav[ing] the force and effect of law;" and

WHEREAS, under Section 418.0 16(a), the "governor may suspend the provisions of any regulatory statute prescribing the procedures for conduct of state business or the orders or rules of a state agency if strict compliance with the provisions, orders, or rules would in any way prevent, hinder, or delay necessary action in coping with a disaster;" and

WHEREAS, under Section 4 18.173, failure to comply with any executive order issued during the COVID-19 disaster is an offense punishable by a fine not to exceed $1,000, confinement in jail for a term not to exceed 180 days, or both fine and confinement.

NOW, THEREFORE, I, Greg Abbott, Governor of Texas, by virtue of the power and authority vested in me by the Constitution and laws of the State of Texas, do hereby order that, beginning now and continuing until 11:59 p.m. on April 21, 2020, all licensed health care professionals and all licensed health care facilities shall postpone all surgeries and procedures that are not immediately medically necessary to correct a serious medical condition of, or to preserve the life of, a patient who without immediate performance of the surgery or procedure would be at risk for serious adverse medical consequences or death, as determined by the patient's physician;

PROVIDED, however, that this prohibition shall not apply to any procedure that, if performed in accordance with the commonly accepted standard of clinical practice, would not deplete the hospital capacity or the personal protective equipment needed to cope with the COVID-19 disaster.

. . . .

This executive order shall remain in effect and in full force until 11:59 p.m. on April 21, 2020, unless it is modified, amended, or rescinded, or superseded by me or by a succeeding governor.

NOTES

1. *Is abortion non-essential?* Although the Texas executive order, like those in other states, generally prohibited non-essential and elective procedures, it was interpreted by state officials to preclude abortion services. As providers maintained, given the regulatory landscape in many of these states, any deferral of abortion services may make it impossible for a woman

to have an abortion. Critically, many of the states that prohibited the performance of non-essential and elective medical procedures are among those that most restrictively regulate abortion services.

2.   *Abortion opportunism?* Professor Rachel Rebouché argues that these emergency abortion bans are opportunistic efforts to use a public health crisis to further restrict abortion. As she explains, including abortion in the group of prohibited medical procedures does not serve the state's interests in preserving hospital capacity and protective gear. "Almost all abortions happen in clinics providing only reproductive health care. For pregnancies before 15 weeks, minimal protective equipment is used. These outpatient procedures, called aspiration abortions, require no sterile field, incision, or general anesthesia." As importantly, the bans have been interpreted to prohibit both surgical *and* medication abortions. The prohibition on medication abortion, Rebouché notes, is especially instrumental. As she notes, "a medication abortion is delivered by ingesting two pills: typically, the first in a health center and the second at home. It requires no protective equipment whatsoever and takes up no hospital space. For both types of abortion, the risks to the pregnant person's health are very low, and complications are extremely rare." Rachel Rebouché, *Anti-abortion Opportunism*, THE NATION, Apr. 15, 2020.

* * *

In May 2021, the Texas Legislature enacted S. B. 8, which bans abortion at just six weeks of pregnancy. Typically, such "heartbeat laws" are challenged on the ground that they ban abortion before viability, in violation of Roe v. Wade *and* Planned Parenthood v. Casey. *These pre-enforcement challenges are usually successful, resulting in an injunction that prevents the law from going into effect while its constitutionality is being litigated (and, in keeping with* Roe *and* Casey, *courts usually invalidate such laws as unconstitutional).*

However, anticipating such an outcome, the Texas legislature created an enforcement mechanism that effectively insulated the law from a pre-enforcement injunction. Unlike most abortion restrictions, which charge the state with the law's enforcement, S.B. 8 specifically precludes the prospect of state enforcement. Instead, it delegates enforcement to private citizens, who are authorized to file suit against any person who provides an abortion in violation of the Act, or who "aids or abets" such an abortion (including by paying for it) regardless of whether they know the abortion is prohibited under the Act, or even intends to engage in such conduct. Further, the law incentivizes private enforcement by requiring courts to award the successful private-citizen plaintiff at least $10,000 in "statutory damages" for each forbidden abortion performed or aided by the defendant and allowing the private-citizen plaintiff to recover attorneys' fees. Notably, successful defendants are not awarded damages, nor are they permitted to recover attorneys' fees.

Some have argued that by prohibiting state officers from enforcing the Act directly and relying instead on private enforcement, the Texas legislature sought to make it more complicated for federal courts to enjoin the Act on a statewide basis.

In an effort to enjoin the law's enforcement, a group of abortion providers filed suit in federal district court, naming Texas state court judges, county clerks, and leaders of anti-choice organizations as defendants. The defendants answered by arguing that the plaintiffs lacked standing to sue them and that, alternatively, they were immune from such suits. The district court scheduled a hearing on the standing question for August 30, 2021, but issued a ruling on the sovereign immunity issue, which was immediately appealed to the United States Court of Appeals for the Fifth Circuit. The Fifth Circuit issued an administrative stay on all proceedings in the litigation, including the hearing on the standing question.

Recognizing that the law would go into effect on September 1, 2021, the abortion providers applied to the Supreme Court, seeking an injunction that would prevent the law from going into effect, or alternatively, an order vacating the Fifth Circuit's administrative stay. However, when the clock struck midnight on September 1, 2021, there was no word from the Court. At around 11 p.m. on September 1, 2021—nearly 23 hours after the deadline elapsed—the Supreme Court announced its decision on the emergency application.

Whole Woman's Health v. Jackson
141 S. Ct. 2494 (2021).

The application for injunctive relief or, in the alternative, to vacate stays of the district court proceedings presented to Justice Alito and by him referred to the Court is denied. To prevail in an application for a stay or an injunction, an applicant must carry the burden of making a "strong showing" that it is "likely to succeed on the merits," that it will be "irreparably injured absent a stay," that the balance of the equities favors it, and that a stay is consistent with the public interest. The applicants now before us have raised serious questions regarding the constitutionality of the Texas law at issue. But their application also presents complex and novel antecedent procedural questions on which they have not carried their burden. For example, federal courts enjoy the power to enjoin individuals tasked with enforcing laws, not the laws themselves. And it is unclear whether the named defendants in this lawsuit can or will seek to enforce the Texas law against the applicants in a manner that might permit our intervention. The State has represented that neither it nor its executive employees possess the authority to enforce the Texas law either directly or indirectly. Nor is it clear whether, under existing precedent, this Court can issue an injunction against state judges asked to decide a lawsuit under Texas's law. Finally, the sole private-citizen respondent before us has filed an affidavit stating that he has no present intention to enforce the law. In light of such issues, we cannot say the applicants have met their burden to prevail in an injunction or stay application. In reaching this conclusion, we stress that we do not purport to resolve definitively any jurisdictional or substantive claim in the applicants' lawsuit. In particular, this order is not based on any conclusion about the constitutionality of Texas's law, and in no way limits other procedurally proper challenges to the Texas law, including in Texas state courts.

■ CHIEF JUSTICE ROBERTS, with whom JUSTICE BREYER and JUSTICE KAGAN join, dissenting.

The statutory scheme before the Court is not only unusual, but unprecedented. The legislature has imposed a prohibition on abortions after roughly six weeks, and then essentially delegated enforcement of that prohibition to the populace at large. The desired consequence appears to be to insulate the State from responsibility for implementing and enforcing the regulatory regime.

. . . I would grant preliminary relief to preserve the status quo ante— before the law went into effect—so that the courts may consider whether a state can avoid responsibility for its laws in such a manner. Defendants argue that existing doctrines preclude judicial intervention, and they may be correct. But the consequences of approving the state action, both in this particular case and as a model for action in other areas, counsel at least preliminary judicial consideration before the program devised by the State takes effect.

. . . .

I would accordingly preclude enforcement of S. B. 8 by the respondents to afford the District Court and the Court of Appeals the opportunity to consider the propriety of judicial action and preliminary relief pending consideration of the plaintiffs' claims.

. . . .

■ JUSTICE BREYER, with whom JUSTICE SOTOMAYOR and JUSTICE KAGAN join, dissenting.

The procedural posture of this case leads a majority of this Court to deny the applicants' request for provisional relief. In my view, however, we should grant that request.

I agree with the Chief Justice, Justice Sotomayor, and Justice Kagan. Texas's law delegates to private individuals the power to prevent a woman from obtaining an abortion during the first stage of pregnancy. But a woman has a federal constitutional right to obtain an abortion during that first stage. And a "State cannot delegate . . . a veto power [over the right to obtain an abortion] which the state itself is absolutely and totally prohibited from exercising during the first trimester of pregnancy." . . . The applicants persuasively argue that Texas's law does precisely that.

The very bringing into effect of Texas's law may well threaten the applicants with imminent and serious harm. One of the clinic applicants has stated on its website that "[d]ue to Texas' SB 8 law," it is "unable to provide abortion procedures at this time." And the applicants, with supporting affidavits, claim that clinics will be unable to run the financial and other risks that come from waiting for a private person to sue them under the Texas law; they will simply close, depriving care to more than half the women seeking abortions in Texas clinics. We have permitted those whom a law threatens with constitutional harm to bring pre-enforcement challenges to the law where the harm is less serious and the threat of enforcement less certain than the harm (and the threat) here.

I recognize that Texas's law delegates the State's power to prevent abortions not to one person (such as a district attorney) or to a few persons (such as a group of government officials or private citizens) but to any person. But I do not see why that fact should make a critical legal difference. That delegation still threatens to invade a constitutional right, and the coming into effect of that delegation still threatens imminent harm. Normally, where a legal right is " 'invaded,' " the law provides " 'a legal remedy by suit or action at law.' " *Marbury v. Madison*, 1 Cranch 137, 163 (1803) (quoting 3 W. Blackstone, Commentaries *23). . . . There may be other not-very-new procedural bottles that can also adequately hold what is, in essence, very old and very important legal wine: The ability to ask the Judiciary to protect an individual from the invasion of a constitutional right—an invasion that threatens immediate and serious injury.

. . . .

■ JUSTICE SOTOMAYOR, with whom JUSTICE BREYER and JUSTICE KAGAN join, dissenting.

The Court's order is stunning. Presented with an application to enjoin a flagrantly unconstitutional law engineered to prohibit women from exercising their constitutional rights and evade judicial scrutiny, a majority of Justices have opted to bury their heads in the sand. Last night, the Court silently acquiesced in a State's enactment of a law that flouts nearly 50 years of federal precedents. Today, the Court belatedly explains that it declined to grant relief because of procedural complexities of the State's own invention. Because the Court's failure to act rewards tactics designed to avoid judicial review and inflicts significant harm on the applicants and on women seeking abortions in Texas, I dissent.

. . . .

The Act is clearly unconstitutional under existing precedents. The respondents do not even try to argue otherwise. Nor could they: No federal appellate court has upheld such a comprehensive prohibition on abortions before viability under current law.

The Texas Legislature was well aware of this binding precedent. To circumvent it, the Legislature took the extraordinary step of enlisting private citizens to do what the State could not. . . .

The Legislature fashioned this scheme because federal constitutional challenges to state laws ordinarily are brought against state officers who are in charge of enforcing the law. By prohibiting state officers from enforcing the Act directly and relying instead on citizen bounty hunters, the Legislature sought to make it more complicated for federal courts to enjoin the Act on a statewide basis.

Taken together, the Act is a breathtaking act of defiance—of the Constitution, of this Court's precedents, and of the rights of women seeking abortions throughout Texas. But over six weeks after the applicants filed suit to prevent the Act from taking effect, a Fifth Circuit panel abruptly stayed all proceedings before the District Court and vacated a preliminary injunction hearing that was scheduled to begin on Monday. The applicants requested emergency relief from this Court, but the Court said nothing. The Act took effect at midnight last night.[1]

Today, the Court finally tells the Nation that it declined to act because, in short, the State's gambit worked. The structure of the State's scheme, the Court reasons, raises "complex and novel antecedent procedural questions" that counsel against granting the application, just as the State intended. This is untenable. It cannot be the case that a State can evade federal judicial scrutiny by outsourcing the enforcement of unconstitutional laws to its citizenry. . . . [T]he Court has rewarded the State's effort to delay federal review of a plainly unconstitutional statute, enacted in disregard of the Court's precedents, through procedural entanglements of the State's own creation.

The Court should not be so content to ignore its constitutional obligations to protect not only the rights of women, but also the sanctity of its precedents and of the rule of law.

. . . .

---

[1] The Court's inaction has had immediate impact. Two hours before the Act took effect, one applicant reported that its waiting rooms were " 'filled with patients' " urgently seeking care while " 'protesters [we]re outside, shining lights on the parking [lot].' " Ariane De Vogue, Texas 6-Week Abortion Ban Takes Effect after Supreme Court Inaction, CNN (Sept. 1, 2021), www. cnn.com/2021/09/01/politics/texas-abortion-supreme-court-sb8-roe-wade/index.html. Then, at midnight, the Act became law, and many abortion providers, including applicants, ceased providing abortion care after more than six weeks from a woman's last menstrual period (LMP). *See, e.g.*, Alamo Women's Reproductive Care (Sept. 1, 2021), https://alamowomensclinic.com ("We cannot provide abortion services to anyone with detectable embryonic or fetal cardiac activity[,] which is typically found at 6 weeks or more from last menstrual period"); Southwestern Women's Surgery Center (Sept. 1, 2021), https://southwesternwomens.com/ southwestern-womens-surgery-center-dallas-texas/ ("In compliance with Texas Senate Bill 8 of 2021, starting on September 1st 2021, our facility cannot provide abortions to patients with detectible embryonic or fetal cardiac activity, which typically starts at 6 weeks LMP"). Since then, at least one applicant has stopped providing abortions entirely. Planned Parenthood South Texas (Sept. 1, 2021), https://www.plannedparenthood.org/planned-parenthood-south-texas ("Due to Texas' SB 8 law, we are unable to provide abortion procedures at this time").

■ JUSTICE KAGAN, with whom JUSTICE BREYER and JUSTICE SOTOMAYOR join, dissenting.

. . . .

Today's ruling illustrates just how far the Court's "shadow-docket" decisions may depart from the usual principles of appellate process. That ruling, as everyone must agree, is of great consequence. Yet the majority has acted without any guidance from the Court of Appeals—which is right now considering the same issues. It has reviewed only the most cursory party submissions, and then only hastily. And it barely bothers to explain its conclusion—that a challenge to an obviously unconstitutional abortion regulation backed by a wholly unprecedented enforcement scheme is unlikely to prevail. In all these ways, the majority's decision is emblematic of too much of this Court's shadow-docket decision-making—which every day becomes more unreasoned, inconsistent, and impossible to defend. I respectfully dissent.

NOTES

1. *The shadow docket.* The Supreme Court's September 1, 2021 ruling on the S.B. 8 challenge was notable in that it did not appear on the Court's merits docket, but rather, its shadow docket. The term "shadow docket" refers to the Court's calendar for resolving emergency appeals and procedural case management issues. The shadow docket differs from the Court's merits docket, the calendar of regular cases for which the Court grants certiorari and requires full briefing, oral argument, and issues lengthy substantive opinions. By contrast, cases come to the shadow docket on an ad hoc, expedited basis, and the issues raised typically are resolved without the benefit of full briefing and oral argument and without much explanation and reasoning. Indeed, most shadow docket decisions, are unsigned orders, making it difficult to discern how each of the justices voted in the dispute. The majority's ruling allowing S.B. 8 to go into effect was notable in that it was lengthier than many shadow docket rulings—it was a full paragraph.

In the S.B. 8 ruling, both the Chief Justice and Justice Kagan registered concerns about using the shadow docket as a vehicle for resolving the "particularly difficult" questions that S.B. 8 presented. Do you agree with this assessment?

2. *A law's fallout.* When S.B. 8 went into effect, some Texas abortion providers in Texas continued providing care for the few individuals who know they are pregnant and seek an abortion within six weeks of pregnancy. However, many providers ceased operations for fear of litigation, forcing clinics to turn away most patients seeking care. Notably, there has been an influx of patients from Texas seeking reproductive healthcare services from clinics in neighboring states. Many of these clinics were already dealing with insufficient resources, especially during the COVID-19 pandemic.

3. *The futility of constitutional adjudication?* Even if S.B. 8 is eventually struck down as unconstitutional, its impact may be difficult to reverse. As

noted, as a result of the law going into effect, many abortion clinics have stopped providing services, for fear of litigation. In 2013, nearly half of Texas' abortion clinics shut down in response to a sweeping abortion restriction law, which the Supreme Court later invalidated in *Whole Woman's Health v. Hellerstedt*, 579 U.S. 582 (2016). Although the decision vindicated abortion providers in Texas, few of the clinics that closed while the law's constitutionality was being litigated reopened in the wake of the Court's decision.

4.   *The United States enters the fray.* Shortly after S.B. 8 went into effect, the United States Department of Justice (DOJ) sued Texas, seeking a declaratory judgment that the law is unconstitutional and an injunction to prevent its enforcement. In announcing the lawsuit, Attorney General Merrick Garland stated that S.B. 8 is "clearly unconstitutional under longstanding Supreme Court precedent" and that the federal government has the responsibility and authority to prevent states from depriving the constitutional rights of individuals. The DOJ complaint maintains that the United States has the authority—and indeed, an obligation—to bring suit against a sovereign state in order to assist individuals in vindicating their constitutional rights. To this end, DOJ argued that Texas violated "settled constitutional law" by intentionally "foreclose[ing] the ability" for individuals to vindicate their constitutional rights under the Fourteenth Amendment. The lawsuit also argued that S.B. 8 violates the Supremacy Clause and is preempted by federal law as it restricts certain abortion services that federal agencies are tasked with facilitating, and that S.B. 8 violates the federal government's intergovernmental immunity, as it "regulates the activities of the federal government and its contractors."

5.   *S.B. 8 returns to the Supreme Court.* The district court issued a lengthy opinion granting the United States' emergency motion and temporarily enjoining the enforcement of S.B. 8. However, the Fifth Circuit granted a stay of the injunction pending appeal. On October 22, 2021, the Supreme Court granted certiorari before judgment in *United States v. Texas* and *Whole Woman's Health v. Jackson*, the abortion providers' lawsuit again Texas state court judges and county clerks and scheduled oral arguments for both cases on the November 1, 2021. Meaningfully, the Court refused to enjoin S.B. 8 and indicated that its grant of certiorari in *United States v. Texas* was limited to the narrow question of whether the United States can bring suit in federal court to obtain declaratory and injunctive relief against Texas and the private defendants. It would not be addressing the substantive merits of S.B. 8's constitutionality. Justice Sotomayor concurred in part and dissented in part to the grant of certiorari, emphasizing the harm to women seeking to exercise their right to abortion care and "the constitutional system as a whole" of the Court's failure to enjoin the law until future adjudication.

6.   *The impact of S.B. 8.* When S.B. 8 went into effect in Texas on September 1, 2021, there were 20 abortion clinics serving the state. While none have permanently closed their doors as a result of S.B. 8, the law's impact on abortion providers has been profound. Fearing litigation, many providers have opted not to perform abortions unless the patient is within the 6-week time period. Prior to S.B. 8, Planned Parenthood's two clinics in

southeast Texas usually provided 25 abortions per day on average. In the week immediately preceding S.B. 8 effective date, those two clinics provided 205 abortions daily, 184 of which daily were for Texas residents. In the two to three weeks following September 1, the clinics provided an average of only five abortions a day. Whole Woman's Health, which operates four clinics in Texas, turned away over 100 patients in the first two weeks of September. Up to 90% of those seeking abortions in have been forced to continue their pregnancies. Clinics in nearby states like Louisiana, Kansas, and Oklahoma have experienced an influx of patients traveling hours from Texas to seek reproductive care. The Hope Medical Group for Women, a clinic in Shreveport, Louisiana, went from having roughly 20% of its patients arrive from Texas prior to S.B. 8 going into effect to roughly 60% after September 1, 2021. *See Advocates track drastic change in 6 months of Texas abortion ban*, MOULTRIE OBSERVER, 2022 WLNR 6053577 (Feb. 27, 2022). Similarly, the Trust Women clinic in Oklahoma City went from seeing 11 patients from Texas in August to seeing 110 patients from Texas in September—a tenfold increase. *Id.*

* * *

In June 2020, almost a year before the Texas legislature enacted S.B. 8, the State of Mississippi submitted a petition of certiorari to the United States Supreme Court seeking review of a challenge to H.B. 1510, Mississippi's Gestational Age Act, a 15-week abortion ban. In its petition for certiorari, Mississippi presented three questions: "(1) Whether all pre-viability prohibitions on elective abortions are unconstitutional; (2) Whether the validity of a pre-viability law that protects women's health, the dignity of unborn children, and the integrity of the medical profession and society should be analyzed under Casey's *"undue burden" standard or* Hellerstedt's *balancing of benefits and burdens; and (3) Whether abortion providers have third party standing to invalidate a law that protects women's health from the dangers of late-term abortions." On May 17, 2021, after considering the petition for nearly a year, the Supreme Court granted review of a single question: Whether all pre-viability abortion bans are unconstitutional. Despite the Court's narrow framing of the issue, in July 2021, when Mississippi filed its first brief before the Court, it went beyond asking the Court to uphold the constitutionality of H.B. 1510. In addition to addressing the constitutionality of pre-viability abortion bans, Mississippi specifically entreated the Court overrule* Roe v. Wade *and* Planned Parenthood v. Casey. *Meaningfully, in the intervening period between June 2020, when Mississippi petitioned the Court for review, and July 2021, when it filed its brief urging the Court to overrule* Roe *and* Casey, *Justice Ruth Bader Ginsburg died. Just a week after Ginsburg's death on September 18, 2020, President Donald Trump nominated Seventh Circuit Judge Amy Coney Barrett to fill Ginsburg's seat on the Court. The U.S. Senate confirmed Barrett by a 52–48 vote on October 26, 2020.*

Dobbs v. Jackson Women's Health Organization
142 S. Ct. 2228 (2022).

For an excerpt of Dobbs v. Jackson Women's Health Organization, *see* supra *p. 976.*

D. REGULATING STERILIZATION

Virginia Acts ch. 394, p. 569
(1924).

CHAP. 304.   *An ACT to provide for the sexual sterilization of inmates of State institutions in certain cases*

Whereas, both the health of the individual patient and the welfare of society may be promoted in certain cases by the sterilization of mental defectives under careful safeguard and by competent and conscientious authority, and

Whereas, such sterilization may be effected in males by the operation of vasectomy and in females by the operation of salpingectomy, both of which said operations may be performed without serious pain or substantial danger to the life of the patient, and

Whereas the Commonwealth has in custodial care and is supporting in various State institutions many defective persons who if now discharged or paroled would likely become by the propagation of their kind a menace to society but who if incapable of procreating might properly and safely be discharged or paroled and become self-supporting with benefit both to themselves and to society, and

Whereas, human experience has demonstrated that heredity plays an important part in the transmission of insanity, idiocy, imbecility, epilepsy and crime, now, therefore

1.   Be it enacted by the general assembly of Virginia, That whenever the superintendent of the Western State Hospital, of the Eastern State Hospital, or of the Southwestern State Hospital, or of the Central State Hospital, or of the State Colony for Epileptics and Feeble-minded, shall be of opinion that it is for the best interests of the patients and of society that any inmate of the institution under his care should be sexually sterilized, such superintendent is hereby authorized to perform, or cause to be performed by some capable physician or surgeon, the operation of sterilization on any such patient confined in such institution afflicted with hereditary forms of insanity that are recurrent, idiocy, imbecility, feeble-mindedness or epilepsy; provided that such superintendent shall have first complied with the requirements of this act.

2.   Such superintendent shall first present to the special board of directors of his hospital or colony a petition stating the facts of the case

the grounds of his opinion, verified by his affidavit to the best of his knowledge and belief, and praying that an order may be entered by said board requiring him to perform or to have performed by some competent physician to be designated by him in his said petition or by said board in its order, upon the inmate of his institution named in such petition, the operation of vasectomy if upon a male and of salpingectomy if upon a female. A copy of said petition must be served upon the inmate together with a notice in writing designating the time and place in the said institution, not less than thirty days before the presentation of such petition to said special board of directors when and where said board may hear and act upon such petition.

A copy of the said petition and notice shall also be so served upon the legal guardian or committee of the said inmate if such guardian or committee to be known to the said superintendent, and if there be no such guardian or committee or none such be known to the said superintendent, then the said superintendent shall apply to the circuit court of the county or city in which his said institution is situated, or to the judge thereof in vacation, who by a proper order entered in the common law order book of the said court shall appoint some suitable person to act as guardian of the said inmate during and for the purposes of proceedings under this act, to defend the rights and interests of the said inmate, and the guardian so appointed shall be paid by the said institution a fee of not exceeding twenty-five dollars as many be determined by the judge of the said court for his services under said appointment and such guardian shall be served likewise with a copy of the aforesaid petition and notice. Such guardian may be removed of discharged at any time by the said court of the judge thereof in vacation and new guardian appointed and substituted in his place.

If the said inmate be an infant having a living parent or parents whose names and addresses are known to the said superintendent, they or either of them as the case may be shall be served likewise with a copy of the said petition and notice.

After the notice required by the act shall have been so given, the said special board at the time and place named therein, with such reasonable continuances from time to time and from place to place as the said special board may determine, shall proceed to hear and consider the said petition and the evidence offered in support of and against the same, provided that the said special board shall see to it that the said inmate shall have opportunity and leave to attend the said hearings in person if desired by him or if required by his committee, guardian or parent served with the notice and petition aforesaid.

The said special board may receive and consider as evidence at the said hearing the commitment papers and other records of the said inmate with or in any of the aforesaid named institutions as certified by the superintendent or superintendents thereof, together with such other legal evidence as may be offered by any party to the proceedings.

. . .

Any party to the said proceeding shall have the right to be represented by counsel at such hearings.

The said special board may deny the prayer of the said petition or if the said special board shall find the said inmate is insane, idiotic, imbecile, feeble-minded or epileptic, and by the laws of heredity is the probable potential parent of social inadequate offspring likewise afflicted, that the said may be sexually sterilized without detriment to his or her general health, and the welfare of the inmate of society will be promoted by such sterilization, the said special board may order the said superintendent to perform or to have performed by some competent physician to be named in the such order upon the said inmate, after not less than thirty days from the date of such order, the operation of vasectomy if a male or salpingectomy if a female; provided that nothing in this act shall be construed to authorize the operation of castration nor the removal of sound organs from the body.

3.   From any order so entered by the said special board the said superintendent or the said inmate or his committee or guardian or parent or next friend shall within thirty days after the date of such order have an appeal of right to the circuit court of the county or city in which the said institution is situated, which appeal may be taken by giving notice thereof in writing to any member of the said special board and to the other parties to the said proceeding. . . .

The said circuit court in determining such appeal may consider the record of the proceedings before the said special board, including the evidence therein appearing together with such other legal evidence as the said court may consider pertinent and proper that may be offered to the said court by the any party to the appeal.

Upon such appeal the said circuit court may affirm, revise, or reverse the orders of the said special board appealed from and enter such order as it deems just and right and which it shall certify to the said special board of directors.

The pendency of such appeal shall stay proceedings under the order of the special board until the appeal be determined.

4.   Any party to such appeal in the circuit court may within ninety days after the date of the final order therein, appeal for an appeal to the supreme court of appeals, which may grant or refuse such appeal and shall have jurisdiction to hear and determine the same upon the record of trial in the circuit court and to enter such order as it may that the circuit court should have entered. The pendency of an appeal in the supreme court of appeals shall operate as a stay of proceedings under any orders of the special board or of the circuit court until the appeal be determined by the said supreme court of appeals.

5. Neither any of said superintendents nor any other person legally participating in the execution of the provisions of this act shall be liable either civil or criminally on account of said participation.

6. Nothing in this act shall be construed so as to prevent the medical or surgical treatment for sound therapeutic reasons of any person in this State, by a physician or surgeon licensed by this State, which treatment may incidentally involve the nullification or destruction of the reproductive functions.

Buck v. Bell

274 U.S. 200 (1927).

■ HOLMES, J.

This is a writ of error to review a judgment of the Supreme Court of Appeals of the State of Virginia, affirming a judgment of the Circuit Court of Amherst County, by which the defendant in error, the superintendent of the State Colony for Epileptics and Feeble Minded, was ordered to perform the operation of salpingectomy upon Carrie Buck, the plaintiff in error, for the purpose of making her sterile. The case comes here upon the contention that the statute authorizing the judgment is void under the Fourteenth Amendment as denying to the plaintiff in error due process of law and the equal protection of the laws.

Carrie Buck is a feeble-minded white woman who was committed to the State Colony above mentioned in due form. She is the daughter of a feeble-minded mother in the same institution, and the mother of an illegitimate feeble-minded child. She was eighteen years old at the time of the trial of her case in the Circuit Court in the latter part of 1924. An Act of Virginia approved March 20, 1924 (Laws 1924, c. 394) recites that the health of the patient and the welfare of society may be promoted in certain cases by the sterilization of mental defectives, under careful safeguard, etc.; that the sterilization may be effected in males by vasectomy and in females by salpingectomy, without serious pain or substantial danger to life; that the Commonwealth is supporting in various institutions many defective persons who if now discharged would become a menace but if incapable of procreating might be discharged with safety and become self-supporting with benefit to themselves and to society; and that experience has shown that heredity plays an important part in the transmission of insanity, imbecility, etc. The statute then enacts that whenever the superintendent of certain institutions including the above named State Colony shall be of opinion that it is for the best interest of the patients and of society that an inmate under his care should be sexually sterilized, he may have the operation performed upon any patient afflicted with hereditary forms of insanity, imbecility, etc., on complying with the very careful provisions by which the act protects the patients from possible abuse.

The superintendent first presents a petition to the special board of directors of his hospital or colony, stating the facts and the grounds for his opinion, verified by affidavit. Notice of the petition and of the time and place of the hearing in the institution is to be served upon the inmate, and also upon his guardian, and if there is no guardian the superintendent is to apply to the Circuit Court of the County to appoint one. If the inmate is a minor notice also is to be given to his parents, if any, with a copy of the petition. The board is to see to it that the inmate may attend the hearings if desired by him or his guardian. The evidence is all to be reduced to writing, and after the board has made its order for or against the operation, the superintendent, or the inmate, or his guardian, may appeal to the Circuit Court of the County. The Circuit Court may consider the record of the board and the evidence before it and such other admissible evidence as may be offered, and may affirm, revise, or reverse the order of the board and enter such order as it deems just. Finally any party may apply to the Supreme Court of Appeals, which, if it grants the appeal, is to hear the case upon the record of the trial in the Circuit Court and may enter such order as it thinks the Circuit Court should have entered. There can be no doubt that so far as procedure is concerned the rights of the patient are most carefully considered, and as every step in this case was taken in scrupulous compliance with the statute and after months of observation, there is no doubt that in that respect the plaintiff in error has had due process at law.

The attack is not upon the procedure but upon the substantive law. It seems to be contended that in no circumstances could such an order be justified. It certainly is contended that the order cannot be justified upon the existing grounds. The judgment finds the facts that have been recited and that Carrie Buck "is the probable potential parent of socially inadequate offspring, likewise afflicted, that she may be sexually sterilized without detriment to her general health and that her welfare and that of society will be promoted by her sterilization," and thereupon makes the order. In view of the general declarations of the Legislature and the specific findings of the Court obviously we cannot say as matter of law that the grounds do not exist, and if they exist they justify the result. We have seen more than once that the public welfare may call upon the best citizens for their lives. It would be strange if it could not call upon those who already sap the strength of the State for these lesser sacrifices, often not felt to be such by those concerned, in order to prevent our being swamped with incompetence. It is better for all the world, if instead of waiting to execute degenerate offspring for crime, or to let them starve for their imbecility, society can prevent those who are manifestly unfit from continuing their kind. The principle that sustains compulsory vaccination is broad enough to cover cutting the Fallopian tubes. Three generations of imbeciles are enough.

But, it is said, however it might be if this reasoning were applied generally, it fails when it is confined to the small number who are in the institutions named and is not applied to the multitudes outside. It is the usual last resort of constitutional arguments to point out shortcomings of this sort. But the answer is that the law does all that is needed when it does all that it can, indicates a policy, applies it to all within the lines, and seeks to bring within the lines all similarly [sic] situated so far and so fast as its means allow. Of course so far as the operations enable those who otherwise must be kept confined to be returned to the world, and thus open the asylum to others, the equality aimed at will be more nearly reached.

Judgment affirmed.

. . . .

NOTES

1.   *Sterilization laws and eugenics.* The links between sterilization laws, like the one challenged in *Buck v. Bell*, and eugenics theories have been well-documented. According to Professor Michael Willrich, the effort to use law to further eugenic goals relied on "a potent hybrid of biological science, statistical method, and cultural assumptions" that reached its height in the early 1900s. Michael Willrich, *The Two Percent Solution: Eugenic Jurisprudence and the Socialization of American Law, 1900–1930*, 16 LAW & HIST. REV. 63, 63 (1998). Eugenics-influenced laws "won a diverse following of academics, animal breeders, social workers, criminologists, psychiatrists, institutional superintendents, philanthropists, and activists spanning the political spectrum from socialists to white supremacists." *Id.* Donning the mantle of "science," eugenics-influenced laws were premised on the idea that the problems of a rapidly industrializing society (in which immigrants were becoming a visible—and troubling—presence) could be traced to the existence of inherited traits such as immorality and drunkenness, or mental "feeblemindedness." Immigrants, the poor, and "immoral" women were the main targets of legal attempts to control their reproduction.

2.   *Constructing* Buck v. Bell. Professor Victoria Nourse calls our attention to two different aspects of *Buck v. Bell* not readily apparent to modern readers. First, the case was itself something of a sham, "constructed precisely because sterilization laws had become a dead letter due to hostile state court constitutional rulings." Further, Carrie Buck's lawyer was affiliated with the hospital being sued, and much of the "evidence" against her was provided by Harry Laughlin, a leading eugenicist. Victoria F. Nourse, Buck v. Bell: *A Constitutional Tragedy from a Lost World*, 39 PEPP. L. REV. 101, 105, 112 (2011).

3.   *Evolving notions of the police power.* Second, Nourse observes that in the early years of the twentieth century, notions of the proper relationship between individual rights and the state's police powers were very different: The state could trump individual rights in order to exercise its police power to regulate health, morals, and safety. Victoria F. Nourse, Buck v. Bell: *A Constitutional Tragedy from a Lost World*, 39 PEPP. L. REV. 101, 109 (2011). How does this historical view square with our contemporary understanding of the state's police power? What, in your view, is the idea of the proper

relationship between individuals and the state? Does that relationship change if the individuals under consideration are male or female?

4. *Carrie Buck's "feeblemindedness"*. There is little hard evidence that Carrie Buck, her mother, or her daughter were mentally impaired, as Justice Oliver Wendell Holmes famously asserted in *Buck v. Bell*. Indeed, there is quite a bit of evidence suggesting that all three were of normal intelligence. However, Carrie was born out of wedlock, and had given birth to a child out of wedlock. In all likelihood, Carrie Buck was institutionalized not because she was feebleminded but because she was the mother of an illegitimate child. Moreover, there is some evidence that Buck's pregnancy was the result of a male relative's sexual coercion. A 1938 review of the sterilization policies at the Virginia institution where Carrie Buck was confined found that the behavior of all of the women who had been recommended for sterilization had been characterized under the rubric of "sexual license." PAUL A. LOMBARDO, THREE GENERATIONS, NO IMBECILES: EUGENICS, THE SUPREME COURT, AND *BUCK V. BELL* 252 (2008). Other scholars have elaborated on the role that "sexual license" played in government-coerced sterilization. *See, e.g.*, DANIEL KEVLES, IN THE NAME OF EUGENICS: GENETICS AND THE USES OF HUMAN HEREDITY 107–08 (1981) (describing common justifications for sterilization as "excessive sexuality" and "sexual deviancy").

5. *Unsavory connections*. Harry Laughlin, the main proponent of the "science" of eugenics, the director of the Eugenics Record Office, and President of the Pioneer Fund, was affiliated with those who wished to use eugenics to maintain the racial superiority of the "white race." As legal historian Paul Lombardo has documented, Laughlin testified in favor of the Virginia Racial Integrity Act of 1924, which was famously invalidated in 1967's *Loving v. Virginia*. Moreover, Laughlin's Pioneer Fund worked with Mississippi's notorious Senator Theodore Bilbo and organizations seeking to limit the Civil Rights Act. *See* Paul Lombardo, *"The American Breed": Nazi Eugenics and the Origins of the Pioneer Fund*, 65 ALB. L. REV. 743, 751–52 (2002). The Pioneer Fund, and/or Laughlin himself, gave expert testimony to restrict immigration in the 1920s, and later worked to keep Jews fleeing Hitler from entering the United States. *Id.* at 757.

However, American eugenics theory was not confined to domestic applications—it was actively exported to other jurisdictions. Critically, Nazi "racial hygiene" policies were modeled on American model sterilization laws. Indeed, Laughlin worked closely with German eugenicists, and was awarded an honorary degree from Heidelberg University. *Id.* at 759, 763–64. Taken together, this history suggests that Laughlin, and the segment of eugenics he represented, was "among the most racist and anti-Semitic of early twentieth century eugenicists," as well as one of the most influential. *Id.* at 822. For more on the connections between eugenics theory and Nazism, see HARRY BRUNIUS, BETTER FOR ALL THE WORLD: THE SECRET HISTORY OF FORCED STERILIZATION AND AMERICA'S QUEST FOR RACIAL PURITY (2007), and STEFAN KÜHL, THE NAZI CONNECTION: EUGENICS, AMERICAN RACISM, AND GERMAN NATIONAL SOCIALISM (1994).

6. *Nazism and the changing view of "eugenic" sterilization*. In the 1930s, Nazi Germany relied on American models of eugenics to craft its "final

solution." As scholars have noted, the recruitment of eugenics theory and practice to support the Holocaust fundamentally changed public opinion about eugenics in the United States, culminating in the Court's 1942 opinion in *Skinner v. Oklahoma. See* PAUL A. LOMBARDO, THREE GENERATIONS, NO IMBECILES: EUGENICS, THE SUPREME COURT, AND *BUCK V. BELL* 227–33 (2008); VICTORIA F. NOURSE, IN RECKLESS HANDS: *SKINNER V. OKLAHOMA* AND THE NEAR TRIUMPH OF AMERICAN EUGENICS 129–31 (2008). For further discussion of *Skinner,* see *supra* p. 16, and *infra* p. 1063.

* * *

The mainstream acceptance of eugenics in the early 1900s is evident in Buck v. Bell. *After* Buck, *the eugenics movement was so successful at passing state-level laws that by 1933, Virginia's sterilization law was not an anomaly. Some 150 million people lived in states with eugenic sterilization laws. Like Oklahoma's Habitual Criminal Sterilization Act, provided below, many of these laws aimed to curb crime by limiting recidivists' ability to procreate.*

Oklahoma Habitual Criminal Sterilization Act
ch. 26, ART. 1 (1935).

. . .

SECT. 3. *Habitual Criminal Defined.*

Where used in this Act and for the purposes of this Act the term "habitual criminal" refers to and shall mean: a person, male or female, who, having been twice or more times convicted to final judgment for the commission of crimes amounting to felonies involving moral turpitude, separately brought and tried, either in a court of competent jurisdiction of this State or in any other state of the United States, is thereafter convicted to final judgment in a court of competent jurisdiction of this State for the commission of a crime amounting to a felony involving moral turpitude, and sentenced therefor to serve a term of imprisonment in the Oklahoma State Penitentiary, or the Oklahoma State Reformatory, or any other like penal institution now or hereafter established and maintained by the State of Oklahoma.

SECT. 4. *Sexual Sterilization.*

Any person proceeded against under and pursuant to the provisions of this Act and adjudged to be an [sic] habitual criminal as herein defined, shall upon the adjudication thereof becoming final be rendered sexually sterile. And to render such person sexually sterile, if a male, there shall be performed upon him an operation of vasectomy, and if a female, there shall be performed upon her an operation of salpingectomy.

. . .

SECT. 24A. *Offenses Exempted From Act.*

Provided, that offenses arising out of the violation of the prohibitory laws, revenue acts, embezzlement, or political offenses, shall not come or be considered within the terms of this Act.

Skinner v. Oklahoma
316 U.S. 535 (1942).

For an excerpt of Skinner v. Oklahoma, *see* supra *p. 16.*

NOTES

1. *Preservation through transformation?* Although many eugenics-based sterilization laws were called into question after *Skinner*, the interest in curbing the reproductive capacities of marginalized communities persisted under other (non-eugenics-based) rationales. During this period, new "indications" for sterilization aimed at poor women and minority women were advanced, this time on the grounds of overpopulation and/or restraining burgeoning welfare costs and curbing "illegitimacy." *See* Julius Paul, *The Return of Punitive Sterilization Proposals: Current Attacks on Illegitimacy and the AFDC Program*, 3 LAW & SOC'Y REV. 77, 78 (1968).

2. *Repealing eugenics laws.* In the 1960s and 1970s, new attention to the rights of the disabled, as well as a growing awareness of the disproportionate effect that eugenics-based laws had on minorities, led to a reappraisal of such laws. During this period, sterilization laws that had been passed after *Buck v. Bell*, and that remained on the books after *Skinner*, were repealed in many states. *See* PAUL A. LOMBARDO, THREE GENERATIONS, NO IMBECILES: EUGENICS, THE SUPREME COURT, AND *BUCK V. BELL* 253 (2008).

1. POPULATION CONTROL RHETORIC AND STERILIZATION

Even as the eugenics movement lost popular favor, the rapid increase in population growth in the twentieth century led to the perception that a population crisis was imminent. Advocates for population control, at least some of whom had ties to the discredited eugenics movement of the 1920s and 1930s, thought that birth control and sterilization were key weapons in the effort to stanch overpopulation. In 1968, Paul Ehrlich, a Stanford professor, wrote the best-selling book The Population Bomb. *In it, he warned that growing rates of population—particularly in less developed countries and regions—would likely lead to global starvation and social turmoil. In an effort to curb population growth, state actors and private medical professionals urged more permanent forms of fertility control— particularly sterilization—as evidenced below in* Relf v. Weinberger *and* Madrigal v. Quilligan.

Complaint, *Relf v. Weinberger*
372 F. Supp. 1196 (D.D.C. 1974).

Facts

1. On June 14, 1973, Mary Alice Relf, age 12, and Minnie Relf, age 14, were surgically sterilized in a Montgomery, Alabama, hospital.

2. These tubal sterilizations took place under the direction of the Family Planning Clinic of the Montgomery Community Action Committee, a project funded and controlled by [the Office of Economic Opportunity (O.E.O.)] through the actions of defendant [Alvin J.] Arnett[, the Acting Director of O.E.O.] and his predecessors in office.

3. In addition to Minnie and Mary Alice, the Relfs have one other daughter, Katie, who is 17 years of age. When Community Action moved the Relfs to a public housing project in 1971, the Family Planning Service began the unsolicited administration of experimental birth control injections to Katie. No parental permissions was sought or given. Indeed, the agency sought out the Relf children as good experimental subjects for their family planning program. The F.D.A. approved this experimental drug [Depo-Provera] for use by the Family Planning Service of the Montgomery Community Action Committee.

4. At a later date, the clinic began the unsolicited administration of the same shots to the two younger Relf girls.

5. In March, 1973, Katie Relf was taken to the Family Planning Clinic for insertion of an "I.U.D." (a contraceptive "intra-uterine device"). Once again, her parents were not asked if they had an objection. Katie, who was under the age of consent, submitted to the directions of the clinic staff that she accept implantation of the device.

6. On June 13, 1973, a family planning nurse from O.E.O's Montgomery Community Action Committee picked up Mrs. Relf and the younger girls and transported them to a doctor's office. Mrs. Relf was told the girls were being taken for some shots. She thought the shots were the same as those all three children had been receiving for some time.

7. Neither Mrs. Relf nor the girls spoke with anyone at the doctor's office. From the doctor's office the children and their mother were transported to the hospital where the girls were assigned a room.

8. It was at this time that Mrs. Relf, who neither reads nor writes, put her mark on what was later learned to be an authorization for surgical sterilization. There was no informed consent to the surgery by Mrs. Relf. Mrs. Relf was then escorted home.

9. Minnie and Mary Alice were left by themselves in a ward. A nurse required Minnie to sign a false document stating that she was over twenty-one years old and gave consent to the operation. Minnie did

not understand what the document meant or authorized. So far, neither child had even seen the physician who was to perform the operation nor had either child been explained what was going to happen to her.

10. Sometime prior to the operation, Minnie got out of bed, borrowed some change from another patient in the ward, and telephone a neighbor's house to speak with her mother. (The Relfs do not have a telephone.) Minnie asked her mother to bring her sister and her home, but her mother had to tell her that she had no transportation to get the girls from the hospital.

11. It was the next morning that both children were placed under a general anesthetic and surgically sterilized. At no point prior to the operation did the children or their mother see or talk with the doctor who performed the operation or any other physician. At no time prior to the operation did any physician discuss with the girls or their parents the nature or consequences of the surgery to which Minnie and Mary Alice were about to be subjected. The girls were released from the hospital after three days.

12. On the afternoon of the day Minnie and Mary Alice were taken to the hospital, the same O.E.O. family planning nurse returned to the Relf home and attempted to take Katie to the hospital to undergo sterilization. Katie locked herself in her room and refused to go.

Relf v. Weinberger

372 F. Supp. 1196 (D.D.C. 1974).

■ GESELL, D.J.

These two related cases, which have been consolidated with the consent of all parties, challenge the statutory authorization and constitutionality of regulations of the Department of Health, Education and Welfare (HEW) governing human sterilizations under programs and projects funded by the Department's Public Health Service and its Social and Rehabilitation Service. 39 Fed.Reg. 4730–34 (1974). Plaintiffs are the National Welfare Rights Organization (NWRO), suing on behalf of its 125,000 members, and five individual women, proceeding by class action on behalf of all poor persons subject to involuntary, sterilization under the challenged regulations. Defendants are the Secretary of HEW, under whose authority the regulations were issued, 42 U.S.C. § 216, and two high-level HEW officials charged with the administration of federal family planning funds.

... Congress has authorized the funding of a full range of family planning services under two basic procedures. The Public Health Service administers federal grants to state health agencies and to public and private projects for the provision of family planning services to the poor, 42 U.S.C. §§ 300 et seq., 708(a), and the Social and Rehabilitation Service provides funds for such services under the Medicaid and Aid to Families of Dependent Children programs, 42 U.S.C. §§ 601 *et seq.*, 1396 *et seq.*

Although there is no specific reference to sterilization in any of the family planning statutes nor in the legislative history surrounding their passage,[1] the Secretary has considered sterilization to fall within the general statutory scheme and Congress has been made aware of this position. But until recently, there were no particular rules or regulations governing the circumstances under which sterilizations could be funded under these statutes.

Sterilization of females or males is irreversible. The total number of these sterilizations is clearly of national significance. Few realize that over 16 percent of the married couples in this country between the ages of 20 and 39 have had a sterilization operation. Over the last few years, an estimated 100,000 to 150,000 low-income persons have been sterilized annually under federally funded programs. Virtually all of these people have been adults: only about 2,000 to 3,000 per year have been under 21 years of age and fewer than 300 have been under 18. There are no statistics in the record indicating what percentage of these patients were mentally incompetent.

Although Congress has been insistent that all family planning programs function on a purely voluntary basis, there is uncontroverted evidence in the record that minors and other incompetents have been sterilized with federal funds and that an indefinite number of poor people have been improperly coerced into accepting a sterilization operation under the threat that various federally supported welfare benefits would be withdrawn unless they submitted to irreversible sterilization. Patients receiving Medicaid assistance at childbirth are evidently the most frequent targets of this pressure, as the experiences of plaintiffs Waters and Walker illustrate. Mrs. Waters was actually refused medical assistance by her attending physician unless she submitted to a tubal ligation after the birth. Other examples were documented.

When such deplorable incidents began to receive nationwide public attention due to the experience of the Relf sisters in Alabama, the Secretary took steps to restrict the circumstances under which recipients of federal family planning funds could conduct sterilization operations. On August 3, 1973, the Department published in the Federal Register a notice of Guidelines for Sterilization Procedures under HEW Supported Programs. The notice directed that the policies set forth in the guidelines be implemented through regulations to be issued by the departmental agencies administering programs which provide federal financial assistance for family planning services. Notices of proposed rule making were duly published in the Federal Register on September 21, 1973. Interested persons were given an opportunity to participate in the rule

---

[1]   Congress merely specified that it intended to support the 'full range of family planning services.' H.R.Rep.No.91–1472, 91st Cong., 2d Sess. 10 (1970), U.S.Code Cong. & Admin. News 1970, p. 5068. Only abortion has been specifically excluded. 42 U.S.C. § 300a–6.

making by submitting comments on the proposed regulations. Approximately 300 comments, including those of plaintiff NWRO, were received and reviewed by the Department. The final regulations here under attack were issued on February 6, 1974.

These regulations provide that projects and programs receiving PHS or SRS funds, whether for family planning or purely medical services, shall neither perform nor arrange for the performance of a nontherapeutic sterilization unless certain procedures are carried out. These vary depending upon whether the patient is, under state law, a legally competent adult, a legally competent person under the age of 18, a legally incompetent minor, or a mental incompetent. Briefly, they are as follows:

(1) Legally competent adults must give their 'informed consent' to sterilization. Such consent must be evidenced by a written and signed document indicating, inter alia, that the patient is aware of the benefits and costs of sterilization and of the fact that he may withdraw from the operation without losing federal benefits.

(2) Legally competent persons under the age of 18 must also give such written consent. In these situations, a special Review Committee of independent persons from the community must also have determined that the proposed sterilization is in the best interest of the patient, taking into consideration (a) the expected mental and physical impact of pregnancy and motherhood on the patient, if female, or the expected mental impact of fatherhood, if male, and (b) the expected immediate and long-term mental and physical impact of sterilization on the patient. The Review Committee must also (a) review appropriate medical, social and psychological information concerning the patient, including the age of the patient, alternative family planning methods, and the adequacy of consent, and (b) interview the patient, both parents of the patient (if available), and such other persons as in its judgment will contribute pertinent information. However, parental consent is not required.

(3) Legally incompetent minors must be afforded the above safeguards, and, in addition, a state court of competent jurisdiction must determine that the proposed sterilization is in the best interest of the patient.

(4) The sterilization of mental incompetents of all ages must also be sanctioned by a Review Committee and a court. However, personal consent is not required—it is enough that the patient's 'representative' requests sterilization. Although defendants interpret the term 'representative' to mean a person empowered under state law to consent to the sterilization on

behalf of the patient, no such definition appears in the regulations themselves.

Plaintiffs do not oppose the voluntary sterilization of poor persons under federally funded programs. However, they contend that these regulations are both illegal and arbitrary because they authorize involuntary sterilizations, without statutory or constitutional justification. They argue forcefully that sterilization of minors or mental incompetents is necessarily involuntary in the nature of things. Further, they claim that sterilization of competent adults under these regulations can be undertaken without insuring that the request for sterilization is in actuality voluntary. The Secretary defends the regulations and insists that only "voluntary" sterilization is permitted under their terms.

. . . .

For the reasons developed below, the Court finds that the Secretary has no statutory authority under the family planning sections[6] of the Social Security or Public Health Services Acts to fund the sterilization of any person incompetent under state law to consent to such an operation, whether because of minority or of mental deficiency. It also finds that the challenged regulations are arbitrary and unreasonable in that they fail to implement the congressional command that federal family planning funds not be used to coerce indigent patients into submitting to sterilization. In short, federally assisted family planning sterilizations are permissible only with the voluntary, knowing and uncoerced consent of individuals competent to give such consent. This result requires an injunction against substantial portions of the proposed regulations and their revision to insure that all sterilizations funded under the family planning sections are voluntary in the full sense of that term and that sterilization of incompetent minors and adults is prevented.

The dispute with regard to minors and mental incompetents centers around two aspects of the statutory language. On the one hand, Congress included in every section mentioning family planning a requirement that such services be voluntarily requested. On the other hand, these sections purport to offer family planning services to all poor people and two of them specifically include minors. The Secretary argues that this juxtaposition indicates that Congress intended that minors personally and incompetents through their representatives would be able to consent to sterilization under these sections. That conclusion is unwarranted.

Although the term "voluntary" is nowhere defined in the statutes under consideration, it is frequently encountered in the law. Even its dictionary definition assumes an exercise of free will and clearly precludes the existence of coercion or force. Webster's Second New International Dictionary 2858 (2d ed. 1961). And its use in the statutory

---

[6]   Sterilizations required by bona fide medical necessity could presumably be funded by other HEW programs. *See, e.g.,* note on pp. 1199–1200 supra. The Court need not reach the issue of what safeguards are required under such programs.

and decisional law, at least when important human rights are at stake, entails a requirement that the individual have at his disposal the information necessary to make his decision and the mental competence to appreciate the significance of that information.

No person who is mentally incompetent can meet these standards, nor can the consent of a representative, however sufficient under state law, impute voluntariness to the individual actually undergoing irreversible sterilization. Minors would also appear to lack the knowledge, maturity and judgment to satisfy these standards with regard to such an important issue, whatever may be their competence to rely on devices or medication that temporarily frustrates procreation. This is the reasoning that provides the basis for the nearly universal common law and statutory rule that minors and mental incompetents cannot consent to medical operations, or be held to contractual obligations.[7]

The statutory references to minors and mental incompetents do not contradict this conclusion, for they appear only in the context of family planning services in general. Minors, for example, are not legally incompetent for all purposes, and many girls of child-bearing age are undoubtedly sufficiently aware of the relevant considerations to use temporary contraceptives that intrude far less on fundamental rights. However, the Secretary has not demonstrated and the Court cannot find that Congress deemed such children capable of voluntarily consenting to an irreversible operation involving the basic human right to procreate. Nor can the Court find, in the face of repeated warnings concerning voluntariness, that Congress authorized the imposition of such a serious deprivation upon mental incompetents at the will of an unspecified "representative."

The regulations also fail to provide the procedural safeguards necessary to insure that even competent adults voluntarily request sterilization. Plaintiffs would require an elaborate hearing process prior to the operation to remedy this problem. The Secretary, however, has determined that the consent document procedure set forth in the existing regulations is adequate in most instances to insure a knowledgeable decision, and the Court finds that this determination is not unreasonable. In one respect, however, the consent procedure must be improved. Even a fully informed individual cannot make a 'voluntary' decision concerning sterilization if he has been subjected to coercion from doctors or project officers. Despite specific statutory language forbidding the recipients of federal family planning funds to threaten a cutoff of program benefits unless the individual submits to sterilization and despite clear evidence that such coercion is actually being applied, the challenged regulations

---

[7]   Most of the state sterilization statutes brought to the attention of the Court appear to have been passed for eugenic rather than family planning purposes and make no pretense that the sterilization of minors or mental incompetents can be considered 'voluntary.' *See, e.g.,* Ind.Stat.Ann. §§ 22–1601 to 22–1618 (1964), IC 1971, 16–13–13–1 to 16–13–15–6; Iowa Code Ann. §§ 145.1–145.22 (1972); N.H.Rev.Stat.Ann. §§ 174:1–174:14 (1964).

contain no clear safeguard against this abuse. Although the required consent document must state that the patient can withdraw his consent to sterilization without losing other program benefits, there is nothing to prohibit the use of such coercion to extract the initial consent.

In order to prevent express or implied threats, which would obviate the Secretary's entire framework of procedural safeguards, and to insure compliance with the statutory language, the Court concludes that the regulations must also be amended to require that individuals seeking sterilization be orally informed at the very outset that not federal benefits can be withdrawn because of a failure to accept sterilization. This guarantee must also appear prominently at the top of the consent document already required by the regulations. To permit sterilization without this essential safeguard is an unreasonable and arbitrary interpretation of the congressional mandate.

Since these conclusions are based on statutory rather than constitutional grounds, the Court need not reach the question of whether involuntary sterilization could be funded by Congress. It is sufficient to note that there is no indication whatever that Congress intended to do so under the existing legislation, and such an intent will not be lightly assumed in light of the fundamental interests at stake. The present statutes were passed to facilitate only voluntary family planning and thus to assist the individual in the exercise of his voluntary right to govern his own procreation. Involuntary sterilization is not only distinguishable from these services, but diametrically so. It invades rather than compliments the right to procreate.

This controversy has arisen during a period of rapid change in the field of birth control. In recent years, through the efforts of dedicated proponents of family planning, birth control information and services have become widely available. Aided by the growing acceptance of family planning, medical science has steadily improved and diversified the techniques of birth prevention and control. Advancements in artificial insemination and in the understanding of genetic attributes are also affecting the decision to bear children. There are even suggestions in the scientific literature that the sex of children may soon be subject to parental control. And over this entire area lies the specter of overpopulation, with its possible impact upon the food supply, interpersonal relations, privacy, and the enjoyment of our "inalienable rights."

Surely the Federal Government must move cautiously in this area, under well-defined policies determined by Congress after full consideration of constitutional and far-reaching social implications. The dividing line between family planning and eugenics is murky. And yet the Secretary, through the regulations at issue, seeks to sanction one of the most drastic methods of population control—the involuntary irreversible sterilization of men and women—without any legislative guidance. Whatever might be the merits of limiting irresponsible reproduction, which each year places increasing numbers of unwanted or mentally defective children into tax supported institutions, it is for Congress and not individual social workers and physicians to determine the manner in which federal funds should be used to support such a program. We should not drift into a policy which has unfathomed implications and which permanently deprives unwilling or immature citizens of their ability to procreate without adequate legal safeguards and a legislative determination of the appropriate standards in light of the general welfare and of individual rights.

. . . .

NOTES

1. *The new face of sterilization.* The Relf sisters represented the new incarnation of eugenic sterilization laws. With federal funding from the Office of Economic Opportunity (OEO), the sisters were subjected to a range of family planning actions (injections of then non-FDA-approved Depo Provera and IUDs) because they were poor, black, and living in public housing, where there were boys "hanging around the girls." Lisa Ikemoto, *Infertile by Force and Federal Complicity: The Story of* Relf v. Weinberger, *in* WOMEN AND THE LAW STORIES 179, 187, 192–94 (Elizabeth Schneider & Stephanie Wildman eds., 2011).

2. *The road not taken.* At the time the Relf sisters were sterilized, Dr. Warren Hern was the Chief of the Program Development and Evaluation Branch of the OEO. Hern testified before Congress that in that capacity, he had drafted guidelines to ensure informed consent to voluntary sterilization, and had requested that the OEO not authorize sterilizations until the guidelines had been approved. "We felt that there were possibilities that people who were not adequately informed, or able to consent for themselves, . . . would perhaps be vulnerable to a procedure which would render them sterile, and in which they were unable to really protect themselves against this kind of thing." *Quality of Health Care-Human Experimentation: Hearings on S. 2071, S. 2072, and H.R. 7724 Before the Subcomm. on Health of the Comm. on Labor & Pub. Welfare,* 93d Cong. 1511 (1973) (statement of Dr. Warren Hern, former chief, Program Development & Evaluation Branch, Family Planning Division, Office of Economic Opportunity). Regrettably, this request was not followed, and Hern was told that the guidelines would not be implemented until after the 1972 election. *Id.* at 1510. When the guidelines were further delayed, Hern resigned his position in protest. *Id.* at 1513.

3. *Race, abortion rights, and sterilization.* A National Fertility Study in 1970 noted that twenty percent of all married black women, and about the same percent of Chicana women, had been sterilized. In Puerto Rico, over thirty-five percent of women of childbearing age had been sterilized by 1970. *See* ANGELA DAVIS, WOMEN, RACE, AND CLASS 219 (1981); *see generally* CHARLES F. WESTOFF & NORMAN B. RYDER, THE CONTRACEPTIVE REVOLUTION (1977) (discussing the results of the National Fertility Study in 1970). The stories of the Relf sisters, and of Warren Hern's resignation, make

clear that sterilization abuses in government-funded health care were common—abuses that white feminist groups largely ignored as they focused their attention on securing abortion rights in the 1970s. DAVIS, *supra* at 221.

4.   *Consent and coercion.* It is not clear that *all* sterilized women were the victims of coercion. As we have seen, until widespread federal funding of contraception, women of color were more likely to report excess fertility than were white women. Women with excess fertility (i.e. women with children who felt that their families were already complete) may have found sterilization particularly attractive as a means of controlling fertility. Given Professor Angela Davis's all-too-warranted warning about the coercive dangers of sterilization, how should policy ensure that women of all races and classes experience sterilization as a choice, rather than as the product of explicit and implicit coercion?

5.   *Sterilization of Native-American women.* At the request of Native-American women, Senator James Abourezk of South Dakota asked the Government Accounting Office (GAO) to investigate stories of coerced or deceptive sterilizations by the Indian Health Service (IHS). The GAO did so, and released its Report in November of 1976. In many ways, the Report was shockingly incomplete. It covered only four of twelve IHS program areas, and did not interview Native women. In addition, obstetrical and gynecological services contracted out to other providers—an IHS common practice—were not investigated. Despite these omissions, the GAO Report documented several troubling occurrences, including several instances of the sterilization of minors, sterilizations undertaken the day the woman had given birth, consent forms signed the day *after* the sterilization had taken place, and noncompliance with the mandated 72-hour waiting period for sterilization procedures. *See* Jane Lawrence, *The Indian Health Service and the Sterilization of Native American Women*, 24 AM. INDIAN Q. 400, 406–09 (2000). The case of Native-American women reveals one of the reasons that government policies fall hardest on certain populations: those who rely on government for the provision of services are uniquely vulnerable to coercion, both because of their frequent interaction with government actors, and the complicating factor of their dependence on the government.

Elena Gutiérrez, Fertile Matters: The Politics of Mexican-Origin Women's Reproduction
36–37 (2008).

The Advent of Surgical Sterilization

Academics and others typically define sterilization abuse as "the misinformed, coerced, or unknowing termination of the reproductive capacity of women and men." The long and well-researched history of sterilization abuse in the United States has demonstrated that practitioners of coercive sterilization have targeted their subjects according to race, class, and gender. As historian Adelaida Del Castillo has noted, sterilization abuse of Mexican-origin peoples for eugenic reasons had occurred previously. Before sterilization was widely available, individual judges would make parole and other conditions of probation dependent upon sterilization. In 1966, for example, Nancy Hernandez was sentenced to jail when she refused to agree to be sterilized for a misdemeanor conviction.

During the 1970s, several circumstances directly precipitated sterilization abuse nationwide. For one thing, medical regulations governing sterilization options for most women had become less restrictive. Earlier sterilization was guided by an age-parity formula, whereby a doctor would only sterilize a woman if her age multiplied by the number of her children exceeded 120. . . . The liberalization of medical guidelines for sterilization was coupled with increased availability of funding . . . most notably through passage of the Family Planning Services and Population Research Act in 1970. While in 1965 only $5 million of federal money was available for family planning services for the poor, in 1979 the government distributed $260 million for this purpose. . . .

Madrigal v. Quilligan
No. CV 75–2057–JWC (C.D. Cal. 1978).

■ CURTIS, J.

This is a civil rights action brought pursuant to Title 42, U.S.C. § 1983, by ten Mexican women claiming violations of their constitutional rights. Specifically, they charge that they were surgically sterilized at the USC-Los Angeles County General Medical Center, allegedly without their voluntary and informed consent.

. . . .

The rather subtle but underlying thrust of plaintiffs' complaint appears to be that they were all victims of a concerted plan by hospital attendants and doctors to push them, as members of a low socio-economic group who tend to ward large families, to consent to sterilization in order to accomplish some sinister, invidious, social purpose. A careful search of the record fails to produce any evidence whatever to support this contention. It did appear that the hospital had received funds for the establishment of a family planning program, and that discussion and encouragement of alternative methods of birth control, including sterilization, were carried on in the outpatient prenatal care clinic. In the obstetrics ward, however, whenever a sterilization procedure was suggested or advised, it was done on the initiative of the individual employee. There was no hospital rule or instruction directed to these employees relative to the encouragement of patients to be sterilized and there was no evidence of concerted or conspiratorial action.

Consequently, this case in its present posture consists of ten separate and distinct claims against the individual doctors who actually performed the sterilization, and the liability of each must be determined by his own conduct.

. . . .

[In the context of an informed consent to sterilization case] in order for the defendant physician to be liable the absence of free and informed consent must be intelligibly communicated to the doctor. If he "negligently interpreted plaintiff's communications to indicate she consented to the operation, he is not liable under the standards enunciated in *Wood*, even if plaintiff did not intend to consent."

Liability, in this context, is predicated upon some conduct which is either malicious or is in wanton disregard of constitutional rights. There would be liability

> . . . if . . . [the doctor] determined that sterilization of the plaintiff was for her own good or the good of society and as a consequence of that belief ignored indications from the plaintiff that she did not consent to the operation, or if . . . he attempted to take advantage of her mental and communication limitations to unduly influence her decisions. . . .

With these legal principles in mind we turn to a consideration of the facts.

This case is essentially the result of a breakdown in communication between the patients and the doctors. All plaintiffs are Spanish speaking women whose ability to understand and speak English is limited. This fact is generally understood by the staff at the Medical Center and most members have acquired enough familiarity with the language to get by. There is also an interpreter available whose services are used when thought to be necessary. But even with these precautions misunderstandings are bound to occur.

Furthermore, the cultural background of these particular women has contributed to the problem in a subtle but very significant way. According to the plaintiffs' anthropological expert, they are members of a traditional Mexican rural subculture, a relatively narrow spectrum of Mexican people living in this country whose lifestyle and cultural background derives from the lifestyle and culture of small rural communities in Mexico. He further testified that a cultural trait which is very important with this group is an extreme dependence upon family. Most come from large families and wish to have large families for their own comfort and support. Furthermore, the status of a women and her husband within that group depends largely upon the woman's ability to produce children. If for any reason she cannot, she is considered an incomplete woman and is apt to suffer a disruption of her relationship with her family and husband. When faced with a decision of whether or not to be sterilized, the decision process is a much more traumatic event with her than it would be with a typical patient and consequently, she would require greater explanation, more patient advice, and greater care in interpreting her consent than persons not members of such a subculture would require.

But this need for such delicate treatment is not readily apparent. The anthropological expert testified that he would not have known that these women possessed these traits had he not conducted tests and a study which required some 450 hours of time. He further stated that a determination by him based upon any less time would not have been worth "beans." It is not surprising therefore that the staff of a busy metropolitan hospital which has neither the time nor the staff to make such esoteric studies would be unaware of these atypical cultural traits.

It is against this backdrop therefore that we must analyze the conduct of the doctors who treated the plaintiffs in this case.

Since these operations occurred between 1971 and 1974, and were performed by the doctors operating in a busy obstetrics ward, it is not surprising that none of the doctors have any independent recollection of the events leading up to the operations. They all testified, however, that it was their custom and practice not to suggest a sterilization procedure unless a patient asked for it or there were medical complications which would require the doctor, in the exercise of prudent medical procedures, to make such suggestion. They further testified that it was their practice when a patient requested sterilization to explain its irreversible result and they stated that they would not perform the operation unless they were certain in their own mind that the patient understood the nature of the operation and was requesting the procedure. The weight to be given to such testimony and the inferences to be drawn therefrom will be determined in the light of all the testimony relating to each doctor's conduct.

. . . .

DOLORES MADRIGAL

The plaintiff Madrigal was born in a small town in Mexico and attended school there through the sixth grade. She does not read or speak English fluently. She had two children and after the birth of her second child she underwent a tubal ligation performed by Dr. Rutland. The medical file contains an early note that Mrs. Madrigal has suffered from a placenta previa during her first pregnancy and rom toxemia during her second. During labor, and having indicated that she did not wish a tubal ligation, her husband was called to the hospital. She overheard an interpreter telling him that because of the complications she might die in the event of future pregnancy. She was then told that her husband had agreed to the operation and she was again presented with a consent form which she signed, inserting in her own handwriting therein a statement that she understood she was not going to have any more children. She complains that some pressure was put upon her to sign the consent, although Nurse Lang, who witnessed the signature, testified that she would not have witnessed a consent for sterilization if the patient had not verified her understanding of the nature of the operation and its consequences. In any event, there is no evidence that Dr. Rutland, who performed the operation, had any part in overzealous solicitation for the sterilization, even if it had occurred. Dr. Rutland, on the other hand, testified that he speaks some Spanish and in accordance with his custom and practice would have explained the nature of the procedure, its permanency and its risks through an interpreter. In any event, he had before him the medical file which indicated an earlier desire on the part of the plaintiff for a tubal ligation and her written consent with the insertion of her own handwriting that she understood that the operation would prevent her from having children ever again.

I find that under the circumstances Dr. Rutland performed the operation in the bona fide belief that Mrs. Madrigal had given her informed and voluntary consent, and that his belief was reasonable.

MARIA HURTADO

Mrs. Hurtado is a forty-two year old Mexican-American born in Mexico and has a sixth grade education. She has five living children and gave birth to three more who were born dead. She has had three cesarean sections and was given a tubal ligation by Dr. Neuman after the birth of her last child. Mrs. Hurtado contends that she was never informed about the nature and effect of the tubal ligation and nothing was ever said about it until she was in labor. She further states that the consent forms were brought to her during labor and she was not aware that she was signing a consent for tubal ligation. Although Mrs. Hurtado denies it, the hospital records indicate that she had made a request to the intern in the clinic some time before that she desired a tubal ligation. A similar note appeared in the medical record made by another doctor during another one of Mrs. Hurtado's clinical visits. At the time of her admission, she was examined by still another doctor to whom she again indicated her desire to have no more children. Consequently, consent forms were prepared and were signed by her before she had had any medication and before she was in active labor. Dr. Neuman, who performed the operation, testified that it was his custom and practice to always ask a patient who had indicated that she wanted a tubal libation to again express her consent. In the light of the contrary evidence, Mrs. Hurtado's statement that she did not remember signing the consent for tubal libation and had not been informed of its nature and results is simply not credible.

I find therefore that the evidence is insufficient to rebut the inferences drawn from the record, and that in any event Dr. Neuman was acting in a bona fide belief that Mrs. Hurtado had consented to the operation and that such belief was reasonable.

JOVITA RIVERA

This plaintiff was born in Mexicali, Mexico, in 1946 and came to the United States to live in 1968. She neither speaks nor understands the English language well. There have been five children of the marriage, one of whom was born dead. Mrs. Rivera obtained prenatal care at the Medical Center. At the time of her admission to the hospital she told the admitting doctor that she wanted her tubes tied. She had previously agreed with her husband that she would have her tubes tied after the fourth child. She understood, however, from her sister-in-law that this operation was reversible and that, at a later date if she decided she wanted more children, she could have tubes untied. She did not tell anyone at the hospital of this belief. While in labor, an emergency situation arose in which it became apparent that Mrs. Rivera could not deliver normally and a cesarean section was necessary within the next ten minutes in order to save the baby's life. Because of the emergency, a resident physician was called in to perform the operation. He again asked the plaintiff if she intended to have her tubes tied and she answered in the affirmative. Because of the emergency nature of the matter, no written consent was obtained from the plaintiff, but as a part of the cesarean section a tubal ligation was performed.

The doctor testified that it was not his practice to ask a patient about a sterilization procedure unless it was suggested by the patient herself or unless some medical reason for doing so arose. After it was determined a cesarean section would have to be performed on Mrs. Rivera, and seeing the note in the hospital record indicating that she had previously asked to have her tubes tied, he again mentioned it to her and got an affirmative answer. The doctor further testified that he would never have performed a tubal ligation had he not fully believed that the plaintiff specifically asked for it.

From these facts, I conclude that the doctor was acting in good faith believing that he had an unequivocal consent and that such belief was reasonable under the circumstances.

MARIA FIGUEROA

Mrs. Figueroa is a thirty-one year old Mexican woman, the mother of three children, all of whom were delivered by cesarean section. At the time of the birth of the first child both Mrs. Figueroa and her husband had executed a consent form for a possible emergency tubal ligation or hysterectomy prior to the delivery of the child by cesarean section. However, this was not necessary and no such operation was performed. At the time of the birth of her last child, Dr. Kreitzer attempted a low transverse cesarean section which he was compelled to abandon in favor of a classical cesarean section when he encountered dense adhesions affecting the uterus and bladder rendering it impossible to mobilize the bladder. The excessive scarring and adhesions and the additional incisions significantly increased the risk in the event of subsequent pregnancy, including uterine rupture. At the time of her most recent pregnancy, multiple adhesions between the interior abdominal wall omentum and uterus were also noted and the lower uterine segment was described as very thin. Since Mrs. Figueroa was already in surgery when these conditions were revealed, her husband was called and the increased risks were discussed with him. He consented to the tubal ligation for his wife and signed a consent for sterilization form and Dr. Kreitzer and senior resident William E. Merritt executed a physician's certificate of emergency certifying that the delay necessary to obtain complete consent for treatment would endanger the patient's life or change of recovery. Mrs. Figueroa now believes that the operation was unnecessary.

I find that Dr. Dreitzer [sic] performed the operation in the bona fide belief that Mrs. Figueroa would have consented had she been able, since she had done so once before when a cesarean procedure seemed imminent. This belief was further supported by the written consent form signed by the husband after the risks had been explained to him. Such a belief I find to be reasonable.

HELENA OROZCO

Helena Orozco was born in Forth [sic] Worth, Texas, and speaks both English and Spanish. She has had four children by a previous marriage and two by her present marriage. She has, in addition, one adopted daughter. She received her prenatal care at the Medical Center and was, on many occasions, advised by personnel that she should have her tubes tied so that she would not have any more children because she already had "too many cesarean sections." Her condition was further complicated by a ruptured hernia which someone attending her indicated would be a serious problem in the event of another pregnancy. She at first indicated that she did not want a tubal ligation but did consent to the cesarean. At a later time, however, she did sign her written consent because, she says, of the insistence of some member of the staff. The defendant Robert Yee performed the cesarean section, bilateral tubal ligation, and umbilical hernia repair, in reliance upon the written consent found in the file. There is no evidence which indicates that Dr. Yee was present or participated in obtaining the written consent, nor that he was aware that the plaintiff was in any way unwilling to have the operation. In fact, he testified that he would not have performed the sterilization procedures if he had any reason whatever to doubt the validity of the written consent.

I conclude therefore as to this defendant, Dr. Yee, that he was acting in the bona fide belief that he had the plaintiff's consent and that this belief was reasonable.

GEORGIA HERNANDEZ

Mrs. Hernandez is a thirty-eight year old Mexican-American woman who understands some English and who had no prenatal care at the medical Center. She first came to the hospital with complications as she was already bleeding and experiencing labor pains. As she progressed it became apparent that a cesarean section was necessary at which time the doctor asked her about having her tubes tied. He told her the Mexican people were very poor and that she should not have any more children because she could not support them. She does not remember signing any consent form although there is one in the file. Plaintiff contends that her handwriting on this consent form shows indications of medication and traumatic shock, especially so when compared with other signatures of hers appearing in the file. The handwriting expert believed this signature was written under abnormal conditions. He testified that this could have been caused in one of several ways. One of these possibilities was that she was in severe labor pains and another possibility, which seems to me to be more credible, was that the consent was signed while she was lying in her hospital bed. In any event, there was nothing about this signature which would suggest to the surgeon that her consent was equivocal. The doctor testified that Mrs. Hernandez had been offered a sterilization operation at the time of her admission but had refused. As the time for delivery arrived and it became apparent that a cesarean section would be required, he again discussed the sterilization process with Mrs. Hernandez, at which time she signed the consent for cesarean but was not yet willing to consent to the sterilization. Shortly before she was going in to the operating room, she indicated the decision to have the operation and this was noted in the file. The doctor denied that at any time he had made the statement that she should not have any more children because the Mexican people were too poor to support them. He also states that such a remark is entirely out of character and that he was certain he did not make it. He further stated that the consent was obtained before any anesthetic was applied and before she had been given any medication which would affect her ability to make a decision. He said that it was his custom and practice never to perform such an operation without a clear, voluntary consent by the patient, and that he would not have performed such an operation on this occasion had he not believed that she had voluntarily consented to it.

I find therefore that in performing a tubal ligation upon this plaintiff, Dr. Mutch was acting in the bona fide belief that he had the voluntary and knowing consent of the plaintiff, and that such a belief was reasonable.

CONSUELO HERMOSILLO

This plaintiff was born in 1949 in Vera Cruz, Mexico, where she was educated through the eighth grade. She had three children, all born by cesarean section. It was at the birth of her third child that a tubal ligation was performed. She had received prenatal care at a County clinic where she was informed that it was advisable, after her third cesarean, to have a sterilization operation because of the risk of serious complications in further pregnancies. She testified that she did not want to give up having more children and that because of this advice given her at the clinic often came home crying. She then discussed the matter with her sister-in-law who told her that she had had her tubes tied and that she thought she could later have them untied. Such a belief was never mentioned to anyone at the hospital. In the early stages of labor it appeared that Mrs. Hermosillo might be able to deliver normally but as the delivery progressed it became apparent that a cesarean section would be necessary, at which time she apparently signed a consent form for tubal ligation. Neither she nor the doctors have any specific recollection of what occurred at the time the consent was actually signed. The form, however, did contain a statement in her own handwriting in Spanish to the effect that she understood the nature of the operation. Both Dr. Muth, who performed the tubal ligation, and the senior resident physician, Allen Luckman, M.D., who assisted in the surgery, both testified that they would not have performed the sterilization process had they not believed that Mrs. Hermosillo had given a free and voluntary consent as indicated by the written form in the hospital record. The evidence amply supports the inference that Mrs. Hermosillo was thoroughly acquainted with the nature of the operation, except possibly for the undisclosed belief that despite what doctors told her she could have her tubes untied.

I conclude therefore that Mrs. Hermosillo was fully aware of the nature and effect of the tubal ligation although she had hoped for a normal delivery in which event such an operation would not have been done. But when it became apparent that cesarean section was necessary she changed her mind and voluntarily consented and, in doing so, signed a consent form upon which the surgeon relied. I find that Dr. Muth performed the tubal ligation in the bona fide belief that Mrs. Hermosillo had consented and that his belief was reasonable under the circumstances.

ESTELLA BENAVIDES

This plaintiff was born in 1942 in the State of Michoacan, Mexico. She does not either speak or read English and has only a sixth grade education in Mexican schools. She and her husband have three children, the first two of which were born normally. When her third child was expected she developed complications which started with profuse bleeding and she eventually asked to be delivered by cesarean section. She was asked by the doctors if she wanted a tubal ligation in view of the potential high risk of future cesarean deliveries. She first refused, but after some persuasion she signed a written consent for she was fearful that if she should become pregnant again she might die and her children would be left alone with no one to care for them. In her written consent she wrote in Spanish in her own handwriting the phrase, "I understand that I will not have any more children after this operation."

I find that the plaintiff was well aware of the nature and effect of the tubal ligation, and the consent form was signed by her after weighing all considerations. I further conclude that the doctor performing the tubal ligation did so in the bona fide belief that the plaintiff had given her free and knowing consent and that this belief was reasonable.

. . . .

The plaintiffs have placed great reliance upon a New York psychiatrist who stated unequivocally that it would be impossible for a woman in labor, after suffering her first pain, to give an intelligent and knowing consent to a sterilization operation. Such a statement completely defies common sense. I prefer as more credible the testimony of the other doctors to the effect that whether a consent represented an informed and voluntary decision depended upon many facts, that a judgment could best be made by someone present at the moment the decision is made. One doctor testified that the fact that a woman was in labor might or might not affect her decision, depending upon the circumstances. There was further evidence that the attending physician was probably in the best position to make a judgment since he would be acutely aware of the necessity of having the patient's consent.

. . . .

This case has not been an easy one to try for it has involved social, emotional, and cultural considerations of great complexity. There is no doubt but that these women have suffered severe emotional and physical stress because of these operations. One can sympathize with them for their inability to communicate clearly, but one can hardly blame the doctors for relying on these indicia of consent which appeared to be unequivocal on their face and which are in constant use in the Medical Center.

Let judgment be entered for the defendants.

NOTES

1.   *The missing* Madrigal. Despite the importance of the issues in *Madrigal v. Quilligan*, access to the decision is limited. As an unpublished opinion, it does not show up in legal databases or in hard copy in most law libraries. Note that the excerpt in this casebook is itself an edited version of the court's decision excerpted in DOROTHY A. BROWN, CRITICAL RACE THEORY: CASES, MATERIALS, AND PROBLEMS 102–11 (2003). While this is not unique to *Madrigal*, why might the court have declined to publish its opinion in this case?

2.   *Communication breakdown?* The *Madrigal* court concludes that the case is "essentially the result of a breakdown in communication between the patients and the doctors." Does this assessment appropriately characterize the dynamic that existed between the *Madrigal* plaintiffs and their doctors? What factors might have contributed to the perceived communication breakdown?

3.   *The physician-patient relationship.* Is the physician-patient relationship depicted in *Madrigal* consistent with other reproductive rights cases, where the courts imagine women exercising their reproductive freedom in close consultation with their doctors? Is there a power differential that exists between the *Madrigal* plaintiffs and their doctors?

4.   *Notes from the trial.* Dr. Carlos G. Vélez-Ibáñez, an anthropologist, served as an expert witness in the *Madrigal* case. He described the trial judge, Jesse William Curtis, Jr., as "a white-haired 70-year old" who "seemed like the stereotype of the paternalistic figure." Carlos G. Vélez-Ibáñez, *The Nonconsenting Sterilization of Mexican Women in Los Angeles, in* TWICE A

MINORITY: MEXICAN AMERICAN WOMEN 235, 243–44 (Margarita B. Melville ed., 1980). According to Vélez-Ibáñez, Judge Curtis was a "conservative judge who lived aboard his yacht in Newport Beach, one of the most prestigious areas in Southern California." *Id.* at 244. By contrast, the plaintiffs were low-income Chicanas with limited English proficiency. The lawyers in the case also spanned the spectrum of race and class. The plaintiffs' two lawyers were a Chicano man and woman "from the local poverty legal centers." *Id.* at 243. The defendants were represented by two white lawyers "from one of the more prestigious Beverly Hill[s] law firms." *Id.* According to Vélez-Ibáñez, the defendants' lawyers "seemed quite relaxed . . . in the courtroom." *Id.*

5.   *Sterilization and race-based eugenics.* As Professor Maya Maniana explains, *Madrigal* is part of a longer history of compulsory and deceptive sterilization practices targeted toward disfavored groups in the United States. *See* Maya Manian, *Coerced Sterilization of Mexican-American Women: The Story of* Madrigal v. Quilligan, *in* REPRODUCTIVE RIGHTS AND JUSTICE STORIES (Melissa Murray, Katherine Shaw, Reva B. Siegel eds., 2019). In 1970, a national study found that roughly twenty percent of all married black women had been sterilized, and that a similar percentage of all Chicana women had been sterilized as well. *Id.* The litigation in *Madrigal* is emblematic of decades of eugenic sterilization abuse towards Mexican-American women that dates back to the 1900s, and still persists today. *Id.* In 2013, an investigation of California prisons found that nearly one hundred and fifty inmates, mostly low-income women and women of color, were improperly sterilized. The prison physician defended the sterilization policy based on reduced welfare costs for "unwanted" children. *Id.*

6.   *Race, class, and gender.* Some scholars have criticized the reproductive rights movement as being unduly focused on access to abortion—a right, they argue, that is more likely to be exercised by women with means. By focusing on abortion, critics contend, the reproductive rights movement has subordinated—and indeed, ignored—the reproductive rights issues that most affect poor women, minorities, lesbians, and transgender women. As Professor Maya Manian argues, *Madrigal* highlights this tension between white feminists who generally opposed restrictions on abortion, sterilization, and contraception, with women of color, particularly Chicana feminist activists, who raised concerns about how those reproductive tools were being used abusively. *See* Maya Manian, *Coerced Sterilization of Mexican-American Women: The Story of* Madrigal v. Quilligan, *in* REPRODUCTIVE RIGHTS AND JUSTICE STORIES (Melissa Murray, Katherine Shaw, Reva B. Siegel eds., 2019). Do you agree with this characterization?

7.   Madrigal *2.0?* In September 2020, a consortium of advocacy groups filed a complaint with the Inspector General of the Department of Homeland Security, condemning the treatment of Immigration and Customs Enforcement (ICE) detainees at the Irwin County Detention Center (ICDC) in Georgia. According to the complaint, one of the facility's nurses, Dawn Wooten, had raised concerns "regarding the rate at which hysterectomies are performed on immigrant women under ICE custody at ICDC." Complaint, https://projectsouth.org/wp-content/uploads/2020/09/OIG-ICDC-Complaint-1.pdf (Sept. 14, 2021). According to Wooten, "a lot of women [at ICDC] go

through a hysterectomy." *Id.* at 18. Although Wooten acknowledged that some conditions might be severe enough to warrant a hysterectomy or tubal ligation, the sheer number of women who were sterilized at ICDC was alarming—"everybody's uterus cannot be that bad." *Id.* at 19. And critically, it was not simply the high rates of hysterectomies that concerned Wooten; it was also that basic protocols around informed consent were not being followed. As Wooten explained, "These immigrant women, I don't think they really, totally, all the way understand [sterilization] is what's going to happen depending on who explains it to them." *Id.* At least initially, there was significant media coverage of the alleged ICE sterilizations. However, the news cycle soon shifted to focus on another event of public significance: the September 18, 2020 death of Justice Ruth Bader Ginsburg.

* * *

Madrigal makes clear that the cultural emphasis on abortion as exhaustive of "reproductive rights" is a troubling development. In the following selections, feminists offer a critique of the emphasis on abortion rights and issue a clarion call for a more expansive understanding of reproductive rights. In what ways do their words comport with—or depart from—your understanding of reproductive justice?

Rosalyn Baxandall and Linda Gordon, *Foreword, in* Dear Sisters: Dispatches from the Women's Liberation Movement

150 (Rosalyn Baxandall & Linda Gordon eds. 2000).

The women's liberation movement popularized the concept of reproductive rights. This slogan contained a critique of the narrow focus on abortion legalization . . . An expanded reproductive rights campaign asserted women's right to bear children in safe and healthy circumstances as well as to choose not to give birth. The movement saw day care and child welfare as equal in importance to birth control. The movement was particularly infuriated by the Hyde Amendments to annual federal government appropriations bills . . . which banned the use of Medicaid funds for abortion except in cases of extreme danger to life; as a result Medicaid could be used to pay for sterilization but not for contraception or abortion.

The new reproductive rights organizations, such as the Committee for Abortion Rights and Against Sterilization Abuse (CARASA), also criticized the population-control establishment for its attempts to use birth control not to strengthen women's autonomy but against overpopulation, which it conceived as the root of poverty. Feminists countered that the causality went the other way—people adopted birth control as they became more prosperous and as women gained autonomy—and criticized the population controllers for not prioritizing women's choice. Two decades later, the most influential population control foundations have been convinced that the best route to lowering population is strengthening women's economic well-being, education, and political rights.

In defending women's rights to have children and be able to provide for them, the reproductive rights movement also attacked the widespread practice of coercive sterilization that continued in the 1970s. CARASA investigated and documented thousands of cases of forced sterilization, especially directed at people of color; welfare recipients were threatened with cut-offs or stipends unless they submitted to sterilization, and women were asked to sign sterilization consent forms while in labor, either in pain or partly anaesthetized. In 1974, responding to the women's movement pressure, the U.S. Department of Health, Education, and Welfare issued guidelines that required informed consent and prohibited sterilization of women under 21. Although it took over a decade to bring most hospitals into compliance with these guidelines, the campaign eventually reduced sterilization abuse considerably, another victory of the women's liberation movement. . . .

Joan Kelly, *Sterilization: Rights and Abuse of Rights, in* Dear Sisters: Dispatches From the Women's Liberation Movement

150–53 (Rosalyn Baxandall & Linda Gordon eds. 2000).

Sterilization is the fastest growing form of birth control. And sterilization-abuse is emerging as the single greatest threat to reproductive freedom. "Forced sterilization" is an ugly phrase. It recalls the race eugenics of the 1930s. . . . [B]ut today it refers to numbers of women—poor, mostly Black, Latin, and Native American—whose control over their own bodies is being legally and surgically terminated by white, middle-class men in the name of the society and government of the United States.

. . . .

. . . [A] report issued recently by the General Accounting Office (GAO) [shows that] [i]n four Indian Health Services Hospitals alone, 3,406 sterilizations were performed between 1973 and 1976. Since Native Americans constitute only half of one percent of the national population, we can understand how facts such as these, and a sterilization rate said to range anywhere from 14 to 25%, revive the spectre of genocide. One study of New York City hospitals in 1973 showed that the proportion of Spanish-speaking women sterilized was almost three times that of the proportion of Black women and almost six times as great as the proportion of white women . . .

. . . .

Several surveys of doctors' attitudes show that an alarmingly high percentage favor compulsory sterilization of welfare mothers. Behind the doctors and the agencies, and certainly behind public agencies such as the Indian Health Service, stand the laws, programs, and policies of the U.S. government. They ultimately will determine this country's course with respect to sterilization and sterilization-abuse. But they are, or should be, subject to our guidance, and they are beginning to attract it.

NOTES

1. *Feminism and sterilization.* The previous dispatches from the women's movement posit sterilization as a critical issue for the women's movement and feminists. If this is the case, why do some, like Professor Angela Davis, criticize the women's movement and feminism as being inattentive to these issues? *See* ANGELA DAVIS, WOMEN, RACE, AND CLASS (1981). To what extent did the women's movement focus on abortion rights minimize these other reproductive rights and justice issues?

2. *Race, class, and gender.* Some scholars have criticized the reproductive rights movement as being unduly focused on access to abortion—a right, they argue, that is often exercised by women with means. By focusing on abortion, they contend, the reproductive rights movement has subordinated—and indeed, ignored—the reproductive rights issues that most affect poor women, minorities, lesbians, and transgender women. Do you agree with this characterization?

* * *

Given the history presented in the previous readings, it is wise to be skeptical of policies that present themselves as being "in the best interests" of others. As we have seen, it is all too easy to view less advantaged people as either not worthy of or interested in having children, rather than investigating the social conditions which make parenthood problematic. Some of the most vexing issues in this domain remain those surrounding reproductive choices—particularly the choice to give up one's reproductive capacity—by people whose ability to consent is limited in some way, particularly people with disabilities and people facing incarceration.

In re Guardianship of Moe

960 N.E.2d 350 (Mass. App. Ct. 2012).

■ GRAINGER, J.

Mary Moe appeals from an order by a judge of the Probate and Family Court Department appointing her parents as guardians for the purpose of consenting to the extraordinary procedures of abortion and sterilization. . . .

The facts are undisputed. Moe, thirty-two years old, is mentally ill, suffering from schizophrenia or schizoaffective disorder and bipolar mood disorder. Moe is pregnant. . . . She has been pregnant twice before. On the first occasion she had an abortion, and on the second she gave birth to a boy who is in the custody of her parents. At some point in the time period between her abortion and the birth of her son, Moe suffered a psychotic break, and has been hospitalized numerous times for mental illness.

The Department of Mental Health (department) filed a petition seeking to have Moe's parents appointed as temporary guardians for purposes of consenting to an abortion. A probate judge appointed counsel for Moe and conducted a hearing at which Moe, her court-appointed attorney, and counsel for the department were present. At the hearing Moe was asked about an abortion and replied that she "wouldn't do that." Moe also asserted that she was not pregnant and that she had met the judge before, although according to the judge, she and Moe had never met. Moe also erroneously stated that she had previously given birth to a baby girl named Nancy.

Based on "several and substantial delusional beliefs," the judge found Moe incompetent to make a decision about an abortion. The judge appointed a guardian ad litem (GAL) to investigate the issue of substituted judgment, and to submit a written report. . . .

The GAL submitted a report noting the following. In October of 2011, Moe visited a hospital emergency room, where a test found that she was two to three months pregnant. A consultation was ordered to determine the effect on the fetus of the medication used to treat Moe's mental illness. The consulting physician determined that the risk of stopping that medication while Moe was pregnant was higher than simply continuing the medication.

The GAL report and the record generally provide additional background. The defendant suffered a psychotic break when she was a college student. Thereafter, she believed people were staring at her and stating that she killed her baby. She becomes agitated and emotional when discussing the pregnancy that ended in an abortion. Consistent with denying that she is now pregnant, she refuses obstetrical care and testing.

Moe also states that she is "very Catholic," does not believe in abortion, and would never have an abortion. Her parents, however, have stated that she is not an "active" Catholic. Moe's parents believe that it is in the best interests of their daughter to terminate her pregnancy. After investigating these facts and Moe's desires, the GAL concluded on a substituted judgment analysis that Moe would decide against an abortion if she were competent.

Without conducting a hearing, the judge concluded to the contrary, notwithstanding Moe's expressed preferences and the recommendations of the GAL. Specifically, the judge "[credited] the facts as reported by the GAL," but found them "inconclusive." The judge reasoned instead that if Moe were competent, she "would not choose to be delusional," and therefore would opt for an abortion in order to benefit from medication that otherwise could not be administered due to its effect on the fetus. The judge ordered that Moe's parents be appointed as coguardians and that Moe could be "coaxed, bribed, or even enticed . . . by ruse" into a hospital where she would be sedated and an abortion performed.

Additionally, *sua sponte*, and without notice, the judge directed that any medical facility that performed the abortion also sterilize Moe at the same time "to avoid this painful situation from recurring in the future."

. . . .

"[T]he personal decision whether to bear or beget a child is a right so fundamental that it must be extended to all persons, including those who are incompetent." *Matter of Mary Moe*, 579 N.E.2d 682, 685 (Mass. App. Ct. 1991). Because of the fundamental nature of this right, in deciding whether a guardian may consent to an abortion or sterilization on behalf of the incapacitated person, we apply the doctrine of substituted judgment.

Because sterilization is the deprivation of the right to procreate, it is axiomatic that an incompetent person must be given adequate notice of the proceedings, an opportunity to be heard in the trial court on the issue of the ability to give informed consent, a determination on the issue of substituted judgment if no such ability is found, and the right to appeal. "[P]ersonal rights implicated in . . . petitions for sterilization require the judge to exercise the *utmost care.* . . . The judge must enter detailed written findings indicating those persuasive factors that determine the outcome" (Emphasis added.) In ordering sterilization *sua sponte* and without notice, the probate judge failed to provide the basic due process that is constitutionally required under the Fourteenth Amendment to the United States Constitution. We reverse the order directing Moe's sterilization.

. . . The judge relied on several undisputed facts to determine that Moe was incompetent to decide whether to abort the fetus. Our examination of the record reveals only one finding that provides evidentiary support for the judge's determination. Specifically, the fact that Moe denied her pregnancy entitled the judge to infer an inability to confront the issue in a realistic manner. The other facts on which the judge relied—that Moe believed she had a daughter or that she had previously met the judge—do not support a determination of incompetency on the issue whether to terminate her current pregnancy. "A person may be adjudicated legally incompetent to make some decisions but competent to make other decisions." *Matter of Moe*, 423 N.E.2d 712, 720 (Mass. 1982). While the judge's finding that Moe does not have the capacity to decide whether to have an abortion is not necessarily one we might have made as a trier of fact, it has support in the record.

Assuming that Moe is incompetent to decide whether to terminate her pregnancy, the substituted judgment standard applies. . . . "In utilizing the doctrine [of substituted judgment,] the court does not decide what is necessarily the best decision but rather what decision would be made by the incompetent person if he or she were competent. 'In short if an individual would, if competent, make an unwise or foolish decision, the judge must respect that decision,' " assuming the judge were required to respect the same decision by a competent person.

In this context the law requires an evidentiary hearing or, failing that, a finding that "extraordinary circumstances [exist] requiring the absence of the incapacitated person." The judge's findings may, however, be based exclusively on "affidavits and other documentary evidence" if the judge makes an additional finding, based on representation of counsel, that there are no contested issues of fact. The order here, issued without a hearing and without any findings to support the failure to conduct a hearing, did not comply with the conditions for its issuance established by law.

We note as well that Moe's "actual preference 'is an important part of the substituted judgment determination.' " *Matter of Mary Moe*, 579 N.E.2d at 686. As stated, Moe has consistently expressed her opposition to abortion, and the GAL report concludes that she would continue to do so if she were competent.

We reverse that portion of the order requiring sterilization of Moe. . . .

We vacate that portion of the order requiring Moe to undergo an abortion. We remand the case for a proper evidentiary inquiry and decision on the issue of substituted judgment. The record indicates that a determination should ensue with all possible speed before a different judge, and that such a determination will benefit from an immediate examination establishing the viability and status of the pregnancy.

We vacate that portion of the order insofar as it makes the appointment of the parents as guardians conditional on the need for them to approve an abortion (which issue is now subject to the preceding paragraph), and the order shall be modified to allow their appointment for general purposes relating to Moe's routine medical care, health and welfare, including, as appropriate, the duration, condition, and viability of her pregnancy.

So ordered.

Vanessa Volz, *A Matter of Choice: Women with Disabilities, Sterilization, and Reproductive Autonomy in the Twenty-First Century*

27 WOMEN'S RTS. L. REP. 203 (2006).

I know I am not expected to have children. I don't know how I know, I just do. Nobody ever said anything; it's probably what they didn't say that made the difference.[1]

The right to decide whether or not to reproduce extends to a broad range of people, but women with disabilities, particularly those with cognitive disabilities, continue to be excluded from this group. . . .

. . . [T]he privacy right to reproductive autonomy in *Roe* appears to be more restrictive for women with disabilities than for women without disabilities. While involuntary sterilization statutes are not used with the regularity with which they were . . . they can still be invoked with the proper judicial consent procedure. Moreover, in some states women with disabilities can be prevented from retaining legal custody of their children on the basis of their disability. . . .

. . . [O]pinions still differ as to whether individuals with disabilities should be afforded equal protection with other persons regarding decisions about their reproductive rights . . . Specifically, the issue revolves around who the decision maker should be in situations where a woman with a disability lives with her family or on her own; should it be the parents or guardians of a disabled woman, the courts, or the woman herself? A few jurisdictions, such as Colorado, have banned the sterilization of incompetent individuals altogether. However, in most states sterilization is still an option as long as appropriate judicial approval is obtained first. The requirements for judicial approval may be considered the most fundamental procedural protection prerequisite for forced sterilization today. . . .

Under most current sterilization reform laws, "the state may authorize sterilization" under its authority "if certain conditions are met." Many of these state laws follow a model derived from *In re Guardianship of Hayes*, a Washington Supreme Court decision [where] a mother petitioned the court to have her sixteen-year-old daughter, Edith Hayes, sterilized. However, the court found that sterilization was not in Hayes's best interests, and it established a two-part inquiry in reaching this decision. First, the court must determine whether the individual is competent to make an informed medical decision about sterilization. . . . "If the court determines the person is incompetent . . . it must then consider specific factors and decide whether sterilization is in the person's 'best interests.' "

---

[1] M. Duffy, *Making Choices, in* MUSTN'T GRUMBLE: WRITING BY DISABLED WOMEN 1, 29 (L. Keith ed., 1994).

Courts rely on varying factors to determine what qualifies as a woman's "best interest". One analysis inquires whether the individual is "able to reproduce and whether she is 'imminently' likely to engage in sexual activity." The petitioner may also be asked to "demonstrate that less drastic forms of contraception have been tried and are not feasible." Moreover, the court must assess the woman's "capacity to care for a child," and in some states the court must also determine if a woman understands her reproductive functions and the "relationship between sexual intercourse, pregnancy, and childbirth." The *Hayes* decision went further than other similar cases in that the court also presumed that sterilization would have detrimental effects on the physical or emotional health of the patient, which is a consideration most other courts have ignored. In *Hayes*, the court found that the evidence failed to illustrate that sterilization was in the patient's best interest; further, it said that the "best interests" requirement will be satisfied only in a "rare and unusual case." It also stated that "[t]here is a heavy presumption against sterilization of an individual incapable of informed consent."

. . . .

. . . Today, it is generally conceded that the interests or desires of the medical patient reign supreme, but this presumption is often disregarded or dismissed as insignificant when considering the desires of a woman with a disability. Should the patient be the sole determinant of sterilization decisions, or should the interests of others weigh into the balance as well? Other interests to consider may include those of parents, the state, and the child. . . .

Women with cognitive disabilities have historically been stereotyped as unable to occupy the sphere of motherhood. Such stereotypes have prevailed into modern day, although this stigma has been in tension with increased examples of parents with mild mental disabilities who successfully raise their children. . . . Competency doctrine is most frequently used to describe the mentally ill or mentally retarded; the latter group in particular endures strict state regulation in termination of parental rights proceedings . . . although parental rights may be considered fundamental, these rights are not absolute, and they can be regulated by legislation that withstands strict scrutiny analysis. Specifically, a conflict arises when the right to bear and raise children comes into tension with the state's interest in protecting those children against incompetent parenting.

. . . .

The state must show a compelling reason why the parent is unfit and unable to raise her own child. . . . While a child's safety and care should be of principal importance, parents who have cognitive or developmental disabilities often can still provide the necessary support for their children. In other words, a mother's right to parent should not be terminated merely because her IQ is below a certain level if she is still able to provide for the child. Courts, however, often determine parental competence solely on the basis of an existence of a disability; or, as previously discussed, they approve sterilization methods that ensure that pregnancy will never occur in the first place.

V.   REDEFINING REPRODUCTIVE CHOICE FOR WOMEN WITH DISABILITIES

. . . .

. . . While the feminist movement, led primarily by non-disabled women, has struggled for women to have the choice not to bear children by advocating for abortion rights, women with disabilities view reproductive rights as more than the right not to have a child. . . . Reproductive freedom for women with disabilities, therefore, parallels abortion rights in this sense; if all women have the right to choose not to bear a child, then all women must also have the right to bear children.

. . . .

Women with disabilities have claimed that the denial of their mothering rights through forced sterilization or general discouragement by doctors, professionals, and family members not to have children, is an experience of oppression . . . Giving birth and raising children can bring that individual a sense of security, an increase in self-esteem, a sense of belonging, and a reason to continue living. These concerns and interests, however, too often seem lost in the mainstream reproductive rights movement that focuses on "choice" as the choice whether or not to abort a fetus. The pro-choice movement, it seems, would benefit by adapting a more comprehensive definition of the term to include the concerns of women who may want to have a child, but have systematically been denied that right.

. . . .

Human Rights Watch, Sterilization of Women and Girls with Disabilities: A Briefing Paper
(2011).

. . . .

Background

Systemic . . . discrimination against women and girls with disabilities continues to result in widespread denial of their right to experience their sexuality, to have sexual relationships and to found and maintain families. The . . . right of a woman to make her own reproductive choices [is] enshrined in a number of international human rights treaties and instruments. However, throughout the world, an alarming number of women and girls with disabilities have been, and continue to be, denied these rights through the practice of forced sterilization. . . .

Across the globe, forced sterilization is performed on young girls and women with disabilities for various purposes, including eugenics-based practices of population control, menstrual management and personal care, and pregnancy prevention (including pregnancy that results from sexual abuse). The practice of forced sterilization is [a] denial of . . . human rights . . . framed within traditional social attitudes that characterize disability as a personal tragedy or a matter for medical management and rehabilitation. The difficulty some women with disabilities may have in understanding or communicating what was done to them increases their vulnerability to forced sterilization. A further aggravating factor is the widespread practice of legal guardians or others making life-altering decisions for persons with disabilities, including consenting to sterilization on their behalf.

. . . [T]he practice of forced sterilization continues to be . . . justified . . . as being in the "best interests" of women and girls with disabilities. However, arguments for their "best interests" often have little to do with the rights of women and girls with disabilities and more to do with social factors, such as avoiding inconvenience to caregivers, the lack of adequate measures to protect against the sexual abuse . . . of women and girls with disabilities, and the lack of adequate . . . services to support women with disabilities in their decision to become parents. . . .

Safeguards to prevent forced sterilization should not infringe the rights of women with disabilities to choose sterilization voluntarily and be provided with the necessary supports to ensure that they can make and communicate a choice based on free and informed consent.

International Human Rights Standards

The *Convention on the Rights of Persons with Disabilities* provides a basis for upholding the rights of persons with disabilities. . . . Article 23 reinforces the right . . . to found and maintain a family and to retain their fertility on an equal basis with others. Article 12 reaffirms the right of persons with disabilities to recognition everywhere as persons before the law . . . including access to the support they may require to exercise their legal capacity. Article 25 clearly articulates that free and informed consent should be the basis for providing health care to persons with disabilities. . . .

. . . [F]orced sterilization of girls and women with disabilities is a breach of Article 10 . . . of the *International Covenant on Economic, Social and Cultural Rights*. The Human Rights Committee addresses the prohibition of forced sterilization in the *International Covenant on Civil and Political Rights* through Article 7, prohibiting torture, cruel, inhuman or degrading treatment; Article 17, ensuring the right to privacy; and Article 24, mandating special protection for children. The Committee Against Torture has recommended that States take urgent measures to investigate promptly, impartially, thoroughly, and effectively all allegations of involuntary sterilization of women, prosecute and punish the perpetrators, and provide the victims with fair and adequate compensation.

The Committee on the Rights of the Child has identified forced sterilization of girls with disabilities as a form of violence and noted that State parties to the *Convention on the Rights of the Child* are expected to prohibit by law the forced sterilization of children with disabilities. The Committee has also explained that the principle of the "best interests of the child" cannot be used to justify practices which conflict with the child's human dignity and right to physical integrity.

. . . .

Recommendations

. . . .

1. The free and informed consent of the woman herself is a requirement for sterilization.

. . . .

2. As part of any process to ensure fully informed choice and consent, women with disabilities must be provided with information that sterilization is a permanent procedure and that alternatives to sterilization exist, such as reversible forms of family planning.

. . . .

3. Sterilization for prevention of future pregnancy does not constitute a medical emergency and does not justify departure from the general principles of free and informed consent. This is the case even if a future pregnancy may endanger a woman's life or health.

4. Sterilization should not be performed on a child.

5. Women and girls with disabilities, including through their representative organizations and networks, must be included in the evaluation and development of legislation . . . to ensure the enjoyment of all their rights, including sexual and reproductive rights and the right to found a family. . . .

Michelle Fine & Adrienne Asch, *Disabled Women: Sexism Without the Pedestal*

8 J. SOC. & SOC. WELFARE 233, 235 (1981).

. . . .

[Many] social factors, including sexual and reproductive relationships, differentially affect disabled women. While empirical data are largely unavailable, a growing grapevine and media coverage indicate that disabled women are often advised by professionals not to bear children, and are (within race and class groupings) more likely to be threatened by or victims of involuntary sterilization than nondisabled women (Committee for Abortion Rights and Against Sterilization Abuse,

1979). Reproductive freedom, child custody as well as domestic violence are particular concerns for these women who are traditionally overlooked when "optimal" social programs are formulated.

Because public opinion assumes disabled women to be inappropriate as mothers or sexual beings (International Rehabilitation Review, 1977), relevant information, counseling, technology and research findings are lacking. Safilios-Rothschild notes, for example, that because coronary research is almost exclusively conducted with men, women heart attack victims who a[sk] physicians about resumption of sexual activity are advised about male-derived standards, or left with no answers (International Rehabilitation Review, 1977). The social neglect of the sexual and reproductive roles of disabled women worsens the circumstances confronted by these women.

. . . .

Adrienne Asch, *Reproductive Technology and Disability, in* Reproductive Laws for the 1990s
69, 105–06 (Sherrill Cohen & Nadine Taub eds. 1989).

Interference with Reproductive Choice

Interference with reproductive choice for disabled women begins long before laws about access to reproductive services and technology. It starts in exclusion from sex education classes and in parental silence about sexuality and motherhood. It continues in the inaccessibility of affordable gynecological services; the lack of safe birth control for some disabled women, who have little choice left but sterilization; and the still-prevalent sterilizations of people with slight and severe degrees of mental retardation in and out of institutions. Authorities on the mentally retarded advance three reasons . . . for considering sterilization, even if involuntary, for persons with some level of retardation: concern for the welfare of the resulting children; concern about the drain on the state's resources entailed by assisting parents and their children; and concern about curbing the sexual expression of retarded people unable to manage safe birth control, but desirous of and able to manage sexual intimacy. As recently as 1983, 15 states had statutes permitting the compulsory sterilization of people with mental illness or mental retardation in or out of institutions, and 4 states authorized sterilizations for persons with epilepsy.

. . . [A]rguably, there may be some people with or without diagnosable disabilities who are inadequate or unfit parents. However, there is no body of evidence to suggest that a parent's disability in itself harms children, and there is some evidence to suggest that raising children enriches the lives of disabled people as it enriches the lives of the nondisabled.

NOTES

1. *Privileging procreation and family ties?* In response to the unsavory history of coerced sterilization, many states have placed substantial procedural and substantive obstacles in the path of sterilization, and some forbid entirely the sterilization of individuals deemed unable to understand and consent to the procedure. Professor Elizabeth Scott contends that this privileges the right to procreate over all other interests that a mentally disabled person might have, such as the interest not to procreate, personal autonomy, and the right to make reproductive choices. Echoing Vanessa Volz, Scott also notes that as "warehousing" of the mentally disabled has waned, families have assumed responsibility for the care of many disabled persons, creating an interest in the stability of the families in which they reside. Elizabeth S. Scott, *The Sterilization of Mentally Retarded Persons: Reproductive Rights and Family Privacy*, 35 DUKE L.J. 806, 807, 815–25 (1986).

2. *Sterilization and disability.* Throughout this casebook, we have looked at how certain forms of inequality come to be seen as "natural." As the above selections detail, it is often assumed that a pregnant woman who discovers that her fetus has a disability would want an abortion, or that girls and women with disabilities should be given the "choice" of having sex without the prospect of pregnancy. As Professor Linda Krieger has argued, however, the Americans with Disabilities Act (ADA) introduced a new model of equality, recognizing that "disability" inheres not in the biological features of individuals, but in the social relations (structures) surrounding the people with those features. In going beyond "formal equality" to insist that employers engage in interactive, good faith measures to accommodate the needs of disabled persons, the ADA reflected a new anti-discrimination paradigm. *See* Linda Hamilton Krieger, *Foreword—Backlash Against the Americans with Disabilities Act: Interdisciplinary Perspectives and Implications for Social Justice Strategies*, 21 BERKELEY J. EMP. & LAB. L. 1, 3 (2000). How might this new paradigm change the way that courts view disabled individuals' reproductive decisions?

* * *

Following Skinner v. Oklahoma, *316 U.S. 535 (1942),* supra *p. 16, criminal statutes prescribing sterilization as a condition of punishment fell into desuetude and were infrequently enforced. However,* Skinner *did not in fact forbid such statutes as a general matter. The decision specifically invalidated Oklahoma's criminal sterilization act on the ground that the Act impermissibly exempted those convicted of white collar crimes, like embezzlement, while subjecting those convicted of "blue collar" crimes, like theft, to sterilization. Although the* Skinner *Court found the Oklahoma statute violated the Equal Protection Clause, it made no judgment concerning whether sterilization laws more generally violated the Constitution. Id. at 537. With this in mind, it is perhaps unsurprising that, since the 1990s, chemical "castration"—a form of sterilization—has become more common as a punishment for those convicted of sexual offenses. As of 2008, several states permitted either chemical or physical castration of sex offenders, including California, Montana, and Oregon.*

<h1 style="text-align:center">Montana Code § 45–5–512</h1>
(2013).

(1) A person convicted of a first offense under 45–5–502(3) [, prescribing punishment for sexual assault where "the victim is less than 16 years old and the offender is 3 or more years older than the victim or if the offender inflicts bodily injury upon anyone in the course of committing sexual assault"], 45–5–503(3)[, prescribing punishment for sexual intercourse without consent where "the victim is less than 16 years old and the offender is 3 or more years older than the victim or if the offender inflicts bodily injury upon anyone in the course of committing sexual intercourse without consent"], or 45–5–507(4)[, prescribing punishment for incest where "the victim is less than 16 years old and the offender is 3 or more years older than the victim or if the offender inflicts bodily injury upon anyone in the course of committing incest"] or (5)[, prescribing punishment for incest "[i]f the victim was 12 years of age or younger and the offender was 18 years of age or older at the time of the offense"] may, in addition to the sentence imposed under those sections, be sentenced to undergo medically safe medroxyprogesterone acetate treatment or its chemical equivalent or other medically safe drug treatment that reduces sexual fantasies, sex drive, or both, administered by the department of corrections or its agent pursuant to subsection (4) of this section.

(2) A person convicted of a second or subsequent offense under 45–5–502(3), 45–5–503, or 45–5–507 may, in addition to the sentence imposed under those sections, be sentenced to undergo medically safe medroxyprogesterone acetate treatment or its chemical equivalent or other medically safe drug treatment that reduces sexual fantasies, sex drive, or both, administered by the department of corrections or its agent pursuant to subsection (4) of this section.

(3) A person convicted of a first or subsequent offense under 45–5–502, 45–5–503, or 45–5–507 who is not sentenced to undergo medically safe medroxyprogesterone acetate treatment or its chemical equivalent or other medically safe drug treatment that reduces sexual fantasies, sex drive, or both, may voluntarily undergo such treatment, which must be administered by the department of corrections or its agent and paid for by the department of corrections.

(4) Treatment under subsection (1) or (2) must begin 1 week before release from confinement and must continue until the department of corrections determines that the treatment is no longer necessary. Failure to continue treatment as ordered by the department of corrections constitutes a criminal contempt of court for failure to comply with the sentence, for which the sentencing court shall impose a term of

incarceration without possibility of parole of not less than 10 years or more than 100 years.

(5)   Prior to chemical treatment under this section, the person must be fully medically informed of its effects.

(6)   A state employee who is a professional medical person may not be compelled against the employee's wishes to administer chemical treatment under this section.

California Penal Code § 645
(2013).

SEC. 645. *Sex offenses; parole; medroxyprogesterone acetate treatment or equivalent; protocols.*

(a)   Any person guilty of a first conviction of any offense specified in subdivision (c)[, which includes various forms of sodomy, lewd and lascivious acts undertaken by force, various forms of oral copulation, and various forcible acts of sexual penetration], where the victim has not attained 13 years of age, may, upon parole, undergo medroxyprogesterone acetate treatment or its chemical equivalent, in addition to any other punishment prescribed for that offense or any other provision of law, at the discretion of the court.

(b)   Any person guilty of a second conviction of any offense specified in subdivision (c), where the victim has not attained 13 years of age, shall, upon parole, undergo medroxyprogesterone acetate treatment or its chemical equivalent, in addition to any other punishment prescribed for that offense or any other provision of law.

(c)   [referring to sections prescribing various statutory offenses]

(d)   The parolee shall begin medroxyprogesterone acetate treatment one week prior to his or her release from confinement in the state prison or other institution and shall continue treatments until the Department of Corrections demonstrates to the Board of Prison Terms that this treatment is no longer necessary.

(e)   If a person voluntarily undergoes a permanent, surgical alternative to hormonal chemical treatment for sex offenders, he or she shall not be subject to this section.

(f)   The Department of Corrections shall administer this section and implement the protocols required by this section. Nothing in the protocols shall require an employee of the Department of Corrections who is a physician and surgeon licensed pursuant to Chapter 5 (commencing with Section 2000) of Division 2 of the Business and Professions Code or the Osteopathic Initiative Act to participate against his or her will in the administration of the provisions of this section. These protocols shall include, but not be limited to, a requirement to inform the person about the effect of hormonal chemical treatment and any side effects that may result from it. A person subject to this section shall acknowledge the receipt of this information.

NOTE

Chemical castration. Because the administration of large doses of Depo-Provera to males is thought to reduce male sexual drive and performance, several states use this so-called "chemical castration" as a punishment for sex offenders. In California, for example, chemical castration is a mandatory condition of parole after a second sexual offense against a person under thirteen years of age, including both forcible and statutory rape. *See* CAL. PENAL CODE § 645(a)–(c) (2014). The treatment continues until the Department of Corrections deems it no longer necessary. Unlike California prisons' nominal procedures for women's sterilization, see note *infra* p. 1100, there are no statutory provisions for medical supervision or informed consent in circumstances involving chemical castration. Inmates can avoid chemical castration only by opting for surgical castration. *See* Audrey Moog, *California Penal Code Section 645: Legislators Practice Medicine on Child Molesters*, 15 J. CONTEMP. HEALTH L. & POL'Y 711, 726–27 (1999). For an overview of current state practices involving chemical castration, see Charles L. Scott & Trent Holmberg, *Castration of Sex Offenders: Prisoners' Rights Versus Public Safety*, 31 J. AM. ACAD. PSYCHIATRY & L. 502 (2003).

* * *

Although they do not technically lose their rights to reproduce and raise children, once in prison, incarcerated individuals rely upon the prisons for their reproductive health care. In this setting, they are vulnerable both to coercion and to policies and practices by prison officials and staff that are grounded in stereotypes of who "should" reproduce that trace back through the United States' eugenic past.

Corey G. Johnson, *Female Inmates Sterilized in California Prisons Without Approval*, Ctr. for Investigative Reporting
(July 7, 2013).

Doctors under contract with the California Department of Corrections and Rehabilitation sterilized . . . female inmates from 2006 to 2010 without required state approvals, the Center for Investigative Reporting has found.

At least [132]* women received tubal ligations in violation of prison rules during those five years—and there are perhaps 100 more dating back to the late 1990s, according to state documents and interviews.

---

*   The article as originally published listed this number as 148, however subsequent investigation by the Center for Investigative Reporting revealed that it was actually 132 women. *See* Corey G. Johnson, *California Doctor Linked to Sterilizations No Stranger to Controversy*, CTR. FOR INVESTIGATIVE REPORTING (Feb. 13, 2014), https://revealnews.org/article/calif-prison-doctor-linked-to-sterilizations-no-stranger-to-controversy-2/.—Eds.

. . . .

The women were signed up for the surgery while they were pregnant and housed at either the California Institution for Women in Corona or Valley State Prison for Women in Chowchilla, which is now a men's prison.

Former inmates and prisoner advocates maintain that prison medical staff coerced the women, targeting those deemed likely to return to prison in the future.

Crystal Nguyen, a former Valley State Prison inmate who worked in the prison's infirmary during 2007, said she often overheard medical staff asking inmates who had served multiple prison terms to agree to be sterilized.

. . . .

One former Valley state inmate who gave birth to a son in October 2006 said the institution's OB-GYN, Dr. James Heinrich, repeatedly pressured her to agree to a tubal ligation.

. . . .

During an interview with CIR, Heinrich said he provided an important service to poor women who faced health risks in future pregnancies because of past cesarean sections. The 69-year-old Bay Area physician denied pressuring anyone and expressed surprise that local contract doctors had charged for the surgeries. He described the $147,460 total as minimal.

"Over a 10-year period, that isn't a huge amount of money," Heinrich said, "compared to what you save in welfare paying for these unwanted children—as they procreated more."

The top medical manager at Valley State Prison from 2005 to 2008 characterized the surgeries as an empowerment issue for female inmates, providing them the same options as women on the outside. Daun Martin, a licensed psychologist, also claimed that some pregnant women, particularly those on drugs or who were homeless, would commit crimes so they could return to prison for better health care.

"Do I criticize those women for manipulating the system because they're pregnant? Absolutely not," Martin, 73, said. "But I don't think it should happen. And I'd like to find ways to decrease that."

Martin denied approving the surgeries, but at least 60 tubal ligations were done at Valley State while Martin was in charge, according to the state contracts database.

. . . .

Federal and state laws ban inmate sterilizations if federal funds are used, reflecting concerns that prisoners might feel pressured to comply. California used state funds instead, but since 1994, the procedure has required approval from top medical officials in Sacramento on a case-by-case basis.

Yet no tubal ligation requests have come before the health care committee responsible for approving such restricted surgeries, said Dr. Ricki Barnett, who tracks medical services and costs for the California Prison Health Care Receivership Corp. Barnett, 65, has led the Health Care Review Committee Since joining the prison receiver's office in 2008.

"When we heard about the tubal ligations, it made us feel slightly queasy," Barnett said. "It wasn't so much that people were conspiratorial or coercive or sloppy. It concerns me that people never took a step back to project what they would feel if they were in the inmate's shoes and what the inmate's future might hold should they do this."

. . . .

NOTES

1. *Sterilization in California prisons.* The practices discovered by the Center for Investigative Reporting were likely in violation of California's own regulations. Indeed, the California Code of Regulations for Prisons states that tubal ligations and sterilizations are not to be provided as part of prison health care unless medically necessary. CAL. CODE REGS. tit. 15 § 3350.1 (2014).

2. *Paternalism and sterilization.* Recall that in *Buck v. Bell*, Justice Holmes intoned that it was "better for all the world" if the "unfit" (broadly defined) refrained from having children. *Buck v. Bell*, 274 U.S. 200, 207 (1927). What is apparent in today's coerced sterilization cases is that the state and/or medical actors need not be evil or ill-intentioned. All that is necessary for vulnerable people to be harmed is a paternalistic assumption that individuals would be "better off" if they did not have children. From *Buck v. Bell*, to *Relf*, to the sterilizations that occurred in California's prisons, state actors have assumed that regardless of the absence of consent, sterilization would provide significant benefits to the individual involved, as well as to society.

3. *Pronatalism: everything old is new again.* It is worth remembering that policies that limit reproduction exist alongside policies intended to *encourage* reproduction. With the notable exception of the United States, many advanced democracies offer family allowances to help parents care for children and encourage population growth. Such pronatalism, however, can target certain populations while ignoring others. In Israel, for example, some groups, such as Arab-Israelis, were effectively excluded from these policies until the 1990s. Likewise, French family policies limited family allowances in the Overseas Departments (Martinique, Guadeloupe, French Guiana, and Réunion)—jurisdictions that were legally a part of the French nation, but that were largely composed of populations of color. Leslie King, *From Pronatalism to Social Welfare? Extending Family Allowances to Minority Populations in France and Israel*, 17 EUROPEAN J. POPULATION 305, 306 (2001).

INDEX

References are to Pages